11 Practice Tests for the

SAT®

& PSAT

2014 Edition

The Staff of The Princeton Review

PrincetonReview.com

Random House, Inc. New York

The Princeton Review, Inc.
111 Speen Street, Suite 550
Framingham, MA 01701
E-mail: editorialsupport@review.com

ISBN 978-0-307-94616-4
ISSN 1550-2791

Editor: Selena Coppock
Production Editor: Lee Elder
Production Artist: John E. Stecyk

Printed in the United States of America on partially recycled paper.
10 9 8 7 6 5 4 3 2 1
2014 Edition

Editorial
Rob Franek, Senior VP, Publisher
Mary Beth Garrick, Director of Production
Selena Coppock, Senior Editor
Calvin Cato, Editor
Kristen O'Toole, Editor
Meave Shelton, Editor
Alyssa Wolff, Editorial Assistant

Random House Publishing Team
Tom Russell, Publisher
Nicole Benhabib, Publishing Director
Ellen L. Reed, Production Manager
Alison Stoltzfus, Managing Editor

Acknowledgments

This book could never have been created without the dedication and collective expertise of the staff and students of The Princeton Review.

Many thanks to Jonathan Chui, the National Content Director for SAT.

Special thanks also to Adam Robinson, who conceived of and perfected the Joe Bloggs approach to standardized tests as well as many other successful techniques used by The Princeton Review.

Contents

Foreword

Congratulations! By picking up this book, you've taken a big step toward earning the highest SAT score that you can achieve.

The Princeton Review was founded in 1981; our first class had 19 New York students. By 1990, we had become the most popular SAT course in the country, and we remain so today. With more than 30 years in the business, we have built proven test-taking strategies and comprehensive content. Our test preparation programs are uniquely engineered to produce higher scores.

We created the practice tests in this book after analyzing tens of thousands of SAT questions and scrutinizing the test writers' strategies in fine detail. Our most experienced and analytical teachers gathered to review every question to ensure that these tests adhere to the length, style, and most importantly, the content that you will see on test day. Many tests in this book have been taken by thousands of Princeton Review students. We continually evaluate the data on each question to ensure validity and to refine the level of difficulty within each test to match that of the SAT even more closely.

We monitor the real test to make certain that you are practicing what you really need to know for a higher score on the SAT. If you've used earlier editions of this book, you'll see that there were vast changes between the 2009 and 2010 editions, and we continue in this edition to refine the material for a genuine testing experience. Hence, these practice tests are just like what you'll see on test day.

If you work through the tests and evaluate your performance with our comprehensive explanations, you'll develop the skills that you need to score higher on the SAT. Just as we have strived to give you the most accurate testing experience possible, you will get the most out of your efforts if you mimic the test setting as closely as you can. Take an entire test using the time limits for each section. You can use any questions you skip during the timed test for extra practice before you move on to the next test. Review the detailed explanations questions to brush up on essential SAT skills.

As you prepare, remember that the SAT measures nothing except for how well you can take an SAT.

- **It doesn't measure the stuff that matters.** It measures neither intelligence nor the depth and breadth of what you're learning in high school. It doesn't predict college grades as well as your high school grades do, and many schools are hesitant to use the score from your 25-minute essay in their application decisions at all. Colleges know there is more to you as a student—and as a person—than what you do at a single four-hour test administration on a random Saturday or Sunday morning.

- **It under-predicts the college performance of women, minorities, and disadvantaged students.** Historically, women have done better than men in college but worse on the SAT. For a test that is used to help predict performance in college for students across the country, that's a pretty poor record.

Of course, this doesn't mean that you shouldn't take the SAT. Although almost every college will accept the ACT (the other admittance test) and many colleges and universities schools have made the SAT optional, most selective colleges still require SAT scores. Always remember, though, that your SAT score is only a measure of how well you perform on the SAT—and nothing else!

Make sure you give yourself enough preparation time so that your hard and smart work will make a significant and substantial difference. Do your research and find out what score you need to get into the school of your dreams. Based on that, determine how much you should prepare—and get to work! Good luck on the SAT and with the college admissions process.

Sincerely,

The Staff of The Princeton Review

Part I
Orientation

Chapter 1
SAT Basics

Hi there—welcome to our book. Before you dive into the practice tests, which constitute the majority of this book, we thought you might have some questions about the SAT. Therefore, we'd like to begin by offering some basic information to help get you started.

WHAT IS THE SAT?

The SAT is a test that many colleges use in their evaluation of applicants for admission. The test runs 3 hours and 45 minutes and is divided into 10 sections (not necessarily in this order):

- one 25-minute Essay section
- two 25-minute Math sections
- two 25-minute Critical Reading sections
- one 25-minute Grammar (Writing) section
- one 20-minute Math section
- one 20-minute Critical Reading section
- one additional 25-minute Writing, Math, or Critical Reading experimental section
- one 10-minute Grammar (Writing) section

The essay is the first section of the SAT and takes 25 minutes. While the real SAT has 10 sections, the practice tests in this book do not include experimental sections, so each practice test is 9 sections long. Be sure to skip the "experimental" section (which varies from test to test) when filling out your answer sheet for each test.

How Is the SAT Scored?

Your Math, Critical Reading, and Writing scores are available online at the College Board's website or by phone about two and a half weeks after you take the real SAT. Four weeks after you take the SAT, you'll receive in the mail a report containing your scores. Each score is reported on a scale from 200 to 800; the average student scores around 500 in each subject area. Scores go up or down in increments of 10 points.

The maximum total score for the SAT is a 2400. You'll also hear about two other kinds of scores in connection with the SAT and other standardized tests: raw scores and percentile scores.

Your *raw score* is simply the number of questions you answered correctly minus a fraction of the number of multiple-choice questions you answered incorrectly; it's used to calculate your final scaled score (from 200 to 800). A *percentile score* is how you did in relation to everyone else who took the test. If your score is in the 60th percentile, it means you did better on the test than 60 percent of the people who took it on the same day as you. Percentile varies from year to year and from test to test. For example, a 550 might put you in the 65th percentile one year but the 55th percentile the next year.

Who Makes the SAT?

The SAT is published by Educational Testing Service (ETS). ETS is a large company that sells not only the SAT but also about 500 other tests, including ones for CIA agents, golf pros, travel agents, firefighters, and barbers. ETS is located outside of Princeton, New Jersey, on a beautiful 400-acre estate that used to be a hunting club. The buildings where the SAT is written are surrounded by woods and hills. There is a swimming pool, a goose pond, a baseball diamond, lighted tennis courts, jogging trails, an expensive house for the company's president, and a private hotel where rooms cost more than $200 a night.

You may have been told that ETS is a government agency or that it's part of Princeton University. It is neither. ETS is just a private company that makes a lot of money by writing and selling tests. The organization that hires ETS to write the SAT is called the College Entrance Examination Board or the College Board.

What Does the SAT Measure?

If you are like many high school students, you might think of the SAT as a test of how smart you are. If you score 800 on the Critical Reading section, you probably think of yourself as a genius. If you score 200, you probably think of yourself as not a genius. You may even think of an SAT score as a permanent label, like your Social Security number. ETS encourages you to think this way by telling you that the test measures your ability to reason and by claiming that you cannot significantly improve your score through special preparation (a strange claim from a company that sells its own preparation materials!).

Nothing could be further from the truth. The SAT doesn't test how smart you are; more than anything else, it's a test that merely tests how good you are at taking the SAT.

Can you learn to be better at taking the SAT? Of course you can. That's what this book is all about. You can improve your SAT score in exactly the same way you would improve your grade in chemistry: by learning the material you are going to be tested on and familiarizing yourself with the test format. Let's get to know the test.

Score Choice!

This is maybe the one nice thing that ETS has ever done for you. Don't let it go to your head, though, they are doing it to compete with the ACT, which has always given students this privilege.

As of March 2009, you can now choose which SAT (by test date) and which SAT Subject Scores (by individual test) you want to sent on to colleges. Previously, colleges would see your whole record. Now they just see what they need to (i.e., your best score). Score Choice is optional and you have to specify by checking a box that you'd like to use it. If you don't check the box, all your scores will be sent automatically.

How Important Are SAT Scores?

The SAT is an important factor when you apply to colleges, but it is not the only factor. A rule of thumb: The larger the college, the more important the SAT score. Small liberal arts colleges will heavily weigh your extracurricular activities, interview, essays, and recommendations. Large state universities, however, often admit students based on formulas consisting mostly of just two ingredients: test scores and grade-point averages.

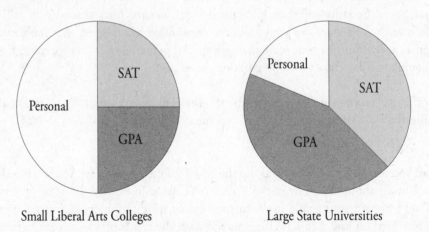

Small Liberal Arts Colleges   Large State Universities

Even at a small liberal arts college, however, SAT scores can be a deciding factor. If your scores fall below a school's usual range, admissions officers will look very critically at other elements in your application. For most college applicants, their SAT scores are the equivalent of a first impression. If your scores fall within the range of their acceptable SAT scores, an admissions officer will be more likely to give you the benefit of the doubt in other areas.

How Important Are the Writing Scores?

Colleges and universities are still working on how best to utilize the Writing score on the SAT. The Math and Critical Reading scores are both extremely familiar to colleges and comparable with the older test's scores, but the Writing score is obviously less familiar. Many schools are using the Writing score for placement purposes, but other schools aren't quite sure what to do with it. So for the time being, expect to see a decent amount of variation in how colleges treat the SAT Writing score.

The best approach to the Writing portions of the test is to do your best, just as you do on the other portions. Don't worry about how colleges may or may not use this score. If you want to know how a college to which you are applying will use the Writing score, contact the admissions office of that college directly, or refer to the college's website for more details.

WHAT IS THE PRINCETON REVIEW?

The Princeton Review is the nation's largest SAT-preparation company. We offer courses in more than 500 locations and online, and we publish best-selling books and software to get students ready for this test. We also prepare students and schools for the PSAT, ACT, GRE, GMAT, LSAT, MCAT, USMLE, TOEFL, and many other national and state standardized tests.

The Princeton Review's techniques and strategies are unique and powerful. Our team of crack experts in Research & Development (R&D) created them after spending countless hours taking and scrutinizing real SATs, analyzing them, and proving our theories in hundreds of classrooms across the country with thousands of real students. Our methods are widely imitated, but no one else achieves our score improvements. Trust us; you're in the right place.

WHAT IS THE BEST WAY TO PREPARE FOR THE SAT?

First off, take your time. Do not try to prep in the week before the test. Ideally, you should spread the work out over a several months. Second, give it some effort. The SAT is important and requires that you prepare diligently and smartly. What does practicing smartly mean? Taking the practice tests in this book cannot singularly help you increase your score. Grading your practice tests and then understanding the explanations for the questions that you missed will immeasurably identify mistakes and raise your score.

Should you take a course or get a tutor? Learning from The Princeton Review's SAT instructors and tutors will always be beneficial. If you don't already have a 2400, then that means there's at least one technique or strategy that you could learn to boost your score! An alternative to courses and tutorials would be our *Cracking the SAT* book in which you can learn many of our techniques and strategies.

Chapter 2
Scoring

HOW TO USE THIS BOOK

Scoring Your Own SAT Practice Test

The College Board figures out your score by using the following formula:

> # of questions you get correct – (# of multiple-choice questions you get incorrect ÷ 4) = Raw Score

They take your Raw Score, along with the Raw Score of every other test taker in the country, and figure out a curve. Finally, they assign each Raw Score to a number on a scale of 200 to 800. This is your Scaled Score.

How Do I Figure Out My Score?

Let's look at the subjects one at a time. Fill in the numbers on your SAT scoring worksheet on page 91.

Writing

Step One   Count up the number of your correct answers for the multiple-choice Writing Skills section. This is the number that goes in the first box.

Step Two   Count up the number of your incorrect answers for the multiple-choice Writing Skills section. Divide this number by four and place the resulting number in the second box.

Step Three   Subtract the second number from the first. This is your Grammar Raw Score. This is the number that goes in the third box.

Step Four   Look up the number from the third box in the Writing Multiple-Choice Subscore Conversion Table on page 92. This is your Grammar Scaled Subscore.

Step Five   The essay is scored on a scale from 2 to 12. It is based on the score that two graders give you, each on a scale from 1 to 6. The number that you should put in the fourth box depends on how it was scored. If your essay is self-graded on a 1 to 6 scale, then double that number so that it is from 2 to 12. Take your 2 to 12 grade and double it so that it is from 4 to 24. This is the number that goes in the fourth box.

Step Six	Add the fourth box to the third. This is your Writing Raw Score. This number goes in the fifth box.
Step Seven	Look up the number from the fifth box in the SAT Score Conversion Table. This is your Writing Scaled Score.

Critical Reading

Step One	Count up the number of your correct answers for the three Critical Reading sections of the test. This is the number that goes in the first box.
Step Two	Count up the number of your incorrect answers for the three Critical Reading sections of the test. Divide this number by four. The resulting number goes in the second box.
Step Three	Subtract the second number from the first. This is your Critical Reading Raw Score. This is the number that goes in the third box.
Step Four	Look up the number from the third box in the SAT Score Conversion Table on page 92. This is your Critical Reading Scaled Score.

Math

Step One	Count up the number of your correct grid-in answers. This is the number that goes in the first box.
Step Two	Count up the number of your correct answers for the multiple-choice questions in the three Math sections of the test. This is the number that goes in the second box.
Step Three	Count up the number of your incorrect answers for the multiple-choice questions in the three Math sections of the test. **Do NOT include any grid-in questions you may have answered incorrectly or left blank.** Divide this number by four and place the resulting number in the third box.
Step Four	Subtract the third number from the second, and then add the first number. This is your Math Raw Score. This is the number that goes in the fourth box.
Step Five	Look up the number from the fourth box in the SAT Score Conversion Table on page 96. This is your Math Scaled Score.

Looking to score your PSAT? Go to page 892.

Getting the Most from Your Tests

We recommend five general approaches to using this book.

1. **Simulate the test experience by taking tests in their entirety under actual time constraints.** It would be pretty foolish to prepare for a marathon by running a few 50-yard dashes just before race day. Likewise, you will not want to risk taking the actual SAT without having trained yourself to test for nearly four hours. As we do in our courses and tutorials, we recommend that you use at least four of the tests in this book as timed test simulations and space them out over your preparation calendar.

2. **Analyze your performance.** Taking test after test will help. But it will help more if you evaluate your scores, learn from your mistakes, and adjust your approach before taking another test.

3. **Review—especially areas of weakness.** Another benefit of the analysis of your performance after each test is that you can isolate your strengths and weaknesses. If you spend your time and energy on those areas of the test on which you need the most improvement, you'll make the most of your preparation time.

4. **When you're not testing, drill.** Although taking full-length tests is critical, it's not the only way to use the tests in this book. If you've been focused on reviewing your math skills, for example, take a timed Math section or two in one of the tests to gauge your improvement.

5. **Use this book in conjunction with additional test-preparation advice and resources.** You'll certainly pick up many of our strategies in the explanations to each question. But we also strongly recommend using the test practice strategies you may have learned elsewhere, perhaps in our *Cracking the SAT* book.

It's finally time to turn you loose. Good luck with the rest of this book, and good luck preparing for the SAT!

Chapter 3
What's on the SAT?
An Insider's Guide

THE TRUTH ABOUT THE SAT

You may not realize it, but you've arrived at what will prove to be a very useful resource for you as you embark on your journey toward the best SAT score you can achieve. There's much to know about the content of the SAT, but we are going to cut right to the chase by giving you an insider's look into what ETS (the company that writes the SAT for the College Board) *says* is on the SAT—and what *really* is on the test.

We aren't going to teach you all the content you need to master for the SAT—if that's what you are looking for, a great companion to this book is our very own *Cracking the SAT*. In this book, we are going to do something a little different. You already know a bunch of math, probably more than you really need to do well on the SAT. You also, we presume, know how to read and write grammatically (more or less). But what you may *not* know is how ETS will test your math knowledge, reading skills, and grammar know-how. Trust us, knowing *how* stuff is tested can be just as valuable as knowing the stuff itself.

The rest of this chapter will provide an overview of the content on the SAT, organized in the following way:

- what you need to know
- what ETS says about the SAT
- what ETS actually *means*
- how ETS will test certain concepts (or, in the case of the essay, how graders will evaluate your work)

Are you ready? Good! Let's start with the first part of the SAT you'll see on test day: the essay.

WHAT DO I NEED TO KNOW ABOUT THE ESSAY?

The Writing portion of the SAT totals 60 minutes and includes two types of assessments that claim to evaluate test takers' writing skills. One type is multiple-choice grammar questions, which make up two sections of the test (we'll deal with those later). But it's the second type—the essay—that has many students sweating. Multiple-choice questions are a piece of cake compared with the chilling sight of a big, blank space that has to be filled up with your own writing. Just because it's intimidating to some doesn't mean that you need to lose sleep over it.

In the next few pages, we'll give you a little more information about the essay and show you how to score your essays after taking the tests in this book. Finally, we'll outfit you with some tips on how you should prepare for the essay so that you nail it on test day.

What Will I Write About?

You will read a pair of quotations or a short passage that states one or more viewpoints on some generic topic, and you will write an essay arguing your position on that topic. You are free to use nearly any kind of evidence, reasons, or examples to support your ideas, as long as they are clearly relevant to the issue at hand and your thesis.

How Will My Essay Be Scored?

In a word, quickly. More specifically, your essay will be scanned into a computer and posted on an Internet server. Two official, trained "readers" will each read your essay online at their own personal computers. Each reader has to be available to score essays for *at least* four hours at a time and must read between 16 and 25 essays per hour. That means that readers will be scoring around one hundred, and possibly more, essays at one sitting. After reading that many timed essays on the exact same topic, it isn't far-fetched to say that readers will probably be a little fatigued. That's why it's important to give readers exactly what they are supposed to be looking for. Your essay may be #103 instead of #4, and by that point in the scoring process, the readers probably just aren't going to have the will or the energy to dig any deeper than necessary to find reasons to award your essay a high score.

Your essay will most likely be scored by high school teachers who have been trained in the College Board's essay-scoring guidelines. High school teachers are favored as readers for two reasons. First, they are familiar with high school students' writing, the common mistakes students make, and the skills they should have developed by the time they take the test. Second, high school teachers, traditionally not the best-paid professionals, are more willing than most others to take the wage offered to people to read and score essays. There will probably be a few college professors who also read SAT essays, but the majority of readers will be high school teachers.

The possible scoring range for each reader is from 1 to 6, for a total combined essay score of 2 to 12. Essays not written on the assigned topic will be awarded a score of 0. If the two readers award your essay significantly different scores (for example, if one gives it a 2 and the other a 6), a third "master" reader will be brought in to, well, settle the score (pun completely intended). You'll receive two subscores for the Writing section: a multiple-choice subscore on a scale of 20 to 80, and an essay subscore on a scale of 2 to 12. Those two subscores will be combined to calculate an overall Writing score on the 200 to 800 scale.

What Your Score Says About Your Essay

According to the College Board, the organization that owns the SAT, a score of 6 is given to an essay that "effectively and insightfully addresses the writing task; is well-organized and fully developed, using clearly appropriate examples to support ideas; and displays consistent facility in the use of language, demonstrating variety in sentence structure and range of vocabulary," although it may have "occasional errors." In contrast, an essay with "very poor organization, very thin development, and usage and syntactical errors so severe that meaning is somewhat obscured" merits a score of 1. There are four gradations between these two extremes. (Visit www.collegeboard.com to read the entire essay-grading rubric.)

Huh? What Does That Really Mean?

The College Board says that essay readers will score essays "holistically." This approach means that they will be grading based on how thorough your essay is as a whole, instead of nitpicking over minor grammar and syntax errors. As we've said, essay graders are on a tight schedule; therefore, writing for an essay grader is much different from writing for your English teacher. In keeping with this holistic approach, the College Board has gone so far as to say that you can get a top essay score even if you make some grammar, punctuation, and spelling mistakes. Besides, they already test you in those specific areas on the multiple-choice portion of the Writing section.

Let's break it down into even simpler terms: Your essay score is a function of the following principles:

How complex are your ideas?

All of the prompts for SAT essays ask questions for which there is no "right" or "easy" answer. Graders are looking to see not only whether you have taken a clear stance on the issue, but also that you discuss the issue with some "insightfulness." Graders look to see whether you provide a context for your discussion and move from idea to idea in a logical, coherent way.

How well do you develop your examples?

"Development" refers to both the level of detail you go into when you present your examples as well as your discussion of those examples. If you do not thoroughly explain your examples—such as what a particular book is about or why a certain historical event supports your thesis—your score will suffer.

How well do you use the language?

Good writing has the ability to conjure an image. It is lively and uses original expressions rather than predictable clichés. You don't have to pepper your essay with words such as *plethora* and *exacerbate* to get a top score, but graders *are* looking for you to use correctly words that clearly express your ideas. The language used in the best essays flows naturally and keeps the reader interested, which is definitely what you are looking to do.

Debunking SAT Essay Myths

Unlike other essays you may have written in school, the SAT essay allows you to present and support your ideas in a number of different ways. Don't listen if anyone tells you that you *have* to write your essay a certain way. In fact, now is as good a time as any to debunk some myths about the SAT essay.

Myth #1: *Never use "I" in the SAT essay.*

Reality #1: Many English teachers tell their students never to use "I" when they write. In certain kinds of writing, this is a good rule to follow. However, there is nothing wrong with using "I" on the SAT essay. In fact, when using a personal example to support your ideas, it's nearly impossible to avoid it.

Myth #2: *Never use personal examples.*

Reality #2: Personal examples are not, in themselves, taboo on the SAT essay. Indeed, there are plenty of examples of essays using personal examples that received scores of 6, the highest score possible. Personal examples can also be the most appropriate kind to use depending on what the prompt is about. The *real* problem with using personal examples lies in how difficult they can be to use really well. If you get too caught up in telling the story and start to get off track, or tell a scintillating story that isn't actually relevant to the topic, your scores will *not* benefit.

Myth #3: *I must write a five-paragraph essay and provide three different examples, plus have a full introduction and conclusion.*

Reality #3: Wrong again. A five-paragraph organizational structure is just one of many you can use to construct your argument. Many students (and teachers) prefer this style because it can help you organize your thoughts, but it is neither penalized nor rewarded on the SAT. Similarly, you don't need three examples. What counts is that your examples are appropriate and well developed; many a top-scoring essay has only two—and sometimes just one—really excellent examples that the writer explains with exceptional thoroughness.

Myth #4: *The longer the essay, the higher the score.*

Reality #4: Though there have been claims that longer essays *always* receive higher scores, this is simply not the case. Longer essays tend to get higher grades only because providing specific, detailed evidence and adequately developing your ideas requires words. Shorter essays also tend to get lower grades because the writers typically don't provide enough detail nor do they develop their ideas very much. However, a relatively short essay, if well organized and succinctly phrased, can earn a top score, while an essay that rambles on for two irrelevant, repetitive pages will not.

SAMPLE ESSAYS WITH SCORES

To illustrate how the College Board will score your essay, we've included a series of sample essays with authentic scores from official SAT graders. These essays will also help you to evaluate your own essay writing on the practice tests in this book. We'll use the following topic and prompt for each of the sample essays.

Think carefully about the issue presented in the following excerpt and the assignment below.

> The only way a government can function, and the only way a people's voice can be expressed, is through a process in which decisions are made by the majority. This is not a perfect way of controlling government, but the alternatives—decisions made by a minority, or by one person—are even worse.
>
> Adapted from Thomas Jefferson

Assignment: Is the opinion of the majority always right? Plan and write an essay in which you develop your point of view on this issue. Support your position with reasoning and examples taken from your reading, studies, experience, or observations.

Essay at Scoring Level 6

The question as to whether the majority is right or wrong is not as easy to answer as it may seem. Depending on the context of the opinion, the voice of the majority—however it is defined—may or may not be a poor guide. The quality depends on the context.

There is a cliché that states the majority is always wrong, and this trope has some credence. "Mob rule" embodies this idea well; the unruly masses, guided by ignorance and unchecked by ethics, create their own rights and wrongs. In the American South in the early 20th century, lynchings of Blacks were commonplace, and Blacks had few, if any, rights. Because the majority there believed it was right to treat Blacks this way, these practices were rarely challenged. Even when the federal and state laws changed, Blacks were mistreated, unprotected by the law. The majority's belief in the South ruled, not the laws of state or country. In retrospect we see that the majority in the South perpetuated crimes that went unpunished, but at the time, no one and nothing could control the racist stranglehold on Blacks in the South.

Even today, the majority—as it is perceived—tends to have poor judgment. But here is where this question gets complicated. Who exactly <u>is</u> the majority? The "majority" of Americans voted for Al Gore in the 2000 presidential election, but George Bush became President. The real "majority" voted one way, but the "official majority" another. Here the voice of the real majority was silenced by an unfair electoral system.

The results of that election are part of the modern-day problem of who the majority really is. If you listen to the news, it sounds as if the "majority" believes war is good, the president is beloved, and that life is just peachy all around. This "majority" is fake and deluded, but it is the fact that it *is* fake that makes it impossible to judge whether its opinions are poor or not.

Evaluation for Essay at Scoring Level 6

ETS says that an essay receiving a score of 6 is "outstanding." This essay received the highest possible score from both readers, so it must be doing *something* right! One of the first things you may notice is that the writer's grasp of the language is very strong. The writer not only uses fairly high-level vocabulary correctly, but also chooses words and sentences that add meaningful expression and emphasis to her writing. Second, the writer takes a unique approach to the prompt by stating that the "answer" to the question depends on context and successfully supports this idea throughout the entire essay without losing focus. This writer "insightfully" develops her ideas, one of the key features of a top essay, by showing that the answer to the question is not as clear cut as it seems. Lastly, the examples provided are apt and well developed, meaning they are discussed in detail, leaving no question in the reader's mind about what they mean or why they prove the writer's point. All in all, this is a strong piece of writing.

Now let's take a look at an essay that received a score of 5. As you read it, think about what the writer did well, but also think about what the writer could have done better.

Essay at Scoring Level 5

I believe that the opinion of the majority isn't always right. Just because many people believe something is right, does not make it right. The examples of the Nazis in World War II, The Scarlet Letter, and Lord of the Flies show this to be true.

One example in which the opinion of the majority was not a good guide is the Nazis in Germany during World War II. This group was following the orders of Adolf Hitler, who they thought was right. The Nazis did terrible things, such as kill innocent people, force people out of their homes and into concentration camps, and rape and pillage. If they had been individuals, certainly they would not have done these things. However, since they were following the majority, they committed deeds that were not right.

Another example of the majority not being a good guide is in the novel The Scarlet Letter. In this story, the young woman Hester Prynne is suspected of committing adultery. The townspeople decide that she should be punished, so she is made an outcast and must wear the letter "A" on her clothes so that people will know that she committed adultery. The majority did not come up with the right conclusion and punished an innocent woman. This shows that the majority is not always right.

A final example that the majority can be a poor guide is in the Lord of the Flies. In this novel, a group of boys becomes stranded on an island. As a group, they elect a leader to follow. Everyone has to follow this decision of the majority, but it eventually turns out to be a bad decision, causing a split in the group. Chaos follows. Had the boys not decided to go with the decision of the majority, they might have been happy and peaceful from the beginning. Clearly, the opinion of the majority was not the best guide in this situation.

The examples above show that the opinion of the majority can be a poor guide. If people would sometimes act as individuals and not part of a herd, they could make better decisions.

Evaluation for Essay at Scoring Level 5

ETS says that an essay receiving a score of 5 is "effective." Overall, this essay is well done: It has a clear thesis, good organization, and relevant examples. But what would need to improve for this writer to score a 6?

For starters, the writer's vocabulary and use of language is not as skilled as it could be. The writer presents his ideas in a very straightforward manner, using less varied kinds of sentences than did the writer who scored a 6. The other place where this essay could be improved is in the development of the examples. The writer chose to use three different examples and provides some discussion of each. However, the examples all seem to say the same thing: When you follow the majority, bad things happen. This is a more simplistic view of the issue than we saw in the first essay and therefore doesn't demonstrate quite the level of "insightfulness" that graders are looking for in a top paper. The writer of this essay may benefit next time by citing only two examples but discussing them in more detail. Better transitions between the examples would also make for a smoother progression of ideas.

If your essays look a lot like this one, remember: A 5 is a very good score on the SAT essay! Only around 10 percent of essays get this score, so if you receive this score, you will be ahead of many other students.

Let's take a look at an essay that received a score of 4.

Essay at Scoring Level 4

I believe that the opinion of the majority is generally not right. It is as true today as it was in 1492—strong and intelligent rulers are needed to avoid mob rule. We are all slaves to our biases and prejudices and, in matters of importance, it takes clear, unbiased thinkers to overpower the majority. This theory can be proved by examining The Constitution of the United States and The Adventures of Huckleberry Finn by Mark Twain.

First, when America's Founding Fathers set forth to create the Constitution, they were very aware of the dangers of majority rule. Because of their studies, they knew that a well run republic can't be a true democracy. Therefore, they created the "Electoral College" who would chose the President. Instead of being chosen directly by the people, the President is technically elected by a group of electors who were in turn chosen by their states. This was a victory for the Anti-Federalists who wanted to guarantee that each state had an equal voice and big states wouldn't dominate policies because of their numbers. This was challenged after the election of 2000 in which Al Gore won the popular vote and George W. Bush won the Electoral Vote. Whether you like Bush or not, you can agree that if the election was decided by majority, the entire South and Midwest would be dominated by Northeast and West States. Thus, the Framers built a safeguard against majority rule into the Constitution because it is a poor guide.

Second, the novel <u>The Adventures of Huckleberry Finn</u> by Mark Twain shows that the majority is not always right. Huck travels with an escaped slave named Jim. The majority of Southerners (Huck's contemporaries) would have thought that Huck should report Jim. But, Huck was a strong individual and knew that slavery was wrong and Jim was a wise man who he could learn a lot from. Thus, Huck showed that the majority is often a poor guide.

In conclusion, through examples of the Electoral College and <u>Huck Finn</u>, I've shown that the majority is poor guide. In the modern age, where pure democracy is easier to find, we all should remember the concerns of our Founders and great authors and distrust the majority and make our own decisions.

Evaluation for Essay at Scoring Level 4

ETS says that an essay receiving a score of 4 is "competent," meaning it does the basic job of conveying the writer's ideas. In this case, the writer does state the thesis clearly and provides two examples in support of that thesis. However, this writer does not present his or her ideas in as smooth and logical a manner as did the writer of the previous essays. In the discussion of the examples, the writer could have provided more detailed explanation, as it is not always clear what the writer means or how the different ideas are connected. For example, what does "they knew that a well run republic can't be a true democracy" mean? A writer should never leave it up to the reader to fill in this kind of gap. The second example is also not as well developed as the first. Lastly, this essay contains some noticeable grammar errors and ambiguous pronoun references that force the reader to work harder to understand what the writer is talking about.

That does it for the top-half scores on the SAT essay. Unlike the top-half scores, which are defined by how well the writer fulfills the requirements of the essay, the bottom half of the scoring spectrum is defined by what is lacking or missing altogether. Let's take a look.

Essay at Scoring Level 3

Thomas Jefferson found that the majority's decision is "the only legitimate foundation of any government." He also thought that the right of freedom of speech is completely necessary and critical in a successful democracy. I believe Jefferson was correct; the will of the majority is the best way to go.

If the most popular vote is chosen, the people will receive what they want. Everyone's opinions will be considered, and the best one will be selected. The public realizes what is beneficial or detrimental to them. When this recognition comes from most of the people, a united bond is formed between them. They know that they stand together in their beliefs.

Every four years it is time to elect a President of the United States. The will of the citizens is made known when they vote on their favorite candidate. If most people choose a certain man, chances are he will be an excellent leader for the job. His ability to campaign, his past actions, and his personal characters shine above the rest enough to make him a winner in the eyes of the Americans.

Free expression is of utmost importance. In school, the student body votes on those who will represent their class, what their class shirt will look like, and how they want to have their activities. The kids make the right decision because they know what will make them happy.

Evaluation for Essay at Scoring Level 3

ETS says that an essay receiving a score of 3 is "inadequate." Although the writer has a clear point of view, the examples provided are repetitive and very general, lacking the kind of specificity and thorough explanation that we saw in the higher-scoring essays. The second example about the student body comes out of nowhere, as does the idea of the importance of free expression. There just isn't a clear connection between ideas. Lastly, the ideas are very simplistic: "If the most popular vote is chosen, the people will receive what they want." Does this sound like the real world to you? Overall, this essay needs better, more specific examples to get to the next level. A conclusion, even a minimal one, would be nice as well.

Essay at Scoring Level 2

The majority is hardly ever right. People may believe that just because they are in the majority they are right. When the first cars came out everyone thought that they wouldn't last very long. But cares have been around for close to a hundred years now and almost everyone has a car.

In my science class the teacher asked for a vote on which way would be better to mix two different chemicals. The majority of the class voted for the wrong way while two or three people, including myself, voted for the right way. And also when Elvis first started to sing the majority of people that did listen to him thought that he wasn't going to make it as a singer and that he should go back to driving trucks.

The majority of people are very seldomly ever right. And just because you are in the majority doesn't make you right.

Evaluation for Essay at Scoring Level 2

ETS says that an essay receiving a score of 2 is "seriously limited." As with the essay that scored a 3, this essay offers a few brief examples but doesn't discuss them at all. The writer presents his ideas in a very disorganized manner, sort of the textual equivalent of wandering aimlessly in circles through a forest. The language is also repetitive and simplistic. This writer needs a better organizational structure and better, more specific examples to get to the next level.

And About Scoring Level 1…

Do you really want to read an essay that would receive a 1? We are not even going there. In practice, readers will score very few essays as a 1. Besides, if you're reading this, you should already be well prepared to surpass the lowest essay score—as long as you write *something* related to the topic and provide some support for your ideas.

How Should You Score Your Essay?

Score it as objectively as possible. Yeah, we know that it's your writing and that you're in love with it, but when it comes to preparing for the SAT, you need to be brutally honest with yourself if you want to spot your weaknesses and improve on them. So that means you need to take a step away from your essay as best you can and score it as though it were written by someone else, someone you've never met.

Better yet, we recommend that you ask your mom or dad, brother or sister, teacher, or most grammatically overachieving friend to review the sample essays and our evaluations of them and apply them to your essays.

WHAT DO I NEED TO KNOW ABOUT MULTIPLE-CHOICE WRITING?

On the multiple-choice portion of the SAT Writing section, ETS is testing your ability to spot errors in sentences. Some are obvious, but others are less so. All you need to know for this part of the SAT is a pretty limited list of grammar rules that are likely already familiar to you. Don't worry. You aren't going to have to know any weird terminology. But you do need to be aware that the rules of written English often differ from the spoken English that we hear every day. Remembering the rules will get you further on the SAT than will trusting your ear.

What Does ETS Say About Grammar?

Not much. ETS claims that the multiple-choice Writing questions on the SAT measure a test-taker's ability to "recognize and correct faults in usage and sentence structure" and "recognize effective sentences that follow the conventions of standard written English." However, ETS does not point to any particular reference or guide that lists all the rules you need to know. The folks at ETS simply state that the questions test a student's "ability to identify sentence errors, improve sentences, and improve paragraphs," which basically just tells you that there are three question formats. Big help they are.

What Does That Mean?

It means good things for you. Trust us, there are hundreds of grammar points on which ETS could test you, but they tend to stick to the most common errors about which no one disagrees. Since there are many grammar "rules" over which experts argue, most SAT grammar questions repeatedly test a relatively small group of rules.

1. **Agreement: Subject/Verb, Pronoun/Noun, Noun/Noun**—Singular goes with singular, and plural goes with plural. So *I am,* but *You are. Those students brought their own books,* but *Each student brought his or her own book.*

2. **Pronoun Case and Ambiguity**—Pronoun case is what tells you to say *I saw him and he saw me. I* and *he* are subject pronouns, while *him* and *me* are object pronouns.
   Ambiguous pronouns create confusion because it isn't clear to what exactly the pronouns refer. For example, who does *she* refer to in the following sentence, Britney or Christina? *Britney told Christina that of all the pop divas out there, she was the most talented.*

3. **Verbs: Tense and Voice**—Past, present, or future? Make sure the verbs in each sentence are in the proper tense based on other information you are given in the sentence.
   The SAT also sometimes tests voice, which pretty much means "passive versus active." The active is always preferable to the passive, so when you see *The book was enjoyed by me* (passive), choose an answer like this: *I enjoyed the book* (active).

4. **Coordinating Clauses: Fragments, Run-ons, and Comma Splices**— Sentence fragments are incomplete sentences that lack a verb: *My brother going to the mall* is a fragment.
   A run-on is a sentence in desperate need of a punctuation mark to separate two or more complete ideas. This is a run-on: *I have a test tomorrow I need to study for it.* You can fix a run-on in a few ways. You can add a period, colon, or semicolon, as such: *I have a test tomorrow; I need to study for it.* Or you can use other punctuation and linking words called conjunctions, as such: *I have a test tomorrow, and I need to study for it.*
   A comma splice is what happens when you try to fix a run-on sentence by adding only a comma: *I have a test tomorrow, I need to study for it.* Not good! Fix comma splices the same way you fix run-ons: Use a period, semicolon, colon, or conjunction.

5. **Idioms**—An idiom is a set of words that must go together. Idioms on the SAT are some of the toughest concepts to master simply because there are so *many* of them that could be tested. Little words called prepositions often must be paired with certain words to create an idiom. For example, you may hear people say, *I am planning on going to the football game,* but the correct idiom is *planning to go.* Familiar phrases such as *neither…nor* are also idioms.

6. **Parallelism**—Parallelism just means that when you have a list of things or actions, each thing in the list should be in the same form. For example, *I studied for my physics test, ate lunch, and I went to gym class* isn't parallel. However, *I studied for my physics test, ate lunch, and went to gym class* is parallel.

7. **Misplaced Modifiers**—Misplaced modifiers are some of the most humorous grammatical errors you'll see on the SAT. Modifiers are words or phrases that describe something else in the sentence. To use them properly, be sure they are right next to the thing they describe. If they are "misplaced"—that is, far away from what they're describing—the meaning of the sentence may be distorted. Read the sentence, *Walking home in the rain without an umbrella, my hair was a mess by the time I got home.* Though you know perfectly well what the writer is trying to say, grammatically this sentence says that *my hair* was *walking home in the rain without an umbrella*!

8. **Comparisons**—This is one of the hardest errors to see. The comparison rule simply says, "Compare similar things." So if you see *I prefer Maya Angelou's novels to Toni Morrison,* you should notice that this sentence incorrectly compares *Maya Angelou's novels* with *Toni Morrison.* Don't compare books to people: Compare books to books. Instead, the sentence should read, *I prefer Maya Angelou's novels to Toni Morrison's* or even *I prefer Maya Angelou's novels to those of Toni Morrison.*

9. **Word Choice**—The SAT also tests your vocabulary on the grammar section by including words that are often misused or confused with other similar words. For example, *John B.'s writing is full of obscure literary illusions that the average reader may not understand* contains a word choice error. The word *illusion* (a false perception or belief) is not the right one—the correct word is *allusion* (an indirect reference).

10. **Other Little Things**—There are lots of smaller rules that the SAT tests involving the use of adjectives, adverbs, pronouns, and other parts of speech. If you want the full list, pick up *Cracking the SAT.* If not, don't worry. If you master the first nine rules in this list, you will master the majority of questions on the multiple-choice portion of the SAT Writing section.

What Makes a Writing Question Hard?

In harder questions, ETS loves to (1) test obscure rules that may not be familiar to you; (2) use turns of phrase that you hear spoken in everyday, or colloquial, language that are officially "ungrammatical"; and (3) test style rather than hard-and-fast rules.

The Obscure

Read this sentence: *Peter Jackson's movies have made him one of the most successful directors working today.* Sounds perfectly fine, right? Wrong. In SAT-land, this sentence is incorrect. Specifically, the pronoun *him* has no antecedent, meaning that there is no noun in the sentence to which *him* refers.

Yes, yes, I know what you are thinking. You and I both understand from context that *him* refers to Peter Jackson, but in formal grammar terms, *Peter Jackson's* is an adjective that describes the noun *movies*, and *movies* can't be the thing to which *him* refers. This is an obscure rule but one that is fair game on hard SAT questions.

The Colloquial

Go back and check out some of the examples of error types that appear on the SAT. How many of those errors do you hear every day from your friends, parents, or even your teachers? Probably many of them. In fact, sometimes the "ungrammatical" version of a sentence sounds more correct than the grammatical one! For instance, the sentence *Everyone has their own likes and dislikes when it comes to music* is actually wrong. The correct phrasing is *Everyone has <u>his or her</u> own likes and dislikes* because the pronoun *everyone* is singular. The fact that so many familiar phrases are wrong on the SAT is why it is so important to know the rules. Don't rely on your ear to tell you what is correct.

Style Over Substance

The last piece in the SAT Writing puzzle concerns writing style rather than concrete rules. On the SAT, there are plenty of occasions when an incorrect answer is wrong because it is considered redundant, awkward, or wordy. ETS faults these answers because they are not "effective." Even if the meaning of a sentence is clear, the expression may be less than ideal. So how do you know what to pick? In general, if you cannot pinpoint a grammar error, simply choose the shortest answer. This won't get you the right answer every time, but it can really help you guess more effectively.

The best way to improve your style sense is to do lots of practice questions, pay attention to the wording of correct answers, and read the explanations provided in the back of this book. Trust us: Familiarity with SAT style comes most directly from working on many SAT questions, not from poring over grammar books that have more information than you really need!

That's about it for SAT Writing. Now let's take a look at SAT Math.

WHAT DO I NEED TO KNOW ABOUT THE MATH?

SAT Math isn't like the math you do in school. There is no partial credit, and ETS doesn't care *how* you get the answer as long as you find it. Therefore, it pays to think about all the different ways you can approach and solve problems. Sometimes using your calculator or working through the answer choices until you find one that works is just as efficient as "doing the math." If you get stumped, try to approach the problem in a different way. Use real values if variables are too hard to work with. Consider plotting some sample points on a graph if working with the equation isn't helpful. Use estimation to eliminate answers you know can't be right. ETS writes questions that encourage a multifaceted approach, so often it pays to think outside the box to get the answer.

What Does ETS Say About the Math?

ETS says, "The content and format of the SAT reflect accepted educational standards and practices. The math section requires students to apply mathematical concepts and to use data literacy skills in interpreting tables, charts, and graphs." Yawn.

What Does That Mean?

ETS is testing concepts that it expects you to know and requires you to use a combination of your math content knowledge, reading abilities, and reasoning skills to solve math problems. In other words, it's not just about "knowing the math."

Doing well in SAT Math means reading carefully, answering the right question, calculating carefully, and using the rules of math to find your way to the right answer. Therefore, if you are ever working on a problem and think, "I have no idea how to even start this problem!" you have likely come across a problem that requires you to use a little reasoning to solve it.

What Makes a Math Question Hard?

ETS determines the difficulty of individual questions by making students do the questions in the "experimental" section on the real SAT, which doesn't count toward your score. Therefore, questions that many students get right are "easy," and questions that few students get right are "hard." However, difficulty is not aligned to content, meaning that the hardest question on the test could just as easily be an algebra, an arithmetic, a data, or a geometry question.

Harder questions require you to follow multiple steps and use multiple concepts to solve them. They also are more likely to involve variables or other unknown values and require that you use your reasoning skills and the rules of math to solve the problem rather than just simply do quick calculations.

In contrast, easier questions involve concrete numbers and fewer steps and tend to give you all or most of the information you need to answer them. As questions become more difficult, ETS gives you less information, meaning you have to come up with the stuff you need to solve these questions on your own. When you're stuck, always think about the rules of math that apply to the problem at hand. In other words, when facing a tough problem involving circles always ask yourself, "What do I know about circles?" One of the rules governing circles will help you get to the next step.

How About Some Examples?

Sure! Knowing the concepts on the test is good, but also being prepared for the different ways those concepts are tested is better. Here is a sampling of how ETS can take the same concepts and make them harder.

Slope

Slope problems on the SAT can be presented as either word problems or visual problems with figures. All you have to remember, though, is that the slope of a line is the relationship of how much the line "rises" to how much it "runs."

- Easy problems involving slope will often give you a picture of a line on a coordinate plane for which you need to identify the slope. Knowing if the slope is positive, negative, or zero helps eliminate most answers. You may need to calculate the slope using the slope formula.
- Medium slope problems may ask for a missing coordinate for a point on a line with a given slope. The slope formula will help you here. Medium problems also may ask you to determine the slope from an equation in the $y = mx + b$ form. As long as you can find the m and the equation is in this form, you can determine slope. Problems with variables instead of numbers as coordinates may also fall into the medium pile.
- Harder slope problems may involve parallel, perpendicular, or reflected lines, so know what the slope rules are for these kinds of lines. A harder question may also provide you with a chart of x and y values from which to calculate the slope. It may seem that you are not given enough information to use the slope formula, but you always are.

Functions

Problems involving functions show up regularly on the SAT and either use the normal $f(x)$ notation or ETS's goofy made-up symbols.

- In easy function problems, your task will be fairly straightforward. You may be required to plug some values into the formula and solve the problem arithmetically. ETS may also give you a list of x and y values and ask you to choose which function satisfies the values given.

- Medium functions may give you a function in $f(x)$ notation and ask you for the value of $2f(x)$ or some other value. ETS makes these problems harder by adding factoring or distribution concepts. In other words, ETS will ask you to use functions in different, less straightforward ways. If you read carefully and always keep in mind what the function notation actually means, these are very doable questions.
- The hardest function problems may involve multiple functions or use many variables instead of actual numbers. Sometimes to solve the hardest function problems, you may find that other concepts—such as quadratic or rational equations—come into play. The hallmark of these questions is that it sometimes gets hard to know where to go next or what you should do with the values.

Graphing Linear Equations

If ETS says linear equation, just think: $y = mx + b$, where m is slope and b is the y-intercept, the point at which the line crosses the y-axis, and $x = 0$.

- Easier problems involving linear equations may require that you know what the variables in the equation above mean. They may also ask you to identify the graph of a given equation, which can easily be solved with a graphing calculator. Without a calculator, these problems can be solved simply by plugging numbers into the equation and plotting points.
- Harder problems involving linear equations may give you an equation that is NOT in $y = mx + b$ form, requiring some factoring to isolate your y. Harder questions may also give you an equation of a line and ask you to find the equation of a line that is perpendicular to, or a reflection of, that line. If you know the rules, great! If not, you can still use a graphing calculator or sketch the line to help find the answer.

That's about it for the SAT Math. If you need a brush-up on the math concepts tested, remember to check out *Cracking the SAT,* which teaches you all the concepts that are tested on the SAT. Now let's move on to the last portion of the SAT: the Reading section.

WHAT DO I NEED TO KNOW ABOUT THE READING SECTIONS?

There are two 25-minute and one 20-minute Reading sections on the SAT. Of the 67 reading questions, 19 are sentence completion questions and 48 are passage-based. It is useful for you to have a strong grasp of vocabulary to tackle both types of questions. The reading passages themselves range from 100 to 850 words and cover a wide variety of subject matter. However, you can always count on seeing at least one fiction passage, one science passage, and one humanities (history, literature, art, and so on) passage on each test.

What Does ETS Say About the Reading Sections?

ETS says that sentence completion questions measure your "knowledge of the meanings of words" and your "ability to understand how the different parts of a sentence fit logically together." Passage-based questions measure your vocabulary knowledge, your ability to understand "significant information stated directly in the passage," and your ability "to synthesize and analyze information as well as to evaluate the assumptions made and the techniques used by the author." In the end, you are always to choose the "best answer" from those provided.

What Does That Mean?

If the SAT is any indication, success in college is still heavily linked to your ability to master obscure words such as *lugubrious, insouciant,* and *quotidian.* (What, doesn't anybody get to use a dictionary in college?) This is an old idea that hasn't died out yet. Do what you can here. Use the context that surrounds vocabulary words to help you decipher the meanings of words, and move on.

When it comes to the passage-based questions, which constitute the majority of the reading questions, you need to be able to understand what the passages say, how and why the authors wrote what they did, and what the passages *don't* say. Many a wrong answer contains something that is sort of related to the content of the passage but that isn't actually mentioned anywhere. Maintaining a sharp focus on what *is* in the passage is crucial to doing well.

In essence, the "best" answers on passage-based questions offend no one and are supported by the passage in such a way that you can point to the *exact* lines in the passage where you got the information. If you can't prove an answer using the passage, you are probably falling for a trap answer.

What Makes a Reading Question Hard?

It depends on the question. Both sentence completion and certain passage-based questions are intended primarily to test your vocabulary knowledge. Easier vocabulary questions ask about more common words and give you more clues to the words' meanings, but harder vocabulary questions may provide little to no context to help you figure out the meaning of high-level words. For example, a hard sentence completion question may say, *A person who works loading and unloading ships is called a _____.* If you spend much time reading eighteenth-century literature rife with stories about *stevedores,* you'll ace this one. If not, there isn't much here to work with. Similarly, harder reading questions that ask about the meaning of a difficult word or phrase in context may be stacked to the rafters with even *more* hard vocabulary in the answers. Lastly, harder sentence completion questions may involve long, complicated sentences with subtle clues that make it more difficult for you to know what needs to go in a particular blank. Don't be afraid to skip hard questions!

Questions that focus primarily on the actual content of reading passages are made harder in a couple of different ways. Similar to how math questions are made harder by requiring lots of steps to solve, harder reading questions often involve multiple tasks. While an easier question may simply ask what the main idea of a passage is, a harder question may ask you to identify what most undermines an author's main point. To solve the harder question, you not only have to correctly identify the author's main point, but you also have to understand the argumentative structure the author uses so you can undermine or weaken it. Yikes!

The other way ETS makes passage-based questions hard is by asking about an author's use of language, particularly when the author uses figurative language. You use this kind of language every day, even if you don't realize it. If you have a really bad day at school and think to yourself, "This was the worst day ever!" you don't really mean that it was, statistically speaking, the worst day of your life. You just mean that you had a bad day. That's figurative language (or in this case, specifically hyperbole, or exaggeration).

Sometimes, figurative language is pretty easy to understand if you understand generally what is going on in the passage. But when ETS includes a reading passage from an older work of fiction, it may be hard to understand what in the world the characters are saying because the language is so unlike that which you are accustomed to hearing. But don't sweat the old school stuff—just read enough to figure out what the story is about and how the characters feel. This is often enough to tackle a number of questions successfully.

Anything Else?

Always remember that, no matter what anyone tells you, there is no such thing as a test that you can't study for. Your SAT score is in your hands. The more you practice taking the SAT, the more familiar you will be with the test on test day.

Even if you don't get your dream score, remember that the SAT is only a part of your application. Prepare. Take the test. Move on with your life. Good luck!

Part II
SAT Practice Tests

Chapter 4
Practice Test 1

Your Name (print) _____

Last   First   Middle

Date _____

IMPORTANT: The following codes should be copied onto your answer sheet exactly as shown.

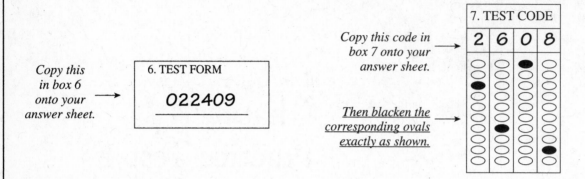

Copy this in box 6 onto your answer sheet. →

6. TEST FORM

022409
_____

Copy this code in box 7 onto your answer sheet. →

Then blacken the corresponding ovals exactly as shown. →

7. TEST CODE

2   6   0   8

General Directions

You will have three hours and 20 minutes to work on this objective test designed to familiarize you with all aspects of the SAT.

This test contains five 25-minute sections, two 20-minute sections, one 10-minute section, and one 25-minute essay. The supervisor will tell you when to begin and end each section. During the time allowed for each section, you may work only on that particular section. If you finish your work before time is called, you may check your work on that section, but you are not to work on any other section.

You will find specific directions for each type of question found in the test. **Be sure you understand the directions before attempting to answer any of the questions.**

YOU ARE TO INDICATE ALL YOUR ANSWERS ON THE SEPARATE ANSWER SHEET:

1. The test booklet may be used for scratchwork. However, no credit will be given for anything written in the test booklet.

2. Once you have decided on an answer to a question, darken the corresponding space on the answer sheet. Give only one answer to each question.

3. There are 40 numbered answer spaces for each section; be sure to use only those spaces that correspond to the test questions.

4. **Be sure each answer mark is dark and completely fills the answer space.** Do not make any stray marks on your answer sheet.

5. If you wish to change an answer, erase your first mark completely—an incomplete erasure may be considered an intended response—and blacken your new answer choice.

Your score on this test is based on the number of questions you answer correctly minus a fraction of the number of questions you answer incorrectly. Therefore, it is improbable that random or haphazard guessing will alter your score significantly. There are no deductions for incorrect answers on the student-produced response questions. However, if you are able to eliminate one or more of the answer choices on any question as wrong, it is generally to your advantage to guess at one of the remaining choices. Remember, however, not to spend too much time on any one question.

Diagnostic Test Form

Use a No. 2 pencil only. Be sure each mark is dark and completely fills the intended oval. Completely erase any errors or stray marks.

1 Your Name:

(Print)

Last   First   M.I.

Signature: Date ___/___/___

Home Address:

Number and Street   City   State   Zip Code

E-Mail: School: Class:

(Print)

2 YOUR NAME

Last Name (First 4 Letters)

				FIRST INIT	MID INIT
	–	–	–		
	'	'	'		
	◯	◯	◯		
Ⓐ	Ⓐ	Ⓐ	Ⓐ	Ⓐ	Ⓐ
Ⓑ	Ⓑ	Ⓑ	Ⓑ	Ⓑ	Ⓑ
Ⓒ	Ⓒ	Ⓒ	Ⓒ	Ⓒ	Ⓒ
Ⓓ	Ⓓ	Ⓓ	Ⓓ	Ⓓ	Ⓓ
Ⓔ	Ⓔ	Ⓔ	Ⓔ	Ⓔ	Ⓔ
Ⓕ	Ⓕ	Ⓕ	Ⓕ	Ⓕ	Ⓕ
Ⓖ	Ⓖ	Ⓖ	Ⓖ	Ⓖ	Ⓖ
Ⓗ	Ⓗ	Ⓗ	Ⓗ	Ⓗ	Ⓗ
Ⓘ	Ⓘ	Ⓘ	Ⓘ	Ⓘ	Ⓘ
Ⓙ	Ⓙ	Ⓙ	Ⓙ	Ⓙ	Ⓙ
Ⓚ	Ⓚ	Ⓚ	Ⓚ	Ⓚ	Ⓚ
Ⓛ	Ⓛ	Ⓛ	Ⓛ	Ⓛ	Ⓛ
Ⓜ	Ⓜ	Ⓜ	Ⓜ	Ⓜ	Ⓜ
Ⓝ	Ⓝ	Ⓝ	Ⓝ	Ⓝ	Ⓝ
Ⓞ	Ⓞ	Ⓞ	Ⓞ	Ⓞ	Ⓞ
Ⓟ	Ⓟ	Ⓟ	Ⓟ	Ⓟ	Ⓟ
Ⓠ	Ⓠ	Ⓠ	Ⓠ	Ⓠ	Ⓠ
Ⓡ	Ⓡ	Ⓡ	Ⓡ	Ⓡ	Ⓡ
Ⓢ	Ⓢ	Ⓢ	Ⓢ	Ⓢ	Ⓢ
Ⓣ	Ⓣ	Ⓣ	Ⓣ	Ⓣ	Ⓣ
Ⓤ	Ⓤ	Ⓤ	Ⓤ	Ⓤ	Ⓤ
Ⓥ	Ⓥ	Ⓥ	Ⓥ	Ⓥ	Ⓥ
Ⓦ	Ⓦ	Ⓦ	Ⓦ	Ⓦ	Ⓦ
Ⓧ	Ⓧ	Ⓧ	Ⓧ	Ⓧ	Ⓧ
Ⓨ	Ⓨ	Ⓨ	Ⓨ	Ⓨ	Ⓨ
Ⓩ	Ⓩ	Ⓩ	Ⓩ	Ⓩ	Ⓩ

3 PHONE NUMBER

⓪	⓪	⓪	⓪	⓪	⓪	⓪
①	①	①	①	①	①	①
②	②	②	②	②	②	②
③	③	③	③	③	③	③
④	④	④	④	④	④	④
⑤	⑤	⑤	⑤	⑤	⑤	⑤
⑥	⑥	⑥	⑥	⑥	⑥	⑥
⑦	⑦	⑦	⑦	⑦	⑦	⑦
⑧	⑧	⑧	⑧	⑧	⑧	⑧
⑨	⑨	⑨	⑨	⑨	⑨	⑨

4 DATE OF BIRTH

MONTH	DAY		YEAR	
◯ JAN				
◯ FEB				
◯ MAR	⓪	⓪		⓪
◯ APR	①	①		①
◯ MAY	②	②		②
◯ JUN	③	③		③
◯ JUL		④		④
◯ AUG		⑤	⑤	⑤
◯ SEP		⑥	⑥	⑥
◯ OCT		⑦	⑦	⑦
◯ NOV		⑧	⑧	⑧
◯ DEC		⑨	⑨	⑨

5 SEX

◯ MALE
◯ FEMALE

IMPORTANT: Fill in items 6 and 7 exactly as shown on the preceding page.

6 TEST FORM
(Copy from back of test book)

7 TEST CODE

⓪	⓪	⓪	⓪
①	①	①	①
②	②	②	②
③	③	③	③
④	④	④	④
⑤	⑤	⑤	⑤
⑥	⑥	⑥	⑥
⑦	⑦	⑦	⑦
⑧	⑧	⑧	⑧
⑨	⑨	⑨	⑨

8 OTHER

1 Ⓐ Ⓑ Ⓒ Ⓓ Ⓔ
2 Ⓐ Ⓑ Ⓒ Ⓓ Ⓔ
3 Ⓐ Ⓑ Ⓒ Ⓓ Ⓔ

PLEASE DO NOT WRITE IN THIS AREA

SERIAL #

THIS PAGE INTENTIONALLY LEFT BLANK

Begin your essay on this page. If you need more space, continue on the next page.

Continue on the next page, if necessary.

SECTION 2

1 Ⓐ Ⓑ Ⓒ Ⓓ Ⓔ
2 Ⓐ Ⓑ Ⓒ Ⓓ Ⓔ
3 Ⓐ Ⓑ Ⓒ Ⓓ Ⓔ
4 Ⓐ Ⓑ Ⓒ Ⓓ Ⓔ
5 Ⓐ Ⓑ Ⓒ Ⓓ Ⓔ
6 Ⓐ Ⓑ Ⓒ Ⓓ Ⓔ
7 Ⓐ Ⓑ Ⓒ Ⓓ Ⓔ
8 Ⓐ Ⓑ Ⓒ Ⓓ Ⓔ
9 Ⓐ Ⓑ Ⓒ Ⓓ Ⓔ
10 Ⓐ Ⓑ Ⓒ Ⓓ Ⓔ

11 Ⓐ Ⓑ Ⓒ Ⓓ Ⓔ
12 Ⓐ Ⓑ Ⓒ Ⓓ Ⓔ
13 Ⓐ Ⓑ Ⓒ Ⓓ Ⓔ
14 Ⓐ Ⓑ Ⓒ Ⓓ Ⓔ
15 Ⓐ Ⓑ Ⓒ Ⓓ Ⓔ
16 Ⓐ Ⓑ Ⓒ Ⓓ Ⓔ
17 Ⓐ Ⓑ Ⓒ Ⓓ Ⓔ
18 Ⓐ Ⓑ Ⓒ Ⓓ Ⓔ
19 Ⓐ Ⓑ Ⓒ Ⓓ Ⓔ
20 Ⓐ Ⓑ Ⓒ Ⓓ Ⓔ

21 Ⓐ Ⓑ Ⓒ Ⓓ Ⓔ
22 Ⓐ Ⓑ Ⓒ Ⓓ Ⓔ
23 Ⓐ Ⓑ Ⓒ Ⓓ Ⓔ
24 Ⓐ Ⓑ Ⓒ Ⓓ Ⓔ
25 Ⓐ Ⓑ Ⓒ Ⓓ Ⓔ
26 Ⓐ Ⓑ Ⓒ Ⓓ Ⓔ
27 Ⓐ Ⓑ Ⓒ Ⓓ Ⓔ
28 Ⓐ Ⓑ Ⓒ Ⓓ Ⓔ
29 Ⓐ Ⓑ Ⓒ Ⓓ Ⓔ
30 Ⓐ Ⓑ Ⓒ Ⓓ Ⓔ

31 Ⓐ Ⓑ Ⓒ Ⓓ Ⓔ
32 Ⓐ Ⓑ Ⓒ Ⓓ Ⓔ
33 Ⓐ Ⓑ Ⓒ Ⓓ Ⓔ
34 Ⓐ Ⓑ Ⓒ Ⓓ Ⓔ
35 Ⓐ Ⓑ Ⓒ Ⓓ Ⓔ
36 Ⓐ Ⓑ Ⓒ Ⓓ Ⓔ
37 Ⓐ Ⓑ Ⓒ Ⓓ Ⓔ
38 Ⓐ Ⓑ Ⓒ Ⓓ Ⓔ
39 Ⓐ Ⓑ Ⓒ Ⓓ Ⓔ
40 Ⓐ Ⓑ Ⓒ Ⓓ Ⓔ

SECTION 3

1 Ⓐ Ⓑ Ⓒ Ⓓ Ⓔ
2 Ⓐ Ⓑ Ⓒ Ⓓ Ⓔ
3 Ⓐ Ⓑ Ⓒ Ⓓ Ⓔ
4 Ⓐ Ⓑ Ⓒ Ⓓ Ⓔ
5 Ⓐ Ⓑ Ⓒ Ⓓ Ⓔ
6 Ⓐ Ⓑ Ⓒ Ⓓ Ⓔ
7 Ⓐ Ⓑ Ⓒ Ⓓ Ⓔ
8 Ⓐ Ⓑ Ⓒ Ⓓ Ⓔ
9 Ⓐ Ⓑ Ⓒ Ⓓ Ⓔ
10 Ⓐ Ⓑ Ⓒ Ⓓ Ⓔ

11 Ⓐ Ⓑ Ⓒ Ⓓ Ⓔ
12 Ⓐ Ⓑ Ⓒ Ⓓ Ⓔ
13 Ⓐ Ⓑ Ⓒ Ⓓ Ⓔ
14 Ⓐ Ⓑ Ⓒ Ⓓ Ⓔ
15 Ⓐ Ⓑ Ⓒ Ⓓ Ⓔ
16 Ⓐ Ⓑ Ⓒ Ⓓ Ⓔ
17 Ⓐ Ⓑ Ⓒ Ⓓ Ⓔ
18 Ⓐ Ⓑ Ⓒ Ⓓ Ⓔ
19 Ⓐ Ⓑ Ⓒ Ⓓ Ⓔ
20 Ⓐ Ⓑ Ⓒ Ⓓ Ⓔ

21 Ⓐ Ⓑ Ⓒ Ⓓ Ⓔ
22 Ⓐ Ⓑ Ⓒ Ⓓ Ⓔ
23 Ⓐ Ⓑ Ⓒ Ⓓ Ⓔ
24 Ⓐ Ⓑ Ⓒ Ⓓ Ⓔ
25 Ⓐ Ⓑ Ⓒ Ⓓ Ⓔ
26 Ⓐ Ⓑ Ⓒ Ⓓ Ⓔ
27 Ⓐ Ⓑ Ⓒ Ⓓ Ⓔ
28 Ⓐ Ⓑ Ⓒ Ⓓ Ⓔ
29 Ⓐ Ⓑ Ⓒ Ⓓ Ⓔ
30 Ⓐ Ⓑ Ⓒ Ⓓ Ⓔ

31 Ⓐ Ⓑ Ⓒ Ⓓ Ⓔ
32 Ⓐ Ⓑ Ⓒ Ⓓ Ⓔ
33 Ⓐ Ⓑ Ⓒ Ⓓ Ⓔ
34 Ⓐ Ⓑ Ⓒ Ⓓ Ⓔ
35 Ⓐ Ⓑ Ⓒ Ⓓ Ⓔ
36 Ⓐ Ⓑ Ⓒ Ⓓ Ⓔ
37 Ⓐ Ⓑ Ⓒ Ⓓ Ⓔ
38 Ⓐ Ⓑ Ⓒ Ⓓ Ⓔ
39 Ⓐ Ⓑ Ⓒ Ⓓ Ⓔ
40 Ⓐ Ⓑ Ⓒ Ⓓ Ⓔ

CAUTION Grid answers in the section below for SECTION 2 or SECTION 3 only if directed to do so in your test book.

Student-Produced Responses ONLY ANSWERS THAT ARE GRIDDED WILL BE SCORED. YOU WILL NOT RECEIVE CREDIT FOR ANYTHING WRITTEN IN THE BOXES.

Quality Assurance Mark ●

9, 10, 11, 12, 13, 14, 15, 16, 17, 18 — grids with digits 0–9 in four columns each.

SECTION 4

1 Ⓐ Ⓑ Ⓒ Ⓓ Ⓔ
2 Ⓐ Ⓑ Ⓒ Ⓓ Ⓔ
3 Ⓐ Ⓑ Ⓒ Ⓓ Ⓔ
4 Ⓐ Ⓑ Ⓒ Ⓓ Ⓔ
5 Ⓐ Ⓑ Ⓒ Ⓓ Ⓔ
6 Ⓐ Ⓑ Ⓒ Ⓓ Ⓔ
7 Ⓐ Ⓑ Ⓒ Ⓓ Ⓔ
8 Ⓐ Ⓑ Ⓒ Ⓓ Ⓔ
9 Ⓐ Ⓑ Ⓒ Ⓓ Ⓔ
10 Ⓐ Ⓑ Ⓒ Ⓓ Ⓔ

11 Ⓐ Ⓑ Ⓒ Ⓓ Ⓔ
12 Ⓐ Ⓑ Ⓒ Ⓓ Ⓔ
13 Ⓐ Ⓑ Ⓒ Ⓓ Ⓔ
14 Ⓐ Ⓑ Ⓒ Ⓓ Ⓔ
15 Ⓐ Ⓑ Ⓒ Ⓓ Ⓔ
16 Ⓐ Ⓑ Ⓒ Ⓓ Ⓔ
17 Ⓐ Ⓑ Ⓒ Ⓓ Ⓔ
18 Ⓐ Ⓑ Ⓒ Ⓓ Ⓔ
19 Ⓐ Ⓑ Ⓒ Ⓓ Ⓔ
20 Ⓐ Ⓑ Ⓒ Ⓓ Ⓔ

21 Ⓐ Ⓑ Ⓒ Ⓓ Ⓔ
22 Ⓐ Ⓑ Ⓒ Ⓓ Ⓔ
23 Ⓐ Ⓑ Ⓒ Ⓓ Ⓔ
24 Ⓐ Ⓑ Ⓒ Ⓓ Ⓔ
25 Ⓐ Ⓑ Ⓒ Ⓓ Ⓔ
26 Ⓐ Ⓑ Ⓒ Ⓓ Ⓔ
27 Ⓐ Ⓑ Ⓒ Ⓓ Ⓔ
28 Ⓐ Ⓑ Ⓒ Ⓓ Ⓔ
29 Ⓐ Ⓑ Ⓒ Ⓓ Ⓔ
30 Ⓐ Ⓑ Ⓒ Ⓓ Ⓔ

31 Ⓐ Ⓑ Ⓒ Ⓓ Ⓔ
32 Ⓐ Ⓑ Ⓒ Ⓓ Ⓔ
33 Ⓐ Ⓑ Ⓒ Ⓓ Ⓔ
34 Ⓐ Ⓑ Ⓒ Ⓓ Ⓔ
35 Ⓐ Ⓑ Ⓒ Ⓓ Ⓔ
36 Ⓐ Ⓑ Ⓒ Ⓓ Ⓔ
37 Ⓐ Ⓑ Ⓒ Ⓓ Ⓔ
38 Ⓐ Ⓑ Ⓒ Ⓓ Ⓔ
39 Ⓐ Ⓑ Ⓒ Ⓓ Ⓔ
40 Ⓐ Ⓑ Ⓒ Ⓓ Ⓔ

SECTION 5

1 Ⓐ Ⓑ Ⓒ Ⓓ Ⓔ
2 Ⓐ Ⓑ Ⓒ Ⓓ Ⓔ
3 Ⓐ Ⓑ Ⓒ Ⓓ Ⓔ
4 Ⓐ Ⓑ Ⓒ Ⓓ Ⓔ
5 Ⓐ Ⓑ Ⓒ Ⓓ Ⓔ
6 Ⓐ Ⓑ Ⓒ Ⓓ Ⓔ
7 Ⓐ Ⓑ Ⓒ Ⓓ Ⓔ
8 Ⓐ Ⓑ Ⓒ Ⓓ Ⓔ
9 Ⓐ Ⓑ Ⓒ Ⓓ Ⓔ
10 Ⓐ Ⓑ Ⓒ Ⓓ Ⓔ

11 Ⓐ Ⓑ Ⓒ Ⓓ Ⓔ
12 Ⓐ Ⓑ Ⓒ Ⓓ Ⓔ
13 Ⓐ Ⓑ Ⓒ Ⓓ Ⓔ
14 Ⓐ Ⓑ Ⓒ Ⓓ Ⓔ
15 Ⓐ Ⓑ Ⓒ Ⓓ Ⓔ
16 Ⓐ Ⓑ Ⓒ Ⓓ Ⓔ
17 Ⓐ Ⓑ Ⓒ Ⓓ Ⓔ
18 Ⓐ Ⓑ Ⓒ Ⓓ Ⓔ
19 Ⓐ Ⓑ Ⓒ Ⓓ Ⓔ
20 Ⓐ Ⓑ Ⓒ Ⓓ Ⓔ

21 Ⓐ Ⓑ Ⓒ Ⓓ Ⓔ
22 Ⓐ Ⓑ Ⓒ Ⓓ Ⓔ
23 Ⓐ Ⓑ Ⓒ Ⓓ Ⓔ
24 Ⓐ Ⓑ Ⓒ Ⓓ Ⓔ
25 Ⓐ Ⓑ Ⓒ Ⓓ Ⓔ
26 Ⓐ Ⓑ Ⓒ Ⓓ Ⓔ
27 Ⓐ Ⓑ Ⓒ Ⓓ Ⓔ
28 Ⓐ Ⓑ Ⓒ Ⓓ Ⓔ
29 Ⓐ Ⓑ Ⓒ Ⓓ Ⓔ
30 Ⓐ Ⓑ Ⓒ Ⓓ Ⓔ

31 Ⓐ Ⓑ Ⓒ Ⓓ Ⓔ
32 Ⓐ Ⓑ Ⓒ Ⓓ Ⓔ
33 Ⓐ Ⓑ Ⓒ Ⓓ Ⓔ
34 Ⓐ Ⓑ Ⓒ Ⓓ Ⓔ
35 Ⓐ Ⓑ Ⓒ Ⓓ Ⓔ
36 Ⓐ Ⓑ Ⓒ Ⓓ Ⓔ
37 Ⓐ Ⓑ Ⓒ Ⓓ Ⓔ
38 Ⓐ Ⓑ Ⓒ Ⓓ Ⓔ
39 Ⓐ Ⓑ Ⓒ Ⓓ Ⓔ
40 Ⓐ Ⓑ Ⓒ Ⓓ Ⓔ

CAUTION   Grid answers in the section below for SECTION 4 or SECTION 5 only if directed to do so in your test book.

Student-Produced Responses   ONLY ANSWERS THAT ARE GRIDDED WILL BE SCORED. YOU WILL NOT RECEIVE CREDIT FOR ANYTHING WRITTEN IN THE BOXES.

Quality Assurance Mark ●

9, 10, 11, 12, 13, 14, 15, 16, 17, 18 — Student-produced response grids (columns 0–9 with fraction and decimal point bubbles)

SECTION 6

1 Ⓐ Ⓑ Ⓒ Ⓓ Ⓔ
2 Ⓐ Ⓑ Ⓒ Ⓓ Ⓔ
3 Ⓐ Ⓑ Ⓒ Ⓓ Ⓔ
4 Ⓐ Ⓑ Ⓒ Ⓓ Ⓔ
5 Ⓐ Ⓑ Ⓒ Ⓓ Ⓔ
6 Ⓐ Ⓑ Ⓒ Ⓓ Ⓔ
7 Ⓐ Ⓑ Ⓒ Ⓓ Ⓔ
8 Ⓐ Ⓑ Ⓒ Ⓓ Ⓔ
9 Ⓐ Ⓑ Ⓒ Ⓓ Ⓔ
10 Ⓐ Ⓑ Ⓒ Ⓓ Ⓔ

11 Ⓐ Ⓑ Ⓒ Ⓓ Ⓔ
12 Ⓐ Ⓑ Ⓒ Ⓓ Ⓔ
13 Ⓐ Ⓑ Ⓒ Ⓓ Ⓔ
14 Ⓐ Ⓑ Ⓒ Ⓓ Ⓔ
15 Ⓐ Ⓑ Ⓒ Ⓓ Ⓔ
16 Ⓐ Ⓑ Ⓒ Ⓓ Ⓔ
17 Ⓐ Ⓑ Ⓒ Ⓓ Ⓔ
18 Ⓐ Ⓑ Ⓒ Ⓓ Ⓔ
19 Ⓐ Ⓑ Ⓒ Ⓓ Ⓔ
20 Ⓐ Ⓑ Ⓒ Ⓓ Ⓔ

21 Ⓐ Ⓑ Ⓒ Ⓓ Ⓔ
22 Ⓐ Ⓑ Ⓒ Ⓓ Ⓔ
23 Ⓐ Ⓑ Ⓒ Ⓓ Ⓔ
24 Ⓐ Ⓑ Ⓒ Ⓓ Ⓔ
25 Ⓐ Ⓑ Ⓒ Ⓓ Ⓔ
26 Ⓐ Ⓑ Ⓒ Ⓓ Ⓔ
27 Ⓐ Ⓑ Ⓒ Ⓓ Ⓔ
28 Ⓐ Ⓑ Ⓒ Ⓓ Ⓔ
29 Ⓐ Ⓑ Ⓒ Ⓓ Ⓔ
30 Ⓐ Ⓑ Ⓒ Ⓓ Ⓔ

31 Ⓐ Ⓑ Ⓒ Ⓓ Ⓔ
32 Ⓐ Ⓑ Ⓒ Ⓓ Ⓔ
33 Ⓐ Ⓑ Ⓒ Ⓓ Ⓔ
34 Ⓐ Ⓑ Ⓒ Ⓓ Ⓔ
35 Ⓐ Ⓑ Ⓒ Ⓓ Ⓔ
36 Ⓐ Ⓑ Ⓒ Ⓓ Ⓔ
37 Ⓐ Ⓑ Ⓒ Ⓓ Ⓔ
38 Ⓐ Ⓑ Ⓒ Ⓓ Ⓔ
39 Ⓐ Ⓑ Ⓒ Ⓓ Ⓔ
40 Ⓐ Ⓑ Ⓒ Ⓓ Ⓔ

SECTION 7

1 Ⓐ Ⓑ Ⓒ Ⓓ Ⓔ
2 Ⓐ Ⓑ Ⓒ Ⓓ Ⓔ
3 Ⓐ Ⓑ Ⓒ Ⓓ Ⓔ
4 Ⓐ Ⓑ Ⓒ Ⓓ Ⓔ
5 Ⓐ Ⓑ Ⓒ Ⓓ Ⓔ
6 Ⓐ Ⓑ Ⓒ Ⓓ Ⓔ
7 Ⓐ Ⓑ Ⓒ Ⓓ Ⓔ
8 Ⓐ Ⓑ Ⓒ Ⓓ Ⓔ
9 Ⓐ Ⓑ Ⓒ Ⓓ Ⓔ
10 Ⓐ Ⓑ Ⓒ Ⓓ Ⓔ

11 Ⓐ Ⓑ Ⓒ Ⓓ Ⓔ
12 Ⓐ Ⓑ Ⓒ Ⓓ Ⓔ
13 Ⓐ Ⓑ Ⓒ Ⓓ Ⓔ
14 Ⓐ Ⓑ Ⓒ Ⓓ Ⓔ
15 Ⓐ Ⓑ Ⓒ Ⓓ Ⓔ
16 Ⓐ Ⓑ Ⓒ Ⓓ Ⓔ
17 Ⓐ Ⓑ Ⓒ Ⓓ Ⓔ
18 Ⓐ Ⓑ Ⓒ Ⓓ Ⓔ
19 Ⓐ Ⓑ Ⓒ Ⓓ Ⓔ
20 Ⓐ Ⓑ Ⓒ Ⓓ Ⓔ

21 Ⓐ Ⓑ Ⓒ Ⓓ Ⓔ
22 Ⓐ Ⓑ Ⓒ Ⓓ Ⓔ
23 Ⓐ Ⓑ Ⓒ Ⓓ Ⓔ
24 Ⓐ Ⓑ Ⓒ Ⓓ Ⓔ
25 Ⓐ Ⓑ Ⓒ Ⓓ Ⓔ
26 Ⓐ Ⓑ Ⓒ Ⓓ Ⓔ
27 Ⓐ Ⓑ Ⓒ Ⓓ Ⓔ
28 Ⓐ Ⓑ Ⓒ Ⓓ Ⓔ
29 Ⓐ Ⓑ Ⓒ Ⓓ Ⓔ
30 Ⓐ Ⓑ Ⓒ Ⓓ Ⓔ

31 Ⓐ Ⓑ Ⓒ Ⓓ Ⓔ
32 Ⓐ Ⓑ Ⓒ Ⓓ Ⓔ
33 Ⓐ Ⓑ Ⓒ Ⓓ Ⓔ
34 Ⓐ Ⓑ Ⓒ Ⓓ Ⓔ
35 Ⓐ Ⓑ Ⓒ Ⓓ Ⓔ
36 Ⓐ Ⓑ Ⓒ Ⓓ Ⓔ
37 Ⓐ Ⓑ Ⓒ Ⓓ Ⓔ
38 Ⓐ Ⓑ Ⓒ Ⓓ Ⓔ
39 Ⓐ Ⓑ Ⓒ Ⓓ Ⓔ
40 Ⓐ Ⓑ Ⓒ Ⓓ Ⓔ

CAUTION Grid answers in the section below for SECTION 6 or SECTION 7 only if directed to do so in your test book.

Student-Produced Responses

ONLY ANSWERS THAT ARE GRIDDED WILL BE SCORED. YOU WILL NOT RECEIVE CREDIT FOR ANYTHING WRITTEN IN THE BOXES.

Quality Assurance Mark ●

9 | 10 | 11 | 12 | 13

(grid boxes with digits 0–9 for each question)

14 | 15 | 16 | 17 | 18

(grid boxes with digits 0–9 for each question)

SECTION 8

1 Ⓐ Ⓑ Ⓒ Ⓓ Ⓔ	11 Ⓐ Ⓑ Ⓒ Ⓓ Ⓔ	21 Ⓐ Ⓑ Ⓒ Ⓓ Ⓔ	31 Ⓐ Ⓑ Ⓒ Ⓓ Ⓔ
2 Ⓐ Ⓑ Ⓒ Ⓓ Ⓔ	12 Ⓐ Ⓑ Ⓒ Ⓓ Ⓔ	22 Ⓐ Ⓑ Ⓒ Ⓓ Ⓔ	32 Ⓐ Ⓑ Ⓒ Ⓓ Ⓔ
3 Ⓐ Ⓑ Ⓒ Ⓓ Ⓔ	13 Ⓐ Ⓑ Ⓒ Ⓓ Ⓔ	23 Ⓐ Ⓑ Ⓒ Ⓓ Ⓔ	33 Ⓐ Ⓑ Ⓒ Ⓓ Ⓔ
4 Ⓐ Ⓑ Ⓒ Ⓓ Ⓔ	14 Ⓐ Ⓑ Ⓒ Ⓓ Ⓔ	24 Ⓐ Ⓑ Ⓒ Ⓓ Ⓔ	34 Ⓐ Ⓑ Ⓒ Ⓓ Ⓔ
5 Ⓐ Ⓑ Ⓒ Ⓓ Ⓔ	15 Ⓐ Ⓑ Ⓒ Ⓓ Ⓔ	25 Ⓐ Ⓑ Ⓒ Ⓓ Ⓔ	35 Ⓐ Ⓑ Ⓒ Ⓓ Ⓔ
6 Ⓐ Ⓑ Ⓒ Ⓓ Ⓔ	16 Ⓐ Ⓑ Ⓒ Ⓓ Ⓔ	26 Ⓐ Ⓑ Ⓒ Ⓓ Ⓔ	36 Ⓐ Ⓑ Ⓒ Ⓓ Ⓔ
7 Ⓐ Ⓑ Ⓒ Ⓓ Ⓔ	17 Ⓐ Ⓑ Ⓒ Ⓓ Ⓔ	27 Ⓐ Ⓑ Ⓒ Ⓓ Ⓔ	37 Ⓐ Ⓑ Ⓒ Ⓓ Ⓔ
8 Ⓐ Ⓑ Ⓒ Ⓓ Ⓔ	18 Ⓐ Ⓑ Ⓒ Ⓓ Ⓔ	28 Ⓐ Ⓑ Ⓒ Ⓓ Ⓔ	38 Ⓐ Ⓑ Ⓒ Ⓓ Ⓔ
9 Ⓐ Ⓑ Ⓒ Ⓓ Ⓔ	19 Ⓐ Ⓑ Ⓒ Ⓓ Ⓔ	29 Ⓐ Ⓑ Ⓒ Ⓓ Ⓔ	39 Ⓐ Ⓑ Ⓒ Ⓓ Ⓔ
10 Ⓐ Ⓑ Ⓒ Ⓓ Ⓔ	20 Ⓐ Ⓑ Ⓒ Ⓓ Ⓔ	30 Ⓐ Ⓑ Ⓒ Ⓓ Ⓔ	40 Ⓐ Ⓑ Ⓒ Ⓓ Ⓔ

SECTION 9

1 Ⓐ Ⓑ Ⓒ Ⓓ Ⓔ	11 Ⓐ Ⓑ Ⓒ Ⓓ Ⓔ	21 Ⓐ Ⓑ Ⓒ Ⓓ Ⓔ	31 Ⓐ Ⓑ Ⓒ Ⓓ Ⓔ
2 Ⓐ Ⓑ Ⓒ Ⓓ Ⓔ	12 Ⓐ Ⓑ Ⓒ Ⓓ Ⓔ	22 Ⓐ Ⓑ Ⓒ Ⓓ Ⓔ	32 Ⓐ Ⓑ Ⓒ Ⓓ Ⓔ
3 Ⓐ Ⓑ Ⓒ Ⓓ Ⓔ	13 Ⓐ Ⓑ Ⓒ Ⓓ Ⓔ	23 Ⓐ Ⓑ Ⓒ Ⓓ Ⓔ	33 Ⓐ Ⓑ Ⓒ Ⓓ Ⓔ
4 Ⓐ Ⓑ Ⓒ Ⓓ Ⓔ	14 Ⓐ Ⓑ Ⓒ Ⓓ Ⓔ	24 Ⓐ Ⓑ Ⓒ Ⓓ Ⓔ	34 Ⓐ Ⓑ Ⓒ Ⓓ Ⓔ
5 Ⓐ Ⓑ Ⓒ Ⓓ Ⓔ	15 Ⓐ Ⓑ Ⓒ Ⓓ Ⓔ	25 Ⓐ Ⓑ Ⓒ Ⓓ Ⓔ	35 Ⓐ Ⓑ Ⓒ Ⓓ Ⓔ
6 Ⓐ Ⓑ Ⓒ Ⓓ Ⓔ	16 Ⓐ Ⓑ Ⓒ Ⓓ Ⓔ	26 Ⓐ Ⓑ Ⓒ Ⓓ Ⓔ	36 Ⓐ Ⓑ Ⓒ Ⓓ Ⓔ
7 Ⓐ Ⓑ Ⓒ Ⓓ Ⓔ	17 Ⓐ Ⓑ Ⓒ Ⓓ Ⓔ	27 Ⓐ Ⓑ Ⓒ Ⓓ Ⓔ	37 Ⓐ Ⓑ Ⓒ Ⓓ Ⓔ
8 Ⓐ Ⓑ Ⓒ Ⓓ Ⓔ	18 Ⓐ Ⓑ Ⓒ Ⓓ Ⓔ	28 Ⓐ Ⓑ Ⓒ Ⓓ Ⓔ	38 Ⓐ Ⓑ Ⓒ Ⓓ Ⓔ
9 Ⓐ Ⓑ Ⓒ Ⓓ Ⓔ	19 Ⓐ Ⓑ Ⓒ Ⓓ Ⓔ	29 Ⓐ Ⓑ Ⓒ Ⓓ Ⓔ	39 Ⓐ Ⓑ Ⓒ Ⓓ Ⓔ
10 Ⓐ Ⓑ Ⓒ Ⓓ Ⓔ	20 Ⓐ Ⓑ Ⓒ Ⓓ Ⓔ	30 Ⓐ Ⓑ Ⓒ Ⓓ Ⓔ	40 Ⓐ Ⓑ Ⓒ Ⓓ Ⓔ

SECTION 10

1 Ⓐ Ⓑ Ⓒ Ⓓ Ⓔ	11 Ⓐ Ⓑ Ⓒ Ⓓ Ⓔ	21 Ⓐ Ⓑ Ⓒ Ⓓ Ⓔ	31 Ⓐ Ⓑ Ⓒ Ⓓ Ⓔ
2 Ⓐ Ⓑ Ⓒ Ⓓ Ⓔ	12 Ⓐ Ⓑ Ⓒ Ⓓ Ⓔ	22 Ⓐ Ⓑ Ⓒ Ⓓ Ⓔ	32 Ⓐ Ⓑ Ⓒ Ⓓ Ⓔ
3 Ⓐ Ⓑ Ⓒ Ⓓ Ⓔ	13 Ⓐ Ⓑ Ⓒ Ⓓ Ⓔ	23 Ⓐ Ⓑ Ⓒ Ⓓ Ⓔ	33 Ⓐ Ⓑ Ⓒ Ⓓ Ⓔ
4 Ⓐ Ⓑ Ⓒ Ⓓ Ⓔ	14 Ⓐ Ⓑ Ⓒ Ⓓ Ⓔ	24 Ⓐ Ⓑ Ⓒ Ⓓ Ⓔ	34 Ⓐ Ⓑ Ⓒ Ⓓ Ⓔ
5 Ⓐ Ⓑ Ⓒ Ⓓ Ⓔ	15 Ⓐ Ⓑ Ⓒ Ⓓ Ⓔ	25 Ⓐ Ⓑ Ⓒ Ⓓ Ⓔ	35 Ⓐ Ⓑ Ⓒ Ⓓ Ⓔ
6 Ⓐ Ⓑ Ⓒ Ⓓ Ⓔ	16 Ⓐ Ⓑ Ⓒ Ⓓ Ⓔ	26 Ⓐ Ⓑ Ⓒ Ⓓ Ⓔ	36 Ⓐ Ⓑ Ⓒ Ⓓ Ⓔ
7 Ⓐ Ⓑ Ⓒ Ⓓ Ⓔ	17 Ⓐ Ⓑ Ⓒ Ⓓ Ⓔ	27 Ⓐ Ⓑ Ⓒ Ⓓ Ⓔ	37 Ⓐ Ⓑ Ⓒ Ⓓ Ⓔ
8 Ⓐ Ⓑ Ⓒ Ⓓ Ⓔ	18 Ⓐ Ⓑ Ⓒ Ⓓ Ⓔ	28 Ⓐ Ⓑ Ⓒ Ⓓ Ⓔ	38 Ⓐ Ⓑ Ⓒ Ⓓ Ⓔ
9 Ⓐ Ⓑ Ⓒ Ⓓ Ⓔ	19 Ⓐ Ⓑ Ⓒ Ⓓ Ⓔ	29 Ⓐ Ⓑ Ⓒ Ⓓ Ⓔ	39 Ⓐ Ⓑ Ⓒ Ⓓ Ⓔ
10 Ⓐ Ⓑ Ⓒ Ⓓ Ⓔ	20 Ⓐ Ⓑ Ⓒ Ⓓ Ⓔ	30 Ⓐ Ⓑ Ⓒ Ⓓ Ⓔ	40 Ⓐ Ⓑ Ⓒ Ⓓ Ⓔ

> **Turn to Section 1 of your answer sheet to write your essay.**

The essay gives you an opportunity to show how effectively you can develop and express ideas. You should, therefore, take care to develop your point of view, present your ideas logically and clearly, and use language precisely.

Your essay must be written on the lines provided on your answer sheet—you will receive no other paper on which to write. You will have enough space if you write on every line, avoid wide margins, and keep your handwriting to a reasonable size. Remember that people who are not familiar with your handwriting will read what you write. Try to write or print so that what you are writing is legible to those readers.

You have twenty-five minutes to write an essay on the topic assigned below. DO NOT WRITE ON ANOTHER TOPIC. AN OFF-TOPIC ESSAY WILL RECEIVE A SCORE OF ZERO.

Think carefully about the issue presented in the following excerpt and the assignment below.

> Society may limit our actions, but it cannot limit our thoughts. Even if society disapproves of our opinions, we are ultimately free to decide whatever we want. Those decisions may, of course, have consequences, but they are still ours to make.

Assignment: Do society's rules limit our decisions such that our choices are not freely made? Plan and write an essay in which you develop your point of view on this issue. Support your position with reasoning and examples taken from your reading, studies, experience, or observations.

DO NOT WRITE YOUR ESSAY IN YOUR TEST BOOK. You will receive credit only for what you write on your answer sheet.

BEGIN WRITING YOUR ESSAY IN SECTION 1 OF THE ANSWER SHEET.

STOP
If you finish before time is called, you may check your work on this section only.
Do not turn to any other section in the test.

SECTION 2
Time — 25 minutes
20 Questions

Turn to Section 2 of your answer sheet to answer the questions in this section.

Directions: For this section, solve each problem and decide which is the best of the choices given. Fill in the corresponding circle on the answer sheet. You may use any available space for scratchwork.

Notes

1. The use of a calculator is permitted.

2. All numbers used are real numbers.

3. Figures that accompany problems in this test are intended to provide information useful in solving the problems. They are drawn as accurately as possible EXCEPT when it is stated in a specific problem that the figure is not drawn to scale. All figures lie in a plane unless otherwise indicated.

4. Unless otherwise specified, the domain of any function f is assumed to be the set of all real numbers x for which $f(x)$ is a real number.

Reference Information

     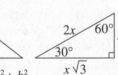

$A = \pi r^2$ $A = lw$ $A = \frac{1}{2}bh$ $V = lwh$ $V = \pi r^2 h$ $c^2 = a^2 + b^2$

$C = 2\pi r$

Special Right Triangles

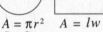

The number of degrees of arc in a circle is 360.

The sum of the measures in degrees of the angles of a triangle is 180.

---

1. Leah is loading supplies from her garage into her truck. If she loads 10 identical water containers that each weigh 20 pounds and 8 identical sacks of food that each weigh 10 pounds, then what is the total weight of supplies that she is loading onto her truck?

(A)   30
(B)   230
(C)   280
(D)   320
(E)   380

2. The midpoint of segment $\overline{PQ}$ is F, and the length of $\overline{FQ}$ is $3m$. What is the length of $\overline{PQ}$ in terms of m ?

(A) $\frac{3}{2}m$

(B) $3m$

(C) $4m$

(D) $\frac{9}{2}m$

(E) $6m$

GO ON TO THE NEXT PAGE ➤

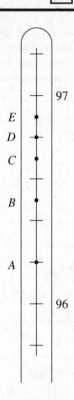

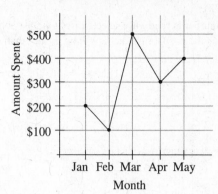

3. In the thermometer above, all the tick marks are equally spaced. Which lettered point is closest to 96.7 ?

(A) *A*
(B) *B*
(C) *C*
(D) *D*
(E) *E*

4. The line graph above shows the amount of money spent on office supplies by Jacksonville Tax Service during the first five months of the year. According to the graph, the amount it spent in May was how many times the amount it spent in January?

(A) 1
(B) 2
(C) 3
(D) 4
(E) 5

5. The cost for a bag of polished stones at a craft fair is $10 for a hand-stitched bag and 50 cents for each polished stone. Which of the following functions represents the total cost, in dollars, for *p* polished stones divided into two bags?

(A) $f(p) = 20 + 2p$

(B) $f(p) = 20 + \dfrac{1}{2}p$

(C) $f(p) = 10p + 2$

(D) $f(p) = 15p$

(E) $f(p) = 10p$

GO ON TO THE NEXT PAGE

−4, −3, −2, −1, 0, 1, 2, 3

6. If a number is randomly selected from the list above, what is the probability that it will be greater than −2 ?

(A) $\dfrac{1}{4}$

(B) $\dfrac{3}{8}$

(C) $\dfrac{1}{2}$

(D) $\dfrac{5}{8}$

(E) $\dfrac{3}{4}$

7. Three times a number is the same as that number subtracted from 12. What is the number?

(A) −6
(B) −2
(C) 2
(D) 3
(E) 4

8. One-half of the water in a pond evaporates each week. There are 2,400 gallons of water in the pond at the end of the third week. In gallons, how much less water is in the pond at the end of the seventh week than at the end of the third week?

(A) 2,250
(B) 1,975
(C) 1,800
(D) 950
(E) 150

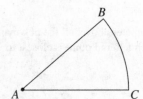

9. In the figure above, the length of arc $\overset{\frown}{BC}$ is $\dfrac{1}{9}$ the circumference of a circle with center A. If AB has length 6, what is the area of the sector of the circle shown above?

(A) $\dfrac{\pi}{9}$

(B) $\dfrac{\pi}{4}$

(C) 2π

(D) 4π

(E) 9π

GO ON TO THE NEXT PAGE

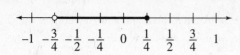

$$-1 \quad -\tfrac{3}{4} \quad -\tfrac{1}{2} \quad -\tfrac{1}{4} \quad 0 \quad \tfrac{1}{4} \quad \tfrac{1}{2} \quad \tfrac{3}{4} \quad 1$$

10. Which of the following equations represents the inequality shown on the number line above?

(A) $-2 \le 4t + 1 \le 2$
(B) $-2 \le 4t + 1 < 2$
(C) $-2 < 4t + 1 \le 2$
(D) $-2 < 4t + 1 < 2$
(E) $-2 \ge 4t + 1 > 2$

11. For any point on line ℓ, the product of the x-coordinate and the y-coordinate is less than or equal to zero. Which of the following could be the equation of line ℓ ?

(A) $y = -2$
(B) $x = -2$
(C) $y = -2x$
(D) $y = -2x - 2$
(E) $y = 2x - 2$

12. If $100 - 2xy - y^2 = x^2$, which of the following must be true?

(A) $x - y = 10$
(B) $x^2 + y^2 = 100$
(C) $(x + y)(x - y) = 100$
(D) $(x + y)^2 = 100$
(E) $(x - y)^2 = 100$

If p is an integer between 1,000 and 1,030, and if the sum of the digits of p is odd, then p must be odd.

13. Which of the following is one possible value of p that proves the above statement FALSE?

(A) 1,017
(B) 1,018
(C) 1,019
(D) 1,020
(E) 1,021

GO ON TO THE NEXT PAGE

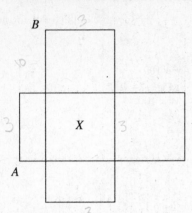

Note: Figure not drawn to scale.

14. In the figure above, rectangle A and rectangle B overlap to form square X and 4 smaller rectangles that surround square X. If A and B each have an area of 30, and all sides of the 4 surrounding rectangles are integers, which of the following is the area of square X ?

(A) 49
(B) 36
(C) 25
(D) 16
(E) 9

15. Right triangle A has base b, height h, and area x.
Rectangle B has length $2b$ and width $2h$. What is the area of rectangle B in terms of x ?

(A) $2x$
(B) $4x$
(C) $6x$
(D) $7x$
(E) $8x$

16. If $a^{\frac{1}{2}} = b^2$ and a and b are both greater than 1, then what is the value of a^2 in terms of b ?

(A) $b^{\frac{1}{4}}$

(B) $b^{\frac{1}{2}}$

(C) b

(D) b^4

(E) b^8

17. Shawn creates a meal by mixing the pastas, sauces, and toppings in his kitchen. Each meal he creates consists of one type of pasta, one sauce, and one type of topping. If Shawn can make exactly 30 different meals, which of the following could NOT be the number of sauces that Shawn has?

(A) 1
(B) 2
(C) 3
(D) 4
(E) 5

GO ON TO THE NEXT PAGE

18. Each student in a cooking class of 50 students is assigned to create a dessert, an appetizer, or both. The total number of students creating an appetizer is seven more than the number of students creating a dessert. If the number of students who create two dishes is the same as the number of students who create exactly one dish, how many students created only a dessert?

(A)   9
(B)   16
(C)   25
(D)   34
(E)   41

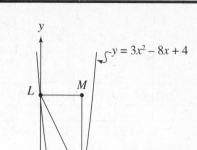

19. In the figure above, the graph of the function $3x^2 - 8x + 4$ is shown. The function intersects the y-axis at L and the x-axis at N. Line segments LM and MN are perpendicular, and LM is parallel to the x-axis. What is the area of triangle LMN?

(A) $\dfrac{1}{2}$

(B) $\dfrac{3}{8}$

(C)   4

(D)   8

(E)   16

20. If $2a = 3b$, $\dfrac{1}{3}c = 6b^2 + 2$, and $b > 0$, what is c in terms of a?

(A) $8a^2 + 6$
(B) $8a^2 + 12$
(C) $12a^2 + 6$
(D) $18a^2 + 6$
(E) $18a^2 + 12$

STOP

If you finish before time is called, you may check your work on this section only.
Do not turn to any other section in the test.

SECTION 4
Time — 25 minutes
24 Questions

Turn to Section 4 of your answer sheet to answer the questions in this section.

Directions: For each question in this section, select the best answer from among the choices given and fill in the corresponding circle on the answer sheet.

Each sentence below has one or two blanks, each blank indicating that something has been omitted. Beneath the sentence are five words or sets of words labeled A through E. Choose the word or set of words that, when inserted in the sentence, best fits the meaning of the sentence as a whole.

Example:

Desiring to ------- his taunting friends, Mitch gave them taffy in hopes it would keep their mouths shut.

(A) eliminate   (B) satisfy   (C) overcome
  (D) ridicule   (E) silence

1. The witness's testimony was truly ------- , rambling and incoherent.

   (A) informative   (B) capricious   (C) disjointed
      (D) indignant   (E) essential

2. The recent addition of members who care less about fundraising than about throwing expensive parties has given rise to ------- that the club's funds will soon be -------.

   (A) recriminations . . enhanced
   (B) suspicions . . traditional
   (C) recommendations . . connected
   (D) concerns . . exhausted
   (E) allegations . . improved

3. The politician's speeches were -------: because he did not take a stand on any issue, voters felt ------- about his position on topics that mattered in the election.

   (A) misleading . . assured
   (B) vague . . uncertain
   (C) predictable . . determined
   (D) passionate . . absolute
   (E) legislative . . reasonable

4. The physicist did not support his theory with adequate -------; nonetheless, he was surprised that his claim was rejected as -------.

   (A) objectivity . . hearsay
   (B) significance . . sympathy
   (C) substantiation . . fallacy
   (D) equivocation . . guesswork
   (E) verification . . treachery

5. Although the candidates were respectful of each other during the debate, they ------- each other's character during their post-debate press conferences.

   (A) celebrated   (B) impugned   (C) elected
      (D) mollified   (E) filibustered

6. The library lends an abundance of science books -------- of technical jargon: the straightforward descriptions in such books help ------- new knowledge about scientific topics to beginners.

   (A) reminiscent . . divulge
   (B) devoid . . convey
   (C) redolent . . grant
   (D) deficient . . duplicate
   (E) indicative . . revive

7. The principal characterized his pupils as ------- because they were pampered and spoiled by their indulgent parents.

   (A) cosseted   (B) disingenuous   (C) corrosive
      (D) laconic   (E) mercurial

8. Greg was extremely ------- , for he carefully accumulated money to ensure that he would have funds during his retirement.

   (A) reticent   (B) assiduous   (C) fallible
      (D) clairvoyant   (E) provident

GO ON TO THE NEXT PAGE

Directions: Each passage below is followed by questions based on its content. Answer the questions on the basis of what is <u>stated</u> or <u>implied</u> in each passage and in any introductory material that may be provided.

Questions 9-10 are based on the following passage.

Since 1970, national parks have had to double the number of signs warning visitors of possible hazards. The new signs have a dual purpose in that they also protect the parks from
Line unnecessary litigation. In 1972, the National Parks Service
5 in Yellowstone was forced to pay more than $87,000 to the victim of a bear attack. This ruling prompted Yellowstone historian Lee Whittlesey to write, "Analogously I could ask, should New York's Central Park have signs every ten feet saying, 'Danger! Muggers!' just because a non-streetwise,
10 non–New Yorker might go walking there?"

9. The reference to "the victim" (lines 5-6) serves primarily to

(A) support a previous claim
(B) summarize a counterargument
(C) restate an inconsistency
(D) suggest a possible solution
(E) elaborate on a hypothesis

10. Lee Whittlesey's attitude toward the "ruling" in line 6 could best be described as

(A) disinterested
(B) apathetic
(C) appreciative
(D) enthusiastic
(E) sarcastic

Questions 11-12 are based on the following passage.

The notion that journalists should strive to remain objective has been challenged in recent years as new reporting styles have come into vogue. For instance, a novel
Line style of journalism, known as "gonzo journalism," emerged
5 in the 1970s. This form, which remains popular today, is characterized by a punchy style, rough and occasionally sarcastic language, and an apparent disregard for conventional journalistic writing customs. Unlike traditional journalists, gonzo journalists use the power of both emotions and
10 personal experience to convey their messages. Rather than adhering to the objectivity prized in standard journalistic writing, they believe in presenting an unedited perspective on a story in "true gonzo" form.

11. The passage suggests that the writing of "traditional journalists" (line 8) is typically

(A) controversial
(B) neutral
(C) superficial
(D) authoritative
(E) subjective

12. The passage primarily focuses on which aspect of gonzo journalism?

(A) Its comedic elements
(B) Its alterations of language
(C) Its editing
(D) Its subject matter
(E) Its unconventionality

GO ON TO THE NEXT PAGE

Questions 13-24 are based on the following passages.

The following passages discuss the possibility of time travel. Passage 1 was written by a physicist, while passage 2 was written by a historian.

Passage 1

Ever since H.G. Wells published his classic novella, *The Time Machine*, in 1895, science fiction fans have been fascinated by the idea of contraptions that could effortlessly
Line transport passengers through time at the push of a button. The
5 truth, however, is that two-way travel from present to past would probably violate both the laws of causality and the laws of physics.

To be sure, certain celebrity scientists have postulated the existence of wormholes, warp drives, and other theoretical
10 constructs that might make time travel a reality. I have to confess that I find these notions rather unconvincing. While I agree with the view expressed by most physicists, which is that Einstein's Theory of Relativity ought to make some form of limited travel to the future possible, I consider it
15 highly implausible that an advanced civilization of the future would be able to send 'time-tourists' back into our own time. Eloquent support for my position comes from the eminent physicist Stephen Hawking, who has published a theory known as the "Chronological Protection Conjecture"
20 that conclusively debunks the concept of moving backwards through time.

Hawking raises two objections to the possibility of time travel. The first is that if time travelers were able to return to their own past, they might be able to alter the future.
25 Among time travel devotees, this conundrum is known as the Grandfather Paradox. Suppose a man was able to travel back in time and kill his own grandfather, thus preventing the man's father from being conceived. As a result, the man himself could never have been born. But since he was not
30 born, he could not have killed his grandfather. Thus, we are forced to conclude that the man both killed and could not have killed his grandfather! The implausibility of this scenario indicates a fundamental flaw in the concept of backwards time travel.

35 Another problem is that, as Hawking has observed, if time travel were possible, wouldn't we be swamped with visitors from the future? The logic of this argument is straightforward. On a grand scale, modern science is still in its infancy, yet the pace of technological advancement has been dramatic. In
40 less than a hundred years, we have gone from horse-drawn carriages to walking on the moon, and the rate of innovation shows no sign of slowing down. If it were possible to travel backwards in time, it seems almost inevitable that our distant descendants would eventually develop the necessary
45 technology, and return to visit their ancestors. The fact that hordes of time travelers are not walking around suggests that backwards time travel is unlikely to occur, no matter how technologically advanced our society becomes.

Passage 2

When the world's most respected physicist expresses
50 skepticism about an issue, his opinion carries a great deal of weight. Stephen Hawking's "Chronological Protection Conjecture," while allowing for the possibility of time travel to the future, presents a formidable logical argument against the possibility of traveling back through time, and has caused
55 many a professional scientist to dismiss the whole concept out of hand.

Not everyone, however, is convinced. Carl Sagan, for example, has called Hawking's argument "very dubious," and asserts that he can think of half a dozen reasons why "we
60 might not be awash in time travelers, and yet time travel is still possible." For one thing, there might be something about time travel that makes it impossible for us to see visitors from the future, even if they are in our midst. Or perhaps they simply don't want to be seen, and have developed the
65 necessary technology to prevent us from catching a glimpse of them. As for the oft-cited Grandfather Paradox, Sagan notes that while the idea of a self-consistent causality is appealing, "inconsistencies might very well be consistent with the universe." Though dismissive of Hawking's argument,
70 Sagan remains noncommittal about the possibility of time travel, preferring to "withhold judgment until there is better evidence."

Physicist Ronald Mallett, a professor at the University of Connecticut, is more optimistic. He believes that time
75 travel can be achieved within the next decade, and has actively pursued funding to build an experimental version of a time travel device. Mallett's time machine, known as the Spacetime Twisting by Light (STL) project, would use a ring laser and Einstein's Theory of Relativity to produce
80 a circulating cylinder of light. In theory, this device could produce "closed spacetime curves," allowing time travel into the past. Mallett's theories are controversial, but have gained adherents within the scientific community. One colleague expressed his support for Mallett's point of view by noting
85 that "while we shouldn't expect time machines to turn up in shops any time soon, we can be confident that one day, they will."

13. Which statement best describes a significant difference between the two passages?

(A) Passage 1 rejects the Chronological Protection Conjecture, while Passage 2 embraces it.

(B) Passage 1 analyzes a work of fiction, while Passage 2 presents scientific evidence.

(C) Passage 1 argues a position, while Passage 2 surveys current opinion about a topic.

(D) Passage 1 defends a point of view, while Passage 2 questions the objectivity of that point of view.

(E) Passage 1 details a phenomenon, while Passage 2 details an ideology that rejects that phenomenon.

GO ON TO THE NEXT PAGE ➡

14. In line 3, the author uses the word "contraptions" in order to

(A) suggest that time travel may soon be within our grasp
(B) imply that science fiction novels have no merit
(C) praise the creativity of science fiction writers
(D) contrast fictional conceptions with a scientific point of view
(E) claim that literature exerts undue influence on scientific research

15. The "celebrity scientists" in line 8, Passage 1, most directly share the attitude of

(A) Stephen Hawking (Passage 1)
(B) H.G. Wells (Passage 1)
(C) "science fiction fans" (line 2, Passage 1)
(D) "a professional scientist" (line 55, Passage 2)
(E) Ronald Mallett (Passage 2)

16. The claim made in Passage 1 that the Chronological Protection Conjecture "conclusively debunks" (line 20) the notion of backwards time travel would most likely be characterized by the author of Passage 2 as

(A) an oversimplification of a complex issue
(B) a revelation of a surprising piece of evidence
(C) an attack on the credibility of reputable scientists
(D) evidence of the innate skepticism of professional physicists
(E) support for a position outlined by Ronald Mallett

17. In line 36, the word "swamped" most nearly means

(A) drenched
(B) invaded
(C) submerged
(D) slowed
(E) overwhelmed

18. The author of Passage 1 refers to "horse-drawn carriages" (lines 40-41) in order to

(A) criticize the primitive methods of transportation used by our ancestors
(B) highlight the need for additional research
(C) underscore the rate of scientific progress
(D) demonstrate the superiority of contemporary science
(E) draw attention to the dangers of modern technology

19. The argument outlined in lines 38-45 ("On a . . . ancestors") depends most directly on which of the following assumptions?

(A) Scientists will require thousands of years to develop time travel devices.
(B) Scientists will eventually solve all problems known to man.
(C) Travelers from the future would be unwilling to share their technology with us.
(D) Travelers from the future would be noticeable to contemporary humans.
(E) Travelers from the future would inevitably use technology for hostile purposes.

20. The author of Passage 2 would most likely characterize the Chronological Protection Conjecture as

(A) misunderstood
(B) perplexing
(C) controversial
(D) convoluted
(E) inaccurate

21. Both Stephen Hawking and the author of Passage 1 would agree that

(A) Einstein's Theory of Relativity demonstrates that time travel is impossible
(B) the Chronological Protection Conjecture is considered a controversial theory
(C) scientists should focus on problems in the present rather than seek to travel through time
(D) time travel in one direction may be theoretically possible
(E) time travel remains unlikely as long as science is publicly funded

22. How would Carl Sagan (line 57, Passage 2) most likely respond to the statement by the author of Passage 1 about "hordes of time travelers" (line 46) ?

(A) The issue of time travel requires further study.
(B) The concept of time travel raises serious moral issues.
(C) Time travelers are invisible because they come from another dimension.
(D) Opponents of time travel have ignored crucial evidence.
(E) The laws of the universe defy all logic.

GO ON TO THE NEXT PAGE

23. The quotation in lines 68-69 ("inconsistencies . . . universe") serves primarily to

    (A) offer an aside
    (B) summarize a difficulty
    (C) pose a riddle
    (D) provide concrete evidence
    (E) question a belief

24. In line 84, "noting" most nearly means

    (A) asserting
    (B) writing
    (C) perceiving
    (D) distinguishing
    (E) recording

STOP

If you finish before time is called, you may check your work on this section only.
Do not turn to any other section in the test.

NO TEST MATERIAL ON THIS PAGE.

SECTION 5
Time — 25 minutes
35 Questions

Turn to Section 5 of your answer sheet to answer the questions in this section.

Directions: For each question in this section, select the best answer from among the choices given and fill in the corresponding circle on the answer sheet.

The following sentences test correctness and effectiveness of expression. Part of each sentence or the entire sentence is underlined; beneath each sentence are five ways of phrasing the underlined material. Choice A repeats the original phrasing; the other four choices are different. If you think the original phrasing produces a better sentence than any of the alternatives, select choice A; if not, select one of the other choices.

In making your selection, follow the requirements of standard written English; that is, pay attention to grammar, choice of words, sentence construction, and punctuation. Your selection should result in the most effective sentence—clear and precise, without awkwardness or ambiguity.

EXAMPLE:

Bobby Flay baked his first cake <u>and he was thirteen years old then</u>.

(A) and he was thirteen years old then
(B) when he was thirteen
(C) at age thirteen years old
(D) upon the reaching of thirteen years
(E) at the time when he was thirteen

Ⓐ●ⒸⒹⒺ

1. <u>To arrest and imprison petty criminals</u> undeniably improved the vitality of each city neighborhood.

   (A) To arrest and imprison petty criminals
   (B) The arrest and imprisonment of petty criminals
   (C) Having arrested and imprisoned petty criminals,
   (D) Petty criminals, as a result of having been arrested and imprisoned,
   (E) The petty criminals, by being arresting and imprisoned,

2. <u>Mark's brother received athletic scholarship offers from all the colleges he applied to, being the national fencing champion.</u>

   (A) Mark's brother received athletic scholarship offers from all the colleges he applied to, being the national fencing champion.
   (B) Mark's brother received athletic scholarship offers from all the colleges he applied to, and he was the national fencing champion.
   (C) Mark's brother, who as the national fencing champion received athletic scholarship offers from all the colleges he applied to.
   (D) Being Mark's brother, the national fencing champion received athletic scholarship offers from all the colleges he applied to.
   (E) Mark's brother, the national fencing champion, received athletic scholarship offers from all the colleges he applied to.

3. Houses in parts of California are frequently destroyed by earthquakes, mudslides and <u>brushfires, because of this fact, many residents pay large premiums for homeowner's insurance</u>.

   (A) brushfires, because of this fact, many residents pay large premiums for homeowner's insurance
   (B) brushfires, with many residents therefore paying large premiums for homeowner's insurance
   (C) brushfires, many residents pay large premiums for homeowner's insurance as a result
   (D) brushfires; and many residents pay large premiums for homeowner's insurance
   (E) brushfires; therefore, many residents pay large premiums for homeowner's insurance

4. The sun-ripened fruits from small orchards on rural farms are popularly used for making both <u>fresh pie but delicious</u> tarts.

   (A) fresh pies but delicious
   (B) fresh pies or delicious
   (C) delicious but fresh pies and
   (D) fresh pie and delicious
   (E) fresh pie being like delicious

GO ON TO THE NEXT PAGE

5. Fearful of the dangerous by-products from combustion engines and factories in urban areas, <u>ecologists suggest that riding bikes, subways, and public buses will</u> help decrease pollution.

(A) ecologists suggest that riding bikes, subways, and public buses will

(B) riding bikes, subways, and public buses, this is what ecologists suggest will

(C) and with suggestions from ecologists that riding bikes, subways, and public buses will

(D) suggestions from ecologists concerning the riding of bikes, subways, and public buses will

(E) ecologists suggesting that riding bikes, subways, and public buses would

6. In her biography of Abraham Lincoln, Goodwin succeeds in her intention not only to illustrate her historical subject <u>and establishing that</u> his leadership was remarkable.

(A) and establishing that

(B) while establishing that

(C) but also to establish that

(D) but also her establishment of how

(E) and also to establish how

7. Rachel Carson, the author of the controversial book *Silent Spring*, <u>was a supporter of environmental protection, a defender of animal conservation, and an opponent of</u> pesticide usage.

(A) was a supporter of environmental protection, a defender of animal conservation, and an opponent of

(B) was a supporter of environmental protection, a defender of animal conservation, and opposing

(C) was a supporter of environmental protection, defended animal conservation, and an opponent of

(D) was a supporter of environmental protection, a defender of animal conservation, and she opposed

(E) was a supporter of environmental protection, a defender of animal conservation, opposing

8. The school's Honor Society accepts students from various majors <u>having earned</u> excellent grades in all their first-year coursework.

(A) having earned

(B) who have earned

(C) to earn

(D) to be earning

(E) and they earned

9. <u>Working in the rafters, the rehearsal came to an abrupt end when a stagehand dropped a heavy camera;</u> thankfully, no one was injured.

(A) Working in the rafters, the rehearsal came to an abrupt end when a stagehand dropped a heavy camera

(B) Working in the rafters, a heavy camera was dropped by a stagehand, abruptly ending all rehearsal

(C) Abruptly ending all rehearsal, a stagehand dropped a heavy camera working in the rafters

(D) The rehearsal came to an abrupt end when a stagehand working in the rafters dropped a heavy camera

(E) When working in the rafters, a heavy camera dropped by the stagehand abruptly ended all rehearsal

10. We have come to acknowledge that history teaches important lessons <u>which, if they are ignored, you put everyone in jeopardy.</u>

(A) which, if they are ignored, you put everyone in jeopardy

(B) and if you ignore them you put everyone in jeopardy

(C) and ignoring it will be perilous

(D) and it puts everyone in jeopardy to ignore them

(E) that we ignore at our own peril

11. The school board's ideas for reforming the curriculum were offered <u>more as general guidelines than as</u> precise prescriptions for change.

(A) more as general guidelines than as

(B) as general guidelines more than

(C) more for general guidelines than

(D) for general guidelines more than as

(E) as more general guidelines than

GO ON TO THE NEXT PAGE

The following sentences test your ability to recognize grammar and usage errors. Each sentence contains either a single error or no error at all. No sentence contains more than one error. The error, if there is one, is underlined and lettered. If the sentence contains an error, select the one underlined part that must be changed to make the sentence correct. If the sentence is correct, select choice E. In choosing answers, follow the requirements of standard written English.

EXAMPLE:

The other players and her significantly improved
   A   B   C

the game plan created by the coaches. No error
              D   E

Ⓐ ● Ⓒ Ⓓ Ⓔ

12. Prior to the invention of the printing press in the 1400s, the

only way to produce duplicates of books has been to
           A   B   C

have copies handwritten by professional scribes. No error
           D   E

13. The least effective supervisors make their subordinates
      A   B

feel worthless and inadequate; as a result they

often find that their subordinates deliberately refuse to
   C   D

comply with directives and requests. No error
                     E

14. During her term at Trinity University studying music
     A

composition, Julia becoming known for her tendency
               B

to incorporate both traditional instruments and industrial
  C

machinery in her remakes of 1980s rock songs. No error
        D   E

15. Trailing behind the marching band, the art club's float
     A

was the most brightest painted display in the parade.
  B   C   D

No error
  E

16. While the speaker showed us her research on
   A

contemporary Chinese architecture, she illustrated

different artistic elements using drawings of her
                         B

own favorite designs influenced by Chinese structures,
  C

giving you a clear understanding of the lecture. No error
   D   E

17. One of the most famous plays from ancient Greece
   A

are The Clouds, a satirical and unusually critical
  B   C

comedy about the teaching styles found in Athens at the
                        D

time. No error
      E

18. An early advocate to the woman's suffrage movement,
        A

Victoria Woodhull was a candidate for President,
           B

although when she tried to vote, election officials would
              C

not accept her ballot. No error
   D   E

19. The city park bounded by North Street, South Street,
           A

First Avenue, and Second Avenue contain a garden and a
                     B

pea patch communally tended by local residents.
       C   D

No error
  E

GO ON TO THE NEXT PAGE

20. For most of her life, Janet has saved money carefully, but
    A

    now that her savings are becoming increasingly plentiful
    B   C

    bankers are encouraging her to invest it. No error
                                          D   E
    .

21. At a time when knowledge of the Maori warrior
              A

    tradition appears on the brink to vanishing, the
              B   C

    contemporary media publications in New Zealand are

    making a valiant attempt to preserve this cultural
                      D

    heritage. No error
              E

22. While visiting New York, the tourist group thought that
    A   B

    the city's smog problem was worse than Los Angeles.
                            C   D

    No error
    E

23. Dr. Cartwright smugly revealed his department's latest
                    A   B

    product, a medication that cures the common cold when
             C

    taking a pill. No error
    D   E

24. As interns, young students work not for companies of
    A   B

    their own choosing but rather for companies chosen by
    C   D

    their professors. No error
                      E

25. Even though the weather was abysmal, Anika arrived
                            A

    twenty minutes early for her class since she had
                          B

    ran quickly all the way from the parking lot. No error
    C   D   E

26. Daily requests for interviews with the mayor of Chicago
                                  A

    number more than twice that of the governor of
    B   C   D

    Illinois. No error
              E

27. To claim that an advertisement persuades whomever one
                                                      A

    wants it to persuade is often discounting the intelligence
    B   C

    and even the aptitude of an audience. No error
        D   E

28. Overuse of chemical fertilizers on farm crops

    both destroys many beneficial organisms in the soil
    A   B

    and weakens the crop's resistance to ever more virulent
        C   D

    diseases. No error
              E

29. Between the two major techniques for culturing bacteria,
    A

    the streaking method tends to be the one preferred by
                         B   C

    scientists because it is the most effective. No error
                               D   E

GO ON TO THE NEXT PAGE ⟩

Directions: The following passage is an early draft of an essay. Some parts of the passage need to be rewritten.

Read the passage and select the best answers for the questions that follow. Some questions are about particular sentences or parts of sentences and ask you to improve sentence structure or word choice. Other questions ask you to consider organization and development. In choosing answers, follow the requirements of standard written English.

Questions 30-35 are based on the following passage.

(1) After eating gelato in Florence, Italy, I was amazed at how different it was from the kind sold in America. (2) Gelato is Italian ice cream, but it is smoother and fluffier than ours. (3) Some American cities sell gelato at shops also called *gelaterias,* and some ice cream manufacturers produce processed gelato. (4) Neither product tastes like Italian gelato. (5) I craved the flavors and texture of the Italian version I had experienced. (6) I decided to make my own gelato.

(7) I discovered that gelato is very, very hard to make as good as they do in Italy. (8) First, it needs to have some air by churning it into liquid to make it fluffy, but too much air will make it too fluffy. (9) American stores and manufacturers add things like emulsifiers to keep the gelato fluffy for an unnaturally long time. (10) Gelato in Italy is made and eaten on the same day so the texture does not need artificial and chemical preservatives.

(11) Flavors of American versions of gelato were bland in comparison. (12) American producers find it easier to use frozen canned or otherwise preserved fruits, but highly processed fruits and other ingredients lose a lot of flavor. (13) Italian producers purchase just enough fresh fruit to make the day's batch of gelato. (14) In conclusion, gelato does not work in America because its nature prevents it from mass production. (15) Good gelato must be created correctly, in the Italian way, in small batches and using the freshest ingredients.

30. In context, which of the following is best placed at the beginning of sentence 4 (reproduced below) ?

Neither product tastes like Italian gelato.

(A) However,
(B) Consequently,
(C) Additionally,
(D) Subsequently,
(E) And,

31. In context, which of the following is the best version of sentences 5 and 6 (reproduced below) ?

I craved the flavors and texture of the Italian version. I decided to make my own gelato.

(A) In order to make my own gelato I experienced the flavors and texture of the Italian version I craved.
(B) The flavors and textures differ, and I craved the Italian version, so I attempted to create my own gelato.
(C) Because I craved the flavors and textures of the Italian version, I decided to make my own gelato.
(D) Since the flavors and textures differ, I craved the Italian version, I decided to make my own gelato.
(E) I decided that my own gelato would be made with the flavors and textures of the Italian version because I craved it.

32. In context, which is the best version of the underlined portion of sentence 7 (reproduced below) ?

I discovered that gelato is very, very hard to make as good as they do in Italy.

(A) (as it is now)
(B) gelato is very hard to make, it is better
(C) because gelato is harder to make as good as it is
(D) it is very difficult to make gelato as good as the kind found
(E) it is more difficult to make gelato as good as they do

33. In context, which of the following is the best revision of sentence 8 (reproduced below) ?

First, it needs to have some air by churning it into liquid to make it fluffy, but too much air will make it too fluffy.

(A) The fluffy texture of gelato is achieved by carefully churning milk or water to ensure the perfect quantity of air is added to the liquid.
(B) To make gelato fluffy, one must churn air into a liquid such as milk or water, and watch the texture so that not too much air is churned in.
(C) Starting with a liquid, such as milk or water, it is churned carefully to add the air that makes it fluffy, though too much air is a bad thing.
(D) Milk or water plus air transforms the liquid into gelato; one must add the proper amount of air for a fluffy consistency.
(E) One can churn air into liquid for fluffy gelato; be careful about excess air which makes the gelato overly fluffy.

GO ON TO THE NEXT PAGE

34. In sentence 9, "things" is best replaced by

(A) stuff
(B) ingredients
(C) processes
(D) objects
(E) manufacturers

35. In context, which of the following is the best revision of sentence 14 (reproduced below) ?

In conclusion, gelato does not work in America because its nature prevents it from mass production.

(A) (As it is now)
(B) Since gelato does not work in America because its nature prevents it from mass production.
(C) However, gelato is not possible in America because its nature makes it difficult to mass-produce.
(D) Simply put, American manufacturers cannot make authentic-tasting gelato because by its nature it is difficult to mass produce.
(E) Being that American manufacturers cannot make authentic-tasting gelato because by nature it is difficult to mass-produce. .

STOP

If you finish before time is called, you may check your work on this section only.
Do not turn to any other section in the test.

SECTION 6
Time — 25 minutes
18 Questions

Turn to Section 6 of your answer sheet to answer the questions in this section.

Directions: This section contains two types of questions. You have 25 minutes to complete both types. For questions 1-8, solve each problem and decide which is the best of the choices given. Fill in the corresponding circle on the answer sheet. You may use any available space for scratchwork.

Notes

1. The use of a calculator is permitted.

2. All numbers used are real numbers.

3. Figures that accompany problems in this test are intended to provide information useful in solving the problems. They are drawn as accurately as possible EXCEPT when it is stated in a specific problem that the figure is not drawn to scale. All figures lie in a plane unless otherwise indicated.

4. Unless otherwise specified, the domain of any function f is assumed to be the set of all real numbers x for which $f(x)$ is a real number.

Reference Information

 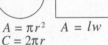

$A = \pi r^2$ $A = lw$ $A = \frac{1}{2}bh$ $V = lwh$ $V = \pi r^2 h$ $c^2 = a^2 + b^2$

Special Right Triangles

The number of degrees of arc in a circle is 360.

The sum of the measures in degrees of the angles of a triangle is 180.

---

1. If one angle in a right triangle is 20, which of the following is the degree measure of another angle in the triangle?

   (A) 30
   (B) 40
   (C) 50
   (D) 60
   (E) 70

2. If $7y = 3$, what is the value of $\frac{21y}{9}$?

   (A) $\frac{3}{7}$

   (B) 1

   (C) $\frac{7}{3}$

   (D) $\frac{14}{3}$

   (E) 9

GO ON TO THE NEXT PAGE

NUMBER OF PARKING VIOLATIONS BY YEAR AND MONTH

Month	2007	2008
August	35	30
September	46	51
October	25	30
November	10	15
December	19	39

3. According to the information given in the table above, what was the overall increase from 2007 to 2008 in the number of parking violations for August through December?

(A) 20
(B) 25
(C) 30
(D) 35
(E) 40

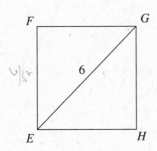

4. In the figure above, *EFGH* is a square. What is the length of side $\overline{EF}$?

(A) 2
(B) $2\sqrt{2}$ (approximately 2.83)
(C) 3
(D) $3\sqrt{2}$ (approximately 4.24)
(E) $3\sqrt{3}$ (approximately 5.20)

5. Which of the following is NOT a possible value of $2 - x$, if x is a one-digit integer?

(A) −8
(B) −6
(C) −4
(D) −2
(E) 2

6. If $a^x = 4$ and $a^c = 64$, what is the value of a^{x-c} ?

(A) −60

(B) −16

(C) $\dfrac{1}{16}$

(D) 16

(E) 32

GO ON TO THE NEXT PAGE

7. Zenia drew a route on a map, starting with a 32 centimeter line from her home due north to Anne's home. She continued the route with a 44 centimeter line due south to Beth's home, a 33 centimeter line due west to Caleb's home, and a 28 centimeter line due east to Damon's home. What is the distance on the map, in centimeters, from Damon's home to Zenia's home?

(A)   5
(B)   12
(C)   13
(D)   33
(E)   55

8. If 60 percent of Jared's jigsaw puzzles have 50 pieces each and 40 percent of his jigsaw puzzles have 30 pieces each, what is the average (arithmetic mean) number of pieces per puzzle?

(A)   36
(B)   38
(C)   40
(D)   42
(E)   44

GO ON TO THE NEXT PAGE

Directions: For Student-Produced Response questions 9-18, use the grids at the bottom of the answer sheet page on which you have answered questions 1-8.

Each of the remaining 10 questions requires you to solve the problem and enter your answer by marking the circles in the special grid, as shown in the examples below. You may use any available space for scratch work.

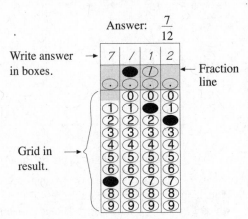

Answer: $\frac{7}{12}$

Write answer in boxes. ← Fraction line

Grid in result.

Answer: 2.5

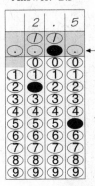

← Decimal point

Answer: 201
Either position is correct.

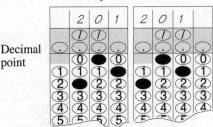

Note: You may start your answers in any column, space permitting. Columns not needed should be left blank.

- Mark no more than one circle in any column.

- Because the answer document will be machine-scored, **you will receive credit only if the circles are filled in correctly.**

- Although not required, it is suggested that you write your answer in the boxes at the top of the columns to help you fill in the circles accurately.

- Some problems may have more than one correct answer. In such cases, grid only one answer.

- No question has a negative answer.

- **Mixed numbers** such as $3\frac{1}{2}$ must be gridded as

  3.5 or 7/2. (If 3 1 / 2 is gridded, it will be

  interpreted as $\frac{31}{2}$, not $3\frac{1}{2}$.)

- **Decimal Answers:** If you obtain a decimal answer with more digits than the grid can accommodate, it may be either rounded or truncated, but it must fill the entire grid. For example, if you obtain an answer such as 0.6666..., you should record your result as .666 or .667. **A less accurate value such as .66 or .67 will be scored as incorrect.**

Acceptable ways to grid $\frac{2}{3}$ are:

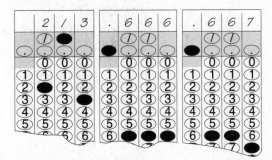

9. Belinda can bike 10 miles in 3 hours. At this rate, how many miles can she bike in 4 hours?

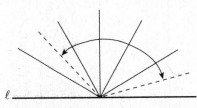

10. In the figure above, line ℓ is intersected by five line segments, creating six angles with equal measures. If the dotted segments bisect two of those angles, what is the measure of the angle indicated by the arrow? (Disregard the degree symbol when gridding your answer.)

GO ON TO THE NEXT PAGE →

11. If $2,500 < x + 1,300 < 5,200$, and x is an integer, what is the greatest possible value of x ?

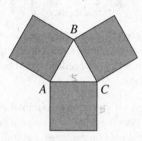

12. In the figure above, ABC is an equilateral triangle formed by the edges of three squares. If triangle ABC has a perimeter of 15, what is the total area of the shaded regions?

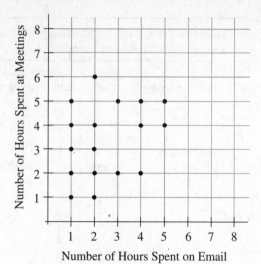

13. Plotted on the graph above are the results of a survey in which 17 office workers were asked how many hours a day they spent composing email and attending meetings. Each dot reflects one office worker. The median number of hours spent composing emails is how much less than the median number of hours spent attending meetings?

14. In a class of 330 students, there are 60 more girls than boys. How many girls are there in the class?

GO ON TO THE NEXT PAGE

15. Maria has 74 pebbles that she wants to divide into 25 piles. If the tenth pile is to have more pebbles than any other pile, what is the least number of pebbles Maria can put into the tenth pile?

16. If $2452 = 60q + 52r$, and q and r are positive integers, what is one possible value for $q + r$?

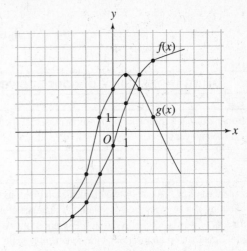

17. Portions of the graphs of functions $f(x)$ and $g(x)$ are shown in the figure above. If $h(x)$ is defined by $h(x) = f(2x) + 2g(x)$ for all values of x, what is the value of $h(1)$?

18. In the xy plane, lines a and c intersect at the point with coordinates $(n, \frac{7}{2})$. If the equation of line a is $y = \frac{1}{2}x + 5$, and the equation of line c is $y = \frac{1}{3}x + b$, what is the value of b?

STOP

If you finish before time is called, you may check your work on this section only.
Do not turn to any other section in the test.

SECTION 7
Time — 25 minutes
24 Questions

Turn to Section 7 of your answer sheet to answer the questions in this section.

Directions: For each question in this section, select the best answer from among the choices given and fill in the corresponding circle on the answer sheet.

Each sentence below has one or two blanks, each blank indicating that something has been omitted. Beneath the sentence are five words or sets of words labeled A through E. Choose the word or set of words that, when inserted in the sentence, <u>best</u> fits the meaning of the sentence as a whole.

Example:

Desiring to ------- his taunting friends, Mitch gave them taffy in hopes it would keep their mouths shut.

(A) eliminate   (B) satisfy   (C) overcome
   (D) ridicule   (E) silence

Ⓐ Ⓑ Ⓒ Ⓓ ●

---

1. Once viewed as ------- , the dream of cars that produce no harmful pollutants may soon be ------- now that prototypes have been built that emit only water vapor.

   (A) fundamental . . imagined
   (B) quixotic . . achieved
   (C) hypothetical . . deluded
   (D) inescapable . . realized
   (E) conclusive . . mysterious

2. Reviewers noted that the autobiography was exceptionally ------- due to the writer's truthful and revealing descriptions of her life.

   (A) candid   (B) didactic   (C) comprehensive
      (D) baroque   (E) languid

3. Some people who are ------- appear to be aloof when in reality they are merely shy.

   (A) belligerent   (B) pliant   (C) timorous
      (D) conspicuous   (E) avuncular

4. Glowing with joy and delight, Laura was positively ------- on her graduation day.

   (A) rapturous   (B) assiduous   (C) nihilistic
      (D) intractable   (E) phlegmatic

5. Conservationists are contemplating a plan to remove the broken crates, washed-up cargo, and other ------- left over from the shipwreck.

   (A) raiment   (B) detritus   (C) periphery
      (D) desolation   (E) trajectory

GO ON TO THE NEXT PAGE

Directions: Each passage below is followed by questions based on its content. Answer the questions on the basis of what is <u>stated</u> or <u>implied</u> in each passage and in any introductory material that may be provided.

Questions 6-9 are based on the following passages.

Passage 1

Charles Ives, the iconoclastic American composer who mixed everything from religious hymns to brass band marches to classical music into his symphonies, would have
Line been right at home in the musical culture of contemporary
5 America. Our musical tastes prove us to be robust explorers, unconstrained by tradition. We mix and match musical styles rather than preserve the preferences of our parents and grandparents. America has no single dominant musical culture. What characterizes our musical taste is how we listen,
10 not what we listen to. As listeners, we commonly amalgamate a wide range of musical styles into our own personal "soundtracks." The whole world's music is our music.

Passage 2

Music is often viewed as one of the most salient indicators of cultural identity. As a little boy, my entire musical universe
15 consisted of Chinese classical music. I thought all kids grew up learning to play instruments such as the Erhu (a two-stringed fiddle) and the Xindi (a bamboo flute). After we immigrated to America, my ideas about music were turned upside down. In school, my classmates seemed to be
20 conversant in every conceivable musical genre. Their tastes rubbed off on me, and I became interested in a broad range of different styles. By the time I graduated from high school, I was as likely to listen to hip-hop or rock as to traditional Chinese music.

6. Which of the following best describes how the two passages differ in their discussions of music?

(A) Passage 1 lists several popular types of music, whereas passage 2 focuses on types that are rarely heard.
(B) Passage 1 suggests that a person's upbringing determines listening habits, whereas Passage 2 implies that listening habits are largely self-determined.
(C) Passage 1 offers a historical analysis of music, whereas Passage 2 presents an abstract theory of music.
(D) Passage 1 emphasizes aspects of music that are common to all cultures, whereas Passage 2 contrasts the music of different cultures.
(E) Passage 1 remarks on a culture's general attitude toward music, whereas Passage 2 discusses the listening habits of a certain individual.

7. The author of Passage 1 would most likely describe the listening habits discussed in the last sentence of Passage 2 (lines 22-24) as

(A) surprisingly bold
(B) regrettably conservative
(C) embarrassingly pretentious
(D) characteristically American
(E) overly tolerant

8. Unlike the author of Passage 1, the author of Passage 2 makes significant use of

(A) literary metaphors
(B) personal experience
(C) historical analysis
(D) direct quotation
(E) hypothetical scenarios

9. Which of the following best describes the relationship between the two passages?

(A) Passage 1 discusses musical styles that are criticized in Passage 2.
(B) Passage 1 provides a broader context for the experiences described in Passage 2.
(C) Passage 1 provides a personal interpretation of the thesis put forth in Passage 2.
(D) Passage 2 cites examples referred to in Passage 1 to correct a common misconception.
(E) Passage 2 raises objections that are resolved in Passage 1.

GO ON TO THE NEXT PAGE

Questions 10-16 are based on the following passage.

The following passage is excerpted from a novel written in 1909. Dr. Karl Hubers, a main character, is a world-famous scientist.

He was one of the men who go before. Out in the great field of knowledge's unsurveyed territory he worked—a blazer of the trail, a voice crying from the wilderness: "I
Line have opened up another few feet. You can come now a little
5 farther." Then the crowd would come in and take possession, soon to become accustomed to the ground, forgetting that only a little while before it had been impassable, scarcely thinking of the little body of men who had opened the way for them. And only the little band itself would ever know how
10 stony that path, how deep the ditches, how thick and thorny the underbrush. "Why this couldn't have been so bad," the crowd said, after it had flocked in - "strange it should have taken so long!"

At the time of his falling in love, Dr. Karl Hubers
15 was thirty-nine years old. He had worked in European laboratories, notably the Pasteur Institute of Paris, and among men of his kind was regarded as one to be reckoned with. Then the president of a great university had spied Karl Hubers, working away over there in Europe. The president
20 had a genius for perceiving when a man stood on the verge of great celebrity, and so he cried out now: "Come over and do some teaching for us! We will give you just as good a laboratory as you have there and plenty of time for your own work." Now, while he would be glad enough to have Dr.
25 Hubers do the teaching, what he wanted most of all was to possess him, so that in the day of victory that young giant of a university would rise up and proclaim: "See! We have done it!" And Dr. Hubers, lured by the promise of time and facility for his own work, liking what he knew of the young
30 university, had come over and established himself in Chicago.

Generations before, his ancestors in Europe had swept things before them with a mighty hand. With defeat and renunciation they did not reckon. If they loved a woman, they picked her up and took her away. And civilisation has not
35 quite washed the blood of those men from the earth. Europe gave to Karl Hubers something more than a scholar's mind. At any rate, he did a very unapproved and most uncivilised thing. When he fell in love and decided he wanted to marry Ernestine Stanley, he asked for his year's leave of absence
40 before he went to find out whether Miss Stanley was kindly disposed to the idea of marrying him. Now why he did that, it is not possible to state, but the thing proving him quite hopeless as a civilised product is that it never struck him that there was anything so very peculiar in his order of procedure.
45 His assistants had to do a great deal of reminding after he came back that week, and they never knew until afterwards that his abstraction was caused by something quite different from germs. They thought—unknowing assistants—that he was on a new trail, and judged from the expression of his face
50 that it was going to prove most productive.

10. Which of the following most resembles the actions of "the crowd" (line 5) ?

(A) A climber who attempts to reach the top of a mountain is forced to stop because of the obstacles in his path

(B) A star athlete who is expected to lead his team suffers a career-ending injury in the first game of the season

(C) A son who inherits a business that his father started is unappreciative of the difficulties that the father faced

(D) A worker who attempts to unionize a group of factory laborers is abruptly fired by his manager

(E) A composer who writes strikingly original music refuses to compromise for the sake of popularity

11. According to the passage, which of the following best describes what the president of the university "wanted most of all" (line 25) ?

(A) To have physical control over Dr. Hubers
(B) To claim credit for Dr. Hubers' achievements
(C) To facilitate Dr. Hubers' spiritual development
(D) To have Dr. Hubers work as an instructor at the university
(E) To make Dr. Hubers feel indebted to him

12. Lines 35-36 ("Europe gave . . . mind") most directly suggest that Dr. Hubers possesses which of the following qualities?

(A) intelligence
(B) brutality
(C) absent-mindedness
(D) cleanliness
(E) impulsiveness

GO ON TO THE NEXT PAGE

13. In line 41, the word "disposed" most nearly means

  (A) inclined
  (B) rejected
  (C) dispensed
  (D) conditioned
  (E) equipped

14. The author uses the phrase "quite hopeless" (lines 42-43) in order to

  (A) emphasize the unlikelihood of Miss Stanley returning his affections
  (B) evoke sympathy for Dr. Hubers' unfortunate predicament
  (C) suggest that Dr. Hubers is oblivious to social conventions
  (D) indicate that Dr. Hubers is accustomed to living in the wilderness
  (E) criticize Dr. Hubers for his overly clinical view of marriage

15. The description in lines 45-48 ("His assistants . . . germs") primarily suggests that Dr. Hubers

  (A) was too great a thinker to be concerned with trivial details
  (B) had discovered a revolutionary cure for a disease
  (C) was afflicted by a condition that caused temporary loss of memory
  (D) was distracted by concerns unrelated to his work
  (E) had never been able to function without the help of others

16. In context, the phrase "unknowing assistants" (line 48) serves to suggest that

  (A) a character was predictable
  (B) an impression was mistaken
  (C) an employee was less than qualified
  (D) a reputation was exaggerated
  (E) an attitude was upsetting

GO ON TO THE NEXT PAGE

Questions 17-24 are based on the following passage.

The following passage considers the reliability of eyewitness testimony in criminal trials and discusses how individual and cultural factors can color visual perception.

Western juries have traditionally found eyewitness testimony to be the most convincing evidence in criminal trials. Seeing is believing, as the saying goes. In numerous
Line cases, when witnesses pointed to the defendant, his or her fate
5 was sealed. But how reliable is eyewitness testimony? Recent cases have suggested that despite our best intentions, we may unwittingly distort what we perceive.

Artists and psychologists have long known that "seeing" is not a simple matter of recording visual input. People
10 perceive the exterior world through a complex matrix of cultural expectations, personality traits, moods, and life experiences. For example, researchers tested the cultural influence on perception by showing a set of optical illusions to various groups, and found that different groups responded
15 in divergent ways. Accustomed to and inundated by perpendicular structures, Western Europeans succumbed easily to illusions based on rectangular lines. On the other hand, the Zulu people of South Africa, whose environment had been comprised almost entirely of circular forms (round
20 houses, doors, etc.) did not fall prey to those linear illusions.

Cultural expectations also influence the selectivity of our seeing. The amount of visual information that exists far exceeds our ability to process it, so we must filter that sensory input into recognizable images. In looking at a face, we do
25 not see elongated ovals set in complex shadows and shading, we see eyes. And that filtering process is informed by what we perceive to be significant, which is influenced by cultural norms. Some cultures may emphasize differences in hair color or texture, others the shape of a nose or mouth, still others the
30 set of the eyes.

But it is not only group expectations that color what we see; personality and mood fluctuation can also alter our perceptions. Orderly minds that shun ambiguity will see an off-center image as firmly fixed in the center. The
35 same photograph of four young men allows for shifting interpretations based on our current feelings: a mood of happiness reveals boys enjoying a relaxing day, while anxiety changes the picture to students worrying about exams.

In addition, numerous prosaic factors affect our ability
40 to record an image accurately. Duration of the encounter, proximity to the subject, lighting, and angle all affect our ability to see, and even stress may further undermine the accuracy of our perceptions.

What will this mean for criminal trials? Juries often have
45 been reluctant to convict without eyewitness identification. Blood samples, fingerprints, and the like frequently require understanding of complex scientific technicalities and do not resonate as deeply with juries as does testimony. But as confidence in eyewitness testimony wanes, such
50 circumstantial evidence may someday replace visual identification as the lynchpin of criminal trials.

---

17. The primary purpose of the passage is to

(A) raise concerns about the reliability of a type of evidence

(B) examine the role of culture in influencing perception

(C) question the reliability of juries in criminal trials

(D) shed light on the differences between perception and reality

(E) offer solutions to the problem of cultural bias

18. The "saying" in line 3 primarily serves to

(A) emphasize an accepted point of view

(B) weaken an opposing position

(C) define a controversial term

(D) explain an apparent contradiction

(E) voice a long-held concern

19. The author refers to "Western Europeans" and the "Zulu" (lines 16-18) in order to suggest that

(A) no two people ever see the same thing

(B) it is often difficult for two people of different backgrounds to agree

(C) cultural differences may affect what one perceives

(D) one's perception is entirely dependent upon one's culture

(E) people from certain cultures may be easily deceived

20. In line 31, "color" most nearly means

(A) modify

(B) brighten

(C) disguise

(D) excuse

(E) adorn

21. The discussion of the "photograph of four young men" (line 35) most directly demonstrates

(A) the psychological need to conform

(B) a link between emotion and perception

(C) the longing for a forgotten childhood

(D) a discrepancy between fiction and reality

(E) the importance of friendship

GO ON TO THE NEXT PAGE

22. The author's mention of "numerous prosaic factors" (line 39) primarily suggests that perception

(A) frequently leads people to make accusations regarding events that did not occur

(B) may sometimes be used to intentionally deceive those on juries

(C) is often hindered by the way the brain interprets images and colors

(D) may be affected by circumstances unrelated to the viewer's mental state

(E) is often a cause of anxiety in eyewitness testimony for civil and criminal trials

23. The author suggests that "blood samples" and "fingerprints" (line 46) are examples of evidence that

(A) can be interpreted only by trained scientists

(B) may be responsible for the conviction of innocent people

(C) are considered infallible by law enforcement officials

(D) may be seen as less convincing than eyewitness accounts

(E) will result in the elimination of eyewitness testimony from trials

24. Lines 49-51 ("But as . . . trials") primarily serve to

(A) offer support for a previous claim

(B) propose a hypothetical outcome

(C) change the focus of the discussion to an unrelated situation

(D) acknowledge a flaw in an influential study

(E) suggest an area for further research

STOP

If you finish before time is called, you may check your work on this section only.
Do not turn to any other section in the test.

SECTION 8
Time — 20 minutes
19 Questions

Turn to Section 8 of your answer sheet to answer the questions in this section.

Directions: For each question in this section, select the best answer from among the choices given and fill in the corresponding circle on the answer sheet.

Each sentence below has one or two blanks, each blank indicating that something has been omitted. Beneath the sentence are five words or sets of words labeled A through E. Choose the word or set of words that, when inserted in the sentence, best fits the meaning of the sentence as a whole.

Example:

Desiring to ------- his taunting friends, Mitch gave them taffy in hopes it would keep their mouths shut.

(A) eliminate   (B) satisfy   (C) overcome
    (D) ridicule   (E) silence

Ⓐ Ⓑ Ⓒ Ⓓ ●

---

1. After her grandchildren spent hours begging her to make cookies for them, Genevieve finally gave in as a result of the children's ------- .

    (A) merriment   (B) persistence   (C) generosity
        (D) friendliness   (E) hostility

2. Plentiful rainfall is essential to the ------- of fruit trees; if the weather is too dry, their health will be -------.

    (A) soundness . . reiterated
    (B) success . . ensured
    (C) finesse . . belittled
    (D) tenacity . . converged
    (E) survival . . compromised

3. Arsenic, best known as a lethal poison, is surprisingly effective at ------- a variety of diseases, a paradox that illustrates that even the most hazardous substances may have ------- effects.

    (A) infecting . . restorative
    (B) curing . . devastating
    (C) diagnosing . . reciprocal
    (D) treating . . beneficial
    (E) spreading . . salutary

4. Andy is ------- in good times and bad: he is confidently optimistic and virtually impossible to discourage.

    (A) morose   (B) facetious   (C) obdurate
        (D) sanguine   (E) controvertible

5. It was clear that the children were ------- at the end of the trip; with droopy eyes and frequent yawning, they began to doze off on the way home.

    (A) vertiginous   (B) inconsolable   (C) sedulous
        (D) somnolent   (E) fractious

6. Although winning large sums often changes one's attitude toward money, the most ------- skinflint is unlikely to shed a ------- entrenched over a lifetime and live opulently.

    (A) inveterate . . disposition
    (B) gracious . . habit
    (C) chronic . . collaboration
    (D) cantankerous . . dilemma
    (E) benevolent . . personality

GO ON TO THE NEXT PAGE

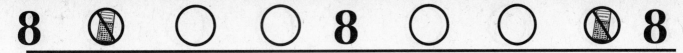

Questions 7-19 are based on the following passage.

The following passage relates some conclusions the author draws after listening to a lecture by a college professor.

Several weeks ago, when the weather was still fine, I decided to eat my lunch on the upper quad, an expanse of lawn stretching across the north end of campus and hedged
Line in by ancient pine trees on one side and university buildings
5 on the other. Depositing my brown paper lunch bag on the grass beside me, I munched in silence, watching the trees ripple in the wind and musing over the latest in a series of "controversial" symposiums I had attended that morning. The speaker, an antiquated professor in suspenders and a
10 mismatched cardigan, had delivered an earnest diatribe against modern tools of convenience like electronic mail and instant messaging programs. I thought his speech was interesting, but altogether too romantic.

My solitude was broken by two girls, deep in conversation,
15 who approached from behind and sat down on the grass about ten feet to my left. I stared hard at my peanut butter sandwich, trying to not eavesdrop, but their stream of chatter intrigued me. They interrupted each other frequently, paused at the same awkward moments, and responded to each
20 other's statements as if neither one heard what the other said. Confused, I stole a glance at them out of the corner of my eye. I could tell that they were college students by their style of dress and the heavy backpacks sinking into the grass beside them. Their body language and proximity also indicated that
25 they were friends. Instead of talking to each other, however, each one was having a separate dialogue on her cell phone.

As I considered this peculiar scene, this morning's bleary-eyed lecturer again intruded into my thoughts. His point in the symposium was that, aside from the disastrous
30 effects of emails and chatting on the spelling, grammar, and punctuation of the English language, these modern conveniences also considerably affect our personal lives. Before the advent of electronic mail, people wrote letters. Although writing out words by hand posed an inconvenience,
35 it also conferred certain important advantages. The writer had time to think about his message, about how he could best phrase it in order to help his reader understand him, about how he could convey his emotions without the use of dancing and flashing smiley-face icons. When he finished
40 his letter, he had created a permanent work of art to which a hurriedly typed email or abbreviated chat room conversation could never compare. The temporary, impersonal nature of computers, Professor Spectacles concluded, is gradually rendering our lives equally temporary and impersonal.

45 And what about cell phones? I thought. I have attended classes where students, instead of turning off their cell phones for the duration of the lecture, leave the classroom to take calls without the slightest hint of embarrassment. I have sat in movie theaters and ground my teeth in frustration at the
50 person behind me who can't wait until the movie is over to give his colleague a scene-by-scene replay. And then I watched each girl next to me spend her lunch hour talking to someone else instead of her friend. Like the rest of the world, these two pay a significant price for the benefits of
55 convenience and the added safety of being in constant contact with the world. When they have a cell phone, they are never alone, but then again, *they are never alone.*

They may not recognize it, but those girls, like most of us, could use a moment of solitude. Cell phones make it so easy
60 to reach out and touch someone that they have us confused into thinking that being alone is the same thing as being lonely. It's all right to disconnect from the world every once in a while; in fact, I feel certain that our sanity and identity as humans necessitates it. And I'm starting to think that maybe
65 the Whimsical Professor ranting about his "technological opiates" is not so romantic after all.

7. The sentence in which "controversial" (lines 5-8) appears indicates that the narrator considers the word to be

(A) a metaphor
(B) a prediction
(C) an impression
(D) an overstatement
(E) an epithet

8. In lines 9-10, the narrator mentions "suspenders and a mismatched cardigan" primarily in order to

(A) point out that college professors are often underpaid
(B) portray the speaker as somewhat eccentric
(C) criticize the speaker's lack of fashion sense
(D) examine the relationship between clothing and technology
(E) praise the speaker for his refusal to conform to society

9. Lines 14-20 suggest that the narrator viewed the conversation between the two girls as

(A) refined
(B) insignificant
(C) disjointed
(D) hostile
(E) tedious

GO ON TO THE NEXT PAGE

10. In line 21, "stole" most nearly means

(A) visited
(B) borrowed
(C) appropriated
(D) illustrated
(E) hazarded

11. The passage as a whole suggests that the narrator regards the conversation between the two girls as

(A) a situation that causes the narrator to reflect on an opinion expressed in the previous paragraph
(B) a typical conversation between two college students
(C) the reasons that modern modes of communication are necessary
(D) an incident that resulted in a confrontation between two students
(E) the narrator's annoyance with inconsiderate students

12. The narrator's reference to "smiley-face icons" (line 39) most directly suggests

(A) nostalgia for an easier way of life
(B) skepticism about certain modes of communication
(C) annoyance at the insensitivity of modern writers
(D) confusion over the complexities of modern conveniences
(E) appreciation for the expressive possibilities of email

13. Which of the following examples, if true, would best illustrate the symposium speaker's reasoning as described in the third paragraph?

(A) A newlywed couple sends copies of a generic thank-you card from an Internet site to wedding guests.
(B) A high school student uses a graphing program for her algebra homework.
(C) A former high school class president uses the Internet to locate and invite members of the class to a reunion.
(D) A publisher utilizes an editing program to proofread texts before they are printed.
(E) A hostess uses her computer to design and print nameplates for all her party guests.

14. The narrator suggests that the "person" (line 50) is

(A) impetuous
(B) languid
(C) tactless
(D) demonstrative
(E) taciturn

15. The author would most likely define the "significant price" (line 54) as the

(A) costs that must be shouldered by people of all nations
(B) charges that result from excessive cell phone use
(C) difficulty of experiencing a certain amount of privacy
(D) satisfaction that comes from close personal relationships
(E) insecurity caused by modern communication devices

16. In line 57, the author italicizes the words "they are never alone" primarily to

(A) draw attention to a social problem
(B) indicate that the phrase is a translation
(C) suggest that the phrase is a metaphor
(D) imply an alternate meaning of the phrase
(E) point out that the phrase is an exaggeration

17. In context, the reference to the "Whimsical Professor" in line 65 suggests that the narrator was experiencing

(A) a sensation of regret
(B) an unforeseen difficulty
(C) a moment of solitude
(D) a feeling of loneliness
(E) a change of heart

18. In the context of the passage, which piece of technology would the narrator disapprove of most?

(A) A wristwatch that automatically updates the time with a global server
(B) A portable gaming device featuring realistic graphics
(C) A device allowing the user to chat with other people at any time
(D) An earpiece that automatically translates languages to English
(E) A digital book reader with a large, bulky screen

19. The primary purpose of the passage is to

(A) criticize an expert
(B) evaluate an argument
(C) describe a conversation
(D) relate an anecdote
(E) defend a technology

STOP
**If you finish before time is called, you may check your work on this section only.
Do not turn to any other section in the test.**

NO TEST MATERIAL ON THIS PAGE.

SECTION 9
Time — 20 minutes
16 Questions

Turn to Section 9 of your answer sheet to answer the questions in this section.

Directions: For this section, solve each problem and decide which is the best of the choices given. Fill in the corresponding circle on the answer sheet. You may use any available space for scratchwork.

Notes

1. The use of a calculator is permitted.

2. All numbers used are real numbers.

3. Figures that accompany problems in this test are intended to provide information useful in solving the problems. They are drawn as accurately as possible EXCEPT when it is stated in a specific problem that the figure is not drawn to scale. All figures lie in a plane unless otherwise indicated.

4. Unless otherwise specified, the domain of any function f is assumed to be the set of all real numbers x for which $f(x)$ is a real number.

Reference Information

$A = \pi r^2$ $A = lw$ $A = \frac{1}{2}bh$ $V = lwh$ $V = \pi r^2 h$ $c^2 = a^2 + b^2$
$C = 2\pi r$

Special Right Triangles

The number of degrees of arc in a circle is 360.

The sum of the measures in degrees of the angles of a triangle is 180.

1. Which of the following represents "the square of the sum of a and b" ?

(A) $a^2 + b^2$
(B) $(a + b)^2$
(C) $a^2 + b$
(D) $2a + 2b$
(E) $a + b^2$

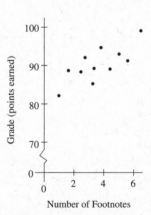

2. Eleven students were instructed to write an essay. The scatterplot above shows the grade and the number of footnotes in each essay. Which of the following is true regarding the line of best fit?

(A) Its slope is negative.
(B) Its slope is positive.
(C) It goes through the point $(0, t)$, where $t \le 0$.
(D) It goes through the point $(s, 0)$, where $s \ge 0$.
(E) It goes through the point $(0, 0)$.

GO ON TO THE NEXT PAGE

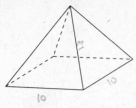

3. The pyramid shown above has a square base with an area of 100 square feet. If each edge from the top of the pyramid to a corner of the base is 13 feet long, what is the sum of the lengths of the 8 edges of the pyramid?

(A) 92
(B) 96
(C) 100
(D) 104
(E) 108

4. Selena has two types of records, worth a total of $41.75. Of her 25 records, b records are worth $1.25 each and the remaining d records are worth $2.30 each. Selena has no other types of records. Which of the following sets of equations can be solved to determine how many of each record type Selena has?

(A) $b + d = 41.75$
$3.55(b + d) = 25$
(B) $3.55(b + d) = 41.75$
$1.25(b + d) = 2.30$
(C) $3.55(b + d) = 41.75$
$1.25b + 2.30d = 25$
(D) $b + d = 25$
$2.30b + 1.25d = 41.75$
(E) $b + d = 25$
$1.25b + 2.30d = 41.75$

5. Eva and Magnus took a road trip and shared the driving. Eva drove four times as many miles as Magnus drove. What percent of the total miles of the trip did Eva drive?

(A) 70%
(B) 75%
(C) 80%
(D) 85%
(E) 90%

6. Cathy's average rate during the Boston Marathon was 10 minutes a mile for the first b hours where $b < 4$. In terms of b, how many more miles does Cathy have to run to complete the 26-mile race?

(A) $26 - 6b$

(B) $26 - 600b$

(C) $6b - 26$

(D) $26 - \dfrac{6}{b}$

(E) $\dfrac{26 - b}{6}$

GO ON TO THE NEXT PAGE

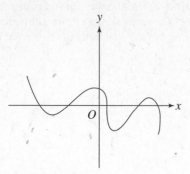

7. What is the total number of *x*- and *y*-intercepts contained in the graph that would result from reflecting the graph above about the *x*-axis?

(A) Three
(B) Four
(C) Five
(D) Six
(E) Seven

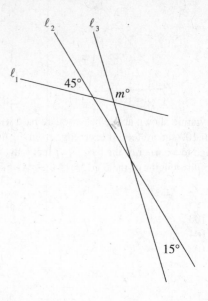

9. Three lines, ℓ_1, ℓ_2, and ℓ_3 intersect as shown. What is the value of *m* ?

(A) 115
(B) 120
(C) 125
(D) 130
(E) 145

8. If $w + x = 5$ and $y + z = 6$, what is the value of $wy + xz + wz + xy$?

(A) 11
(B) 22
(C) 30
(D) 41
(E) 60

$$a^3 \times a^6 = a^c$$

$$\frac{\left(b^5\right)^d}{b^d} = b^{40}$$

10. In the equations above, $a > 1$ and $b > 1$. What is the sum of *c* and *d* ?

(A) 8
(B) 9
(C) 15
(D) 17
(E) 19

GO ON TO THE NEXT PAGE

11. If $a + b - c = d + 6$, $c - b = 8$, and $3a = 2 - d$, what is the value of a ?

(A) 2
(B) 4
(C) 8
(D) 12
(E) 16

12. If $\dfrac{z}{3} - \dfrac{5}{6} = \left| \dfrac{z}{3} - \dfrac{5}{6} \right|$, what is the least possible integer value of z ?

(A) −3
(B) 0
(C) 2
(D) 3
(E) 6

13. The number represented by $\dfrac{1}{x}$ has a tens digit larger than its units digit. If the tens digit of $\dfrac{1}{x}$ is odd, what is the greatest possible value of x ?

(A) 0.010204. . .
(B) 0.027027 . . .
(C) 0.03333333 . . .
(D) 0.09090909 . . .
(E) 0.1

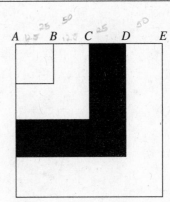

Note: Figure not drawn to scale.

14. In the figure above, four squares share a vertex at point A. If B is the midpoint of $\overline{AC}$, C is the midpoint of $\overline{AD}$, and D is the midpoint of $\overline{AE}$, what fractional part of the largest square is shaded?

(A) $\dfrac{1}{16}$

(B) $\dfrac{1}{8}$

(C) $\dfrac{3}{16}$

(D) $\dfrac{1}{4}$

(E) $\dfrac{5}{16}$

GO ON TO THE NEXT PAGE

$$\frac{5}{\sqrt{x-3}} = 3$$

15. For $x > 3$, which of the following equations is equivalent to the equation above?

(A) $5 = 3(x - 3)$
(B) $3 = 9(x - 3)$
(C) $25 = 3(x - 9)$
(D) $25 = 9(x - 3)$
(E) $25 = 3(x - 3)$

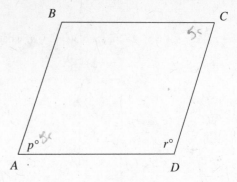

Note: Figure not drawn to scale.

16. In the figure above, $AB\|CD$ and $AD\|BC$. If $p = 5r$, what is the value of p ?

(A) 15
(B) 30
(C) 75
(D) 90
(E) 150

S T O P
If you finish before time is called, you may check your work on this section only.
Do not turn to any other section in the test.

NO TEST MATERIAL ON THIS PAGE.

SECTION 10
Time — 10 minutes
14 Questions

Turn to Section 10 of your answer sheet to answer the questions in this section.

Directions: For each question in this section, select the best answer from among the choices given and fill in the corresponding circle on the answer sheet.

The following sentences test correctness and effectiveness of expression. Part of each sentence or the entire sentence is underlined; beneath each sentence are five ways of phrasing the underlined material. Choice A repeats the original phrasing; the other four choices are different. If you think the original phrasing produces a better sentence than any of the alternatives, select choice A; if not, select one of the other choices.

In making your selection, follow the requirements of standard written English; that is, pay attention to grammar, choice of words, sentence construction, and punctuation. Your selection should result in the most effective sentence—clear and precise, without awkwardness or ambiguity.

EXAMPLE:

Bobby Flay baked his first cake <u>and he was thirteen years old then</u>.

(A) and he was thirteen years old then
(B) when he was thirteen
(C) at age thirteen years old
(D) upon the reaching of thirteen years
(E) at the time when he was thirteen

1. <u>The International Students' Club sponsoring bake sales last month</u> in order to raise funds for foreign exchange students to visit their families during the holidays.

(A) The International Students' Club sponsoring bake sales last month
(B) The International Students' Club would sponsor bake sales last month
(C) Sponsoring bake sales last month, the International Students' Club
(D) The International Students' Club sponsored bake sales last month
(E) Bake sales sponsored last month by the International Students' Club

2. <u>As an area that is a habitat for 40,000 varieties of plants, the Amazon Rainforest is growing</u> across 1.7 billion acres in the center of South America.

(A) As an area that is a habitat for 40,000 varieties of plants, the Amazon Rainforest is growing
(B) An area that is a habitat for 40,000 varieties of plants, the growth of the Amazon Rain forest
(C) A habitat for 40,000 varieties of plants, the Amazon Rainforest grows
(D) It is a habitat for 40,000 varieties of plants but the Amazon Rainforest also grows
(E) A habitat for 40,000 varieties of plants, the Amazon Rainforest, growing

3. Albert Einstein, who won a Nobel prize for physics, <u>dedicated the last years of his life and searched</u> for a unified field theory.

(A) dedicated the last years of his life and searched
(B) dedicated the last years of his life having searched
(C) having dedicated the last years of his life doing his searching
(D) dedicated the last years of his life to searching
(E) dedicating the last years of his life searching

4. <u>The Beatles, remembered for their groundbreaking music, which</u> dramatically affected the new, burgeoning teen culture of the band's biggest fans.

(A) The Beatles, remembered for their groundbreaking music, which
(B) The Beatles are remembered for their groundbreaking music, it
(C) The Beatles are remembered for their groundbreaking music, which
(D) The Beatles, with their groundbreaking music that
(E) The Beatles, their groundbreaking music is remembered to have

GO ON TO THE NEXT PAGE

5. Mastering the dozens of recipes for stocks and sauces found in many French cookbooks <u>are essential for young cooks when they work</u> in four-star kitchens.

(A) are essential for young cooks when they work
(B) is essential for young cooks working
(C) is the essential thing young cooks make when they work
(D) for young working cooks, are essential
(E) and which are essential for young cooks who work

6. The manager's directions for the project described how to organize the team, <u>meeting the deadline, and satisfying the client</u>.

(A) meeting the deadline, and satisfying the client
(B) both meeting the deadline, and satisfying the client
(C) with meeting the deadline and then satisfying the client
(D) meet and satisfy the deadline and the client
(E) meet the deadline, and satisfy the client

7. In the mid-nineteenth century, English novelists and political theorists described cities full of workers <u>experiencing a world of misery and struggling</u> against extreme poverty for their survival.

(A) experiencing a world of misery and struggling
(B) experiencing a world of misery, and they struggle
(C) who were experiencing a world of misery, to struggle
(D) who experienced a world of misery, then they struggled
(E) they experienced a world of misery to struggle

8. Most troublesome of the anthracnose fungi, *Discula destructiva*, if untreated, kills its host tree <u>gradually, and they are also known to cause</u> symptoms that resemble those of other diseases.

(A) gradually, and they are also known to cause
(B) gradually, and it is known that they cause
(C) gradually and is also known to cause
(D) gradually also causing their
(E) gradually, in addition, it causes its

9. The reason Mark Twain's writings utilize satire to address social questions is <u>that satire can both entertain readers and provoke</u> thought and controversy.

(A) that satire can both entertain readers and provoke
(B) it both entertained readers and it could provoke
(C) because satire entertain readers and provoke
(D) because of it entertaining readers and provoking
(E) that of entertaining readers and provoking

10. The admissions officers reported that applying for scholarships and other types of financial aid <u>neither increase or decrease</u> a student's chance of being accepted into the program.

(A) neither increase or decrease
(B) neither increase nor decrease
(C) neither increases nor decreases
(D) do not increase or decrease
(E) does nor increase or decreases

11. <u>Since they are instructed to avoid controversial statement-making</u>, political speeches are usually bland and innocuous.

(A) Since they are instructed to avoid controversial statement making
(B) Being instructed to avoid making controversial statements
(C) Based on instructions to speechwriters to avoid making controversial statements
(D) Advising speechwriters to avoid making controversial statements
(E) Because speechwriters are instructed to avoid making controversial statements

12. Playwrights convey the range of human emotions <u>by combining the comedic with the tragedy</u> in their plays.

(A) by combining the comedic with the tragedy
(B) by combining the comedic with the tragic
(C) in a combining of comedy with the tragic
(D) when their combining comedy with the tragic
(E) through combinations of comedy and tragic

GO ON TO THE NEXT PAGE

13. The school's stringent dress codes and guidelines for proper conduct <u>were not impulsive but a need</u> to prevent lewd and offensive behavior from distracting the student population.

   (A) were not impulsive but a need
   (B) were not impulsive but needed
   (C) were not because of impulse, it needed
   (D) resulted not from impulse, but it needed
   (E) resulted not from impulse but from a need

14. Despite its efficient and widespread use in America, the synthetic pesticide DDT was <u>banned: its effects were</u> found to be extremely dangerous for humans and the environment.

   (A) banned: its effects were
   (B) banned, its effects were
   (C) banned; its effects being
   (D) banned; its effects were being
   (E) banned, yet its effects were

STOP

If you finish before time is called, you may check your work on this section only.
Do not turn to any other section in the test.

NO TEST MATERIAL ON THIS PAGE.

PRACTICE TEST 1: ANSWER KEY

2 Math	4 Reading	5 Writing	6 Math	7 Reading	8 Reading	9 Math	10 Writing
1. C	1. C	1. B	1. E	1. B	1. B	1. B	1. D
2. E	2. D	2. E	2. B	2. A	2. E	2. B	2. C
3. C	3. B	3. E	3. C	3. C	3. D	3. A	3. D
4. B	4. C	4. D	4. D	4. A	4. D	4. E	4. C
5. B	5. B	5. A	5. A	5. B	5. D	5. C	5. B
6. D	6. B	6. C	6. C	6. E	6. A	6. A	6. E
7. D	7. A	7. A	7. C	7. D	7. D	7. D	7. A
8. A	8. E	8. B	8. D	8. B	8. B	8. C	8. C
9. D	9. A	9. D	9. $\dfrac{40}{3}$ or 13.3	9. B	9. C	9. B	9. A
10. C	10. E	10. E	10. 120	10. C	10. E	10. E	10. C
11. C	11. B	11. A	11. 3,899	11. B	11. A	11. B	11. E
12. D	12. E	12. C	12. 75	12. E	12. B	12. D	12. B
13. D	13. C	13. E	13. 2	13. A	13. A	13. E	13. E
14. E	14. D	14. B	14. 195	14. C	14. C	14. C	14. A
15. E	15. E	15. C	15. 4	15. D	15. C	15. D	
16. E	16. A	16. D	16. 41, 43, 45, 47	16. B	16. D	16. E	
17. D	17. E	17. B	17. 12	17. A	17. E		
18. A	18. C	18. A	18. $\dfrac{9}{2}$ or 4.5	18. A	18. C		
19. C	19. D	19. B		19. C	19. B		
20. A	20. C	20. D		20. A			
	21. D	21. C		21. B			
	22. A	22. D		22. D			
	23. E	23. D		23. D			
	24. A	24. E		24. B			
		25. C					
		26. D					
		27. C					
		28. E					
		29. D					
		30. A					
		31. C					
		32. D					
		33. A					
		34. B					
		35. D					

SAT SCORING WORKSHEET

For directions on how to score your SAT practice test, see pages 10–11.

SAT Writing Section

Total Writing Multiple-Choice Questions Correct: ☐

−

Total Writing Multiple-Choice Questions Incorrect: _____ ÷ 4 = ☐

Grammar Scaled Subscore

Grammar Raw Score: ☐ ▬ ☐

Compare the Grammar Raw Score with the Writing Multiple-Choice Subscore Conversion Table on page 92 to find the Grammar Scaled Subscore.

+

Your Essay Score (2–12): _____ × 2 = ☐

Writing Raw Score: ☐

Writing Scaled Score

Compare Raw Score with SAT Score Conversion Table on page 92 to find the Writing Scaled Score. ▬ ☐

SAT Critical Reading Section

Total Critical Reading Questions Correct: ☐

−

Total Critical Reading Questions Incorrect: _____ ÷ 4 = ☐

Critical Reading Raw Score: ☐

Critical Reading Scaled Score

Compare Raw Score with SAT Score Conversion Table on page 92 to find the Critical Reading Scaled Score. ▬ ☐

SAT Math Section

Total Math Grid-In Questions Correct: ☐

+

Total Math Multiple-Choice Questions Correct: ☐

−

Total Math Multiple-Choice Questions Incorrect: _____ ÷ 4 = ☐

Don't include wrong answers from grid-ins!

Math Raw Score: ☐

Math Scaled Score

Compare Raw Score with SAT Score Conversion Table on page 92 to find the Math Scaled Score. ▬ ☐

SAT SCORE CONVERSION TABLE

Raw Score	Writing Scaled Score	Reading Scaled Score	Math Scaled Score	Raw Score	Writing Scaled Score	Reading Scaled Score	Math Scaled Score	Raw Score	Writing Scaled Score	Reading Scaled Score	Math Scaled Score
73	800			47	590–630	600–640	660–700	21	400–440	410–450	440–480
72	790–800			46	590–630	590–630	650–690	20	390–430	400–440	430–470
71	780–800			45	580–620	580–620	650–690	19	380–420	400–440	430–470
70	770–800			44	570–610	580–620	640–680	18	370–410	390–430	420–460
69	770–800			43	570–610	570–610	630–670	17	370–410	380–420	410–450
68	760–800			42	560–600	570–610	620–660	16	360–400	370–410	400–440
67	760–800	800		41	560–600	560–600	610–650	15	350–390	360–400	400–440
66	760–800	770–800		40	550–590	550–590	600–640	14	340–380	350–390	390–430
65	750–790	760–800		39	540–580	550–590	590–630	13	330–370	340–380	380–420
64	740–780	750–790		38	530–570	540–580	590–630	12	320–360	340–380	360–400
63	730–770	740–780		37	530–570	530–570	580–620	11	320–360	330–370	350–390
62	720–760	730–770		36	520–560	530–570	570–610	10	310–350	320–360	340–380
61	710–750	720–760		35	510–550	520–560	560–600	9	300–340	310–350	330–370
60	700–740	710–750		34	500–540	520–560	560–600	8	290–330	300–340	320–360
59	690–730	700–740		33	490–530	510–550	550–590	7	280–320	300–340	310–350
58	680–720	690–730		32	480–520	500–540	540–580	6	270–310	290–330	300–340
57	680–720	680–720		31	470–510	490–530	530–570	5	260–300	280–320	290–330
56	670–710	670–710		30	470–510	480–520	520–560	4	240–280	270–310	280–320
55	660–720	670–710		29	460–500	470–510	520–560	3	230–270	250–290	280–320
54	650–690	660–700	760–800	28	450–490	470–510	510–550	2	230–270	240–280	270–310
53	640–680	650–690	740–780	27	440–480	460–500	500–540	1	220–260	220–260	260–300
52	630–670	640–680	730–770	26	430–470	450–490	490–530	0	210–250	200–240	250–290
51	630–670	630–670	710–750	25	420–460	440–480	480–520	–1	200–240	200–230	230–270
50	620–660	620–660	690–730	24	410–450	430–470	470–510	–2	200–230	200–220	220–260
49	610–650	610–650	680–720	23	410–450	430–470	460–500	–3	200–220	200–210	200–240
48	600–640	600–640	670–710	22	400–440	420–460	450–490				

WRITING MULTIPLE-CHOICE SUBSCORE CONVERSION TABLE

Grammar Raw Score	Grammar Scaled Subscore	Grammar Raw Score	Grammar Scaled Subscore	Grammar Raw Score	Grammar Scaled Subscore	Grammar Raw Score	Grammar Scaled Subscore	Grammar Raw Score	Grammar Scaled Subscore
49	78–80	38	67–71	27	55–59	16	42–46	5	30–34
48	77–80	37	66–70	26	54–58	15	41–45	4	29–33
47	75–79	36	65–69	25	53–57	14	40–44	3	28–32
46	74–78	35	64–68	24	52–56	13	39–43	2	27–31
45	72–76	34	63–67	23	51–55	12	38–42	1	25–29
44	72–76	33	62–66	22	50–54	11	36–40	0	24–28
43	71–75	32	61–65	21	49–53	10	35–39	–1	22–26
42	70–74	31	60–64	20	47–51	9	34–38	–2	20–23
41	69–73	30	59–63	19	46–50	8	33–37	–3	20–22
40	68–72	29	58–62	18	45–49	7	32–36		
39	68–72	28	56–60	17	44–48	6	31–35		

Chapter 5
Practice Test 1:
Answers and
Explanations

SECTION 2

1. **C** Start by finding the total weight of the water containers. If there are 10 water containers that weigh 20 pounds each, then there is a total water container weight of 200 pounds. Similarly, if there are 8 identical sacks of food, then there is a total of 80 pounds of food. Taken together, there is a total weight of 280 pounds, or answer choice (C).

2. **E** Draw segment $\overline{PQ}$ and Plug In the information from the question. $3m$ is half of the total length, which is therefore $6m$, answer (E). We can Plug In our own number for m as well: if $m = 2$, then $\overline{FQ}$ is 6 and the whole length of $\overline{PQ}$ is 12. Among the answers, only (E) gives 12 when $m = 2$. The result is (A) if $\overline{FQ}$ is divided rather than multiplied by 2, while (B) is the length of $\overline{PF}$.

3. **C** On the number line, the space between the 96 and the 97 is divided into 5 equal parts. The first tick mark is equal to 96.2, the second equals 96.4, the third equals 96.6, the fourth equals 96.8. Since we are looking for which point is equal to 96.7, we need the one that is between the third and fourth lines after 96, which is where point C is located.

4. **B** In January, Jacksonville Tax Service spent $200 on office supplies and spent $400 on supplies in May. This is double what it was in January, so (B) 2 is the correct answer.

5. **B** It costs $10 to buy a hand-stitched bag and $.50 for each polished stone, represented by p. So in dollars, each polished stone would cost $.5p$ or $\frac{1}{2}p$. The stones are going into 2 bags that cost $20 together, so the total cost for the bag of polished stones would be $20 + \frac{1}{2}p$, as in (B). We can also replace the variable with a number. If $p = 4$, the stones would cost $2, for a total of $22 with the bag. Only (B) gives an answer of $22 when the p is replaced with a 4 in the answer choices. (A) gives $28, (C) gives $42, (D) gives $60, and (E) gives $40.

6. **D** Five of the numbers are greater than –2, and there are a total of 8 numbers, so the correct fraction is (D) $\frac{5}{8}$. The answer in (E) incorrectly includes –2; (A) is the probability that the number would be less than –2; (B) is the probability that the number is –2 or less.

7. **D** Translate the question into math. Three times a number is the same as $3x$. That number subtracted from 12 is the same as $12 - x$. So $3x = 12 - x$. Now solve: Add x to each side: $4x = 12$, and $x = 3$. The answer is (D).

8. **A** Begin by finding how much water is left in the pond at the end of the seventh week. Half of the water evaporates each week, which means that there's half as much water left at the end of each week. There are 2,400 gallons at the end of the third week, so there are 1,200 gallons in the pond at the end of the fourth week, 600 gallons at the end of the fifth week, 300 gallons at the end of the sixth week, and 150 gallons at the end of the seventh week. To find how much more water was in the pond in the third week, subtract this from the 2,400 gallons from the third week: $2,400 - 150 = 2,250$, answer (A).

9. **D** Because AB is a radius of the circle, use the area formula, πr^2, to find that the area of the whole circle is 36π. The question states that the arc is $\frac{1}{9}$ of the circumference so the sector is $\frac{1}{9}$ of the total area. $\frac{36\pi}{9}$ gives the area of the sector, 4π (D).

10. **C** Because all the answer choices have the value –2 on the left, $4t + 1$ in the middle, and 2 on the right, all we need to do is focus on the inequality signs. We can eliminate (E) off the bat, because it is saying that –2 is greater than 2. On the number line, a hollow dot indicates that the number is **not** included in the range of values, so for the first inequality symbol in each number sentence, eliminate the answers that have a ≤ rather than <. (A) and (B) are out. A solid dot indicates that the number is included and should be represented by ≤, so eliminate (D). The correct answer is (C).

11. **C** Only in (C) is a positive y guaranteed a negative x and vice-versa. Start by drawing the lines in the answer choices. (A) is a horizontal line in which all the y values are –2. When the x value is also negative, the product of the coordinates is positive. (B) is a vertical line in which all the x values are –2. When the y value is also negative, the product of the coordinates is positive. To disprove (D) use the equation to find points on the line. Using $x = 2$ and $x = -2$, gives coordinate pairs $(2, -6)$ and $(-2, 2)$, which if connected cut through the portion of the coordinate plane where x and y are both negative, thus giving a positive product. (E) can be disproved because if $x = -2$ in the equation, the y value is –6, which gives a positive product.

12. **D** Collect like terms by getting all the variables onto one side: $100 = x^2 + 2xy + y^2$. The right side of the equation is a commonly used quadratic equation: $x^2 + 2xy + y^2 = (x + y)^2$. Use this to factor the right side of the equation and get $(x + y)^2 = 100$, as seen in (D).

13. **D** To prove the statement false, we need to find a number in which the sum of the digits is odd, but p is even (opposite of *must be odd*). Eliminate (A), (C), and (E) because they are odd and we are looking for an even number. (D) is correct because the sum of the digits in 1,020 is odd, but the number itself is even. The sum of the digits in (B) is even, and therefore does not prove the statement false.

14.   E   One way to solve this is to use each answer as the area of the square and see if the surrounding rectangles can be made to have sides that are all integers. Eliminate (A) and (B) because the area of the square cannot be larger than the area of one of the rectangles. In (C) the short side of rectangles A and B is 5 and the long side is 6, but this leaves only 1 unit, which cannot be split into two integers. In (D), an area of 16 means the short side of rectangles A and B is 4, but the long side of would have to be 7.5, which cannot be split into two integers. Only (E) works: rectangles A and B would have dimensions of 3×10, leaving 7 units for sides of the surrounding rectangles. 7 can be split into 1 and 6, 2 and 5, or 3 and 4.

15.   E   We can find the answer by replacing b and h with real numbers. Let's say $b = 3$ and $h = 4$. Since the area of a triangle is $\frac{1}{2}$ base times height, the area of triangle A is $\frac{1}{2} \times 3 \times 4 = 6$. The area of the triangle is x, so $x = 6$. Now find the area of the rectangle, where $b = 3$ and $h = 4$: each quantity is doubled, so the rectangle is 6 by 8. The area of a rectangle is length times width, so the area of rectangle B is 48. Choice (E) represents 48 when $x = 6$. To solve this question algebraically, use the triangle area formula, $A = \frac{1}{2}bh$, to find the area of triangle A: $x = \frac{1}{2}bh$. The area of rectangle B (length × width) is $2b \times 2h$, or $4bh$. Since $4bh$ is $8 \times \frac{1}{2}bh$, the area of rectangle B is $8x$, as seen in (E). Watch out for (B); that's the area of a triangle with those dimensions.

16.   E   Plug In a value for a. Let's say $a = 16$; therefore, $a^{\frac{1}{2}}$ is $16^{\frac{1}{2}}$, or 4. So the equation is now $4 = b^2$, which means that $b = 2$. The question asks for the value of a^2, which would be 16^2, or 256. Find the values in the answer choices for when $b = 2$. Choice (E) gives 2^8, which is 256. To solve this question algebraically, first find a^2, which results from raising $a^{\frac{1}{2}}$ to the fourth power. When we raise a number with an exponent to another power, we multiply the exponents. So $\left(a^{\frac{1}{2}}\right)^4 = a^{\frac{4}{2}} = a^2$. Now do the same on the other side of the equal sign for b^2: $\left(b^2\right)^4 = b^8$, the answer in (E).

17. **D** We can determine how many different meals Shawn can make by multiplying the number of pastas, sauces, and toppings; the product is the number of meals Shawn can make. Since Shawn can make 30 different meals, the number of sauces available to Shawn must be a factor of 30. Only choice (D) gives a number that is not a factor of 30. For example, choice (C) is incorrect because Shawn could have 3 sauces available. He could also have, say, 2 types of pasta and 5 types of toppings; the product of 2, 3, and 5 is 30. Choice (D) is correct because he can't have 4 choices of sauces to make 30 different meals. If the product of the number of pastas, sauces (4), and toppings is 30, then the product of the number of pastas and toppings is $\frac{30}{4}$, and there's no number of pastas and toppings that, when multiplied, will give you $\frac{30}{4}$.

18. **A** This question is most easily answered using the group formula: group 1 + group 2 – both + neither = total number. In this case, we don't need the "neither" portion. We know that the number of appetizers is 7 more than the number of deserts, and that half of the entire class made both dishes. This gives us $d + (d + 7) - 25 = 50$. Solving the equation gives $d = 34$, but that is the number of everyone who made a dessert, not those who made *only* dessert. Subtract the "both" number from this to get $34 - 25 = 9$, answer (A). (B) is the number of students who made only an appetizer, (C) is the number of students who made both dishes, (D) is the total number of desserts made and (E) is the total number of appetizers made.

19. **C** To find the sides of the triangle, find the x- and y-intercepts of the function. To find the y-intercept, substitute 0 for all the x-values: $y = 3x^2 - 8x + 4 = 3(0) - 8(0) + 4 = 4$. Thus, the side MN in the figure has a measure of 4. To find the x-intercept, set $y = 0$: $0 = 3x^2 - 8x + 4 = (3x - 2)(x - 2)$. The x-intercept, therefore, has two values: $x = \frac{2}{3}$ and $x = 2$. Note, however, that the point N on the figure is the x-intercept farther from the origin, so N must be the x-intercept given by the point $(2, 0)$. Accordingly, the length of side LM is 2. To find the area of this triangle, use the area formula $A = \frac{1}{2}bh = \frac{1}{2}(2)(4) = 4$, answer (C).

20. **A** The easiest way to work this question is to Plug In numbers for the variables. Since b is in both equations, let's say $b = 2$. Then solve for a and c. $2a = 3(2)$, so $a = 3$. $\frac{1}{3}c = 6(2^2) + 2$, so $c = 78$. The question asks for c, so look for an answer that equals 78. Remember that $a = 3$. Choice (A) is equal to 78, so that's the answer. Choice (B) is equal to 84, (C) is 114, (D) is 168, and (E) is 174, so they're all wrong. To work the question algebraically, solve for b in the first equation by dividing both sides by 3 to get $\frac{2a}{3} = b$. Now, to solve for c, factor the second equation to get $\frac{1}{3}c = (2b)(3b) + 2$. Substitute for $2b$ and $3b$, using the value of b from the first equation, to get $\frac{1}{3}c = \left(2 \times \frac{2a}{3}\right)(2a) + 2$. Now collect like terms and simplify the equation: $\frac{1}{3}c = \left(\frac{4a}{3}\right)(2a) + 2$, $\frac{1}{3}c = \frac{8a^2}{3} + 2$, and multiply both sides by 3 to get $c = 8a^2 + 6$, answer (A).

SECTION 4

1. **C** Since we know that the *witness's testimony* was *rambling and incoherent*, we want something that means "rambling." (C), *disjointed*, means "not connected," or "out of order," which matches what we know about the witness's testimony.

2. **D** Most of the words (except *recommendations*) work for the first blank, so focus on the second blank. There is a time trigger in the sentence: a *recent addition* will *soon* change something about the funds. The new *members* don't care about *fundraising* but throw *expensive parties*. A good word for the second blank is "gone." Only (D) *exhausted* is anything like "gone."

3. **B** The clue for the first blank is that *he did not take a stand on any issue*. His speeches must mean something like "not taking a position." This eliminates choices (C), (D), and (E). If he is *misleading* or *vague*, how do voters feel about his *position on topics*? The word *uncertain* (B) fits the sentence better than *assured*.

4. **C** For the first blank we need a word for something that would *support his theory*, such as "proof." Both (C) *substantiation* and (E) *verification* could mean "proof." A clue for the second blank, *nonetheless, he was surprised*, lets us know that the *claim was rejected* because of his lack of *support*. So the second blank must mean or be something "unsupported" or "unproven." (A) *hearsay* is close, because gossip is often not substantiated; (C) *fallacy* means "an erroneous or false idea" that would be unable to be proven. (E) *treachery* has to do with dishonesty, but *treachery* is a more serious type of betrayal than the sentence calls for. Only (C) matches both blanks.

5. **B** *Although* indicates that the blank is the opposite of *respectful. Impugned,* which means "attacked," is the only word that fits. The correct answer is (B).

6. **B** In the sentence, *straightforward descriptions* is opposite of *technical jargon,* and that these *books help beginners* tells us the book has no *technical jargon.* The first blank should mean *without* when combined with *of.* Both (B) and (D) work for the first blank. The second blank is a verb that means "teach" or "provide" *new knowledge…to beginners.* (B), (C), and maybe (A) could work in the second blank; eliminate (D) and (E); (B) is the only one that matches in both blanks.

7. **A** The word *because* tells us we're looking for a synonym for *pampered and spoiled.* Only *cosseted* fits. The correct answer is (A).

8. **E** So Greg *carefully accumulated money,* which means the blank must mean that *Greg was extremely* "good at saving money for the future." (A) *reticent* means that Greg wouldn't talk much, which doesn't work. (B) *assiduous* means that he pays careful attention to detail, which isn't the same as saving money. (C) *fallible* means he can makes mistakes, which isn't supported by the sentence, and (D) *clairvoyant* means that he can see the future. So (E), the only answer left, is correct. *Provident* means "frugal" or "saves money for a rainy day."

9. **A** The author of the passage brings up the victim in order to show a time when the National Parks had to pay a huge lawsuit because they didn't have enough warning signs. (A), *support a previous claim,* matches up with this: he had previously claimed that the signs were there to *protect the parks from unnecessary litigation,* and the reference to the victim gives an example of the unnecessary litigation the Parks are trying to avoid.

10. **E** Whittlesey compares the National Parks to Central Park, commenting that it would be ridiculous to put up as many warning signs in Central Park as the National Park is required to put up. He is not a fan of the ruling. (E), *sarcastic,* means he is making fun of it, which is exactly what he is doing.

11. **B** The passage states that *unlike traditional journalists, gonzo journalists use the power of both emotions and personal experience,* meaning that traditional journalists normally do not use emotions or personal experience—they remain objective in their writings. (B), *neutral,* comes closest to meaning "objective." (A), (C), and (D) are not synonyms for objective and (E), *subjective,* is the opposite of objective.

12. **E** The author mentions that gonzo journalism is different in many ways from standard journalistic writing: it can be sarcastic, emotional, rough, or personal. The only answer that matches this is (E), *its unconventionality*. (C) is wrong because although it mentions editing, it is not the focus of the passage. (D) is wrong because the passage states that gonzo journalism is different because of how it is written, not what is written about.

13. **C** The author of Passage 1 clearly argues one position: that time travel is unlikely. The author of Passage 2, on the other hand, has no position; he simply presents three opinions, ranging from skeptical (Stephen Hawking) to noncommittal (Carl Sagan) to optimistic (Ronald Mallett). (A), (B), (D), and (E) all mention things that are contradicted by the passages.

14. **D** The author brings up *contraptions* to show that in science fiction, time travel is easy. This contrasts sharply with the view he expresses in the next sentence. (D) paraphrases this contrast nicely. (A) contradicts the author's point of view, while (B), (C), and (E) are not mentioned in the passage.

15. **E** The "celebrity scientists" mentioned in the passage have postulated or hypothesized about the existence of wormholes, warp drives, and other theoretical constructs that might make time travel a reality. So the correct answer should be about someone who is thinking of a way to make time travel real. Only Ronald Mallett, at the end of Passage 2, does this, so answer (E) is correct. H.G. Wells and the science fiction fans (C) in Passage 1, are certainly fascinated by time travel, but they are not doing anything to make time travel a reality.

16. **A** The author of Passage 2 begins by acknowledging the importance of the Conjecture, but then notes that *Not everyone…is convinced* (line 57). He then goes on to outline two positions that differ, in varying degrees, with Hawking's Conjecture. Thus, he would regard the claim by the author of Passage 1 as *an oversimplification of a complex issue*, as in (A). (B), (C), and (D) are not mentioned in Passage 2, while (E) contradicts the passage.

17. **E** The passage mentions *hordes of time travelers,* suggesting *overwhelmed*, (E). (A) and (C) are the overly literal traps, (D) doesn't make sense, and (B) is extreme; they're *time-tourists*, so they're not coming to attack us!

18. **C** The author states that *the pace of technological advancement has been dramatic*, and then illustrates his point with an example: *In less than a hundred years, we have gone from horse-drawn carriages to walking on the moon.* (C) is a nice paraphrase of the author's point. The other answers are not indicated in the passage.

19. **D** The *argument* is stated as *if time travel were possible, wouldn't we be swamped with visitors from the future?* But, we would know if we were *swamped* only if we could see the visitors from the future. What if they are invisible? The author doesn't consider this possibility, because he is assuming that we would be able to see or somehow *notice* these visitors, as described in (D).

20. **C** After noting that Stephen Hawking's opinion *carries a great deal of weight*, the author states that the Conjecture *has caused many a professional scientist to dismiss the whole concept.* The next paragraph begins, *Not everyone, however, is convinced.* The passage as a whole shows two opposing reactions to the *Chronological Protection Conjecture*, thus showing the concept to be *controversial*, (C).

21. **D** The author of Passage 1 states *I agree…that Einstein's Theory of Relativity ought to make some form of limited travel to the future possible.* The author of Passage 2 states *Stephen Hawking's "Chronological Protection Conjecture,"…allow[s] for the possibility of time travel to the future.* These two statements support choice (D). (A) is false, while (B), (C), and (E) are not indicated in the passage.

22. **A** The statement about *hordes of time travelers* shows that the author of Passage 1 doesn't believe that time travel is possible. How would Sagan respond to this? We don't have to read his mind; we just have to know what he's already said which is that he *prefer[s] to "withhold judgment until there is better evidence."* (A) paraphrases this nicely.

23. **E** The quote is clearly used to throw into doubt the *Grandfather Paradox*, which (as we learned in Passage 1) claims that the universe must obey the laws of causality. (E) summarizes the purpose of the statement accurately.

24. **A** The word *noting* in the passage means something like "saying" or "stating an opinion." The colleague is stating his opinion as to the likelihood of time travel. The only answer that matches with this is (A), *asserting*, which means "to state an opinion."

SECTION 5

1. **B** As written, the sentence has no subject: *to arrest and imprison* are verbs, so eliminate (A). (B) fixes this problem with nouns *the arrest and imprisonment.* (D) and (E) change the meaning to state that the *petty criminals* themselves *improve the vitality*, rather than their arrest and imprisonment. (C) is an incomplete sentence.

2. **E** (A) and (D) use the unnecessary verb form *being* to modify *Mark's brother.* (C) is a sentence fragment. (B) changes the meaning of the sentence: the fact that he is *the national fencing champion* is not a new point, it is the reason for the scholarship. (E) keeps *the national fencing champion* as a modifier and places it closest to the person it is modifying.

3. **E** (A), (C), and (D) contain incorrect punctuation: two independent clauses cannot be joined by a comma and a dependent clause cannot follow a semicolon. (B) changes the meaning of the original sentence by adding *with.* (E) fixes the comma splice and keeps the original meaning.

4. **D** The conjunction *both* requires "and" between the conjoined elements. The absence of "and" from (A), (B), and (E) is reason enough to eliminate them. (C) lacks parallel structure, making (D) the better choice.

5. **A** The sentence is correct as written. (C) and (E) are sentence fragments. (D) has a misplaced modifier. In (B) the comma between two independent clauses creates a comma splice. (A) has the verbs in the proper tense and has the modified noun, *ecologists*, right next to its modifier.

6. **C** The sentence as written has an idiom error: the correct form is *not only…but also*. Eliminate (A), (B), and (E). The original sentence also has a parallelism error in *to illustrate…establishing*. Only (C) has the correct idiom and parallel structure.

7. **A** (A) contains all nouns—*a supporter, a defender, an opponent*—in parallel form. (B), (C), (D), and (E) all contain parallelism errors because they each change one of these to a gerund, such as *opposing* in (B) and (E) or a verb, such as *defended* in (C) and *opposed* in (D).

8. **B** (A) and (D) have incorrect verb tenses. (C) changes the meaning of the sentence with an unnecessary preposition and (E) adds an unnecessary conjunction. (B) uses the correct verb tense and the correct pronoun to start a modifying clause.

9. **D** As written the sentence has a misplaced modifier: *the rehearsal* could not have *been working in the rafters*. Nor could *a heavy camera* (B), (C), and (E). The only sentence that correctly identifies the stagehand as the one working in the rafters is (D).

10. **E** The sentence as written switches the pronoun from *We* to *you*, as does answer (B). The pronoun *it* in (C) does not agree with *lessons* in the non-underlined portion of the sentence. In (D) it is not clear what *it* refers to. (E) has pronouns that agree with the rest of the sentence (*we, our*) and eliminates unnecessary wordiness.

11. **A** This sentence is correct as written. The word *more* is appropriate because two things are being compared. The idiom *more…than* is correct, as is the parallel use of *as* after each word to go along with *offered*.

12. **C** The correct choice is (C) because of a verb tense error. The modifying phrase refers to a time in the past, so the main verb must be in the past tense. Since *has been* is in the present perfect tense, it is incorrect.

13. **E** There is no error in the sentence. (B) is the correct possessive pronoun to use with the plural noun *supervisors*. (C) has the correct plural form of the verb, since the subject of *find* is they.

14. **B** The correct choice is (B) because of a verb tense error. The verb *becoming* should be "became." As it stands, without the verb form the sentence is a fragment.

15. **C** The correct choice is (C) because *most brightest* is redundant. The correct phrasing would be *most brightly painted*.

16. **D** There is a pronoun error in answer choice (D). The pronoun *you* does not match *us*, causing an agreement error. It might be tempting to choose (C) because *own favorite* sounds weird, but that phrase does not break a grammar rule.

17. **B** The correct choice is (B) because of a subject-verb agreement error. The subject of the sentence is *one of the most famous plays* which refers to *The Clouds*. Since the subject is singular, the verb should be as well.

18. **A** Answer (A) contains an idiom error. *Advocate to* should be *advocate of*. Be sure to go through each answer choice carefully with grammar rules for each part of speech in mind when trying to spot an error.

19. **B** Choice (B) includes an agreement error. The subject of the sentence is *city park* which is singular, so the verb should be *contains* in order to agree. Choice (A) is an example of the way ETS will throw in uncommon usage which may sound wrong but doesn't break a rule.

20. **D** There is a pronoun error in choice (D). Remember, any time a pronoun is underlined, check that it agrees with the subject. In this case, *savings* is plural and the pronoun *it* is singular.

21. **C** Answer (C) contains an idiom error. The correct phrase is *brink of* not *brink to*. Remember that most idiom errors can be spotted by the misuse of a preposition, so when prepositions are underlined, always check for idioms.

22. **D** The correct choice is (D) because of a comparison error. The sentence is comparing New York City's smog problem to the actual city of Los Angeles instead of comparing it to Los Angeles' smog problem.

23. **D** This sentence contains a misplaced modifier in answer (D). As written, it sounds as if the *medication* takes the pill, which is not the intended meaning of the sentence.

24. **E** There is no error in this sentence. Don't rely on what the sentence "sounds" like when trying to find an error.

25. **C** Answer (C) contains a verb error. *Had ran* is incorrect; it would be correct as *had run*. When two things both start and stop in the past, we need the past perfect tense, which uses the helping verb *had* and the present tense of the verb.

26. **D** Choice (D) contains an agreement error. The subject is *requests*, which is plural, so the pronoun that replaces it should be *those* rather than *that*. Answer (C) might be tempting, since using *number* as a verb is slightly uncommon; however, it is grammatical, so (C) can't be correct.

27. **C** Answer (C) contains a parallelism error; the tense is inconsistent with that of the rest of the sentence. *Discounting* does not match *to claim*. To be parallel, (C) should read "to discount."

28. **E** There is no error in this sentence, so (E) is correct. There are some phrases like *ever more virulent* or *both destroys* that may sound awkward, but there are no grammar rules broken in this sentence.

29. **D** The correct choice is (D) because of a comparison error. The superlative *most* can be used only when comparing more than two things. When comparing only two things, "more" must be used.

30. **A**   (B), (C), (D), and (E) suggest that sentence 4 stems from the prior sentences as a natural conclusion. However, sentence 4 opposes the previous sentences, so (A), *However*, is the best option. Understanding this sentence requires understanding these transition words.

31. **C**   (A) is awkward and questionable in meaning. (B) is close, but does not flow very well due to the short phrases separated by commas. (D) creates a comma splice by having two complete phrases connected by a comma. (E) is passive and has the ambiguous pronoun *it*. This leaves only (C) as the correct answer.

32. **D**   As written, the sentence has an ambiguous pronoun, *they,* and the sentence is made awkward by the repeated *very* and the phrase *make as good*. (B) creates a comma splice by joining two complete sentences with a comma. (C) creates an incomplete sentence by starting a phrase with the word *because* without providing the result. (E) does not clear up the ambiguous pronoun, and adds an extra comparison with *more*. (D) is the clearest form of the sentence.

33. **A**   (B) is awkward and wordy. (C) is awkward: The sentence would not need the unclear pronoun *it* if *liquid* were the subject, rather than *Starting with a liquid*. (D) leaves out the churning process, and is not as clear as (A) about how the air is added to the liquid. In (E), the person speaking changes halfway through the sentence; the first clause is in the third person and the second clause is in the second person command form. The end of (E) in unnecessarily repetitive.

34. **B**   (A) does not clarify the sentence at all; (B) is a better choice. (C), (D), and (E) aren't things that could be added to the gelato, so (B) is indeed the correct answer.

35. **D**   In the original sentence, *In conclusion* is a stiff and obvious way of presenting a point, and the awkward phrase *gelato does not work in America because its nature prevents it from mass production* is unclear about who or what *prevents it*. Choice (B) becomes a sentence fragment when *Since*, a word that introduces a dependent clause, replaces *In conclusion*. The awkward phrase is replaced by a somewhat less awkward one in (C), but the word *However* incorrectly indicates a change of direction in the sentence or a contrast to the previous idea. Both (D) and (E) replace the awkward phrase with clearer ones, however, (E) introduces the sentence with *Being that*, which makes the sentence a fragment, leaving (D) as the correct answer.

SECTION 6

1.   **E**   The sum of the measures of the angles of a triangle must be 180 degrees. The question gives us two angles: 90 degrees (it's a right triangle) and 20 degrees. 180 − 90 − 20 = 70, the measure of the third angle. (E) is correct.

2. **B** Although we can solve for y and plug that value into the fraction, it is easier to change the equation to match the fraction. You may notice that 21 is 3×7 and 9 is 3×3. So, multiply both sides of $7y = 3$ by 3, to get $21y = 9$ and then divide both sides by 9 to see that $\frac{21y}{9} = 1$, answer (B). (A) gives the value of y. Answer choice (C) is the reciprocal of y.

3. **C** Add the two columns and subtract: The total number of parking violations for 2007 is 135. The total for 2008 is 165. So, they increase from 135 to 165, which is 30, (C).

4. **D** As the diagonal of the square, $\overline{EG}$ divides the square into two 45-45-90-degree triangles. In such a triangle, the legs have length s and the hypotenuse has length $s\sqrt{2}$. In ΔEFG, the hypotenuse is 6, which means that $s\sqrt{2} = 6$. To find the length of the sides, solve for s: $s = \frac{6}{\sqrt{2}} = \frac{6\sqrt{2}}{\sqrt{2}\sqrt{2}} = \frac{6\sqrt{2}}{2} = 3\sqrt{2}$, answer (D).

5. **A** The easiest way to find out which answer choice is NOT equal to $2 - x$ is to try each answer, and eliminate the ones that do work. If $2 - x = -8$, is there a one-digit integer we could Plug In for x that would work? To make the equation work, x would have to be 10, which isn't a one-digit integer, so (A) does not work. All the other answers do work: for (B), x would be 8, for (C) x would be 6, for (D) x would be 4, and for (E) x would be 0.

6. **C** This could be solved using $a = 2$ or $a = 4$, and either way (C) $\frac{1}{16}$ is the correct answer. If $a = 4$, then $x = 1$ and $c = 3$. This gives $ax^{-c} = 4^{-2}$. A negative exponent means that we put the expression (without the negative sign) as the denominator of a fraction with 1 as the numerator. $\frac{1}{4^2} = \frac{1}{16}$, making (C) the correct answer.

7. **C** Draw this one out. Because Anne's, Zenia's, and Beth's all lie in that order on a vertical line with a length of 44, and we know the length between and Anne's and Zenia's is 32, the length between Zenia's and Beth's is 12. Moving due west from Beth's creates a right angle. Caleb's, Damon's, and Beth's all lie on the horizontal line in that order. The length between Caleb's and Beth's is 33, so subtract the length between Caleb's and Damon's to see that the length between Damon's and Beth's is 5. Now we have a right triangle with legs of 5 and 12. Use the Pythagorean theorem or remember the 5-12-13 triplet to find that the diagonal distance between Damon's and Zenia's home is 13, (C).

8. **D** Since the problem never indicates how many jigsaw puzzles Jared has, we can make up our own number. Assuming Jared has 10 puzzles, 6 puzzles have 50 pieces and 4 puzzles have 30 pieces. The average is $\frac{\text{total number of pieces}}{\text{total number of puzzles}} = \frac{6(50) + 4(30)}{10} = 42$, answer (D). Choice (B) mixes up the percentages. Choice (C) ignores the percentages and just finds the average of 50 and 30 pieces.

9. $\dfrac{40}{3}$ or 13.3

First, find the rate given: $\dfrac{10 \text{ miles}}{3 \text{ hours}}$ = 3.33 mph; then find the miles covered in four hours: 3.33 mph × 4 hours = 13.3 miles.

10. 120   To find the measure of each individual angle, remember that we're really just dealing with a straight line, and that 6 equal angles form that line. There are 180° in a straight line, therefore $6x = 180°$ and each individual angle (x in this case) is 30°. If two angles are "bisected," that simply means they are split in half, so any bisected 30° angle will be split into two 15° angles. To find the measure of the angle indicated by the arrow, count the smaller angles contained therein. There are three 30° angles and two 15° angles, so 30 + 30 + 30 + 15 + 15 = 120.

11. 3,899   First, find the range of x by subtracting 1,300 from all parts of the inequality: $1,200 < x < 3,900$. In this case, the largest possible value for x is 3,899, because x must be an integer *less than* (NOT *less than or equal to*) 3,900.

12. 75   Since the perimeter of the equilateral triangle is 15, each side is 5. That means each side of the three squares is 5. Area of a square is side squared, so the area of each square is 25. The total area of the three squares is 75.

13. 2   The median is the middle number when all the items in a list are organized in ascending order. List out the numbers: 5 people spent one hour on email, so 1, 1, 1, 1, 1 are our first five numbers. 5 spent two hours on email, so we add 2, 2, 2, 2, 2. Continuing on, the full list is 1 1 1 1 1 2 2 2 2 2 3 3 4 4 4 5 5. The median here is 2. Do the same thing for Meeting Attendance, and we get a list of 1 1 2 2 2 2 3 3 4 4 4 4 5 5 5 5 6. The median for this list is 4, so the difference between the medians is 2.

14. 195   Set a variable g for girls, and translate the information in the problem into an equation: $g + (g - 60) = 330$. Therefore, $2g - 60 = 330$; $2g = 390$; and $g = 195$.

15. 4   One pile of 4 pebbles will leave 70 pebbles to divide among the remaining 24 piles, which we can do with a combination of piles of 1, 2, and/or 3 pebbles. 3 couldn't be the biggest pile because we would need more than one pile of 3 to get to 74 in only 25 piles. This question hinges upon the fact that we can't have fractional pebbles, and that we're allowed only one pile of the highest number.

16. 41, 43, 45, and 47   The easiest way to answer this question is to make a guess as to what the numbers might be and check to make sure it works with the information in the question. The 52 in 2,452 and 52r reveals an opportunity to break 2,452 into 2,400 + 52, which are individually multiples of 60 and 52, respectively. The equation will look like this: $2,400 + 52 = 60q + 52r$. We can then determine possible values for q and r by creating two equations: $2,400 = 60q$ and $52 = 52r$. In this case, $q = 40$ and $r = 1$. Remember, we need to find only one answer for a question that asks for "one possible value."

17. **12** The first step is to simplify the expression into $h(1) = f(2) + 2 \times g(1)$. Next, use the graphs to determine the values of $f(2)$ and $g(1)$. The value of $f(2)$ is 4, and the value of $g(1)$ is 4, which yields $h(1) = 4 + 2 \times 4$, which equals 12.

18. $\dfrac{9}{2}$ **or 4.5**

Solve for n in the equation for line a by replacing x with n and y with $\dfrac{7}{2}$; $n = -3$. Since the point of intersection is now $(-3, \dfrac{7}{2})$ we can use those two values in the second equation to find b by replacing x with -3 and y with $\dfrac{7}{2}$ to give us $\dfrac{7}{2} = \dfrac{1}{3} \times (-3) + b$, solving for $b = \dfrac{9}{2}$.

SECTION 7

1. **B** Start with the second blank. The phrase *now that prototypes have been built that emit only water vapor* tells us that the *dream* is likely to come true. A good word for the second blank is something like "reality." Therefore, eliminate (A), (C), and (E). Now tackle the first blank. The word *once* tells us that the first blank is opposed in meaning to the second blank, so eliminate (D). The first blank should mean something like "unrealistic," which is a synonym for *quixotic* (B).

2. **A** We know that the autobiography was *truthful* and *revealing*. (A), *candid*, matches this description. (B), *didactic*, means "instructive," which doesn't match with what we know about the autobiography. (C) means "overly sentimental," (D) means "extravagant or complex," and (E) means "immature," none of which works.

3. **C** The *people* are not *aloof*; they are *merely shy*. So we need a synonym for *shy*. *Timorous*, which means nervous or timid, is the only word that matches. The correct answer is (C).

4. **A** Laura was *Glowing with joy and delight*—so that is what the blank means. We want something positive. We can eliminate (C) because it is negative. While (A) and (B) are both positive, (A) means "happy" while (B) means "hard working." (A) *rapturous* is the best choice for the blank.

5. **B** We know that the conservationists are trying to remove all those *broken crates* and *washed up junk* from the shipwreck so the blank must mean something like "garbage leftover from a shipwreck." (B), *detritus*, means this. The other tough word here is (A), *raiment*, which means clothing.

6. **E** Process of Elimination is a good strategy for this question. Eliminate (A) because *popular* is not an apt description of the types listed in Passage 1, and we don't know if the types listed in Passage 2 are *rarely heard*. Eliminate (B) because it directly contradicts the passage; we *mix and match musical styles rather than preserve the preferences of our parents and grandparents*. Get rid of (C) because there's neither a *historical analysis* in Passage 1, nor an *abstract theory* in Passage 2. Eliminate (D) because Passage 1 discusses only American culture, not *all cultures*. (E) nicely summarizes a difference between the two passages.

7. **D** The author of Passage 1 states that we *mix and match musical styles rather than preserve the preferences of our parents and grandparents.* Therefore, he or she would describe the listening habits as typical of an American, which is a good match for (D).

8. **B** The author of Passage 2 discusses his or her own experiences, whereas Passage 1 is entirely in the third person. Therefore, Passage 2 makes significant use of *personal experience*, (B).

9. **B** Process of Elimination is a good strategy for this question. Eliminate (A) because Passage 2 doesn't *criticize.* (B) sounds good. (C) is a trap because it switches the order of the passages. (D) doesn't work because there's no attempt to *correct a common misconception.* Eliminate (E) because there are no *objections* and no *resolving.* (B) is indeed the correct answer.

10. **C** This question asks us to draw an analogy between the actions of the crowd and the situations in the answer choices. Begin by describing the crowd in general terms. The crowd *come(s) in and take(s) possession* after someone else has *opened the way*; they also don't appreciate how tough it was for the persons who paved the way, as shown by the statements *Why this couldn't have been so bad,… strange it should have taken so long!* Of the answer choices, only (C) is similar to the crowd.

11. **B** The president knew that Dr. Hubers *stood on the verge of great celebrity,* meaning he was going to do great things. The president also promised him *just as good a laboratory as you have there and plenty of time for your own work.* Why? Because he wanted to be able to *rise up and proclaim: "See! We have done it!"* In other words, *claim credit for Dr. Hubers' achievements* (B). (A) and (C) are traps that exploit the literal meaning of *possess.* (D) is NOT what he *wanted most of all,* and (E) is not indicated.

12. **E** The beginning of the paragraph describes Dr. Hubers' ancestors and suggests that Dr. Hubers retained certain of their characteristics. And what were these characteristics? The phrase *If they loved a woman, they picked her up and took her away* indicates *impulsiveness* (E). (B) is close, but there is no evidence of *brutality*—it's a little too strong. (A) and (C) may be characteristics of Dr. Hubers, but not the ones asked about in this question. (D) is never indicated in the passage.

13. **A** Go back to the passage and come up with a word to replace *disposed* based on the context of the sentence. Something like "willing" or "receptive" fits the meaning well. Only *inclined* (A) is a good match. Don't go for the primary meaning of the word in these questions; (C) is a blatant trap answer.

14. **C** The author states that what made Hubers *quite hopeless as a civilised product* was that *it never struck him that there was anything so very peculiar* with his taking a year off to get married before he had even asked Miss Stanley to marry him. The author's not talking about Miss Stanley, so we can remove (A). He's not trying to make us feel bad for Hubers, so we can remove (B). (C) matches up with Hubers' *very unapproved and most uncivilised thing* of neglecting to get Miss Stanley's opinion before taking action. (D) is not mentioned at all, so eliminate it. (E) is wrong because the passage doesn't state that Hubers has an *overly clinical view of marriage.*

15. **D** The phrase *His assistants had to do a great deal of reminding after he came back that week* tells us that Dr. Hubers was *distracted*, and from the previous paragraph we know it was because he proposed to Miss Stanley, so his distraction was *unrelated to his work*. (D) does a good job of paraphrasing this point. The other answers are not indicated in the passage.

16. **B** The assistants believed Dr. Hubers was distracted because *he was on a new trail,* when actually he was distracted by his relationship with Miss Stanley (as explained in the previous paragraph). Thus, their *impression was mistaken* (B).

17. **A** The purpose of the passage is to show how eyewitness testimony is not always reliable, which matches (A). (B) is too narrow; it applies only to the second and third paragraphs. (C) is not mentioned in the passage, and (D) and (E) are too sweeping (and also are not supported by the passage).

18. **A** The author of the passage explains that juries have traditionally found eyewitness testimony to be the most convincing evidence and that, after all, seeing is believing. So the author uses the saying to *emphasize an accepted point of view,* (A).

19. **C** Western Europeans and the Zulu are used as examples of how, when shown the same images, *different groups responded in divergent ways.* (C) summarizes this point succinctly. (A) and (D) are too extreme, while (B) and (E) are not supported by the passage.

20. **A** The clue to the meaning of *color* is the following phrase: *personality and mood fluctuation can also alter our perceptions.* Substitute *alter* for *color* and then eliminate any choices that don't match. (A) *modify* is closest to "alter."

21. **B** The *photograph of four young men* is used by the author to show that happy people believe the photograph is of four happy kids, but people who are anxious assume those in the photo are anxious. So the author is showing how the viewer's emotion can change their perception, answer choice (B).

22. **D** The *numerous prosaic factors* mentioned include ordinary things that can affect the accuracy of perception such as *duration of the encounter, proximity to the subject, lighting, and angle.* So the author is saying that it's not just the mental things he has mentioned previously that can affect the accuracy of perception. (D) mentions these *circumstances unrelated to the viewer's mental state.*

23. **D** The author states that *[blood samples and fingerprints] do not resonate as deeply with juries as does testimony.* (D) paraphrases this sentence nicely. (A), (C), and (E) are all too absolute, while (B) is not indicated in the passage.

24. **B** The author concludes the passage by saying that, because of the problems with eyewitness testimony, it may no longer be as important as things like blood samples and fingerprints. The author is not supporting a previous claim, but making a new one so (A) is out. (B) is exactly what the author is doing: saying what could happen in the future. (C) is wrong because he is not talking about *an unrelated situation.* (D) is wrong because he does not mention any study in this paragraph. (E) is incorrect because he is not telling anyone what should be studied.

SECTION 8

1. **B** The clue is that they *spent hours begging*. So the blank must mean continuing to do something. The closest word in the choices is *persistence*, (B). Choice (C) may be appealing, but it is the grandmother who is generous, not the *grandchildren*.

2. **E** We know we are worried about the trees' *health* from the last half of the sentence. Recycle that clue for the first blank. Keep (A), (B), (E), and maybe (D). The second blank should be negative; (A), (B), and (D) don't match because their words for the second blank are neutral. *Compromised* may not seem negative, but it has a secondary definition that works. (E) is the best answer.

3. **D** *Surprisingly* indicates that the first blank contradicts *lethal poison*, so eliminate (A) and (E), and note that (C) is weak. We now know we're looking for a positive word for the second blank, so eliminate (B) and (C). The correct answer is (D).

4. **D** The semicolon indicates that we're looking for a synonym for *confidently optimistic*. Only *sanguine* matches. The correct answer is (D).

5. **D** The clue is that the children had *droopy eyes and frequent yawning*. The semicolon serves as a same direction trigger, which tells us we can recycle the clue. The blank must mean "sleepy." The only word that means "sleepy" is *somnolent*, (D). Although *sedulous* sounds close to "sedated," it does not mean tired.

6. **A** The second part of the sentence tells us that the *skinflint is unlikely to* do something. That "something" is in the first part of the sentence: *changes one's attitude*. A good word for the second blank is a synonym for *attitude*. (A), (E), and maybe (B) work. The clue for the first blank is [*attitude*] *entrenched over a lifetime*, so we're looking for something that means "habitual." Answers (A) and (C) both work for the first blank, but only (A) fits in both blanks.

7. **D** The quotes around "*controversial*," and his description of the speaker indicate that the author does not think that the symposiums were particularly controversial. So calling it controversial is *an overstatement*, (D).

8. **B** We know that the speaker is opposed to *modern conveniences*, which makes him rather unusual, especially in front of a group of college students. The author mentions his wardrobe, which is also clearly out of step with the times, to accentuate the impression that the speaker is a little unusual. (B) *eccentric* captures this "unusualness" best. (C) is too much of a stretch; the author doesn't really *criticize*, and anyway that's not *why* he mentions the speaker's apparel. (E) is off because he's not praising the professor at this point. (A) and (D) are not supported by the passage.

9. **C** The author notes that the girls interrupted each other frequently, paused at the same awkward moments, and responded to each other's statements as if neither one heard what the other said. The word *disjointed* (C) sums this up accurately. The conversation might be *insignificant* (B), but it doesn't say so in the passage.

10.   E   Go back to the passage and come up with a word to replace *stole* based on the context of the sentence. To "steal" a glance means to glance quickly to avoid the glance being noticed by its subject. "Risked" would be a good choice because he runs the risk of being caught looking. Only *hazarded* is a good match—hazard means "take a chance; risk." (B) and (C) are traps based on the usual meanings of the word, while (A) and (D) don't fit at all.

11.   A   Why does the author tell the story about the girls? He's just told us about the symposium speaker's point, which is that the speaker is *against modern tools of convenience.* The narrator felt the *speech* was *altogether too romantic.* Observing the girls' conversations led him to reconsider or *reflect,* as in (A). By the end of the passage, the narrator feels the professors' speech was *not so romantic after all.*

12.   B   The reference to *smiley-faced icons* is used to show that old-fashioned letter writing had *certain important advantages* over modern ways of communication. Thus, the reference expresses *skepticism about certain modes of communication.* Although the narrator does seem *nostalgic* for the old days, there's nothing about an *easier way of life,* so (A) can't work. (C) is too sweeping; the narrator is not discussing *modern writers.* (D) is not indicated in the passage, and (E) directly contradicts the passage.

13.   A   The symposium speaker's reasoning is that *The temporary, impersonal nature of computers,…is gradually rendering our lives equally temporary and impersonal.* In the answers, (A) is an example of a newlywed couple using technology to make communication more impersonal. None of the other answers use technology in a way that could be called impersonal.

14.   C   The person in the movie theater was clearly not thinking about anyone else around him. So he was *tactless,* "unthinking or careless," answer (C). If he were *impetuous* (A), he would be suddenly energetic or impulsive. If he were *languid* (B), he would be tired and unmoving. The person in the theater was not necessarily *demonstrative* (D); he just talked a lot. To be demonstrative is to openly demonstrate one's emotions. He also wasn't *taciturn,* (E), which means not talkative.

15.   C   The author states that the *significant price* is that the girls *are never alone,* and elaborates by noting that the girls *could use a moment of solitude.* Thus, they have *difficulty experiencing a certain amount of privacy.* (A) and (B) are overly literal traps—we're not talking about a monetary price. (D) contradicts the passage, while (E) is not supported.

16.   D   The first time the narrator states *they are never alone,* he uses the phrase to show that the girls never have to be out of touch. But the second iteration, in italics, is used to show that the girls are unable to experience solitude. Thus, the italics are used to *imply an alternate meaning of the phrase.* Though (A) is true, it's no reason to use italics, and (B), (C), and (E) are not supported.

17. **E** The last sentence makes it clear that the narrator is now in sympathy with the professor. Whereas previously, he thought the professor was out of touch, he now feels that the professor had a valid point. The narrator therefore had *a change of heart* (E). (A) refers to the situation caused by modern technology. There is no *unforeseen difficulty* as mentioned in (B). (C) is mentioned in the paragraph, but as a quality that *the girls* lack. (D) is also mentioned, but not as something that the narrator is experiencing.

18. **C** The narrator's biggest problem with technology is when it doesn't allow a person to disconnect from the world. (C) would keep everyone in constant contact, which is what the narrator warns about in his discussion of cell phones.

19. **B** The narrator starts out unconvinced by the speaker, but by the end of the passage, after considering the argument carefully, he's in agreement. Thus, he *evaluates an argument*. He doesn't primarily *criticize*, so eliminate (A). (C) and (D) deal with the second paragraph only, so they're too specific. (E) is not supported by the passage.

SECTION 9

1. **B** Start with the sum of a and b: $a + b$. The square of this would be $(a + b)^2$, making (B) the correct answer. (A) is "the sum of the squares of a and b."

2. **B** The line of best fit is a straight line that best approximates the data. If you draw a line to approximate the trend in the scatterplot, you see that as the number of citations increases, the grade increases. This means that the line of best fit has a positive slope: choice (B). Choice (A) indicates that as citations increase, grade decreases. Choice (C) says the line of best fit has a negative y-intercept, but the line in the graph has a positive y-intercept. Choice (D) says line of best fit has a positive x-intercept; if this line continued in both directions, it would have a negative x-intercept. Choice (E) says the line of best fit passes through the origin, but you already know that the line has a positive y-intercept.

3. **A** Since the base is square, and the area is 100, each edge must be 10. Because there are 4 edges along the square base, multiply 4 by 10 to get 40, the total length of the base edges. There are four edges from the top of the pyramid to a corner and each is 13 feet, so $4 \times 13 = 52$, the total length of those four edges. Add 40 and 52 to get 92, (A) the total length of all 8 edges of the pyramid.

4. **E** Do not solve the equation sets, as the question does not seek the actual values of b and d. Deal with the number of albums first. Because b and d represent the number of each type of album and there are a total of 25 albums, $b + d = 25$. Eliminate (A), (B), and (C). Now address the value. The b albums cost $1.25 each and the d albums cost $2.30 each; the grand total is $41.75. Answer choice (E) reflects this equation. If you picked (D), you reversed the costs of b and d.

5. **C** Since we have a ratio, but no real numbers, let's make up some distances. Let's say that Magnus drove 10 miles. This means that Eva drove 4 times as many miles, so Eva drove 40 miles. The trip was therefore 50 miles altogether. Eva drove 40 miles out of 50 total miles, which is 80%.

6. **A** Make up a number for b. Suppose $b = 2$, which means that Cathy runs for 2 hours at 10 minutes per mile. First, convert 2 hours to 120 minutes and then set up as a proportion to find how many miles she travels. So, $\dfrac{10 \text{ min}}{1 \text{ mile}} = \dfrac{120 \text{ min}}{x \text{ miles}}$. Cross-multiply to get $10x = 120$ or $x = 12$ miles. Now, $26 - 12 \doteq 14$ miles left. Replace b with 2 in the answer choices, and the one that gives 14 is the correct answer. To also solve this algebraically, if Cathy runs a mile in 10 minutes, she runs 6 miles per hour for b hours. So for the first b hours she runs $6b$ miles. Subtract this from 26 to get the distance remaining after b hours: $26 - 6b$, as in (A).

7. **D** In the image, the graph hits the x- and y- axes six times. The reflected version of the graph would be a mirror image graph, such that the curves are shifted to the opposite sides of the x-axis. Thus, the new graph will have exactly the same number of intercept points: (D) Six. If you picked (C), you counted only the x-intercept points.

8. **C** One easy way to work this problem is to Plug In numbers for the variables. Since $w + x = 5$, make $w = 2$ and $x = 3$ and since $y + z = 6$, make $y = 1$ and $z = 5$. Now use the values to find the products being added together: $wy = 2$, $xz = 15$, $wz = 10$, $xy = 3$. $2 + 15 + 10 + 3 = 30$, answer (C). We can solve it algebraically by putting the terms $w + x$ and $y + z$ into parentheses and using FOIL; you get $wy + wz + xy + xz$, which is slightly different from the order of the pairs listed in the question, but the pairs are the same ones and adding in any order gives the same answer. Since you know the value of the expressions in the parentheses, just multiply those numbers: $(w + x)(y + z) = (5)(6) = 30$, answer (C).

9. **B** The three lines form a triangle, and each of the degree measurements given are vertical angles of the triangle. Therefore, the three angles of the triangle are, 45°, 15°, and $m°$. $45 + 15 + m = 180$, and $m = 120$. The answer is (B).

10. **E** When you multiply numbers with the same bases, you add the exponents. This means this first equation can be simplified to $a^9 = a^c$; therefore, $c = 9$. When you raise a number with an exponent to another power, you multiply the exponents, so the top half of the second equation becomes b^{5d} and the second equation becomes $\dfrac{b^{5d}}{b^d} = b^{40}$. When you divide numbers with the same bases, you subtract the exponents; therefore, the second equation becomes $b^{4d} = b^{40}$ and $4d = 40$, so $d = 10$. Then add c and d to get the answer seen in (E): $9 + 10 = 19$.

11. **B**   Stack the three equations and add, like this:

$$\begin{aligned} a + b - c &= d + 6 \\ -b + c &= 8 \\ + 3a &= -d + 2 \\ \hline 4a &= 16 \end{aligned}$$

On the left side of the equation, $a + 3a$ is $4a$, $b + (-b)$ is 0, and $-c + c$ is 0, so the sum of the left sides of the equations is $4a$. The sum of the right sides of the equations is 16 (the b's, c's, and d's cancel out). So $4a = 16$; therefore, $a = 4$, as in (B).

12. **D**   Try out the answer choices in the question and see which is the smallest value for z that makes the equation true. Answer choices (A), (B), and (C) create a negative number on the left side of the equation and a positive number on the right side. With (D) and (E), both sides of the equation are positive, and since 3 is smaller than 6, the correct answer is (D).

13. **E**   Begin with the description of $\frac{1}{x}$: its tens digit is odd and larger than its units digit. 10 fits the description and is an easy number to work with. So say $\frac{1}{x}$ is 10 and solve for x: $\frac{1}{x} = 10$, so $1 = 10x$, and $x = \frac{1}{10}$. In decimals, this is 0.1, so choice (E) works. Since the question asks for the largest possible value and this is the biggest number in the answers, you've found the credited response. If 0.1 weren't the biggest number you could try another number, like 31. If $\frac{1}{x}$ were 31, then $x = \frac{1}{31} = 0.0322580...$ and you could continue trying numbers until you found the biggest number that worked. Plug In The Answers. (B) gives 37 and (D) gives 11, in conflict with the description that $\frac{1}{x}$ should give a number with a tens digit larger than the units digit. All of the numbers in the answer choices are possible values of x in that they give you numbers with a larger, odd tens digit, but (E) has the greatest value of x. Be careful! (A) gives the largest value in the list for $\frac{1}{x}$ not x.

14. **C**   Since there are no values for the lengths in the figure, let's say AB is 1. And since B, C, and D are the midpoints mentioned in the question, $AC = 2$, $AD = 4$, and $AE = 8$. Find the area of the shaded region by subtracting the areas of the squares with sides $\overline{AD}$ and $\overline{AC}$. The area of a square is the length of the side of the square raised to the second power, so the area of the square with side $\overline{AD}$ is 16 and the area of the square with side $\overline{AC}$ is 4; therefore the area of the shaded region is $16 - 4 = 12$. To find the answer, you'll need the area of the largest square. Its side has length 8, so its area is 64. The fractional part that is shaded is the area of the shaded region divided by the area of the large square: $\frac{12}{64} = \frac{3}{16}$, the fraction in (C).

15. **D** To find an equivalent equation, simplify. One clue is that none of the answers has a root, go get rid of that by squaring both sides of the equation, which gives $\dfrac{25}{x-3} = 9$. None of the answers has a fraction, so get rid of that by multiplying both sides of the equation by the denominator, which gives $25 = 9(x-3)$, which is seen in answer (D).

16. **E** When a line passes through two parallel lines, all the small angles are the same, all the big angles are the same, and any big angle plus any small angle adds up to 180. So, $p + r = 180$. Replace p with $5r$, such that $5r + r = 180$. Thus, r is 30, and $5r$ is 150, which is the value of p, making (E) the correct choice. If you picked (B) you stopped solving when you found the value of r, not p. If you picked (A) or (C), you mistakenly solved for $p + r = 90$.

SECTION 10

1. **D** (A), (C), and (E) are sentence fragments because of incorrect verb forms and structures. (B) contains a verb tense error: *would* cannot be used with *last month*. (D) has the proper form of the verb to agree with the event occurring *last month*.

2. **C** The sentence as written is passive and wordy. (B) has a misplaced modifier: *An area* cannot describe *the growth*. (C) removes the passive voice from the phrase, "As an area…plants." (D) has an unnecessary *also* that does not link two ideas. (E) is an incomplete sentence.

3. **D** The original sentence contains a verb error. The verb *dedicated* requires a prepositional phrase or a verb phrase to follow it. This eliminates (A). (B) and (E) introduce verb tense errors. (C) has a wordy and awkward construction. (D) has the necessary prepositional phrase *to searching* and correct verb tense.

4. **C** The sentence as written lacks a verb; both (B) and (C) fix that problem by making *The Beatles* the subject and *are* the verb of the sentence. (B), however, contains a comma splice, leaving only (C).

5. **B** This sentence has a subject-verb agreement error. The subject *Mastering*—a gerund that is used as a noun for the process or action—is singular. Eliminate (A), (D), and (E) for using the plural verb. (C) is wordier and doesn't make sense: *Mastering* isn't something that *young cooks make*. Only (B) is grammatically correct.

6. **E** The list of actions in the sentence as written is not parallel. The verbs must all have the same form as *organize*. (D) and (E) both use *meet* and *satisfy* but (D) changes the meaning by separating the verbs from their objects, leaving (E) as the correct answer choice.

7. **A** The sentence is correct as written. (B) is not parallel. (C) changes the meaning of the sentence, indicating that *novelists and political theorists* wrote in order *to struggle*. (D) changes the meaning of the sentence. (E) creates a run-on sentence and changes the meaning.

8. **C** The sentence as written has an agreement problem: *they* does not agree with the singular *Discula destructiva,* so eliminate (A). (B) and (D) also have agreement problems. (E) creates a comma splice.

9. **A** The sentence is correct as written. (B) is not parallel; (C) and (D) have redundant use of *because* following *The reason,* which requires *that.* The "ing" words in (E) together are plural, and do not agree with *is* in the non-underlined part.

10. **C** The correct idiom is *neither...nor.* The sentence as written use *or.* The phrase *applying for* is a singular subject, and so needs verbs *increases* and *decreases.* Only (C) has the correct idiom and verb structure.

11. **E** In the sentence as written, *they* is an ambiguous pronoun. (B) and (D) have misplaced modifiers: *speeches* cannot be *instructed to avoid* something nor can they advise *speechwriters.* (C) is wordy and awkward. (E) correctly sets up a cause for the effect given in the non-underlined portion of the sentence.

12. **B** The sentence as written compares an adjective (*comedic*) and a noun (*tragedy*). Eliminate (A). All the other answers use *tragic,* so compare the rest of the choices, looking for other errors. The correct answer will match comedic with tragic. (B) adds no additional errors. The phrase *in a combining of* in (C) is awkward and ungrammatical. (D) is incomplete due to the addition of *when* and (E) mismatches *comedy* and *tragic.*

13. **E** (A) and (B) contain adjective errors: the subject of the sentence, the *dress codes,* cannot be described as *impulsive,* only the reason for establishing them can be. (C) creates a comma splice. (D) creates a parallelism error. (E) is parallel and corrects the adjective error.

14. **A** (A) correctly joins two independent clauses with a colon. (B) creates a comma splice error. (C) incorrectly joins a dependent clause to an independent clause with a semicolon. (D) introduces the unnecessary verb *being,* and (E) uses the redundant conjunction *yet.*

Chapter 6
Practice Test 2

Your Name (print) _____

Last   First   Middle

Date _____

IMPORTANT: The following codes should be copied onto your answer sheet exactly as shown.

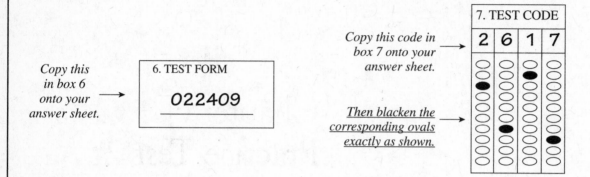

Copy this in box 6 onto your answer sheet. →

6. TEST FORM

022409

Copy this code in box 7 onto your answer sheet. →

Then blacken the corresponding ovals exactly as shown. →

7. TEST CODE

2 6 1 7

General Directions

You will have three hours and 20 minutes to work on this objective test designed to familiarize you with all aspects of the SAT.

This test contains five 25-minute sections, two 20-minute sections, one 10-minute section, and one 25-minute essay. The supervisor will tell you when to begin and end each section. During the time allowed for each section, you may work only on that particular section. If you finish your work before time is called, you may check your work on that section, but you are not to work on any other section.

You will find specific directions for each type of question found in the test. **Be sure you understand the directions before attempting to answer any of the questions.**

YOU ARE TO INDICATE ALL YOUR ANSWERS ON THE SEPARATE ANSWER SHEET:

1. The test booklet may be used for scratchwork. However, no credit will be given for anything written in the test booklet.

2. Once you have decided on an answer to a question, darken the corresponding space on the answer sheet. Give only one answer to each question.

3. There are 40 numbered answer spaces for each section; be sure to use only those spaces that correspond to the test questions.

4. **Be sure each answer mark is dark and completely fills the answer space.** Do not make any stray marks on your answer sheet.

5. If you wish to change an answer, erase your first mark completely—an incomplete erasure may be considered an intended response—and blacken your new answer choice.

Your score on this test is based on the number of questions you answer correctly minus a fraction of the number of questions you answer incorrectly. Therefore, it is improbable that random or haphazard guessing will alter your score significantly. There are no deductions for incorrect answers on the student-produced response questions. However, if you are able to eliminate one or more of the answer choices on any question as wrong, it is generally to your advantage to guess at one of the remaining choices. Remember, however, not to spend too much time on any one question.

Diagnostic Test Form

Use a No. 2 pencil only. Be sure each mark is dark and completely fills the intended oval. Completely erase any errors or stray marks.

1 Your Name:

(Print) _____
Last   First   M.I.

Signature: _____ Date ___/___/___

Home Address: _____
Number and Street   City   State   Zip Code

E-Mail: _____ School: _____ Class: _____
(Print)

---

2 YOUR NAME

Last Name
(First 4 Letters)

				FIRST INIT	MID INIT
	⊖	⊖	⊖		
	˙	˙	˙		
	◯	◯	◯		
Ⓐ	Ⓐ	Ⓐ	Ⓐ	Ⓐ	Ⓐ
Ⓑ	Ⓑ	Ⓑ	Ⓑ	Ⓑ	Ⓑ
Ⓒ	Ⓒ	Ⓒ	Ⓒ	Ⓒ	Ⓒ
Ⓓ	Ⓓ	Ⓓ	Ⓓ	Ⓓ	Ⓓ
Ⓔ	Ⓔ	Ⓔ	Ⓔ	Ⓔ	Ⓔ
Ⓕ	Ⓕ	Ⓕ	Ⓕ	Ⓕ	Ⓕ
Ⓖ	Ⓖ	Ⓖ	Ⓖ	Ⓖ	Ⓖ
Ⓗ	Ⓗ	Ⓗ	Ⓗ	Ⓗ	Ⓗ
Ⓘ	Ⓘ	Ⓘ	Ⓘ	Ⓘ	Ⓘ
Ⓙ	Ⓙ	Ⓙ	Ⓙ	Ⓙ	Ⓙ
Ⓚ	Ⓚ	Ⓚ	Ⓚ	Ⓚ	Ⓚ
Ⓛ	Ⓛ	Ⓛ	Ⓛ	Ⓛ	Ⓛ
Ⓜ	Ⓜ	Ⓜ	Ⓜ	Ⓜ	Ⓜ
Ⓝ	Ⓝ	Ⓝ	Ⓝ	Ⓝ	Ⓝ
Ⓞ	Ⓞ	Ⓞ	Ⓞ	Ⓞ	Ⓞ
Ⓟ	Ⓟ	Ⓟ	Ⓟ	Ⓟ	Ⓟ
Ⓠ	Ⓠ	Ⓠ	Ⓠ	Ⓠ	Ⓠ
Ⓡ	Ⓡ	Ⓡ	Ⓡ	Ⓡ	Ⓡ
Ⓢ	Ⓢ	Ⓢ	Ⓢ	Ⓢ	Ⓢ
Ⓣ	Ⓣ	Ⓣ	Ⓣ	Ⓣ	Ⓣ
Ⓤ	Ⓤ	Ⓤ	Ⓤ	Ⓤ	Ⓤ
Ⓥ	Ⓥ	Ⓥ	Ⓥ	Ⓥ	Ⓥ
Ⓦ	Ⓦ	Ⓦ	Ⓦ	Ⓦ	Ⓦ
Ⓧ	Ⓧ	Ⓧ	Ⓧ	Ⓧ	Ⓧ
Ⓨ	Ⓨ	Ⓨ	Ⓨ	Ⓨ	Ⓨ
Ⓩ	Ⓩ	Ⓩ	Ⓩ	Ⓩ	Ⓩ

---

3 PHONE NUMBER

⓪	⓪	⓪	⓪	⓪	⓪	⓪
①	①	①	①	①	①	①
②	②	②	②	②	②	②
③	③	③	③	③	③	③
④	④	④	④	④	④	④
⑤	⑤	⑤	⑤	⑤	⑤	⑤
⑥	⑥	⑥	⑥	⑥	⑥	⑥
⑦	⑦	⑦	⑦	⑦	⑦	⑦
⑧	⑧	⑧	⑧	⑧	⑧	⑧
⑨	⑨	⑨	⑨	⑨	⑨	⑨

---

4 DATE OF BIRTH

MONTH	DAY		YEAR	
◯ JAN				
◯ FEB				
◯ MAR	⓪	⓪		⓪
◯ APR	①	①		①
◯ MAY	②	②		②
◯ JUN	③	③		③
◯ JUL		④		④
◯ AUG		⑤	⑤	⑤
◯ SEP		⑥	⑥	⑥
◯ OCT		⑦	⑦	⑦
◯ NOV		⑧	⑧	⑧
◯ DEC		⑨	⑨	⑨

---

5 SEX

◯ MALE
◯ FEMALE

IMPORTANT: Fill in items 6 and 7 exactly as shown on the preceding page.

6 TEST FORM
(Copy from back of test book)

---

7 TEST CODE

⓪	⓪	⓪	⓪
①	①	①	①
②	②	②	②
③	③	③	③
④	④	④	④
⑤	⑤	⑤	⑤
⑥	⑥	⑥	⑥
⑦	⑦	⑦	⑦
⑧	⑧	⑧	⑧
⑨	⑨	⑨	⑨

---

8 OTHER

1 Ⓐ Ⓑ Ⓒ Ⓓ Ⓔ
2 Ⓐ Ⓑ Ⓒ Ⓓ Ⓔ
3 Ⓐ Ⓑ Ⓒ Ⓓ Ⓔ

OpScan *i*NSIGHT™ forms by Pearson NCS EM-253760-3:654321   Printed in U.S.A.   © TPR Education IP Holdings, LLC

PLEASE DO NOT WRITE IN THIS AREA

◯◯◯◯◯◯◯◯◯◯◯◯◯◯◯◯◯◯◯◯◯◯◯

SERIAL #

THIS PAGE INTENTIONALLY LEFT BLANK

SECTION 1

IMPORTANT: USE A NO. 2 PENCIL. DO NOT WRITE OUTSIDE THE BORDER!
Words written outside the essay box or written in ink **WILL NOT APPEAR** in the copy sent to be scored and your score will be affected.

Begin your essay on this page. If you need more space, continue on the next page.

Continue on the next page, if necessary.

SECTION 2

1 Ⓐ Ⓑ Ⓒ Ⓓ Ⓔ
2 Ⓐ Ⓑ Ⓒ Ⓓ Ⓔ
3 Ⓐ Ⓑ Ⓒ Ⓓ Ⓔ
4 Ⓐ Ⓑ Ⓒ Ⓓ Ⓔ
5 Ⓐ Ⓑ Ⓒ Ⓓ Ⓔ
6 Ⓐ Ⓑ Ⓒ Ⓓ Ⓔ
7 Ⓐ Ⓑ Ⓒ Ⓓ Ⓔ
8 Ⓐ Ⓑ Ⓒ Ⓓ Ⓔ
9 Ⓐ Ⓑ Ⓒ Ⓓ Ⓔ
10 Ⓐ Ⓑ Ⓒ Ⓓ Ⓔ

11 Ⓐ Ⓑ Ⓒ Ⓓ Ⓔ
12 Ⓐ Ⓑ Ⓒ Ⓓ Ⓔ
13 Ⓐ Ⓑ Ⓒ Ⓓ Ⓔ
14 Ⓐ Ⓑ Ⓒ Ⓓ Ⓔ
15 Ⓐ Ⓑ Ⓒ Ⓓ Ⓔ
16 Ⓐ Ⓑ Ⓒ Ⓓ Ⓔ
17 Ⓐ Ⓑ Ⓒ Ⓓ Ⓔ
18 Ⓐ Ⓑ Ⓒ Ⓓ Ⓔ
19 Ⓐ Ⓑ Ⓒ Ⓓ Ⓔ
20 Ⓐ Ⓑ Ⓒ Ⓓ Ⓔ

21 Ⓐ Ⓑ Ⓒ Ⓓ Ⓔ
22 Ⓐ Ⓑ Ⓒ Ⓓ Ⓔ
23 Ⓐ Ⓑ Ⓒ Ⓓ Ⓔ
24 Ⓐ Ⓑ Ⓒ Ⓓ Ⓔ
25 Ⓐ Ⓑ Ⓒ Ⓓ Ⓔ
26 Ⓐ Ⓑ Ⓒ Ⓓ Ⓔ
27 Ⓐ Ⓑ Ⓒ Ⓓ Ⓔ
28 Ⓐ Ⓑ Ⓒ Ⓓ Ⓔ
29 Ⓐ Ⓑ Ⓒ Ⓓ Ⓔ
30 Ⓐ Ⓑ Ⓒ Ⓓ Ⓔ

31 Ⓐ Ⓑ Ⓒ Ⓓ Ⓔ
32 Ⓐ Ⓑ Ⓒ Ⓓ Ⓔ
33 Ⓐ Ⓑ Ⓒ Ⓓ Ⓔ
34 Ⓐ Ⓑ Ⓒ Ⓓ Ⓔ
35 Ⓐ Ⓑ Ⓒ Ⓓ Ⓔ
36 Ⓐ Ⓑ Ⓒ Ⓓ Ⓔ
37 Ⓐ Ⓑ Ⓒ Ⓓ Ⓔ
38 Ⓐ Ⓑ Ⓒ Ⓓ Ⓔ
39 Ⓐ Ⓑ Ⓒ Ⓓ Ⓔ
40 Ⓐ Ⓑ Ⓒ Ⓓ Ⓔ

SECTION 3

1 Ⓐ Ⓑ Ⓒ Ⓓ Ⓔ
2 Ⓐ Ⓑ Ⓒ Ⓓ Ⓔ
3 Ⓐ Ⓑ Ⓒ Ⓓ Ⓔ
4 Ⓐ Ⓑ Ⓒ Ⓓ Ⓔ
5 Ⓐ Ⓑ Ⓒ Ⓓ Ⓔ
6 Ⓐ Ⓑ Ⓒ Ⓓ Ⓔ
7 Ⓐ Ⓑ Ⓒ Ⓓ Ⓔ
8 Ⓐ Ⓑ Ⓒ Ⓓ Ⓔ
9 Ⓐ Ⓑ Ⓒ Ⓓ Ⓔ
10 Ⓐ Ⓑ Ⓒ Ⓓ Ⓔ

11 Ⓐ Ⓑ Ⓒ Ⓓ Ⓔ
12 Ⓐ Ⓑ Ⓒ Ⓓ Ⓔ
13 Ⓐ Ⓑ Ⓒ Ⓓ Ⓔ
14 Ⓐ Ⓑ Ⓒ Ⓓ Ⓔ
15 Ⓐ Ⓑ Ⓒ Ⓓ Ⓔ
16 Ⓐ Ⓑ Ⓒ Ⓓ Ⓔ
17 Ⓐ Ⓑ Ⓒ Ⓓ Ⓔ
18 Ⓐ Ⓑ Ⓒ Ⓓ Ⓔ
19 Ⓐ Ⓑ Ⓒ Ⓓ Ⓔ
20 Ⓐ Ⓑ Ⓒ Ⓓ Ⓔ

21 Ⓐ Ⓑ Ⓒ Ⓓ Ⓔ
22 Ⓐ Ⓑ Ⓒ Ⓓ Ⓔ
23 Ⓐ Ⓑ Ⓒ Ⓓ Ⓔ
24 Ⓐ Ⓑ Ⓒ Ⓓ Ⓔ
25 Ⓐ Ⓑ Ⓒ Ⓓ Ⓔ
26 Ⓐ Ⓑ Ⓒ Ⓓ Ⓔ
27 Ⓐ Ⓑ Ⓒ Ⓓ Ⓔ
28 Ⓐ Ⓑ Ⓒ Ⓓ Ⓔ
29 Ⓐ Ⓑ Ⓒ Ⓓ Ⓔ
30 Ⓐ Ⓑ Ⓒ Ⓓ Ⓔ

31 Ⓐ Ⓑ Ⓒ Ⓓ Ⓔ
32 Ⓐ Ⓑ Ⓒ Ⓓ Ⓔ
33 Ⓐ Ⓑ Ⓒ Ⓓ Ⓔ
34 Ⓐ Ⓑ Ⓒ Ⓓ Ⓔ
35 Ⓐ Ⓑ Ⓒ Ⓓ Ⓔ
36 Ⓐ Ⓑ Ⓒ Ⓓ Ⓔ
37 Ⓐ Ⓑ Ⓒ Ⓓ Ⓔ
38 Ⓐ Ⓑ Ⓒ Ⓓ Ⓔ
39 Ⓐ Ⓑ Ⓒ Ⓓ Ⓔ
40 Ⓐ Ⓑ Ⓒ Ⓓ Ⓔ

CAUTION Grid answers in the section below for SECTION 2 or SECTION 3 only if directed to do so in your test book.

Student-Produced Responses

ONLY ANSWERS THAT ARE GRIDDED WILL BE SCORED. YOU WILL NOT RECEIVE CREDIT FOR ANYTHING WRITTEN IN THE BOXES.

Quality Assurance Mark ●

9 10 11 12 13

14 15 16 17 18

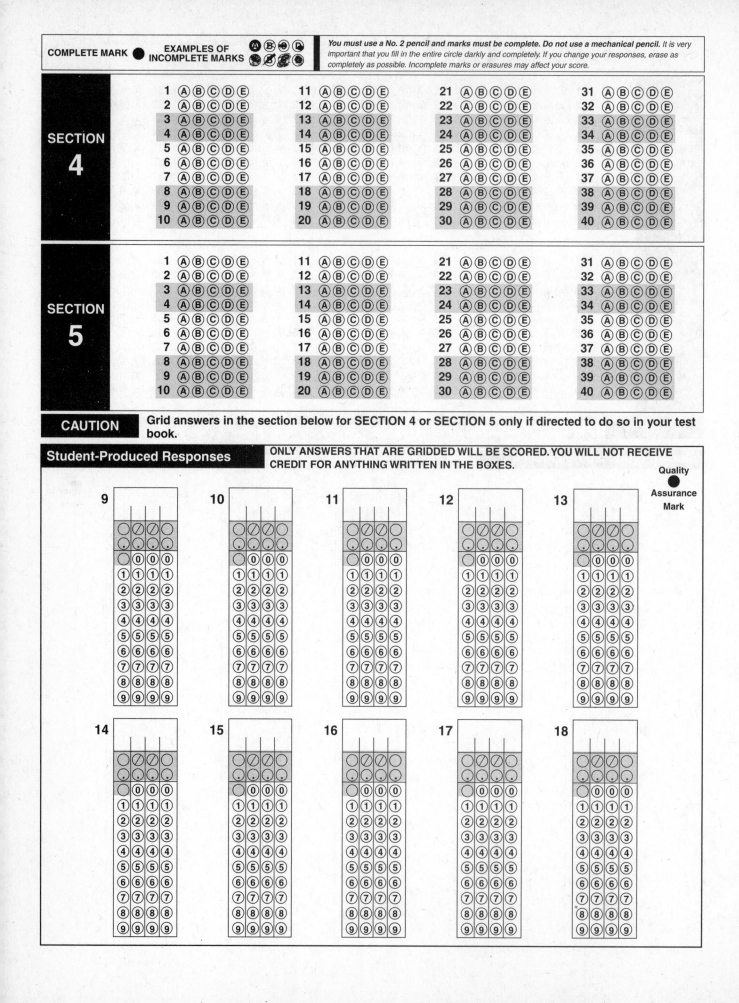

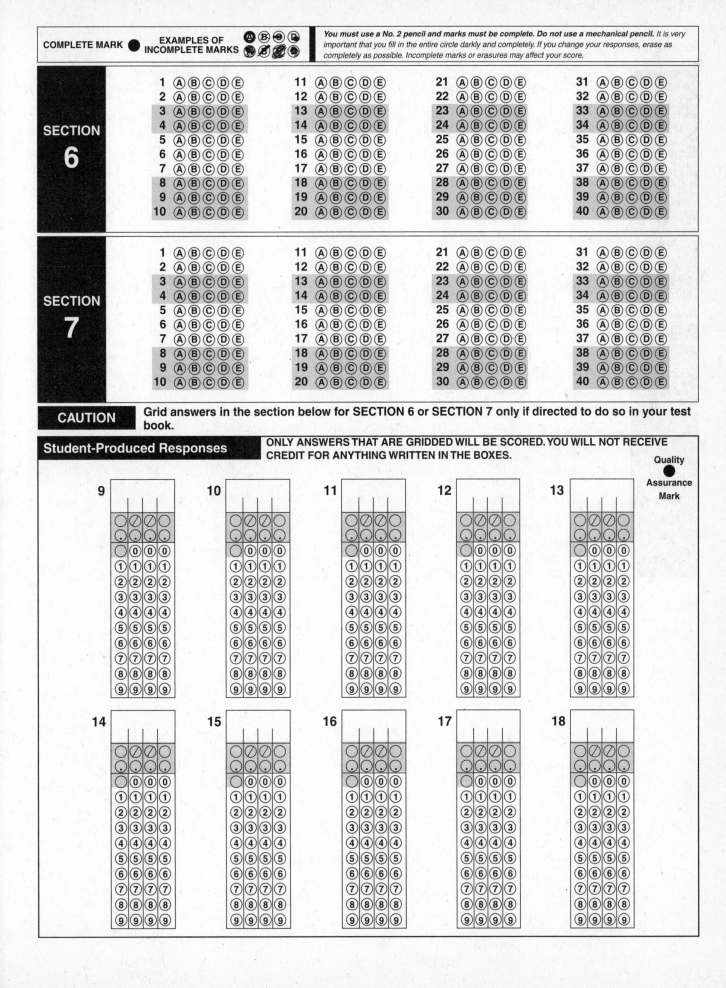

COMPLETE MARK ●

EXAMPLES OF INCOMPLETE MARKS Ⓐ Ⓑ ⊖ Ⓓ ⊗ ∅ ⊘ ⊛

You must use a No. 2 pencil and marks must be complete. Do not use a mechanical pencil. It is very important that you fill in the entire circle darkly and completely. If you change your responses, erase as completely as possible. Incomplete marks or erasures may affect your score.

SECTION 8

1 Ⓐ Ⓑ Ⓒ Ⓓ Ⓔ	11 Ⓐ Ⓑ Ⓒ Ⓓ Ⓔ	21 Ⓐ Ⓑ Ⓒ Ⓓ Ⓔ	31 Ⓐ Ⓑ Ⓒ Ⓓ Ⓔ
2 Ⓐ Ⓑ Ⓒ Ⓓ Ⓔ	12 Ⓐ Ⓑ Ⓒ Ⓓ Ⓔ	22 Ⓐ Ⓑ Ⓒ Ⓓ Ⓔ	32 Ⓐ Ⓑ Ⓒ Ⓓ Ⓔ
3 Ⓐ Ⓑ Ⓒ Ⓓ Ⓔ	13 Ⓐ Ⓑ Ⓒ Ⓓ Ⓔ	23 Ⓐ Ⓑ Ⓒ Ⓓ Ⓔ	33 Ⓐ Ⓑ Ⓒ Ⓓ Ⓔ
4 Ⓐ Ⓑ Ⓒ Ⓓ Ⓔ	14 Ⓐ Ⓑ Ⓒ Ⓓ Ⓔ	24 Ⓐ Ⓑ Ⓒ Ⓓ Ⓔ	34 Ⓐ Ⓑ Ⓒ Ⓓ Ⓔ
5 Ⓐ Ⓑ Ⓒ Ⓓ Ⓔ	15 Ⓐ Ⓑ Ⓒ Ⓓ Ⓔ	25 Ⓐ Ⓑ Ⓒ Ⓓ Ⓔ	35 Ⓐ Ⓑ Ⓒ Ⓓ Ⓔ
6 Ⓐ Ⓑ Ⓒ Ⓓ Ⓔ	16 Ⓐ Ⓑ Ⓒ Ⓓ Ⓔ	26 Ⓐ Ⓑ Ⓒ Ⓓ Ⓔ	36 Ⓐ Ⓑ Ⓒ Ⓓ Ⓔ
7 Ⓐ Ⓑ Ⓒ Ⓓ Ⓔ	17 Ⓐ Ⓑ Ⓒ Ⓓ Ⓔ	27 Ⓐ Ⓑ Ⓒ Ⓓ Ⓔ	37 Ⓐ Ⓑ Ⓒ Ⓓ Ⓔ
8 Ⓐ Ⓑ Ⓒ Ⓓ Ⓔ	18 Ⓐ Ⓑ Ⓒ Ⓓ Ⓔ	28 Ⓐ Ⓑ Ⓒ Ⓓ Ⓔ	38 Ⓐ Ⓑ Ⓒ Ⓓ Ⓔ
9 Ⓐ Ⓑ Ⓒ Ⓓ Ⓔ	19 Ⓐ Ⓑ Ⓒ Ⓓ Ⓔ	29 Ⓐ Ⓑ Ⓒ Ⓓ Ⓔ	39 Ⓐ Ⓑ Ⓒ Ⓓ Ⓔ
10 Ⓐ Ⓑ Ⓒ Ⓓ Ⓔ	20 Ⓐ Ⓑ Ⓒ Ⓓ Ⓔ	30 Ⓐ Ⓑ Ⓒ Ⓓ Ⓔ	40 Ⓐ Ⓑ Ⓒ Ⓓ Ⓔ

SECTION 9

1 Ⓐ Ⓑ Ⓒ Ⓓ Ⓔ	11 Ⓐ Ⓑ Ⓒ Ⓓ Ⓔ	21 Ⓐ Ⓑ Ⓒ Ⓓ Ⓔ	31 Ⓐ Ⓑ Ⓒ Ⓓ Ⓔ
2 Ⓐ Ⓑ Ⓒ Ⓓ Ⓔ	12 Ⓐ Ⓑ Ⓒ Ⓓ Ⓔ	22 Ⓐ Ⓑ Ⓒ Ⓓ Ⓔ	32 Ⓐ Ⓑ Ⓒ Ⓓ Ⓔ
3 Ⓐ Ⓑ Ⓒ Ⓓ Ⓔ	13 Ⓐ Ⓑ Ⓒ Ⓓ Ⓔ	23 Ⓐ Ⓑ Ⓒ Ⓓ Ⓔ	33 Ⓐ Ⓑ Ⓒ Ⓓ Ⓔ
4 Ⓐ Ⓑ Ⓒ Ⓓ Ⓔ	14 Ⓐ Ⓑ Ⓒ Ⓓ Ⓔ	24 Ⓐ Ⓑ Ⓒ Ⓓ Ⓔ	34 Ⓐ Ⓑ Ⓒ Ⓓ Ⓔ
5 Ⓐ Ⓑ Ⓒ Ⓓ Ⓔ	15 Ⓐ Ⓑ Ⓒ Ⓓ Ⓔ	25 Ⓐ Ⓑ Ⓒ Ⓓ Ⓔ	35 Ⓐ Ⓑ Ⓒ Ⓓ Ⓔ
6 Ⓐ Ⓑ Ⓒ Ⓓ Ⓔ	16 Ⓐ Ⓑ Ⓒ Ⓓ Ⓔ	26 Ⓐ Ⓑ Ⓒ Ⓓ Ⓔ	36 Ⓐ Ⓑ Ⓒ Ⓓ Ⓔ
7 Ⓐ Ⓑ Ⓒ Ⓓ Ⓔ	17 Ⓐ Ⓑ Ⓒ Ⓓ Ⓔ	27 Ⓐ Ⓑ Ⓒ Ⓓ Ⓔ	37 Ⓐ Ⓑ Ⓒ Ⓓ Ⓔ
8 Ⓐ Ⓑ Ⓒ Ⓓ Ⓔ	18 Ⓐ Ⓑ Ⓒ Ⓓ Ⓔ	28 Ⓐ Ⓑ Ⓒ Ⓓ Ⓔ	38 Ⓐ Ⓑ Ⓒ Ⓓ Ⓔ
9 Ⓐ Ⓑ Ⓒ Ⓓ Ⓔ	19 Ⓐ Ⓑ Ⓒ Ⓓ Ⓔ	29 Ⓐ Ⓑ Ⓒ Ⓓ Ⓔ	39 Ⓐ Ⓑ Ⓒ Ⓓ Ⓔ
10 Ⓐ Ⓑ Ⓒ Ⓓ Ⓔ	20 Ⓐ Ⓑ Ⓒ Ⓓ Ⓔ	30 Ⓐ Ⓑ Ⓒ Ⓓ Ⓔ	40 Ⓐ Ⓑ Ⓒ Ⓓ Ⓔ

SECTION 10

1 Ⓐ Ⓑ Ⓒ Ⓓ Ⓔ	11 Ⓐ Ⓑ Ⓒ Ⓓ Ⓔ	21 Ⓐ Ⓑ Ⓒ Ⓓ Ⓔ	31 Ⓐ Ⓑ Ⓒ Ⓓ Ⓔ
2 Ⓐ Ⓑ Ⓒ Ⓓ Ⓔ	12 Ⓐ Ⓑ Ⓒ Ⓓ Ⓔ	22 Ⓐ Ⓑ Ⓒ Ⓓ Ⓔ	32 Ⓐ Ⓑ Ⓒ Ⓓ Ⓔ
3 Ⓐ Ⓑ Ⓒ Ⓓ Ⓔ	13 Ⓐ Ⓑ Ⓒ Ⓓ Ⓔ	23 Ⓐ Ⓑ Ⓒ Ⓓ Ⓔ	33 Ⓐ Ⓑ Ⓒ Ⓓ Ⓔ
4 Ⓐ Ⓑ Ⓒ Ⓓ Ⓔ	14 Ⓐ Ⓑ Ⓒ Ⓓ Ⓔ	24 Ⓐ Ⓑ Ⓒ Ⓓ Ⓔ	34 Ⓐ Ⓑ Ⓒ Ⓓ Ⓔ
5 Ⓐ Ⓑ Ⓒ Ⓓ Ⓔ	15 Ⓐ Ⓑ Ⓒ Ⓓ Ⓔ	25 Ⓐ Ⓑ Ⓒ Ⓓ Ⓔ	35 Ⓐ Ⓑ Ⓒ Ⓓ Ⓔ
6 Ⓐ Ⓑ Ⓒ Ⓓ Ⓔ	16 Ⓐ Ⓑ Ⓒ Ⓓ Ⓔ	26 Ⓐ Ⓑ Ⓒ Ⓓ Ⓔ	36 Ⓐ Ⓑ Ⓒ Ⓓ Ⓔ
7 Ⓐ Ⓑ Ⓒ Ⓓ Ⓔ	17 Ⓐ Ⓑ Ⓒ Ⓓ Ⓔ	27 Ⓐ Ⓑ Ⓒ Ⓓ Ⓔ	37 Ⓐ Ⓑ Ⓒ Ⓓ Ⓔ
8 Ⓐ Ⓑ Ⓒ Ⓓ Ⓔ	18 Ⓐ Ⓑ Ⓒ Ⓓ Ⓔ	28 Ⓐ Ⓑ Ⓒ Ⓓ Ⓔ	38 Ⓐ Ⓑ Ⓒ Ⓓ Ⓔ
9 Ⓐ Ⓑ Ⓒ Ⓓ Ⓔ	19 Ⓐ Ⓑ Ⓒ Ⓓ Ⓔ	29 Ⓐ Ⓑ Ⓒ Ⓓ Ⓔ	39 Ⓐ Ⓑ Ⓒ Ⓓ Ⓔ
10 Ⓐ Ⓑ Ⓒ Ⓓ Ⓔ	20 Ⓐ Ⓑ Ⓒ Ⓓ Ⓔ	30 Ⓐ Ⓑ Ⓒ Ⓓ Ⓔ	40 Ⓐ Ⓑ Ⓒ Ⓓ Ⓔ

SECTION 1
ESSAY
Time — 25 minutes

Turn to Section 1 of your answer sheet to write your essay.

The essay gives you an opportunity to show how effectively you can develop and express ideas. You should, therefore, take care to develop your point of view, present your ideas logically and clearly, and use language precisely.

Your essay must be written on the lines provided on your answer sheet—you will receive no other paper on which to write. You will have enough space if you write on every line, avoid wide margins, and keep your handwriting to a reasonable size. Remember that people who are not familiar with your handwriting will read what you write. Try to write or print so that what you are writing is legible to those readers.

You have twenty-five minutes to write an essay on the topic assigned below. DO NOT WRITE ON ANOTHER TOPIC. AN OFF-TOPIC ESSAY WILL RECEIVE A SCORE OF ZERO.

Think carefully about the issue presented in the following excerpt and the assignment below.

> Although we often think of armies and countries as if they were led by a solitary person of authority, in reality they are run by a great many people. A single person can keep track of only a few things, so complicated systems and groups must be run by many people, each of whom controls a tiny piece of the whole. Not even the smartest person could take responsibility for every action necessary to keep things running smoothly.

Assignment: Are many leaders necessary for a group of people to function effectively? Plan and write an essay in which you develop your point of view on this issue. Support your position with reasoning and examples taken from your reading, studies, experience, and observations.

DO NOT WRITE YOUR ESSAY IN YOUR TEST BOOK. You will receive credit only for what you write on your answer sheet.

BEGIN WRITING YOUR ESSAY IN SECTION 1 OF THE ANSWER SHEET.

STOP
**If you finish before time is called, you may check your work on this section only.
Do not turn to any other section in the test.**

SECTION 2
Time — 25 minutes
24 Questions

Turn to Section 2 of your answer sheet to answer the questions in this section.

Directions: For each question in this section, select the best answer from among the choices given and fill in the corresponding circle on the answer sheet.

Each sentence below has one or two blanks, each blank indicating that something has been omitted. Beneath the sentence are five words or sets of words labeled A through E. Choose the word or set of words that, when inserted in the sentence, best fits the meaning of the sentence as a whole.

Example:

Desiring to ------- his taunting friends, Mitch gave them taffy in hopes it would keep their mouths shut.

(A) eliminate   (B) satisfy   (C) overcome
   (D) ridicule   (E) silence

Ⓐ Ⓑ Ⓒ Ⓓ ●

---

1. Some readers consider the novels of Ellis Peters ------- because the plots of the stories repeat, often ------- the same pattern.

   (A) systematic . . rendering of
   (B) disturbing . . adhering to
   (C) inviting . . offering up
   (D) formulaic . . conforming to
   (E) prescriptive . . gravitating toward

2. The prosecutor was not convinced solely by the defendant's testimony; he required statements from two other witnesses that ------- the information.

   (A) introduced   (B) suppressed   (C) compromised
      (D) impugned   (E) corroborated

3. While the number of antibiotic-resistant bacteria species is increasing, scientists still see these mutations as ------- because they constitute a tiny fraction of all bacteria.

   (A) anomalies   (B) extensions   (C) antibodies
      (D) therapies   (E) bifurcations

4. The detective had solved every other case easily, but this case would severely test his crime-solving ------- .

   (A) subtlety   (B) flamboyance   (C) faculty
      (D) effrontery   (E) exoneration

5. Although the counselors are habitually lax, when the camp owner is around they ------- their usual approach and are far more ------- than the campers prefer.

   (A)   augment . . exacting
   (B)   perpetuate . . dissolute
   (C)   renounce . . sedentary
   (D)   accommodate . . itinerant
   (E)   eschew . . stringent

GO ON TO THE NEXT PAGE

Directions: Each passage below is followed by questions based on its content. Answer the questions on the basis of what is <u>stated</u> or <u>implied</u> in each passage and in any introductory material that may be provided.

Questions 6-9 are based on the following passages.

Passage 1

The Taj Mahal, located in Agra, India, is one of the most magnificent examples of Islamic architecture. Shah Jahan, a Muslim ruler, built it in the seventeenth century as a tribute to
Line his late wife. The style of the building seems to reflect that it
5 was built for a beloved woman. Delicate white marble walls, accented by lofty arches and lacy scrollwork, support a series of domes. Four slender towers stand guard near the corners of the building. Overall, the style of the structure gives a striking impression of lightness, despite the heavy stone material. All
10 of these characteristics lead to an almost otherworldly beauty, worthy of any queen.

Passage 2

Although the Taj Mahal has long been recognized for its architectural beauty, it is often overlooked that Shah Jahan commissioned the building in 1632 as a tomb for his most
15 beloved wife. The tomb is flanked on the west by a mosque, a Muslim place of worship. Arabic script is inlaid along the walls of the Taj Mahal, and it is rumored that the entire Muslim holy book, the Koran, is written along the structure's walls and supports. The architectural wonder of the Taj Mahal
20 cannot be denied; however, it is vital to recognize the spiritual aspects that pervade one of the world's most recognizable buildings.

6. Compared to Passage 2, Passage 1 is more concerned with the Taj Mahal's

(A) enduring popularity
(B) aesthetic qualities
(C) spiritual function
(D) controversial history
(E) enormous cost

7. The primary purpose of Passage 2 is to

(A) highlight the religious nature of a structure
(B) criticize an obsession with physical beauty
(C) define the historical importance of a building
(D) explain an architectural paradox
(E) identify a source of inspiration

8. The authors of both passages would most likely agree that the Taj Mahal

(A) is the most famous example of Islamic architecture
(B) was primarily designed to be a place of worship
(C) was originally intended as a memorial
(D) is not typical of buildings in India
(E) is both graceful and solidly constructed

9. Unlike the author of Passage 1, the author of Passage 2 acknowledges that the Taj Mahal is

(A) widely known
(B) located in India
(C) architecturally significant
(D) extremely old
(E) frequently overlooked

GO ON TO THE NEXT PAGE

Questions 10-18 are based on the following passage.

The following passage, adapted from a recent article, focuses on Europa, one of Jupiter's moons. Europa is one of the few objects in our solar system that may contain water.

Imagine you are a diver, descending through Europa's outer shield of ice into the protected ocean below. You will not see plants, arching their way towards a distant sun. You
Line will not see fish, darting towards a piece of flotsam spotted
5 floating through the current. You will not see the sparkling plane of light above that tells you "this is up" and "this is down." You are floating, alone, in darkness. This is Europa's ocean.

Scientists want desperately to see this shadowed oceanic
10 world for one simple reason: it may have water, and with water may come life. Europa's water, if indeed it is there, slips under a sheet of ice 5 to 20 miles thick that blocks all incoming light. To find life there, even if only a single-celled organism, clinging to a small undersea volcano for warmth
15 and energy, would mean that the building blocks that made us are not unique, but more plentiful and varied than we thought, spread through solar systems we will never reach. If there is no life in those covered murky depths, then new questions will have to be asked. Could life survive there? If so, why
20 didn't it develop? What key ingredient was missing? The more we know about Europa's hidden oceans, the more we will understand about Earth.

It has long been known that Europa is essentially a ball of ice, crisscrossed with lines and freckled like an orange. These
25 lines and freckles led some to postulate that the Europa's ice was constantly shifting and buckling, perhaps due to a sea below the shell of ice. In 1977, in the Galapagos Rift, deep in the Pacific Ocean, scientists discovered creatures that live far from the sun's reach and derive their energy entirely from
30 small undersea thermal vents. As we discovered hardier and stranger creatures such as these thriving in harsh, sunless environments, the possibility of life in Europa's bleak abyss blossomed. Science fiction writers, such as Arthur C. Clarke, wrote tales about hypothetical creatures living in the dark
35 depths below. It was not, however, until the Galileo spacecraft was able to observe Europa up close in 1995 that scientists had solid evidence of an ocean below Europa's crust of ice.

If there is an ocean, then there may be alien ecosystems. And here is the paradox: to look for these organisms,
40 we would have to enter their world and risk disrupting it permanently. If Europa is home to life, then that life could be tied so closely to its current environment that the addition of anything new could be as harmful as pouring a cup of salt into a goldfish's bowl. The National Academy of Sciences
45 has warned against the possibility of microbes that could preserve themselves in the vacuum of interplanetary travel and, hitched on to one of our probes, contaminate Europa's ocean. Since Europa's ocean, should it exist, is one continuous whole, damage to one part of Europa's ecosystem could not be
50 contained.

Is exploring Europa worth the risk? It would require billions of dollars of research and construction, and take at least a decade, to complete any sort of probe to Europa's depths. So far, although many expeditions have been planned
55 both by NASA and by the European Space Agency, few have made it past the planning stages. The risks of contaminating an entire ecosystem have added further roadblocks. But even though we have, in the words of one scientist, "a scientific, moral, and legal responsibility" to preserve Europa, we also
60 have a responsibility to search for knowledge. As alien as Europa is, understanding the life that may live there could help us understand similarly "alien" life here on Earth, such as the mysterious creatures inhabiting the isolated subglacial lakes of Vostok, Untersee, and Ellsworth. Unlike the
65 discoverers of centuries past, we cannot rush into a pristine wilderness unprepared, but must find a way to observe without disrupting.

10. The primary purpose of the passage is to

(A) explain the experiences of a hypothetical visitor to Europa
(B) discourage travel to other planets and moons
(C) describe current theories and dilemmas about Europa
(D) compare possible life forms on Europa with those in subglacial lakes
(E) emphasize the legal obligations of the scientific community

11. In lines 13-17 ("To find . . . reach") the author does which of the following?

(A) Describes an actual organism
(B) References an influential authority
(C) Presents a location to investigate
(D) Warns of a possible danger
(E) Speculates about a possibility

12. The author introduces the example of the Galapagos Rift (line 27) in order to

(A) suggest that seemingly inhospitable places are capable of supporting life
(B) highlight the strangeness of deep-sea fish compared to other types of fish
(C) underscore the improbability of discovering life beneath the surface of Europa
(D) explain the difficulty of conducting scientific experiments in inaccessible places
(E) contrast the creatures that live in the Pacific Ocean with those that live in Europa's ocean

GO ON TO THE NEXT PAGE

13. In line 37, "solid" most nearly means

   (A) upstanding
   (B) homogenous
   (C) definitive
   (D) continuous
   (E) hearty

14. In context, the comment in lines 39-41 ("And here . . . permanently") primarily serves to

   (A) support an earlier claim
   (B) offer a short aside
   (C) illustrate a likely advantage
   (D) change the focus of the discussion
   (E) contest a possible objection

15. The sentence in lines 41-44 ("If Europa . . . bowl") emphasizes Europa's

   (A) mystery
   (B) fragility
   (C) desolation
   (D) impurity
   (E) distance

16. The author most likely mentions "a goldfish's bowl" in line 44 in order to

   (A) highlight the necessity of instruments that can precisely measure quantities
   (B) point out an unfortunate but inevitable consequence
   (C) illustrate the relative size of Europa's ocean in comparison to our own
   (D) convey the sensitivity of fish to the mineral content of water
   (E) emphasize the possible implications of an undertaking

17. The author's attitude in lines 57-60 ("But even . . . knowledge") is best described as

   (A) perplexed
   (B) resolute
   (C) optimistic
   (D) indignant
   (E) restrained

18. The author indicates all of the following in the final paragraph EXCEPT

   (A) any plant life on Europa could be in danger of infection from a previously unknown virus
   (B) a further investigation of Europa would call for sizeable investments of time and money
   (C) investigating life on Europa could supply information about life on Earth
   (D) a variety of missions to Europa have been planned by more than one agency
   (E) there may be locations on Europa that share similarities to locations on Earth

GO ON TO THE NEXT PAGE

Questions 19-24 are based on the following passages.

Passage 1 is adapted from a 2008 essay. Passage 2, adapted from an 1857 novel, is about a self-proclaimed "herb doctor," who is actually a salesman of a sham medicine. The herb doctor has just sold his medicine to an old man, and is now trying to sell it to a hunter from Missouri.

Passage 1

A couple years ago, I was diagnosed with a minor joint inflammation in my right knee. It was nothing serious, although I wasn't able to hike for a while, but soon friends
Line and family were telling me about all sorts of treatments. Some
5 were variations on what my doctor had told me: bed rest, ice, wearing a knee brace. But many of the other treatments were so bizarre that I wondered how my friends could honestly believe them: standing on my head, putting magnets in my shoes, eating 20 figs a day. Anything that started with the
10 words "this will definitely work" I ignored immediately, assuming it was definitely ridiculous.

Medicine is a science of uncertainties. We try things, and see if they tend to work. If they don't, we try something else. Even the treatments we are "sure" about don't work
15 all the time. Aspirin helps headaches most of the time, but sometimes there's nothing we can do. That's why the cure-all is so tempting. It is hard to admit that, with all we are capable of, there are still things that mankind cannot fix or heal. Phony treatments fill that need; a bogus cure
20 is a security blanket. In the nineteenth century, when the confidence man* roamed the US, there was no patent tonic too patently ridiculous to find a buyer. The best the patient of such medicines could hope for is to feel no worse. For most, however, the medicines were essentially poisons, and could
25 cause damage far worse than the original ailment. What is most remarkable is that many of those duped and damaged by one potion would then seek to cure these new symptoms with the next cure-all that came along.

Passage 2

"Sir," the herb doctor said with unimpaired affability,
30 producing one of his boxes, which was small, tin, and filled with whatever bits of grass and dirt had happened to be close by, "though your manner is refined your voice is rough; in short, you seem to have a sore throat. In the name of Nature, I present you with this box; my venerable friend here has a
35 similar one; but to you, a free gift, sir."

"I tell you I want none of your boxes," said the hunter, snapping his rifle.

"Oh, take it! Do take it," chimed in the old man; "I wish he would give me one for nothing."
40 "You find it lonely, eh," said the hunter, turning around; "tricked yourself, you would have a companion."

"How can he find it lonely," returned the herb doctor, "or desire a companion, when here I stand by him; I, even I, in whom he has trust. As for the tricking, tell me, is it humane
45 to talk so to this poor old man? Granting that his dependence on my medicine is vain, is it kind to deprive him of what, in mere imagination, if nothing more, may help him last out his disease? For you, if you have no faith, and, thanks to your native health, can get along without it, fine; yet, how cruel
50 an argument to use, with this afflicted one here. Is it not for all the world as if some brawny boxer, aglow in December, should rush in and put out a hospital-fire, because, since he feels no need of artificial heat, the shivering patients shall have none? Put it to your conscience, sir, and you will admit,
55 that, whatever be the nature of this afflicted one's trust, you, in opposing it, show either a confused head or a heart amiss. Are you so pitiless?

* A conman, particularly common in the United States in the nineteenth-century, who often traveled from town to town and sold fake medicines.

GO ON TO THE NEXT PAGE

19. The reference to "a security blanket" (line 20) can be best understood to mean that the "bogus cure"

    (A) can be used to cover up symptoms

    (B) is harmful to the person who takes it, but harmless to others

    (C) can be comforting even if it is not effective

    (D) is used by doctors only when other methods have failed

    (E) can help children and adults alike

20. The "confidence man" (line 21) is closest to which of the following in Passage 2 ?

    (A) the old man

    (B) the hunter

    (C) the herb doctor

    (D) the brawny boxer

    (E) shivering patients

21. What do the "patent tonic" (line 21) and the "box" (line 34) have in common?

    (A) Both were actually toxic in small quantities.

    (B) Both were advertised to cure an ailment.

    (C) Both were based on earlier folk remedies.

    (D) Both were given away for free to attract customers.

    (E) Both were rejected by the medical establishment.

22. The herb doctor refers to the "brawny boxer" (line 51) in order to point out that

    (A) the hunter should buy the box of medicine

    (B) the medicine is useful to patients who are experiencing chills

    (C) athletes generally do not need medicine

    (D) the herb doctor knows that the medicine will not work

    (E) the hunter should not disparage the old man's belief in the medicine

23. The author's observations in Passage 1 compared with the herb doctor's observations in Passage 2 are

    (A) less joyous

    (B) less humorous

    (C) more deceptive

    (D) more realistic

    (E) more perplexed

24. Which of the following is an observation offered by the author of Passage 1 that is NOT exhibited by a character in Passage 2 ?

    (A) A medicine, even if it does not physically heal, can bring mental relief.

    (B) Medicines are sometimes based on plants found in nature.

    (C) Some people were willing to purchase medicines with no medical support.

    (D) Buyers, after purchasing a medicine, often feel they have been swindled.

    (E) Medicine is generally based on trial and error.

STOP

If you finish before time is called, you may check your work on this section only.
Do not turn to any other section in the test.

SECTION 3
Time — 25 minutes
18 Questions

Turn to Section 3 of your answer sheet to answer the questions in this section.

Directions: This section contains two types of questions. You have 25 minutes to complete both types. For questions 1-8, solve each problem and decide which is the best of the choices given. Fill in the corresponding circle on the answer sheet. You may use any available space for scratchwork.

Notes

1. The use of a calculator is permitted.

2. All numbers used are real numbers.

3. Figures that accompany problems in this test are intended to provide information useful in solving the problems. They are drawn as accurately as possible EXCEPT when it is stated in a specific problem that the figure is not drawn to scale. All figures lie in a plane unless otherwise indicated.

4. Unless otherwise specified, the domain of any function f is assumed to be the set of all real numbers x for which $f(x)$ is a real number.

Reference Information

 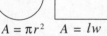

$A = \pi r^2$ $A = lw$ $A = \frac{1}{2}bh$ $V = lwh$ $V = \pi r^2 h$ $c^2 = a^2 + b^2$ Special Right Triangles

$C = 2\pi r$

The number of degrees of arc in a circle is 360.

The sum of the measures in degrees of the angles of a triangle is 180.

1. If $\dfrac{a-b-5}{2} = 10$, then what is the value of $a - b$?

   (A) 20
   (B) 25
   (C) 30
   (D) 35
   (E) 40

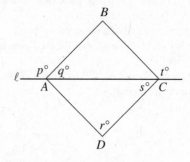

2. In the figure above, line ℓ forms the diagonal of square *ABCD*. Which of the following must be true?

   (A) $p = t$
   (B) $q = r$
   (C) $q = t$
   (D) $r = s$
   (E) $r = t$

GO ON TO THE NEXT PAGE

$$r = 4c - d$$
$$t = (c + 1)r$$

3. If r and t are defined by the equations above, what is the value of t when $c = 3$ and $d = 2$?

(A)   10
(B)   12
(C)   30
(D)   40
(E)   80

RATE OF EVAPORATION						
Time Elapsed (in hours)	0	2	4	6	8	10
Volume of Water (in ml)	14	10	7	5	4	3.5

4. Which of the following graphs best represents the information in the table above?

(A)
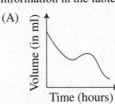

(B)
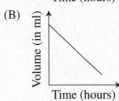

(C)
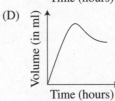

(D)
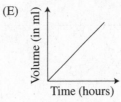

(E)
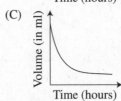

GO ON TO THE NEXT PAGE

$f(x)$	x
25	0
26	1
29	2

5. Which of the following functions satisfies each pair of numbers in the table above?

(A) $f(x) = 25 + 25x$
(B) $f(x) = 25 + 13x$
(C) $f(x) = 25 + 5x$
(D) $f(x) = 25 + x$
(E) $f(x) = 25 + x^2$

$$p = y^8$$
$$q = y^5$$

7. If the above statements are true and $y > 1$, which of the following is equal to y^9 ?

(A) $(p - q)^3$

(B) $(pq)^3$

(C) $\left(\dfrac{p}{q}\right)^3$

(D) $p - 3q$

(E) $p - q^3$

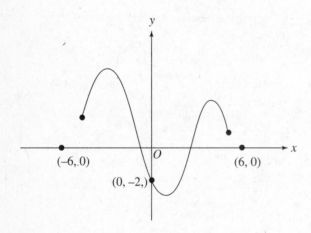

6. The figure above shows the graph of $y = g(x)$. For how many values of x between -6 and 6 does $g(x) = 0$?

(A) One
(B) Two
(C) Three
(D) Four
(E) More than four

8. If $\dfrac{4}{5}p$ is two times the value of $\dfrac{q}{10}$, where p and q are both positive integers, then p is what percent of q ?

(A) 625%
(B) 400%
(C) 80%
(D) 25%
(E) 4%

GO ON TO THE NEXT PAGE

Directions: For Student-Produced Response questions 9-18, use the grids at the bottom of the answer sheet page on which you have answered questions 1-8.

Each of the remaining 10 questions requires you to solve the problem and enter your answer by marking the circles in the special grid, as shown in the examples below. You may use any available space for scratch work.

Answer: $\frac{7}{12}$

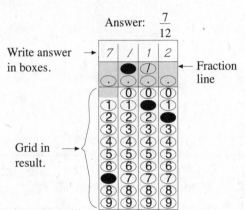

Write answer → in boxes.

Fraction line

Grid in → result.

Answer: 2.5

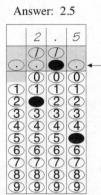

Decimal point

Answer: 201
Either position is correct.

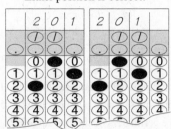

Note: You may start your answers in any column, space permitting. Columns not needed should be left blank.

• Mark no more than one circle in any column.

• Because the answer document will be machine-scored, **you will receive credit only if the circles are filled in correctly.**

• Although not required, it is suggested that you write your answer in the boxes at the top of the columns to help you fill in the circles accurately.

• Some problems may have more than one correct answer. In such cases, grid only one answer.

• No question has a negative answer.

• **Mixed numbers** such as $3\frac{1}{2}$ must be gridded as

3.5 or 7/2. (If 3 | 1 | / | 2 is gridded, it will be

interpreted as $\frac{31}{2}$, not $3\frac{1}{2}$.)

• **Decimal Answers:** If you obtain a decimal answer with more digits than the grid can accommodate, it may be either rounded or truncated, but it must fill the entire grid. For example, if you obtain an answer such as 0.6666..., you should record your result as .666 or .667. **A less accurate value such as .66 or .67 will be scored as incorrect.**

Acceptable ways to grid $\frac{2}{3}$ are:

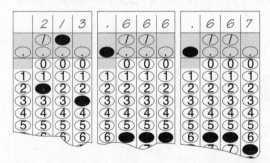

9. The price of item *A* increased from 36 dollars to 50 dollars in a week. The price of item *B* increased by half as many dollars as the price of item *A* did during the same week. If the price of item *B* was 52 dollars at the beginning of the week, what was the price, in dollars, of item *B* at the end of the week?

10. Since the beginning of the year, the number of articles on Randy's website has doubled during every 2-month period of time. If there were 7,200 articles on Randy's website at the beginning of July, how many articles were on Randy's website at the beginning of January of the same year?

GO ON TO THE NEXT PAGE →

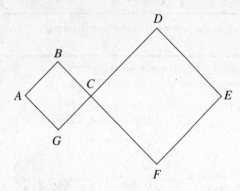

11. In the figure above, squares *ABCG* and *CDEF* share point *C*, and line segment $\overline{DG}$ has length 15. What is the sum of the perimeters of the two squares?

12. If $a = 4b$, $b = 5c$, $a = dc$, and $a \neq 0$, what is the value of *d* ?

13. Rebecca is removing DVDs from a shelf that has 15 dramas and 15 comedies on it. What is the least number of DVDs that Rebecca could remove so that the ratio of dramas to comedies left on the shelf will be 3 to 5 ?

14. If $|2 - 3y| < 2$, what is one possible value of *y* ?

GO ON TO THE NEXT PAGE

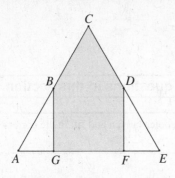

15. In the figure above, $\triangle ACE$ is equilateral. If $\overline{AB} = \overline{BC}$, $\overline{CD} = \overline{DE}$, and $BDFG$ is a rectangle, what fraction of the area of $\triangle ACE$ is shaded?

16. For what positive number is the cube root of the number the same as the number divided by 100 ?

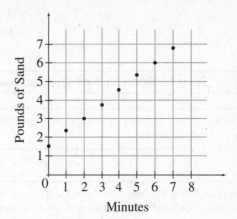

17. As represented by the graph above, sand is added at a constant rate of x pounds per minute to a container that already contains $1\frac{1}{2}$ pounds of sand. If after 7 minutes there are $6\frac{3}{4}$ pounds of sand in the container, what is the value of x ?

$$(a + b)^2 \leq (a - b)^2 + 36$$

18. In the equation above, $0 \leq a \leq b$. What is the <u>greatest</u> possible value of a ?

STOP
If you finish before time is called, you may check your work on this section only.
Do not turn to any other section in the test.

SECTION 4
Time — 25 minutes
25 Questions

Turn to Section 4 of your answer sheet to answer the questions in this section.

Directions: For each question in this section, select the best answer from among the choices given and fill in the corresponding circle on the answer sheet.

Each sentence below has one or two blanks, each blank indicating that something has been omitted. Beneath the sentence are five words or sets of words labeled A through E. Choose the word or set of words that, when inserted in the sentence, best fits the meaning of the sentence as a whole.

Example:

Desiring to ------- his taunting friends, Mitch gave them taffy in hopes it would keep their mouths shut.

(A) eliminate   (B) satisfy   (C) overcome
    (D) ridicule   (E) silence

1. As proponents of environmental preservation begin to outnumber those who engage in deforestation, there is hope that destruction of the rainforest will soon -------.

   (A) acquiesce   (B) flourish   (C) concur
       (D) abate   (E) mediate

2. Unlike other early comedians who preferred to follow scripts, Ernie Kovacs often ------- during his sketches, ------- mixing in new lines as they came to him.

   (A) internalized . . skillfully
   (B) ad-libbed . . spontaneously
   (C) dictated . . cautiously
   (D) improvised . . soberly
   (E) extemporized . . inappropriately

3. The professor's ------- and seemingly irrelevant digressions actually illustrated how the ancient theories were ------- current research.

   (A) random . . built upon
   (B) jarring . . baffled by
   (C) focused . . essential to
   (D) tangential . . vital to
   (E) bizarre . . dessicated by

4. John's novels were inspired by the hostile and combative nature of ------- characters in historical war stories.

   (A) perfidious   (B) abstract   (C) docile
       (D) jaunty   (E) bellicose

5. The city's tax laws were both ------- and -------: incredibly complicated and completely out of date.

   (A) byzantine . . antiquated
   (B) bereft . . inconsequential
   (C) obfuscated . . ubiquitous
   (D) quiescent . . fossilized
   (E) cosmopolitan . . obsolete

6. The admiration shown for the new president by people everywhere was so pronounced that it could be described as -------.

   (A) adulation   (B) exasperation   (C) commiseration
       (D) enervation   (E) extirpation

7. Once forthright and blunt, Keisha has become increasingly ------- and inscrutable over the past several years.

   (A) candid   (B) brusque   (C) unswerving
       (D) enigmatic   (E) cultured

8. As the Spanish Civil War progressed, it became increasingly marked by foreign interventions and shifting alliances, making for a ------- situation that belied the war's ------- beginnings.

   (A) beleaguered . . serendipitous
   (B) intricate . . auspicious
   (C) convoluted . . straightforward
   (D) canonical . . abrogated
   (E) retrenched . . somber

GO ON TO THE NEXT PAGE

Directions: Each passage below is followed by questions based on its content. Answer the questions on the basis of what is <u>stated</u> or <u>implied</u> in each passage and in any introductory material that may be provided.

Questions 9-10 are based on the following passage.

As a music critic, I have sifted through more horrible albums than most people would foist upon their worst enemy. But it is when I must review a concept album, a CD-length set

Line of songs with a single unifying theme, that I feel that I must
5 truly have a very powerful enemy indeed. A concept album is simply too long and too repetitive: every song is leading towards one single point, so you're guaranteed to hear the same idea, over and over. It is like reading a series of stories in which each story has the exact same moral, or watching
10 a detective show in which the killer is the same person each week.

9. The author makes the statement in lines 4-5 ("I feel . . . indeed") in order to

   (A) challenge a belief with a comical example
   (B) explain a grievance by quoting a conflicting source
   (C) cite an authority to justify a bold assertion
   (D) advance a negative opinion using humorous terms
   (E) offer an amusing anecdote to support a claim

10. In lines 8-11, ("It is . . . week"), the author makes use of

    (A) analogy
    (B) generalization
    (C) allusion
    (D) exaggeration
    (E) personification

Questions 11-12 are based on the following passage.

Although many people associate slavery exclusively with the plight of African Americans in eighteenth- and nineteenth-century America, many different races and

Line ethnicities have been enslaved throughout history. The Slavs,
5 an Eastern European people, were among the many historical victims. The term "Slav" originally meant "those who speak," while the old Latin word "servus" was used to refer to unfree laborers. In the Holy Roman Empire, Slavs were so frequently subjugated that "slav," or "slave," came to refer to people who
10 were forced to work for no wages, while "servant" (derived from "servus") became the preferred term for those who served more willingly. Thus, the modern meaning of both terms arose from the unfortunate situation of the Slavs.

11. The author most likely mentions the plight of African Americans in order to

    (A) contrast a commonly held view with a broader historical perspective
    (B) indicate that African Americans were treated as poorly as the Slavs were
    (C) explain why the institution of slavery has persisted over the centuries
    (D) emphasize the contemporary relevance of a historical injustice
    (E) examine the cultural ties between two distinct groups

12. The passage is primarily concerned with

    (A) suggesting that the use of certain words may be inappropriate
    (B) tracing the history of the Slavs from ancient to modern times
    (C) offering an explanation for the root causes of slavery
    (D) relating a particular linguistic usage to historical events
    (E) criticizing the brutality of the ancient Romans

GO ON TO THE NEXT PAGE

Questions 13-25 are based on the following passage.

The following passage, from a novel set in the late nineteenth-century, depicts a first meeting of two families.

Aphra Edwards grew accustomed to her new economic position and got on quite well with the other women of similar social standing in the town, meeting for lunch or tea when
Line there was little to be done around the house. Even though
5 the Edwards family had lost its estate and servants when the business collapsed, Aphra was happy in this provincial role and not often bothered by the domestic disturbances of her simpler life. It all seemed so trivial compared to the heartache she had already endured.

10 Her daughter Rachel would often join her at these social gatherings and therefore was also well known in the community. Rachel had adjusted quite beautifully, as it was in this new location that she was able to develop the cutting-edge sharpness she was once known for and shape it into
15 a savvy gracefulness envied by all the other young ladies. Rachel's acquaintance was in fact desired by many in this new town's social circle. She had, on occasion, been called upon by members of the upper echelons of society that had heard of her, this wise and graceful beauty, daughter of the great
20 fallen Phineas Edwards. So, though it stunned Rachel a little (who had yet to develop the egotism that often accompanied such attention), it was no surprise to her mother when they received an invitation to tea at the Hamilton estate with Ginny Hamilton, sister of the well-known Nathaniel Hamilton.

25 Aphra and Rachel no longer fussed over society as they once did because they could rest in the knowledge that everyone knew of their tragic downfall and there was no need to pretend otherwise. With only modest preparations made, the day soon came, and Aphra and Rachel maintained
30 their mild excitement as they stepped into the carriage. It was a pleasant but brisk fall afternoon, the wind blowing the leaves off the trees and giving Aphra only minor difficulties as she gathered her clothing into the carriage. Rachel had no such trouble, as it seemed her heightened sense of grace and
35 elegance had translated to her physical being as well.

"Mother, I do hope that Ginny Hamilton is as pleasant as her brother made her out to be at the train station."

"I'm sure she will be. I have heard only good things about the Hamilton family, and Ginny especially is known for
40 having a kind and gentle heart. But Rachel, dear, are you sure it is Ginny whose acquaintance you are anticipating?"

"Why, Mother, you know me better than that, to think I would get my hopes up over a silly little thing like this. I have no intentions beyond those of tea and a sociable time."

45 Sure enough, as if to spite her efforts of denial, there was Nathaniel Hamilton standing on the porch. He stood flanked by stately columns and two servants, speaking to them with his back turned to the drive. The servants then quickly entered the house and Nathaniel turned around gracefully to
50 greet his guests with a genuine, spontaneous smile, as if their coming was a pleasant surprise.

"Good afternoon, ladies. I have just come home myself from the office and figured I could stand a moment or two in this lovely fall afternoon waiting your arrival." He gestured to
55 the amber trees around him.

"Good afternoon, Mister Hamilton. Rachel and I, too, have been enjoying this lovely weather. It was so nice of your sister to invite us here for tea."

"Indeed. Won't you come in? Ginny is waiting in the
60 parlor."

"With pleasure."

Nathaniel escorted them through the airy entryway to the parlor silently, not knowing exactly what to say. The parlor was filled with afternoon sun and vibrant colors, and in the
65 center stood Ginny Hamilton, pleasant as the setting that surrounded her.

"Ginny, Rachel and Aphra are here to make your acquaintance. Rachel, Aphra, this is my sister Ginny." Ginny curtsied politely. It was obvious that she was Nathaniel's
70 sister. Impeccably dressed with a clean, fresh, youthful look about her face, one could not discern which was the older of the two, though in fact Ginny was several years older than her brother. Her satiny brunette hair and creamy skin made her beautiful in the uncommon way, unlike Rachel's classically
75 beautiful light features. Aphra took an instant liking to her.

13. The first paragraph primarily focuses on

(A) a heartbreaking account of disaster
(B) the joy of socializing with friends
(C) a character's emotional state
(D) the difficulties of rural life
(E) Aphra's love for her family·

14. The word "heartache" (line 8) refers to

(A) an unexpected illness
(B) an emotional encounter
(C) a romantic entanglement
(D) a bittersweet memory
(E) a financial misfortune

15. The author's depiction of Rachel in lines 10-20 ("Her daughter . . . Edwards") primarily serves to illustrate her

(A) prospects for a fortunate marriage
(B) resemblance to Phineas Edwards
(C) enviable style and intelligence
(D) recognition of the contrast between her and Aphra
(E) desire to excite jealousy in her friends

16. In line 12, "beautifully" most nearly means

(A) successfully
(B) exotically
(C) attractively
(D) vainly
(E) strikingly

GO ON TO THE NEXT PAGE

17. The parenthetical phrase in lines 21-22 ("who had . . . attention") suggests that Rachel lacks

    (A) self-esteem
    (B) vanity
    (C) common sense
    (D) impassivity
    (E) ambition

18. For Rachel, "tea" (line 23) represents

    (A) an awkward encounter
    (B) an unexpected opportunity
    (C) an onerous duty
    (D) a dangerous development
    (E) a long-desired invitation

19. The author employs the phrase "no longer fussed over society" (line 25) to imply that the women had previously

    (A) given consideration to impressing and pleasing others
    (B) passed judgment on those of lower social classes
    (C) taken great pains to find a husband for Rachel
    (D) dressed extravagantly to announce their superiority
    (E) tried to appear grander than their finances allowed

20. In line 28, "modest" most nearly means

    (A) bashful
    (B) slight
    (C) demure
    (D) stingy
    (E) delicate

21. In the context of the passage, "translated" (line 35) suggests that

    (A) grace and elegance are difficult to achieve
    (B) true beauty reveals the presence of inherent characteristics
    (C) an individual's demeanor can mirror that person's character
    (D) sophisticated individuals can transform their appearances
    (E) ethereal qualities such as grace are connected to class

22. In lines 38-41 ("I'm sure . . . anticipating"), Aphra responds to Rachel's remark by

    (A) comparing Ginny to some of Rachel's other friends
    (B) suggesting that Rachel secretly dislikes members of the Hamilton family
    (C) questioning the reliability of certain statements about Ginny's character
    (D) worrying that Rachel is overly concerned with other people's opinions
    (E) implying that there is an alternative reason for Rachel's interest in their visit

23. In lines 42-44, Rachel deflects Aphra's question by

    (A) misinterpreting the meaning of a phrase
    (B) questioning the motives of an individual
    (C) minimizing the significance of an occasion
    (D) lamenting the difficulties of a situation
    (E) justifying a response to an accusation

24. The conversation between Aphra and Nathaniel in lines 52-61 is best characterized as

    (A) an easy conversation between close friends
    (B) an earnest discussion between lovers
    (C) a formal negotiation between colleagues
    (D) a polite exchange between acquaintances
    (E) a playful argument between adversaries

25. Lines 73-75 ("Her . . . features") primarily serve to

    (A) offer an example
    (B) draw a comparison
    (C) make a prediction
    (D) present a theory
    (E) recount an anecdote

STOP

If you finish before time is called, you may check your work on this section only.
Do not turn to any other section in the test.

SECTION 5
Time — 25 minutes
20 Questions

Turn to Section 5 of your answer sheet to answer the questions in this section.

Directions: For this section, solve each problem and decide which is the best of the choices given. Fill in the corresponding circle on the answer sheet. You may use any available space for scratchwork.

Notes

1. The use of a calculator is permitted.

2. All numbers used are real numbers.

3. Figures that accompany problems in this test are intended to provide information useful in solving the problems. They are drawn as accurately as possible EXCEPT when it is stated in a specific problem that the figure is not drawn to scale. All figures lie in a plane unless otherwise indicated.

4. Unless otherwise specified, the domain of any function f is assumed to be the set of all real numbers x for which $f(x)$ is a real number.

Reference Information

   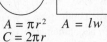 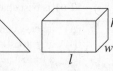 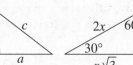

$A = \pi r^2$ $A = lw$ $A = \frac{1}{2}bh$ $V = lwh$ $V = \pi r^2 h$ $c^2 = a^2 + b^2$

Special Right Triangles

$C = 2\pi r$

The number of degrees of arc in a circle is 360.

The sum of the measures in degrees of the angles of a triangle is 180.

---

1. If Donald can type w words in m minutes, which of the following represents his average typing speed, in words per minute?

(A) $\dfrac{m}{w}$

(B) $\dfrac{w}{m}$

(C) $\dfrac{1}{2}mw$

(D) mw

(E) $2mw$

2. Angelique invited 42 people to a conference. Of the invitees, 8 people declined, and the rest accepted. On the day of the conference, a snowstorm prevented half of those who accepted from making it to the conference. If no other people accepted or declined, what fraction of Angelique's original 42 invitees attended the conference?

(A) $\dfrac{13}{42}$

(B) $\dfrac{1}{3}$

(C) $\dfrac{5}{14}$

(D) $\dfrac{8}{21}$

(E) $\dfrac{17}{42}$

GO ON TO THE NEXT PAGE

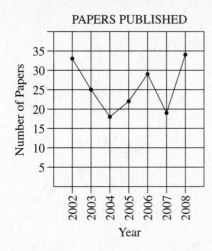

PAPERS PUBLISHED

3. The line graph above shows the number of papers published by the economics department at a major university for the years 2002 through 2008. For which of the following years was the number of papers published closest to the average (arithmetic mean) number of papers published in 2002 and 2003 ?

(A) 2004
(B) 2005
(C) 2006
(D) 2007
(E) 2008

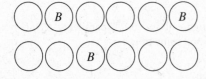

4. Jean-Paul is making place settings for Sunday brunch. He wants to make sure no two plates next to each other on the same side of the table and no two plates directly across from each other on the table are the same color. If the settings labeled *B* are blue, how many of the nine remaining settings <u>cannot</u> be blue?

(A) Two
(B) Three
(C) Four
(D) Five
(E) Six

5. If $x > 0$ and $y < 0$, which of the following must be positive?

(A) $2y$
(B) $-2x$
(C) $-4xy$
(D) $x + 2y$
(E) $4(x + y)$

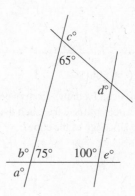

6. In the figure above, which of the following is greatest?

(A) a
(B) b
(C) c
(D) d
(E) e

GO ON TO THE NEXT PAGE

7. Albert's diet allows him to consume no more than 450 calories for breakfast. He decides to have 3 mini-muffins, which each contain 140 calories, and a drink. If n represents the number of calories that his drink can contain, which of the following inequalities could be used to find all possible values for n?

    (A) $n \geq 3(140)$
    (B) $3(140) + n \leq 450$
    (C) $3(140) + n \geq 450$
    (D) $3(140) - n \leq 450$
    (E) $3(140) - n \geq 450$

8. How many lines can be drawn from one vertex of a cube to the other vertices of the cube, such that the lines are not parallel to any edge of the cube?

    (A)   4
    (B)   6
    (C)   7
    (D)   24
    (E)   42

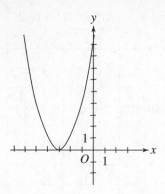

9. Which of the following could be the equation of the graph above?

    (A) $y = (x + 3)^2$
    (B) $y = x^2 + 3$
    (C) $y = (x - 3)^2$
    (D) $y = x^2 - 3$
    (E) $y = 3x^2$

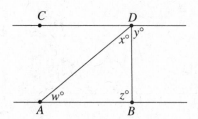

10. In the figure above, $\overline{AB}$ is parallel to $\overline{CD}$. If $y = 88$, then what is the value of $w + x$?

    (A) 88
    (B) 89
    (C) 90
    (D) 91
    (E) 92

GO ON TO THE NEXT PAGE

$$h(x) = \frac{3}{2}x + 1$$

$$f(x) = \frac{4}{3}x$$

11. The functions h and f are defined above. What is the value of $h(5) - f(3)$?

(A) 8.5
(B) 5
(C) 4.5
(D) 4
(E) 3

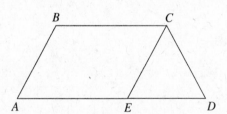

12. In the figure above, $ABCE$ is a parallelogram and $\triangle ECD$ is equilateral. If $AE = 8$ and the perimeter of $\triangle ECD$ is 18, what is the perimeter of $ABCE$?

(A) 42
(B) 32
(C) 30
(D) 28
(E) 18

13. A class of 8 students had an average (arithmetic mean) test score of 76 on its first test. On the second test, all but two students received the same score as they did on the first test. One student received a 96 instead of a 72, and another received a 70 instead of a 62. What was the average score on the second test?

(A) 80
(B) 78
(C) 76
(D) 74
(E) 72

NUMBER OF ANIMALS AT THE PET STORE		
	Cats	Dogs
Less than 3 months old	26	8
3 or more month old	6	24

14. The table above shows the number of animals at a particular pet store according to the type of animal and age. If a dog is to be chosen at random, what is the probability that the dog is less than 3 months old?

(A) $\dfrac{1}{3}$

(B) $\dfrac{1}{4}$

(C) $\dfrac{3}{8}$

(D) $\dfrac{3}{4}$

(E) $\dfrac{3}{5}$

GO ON TO THE NEXT PAGE

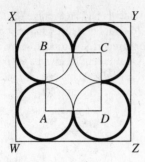

15. Four congruent circles with centers A, B, C, and D are inscribed in square $WXYZ$, as shown above. If the area of square $WXYZ$ is 4, what is the total length of the darkened curves?

(A) 3π
(B) 4π
(C) 6π
(D) 8π
(E) 16π

16. If a is a nonnegative integer, and b is a positive multiple of 4, how many possible distinct values of ab are less than 10 ?

(A) None
(B) One
(C) Two
(D) Three
(E) Five

17. For all numbers a and b, let $a\ \Phi\ b = a^2b + ab^2$. What is the value of $(1\ \Phi\ 2)\ \Phi\ 3$?

(A) 6
(B) 12
(C) 54
(D) 108
(E) 162

18. In a sequence of numbers, the first term is x and the ratio of each subsequent term to the previous term is 3 to 1. Which of the following expressions represents the difference between the fourth term and the second term?

(A) $3x$
(B) $9x$
(C) $12x$
(D) $24x$
(E) $27x$

GO ON TO THE NEXT PAGE

19. The length of a line segment with endpoints L and P is a positive integer less than 24. N is the midpoint of $\overline{LP}$, M is the midpoint of $\overline{LN}$, and O is the midpoint of $\overline{NP}$. Which of the following could be the distance between M and P ?

(A) 18
(B) 17
(C) 16
(D) 15
(E) 14

20. If $y < 0$ and $z \neq 0$, each of the following could be true EXCEPT

(A) $y^2z^2 < 0$
(B) $yz^2 < 0$
(C) $y^2z < 0$
(D) $yz < 0$
(E) $y^3z < 0$

STOP

If you finish before time is called, you may check your work on this section only.
Do not turn to any other section in the test.

SECTION 7
Time — 25 minutes
35 Questions

Turn to Section 7 of your answer sheet to answer the questions in this section.

Directions: For each question in this section, select the best answer from among the choices given and fill in the corresponding circle on the answer sheet.

The following sentences test correctness and effectiveness of expression. Part of each sentence or the entire sentence is underlined; beneath each sentence are five ways of phrasing the underlined material. Choice A repeats the original phrasing; the other four choices are different. If you think the original phrasing produces a better sentence than any of the alternatives, select choice A; if not, select one of the other choices.

In making your selection, follow the requirements of standard written English; that is, pay attention to grammar, choice of words, sentence construction, and punctuation. Your selection should result in the most effective sentence—clear and precise, without awkwardness or ambiguity.

EXAMPLE:

Bobby Flay baked his first cake <u>and he was thirteen years old then</u>.

(A) and he was thirteen years old then
(B) when he was thirteen
(C) at age thirteen years old
(D) upon the reaching of thirteen years
(E) at the time when he was thirteen

---

1. <u>The curry had a lot of spiciness, this made Toby drink</u> a pitcher of water.

(A) The curry had a lot of spiciness, this made Toby drink
(B) The curry, which was spicy, making Toby drink
(C) The spiciness of the curry made Toby drink
(D) Because of how spicy the curry was, this is what made Toby drink
(E) Having a lot of spiciness, Toby discovered that the curry made him drink

2. Once experiments confirmed <u>the way ultrasounds were reliable screening techniques</u>, doctors depended less frequently on invasive measures, which were often more dangerous.

(A) the way ultrasounds were reliable screening techniques
(B) the way in which reliability of ultrasound screening techniques
(C) that ultrasounds, which were reliable screening techniques
(D) that ultrasounds, and they were reliable screening techniques
(E) that ultrasounds were reliable screening techniques

3. <u>Moving on to other topics, the dispute was abandoned by the editors</u> in order to accomplish a greater amount of work at the meeting.

(A) Moving on to other topics, the dispute was abandoned by the editors
(B) After having had moved on to other topics, the editors abandoned the dispute
(C) Other topics were moved on to, and the editors abandon the dispute
(D) The editors moved on to other topics, the dispute was abandoned
(E) Moving on to other topics, the editors abandoned the dispute

4. Scientists have found that foods such as pomegranates and spinach contain beneficial <u>antioxidants, which help prevent heart disease</u>.

(A) antioxidants, which help prevent heart disease
(B) antioxidants; heart disease can be prevented
(C) antioxidants, that is what helps prevent heart disease
(D) antioxidants, they help prevent heart disease
(E) antioxidants, and they help prevent heart disease

GO ON TO THE NEXT PAGE

5. Heart disease, <u>it having developed often unnoticed for many years,</u> is sometimes the result of a poor diet.

(A) it having developed often unnoticed for many years,
(B) often developing unnoticed for many years,
(C) being often unnoticed, will develop for many years, as it
(D) with often unnoticed developing for many years,
(E) developed for many years and often unnoticed

6. For the next history project, each student will need to produce a colorful poster, a class presentation, <u>and researching a paper</u>.

(A) and researching a paper
(B) and a research paper
(C) with a research paper
(D) and to research a paper
(E) including each student's research paper

7. More common than right whales, some humpback whales <u>becoming as large as</u> 60 feet in length and are carefully protected in American coastal waters.

(A) becoming as large as
(B) that become largely up to
(C) has become the size of
(D) become as large as
(E) became as largely as

8. The bank <u>has changed their policies to allow</u> customers to write as many checks as they want without additional fees.

(A) has changed their policies to allow
(B) has changed their policies, allowing
(C) changes its policies, it allows
(D) changing the policies to allow
(E) has changed its policies to allow

9. The Selous Game Reserve, one of the world's largest natural preserves, <u>protects many endangered species that are</u> threatened by poachers and environmental damage.

(A) protects many endangered species that are
(B) protecting many endangered species,
(C) and it protects many endangered species, which are
(D) which protects many endangered species,
(E) is the protector of endangered species, being

10. Found attached to the colon, the <u>organ known as the appendix losing importance</u> thousands of years ago through the process of evolution.

(A) the organ known as the appendix losing importance
(B) the organ known as the appendix has lost importance
(C) importance of the organ known as the appendix losing
(D) the organ known as the appendix lost importance
(E) importance of the organ known as the appendix was lost

11. A true friend is someone to whom <u>you can turn when one's day has been a disaster and they need someone to listen</u>.

(A) you can turn when one's day has been a disaster and they need someone to listen
(B) a person can turn to when their day has been a disaster and they need someone to listen
(C) they can turn, they need someone to listen
(D) one can turn when one's day has been a disaster and you need someone to listen to them
(E) you can turn when your day has been a disaster and you need someone to listen to you

GO ON TO THE NEXT PAGE

The following sentences test your ability to recognize grammar and usage errors. Each sentence contains either a single error or no error at all. No sentence contains more than one error. The error, if there is one, is underlined and lettered. If the sentence contains an error, select the one underlined part that must be changed to make the sentence correct. If the sentence is correct, select choice E. In choosing answers, follow the requirements of standard written English.

EXAMPLE:

The other players and her significantly improved
     A   B   C

the game plan created by the coaches. No error
            D   E

Ⓐ ● Ⓒ Ⓓ Ⓔ

12. The boy saw that his sick puppy was becoming
                             A

more healthier , with a higher activity level and more
   B   C

energy for playing fetch and chasing squirrels. No error
         D   E

13. Research has indicated that eating fewer fats—trans fats
         A

in particular—may help to reduce the risk of diabetes in
                B

some people and decreasing the chance of heart attacks
            C

by lowering blood pressure. No error
   D   E

14. The recently selected general manager,
      A

to the disappointment of players on the team, have asked
   B   C

for the immediate resignation of the head coach.
           D

No error
E

15. The MoMA, the Museum of Modern Art, displays
                              A

paintings that are representative of contemporary art,
         B   C

providing an excellent opportunity to study the current
                  D

era of artwork. No error
           E

16. Because the parking lot was filthy, the waterfront had no
                    A   B

lifeguard, and the sand covered with trash, tourists
                C

walking by the beach realized that it was closed. No error
   D   E

17. In the 1990s, many analysts starting their careers
                     A

believe that long hours were a worthwhile sacrifice to
  B   C

make for the opportunity to enter a lucrative industry.
     D

No error
E

18. Among American swimmers, Michael Phelps is an
   A

excellent example of an athlete who, while contributing
                        B

to the success of his teammates, has earned many
          C

accolades himself. No error
      D   E

19. When my sister won the student body election in her

senior year, it immediately established herself as one of
       A   B   C

the most influential students in her class. No error
    D   E

GO ON TO THE NEXT PAGE

20. The meeting minutes revealed that employees at the bank

hope that his or her benefits will increase thanks to a
A   B   C

change in medical coverage. No error
D   E

21. Not many teachers have explained the causes of the
A   B

Spanish-American war as extensive as Mr. Wilcox,
C

whose lectures are still an inspiration to his colleagues.
D

No error
E

22. It was a Hungarian interior designer who initially
A

succeeded with introducing the now iconic Rubik's
B   C

cube to toy stores worldwide. No error
D   E

23. Incessant monitoring via surveillance cameras reveal
A   B

that the majority of customers browse the shelves and
C

are likely to purchase more items than they originally
D

intended. No error
E

24. At Ralph's, the town's only grocery store, a clever
A

developed marketing campaign, including television and

radio ads, increased sales and helped the store promote
B   C   D

its selection of organic produce. No error
E

25. Because the old version of the instruction manual

contains as many as 300 omissions and errors, they are
A   B

considered less reliable than the version of the manual
C   D

now used by the company. No error
E

26. Only by camping outside overnight was the fan able
A   B

to reserve what was beginning to look like the last
C   D

available concert ticket. No error
E

27. Last year, when diplomats flew from foreign countries
A

to visit our campus and lecture at neighboring colleges,
B

the dean called my classmates and I to his office to greet
C   D

the visitors. No error
E

28. Thanks to the rapid growth of the internet, the internet
A

service provider gained three million subscribers by
B

1996 and, by 1996, was gaining as many as a thousand
C   D

new customers each week. No error
E

29. A decade in the making, the documentary on penguins is
A

both a response to widespread misinformation with
B   C

their mating habits and an investigation into their
D

behaviors. No error
E

GO ON TO THE NEXT PAGE

Directions: The following passage is an early draft of an essay. Some parts of the passage need to be rewritten.

Read the passage and select the best answers for the questions that follow. Some questions are about particular sentences or parts of sentences and ask you to improve sentence structure or word choice. Other questions ask you to consider organization and development. In choosing answers, follow the requirements of standard written English.

Questions 30-35 are based on the following passage.

(1) Although half a million people suffer from chronic fatigue syndrome, or CFS, the disease has been frequently dismissed. (2) The medical community doesn't know the cause, has difficulty diagnosing it, and it is hard to test. (3) CFS used to be called "yuppie flu" because many young professionals struggled with it and made their suffering known in the 1980s. (4) Later on it was thought to have been caused by Epstein-Barr virus. (5) Because the victims often get depression because of their symptoms, some doctors used to believe it was psychological. (6) Nowadays, doctors think it is caused by a virus because it shows up after many virus-based diseases.

(7) The only way to diagnose CFS is to eliminate everything else; there is no diagnostic test to see if you have it. (8) The symptoms can resemble the flu and depression. (9) Additionally, there is no cure and because there's no cure doctors treat the symptoms.

(10) It is easy to see why this disease has been dismissed and ignored. (11) It's because of its vagueness and mystery. (12) The stereotypes that have been attached to CFS make it hard for sufferers to be believed and to get help. (13) Additionally, just because a disease isn't understood or curable doesn't mean those who have it shouldn't get assistance. (14) Chronic fatigue syndrome has afflicted both the public and the medical community: The public suffers from the symptoms and the medical community suffers from a lack of knowledge.

30. Which of the following is the best version of sentence 2 (reproduced below) ?

The medical community doesn't know the cause, has difficulty diagnosing it, and it is hard to test.

(A) The medical community does not know the cause of the disease, has difficulty diagnosing it, and cannot test for it.

(B) Because the medical community does not know the cause, they cannot diagnose or test for it.

(C) The medical community does not know the cause and has difficulty diagnosing it, so it is hard to test.

(D) The medical community does not know the cause, diagnosis, or test.

(E) Additionally, the medical community cannot cause, diagnose, or test for the disease.

31. In context, which version of the underlined portion of sentence 5 (reproduced below) is the best?

Because the victims often get depression because of their symptoms, other doctors used to believe it was psychological.

(A) those symptoms were

(B) their depression was

(C) the victims were

(D) chronic fatigue syndrome was

(E) they were

32. Which of the following is the best version of sentence 9 (reproduced below) ?

Additionally, there is no cure and because there's no cure doctors treat the symptoms.

(A) However, doctors treat the symptoms with the cure for CFS.

(B) Currently, doctors treat the symptoms because there is no cure for CFS.

(C) But doctors know there is no cure and because of that they treat the symptoms.

(D) Since there is no cure for CFS, doctors treat the symptoms without the cure.

(E) When there are symptoms, doctors treat them without the cure for CFS.

GO ON TO THE NEXT PAGE

33. The writer's analysis would have been strengthened most by the inclusion of

(A) the number of people who struggle with CFS

(B) a further explanation of "yuppie flu"

(C) the names and backgrounds of the doctors who treat CFS

(D) a description of experimental CFS therapies

(E) more details about the symptoms and stereotypes of CFS

34. Which of the following is the best version of sentences 10 and 11 (reproduced below) ?

It is easy to see why this disease has been dismissed and ignored. It's because of its vagueness and mystery.

(A) This disease has been dismissed and ignored because of its vagueness and mystery.

(B) It is easy to see that why this disease has been dismissed and ignored is because of the vagueness and the mystery.

(C) Vagueness and mystery cause people to dismiss and ignore this disease.

(D) Why this disease has been dismissed and ignored is because of its vagueness and mystery.

(E) It is easy for you to see why this disease has been dismissed and ignored: because of vagueness and mystery.

35. Of the following, which is the best replacement for "Additionally" in sentence 13 ?

(A) And so

(B) Furthermore

(C) However

(D) Therefore

(E) When

STOP
If you finish before time is called, you may check your work on this section only.
Do not turn to any other section in the test.

SECTION 8
Time — 20 minutes
16 Questions

Turn to Section 8 of your answer sheet to answer the questions in this section.

Directions: For this section, solve each problem and decide which is the best of the choices given. Fill in the corresponding circle on the answer sheet. You may use any available space for scratchwork.

Notes

1. The use of a calculator is permitted.

2. All numbers used are real numbers.

3. Figures that accompany problems in this test are intended to provide information useful in solving the problems. They are drawn as accurately as possible EXCEPT when it is stated in a specific problem that the figure is not drawn to scale. All figures lie in a plane unless otherwise indicated.

4. Unless otherwise specified, the domain of any function f is assumed to be the set of all real numbers x for which $f(x)$ is a real number.

Reference Information

     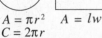 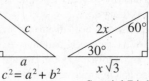

$A = \pi r^2$ $A = lw$
$C = 2\pi r$ $A = \frac{1}{2}bh$ $V = lwh$ $V = \pi r^2 h$ $c^2 = a^2 + b^2$

Special Right Triangles

The number of degrees of arc in a circle is 360.

The sum of the measures in degrees of the angles of a triangle is 180.

---

1. Each of the following is a factor of 120 EXCEPT

(A)   4
(B)   10
(C)   18
(D)   24
(E)   60

2. If $y < 0$ and $(x + 2)(y - 4) = 0$, then $x =$

(A)   −4
(B)   −2
(C)   0
(D)   2
(E)   4

GO ON TO THE NEXT PAGE

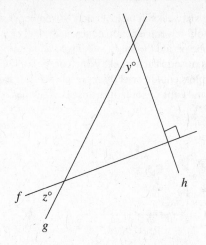

Note: Figure not drawn to scale.

	MERCHANDISE PRICES	
	Bracelet	**Scarf**
California	$3.50	$15.00
Illinois	$2.40	$10.00
New York	$5.25	$21.00

CAPACITY OF SHIPPING BOXES			
	A	**B**	**C**
Bracelets	150	130	120
Scarves	10	15	20

3. Lines f, g, and h intersect as shown in the figure above. If $z = 35$, what is the value of y ?

(A) 40
(B) 45
(C) 50
(D) 55
(E) 60

4. An accessories manufacturer makes one style each of bracelets and scarves that are shipped to stores in three different states. The chart on the left above gives the prices the manufacturer charges for each bracelet and scarf to the stores in the three states. The chart on the right gives the maximum number of bracelets and scarves that can fit in each of three shipping boxes, A, B, and C. Based on the prices shown, what is the maximum possible value of the bracelets and scarves that can be shipped to New York in shipping box A ?

(A) $920.00
(B) $997.50
(C) $1020.50
(D) $1080.00
(E) $1890.50

5. If $\dfrac{5^a}{5^4} = 5^{16}$, what is the value of a ?

(A)   4
(B) 12
(C) 20
(D) 64
(E) 68

GO ON TO THE NEXT PAGE

6. Square *ABCD* in the coordinate plane has points *A*(1, 3), *B*(5, 7), and *C*(9, 3). Which of the following could be the coordinates of point *D* ?

(A) (3, 1)
(B) (3, –3)
(C) (5, –1)
(D) (5, 3)
(E) (7, –5)

7. If *a*, *b*, and *c* are distinct positive odd integers less than 6, how many different values of $a(b^c)$ are possible?

(A) Two
(B) Three
(C) Four
(D) Five
(E) Six

8. During six weeks in October and November, a snack stand sold fewer ice cream cones each week. During this same period the snack stand sold a greater number of cups of soup each week. Which of the following scatterplots could correctly represent sales of ice cream cones and cups of soup over this six week period?

(A)

(B)

(C)

(D)

(E)

GO ON TO THE NEXT PAGE

9. A line passes through the points $(0, a)$ and $(b, 0)$. Which of the following is the slope of the line?

(A) $-\dfrac{a}{b}$

(B) $-\dfrac{b}{a}$

(C) $\dfrac{a}{b}$

(D) $\dfrac{b}{a}$

(E) $\dfrac{a}{ab}$

10. Container A and container B are right circular cylinders. Container A has a radius of 4 inches and a height of 5 inches while container B has a radius of 2 inches and a height of 10 inches. Sarah pours equal amounts of oil into both containers and finds that the height of the oil in container A is 2 inches. What is the height of the oil in container B ?

(A) 8 inches
(B) 8.5 inches
(C) 9 inches
(D) 9.5 inches
(E) 10 inches

$$\frac{w-x}{y+z} = \frac{3}{4}$$

11. In the equation above, w, x, y, and z are distinct numbers. What is the value of $\dfrac{7w-7x}{15y+15z}$?

(A) $\dfrac{3}{4}$

(B) $\dfrac{3}{5}$

(C) $\dfrac{7}{15}$

(D) $\dfrac{7}{20}$

(E) $\dfrac{28}{45}$

12. Tick marks are equally spaced on the number line above. Which of the lettered points is equivalent to the value of $-x^2$?

(A) A
(B) B
(C) C
(D) D
(E) E

GO ON TO THE NEXT PAGE

13. If the sum of a and b is c, what is the average (arithmetic mean) of a, b, and c ?

(A) $2c$

(B) $\dfrac{2c}{3}$

(C) $\dfrac{a+b}{c}$

(D) $\dfrac{3c}{a+b}$

(E) $c-(a+b)$

14. Points A, B, and C are the three vertices of a triangle. The location of point X is such that $AX = BX$. Which of the following could be true?

    I.   X is on $\overline{AB}$
    II. X is inside $\triangle ABC$
    III. X is outside $\triangle ABC$

(A) I only
(B) III only
(C) I and II only
(D) II and III only
(E) I, II, and III

15. The wholesale price of a car is w dollars. The retail price of this car is r percent greater than the wholesale price. During a special promotion, the retail price of the car is then discounted by s percent. Which of the following expressions represents the price, in dollars, of this car during the special promotion?

(A) $w\left(\dfrac{r}{100}\right)\left(\dfrac{s}{100}\right)$

(B) $w\left(1+\dfrac{r}{100}\right)\left(1-\dfrac{s}{100}\right)$

(C) $w\left(\dfrac{rs}{100}\right)$

(D) $w+\dfrac{wr}{100}-\dfrac{ws}{100}$

(E) $w\left(\dfrac{wr}{100}-\dfrac{ws}{100}\right)$

16. In rectangle $EFGH$, $\overline{EF} \perp \overline{EH}$ and $GH = 4$. Which of the following could be the length of $\overline{EG}$?

(A) 1
(B) 2
(C) 3
(D) 4
(E) 5

STOP

If you finish before time is called, you may check your work on this section only.
Do not turn to any other section in the test.

NO TEST MATERIAL ON THIS PAGE.

SECTION 9
Time — 20 minutes
18 Questions

Turn to Section 9 of your answer sheet to answer the questions in this section.

Directions: For each question in this section, select the best answer from among the choices given and fill in the corresponding circle on the answer sheet.

Each sentence below has one or two blanks, each blank indicating that something has been omitted. Beneath the sentence are five words or sets of words labeled A through E. Choose the word or set of words that, when inserted in the sentence, best fits the meaning of the sentence as a whole.

Example:

Desiring to ------- his taunting friends, Mitch gave them taffy in hopes it would keep their mouths shut.

(A) eliminate   (B) satisfy   (C) overcome
    (D) ridicule   (E) silence

Ⓐ Ⓑ Ⓒ Ⓓ ●

---

1. Lavender oil is said to have ------- effects: in recent years people have been using lavender in sleep aids and for relaxing aromatherapy.

    (A) questionable   (B) sedative   (C) allergic
        (D) irritating   (E) invigorating

2. His nonprofit agency has served as a ------- in the community, bringing about many changes and developing new programs in local schools.

    (A) mandate   (B) curiosity   (C) disposition
        (D) hypothesis   (E) catalyst

3. Just as financial advisors for the company predicted, the company's ability to expand into new markets has -------, even though its profits are not very -------.

    (A) diminished . . incremental
    (B) accumulated . . inadequate
    (C) deteriorated . . abundant
    (D) endured . . deficient
    (E) increased . . substantial

4. The old man was practically the definition of ------- : ill-tempered and mean to every person he met.

    (A) arcane   (B) profligate   (C) bureaucratic
        (D) cantankerous   (E) ancient

5. Unwilling to -------, the commissioner ------- to keep his job despite the accusations of wrongdoing that could end his career.

    (A) resign . . endeavored
    (B) extend . . innovated
    (C) adapt . . emerged
    (D) retire . . advanced
    (E) persist . . compromised

6. The professor recommended that his students rely on modern research into eighteenth century literature rather than use commentaries from ------- authors.

    (A) bombastic   (B) prodigious   (C) pedantic
        (D) obsolescent   (E) esoteric

GO ON TO THE NEXT PAGE

Directions: Each passage below is followed by questions based on its content. Answer the questions on the basis of what is <u>stated</u> or <u>implied</u> in each passage and in any introductory material that may be provided.

Questions 7-18 are based on the following passage.

The following passage recalls an art historian's lifelong love of pre-modern art and his first encounter with contemporary sculpture.

By the time I had completed my second year at college, I knew all that was important to know about the world of art. After all, hadn't I been steeped in paintings and sculptures
Line ever since I could walk? My mother came from a family of
5 professors, and when she married my father, she made it clear that her children would be exposed to all that New York had to offer. And so, by the tender age of seven, I had spent what seemed like years in New York's great art museums: The Metropolitan, the Frick, and the Cloisters.
10 "Do you see the exquisite lace and beadwork on her gown?" My mother was my constant companion and guide on these artistic expeditions. I dutifully admired the amazingly detailed work. Indeed, regal and beautiful society portraits, powerful stormy seascapes, graceful Grecian sculptures—
15 they all enthralled me. I became an ardent art lover. But with a child's stubborn intensity, I insisted that good art must be *old*. In rendering judgment of any piece, I would study that small white card they helpfully provided next to each painting detailing the artist, title, and most important, the
20 year of creation. The later the date on that little card, the more contempt I heaped upon it. I was suspicious of anything from my own century, and I absolutely balked at anything that was not older than I was.
When I entered the university, my prejudices had not
25 changed. With my mother's enthusiastic support, I enrolled in the art history department. For two years, I studied the old masters. I could picture the studio apprentices patiently grinding pigments, painstakingly creating the palettes from which masterpieces would be constructed. Their meticulous
30 and time-consuming efforts set the benchmark for me. What could modern artists—whose colors were simply squeezed from a tube—do to compare?
And so it was with great reluctance that I endured Ms. Wright's required contemporary art class in my junior year.
35 For weeks, I watched slide shows of twentieth-century art celebrities and listened to Ms. Wright's commentaries with a stony indifference. I was not about to abandon my hard-earned opinions. "Notice this painting's remarkable sense of light and color." I scoffed. How could this juvenile painting
40 claim to compare its use of light to the luminous quality of a Johannes Vermeer* I looked at her slides, but I did not want to see. My dismay with the class only heightened when Ms. Wright announced that our class would be making a trip to the local gallery to view a contemporary sculpture
45 installation.

The day arrived and I trooped off with my fellow classmates to the gallery. I could see at once that it would be exactly as I predicted. The front room of the gallery featured a series of monochromatic paintings, creatures of varying
50 shades of black or red or white. Ms Wright then led us to the back room where the sculptures were installed. The large room was a sea of gray walls and gray carpet punctuated at intervals by the sculptures. The pieces themselves were also an uninspired gray. They were large simple shapes, virtually
55 unadorned. As I studied one, I was highly unimpressed—where was the detail, the figure, the work? Then Ms. Wright said something unexpected. She showed us to an area in the middle of the room and told us to sit down.
"Try not to think of each sculpture as an isolated work.
60 Rather, consider the installation a series of pieces meant to make up a whole." Despite myself, I found the room around me transforming. I was no longer seeing a number of disconnected and disappointing sculptures. The size and simplicity of each piece began to make sense. They worked
65 together, perfectly placed within the empty spaces to create one of the most remarkable feats of artistic harmony I had ever experienced. I was transformed. In that one day, Ms. Wright brought down the walls of a lifetime.

* A seventeenth-century Dutch painter.

7. The question in lines 3-4 ("After . . . walk") serves primarily to

   (A) evoke a painful memory
   (B) discredit a family member
   (C) call attention to paradoxical behavior
   (D) lend support to an assertion
   (E) describe a stressful situation

8. The author's observation in lines 7-9 ("And so . . . Cloisters") most directly suggests that he was

   (A) bored by his repeated visits to art museums
   (B) annoyed at being constantly accompanied by his mother
   (C) proud of his ability to imitate famous painting
   (D) resentful of not being able to spend more time outdoors
   (E) confident about his extensive knowledge of art

GO ON TO THE NEXT PAGE

9. In lines 12-17 ("I dutifully . . .old"), the author suggests that he valued works of art that do all of the following EXCEPT

(A) appeal to a diverse audience
(B) depict turbulent natural scenes
(C) appear elegant and refined
(D) portray individuals in a dignified manner
(E) display intricate craftsmanship

10. The author's "judgment" (line 17) is based on which of the following assumptions?

(A) Paintings affect adults and children in different ways.
(B) People often have a superficial understanding of art.
(C) Artists have difficulty assessing the value of their own works.
(D) Artworks from the same period are of similar quality.
(E) Information provided by museums may be misleading.

11. The third paragraph suggests that which of the following might best fit the author's idea of a masterpiece?

(A) A watercolor that was created in a flash of inspiration
(B) A painting that was exceptionally valuable
(C) A sculpture that was slowly and carefully carved
(D) A sketch produced by an untrained artist
(E) A mural that revealed the artist's political leanings

12. The sentence in lines 33-34 ("And so . . . year") functions as a transition in the passage from

(A) a discussion of the history of pre-modern art to a consideration of the contemporary relevance of that art
(B) an explication of the author's views on art to a description of an encounter that challenged those views
(C) a consideration of the virtues of traditional art to a reflection on the limitations of that type of art
(D) a chronicle of a specific event in the author's life to a discussion of the larger significance of that event
(E) a reminiscence about the author's childhood to a remembrance of the author's college years

13. In lines 33-38, the author's attitude toward contemporary art is best described as

(A) angry and bewildered
(B) unsympathetic and inflexible
(C) defeated and resigned
(D) indecisive and uneasy
(E) ill-considered and myopic

14. In line 39, "juvenile" most nearly means

(A) indifferent
(B) spoiled
(C) inexpert
(D) pure
(E) delinquent

15. The author's statement that he "did not want to see" (line 41-42) emphasizes the idea that his

(A) response was colored by deeply ingrained beliefs
(B) goals were thwarted by an unplanned excursion
(C) judgment was influenced by a desire for attention
(D) ideals were compromised by a hasty decision
(E) vision was affected by his animosity for the instructor

16. In lines 46-56 ("The day . . .work"), the author indicates that the "sculptures" lack both

(A) impulsiveness and rigor
(B) accessibility and originality
(C) preparation and research
(D) directness and bulk
(E) complexity and variety

17. The last paragraph introduces the idea that

(A) contemporary art can be disturbing and disorienting
(B) modern sculptors have lost interest in traditional subject matter
(C) unskilled artists are capable of producing interesting works
(D) context may affect the impression that an artwork makes
(E) teachers usually know more about a subject than their students do

18. In line 68, "walls" refers to the

(A) gallery's interior
(B) author's preconceptions
(C) instructor's classroom
(D) artist's vision
(E) university's requirements

STOP

If you finish before time is called, you may check your work on this section only.
Do not turn to any other section in the test.

NO TEST MATERIAL ON THIS PAGE.

SECTION 10
Time — 10 minutes
14 Questions

Turn to Section 10 of your answer sheet to answer the questions in this section.

Directions: For each question in this section, select the best answer from among the choices given and fill in the corresponding circle on the answer sheet.

The following sentences test correctness and effectiveness of expression. Part of each sentence or the entire sentence is underlined; beneath each sentence are five ways of phrasing the underlined material. Choice A repeats the original phrasing; the other four choices are different. If you think the original phrasing produces a better sentence than any of the alternatives, select choice A; if not, select one of the other choices.

In making your selection, follow the requirements of standard written English; that is, pay attention to grammar, choice of words, sentence construction, and punctuation. Your selection should result in the most effective sentence—clear and precise, without awkwardness or ambiguity.

EXAMPLE:

Bobby Flay baked his first cake <u>and he was thirteen years old then</u>.

(A) and he was thirteen years old then
(B) when he was thirteen
(C) at age thirteen years old
(D) upon the reaching of thirteen years
(E) at the time when he was thirteen

Ⓐ ● Ⓒ Ⓓ Ⓔ

1. The final exam was <u>easier than it but far more comprehensive than the midterm</u>.

(A) easier than it but far more comprehensive than the midterm
(B) easier and it is far more comprehensive than the midterm
(C) easier than the midterm; it is far more comprehensive than it
(D) easier than the midterm but far more comprehensive
(E) far more comprehensive than the midterm and it was easier than it

2. When the Vietnam War, one of the most controversial wars in history, led to an escalation of the military draft, thousands of students gathered in large cities <u>to protest it</u>.

(A) to protest it
(B) for their protests
(C) to protest
(D) in protest of it
(E) in protesting

3. <u>Because of asking to no effect for better health coverage, the union members decided</u> to walk out until company management responded to their complaints.

(A) Because of asking to no effect for better health coverage, the union members decided
(B) Having asked to no effect for better health coverage, the union members decided
(C) The union members asked to no effect for better health coverage, thus, finally, deciding
(D) The union members asked to no effect for health coverage to get better, then deciding
(E) Asking for health care coverage to get better was to no effect, which eventually caused the union members to decide

4. The emergency management team members do their utmost <u>with alerts to the public of imminent storms threatening the coast; however, it being its responsibility</u> to obey all warnings and instructions.

(A) with alerts to the public of imminent storms threatening the coast; however, it being its responsibility
(B) to alert the public about imminent storms threatening the coast, then it is its responsibility
(C) to alert the public of imminent storms threatening the coast: however, it is the public's responsibility
(D) when alerting the public about imminent threatening storms to the coast, and it is its responsibility
(E) about alerting the public of their imminent storms threatening the coast, as it is responsible

GO ON TO THE NEXT PAGE

5. Permission to enroll in biology honors classes requires a recommendation from the department chairperson.

    (A) Permission to enroll in biology honors classes requires a recommendation from the department chairperson.

    (B) For biology honors classes, permission to enroll requires the department chairperson recommending them.

    (C) Permission to enroll in biology honors classes require a recommending by the department chairperson.

    (D) Permission to enroll in biology honors classes requires to be recommended by the department chairperson.

    (E) Requiring a recommendation from the department chairperson is permission to enroll in biology honors classes.

6. As a little girl, Agnes walked to the studio twice a week, and she was dragging her cello in order to learn musical technique from a renowned teacher.

    (A) and she was dragging

    (B) when she drags

    (C) to drag

    (D) dragging

    (E) where she dragged

7. New rules designed to decrease truancy requires homeroom teachers to take attendance twice per day.

    (A) requires homeroom teachers to take

    (B) require homeroom teachers to take

    (C) require homeroom teachers taking

    (D) that requires homeroom teachers to take

    (E) are requiring homeroom teachers taking

8. Remind her of what you have done and a report of your progress.

    (A) a report of

    (B) your reporting of

    (C) what you report of

    (D) what report you had made of

    (E) give her a report of

9. Unlike other children's films, the animated feature *The Nightmare Before Christmas* glorified abnormality and eccentricity; its creator, Tim Burton, became famous for these themes.

    (A) Unlike

    (B) Not as with

    (C) Unlike what was seen in

    (D) Unlike the case of

    (E) In contrast with

10. Great jazz music and delicious Cajun cuisine at Jonathan's Mardi Gras party was hindering our effort to leave the party.

    (A) was hindering

    (B) were hindering

    (C) hindering

    (D) they hindered

    (E) hindering us in

11. A Category 4 hurricane landed at Galveston on September 8, 1900, devastating the lives of thousands in the city, the population was caught unprepared because of storm-tracking being imprecise at the time.

    (A) city, the population was caught unprepared because of storm-tracking being imprecise at the time

    (B) city, because storm-tracking was imprecise at the time, the population was caught unprepared

    (C) city; catching the population unprepared because storm-tracking was imprecise at the time

    (D) city; the population was caught unprepared because storm-tracking was imprecise at the time

    (E) city and catching the population unprepared, which was caused by storm-tracking being imprecise at the time

12. The disregard shown by the government in addressing the harmful consequences of a variety of industrial practices have earned them their poor reputation among environmentalists.

    (A) have earned them their

    (B) have earned them a

    (C) have earned it its

    (D) has earned for it their

    (E) has earned it a

GO ON TO THE NEXT PAGE

13. Many schools are drawn to programs that reward students monetarily for attendance and good grades; adopting these programs can lead to an increase in a school's graduation rate.

(A) good grades; adopting these programs can lead to an increase in

(B) good grades, which can lead to an increase in

(C) good grades, it can lead to an increase in

(D) good grades, while these programs can lead to an increase in

(E) good grades that can lead to an increase in

14. Scientists have discovered that young animals are most likely to adapt to the effects of injury than older animals.

(A) are most likely to adapt to the effects of injury than older animals

(B) are more likely to adapt to the effects of injury compared to older animals

(C) are more likely than older animals to adapt to the effects of injury

(D) compared with older animals most likely adapt to the effects of injury

(E) more likely adapt to the effects of injury than in older animals

STOP
If you finish before time is called, you may check your work on this section only.
Do not turn to any other section in the test.

NO TEST MATERIAL ON THIS PAGE.

PRACTICE TEST 2: ANSWER KEY

2 Reading	3 Math	4 Reading	5 Math	7 Writing	8 Math	9 Reading	10 Writing
1. D	1. B	1. D	1. B	1. C	1. C	1. B	1. D
2. E	2. A	2. B	2. E	2. E	2. B	2. E	2. C
3. A	3. D	3. D	3. C	3. E	3. D	3. E	3. B
4. C	4. C	4. E	4. E	4. A	4. B	4. D	4. C
5. E	5. E	5. A	5. C	5. B	5. C	5. A	5. A
6. B	6. B	6. A	6. D	6. B	6. C	6. D	6. D
7. A	7. C	7. D	7. B	7. D	7. D	7. D	7. B
8. C	8. D	8. C	8. A	8. E	8. E	8. E	8. E
9. A	9. 59	9. D	9. A	9. A	9. A	9. A	9. A
10. C	10. 900	10. A	10. E	10. D	10. A	10. D	10. B
11. E	11. 60	11. A	11. C	11. E	11. D	11. C	11. D
12. A	12. 20	12. D	12. D	12. B	12. C	12. B	12. E
13. C	13. 6	13. C	13. A	13. C	13. B	13. B	13. A
14. D	14. $0 < y < \frac{4}{3}$ or $0 < y < 1.33$	14. E	14. B	14. C	14. E	14. C	14. C
15. B		15. C	15. A	15. E	15. B	15. A	
16. E		16. A	16. D	16. C	16. E	16. E	
17. B	15. $\frac{3}{4}$ or .75	17. B	17. E	17. B		17. D	
18. A	16. 1,000	18. B	18. D	18. E		18. B	
19. C	17. $\frac{3}{4}$ or .75	19. A	19. D	19. A			
20. C	18. 3	20. B	20. A	20. B			
21. B		21. C		21. C			
22. E		22. E		22. B			
23. D		23. C		23. B			
24. E		24. D		24. A			
		25. B		25. B			
				26. E			
				27. C			
				28. B			
				29. C			
				30. A			
				31. D			
				32. B			
				33. E			
				34. A			
				35. C			

SAT SCORING WORKSHEET

For directions on how to score your SAT practice test, see pages 10–11.

SAT Writing Section

Total Writing Multiple-Choice Questions Correct: [   ]

$-$

Total Writing Multiple-Choice Questions Incorrect: _____ ÷ 4 = [   ]

Grammar Raw Score: [   ]

Grammar Scaled Subscore
[   ]

Compare the Grammar Raw Score with the Writing Multiple-Choice Subscore Conversion Table on page 172 to find the Grammar Scaled Subscore.

$+$

Your Essay Score (2–12): _____ × 2 = [   ]

Writing Raw Score: [   ]

Compare Raw Score with SAT Score Conversion Table on page 172 to find the Writing Scaled Score.

Writing Scaled Score
[   ]

SAT Critical Reading Section

Total Critical Reading Questions Correct: [   ]

$-$

Total Critical Reading Questions Incorrect: _____ ÷ 4 = [   ]

Critical Reading Raw Score: [   ]

Compare Raw Score with SAT Score Conversion Table on page 172 to find the Critical Reading Scaled Score.

Critical Reading Scaled Score
[   ]

SAT Math Section

Total Math Grid-In Questions Correct: [   ]

$+$

Total Math Multiple-Choice Questions Correct: [   ]

$-$

Total Math Multiple-Choice Questions Incorrect: _____ ÷ 4 = [   ]

Don't include wrong answers from grid-ins!

Math Raw Score: [   ]

Compare Raw Score with SAT Score Conversion Table on page 172 to find the Math Scaled Score.

Math Scaled Score
[   ]

SAT SCORE CONVERSION TABLE

Raw Score	Writing Scaled Score	Reading Scaled Score	Math Scaled Score	Raw Score	Writing Scaled Score	Reading Scaled Score	Math Scaled Score	Raw Score	Writing Scaled Score	Reading Scaled Score	Math Scaled Score
73	800			47	590–630	600–640	660–700	21	400–440	410–450	440–480
72	790–800			46	590–630	590–630	650–690	20	390–430	400–440	430–470
71	780–800			45	580–620	580–620	650–690	19	380–420	400–440	430–470
70	770–800			44	570–610	580–620	640–680	18	370–410	390–430	420–460
69	770–800			43	570–610	570–610	630–670	17	370–410	380–420	410–450
68	760–800			42	560–600	570–610	620–660	16	360–400	370–410	400–440
67	760–800	800		41	560–600	560–600	610–650	15	350–390	360–400	400–440
66	760–800	770–800		40	550–590	550–590	600–640	14	340–380	350–390	390–430
65	750–790	760–800		39	540–580	550–590	590–630	13	330–370	340–380	380–420
64	740–780	750–790		38	530–570	540–580	590–630	12	320–360	340–380	360–400
63	730–770	740–780		37	530–570	530–570	580–620	11	320–360	330–370	350–390
62	720–760	730–770		36	520–560	530–570	570–610	10	310–350	320–360	340–380
61	710–750	720–760		35	510–550	520–560	560–600	9	300–340	310–350	330–370
60	700–740	710–750		34	500–540	520–560	560–600	8	290–330	300–340	320–360
59	690–730	700–740		33	490–530	510–550	550–590	7	280–320	300–340	310–350
58	680–720	690–730		32	480–520	500–540	540–580	6	270–310	290–330	300–340
57	680–720	680–720		31	470–510	490–530	530–570	5	260–300	280–320	290–330
56	670–710	670–710		30	470–510	480–520	520–560	4	240–280	270–310	280–320
55	660–720	670–710		29	460–500	470–510	520–560	3	230–270	250–290	280–320
54	650–690	660–700	760–800	28	450–490	470–510	510–550	2	230–270	240–280	270–310
53	640–680	650–690	740–780	27	440–480	460–500	500–540	1	220–260	220–260	260–300
52	630–670	640–680	730–770	26	430–470	450–490	490–530	0	210–250	200–240	250–290
51	630–670	630–670	710–750	25	420–460	440–480	480–520	–1	200–240	200–230	230–270
50	620–660	620–660	690–730	24	410–450	430–470	470–510	–2	200–230	200–220	220–260
49	610–650	610–650	680–720	23	410–450	430–470	460–500	–3	200–220	200–210	200–240
48	600–640	600–640	670–710	22	400–440	420–460	450–490				

WRITING MULTIPLE-CHOICE SUBSCORE CONVERSION TABLE

Grammar Raw Score	Grammar Scaled Subscore	Grammar Raw Score	Grammar Scaled Subscore	Grammar Raw Score	Grammar Scaled Subscore	Grammar Raw Score	Grammar Scaled Subscore	Grammar Raw Score	Grammar Scaled Subscore
49	78–80	38	67–71	27	55–59	16	42–46	5	30–34
48	77–80	37	66–70	26	54–58	15	41–45	4	29–33
47	75–79	36	65–69	25	53–57	14	40–44	3	28–32
46	74–78	35	64–68	24	52–56	13	39–43	2	27–31
45	72–76	34	63–67	23	51–55	12	38–42	1	25–29
44	72–76	33	62–66	22	50–54	11	36–40	0	24–28
43	71–75	32	61–65	21	49–53	10	35–39	–1	22–26
42	70–74	31	60–64	20	47–51	9	34–38	–2	20–23
41	69–73	30	59–63	19	46–50	8	33–37	–3	20–22
40	68–72	29	58–62	18	45–49	7	32–36		
39	68–72	28	56–60	17	44–48	6	31–35		

Chapter 7
Practice Test 2:
Answers and
Explanations

SECTION 2

1. **D** The clues here are *repeat* and *same pattern*. That is really all we know about the novels. Use that information in the first blank, and look for a word that means "with a repetitive pattern," which is what the first word in (A) and (D) mean. For the second blank, since the stories repeat they must "stick to" the same pattern. (B), (D), and (E) all work, but (D) is the only answer choice that works with both blanks.

2. **E** The prosecutor needed more evidence; he wanted two people to back up the defendant. You need a word that means "supporting someone else's story." (E) *corroborated* is the only one that works. If you didn't get this one, hit the vocab.

3. **A** The blank describes how scientists characterize bacterial *mutations*. If the number of antibiotic resistant species is increasing, we might expect that scientists would be concerned, but the word *While* signals a change of direction. The phrase *tiny fraction of all bacteria* tells us that scientists see the mutations as "exceptions." Choices (C) and (D) might be attractive because they sound related to antibiotics and bacteria, but they don't match our word. (B) and (E) don't fit; only (A) *anomalies* means "exceptions."

4. **C** The word *but* tells us that this case is going to be different from all the other, easy cases. The blank probably means something like "being good at." Only (C) means this; *faculty* has the meaning we're used to (the teachers at a college or school), and a second meaning, which means "strong mental powers" or "ability."

5. **E** Look at the second blank first. Earlier in the sentence, the counselors are described as *habitually lax*. The words *Although* and *far more* indicate that the second blank will be the opposite of *lax*, something like "strict." There are a lot of tough words; don't eliminate any words you don't know the meaning of. Of the words in the answer choices, both (A) *exacting*, and (E) *stringent* mean "strict." For the first blank, something like "get rid of" is the meaning to look for. (C) *renounce* and (E) *eschew* both work, making (E) the best answer.

6. **B** The author of Passage 1 is primarily concerned with the Taj Mahal's *otherworldly beauty*. Answer (B), *aesthetic qualities,* matches this. The author of Passage 2, while acknowledging the Taj Mahal's beauty, is NOT primarily concerned with beauty, as evidenced by the first and last sentence. Answer (C) is emphasized in Passage 2, not Passage 1. The other answers are not mentioned in either passage.

7. **A** The author of Passage 2 is primarily concerned with the *spiritual aspects* of the Taj Mahal. (A) paraphrases this point. (B) is too strong. (C) and (D) are not mentioned. (E) is mentioned, but it is not the *primary* purpose of the passage.

8. **C** Passage 1 states that the Taj Mahal was built *as a tribute*. Passage 2 states that *Shah Jahan commissioned the building…as a tomb.* Thus, both authors agree that the building *was originally intended as a memorial* (C). (A) is extreme and not mentioned in either passage; (B) is mentioned only in Passage 2; (D) is not mentioned in either passage; and (E) is mentioned only in Passage 1.

9.　A　The author of Passage 2 notes that the Taj Mahal is *one of the world's most recognizable buildings.* This matches (A), *widely known.* Although the author of Passage 1 praises the Taj Mahal as one of *the* most magnificent examples, he never mentions whether anyone else knows of it. Answer (B) is mentioned in Passage 1 only. (C) is mentioned in both passages, while (D) and (E) are not mentioned.

10.　C　The passage mostly talks about Europa, and how we need to preserve any life that may live there. (A) is true only of the first paragraph, and (D) and (E) are true only of the last paragraph, so they can be eliminated. (B) is too strong; the author is trying to warn of the possibility that we may infect Europa, not trying to keep us from going there. (C) is correct. The passage describes some *current theories,* and the last half of the passage discusses the *dilemmas* regarding the exploration of Europa.

11.　E　The author states that finding an organism living on Europa, no matter what it is, would be important because it means that life is *more plentiful and varied than we thought* (line 16). But he's not sure if life is there, so he instead *speculates about a possibility* (E): the possibility that there is life on Europa.

12.　A　The author uses the example of the *Galapagos Rift* to show that life can persist even in the harshest environments, as evidenced by the phrase *As we discovered hardier and stranger creatures such as these thriving in harsh, sunless environments, the possibility of life in Europa's bleak abyss blossomed.* (A) paraphrases this point accurately. (B) is out because we're not comparing different types of fish. (C) is the opposite of what the author means (D) is not the point of the example, and the passage is not specifically discussing *scientific experiments.* (E) is no good because we don't know if there are creatures that *live in Europa's ocean.*

13.　C　The passage states that the *scientists had solid evidence of an ocean.* If we eliminate the word *solid,* then something like "confirming" or "supporting" would fit. Only (C) *definitive* matches with this.

14.　D　After discussing current theories regarding Europa, the author then mentions the paradox: investigating Europa could actually hurt any possible creatures living there. The author then discusses how we could hurt these creatures, and how to avoid it. So the sentence serves to (D) *change the focus of the discussion.* It's not to (B) *offer a short aside,* because if it was a short aside then the author would be mentioning an idea that he doesn't plan to investigate.

15.　B　The author is making a comparison trying to show that we *could* damage Europa's ecosystem by exploring it, just as *pouring a cup of salt into a goldfish's bowl could* hurt the goldfish. So although the author is trying to say that Europa could be easily damaged, that it is fragile, the uncertainty expressed in the comparison emphasizes just how little is known about Europa making (B), *fragility,* the best answer.

16. **E**   The author mentions a goldfish's bowl to show that we may end up hurting any life on Europa while looking for it. He doesn't care about instruments, so eliminate (A). We don't know that damaging life on Europa is an *inevitable consequence*, so we can eliminate (B). He's not saying anything about the size of the oceans, he is merely using the goldfish bowl to make a point about how delicate Europa's life may be, so eliminate (C). We can eliminate (D) because the author mentions the goldfish simply as a point of comparison, not to make any statement about the *sensitivity of fish*. (E) is correct. He is using the simile to *emphasize the possible implications of an undertaking*, specifically the undertaking of exploring Europa.

17. **B**   Despite the many possible drawbacks and consequences of exploring Europa, the author states that we have a *responsibility to search for knowledge* (line 60). So he is determined that we should investigate Europa, which means he is (B) *resolute*. He is not (A) *perplexed*, which would mean he was confused, nor is he (C) *optimistic*, because he doesn't know whether or not there will be life. (D) *indignant* would mean he is angry about something. (E) *restrained* would mean he is holding back in some way, although he is actually directly stating what he believes.

18. **A**   (A) is not mentioned in the final paragraph. (B) is mentioned in lines 51–53, (C) is mentioned in lines 61–62, (D) is mentioned in lines 54–56, and (E) is mentioned in lines 63–64.

19. **C**   The *bogus cure is a security blanket* because it convinces people that *things that mankind cannot fix or heal* do not exist. So the bogus cure is (C) *comforting even if it is not effective*. (A), (D), and (E) are not mentioned in the passage, and (B) is mentioned later, unrelated to the security blanket comment.

20. **C**   The *confidence man* sold fake medicines. The only person in Passage 2 who sells fake medicines is (C) *the herb doctor*, who sells a box *filled with whatever bits of grass and dirt happened to be close by*.

21. **B**   Both the tonic and the box are supposed to be medicines and are sold as such. (B), *Both were advertised to cure an ailment*, matches this. (C) and (E) are not mentioned in the passage. (A) is mentioned only in Passage 1, and (D) is mentioned only in Passage 2.

22. **E**   The herb doctor brings up the brawny boxer to say that just because the hunter doesn't need the medicine doesn't mean he should badmouth it to the old man. The medicine, after all, will *in mere imagination, if nothing more*, help the old man. So how could the hunter be *so pitiless?* (E), *the hunter should not disparage the old man's belief in the medicine*, basically says this. (B) and (C) are too literal, because the herb doctor mentions the boxer only to make a larger point. (A) and (D) are not mentioned in the passage.

23. **D**   The author of Passage 1 is against the cure medicines because they can do harm, but he realizes that they can occasionally have some use. So he is (D) *more realistic* than the herb doctor, who is trying his best to lie his way into making a sale.

24. **E** We're looking for something mentioned by the author of Passage 1, but not mentioned anywhere in Passage 2. (A) is mentioned in Passage 1 and by the herb doctor near the end of Passage 2, so we can eliminate it. (B) is only sort of mentioned in Passage 2. (C) is mentioned in Passage 1 and shown by the fact that the old man in Passage 2 just bought the medicine. (D) is not mentioned in either passage. This leaves (E), *medicine is generally based on trial and error*, which is mentioned by the author of Passage 1, *we try things, and see if they tend to work*, but nowhere in Passage 2.

SECTION 3

1. **B** Solve for $a - b$ by first multiplying both sides of the equation by 2: you get $a - b - 5 = 20$. Then add 5 to both sides: $a - b = 25$. Don't solve for a and b individually because you've already found the answer.

2. **A** Because $ABCD$ is a square, $r = 90°$. Line ℓ forms the diagonal of square $ABCD$, so it splits the angle in half, making $q = 45$ and $s = 45$. Because there are 180° in a line, $p = 135$ and $t = 135$. Of the pairs listed in the answer choices, only (A) $p = t$ is true.

3. **D** Find the value of t by using the values given in the question. If $c = 3$ and $d = 2$, then $r = 4(3) - 2 = 12 - 2 = 10$ for the first equation. Using $r = 10$ in the second equation: $t = (3 + 1)10 = (4)(10) = 40$. If you accidentally found r instead of solving for t, (A) 10 would be your solution. If you used d instead of c in the 2nd equation, $t = (2 + 1)10 = (3)(10) = 30$, (C), would be your solution. The correct answer is (D).

4. **C** Eliminate graphs that do not express the relationship between time and volume as expressed in the chart. At zero hours, there are 14 milliliters of water. Eliminate (D) and (E), since the graphs start at the origin, where both time and volume equal zero. Consider (A): This graph shows the volume of water decreasing, then increasing slightly, then decreasing again. Since this relationship is not mirrored in the values given in the table, eliminate it. Look at (B): This says that time and volume of water vary inversely, meaning when time increases, volume decreases proportionately. This is not the case here, since more water is lost between hours 0 and 2 than are lost between hours 8 and 10. That leaves (C).

5. **E** Plug In numbers from the grid. Plugging In 0 doesn't allow us to eliminate any answer choices. If you Plug In 1, however, only (D) and (E) produce $f(x) = 26$, so eliminate (A), (B), and (C). Plug In 2, and only (E) produces the proper $f(x)$ value of 29. The correct answer is (E).

6. **B** Since $y = g(x)$ and the question is asking how many times $g(x) = 0$, it's really asking how many times $y = 0$. Since the graph touches the x-axis twice, there are two values of x that give the graph a y-value of 0. If you chose (A), you counted the number of times that $x = 0$ rather than the number of times that $y = 0$.

7. C   One way to work this question is to Plug In a number for y. Let's say $y = 2$; therefore $p = 2^8 = 256$, $q = 2^5 = 32$, and $y^9 = 512$. Now resolve each answer choice to see which has a value of 512 using $p = 256$ and $q = 32$ (it helps to have a calculator handy): (A) $(256 - 32)^3 = 224^3 = 11{,}239{,}424$, (B) $(256 \times 32)^3 = 8192^3 = 549{,}755{,}813{,}888$; (C) $\left(\dfrac{256}{32}\right)^3 = 8^3 = 512$; (D) $256 - 3(32) = 256 - 96 = 160$, (E) $256 - 32^3 = 256 - 32{,}768 = -32{,}512$. Only (C) matches what we came up with for y^9. The algebraic way to solve this question would be to see that $y^9 = (y^3)^3$. $\dfrac{p}{q} = \dfrac{y^8}{y^5} = y^3$ because when you divide numbers with the same base, you subtract the exponents. So $\left(y^3\right)^3 = \left(\dfrac{p}{q}\right)^3$.

8. D   The easiest way to deal with this question is to come up with your own number for p and determine the value of q. If you Plug In 10 for p, then you can translate the first half of the question into the equation $\left(\dfrac{4}{5}\right)(10) = \dfrac{q}{10} \times 2$, which means q equals 40. Translate the phrase "p is what percent of q" into the equation $p = \dfrac{x}{100} \times q$. Fill in the values you obtained to get $10 = \dfrac{x}{100} \times 40$. Solve for x, which will work out to 25, giving (D), as "percent" means "out of 100," and thus $\dfrac{25}{100} = 25\%$.

To solve the problem algebraically, translate the phrase "$\dfrac{4}{5}p$ is equal to $\dfrac{q}{10}$ multiplied by 2" into the equation $\dfrac{4}{5}p = \dfrac{2q}{10}$. This can be simplified to $\dfrac{4}{5}p = \dfrac{q}{5}$ then further simplified to $4p = q$, or $\dfrac{p}{q} = \dfrac{1}{4}$. Next, use the equation $p = \dfrac{x}{100} \times q$. Solving the equation for x yields $x = 100 \times \dfrac{p}{q}$. Substituting the value of $\dfrac{p}{q}$ from above, you get $x = 100 \times \dfrac{1}{4}$, or 25%. If you answered (B), you solved for q percent of p. If you answered (A) or (E), you inversed one of the fractions.

9. 59   The difference between the beginning and end prices of item A is 14, so it increased 14 dollars that week. The price of item B increased by half as much, so divide 14 by 2: the price of B increased 7 dollars. Add 7 to 52, the original price of B, to get the final price of B: 59.

10. **900** Since the number of articles doubles every two months, divide 7,200 by 2 to find the number of articles two months earlier: there were 3,600 articles at the beginning of May. Do this again to find the number of articles at the beginning of March: 1,800. Divide 1,800 by 2 to find that there were 900 articles at the beginning of January.

11. **60** $\overline{DG}$ = 15, so pick values for $\overline{CD}$ and $\overline{CG}$: you could say $\overline{CD}$ = 10 and $\overline{CG}$ = 5. Then find the perimeter of each square by adding all four of its sides: the perimeter of *ABCG* is 20 and the perimeter of *CDEF* is 40. Add them together to get 60.

12. **20** A great way to solve this problem is to Plug In numbers. Say b = 2. Then a = 8. 2 = 5c, so $c = \dfrac{2}{5}$ or 0.4. Now, $8 = d(\dfrac{2}{5})$, so d = 20.

13. **6** Since the question asks for the <u>least</u> number of DVDs that could be removed, remove only dramas. If you remove one drama, then the ratio of drama to comedy is 14:15; remove another and it's 13:15; remove another and it's 12:15, which reduces to 4:5. Remove another 3 dramas and you have 9 dramas and 15 comedies: a 3:5 drama-to-comedy ratio. To get there, you've removed a total of 6 DVDs.

14. $\mathbf{0 < y < \dfrac{4}{3}}$ **or** $\mathbf{0 < y < 1.33}$

   The absolute value complicates this problem in that you'll have to solve twice: once assuming that $2 - 3y$ is less than 2 and another time for when $-(2 - 3y)$ is less than 2. Start with the first one: $2 - 3y < 2$, so $-3y < 0$, so $y > 0$. Solve the second scenario: $-(2 - 3y) < 2$, so $-2 + 3y < 2$, so $3y < 4$, so $y < \dfrac{4}{3}$. Therefore, y can be any number less than $\dfrac{4}{3}$ and greater than 0.

15. $\dfrac{3}{4}$ **or .75**

   Begin by drawing a line connecting points B and D. Then add point M, the midpoint of $\overline{AE}$, to the figure. Now draw $\overline{BM}$ and $\overline{DM}$. Now you've divided ACE into four smaller triangles: ABM, BCD, BDM, and DEM. Each small triangle is $\dfrac{1}{4}$ of ACE. BCD is entirely shaded, so that's $\dfrac{1}{4}$ of ACE. BDM is also shaded, so that's another $\dfrac{1}{4}$ of the triangle. Half of ABM is shaded, and $\dfrac{1}{2}$ of $\dfrac{1}{4}$ is $\dfrac{1}{8}$. Half of DEM is shaded, so that's another $\dfrac{1}{8}$. Add these fractions together to get the fraction of ACE that's shaded: $\dfrac{1}{4} + \dfrac{1}{4} + \dfrac{1}{8} + \dfrac{1}{8} = \dfrac{2}{8} + \dfrac{2}{8} + \dfrac{1}{8} + \dfrac{1}{8} = \dfrac{6}{8} = \dfrac{3}{4}$.

16. **1,000** Begin by writing the equation described in the question: $\sqrt[3]{x} = \dfrac{x}{100}$, then solve for x. Cube both

sides: $x = \dfrac{x^3}{1,000,000}$. Cross-multiply: $1,000,000x = x^3$. Divide both sides by x: $1,000,000 = x^2$.

Take the square root of both sides: $1,000 = x$.

17. $\dfrac{3}{4}$ **or .75**

There are $1\frac{1}{2}$ pounds of sand at start, so a total of $5\frac{1}{4}$ pounds is added after 7 minutes. Turning

$5\frac{1}{4}$ into the improper fraction $\dfrac{21}{4}$ makes it easier to divide by 7 and see that the rate is $\dfrac{3}{4}$ pound

of sand per minute. Look at the graph for the amount of pounds of sand given in whole numbers,

which are easier to use: At 2 minutes, the amount of sand is 3 pounds. The next time the num-

ber of pounds of sand is a whole number is at 6 minutes, when there is 6 pounds of sand. So in

4 minutes, the amount of sand increased by 3 pounds. To determine the rate, divide 3 pounds by

4 minutes, giving you $\dfrac{3}{4}$.

18. **3** Expand the left and right sides of the inequality to get $a^2 + 2ab + b^2 \le a^2 - 2ab + b^2 + 36$. Subtract
$a^2 - 2ab + b^2$ from both sides to get $4ab \le 36$. Divide both sides by 4 to get $ab \le 9$. To make a as big
as possible, b must be as small as possible, but still equal to or greater than a. If a and b are equal,
then you can take the square root of both sides to see that $a \le 3$, meaning that the biggest value is
of a is 3.

SECTION 4

1. **D** Since the sentence describes more people who are in favor of *preservation* than *deforestation*, the
blank must mean something like "decrease" or "stop." The closest choice is *abate* in (D).

2. **B** Kovacs is *unlike other comedians*, who use scripts. That means he talks off the top of his head. Here,
(B), (C), (D), and (E) all work pretty well for the first blank. For the second blank, how does he
mix in new lines? *As they come to him.* (B) *spontaneously* is the only one that still works.

3. **D** First let's look at the second blank. The words *seemingly irrelevant* and *actually* lets you know that
the second blank means something like "relevant to" or "connected to." Both (C) and (D) could
fit this meaning. The first blank will be similar to the *seemingly irrelevant digressions*, so the blank
probably means "way off-topic." (D), *tangential*, has this meaning while (C) *focused* is the opposite,
leaving (D) as the best answer.

4. **E** The clue for the blank is *the hostile and combative nature* and *war stories*. The blank must mean something close to "warlike." The closest choice is *bellicose*, (E).

5. **A** Let's reuse the words that follow the colon: the first blank means *incredibly complicated*. Eliminate (B), (D), and (E). (C), *obfuscated*, could fit, but it implies that it was purposefully made complicated, which is probably not the case. Let's leave it as a weak answer. We can reuse words from the sentence for the second blank as well: it must mean *completely out of date*. (C), *ubiquitous*, which means "present everywhere," doesn't fit, leaving answer (A).

6. **A** The sentence is about the people's *admiration*. Because this admiration *was so pronounced*, the blank must mean something close to "extreme admiration." The closest choice is *adulation* (A).

7. **D** The phrase *once forthright and blunt* indicates that the blank should be opposite in meaning of *forthright* ("direct"). "Indirect" and "ambiguous" would both be good words to fill that blank, making (D) *enigmatic* ("puzzling") the best choice. (A), (B), and (C) all mean "direct," and (E) does not match the clue.

8. **C** (C) is correct, since the word *belied* indicates opposition between the blanks. The words in the sentence indicate that the first blank means something like "complicated." Both (B) and (C) work for the first blank, but only (C) has a second word that is the opposite of the first. (A) is incorrect because *serendipitous* means "having made a fortunate discovery by accident"—an unlikely start for a war. (E) and (D) are trap answers because *canonical* and *retrenched* may lead one to think of war but the words don't make sense in context.

9. **D** The author is making a joke that he must *have a very powerful enemy indeed* if he must undergo the torture of listening to a concept album. (A) is wrong because he is not *challenging a belief*. Nor is he (B) *quoting a conflicting source*, nor does he (C) *cite an authority*. The author is also not offering (E) *an amusing anecdote*, because he is not actually telling a small story here. Instead, he is saying he doesn't like the concept albums (*advance a negative opinion*) and he does so through a joke (*using humorous terms*), so (D) is the answer.

10. **A** The author is comparing a concept album with reading repetitive stories or watching a bad detective show. So we want an answer that means "to make a comparison," which is what (A), *analogy*, means.

11. **A** The author is contrasting the view held by *many people,* which pertains exclusively to *eighteenth- and nineteenth-century America,* with the view that *many different races and ethnicities have been enslaved throughout history.* Answer (A) expresses this point accurately. (B) is false because the *treatment* of these two groups is not discussed. (C) is tempting, but the author merely notes that slavery has persisted for a long time; he doesn't explain why. (D) is no good because there's no mention of *contemporary relevance.* Eliminate (E) because *cultural ties* between African Americans and Slavs are never even hinted at; the author is merely noting that both groups were enslaved.

12. **D** The main purpose of the passage is to show the use of the terms *Slav* and *servus* changed over time due to the enslavement of the Slavs. (D) paraphrases this nicely. Eliminate (A) because it's not

mentioned in the passage. (B) is out because we don't discuss the Slavs in *modern times.* (C) is no good because the author doesn't discuss *the root causes of slavery.* (E) is too strong, and the *ancient Romans* are only a minor part of the passage.

13.   **C**   The primary focus of the first paragraph is on how Aphra is feeling, or *a character's emotional state* (C). We learn that she *grew accustomed…got on quite well…was happy and not often bothered. Heartache* is mentioned in the paragraph and in (A), but it's too strong and not the *primary* focus. (B), (D), and (E) are not indicated in the passage.

14.   **E**   *Heartache* refers directly to the fact that *the Edwards family had lost its estate and servants when the business collapsed.* (E) is the only answer that matches.

15.   **C**   This part of the passage says that Rachel was considered *wise* and *graceful* (line 19) and that she was *envied* for her *savvy gracefulness* (line 15). This is best paraphrased in (C). The referenced part of the passage never mentions marriage, so (A) is incorrect; nor do we know if she resembled her father, so (B) is also incorrect. (D) is incorrect because the reference discusses only Rachel, and we do not know if she is similar to Aphra (although one similarity, their shared ability to adjust, has already been mentioned). (E) is incorrect because although Rachel did excite jealousy among her friends, the passage never says that she intended to.

16.   **A**   Insert your own word. It's clear that Rachel has adjusted well, so "well" would be a good choice. (A), *successfully,* is the best match. (C) and (E), which are the more conventional meanings of *beautifully,* are traps, while (B) and (D) are in no way supported by the passage.

17.   **B**   The phrase tells us that Rachel *had yet to develop…egotism.* Thus, she lacked *vanity* (B). The other answers are not indicated in the passage.

18.   **B**   According to the passage, *it stunned Rachel a little…when they received an invitation to tea at the Hamilton estate* (lines 20–23). Thus, the invitation was *unexpected.* In the carriage, she feels *mild excitement* and talks with her mother about the possibility of getting to know Ginny (and, it's implied, Nathaniel). (B) best expresses these feelings. (A), (C), and (D) are too negative; Rachel takes pleasure in the chance to meet the Hamiltons. (E) is incorrect because we don't know what Rachel had previously thought about going to the Hamiltons'.

19.   **A**   Rachel and Aphra *no longer fussed over society.* Why not? *Because they could rest in the knowledge that everyone knew of their tragic downfall and there was no need to pretend otherwise* (lines 26–28). The combination of these two phrases tells us that they no longer worry about hiding their poverty for social reasons. The phrases *no longer* and *as they once did* (lines 25–26) tell us that they used to care more about fitting in. This is best paraphrased in (A). (B) is incorrect, since the passage never says that they looked down on members of *lower social classes.* (C) is incorrect since marriage is never mentioned in this paragraph. (D) is tempting, but the reference never mentions how they dressed, nor does it indicate that Rachel and Aphra thought of themselves as better than others, so eliminate this answer. (E) is close, but, as with (D), the passage never indicates that Rachel

and Aphra tried to appear richer than they were. There is not enough information to support this answer.

20. **B** The fact that *Aphra and Rachel no longer fussed over society* indicates that their preparations were "minimal," or "little." *Slight* is the best match. (A) and (C) are traps because they are more common meanings of *modest*.

21. **C** The sentence referenced describes Rachel's ease as she climbs into the carriage: *it seemed that her heightened sense of grace and elegance had translated to her physical being* (lines 34–35). In other words, her natural grace carries over into her body, allowing her to smoothly enter the carriage. This is best paraphrased in (C). (A) is incorrect because we do not know whether grace and elegance are *difficult to achieve*. (B) is incorrect because we are not discussing *beauty*. (D) is incorrect because there is no indication that anyone has changed her appearance. (E) is incorrect because these lines don't deal with Rachel's social class.

22. **E** Aphra does two things here. First, she assures Rachel that Ginny is okay. However, none of the answers refer to this part of her statement. The second thing she does is to ask *are you sure it is Ginny whose acquaintance you are anticipating?* She does this to suggest that the real reason for Rachel's concern is her interest in Ginny's brother. Thus, Aphra is *implying that there is an alternative reason for Rachel's interest in their visit* (E). None of the other answers are supported by the passage.

23. **C** Rachel responds to Aphra's question by referring to the meeting with the Hamiltons as a *silly little thing*. Thus, she minimizes *the significance of an occasion*. The other answers are not supported by the passage.

24. **D** The conversation between Aphra and Nathaniel is polite. Nathaniel welcomes the women to his home, and Aphra thanks him. This is best paraphrased by (D). (A) is incorrect because the passage does not imply that Aphra and Nathaniel are close friends. Nathaniel and Aphra are not lovers (instead, we have reason to believe that he and her daughter may get together) so (B) is incorrect. (C) is incorrect because the passage does not indicate that Aphra and Nathaniel work together, so they're not *colleagues*. (E) is incorrect because Aphra and Nathaniel are not rivals or enemies.

25. **B** The sentence describes Ginny's beauty, and notes that it was *unlike Rachel's classically beautiful light features*. Thus, it *draw[s] a comparison* between Rachel and Ginny. The other answers are not supported by the passage.

SECTION 5

1. **B** The safest way to solve this problem is to Plug In numbers for the variables. Let's say Donald can type 20 words in 2 minutes, so $w = 20$ and $m = 2$. At this rate, he types 10 words per minute. To find that number, you divided 20 by 2, or w by m, as seen in (B). If you replace the variables in the answer choices with the numbers you chose for m and w, you'll see that only (B) gives an answer of 10, as well.

2. **E** Of the 42 people originally invited, 8 declined, leaving 34 people. Half of those people were unable to make it due to the snowstorm, so that left only 17 people out of the original 42, or $\frac{17}{42}$ (E).

3. **C** First find the average number of papers for 2002–2003. The dot is a little below 35 for 2002, so let's call it 33. The dot for 2003 is at 25. $33 + 25 = 58$, so the average is 29. Only the dot for 2006 is close to 30, so that is the year in which the number of papers was closest to the average. You can also do this visually: the dot for 2006 is the only one that falls between the dot for 2002 and the dot for 2003.

4. **E** Cross out any of the plates to the left or right of the circles marked with B as well as any plates across from them, since these cannot be blue. On the top row, the first, third, and fifth plates should be crossed out. On the bottom row, the second, fourth, and sixth plates should be crossed out. These are the plates that cannot be blue. Add them up to find that six cannot be blue.

5. **C** Plug In numbers for the variables: Let's say $x = 2$ and $y = -3$. Choice (A) is $(2)(-3) = -6$, so eliminate it. (B) is $(-2)(2) = -4$, so eliminate it. (C) is $(-4)(2)(-3) = 12$, a positive, so hold onto that. Check the rest of the answers to be sure: (D) is $2 + 2(-3) = 2 - 6 = -4$, so eliminate it. (E) is $4(2 - 3) = 4(-1) = -4$, so eliminate it as well. If you didn't Plug In numbers for the variables, you'd have to see that a negative times a positive, such as in (A) and (B), is always negative, whereas a negative times a negative number, such as in (C) is always positive. (D) and (E) are sometimes positive, sometimes negative, but the question asks for the choice that is *always* positive.

6. **D** Because of vertical angles, a must be 75°. Use the rule of 180 for b, c, and e—there are 180° in a straight line: b must be $180 - 75 = 105°$. c must be $180 - 65 = 115°$. e must be $180 - 100 = 80$. Because d exists within a quadrilateral and all quadrilaterals (a shape with 4 sides) contain 360°, d must be $360 - (100 + 75 + 65) = 360 - 240 = 120$. So, $a = 75$, $b = 105$, $c = 115$, $d = 120$, $e = 80$, and (D) d is greatest.

7. **B** You know that the total number of calories is no greater than 450. In each of the answer choices n represents the drink and 3(140) represents the mini-muffins. We need an inequality that shows the total number of calories as less than or equal to 450, so get rid of (C) and (E) because the inequality sign is pointed the wrong way from 450. (B) is correct because it shows the sum of the calories instead of the difference seen in (D). (A) cannot be used to determine the value of n because it is missing information (the total number of calories) necessary to solving the value correctly.

8.   **A**   A cube has 6 faces and 8 vertices. From one vertex of the square, there are 7 potential lines that could be drawn, but some of them will be parallel to an edge, and therefore not count. Of the 7 potential lines, three are parallel to an edge, leaving 4 lines that fit the requirements stated in the question. The correct answer is (A).

9.   **A**   Plug the equations in the answers into a graphing calculator to find out which one matches the graph. Or, choose a point on the graph and use the coordinates of that point to test the equations to find out which one is correct. For example, the graph hits $(-3, 0)$ where $x = -3$ and $y = 0$. For (A), $0 = (-3 + 3)^2$; $0 = 0^2$; $0 = 0$. This is true, so keep it. For (B), $0 = (-3)^2 + 3$; $0 = 9 + 3$; $0 \neq 12$. Eliminate (B). For (C), $0 = (-3 - 3)^2$; $0 = (-6)^2$; $0 \neq 36$, so get rid of (C). For (D), $0 = (-3)^2 - 3$; $0 = 9 - 3$; $0 \neq 6$, so eliminate (D), too. For (E), $0 = 3(-3)^2$; $0 = 3(9)$; $0 \neq 27$. Eliminate (E). The only one that worked was (A).

10. **E**   When a line crosses two parallel lines, it creates two distinct angles, one big and one small. The big angles are equal to each other and the small angles are equal to each other. The small angles created by $\overline{BD}$ are y and z. Since $y = z$, $z = 88$. Because the degrees in a triangle add to 180, we know that $w + x + z = 180$, so $w + x = 92$. If you chose (C), you assumed z was 90. The correct answer is (E).

11. **C**   By plugging the values from the question into the functions, you get $h(5) = 8.5$ and $f(3) = 4$. Thus, the difference is 4.5. If you answered (A) or (D), you chose a partial answer. (B) and (E) are the numbers to plug into the functions, not the numbers you get out.

12. **D**   If ECD is an equilateral triangle with perimeter 18, each side length is equal to 6. Since opposite sides of a parallelogram have equal lengths, $AB = CE = 6$ and $BC = AE = 8$, so the perimeter of the parallelogram is $8 + 6 + 8 + 6 = 28$.

13. **A**   If 8 students received an average score of 76, the sum of the scores must be 8×76, or 608. The two students improved a total of 32 points, so the sum of scores on the second test must be 640. Divide 640 by the 8 students to calculate the average score of 80. If you answered (E), you subtracted the score improvements for the second test instead of adding them.

14. **B**   The probability that a randomly selected dog is less than 3 months old is the number of dogs that are less than 3 months old divided by the total number of dogs. According to the table, there are 8 dogs less than 3 months old; $8 + 24 = 32$, so there are 32 dogs total. The probability of selecting a dog that is less than 3 months old is $\frac{8}{32} = \frac{1}{4}$.

15. **A**   Use the area of a square formula ($A = s^2$, when A is area and s is the length of the side) to find the length of the side of square $WXYZ$: $4 = s^2$, so $s = 2$. Since all four circles are congruent, the diameter of each is 1; therefore, the radius of each circle is $\frac{1}{2}$. Use the circumference formula from the box at the beginning of the math section ($C = 2\pi r$) to find the circumference of one circle:

$C = 2 \times \pi \times \dfrac{1}{2} = \pi$. Since the darkened curves cover only $\dfrac{3}{4}$ of each circle, the length of the darkened curve of one circle is $\dfrac{3}{4}\pi$. Multiply this by 4 to get the darkened curves of all 4 circles: $4 \times \dfrac{3}{4}\pi = 3\pi$, answer (A).

16. **D**   Plug In values for a and b. Because ab must be less than 10, you should start with the lowest possible values for each. The smallest possible value of a is 0, and the smallest possible value of b is 4. With these values for a and b, ab is 0. Next, Plug In 1 and 2 for a, which produces new values for ab of 4 and 8 respectively, both of which are less than 10. If we try $a = 3$, however, ab is 12, which is more than 10. If we use another positive multiple of 4, say $b = 8$, $0 \times 8 = 0$, a value of ab that we have already accounted for. If $a = 1$ when $b = 8$, $1 \times 8 = 8$, another value for ab that has been accounted for. Thus, 0, 4, and 8 are the only possible values of values of ab less than 10, and the answer is (D). If you chose (C), you confused "nonnegative" and "positive."

17. **E**   Start within the parentheses—Use 1 in place of a and 2 in place of b. $1 \Phi 2 = (1^2 \times 2) + (1 \times 2^2) = 2 + 4 = 6$. Now 6 is the a value and 3 will be the b value. $(6^2 \times 3) + (6 \times 3^2) = 108 + 54 = 162$, answer (E). If you just added the 1 and 2 in the parentheses and solved for $3 \Phi 3$ instead, you would get caught by the trap answer in (C). You can see that the choices include many partial answers, but only (E) is correct.

18. **D**   The easiest way to work this question is to Plug In a number for x: let's say $x = 2$. You want to find the second term (which we'll call a) and the question says that the ratio of the second to the first term is 3 to 1, so set up that proportion: $\dfrac{a}{2} = \dfrac{3}{1}$. Now cross-multiply to solve for a: $a = 6$. Continue setting up and solving proportions like this. Let's call the third term b: $\dfrac{b}{6} = \dfrac{3}{1}$, so $b = 18$. Let's call the fourth term c: $\dfrac{c}{18} = \dfrac{3}{1}$, so $c = 54$. The difference of c and a is 48. Remember that $x = 2$ as you review the answer choices: (D) is $24 \times 2 = 48$. To solve this question without Plugging In a number for x, you'd have to see that each term is 3 times the previous term: so the second term is $3x$; the third term is $3 \times 3x$, or $9x$; and the fourth term is $27x$. $27x - 3x = 24x$, answer (D).

19. **D**   It is best to draw the line and plot the points according to what is described. If we do this carefully, we should see that $\overline{MP} = \dfrac{3}{4}\overline{LP}$, and remember that the length of $\overline{LP}$ must be an integer less than 24. If we use the answer choices for values of $\overline{MP}$, we get the following lengths for $\overline{LP}$: For (A), $\overline{LP}$ would be 24; for (B), $\overline{LP}$ would be $22\dfrac{2}{3}$; for (C), $\overline{LP}$ would be $21\dfrac{1}{3}$; for (D), $\overline{LP}$ would be 20; and for (E), $\overline{LP}$ would be $18\dfrac{2}{3}$. (A) and (D) are both integers, but only (D) is less than 24, making (D) the correct answer.

20.   **A**   The easiest way to solve this problem is to Plug In numbers for y and z. Let's say $y = -2$ and $z = 3$. The left side of the inequality in (A) is $(-2)^2(3)^2 = (4)(9) = 36$, in (B) is $(-2)(3)^2 = (-2)(9) = -18$, in (C) is $(-2)^2(3) = (4)(3) = 12$, in (D) is $(-2)(3) = -6$, and in (E) is $(-2)^3(3) = (-8)(3) = -24$. Since choices (B), (D), and (E) are all true, you can eliminate them from consideration (you're looking for the one that CANNOT be true). Now let's try $y = -2$ and $z = -3$. The left side of (A) is $(-2)^2(-3)^2 = (4)(9) = 36$ and the left side of (C) is $(-2)^2(-3) = (4)(-3) = -12$. Since (C) is now true, you can eliminate it as well; therefore, through Process of Elimination, (A) cannot be true. The reason (A) cannot be true is: any positive number squared is positive and any negative number squared is positive; therefore, y^2 will always be positive and (it doesn't matter whether z is positive or negative) z^2 will always be positive, and the product of two positive numbers is positive. If you didn't Plug In numbers for the variables, you'd have to deduce this for every answer choice. For (B), y is negative and z^2 is positive, so their product is negative; therefore, (B) is always true. For (C), y^2 is positive and z could be positive or negative; the product of these two would be positive or negative (depending on z), so (C) is true sometimes. For (D), y is negative and z is positive or negative, so their product would be positive or negative (depending on z again); therefore, (D) is true sometimes. For (E) y^3 is negative and z could again be positive or negative; therefore, (E) is sometimes true for the same reason as (C) and (D).

SECTION 7

1.   **C**   As written, this sentence contains a comma splice, so eliminate (A). (B), on the other hand, is a sentence fragment; changing the verb to *making* makes the sentence incomplete. (D) is overly wordy, and (E) is a misplaced modifier that describes *Toby* as what's spicy. Only (C) clearly defines the relationship in a complete and correctly punctuated sentence.

2.   **E**   The original sentence contains a conjunction error. *The way* is not the correct conjunction to use with a subordinate clause, so (A) and (B) must be eliminated. (C) and (D) do not contain complete clauses after the use of *that* and also must be eliminated. (E) correctly uses *that* to link what was confirmed (the *techniques*) to the verb *confirmed*.

3.   **E**   The original sentence is passive and contains a misplaced modifier: *the dispute* cannot move *on to other topics*—the editors were the ones who moved on. (B) fixes this error but changes the meaning by adding *by*. (C) has mismatched verb tenses. (D) contains a comma splice. (E) correctly attributes the *moving on* to *the editors*.

4.   **A**   This sentence is correct as it stands, clearly indicating that it is *antioxidants* that *help prevent heart disease*. The change of conjunctions in (B) makes the relationship of the *antioxidants* and heart disease unclear. (C) and (D) contain comma splices, and (E) contains an ambiguous pronoun: it is unclear whether *they* refers to *pomegranates and spinach* or *antioxidants*.

5. **B** (A) has a redundant pronoun and the unnecessary verb form *having*. (B) has the correct verb form for a modifying phrase. (C) has the unnecessary verb form, *being*. (D) is awkward and not as good as (B). (E) has the wrong verb tense for the modifying phrase.

6. **B** The sentence contains a parallelism error. Everything else in the list is an adjective-noun combination, while the underlined portion contains a gerund. This eliminates (A), (D), and (E). (C) contains the wrong conjunction. Only (B) has the same construction as the other items on the list.

7. **D** Both (A) and (B) are missing verbs. (A) contains a gerund (*becoming*) and (B) has a verb in the subordinate clause created by *that*…but not in the sentence itself. (C) and (E) both use the wrong tense of the verb *become*, among other problems. Therefore, (D) is the best answer.

8. **E** The sentence contains a pronoun agreement error. The subject *the bank* is singular while the pronoun *their* is plural. This eliminates (A) and (B). (C) creates a comma splice error. (D) creates a verb tense error. (E) has the correct pronoun and introduces no other errors.

9. **A** This sentence contains no error. In (B) the comma creates an incomplete clause at the end of the sentence. (C) uses the unnecessary conjunction *and*. (D) creates an incomplete sentence, and (E) is awkward and passive, and uses *being* which is usually an incorrect answer on the SAT.

10. **D** (C) and (E) are both incorrect because they contain misplaced modifiers. The difference seen in (A), (B), and (D) is the way the verb "to lose" is conjugated. The phrase *thousands of years ago* lets us know we need the past tense, but (A) has *losing*, which does not function as a verb and creates a sentence fragment, and (B) uses the present perfect *has lost*. In (D), the simple past *lost* is correct. The best answer is therefore (D).

11. **E** The sentence as written has a pronoun agreement error: either *you* or *one* is correct when used consistently in a sentence, but the pronouns cannot mix as they do in (A) and (D). In (B) there is a lack of agreement between the plural pronoun *their* and *a person*. (C) is missing information that would make the sentence complete, and there is no noun that connects to the pronoun *they*. Only (E) has consistent pronouns in agreement and is correct.

12. **B** The phrase *more healthier* is redundant. *Healthier* already means *more healthy*, so to say *more healthier* would be like saying *more more healthy*: both are redundant.

13. **C** This is an example of a list that is not parallel. There are two things eating less fats may help to do. As written, the first is *to reduce* (the risk of diabetes). As written, the second is *decreasing* (the chance of heart attacks). Because *to* is not underlined, it is not possible to change *to reduce*. Therefore, *decreasing* is not grammatical, and is the answer. Correctly written, the sentence should say *to decrease the chance of heart attacks*.

14. C   SAT questions often separate the subject and the verb with a prepositional phrase (*to the disappointment…team*). The subject of the sentence is the *general manager*. The *general manager* is singular, but *have asked* is plural. Therefore, (C) is the answer because it violates the rules of subject/verb agreement.

15. E   This sentence is correct as written. Remember, just because it "sounds funny," doesn't mean it's wrong. Make sure you identify the error before you select an answer. (E) is going to be right approximately $\frac{1}{5}$ of the time, so if you've checked all the underlined portions and haven't identified an error, don't be afraid to pick (E).

16. C   (C) is incorrect because the verb is in its active form, suggesting that the *sand* actually did the covering, whereas the sand is being covered by something else (it tells us *with trash*). The passive *was covered* would be correct because the sand is being covered by the trash. This would also make it parallel with the other verbs in the list, each of which uses a helping verb (*was* and *had*).

17. B   The time indicator *In the 1990s* tells us that the action of the *analysts starting their careers* in this sentence took place in the past. Therefore, (C) *believe* is the wrong tense, because it is in the present tense, and should be *believed*.

18. E   This sentence is correct as written. Remember, just because it "sounds funny," doesn't mean it's wrong. Make sure you identify the error before you select an answer. (E) is going to be right approximately $\frac{1}{5}$ of the time, so if you've checked all the underlined portions and haven't identified an error, don't be afraid to pick (E).

19. A   This question is testing pronouns. In (A) *it* should instead be *she* to make the sentence make sense and agree with the non-underlined *herself*, to read *she established herself*.

20. B   This question is testing agreement between the subject and the pronouns. The subject is *employees*, which is plural, but *his or her* is singular; the correct pronoun would be *their*.

21. C   Answer (C) contains the error: the word *extensive* should be *extensively*. An adjective cannot be used to describe a verb: you almost always need to add -*ly* to an adjective in order to create an adverb. (How were the causes described? Extensive*ly*.)

22. B   In this question, the error is found in the preposition *with*, which is the wrong preposition for the word *succeeded*. The designer succeeded *in* introducing the toy. This is an example of an idiom error, which often can be found by looking carefully at the underlined prepositions.

23. B   The verb in (B) is incorrect; it should be *reveals* to agree with the subject *monitoring*. Don't be confused by the noun right next to the verb, in this case *cameras*. On the test there is often a noun next to a verb that makes a wrong answer sound right. In this case, you can "trim the fat." Take out extra words between the subject and verb; here, you'd get the phrase *incessant monitoring reveal* which should make the error more obvious.

24. **A** The error here is an adjective/adverb error. The word *clever* should instead be *cleverly*. Remember to use an adverb (add *-ly*) when you're describing a verb.

25. **B** Since the subject of the sentence is *the instruction manual*, the pronoun that replaces the manual should be *it is* rather than *they are*.

26. **E** The sentence is correct as written. The sentence could be confusing, since the structure is a bit complicated, but there is nothing grammatically wrong.

27. **C** The error here is a pronoun case error. To decide whether to choose *I* or *me* (the subject or object case), the easiest thing is to take out the words between the subject and the pronoun and test the sentence. Would you say the *dean called me* or *the dean called I*? That test usually makes the answer pretty clear.

28. **B** Since both of the events (*gained* and *was gaining*) happened in the past, you need the past perfect tense, which uses the helping verb *had*. The sentence should read *the internet service provider had gained three million subscribers.*

29. **C** This sentence has an idiom error. The preposition that goes with *misinformation* should be *about* rather than *with*.

30. **A** (A) restates the sentence more clearly and concisely than do the other choices. (B) and (E) change the meaning of the sentence. (C) contains the ambiguous pronoun *it*. (D) loses the meaning in oversimplifying the grammar.

31. **D** This sentence incorrectly uses the pronoun *it* because *it* does not represent any of the four previous nouns in the sentence. (A), (B), (C), and (E) are all other nouns in the sentence, but in context of the passage the author is referring to *chronic fatigue syndrome*, (D).

32. **B** (A) changes the meaning of the sentence. (C) is attractive, but wordy. (D) is repetitive. (E) is awkward and wordy. (B) is the best choice because it flows smoothly and is concise.

33. **E** (A) is already mentioned in sentence 1. (B) is not very necessary. (C) would not have added to the analysis and would take up too much space in the essay. (D) might seem like a good choice, but that would be unnecessarily specific information when we haven't been told the details about things the author alludes to but does not explain, such as the *symptoms* and *stereotypes*. (E) is the most specific way to enhance the analysis.

34. **A** (A) is the most concise combination of the sentences. Both (B) and (D) are redundant in using *why* and *because*. (C) changes the meaning of the sentence. (E) uses the pronoun *you*, which is not present in the rest of the passage, and it is ambiguous what exactly is vague and mysterious.

35. **C** In the sentences before sentence 13, the author states that sufferer's concerns had been *dismissed and ignored* and that it's hard *to be believed and to get help*. Sentence 13 puts forth the idea that sufferers should get help, so we need a word that indicates a change. Only (C) *However* creates such a transition.

SECTION 8

1. **C** Divide 120 by the answer choices. Starting with (A), $\dfrac{120}{4} = 30$. 4 is a factor, so eliminate (A). In (B), $\dfrac{120}{10} = 12$. 10 is a factor so eliminate (B). For (C), $\dfrac{120}{18} = 6\dfrac{2}{3}$. 18 is not a factor, so keep (C). In (D), $\dfrac{120}{24} = 5$. 24 is a factor so eliminate (D). Lastly, $\dfrac{120}{60} = 2$. 60 is a factor, so eliminate (E). (C) is the correct answer.

2. **B** Either $(x + 2)$ or $(y - 4)$ must equal 0. Because $y < 0$, you know that $(y - 4)$ cannot equal 0. Therefore, $(x + 2)$ must equal 0, and x must be –2. If you chose (E), you chose the value for y to make $(y - 4) = 0$. If you chose (D), you confused your signs. The correct answer is (B).

3. **D** Since vertical angles are congruent, the measure of the bottom-left angle formed by lines f and g is 35°. The sum of the measures of the angles of a triangle is 180°; therefore, you can determine y by subtracting the measures of the two angles you know from 180: $180 - 90 - 35 = 55$.

4. **B** Use the charts in order to find out how much a bracelet and a scarf cost in New York ($5.25 for a bracelet and $21.00 for a scarf). Then, find out how many things fit in shipping box A (150 bracelets and 10 scarves). Multiply the information to find the total. (150 bracelets × $5.25) + (10 scarves × $21.00). This makes $787.50 + $210.00, which adds up to (B) $997.50.

5. **C** When a base number with an exponent is divided by a number that has the same base, subtract the bottom exponent from the top exponent. In other words, $a - 4 = 16$, so $a = 20$. Or, use the answers to find out which one is the value of a. Subtracting 4 from the value in the answers (A), $4 - 4 = 0$, resulting in 5^0, which equals 1, not 5^{16}. (B) would result in 5^8 (C) gives the 5^{16} seen in the question, and you could stop there, having found the correct answer. If you had incorrectly tried dividing the exponents, the result would be (D): $\dfrac{a}{4} = 16$, and $a = 64$. The correct answer is (C)

6. **C** Begin sketching square $ABCD$ by plotting the three given points. This square has been rotated 45° from what we normally think of, so it looks like a diamond: points A and C have the same y-value, so points B and D must have the same x-value. Therefore, you can eliminate choices (A), (B), and (E). The distance from A to C is 8 (subtract their x-values: $9 - 1 = 8$); because the diagonals of a square are equal in length, the distance from B to D must also be 8. Subtract 8 from the y-value of B: $7 - 8 = -1$, the y-value of D, making the correct answer (C).

7. **D** The positive odd integers less than 6 are 1, 3, and 5, so those are the possible values of a, b, and c. The question mentioned that a, b, and c are *distinct*, which means they're each a different integer. Now try out all the possible arrangements. There's $1(3^5) = 1(243) = 243$; $1(5^3) = 1(125) = 125$; $3(1^5) = 3(1) = 3$; $3(5^1) = 3(5) = 15$; $5(1^3) = 5(1) = 5$; $5(3^1) = 5(3) = 15$. So the possible values of $a(bc)$ are 243, 125, 3, 15, 5, and 15. Since the question asks how many *different* values there are, don't count 15 twice. There are five different values total.

8. **E** First eliminate any graphs in which the number of ice cream cones does not decrease each week over the six week period. We can get rid of (B) because the number of ice cream cones is increasing. We can eliminate (C) because it shows the number of ice cream cones decreasing every two weeks. Now eliminate graphs in which the number of cups of soup does not increase each week. Eliminate (A) because it shows the number of cups of soup decreasing each week. Get rid of (D) because the number of cups of soup stays the same each week. Only in (E) does the number of ice cream cones get smaller each week while the number of cups of soup gets bigger every week.

9. **A** Use the slope formula: $\frac{y_2 - y_1}{x_2 - x_1}$. Plugging In the points given in the problem, you get $\frac{a-0}{0-b}$, or $-\frac{a}{b}$. If you chose (C), you reversed either x_1 and x_2 or y_1 and y_2. If you chose (B) or (D), you inversed the slope formula by putting the x values on top of the fraction instead of the y values. The correct answer is (A).

10. **A** You'll need the volume of a cylinder formula from the box at the beginning of the math section: $V = \pi r^2 h$ when V is the volume, r is the radius, and h is the height. For container A, the radius is 4 inches and the height of the oil is 2 inches, so the volume of oil is $V = \pi \times 4^2 \times 2 = \pi \times 16 \times 2 = 32\pi$. For container B, the volume of the oil is the same but the radius is 2 inches, so put those numbers into the cylinder equation and solve for the height: $32\pi = \pi \times 2^2 \times h$, so $32\pi = 4\pi h$. Divide both sides by 4π to get $h = 8$.

11. **D** From the original equation, you know that when $w - x = 3$, $y + z = 4$. Use these values in the fraction in the question: $7w - 7x$ can be factored to $7(w - x)$. $7(3) = 21$, so the top of the fraction has a value of 21. Similarly, for the bottom of the fraction, $15(y + z) = 15(4) = 60$, giving a denominator of 60. $\frac{21}{60}$ reduces to $\frac{7}{20}$, answer (D).

12. **C** Plug In a value for x, such as .5. $-(.5)^2$ is $-.25$, which is closest to point C. If you answered (D), you forgot to take the negative of your square. If you answered (B) or (E), you doubled the value of x, leaving off the negative in one case. The correct answer is (C).

13. **B** When there are variables in the question and in the answer choices, try making up your own numbers. Let $a = 4$ and $b = 5$. That means c, the sum of a and b, is 9. The question asks for the average of a, b, and c: $\dfrac{a+b+c}{3} = \dfrac{18}{3} = 6$. Plug In $a = 4$, $b = 5$, and $c = 9$ in the answer choices and eliminate any that don't equal 6. Only (B) works. If you use algebra to solve, the average of a and b and their sum, c, is the same as $2c$ divided by 3.

14. **E** Draw the triangle, and then check each statement. Could X be on $\overline{AB}$? Sure, if it is the midpoint. Eliminate (B) and (D). Check statement II—could X be inside $\triangle ABC$? Yes, the only restriction on X is that it is equidistant from A and B. Eliminate (A). Although statement III seems "opposite" of statement II, due to the *inside* and *outside* locations, a point outside of the triangle could also be equidistant from A and B. The correct answer is (E).

15. **B** When you see variables in the answer choices, try making up your own numbers to make the math easier. Let's say that $w = \$100$, and that the retail price is 20% greater than the wholesale price, so $r = 20$. Lastly, let's say that the special promotion provides a 15% discount, so $s = 15$. Now work through the problem with these numbers: The markup on a \$100 car would be 20%, or \$20, so the retail price is \$120. During the special promotion, the \$120 is discounted by 15%. What is 15% of \$120? $120 \times \dfrac{15}{100} = \$18$, so the special promotion price is $\$120 - \$18 = \$102$. Plug the values for the variables we used above into the answer choices and choose the one that results in \$102. Only (B) works: $\$100 \times \left(1 + \dfrac{20}{100}\right) \times \left(1 - \dfrac{15}{100}\right) = \$102$.

16. **E** Begin by drawing rectangle *EFGH* as described. If you draw $\overline{EG}$, you'll see that it's the diagonal of the rectangle. The diagonal divides a rectangle into two right triangles: in this case, triangles *EFG* and *EGH*. Since the hypotenuse is the longest side of a triangle and $\overline{EG}$ is the hypotenuse of both of these right triangles, $\overline{EG}$ must be longer than 4.

SECTION 9

1. **B** The clue to the blank is that lavender oil has been used in *sleep aids and for relaxing aromatherapy.* The colon indicates that the word for the blank should mean roughly the same thing as the clue. Thus, the blank should mean something like "relaxing." The closest choice is *sedative* (B).

2. **E** What did his nonprofit do? It brought *about many changes* and developed *new programs.* You need a word that means change. (E) is the only one that comes close here. If you didn't know at least 3 of the words in the answer choices, this is probably a good question to skip.

3.   E   The sentence is about *the company's ability to expand*. The first blank could mean either "increased" or "decreased," so we must look at the second blank to determine which one. The words *even though* and *not* cancel each other out, and so both blanks must be positive or both negative. Thus, we are looking for an answer choice in which both words are going in the same direction. The only choice that accomplishes this is choice (E).

4.   D   The blank has to be a word that means *ill-tempered and mean*. Only option (D), *cantankerous*, fits. Although (E), *ancient*, could be used to describe an old man, it would not make him *the definition of…ill-tempered and mean.*

5.   A   The commissioner was *unwilling to* do something. It seems he wanted *to keep his job despite* something *that could end his career.* The first blank should suggest the loss of a job. We can keep (A) and (D), and any other answer choices with words you aren't sure about. For the second blank we need a word that means "attempted." Of all the choices, (A) is the best match for both blanks.

6.   D   The word "rather" tells us that the blank has to mean the opposite of *modern*. The blank should then mean something like "historical" or "old-fashioned." The closest word in the choices is (D), *obsolescent*, which means "obsolete" or "old-fashioned."

7.   D   The question in lines 3–4 is rhetorical; the author already knows the answer. The purpose is to back up his claim that *I knew all that was important to know about the world of art.* Answer choice (D) summarizes this nicely. None of the other answers are supported by the passage.

8.   E   The sentence in lines 7–9 provides more support for the author's claim that he *knew all that was important to know about the world of art.* Thus, it shows that he was *confident about his extensive knowledge of art* (E). The other answers are not supported by the passage.

9.   A   Use Process of Elimination on this one by eliminating everything that's mentioned in the passage. *Powerful stormy seascapes* gets rid of (B). *Graceful Grecian sculptures* and *regal and beautiful society portraits* get rid of (C) and (D). *Amazingly detailed work* gets rid of (E). Only (A) is never mentioned.

10.   D   The author's *judgment* is based primarily on age. He *insisted that good art must be old*, and even more importantly, *the later the date…the more contempt I heaped upon it.* This indicates that the author views all works from the same time period as equal. (D) paraphrases this nicely. The other answers are not supported by the passage.

11.   C   The author expresses his admiration for *masterpieces* by using words such as *patiently, painstakingly, meticulous,* and *time-consuming.* Thus, the correct answer must refer to these qualities as well. Only (C) accomplishes this. (A) indicates speed and impulsiveness, which is the opposite of what the author admires. (B) is out because the passage never mentions *value*, monetary or otherwise. The mention of *masters* and *apprentices* indicates that the author would frown upon *an untrained artist* (D). *Political leanings* (E) are never mentioned.

12. **B** The first three paragraphs lay out the author's love of old art and dislike of contemporary art. Beginning with the fourth paragraph, the author discusses Ms. Wright's class, which challenges and eventually transforms his views about contemporary art. Answer choice (B) paraphrases this nicely. The other answers are not supported by the passage.

13. **B** The key phrases in the paragraph are *stony indifference* and *I was not about abandon my…opinions*. These two points add up to *unsympathetic and inflexible* (B). The other answers are not supported by the passage.

14. **C** Substitute your own word for *juvenile*. "Basic" or "unskilled" would be appropriate choices. Both of these are closest to *inexpert*. Watch out for *spoiled* and *delinquent*, which are traps.

15. **A** The statement suggests that the author's prejudices prevented him from "seeing" the slides in an unbiased way. (A) is a succinct summary of this point. No *goals were thwarted* (B); he doesn't have a *desire for attention* (C); there's no *hasty decision* (D); there's no indication that his *vision was affected* (E).

16. **E** The author states that the *sculptures* were *simple* and *unadorned*, and asks *where was the detail?* He also emphasizes the uniform *gray* of both the room and the sculptures. These remarks support (E), a lack of *complexity and variety*. (A) and (B) are both half-right (which makes them all wrong), while (C) and (D) are not mentioned at all.

17. **D** Ms. Wright urges the class to *try not to think of each sculpture as an isolated work*. The author then realizes that the sculptures *worked together, perfectly placed within the empty spaces*. Thus, the relationship of a work of art to other works, as well as their placement within a room, affects how the work is perceived. Answer choice (D) sums up this point. The other answers are not supported by the passage.

18. **B** In the last paragraph, the author realizes that contemporary art might have some positive qualities after all. In context, the statement *Ms. Wright brought down the walls of a lifetime* clearly refers to the *author's preconceptions* (B).

SECTION 10

1. **D** The original sentence contains a pronoun error. The pronoun *it* cannot be used before the noun that it is replacing. This eliminates (A) and (B). (C) and (E) add a pronoun ambiguity error and must be eliminated as well. This leaves (D) as the best choice.

2. **C** The sentence contains a redundancy error. The use of *it* at the end of the sentence is redundant following the statement of the event itself. This eliminates (A) and (D). (E) introduces a verb tense error. (B) is more awkward and changes the meaning of the sentence in comparison to (C).

3. **B** The sentence as written uses the conjunction *because* incorrectly. (A) is therefore wrong. (C) is redundant, among other problems (*thus* and *finally* are unnecessarily repetitive). *Deciding* in (D) is a gerund when it should be the simple past *decided*, so (D) is incorrect. (E) is unnecessarily wordy. Therefore, (B) is the best answer.

4. **C** This sentence and its answers are full of problems. Focusing on one issue, ambiguous pronouns, will help you quickly arrive at the right answer. In the sentence as written, *its responsibility* is unclear: *its* is ambiguous. *It* could refer to the announcement, the public, or the coast. This problem is repeated in all of the answers except (C), which replaces *its* with *the public's*, thus removing the ambiguous pronoun.

5. **A** The sentence is correct as written. (B) is awkward and contains a vague pronoun. In (C) the sentence has a subject-verb agreement error: *permission* is singular, but the verb *require* is plural. There is also a diction error: *recommending* is not the proper noun form. (D) introduces a verb tense error—*requires* cannot be followed by an infinitive verb.

6. **D** The conjunction *and* makes this sentence awkward and the verb construction *was dragging* does not agree with the verb in the non-underlined portion of the sentence. (B) improves the conjunction, but the verb is in the wrong tense. (C) changes the meaning of the sentence, indicating that the reason *Agnes walked to the studio* was *to drag her cello*. Although (D) *dragging* partly has the same verb form as the original, it is a legitimate way to repair the sentence: without the *was*, the word *dragging* appropriately describes Agnes's action. (E) is incorrect because it changes the meaning to indicate that the studio was the place **in** which she dragged her cello, rather than the place **to** which she dragged her cello.

7. **B** This sentence has a subject-verb agreement error. *New rules* is a plural subject, while *requires* belongs with a singular subject. Eliminate (A) and (D). Of the three remaining choices, (B) is the best choice because it uses the correct idiom *require to* and avoids the *ing* words in (C) and (E).

8. **E** The sentence as written has a parallelism error. This is a very short list of two things the speaker is asking the listener to do. The first is *remind* (*her of what you have done*). The second is *a report* (*of your progress*). One is a verb, the other is a noun. Therefore, this list is not parallel. The only answer that offers a verb to parallel the verb in the non-underlined portion of the sentence is (E), *give*. None of the other answers is parallel.

9. **A** The sentence as written correctly sets up a comparison between nouns. (B) is awkward and not idiomatically correct. (C) and (D) contain comparison errors. (E) contains an idiom error. Only (A) clearly and concisely expresses that Burton's film is different from other films.

10. **B** The sentence as written has a subject/verb agreement problem (*great jazz music and delicious Cajun cuisine* are plural, *was* is singular). Eliminate (A). (B) fixes the problem. (C) and (E) have no verb and are therefore sentence fragments (the gerund *hindering* does not function as a verb). As (D) is written, we have the subject repeated twice, once as *great jazz music and delicious Cajun cuisine* and again as *they*, which is redundant.

11. **D** The sentence has a comma splice: two complete sentences cannot be joined by a comma. (B) also has a comma splice. (C) uses a semicolon, but the second half of the sentence is not a complete sentence on its own, so the semicolon is inappropriate. (D) correctly uses the semicolon to join two complete sentences that are related in content. (E) contains a misplaced modifier: the sentence says the *Category 4 hurricane…was caused by storm tracking being imprecise.*

12. **E** In the underlined portion, *them* refers to *the government* and is the incorrect pronoun to use because *the government* is a collective noun, and is singular. Eliminate (A) and (B) for incorrect pronouns. The singular subject *The disregard* does not match the plural verb *have* in the underlined portion of the sentence: it should be *has*. Eliminate (C). Of the two remaining answer choices, (D) brings a plural possessive *their* into the sentence unnecessarily. (E) is the only grammatically correct choice.

13. **A** The sentence as written correctly uses a semicolon to join two related thoughts that could stand on their own as complete sentences. (B) and (E) have misplaced modifiers: they indicate that *good grades…can lead to an increase in the graduation rate* when the sentence seems to mean that the *programs* are what lead to the increased graduation rate. (C) creates a comma splice. (D) forms an incomplete sentence due to the phrase that begins *while…*

14. **C** The sentence as written incorrectly uses "most" to compare two things (*young animals* and *older animals*). (D) can be eliminated for the same reason. (B) incorrectly uses the word *compared*, and, when in doubt, remember, K.I.S.S, Keep It Short and Simple, another reason to pick (C) over (B). (E) uses a false comparison (*young animals* to *in older animals*).

Chapter 8
Practice Test 3

Your Name (print)			
	Last	First	Middle
Date			

IMPORTANT: The following codes should be copied onto your answer sheet exactly as shown.

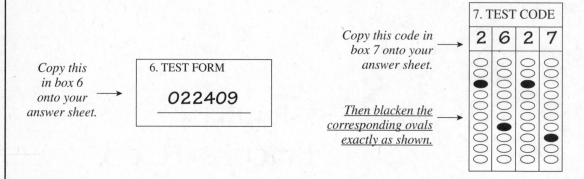

Copy this in box 6 onto your answer sheet. →

6. TEST FORM

022409

Copy this code in box 7 onto your answer sheet. →

Then blacken the corresponding ovals exactly as shown. →

7. TEST CODE

2 6 2 7

General Directions

You will have three hours and 20 minutes to work on this objective test designed to familiarize you with all aspects of the SAT.

This test contains five 25-minute sections, two 20-minute sections, one 10-minute section, and one 25-minute essay. The supervisor will tell you when to begin and end each section. During the time allowed for each section, you may work only on that particular section. If you finish your work before time is called, you may check your work on that section, but you are not to work on any other section.

You will find specific directions for each type of question found in the test. **Be sure you understand the directions before attempting to answer any of the questions.**

YOU ARE TO INDICATE ALL YOUR ANSWERS ON THE SEPARATE ANSWER SHEET:

1. The test booklet may be used for scratchwork. However, no credit will be given for anything written in the test booklet.

2. Once you have decided on an answer to a question, darken the corresponding space on the answer sheet. Give only one answer to each question.

3. There are 40 numbered answer spaces for each section; be sure to use only those spaces that correspond to the test questions.

4. **Be sure each answer mark is dark and completely fills the answer space.** Do not make any stray marks on your answer sheet.

5. If you wish to change an answer, erase your first mark completely—an incomplete erasure may be considered an intended response—and blacken your new answer choice.

Your score on this test is based on the number of questions you answer correctly minus a fraction of the number of questions you answer incorrectly. Therefore, it is improbable that random or haphazard guessing will alter your score significantly. There are no deductions for incorrect answers on the student-produced response questions. However, if you are able to eliminate one or more of the answer choices on any question as wrong, it is generally to your advantage to guess at one of the remaining choices. Remember, however, not to spend too much time on any one question.

Diagnostic Test Form

Use a No. 2 pencil only. Be sure each mark is dark and completely fills the intended oval. Completely erase any errors or stray marks.

1 Your Name:

(Print) _____
Last   First   M.I.

Signature: _____   Date ___/___/___

Home Address: _____
Number and Street   City   State   Zip Code

E-Mail: _____   School: _____   Class: _____
(Print)

2 YOUR NAME

Last Name
(First 4 Letters)

				FIRST INIT	MID INIT
	⊖	⊖	⊖		
	⊙	⊙	⊙		
	◯	◯	◯		
Ⓐ	Ⓐ	Ⓐ	Ⓐ	Ⓐ	Ⓐ
Ⓑ	Ⓑ	Ⓑ	Ⓑ	Ⓑ	Ⓑ
Ⓒ	Ⓒ	Ⓒ	Ⓒ	Ⓒ	Ⓒ
Ⓓ	Ⓓ	Ⓓ	Ⓓ	Ⓓ	Ⓓ
Ⓔ	Ⓔ	Ⓔ	Ⓔ	Ⓔ	Ⓔ
Ⓕ	Ⓕ	Ⓕ	Ⓕ	Ⓕ	Ⓕ
Ⓖ	Ⓖ	Ⓖ	Ⓖ	Ⓖ	Ⓖ
Ⓗ	Ⓗ	Ⓗ	Ⓗ	Ⓗ	Ⓗ
Ⓘ	Ⓘ	Ⓘ	Ⓘ	Ⓘ	Ⓘ
Ⓙ	Ⓙ	Ⓙ	Ⓙ	Ⓙ	Ⓙ
Ⓚ	Ⓚ	Ⓚ	Ⓚ	Ⓚ	Ⓚ
Ⓛ	Ⓛ	Ⓛ	Ⓛ	Ⓛ	Ⓛ
Ⓜ	Ⓜ	Ⓜ	Ⓜ	Ⓜ	Ⓜ
Ⓝ	Ⓝ	Ⓝ	Ⓝ	Ⓝ	Ⓝ
Ⓞ	Ⓞ	Ⓞ	Ⓞ	Ⓞ	Ⓞ
Ⓟ	Ⓟ	Ⓟ	Ⓟ	Ⓟ	Ⓟ
Ⓠ	Ⓠ	Ⓠ	Ⓠ	Ⓠ	Ⓠ
Ⓡ	Ⓡ	Ⓡ	Ⓡ	Ⓡ	Ⓡ
Ⓢ	Ⓢ	Ⓢ	Ⓢ	Ⓢ	Ⓢ
Ⓣ	Ⓣ	Ⓣ	Ⓣ	Ⓣ	Ⓣ
Ⓤ	Ⓤ	Ⓤ	Ⓤ	Ⓤ	Ⓤ
Ⓥ	Ⓥ	Ⓥ	Ⓥ	Ⓥ	Ⓥ
Ⓦ	Ⓦ	Ⓦ	Ⓦ	Ⓦ	Ⓦ
Ⓧ	Ⓧ	Ⓧ	Ⓧ	Ⓧ	Ⓧ
Ⓨ	Ⓨ	Ⓨ	Ⓨ	Ⓨ	Ⓨ
Ⓩ	Ⓩ	Ⓩ	Ⓩ	Ⓩ	Ⓩ

3 PHONE NUMBER

⓪	⓪	⓪	⓪	⓪	⓪	⓪
①	①	①	①	①	①	①
②	②	②	②	②	②	②
③	③	③	③	③	③	③
④	④	④	④	④	④	④
⑤	⑤	⑤	⑤	⑤	⑤	⑤
⑥	⑥	⑥	⑥	⑥	⑥	⑥
⑦	⑦	⑦	⑦	⑦	⑦	⑦
⑧	⑧	⑧	⑧	⑧	⑧	⑧
⑨	⑨	⑨	⑨	⑨	⑨	⑨

4 DATE OF BIRTH

MONTH	DAY		YEAR	
◯ JAN				
◯ FEB				
◯ MAR	⓪	⓪		⓪
◯ APR	①	①		①
◯ MAY	②	②		②
◯ JUN	③	③		③
◯ JUL		④		④
◯ AUG		⑤	⑤	⑤
◯ SEP		⑥	⑥	⑥
◯ OCT		⑦	⑦	⑦
◯ NOV		⑧	⑧	⑧
◯ DEC		⑨	⑨	⑨

5 SEX
◯ MALE
◯ FEMALE

IMPORTANT: Fill in items 6 and 7 exactly as shown on the preceding page.

6 TEST FORM
(Copy from back of test book)

7 TEST CODE

⓪	⓪	⓪	⓪
①	①	①	①
②	②	②	②
③	③	③	③
④	④	④	④
⑤	⑤	⑤	⑤
⑥	⑥	⑥	⑥
⑦	⑦	⑦	⑦
⑧	⑧	⑧	⑧
⑨	⑨	⑨	⑨

8 OTHER
1 Ⓐ Ⓑ Ⓒ Ⓓ Ⓔ
2 Ⓐ Ⓑ Ⓒ Ⓓ Ⓔ
3 Ⓐ Ⓑ Ⓒ Ⓓ Ⓔ

PLEASE DO NOT WRITE IN THIS AREA

◻ ◯◯◯◯◯◯◯◯◯◯◯◯◯◯◯◯◯

SERIAL #

THIS PAGE INTENTIONALLY LEFT BLANK

SECTION 1

IMPORTANT: **USE A NO. 2 PENCIL. DO NOT WRITE OUTSIDE THE BORDER!**
Words written outside the essay box or written in ink **WILL NOT APPEAR** in the copy
sent to be scored and your score will be affected.

Begin your essay on this page. If you need more space, continue on the next page.

Continue on the next page, if necessary.

Continuation of ESSAY Section 1 from previous page. Write below only if you need more space.
IMPORTANT: DO NOT START on this page—if you do, your essay may appear blank and your score may be affected.

SERIAL #

SECTION 2

1 Ⓐ Ⓑ Ⓒ Ⓓ Ⓔ
2 Ⓐ Ⓑ Ⓒ Ⓓ Ⓔ
3 Ⓐ Ⓑ Ⓒ Ⓓ Ⓔ
4 Ⓐ Ⓑ Ⓒ Ⓓ Ⓔ
5 Ⓐ Ⓑ Ⓒ Ⓓ Ⓔ
6 Ⓐ Ⓑ Ⓒ Ⓓ Ⓔ
7 Ⓐ Ⓑ Ⓒ Ⓓ Ⓔ
8 Ⓐ Ⓑ Ⓒ Ⓓ Ⓔ
9 Ⓐ Ⓑ Ⓒ Ⓓ Ⓔ
10 Ⓐ Ⓑ Ⓒ Ⓓ Ⓔ

11 Ⓐ Ⓑ Ⓒ Ⓓ Ⓔ
12 Ⓐ Ⓑ Ⓒ Ⓓ Ⓔ
13 Ⓐ Ⓑ Ⓒ Ⓓ Ⓔ
14 Ⓐ Ⓑ Ⓒ Ⓓ Ⓔ
15 Ⓐ Ⓑ Ⓒ Ⓓ Ⓔ
16 Ⓐ Ⓑ Ⓒ Ⓓ Ⓔ
17 Ⓐ Ⓑ Ⓒ Ⓓ Ⓔ
18 Ⓐ Ⓑ Ⓒ Ⓓ Ⓔ
19 Ⓐ Ⓑ Ⓒ Ⓓ Ⓔ
20 Ⓐ Ⓑ Ⓒ Ⓓ Ⓔ

21 Ⓐ Ⓑ Ⓒ Ⓓ Ⓔ
22 Ⓐ Ⓑ Ⓒ Ⓓ Ⓔ
23 Ⓐ Ⓑ Ⓒ Ⓓ Ⓔ
24 Ⓐ Ⓑ Ⓒ Ⓓ Ⓔ
25 Ⓐ Ⓑ Ⓒ Ⓓ Ⓔ
26 Ⓐ Ⓑ Ⓒ Ⓓ Ⓔ
27 Ⓐ Ⓑ Ⓒ Ⓓ Ⓔ
28 Ⓐ Ⓑ Ⓒ Ⓓ Ⓔ
29 Ⓐ Ⓑ Ⓒ Ⓓ Ⓔ
30 Ⓐ Ⓑ Ⓒ Ⓓ Ⓔ

31 Ⓐ Ⓑ Ⓒ Ⓓ Ⓔ
32 Ⓐ Ⓑ Ⓒ Ⓓ Ⓔ
33 Ⓐ Ⓑ Ⓒ Ⓓ Ⓔ
34 Ⓐ Ⓑ Ⓒ Ⓓ Ⓔ
35 Ⓐ Ⓑ Ⓒ Ⓓ Ⓔ
36 Ⓐ Ⓑ Ⓒ Ⓓ Ⓔ
37 Ⓐ Ⓑ Ⓒ Ⓓ Ⓔ
38 Ⓐ Ⓑ Ⓒ Ⓓ Ⓔ
39 Ⓐ Ⓑ Ⓒ Ⓓ Ⓔ
40 Ⓐ Ⓑ Ⓒ Ⓓ Ⓔ

SECTION 3

1 Ⓐ Ⓑ Ⓒ Ⓓ Ⓔ
2 Ⓐ Ⓑ Ⓒ Ⓓ Ⓔ
3 Ⓐ Ⓑ Ⓒ Ⓓ Ⓔ
4 Ⓐ Ⓑ Ⓒ Ⓓ Ⓔ
5 Ⓐ Ⓑ Ⓒ Ⓓ Ⓔ
6 Ⓐ Ⓑ Ⓒ Ⓓ Ⓔ
7 Ⓐ Ⓑ Ⓒ Ⓓ Ⓔ
8 Ⓐ Ⓑ Ⓒ Ⓓ Ⓔ
9 Ⓐ Ⓑ Ⓒ Ⓓ Ⓔ
10 Ⓐ Ⓑ Ⓒ Ⓓ Ⓔ

11 Ⓐ Ⓑ Ⓒ Ⓓ Ⓔ
12 Ⓐ Ⓑ Ⓒ Ⓓ Ⓔ
13 Ⓐ Ⓑ Ⓒ Ⓓ Ⓔ
14 Ⓐ Ⓑ Ⓒ Ⓓ Ⓔ
15 Ⓐ Ⓑ Ⓒ Ⓓ Ⓔ
16 Ⓐ Ⓑ Ⓒ Ⓓ Ⓔ
17 Ⓐ Ⓑ Ⓒ Ⓓ Ⓔ
18 Ⓐ Ⓑ Ⓒ Ⓓ Ⓔ
19 Ⓐ Ⓑ Ⓒ Ⓓ Ⓔ
20 Ⓐ Ⓑ Ⓒ Ⓓ Ⓔ

21 Ⓐ Ⓑ Ⓒ Ⓓ Ⓔ
22 Ⓐ Ⓑ Ⓒ Ⓓ Ⓔ
23 Ⓐ Ⓑ Ⓒ Ⓓ Ⓔ
24 Ⓐ Ⓑ Ⓒ Ⓓ Ⓔ
25 Ⓐ Ⓑ Ⓒ Ⓓ Ⓔ
26 Ⓐ Ⓑ Ⓒ Ⓓ Ⓔ
27 Ⓐ Ⓑ Ⓒ Ⓓ Ⓔ
28 Ⓐ Ⓑ Ⓒ Ⓓ Ⓔ
29 Ⓐ Ⓑ Ⓒ Ⓓ Ⓔ
30 Ⓐ Ⓑ Ⓒ Ⓓ Ⓔ

31 Ⓐ Ⓑ Ⓒ Ⓓ Ⓔ
32 Ⓐ Ⓑ Ⓒ Ⓓ Ⓔ
33 Ⓐ Ⓑ Ⓒ Ⓓ Ⓔ
34 Ⓐ Ⓑ Ⓒ Ⓓ Ⓔ
35 Ⓐ Ⓑ Ⓒ Ⓓ Ⓔ
36 Ⓐ Ⓑ Ⓒ Ⓓ Ⓔ
37 Ⓐ Ⓑ Ⓒ Ⓓ Ⓔ
38 Ⓐ Ⓑ Ⓒ Ⓓ Ⓔ
39 Ⓐ Ⓑ Ⓒ Ⓓ Ⓔ
40 Ⓐ Ⓑ Ⓒ Ⓓ Ⓔ

CAUTION Grid answers in the section below for SECTION 2 or SECTION 3 only if directed to do so in your test book.

Student-Produced Responses

ONLY ANSWERS THAT ARE GRIDDED WILL BE SCORED. YOU WILL NOT RECEIVE CREDIT FOR ANYTHING WRITTEN IN THE BOXES.

Quality Assurance Mark ●

9, 10, 11, 12, 13, 14, 15, 16, 17, 18 — grid answer boxes with digits 0–9.

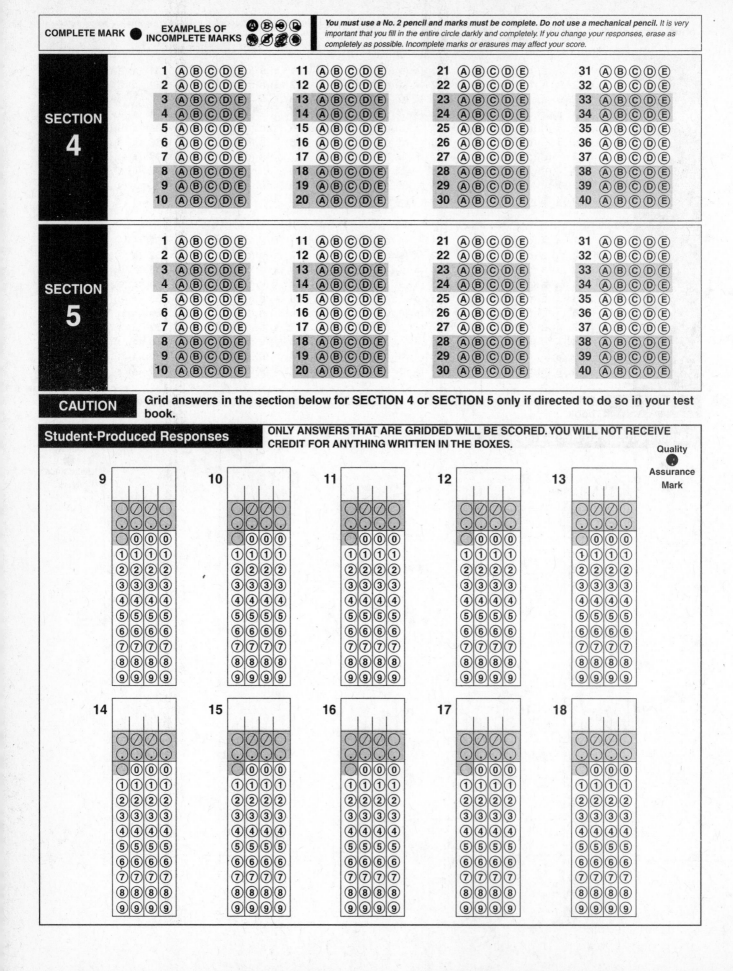

SECTION 6

1 Ⓐ Ⓑ Ⓒ Ⓓ Ⓔ
2 Ⓐ Ⓑ Ⓒ Ⓓ Ⓔ
3 Ⓐ Ⓑ Ⓒ Ⓓ Ⓔ
4 Ⓐ Ⓑ Ⓒ Ⓓ Ⓔ
5 Ⓐ Ⓑ Ⓒ Ⓓ Ⓔ
6 Ⓐ Ⓑ Ⓒ Ⓓ Ⓔ
7 Ⓐ Ⓑ Ⓒ Ⓓ Ⓔ
8 Ⓐ Ⓑ Ⓒ Ⓓ Ⓔ
9 Ⓐ Ⓑ Ⓒ Ⓓ Ⓔ
10 Ⓐ Ⓑ Ⓒ Ⓓ Ⓔ

11 Ⓐ Ⓑ Ⓒ Ⓓ Ⓔ
12 Ⓐ Ⓑ Ⓒ Ⓓ Ⓔ
13 Ⓐ Ⓑ Ⓒ Ⓓ Ⓔ
14 Ⓐ Ⓑ Ⓒ Ⓓ Ⓔ
15 Ⓐ Ⓑ Ⓒ Ⓓ Ⓔ
16 Ⓐ Ⓑ Ⓒ Ⓓ Ⓔ
17 Ⓐ Ⓑ Ⓒ Ⓓ Ⓔ
18 Ⓐ Ⓑ Ⓒ Ⓓ Ⓔ
19 Ⓐ Ⓑ Ⓒ Ⓓ Ⓔ
20 Ⓐ Ⓑ Ⓒ Ⓓ Ⓔ

21 Ⓐ Ⓑ Ⓒ Ⓓ Ⓔ
22 Ⓐ Ⓑ Ⓒ Ⓓ Ⓔ
23 Ⓐ Ⓑ Ⓒ Ⓓ Ⓔ
24 Ⓐ Ⓑ Ⓒ Ⓓ Ⓔ
25 Ⓐ Ⓑ Ⓒ Ⓓ Ⓔ
26 Ⓐ Ⓑ Ⓒ Ⓓ Ⓔ
27 Ⓐ Ⓑ Ⓒ Ⓓ Ⓔ
28 Ⓐ Ⓑ Ⓒ Ⓓ Ⓔ
29 Ⓐ Ⓑ Ⓒ Ⓓ Ⓔ
30 Ⓐ Ⓑ Ⓒ Ⓓ Ⓔ

31 Ⓐ Ⓑ Ⓒ Ⓓ Ⓔ
32 Ⓐ Ⓑ Ⓒ Ⓓ Ⓔ
33 Ⓐ Ⓑ Ⓒ Ⓓ Ⓔ
34 Ⓐ Ⓑ Ⓒ Ⓓ Ⓔ
35 Ⓐ Ⓑ Ⓒ Ⓓ Ⓔ
36 Ⓐ Ⓑ Ⓒ Ⓓ Ⓔ
37 Ⓐ Ⓑ Ⓒ Ⓓ Ⓔ
38 Ⓐ Ⓑ Ⓒ Ⓓ Ⓔ
39 Ⓐ Ⓑ Ⓒ Ⓓ Ⓔ
40 Ⓐ Ⓑ Ⓒ Ⓓ Ⓔ

SECTION 7

1 Ⓐ Ⓑ Ⓒ Ⓓ Ⓔ
2 Ⓐ Ⓑ Ⓒ Ⓓ Ⓔ
3 Ⓐ Ⓑ Ⓒ Ⓓ Ⓔ
4 Ⓐ Ⓑ Ⓒ Ⓓ Ⓔ
5 Ⓐ Ⓑ Ⓒ Ⓓ Ⓔ
6 Ⓐ Ⓑ Ⓒ Ⓓ Ⓔ
7 Ⓐ Ⓑ Ⓒ Ⓓ Ⓔ
8 Ⓐ Ⓑ Ⓒ Ⓓ Ⓔ
9 Ⓐ Ⓑ Ⓒ Ⓓ Ⓔ
10 Ⓐ Ⓑ Ⓒ Ⓓ Ⓔ

11 Ⓐ Ⓑ Ⓒ Ⓓ Ⓔ
12 Ⓐ Ⓑ Ⓒ Ⓓ Ⓔ
13 Ⓐ Ⓑ Ⓒ Ⓓ Ⓔ
14 Ⓐ Ⓑ Ⓒ Ⓓ Ⓔ
15 Ⓐ Ⓑ Ⓒ Ⓓ Ⓔ
16 Ⓐ Ⓑ Ⓒ Ⓓ Ⓔ
17 Ⓐ Ⓑ Ⓒ Ⓓ Ⓔ
18 Ⓐ Ⓑ Ⓒ Ⓓ Ⓔ
19 Ⓐ Ⓑ Ⓒ Ⓓ Ⓔ
20 Ⓐ Ⓑ Ⓒ Ⓓ Ⓔ

21 Ⓐ Ⓑ Ⓒ Ⓓ Ⓔ
22 Ⓐ Ⓑ Ⓒ Ⓓ Ⓔ
23 Ⓐ Ⓑ Ⓒ Ⓓ Ⓔ
24 Ⓐ Ⓑ Ⓒ Ⓓ Ⓔ
25 Ⓐ Ⓑ Ⓒ Ⓓ Ⓔ
26 Ⓐ Ⓑ Ⓒ Ⓓ Ⓔ
27 Ⓐ Ⓑ Ⓒ Ⓓ Ⓔ
28 Ⓐ Ⓑ Ⓒ Ⓓ Ⓔ
29 Ⓐ Ⓑ Ⓒ Ⓓ Ⓔ
30 Ⓐ Ⓑ Ⓒ Ⓓ Ⓔ

31 Ⓐ Ⓑ Ⓒ Ⓓ Ⓔ
32 Ⓐ Ⓑ Ⓒ Ⓓ Ⓔ
33 Ⓐ Ⓑ Ⓒ Ⓓ Ⓔ
34 Ⓐ Ⓑ Ⓒ Ⓓ Ⓔ
35 Ⓐ Ⓑ Ⓒ Ⓓ Ⓔ
36 Ⓐ Ⓑ Ⓒ Ⓓ Ⓔ
37 Ⓐ Ⓑ Ⓒ Ⓓ Ⓔ
38 Ⓐ Ⓑ Ⓒ Ⓓ Ⓔ
39 Ⓐ Ⓑ Ⓒ Ⓓ Ⓔ
40 Ⓐ Ⓑ Ⓒ Ⓓ Ⓔ

CAUTION Grid answers in the section below for SECTION 6 or SECTION 7 only if directed to do so in your test book.

Student-Produced Responses

ONLY ANSWERS THAT ARE GRIDDED WILL BE SCORED. YOU WILL NOT RECEIVE CREDIT FOR ANYTHING WRITTEN IN THE BOXES.

Quality Assurance Mark

9 10 11 12 13

14 15 16 17 18

COMPLETE MARK ● **EXAMPLES OF INCOMPLETE MARKS** Ⓐ Ⓑ ⊖ Ⓓ ⊗ ∅ ⊘ ⊙

You must use a No. 2 pencil and marks must be complete. Do not use a mechanical pencil. It is very important that you fill in the entire circle darkly and completely. If you change your responses, erase as completely as possible. Incomplete marks or erasures may affect your score.

SECTION 8

1 Ⓐ Ⓑ Ⓒ Ⓓ Ⓔ	11 Ⓐ Ⓑ Ⓒ Ⓓ Ⓔ	21 Ⓐ Ⓑ Ⓒ Ⓓ Ⓔ	31 Ⓐ Ⓑ Ⓒ Ⓓ Ⓔ
2 Ⓐ Ⓑ Ⓒ Ⓓ Ⓔ	12 Ⓐ Ⓑ Ⓒ Ⓓ Ⓔ	22 Ⓐ Ⓑ Ⓒ Ⓓ Ⓔ	32 Ⓐ Ⓑ Ⓒ Ⓓ Ⓔ
3 Ⓐ Ⓑ Ⓒ Ⓓ Ⓔ	13 Ⓐ Ⓑ Ⓒ Ⓓ Ⓔ	23 Ⓐ Ⓑ Ⓒ Ⓓ Ⓔ	33 Ⓐ Ⓑ Ⓒ Ⓓ Ⓔ
4 Ⓐ Ⓑ Ⓒ Ⓓ Ⓔ	14 Ⓐ Ⓑ Ⓒ Ⓓ Ⓔ	24 Ⓐ Ⓑ Ⓒ Ⓓ Ⓔ	34 Ⓐ Ⓑ Ⓒ Ⓓ Ⓔ
5 Ⓐ Ⓑ Ⓒ Ⓓ Ⓔ	15 Ⓐ Ⓑ Ⓒ Ⓓ Ⓔ	25 Ⓐ Ⓑ Ⓒ Ⓓ Ⓔ	35 Ⓐ Ⓑ Ⓒ Ⓓ Ⓔ
6 Ⓐ Ⓑ Ⓒ Ⓓ Ⓔ	16 Ⓐ Ⓑ Ⓒ Ⓓ Ⓔ	26 Ⓐ Ⓑ Ⓒ Ⓓ Ⓔ	36 Ⓐ Ⓑ Ⓒ Ⓓ Ⓔ
7 Ⓐ Ⓑ Ⓒ Ⓓ Ⓔ	17 Ⓐ Ⓑ Ⓒ Ⓓ Ⓔ	27 Ⓐ Ⓑ Ⓒ Ⓓ Ⓔ	37 Ⓐ Ⓑ Ⓒ Ⓓ Ⓔ
8 Ⓐ Ⓑ Ⓒ Ⓓ Ⓔ	18 Ⓐ Ⓑ Ⓒ Ⓓ Ⓔ	28 Ⓐ Ⓑ Ⓒ Ⓓ Ⓔ	38 Ⓐ Ⓑ Ⓒ Ⓓ Ⓔ
9 Ⓐ Ⓑ Ⓒ Ⓓ Ⓔ	19 Ⓐ Ⓑ Ⓒ Ⓓ Ⓔ	29 Ⓐ Ⓑ Ⓒ Ⓓ Ⓔ	39 Ⓐ Ⓑ Ⓒ Ⓓ Ⓔ
10 Ⓐ Ⓑ Ⓒ Ⓓ Ⓔ	20 Ⓐ Ⓑ Ⓒ Ⓓ Ⓔ	30 Ⓐ Ⓑ Ⓒ Ⓓ Ⓔ	40 Ⓐ Ⓑ Ⓒ Ⓓ Ⓔ

SECTION 9

1 Ⓐ Ⓑ Ⓒ Ⓓ Ⓔ	11 Ⓐ Ⓑ Ⓒ Ⓓ Ⓔ	21 Ⓐ Ⓑ Ⓒ Ⓓ Ⓔ	31 Ⓐ Ⓑ Ⓒ Ⓓ Ⓔ
2 Ⓐ Ⓑ Ⓒ Ⓓ Ⓔ	12 Ⓐ Ⓑ Ⓒ Ⓓ Ⓔ	22 Ⓐ Ⓑ Ⓒ Ⓓ Ⓔ	32 Ⓐ Ⓑ Ⓒ Ⓓ Ⓔ
3 Ⓐ Ⓑ Ⓒ Ⓓ Ⓔ	13 Ⓐ Ⓑ Ⓒ Ⓓ Ⓔ	23 Ⓐ Ⓑ Ⓒ Ⓓ Ⓔ	33 Ⓐ Ⓑ Ⓒ Ⓓ Ⓔ
4 Ⓐ Ⓑ Ⓒ Ⓓ Ⓔ	14 Ⓐ Ⓑ Ⓒ Ⓓ Ⓔ	24 Ⓐ Ⓑ Ⓒ Ⓓ Ⓔ	34 Ⓐ Ⓑ Ⓒ Ⓓ Ⓔ
5 Ⓐ Ⓑ Ⓒ Ⓓ Ⓔ	15 Ⓐ Ⓑ Ⓒ Ⓓ Ⓔ	25 Ⓐ Ⓑ Ⓒ Ⓓ Ⓔ	35 Ⓐ Ⓑ Ⓒ Ⓓ Ⓔ
6 Ⓐ Ⓑ Ⓒ Ⓓ Ⓔ	16 Ⓐ Ⓑ Ⓒ Ⓓ Ⓔ	26 Ⓐ Ⓑ Ⓒ Ⓓ Ⓔ	36 Ⓐ Ⓑ Ⓒ Ⓓ Ⓔ
7 Ⓐ Ⓑ Ⓒ Ⓓ Ⓔ	17 Ⓐ Ⓑ Ⓒ Ⓓ Ⓔ	27 Ⓐ Ⓑ Ⓒ Ⓓ Ⓔ	37 Ⓐ Ⓑ Ⓒ Ⓓ Ⓔ
8 Ⓐ Ⓑ Ⓒ Ⓓ Ⓔ	18 Ⓐ Ⓑ Ⓒ Ⓓ Ⓔ	28 Ⓐ Ⓑ Ⓒ Ⓓ Ⓔ	38 Ⓐ Ⓑ Ⓒ Ⓓ Ⓔ
9 Ⓐ Ⓑ Ⓒ Ⓓ Ⓔ	19 Ⓐ Ⓑ Ⓒ Ⓓ Ⓔ	29 Ⓐ Ⓑ Ⓒ Ⓓ Ⓔ	39 Ⓐ Ⓑ Ⓒ Ⓓ Ⓔ
10 Ⓐ Ⓑ Ⓒ Ⓓ Ⓔ	20 Ⓐ Ⓑ Ⓒ Ⓓ Ⓔ	30 Ⓐ Ⓑ Ⓒ Ⓓ Ⓔ	40 Ⓐ Ⓑ Ⓒ Ⓓ Ⓔ

SECTION 10

1 Ⓐ Ⓑ Ⓒ Ⓓ Ⓔ	11 Ⓐ Ⓑ Ⓒ Ⓓ Ⓔ	21 Ⓐ Ⓑ Ⓒ Ⓓ Ⓔ	31 Ⓐ Ⓑ Ⓒ Ⓓ Ⓔ
2 Ⓐ Ⓑ Ⓒ Ⓓ Ⓔ	12 Ⓐ Ⓑ Ⓒ Ⓓ Ⓔ	22 Ⓐ Ⓑ Ⓒ Ⓓ Ⓔ	32 Ⓐ Ⓑ Ⓒ Ⓓ Ⓔ
3 Ⓐ Ⓑ Ⓒ Ⓓ Ⓔ	13 Ⓐ Ⓑ Ⓒ Ⓓ Ⓔ	23 Ⓐ Ⓑ Ⓒ Ⓓ Ⓔ	33 Ⓐ Ⓑ Ⓒ Ⓓ Ⓔ
4 Ⓐ Ⓑ Ⓒ Ⓓ Ⓔ	14 Ⓐ Ⓑ Ⓒ Ⓓ Ⓔ	24 Ⓐ Ⓑ Ⓒ Ⓓ Ⓔ	34 Ⓐ Ⓑ Ⓒ Ⓓ Ⓔ
5 Ⓐ Ⓑ Ⓒ Ⓓ Ⓔ	15 Ⓐ Ⓑ Ⓒ Ⓓ Ⓔ	25 Ⓐ Ⓑ Ⓒ Ⓓ Ⓔ	35 Ⓐ Ⓑ Ⓒ Ⓓ Ⓔ
6 Ⓐ Ⓑ Ⓒ Ⓓ Ⓔ	16 Ⓐ Ⓑ Ⓒ Ⓓ Ⓔ	26 Ⓐ Ⓑ Ⓒ Ⓓ Ⓔ	36 Ⓐ Ⓑ Ⓒ Ⓓ Ⓔ
7 Ⓐ Ⓑ Ⓒ Ⓓ Ⓔ	17 Ⓐ Ⓑ Ⓒ Ⓓ Ⓔ	27 Ⓐ Ⓑ Ⓒ Ⓓ Ⓔ	37 Ⓐ Ⓑ Ⓒ Ⓓ Ⓔ
8 Ⓐ Ⓑ Ⓒ Ⓓ Ⓔ	18 Ⓐ Ⓑ Ⓒ Ⓓ Ⓔ	28 Ⓐ Ⓑ Ⓒ Ⓓ Ⓔ	38 Ⓐ Ⓑ Ⓒ Ⓓ Ⓔ
9 Ⓐ Ⓑ Ⓒ Ⓓ Ⓔ	19 Ⓐ Ⓑ Ⓒ Ⓓ Ⓔ	29 Ⓐ Ⓑ Ⓒ Ⓓ Ⓔ	39 Ⓐ Ⓑ Ⓒ Ⓓ Ⓔ
10 Ⓐ Ⓑ Ⓒ Ⓓ Ⓔ	20 Ⓐ Ⓑ Ⓒ Ⓓ Ⓔ	30 Ⓐ Ⓑ Ⓒ Ⓓ Ⓔ	40 Ⓐ Ⓑ Ⓒ Ⓓ Ⓔ

SECTION 1
ESSAY
Time — 25 minutes

Turn to Section 1 of your answer sheet to write your essay.

The essay gives you an opportunity to show how effectively you can develop and express ideas. You should, therefore, take care to develop your point of view, present your ideas logically and clearly, and use language precisely.

Your essay must be written on the lines provided on your answer sheet—you will receive no other paper on which to write. You will have enough space if you write on every line, avoid wide margins, and keep your handwriting to a reasonable size. Remember that people who are not familiar with your handwriting will read what you write. Try to write or print so that what you are writing is legible to those readers.

You have twenty-five minutes to write an essay on the topic assigned below. DO NOT WRITE ON ANOTHER TOPIC. AN OFF-TOPIC ESSAY WILL RECEIVE A SCORE OF ZERO.

Think carefully about the issue presented in the following excerpt and the assignment below.

> If the First Amendment means anything, it means that a State has no business telling a man, sitting alone in his own home, what books he may read or what films he may watch. Our whole constitutional heritage rebels at the thought of giving government the power to control men's minds.
>
> U.S. Supreme Court Justice Thurgood Marshall

Assignment: Can censorship limit people's rights? In an essay, support your position by discussing an example (or examples) from literature, the arts, science and technology, history, current events, or your own experience or observation.

DO NOT WRITE YOUR ESSAY IN YOUR TEST BOOK. You will receive credit only for what you write on your answer sheet.

BEGIN WRITING YOUR ESSAY IN SECTION 1 OF THE ANSWER SHEET.

STOP
**If you finish before time is called, you may check your work on this section only.
Do not turn to any other section in the test.**

SECTION 2
Time — 25 minutes
20 Questions

Turn to Section 2 of your answer sheet to answer the questions in this section.

Directions: For this section, solve each problem and decide which is the best of the choices given. Fill in the corresponding circle on the answer sheet. You may use any available space for scratchwork.

Notes

1. The use of a calculator is permitted.

2. All numbers used are real numbers.

3. Figures that accompany problems in this test are intended to provide information useful in solving the problems. They are drawn as accurately as possible EXCEPT when it is stated in a specific problem that the figure is not drawn to scale. All figures lie in a plane unless otherwise indicated.

4. Unless otherwise specified, the domain of any function f is assumed to be the set of all real numbers x for which $f(x)$ is a real number.

Reference Information

   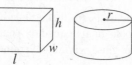 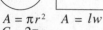 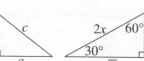

$A = \pi r^2$ $A = lw$ $A = \frac{1}{2}bh$ $V = lwh$ $V = \pi r^2 h$ $c^2 = a^2 + b^2$ Special Right Triangles
$C = 2\pi r$

The number of degrees of arc in a circle is 360.

The sum of the measures in degrees of the angles of a triangle is 180.

---

1. What number increased by 4 is equal to 19 decreased by 4 ?

(A) 10
(B) 11
(C) 15
(D) 19
(E) 27

2. Marvin eats 3 bananas and 1 apple every day. If the cost of each banana is b dollars and the cost of each apple is a dollars, which of the following represents the total cost, in dollars, of the bananas and apples Marvin eats in 1 week? (1 week = 7 days)

(A) $7b + a$
(B) $21b + a$
(C) $7(b + a)$
(D) $7(b + 3a)$
(E) $7(3b + a)$

GO ON TO THE NEXT PAGE

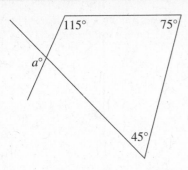

3. In the figure above, what is the value of *a* ?

(A) 105
(B) 110
(C) 115
(D) 120
(E) 125

4. What is the value of *m* if $\dfrac{4}{3m-2} = \dfrac{4}{m+6}$?

(A) −4
(B) −2
(C) 0
(D) 2
(E) 4

5. Given the five pairs of numbers below, for which pair is the ratio of the smaller number to the larger number 2 to 3 ?

(A) 3, 6
(B) 4, 9
(C) 5, 15
(D) 6, 10
(E) 8, 12

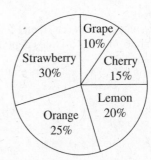

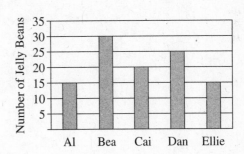

6. Susannah buys a bag containing 700 jelly beans that come in 5 assorted flavors. The circle graph above shows each flavor as a percent of the total amount of jelly beans. The bar graph shows the number of one flavor of jelly beans that Susannah gave to each of five friends. Which flavor is represented by the bar graph?

(A) Strawberry
(B) Orange
(C) Lemon
(D) Cherry
(E) Grape

GO ON TO THE NEXT PAGE

7. In the xy-plane, a line contains the points $(-3, 7)$, $(1, -3)$, and $(3, t)$. What is the value of t ?

(A) −13
(B) −11
(C) −10
(D) −9
(E) −8

9. If, for all integers x and y, $x \ddagger y$ is defined by $x \ddagger y = x + y \times x$, what is the value of $3 \ddagger 4$?

(A) 10
(B) 12
(C) 15
(D) 21
(E) 36

8. For how many integers between 10 and 100 is the tens digit equal to 5, 6, or 7 and the units digit (ones digit) equal to 2, 3, or 4 ?

(A) Three
(B) Four
(C) Six
(D) Nine
(E) Ten

10. A certain fruit salad contains only grapes, strawberries, and orange slices. If the grapes have a weight equal to that of the orange slices, and the weight of the strawberries is three times the weight of the grapes, how many grams of grapes are there in 400 grams of fruit salad?

(A) 44.4
(B) 80
(C) 100
(D) 133.3
(E) 240

GO ON TO THE NEXT PAGE

11. If $7^{x+3} + 7^2 = 98$, what is x ?

(A) −5
(B) −3
(C) −1
(D) 1
(E) 3

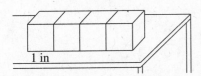

12. Harvey begins lining up 1-inch cubes in a row on a table, as shown above. Each cube, except the first and last, shares two of its faces with adjacent cubes. If Harvey continues until he has lined up 13 cubes on the table, what is the surface area, in square inches, of the cubes' faces that do not touch the table or another cube?

(A) 38
(B) 39
(C) 41
(D) 43
(E) 45

Lisa sometimes works on Saturday.
Michael always cooks dinner on Tuesday.

13. If both statements above are true, which of the following statements CANNOT be true?

(A) Lisa cooks dinner on Tuesday.
(B) Michael works on Saturday.
(C) Neither Lisa nor Michael cooks dinner on Tuesday.
(D) Neither Lisa nor Michael worked last Saturday.
(E) Both Lisa and Michael cook dinner on Tuesday.

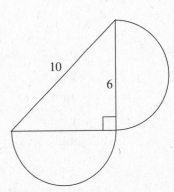

Note: Figure not drawn to scale

14. The figure above is composed of two semicircles and one triangle. What is the perimeter of the figure?

(A) $6\pi + 10$
(B) $7\pi + 7$
(C) $7\pi + 10$
(D) $14\pi + 7$
(E) $14\pi + 10$

GO ON TO THE NEXT PAGE ⟶

$$ts < 0 < t - s$$

15. If the statement above is true, which of the following must also be true?

    (A) $t > s$
    (B) $s > t$
    (C) $t = s$
    (D) $t > 0$ and $s > 0$
    (E) $t < 0$ and $s < 0$

OUTCOME OF CARMEN'S TENNIS MATCHES

Month	Wins	Losses
March	5	6
April	4	8
May	8	2
June	7	6
July	6	6

17. Carmen's tennis club posts the names of those players who compete in at least 12 matches per month and win more matches than they lose. For how many of the months listed in the table above was Carmen's name posted by the tennis organization?

    (A) None
    (B) One
    (C) Two
    (D) Three
    (E) Four

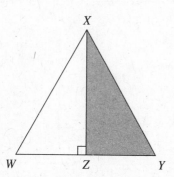

16. In the figure above, $\triangle WXY$ has three congruent sides and has a perimeter of 12. What is the area of the shaded portion of the figure?

    (A) 2
    (B) $2\sqrt{3}$
    (C) 4
    (D) $4\sqrt{3}$
    (E) 6

GO ON TO THE NEXT PAGE

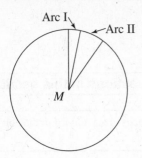

18. The circumference of circle M, above, is to be divided into nonoverlapping arcs. If the first arc is $\frac{1}{30}$ of the circumference of the circle and the length of each arc after the first is twice the length of the previous arc, into how many arcs can the circle be divided?

(A) Two
(B) Three
(C) Four
(D) Five
(E) Six

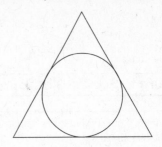

20. In the figure above, a circle with radius 1 is inscribed in an equilateral triangle. What is the area of the triangle?

(A) 3
(B) 4
(C) $2\sqrt{3}$ (approximately 3.46)
(D) $3\sqrt{2}$ (approximately 4.24)
(E) $3\sqrt{3}$ (approximately 5.20)

19. If $a = 2b = 3c = 4d$ and $abcd \neq 0$, what is the average (arithmetic mean) of a, b, and c in terms of d ?

(A) $\dfrac{26d}{9}$

(B) $\dfrac{25d}{9}$

(C) $\dfrac{8d}{3}$

(D) $\dfrac{23d}{9}$

(E) $\dfrac{22d}{9}$

STOP
If you finish before time is called, you may check your work on this section only.
Do not turn to any other section in the test.

SECTION 3
Time — 25 minutes
25 Questions

Turn to Section 3 of your answer sheet to answer the questions in this section.

Directions: For each question in this section, select the best answer from among the choices given and fill in the corresponding circle on the answer sheet.

Each sentence below has one or two blanks, each blank indicating that something has been omitted. Beneath the sentence are five words or sets of words labeled A through E. Choose the word or set of words that, when inserted in the sentence, best fits the meaning of the sentence as a whole.

Example:

Desiring to ------- his taunting friends, Mitch gave them taffy in hopes it would keep their mouths shut.

(A) eliminate   (B) satisfy   (C) overcome
    (D) ridicule   (E) silence

Ⓐ Ⓑ Ⓒ Ⓓ ●

1. Palm trees are ------- on Jei's college campus, so much so that they are almost as abundant as students and professors.

    (A) bountiful   (B) revered   (C) embellished
        (D) exorbitant   (E) abashed

2. By pleading with Justin to ------- his choice and urging him to investigate other options, Mrs. Weathersby made Justin feel ------- his ability to make suitable decisions for his future.

    (A) synthesize . . incompatible with
    (B) modify . . satisfied with
    (C) invalidate . . confident in
    (D) eliminate . . accustomed to
    (E) reconsider . . dubious of

3. Kendra set her novel in the -------, because she hoped to capture the atmosphere of the bustling, densely populated place.

    (A) neighborhood   (B) farmstead   (C) metropolis
        (D) prohibition   (E) conflict

4. Although the alchemists of the fifteenth and sixteenth centuries who claimed the ability to create gold were -------, their experiments with materials and chemicals actually helped ------- the scientific field of modern chemistry.

    (A) charlatans . . eschew
    (B) frauds . . spawn
    (C) amateurs . . depreciate
    (D) physicists . . chronicle
    (E) craftsmen . . reiterate

5. Music that is made up as it is performed is, by definition, -------.

    (A) beauteous   (B) prevailing   (C) improvisational
        (D) composed   (E) melodious

6. Kurt Vonnegut, one of the most ------- writers of his generation, has garnered a reputation that highlights this ------- characteristic and downplays his narrative abilities.

    (A) extroverted . . reclusive
    (B) ingenious . . limited
    (C) political . . aggressive
    (D) cynical . . sardonic
    (E) reserved . . complex

7. In spite of the ------- of microbes resistant to Penicillin, many people still believe that the drug is -------, a cure-all treatment for infections.

    (A) abstruseness . . a remedy
    (B) profusion . . a panacea
    (C) proliferation . . an enigma
    (D) ardor . . an icon
    (E) whimsicality . . a paradox

8. Professor Jackson was constantly praised by many over-eager graduate students trying to flatter him, but these ------- students could not win the approval that more ------- students would receive.

    (A) sycophantic . . sincere
    (B) impressionable . . gregarious
    (C) ostentatious . . eccentric
    (D) pernicious . . dilatory
    (E) realistic . . rigorous

GO ON TO THE NEXT PAGE

Directions: Each passage below is followed by questions based on its content. Answer the questions on the basis of what is <u>stated</u> or <u>implied</u> in each passage and in any introductory material that may be provided.

Questions 9-10 are based on the following passage.

While virtually all scientists accept the principles of evolutionary theory, there remains great uncertainty concerning the mechanism of rapid and drastic change
Line between successive species. In the past, interspecies
5 hybridization was dismissed as a possible solution, since hybrids are rarely as vigorous as purebred species. However, current research on hybridization suggests that although some hybrids are not as virile as either of the parent species, they are often strong enough to pass their traits on. Scientists have
10 also found hybrid species, such as certain types of corn, that are stronger than their parent species, a phenomenon known as "hybrid vigor." These findings suggest that hybridization plays a far more important role in evolution than previously suspected.

9. It can be inferred that some scientists previously believed that

   (A) the details of evolutionary theory may never be fully understood
   (B) hybrid plants lack the ability to reproduce by themselves
   (C) plants that are robust possess an evolutionary advantage
   (D) purebred plants play a relatively minor role in evolution
   (E) climate affects the ability of plants to adapt to their environment

10. The passage implies that most scientists will adopt a theory that

   (A) includes elements about which little is known
   (B) cannot be proven by experimental means
   (C) involves ideas which will likely be disproved later
   (D) has limited real-world applications
   (E) are unlikely to be contradicted by later evidence

Questions 11-12 are based on the following passage.

Art critic Walter Benjamin defined Modernism as "a movement that constructed itself in opposition to the home." It is no wonder, then, that many modern art museums adopt an angular, bare, or industrial design. They do not attempt
Line
5 to create a neutral space for the art; rather, they provide the distinctively un-cozy, anti-domestic space modern art requires. These spaces allow the artists to discuss aesthetic ideas, but, more importantly, they create a proper setting for subversive, socially deconstructive art.

11. The author would most likely agree with which of the following statements about modern art?

   (A) It mocks the design of the typical home.
   (B) It can have both artistic and social impact.
   (C) It often alienates people who are used to traditional art.
   (D) It is more concerned with design elements than with social commentary.
   (E) It is most effective when displayed in a person's home.

12. The passage implies that the "spaces" (line 7) in which modern art is displayed

   (A) inspire artists to create innovative works of art
   (B) prevent people from displaying art in their homes
   (C) complement the attitudes expressed by much modern art
   (D) provide a place for people to discuss subversive political ideas
   (E) are incapable of influencing people's perception of art

GO ON TO THE NEXT PAGE

Questions 13-25 are based on the following passage.

This passage is adapted from a recent book about the relationship between food production and the environment.

As I sat in my car, eating a cheeseburger and fries, I suddenly found it difficult to fathom the chain of events that had led me to this point, since the project that became so
Line complex and multifaceted had once seemed so simple and
5 straightforward. I had set out to write a book about food. I had long known that human beings, due to their omnivorous nature, have a complicated relationship with food. For a cow, the decision of what to have for lunch is a simple one: If it's grass, it must be good to eat. But for humans (and other
10 omnivores), an enormous amount of time and effort must be expended on deciding exactly what to eat. People have always relied on their powers of cognition and memory to steer them away from foods that are harmful or unpleasant, and toward foods that are nourishing and enjoyable. In fact, some
15 anthropologists theorize that the reason humans originally developed such large and complex brains was to help solve the riddle of what to have for lunch. I decided that pondering this seemingly simple question would be the best way to begin my inquiry into our relationship with food.
20 My original plan was to follow the paths of several food chains, from beginning to end: from farm or ranch to dinner table. Since American cuisine is so commonly associated with fast food, I started by attempting to trace the ingredients that make up a typical fast food meal, from their presumably
25 pastoral points of origin to their final destination as a cheeseburger and fries, consumed while I drove down the freeway. I was attracted to this particular plan for its variety and for its extremes. In the same way that following a river from alpine peaks to desert floor exposes the traveler to every
30 conceivable climate, I assumed that tracing these routes would afford me a glimpse of all the myriad sources of our food.
What I didn't realize was that following these paths would be more complex than I had ever imagined. The complexity arose, at least in part, from the sheer magnitude of the task. In
35 retrospect, I should have known that tracing the precise route of any single food item was about as realistic as following the route of a glass of water after it's been poured into a stream. Eventually, I realized that the only way to surmount this difficulty was to follow the stream itself rather than what was
40 floating in it: To follow "potatoes" rather than "this bag of potatoes."
Unfortunately, this took care of only part of my problem. The greater difficulty arose not from the stream itself, but from all the tributaries, inlets, and channels that crisscrossed
45 or diverged from my chosen path. I had believed that the particular stream I was following existed in splendid isolation, while in reality it was hopelessly intertwined with all sorts of other streams, in such a way that it was often impossible to tell where one left off and another began. There was no
50 way to consider the stream labeled "corn," for example, without taking into account the stream that was "industrial fertilizer production." That stream, in turn, was impossible to contemplate without a side trip down the tributary named

"fossil fuels," and so on. It didn't take many of these side trips
55 to feel as if I'd lost sight of my original goal.
Looking back, I think I must have known all along that my plan wouldn't survive the journey in its original form. Certainly, I always had an inkling that the production of food was just a small part of a much greater ecosystem, even if I
60 hadn't consciously understood that pursuing the stream that represented agriculture would lead me onto so many other related pathways. In the end, I came to realize that no part of an ecosystem can be isolated and studied without considering the broad framework that supports it.

13. In context, the author's statement that he "found it difficult" (line 2) emphasizes the idea that

(A) a plan changed unexpectedly
(B) a problem became impossible to solve
(C) a question was resolved through investigation
(D) an emotional approach to research obstructed progress
(E) an error in calculations compromised research findings

14. Which statement best describes the function of the sentence in lines 7-9 ("For a . . . eat") ?

(A) It identifies a further reason humans have a complicated relationship with what they eat.
(B) It provides a contrast to a situation described in the rest of the paragraph.
(C) It reveals the author's ability to adapt his argument to include additional species.
(D) It highlights the similarity between two methods of choosing what to eat.
(E) It expresses regret about the outcome of the author's investigations.

15. The "riddle" (line 17) is best described as a

(A) puzzle that is relatively trivial
(B) mystery that is unlikely to be solved
(C) topic of little interest
(D) subject of compelling significance
(E) question that is easily answered

16. In line 22, the author's reference to American cuisine primarily serves to

(A) illustrate the necessity of food choices in contemporary culture
(B) describe an alternative theory of food production
(C) justify a controversial way of doing of research
(D) underline important differences between the author and other food writers
(E) explain the logic behind a particular course of action

GO ON TO THE NEXT PAGE

17. The sentence in lines 22-27 ("Since . . . freeway") conveys the author's

(A) dislike of popular stereotypes
(B) uncertainty about a source
(C) distaste for a particular meal
(D) appreciation for the surrounding scenery
(E) concern for a lack of nutritional value

18. The statement in lines 32-33 ("What I . . . imagined") functions primarily to

(A) provide a lengthy aside in order to give context for an earlier discovery
(B) indicate an important and unforeseen issue with the author's methodology
(C) express dismay at the lack of a suitable information for a book
(D) foreshadow the eventual resolution of an apparent flaw in the author's plan
(E) suggest that some of the author's findings are not as trustworthy as initially supposed

19. In context, the reference to a "glass of water" (line 37) primarily serves to

(A) emphasize the author's increasing awareness of the complications of a project
(B) suggest that few people appreciate the difficulty of writing about food
(C) describe specific research methods used by the author
(D) convey the author's success in tracing a particular food chain
(E) indicate the importance of a rigorous methodology for collecting information

20. In line 43, the "greater difficulty" is best understood as the

(A) absence of evidence to support the author's claims
(B) problems caused by the environmental practices of food producers
(C) confusion caused by the intentionally deceptive labels on food products
(D) likelihood of becoming sidetracked by secondary pursuits
(E) hardship of traveling through unfamiliar territory

21. The list of "tributaries, inlets, and channels" (line 44) primarily serves to

(A) emphasize the many areas unrelated to the author's goal
(B) specify a way to navigate a convoluted topic
(C) illustrate the complexities of a particular undertaking
(D) enumerate the similarities between research and streams
(E) hint at the strengths of the subject chosen

22. In line 46, "splendid" most nearly means

(A) perplexing
(B) optimistic
(C) accessible
(D) attractive
(E) absolute

23. The author views the "side trip" (line 53) primarily as

(A) offering a useful diversion from work on a complex problem
(B) illustrating the flow of information from one group to another
(C) adding to his loss of focus on community food sources
(D) contributing an important component of a process under investigation
(E) increasing the availability of resources to a greater number of people

24. The author presents the final sentence (lines 62-64) as

(A) a commentary infused with hope
(B) a lesson drawn from personal experience
(C) an admonition filled with grim foreboding
(D) a challenge to recent scholarship
(E) an afterthought laced with irony

25. The primary purpose of the passage is to report on the

(A) various ways in which corn is used in industrial farming techniques
(B) author's theory about the industrialization of food in North America
(C) amount of energy required to process most food currently consumed
(D) thought processes of a researcher contemplating issues in food production
(E) significance of research studies in altering our perceptions of food

STOP

If you finish before time is called, you may check your work on this section only.
Do not turn to any other section in the test.

SECTION 5
Time — 25 minutes
35 Questions

Turn to Section 5 of your answer sheet to answer the questions in this section.

Directions: For each question in this section, select the best answer from among the choices given and fill in the corresponding circle on the answer sheet.

The following sentences test correctness and effectiveness of expression. Part of each sentence or the entire sentence is underlined; beneath each sentence are five ways of phrasing the underlined material. Choice A repeats the original phrasing; the other four choices are different. If you think the original phrasing produces a better sentence than any of the alternatives, select choice A; if not, select one of the other choices.

In making your selection, follow the requirements of standard written English; that is, pay attention to grammar, choice of words, sentence construction, and punctuation. Your selection should result in the most effective sentence—clear and precise, without awkwardness or ambiguity.

EXAMPLE:

Bobby Flay baked his first cake <u>and he was thirteen years old then</u>.

(A) and he was thirteen years old then
(B) when he was thirteen
(C) at age thirteen years old
(D) upon the reaching of thirteen years
(E) at the time when he was thirteen

1. During the early 1980s, after performing in numerous local talent shows, my <u>cousin, who had demonstrated</u> her talent on the television show "Star Search."

   (A) cousin, who had demonstrated
   (B) cousin, the demonstrator of
   (C) cousin demonstrating
   (D) cousin demonstrated
   (E) cousin, as a result of demonstrating

2. Written by John Patrick Shanley in 2004, <u>the Pulitzer Prize was awarded in 2005 to the play *Doubt: A Parable* for its challenging themes</u>.

   (A) the Pulitzer Prize was awarded in 2005 to the play *Doubt: A Parable* for its challenging themes
   (B) the Pulitzer Prize, awarded to the play *Doubt: A Parable* in 2005 for its challenging themes
   (C) the play *Doubt: A Parable*'s challenging themes were the reason it was awarded the Pulitzer Prize in 2005
   (D) its challenging themes got the play *Doubt: A Parable* the award of the Pulitzer Prize in 2005
   (E) the play *Doubt: A Parable* was awarded the Pulitzer Prize in 2005 for its challenging themes

3. Throughout the twisting streets that she can see from her apartment <u>curve an extended row of ruined old buildings</u>.

   (A) curve an extended row of ruined old buildings
   (B) curves an extended row of ruined old buildings
   (C) curves ruined old buildings in an extended row
   (D) there curves ruined old buildings in an extended row
   (E) there curve an extended row of ruined old buildings

4. The Americans with Disabilities Act, or ADA, <u>codifies laws that guarantee equal access</u> for people who have physical or mental impairments.

   (A) codifies laws that guarantee equal access
   (B) it codifies laws, and it guarantees equal access
   (C) the laws codified by it are for guaranteed equal access
   (D) codifying laws that guarantee equal access
   (E) which codify laws that guarantee equal access

GO ON TO THE NEXT PAGE

5. A class of fresh faced, eager kindergartners arriving each September by school bus to begin learning in the public school system.

    (A) A class of fresh faced, eager kindergartners arriving each September by school bus

    (B) A class of fresh faced, eager kindergartners from school buses, each September they arrive

    (C) When each September a class of fresh faced, eager kindergartners arrives by school bus

    (D) Each September a class of fresh faced, eager kindergartners arrives by school bus

    (E) A class of fresh faced, eager kindergartners who arrive by school bus each year

6. Once considered to be a vast and insignificant jungle, biologists, who treasure its diverse wildlife and rich foliage, are intrigued by the Amazon rainforest.

    (A) biologists, who treasure its diverse wildlife and rich foliage, are intrigued by the Amazon rainforest

    (B) diverse wildlife and rich foliage are treasured by biologists now intrigued by the Amazon rainforest

    (C) diverse wildlife and rich foliage are treasured by biologists, who are intrigued by the Amazon rainforest

    (D) it intrigues biologists, who treasure the diverse wildlife and rich foliage of the Amazon rainforest

    (E) the Amazon rainforest intrigues biologists, who treasure its diverse wildlife and rich foliage

7. With their protest lyrics and their unapologetic stories of working-class life often avoided in popular music, Bob Dylan's timeless songs are often regarded as the poetry of the people.

    (A) Bob Dylan's timeless songs are often regarded

    (B) Bob Dylan has recorded timeless songs that are often regarded

    (C) the timeless songs of Bob Dylan often regarded

    (D) people often regard the timeless songs of Bob Dylan

    (E) people often regard that Bob Dylan's timeless songs are

8. To predict a definite outcome of a financial investment is assuming a nearly impossible task.

    (A) investment is assuming

    (B) investment is to assume

    (C) investment assumes

    (D) investment, it assumes

    (E) investment, therefore assuming

9. By running an additional performance, the drama club members raised a profit larger in ticket sales than if they added the profits from bake sales, car washes, raffles, and donations.

    (A) profit larger in ticket sales than if they added the profits from bake sales, car washes, raffles, and donations

    (B) profit larger in ticket sales than adding the profits from bake sales, car washes, raffles, and donations

    (C) larger profit from ticket sales than the total profits from bake sales, car washes, raffles, and donations

    (D) larger profit from ticket sales than from bake sales, car washes, raffles, and donations added together

    (E) larger profit from sales of tickets than the adding of profits from bake sales, car washes, raffles, and donations

10. There is an unpredictable connection between an artist and the source of her inspiration, when at its height can be revelatory and at its depths, demoralizing.

    (A) when at its height can be revelatory and at its depths, demoralizing

    (B) when at their height can be revelatory and at their depths, demoralizing

    (C) who at heights is revelatory and at depths, demoralizing

    (D) which at its height can be revelatory and at its depths, demoralizing

    (E) while at their height is revelatory and at their depths is demoralizing

11. The locksmith disliked his apprentice not so much for his lack of interest in key cutting, but because he regarded every locked door with fear and anxiety.

    (A) but because he regarded every locked door with fear and anxiety

    (B) but because of his regarding every locked door with fear and anxiety

    (C) but for being fearful and anxious in regarding every locked door

    (D) as for him regarding every locked door fearfully and anxiously

    (E) as for his fearful and anxious regard for every locked door

GO ON TO THE NEXT PAGE

The following sentences test your ability to recognize grammar and usage errors. Each sentence contains either a single error or no error at all. No sentence contains more than one error. The error, if there is one, is underlined and lettered. If the sentence contains an error, select the one underlined part that must be changed to make the sentence correct. If the sentence is correct, select choice E. In choosing answers, follow the requirements of standard written English.

EXAMPLE:

The other players and her significantly improved
   A   B   C

the game plan created by the coaches. No error
             D   E

Ⓐ ● Ⓒ Ⓓ Ⓔ

12. After receiving our degrees in English literature, my

roommate and I developed the skills to analyze complex
           A   B

novels more deep than we could
       C

in high school. No error
    D   E

13. Before taking his cat to the vet, David moved the
    A

furniture and vacuuming the carpet, causing the cat to
        B   C

run away and hiss angrily. No error
            D   E

14. Once the week of final exams arrived, Brian needed to
                 A

read several history chapters, to study and prepare
                        B

himself for a biology test, and he should revise his
 C   D

paper on Shakespeare. No error
           E

15. The writings of economist and humanist Karl
    A

Marx influenced many 20th century theorists of
       B

postmodernism, a philosophy that deconstructed
           C

traditional beliefs and aims to reconsider social values
             D

and morals. No error
       E

16. Because biology labs focus on hands-on learning

and promote skills needed for solving common
      A

problems is why they have been generally required by
    B   C   D

medical and health-related programs. No error
           E

17. On the shelf in the garage are a collection of tools
                 A

freely available to any woodworkers who desire to add
    B   C

details to their creations. No error
      D   E

18. At the annual dessert festival, carefully crafted pastries
                A

are presented in elegant displays, drawing people from
 B

near and far to take part in this yearly event. No error
              C   D   E

19. The only student to be awarded a community service
            A

medal, the senior class president has accumulated the
                B

most hours of service when he helped build homes in
                    C

Guatemala last summer. No error
      D   E

GO ON TO THE NEXT PAGE →

20. When *Star Wars* had their 20th anniversary, many
                            A   B

fans worldwide sought to collect new pieces of movie
                        C   D

memorabilia. No error
              E

21. Incompatible with newer programs and deemed useless,
                      A   B

the company's software has been updated unsuccessful
                              C   D

for modern consumers. No error
                        E

22. Though originally unpopular among taxpayers, the
           A

housing fee increase was implemented in order to build
                                                    B

more safer playgrounds for the community. No error
     C   D   E

23. Since J. S. Bach's compositions were performed in
    A   B

numerous cities in Germany during his lifetime, his
     C

music did not gain recognition until centuries after his
              D

death. No error
       E

24. After many years of dedicated training, some martial
          A

artists are so skilled in reacting at any stimulus that they
                        B

can quickly retaliate if attacked; this skill makes them
     C

extremely dangerous opponents. No error
     D   E

25. Most of the paintings throughout this gallery
                          A

appear to be uncared for, and if you examine one
     B

closely, you will see that the paint has faded and
                                     C

their frames have cracked. No error
     D   E

26. A person who uses hand tools to accomplish only
                                A

such tasks as hanging pictures and fixing window shades
     B

need not purchase the most cutting-edge power tools
     C   D

developed for professionals. No error
                              E

27. In addition to possessing a deep knowledge of world
                   A

history, diplomats must have practice in dealing with
                                     B

foreign cultures if he or she is to begin to build strong
                    C   D

relationships with foreign leaders. No error
                                     E

28. Janet sent Howard to Richard's camp for the summer,
                                        A

never dreaming that three weeks would go by before
     B   C

hearing from Howard. No error
     D   E

29. In spite of the fact that handwriting on rare books usually
    A

causes a decrease in sale price, the value of autographed
     B

books is actually greater than books that have not been
       C   D

signed. No error
        E

Directions: The following passage is an early draft of an essay. Some parts of the passage need to be rewritten.

Read the passage and select the best answers for the questions that follow. Some questions are about particular sentences or parts of sentences and ask you to improve sentence structure or word choice. Other questions ask you to consider organization and development. In choosing answers, follow the requirements of standard written English.

Questions 30-35 are based on the following passage.

(1) People who live on the East and West Coasts often assume that the Midwest has nothing interesting in it. (2) They are wrong. (3) One example is Branson, Missouri. (4) Branson, Missouri is a tiny town in the Ozark Mountains on the border of Missouri and Arkansas. (5) Branson is a tourist town, like ski towns and beach resorts, it is visited by hundreds of thousands of people every year during the months when its shows are in season. (6) People come to Branson for affordable family fun.

(7) Branson might seem overly commercial or even tacky. (8) There are hundreds of stores and outlets and places that sell not only regular merchandise but also unique and even strange local crafts and tourist items. (9) Huge billboards—surrounding hotels, motels, and tour buses, which are everywhere and full of tourists—advertise shows, shops, and malls. (10) Visitors often come in search of country music and old-fashioned music that is hard to find on the radio nowadays.

(11) But the critics don't understand everything there is to know about Branson. (12) There are many recreations and natural attractions in this area, like golf courses, lakes, rivers, caverns, and mountains. (13) People really don't know what the place has to offer. (14) Some of America's most famous and beloved entertainers, such as the Osmonds, perform regularly in this location. (15) It also features performers most famous for their work there, like Shoji Tabuchi, a performer from Japan who has been delighting audiences in Branson for fourteen years. (16) And, it's safer and more reasonably priced than Las Vegas or Nashville with some of the same assets.

30. What is the primary purpose of sentence 1 ?

(A) To present a commonly held view.
(B) To describe the geography of a region.
(C) To introduce an idea that the author will contest.
(D) To provide an example of bias.
(E) To express the writer's beliefs.

31. In context, which of the following is the best revision of sentence 5 (reproduced below) ?

Branson is a tourist town, like ski towns and beach resorts, it is visited by hundreds of thousands of people every year during the months when its shows are in season.

(A) Branson is a tourist town, like those near ski or beach resorts: each year, hundreds of thousands of travelers visit during the months when its shows are in season.
(B) Branson is a tourist town like ski and beach resorts; it is visited by hundreds of thousands of people every year during the months when its shows are in season.
(C) Like the ones near ski and beach resorts, Branson is a tourist town, visited by hundreds of thousands of seasonal travelers during the months when their shows are in it.
(D) Visited by hundreds of thousands of travelers during the months when its shows are in season, every year Branson is like a tourist town near beach or ski resorts.
(E) Branson is a tourist town: hundreds of thousands of travelers like those who visit ski or beach resorts visit Branson during the months each year when its shows are in season.

32. Which of the following additions would most improve the first paragraph (sentences 1-6) ?

(A) Listing mundane tourist attractions available on the East Coast
(B) Providing an overview of live performances that Branson offers
(C) Explaining the settlement of the Ozarks and the founding of Branson
(D) Placing sentence 6 immediately after sentence 2
(E) Deleting sentence 2

GO ON TO THE NEXT PAGE

33. Of the following, which is the best version of sentence 9 (reproduced below) ?

Huge billboards—surrounding hotels, motels, and tour buses, which are everywhere and full of tourists—advertising shows, shops, and malls.

(A) Huge billboards surrounding hotels, motels, and tour buses, which are everywhere and full of tourists, advertise shows, shops, and malls.

(B) The streets are lined with hotels, motels, and tour buses whose occupants take in huge billboards that are everywhere advertising shows, shops, and malls.

(C) The streets are lined with hotels, motels, and tour buses full of tourists, as well as huge billboards advertising shows, shops, and malls to the visitors.

(D) Huge billboards advertise shows, shops, and malls and surround hotels, motels, and tour buses, which are everywhere filled with tourists taking it in.

(E) The streets are lined: hotels, motels, and tour buses are everywhere, and their occupants take in huge billboards advertising shows, shops, and malls.

34. In context, which version of sentences 12 and 13 (reproduced below) best combines them into a single sentence?

There are many recreations and natural attractions in this area, like golf courses, lakes, rivers, caverns, and mountains. People really don't know what the place has to offer.

(A) You might not realize that this area offers a range of recreations activities and natural attractions, including golf courses, lakes, rivers, caverns, and mountains.

(B) People unfamiliar with Branson might not realize that this area offers a range of recreational activities and natural attractions, including golf courses, lakes, rivers, caverns, and mountains.

(C) People might not realize that golf courses, lakes, rivers, caverns, and mountains might all be found in Branson if they were to visit.

(D) People unfamiliar with Branson do not know that golf courses, lakes, rivers, caverns, and mountains can all be found in the Branson area if they were to visit.

(E) You might not realize, if unfamiliar with Branson, the range of recreational and natural resources available in the city, golf courses, lakes, rivers, caverns, and mountains being just a few.

35. In context, which of the following is the best revision for the underlined part of sentence 16 (reproduced below) ?

And, it's safer and more reasonably priced than Las Vegas or Nashville with some of the same assets.

(A) (As it is now)

(B) And, even though it is safer and more reasonably priced than Las Vegas or Nashville, it has

(C) And, because it is safer and more reasonably priced than Las Vegas or Nashville, it has

(D) However, it is safer and more reasonably priced than Las Vegas or Nashville, and it also has

(E) Lastly, Branson is safer and more reasonably priced than either Las Vegas or Nashville, but has

STOP

If you finish before time is called, you may check your work on this section only.
Do not turn to any other section in the test.

SECTION 6
Time — 25 minutes
18 Questions

Turn to Section 6 of your answer sheet to answer the questions in this section.

Directions: This section contains two types of questions. You have 25 minutes to complete both types. For questions 1-8, solve each problem and decide which is the best of the choices given. Fill in the corresponding circle on the answer sheet. You may use any available space for scratchwork.

Notes

1. The use of a calculator is permitted.

2. All numbers used are real numbers.

3. Figures that accompany problems in this test are intended to provide information useful in solving the problems. They are drawn as accurately as possible EXCEPT when it is stated in a specific problem that the figure is not drawn to scale. All figures lie in a plane unless otherwise indicated.

4. Unless otherwise specified, the domain of any function f is assumed to be the set of all real numbers x for which $f(x)$ is a real number.

Reference Information

$A = \pi r^2$ $A = lw$ $A = \frac{1}{2}bh$ $V = lwh$ $V = \pi r^2 h$ $c^2 = a^2 + b^2$ Special Right Triangles

$C = 2\pi r$

The number of degrees of arc in a circle is 360.

The sum of the measures in degrees of the angles of a triangle is 180.

1. Which of the following is NOT a factor of $9^2 - 9$?

   (A)   6
   (B)   8
   (C)   12
   (D)   18
   (E)   32

2. A chef prepares a multicourse meal at a client's home. For this service, she charges a base price of $150, and adds an additional $20 for each course ordered. If a client orders c courses, which of the following represents the total charge, in dollars, for the meal?

   (A) $170c$
   (B) $150 + c$
   (C) $150c + 20$
   (D) $150 + 20c$
   (E) $170 + 20c$

GO ON TO THE NEXT PAGE

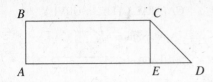

3. In the figure above, *CDE* is an isosceles triangle and *ABCE* is a rectangle. If *AD* = 16 and *DE* = 4, what is the area of rectangle *ABCE* ?

(A) 48
(B) 56
(C) 64
(D) 72
(E) 80

$$a + b + c = 4$$
$$d + e = 5$$

4. What is the value of $ae + ce + bd + be + cd + ad$?

(A)   6
(B)   9
(C)   14
(D)   20
(E)   34

YEAR	RESIDENTS
2000	550
2001	725
2002	950
2003	1125
2004	1350

5. The chart above shows the number of residents of the Sunny Forest housing development from 2000 to 2004. Starting in 2000, the number of residents increased a constant amount every 2 years. If the number of residents continued to increase at this rate, how many residents were there in 2006 ?

(A) 1525
(B) 1700
(C) 1750
(D) 1800
(E) 1875

GO ON TO THE NEXT PAGE

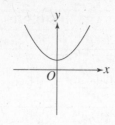

6. If the figure above shows the graph of $y = |g(x)|$, which of the following could be the graph of $y = g(x)$?

(A)

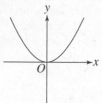

(B)

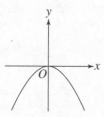

(C)

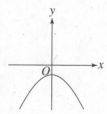

(D)

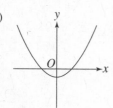

(E)

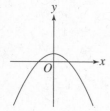

CAPITAL CITIES SURVEY

Apia, Samoa	23%
Brasilia, Brazil	41%
Colombo, Sri Lanka	52%
Dakar, Senegal	39%
Yerevan, Armenia	37%
Zagreb, Croatia	20%

7. For each of six capital cities, the graph above shows the percent of 500 people who said they would be interested in winning a trip to that city. According to the information in the graph, which of the following statements must be true?

   I.   All people who were interested in Zagreb were also interested in Brasilia.

  II.   More than half of the people said they were interested in Colombo.

 III.   No person said he or she was interested in more than one city.

(A) I only
(B) II only
(C) III only
(D) I and III only
(E) II and III only

8. If $a^{\frac{2}{5}} = b$, what does a^6 equal in terms of b ?

(A) b^2

(B) $b^{\frac{12}{5}}$

(C) b^6

(D) b^{10}

(E) b^{15}

GO ON TO THE NEXT PAGE

Directions: For Student-Produced Response questions 9-18, use the grids at the bottom of the answer sheet page on which you have answered questions 1-8.

Each of the remaining 10 questions requires you to solve the problem and enter your answer by marking the circles in the special grid, as shown in the examples below. You may use any available space for scratch work.

Answer: $\frac{7}{12}$

Write answer in boxes. → Fraction line

Grid in result. →

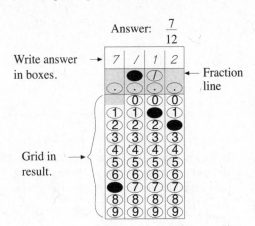

Answer: 2.5

← Decimal point

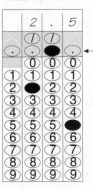

Answer: 201
Either position is correct.

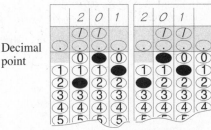

Note: You may start your answers in any column, space permitting. Columns not needed should be left blank.

- Mark no more than one circle in any column.

- Because the answer document will be machine-scored, **you will receive credit only if the circles are filled in correctly.**

- Although not required, it is suggested that you write your answer in the boxes at the top of the columns to help you fill in the circles accurately.

- Some problems may have more than one correct answer. In such cases, grid only one answer.

- No question has a negative answer.

- **Mixed numbers** such as $3\frac{1}{2}$ must be gridded as

  3.5 or 7/2. (If [3 1 / 2] is gridded, it will be

  interpreted as $\frac{31}{2}$, not $3\frac{1}{2}$.)

- **Decimal Answers:** If you obtain a decimal answer with more digits than the grid can accommodate, it may be either rounded or truncated, but it must fill the entire grid. For example, if you obtain an answer such as 0.6666..., you should record your result as .666 or .667. **A less accurate value such as .66 or .67 will be scored as incorrect.**

Acceptable ways to grid $\frac{2}{3}$ are:

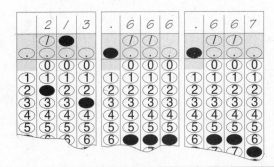

521,346.98

9. In the xy-coordinate plane, point (2, 9) is on the line whose equation is $y = 4x + b$. What is the value of b ?

10. If the number above is modified by switching the order of the digit 3 and the digit 4, then the resulting number will be how much more than the original number?

GO ON TO THE NEXT PAGE

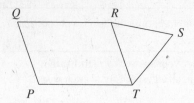

11. In the figure above, figure *PQRT* is a parallelogram and triangle *RST* is equilateral. If angle *P* is 110 degrees, what is the degree measure of angle *PTS*? (Disregard the degree symbol when gridding your answer.)

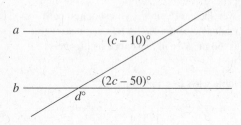

12. In the figure above, $a \parallel b$. What is the value of *d*?

13. If $0 < 5q - 4 < 2$, what is one possible value for *q*?

14. In the *xy*-plane, a circle has its center at the origin. If the shortest line segment that can be drawn from a point on the circle to the point $(0, -9)$ has a length of 3, and point $(0, -9)$ is outside the circle, what is the radius of the circle?

GO ON TO THE NEXT PAGE

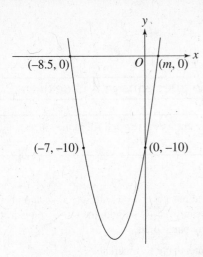

15. The graph of a quadratic function is shown in the figure above. What is the value of m ?

16. Jessica prepares rock samples of 3 different weights for a science experiment. She has 15 rocks that weigh 50 pounds each, x rocks that weigh 70 pounds each, and 6 rocks that weigh 110 pounds each. If the median weight of all of the rocks is 70 pounds, and x is a positive integer, what is the least possible value of x ?

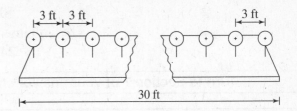

17. A landscaper plants flowers in a 30-foot flower bed as represented by the figure above. If a flower is planted at each end and also planted every 3 feet along the flower bed, how many flowers will the farmer plant altogether in the flower bed?

18. A turtle walked 5 feet at an average speed of 10 feet per minute. It then walked the next 5 feet at an average speed of 20 feet per minute. What was the average speed, in feet per minute, of the turtle for the 10 feet?

STOP

If you finish before time is called, you may check your work on this section only.
Do not turn to any other section in the test.

SECTION 7
Time — 25 minutes
24 Questions

Turn to Section 7 of your answer sheet to answer the questions in this section.

Directions: For each question in this section, select the best answer from among the choices given and fill in the corresponding circle on the answer sheet.

Each sentence below has one or two blanks, each blank indicating that something has been omitted. Beneath the sentence are five words or sets of words labeled A through E. Choose the word or set of words that, when inserted in the sentence, best fits the meaning of the sentence as a whole.

Example:

Desiring to ------- his taunting friends, Mitch gave them taffy in hopes it would keep their mouths shut.

(A) eliminate   (B) satisfy   (C) overcome
  (D) ridicule   (E) silence

---

1. To address her teacher's criticisms, Calla chose to ------- her research paper by adding more detailed footnotes.

   (A) promote   (B) improvise   (C) amend
     (D) reiterate   (E) professionalize

2. The candidate thought his ------- popularity would guarantee a victory, but after losing the election, he realized how ------- the support for his campaign had really been.

   (A) interested . . incidental
   (B) conventional . . neglected
   (C) positive . . experimental
   (D) conscientious . . suspicious
   (E) extensive . . narrow

3. The band has never won widespread acclaim because its output, sadly, is -------, with the ------- songs lost among the many banal ones.

   (A) amendable . . remarkable
   (B) mixed . . profound
   (C) enthralling . . vapid
   (D) flippant . . superior
   (E) obnoxious . . memorable

4. Most of Edgar Allan Poe's stories have a ------- tone because their plots are often shaded by dark and gloomy circumstances with dismal endings.

   (A) doleful   (B) fortuitous   (C) metaphorical
     (D) provocative   (E) scintillating

5. "The greatest wealth is contentment with a little" is ------- of this philosophical camp, a fundamental principle accepted by most of its members.

   (A) an eccentricity   (B) an acronym   (C) a maxim
     (D) a prospectus   (E) a contrivance

GO ON TO THE NEXT PAGE

Directions: Each passage below is followed by questions based on its content. Answer the questions on the basis of what is <u>stated</u> or <u>implied</u> in each passage and in any introductory material that may be provided.

Questions 6-9 are based on the following passages.

Passage 1

The notion that cats are more intelligent than dogs originates in human presumption. From our observations of other humans, we infer that independence and reluctance
Line to follow orders correlate with intelligence. So, when we
5 see dogs slavishly obeying their owner's commands, we leap to the conclusion that dogs must lack intelligence. By comparison, cats, with their Olympian detachment and cool disregard of their owner's wishes, seem dignified, and therefore smart. Following this line of reasoning, we might
10 be tempted to conclude that pigs are particularly dim-witted, since they spend most of their days wallowing in mud and filth.

Passage 2

Are cats more intelligent than dogs? The typical cat owner would probably answer with a resounding YES! Such people
15 usually dismiss dogs as servile lackeys, while praising cats for their noble sense of self-determination. This thinking presupposes a complete understanding of the nature of animal intelligence and how it relates to human intelligence – a level of understanding that we have not yet acquired. Intelligence
20 is often assumed to be associated with certain behavioral characteristics. Cat-lover's theories about the braininess of their pets revolve around the belief that cats have too much self-respect to obey their owner's whims. Dogs, with their constant need to please their masters, are obviously less
25 intelligent. Or are they?

6. The authors would most likely agree on which of the following points?

(A) People are fascinated by the subject of animal intelligence.
(B) Theories about cats have created false impressions in the minds of their owners.
(C) People view the topic of animal intelligence from an overly narrow perspective.
(D) Cats are not the only animals that are highly intelligent.
(E) Dogs are significantly more intelligent than cats.

7. The author of Passage 2 suggests that the "line of reasoning" discussed in line 9, Passage 1 arises because people

(A) are unaware of the behavioral characteristics of cats
(B) believe that cats are unlike any other animals
(C) assume they know more than they actually do
(D) find cats less enjoyable to own than other pets
(E) frequently ignore important information about their animals

8. Passage 2, unlike Passage 1, refers to

(A) explanations for the behavior of cats
(B) the current state of scientific knowledge
(C) dogs' tendency to comply with their owner's wishes
(D) the beliefs of dog owners about their pets' intelligence
(E) the connection between intelligence and certain types of behavior

9. Which of the following is implied in both passages but explicitly stated in neither?

(A) Some pet owners base their choice of pet on its self-sufficiency.
(B) Cats are likely more intelligent than is assumed.
(C) Cats usually pay closer attention to their masters than do dogs.
(D) People often determine intelligence by assessing conduct.
(E) Cat owners lavish too much attention upon their pets.

GO ON TO THE NEXT PAGE

Questions 10-17 are based on the following passage.

The following passage is taken from a novel set in 1905 in New York City. Una Golden, the main character, has moved to New York from Panama, Pennsylvania, and enrolled in a commercial school.

Whiteside and Schleusner's College of Commerce, where Una learned the art of business, occupied only five shabby rooms of crepuscular windows and perpetually dusty corners
Line in a converted (but not sanctified) old dwelling house on West
5 Eighteenth Street. The faculty was considered competent enough, and among them they ground out instruction in shorthand, typewriting, book-keeping, English grammar, spelling, composition, and commercial geography. Once or twice a week, language-masters from a linguistics mill down
10 the street were had in to chatter the more vulgar phrases of French, German, and Spanish.

Most of the girls in the school learned nothing but shorthand and typewriting, but to these Una added English grammar, spelling, and letter-composition. After breakfast at
15 the little flat which she had taken with her mother, she fled to the school. She drove into her books, she delighted in the pleasure of her weary teachers when she snapped out a quick answer to questions, or typed a page correctly, or was able to remember the shorthand symbol for a difficult word like
20 "psychologize."

Panama, Pennsylvania, had never regarded Una as a particularly capable young woman. Dozens of others were more masterful at trimming the Christmas tree, preparing for the annual picnic of the Needlework Coterie, arranging
25 a surprise donation party for the pastor, even spring house-cleaning. But she had been well spoken of as a marketer, a cook, a neighbor who would take care of your baby while you went visiting—because these tasks had seemed worthwhile to her. She was more practical than either Panama or herself
30 believed. All these years she had, without knowing that she was philosophizing, without knowing that there was a world-wide inquiry into a woman's place, been trying to find work that needed her. And now, something had freed her—she had become a feminist, demanding the world and all the fullness
35 thereof as her field of labor.

Where Una found her new vision of the world, it cannot be said. Certainly not in the lectures of her teachers, humorless and unvisioned grinds, who droned that by divine edict letters must end with a "yours truly" one space to the left of
40 the middle of the page; who sniffed at card-ledgers as new-fangled nonsense, and, at their most inspired, croaked out such platitudes as: "Look out for the pennies and the pounds will look out for themselves," or "The man who fails is the man who watches the clock."

45 Nor was her new understanding to be found in the books over which Una labored—the flat, maroon-covered, dusty, commercial geography, the arid book of phrases and rules-of-the-thumb called "Fish's Commercial English," the manual of touch-typewriting, or the shorthand primer that, with its
50 grotesque symbols and numbered exercises and yellow pages dog-eared by many owners, looked like an old-fashioned grammar headachily perused in some divinity-school library.

Least of all did her new sensibility come from the other girls of the commercial college. They seemed alternately
55 third-rate stenographers and very haughty urbanites who knew all about "fellows" and "shows" and "glad rags." Except for good-natured Miss Moynihan, and the oldish, anxious, industrious Miss Ingalls, who, like Una, came from a small town, Una saw the girls of the school only in a mass.

10. In line 5, the "faculty" is described as

(A) mysterious
(B) cultured
(C) adequate
(D) antiquated
(E) wise

11. The use of the word "fled" in line 15 most directly suggests that Una is

(A) irritated by the slow pace of instruction
(B) proud of her ability to outshine her classmates
(C) anxious to free herself from her mother's influence
(D) eager to immerse herself in learning
(E) delighted by the prospect of landing a high-paying job

12. The sentence in lines 22-26 ("Dozens . . . house-cleaning") is best understood as a list of

(A) skills that every young women should master
(B) anecdotes about a painful period in Una's life
(C) duties that Una views as beneath a person of her social status
(D) amusements that distract women from their oppression
(E) activities that Una shows little interest in

13. The primary purpose of the third paragraph is to show Una's

(A) evolving understanding of her own abilities
(B) increasing disenchantment with her living situation
(C) changing relationship with her childhood friends
(D) growing nostalgia for the town she grew up in
(E) continuing anxiety about her lack of marketable skills

GO ON TO THE NEXT PAGE →

14. The description in lines 37-44 ("Certainly not . . . clock") serves to suggest that Una found her lectures to be

(A) hilarious
(B) tedious
(C) captivating
(D) malicious
(E) profound

15. In line 40, "sniffed" most nearly means

(A) whistled
(B) sampled
(C) wept
(D) inhaled
(E) scoffed

16. The author's use of the word "inspired" (line 41) is best described as

(A) excessive
(B) metaphorical
(C) ironic
(D) tolerant
(E) defensive

17. In the last paragraph, the author suggests that Una views the girls as

(A) particularly memorable
(B) embarrassingly inappropriate
(C) surprisingly sophisticated
(D) regrettably underhanded
(E) largely indistinguishable

GO ON TO THE NEXT PAGE

Questions 18-24 are based on the following passage.

A favela is a slum neighborhood in Rio de Janeiro. The following passage discusses the political activism of citizens in one favela.

The favela of Vidigal is situated at the base of towering cliffs that overlook the Atlantic Ocean. The population of the favela is fairly homogenous: most residents work
Line in the service sector, and only about 30 percent of them
5 have completed primary school. With somewhere in the neighborhood of 6,500 inhabitants, it is one of the largest favelas in Rio de Janeiro. Despite its size, Vidigal is an unusually close-knit and cohesive community. The unique past of the favela has taught its residents the value of unity
10 and organization.

The defining moment in Vidigal's political history occurred in October of 1977. Vidigal had the unfortunate luck of being located between two of Rio de Janeiro's wealthiest neighborhoods. One of Rio de Janeiro's most expensive
15 resorts was literally around the corner from the favela, and developers wished to extirpate Vidigal and use the land for the construction of luxury condominiums. On October 25th, government emissaries, with a contingent of military police in tow, arrived in the favela and announced that the first group
20 of houses would be torn down.

Most residents of Vidigal acquiesced to the government's demands, relocating to a new neighborhood in Santa Cruz, a favela hours away from their jobs and families. But some members of the community decided to stay and fight. At the
25 time, the representative in charge of Vidigal's district was Paolo Duque, a petty politician who made token gestures— such as new shirts for the local soccer team—to the favela in order to maintain votes, while neglecting to bring about any real change in the living conditions in the slum. The
30 concerned residents of Vidigal journeyed to Duque's office and pleaded for help. Duque was unresponsive, saying that his hands were tied, at least until the next election. His message to the community was clear: With no votes at stake, no help would be forthcoming.
35 Instead of giving up, the leaders of Vidigal sought out a new form of political action. First, members of the community contacted various prominent social organizations in Rio de Janeiro, including the Brazilian Bar Association, the Catholic Church, and the Brazilian Institute of Architects, and enlisted
40 their support and political expertise. Next, community leaders rallied the remaining population of Vidigal to the cause, giving a political voice to people who for years had none. Facing an organized, unified, and passionate neighborhood organization with connections to strong social institutions,
45 the governor of Rio de Janeiro had no choice but to cancel the proposed demolition.

In later years, the residents of Vidigal succeeded in lobbying for an independent electrical supply, paved roads, a rudimentary sewage system, and a medical clinic. Each of
50 these civil projects resulted from the lobbying of an active and unified citizenry, a citizenry that had rejected a corrupt political system for an empowering one.

18. The first paragraph reveals which of the following about Vidigal?

(A) Its children do not have access to educational opportunities.
(B) Its citizens have learned from the favela's history.
(C) Its residents suffer from exploitative working conditions.
(D) It is unlike any of the communities that surround it.
(E) It provides a dramatic view of the Atlantic Ocean.

19. The last sentence of the opening paragraph (lines 8-10) principally serves to

(A) emphasize an interesting discrepancy
(B) introduce an idea to be explored
(C) provide an explanation for Vidigal's location
(D) contrast Vidigal's size with its closeness and unity
(E) illustrate the need for a democratic system

20. The author mentions the "new shirts" (line 27) primarily in order to

(A) clarify the beneficial actions of a politician
(B) illustrate the relatively minor actions of an individual
(C) undermine a description presented earlier
(D) offer evidence that small expressions may have large effects
(E) praise the ability of the soccer team to get new uniforms

21. In lines 31-32, the attitude of Paolo Duque can best be described as

(A) paternalistic
(B) belligerent
(C) morose
(D) benevolent
(E) apathetic

GO ON TO THE NEXT PAGE

22. On the basis of information provided later in the passage, the word "fight" (line 24) best conveys

(A) avoiding politics
(B) embracing change
(C) finding support
(D) attacking the government
(E) slandering the representatives

23. In lines 24-34, the author's portrayal of Paolo Duque is best described as

(A) a cautionary tale
(B) an unwarranted attack
(C) an emotional plea
(D) a frank assessment
(E) a familiar complaint

24. The "new form of political action" (line 36) is best understood as a strategy of

(A) abiding by and agreeing to the government's regulations
(B) organizing a voting community with strong political participation
(C) aligning community groups with influential social institutions
(D) electing educated leaders to represent the neighborhood
(E) presenting a compelling story to the national press organizations

STOP

If you finish before time is called, you may check your work on this section only.
Do not turn to any other section in the test.

SECTION 8
Time — 20 minutes
16 Questions

Turn to Section 8 of your answer sheet to answer the questions in this section.

Directions: For this section, solve each problem and decide which is the best of the choices given. Fill in the corresponding circle on the answer sheet. You may use any available space for scratchwork.

Notes

1. The use of a calculator is permitted.

2. All numbers used are real numbers.

3. Figures that accompany problems in this test are intended to provide information useful in solving the problems. They are drawn as accurately as possible EXCEPT when it is stated in a specific problem that the figure is not drawn to scale. All figures lie in a plane unless otherwise indicated.

4. Unless otherwise specified, the domain of any function f is assumed to be the set of all real numbers x for which $f(x)$ is a real number.

Reference Information

  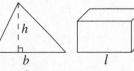 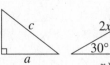

$A = \pi r^2$ $A = lw$ $A = \frac{1}{2}bh$ $V = lwh$ $V = \pi r^2 h$ $c^2 = a^2 + b^2$ Special Right Triangles

$C = 2\pi r$

The number of degrees of arc in a circle is 360.

The sum of the measures in degrees of the angles of a triangle is 180.

---

1. If $6a + 3b = 32$ and $b = 4$, then what is the value of $3a$?

   (A) 5
   (B) 9
   (C) 10
   (D) 12
   (E) 20

2. Points Q, R, and S lie on $\overline{XZ}$ in such a way that Q is the midpoint of $\overline{XZ}$, R is the midpoint of $\overline{XQ}$ and S is the midpoint of $\overline{QZ}$. If $QS = 4$, what is length RZ ?

   (A) 8
   (B) 12
   (C) 16
   (D) 20
   (E) 24

GO ON TO THE NEXT PAGE

3. Set *A* consists of all even numbers between 10 and 20, inclusive. Set *B* consists of all multiples of 3 between 7 and 19, inclusive. If set *C* consists of all the numbers that appear both in set *A* and set *B*, how many members does set *C* have?

   (A) Two
   (B) Five
   (C) Seven
   (D) Eight
   (E) Ten

   $$y = cx$$

4. In the equation above, *c* is a constant. When $y = 9$, then $x = 4$. When $y = 36$, what does *x* equal?

   (A)   8
   (B)   10
   (C)   13
   (D)   16
   (E)   81

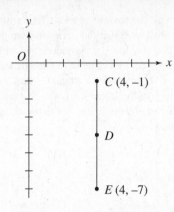

5. In the figure above $\overline{CE}$ is the diameter of a circle with center *D* (not shown). Which of the following are the coordinates of one point on the circumference of the circle?

   (A) (1, –1)
   (B) (4, –4)
   (C) (7, –4)
   (D) (5, –5)
   (E) (7, –7)

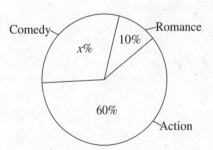

6. The circle graph above shows the inventory of movie genres in a certain DVD rental store. What is the ratio of the number of romance movies to the number of comedy movies?

   (A) 1 to 2
   (B) 1 to 3
   (C) 1 to 4
   (D) 1 to 6
   (E) 1 to 9

GO ON TO THE NEXT PAGE →

7. A survey of all the students who attend Central Valley High School showed that there was an average (arithmetic mean) of 33.6 students per classroom and an average of 22.4 electronic devices brought to class by students per classroom. If 4,200 students attend Central Valley High School, which of the following is the best estimate of the total number of electronic devices in the classrooms of Central Valley?

(A) 1,680
(B) 2,520
(C) 2,800
(D) 4,075
(E) 6,300

Sequence Y: 5, 10, 15, . . .
Sequence Z: 3, 6, 12, . . .

8. The first term in sequence Y is 5, and each term after the first is 5 more than the preceding term. The first term in Sequence Z is 3, and each term after the first is 2 times the preceding term. What is the least value of x such that the xth term of Sequence Z is more than three times the xth term of Sequence Y?

(A) 5
(B) 6
(C) 7
(D) 8
(E) 9

9. If x, y, and z are consecutive positive integers and $x < y < z$, which of the following could be true?

    I. $y = 2x$
    II. $z = 2x$
    III. $z = 2y$

(A) I only
(B) II only
(C) III only
(D) I and II only
(E) I, II and III

10. There are y sculptures in a gallery. If one is to be selected at random from the collection, the probability that a bronze statue will be selected is $\dfrac{2}{5}$. In terms of y, how many of the sculptures are bronze statues?

(A) $\dfrac{y}{5}$

(B) $\dfrac{2y}{5}$

(C) $\dfrac{5y}{2}$

(D) $\dfrac{7y}{5}$

(E) $5y$

GO ON TO THE NEXT PAGE

x	–2	–1	0	1	2
$f(x)$	4	2	3	1	–1
$g(x)$	1	–1	2	3	4

11. The table above shows the values of two functions. What is the value of $f(2) - g(-2)$?

(A) –2
(B) 0
(C) 1
(D) 3
(E) 4

12. If three angles of a quadrilateral are congruent and the average (arithmetic mean) of the measures of two angles of the quadrilateral is 80°, which of the following could NOT be the measure of an angle of the quadrilateral?

(A) 60°
(B) 80°
(C) 100°
(D) 120°
(E) 140°

13. On the number line shown above, all the tick marks are equally spaced. What is the value of m ?

(A) –2
(B) –1
(C) 0
(D) 3
(E) 4

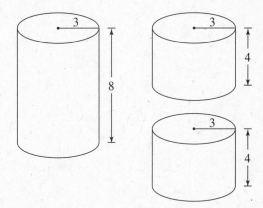

14. If a right circular cylinder with radius 3 and height 8 were divided into 2 identical right circular cylinders as shown above, then the total surface area of the two smaller cylinders would be how much <u>greater</u> than the surface area of the original cylinder?

(A) 14π
(B) 16π
(C) 18π
(D) 20π
(E) 22π

GO ON TO THE NEXT PAGE

15. If c and d are integers and $c^2 - d^2$ is even, which of the following must be true?

   (A) cd is odd.
   (B) cd is even.
   (C) $c + d$ is odd.
   (D) $c + d$ is even.
   (E) $c - d$ is odd.

16. If m and n are constants, what is the value of n if the equation $(x + 9)(x + m) = x^2 + 4mx + n$ is true for all values of x ?

   (A)   9
   (B) 18
   (C) 27
   (D) 36
   (E) 48

STOP

If you finish before time is called, you may check your work on this section only.
Do not turn to any other section in the test.

NO TEST MATERIAL ON THIS PAGE.

SECTION 9
Time — 20 minutes
18 Questions

Turn to Section 9 of your answer sheet to answer the questions in this section.

Directions: For each question in this section, select the best answer from among the choices given and fill in the corresponding circle on the answer sheet.

Each sentence below has one or two blanks, each blank indicating that something has been omitted. Beneath the sentence are five words or sets of words labeled A through E. Choose the word or set of words that, when inserted in the sentence, best fits the meaning of the sentence as a whole.

Example:

Desiring to ------- his taunting friends, Mitch gave them taffy in hopes it would keep their mouths shut.

(A) eliminate   (B) satisfy   (C) overcome
    (D) ridicule   (E) silence

Ⓐ Ⓑ Ⓒ Ⓓ ●

1. Many vacationers in Brazil and Costa Rica are attracted to the vibrant flowers and trees that compose the ------- rainforests of these countries.

    (A) isolated   (B) lush   (C) extensive
        (D) barren   (E) monumental

2. Many business models that economists once lauded as ------- are now widely derided as failures by the business community.

    (A) definitive   (B) commendable   (C) constructive
        (D) obscure   (E) circuitous

3. Even though many actors have artistic motives for performing, some are attracted by the recognition, because success in acting can be very ------- .

    (A) diverting   (B) acquisitive   (C) fulfilling
        (D) prestigious   (E) invigorating

4. Testing new drugs in large clinical trials often yields ------- results: scientists that do so can eliminate dangerous effects better than those at companies in which this type of experimentation is -------.

    (A) unsuccessful . . cultivated
    (B) viable . . supported
    (C) failed . . protested
    (D) positive . . avoided
    (E) catastrophic . . disfavored

5. In some elderly people, bone structures have a ------- that renders them vulnerable to breakages caused by falls and other traumas.

    (A) convolution   (B) plasticity   (C) morbidity
        (D) insidiousness   (E) frailty

6. Most of the university's students regarded the cancellation of hands-on training programs as -------, even senseless, and some have gone as far as submitting formal letters of ------- to administrators.

    (A) absurd . . remonstrance
    (B) inane . . abetment
    (C) logical . . grievance
    (D) misguided . . endorsement
    (E) plausible . . pedantry

GO ON TO THE NEXT PAGE ➔

Directions: Each passage below is followed by questions based on its content. Answer the questions on the basis of what is <u>stated</u> or <u>implied</u> in each passage and in any introductory material that may be provided.

Questions 7-18 are based on the following passages.

Passage 1

The following passages relate to Theodore Roosevelt's participation in the Battle of San Juan Hill, the pivotal battle of the Spanish-American War. Roosevelt was the commander of a group of volunteers known as the Rough Riders. Their "charge up San Juan Hill," which became the subject of articles, books, and even paintings, led directly to Roosevelt's political rise. But what really happened during the battle? An account by war correspondent Richard Harding Davis, written after the battle in July 1898, appears in Passage 1. A contemporary historian provides another version in Passage 2.

Our troops could not retreat, as the trail for two miles behind them was wedged with men. They could not remain where they were, for they were being shot to pieces. There
Line was only one thing they could do—go forward and take the
5 San Juan hills by assault. It was as desperate as the situation itself. To charge earthworks held by men with modern rifles and artillery is an impossible military proposition. But this campaign had not been conducted according to military rules, and a series of blunders had brought seven thousand
10 American soldiers into a chute of death from which there was no escape, except by taking the enemy who held them by the throat and driving him out. So the generals stepped back and relinquished their command to the regimental officers and the enlisted men.
15 "We can do nothing more," they virtually said. "There is the enemy."
Colonel Roosevelt, on horseback, broke from the woods and shouted: "If you don't wish to go forward, let my men pass." The junior officers of the Ninth instantly sprang into
20 line with the Rough Riders, and charged at the blue block-house on the right. No one who saw Roosevelt take that ride expected he would finish it alive. As the only mounted man, he was the most conspicuous object in range of the rifle pits, then only 200 yards ahead. Mounted high on horseback and
25 charging at a gallop and quite alone, he made you feel you would like to cheer.
The men held their guns pressed across their chests and stepped heavily as they climbed. They walked to greet death at every step, forming a thin blue line that kept creeping
30 higher and higher up the hill. It was as inevitable as the rising tide. The fire of the Spanish riflemen, who still stuck bravely to their posts, doubled and trebled in fierceness, the hills crackled and burst in amazed roars, and rippled with waves of tiny flame. But the blue line crept steadily on, and then, near
35 the top, the Spaniards appeared for a moment outlined against the sky and poised for instant flight, fired a last volley, and fled before the swift-moving wave that leaped and sprang after them.

Passage 2

There is no doubt that Roosevelt was a courageous and
40 inspired leader of men. In his brief military career, he braved extraordinary danger while showing little regard for his own safety. He regularly placed the welfare of ordinary enlisted men before that of himself and his officers.
But the legend of the charge up San Juan Hill is more
45 myth than fact.
Roosevelt and his Rough Riders charged not up San Juan Hill, where the vast majority of Spanish defenders were dug in, but rather up Kettle Hill, which was hardly defended at all. Roosevelt and his Rough Riders were able to climb Kettle hill
50 almost unopposed and take the handful of Spanish defenders by surprise. From Kettle Hill, the Rough Riders were eventually able to make their way over to San Juan Hill. By that time, however, most of the Spanish defenders had already been driven out by General Kent and his troops. The actions
55 of Roosevelt and the Rough Riders had almost no impact on the outcome of the battle.
The myth of Roosevelt's heroic charge was largely created by Richard Harding Davis, a reporter who was also a close friend of Roosevelt. Although Davis' accounts were written
60 in the first person, he did not actually witness the events he described in such vivid detail. At the time of the assault, Davis was nearly a mile away, his view obscured by dense jungle. After the fighting was over, Roosevelt gave his version of the battle to Davis, who embellished Roosevelt's account
65 considerably. Other reporters, even less scrupulous than Davis, further embroidered the story, claiming that Roosevelt cut down enemy soldiers with his sword, and that his prize stallion was shot from under him during the battle.
Roosevelt himself did not make these claims. But he did
70 not contradict them, either. When reporters praised him for his charge up San Juan Hill, he declined to correct them. Even years later, he did not bother to mention that his sword had remained tied to his luggage for the duration of the war, or that his prized stallion had died of natural causes. Roosevelt
75 had gone to war determined to emerge a hero, and in this he succeeded, at least in the court of public opinion.

7. In line 2, the word "wedged" most nearly means

(A) fastened
(B) crowded
(C) levered
(D) breached
(E) arrayed

GO ON TO THE NEXT PAGE

8. In lines 8-9, the author of Passage 1 refers to "military rules" in order to suggest that

(A) an undisciplined army required strict regulation
(B) an unfortunate situation might have been prevented
(C) a carefully laid plan had been thoughtlessly ignored
(D) a specific response was out of character
(E) a lapse in judgment was easily explained

9. In the opening paragraph of Passage 1, the mood Davis portrays is primarily one of

(A) definite failure
(B) feigned indignation
(C) optimistic confidence
(D) patriotic pride
(E) overwhelming difficulty

10. The author of Passage 1 uses the words "crackled" and "burst" (line 33) in order to

(A) emphasize the damage done to the surrounding landscape
(B) identify the root causes of the hostilities
(C) criticize an apparent disregard for human life
(D) portray the intensity of the Spanish resistance
(E) deplore the behavior of the officers during the battle

11. The author of Passage 2 notes the "vivid detail" (line 61) of Davis' writings in order to

(A) praise an author
(B) justify a decision
(C) highlight an inconsistency
(D) condemn a crime
(E) describe a friendship

12. In Passage 2, the reference to "other reporters" (line 65) primarily serves to

(A) illustrate the exaggerations attached to Roosevelt's story
(B) provide additional examples of Roosevelt's bravery
(C) suggest that journalists are unreliable wartime observers
(D) explain how Roosevelt had an impact in a large battle
(E) defend reports by Davis as less misleading than others

13. The primary purpose of Passage 2 is to

(A) contradict a commonly held opinion
(B) analyze a single historical event
(C) discredit the heroism of an individual
(D) offer a description of a historical character
(E) defend an unpopular belief

14. In contrast to the author of Passage 1, the author of Passage 2 suggests that Roosevelt acted primarily out of

(A) cowardice
(B) cynicism
(C) patriotism
(D) malice
(E) self-interest

15. In contrast to the author of Passage 2, the author of Passage 1 suggests that Roosevelt

(A) allowed journalists to exaggerate his military accomplishments
(B) deliberately disobeyed the orders of his superiors
(C) encountered stiff resistance on San Juan Hill
(D) was a brave and selfless military figure
(E) was elected president based on his war record

16. The author of Passage 2 would most likely cite which of the following, referred to in Passage 1, as evidence of something that was "largely created by Richard Harding Davis" (lines 57-58) ?

(A) "they were being shot to pieces" (line 3)
(B) "a series of blunders" (line 9)
(C) "let my men pass" (lines 18-19)
(D) "their guns pressed across their chests" (line 27)
(E) "fled before the swift-moving wave" (line 37)

17. The authors of both passages agree that

(A) Roosevelt was not always truthful
(B) San Juan Hill was heavily defended
(C) the generals did have much of an effect on the battle
(D) some accounts of Roosevelt's assault were exaggerated
(E) Roosevelt's stallion survived the battle

18. Compared to that of Passage 2, the tone of Passage 1 is more

(A) sardonic
(B) analytical
(C) conversational
(D) dramatic
(E) severe

STOP

If you finish before time is called, you may check your work on this section only.
Do not turn to any other section in the test.

NO TEST MATERIAL ON THIS PAGE.

SECTION 10
Time — 10 minutes
14 Questions

Turn to Section 10 of your answer sheet to answer the questions in this section.

Directions: For each question in this section, select the best answer from among the choices given and fill in the corresponding circle on the answer sheet.

The following sentences test correctness and effectiveness of expression. Part of each sentence or the entire sentence is underlined; beneath each sentence are five ways of phrasing the underlined material. Choice A repeats the original phrasing; the other four choices are different. If you think the original phrasing produces a better sentence than any of the alternatives, select choice A; if not, select one of the other choices.

In making your selection, follow the requirements of standard written English; that is, pay attention to grammar, choice of words, sentence construction, and punctuation. Your selection should result in the most effective sentence—clear and precise, without awkwardness or ambiguity.

EXAMPLE:

Bobby Flay baked his first cake <u>and he was thirteen years old then</u>.

(A) and he was thirteen years old then
(B) when he was thirteen
(C) at age thirteen years old
(D) upon the reaching of thirteen years
(E) at the time when he was thirteen

Ⓐ●ⒸⒹⒺ

1. Delivery of gasoline to the Texas peninsula <u>being provided mostly by officials who were wanting recovery efforts at the site to go on</u>.

   (A) being provided mostly by officials that were wanting recovery efforts at the site to go on
   (B) provided mostly by officials, they wanted the site's recovery effort to go on
   (C) mostly provided by officials wanting the site's going on with its recovery efforts
   (D) was provided mostly by officials who wanted recovery efforts at the site to go on
   (E) were provided by officials mostly wanting the site's recovery efforts going on

2. The John Hancock Center, <u>which was designed</u> by Faziur Khan, is one of the most distinctive features of the Chicago skyline.

   (A) which was designed
   (B) when it was designed
   (C) having designed it
   (D) being designed
   (E) since having been designed

3. If you have read the assigned chapters, you will be prepared <u>as to the material if tested</u>.

   (A) as to the material if tested
   (B) if someone tests you on the material
   (C) if tested regarding material read by you
   (D) if there are tests with the material
   (E) about the material where someone tests you

4. In the eighteenth <u>century was when the growth of the aspiring middle classes fueled</u> a corresponding rise in the number of books on conduct and manners.

   (A) century was when the growth of the aspiring middle classes fueled
   (B) century was when the aspiring middle classes were growing, fueling
   (C) century the growth of the aspiring middle classes fueled
   (D) century, when the growth of the aspiring middle classes began to fuel
   (E) century the aspiring middle classes grew and were fueling

GO ON TO THE NEXT PAGE

5. The author has received more requests for interviews lately because the recent reviews of <u>his novel's bone-chilling plots are rapidly attracting new readers</u>.

(A) his novel's bone-chilling plots are rapidly attracting new readers

(B) his novel's bone-chilling plots rapidly attract them, the new readers

(C) the bone-chilling plots of his novel to new readers are attracting them rapidly

(D) the bone-chilling plots of his novel for new readers are rapidly attracting them

(E) the bone-chilling plots set out in the novel rapidly attract them as new readers

6. <u>Archaeologists have discovered a fossil of an ancient bird preserved in a clay pit, it could reveal</u> crucial new information about prehistoric bird species.

(A) Archaeologists have discovered a fossil of an ancient bird preserved in a clay pit, it could reveal

(B) Archaeologists who have discovered of an ancient bird preserved in a clay pit that could reveal

(C) A fossil that archaeologists have discovered of an ancient bird preserved in a clay pit could reveal

(D) A fossil, which archaeologists have discovered of an ancient bird preserved in a clay pit, perhaps revealing

(E) Perhaps a fossil, which archaeologists discovered of an ancient bird preserved in a clay pit, revealing

7. Elaine was certain that <u>if someone else would have saw</u> the accident, she would have been able to press charges.

(A) if someone else would have saw

(B) if someone else would see

(C) if someone else had seen

(D) had someone else saw

(E) were someone else to see

8. In television sitcoms, the plots are riddled with unlikely twists, many quite ridiculous, often caused <u>by the protagonist lies</u> and the lies build upon one another.

(A) by the protagonist lies

(B) by the protagonist lying

(C) when the protagonist lies

(D) where they lie to the protagonist

(E) through the protagonist lying

9. <u>Because department stores need to maintain a wide range of inventory</u> on their shelves, wholesalers have quick and easy ordering forms online for stores to instantly request more stock when needed.

(A) Because department stores need to maintain a wide range of inventory

(B) Due to department stores which maintain a wide range of inventory

(C) Though department stores need constant maintaining of widely ranging inventory

(D) The need of department stores to maintain a wide range of inventory

(E) The reason that department stores maintain a wide range of inventory

10. Construction on the top floors <u>have finally been completed, for which the management can start</u> to look for tenants who desire to move into the new apartments.

(A) have finally been completed, for which the management can start

(B) have finally been completed, and the management can start

(C) has finally been completed, the management can start

(D) has finally been completed, so the management can start

(E) having finally been completed to where the management can start

11. <u>The African Pygmy hedgehog is starting to become a popular household pet, it having been domesticated only in the last decade or so.</u>

(A) The African Pygmy hedgehog is starting to become a popular household pet, it having been domesticated only in the last decade or so.

(B) The African Pygmy hedgehog, which is starting to become a popular household pet, was domesticated only in the last decade or so.

(C) The African Pygmy hedgehog is starting to become a popular household pet, it was domesticated only in the last decade or so.

(D) Only in the last decade or so, being domesticated, the African Pygmy hedgehog is starting to become a popular household pet.

(E) The African Pygmy hedgehog is starting to become a popular household pet, in the last decade or so being domesticated.

GO ON TO THE NEXT PAGE

12. President Herbert Hoover was originally popular with the American people in the 1920s, <u>his esteem was being</u> ruined after the Great Depression started in 1929.

    (A) his esteem was being
    (B) his esteem is
    (C) his esteem was
    (D) but his esteem was
    (E) but his esteem was being

13. While researching philosophers from Ancient Greece, where fields like philosophy and science are said to have their origins, <u>the works of Aristotle attracted Jesse with their complexity and insight</u>.

    (A) the works of Aristotle attracted Jesse with their complexity and insight
    (B) the works of Aristotle was attractively complex and insightful to Jesse
    (C) Jesse was attracted to the complexity and insight of the works of Aristotle
    (D) attractive to Jesse, the works of Aristotle were complex and insightful
    (E) the complexity and insight of the works of Aristotle attracted Jesse

14. The skills required of a computer animator <u>differs greatly from</u> the skills used for traditional hand-drawn cartoons.

    (A) differs greatly from
    (B) differs greatly to
    (C) differ greatly with
    (D) differ greatly to
    (E) differ greatly from

STOP

If you finish before time is called, you may check your work on this section only.
Do not turn to any other section in the test.

NO TEST MATERIAL ON THIS PAGE.

PRACTICE TEST 3: ANSWER KEY

2 Math	3 Reading	5 Writing	6 Math	7 Reading	8 Math	9 Reading	10 Writing
1. B	1. A	1. D	1. E	1. C	1. C	1. B	1. D
2. E	2. E	2. E	2. D	2. E	2. B	2. B	2. A
3. E	3. C	3. B	3. A	3. B	3. A	3. D	3. B
4. E	4. B	4. A	4. D	4. A	4. D	4. D	4. C
5. E	5. C	5. D	5. C	5. C	5. C	5. E	5. A
6. D	6. D	6. E	6. B	6. C	6. B	6. A	6. C
7. E	7. B	7. A	7. B	7. C	7. C	7. B	7. C
8. D	8. A	8. B	8. E	8. B	8. B	8. B	8. C
9. C	9. C	9. C	9. 1	9. D	9. D	9. E	9. A
10. B	10. A	10. D	10. 90	10. C	10. B	10. D	10. D
11. C	11. B	11. E	11. 130	11. D	11. A	11. C	11. B
12. C	12. C	12. C	12. 150	12. E	12. E	12. A	12. D
13. C	13. A	13. B	13. $\frac{4}{5} < q < \frac{6}{5}$ or $.8 < q < 1.2$	13. A	13. C	13. A	13. C
14. C	14. B	14. D	14. 6	14. B	14. C	14. E	14. E
15. A	15. D	15. D	15. $\frac{3}{2}$ or 1.5	15. E	15. D	15. C	
16. B	16. E	16. B	16. 10	16. C	16. C	16. C	
17. B	17. B	17. A	17. 11	17. E		17. B	
18. D	18. B	18. E	18. $\frac{40}{3}$ or 13.3	18. B		18. D	
19. E	19. A	19. B		19. B			
20. E	20. D	20. A		20. B			
	21. C	21. D		21. E			
	22. E	22. C		22. C			
	23. D	23. A		23. D			
	24. B	24. B		24. C			
	25. D	25. D					
		26. E					
		27. C					
		28. D					
		29. D					
		30. C					
		31. A					
		32. B					
		33. C					
		34. B					
		35. E					

SAT SCORING WORKSHEET

For directions on how to score your SAT practice test, see pages 10–11.

SAT Writing Section

Total Writing Multiple-Choice Questions Correct: [ ]

−

Total Writing Multiple-Choice Questions Incorrect: _____ ÷ 4 = [ ]

Grammar Raw Score: [ ]

_____

Grammar Scaled Subscore

[ ]

Compare the Grammar Raw Score with the Writing Multiple-Choice Subscore Conversion Table on page 258 to find the Grammar Scaled Subscore.

+

Your Essay Score (2–12): _____ × 2 = [ ]

_____

Writing Raw Score: [ ]

> Compare Raw Score with SAT Score Conversion Table on page 258 to find the Writing Scaled Score.

Writing Scaled Score

[ ]

SAT Critical Reading Section

Total Critical Reading Questions Correct: [ ]

−

Total Critical Reading Questions Incorrect: _____ ÷ 4 = [ ]

_____

Critical Reading Raw Score: [ ]

> Compare Raw Score with SAT Score Conversion Table on page 258 to find the Critical Reading Scaled Score.

Critical Reading Scaled Score

[ ]

SAT Math Section

Total Math Grid-In Questions Correct: [ ]

+

Total Math Multiple-Choice Questions Correct: [ ]

−

Total Math Multiple-Choice Questions Incorrect: _____ ÷ 4 = [ ]

Don't include wrong answers from grid-ins!

_____

Math Raw Score: [ ]

> Compare Raw Score with SAT Score Conversion Table on page 258 to find the Math Scaled Score.

Math Scaled Score

[ ]

SAT SCORE CONVERSION TABLE

Raw Score	Writing Scaled Score	Reading Scaled Score	Math Scaled Score
73	800		
72	790–800		
71	780–800		
70	770–800		
69	770–800		
68	760–800		
67	760–800	800	
66	760–800	770–800	
65	750–790	760–800	
64	740–780	750–790	
63	730–770	740–780	
62	720–760	730–770	
61	710–750	720–760	
60	700–740	710–750	
59	690–730	700–740	
58	680–720	690–730	
57	680–720	680–720	
56	670–710	670–710	
55	660–720	670–710	
54	650–690	660–700	760–800
53	640–680	650–690	740–780
52	630–670	640–680	730–770
51	630–670	630–670	710–750
50	620–660	620–660	690–730
49	610–650	610–650	680–720
48	600–640	600–640	670–710
47	590–630	600–640	660–700
46	590–630	590–630	650–690
45	580–620	580–620	650–690
44	570–610	580–620	640–680
43	570–610	570–610	630–670
42	560–600	570–610	620–660
41	560–600	560–600	610–650
40	550–590	550–590	600–640
39	540–580	550–590	590–630
38	530–570	540–580	590–630
37	530–570	530–570	580–620
36	520–560	530–570	570–610
35	510–550	520–560	560–600
34	500–540	520–560	560–600
33	490–530	510–550	550–590
32	480–520	500–540	540–580
31	470–510	490–530	530–570
30	470–510	480–520	520–560
29	460–500	470–510	520–560
28	450–490	470–510	510–550
27	440–480	460–500	500–540
26	430–470	450–490	490–530
25	420–460	440–480	480–520
24	410–450	430–470	470–510
23	410–450	430–470	460–500
22	400–440	420–460	450–490
21	400–440	410–450	440–480
20	390–430	400–440	430–470
19	380–420	400–440	430–470
18	370–410	390–430	420–460
17	370–410	380–420	410–450
16	360–400	370–410	400–440
15	350–390	360–400	400–440
14	340–380	350–390	390–430
13	330–370	340–380	380–420
12	320–360	340–380	360–400
11	320–360	330–370	350–390
10	310–350	320–360	340–380
9	300–340	310–350	330–370
8	290–330	300–340	320–360
7	280–320	300–340	310–350
6	270–310	290–330	300–340
5	260–300	280–320	290–330
4	240–280	270–310	280–320
3	230–270	250–290	280–320
2	230–270	240–280	270–310
1	220–260	220–260	260–300
0	210–250	200–240	250–290
–1	200–240	200–230	230–270
–2	200–230	200–220	220–260
–3	200–220	200–210	200–240

WRITING MULTIPLE-CHOICE SUBSCORE CONVERSION TABLE

Grammar Raw Score	Grammar Scaled Subscore
49	78–80
48	77–80
47	75–79
46	74–78
45	72–76
44	72–76
43	71–75
42	70–74
41	69–73
40	68–72
39	68–72
38	67–71
37	66–70
36	65–69
35	64–68
34	63–67
33	62–66
32	61–65
31	60–64
30	59–63
29	58–62
28	56–60
27	55–59
26	54–58
25	53–57
24	52–56
23	51–55
22	50–54
21	49–53
20	47–51
19	46–50
18	45–49
17	44–48
16	42–46
15	41–45
14	40–44
13	39–43
12	38–42
11	36–40
10	35–39
9	34–38
8	33–37
7	32–36
6	31–35
5	30–34
4	29–33
3	28–32
2	27–31
1	25–29
0	24–28
–1	22–26
–2	20–23
–3	20–22

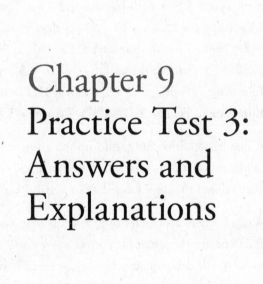

Chapter 9
Practice Test 3:
Answers and
Explanations

SECTION 2

1. **B** Create an equation: if $x + 4 = 19 - 4$, then $x + 4 = 15$. Subtract 4 from both sides to find that $x = 11$. Adding 4 to the right side of the equation, instead of subtracting it gives the incorrect answer in (D). Adding 4 to 19 initially, then adding 4 again gives the incorrect answer in (E). Only (B) fits correctly with the information given in the question.

2. **E** Make up numbers for b and a to make this easier. If $b = 2$ and $a = 3$, for example, then Marvin must spend \$2 on each banana and \$3 on each apple every day, so \$2 × 3 bananas = \$6 and \$3 × 1 apple = \$3. \$6 + \$3 = \$9 per day. \$9 × 7 days = \$63. \$63 is the target number. In the answers, replace b with 2 and replace a with 3. We're looking for the answer choice that gives us a total of 63. For (A), then, $7(2) + 3 = 14 + 3 = 17$. Get rid of it. For (B), $21(2) + 3 = 42 + 3 = 45$. Eliminate it. For (C), $7(2 + 3) = 7(5) = 35$. Eliminate it. For (D), $7[2 + 3(3)] = 7(2 + 9) = 7(11) = 77$. Eliminate it. For (E), $7[3(2) + 3] = 7(6 + 3) = 7(9) = 63$. (E) is correct.

3. **E** A quadrilateral has 360°. Add up the given angles. $115 + 75 + 45 = 235$. To find the remaining angle, subtract 235 from 360 to find that $360 - 235 = 125$. Since the unmarked angle of the quadrilateral and the angle labeled $a°$ are vertical angles, they must be equal to each other and $a = 125$.

4. **E** A good way to approach this problem is to test out the answers. Because the numerators of the two fractions are the same, the correct answer will cause the denominators to be the same. In (A), if $m = -4$, the denominators become −14 and 2, which are not equal. In (B), if $m = -2$, the denominators are unequal at −8 and 4. In (C), if $m = 0$, −2 does not equal 6. In (D), if $m = 2$, 4 does not equal 8, so (E) must be the answer. Testing (E) gives 10 = 10. To solve algebraically, set the denominators equal to each other and solve for m: $3m - 2 = m + 6$, so $2m = 8$ and $m = 4$.

5. **E** Ratios can be written as fractions by putting the first number on top. The pair of numbers that can be reduced to a fraction of $\frac{2}{3}$ is the one with the ratio of 2 to 3. $\frac{3}{6} = \frac{1}{2}$, eliminate (A). $\frac{4}{9}$ is as reduced as it can be, eliminate (B). (C) reduces to $\frac{1}{3}$, (D) reduces to $\frac{3}{5}$, and only (E) reduces to $\frac{2}{3}$.

6. **D** Susannah gave 15 of this flavor of jelly bean to Al. She gave 30 to Bea, 20 to Cai, 25 to Dan and 15 to Ellie. $15 + 30 + 20 + 25 + 15 = 105$. Now, set up the equation. These 105 jelly beans represent what percent of the 700 jelly beans? As an equation, write out $105 = \frac{x}{100}(700)$. This simplifies to $105 = 7x$. So $x = 15$, and the answer is (D), because the portion of the circle graph that equals 15% is the sector labeled "Cherry."

7. **E** Use slope formula, $m = \dfrac{y_2 - y_1}{x_2 - x_1}$ to find the slope, using $(-3, 7)$ and $(1, -3)$. $\dfrac{(-3) - 7}{1 - (-3)} = \dfrac{-10}{4} = -\dfrac{5}{2}$.

Since we know the slope is $-\dfrac{5}{2}$, now we can set up the slope formula again using $(1, -3)$ and $(3, t)$.

$-\dfrac{5}{2} = \dfrac{t - (-3)}{3 - 1} = \dfrac{t + 3}{2}$. Cross multiply to see that $2(t + 3) = -10$. Simplify so that $2t + 6 = -10$ and

$2t = -16$. Divide both sides by 2 so that $t = -8$.

8. **D** The three tens digit numbers (5_, 6_, and 7_) can each have any one of the three units digits numbers (_2, _3, and _4). Write them out or simply multiply 3 by 3.

9. **C** For questions with a weird symbol, just follow the instructions. In this case, plug 3 and 4 into the given equation with $x = 3$ and $y = 4$: $x + y \times y = 3 + 4 \times 3 = 15$, answer (C). Answer (D), 21, is the answer when PEMDAS is executed in the wrong order: any Multiplication and Division must happen before any Addition or Subtraction. Adding first leads to a different, and incorrect, answer.

10. **B** This is a classic Plugging In The Answers problem. Start with answer choice (C) and plug in that there are 100 g of grapes. Once we know the mass of grapes, we can look for other information in the problem to calculate the masses for the other fruits. Since the grapes have an equal mass to that of the orange slices, the orange slices also have a mass of 100 g. The mass of the strawberries is three times the mass of the grapes, so the mass of the strawberries is 300 g. Totaling these together, the total mass is 500 g and greater than the 400 g that we need the salad to be. Thus, if answer choice (C) is too big, then answer choices (D) and (E) will also be too big. We therefore move to answer choice (B), and by repeating the same calculations as those for (C), we get 400 g of salad. Therefore, answer choice (B) is correct.

11. **C** The easiest part of the equation is squaring 7, which gives 49. Subtracting 49 from both sides of the equation leaves $7^{x+3} = 49$, meaning that 7^{x+3} must equal 7^2. Solving for x in $x + 3 = 2$ gives $x = -1$, answer (C).

12. **C** The face of a cube is a square and since the length, width, and height of every cube is 1 inch, the area of each face is 1 square inch. Now we can just count how many faces are exposed. The first cube has 4 exposed faces; the faces not exposed are the one adjacent to the next cube and the one touching the table. The second cube has 3 exposed faces: the top, front, and back. In fact, the second through twelfth cubes (that's 11 cubes) all have 3 exposed faces each. And the final cube (like the first cube) has 4 exposed faces. Now add up all the faces: 4 from the first; $3 \times 11 = 33$, so 33 exposed faces on the middle 11 cubes; and 4 from the final cube. So $4 + 33 + 4 = 41$ exposed faces. And since the area of each exposed face is 1 square inch, the area of the exposed faces is 41 square inches.

13. **C** Compare each answer to the two statements above the question; choose the one that violates a rule. (A) can be true: We don't know anything about when Lisa cooks; likewise, (B) can be true because we don't know anything about Michael's work. For (C), it's possible that Lisa does not cook dinner on Tuesday for the same reason (A) can be true; however, Michael must cook dinner on Tuesday, as mentioned in the second statement, so (C) cannot be true. (D) can be true: Lisa only *sometimes* works on Saturday, so she might not have worked on that particular Saturday, and we don't know anything about Michael's work. (E) can also be true: we don't know about when Lisa cooks and we already know that Michael is cooking on Tuesday. Only (C) is impossible given the statements provided.

14. **C** This is a 6:8:10 right triangle. The circumference of the semicircle with diameter 6 is $\dfrac{\pi d}{2}$, which equals $\dfrac{\pi \times 6}{2} = 3\pi$. Likewise, the circumference of the semicircle with diameter 8 is $\dfrac{\pi d}{2} = \dfrac{\pi \times 8}{2} = 4\pi$. Therefore, the total perimeter is $3\pi + 4\pi + 10 = 7\pi + 10$. (E) is a distracter that might be chosen if the individual circumferences are not divided by 2 to account for half of a circle.

15. **A** We can solve this by Plugging In values for the variables. Just make sure to choose values for t and s that make the given inequality true. (For example, if $t = -2$ and $s = 3$, then the second part of the inequality is $0 < (-2) - 3$, or $0 < -5$, which is not true.). If $t = 2$ and $s = -3$, then $t - s = 2 - (-3) = 2 + 3 = 5$. Replace the variables in the answers with 2 and -3, and only (A) is true.

16. **B** The height of an equilateral triangle divides the triangle into two 30-60-90 special right triangles. Recall from the box of formulas at the beginning of the math section that the proportion of the sides in a 30-60-90 triangle is x, $x\sqrt{3}$, $2x$. In the case of triangle WXY, since we know the perimeter is 12, each side is 4, and, as we can see that side WX is opposite the 90° angle WX has a value of $2x$; thus, $x = 2$ and is the base of XYZ, the triangle we need to find the area of. Having found $x = 2$, we know the height is $2\sqrt{3}$. Using these values in the area formula gives us $\dfrac{1}{2}bh = \dfrac{1}{2} \times 2 \times 2\sqrt{3} = 2\sqrt{3}$.

17. **B** The first rule Carmen must satisfy in order to have her name posted is to compete in at least 12 matches, so eliminate from consideration the months in which she didn't do that: she competed in fewer than 12 matches in March and May, so she didn't get her name posted in those months. We can also eliminate those months in which she didn't win more than she lost: March (if we hadn't eliminated it already), April, and July are eliminated. That leaves only one month, June, in which she played in at least 12 matches and won more than she lost.

18. **D** The first arc is $\dfrac{1}{30}$ of the circumference of the circle, the second is $\dfrac{2}{30}$, the third is $\dfrac{4}{30}$, and the fourth is $\dfrac{8}{30}$. These four arcs account for $\dfrac{1}{30} + \dfrac{2}{30} + \dfrac{4}{30} + \dfrac{8}{30} = \dfrac{15}{30} = \dfrac{1}{2}$ of the circle. It is impossible to construct another arc in the same fashion because it would be bigger than the undivided part of the circle. So, there are four arcs constructed as described plus the semicircle, which also counts as an arc for a total of five arcs.

19. **E** The easiest way to work this problem is to Plug In numbers for the variables. If each part of the system of equalities equals 12, then $a = 12$, $b = 6$, $c = 4$, and $d = 3$. Then find the average of a, b, and c by adding those three values and dividing by three: $\dfrac{12+6+4}{3} = \dfrac{22}{3}$. Now resolve each answer (remember, $d = 3$); only (E) gives $\dfrac{22}{3}$. Solving the question algebraically takes more work. Begin by expressing each variable in terms of d: $a = 4d$; $2b = 4d$, so $b = 2d$; $3c = 4d$, so $c = \dfrac{4d}{3}$. Now add these up and divide by three: $\dfrac{a+b+c}{3} = \dfrac{4d + 2d + \dfrac{4d}{3}}{3}$. We can simplify this multiplying the top and bottom of the fraction by 3: $\dfrac{4d + 2d + \dfrac{4d}{3}}{3} \times \dfrac{3}{3} = \dfrac{12d + 6d + 4d}{9} = \dfrac{22d}{9}$.

20.   E   Begin by drawing each radius from the center of the circle to the points where the sides of the triangle touch the circle; there are 3 of these radii, and we know that each has length 1. Radii (such as these) are perpendicular to tangents, so they all form right angles with the sides of the triangle. The formula for area of a triangle is $A = \frac{1}{2}bh$, where b is the base and h is the height, so draw the height of the triangle, from the top point down to the base. An equilateral triangle has three 60° angles, so the top angle has just been cut in half: each smaller angle has a measure of 30°. Now we know that the two small triangles formed at the top of the original equilateral triangle are 30-60-90 triangles (30° at the top, 90° at the tangent point, and a 60° angle at the center of the circle.) The proportions of the legs of 30-60-90 triangles are x, $x\sqrt{3}$, and $2x$. In this case, x (across from the 30° angle, the radius of the circle) equals 1, so the longer leg (across from the 60° angle, the part of the original triangle from the tangent point to the top) has length $\sqrt{3}$, and the hypotenuse (from the center of the circle up to the top of the original triangle) has length 2. The height of the original, equilateral triangle is the sum of this hypotenuse and the length from the center of the circle down to the base (the radius of the circle, which is 1); therefore, the height is 3. The longer leg of the 30-60-90 triangle is half the length of the side of the original triangle; therefore, each side of the original equilateral triangle (including the base) is $2\sqrt{3}$. Now use these values in the area of a triangle formula: $\frac{1}{2}bh = \frac{1}{2} \times 2\sqrt{3} \times 3 = 3\sqrt{3}$.

SECTION 3

1.   A   The word in the blank must mean *abundant*, or "plentiful," making (A) the best answer. Eliminate (B), (C), and (E), which don't mean "plentiful." (D) is tempting, but *exorbitant* means "excessive," which does not match as well with "plentiful."

2.   E   The fact that Mrs. Weathersby was *urging him to investigate other options* suggests that the first blank should mean something like "change." This eliminates (A) and (D), but (B), (C), and (E) could all potentially fit. For the second blank, Justin probably does not feel positively about his decision-making abilities, since *his choice* reduces Mrs. Weathersby to *pleading with Justin* to change his choice. The second-blank words in (B), (C), and (D) are all positive and can be eliminated, leaving only (E) with words that fit both blanks.

3.   C   Kendra's novel is set in a *bustling, densely populated place. Metropolis* is another word for a large, busy city. (A) *neighborhood* is tempting, but a neighborhood is not bustling and densely populated by definition. (D) *prohibition* and (E) *conflict* might seem attractive because they sound like good settings for a novel, but they are not supported by the sentence.

4. **B** The clue for the first blank is that the alchemists *claimed the ability to create gold*. (A) and (B) are best supported by this clue. The word *actually helped* indicates that the second blank is in contrast to what is indicated in the first part of the sentence. Therefore *spawn* (or "create") is the remaining choice that is best supported by the question, and *eschew* does not fit, so (B) is the best match.

5. **C** The clue is that the music *is made up as it is performed*, so the blank must mean "made up on the spot." (C) *improvisational* is the only word that matches that definition. (D) *composed* and (E) *melodious* are attractive wrong answers because they both are words associated with music. (A) *beauteous* can also be used to describe music, and is an attractive wrong answer for that reason.

6. **D** There is not enough evidence in the sentence to reveal the meaning of each blank. In such a case, think instead about how the two blanks are related to each other. The words surrounding the second blank, *this...characteristic*, indicate that the two blanks have similar meanings. (A) and (B) contain words that are opposite in meaning, while (C) and (E) contain words that are unrelated. Only (D) offers words with similar meanings.

7. **B** The clue for the second blank, *a cure-all treatment* is the definition of *panacea*. (A) *remedy* could also fit, although *panacea* is the better choice because its definition more closely matches the clue. Regardless, the phrase *in spite of* suggests that the first blank means the opposite of the second part of the sentence. Therefore, (B) *profusion* fits, whereas (A) *abstruseness* does not.

8. **A** The clue for the first blank is that the students are *over-eager*, and that they *flatter* Professor Jackson. This clue makes a good case for *sycophantic*, which is an adjective meaning "having the quality of a sycophant," or, in other words, a "flatterer." (C) *ostentatious*, is the only other answer choice that one could possibly make an argument for, based on the clue, but its definition is not as supported by the sentence. The second blank describes students who would have had more luck winning the professor's approval. Therefore, the second blank needs to contrast with the first. In (A) *sincere* contrasts with *sycophantic*, whereas in (C) *eccentric* does not contrast with *ostentatious*.

9. **C** The passage states that in the past, *interspecies hybridization was dismissed as a possible solution, since hybrids are rarely as vigorous as purebred species*. Thus, it must have been believed that "vigor" was an essential trait for evolution. *Robust* means "vigorous." Answer choices (A), (B), (D), and (E) are not indicated in the passage.

10. **A** The passage states that *virtually all scientists accept the principles of evolutionary theory*, even though there are parts of it that are still mysterious, like the *mechanism of rapid and drastic change between species*. (A) states that scientists will adopt a theory that *includes elements about which little is known*, which matches the first sentence. None of the other answers are mentioned in the passage.

11. **B** The author states that modern art is *subversive* and *socially deconstructive*. Thus, in addition to an artistic function, modern art serves a social function, though not necessarily a positive one (depending on your point of view). (A) is too strong and not indicated in the passage, while (C), (D), and (E) state value judgments that are not explicitly supported by the passage.

12. **C**   We know that the spaces *provide the distinctively un-cozy, anti-domestic space modern art requires.* (C) is a good paraphrase of this. (A) and (B) are too strong and not supported by the passage. (D) is deceptive; the spaces provide a place for *artists to discuss aesthetic ideas*, which are not necessarily subversive political ideas. (E) is not supported by the passage.

13. **A**   The author states that he *found it difficult..., since the project that became so complex and multifaceted had once seemed so simple.* Thus, he did not anticipate the *unexpected changes to* (his) *plan* (A). The other answers are not indicated in the passage.

14. **B**   The author's main point in the paragraph is to talk about how *omnivores* have a *complicated relationship with food.* The sentence about *a cow* describes an animal that has *a simple decision* about what to eat. The following sentence, which begins with *but* and returns to the theme of people's difficult decisions regarding food is an additional clue that what is happening is a *contrast* (B).

15. **D**   According to the passage, solving the riddle is *the reason humans originally developed such large and complex brains.* So, it must be pretty important, as (D) indicates. Line 18 says *seemingly simple,* which means it isn't really simple; this eliminates (A) and (E). The other answers are not supported by the passage.

16. **E**   The author refers to American cuisine to explain why he wanted to *trace the ingredients that make up a typical fast food meal.* (E) paraphrases this nicely. (A) might be true, but doesn't answer the question. (B), (C), and (D) are not indicated in the passage.

17. **B**   The author refers to the *presumably pastoral origins,* so he is *uncertain about a source* (B). Answers (A), (C), (D), and (E) are not supported by the passage.

18. **B**   The author says that he *didn't realize that following these paths would be more complex than ever imagined.* The sentence separates the first part of the passage from the second half. In the first half, he mentions his plan, and in the second, he talks about the problems. (A) is wrong because the paragraph isn't an *aside,* it's a major point. (B) is the correct answer: he is saying that there was an *unforeseen issue,* namely that the whole thing was *more complex* than he thought. (C) is wrong because he isn't sad that he didn't have facts for his book. (D) is wrong because there isn't an *eventual resolution of the apparent flaw,* in fact that author can't resolve the complexity of his undertaking. (E) is wrong because the author didn't even specify any findings that are *not as trustworthy as initially supposed.*

19. **A**   The author uses the reference to *a glass of water* to show how hard it is to follow a specific food chain. (A) paraphrases this point successfully. The other answers are not indicated in the passage.

20. **D**   The *greater difficulty* is that the author believed his path *existed in splendid isolation,* when it was actually *hopelessly intertwined* with other paths, leading to side trips. In other words, it was easy to become *sidetracked by secondary pursuits.* (A), (B), and (C) are not mentioned in the passage, while (E) is an overly literal choice (and there's no hardship).

21. C The author mentions the *tributaries, inlets, and channels* in order to point out that the topic he had chosen to study *was hopelessly intertwined with all sorts of other streams*. In other words, he's trying to show how complex his study became, which is what (C) says. None of the other answers are mentioned in the passage.

22. E Go back to the passage and use the context to come up with a word to replace *splendid*. It should be something like "total," because we know that *splendid isolation* is strongly opposed to *hopelessly intertwined*. Only *absolute* is a good match.

23. D The author *felt like he had lost sight of* his *original goal* but, in the last paragraph, states that *in the end*, he realizes *that no part of an ecosystem...can be studied without considering the broad framework*—in other words, he found that the *side trips* provided or contained information that was necessary to truly understand the *process* he was tracing of food as it travels down food chains.

24. B The last sentence is a conclusion based on the experience the author has just described. Eliminate (A) because there's no *hope*; get rid of (C) because the sentence does not suggest *grim foreboding*, eliminate (D) since *recent scholarship* is never mentioned; cross off (E) because the sentence is not an *afterthought* and not *ironic*.

25. D The passage spends most of the time just discussing the things the author studied, and how complicated that study became. (A) is too limited; *corn* is really mentioned in only one paragraph. (B) is wrong because the author doesn't really have a *theory*, instead he is just describing how he hoped to investigate food. (C) and (E) aren't mentioned in the passage. (D) is correct. We definitely know about the author's *thought processes*, as he *contemplates issues in food production*.

SECTION 5

1. D The sentence as written is a sentence fragment. Answer choices (B), (C), and (E) are sentence fragments as well, leaving only (D). The verb form *demonstrated* is required to show that an event started in the past *During the early 1980s*.

2. E This sentence has a misplaced modifier issue. The modifying phrase is "*Written by John Patrick Shanley in 2004*," which is meant to refer to "*the play* Doubt: A Parable." In the original, however, *the Pulitzer Prize* is the closest noun to the phrase, and is therefore incorrectly being modified by the phrase. While it seems that both (C) and (E) fix the problem, only (E) refers to the play itself. (C) actually refers to just a part of the play, the *challenging themes* thus making (E) the correct answer.

3. **B** As written, the verb in the sentence is *curve* (plural), and the subject is *row* (singular), so (A) is incorrect. (B) fixes the problem. (C) changes the subject from *row* to *ruined old buildings* (plural). The phrase *ruined old buildings* does not agree with the singular *curves*, and also creates a change in meaning (do the buildings themselves actually curve?). (D) contains the same problems. (E) has a subject/verb agreement problem (*row* is singular, and *curve* is plural). Therefore, (B) must be the correct answer.

4. **A** The sentence is correct as written. In (B) the pronoun *it* is not necessary and is redundant with the subject of the sentence. (C) is unnecessarily passive. (D) creates a sentence fragment by replacing the verb *codifies* with the gerund *codifying*. (E) creates a sentence fragment by starting the clause with *which*.

5. **D** The sentence as written is a fragment, so eliminate (A). In choosing a verb that will make this a complete sentence, remember that collective nouns take a singular verb. *A class* is the subject of the sentence, and is singular. The correct verb should be *arrives*, eliminating (B) and (E). (C) is a sentence fragment; the second half of the sentence would need a verb parallel to *arrives* to make sense.

6. **E** The sentence contains a misplaced modifier. The modifying statement *once considered to be a vast and insignificant jungle* describes the *Amazon rainforest*. The modifier must be right next to what it is modifying. All the choices except for (E) have something else next to the modifier.

7. **A** The sentence is correct as written. Eliminate (D) and (E) because they contain misplaced modifiers, making it sound as if the lyrics and stories refer to people, not *Bob Dylan's songs*. (B) also changes the subject of the sentence from *songs* to *Bob Dylan*, which isn't correct. (C) omits the verb *are* which is necessary to the sentence.

8. **B** This question is testing parallel structure. The non-underlined verb is *to predict*; eliminate all verbs that aren't parallel, and only (B), *to assume* remains. Elimination based on verb endings also leads to the same answer.

9. **C** The adjective *larger* would more clearly modify *profit* if *larger* came before the word *profit*. This eliminates choice (A) and (B), which each contain a comparison error as well. (D) has a comparison error by not identifying the *profits* of all the activities as the point of comparison. (E) makes the sentence more wordy. (C) correctly compares a modified noun (*larger profit*) with another modified noun (*total profits*) leaving (C) as the best choice.

10. **D** Take a look at the beginnings of the sentences. The words *when, who, which,* or *while* are meant to replace the word *connection*. A connection is not a time, so get rid of (A) and (B). A connection is not a person, so get rid of (C). You're left with (D) and (E); if you're not sure which to pick, look at pronouns. (E) uses "their" which is incorrect since *connection* is singular, so it can't be right.

11. **E** This is an idiom question. Though many idioms can be spotted by the use of prepositions, that's not always the case. Here, the question is testing the phrase *not so much for…as for*. Since we're looking for *as* rather than *but*, we can eliminate (A), (B), and (C). From there, eliminate (D), since the phrase *as for him regarding* isn't parallel with *his…interest*.

12. **C** In (C), the adjective *deep* cannot be used to modify a verb: it needs to be in adverb form. (A) is correct in using the pronoun in subject case.

13. **B** Choice (B) contains a verb agreement error. Verbs need to be parallel in form, and since *moved* is in the past tense, *vacuuming* should agree, and would be correct as *vacuumed*.

14. **D** The verb in (A) is grammatically correct because it is in the same tense as *needed*. The verb in (B) is also fine because it is parallel to *study*. (C) contains the proper reflexive pronoun to refer to *Brian*. (D), however, contains a parallelism error: *he should* is not parallel to *to read* and *to study and prepare*.

15. **D** The verb in (D), *aims*, is in present tense and is not parallel to the previous verb *deconstructed* which is in past tense.

16. **B** (A) has no error because the verb *promote* is parallel in tense to *focus* earlier in the sentence. (B) is grammatically incorrect because *is why* is redundant when *Because* is already used at the beginning of the sentence.

17. **A** The verb in (A) does not agree with its subject which is *a collection of tools*. Even though *tools* is plural, the actual subject is *a collection*, which is singular. Thus, the verb should be the singular *is*.

18. **E** This sentence is correct as written.

19. **B** The verb in (B) is in the present perfect tense and is not parallel to the past tense verb *helped*.

20. **A** The pronoun *their* in (A) does not agree with *Star Wars*. Since it is the title of a movie, it is a singular subject and requires a singular pronoun to refer to it.

21. **D** The adjective *unsuccessful* in (D) is incorrect because it is modifying the verb *updated*. It must be in adverb form to be able to modify a verb.

22. **C** There is a double comparison in (C). The suffix on *safer* serves the same purpose as *more* and is considered redundant.

23. **A** The conjunction in (A) is used incorrectly. The fact that Bach's music *did not gain recognition* is not a result of being *performed in numerous cities*. Something like "Although" would be more appropriate.

24. **B** The verb *reacting* in (B) is used with the incorrect preposition. The correct version of the idiom is *reacting to*.

25. **D** There are pronoun agreement and verb agreement errors in (D). The non-underlined portion indicates a single painting in the phrase *if you examine one.* In (D), *their* is plural, but we are referring back to *one,* which is singular. The verb *have* agrees with the incorrect pronoun, *their.* To agree with *one*, it should be singular, *has.*

26. **E** This sentence is correct as written. Remember, just because it "sounds funny," doesn't mean it's wrong. Always identify the error before selecting an answer. (E) is going to be right approximately $\frac{1}{5}$ of the time, so if you've checked all the underlined portions and haven't identified an error, don't be afraid to pick (E).

27. **C** The pronouns in (C) *he* and *she* are singular, and *or* indicates that only one is applicable at a time. The noun that is replaced, *diplomats*, is plural. Therefore (C) is grammatically incorrect because it fails to follow the rules of pronoun agreement.

28. **D** The way the sentence is written, it sounds like the *three weeks* weren't going to hear from Howard. The author intends to say that the three weeks went by before Janet heard from Howard, and the difference is a grammatically significant error.

29. **D** The error here is (D) because it is a faulty comparison. The author is comparing the *value* of autographed books to *books.* These things are not comparable, and should be correctly be written *greater than that of books,* so (D) is the correct answer.

30. **C** It may or may not be a commonly held view that the *Midwest* is boring (A), but even if it is, the author isn't mentioning this for its own sake; the purpose is to introduce the idea the author wants to shoot down. The author never describes any geographical features of the Midwest, so eliminate (B). Just because some people on the coasts believe that the Midwest is boring does not mean that they actually have a bias, as (D) says, and that's certainly not the purpose of sentence 1, which is what the correct answer must describe. The first sentence expresses the belief of those on the coasts, not the writer's belief as in (E). The author introduces the belief that the Midwest is boring in order to show disagreement in sentence 2 as (C) says.

31. **A** The version in (A) features a well-structured comparison between *Branson* (a town) and those near ski or beach resorts. Also, the original run-on sentence has been corrected with a colon and better structure. (B) contains the same faulty comparison as the original sentence: *Branson* can't be compared with *ski and beach resorts.* (C) contains a pronoun error; plural *their* should refer back to *Branson,* which is singular. In (D), the placement of *every year* implies that this phrase refers to Branson itself, not to travelers who visit annually. (E) changes meaning by comparing different groups of travelers instead of different towns.

32. **B** The paragraph discusses the tourist appeal of Branson, so information that details what is interesting about would be supportive after sentence 4. Sentence 5 refers to *its shows* as if the reader knows that Branson offers *live performances* as mentioned in (B), the correct answer. Information about uninteresting attractions elsewhere does not describe Branson's appeal in (A). As for (C), the general history of Branson is not as relevant to the paragraph's topic. Moving sentence 6 as in (D) results in a sentence that references the more familiar *Branson* immediately before a sentence that refers to *Branson, Missouri*, which should be the more complete first reference. Deleting sentence 2 as in (E) could change the meaning of sentence 3, making *One example* equate *Branson* with *nothing interesting* rather than describing that view as erroneous.

33. **C** The paragraph is about Branson, so it makes sense for the subject of the sentence to refer more closely to the city than to *Huge billboards*—eliminate (A) and (D). (B)'s structure makes it unclear whether *billboards that are everywhere advertising shows, shops, and malls* are seen only by tour bus occupants or occupants of the hotels and motels as well. In (E), the statement *the streets are lined* makes *are everywhere* redundant. (C) is correct because it focuses on *the streets* of Branson and clearly describes the relationships of where things are and who the object of the billboard's advertising is.

34. **B** In (B), the phrase *people unfamiliar with Branson* is more specific than the word *people* in the original sentence, *recreational activities* is more idiomatically correct than *recreations*, and a comma followed by *including* links these two items well. (A) is not good because the passage's tone supports using *people* rather than *you*. In (C), *people* is vague, and the repetition of *might* weakens the sentence. In (D), *can all be found* is passive, and *they* is vague. (E) is an awkward run-on sentence and goes against the tone of the passage with *you*.

35. **E** The use of the word *Lastly* in (E) creates a smoother transition from the previous sentence since this is the last item in a list. The original sentence (A) is somewhat ambiguous, since it is unclear exactly what *it* refers to. (B) contains the phrase *even though*, which sets up a contrast that does not exist in the sentence. The use of *because* in (C) is misleading; the towns don't have the same assets because of the greater safety. In (D) the use of *however* as a transition from the previous sentence doesn't make sense.

SECTION 6

1. **E** $9^2 - 9 = 81 - 9 = 72$. Use each answer choice to find out which one does not go into 72 fully. $72 \div 6 = 12$, for example. So, (A) 6 and (C) 12 are both factors—eliminate them. $72 \div 8 = 9$, so eliminate (B). $72 \div 18 = 4$. Eliminate (D). Only (E) 32 does not go in evenly $72 \div 32 = 2.25$. making it the correct answer.

2. **D** Make up a number for c. If $c = 2$, the total cost of the meal would be $190 ($150 for the up-front fee and $20 for each of the two courses). Plugging $c = 2$ into all five answer choices shows that (D) is the correct answer.

3. **A** If CDE is an isosceles triangle and $DE = 4$, this means the width of the rectangle, CE must equal 4 as well, since CD is the hypotenuse (it's across from the 90° angle and the side across from the longest angle must be the longest side). Subtract 4 from 16 to get 12 as the length of AE, the length of the rectangle. Area of a rectangle = length × width, so the area of rectangle $ABCE = 12 \times 4 = 48$, choice (A).

4. **D** Let's start by pulling out as many "$d + e$" terms as we can. In the middle of the list is $bd + be$, which we can change to $b(d + e)$. Since $d + e = 5$, this is the same as $5b$. There's also ad at the end, and ae at the beginning, and we can change $a(d + e)$ to $5a$. Now all that's left is ce and cd, which become $5c$. Now we have $5a + 5b + 5c$. Factor out the 5 that's in all three terms, and we're left with $5(a + b + c)$, or $5(4) = 20$, answer (D).

5. **C** The problem states that *the number of residents increased a constant amount every 2 years*. If we look at the years 2000 and 2002, the population went up by 400 residents. That number increased from 2002 to 2004 by 400, so there were 1,350 residents in 2004, in 2006 there will be 400 more, for a total of (C) 1,750. Answers (B) and (D) reflect the increase over a period of 1 year rather than 2.

6. **B** The absolute value around $g(x)$ means that all y-values of the graph become positive. The correct graph of $g(x)$ must either look exactly like the graph above the question, if $g(x)$ is positive, or is the reflection of that graph across the x-axis if $g(x)$ is negative. None of the answers match the question image, but if the graph in (B) were reflected across the x-axis, it would match the figure in the question, so this is the correct answer.

7. **B** Check each statement, one at a time, and eliminate any answers that don't reflect whether a statement is true or false. Statement I is not necessarily true, because we do not know which people were interested in each city, just overall percentages of total people. Eliminate (A) and (D), because they both contain I. Statement II is true: 52% of the people were interested in Colombo, so eliminate (C) because it does not contain II. At first statement III might seem to be true, but the six percentage figures total more than 100%, which means that at least some people said they were interested in more than one city. Eliminate (E), because it contains III. As only statement II is true, (B) is correct.

8. **E** Calculate what the exponent of the original a is multiplied by to make it a^6. So, if $\frac{2}{5}x = 6$, what is the value of x? Multiply both sides by 5, then divide by 2 to find that $x = 15$. What this means is that $(a^{\frac{2}{5}})^{15} = a^6$. Since $a^{\frac{2}{5}} = b$, $(a^{\frac{2}{5}})^{15} = b^{15}$, and (E) is correct.

9. **1** The point $(2, 9)$ is an ordered pair that will produce a solution for b in the given equation. The equation should be $9 = 4 \times 2 + b$. Solving for b yields $b = 1$.

10. **90** Reversing the two specified digits would give us a new number: 521,436.98. Find the difference by subtracting the original number (521,346.98) from the new number (521,436.98).

11. **130** There are 360 degrees in a quadrilateral and opposite sides and angles are equal in a parallelogram. Therefore, if a large angle (angle P) of a parallelogram is 110°, the small angle (angle PTR) is 70°. We need to find the measure of angle PTS, so we need to add the 60° of angle RTS in the equilateral triangle, giving a total of 130° for angle PTS.

12. **150** When two parallel lines are cut by a third line, the measures of the alternate interior angles (the two small angles, in this case) are equal; therefore, $c - 10 = 2c - 50$. Solve for c: subtract c from both sides to get $-10 = c - 50$. Then add 50 to both sides: $40 = c$. Therefore, both angles ($c - 10$) and ($2c - 50$) equal 30°. Because the angle ($2c - 50$) and d form a straight line, their measures must add up to 180°. Since ($2c - 50$) is 30, then subtract that from 180 to find d: $d = 180 - 30 = 150$.

13. $\dfrac{4}{5} < q < \dfrac{6}{5}$ **or .8 < q < 1.2**

    Split the question into two separate inequalities and solve independently. $0 < 5q - 4$ yields $\dfrac{4}{5} < q$. $5q - 4 < 2$ yields $q < \dfrac{6}{5}$. Any fraction between $\dfrac{4}{5}$ and $\dfrac{6}{5}$ or decimal between .8 and 1.2 that fits in the spaces available in the grid-in box counts as a correct answer.

14. **6** The fact that there is no figure makes this one more difficult. The referenced point is 3 units below the lowest point of the circle. Since distance is measured in a straight line, just count the distance on the y-axis. This tells us that the point $(0, -6)$ is on the circle, so from there to the origin is a distance of 6.

15. $\dfrac{3}{2}$ **or 1.5**

    A parabola (the shape of the graph of a quadratic function) is symmetrical: therefore, the x-value of the vertex must be half-way between $(-7, -10)$ and $(0, -10)$. The average of the x-values of these points is the x-value of the vertex: $\dfrac{-7 + 0}{2} = -\dfrac{7}{2}$, or -3.5. The vertex is also half-way between $(-8.5, 0)$ and $(m, 0)$. Since the distance from -8.5 to -3.5 is 5, the distance from -3.5 to m must also be 5: $-3.5 + 5 = 1.5$, which is the value of m.

16. **10** Imagine lining up all the rocks in order of value: the 15 50-pound rocks, followed by the x 70-pound rocks, followed by the 6 110-pound rocks. The median weight is the weight of the middle rock; to get the fewest number of 70-pound rocks, say that the first 70-pound rock is the median (middle). That means there are 15 50-pound rocks before the median, so there must be 15 rocks after the median as well. We know that 6 of those rocks weigh 110 pounds, so the other 9 must weigh 70 pounds. Add those 9 to the 1 we used as the median, and there are 10 rocks that weigh 70 pounds.

17. **11** Since a flower must be planted every three feet, simply divide 30 by 3 to yield 10 flowers. However, this question is tough because it's easy to forget the first flower. There are 10 "jumps" between flowers, not 10 flowers. Remember to tack the first flower back on to the total.

18. $\dfrac{40}{3}$ or 13.3

We're going to use the distance = rate × time formula a few times here. Substitute the given information for the first part of the turtle's walk into the formula: $5 = 10t_1$. Solve for the time spent on the first leg: $t_1 = \dfrac{5}{10} = \dfrac{1}{2}$. That means the turtle spent half a minute on the first part. Do this for the second part as well: $5 = 20t_2$, so $t_2 = \dfrac{5}{20} = \dfrac{1}{4}$. Add these two times to get the total time for the trip: $\dfrac{1}{2} + \dfrac{1}{4} = \dfrac{2}{4} + \dfrac{1}{4} = \dfrac{3}{4}$. Then use the $d = rt$ formula a third time to find the rate for the entire 10-foot walk: $10 = r \times \dfrac{3}{4}$. Solve for r: $r = \dfrac{40}{3}$, or 13.3.

SECTION 7

1. **C** The clue is that Calla wants to *add more detailed footnotes*. The word for the blank must mean something like "add to." Only (C), *amend* has this meaning. (E) may be tempting because it is positive, but it does not have a direct connection to anything specific in the sentence.

2. **E** The candidate thought he would win, so a good word for the first blank means "a lot." Eliminate any answers with a drastically different meaning. The word *but* means the sentence changes direction, so instead of "a lot," a word for the second blank means "a little." Note that *narrow* is being used with one of its secondary definitions here, and is a good opposite to *extensive,* making (E) the best answer.

3. **B** The clue for the first blank is the description *sadly.* Therefore, (C) *enthralling* doesn't make sense because it's a positive description and (A) *amendable* is not an explicitly negative description. The word *banal* from the second part of the sentence means "commonplace, tired, or predictable." We know the second blank contrasts with *banal* because the songs described by that blank are *lost among* the banal ones. (B) is the best choice because *mixed* is supported by *with the profound songs lost among the many banal ones.*

4. **A** The clue to help us figure out what the *tone* could be is *dark and gloomy circumstances with dismal endings.* Thus, the blank should mean something close to *dark and gloomy.* The closest choice is *doleful,* which means "sorrowful; mournful; melancholy."

5.　**C**　There is a clue to the meaning of the blank in that the statement is *a fundamental principle*. This describes a *maxim*. All of the other answers could describe an aspect of a philosophical camp but none are supported by the sentence itself.

6.　**C**　Eliminate answers that do not work for both passages. Eliminate (A) as it is not indicated in either passage. Only Passage 2 mentions *theories about cats*, so eliminate (B). Neither passage really supports the idea that *cats...are highly intelligent*, so eliminate (D). Similarly, neither passage goes so far as to say that *dogs are significantly more intelligent than cats*, so get rid of (E). The correct answer is (C). Passage 1 mentions *The notion...originates in human presumption* and that *we leap to conclusions*. Passage 2 describes a group (*typical cat owners*) who have a strong view that opposes that probably held by dog owners.

7.　**C**　The *line of reasoning* can be summarized as basing conclusions about animal intelligence on *our observations of other humans*. The author of Passage 2 suggests that *this thinking presupposes a complete understanding of the nature of animal intelligence...a level of understanding that we have not yet acquired*. Answer (C) paraphrases this nicely. The other answers are not supported by the passage. The correct answer is (C).

8.　**B**　Passage 2 notes that *a complete understanding of the nature of animal intelligence...(is) a level of understanding that we have not yet acquired*. Thus, the passage refers to the *current state of scientific knowledge*. (A) is false because neither passage explains the behavior of cats (though both mention it). (C) and (E) are out because they're mentioned in both passages. Neither passage explicitly discusses the *beliefs of dog owners*, so eliminate (D). This leaves only answer (B).

9.　**D**　The first passage states that *From our observations of other humans, we infer that independence and reluctance to follow orders correlate with intelligence*. The second passage implies this same idea, by stating that *Cat-lover's theories about the braininess of their pets revolve around the belief that cats have too much self-respect to obey their owner's whims*. So people *determine intelligence* by *assessing conduct*, (D). (A), (B), and (E) are not mentioned in the passage. The opposite of (C) is mentioned in both passages.

10.　**C**　The faculty is described as *competent enough*. The passage further states that they *ground out instruction*, strongly suggesting that the faculty is merely "acceptable." *Adequate* is a good match. The correct answer is (C).

11.　**D**　Una is clearly a big fan of going to school, even if she doesn't respect her teachers. The author uses "fled" to dramatize that she is *eager to immerse herself in learning*. Answers (A) and (B) might be true (although we don't know for sure), but they don't answer the question. (C) and (E) are not indicated in the passage.

12. **E**   Eliminate any answers that are not supported by the passage. (A) is extreme (and false, since Una doesn't seem to think these skills are important). Eliminate (B) because it's not a list of *anecdotes*. (C) is out because while Una doesn't think much of these activities, we don't know if that's related to her *social status*. (D) is a poor answer because the list is not one of *amusements*, and *oppression* is much too strong. The correct answer is (E).

13. **A**   After painting a picture of how Una didn't really "fit in" in Panama, the author goes on to state that she was *more practical than either Panama or herself had believed*. In other words, she's capable of more than she thought. (A) paraphrases this succinctly. The other answers are not indicated in the passage.

14. **B**   The passage states that the teachers who gave the lectures were *humorless and unvisioned grinds* who *croaked out platitudes*. So her lectures were boring. The only word that means "boring" is (B) *tedious*.

15. **E**   Go back to the passage and use the context to come up with a word to replace *sniffed*. Since the professors viewed the card-ledgers as *new-fangled nonsense*, something like "looked down on" would work. (E), *scoffed*, is the only answer that matches.

16. **C**   The author deliberately uses the word *inspired* to show that the professors are anything but inspired; phrases such as *humorless and unvisioned grinds* and *croaked out such platitudes* make this clear. Using words to suggest their opposite meaning is one definition of irony. The correct answer is (C).

17. **E**   The key phrase is that *Una saw the girls…in a mass*, meaning they were *largely indistinguishable*. None of the other answers are indicated in the passage.

18. **B**   The last sentence of the paragraph states that *the unique past of the favela has taught its residents the value of unity and organization*. (B) is an accurate paraphrase of this. (A), (C), and (E) are all inferences that we don't know to be true, while (D) is extreme and not supported by the passage.

19. **B**   The last sentence is the author's way of explaining why Vidigal is *an unusually close-knit community*: because of its *unique past*. The author then goes on to describe Vidigal's unique past. So he is (B) *introducing an idea* (the unique past of Vidigal) *to be explored*. (A) is wrong because he's not emphasizing an *interesting discrepancy*.

20. **B**   The author mentions the *new shirts* to show that Paolo Duque didn't do a whole lot for the citizens of Vidigal. His actions were, in other words, *relatively minor*, and the answer is (B). The other answers are not mentioned in the passage.

21. **E**   Paolo Duque says that *his hands were tied, at least until the next election*. So he doesn't care too much about the citizens of Vidigal, because there isn't a reason for him to care. (E), *apathetic*, means to not care. (B), *belligerent*, is wrong because he isn't trying to pick a fight with the citizens, but is instead simply brushing them off.

22. C   The *fight* that the citizens of Vidigal decided on was mostly about getting others to help them out, especially the many *prominent social organizations*, and the *remaining population*. So their fight was really about (C) *finding support*.

23. D   The description evaluates Duque, noting that he made *token gestures...while neglecting to bring about real change*. (D), a *frank assessment*, accurately describes this. (A), (C), and (E) are not supported, and (B) is much too strong.

24. C   The fourth paragraph discusses the importance of *prominent social organizations* as well as *an organized, unified, and passionate neighborhood organization*. (C) paraphrases the mention of these two groups. (A) is the opposite of what is indicated by the passage. (B) is no good because *voting* is not mentioned. (D) is out because we have no idea whether the leaders were *educated*. Eliminate (E) because *national press organizations* are not discussed.

SECTION 8

1. C   Plug $b = 4$ into the equation, giving $6a + 12 = 32$. Isolate $6a = 20$, and divide each side by 2 to find $3a = 10$.

2. B   Draw the line, with the points in the order X, R, Q, S, Z. Write 4 over QS. Because Q splits $\overline{XZ}$ exactly in half, and R and S are midpoints of each half, XR, RQ, QS, and SZ each has a length of 4. Thus, since RZ is made up of 3 segments, the total length is 12.

3. A   Set $A = \{10, 12, 14, 16, 18, 20\}$. Set $B = \{9, 12, 15, 18\}$. Both sets include 12 and 18, so there are two members in set C. Be careful: (D) is the number of members in a set that consists of all the members of set A and set B (without repeats). (E) is the number of members in set A plus the number of members in set B.

4. D   Use the first values given in the problem for x and y in the equation to find the value of c. $9 = 4c$, so $c = 2.25$. Now use that and second value of y given in the problem to find the value of x when y is 36. $36 = 2.25x$, so $x = 16$. Because x is multiplied by a constant, c, we can also set this up as proportions with the values of y and x: $\dfrac{9}{36} = \dfrac{4}{x}$, again resulting in $x = 16$.

5. C   The coordinates in (A) and (E) are outside of the circle. The pair in (B) is at the center of the circle. (D) is inside of the circle. (C) is a point on the circumference and on horizontal diameter. The center of the circle is at $(4, -4)$. From -1 to -7 on the y-axis is a distance of 6, and half that gives a radius of 3. $(7, -4)$ is 3 units to the right of the center of the circle.

6. **B** Because the percents on a circle graph must add up to 100%, the value of x must be 30. The ratio of 10% to 30% is equal to a ratio of 1 to 3. (A) gives the ratio of comedies to action movies. (C) gives a ratio of romance to the total of romance and comedy. (D) gives the ratio of romance to action. (E) gives the ratio of romance to the total of comedy and action.

7. **C** There are a total of 4,200 students at Central Valley High School, so divide this by the average number of students per classroom to find out how many classrooms there are: $4,200 \div 33.6 = 125$. Now that we know there are 125 classrooms total in Central Valley High School, we can multiply this number by the average number of electronic devices brought by students to class per classroom $125 \times 22.4 = 2,800$, answer (C). Dividing by 22.4 and multiplying by 33.6 give the incorrect result found in (E). (D) is the number of classrooms subtracted from the total number of students $(4,200 - 125 = 4,075)$.

8. **B** Continue each sequence, one term at a time. The fourth term of Y is 20 $(15 + 5)$. The fourth term of Z is 24 (12×2), which is greater, but not more than three times greater. The fifth term of Y is 25 $(20 + 5)$ while the fifth term of Z is 48 (24×2). This is almost twice as much as the fifth term of Y, but not big enough. Eliminate (A). The sixth term of Y is 30, while the sixth term of Z is 96, which is more than three times 30. The answer is (B).

9. **D** Try Plugging In numbers for the variables. If x, y, and z were 2, 3, and 4, then statement II would be true because $4 = 2 \times 2$. Eliminate any answers that don't include II: (A) and (C). If we try larger values (like 3, 4, and 5), then none of the statements are true, so try smaller values. If x, y, and z were 1, 2, and 3, then statement I would be true: $2 = 2 \times 1$. Eliminate (B) because it doesn't include I. Statement III can never be true because y would have to be 1 and z would have to be 2. That means that x would be 0, but the question states that all three must be positive. Eliminate (E) because it contains III, leaving only (D) as the correct answer.

10. **B** If the probability that a bronze statue will be selected at random is $\frac{2}{5}$, then $\frac{2}{5}$ of the sculptures are bronze statues. Since there are a total of y sculptures, multiplying y by $\frac{2}{5}$ gives the number of bronze statues. We could also Plug In a number for y. If there are a total of 10 sculptures, then 4 of them are bronze sculptures. Only (B) gives a result of 4 when y is replaced with 10.

11. **A** The value of the functions of $f(x)$ and $g(x)$ can be found in the table. To answer the question we need to find the value of $f(x)$ when x is 2, which is –1. Now find the value of $g(x)$ when x is –2, which is 1. The question asks us to subtract the value of $g(x)$ from $f(x)$: $(-1) - 1 = -2$, answer (A). (B) may incorrectly be chosen if the values were added rather than subtracted. (C) is the value of $g(-2)$, (E) is the result of subtracting the x-values listed in the question without finding the y-value [the $f(x)$ value] on the table.

12. **E** The average of the measures of two angles is 80°, so their sum is 160°. Since the sum of the measures of all four angles of a quadrilateral is 360°, the sum of the other two angles is 360 – 160 = 200°. The question says that three angles are equal; if the first two angles (average 80°, sum 160°) are equal, then they both measure 80°. That means a third angle also measures 80°, so the fourth angle measures 200 – 80 = 120°. Eliminate (B) and (D) because you've just shown that both could be the measure of an angle in the quadrilateral. Now, if the last two angles (sum 200°) are equal, then they both measure 100°. One of the first two angles must also measure 100°, so the fourth angle measures 160 – 100 = 60°. Eliminate (A) and (C) because we just showed that they could work, too. Only (E) cannot work: if 140° is the measure of the three congruent angles, their sum is 140 × 3 = 420°, more than the sum of the measures of the four angles of a quadrilateral. If 140° is the measure of the one angle that is not congruent to the other three, then the sum of the measures of the other three angles is 360 – 140 = 220°; the measure of each of those angles would be $\frac{220}{3} = 73\frac{1}{3}°$, and the measures of no two angles in the quadrilateral would have an average of 80°.

13. **C** For x^2 to be greater than x, yet x^3 less than x suggests that we are dealing with a negative integer for x. (A negative times a negative is positive, and a positive times a negative is negative). We can test the values in the answers as replacements for m. For (A), if m were –2, then since there are three "jumps" to the tick mark labeled 6, dividing a distance of 8 by 3 gives a distance of about 2.67 between tick marks. This gives the tick mark labeled x^2 a value of 3.33, which is not a square of –4.67 (which the value of x if m is –2). (B) doesn't work either: if m = –1, the distance between tick marks is 2.33 and x^2 would have a value of 3.67 which is not the square of –3.33 (the value of x if m is –1). Only (C) does work. If m = 0, then there is a distance of 2 between each tick mark. x^2 would have a value of 4, which is the square of –2 (which the value of x if m is 0).

14. **C** Find the surface area by adding the areas of the circular top and base (the area of each is πr^2, where r is the radius) to the area of the long side of the cylinder (the area of that is $2\pi rh$, where r is the radius and h is the height of the cylinder: it's the circumference times the height). First, find the surface area of the original cylinder: $\pi r^2 = \pi 3^2 = 9\pi$; since there are two of these circles (top and bottom), their total area is 18π. Then the area of the side: $2\pi rh = 6\pi \times 8 = 48\pi$. Add these together to get the total surface area of the original cylinder: $18\pi + 48\pi = 66\pi$. Now find the surface area of one of the small cylinders. Circular base: $\pi r^2 = \pi 3^2 = 9\pi$. Again, double this to 18π because the small cylinder has a top and bottom. Now the area of the small cylinder's side: $2\pi rh = 6\pi \times 4 = 24\pi$. Add them to get the surface area of a small cylinder: $18\pi + 24\pi = 42\pi$. Double this to get the total surface area of the two smaller cylinders: 84π. To find how much greater this is than the surface area of the original cylinder, subtract: $84\pi - 66\pi = 18\pi$.

15. **D** Plug In numbers for the variables: let's say $c = 4$ and $d = 2$. These numbers are acceptable because $c^2 - d^2$ is even: $4^2 - 2^2 = 16 - 4 = 12$. Then $cd = 4 \times 2 = 8$, so eliminate choice (A); $c + d = 4 + 2 = 6$, so eliminate (C); and $c - d = 4 - 2 = 2$, so eliminate (E). Now try different numbers: let's say $c = 5$ and $d = 3$. $c^2 - d^2$ is still even because $5^2 - 3^2 = 25 - 9 = 16$. Now $cd = 5 \times 3 = 15$, so eliminate (B). Choice (D) is still true: $c + d = 5 + 3 = 8$. This method is much easier than approaching the question by analyzing number theory: since the difference of two even numbers is even, the difference of two odd numbers is even, and the difference of one even and one odd number is odd, c^2 and d^2 must be both even or both odd. And since the square of an even number is even and the square of an odd number is odd, c and d must also be either both even or both odd. Now, the product of two even numbers is even and the product of two odd numbers is odd; therefore, neither (A) nor (B) will always be true. The sum and difference of two odd numbers is even and the sum and difference of two even numbers is even; therefore, (C) and (E) will never be true, but (D) will always be true.

16. **C** For any equation of the form $(x + p)(x + q) = x^2 + bx + c$, in which p, q, b, and c are constants, p and q must add to b and multiply to c. Thus, using the numbers and variables from the equation, we can form two equations: $9 + m = 4m$, and $9m = n$. From the first equation, we can derive that $3m = 9$, or $m = 3$. By plugging that value for m into the second equation, we get $n = 9 \times 3 = 27$. Alternately, if we use FOIL for the values in parentheses, we find that $(x + 9)(x + m) = x^2 + 9x + mx + 9m$. Thus, $x^2 + 9x + mx + 9m = x^2 + 4mx + n$. Matching the equivalent parts of the two halves of the equation shows us that $9x + mx = 4mx$ and $9m = n$. First find the value of m: $9x + mx = 4mx$, $9x = 3mx$, $9 = 3m$, $m = 3$. Since $9m = n$, then $n = 27$, answer (C).

SECTION 9

1. **B** The clue is *vibrant flowers and trees*. The blank must mean something close to "having a lot of greenery." The closest answer choice is *lush*.

2. **B** *Lauded* indicates that these models were praised; the word *derided* means that they are praised no longer. (B) is a positive word meaning "worthy of praise," and is correct. While (A) *definitive* and (C) *constructive* can be positive qualities, neither fits as an opposite of *failures*. (D) and (E) both have negative connotations.

3. **D** The clue is that some actors are attracted by *recognition*. The only answer choice supported by this clue is (D) *prestigious*, which means "reputation or influence arising from success." (C) *fulfilling* might sound good because acting can be fulfilling, but it's not justified by what's actually in the sentence. Remember, the right answer always has justification in the sentence.

4.   **D**   For the first blank, the colon serves as a sort of equal sign between the blank and the clue that *scientists can eliminate dangerous effects*. This must mean that the first blank means something good, eliminate (A), (C), and (E). For the second blank, the clue is that *scientists* are able to *eliminate dangerous effects better*. The second blank must mean that scientists at other companies do not do *large clinical trials*. The second word in (C), (D), and (E) is close. The choice that most closely fits both blanks is (D) *positive* and *avoided*.

5.   **E**   In the sentence, the bone structures are described as *vulnerable to breakages*. (E) *frailty*, meaning "the state of being weak" is the only option that reflects the description. While *morbidity* (C) is a negative word, it goes further than describing a *vulnerable bone structure*. There is some tough vocabulary here: look up any unfamiliar words.

6.   **A**   The first blank must mean something close to *senseless* since the blank is followed by the word *even*. The clue for the second blank is that the *students regarded the cancellation* as *senseless*. This means that the second blank should mean something close to "complaint." *Absurd* means "utterly or obviously senseless" and to remonstrate means "to say or plead in protest, objection, or disapproval" so a *remonstrance* is a protest or complaint, making (A) the best answer.

7.   **B**   Go back to the passages and come up with a word to replace *wedged* based on the context. If the men *could not retreat*, the trail must have been "blocked." (B), *crowded*, is a good fit. The correct answer is (B).

8.   **B**   Because the campaign *had not been conducted according to military rules*, American soldiers had been placed in a dangerous situation (*a series of blunders had brought seven thousand American soldiers into a chute of death from which there was no escape*). Answer choice (B) accurately summarizes this state of affairs. We don't know if the army was *undisciplined* (A), or if the plan was *carefully laid* (C), or if something was *out of character* (D), or if a lapse was *easily explained* (E).

9.   **E**   The first paragraph describes all the problems the soldiers faced: *they were being shot to pieces* and they were in *a chute of death from which there was no escape*. It's not a mood of (A) *definite failure*, because we don't know that their failure is definite: in fact, they don't fail at all. (B) and (C) are not mentioned at all in the passage. (D) *patriotic pride*, may work for his later description of Roosevelt, but it's not the mood in the first paragraph. That leaves (E), *overwhelming difficulty*.

10. **D**   The hills *crackled* and *burst* because *the fire of the Spanish rifleman, who still stuck bravely to their posts, doubled and trebled in fierceness*. Thus, the reference emphasizes the *intensity of the Spanish resistance* (D). The other answers are not supported by the passage.

11. **C**   Although Davis' accounts were full of *vivid detail*, Davis wasn't actually there. Thus, the author is attempting to *highlight an inconsistency*. None of the other answers are supported by the passage.

12. **A** The author mentions the *other reporters* to show how they *further embroidered the story*. (A) matches this. (B) is wrong because they are not *additional examples of Roosevelt's bravery*, they are made up. The author is not trying to say that all *journalists are unreliable wartime observers*, just that certain journalists fudged the details. (D) is not mentioned in the passage. (E) is wrong because the author doesn't bring up the other reporters to show how great Davis was, but to show how extreme the myths about Roosevelt often were.

13. **A** Passage 2 is primarily concerned with showing that *the legend of the charge up San Juan Hill is more myth than fact*. So he is trying to (A) *contradict a commonly held opinion*, that Roosevelt was a key part of the battle. (B) is wrong because he is not analyzing the Battle of San Juan Hill, but merely describing part of it. (C) is wrong because he actually states that Roosevelt was heroic in the first paragraph, but he just didn't do one of the things some people claim he did. (D) is wrong because it's not about describing Roosevelt, but about showing what he didn't do. (E) is wrong because we won't know that it's an *unpopular belief*.

14. **E** The author of Passage 2 tells us that *Roosevelt had gone to war determined to emerge a hero*. This explains why he allowed journalists to overstate his heroism during the battle of San Juan: he was acting out of *self-interest*.

15. **C** We need something that's done by Passage 1, but not Passage 2. The second and third paragraphs of Passage 1 make it clear that Roosevelt and the American forces *encountered stiff resistance* (C). However, the author of Passage 2 notes that when Roosevelt and his Rough Riders assaulted Kettle Hill, they were *almost unopposed*. Thus, (C) is correct. (A) is mentioned in Passage 2, but not in Passage 1. (D) is mentioned in both passages. (B) and (E) are not mentioned at all.

16. **C** The author of Passage 2 calls into question the fact that Roosevelt was crucial to the battle, and points out that Davis wasn't even there, so describing the battle as if he was there is misleading. (A), (B), (D), and (E) are all things that could have happened at the battle, since we have no evidence to contradict them. (C), however, states that Roosevelt shouted *let my men pass*, and the other soldiers *sprang into line with the Rough Riders*, then they all proceeded to charge San Juan Hill together. All of this is directly contradicted by the author Passage 2.

17. **B** The author of Passage 1 states that *charging earthworks* was *an impossible military proposition*. The author of Passage 2 states that the *vast majority of Spanish defenders were dug in* at San Juan Hill. So both authors agree that (B) *San Juan Hill was heavily defended*. (A) and (D) are mentioned only in Passage 2, and (C) is mentioned only in Passage 1. (E) is not mentioned in either passage. We know in Passage 2 that his stallion *died of natural causes*, but the passage does not mention if it was before, during, or after the battle.

18. **D** The author of Passage 1 is much more excited than the author of Passage 2: he breathlessly describes the charge of San Juan Hill. (D), *dramatic*, matches this. (C) is wrong because he not writing as if he is talking to the reader. (B) may work for Passage 2, but not Passage 1.

SECTION 10

1. **D** It's possible for a right answer to contain *being*, but be very skeptical of any answer that contains it. (A) does not have a verb (*being* is a gerund, which doesn't function as a verb), and is a sentence fragment as a result. (B) is missing a verb from the first half of the sentence (*Delivery...officials*). (C) is also missing a verb. (E) has a subject/verb agreement problem: *were* (plural) does not agree with the subject, which is *delivery* (singular). The only answer left is (D).

2. **A** The sentence is correct as written. Eliminate (B) because *when* refers to a time not a person. (C) creates an ambiguous pronoun and changes the meaning of the sentence. (D) and (E), by changing the form of the verb, obscure the meaning of the sentence.

3. **B** Eliminate (A) and (E) because they don't include *if*; and the structure must be parallel to the beginning of the sentence. (C) uses passive voice and is unclear compared to (B). (D) changes the meaning with the phrase *tests with the material.*

4. **C** The sentence as written includes the redundant words *was when* as does (B): because *eighteenth century* appears in the sentence, *when* is unnecessary. Only (C) eliminates them without introducing any other errors. (D) creates an incomplete sentence because *when* turns the second part of the sentence into a dependent clause. (E) changes the meaning of the sentence: the *aspiring middle class* people themselves were not *fueling* a *rise in the number of books,* but the *growth* of a particular audience for the books.

5. **A** The underlined portion contains no error. Choices (B), (C), (D), and (E) are unnecessarily wordy.

6. **C** Answer choice (C) is the best of the given choices. Eliminate (A) because it contains a comma splice. Answer (B) is a sentence fragment, and (D) and (E) change the verb to *revealing,* which is not parallel with the rest of the sentence.

7. **C** The underlined portion contains the wrong verb form. After the verb *have*, the past participle must be used, not the past tense of the verb. Thus, we can eliminate (A), (B), and (D) as possible choices. (C) retains the meaning of the original sentence, while (E) unnecessarily alters the sentence.

8. **C** The sentence is incorrect as written. To start the phrase with *by*, the noun *protagonist* would have to be possessive, but even so, *by the protagonist's lies* or *by the protagonist's lying* does not fit with the end of the sentence. Eliminate (A) and (B), *Where* refers only to place, so get rid of (D). (E) also uses the wrong preposition. This leaves (C), which fits because *when* correctly sets up the conditions that cause the *unlikely twists.*

9. **A** There is nothing grammatically wrong with (A), so it is the correct answer. (B) changes the meaning of the sentence, making *department stores* the reason, rather than their *need to maintain a wide range of inventory.* (C) uses the wrong conjunction. (D) makes the sentence more wordy and changes the meaning of the original sentence and (E) creates an incomplete sentence.

10. **D** The sentence contains a subject-verb agreement error. The subject *construction* is singular while the verb *have* is plural. This means that (A), (B), and (E) can be eliminated. (C) introduces a comma splice error, leaving (D) as the correct answer.

11. **B** The sentence as written contains an awkward phrase *it having been*, so eliminate (A). (D) is also awkwardly phrased with *being domesticated*, and (E) changes the meaning of the sentence. Choice (C) contains a comma splice error. (B) is the correct answer because it avoids awkward constructions and has proper verb form.

12. **D** The sentence as written contains a comma splice; additionally the word *being* is often problematic on the SAT. In order for both clauses to be joined grammatically, there must be other punctuation or a conjunction used in between *the 1920s* and *his*. This eliminates choice (A), (B), and (C). (E) can also be eliminated because of the unnecessary use of the word *being*. Only (D) adds the proper conjunction and avoids any other problems.

13. **C** The underlined portion contains a misplaced modifier error. The modifier *while researching philosophers from Ancient Greece* should be modifying *Jesse*, not the *works of Aristotle*. Thus, the only choice that corrects this error is (C).

14. **E** The underlined portion contains a subject-verb agreement error. The subject of the sentence is *skills*, so the verb must be singular, not plural. This eliminates (A) and (B). Comparing the remaining choices, the correct preposition to use with *differ* is *from* and so (E) is the correct answer.

Chapter 10
Practice Test 4

Your Name (print) _____

Last   First   Middle

Date _____

IMPORTANT: The following codes should be copied onto your answer sheet exactly as shown.

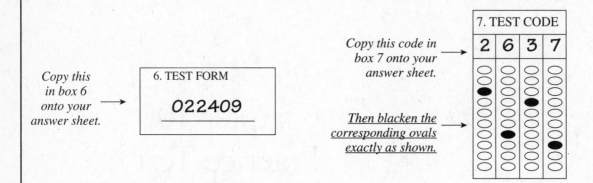

Copy this in box 6 onto your answer sheet. →

6. TEST FORM

022409

Copy this code in box 7 onto your answer sheet. →

Then blacken the corresponding ovals exactly as shown. →

7. TEST CODE

2 6 3 7

General Directions

You will have three hours and 20 minutes to work on this objective test designed to familiarize you with all aspects of the SAT.

This test contains five 25-minute sections, two 20-minute sections, one 10-minute section, and one 25-minute essay. The supervisor will tell you when to begin and end each section. During the time allowed for each section, you may work only on that particular section. If you finish your work before time is called, you may check your work on that section, but you are not to work on any other section.

You will find specific directions for each type of question found in the test. **Be sure you understand the directions before attempting to answer any of the questions.**

YOU ARE TO INDICATE ALL YOUR ANSWERS ON THE SEPARATE ANSWER SHEET:

1. The test booklet may be used for scratchwork. However, no credit will be given for anything written in the test booklet.

2. Once you have decided on an answer to a question, darken the corresponding space on the answer sheet. Give only one answer to each question.

3. There are 40 numbered answer spaces for each section; be sure to use only those spaces that correspond to the test questions.

4. **Be sure each answer mark is dark and completely fills the answer space.** Do not make any stray marks on your answer sheet.

5. If you wish to change an answer, erase your first mark completely—an incomplete erasure may be considered an intended response—and blacken your new answer choice.

Your score on this test is based on the number of questions you answer correctly minus a fraction of the number of questions you answer incorrectly. Therefore, it is improbable that random or haphazard guessing will alter your score significantly. There are no deductions for incorrect answers on the student-produced response questions. However, if you are able to eliminate one or more of the answer choices on any question as wrong, it is generally to your advantage to guess at one of the remaining choices. Remember, however, not to spend too much time on any one question.

Diagnostic Test Form

Use a No. 2 pencil only. Be sure each mark is dark and completely fills the intended oval. Completely erase any errors or stray marks.

1 Your Name:

(Print) _____
Last   First   M.I.

Signature: _____ Date __/__/__

Home Address: _____
                    Number and Street   City   State   Zip Code

E-Mail: _____ School: _____ Class: _____
      (Print)

2 YOUR NAME

Last Name (First 4 Letters) | FIRST INIT | MID INIT

A B C D E F G H I J K L M N O P Q R S T U V W X Y Z

3 PHONE NUMBER

0 1 2 3 4 5 6 7 8 9

IMPORTANT: Fill in items 6 and 7 exactly as shown on the preceding page.

6 TEST FORM
(Copy from back of test book)

7 TEST CODE

0 1 2 3 4 5 6 7 8 9

4 DATE OF BIRTH

MONTH	DAY	YEAR
○ JAN		
○ FEB		
○ MAR	0 0	0
○ APR	1 1	1
○ MAY	2 2	2
○ JUN	3 3	3
○ JUL	4	4
○ AUG	5 5	5
○ SEP	6 6	6
○ OCT	7 7	7
○ NOV	8 8	8
○ DEC	9 9	9

8 OTHER

1 A B C D E
2 A B C D E
3 A B C D E

5 SEX

○ MALE
○ FEMALE

PLEASE DO NOT WRITE IN THIS AREA

SERIAL #

THIS PAGE INTENTIONALLY LEFT BLANK

***IMPORTANT:* USE A NO. 2 PENCIL. DO NOT WRITE OUTSIDE THE BORDER!**
Words written outside the essay box or written in ink **WILL NOT APPEAR** in the copy sent to be scored and your score will be affected.

Begin your essay on this page. If you need more space, continue on the next page.

Continue on the next page, if necessary.

Continuation of ESSAY Section 1 from previous page. Write below only if you need more space.
IMPORTANT: **DO NOT START** on this page—if you do, your essay may appear blank and your score may be affected.

SECTION 2

1 Ⓐ Ⓑ Ⓒ Ⓓ Ⓔ	11 Ⓐ Ⓑ Ⓒ Ⓓ Ⓔ	21 Ⓐ Ⓑ Ⓒ Ⓓ Ⓔ	31 Ⓐ Ⓑ Ⓒ Ⓓ Ⓔ
2 Ⓐ Ⓑ Ⓒ Ⓓ Ⓔ	12 Ⓐ Ⓑ Ⓒ Ⓓ Ⓔ	22 Ⓐ Ⓑ Ⓒ Ⓓ Ⓔ	32 Ⓐ Ⓑ Ⓒ Ⓓ Ⓔ
3 Ⓐ Ⓑ Ⓒ Ⓓ Ⓔ	13 Ⓐ Ⓑ Ⓒ Ⓓ Ⓔ	23 Ⓐ Ⓑ Ⓒ Ⓓ Ⓔ	33 Ⓐ Ⓑ Ⓒ Ⓓ Ⓔ
4 Ⓐ Ⓑ Ⓒ Ⓓ Ⓔ	14 Ⓐ Ⓑ Ⓒ Ⓓ Ⓔ	24 Ⓐ Ⓑ Ⓒ Ⓓ Ⓔ	34 Ⓐ Ⓑ Ⓒ Ⓓ Ⓔ
5 Ⓐ Ⓑ Ⓒ Ⓓ Ⓔ	15 Ⓐ Ⓑ Ⓒ Ⓓ Ⓔ	25 Ⓐ Ⓑ Ⓒ Ⓓ Ⓔ	35 Ⓐ Ⓑ Ⓒ Ⓓ Ⓔ
6 Ⓐ Ⓑ Ⓒ Ⓓ Ⓔ	16 Ⓐ Ⓑ Ⓒ Ⓓ Ⓔ	26 Ⓐ Ⓑ Ⓒ Ⓓ Ⓔ	36 Ⓐ Ⓑ Ⓒ Ⓓ Ⓔ
7 Ⓐ Ⓑ Ⓒ Ⓓ Ⓔ	17 Ⓐ Ⓑ Ⓒ Ⓓ Ⓔ	27 Ⓐ Ⓑ Ⓒ Ⓓ Ⓔ	37 Ⓐ Ⓑ Ⓒ Ⓓ Ⓔ
8 Ⓐ Ⓑ Ⓒ Ⓓ Ⓔ	18 Ⓐ Ⓑ Ⓒ Ⓓ Ⓔ	28 Ⓐ Ⓑ Ⓒ Ⓓ Ⓔ	38 Ⓐ Ⓑ Ⓒ Ⓓ Ⓔ
9 Ⓐ Ⓑ Ⓒ Ⓓ Ⓔ	19 Ⓐ Ⓑ Ⓒ Ⓓ Ⓔ	29 Ⓐ Ⓑ Ⓒ Ⓓ Ⓔ	39 Ⓐ Ⓑ Ⓒ Ⓓ Ⓔ
10 Ⓐ Ⓑ Ⓒ Ⓓ Ⓔ	20 Ⓐ Ⓑ Ⓒ Ⓓ Ⓔ	30 Ⓐ Ⓑ Ⓒ Ⓓ Ⓔ	40 Ⓐ Ⓑ Ⓒ Ⓓ Ⓔ

SECTION 3

1 Ⓐ Ⓑ Ⓒ Ⓓ Ⓔ	11 Ⓐ Ⓑ Ⓒ Ⓓ Ⓔ	21 Ⓐ Ⓑ Ⓒ Ⓓ Ⓔ	31 Ⓐ Ⓑ Ⓒ Ⓓ Ⓔ
2 Ⓐ Ⓑ Ⓒ Ⓓ Ⓔ	12 Ⓐ Ⓑ Ⓒ Ⓓ Ⓔ	22 Ⓐ Ⓑ Ⓒ Ⓓ Ⓔ	32 Ⓐ Ⓑ Ⓒ Ⓓ Ⓔ
3 Ⓐ Ⓑ Ⓒ Ⓓ Ⓔ	13 Ⓐ Ⓑ Ⓒ Ⓓ Ⓔ	23 Ⓐ Ⓑ Ⓒ Ⓓ Ⓔ	33 Ⓐ Ⓑ Ⓒ Ⓓ Ⓔ
4 Ⓐ Ⓑ Ⓒ Ⓓ Ⓔ	14 Ⓐ Ⓑ Ⓒ Ⓓ Ⓔ	24 Ⓐ Ⓑ Ⓒ Ⓓ Ⓔ	34 Ⓐ Ⓑ Ⓒ Ⓓ Ⓔ
5 Ⓐ Ⓑ Ⓒ Ⓓ Ⓔ	15 Ⓐ Ⓑ Ⓒ Ⓓ Ⓔ	25 Ⓐ Ⓑ Ⓒ Ⓓ Ⓔ	35 Ⓐ Ⓑ Ⓒ Ⓓ Ⓔ
6 Ⓐ Ⓑ Ⓒ Ⓓ Ⓔ	16 Ⓐ Ⓑ Ⓒ Ⓓ Ⓔ	26 Ⓐ Ⓑ Ⓒ Ⓓ Ⓔ	36 Ⓐ Ⓑ Ⓒ Ⓓ Ⓔ
7 Ⓐ Ⓑ Ⓒ Ⓓ Ⓔ	17 Ⓐ Ⓑ Ⓒ Ⓓ Ⓔ	27 Ⓐ Ⓑ Ⓒ Ⓓ Ⓔ	37 Ⓐ Ⓑ Ⓒ Ⓓ Ⓔ
8 Ⓐ Ⓑ Ⓒ Ⓓ Ⓔ	18 Ⓐ Ⓑ Ⓒ Ⓓ Ⓔ	28 Ⓐ Ⓑ Ⓒ Ⓓ Ⓔ	38 Ⓐ Ⓑ Ⓒ Ⓓ Ⓔ
9 Ⓐ Ⓑ Ⓒ Ⓓ Ⓔ	19 Ⓐ Ⓑ Ⓒ Ⓓ Ⓔ	29 Ⓐ Ⓑ Ⓒ Ⓓ Ⓔ	39 Ⓐ Ⓑ Ⓒ Ⓓ Ⓔ
10 Ⓐ Ⓑ Ⓒ Ⓓ Ⓔ	20 Ⓐ Ⓑ Ⓒ Ⓓ Ⓔ	30 Ⓐ Ⓑ Ⓒ Ⓓ Ⓔ	40 Ⓐ Ⓑ Ⓒ Ⓓ Ⓔ

CAUTION Grid answers in the section below for SECTION 2 or SECTION 3 only if directed to do so in your test book.

Student-Produced Responses ONLY ANSWERS THAT ARE GRIDDED WILL BE SCORED. YOU WILL NOT RECEIVE CREDIT FOR ANYTHING WRITTEN IN THE BOXES.

Quality Assurance Mark ●

Grids numbered: 9, 10, 11, 12, 13, 14, 15, 16, 17, 18 — each with digit bubbles 0–9.

SECTION 4

1 Ⓐ Ⓑ Ⓒ Ⓓ Ⓔ	11 Ⓐ Ⓑ Ⓒ Ⓓ Ⓔ	21 Ⓐ Ⓑ Ⓒ Ⓓ Ⓔ	31 Ⓐ Ⓑ Ⓒ Ⓓ Ⓔ
2 Ⓐ Ⓑ Ⓒ Ⓓ Ⓔ	12 Ⓐ Ⓑ Ⓒ Ⓓ Ⓔ	22 Ⓐ Ⓑ Ⓒ Ⓓ Ⓔ	32 Ⓐ Ⓑ Ⓒ Ⓓ Ⓔ
3 Ⓐ Ⓑ Ⓒ Ⓓ Ⓔ	13 Ⓐ Ⓑ Ⓒ Ⓓ Ⓔ	23 Ⓐ Ⓑ Ⓒ Ⓓ Ⓔ	33 Ⓐ Ⓑ Ⓒ Ⓓ Ⓔ
4 Ⓐ Ⓑ Ⓒ Ⓓ Ⓔ	14 Ⓐ Ⓑ Ⓒ Ⓓ Ⓔ	24 Ⓐ Ⓑ Ⓒ Ⓓ Ⓔ	34 Ⓐ Ⓑ Ⓒ Ⓓ Ⓔ
5 Ⓐ Ⓑ Ⓒ Ⓓ Ⓔ	15 Ⓐ Ⓑ Ⓒ Ⓓ Ⓔ	25 Ⓐ Ⓑ Ⓒ Ⓓ Ⓔ	35 Ⓐ Ⓑ Ⓒ Ⓓ Ⓔ
6 Ⓐ Ⓑ Ⓒ Ⓓ Ⓔ	16 Ⓐ Ⓑ Ⓒ Ⓓ Ⓔ	26 Ⓐ Ⓑ Ⓒ Ⓓ Ⓔ	36 Ⓐ Ⓑ Ⓒ Ⓓ Ⓔ
7 Ⓐ Ⓑ Ⓒ Ⓓ Ⓔ	17 Ⓐ Ⓑ Ⓒ Ⓓ Ⓔ	27 Ⓐ Ⓑ Ⓒ Ⓓ Ⓔ	37 Ⓐ Ⓑ Ⓒ Ⓓ Ⓔ
8 Ⓐ Ⓑ Ⓒ Ⓓ Ⓔ	18 Ⓐ Ⓑ Ⓒ Ⓓ Ⓔ	28 Ⓐ Ⓑ Ⓒ Ⓓ Ⓔ	38 Ⓐ Ⓑ Ⓒ Ⓓ Ⓔ
9 Ⓐ Ⓑ Ⓒ Ⓓ Ⓔ	19 Ⓐ Ⓑ Ⓒ Ⓓ Ⓔ	29 Ⓐ Ⓑ Ⓒ Ⓓ Ⓔ	39 Ⓐ Ⓑ Ⓒ Ⓓ Ⓔ
10 Ⓐ Ⓑ Ⓒ Ⓓ Ⓔ	20 Ⓐ Ⓑ Ⓒ Ⓓ Ⓔ	30 Ⓐ Ⓑ Ⓒ Ⓓ Ⓔ	40 Ⓐ Ⓑ Ⓒ Ⓓ Ⓔ

SECTION 5

1 Ⓐ Ⓑ Ⓒ Ⓓ Ⓔ	11 Ⓐ Ⓑ Ⓒ Ⓓ Ⓔ	21 Ⓐ Ⓑ Ⓒ Ⓓ Ⓔ	31 Ⓐ Ⓑ Ⓒ Ⓓ Ⓔ
2 Ⓐ Ⓑ Ⓒ Ⓓ Ⓔ	12 Ⓐ Ⓑ Ⓒ Ⓓ Ⓔ	22 Ⓐ Ⓑ Ⓒ Ⓓ Ⓔ	32 Ⓐ Ⓑ Ⓒ Ⓓ Ⓔ
3 Ⓐ Ⓑ Ⓒ Ⓓ Ⓔ	13 Ⓐ Ⓑ Ⓒ Ⓓ Ⓔ	23 Ⓐ Ⓑ Ⓒ Ⓓ Ⓔ	33 Ⓐ Ⓑ Ⓒ Ⓓ Ⓔ
4 Ⓐ Ⓑ Ⓒ Ⓓ Ⓔ	14 Ⓐ Ⓑ Ⓒ Ⓓ Ⓔ	24 Ⓐ Ⓑ Ⓒ Ⓓ Ⓔ	34 Ⓐ Ⓑ Ⓒ Ⓓ Ⓔ
5 Ⓐ Ⓑ Ⓒ Ⓓ Ⓔ	15 Ⓐ Ⓑ Ⓒ Ⓓ Ⓔ	25 Ⓐ Ⓑ Ⓒ Ⓓ Ⓔ	35 Ⓐ Ⓑ Ⓒ Ⓓ Ⓔ
6 Ⓐ Ⓑ Ⓒ Ⓓ Ⓔ	16 Ⓐ Ⓑ Ⓒ Ⓓ Ⓔ	26 Ⓐ Ⓑ Ⓒ Ⓓ Ⓔ	36 Ⓐ Ⓑ Ⓒ Ⓓ Ⓔ
7 Ⓐ Ⓑ Ⓒ Ⓓ Ⓔ	17 Ⓐ Ⓑ Ⓒ Ⓓ Ⓔ	27 Ⓐ Ⓑ Ⓒ Ⓓ Ⓔ	37 Ⓐ Ⓑ Ⓒ Ⓓ Ⓔ
8 Ⓐ Ⓑ Ⓒ Ⓓ Ⓔ	18 Ⓐ Ⓑ Ⓒ Ⓓ Ⓔ	28 Ⓐ Ⓑ Ⓒ Ⓓ Ⓔ	38 Ⓐ Ⓑ Ⓒ Ⓓ Ⓔ
9 Ⓐ Ⓑ Ⓒ Ⓓ Ⓔ	19 Ⓐ Ⓑ Ⓒ Ⓓ Ⓔ	29 Ⓐ Ⓑ Ⓒ Ⓓ Ⓔ	39 Ⓐ Ⓑ Ⓒ Ⓓ Ⓔ
10 Ⓐ Ⓑ Ⓒ Ⓓ Ⓔ	20 Ⓐ Ⓑ Ⓒ Ⓓ Ⓔ	30 Ⓐ Ⓑ Ⓒ Ⓓ Ⓔ	40 Ⓐ Ⓑ Ⓒ Ⓓ Ⓔ

CAUTION Grid answers in the section below for SECTION 4 or SECTION 5 only if directed to do so in your test book.

Student-Produced Responses ONLY ANSWERS THAT ARE GRIDDED WILL BE SCORED. YOU WILL NOT RECEIVE CREDIT FOR ANYTHING WRITTEN IN THE BOXES.

Quality Assurance Mark ●

Grids 9, 10, 11, 12, 13, 14, 15, 16, 17, 18 — each with columns for digits 0–9 and fraction/decimal markers.

SECTION 6

1 Ⓐ Ⓑ Ⓒ Ⓓ Ⓔ	11 Ⓐ Ⓑ Ⓒ Ⓓ Ⓔ	21 Ⓐ Ⓑ Ⓒ Ⓓ Ⓔ	31 Ⓐ Ⓑ Ⓒ Ⓓ Ⓔ
2 Ⓐ Ⓑ Ⓒ Ⓓ Ⓔ	12 Ⓐ Ⓑ Ⓒ Ⓓ Ⓔ	22 Ⓐ Ⓑ Ⓒ Ⓓ Ⓔ	32 Ⓐ Ⓑ Ⓒ Ⓓ Ⓔ
3 Ⓐ Ⓑ Ⓒ Ⓓ Ⓔ	13 Ⓐ Ⓑ Ⓒ Ⓓ Ⓔ	23 Ⓐ Ⓑ Ⓒ Ⓓ Ⓔ	33 Ⓐ Ⓑ Ⓒ Ⓓ Ⓔ
4 Ⓐ Ⓑ Ⓒ Ⓓ Ⓔ	14 Ⓐ Ⓑ Ⓒ Ⓓ Ⓔ	24 Ⓐ Ⓑ Ⓒ Ⓓ Ⓔ	34 Ⓐ Ⓑ Ⓒ Ⓓ Ⓔ
5 Ⓐ Ⓑ Ⓒ Ⓓ Ⓔ	15 Ⓐ Ⓑ Ⓒ Ⓓ Ⓔ	25 Ⓐ Ⓑ Ⓒ Ⓓ Ⓔ	35 Ⓐ Ⓑ Ⓒ Ⓓ Ⓔ
6 Ⓐ Ⓑ Ⓒ Ⓓ Ⓔ	16 Ⓐ Ⓑ Ⓒ Ⓓ Ⓔ	26 Ⓐ Ⓑ Ⓒ Ⓓ Ⓔ	36 Ⓐ Ⓑ Ⓒ Ⓓ Ⓔ
7 Ⓐ Ⓑ Ⓒ Ⓓ Ⓔ	17 Ⓐ Ⓑ Ⓒ Ⓓ Ⓔ	27 Ⓐ Ⓑ Ⓒ Ⓓ Ⓔ	37 Ⓐ Ⓑ Ⓒ Ⓓ Ⓔ
8 Ⓐ Ⓑ Ⓒ Ⓓ Ⓔ	18 Ⓐ Ⓑ Ⓒ Ⓓ Ⓔ	28 Ⓐ Ⓑ Ⓒ Ⓓ Ⓔ	38 Ⓐ Ⓑ Ⓒ Ⓓ Ⓔ
9 Ⓐ Ⓑ Ⓒ Ⓓ Ⓔ	19 Ⓐ Ⓑ Ⓒ Ⓓ Ⓔ	29 Ⓐ Ⓑ Ⓒ Ⓓ Ⓔ	39 Ⓐ Ⓑ Ⓒ Ⓓ Ⓔ
10 Ⓐ Ⓑ Ⓒ Ⓓ Ⓔ	20 Ⓐ Ⓑ Ⓒ Ⓓ Ⓔ	30 Ⓐ Ⓑ Ⓒ Ⓓ Ⓔ	40 Ⓐ Ⓑ Ⓒ Ⓓ Ⓔ

SECTION 7

1 Ⓐ Ⓑ Ⓒ Ⓓ Ⓔ	11 Ⓐ Ⓑ Ⓒ Ⓓ Ⓔ	21 Ⓐ Ⓑ Ⓒ Ⓓ Ⓔ	31 Ⓐ Ⓑ Ⓒ Ⓓ Ⓔ
2 Ⓐ Ⓑ Ⓒ Ⓓ Ⓔ	12 Ⓐ Ⓑ Ⓒ Ⓓ Ⓔ	22 Ⓐ Ⓑ Ⓒ Ⓓ Ⓔ	32 Ⓐ Ⓑ Ⓒ Ⓓ Ⓔ
3 Ⓐ Ⓑ Ⓒ Ⓓ Ⓔ	13 Ⓐ Ⓑ Ⓒ Ⓓ Ⓔ	23 Ⓐ Ⓑ Ⓒ Ⓓ Ⓔ	33 Ⓐ Ⓑ Ⓒ Ⓓ Ⓔ
4 Ⓐ Ⓑ Ⓒ Ⓓ Ⓔ	14 Ⓐ Ⓑ Ⓒ Ⓓ Ⓔ	24 Ⓐ Ⓑ Ⓒ Ⓓ Ⓔ	34 Ⓐ Ⓑ Ⓒ Ⓓ Ⓔ
5 Ⓐ Ⓑ Ⓒ Ⓓ Ⓔ	15 Ⓐ Ⓑ Ⓒ Ⓓ Ⓔ	25 Ⓐ Ⓑ Ⓒ Ⓓ Ⓔ	35 Ⓐ Ⓑ Ⓒ Ⓓ Ⓔ
6 Ⓐ Ⓑ Ⓒ Ⓓ Ⓔ	16 Ⓐ Ⓑ Ⓒ Ⓓ Ⓔ	26 Ⓐ Ⓑ Ⓒ Ⓓ Ⓔ	36 Ⓐ Ⓑ Ⓒ Ⓓ Ⓔ
7 Ⓐ Ⓑ Ⓒ Ⓓ Ⓔ	17 Ⓐ Ⓑ Ⓒ Ⓓ Ⓔ	27 Ⓐ Ⓑ Ⓒ Ⓓ Ⓔ	37 Ⓐ Ⓑ Ⓒ Ⓓ Ⓔ
8 Ⓐ Ⓑ Ⓒ Ⓓ Ⓔ	18 Ⓐ Ⓑ Ⓒ Ⓓ Ⓔ	28 Ⓐ Ⓑ Ⓒ Ⓓ Ⓔ	38 Ⓐ Ⓑ Ⓒ Ⓓ Ⓔ
9 Ⓐ Ⓑ Ⓒ Ⓓ Ⓔ	19 Ⓐ Ⓑ Ⓒ Ⓓ Ⓔ	29 Ⓐ Ⓑ Ⓒ Ⓓ Ⓔ	39 Ⓐ Ⓑ Ⓒ Ⓓ Ⓔ
10 Ⓐ Ⓑ Ⓒ Ⓓ Ⓔ	20 Ⓐ Ⓑ Ⓒ Ⓓ Ⓔ	30 Ⓐ Ⓑ Ⓒ Ⓓ Ⓔ	40 Ⓐ Ⓑ Ⓒ Ⓓ Ⓔ

CAUTION Grid answers in the section below for SECTION 6 or SECTION 7 only if directed to do so in your test book.

Student-Produced Responses

ONLY ANSWERS THAT ARE GRIDDED WILL BE SCORED. YOU WILL NOT RECEIVE CREDIT FOR ANYTHING WRITTEN IN THE BOXES.

Quality Assurance Mark ●

Grids 9–18, each with digits 0–9.

SECTION 8

1 Ⓐ Ⓑ Ⓒ Ⓓ Ⓔ
2 Ⓐ Ⓑ Ⓒ Ⓓ Ⓔ
3 Ⓐ Ⓑ Ⓒ Ⓓ Ⓔ
4 Ⓐ Ⓑ Ⓒ Ⓓ Ⓔ
5 Ⓐ Ⓑ Ⓒ Ⓓ Ⓔ
6 Ⓐ Ⓑ Ⓒ Ⓓ Ⓔ
7 Ⓐ Ⓑ Ⓒ Ⓓ Ⓔ
8 Ⓐ Ⓑ Ⓒ Ⓓ Ⓔ
9 Ⓐ Ⓑ Ⓒ Ⓓ Ⓔ
10 Ⓐ Ⓑ Ⓒ Ⓓ Ⓔ

11 Ⓐ Ⓑ Ⓒ Ⓓ Ⓔ
12 Ⓐ Ⓑ Ⓒ Ⓓ Ⓔ
13 Ⓐ Ⓑ Ⓒ Ⓓ Ⓔ
14 Ⓐ Ⓑ Ⓒ Ⓓ Ⓔ
15 Ⓐ Ⓑ Ⓒ Ⓓ Ⓔ
16 Ⓐ Ⓑ Ⓒ Ⓓ Ⓔ
17 Ⓐ Ⓑ Ⓒ Ⓓ Ⓔ
18 Ⓐ Ⓑ Ⓒ Ⓓ Ⓔ
19 Ⓐ Ⓑ Ⓒ Ⓓ Ⓔ
20 Ⓐ Ⓑ Ⓒ Ⓓ Ⓔ

21 Ⓐ Ⓑ Ⓒ Ⓓ Ⓔ
22 Ⓐ Ⓑ Ⓒ Ⓓ Ⓔ
23 Ⓐ Ⓑ Ⓒ Ⓓ Ⓔ
24 Ⓐ Ⓑ Ⓒ Ⓓ Ⓔ
25 Ⓐ Ⓑ Ⓒ Ⓓ Ⓔ
26 Ⓐ Ⓑ Ⓒ Ⓓ Ⓔ
27 Ⓐ Ⓑ Ⓒ Ⓓ Ⓔ
28 Ⓐ Ⓑ Ⓒ Ⓓ Ⓔ
29 Ⓐ Ⓑ Ⓒ Ⓓ Ⓔ
30 Ⓐ Ⓑ Ⓒ Ⓓ Ⓔ

31 Ⓐ Ⓑ Ⓒ Ⓓ Ⓔ
32 Ⓐ Ⓑ Ⓒ Ⓓ Ⓔ
33 Ⓐ Ⓑ Ⓒ Ⓓ Ⓔ
34 Ⓐ Ⓑ Ⓒ Ⓓ Ⓔ
35 Ⓐ Ⓑ Ⓒ Ⓓ Ⓔ
36 Ⓐ Ⓑ Ⓒ Ⓓ Ⓔ
37 Ⓐ Ⓑ Ⓒ Ⓓ Ⓔ
38 Ⓐ Ⓑ Ⓒ Ⓓ Ⓔ
39 Ⓐ Ⓑ Ⓒ Ⓓ Ⓔ
40 Ⓐ Ⓑ Ⓒ Ⓓ Ⓔ

SECTION 9

1 Ⓐ Ⓑ Ⓒ Ⓓ Ⓔ
2 Ⓐ Ⓑ Ⓒ Ⓓ Ⓔ
3 Ⓐ Ⓑ Ⓒ Ⓓ Ⓔ
4 Ⓐ Ⓑ Ⓒ Ⓓ Ⓔ
5 Ⓐ Ⓑ Ⓒ Ⓓ Ⓔ
6 Ⓐ Ⓑ Ⓒ Ⓓ Ⓔ
7 Ⓐ Ⓑ Ⓒ Ⓓ Ⓔ
8 Ⓐ Ⓑ Ⓒ Ⓓ Ⓔ
9 Ⓐ Ⓑ Ⓒ Ⓓ Ⓔ
10 Ⓐ Ⓑ Ⓒ Ⓓ Ⓔ

11 Ⓐ Ⓑ Ⓒ Ⓓ Ⓔ
12 Ⓐ Ⓑ Ⓒ Ⓓ Ⓔ
13 Ⓐ Ⓑ Ⓒ Ⓓ Ⓔ
14 Ⓐ Ⓑ Ⓒ Ⓓ Ⓔ
15 Ⓐ Ⓑ Ⓒ Ⓓ Ⓔ
16 Ⓐ Ⓑ Ⓒ Ⓓ Ⓔ
17 Ⓐ Ⓑ Ⓒ Ⓓ Ⓔ
18 Ⓐ Ⓑ Ⓒ Ⓓ Ⓔ
19 Ⓐ Ⓑ Ⓒ Ⓓ Ⓔ
20 Ⓐ Ⓑ Ⓒ Ⓓ Ⓔ

21 Ⓐ Ⓑ Ⓒ Ⓓ Ⓔ
22 Ⓐ Ⓑ Ⓒ Ⓓ Ⓔ
23 Ⓐ Ⓑ Ⓒ Ⓓ Ⓔ
24 Ⓐ Ⓑ Ⓒ Ⓓ Ⓔ
25 Ⓐ Ⓑ Ⓒ Ⓓ Ⓔ
26 Ⓐ Ⓑ Ⓒ Ⓓ Ⓔ
27 Ⓐ Ⓑ Ⓒ Ⓓ Ⓔ
28 Ⓐ Ⓑ Ⓒ Ⓓ Ⓔ
29 Ⓐ Ⓑ Ⓒ Ⓓ Ⓔ
30 Ⓐ Ⓑ Ⓒ Ⓓ Ⓔ

31 Ⓐ Ⓑ Ⓒ Ⓓ Ⓔ
32 Ⓐ Ⓑ Ⓒ Ⓓ Ⓔ
33 Ⓐ Ⓑ Ⓒ Ⓓ Ⓔ
34 Ⓐ Ⓑ Ⓒ Ⓓ Ⓔ
35 Ⓐ Ⓑ Ⓒ Ⓓ Ⓔ
36 Ⓐ Ⓑ Ⓒ Ⓓ Ⓔ
37 Ⓐ Ⓑ Ⓒ Ⓓ Ⓔ
38 Ⓐ Ⓑ Ⓒ Ⓓ Ⓔ
39 Ⓐ Ⓑ Ⓒ Ⓓ Ⓔ
40 Ⓐ Ⓑ Ⓒ Ⓓ Ⓔ

SECTION 10

1 Ⓐ Ⓑ Ⓒ Ⓓ Ⓔ
2 Ⓐ Ⓑ Ⓒ Ⓓ Ⓔ
3 Ⓐ Ⓑ Ⓒ Ⓓ Ⓔ
4 Ⓐ Ⓑ Ⓒ Ⓓ Ⓔ
5 Ⓐ Ⓑ Ⓒ Ⓓ Ⓔ
6 Ⓐ Ⓑ Ⓒ Ⓓ Ⓔ
7 Ⓐ Ⓑ Ⓒ Ⓓ Ⓔ
8 Ⓐ Ⓑ Ⓒ Ⓓ Ⓔ
9 Ⓐ Ⓑ Ⓒ Ⓓ Ⓔ
10 Ⓐ Ⓑ Ⓒ Ⓓ Ⓔ

11 Ⓐ Ⓑ Ⓒ Ⓓ Ⓔ
12 Ⓐ Ⓑ Ⓒ Ⓓ Ⓔ
13 Ⓐ Ⓑ Ⓒ Ⓓ Ⓔ
14 Ⓐ Ⓑ Ⓒ Ⓓ Ⓔ
15 Ⓐ Ⓑ Ⓒ Ⓓ Ⓔ
16 Ⓐ Ⓑ Ⓒ Ⓓ Ⓔ
17 Ⓐ Ⓑ Ⓒ Ⓓ Ⓔ
18 Ⓐ Ⓑ Ⓒ Ⓓ Ⓔ
19 Ⓐ Ⓑ Ⓒ Ⓓ Ⓔ
20 Ⓐ Ⓑ Ⓒ Ⓓ Ⓔ

21 Ⓐ Ⓑ Ⓒ Ⓓ Ⓔ
22 Ⓐ Ⓑ Ⓒ Ⓓ Ⓔ
23 Ⓐ Ⓑ Ⓒ Ⓓ Ⓔ
24 Ⓐ Ⓑ Ⓒ Ⓓ Ⓔ
25 Ⓐ Ⓑ Ⓒ Ⓓ Ⓔ
26 Ⓐ Ⓑ Ⓒ Ⓓ Ⓔ
27 Ⓐ Ⓑ Ⓒ Ⓓ Ⓔ
28 Ⓐ Ⓑ Ⓒ Ⓓ Ⓔ
29 Ⓐ Ⓑ Ⓒ Ⓓ Ⓔ
30 Ⓐ Ⓑ Ⓒ Ⓓ Ⓔ

31 Ⓐ Ⓑ Ⓒ Ⓓ Ⓔ
32 Ⓐ Ⓑ Ⓒ Ⓓ Ⓔ
33 Ⓐ Ⓑ Ⓒ Ⓓ Ⓔ
34 Ⓐ Ⓑ Ⓒ Ⓓ Ⓔ
35 Ⓐ Ⓑ Ⓒ Ⓓ Ⓔ
36 Ⓐ Ⓑ Ⓒ Ⓓ Ⓔ
37 Ⓐ Ⓑ Ⓒ Ⓓ Ⓔ
38 Ⓐ Ⓑ Ⓒ Ⓓ Ⓔ
39 Ⓐ Ⓑ Ⓒ Ⓓ Ⓔ
40 Ⓐ Ⓑ Ⓒ Ⓓ Ⓔ

SECTION 1
ESSAY
Time — 25 minutes

Turn to Section 1 of your answer sheet to write your essay.

The essay gives you an opportunity to show how effectively you can develop and express ideas. You should, therefore, take care to develop your point of view, present your ideas logically and clearly, and use language precisely.

Your essay must be written on the lines provided on your answer sheet—you will receive no other paper on which to write. You will have enough space if you write on every line, avoid wide margins, and keep your handwriting to a reasonable size. Remember that people who are not familiar with your handwriting will read what you write. Try to write or print so that what you are writing is legible to those readers.

You have twenty-five minutes to write an essay on the topic assigned below. DO NOT WRITE ON ANOTHER TOPIC. AN OFF-TOPIC ESSAY WILL RECEIVE A SCORE OF ZERO.

Think carefully about the issue presented in the following excerpt and the assignment below.

> Until every soul is freely permitted to investigate every book, creed, and dogma for itself, the world cannot be free. Mankind will be enslaved until there is wisdom enough to allow each man to have his thought and say. It is amazing to me that a difference of opinion upon subjects that we know nothing about should make us hate, persecute, and despise each other.
>
> Adapted from Robert Green Ingersoll

Assignment: Does a lack of knowledge cause conflict? Plan and write an essay in which you develop your point of view on this issue. Support your position with reasoning and examples taken from your reading, studies, experience, and observations.

DO NOT WRITE YOUR ESSAY IN YOUR TEST BOOK. You will receive credit only for what you write on your answer sheet.

BEGIN WRITING YOUR ESSAY IN SECTION 1 OF THE ANSWER SHEET.

S T O P
If you finish before time is called, you may check your work on this section only.
Do not turn to any other section in the test.

SECTION 2
Time — 25 minutes
24 Questions

Turn to Section 2 of your answer sheet to answer the questions in this section.

Directions: For each question in this section, select the best answer from among the choices given and fill in the corresponding circle on the answer sheet.

Each sentence below has one or two blanks, each blank indicating that something has been omitted. Beneath the sentence are five words or sets of words labeled A through E. Choose the word or set of words that, when inserted in the sentence, **best** fits the meaning of the sentence as a whole.

Example:

Desiring to ------- his taunting friends, Mitch gave them taffy in hopes it would keep their mouths shut.

(A) eliminate   (B) satisfy   (C) overcome
    (D) ridicule   (E) silence

---

1. Douglas's habit of missing deadlines and finishing projects late has earned him the well-deserved reputation of being -------.

    (A) an authority   (B) a diplomat   (C) an eliminator
        (D) a procrastinator   (E) an altruist

2. Unfortunately, the referee's decision to cancel the game was -------; after about fifteen minutes the rain cleared up and the conditions were ------- for playing.

    (A) varied . . . mandated
    (B) rash . . . implicit
    (C) similar . . . versatile
    (D) premature . . . suitable
    (E) mysterious . . . ensured

3. Most fish can only take in oxygen from the water, so the labyrinth fish must be considered ------- because it is ------- breathing air as well.

    (A) explosive . . aware of
    (B) harsh . . edified by
    (C) insightful . . proficient at
    (D) united . . precluded from
    (E) atypical . . capable of

4. Chronic pain can have ------- effect on sufferers, sapping one's strength and depriving one of energy.

    (A) an evocative   (B) a cathartic   (C) an enervating
        (D) a pejorative   (E) a disingenuous

5. African American artist Romare Bearden had a remarkably ------- set of talents: he was a painter, a composer, and a player in the Negro Baseball League.

    (A) disaffected   (B) eclectic   (C) regressive
        (D) impugned   (E) corresponding

GO ON TO THE NEXT PAGE

Directions: Each passage below is followed by questions based on its content. Answer the questions on the basis of what is <u>stated</u> or <u>implied</u> in each passage and in any introductory material that may be provided.

Questions 6-7 are based on the following passage.

I have always viewed a chairmaker's shop as a place alive with sounds. Curly wood shavings crackle like popcorn under the stomp of heavy work boots. Sharp drawknives sing shrilly
Line as they skate across the surface of rough-sawn spindles.
5 Coarse files cough and wheeze as they scrape away, while the table saw hums contentedly in the center of the room. The true craftsman listens intently to these sounds; one might say that he engages in an ongoing conversation with them. The slightest variation in a tool's familiar tune will cause him to
10 alter his stroke, or pause to sharpen the tool's blade.

6. The author implies that a "true craftsman" is one who

   (A) enjoys conversing with coworkers
   (B) possesses manual dexterity
   (C) appreciates the fine arts
   (D) responds to subtle changes
   (E) accepts occasional imperfections

7. The rhetorical device featured most prominently in the passage is

   (A) metaphorical language
   (B) flashback
   (C) irony
   (D) veiled allusion
   (E) deliberate understatement

Questions 8-9 are based on the following passage.

Theodore Roosevelt, the 26th President of the United States, was fond of the saying "speak softly but carry a big stick." Interestingly, the same president who was renowned
Line for his "big-stick" approach to foreign affairs was awarded a
5 Nobel Peace Prize in 1906 for his diplomatic efforts to bring about an end to the Russo-Japanese war. Roosevelt also had a profound impact on domestic politics: he used his executive authority to break up the monopolies of large companies, curbed the abuse and exploitation of workers in the meat-
10 packing industry, and created the system of national parks long before environmentalism was fashionable.

8. The author would most probably disagree with which of the following statements about Theodore Roosevelt?

   (A) He took no interest in regulating businesses.
   (B) He was an advocate of an assertive foreign policy.
   (C) He sought to protect the rights of employees.
   (D) His interest in preserving open spaces was unusual at the time.
   (E) His efforts to work for peace brought him public recognition.

9. The primary purpose of the passage is to

   (A) describe the spectrum of activities that is expected of United States presidents
   (B) explain Theodore Roosevelt's interest in foreign affairs
   (C) prove how Theodore Roosevelt was one of the greatest presidents in United States history
   (D) summarize a number of Theodore Roosevelt's accomplishments
   (E) provide a character analysis of Theodore Roosevelt

GO ON TO THE NEXT PAGE

Questions 10-15 are based on the following passage.

The following passage is an excerpt from the memoir of a well-known African American singer and community leader. It is set in New York and Philadelphia in the 1920s.

I now had what amounted to a complex about music. Hopes had been raised too high, and when they crashed too low, I could not be objective. Perhaps I had not admitted it
Line to myself, but Town Hall in New York had represented the
5 mainstream of American musical life, and I had plunged into it hoping to become one of the fortunate swimmers.

I kept rehashing the concert in my mind, lingering on some points and thrusting others so thoroughly aside that I do not remember to this day which dress I wore, whether it was
10 the one Mrs. Patterson had made over for me or a special one. I don't remember what financial arrangements were made with the young man who managed the event, but I do know that I received nothing and that he must have lost money. I thought then, and still do, that I might have done better
15 if I had not been told that auditorium was full. If you are sensitive, and I was perhaps too sensitive, a misrepresentation like that can throw you off balance, particularly if you feel that you have a great deal at stake.

I stopped going regularly to Mr. Boghetti's studio. I
20 appeared once in a while, and things must have gone very indifferently. He realized how much the fiasco had shaken me, and he did not make an issue of my irregular attendance.

Mother and I talked about the whole thing, and with her patience and understanding she helped me out of my trouble.
25 I knew that the criticism was right and that I should not have given the critics the opportunity to write as they did. I kept reiterating that I had wanted so very much to sing well enough to please everybody.

"Listen my child," Mother said. "Whatever you do in this
30 world, no matter how good it is, you will never be able to please everybody. All you can strive for is to do the best it is humanly possible for you to do."

As the months went by I was able again to consider singing as a career. "Think about it for a while," Mother
35 advised, "and think of other things you might like to do."

I thought about it. It took a long time before I could confront singing again with enthusiasm, before the old conviction returned that nothing in life could be as important as music.

10. The passage as a whole best supports which explanation of the narrator's "complex about music" (line 1) ?

(A) Her taste in musical styles became more varied as she grew older.
(B) A critical review of a performance caused her to change careers.
(C) Becoming an accomplished singer was not her primary ambition.
(D) A formidable experience led her to question her aspirations.
(E) Performing in Town Hall was the pinnacle of her early musical career.

11. In line 6, "fortunate swimmers" refers to the author's

(A) obsession with music
(B) desire to be a popular singer
(C) confusion about specifics
(D) respect for other famous singers
(E) rapid change of fortune

12. The use of the phrase "thrusting . . . aside" (line 8) conveys a sense of the narrator's

(A) distress
(B) resentment
(C) instability
(D) sentimentality
(E) perseverance

13. According to the passage, the "misrepresentation" (line 16) refers to a discrepancy between

(A) the narrator's actual proficiency at singing and her performance at the Town Hall
(B) the amount of money the narrator was promised and what she received
(C) the stated number of people in the attendance and the actual number
(D) the reaction of the audience to the Town Hall performance and the reviews of it
(E) the narrator's desire to please everybody and her inability to do so

14. The third paragraph (lines 19-22) primarily focuses on

(A) the importance of rehearsals
(B) the kindness of strangers
(C) an observation about motherhood
(D) a return to a musical career
(E) the consequences of a performance

15. In line 26, the narrator's comment about giving critics "the opportunity" suggests that she

(A) acknowledged that the unfavorable reviews were warranted
(B) intended to switch careers from music to journalism
(C) doubted that the critics who reviewed her did so objectively
(D) recognized the influence critics exert on a singer's career
(E) gave generously even when others insulted her

GO ON TO THE NEXT PAGE

Questions 16-24 are based on the following passages.

The following passages, adapted from books published in 2004 and 2008 respectively, discuss an image, known as "The Scream," painted by Norwegian artist Edvard Munch (1863–1944).

Passage 1

Edvard Munch created it at least four times, using whatever materials were handy. He then created a lithographic version, so that he could make limitless clones of the original.
Line After his death, the copies continued. Andy Warhol made silk
5 screened prints of it. Poster companies sold millions of copies of it. It is *The Scream*, one of the most reproduced works of art ever created.

Broad, wide strokes define *The Scream*. A red sky floats oppressively above a dark green and brown bridge. A dark
10 blue river flows from below the bridge, but also seemingly out of the head of the painting's key element: a pale, androgynous human, clad in black, mouth open, hands against his cheeks. The background is vague, and deliberately undefined in such a way that the entire composition seems to squash and
15 dominate the painting's key figure The figure's vague shape, contorted in apparent pain, would later be seen a signpost for the Expressionist movement to come. And it is crude, seemingly unfinished: exactly as the artist intended.

Of course, then there is the scream itself. Through the
20 stillness of image, we cannot actually know if the main figure is screaming, or merely reacting to, as Munch himself described it, "the infinite scream passing through nature." But the eye invariably falls upon that odd, skull-like face, with its open mouth and eyes round and wide with fear. There are no
25 lines upon the face, just the broad contours of a pallid brown flecked with blue. This is the true power of the painting: in one simple shape, a distorted and oblong head, Munch has captured a raw, gut feeling.

Passage 2

Edvard Munch's *The Scream* is one of those works of
30 art that transcends art itself. Even those who have never placed one foot inside a museum often recognize, and claim an appreciation for, *The Scream*. Simple but surprisingly deep, the painting holds the weight of many differing interpretations. The hopeless struggle of modern man. The
35 realization that we are all ultimately alone. The moment of dread and fear that every person has felt at some point. For some critics, the mere fact that so many people react to *The Scream* in such a primal way justifies the painting's reputation.

40 It is worth pointing out, however, that the initial reaction to Munch's work was less than favorable. Critics tended to either dismiss the crude smears of paint as no better than the aimless "masterpieces" of a bored child, or express mock concern for the emotional well-being of the painter. *The*
45 *Scream* certainly had fans who championed its bleak but direct power, but to most viewers it was simply a poorly-executed painting of a cartoonish mummy in an awkward pose. Munch, however, felt he had stumbled upon a motif that demanded more attention, and began to create prints
50 of *The Scream* in stark black ink. Historian Monica Bohm-Duchen has noted that it was these copies, which in turn were reproduced in several art magazines, that began *The Scream*'s canonization among the Great Works. The effect is almost mathematically direct: as the painting became more
55 accessible, it was more widely admired.

With copies of *The Scream* came variations on *The Scream*. Scholars, such as Leonard Bartin, have pointed out that it has been copied so often because it speaks to an emotion that is common to us all. According to Bartin, if a
60 college student wants to hang a poster in which a cartoonish speech balloon has been superimposed over Munch's masterpiece, it is evidence that *The Scream* is a work of art able to provoke a response, and therefore great. If children want to wear masks that look like the face of the figure in the
65 painting, it is because "something in that face . . . holds us rapt."

The Scream has been reproduced often, true. But these bland, spare reproductions hold no relevance to the actual painting, just as whistling a few notes of a melody from
70 Mozart is not the same as listening to a performance of his *Requiem*. Devoid of context, the central figure is no longer a piece functioning in a larger work of art, he is simply a logo, a brand. It is this logo that adorns coffee cups and movie posters. The simplicity of a logo, the ease at which a
75 simplified version of art can be digested and processed, can quickly allow the watered-down version eclipse the original. Is *The Scream* a great work of art? I will gladly step aside and let the reader judge: but judge the painting itself, and nothing else.

16. Which feature of *The Scream* is mentioned in both passages?

(A) The figure's face
(B) The figure's hands
(C) The composition
(D) The color of the sky
(E) The materials used to create it

GO ON TO THE NEXT PAGE

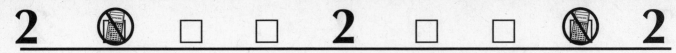

17. The details described in lines 4-7 of Passage 1 ("After his . . . created") would mostly likely be regarded by Monica Bohm-Duchen (lines 50-53, Passage 2) as

(A) incidents that must be considered in any appreciation of *The Scream*
(B) situations that have served to hinder criticism from art enthusiasts
(C) events that may themselves have added to the renown of *The Scream*
(D) facts that have proved troublesome for several art historians
(E) circumstances that have hindered art critics ability to judge *The Scream* objectively

18. Both authors would most likely agree that *The Scream*

(A) is Edvard Munch's masterpiece
(B) has been copied too many times
(C) was an artistic breakthrough
(D) ought to be viewed and analyzed
(E) takes years of study to understand

19. The quotation from Edvard Munch in line 22 serves primarily to

(A) settle a dispute
(B) establish a context
(C) defend a theory
(D) simplify an interpretation
(E) downplay a misconception

20. In line 28, "raw" most nearly means

(A) fresh
(B) inexperienced
(C) stark
(D) exposed
(E) cruel

21. The quotation marks in line 43 of Passage 2 are used by the author primarily to suggest that the critics were

(A) skeptical of *The Scream*'s aesthetic properties
(B) interested in the simplicity of *The Scream*'s composition
(C) incorrect in their analysis of *The Scream*
(D) tired of seeing paintings by children receive praise
(E) commenting on the connection between mental illness and creativity

22. Both the author of Passage 1 and Leonard Bartin (line 57, Passage 2) make which of the following points regarding *The Scream* ?

(A) Its simple shapes make it relatively easy to reproduce.
(B) Its key features are often overlooked in scholarly interpretations.
(C) Its idiosyncrasies are what make it an important painting.
(D) It has inspired several generations of artists.
(E) It tends to elicit a strong instinctive reaction from viewers.

23. The author of Passage 2 mentions "*Mozart's Requiem*" primarily in order to

(A) show that many works of art are often best known in shorter versions
(B) illustrate that a simplified version of a work of art can lack crucial elements
(C) emphasize the universal features those works of art share with *The Scream*
(D) remind readers that works of art can take many different forms
(E) suggest that *The Scream* is also a work of art on a par with *Mozart's Requiem*

24. Which of the following statements best characterizes the different ways in which the authors of Passage 1 and Passage 2 approach *The Scream* ?

(A) The first focuses on its emotional content, while the second argues for a purely intellectual interpretation.
(B) The first stresses its stylistic features, while the second emphasizes possible reasons for its cultural significance.
(C) The first references its repercussions in the larger world, while the second debates its artistic merits.
(D) The first speculates about its intended meaning, while the second examines the variety of attitudes about it.
(E) The first alludes to its unique place in art history, while the second downplays its importance.

STOP

If you finish before time is called, you may check your work on this section only.
Do not turn to any other section in the test.

NO TEST MATERIAL ON THIS PAGE.

SECTION 3
Time — 25 minutes
20 Questions

Turn to Section 3 of your answer sheet to answer the questions in this section.

Directions: For this section, solve each problem and decide which is the best of the choices given. Fill in the corresponding circle on the answer sheet. You may use any available space for scratchwork.

Notes

1. The use of a calculator is permitted.

2. All numbers used are real numbers.

3. Figures that accompany problems in this test are intended to provide information useful in solving the problems. They are drawn as accurately as possible EXCEPT when it is stated in a specific problem that the figure is not drawn to scale. All figures lie in a plane unless otherwise indicated.

4. Unless otherwise specified, the domain of any function f is assumed to be the set of all real numbers x for which $f(x)$ is a real number.

Reference Information

  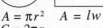 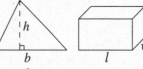 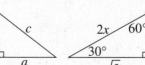

$A = \pi r^2$ $A = lw$
$C = 2\pi r$ $A = \frac{1}{2}bh$ $V = lwh$ $V = \pi r^2 h$ $c^2 = a^2 + b^2$ Special Right Triangles

The number of degrees of arc in a circle is 360.

The sum of the measures in degrees of the angles of a triangle is 180.

---

1. A snail travels 1 foot in 48 minutes. If the snail travels at a constant rate, how many minutes does it take to travel 1 inch? (1 foot = 12 inches)

   (A) One
   (B) Two
   (C) Three
   (D) Four
   (E) Five

66, 34, 18, m, 6, . . .

2. The first five terms of a sequence are shown above. In this sequence, the first term is 66 and each term after it is 1 more than $\frac{1}{2}$ the previous term. What is the value of m ?

   (A)   9
   (B)   10
   (C)   12
   (D)   13
   (E)   14

GO ON TO THE NEXT PAGE

3. What is nine times y if 4 more than three times y is equal to 11 ?

(A) $2\frac{1}{3}$

(B) 7

(C) $9\frac{2}{3}$

(D) 14

(E) 21

Questions 4-5 refer to the following graph

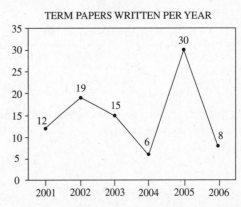

TERM PAPERS WRITTEN PER YEAR

The line graph above shows the number of term papers Joana wrote in each of the years 2001 through 2006.

4. How many more term papers did Joana write in the years 2001 and 2003 combined than she wrote in the year 2002 ?

(A)   6
(B)   8
(C)   10
(D)   12
(E)   14

5. If the data about Joana's term papers were shown in a circle graph, what would be the measure of the central angle of the sector that illustrates the year 2005 ?

(A)   30
(B)   45
(C)   90
(D)   120
(E)   135

GO ON TO THE NEXT PAGE

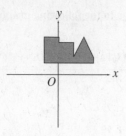

6. Which of the following graphs is the reflection of the shape above about the *x*-axis?

(A)
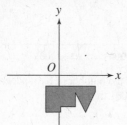

(B)
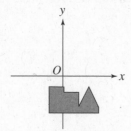

(C)
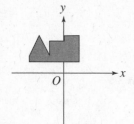

(D)
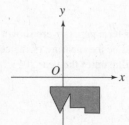

(E)
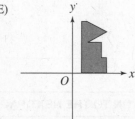

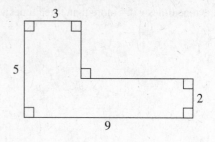

7. What is the area of the figure above?

(A) 27
(B) 29
(C) 33
(D) 35
(E) 39

8. If $a < 0$ and $(a - 4)^2 = 36$, what is a ?

(A) −32
(B) −10
(C) −6
(D) −4
(E) −2

GO ON TO THE NEXT PAGE

$$-5p, -3p, p, 3p$$

9. If $p < 0$, which of the numbers above has the least value?

(A) $-5p$
(B) $-3p$
(C) p
(D) $3p$
(E) It cannot be determined from the information given.

$$a = b^2 + b^3$$

11. In the equation above, $b = c^2$ for any integer c. What is a in terms of c ?

(A) c^5
(B) $c^4 + c^9$
(C) $c^4 + c^6$
(D) $c^3 + c^4$
(E) $c^2 + c^3$

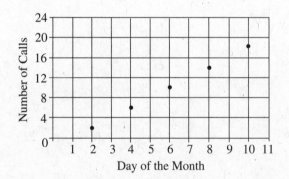

10. A mechanic created a graph showing the number of calls he received about stalled cars during the first 10 days of January. Let C represent the number of calls he received and D represent the number of the day of the month. Which of the following equations represents the data shown above?

(A) $C = 2$
(B) $C = D - 2$
(C) $C = 2D - 2$
(D) $C = D + 4$
(E) $C = 2D$

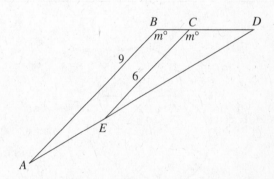

12. In the figure above, what is the ratio of BC to BD ?

(A) 5 to 6
(B) 2 to 3
(C) 1 to 2
(D) 1 to 3
(E) 1 to 6

GO ON TO THE NEXT PAGE

8, 10, x, 12, 8, 10, 8, 10, 10

13. If the set of numbers above has both a median and a single mode of 10, then each of the numbers below could be the value of x EXCEPT

(A) 4
(B) 5
(C) 6
(D) 7
(E) 8

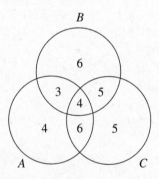

14. The numbers in the Venn diagram indicate the number of elements in sets A, B and C that belong in each region. How many total items are in sets A and C combined?

(A) 41
(B) 37
(C) 33
(D) 27
(E) 10

15. If x is directly proportional to $\sqrt{y}$, then y is inversely proportional to

(A) x^2

(B) $\sqrt{x}$

(C) $\dfrac{1}{\sqrt{x}}$

(D) $\dfrac{1}{x}$

(E) $\dfrac{1}{x^2}$

GO ON TO THE NEXT PAGE

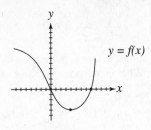

y = f(x)

16. The function f is graphed in the xy-plane above. If the function g is defined by $g(x) = |f(x)|$, which of the following is the graph of function g ?

(A)

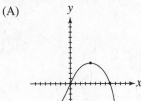

(B)

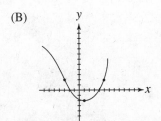

(C)

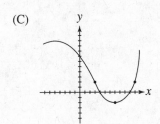

(D)

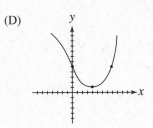

(E)

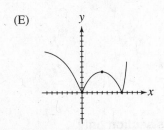

17. The values of x and y are such that $f(x) = f(2y)$ for a certain function f. Which of the following is equivalent to $f(x) + f(x)$?

   I. $2f(2y)$
   II. $f(4y)$
   III. $2[f(y) + f(y)]$

(A) I only
(B) II only
(C) I and III
(D) II and III
(E) I, II, and III

18. A right circular cylinder vase with an inner base radius of 6 inches is filled with water to a height of 20 inches. After a smaller solid right circular cylinder with base radius of 4 inches is then completely submerged in the water, the height of the water is 24 inches. What is the height, in inches, of the smaller cylinder?

(A)   8
(B)   9
(C) 10
(D) 11
(E) 12

GO ON TO THE NEXT PAGE

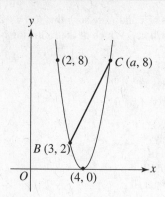

19. Points B and C lie on the parabola above. What is the slope of segment $\overline{BC}$?

(A)   2

(B) $\dfrac{5}{4}$

(C)   1

(D) $\dfrac{4}{5}$

(E) $\dfrac{1}{2}$

$$\frac{1}{x^2}, \frac{1}{x}, x, x^2, x^3$$

20. In the set of numbers above, there is no mode and the median is x^3. What is one possible value of x ?

(A)   2

(B)   1

(C) $\dfrac{1}{2}$

(D) $-\dfrac{1}{2}$

(E) -1

STOP

If you finish before time is called, you may check your work on this section only.
Do not turn to any other section in the test.

NO TEST MATERIAL ON THIS PAGE.

SECTION 5
Time — 25 minutes
24 Questions

Turn to Section 5 of your answer sheet to answer the questions in this section.

Directions: For each question in this section, select the best answer from among the choices given and fill in the corresponding circle on the answer sheet.

Each sentence below has one or two blanks, each blank indicating that something has been omitted. Beneath the sentence are five words or sets of words labeled A through E. Choose the word or set of words that, when inserted in the sentence, <u>best</u> fits the meaning of the sentence as a whole.

Example:

Desiring to ------- his taunting friends, Mitch gave them taffy in hopes it would keep their mouths shut.

(A) eliminate (B) satisfy (C) overcome
   (D) ridicule (E) silence

Ⓐ Ⓑ Ⓒ Ⓓ ●

1. The randomly occurring chemical reactions observed in nature are proof that some reactions can be -------.

   (A) spontaneous (B) hazardous (C) experimental
      (D) deliberate (E) constructive

2. The doctor regarded her patient's condition with -------, but after the surgery the patient ------- and was able to return home much sooner than anticipated.

   (A) hesitation . . benefited
   (B) apprehension . . recuperated
   (C) enthusiasm . . deliberated
   (D) apathy . . installed
   (E) concern . . approved

3. None of the petitioners was able to gather enough signatures in support of keeping the city's nuclear power plant open, an obvious ------- of the community's -------.

   (A) avoidance . . concealment
   (B) experiment . . resistance
   (C) rejection . . sponsorship
   (D) sponsorship . . espousal
   (E) demonstration . . opposition

4. In order to ensure that the children were -------, the school administrators enforced a code of conduct designed to promote ------- behavior among the students.

   (A) balanced . . extreme
   (B) obedient . . tractable
   (C) docile . . prestigious
   (D) studious . . boisterous
   (E) diverse . . spontaneous

5. The article "Tyranny of the Test" ------- the ------- of recent educational legislation, ridiculing the procedures used to formulate school policy.

   (A) reaffirms . . inflexibility
   (B) glorifies . . hypothesis
   (C) invalidates . . pitfalls
   (D) lampoons . . methodology
   (E) avoids . . dictates

6. Even though many doctors warn patients that high-cholesterol foods can increase risk of heart disease, some types of cholesterol are known to have ------- effects.

   (A) detrimental (B) affable (C) negligible
      (D) salutary (E) peripheral

7. The physics professor designed his lectures to avoid ------- the material: his goal was to clarify difficult topics, not make them more confusing.

   (A) theorizing (B) elucidating (C) obfuscating
      (D) delineating (E) accosting

8. Many voters believed that the new candidate ------- too often in his speeches: it seemed like he never chose one side of an issue and intentionally misled his audience

   (A) capitulated (B) equivocated (C) berated
      (D) vituperated (E) debated

GO ON TO THE NEXT PAGE ⟶

Directions: Each passage below is followed by questions based on its content. Answer the questions on the basis of what is <u>stated</u> or <u>implied</u> in each passage and in any introductory material that may be provided.

Questions 9-12 are based on the following passages.

Passage 1

Educated by her father (the village rector), living out her days in secluded rural parishes, known as "Aunt Jane" to all her relations, Jane Austen seemed to embody the same
Line provincial and genteel way of life that she portrayed in her
5 novels. Generations of adoring fans have embraced her works, including *Emma* and *Pride and Prejudice*, as affectionate and witty portraits of the English gentry. For these readers, Austen's novels evoke an idyllic past, suffused with the classically English values of elegant charm and self-effacing
10 modesty, and refreshingly free of weighty political or philosophical concerns.

Passage 2

Often ignored in accounts of Austen's insular environment is the influence of her brother Henry, who introduced her to a sophisticated circle of London artists, writers, and other
15 intellectuals; these acquaintances gave Austen insight into social worlds not usually glimpsed from her small rural parish. She was acutely aware of the contradictions and hypocrisies of the British upper class, which she frequently subjected to withering criticism. Her irony is not humorous;
20 it is caustic and subversive, and seeks to undermine the assumptions of the society she lived in. In this sense, her work is profoundly political.

9. The author of Passage 1 would most likely argue that the interpretation of Jane Austen's work offered in Passage 2

   (A) is not representative of the way enthusiasts often view Austen's novels
   (B) exaggerates the impact of Austen's isolation from the outside world
   (C) is more reflective of how Austen was perceived in her own time than of how she is perceived today
   (D) is overly influenced by the popular interpretation of Austen's writing style
   (E) ignores the influence of the people she met through her brother Henry

10. The author of Passage 2 would probably argue that the "readers" (line 7, Passage 1) are likely to

    (A) support the notion that Austen expresses contempt for the British upper class
    (B) underestimate the degree to which Austen's works have a political purpose
    (C) dismiss the theory that Austen's works were influenced by her rural upbringing
    (D) identify with the difficulties that Austen faced as a female writer
    (E) exaggerate the relevance that Austen's novels have for the modern reader

11. Passage 1 suggests that Austen's depiction of the "British upper class" referred to in line 18, Passage 2, was

    (A) overly provincial
    (B) largely sympathetic
    (C) harshly critical
    (D) rigorously objective
    (E) highly unrealistic

12. The author of Passage 2 and the "adoring fans" mentioned in line 5, Passage 1, would most likely disagree about which of the following concerning Jane Austen?

    (A) Whether her family was a significant influence on her work
    (B) Whether her work accurately portrays the British upper class
    (C) Whether English society was a central topic of her novels
    (D) The extent to which her work is critical of certain segments of society
    (E) The extent to which she should be considered an important author

GO ON TO THE NEXT PAGE

Questions 13-24 are based on the following passage.

The following passage, adapted from a 2005 article, discusses the common garden slug.

As a professional ecologist, I find one image held by amateur gardeners to be particularly irksome: the idea that a "pest-free" garden, cleansed of any creatures that might
Line threaten the gardener's precious plants, is a healthy garden.
5   As an example, consider *Deroceras reticulatum*, otherwise known as the common garden slug. The average gardener believes that this creature is nothing more than an enemy to be exterminated. In attempting to beautify their yards, gardeners utilize an impressive arsenal of chemical
10 weapons designed to bombard the slugs from the air as well as attack them on the ground. Success is attained only when no trace of slugs can be found, although the wary gardener must watch and wait for their return, since permanently ridding a garden of slugs can prove nearly impossible.
15   There are important consequences that result from viewing the slug as mortal enemy. Repeated spraying of chemicals damages topsoil and saps it of essential nutrients. To compensate, gardeners frequently apply artificial fertilizers, which encourage plant growth in the short
20 term, but damage the soil in the long term. As a result, the weakened garden is left susceptible to invasion by all sorts of pests, requiring further application of chemical sprays. Thus, in attempting to attain the cherished ideal of a pristine, pest-free garden, amateur gardeners create a vicious circle:
25 contamination, followed by artificial regeneration and a slow depletion of natural resources, followed by more contamination.
It seems to me that a solution to this dilemma starts with the recognition that a healthy garden is not one that has been
30 emptied of every organism that we find objectionable. Even creatures as repulsive as slugs have a role to play in a properly functioning ecosystem. Instead of trying to rid ourselves of slugs, wouldn't we be better off coming to some sort of accommodation with them?
35   The gardener who decides to coexist with the garden slug soon discovers that its nefarious reputation is at least partially unwarranted. Although it is true that the slug can devour garden plants from the roots up with frightening efficiency, it also produces nutrients for the soil, helping other plants to
40 grow. The diet of a slug consists not just of living plants, but also of plant waste and mold, making this diminutive creature into a sort of natural recycling center. The unique structure of a slug's digestive system enables it to take these discarded products, transform them into the nutrients that plants need to
45 thrive, and then release these nutrients into the soil by means of viscous, slime-like excretions.
In order to reap the benefits that slugs provide while at the same time minimizing the slug's destructive effects, the gardener should focus on two tasks: reducing the slug
50 population to manageable proportions, and diverting the slug's efforts into activities that do the least harm. There are a number of ways to control the population of slugs without resorting to noxious chemicals, but one of the easiest

is to welcome a few of the slug's natural predators into
55 the garden. Ground beetles, toads, and hedgehogs are all naturally predisposed to hunt slugs. Providing a habitat for these creatures will ensure that the slug population is held to reasonable levels.
To limit the slug's destructive effects, the gardener should
60 provide sacrificial plants for the slug to dine on. Lettuce, Zinnias, and Marigolds are all considered delicacies by slugs; the loss of a few of these plants will not distress the typical gardener. At the same time, natural barriers of white ash or diatomaceous earth should be placed around plants that are
65 held in higher esteem by the gardener. These barriers will naturally deter slugs, especially if tastier and more accessible treats are available nearby.
It is true that these measures may seem cumbersome, but in the long run the benefits outweigh the temporary
70 inconvenience to the gardener. A garden should not be a place devoid of all creatures that the gardener finds troublesome; it should be a place in which competing forces balance each other out. By exchanging the ideal of a pest-free garden for one in which pests are tolerated and managed, the gardener
75 ensures a healthier garden and minimizes the hazards associated with chemical pesticides.

13. In line 1, "image" most nearly means

(A) resemblance
(B) apparition
(C) correspondent
(D) perception
(E) reputation

14. In the second paragraph, the author critiques "the average gardener" (lines 6-7) by describing the situation in terms of a

(A) political campaign
(B) sporting event
(C) military strategy
(D) scientific experiment
(E) criminal trial

15. The author would most likely describe the "important consequences" (line 15) as

(A) a decisive victory
(B) a complicated affair
(C) a superior result
(D) an unintended reaction
(E) an idealistic attitude

GO ON TO THE NEXT PAGE ➡

5 ▢ 5 ▭ 5 ▭ 5 ▢ 5

16. The author would most probably characterize the "cherished ideal" (line 23) as

(A) carefully planned
(B) deeply insightful
(C) inconclusive
(D) unintelligible
(E) misguided

17. The primary purpose of lines 28-34 (It seems . . . with them) is to

(A) explain people's responses to certain animals
(B) propose an alternative course of action
(C) offer evidence of environmental destruction
(D) praise the scope of a comprehensive effort
(E) argue in favor of an unpopular position

18. The discussion in lines 35-46 ("The gardener . . . excretions") is best characterized as

(A) a defense
(B) a theory
(C) an exception
(D) an allusion
(E) a comparison

19. The author uses the phrase "natural recycling center" (line 42) to suggest that slugs can

(A) provide a model of environmentalism that people can emulate
(B) help gardeners save money and increase productivity
(C) heal a garden by absorbing and neutralizing harmful chemicals
(D) eliminate all of the problems associated with artificial fertilizers
(E) enable plants to make productive use of waste materials

20. The author's attitude toward the "viscous, slime-like excretions" (line 46) is best described as one of

(A) ambivalence
(B) revulsion
(C) appreciation
(D) uncertainty
(E) irritation

21. In line 54, "welcome" most nearly means

(A) acknowledge
(B) thank
(C) return
(D) introduce
(E) please

22. Lines 59-63 ("To limit . . . gardener") imply that

(A) predators will inevitably destroy a garden unless the gardener takes drastic action
(B) plants that appeal to slugs are not necessarily considered valuable by gardeners
(C) slugs prefer Lettuce, Zinnias, and Marigolds to all other types of plants
(D) gardeners should be sensitive to the needs of other species
(E) people are often unwilling to compromise until forced to do so by circumstances

23. The implication of the phrase "It is true" (line 68) is that the author

(A) recognizes that his suggestions may be viewed as burdensome
(B) agrees with the conventional approach to an issue
(C) is concerned that his ideas will not be taken seriously
(D) is pleased by the willingness of gardeners to change their opinions
(E) accepts that a solution to a problem may never be found

24. The last paragraph chiefly serves to

(A) restate the author's evidence
(B) suggest a direction for further study
(C) intensify an emotional effect
(D) downplay the impact of an approach
(E) underscore the author's position

STOP
If you finish before time is called, you may check your work on this section only.
Do not turn to any other section in the test.

SECTION 6
Time — 25 minutes
35 Questions

Turn to Section 6 of your answer sheet to answer the questions in this section.

Directions: For each question in this section, select the best answer from among the choices given and fill in the corresponding circle on the answer sheet.

The following sentences test correctness and effectiveness of expression. Part of each sentence or the entire sentence is underlined; beneath each sentence are five ways of phrasing the underlined material. Choice A repeats the original phrasing; the other four choices are different. If you think the original phrasing produces a better sentence than any of the alternatives, select choice A; if not, select one of the other choices.

In making your selection, follow the requirements of standard written English; that is, pay attention to grammar, choice of words, sentence construction, and punctuation. Your selection should result in the most effective sentence—clear and precise, without awkwardness or ambiguity.

EXAMPLE:

Bobby Flay baked his first cake <u>and he was thirteen years old then</u>.

(A) and he was thirteen years old then
(B) when he was thirteen
(C) at age thirteen years old
(D) upon the reaching of thirteen years
(E) at the time when he was thirteen

Ⓐ ● Ⓒ Ⓓ Ⓔ

1. Although the senator <u>has been involved</u> in unethical behavior, her constituents continue to show strong support for her.

   (A) has been involved
   (B) involved
   (C) being involved
   (D) has yet to be involved
   (E) is involving

2. Like many freshmen, <u>a sense of homesickness was felt by my roommates</u> for the first few weeks of college.

   (A) a sense of homesickness was felt by my roommates
   (B) a sense of homesickness feeling by my roommates
   (C) my roommates felt homesick
   (D) my roommates, who felt a sense of homesickness
   (E) there was a sense of homesickness felt by my roommates

3. Because <u>Alberto set a state record in the 400-meter dash is the reason why</u> the university offered him a full athletic scholarship.

   (A) Alberto set a state record in the 400-meter dash is the reason why
   (B) Alberto set a state record in the 400-meter dash,
   (C) Alberto set a state record in the 400-meter dash and is why
   (D) Alberto setting a state record in the 400-meter dash,
   (E) Alberto set a state record in the 400-meter dash is why

4. Exceptional teachers not only convey information about subjects such as history, literature, and mathematics, <u>but instill in their students a love for learning</u> that leads them to investigate concepts beyond the classroom walls.

   (A) but instill in their students a love for learning
   (B) and instill in their students also a love of learning
   (C) but instill in their students a love to learn
   (D) but also instill in their students a love of learning
   (E) and instill in their students loving for learning

5. A comedic outlet well-suited to Meadowlark Lemon was the Harlem Globetrotter's brand of <u>basketball, it let him reinterpret</u> the sport without the limitations required by official regulations.

   (A) basketball, it let him reinterpret
   (B) basketball, which let him reinterpret
   (C) basketball that lets him reinterpret
   (D) basketball; letting him reinterpret
   (E) basketball by letting him do reinterpretation of

6. The success of many start up companies may depend on both the regulation of taxes on small businesses <u>and the education of the public</u> about the security of internet commerce.

   (A) and the education of the public
   (B) educating the public
   (C) and the public being educated
   (D) along with the education of the public
   (E) in combination with public education

GO ON TO THE NEXT PAGE →

7. No one reason given for the fall of Rome, though many causes have been proposed over the centuries, <u>are adequate explanations for</u> why the mighty empire did not last.

   (A) are adequate explanations for
   (B) are an adequate explanation for
   (C) adequately explain
   (D) an adequate explanation of
   (E) is an adequate explanation for

8. The architect visited the remote village because <u>many were known there to construct</u> homes much like their predecessors had built.

   (A) many were known there to construct
   (B) many were known there for constructing
   (C) many of the people there were known to construct
   (D) of the many people, they were there constructing
   (E) of knowing that many people constructed there

9. During the Great Depression of 1929, Roosevelt's program to boost the failing economy by implementing the New Deal <u>were met with</u> overwhelming support.

   (A) were received with
   (B) having been met with
   (C) it met
   (D) was met with
   (E) met their

10. When for the past week the weather service warned of a hurricane, island residents should have realized that a storm <u>was imminent and could strike very soon</u>.

    (A) was imminent and could strike very soon
    (B) could happen imminently very soon
    (C) will be imminent and happening soon
    (D) is an imminent thing
    (E) might be imminent

11. Speaking, writing, and body language are <u>all effective, if disparate, forms of communication</u>.

    (A) all effective, if disparate, forms of communication
    (B) effective forms of communication, being, however, disparate
    (C) disparate forms of communications, whereas they are effective
    (D) disparate forms of communication when effective
    (E) forms of communication that are different although being effective

GO ON TO THE NEXT PAGE

The following sentences test your ability to recognize grammar and usage errors. Each sentence contains either a single error or no error at all. No sentence contains more than one error. The error, if there is one, is underlined and lettered. If the sentence contains an error, select the one underlined part that must be changed to make the sentence correct. If the sentence is correct, select choice E. In choosing answers, follow the requirements of standard written English.

EXAMPLE:

The other players and her significantly improved
    A   B   C

the game plan created by the coaches. No error
           D   E

Ⓐ ● Ⓒ Ⓓ Ⓔ

12. Harper Lee's first novel, which was published in 1960
                            A

    by J.B. Lippincott, and translated into editions in over
                    B   C   D

    forty languages. No error
              E

13. Over the last four months, Steven has fought to funding
    A   B   C

    the reconstruction of the recreation center for the purpose
                                    D

    of creating a venue for after-school programs. No error
                                  E

14. Taking a small dose of aspirin causes thinning of the
                           A

    blood but delay the moment when a heart attack
         B   C

    may occur. No error
        D   E

15. According to the results of the questionnaire, most

    audience members were supportive of magicians'
                  A   B

    unwillingness revealing secrets of the trade. No error
              C   D   E

16. Those body builders who competed in the Mr. Universe
                     A   B

    Contest were either on steroids or incredible strong.
              C   D

    No error
    E

17. The reviews for the restaurant are so good that even with
                         A   B

    the option of calling ahead, most patrons can rarely get
                         C   D

    a table within two hours. No error
                      E

18. When Gordon baked the pecan pie and served slices of it
    A

    with various toppings—including vanilla ice cream and
         B

    sprinkles—he had been the first to eat a slice. No error
              C   D   E

19. Ever since her promotion to manager last year,
              A

    Bretney is the hardest-working employee of this small
         B   C

    and highly industrious company. No error
        D   E

GO ON TO THE NEXT PAGE ⟶

20. One of the <u>dangers</u> facing the Kemp's ridley turtle, the
                 A

    smallest <u>of all sea turtles,</u> is that the female nests only
                    B

    <u>on a small stretch</u> <u>of beach</u> in Mexico that is now the
            C   D

    target of developers. <u>No error</u>
                              E

21. The salve made from the leaves of cactus plants <u>are</u>
                                                      A

    highly efficient <u>in healing</u> minor sunburns, <u>thus</u>
                         B   C

    offering a solution <u>to small desert</u> camping fiascos.
                             D

    <u>No error</u>
       E

22. <u>The preferred</u> music genres of members of one
        A

    generation are often <u>much</u> <u>different from</u> <u>those</u> of
                             B   C   D

    another generation. <u>No error</u>
                            E

23. Most of the residents of Heard County <u>no longer</u> attend
                                              A

    church on Sunday, an activity that <u>formerly</u> <u>served</u> to
                                          B   C

    <u>tie the community's</u> families together. <u>No error</u>
            D   E

24. <u>In order</u> for the class to pay attention to and
        A

    <u>be respectful of</u> the substitute teacher, <u>they have</u> to be
           B   C

    convinced that the <u>instructor</u> is knowledgeable.
                           D

    <u>No error</u>
       E

25. The accounting department <u>is presenting</u> requests
                                  A

    <u>to both</u> vice presidents <u>in</u> the hope <u>to receive</u>
        B   C   D

    permission to create a company spa. <u>No error</u>
                                            E

26. <u>Rather than</u> view her <u>glass as</u> either half full <u>or</u> half
        A   B   C

    empty, Reneé chose to see it as <u>overflowing from</u>
                                        D

    possibilities. <u>No error</u>
                       E

27. At the concert, Lucy <u>enjoyed listening</u> to her friend
                            A

    Noah's experimental music, <u>which she</u> thought was
                                   B

    <u>more original</u> than <u>the other bands.</u> <u>No error</u>
        C   D   E

28. The reason for <u>dramatically raising</u> fines for litering
                       A

    <u>is that</u> many pet owners would simply decide <u>to pay it</u>
        B   C

    <u>rather than</u> pick up their pet's waste. <u>No error</u>
        D   E

29. No matter how many times a person <u>has driven</u> in
                                          A

    inclement weather, <u>they should</u> be <u>especially</u> careful
                           B   C

    when driving down a road <u>that</u> is covered with wet snow.
                                 D

    <u>No error</u>
       E

GO ON TO THE NEXT PAGE

Questions 30-35 are based on the following passage.

(1) Puccini's opera *La Bohème* is a timeless tale of love and art and tenderness in trying times and situations. (2) The epic is timeless for many reasons, one of the reasons is that people still relate to it, some even cry over the characters' fates. (3) Because it is timeless, recent artists have tried to bring the story to today's audiences.

(4) Director Baz Lurhmann brought the opera to the musical stage in 2002. (5) He did not change the words or the Italian language in which they were sung. (6) To reach his young audience, he jazzed up the costumes, set, and choreography. (7) The vibrant costumes, including black leather jackets, reflected the 1950s, the time period Lurhmann uses. (8) The set was stark and more reminiscent of the modern day than of a Bohemian ghetto. (9) The choreography transformed the singers into performers, so the show had the dynamic energy of a musical than the stilted movements of traditional opera; the show generally got rave reviews.

(10) Composer Jonathan Larson created the musical *Rent* in 1996, it takes much of the storyline and characters from *La Bohème*. (11) *Rent* was written in the 1990s; accordingly, it talks about issues relating to modern city youth. For example, tuberculosis in the original show became AIDS in the new one. (12) However, despite the rock music and modern slang, starving artists were still starving artists and greedy landlords were still greedy landlords; the musical was a huge success.

(13) Although all these updates of *La Bohème* have come to being, the original by Puccini is still incredibly popular. (14) Performances are given around the world and sell out frequently. (15) Interestingly, even though it is timeless, modern artists have still felt the need to update it.

30. Of the following, which would most improve the first paragraph (sentences 1-3) ?

   (A) a plot synopsis of *La Bohème*
   (B) a history of Puccini's life
   (C) a comparison of Puccini, Lurhmann, and Larson's backgrounds
   (D) an analysis of what audiences appreciate in theater
   (E) a description of tuberculosis and AIDS

31. Which of the following is the best version of sentence 7 (reproduced below) ?

   The vibrant costumes, including black leather jackets, reflected the 1950s, the time period Lurhmann uses.

   (A) The vibrant costumes and black leather jackets, reflected the 1950s, the time period Lurhmann uses.
   (B) The black leather jackets and other vibrant costumes reflected 0 the 1950s, the time period Lurhmann used in his production.
   (C) Lurhmann uses black leather jackets and other vibrant costumes of the 1950s in his production to suggest the time period of the production.
   (D) The vibrant costumes, and jackets imitated those of the 1950s, the time period Lurhmann uses in his production.
   (E) The black leather jackets and other vibrant costumes reproduced the time period of the 1950s of which Lurhmann uses in his production.

32. The purpose of the second paragraph is to

   (A) illustrate the way an artist transformed *La Bohème*
   (B) show how artists have updated *La Bohème* for modern audiences
   (C) explain the differences between *Rent* and *La Bohème*
   (D) explore the plight of tuberculosis victims
   (E) update Puccini's opera for today's youth

33. Which of the following is the best version of sentence 10 (reproduced below) ?

   Composer Jonathan Larson created the musical Rent *in 1996, it takes much of the storyline and characters from* La Bohème.

   (A) (As it is now)
   (B) Composer Jonathan Larson, who created the musical *Rent* in 1996, taking much of the storyline and characters from *La Bohème*.
   (C) Much of the storyline and characters from *La Bohème* were included in *Rent*, which is a musical created by composer Jonathan Larson in 1996.
   (D) *Rent*, a musical by composer Jonathan Larson in 1996, was created by using much of the storyline and characters from *La Bohème*.
   (E) Composer Jonathan Larson created the musical *Rent* in 1996 using much of the storyline and many of the characters from *La Bohème*.

GO ON TO THE NEXT PAGE

34. What is the primary purpose of sentence 12 (reproduced below) ?

However, despite the rock music and modern slang, starving artists were still starving artists and greedy landlords were still greedy landlords; the musical was a huge success.

(A) To demonstrate that all cultures use modern slang

(B) To focus on the tribulations of starving artists who cannot pay their rent

(C) To convey that certain constants attract audiences, regardless of presentation

(D) To show that cultures frequently change and reinvent themselves

(E) To determine that artists, regardless of era, evolve into different forms and appearance

35. Which is the best sentence to put after sentence 15 ?

(A) *Rent* has grossed over $280 million, far more than Lurhmann's *La Bohème*.

(B) Unlike *Rent*, *La Bohème* was first put on by Lurhmann in Australia before traveling to New York.

(C) Lurhmann's *La Bohème* garnered 7 Tony Award nominations in addition to other honors.

(D) Seemingly, artists are as compelled to revisit the story of Puccini's opera as are audiences worldwide.

(E) Lastly, the new interpretations of Puccini's opera, *La Bohème*, show no signs of slowing.

STOP

If you finish before time is called, you may check your work on this section only.
Do not turn to any other section in the test.

SECTION 7
Time — 25 minutes
18 Questions

Turn to Section 7 of your answer sheet to answer the questions in this section.

Directions: This section contains two types of questions. You have 25 minutes to complete both types. For questions 1-8, solve each problem and decide which is the best of the choices given. Fill in the corresponding circle on the answer sheet. You may use any available space for scratchwork.

Notes

1. The use of a calculator is permitted.

2. All numbers used are real numbers.

3. Figures that accompany problems in this test are intended to provide information useful in solving the problems. They are drawn as accurately as possible EXCEPT when it is stated in a specific problem that the figure is not drawn to scale. All figures lie in a plane unless otherwise indicated.

4. Unless otherwise specified, the domain of any function f is assumed to be the set of all real numbers x for which $f(x)$ is a real number.

Reference Information

 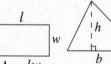 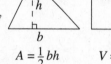

$A = \pi r^2$ $A = lw$ $A = \frac{1}{2}bh$ $V = lwh$ $V = \pi r^2 h$ $c^2 = a^2 + b^2$ Special Right Triangles

$C = 2\pi r$

The number of degrees of arc in a circle is 360.

The sum of the measures in degrees of the angles of a triangle is 180.

---

1. If $x^3 = 1$, what is the value of $\dfrac{x^2 + 3}{x}$?

(A) 0

(B) $\dfrac{1}{3}$

(C) $\dfrac{7}{2}$

(D) 2

(E) 4

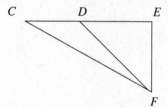

2. In the figure above, $\angle DEF$ of $\triangle CEF$ is a right angle. Of the following lengths, which is the largest?

(A) CE
(B) CF
(C) DE
(D) DF
(E) EF

GO ON TO THE NEXT PAGE

3. The average (arithmetic mean) of the numbers in set A is 8. If a second set of numbers, B, if created by dividing each of the numbers in set A by two, then what is the average of the numbers in set B ?

(A) $\dfrac{1}{2}$

(B) 4

(C) 8

(D) 12

(E) 16

4. If the positive four-digit integer JKLM contains the digits J, K, L, and M, what is the decimal equivalent of JKLM $\times$ 10^{-3} ?

(A) 0.JKLM

(B) J.KLM

(C) JK.LM

(D) JK,LM0

(E) J,KLM,000

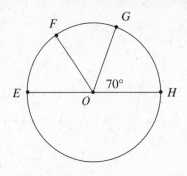

5. In the figure above, $\overline{EH}$ is a diameter of the circle with center O. If $\overline{FO}$ bisects $\angle EOG$, what is the measure of $\angle FOH$?

(A) 180

(B) 125

(C) 110

(D) 105

(E) 90

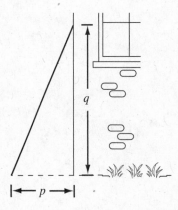

6. The figure above illustrates a ladder extended from a vertical wall to the ground. If the ladder has a slope of $\dfrac{5}{3}$ feet and p is 9 feet, what is q, in feet?

(A) 15

(B) 10

(C) 7.5

(D) 5

(E) 4.5

GO ON TO THE NEXT PAGE

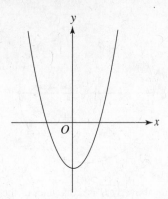

7. The parabola in the graph above is given by the equation $y = ax^2 - 3$. If a new parabola, given by the equation $y = 2ax^2 - 3$, is graphed on the same axes, which of the following best describes the resulting parabola as compared with the parabola above?

   (A) It will move 2 units upward.
   (B) It will be wider.
   (C) It will be narrower.
   (D) It will be moved to the left.
   (E) It will be moved to the right.

8. Serena has three photographs from Brazil—a landscape, a street scene, and a portrait. She also has three photographs from Kenya—a landscape, a street scene, and a portrait—and three photographs from Istanbul—a landscape, a street scene, and a portrait. Serena wants to display three photographs: one landscape, one street scene, and one portrait, and also wants to use one each from Brazil, Kenya, and Istanbul. How many different possibilities does she have?

   (A) 1
   (B) 3
   (C) 6
   (D) 9
   (E) 27

GO ON TO THE NEXT PAGE

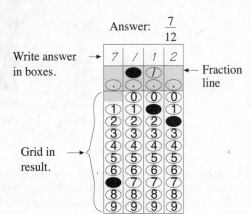

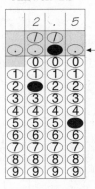

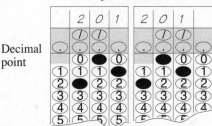

Directions: For Student-Produced Response questions 9-18, use the grids at the bottom of the answer sheet page on which you have answered questions 1-8.

Each of the remaining 10 questions requires you to solve the problem and enter your answer by marking the circles in the special grid, as shown in the examples below. You may use any available space for scratch work.

Answer: $\frac{7}{12}$

Write answer in boxes. → ← Fraction line

Grid in result. →

Answer: 2.5

← Decimal point

Answer: 201
Either position is correct.

Note: You may start your answers in any column, space permitting. Columns not needed should be left blank.

- Mark no more than one circle in any column.

- Because the answer document will be machine-scored, **you will receive credit only if the circles are filled in correctly.**

- Although not required, it is suggested that you write your answer in the boxes at the top of the columns to help you fill in the circles accurately.

- Some problems may have more than one correct answer. In such cases, grid only one answer.

- No question has a negative answer.

- **Mixed numbers** such as $3\frac{1}{2}$ must be gridded as

  3.5 or 7/2. (If $\boxed{3\ 1\ /\ 2}$ is gridded, it will be

  interpreted as $\frac{31}{2}$, not $3\frac{1}{2}$.)

- **Decimal Answers:** If you obtain a decimal answer with more digits than the grid can accommodate, it may be either rounded or truncated, but it must fill the entire grid. For example, if you obtain an answer such as 0.6666..., you should record your result as .666 or .667. **A less accurate value such as .66 or .67 will be scored as incorrect.**

Acceptable ways to grid $\frac{2}{3}$ are:

9. When half of a number is decreased by 7, the result is 8. What is the number?

Cylindrical Containers — Coaster

10. Each of the 3 right cylindrical containers shown has interior dimensions measuring 5 inches in height and 4 inches in diameter. At most, how many circular coasters, each with a 4-inch diameter and a height of $\frac{1}{3}$ inches, can fit inside the three containers altogether?

GO ON TO THE NEXT PAGE →

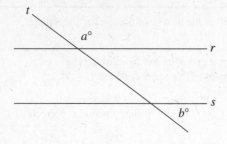

11. In the figure above, $r \parallel s$ and $a = 4b$. What is the value of a ?

12. Let the function $f(x)$ be defined by $f(x) = |2x - 3|$. If p is a real number, what is one possible value of p for which $f(p) < p$?

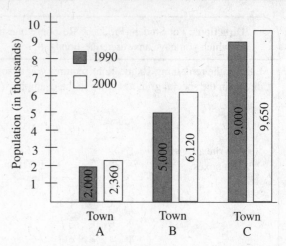

13. The bar graph shown above gives the populations for Town A, Town B, and Town C in 1990 and 2000. What is the average (arithmetic mean) population increase of the three towns from 1990 to 2000 ?

14. A bowl contains 30 blue marbles and 30 green marbles. If 17 blue marbles are removed, what is the maximum number of green marbles that can be removed so that there are at least twice as many green marbles as there are blue marbles?

GO ON TO THE NEXT PAGE

15. If $\dfrac{4a+3b}{2b} = \dfrac{5}{3}$, what is the value of $\dfrac{b}{a}$?

16. At shipping company A, sending a package costs a flat rate of $10 for any package weighing up to and including 10 pounds, plus an additional $0.60 per pound for every pound over 10 pounds. The cost of sending a package using shipping company B is $0.80 per pound for any weight. If the cost of sending a package using Company 1 is the same as the cost of sending a package using Company 2, then how much does the package weigh?

17. A number is considered "odd-mult" if it is the multiple of exactly two consecutive odd numbers. How many positive numbers less than 400 are "odd-mult"?

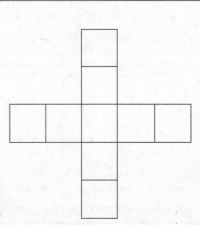

18. The figure above shows an arrangement of 9 squares, each with a side of length s inches. The perimeter of the figure is p inches and the area of the figure is a inches. If $p = a$, then what is the value of s ?

STOP

If you finish before time is called, you may check your work on this section only.
Do not turn to any other section in the test.

SECTION 8
Time — 20 minutes
16 Questions

Turn to Section 8 of your answer sheet to answer the questions in this section.

Directions: For this section, solve each problem and decide which is the best of the choices given. Fill in the corresponding circle on the answer sheet. You may use any available space for scratchwork.

Notes

1. The use of a calculator is permitted.

2. All numbers used are real numbers.

3. Figures that accompany problems in this test are intended to provide information useful in solving the problems. They are drawn as accurately as possible EXCEPT when it is stated in a specific problem that the figure is not drawn to scale. All figures lie in a plane unless otherwise indicated.

4. Unless otherwise specified, the domain of any function f is assumed to be the set of all real numbers x for which $f(x)$ is a real number.

Reference Information

$A = \pi r^2$
$C = 2\pi r$
$A = lw$
$A = \frac{1}{2}bh$
$V = lwh$
$V = \pi r^2 h$
$c^2 = a^2 + b^2$

Special Right Triangles

The number of degrees of arc in a circle is 360.

The sum of the measures in degrees of the angles of a triangle is 180.

1. It takes 72 minutes to drive along a certain route at a constant speed. What fraction of the ride is completed after 12 minutes?

(A) $\dfrac{1}{4}$

(B) $\dfrac{1}{5}$

(C) $\dfrac{1}{6}$

(D) $\dfrac{1}{7}$

(E) $\dfrac{1}{12}$

x	1	2	3	4	5	6
$f(x)$	9	16	t	30	37	44

2. If the table above defines a linear function, what is the value of t ?

(A) 23
(B) 24
(C) 25
(D) 26
(E) 27

GO ON TO THE NEXT PAGE

3. The diameter of a basketball is 4 times the diameter of a racquetball. What is the ratio of the radius of the basketball to that of the racquetball?

(A) 1 : 2
(B) 3 : 2
(C) 4 : 1
(D) 4 : 3
(E) 8 : 1

SHORT STORY GENRES

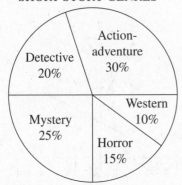

4. In a creative-writing course, 60 students chose from among 5 genres for each assignment. The graph above shows the distribution of the stories turned in for one assignment. If there were 6 assignments during the semester, and the same number of students turned in Detective stories for each assignment, what is the total number of Detective stories turned in during the semester?

(A) 72
(B) 100
(C) 120
(D) 240
(E) 300

5. Janet produced 4 more paintings than three times the number of paintings Sam produced. Last year, Sam produced p paintings. Of the expressions below, which represents the number of paintings Janet produced last year?

(A) $4 - 3p$
(B) $4p - 3$
(C) $4p + 3$
(D) $3p - 4$
(E) $3p + 4$

6. For the inequality $c - d > c$, which of the following must be true?

(A) $c < 0$
(B) $c > 0$
(C) $c < d$
(D) $d < 0$
(E) $d > 0$

GO ON TO THE NEXT PAGE

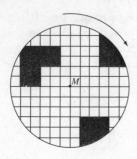

7. Which of the following is a representation of the result if the figure above were rotated 270° clockwise about point *M* ?

(A)

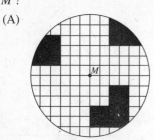

(B)

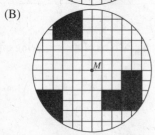

(C)

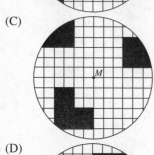

(D)

(E)

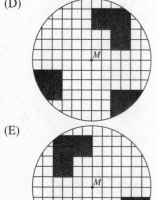

8. If $a > 0$ and $b < 0$, which of the following must be true?

(A) $a + b = 0$

(B) $\dfrac{a}{b} < 0$

(C) $a + b < 0$

(D) $a + b > 0$

(E) $ab > 0$

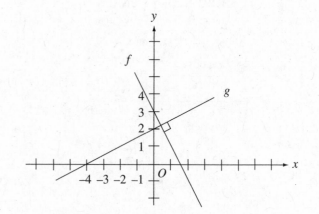

9. In the *xy*-coordinate plane above, line *f* and line *g* are perpendicular to one another. What is the slope of line *f* ?

(A) -2

(B) $-\dfrac{1}{2}$

(C) $\dfrac{1}{2}$

(D) 2

(E) 3

GO ON TO THE NEXT PAGE

10. A bag of candy contains chocolate hearts, vanilla hearts and gumballs. The number of pieces of heart shaped candy is 5 times the number of gumballs. If one piece of candy is to be chosen at random from the bag, the probability that a vanilla heart will be chosen is 4 times the probability that a chocolate heart will be chosen. If there are 16 vanilla hearts in the bag, what is the total number of pieces of candy in the bag?

    (A) 48
    (B) 44
    (C) 36
    (D) 24
    (E) 20

11. If $ab = 8$, $bc = 4$ and $ac = 2$, and $c > 0$, then what is the value of abc ?

    (A) 2
    (B) 4
    (C) 8
    (D) 32
    (E) 64

12. If six less than four times a number is greater than or equal to -2, which of the following represents all possible values of that number?

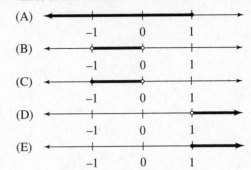

13. In a certain polygon, all of the angles are equal and all of the sides are of equal length. Point Q is a vertex of the polygon. If four diagonals can be drawn from point Q to the other vertices of the polygon, how many sides does the polygon have?

    (A) Eight
    (B) Seven
    (C) Six
    (D) Five
    (E) Four

GO ON TO THE NEXT PAGE

14. When n is a positive integer, $9 + 3^{n+2} = m$. What is the value of 3^n in terms of m ?

(A) $m + 3$

(B) $m^2 - 3$

(C) $\dfrac{m+1}{9}$

(D) $\dfrac{m-9}{9}$

(E) $\dfrac{1}{3} m$

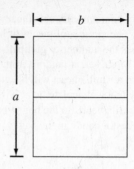

16. A gardener wants to enclose a patch of soil with length a and width b with fencing. He also wants to put a fence down the middle of the patch, to divide it into two smaller rectangular gardens, as seen in the figure above. If the area of the patch is 20 square feet, how many feet of fence, in terms of b, must the gardener use?

(A) $b + \dfrac{20}{b}$

(B) $b + \dfrac{40}{b}$

(C) $3b + \dfrac{40}{b}$

(D) $3b + \dfrac{20}{3b}$

(E) $3b + \dfrac{40}{3b}$

15. In $\triangle ABC$ two sides, AB and BC, are equal. Side AC has a length of 5, and the perimeter of $\triangle ABC$ is 13. If the measure of angle ABC is x , which of the following must be true about x ?

(A) $x < 60$
(B) $60 < x < 90$
(C) $x = 90$
(D) $x > 90$
(E) It cannot be determined from the information given.

STOP
If you finish before time is called, you may check your work on this section only.
Do not turn to any other section in the test.

NO TEST MATERIAL ON THIS PAGE.

SECTION 9
Time — 20 minutes
19 Questions

Turn to Section 9 of your answer sheet to answer the questions in this section.

Directions: For each question in this section, select the best answer from among the choices given and fill in the corresponding circle on the answer sheet.

Each sentence below has one or two blanks, each blank indicating that something has been omitted. Beneath the sentence are five words or sets of words labeled A through E. Choose the word or set of words that, when inserted in the sentence, best fits the meaning of the sentence as a whole.

Example:

Desiring to ------- his taunting friends, Mitch gave them taffy in hopes it would keep their mouths shut.

(A) eliminate   (B) satisfy   (C) overcome
    (D) ridicule   (E) silence

1. The star football player apparently was the victim of an elaborate -------: he had no idea that his girlfriend did not actually exist.

   (A) organization
   (B) determination
   (C) hoax
   (D) belief
   (E) perception

2. Because Donald frequently involved himself in the affairs of others, he gained the reputation of a -------, and even his own friends regarded him as an -------.

   (A) meddler . . interloper
   (B) traitor . . authority
   (C) mediator . . impostor
   (D) negotiator . . arbiter
   (E) conciliator . . intruder

3. Although Devon was viewed by his coworkers as a ------- and reliable employee, his boss viewed him as undependable and easily swayed.

   (A) staunch   (B) apprehensive   (C) incessant
       (D) diffident   (E) singular

4. The safety expert argued that even though the new helmet designs were ------ for their superior protective structures, the unreliable materials suggested for production made the helmets more -------.

   (A) banned . . prohibitive
   (B) lauded . . precarious
   (C) extolled . . advantageous
   (D) analyzed . . useless
   (E) tested . . functional

5. The prosecutor mocked the defendant's lack of -------, noting the lack of evidence or testimony to support the version of events offered by the defense.

   (A) respectability   (B) objection   (C) fidelity
       (D) eloquence   (E) corroboration

6. In spite of the ------- atmosphere at the gathering, John seemed unhappy and detached from the rest of the group.

   (A) reticent   (B) quixotic   (C) despondent
       (D) fortuitous   (E) convivial

GO ON TO THE NEXT PAGE

Directions: Each passage below is followed by questions based on its content. Answer the questions on the basis of what is <u>stated</u> or <u>implied</u> in each passage and in any introductory material that may be provided.

Questions 7-19 are based on the following passage.

This passage, adapted from a novel written in the nineteenth century, portrays two characters—William Crimsworth and Mr. Hunsden, a business associate. At the beginning of the passage, William is out for a walk.

No man likes to acknowledge that he has made a mistake in the choice of his profession, and any human being, worthy of the name, will row long against wind and tide before he
Line allows himself to cry out, "I am baffled!" and submits to be
5 floated passively back to land. From the first week, I felt my occupation oppressive. The thing itself—the work of copying and translating business-letters—was a dry and tedious task enough, but had that been all, I should long have borne with the nuisance. But this was not all; the antipathy which had
10 sprung up between myself and Mr. Crimsworth struck deeper root and spread denser shade daily, excluding me from every glimpse of the sunshine of life.

Antipathy is the only word which can express the feeling Edward Crimsworth had for me. My accent annoyed him; the
15 degree of education evinced in my language irritated him; my punctuality and industry fixed his dislike, and gave it the high flavour and poignant relish of envy. Had I been in anything inferior to him, he would not have hated me so thoroughly. I had long ceased to regard Mr. Crimsworth as my brother—he
20 was a hard, grinding master; he wished to be an inexorable tyrant: that was all. Thoughts, not varied but strong, occupied my mind; two voices spoke within me; again and again they uttered the same monotonous phrases. One said: "William, your life is intolerable." The other: "What can you do to alter
25 it?"

I had received my weekly wages, and was returning to my lodgings, speculating on the general state of my affairs, when I encountered a familiar figure.

"Mr. Hunsden! Good evening."
30 "Good evening, indeed!"

For a moment, Mr. Hunsden fell silent. He seemed possessed of a great urge to speak, yet unsure of how to proceed. Presently, he recovered his composure, and starting from his silent fit, began:
35 "William! What a fool you are to live in those dismal lodgings of Mrs. King's, when you might take rooms in Grove Street, and have a garden like me!"

"I should be too far from the mill."

"What of that? It would do you good to walk there and
40 back two or three times a day; besides, are you such a fossil that you never wish to see a flower or a green leaf?"

"I am no fossil."

"What are you then? You sit at that desk in Crimsworth's counting-house day by day and week by week, scraping
45 with a pen on paper; you never get up; you never say you are tired; you never ask for a holiday; you never take change or relaxation; you give way to no excess of an evening; you neither keep wild company, nor indulge in strong drink."

"Do you, Mr. Hunsden?"
50 "Don't think to pose me with short questions; your case and mine are diametrically different, and it is nonsense attempting to draw a parallel. I say, that when a man endures patiently what ought to be unendurable, he is a fossil."

"Whence do you acquire the knowledge of my patience?"
55 "Why, man, do you suppose you are a mystery? What do you think I do with my eyes and ears? I've been in your counting-house more than once when Crimsworth has treated you like a dog; called for a book, for instance, and when you gave him the wrong one, or what he chose to consider the
60 wrong one, flung it back almost in your face!"

"Well, Mr. Hunsden, what then?"

"I can hardly tell you what then; the conclusion to be drawn as to your character depends upon the nature of the motives that guide your conduct; if you are patient because
65 you expect to make something eventually out of Crimsworth, notwithstanding his tyranny, you are what the world calls interested and mercenary, but if you are patient because you think it a duty to meet insult with submission, you are an essential sap, and in no shape the man for my money."
70 His brow darkened, his thin nostrils dilated a little.

"You'll make nothing by trade," continued he; "nothing more than the crust of dry bread on which you now live; your only chance of getting a competency lies in marrying a rich widow, or running away with an heiress."
75 "I leave such shifts to be put in practice by those who devise them," said I.

"And even that is hopeless," he went on coolly. "What widow would have you? Much less, what heiress? You're not bold and venturesome enough for the one, nor handsome and
80 fascinating enough for the other."

Hunsden saw his advantage; he followed it up.

"You should have been a nobleman, William Crimsworth! You are cut out for one; pity Fortune has cheated Nature! Now, if you'd only an estate, a mansion, and a title, how you
85 could play the part! As it is, you've no power; you're wrecked and stranded on the shores of commerce; forced into collision with practical men, with whom you cannot cope. You'll never succeed as a tradesman!"

GO ON TO THE NEXT PAGE

7. The episode in the passage is best described as a

   (A) dispute between two enemies
   (B) collaboration between two coworkers
   (C) disagreement between two friends
   (D) conversation between two brothers
   (E) confrontation between two acquaintances

8. Lines 1-5 ("No man . . . land") suggest that a person who is "worthy of the name" is one who

   (A) enjoys the challenge of navigating in adverse conditions
   (B) is determined to achieve wealth and respectability in business
   (C) is reluctant to abandon a plan once it has been chosen
   (D) is unwilling to work hard to attain his goals
   (E) has difficulty expressing feelings and emotions

9. William's comments in lines 5-12 ("From . . . life") suggest that his primary objection to his job is his

   (A) increasing resentment of his fellow employees
   (B) growing disenchantment with his employer
   (C) frequent conflicts with demanding customers
   (D) annoyance with the tedious nature of the work
   (E) frustration with working long hours for low pay

10. The list in lines 14-17 ("My accent . . . envy") indicates that Edward Crimsworth is

    (A) angered by William's condescending and scornful manner
    (B) exasperated by William's casual attitude toward his work
    (C) jealous of William's cultivated and professional demeanor
    (D) resentful of the fact that William was favored by their parents
    (E) bewildered by William's tendency to speak in an affected accent

11. In line 42, Mr. Hunsden uses the word "fossil" to suggest that William is

    (A) incapable of walking long distances
    (B) suspicious of anything out of the ordinary
    (C) inhibited by his strict sense of morality
    (D) desensitized by his unvarying routine
    (E) older than the other workers at the counting-house

12. Mr. Hunsden responds to the question posed by William in line 49 by

    (A) denying that the same criteria apply to both of them
    (B) complaining that William's responses are ill-considered
    (C) demanding that William stop questioning his character
    (D) deliberately misunderstanding the meaning of the question
    (E) casually dismissing the importance of the topic

13. Lines 62-69 ("I can . . . money") indicate that Mr. Hunsden is

    (A) uncertain about the reasons underlying William's actions
    (B) confused about whether William really likes his brother
    (C) suspicious about William's plan to take over the family business
    (D) surprised that William refuses to accept his offer of financial assistance
    (E) pleased that William has finally decided to make something of his life

14. Mr. Hunsden's statement in lines 71-74 ("You'll make . . . heiress") is best described as a

    (A) criticism of unconventional relationships
    (B) warning about romantic illusions
    (C) confession of his own failures
    (D) prediction of a bleak future
    (E) confession of secret desires

15. William responds to the statement in lines 71-74 ("You'll make . . . heiress") by implying that

    (A) a goal remains out of reach
    (B) an outcome appears uncertain
    (C) a plan is considered promising
    (D) a strategy is unlikely to succeed
    (E) an idea is unworthy of consideration

16. In line 75, "shifts" most nearly means

    (A) substitutions
    (B) occupations
    (C) schemes
    (D) directions
    (E) adjustments

GO ON TO THE NEXT PAGE

17. In lines 77-80 ("And even . . . other"), Mr. Hunsden suggests that William is

(A) clever but unattractive
(B) drab but appealing
(C) timid and bland
(D) assertive and impoverished
(E) dashing and mysterious

18. In context, the phrase "Fortune has cheated Nature" (line 83) refers to the idea that William is

(A) cruel to members of the lower classes
(B) ill-suited to his chosen profession
(C) prone to making reckless decisions
(D) accustomed to insults from Mr. Hunsden
(E) envious of those who have power and wealth

19. William and Mr. Hunsden most likely agree on which point?

(A) William needs to think more carefully about his future.
(B) William will never succeed as a tradesman.
(C) William should feel fortunate to have a career.
(D) William is treated poorly by his employer.
(E) William should seek marriage with an aristocratic woman.

STOP

If you finish before time is called, you may check your work on this section only.
Do not turn to any other section in the test.

SECTION 10
Time — 10 minutes
14 Questions

Turn to Section 10 of your answer sheet to answer the questions in this section.

Directions: For each question in this section, select the best answer from among the choices given and fill in the corresponding circle on the answer sheet.

The following sentences test correctness and effectiveness of expression. Part of each sentence or the entire sentence is underlined; beneath each sentence are five ways of phrasing the underlined material. Choice A repeats the original phrasing; the other four choices are different. If you think the original phrasing produces a better sentence than any of the alternatives, select choice A; if not, select one of the other choices.

In making your selection, follow the requirements of standard written English; that is, pay attention to grammar, choice of words, sentence construction, and punctuation. Your selection should result in the most effective sentence—clear and precise, without awkwardness or ambiguity.

EXAMPLE:

Bobby Flay baked his first cake <u>and he was thirteen years old then</u>.

(A) and he was thirteen years old then
(B) when he was thirteen
(C) at age thirteen years old
(D) upon the reaching of thirteen years
(E) at the time when he was thirteen

1. In everything from obedience training to home protection, pet owners have become so <u>knowledgeable, and</u> professional trainers often adopt their methods.

   (A) knowledgeable, and
   (B) knowledgeable, also
   (C) knowledgeable that
   (D) knowledgeable therefore
   (E) knowledgeable when

2. Since hiking trails need to be clearly marked, <u>parks departments requiring significant funds</u>.

   (A) parks departments requiring significant funds
   (B) parks departments being what requires significant funds
   (C) parks departments require significant funds
   (D) significant funds are required by parks departments
   (E) significant funds is what they require in parks departments

3. To commemorate its centennial, the town has installed an <u>exhibit, it consists of</u> five parts, each focusing on twenty years of the community's history.

   (A) exhibit, it consists of
   (B) exhibit, it consisting
   (C) exhibit, and it will consist of
   (D) exhibit that consists of
   (E) exhibit, they consist of

4. With audiences following reality shows with unprecedented frequency, <u>producers are urging networks to increase their reality programming, which</u> may ultimately replace other, more substantive, programs.

   (A) producers are urging networks to increase their reality programming
   (B) producers have been urging that networks increase its programming of reality television; those
   (C) the networks ought to increase their programming of reality television, as urged by producers, because they
   (D) producers urge about increasing reality television programming, which
   (E) more reality television should be programmed by networks, urge producers, which

GO ON TO THE NEXT PAGE

5. Contest judges argue about <u>what is the determination of the ultimate Halloween costume and how to critique it</u>.

 (A) what is the determination of the ultimate Halloween costume and how to critique it
 (B) how to determine the ultimate Halloween costume, and also its critique
 (C) how to determine and critique the ultimate Halloween costume
 (D) determining the ultimate Halloween costume as well as critique it
 (E) the determination of the ultimate Halloween costume and critiquing it

6. In the sixteenth century Michelangelo was as celebrated for his sculpture <u>and also for his</u> painting, and he furthermore found success in architecture, poetry and engineering.

 (A) and also for his
 (B) as well as for his
 (C) as he was for his
 (D) but for his
 (E) but also for his

7. Although she had previously been pleased to be photographed and written about, <u>it was after her brief and mysterious disappearance that Agatha Christie had an avoidance of publicity</u>.

 (A) it was after her brief and mysterious disappearance that Agatha Christie had an avoidance of publicity
 (B) it was after her brief and mysterious disappearance that Agatha Christie avoided publicity
 (C) the brief and mysterious disappearance of Agatha Christie who then avoided publicity
 (D) Agatha Christie's brief and mysterious disappearance an avoidance of publicity
 (E) Agatha Christie avoided publicity after her brief and mysterious disappearance

8. One of the most unusual animals in the world, <u>eggs are laid by the platypus, which is a mammal</u>.

 (A) eggs are laid by the platypus, which is a mammal
 (B) the platypus, who is a mammal, lays eggs
 (C) the platypus who is an egg-laying mammal
 (D) the platypus is a mammal that lays eggs
 (E) the mammal which lays eggs is the platypus

9. Many pre- and post-World War II military pilots <u>were believers in their commanding officers' authority, demonstrate national pride</u>, and the importance of discipline.

 (A) were believers in their commanding officers' authority, demonstrate national pride
 (B) are believers in the authority of their commanding officers, national pride being demonstrated
 (C) who believed in the authority of their commanding officers, demonstrate national pride
 (D) believed in the authority of their commanding officers, to demonstrate national pride
 (E) believed in the authority of their commanding officers, the demonstration of national pride

10. A psychological novel, such as George Eliot's *Middlemarch*, is characterized by its focus on the ways the characters' internal states can trigger <u>events in the external</u>.

 (A) events in the external
 (B) external events
 (C) events external
 (D) events externally
 (E) in external events

11. Many of William Blake's <u>etchings were inspired by his notions of good and evil, accompanied by</u> subject-appropriate writings.

 (A) etchings were inspired by his notions of good and evil, accompanied by
 (B) etchings had their inspiration from his notions of good and evil, accompanied by
 (C) etchings, inspired by his notions of good and evil, were accompanied by
 (D) etchings, which were inspired by his notions of good and evil and which are accompanied by
 (E) etchings, being inspired by his notions of good and evil, accompanied by

12. Among the most inspirational and humanitarian films of all time, <u>Frank Capra has long been known for his</u> uplifting messages about the basic goodness within people.

 (A) Frank Capra has long been known for his
 (B) Frank Capra, having become well-known for long
 (C) and the films of Frank Capra are known for
 (D) films by Frank Capra have become known because they have
 (E) the films of Frank Capra have long been known for their

GO ON TO THE NEXT PAGE ⟩

13. When the students take a trip on the intracoastal waterway system next month, they will learn <u>facts with which they have heretofore been unacquainted</u>.

(A) facts with which they have heretofore been unacquainted

(B) facts with which they haven't been acquainted with yet

(C) facts, being, heretofore, unacquainted with them

(D) facts with which they haven't never been acquainted

(E) facts, being unacquainted with them heretofore beforehand

14. The painting style of Picasso, a mix of classical composition and innovative techniques, was regarded as more <u>progressive than his contemporaries</u>.

(A) progressive than his contemporaries

(B) progressive than his contemporaries were painting

(C) progressive than were his contemporaries

(D) progressive than that of his contemporaries

(E) progressive than his contemporaries, when it came to painting

STOP
If you finish before time is called, you may check your work on this section only.
Do not turn to any other section in the test.

NO TEST MATERIAL ON THIS PAGE.

PRACTICE TEST 4: ANSWER KEY

2 Reading	3 Math	5 Reading	6 Writing	7 Math	8 Math	9 Reading	10 Writing
1. D	1. D	1. A	1. A	1. E	1. C	1. C	1. C
2. D	2. B	2. B	2. C	2. B	2. A	2. A	2. C
3. E	3. E	3. E	3. B	3. B	3. C	3. A	3. D
4. C	4. B	4. B	4. D	4. B	4. A	4. B	4. A
5. B	5. D	5. D	5. B	5. B	5. E	5. E	5. C
6. D	6. A	6. D	6. A	6. A	6. D	6. E	6. C
7. A	7. A	7. C	7. E	7. C	7. C	7. E	7. E
8. A	8. E	8. B	8. C	8. C	8. B	8. C	8. D
9. D	9. D	9. A	9. D	9. 30	9. A	9. B	9. E
10. D	10. C	10. B	10. E	10. 45	10. D	10. C	10. B
11. B	11. C	11. B	11. A	11. 144	11. C	11. D	11. C
12. A	12. D	12. D	12. B	12. $1 < x < 3$	12. E	12. A	12. E
13. C	13. E	13. D	13. C	13. 710	13. B	13. A	13. A
14. E	14. D	14. C	14. B	14. 4	14. D	14. D	14. D
15. A	15. E	15. D	15. C	15. 12	15. B	15. E	
16. A	16. E	16. E	16. D	16. 20	16. C	16. C	
17. C	17. A	17. B	17. E	17. 10		17. C	
18. D	18. B	18. A	18. C	18. $\frac{20}{9}$ or 2.22		18. B	
19. B	19. A	19. E	19. B			19. D	
20. C	20. D	20. C	20. E				
21. A		21. D	21. A				
22. E		22. B	22. E				
23. B		23. A	23. E				
24. B		24. E	24. C				
			25. D				
			26. D				
			27. D				
			28. C				
			29. B				
			30. A				
			31. B				
			32. A				
			33. E				
			34. C				
			35. D				

SAT SCORING WORKSHEET

For directions on how to score your SAT practice test, see pages 10–11.

SAT Writing Section

Total Writing Multiple-Choice Questions Correct: ☐

—

Total Writing Multiple-Choice Questions Incorrect: _____ ÷ 4 = ☐

Grammar Raw Score: ☐ ——— Grammar Scaled Subscore ☐

Compare the Grammar Raw Score with the Writing Multiple-Choice Subscore Conversion Table on page 342 to find the Grammar Scaled Subscore.

+

Your Essay Score (2–12): _____ × 2 = ☐

Writing Raw Score: ☐

Writing Scaled Score ☐

Compare Raw Score with SAT Score Conversion Table on page 342 to find the Writing Scaled Score.

SAT Critical Reading Section

Total Critical Reading Questions Correct: ☐

—

Total Critical Reading Questions Incorrect: _____ ÷ 4 = ☐

Critical Reading Raw Score: ☐

Critical Reading Scaled Score ☐

Compare Raw Score with SAT Score Conversion Table on page 342 to find the Critical Reading Scaled Score.

SAT Math Section

Total Math Grid-In Questions Correct: ☐

+

Total Math Multiple-Choice Questions Correct: ☐

—

Total Math Multiple-Choice Questions Incorrect: _____ ÷ 4 = ☐

Don't include wrong answers from grid-ins!

Math Raw Score: ☐

Math Scaled Score ☐

Compare Raw Score with SAT Score Conversion Table on page 342 to find the Math Scaled Score.

SAT SCORE CONVERSION TABLE

Raw Score	Writing Scaled Score	Reading Scaled Score	Math Scaled Score	Raw Score	Writing Scaled Score	Reading Scaled Score	Math Scaled Score	Raw Score	Writing Scaled Score	Reading Scaled Score	Math Scaled Score
73	800			47	590–630	600–640	660–700	21	400–440	410–450	440–480
72	790–800			46	590–630	590–630	650–690	20	390–430	400–440	430–470
71	780–800			45	580–620	580–620	650–690	19	380–420	400–440	430–470
70	770–800			44	570–610	580–620	640–680	18	370–410	390–430	420–460
69	770–800			43	570–610	570–610	630–670	17	370–410	380–420	410–450
68	760–800			42	560–600	570–610	620–660	16	360–400	370–410	400–440
67	760–800	800		41	560–600	560–600	610–650	15	350–390	360–400	400–440
66	760–800	770–800		40	550–590	550–590	600–640	14	340–380	350–390	390–430
65	750–790	760–800		39	540–580	550–590	590–630	13	330–370	340–380	380–420
64	740–780	750–790		38	530–570	540–580	590–630	12	320–360	340–380	360–400
63	730–770	740–780		37	530–570	530–570	580–620	11	320–360	330–370	350–390
62	720–760	730–770		36	520–560	530–570	570–610	10	310–350	320–360	340–380
61	710–750	720–760		35	510–550	520–560	560–600	9	300–340	310–350	330–370
60	700–740	710–750		34	500–540	520–560	560–600	8	290–330	300–340	320–360
59	690–730	700–740		33	490–530	510–550	550–590	7	280–320	300–340	310–350
58	680–720	690–730		32	480–520	500–540	540–580	6	270–310	290–330	300–340
57	680–720	680–720		31	470–510	490–530	530–570	5	260–300	280–320	290–330
56	670–710	670–710		30	470–510	480–520	520–560	4	240–280	270–310	280–320
55	660–720	670–710		29	460–500	470–510	520–560	3	230–270	250–290	280–320
54	650–690	660–700	760–800	28	450–490	470–510	510–550	2	230–270	240–280	270–310
53	640–680	650–690	740–780	27	440–480	460–500	500–540	1	220–260	220–260	260–300
52	630–670	640–680	730–770	26	430–470	450–490	490–530	0	210–250	200–240	250–290
51	630–670	630–670	710–750	25	420–460	440–480	480–520	–1	200–240	200–230	230–270
50	620–660	620–660	690–730	24	410–450	430–470	470–510	–2	200–230	200–220	220–260
49	610–650	610–650	680–720	23	410–450	430–470	460–500	–3	200–220	200–210	200–240
48	600–640	600–640	670–710	22	400–440	420–460	450–490				

WRITING MULTIPLE-CHOICE SUBSCORE CONVERSION TABLE

Grammar Raw Score	Grammar Scaled Subscore	Grammar Raw Score	Grammar Scaled Subscore	Grammar Raw Score	Grammar Scaled Subscore	Grammar Raw Score	Grammar Scaled Subscore	Grammar Raw Score	Grammar Scaled Subscore
49	78–80	38	67–71	27	55–59	16	42–46	5	30–34
48	77–80	37	66–70	26	54–58	15	41–45	4	29–33
47	75–79	36	65–69	25	53–57	14	40–44	3	28–32
46	74–78	35	64–68	24	52–56	13	39–43	2	27–31
45	72–76	34	63–67	23	51–55	12	38–42	1	25–29
44	72–76	33	62–66	22	50–54	11	36–40	0	24–28
43	71–75	32	61–65	21	49–53	10	35–39	–1	22–26
42	70–74	31	60–64	20	47–51	9	34–38	–2	20–23
41	69–73	30	59–63	19	46–50	8	33–37	–3	20–22
40	68–72	29	58–62	18	45–49	7	32–36		
39	68–72	28	56–60	17	44–48	6	31–35		

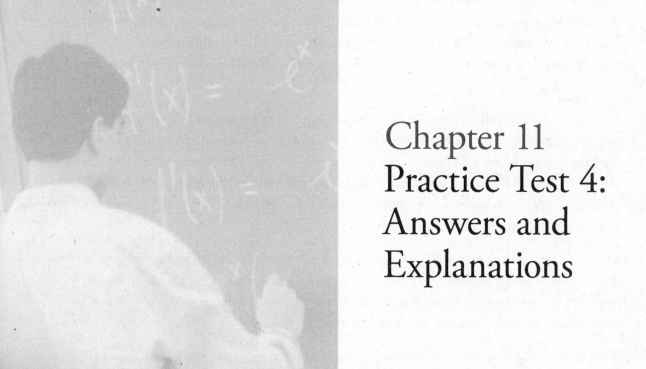

Chapter 11
Practice Test 4:
Answers and
Explanations

SECTION 2

1. **D** Who is Douglas? Someone who *misses deadlines and finishes projects late*. He puts things off. He is a *procrastinator*.

2. **D** What do we know about the referee's decision? Well, after fifteen minutes the rain cleared up, so the decision was probably made too early. (B) and (D) work, but keep any answer choices that you don't know. Considering the second blank, the game was canceled, so conditions must have been bad originally, which means that now they are good. Only (C) and (D) work, so (D) must be the right answer.

3. **E** *Most fish* are one way, and the *labyrinth fish* is another way. Since the *labyrinth fish* is different from *most fish*, a good word for the first blank would be "different" or "unusual." Since it is different from the majority of fish who breathe only water, it must be able to breathe air as well. So it is "able to" breathe air. We have a word for the second blank. The phrase "able to" is a little awkward alongside *breathing*, but as long as its meaning matches the sentence, it is fine. (E) most closely matches the meanings of "different" and "able to."

4. **C** We know we are looking for a word that means something negative because of *sapping strength* and *depriving one of energy*. Hopefully that helps you eliminate a few answers, but the words here are tough. If you don't know the meaning of at least three words, this probably a good one to skip. (C) is the only answer choice here that means *sapping strength*.

5. **B** What do we know about Bearden's talents? He produced paintings, wrote music, and was a baseball player. That is a really wide range of abilities; so our word must mean "wide ranging." Only (B) *eclectic* fits. The words here are really tough, if you don't know the vocab, or you can't eliminate anything, skip this question.

6. **D** The author states that for a *true craftsman…the slightest variation* (in the sound a tool makes) *will cause him to alter his stroke, or pause to sharpen the tool's blade*. In other words, *subtle changes* cause him to *respond* (D). The other answers are not supported by the passage.

7. **A** A metaphor is a comparison that is literally untrue, but conveys the author's point. Tools don't actually *sing, cough, wheeze,* or *hum*. Therefore (A) is the correct answer.

8. **A** Use Process of Elimination to cross off all answers that are true. *Big-stick approach* tells us (B) is true. *Curbed the abuse and exploitation of workers* shows that (C) is true. *Created the system of national parks long before environmentalism was fashionable* means that (D) is true. *Was awarded a Nobel Prize in 1906 for his diplomatic efforts* shows that (E) is true. Only (A) is false, because *used his executive authority to break up the monopolies of large companies* shows that he did have an *interest in regulating businesses*.

9. **D** Eliminate wrong answers. (A) is incorrect because Theodore Roosevelt's accomplishments are not necessarily expected from other United States presidents. (B) is too narrow, because *foreign affairs* is only part of the passage (and *interest* is not really discussed). (C) can be eliminated because *prove* is too extreme. Listing many of Roosevelt's accomplishments does not necessarily mean that he is one of the greatest presidents in United States history. (E) is no good because there's no *character analysis*. (D) is the best answer.

10. **D** The narrator's *complex about music* involves *hopes* that *crashed too low* (lines 1–3), making her obsess negatively about the concert she performed in. Why is she so upset? The narrator relates that her poor performance at Town Hall made her doubt her ambition to be a singer, but she eventually resolved to do it anyway. This is best paraphrased in answer (D). The *complex* in this passage refers to an exaggerated concern or fear, and (A) is a trap answer that uses a different meaning of *complex*—complicated. In addition, the passage never mentions the narrator's musical tastes, so eliminate this answer choice. (B) is incorrect because the passage doesn't tell us if she changed careers, although it implies she did not. (C) may be true, but it does not explain the *complex*. (E) is incorrect because it contradicts the main idea.

11. **B** The author had wanted to be *one of the fortunate swimmers* in the *mainstream of American musical life*. She had wanted, in other words, to be famous. (B), *desire to be a popular singer*, is basically saying that she wanted to be famous.

12. **A** This sentence describes the narrator's memories of the performance at Town Hall: Some are vivid, while she pushes (thrusts) others aside. What emotions does this image reveal? She keeps *rehashing the concert in my mind*—not because she's thrilled (the performance *lost money* and *she might have done better*)—but because, we find, she's upset (*the fiasco had shaken me*) (lines 7–22). (A) most nearly means "upset."

13. **C** The question asks which two contradictory statements or facts constitute the *misrepresentation*. Reading the reference in context, we find that the narrator believes she might have performed better if she *had not been told the auditorium was full*, and that *a misrepresentation like that can throw you off balance*. Tying together these two statements, we can conclude that the misrepresentation refers to the number of people actually in attendance versus those the narrator expected to see. (C) best expresses this relationship. (A) is incorrect because the author's actual skill as a singer is not mentioned here. (B) is incorrect because the narrator states that she does not know how much money she was promised. (D) is incorrect because the reaction of the audience is never mentioned. (E) is incorrect because the narrator's desire to please everyone is not mentioned in this paragraph.

14. **E** The third paragraph says that, after the Town Hall performance, the author *stopped going regularly to Mr. Boghetti's studio*, because *the fiasco had shaken* her. So the paragraph is giving us some details about what happened to the author as a result of her Town Hall performance. (E), *the consequences of a performance*, matches this. (A), *the importance of rehearsals*, is not mentioned in the passage.

15.   **A**   According to the sentence, the author realizes that *the criticism was right* and that she had *given the critics the opportunity* to write negative reviews of her performance. This suggests that the author knows that she had a role in earning the unfavorable criticism. This is best paraphrased in (A). Answers (C) and (E) contradict the author's point in this sentence; she does not blame the critics, as far as we know, and she does take responsibility for her mediocre performance. (B) and (D) are incorrect because her career isn't mentioned at all in this reference.

16.   **A**   *The figure's face* is the only feature mentioned in both passages. Passage 1 mentions *that odd, skull-like face*, and Passage 2 mentions that *something in that face holds us rapt*.

17.   **C**   Monica Bohm-Duchen argues that *as the painting became more accessible, it became more admired*. The lines in Passage 1 refer to ways in which the painting was copied; Monica Bohm-Duchen believes it was those copies that helped to make *The Scream* well-known. So she would probably view the copying of the painting as (C) *events that may themselves have added to the renown of The Scream*. (E) is incorrect because we don't know that the copies have *hindered art critics ability to judge The Scream objectively*, the copies have simply made more people view *The Scream* favorably.

18.   **D**   Both authors believe that *The Scream* (D) *ought to be viewed and analyzed*. The author of Passage 1 spends most of the passage describing what it's like to view *The Scream*, and the author of Passage 2 states that *the reader* should *judge the painting itself*. (A) and (C) are not mentioned in either passage. (B) is referred to only in the second passage. (E) is contradicted by both passages: the main features of *The Scream* are actually immediately understandable.

19.   **B**   The quote from Edvard Munch serves to tell us a little about the scream that gave *The Scream* its name. In other words, it's trying to (B) *establish a context*.

20.   **C**   The passage states that Munch has captured a *raw, gut feeling*. So we want a word that means something along the lines of *gut feeling*, or "direct and obvious." Only (C), *stark* matches this.

21.   **A**   The quotation marks are there to hint that the *aimless "masterpieces" of a bored child* are not actually masterpieces at all, and that the critics did not think too much of *The Scream*. So they were (A) *skeptical of The Scream's aesthetic properties*. The passage does not indicate whether or not the author of Passage 2 thought they were (C) *incorrect*.

22.   **E**   Leonard Bartin points out that *The Scream* is *able to provoke a response, and therefore great*, and that *something in that face holds us rapt*. The author of Passage 1 seems to agree, because he says that *the eye invariably falls upon that odd, skull-like face*, and that *Munch has captured a raw, gut feeling*. So they both agree that people (E) *tends to elicit a strong involuntary response from viewers*. None of the other answers are mentioned by both the author of Passage 1 and Leonard Bartin.

23. **B** The author of Passage 2 mentions *Mozart's Requiem* to show that *Devoid of context, the central figure is no longer a piece functioning in a larger work of art*. So just taking one little part of a work of art isn't enough to really understand it; we need to look at the whole thing. Viewing just the main figure of *The Scream* isn't the same as viewing the full painting, because it's lacking all those other things that the author of Passage 1 mentioned: the sky, the river, the overall composition, et cetera. So the author is trying to (B) *illustrate that a simplified version* (like just seeing the main figure of *The Scream*) *can lack crucial elements* (the rest of the painting). (A) is wrong because the author isn't simply listing works of art that *are often best known in shorter forms*, he's mentioning another work of art that is missing something when shortened.

24. **B** Let's cross off some wrong answers. (A) is wrong because the second passage does not *argue for a purely intellectual interpretation*, it instead argues that the painting should be judged on its own merits. Similarly, (C) is wrong because the second passage does not *debate its artistic merits*. (D) is incorrect because the first passage does not *speculate about its intended meaning*. (E) is wrong because the first passage does not mention anything about *its unique place in art history*. (B) is the correct answer. The first passage *stresses its stylistic features*, because it talks for two paragraphs about what *The Scream* looks like. The second passage *emphasizes possible reasons for its cultural significance*, because it talks about why *The Scream* became so popular: it was copied a lot.

SECTION 3

1. **D** Begin by converting the 1 foot the snail traveled into 12 inches. Now set up a proportion: $\dfrac{12 \text{ inches}}{48 \text{ minutes}} = \dfrac{1 \text{ inch}}{x \text{ minutes}}$. Cross-multiply and solve for x: $12x = 48$, so $x = 4$.

2. **B** The question tells you that to get each term after the first, you multiply the previous by $\dfrac{1}{2}$ and add 1. For example, $\dfrac{1}{2} \times 66 + 1 = 33 + 1 = 34$, the second term. So $m = \dfrac{1}{2} \times 18 + 1 = 9 + 1 = 10$. You can double-check this by predicting that the next term will be $\dfrac{1}{2} \times 10 + 1 = 5 + 1 = 6$, which indeed it is.

3. **E** Translate the equation from English into math. It will read $3y + 4 = 11$. Although you can solve for y and then find $9y$, you can also solve for $3y$ and then triple the value to find $9y$. Because $3y = 7$, that means $9y = 21$. If you selected answer choice (A), you chose the value of y. If you selected answer choice (B), you chose the value of $3y$.

4. **B** Add the amounts given for 2001 and 2003: $12 + 15 = 27$. Subtract from that the amount given for 2002: $27 - 19 = 8$.

5. **D** A circle graph contains 360 degrees, so you need to determine the proportion of the circle that year 2005 will take up. So, add up all of the values from 2001 through 2006. The total is 90. The amount in 2005 (30) is one-third of the total, the central angle of the sector for 2005 must be one-third of the circle, or 120 degrees. If you selected (A), you chose the number from 2005, rather than its proportion of the whole. If you selected (C), you chose the total value of all years, rather than the proportion.

6. **A** A reflection means that the figure is simply flipped over the line of reflection, so a reflection about the x-axis means that the figure should end up like a mirror image below the x-axis. The figures in (C) and (E) are above the x-axis, so eliminate them. Of the three remaining, we need the flat edge of the figure facing the x-axis, so eliminate (C). Lastly, we need the figure that has the triangle on the right portion of the figure, as it is in the original graph. (A) is the only graph that has all the qualities of a figure flipped over the x-axis.

7. **A** Draw a line to divide the figure into two rectangles. Then identify the lengths of all the sides. If you drew a horizontal line, the upper rectangle will measure 3 by 3, and the lower rectangle will measure 9 by 2. Find the area of both rectangles (9 and 18), and add the areas. If you drew a vertical line, the left rectangle will measure 3 by 5, and the right rectangle will measure 6 by 2. Find the area of both rectangles (15 and 12), and add them. Either way, the area is 27 (A).

8. **E** We need a value for a that results in either 6 or -6 in the parentheses so that the squared value is 36. Only (E), -2, gives us -6 in the parentheses. All the other answers give a much greater value than 36 when replacing a in the equation above.

9. **D** The easiest way to solve this problem is to fill in the variable with a number that fits the requirement $p < 0$. If $p = -2$, the four numbers from left to right are: 10, 6, -2, -6. Thus (D) has the least value. If you selected answer choice (A), you selected a positive p or missed that the two negative signs cancel out.

10. **C** Plug In the day value of any point from the graph into the equations in the answers to see which equation yields the corresponding calls value. Whatever point you select, the answer will be (C). For example, if you select day 4 ($D = 4$), you need an equation that yields 6 calls ($C = 6$). The four wrong equations, however, will yield C values of 2 or 8.

11. **C** The easiest way to tackle this is to come up with your own numbers for the variables. Of the two equations, $b = c^2$ is easier to work with. If $c = 2$, then $b = 4$. Use this value for b in the equation above the question. $a = (4)^2 + (4)^3 = 16 + 64 = 80$. Now use $c = 2$ in the answer choices and see which gives 80: (A) equals 32 and (B) will definitely be larger than 80. (C) gives $16 + 64 = 80$, a match, but check the rest: (D) gives $8 + 16 = 24$; (E) gives $4 + 8 = 12$. Only (C) matches. You could also use exponent rules to solve this. Replace b in the equation $a = b^2 + b^3$ with c^2 to get $a = (c^2)^2 + (c^2)^3 = c^4 + c^6$, answer (C).

12. **D** Note that triangle *ABD* and *ECD* share angle *D*. Also, angle *C* and angle *B* both have the measure *m*. Because two sets of the three pairs of angles are the same, the third set of angles must also be the same, meaning the triangles are similar. In similar triangles, the ratio of the lengths of any two common sides is the same as the ratio of the lengths of any other two common sides. Because the ratio of *EC* to *AB* is 6 to 9, the ratio of *CD* to *BD* will also be 6 to 9. However, the question asks for the ratio of *BC* to *BD*, so that ratio would be 3 to 9, which reduces to 1 to 3. If you selected answer choice (B), you found the ratio of *CD* to *BD*.

13. **E** Because the median is the middle number, write the numbers in order: 8, 8, 8, 10, 10, 10, 10, 12. Then, try out the answer choices. Although each of the five answer choices will result in a median of 10, answer choice (E) will create a second mode. The mode is number that appears most. There are four 10s; if $x = 8$, there would also be four 8s.

14. **D** To find the total number of items in *A* and *C* we need to add up all six numbers that are in any of the regions within *A* or *C*. $3 + 4 + 4 + 6 + 5 + 5 = 27$, answer (D) is correct. (B) is the sum of the number of elements in *A* and *C* and the intersection of *A* and *C*. (C) is the total number of items in sets *A*, *B*, and *C*. (E) is the number of elements in the intersection of *A* and *C*.

15. **E** Plug In numbers for *x* and *y*. If *x* is directly proportional to $\sqrt{y}$, then it follows that $\dfrac{x_1}{\sqrt{y_1}} = \dfrac{x_2}{\sqrt{y_2}}$. Some good numbers to Plug In would be $\dfrac{10}{\sqrt{25}} = \dfrac{8}{\sqrt{16}}$. Using these numbers, check the answers to see which is inversely proportional to your value of *y*, which we found to be 25 when *x* is 10.

    The inverse proportion takes the form of $x_1 y_1 = x_2 y_2$. With answer choice (E), the inverse proportion would be $y_1 \times \dfrac{1}{x_1^2} = y_1 \times \dfrac{1}{x_2^2}$. If you Plug In your initial values for *x* and *y*, you get $25 \times \dfrac{1}{100} = 16 \times \dfrac{1}{64} = \dfrac{1}{4}$. Because sides of the equation are equal, (E) is the correct answer. If you chose (A), you used direct instead of inverse variation.

16. **E** Because function *g* is the absolute value of function *f*, no negative points can appear on the graph of function *g*. Eliminate (A), (B), and (C). Nothing else changed between *f*(*x*) and *g*(*x*), so the graph of *g* should be the same as in *f* except any negative points will appear as a mirror image reflected about the *x* axis, as in (E).

17. **A** Check each statement one at a time and eliminate answer choices. Because $f(x) = f(2y)$, you know $f(x) + f(x)$ is the same as $f(2y) + f(2y)$, which can be simplified as $2f(2y)$. Thus, statement I must be true—eliminate answer choices (B) and (D). Is $2f(2y)$ the same thing as $f(4y)$? Not necessarily—consider the function $f(x) = x^2$. In that case $2f(2y) = 2 \times 4y^2 = 8y^2$ while $f(4y) = 16y^2$. Thus, statement II is incorrect—eliminate (E). Now check statement III to see if $2f(2y)$ is the same thing as $2[f(y) + f(y)]$. The 2 in statement III must be distributed to both functions within the brackets, resulting in $2f(y) + 2f(y)$ is not equivalent to $2f(2y)$ if again, the function happens to be $f(x) = x^2$: $2y^2 + 2y^2 = 4y^2$ whereas previously we found $2f(2y) = 8y^2$. Only statement I is true, so (A) is correct.

18. **B** The formula for the volume of a cylinder is at the beginning of every SAT math section. $V = \pi r^2 h$. We need to know the increase in volume when the smaller cylinder is added to the water in the vase. One way to so this is to find the volume of the water without the smaller cylinder and the volume with the cylinder added and subtract to find the difference. A more straightforward way, since we know that the height of the water in the larger cylinder rises by 4 inches, is to use that height and the base measurement of the vase in the volume formula to find that $\pi 6^2 \times 4 = 36\pi \times 4 = 144\pi$ —which equals the volume of the cylinder that was dropped into the larger cylinder. The question asks for the height of the smaller cylinder, which we can find since we know the base radius of the smaller cylinder and the volume: $144\pi = \pi 4^2 \times h = 16\pi h$. Divide both sides by 16π to get h alone and find that $\dfrac{144\pi}{16\pi} = h$, s = 9, choice (B).

19. **A** Let's figure out the coordinates of point C. Parabolas are symmetrical, so the left side looks like the right side. Since the point at (2, 8) is 2 to the left of the middle point of the parabola, the point $(a, 8)$ will be 2 to the right of the middle point, so it's at (6, 8). Now use the slope formula to find the slope of $\overline{BC}$, which is $\dfrac{2-8}{3-6} = \dfrac{-6}{-3} = 2$.

20. **D** Try each number for x. There is no mode, which means that no numbers can repeat themselves. Eliminate (B) and (E). Now try each number left. If $x = 2$, then $x^3 = 8$, which is not the median of $\dfrac{1}{4}, \dfrac{1}{2}, 2, 4$, and 8, respectively. Eliminate (A). If $x = \dfrac{1}{2}$, then $x^3 = \dfrac{1}{8}$, which is not the median of 4, 2, $\dfrac{1}{2}, \dfrac{1}{4}$, and $\dfrac{1}{8}$. Eliminate (C). (D) is the only answer left. If $x = -\dfrac{1}{2}$, then $x^3 = -\dfrac{1}{8}$, which is the median of 4, –2, $-\dfrac{1}{2}, \dfrac{1}{4}$, and $-\dfrac{1}{8}$.

SECTION 5

1. **A** The clue for the blank is *randomly occurring*. Since these reactions are *proof*, the blank should mean close to the clue. *Spontaneous* means *randomly occurring*, so (A) is the best choice.

2. **B** We don't know what is going on with the *patient* until the end of the sentence when we find out that the patient was able to go home, even sooner *than anticipated*. So originally the doctor must have been worried, *but after the surgery the patient* must have been better. The first blank must mean "worry," so eliminate (A), (C), and (D). The second blank should mean "got better," so eliminate (E), leaving (B) as the only answer that fits.

3. **E** The clue for the second blank is that *none of the petitioners were able to gather signatures*. The blank must mean something close to "not supporting." This eliminates choices (A), (C), and (D). The word that precedes the first blank, *obvious*, with the clue for the second blank tells us that the first blank must mean something close to "a showing." Between (B) and (E), choice (E) is closest.

4. **B** The clue *code of conduct* tells us that the meaning of the first blank should be something related to the kind of conduct *school administrators* would approve of. (A), and (E) are completely unrelated to the clue and can be eliminated. The use of *in order to* tells us that the second blank should also be similar to the first blank. *Obedient* and *tractable* are close in meaning while the pairs of words in (C) and (D) are not synonymous. Thus (B) is the best answer.

5. **D** The second half of the sentence serves as a clue that parallels the first half of the sentence. *Ridiculing* is the clue for the first blank. This alone points us to *lampoons*, which means "to mock" or "satirize." The word *procedures* is the clue for the second blank. The word *methodology* fits this clue best. All of the remaining answer choices "sound good." The words could all make sense in reference to an article and a piece of legislation, respectively. Remember not to go by how things "sound." Only one answer will agree with the clue.

6. **D** The words *even though* tell us that the blank should mean something opposite of the clue *increase risk of heart disease*. A good word to use would be "beneficial." (A) is opposite of what we are looking for and (B), (C), and (E) do not mean "beneficial." *Salutary* in (D) means "beneficial to health" and is the best answer.

7. **C** The use of the colon tells us that the meaning of the first half of the sentence must mean something similar to the second half. The clue here is *clarify difficult topics*. Since the word before the blank is *avoid*, we need a word in combination with this one to produce the same thing as the clue. The word for the blank should mean something close to "making difficult." The closest in meaning is *obfuscating* in (C).

8. **B** The clue for the blank is *never chose one side* and *intentionally misled*. The blank must mean something similar because of the colon, which tells us that the first and second part of the sentence must have similar meanings. The best choice is *equivocated* which means "to use deliberately unclear language."

9.   A   Passage 2 says that Austen's work *is caustic and subversive, and seeks to undermine the assumptions of the society she lived in.* Passage 1, however, tells us that fans view Austen's works as *affectionate and witty portraits of the English gentry.* Therefore, the view offered in Passage 2 doesn't represent the view of most fans. (A) paraphrases this nicely. None of the other answers are supported by the passages.

10. B   Passage 1 says that for the *readers, Austen's novels evoke an idyllic past…refreshingly free of weighty political or philosophical concerns.* However, the author of Passage 2 states that Austen's works are *profoundly political.* (B) clearly expresses this difference between the 2 passages. The other answers are not supported by the passages.

11. B   The reference to Passage 2 in this question is mostly a distraction. We want to know what Passage 1 says about *Austen's depiction of the British upper class.* Passage 1 states that for fans, Austen's works are *affectionate and witty portraits of the English gentry.* Thus, they are *largely sympathetic* (B).

12. D   Passage 1 states that for the *adoring fans,* Austen's works are *affectionate and witty portraits of the English gentry.* Passage 2 states that Austen *frequently subjected* (the British upper class) *to withering criticism.* Therefore, the 2 passages disagree about *the extent to which her work is critical…of society* (D). We can also use process of elimination: Both passages suggest her family was important, so eliminate (A). Neither passage mentions the *accuracy* of her depictions, so eliminate (B). Both passages suggest that *English society was a central topic,* so eliminate (C). Both passages indicate Austen is an important author, so eliminate (E).

13. D   Come up with your own word to replace *image.* An important clue is the word *idea* right after the colon. So, something like "idea" or "belief" would work well. Only (D), *perception,* is a match.

14. C   In the second paragraph, the author uses words such as *enemy, arsenal, chemical weapons, bombard,* and *attack* to suggest that the gardener wages war on slugs. Thus (C), a *military strategy,* fits best. The other answers are not supported by the passage.

15. D   The author describes the *important consequences* as a vicious circle: *contamination, followed by…a slow depletion…, followed by more contamination.* (D), an unintended reaction, is a good match. The other answers are not supported by the passage.

16. E   Pursuing the *cherished ideal* leads to the vicious circle discussed in the explanation to question 15. Therefore, the author sees it as *misguided* (E).

17. B   In the previous paragraph, the author shows how trying to wipe out slugs doesn't work. In this paragraph, the author *proposes an alternative course of action:* learning to live with the slugs. Thus, the correct answer is (B). The author doesn't *explain people's responses* (A) or *offer evidence of destruction* (C); he doesn't *praise* anything (D), and there is no position that we know is *unpopular* (E).

18. A   The lines provide evidence that the slug's *nefarious reputation is at least partially unwarranted.* (A), a *defense,* is the best answer. The other answer choices are not supported by the passage.

19.   **E**   The slug is like a recycling center in that it can take discarded products, transform them into the nutrients that plants need to thrive, and release these nutrients into the soil. (E) paraphrases this sentence. (A) and (B) are not supported at all. (C) looks good except for the part about harmful chemicals, which are not mentioned in this paragraph. (D) is extreme, and there's no direct discussion of artificial fertilizers in this paragraph.

20.   **C**   The author's attitude is positive because the *viscous, slime-like excretions* are beneficial; they provide the *nutrients that plants need to thrive.* (C) is the only answer choice that expresses a positive sentiment.

21.   **D**   Come up with your own word to replace *welcome.* Something like "bring" would work, because the author states that *providing a habitat for these creatures* would help to hold down the slug population. (D), *introduce,* is the best match. (C), return, is close, but we don't know that the natural predators had been in the garden before now, so there's no way of knowing if they are returning to the garden.

22.   **B**   The author tells us not only that slugs like certain plants (*Lettuce, Zinnias, and Marigolds are all considered delicacies*), but also that gardeners don't view these plants as terribly valuable (*the loss of a few of these plants will not distress the typical gardener*). Answer choice (B) paraphrases this nicely. (A) and (C) are too extreme, while (D) and (E) are not mentioned.

23.   **A**   The phrase *it is true* applies to the statement that *these measures may seem cumbersome* (if you don't know what cumbersome means, the word *inconvenience* can help you out). Thus, the author *recognizes that his suggestions may be viewed as burdensome* (A). (B) is the opposite of what the author believes, while (C), (D), and (E) are not mentioned in the passage.

24.   **E**   The purpose of the last paragraph is to reiterate the author's main point, as stated in the first and fourth paragraphs. (E) is a good match. The last paragraph doesn't have *evidence* (A); it doesn't refer to *further study* (B); it doesn't *intensify* (C), and it doesn't *downplay the impact of an approach* (D).

SECTION 6

1.   **A**   The sentence is correct as written. (B) lacks a necessary helping verb to use with *involved.* (C) and (E) both use -ing forms, which are usually wrong, as they are here. (D) changes the direction and meaning of the sentence.

2.   **C**   The original sentence contains a misplaced modifier error and is passive. According to the original construction *a sense of homesickness* is *like many freshmen.* It should be *my roommates* who are *like many freshmen.* This eliminates (A) and (B). (D) is not a complete sentence, so we can eliminate it. (E) is redundant and passive and, therefore, not as good an answer as (C).

3. **B** The phrase *is the reason why* in the original sentence is redundant and therefore incorrect. (B) eliminates this construction and simplifies the sentence. (C) and (E) repeat the error found in (A). (D) awkwardly uses *resulting from*, which creates a modifying error.

4. **D** The correct idiom is *not only...but also*. (A), (B), (C), and (E) lack the correct idiom. (D) uses the idiom correctly and keeps *convey* and *instill* parallel.

5. **B** The easiest way to find the right answer in this one is to compare the verbs. You want the past tense *let*, so eliminate (C), (D), and (E). Answer (A) contains a comma splice which makes the sentence a run-on. You're then left with (B).

6. **A** The sentence is correct as written: it keeps the list parallel and has the proper idiom *both...and*. The first thing *success* depends on is *regulation of taxes for small businesses*, a noun followed by prepositional phrases. (C) and (E) don't fit the pattern. (D) doesn't join the parts of the list correctly; it sounds as if *education of the public* must be regulated. (B) is missing an "and" needed to join the parts of the list. (A) joins the parts correctly and has the same structure as the first part of the list.

7. **E** Watch out for subject-verb agreement errors when a lot of words separate the subject and the verb. In this case the phrase enclosed by the commas *though many causes...centuries* separate the singular subject *one reason* from the plural verb *are*. (A), (B), and (C) contain verb agreement errors. (D) creates an incomplete sentence. (E) correctly matches a singular verb to the singular noun *reason*.

8. **C** In the underlined portion of the sentence, it's unclear what *many* refers to, so you can eliminate (A), (B), and (E) because they don't include *people*. Between the two answers left, (C) is preferable because it's a clearer construction. The extra *they* and the *-ing* ending in answer (D) make the sentence awkward and confusing.

9. **D** Watch out for subject-verb agreement errors. (A) can't be right because the subject *program* doesn't agree with the verb *were met*. (E) is wrong because the singular subject can't be paired with a plural pronoun. (B) uses the wrong verb tense, and you don't need the pronoun *it* in (C). The lone remaining answer choice is (D), which is grammatically correct because the singular verb *was* agrees with the subject *program*. Thus, (D) is correct.

10. **E** Eliminate (A), (B), and (C) because they're redundant. *Imminent* means something is about to happen, so you don't need to say it twice. (E) is a better choice than (D) because it's a clearer construction; there's no need for the word *thing* in (D).

11. **A** This sentence is correct as written. All the others use incorrect conjunctions.

12. **B** The sentence as written is a sentence fragment. The error is in (B) because it is missing a verb. You'd need to say it *was* translated in order for this to be a complete sentence.

13. **C** The wrong verb form is in (C). This sentence should use the infinitive form of "fund" in order to read *Steven has fought to fund*.

14. **B** Each verb should be in the same tense, so if aspirin *causes thinning* then it also "delays," instead of *delay*, as in (B).

15. **C** The underlined portion (C) is incorrect: *revealing* should be the infinitive form of "reveal" rather than the gerund. This sentence should read *magicians' unwillingness to reveal secrets of the trade*.

16. **D** *Incredible* modifies *strong*, so *incredible* needs to be in its adverb form: "incredibly" in (D).

17. **E** There are no errors in the sentence as it is written.

18. **C** *Had been* would mean that she had been the first to eat a slice, but now something changed, and she wasn't the first person any longer. Had been is called the "past perfect tense," and is used when something had gone on for a while, but then changed. Gordon ate a slice at one point in time, however, so we want "was" instead.

19. **B** Always check that verbs are in the correct tense. The verb *is* is in the simple present tense, yet the context tells us that Bretney was promoted *last year* and has been a hard worker *ever since*. To indicate that an action began in the past and continues to the present, use the present perfect tense, "has been."

20. **E** There are no errors in the sentence as it is written.

21. **A** The verb after *plants* refers to *the salve an*d, therefore, *are* must be singular *is* to read *The salve made from the leaves of cactus plants is highly efficient*.

22. **E** There are no errors in the sentence as it is written.

23. **E** There are no errors in the sentence as it is written.

24. **C** This sentence has a noun-pronoun agreement error. *The class* is a singular noun, but (C) contains the pronoun *they*. A collective noun like *group* agrees with the singular pronoun "it."

25. **D** This sentence has an idiom error in (D): the wrong preposition follows *hope*. The idiomatically correct phrase is *in the hope of receiving permission*.

26. **D** The correct idiom is phrased *overflowing with* rather than *overflowing from*.

27. **D** The words *more…than* tell us that the sentence compares two things, and the parts of the comparison need to be parallel. (D) is incorrect because it compares Noah's *music* to *other bands*, not to the music of other bands.

28. **C** This sentence has noun-pronoun agreement problem: Because the noun *fines* is plural, the singular pronoun *it* cannot be used to replace *fines*.

29. **B** The plural pronoun *they* refers to the singular noun person and is therefore incorrect. It should be replaced with "he or she."

30.   A   (B) would least help the paragraph. (D) and (E) might be interesting footnotes, but they would not add as much to the paragraph as (C) or (A). (C) would add another dimension to the passage but (B) is the most straightforward way to enhance the essay.

31.   B   (A) has the wrong verb tense compared to the past tense of the rest of the passage and has misplaced commas. (C) has redundant use of *production*. (D) changing the verb from something that means "were influenced by" for the more direct and active *imitated* changes the meaning of the sentence and the verb *uses* is in the wrong tense. (E) is wordy and uses the incorrect verb tense.

32.   A   (B) is tempting because it there is more than one artist mentioned in the passage, but this asks about a single paragraph. (C) is mentioned only in the third paragraph. (D) is the least supported answer. (E) is tempting, until one looks at the subject of the sentence—the essay's writer is not updating the opera; he's writing about Baz Lurhmann's updated version.

33.   E   The original sentence presented is actually a comma splice: It contains two complete ideas without any punctuation. (B) has an independent descriptive phrase between the commas, but the rest of the sentence cannot stand alone. The other problem with the original sentence is that it uses the phrase *much of* to refer to both something uncountable (the *storyline*) and something countable (the *characters*); *much of* can refer only to uncountable things. (C) and (D) don't fix this problem. (E) does without introducing any new problems that would disqualify it from being the credited response.

34.   C   (A) and (E) are not supported by the text. (D) is the opposite of the sentence. (B) looks appealing; however, the passage never discusses the actual tribulations of artists. (C) is the best answer in terms of finding the sentence's function.

35.   D   In deciding on what sentence fits best at the end of the passage we need to focus on flow. Sentence 15 introduces the idea that artists felt the need to change *La Bohème*. (D) correctly references this idea, while the rest of the answers do not. (E) starts well for the last sentence of a passage, but the content of the rest of the sentence do not fit with the paragraph.

SECTION 7

1.   E   Because 1 raised to the third power is still 1, we know that x is 1 (with x^2 we wouldn't be sure if 1 were negative or positive). Knowing this, we can replace x in the fraction in the question with 1:

$$\frac{1^2 + 3}{1} = \frac{4}{1} = 4, \text{ answer (E).}$$

2. **B** Indicate on the figure that $\angle DEF$ is a right angle. You will see that there are two right triangles contained in the figure—$\triangle CEF$ and $\triangle DEF$. The hypotenuse of a right triangle is the largest side of that triangle, meaning that CF is the largest side of $\triangle CEF$ and DF is the largest side of $\triangle DEF$. Note that the two triangles share side EF in common and that side DE is contained within side CE. Because $\triangle CEF$ has the larger second side, it will also have a larger hypotenuse.

3. **B** A good way to approach this problem is to make up simple numbers with an average of 8 for set A, such as 6, 8, and 10. When you cut these in half for set B, you have 3, 4, and 5. The average of those numbers is 4. If you picked (E), you doubled the numbers in set A.

4. **B** Because a negative exponent can be rewritten as a fraction with a positive exponent in the denominator, 10^{-3} is equivalent to $\dfrac{1}{10^3}$ or $\dfrac{1}{1,000}$. Thus, JKLM must be divided by 1,000. This requires moving the decimal point back three spaces, resulting in J.KLM. If you picked (E), you multiplied JKLM by 10^3.

5. **B** Because $\overline{EH}$ is a diameter, the measures of the three angles in the top half of the circle must add to 180°. The measure of $\angle EOG$ is $180 - 70 = 110°$. $\overline{FO}$ bisects it into two angles of 55° each. Now we can find the measure of $\angle FOH$: $70 + 55 = 125°$, answer (B).

6. **A** The wall and ground are at right angles, much like a coordinate plane. The slope formula can be simplified as "rise over run," or, in this case, the height where the ladder hits the wall over the length of ground between the ladder and the wall. A slope of $\dfrac{5}{3}$ indicates that for every 5 feet of height, there is a corresponding 3 feet distance from the wall. Because $p = 9$, or three times the of 3 units indicated by the slope, q must equal three times the 5 units indicated by the slope, so the correct answer is (A), 15.

7. **C** It is useful to know the transformative properties of parabolas, including that an increased coefficient a narrows the parabola. You can also pick an a and x value for each formula and compare the resulting y values. Using $a = 2$ and $x = 3$, the original graph would have a y value of 15. Using the same a and x values in the new formula yields a y value of 33. If you roughly plot these points on the graph, you will see that the higher y value in the new formula generates a narrower parabola.

8. **C** Take each photograph type one at a time in any order. For her landscape photograph, Serena has three choices—one each from Brazil, Kenya and Istanbul. For her street scene, however, she has only two choices, because one of the three countries is already represented by the landscape photograph. Thus, so far, there are six possible arrangements, because any of three landscape photographs could be paired with either of the two museum photographs. For the portrait, Serena has only one option, whichever country is not yet represented. Thus, the total number of possible arrangements is $3 \times 2 \times 1 = 6$, (C). If you picked (E), you did not account for the fact that each country (as well as each photograph type) limits what can be included for each spot.

9. **30** Translate the word problem into the equation $\frac{1}{2}x - 7 = 8$. Solve this equation to get $x = 30$.

10. **45** Divide 5, the height of the container, by $\frac{1}{3}$, the height of a coaster, to get 15. Since there are 3 containers, multiply by three to find the total number of coasters that can fit into the containers.

11. **144** When 2 parallel lines are intersected by a third line, 2 kinds of angles are created: Big angles and small angles. All the big angles are equal, all the small angles are equal, and any big angle plus any small angle equals 180. Therefore, $a + b = 180$. Substituting $4b$ for a yields the equation $b + 4b = 180$. $5b = 180$ so $b = 36$ and from the equation in the question, $a = 4b = 144$.

12. **$1 < x < 3$**

    The easiest way to solve this problem is just to try small values for x. Substituting 2 for x yields $|2(2) - 3| < 2$, which is true. Another way to solve the problem is to write an equation: $|2x - 3| < x$. Remove the absolute value bars by turning this into two separate equations: $2x - 3 < x$, and $-(2x - 3) < x$. Solving both of these equations gives two solutions: $x > 1$, and $x < 3$.

13. **710** The increase in Town A is 360 (2,360 – 2,000); the increase in Town B is 1,120 (6,120 – 5,000); and the increase in Town C is 650 (9,650 – 9,000). The total population increase is 2,130. To get the average, divide the total by 3 to get 710.

14. **4** If 17 blue marbles are removed, there are 13 blue marbles left. Twice 13 is 26, so at most 4 green marbles can be removed to ensure that there are at least 26 green marbles, which is twice the number of blue marbles.

15. **12** One way to solve this problem is to Plug In values for b. If we say $b = 2$, then $\frac{4a+6}{4} = \frac{5}{3}$. Cross multiply to get $12a + 18 = 20$. Now solve to get $a = \frac{1}{6}$. Thus, $\frac{a}{b} = \frac{2}{\frac{1}{6}} = 12$. Alternatively, you could cross-multiply to get $12a + 9b = 10b$. Now combine like terms to get $12a = b$. Dividing by a yields $12 = \frac{b}{a}$.

16. **20** You can use some simple algebra to represent the information. If w represents the weight of the package, then the cost of using Company 1 is $\$10 + \$0.60(w - 10)$. The cost of using Company 2 is $\$0.80w$. You can set the two expressions equal to each other and solve for w. Initially, $10 + 0.60(w - 10) = 0.80w$. Distribute on the left side and combine like terms to get $4 = 0.20w$. Solve for w and you get 20.

17. **10** The smallest *odd-mult* is 3 (1 × 3). You can continue to generate *odd-mults* by multiplying consecutive odd numbers: 15 (3 × 5), 35 (5 × 7), 63 (7 × 9), 99 (9 × 11), 143 (11 × 13), 195 (13 × 15), 255 (15 × 17), 323 (17 × 19), and 399 (19 × 21). There are a total of 10 less than 400: 21 × 23 is too big at 483.

18. $\dfrac{20}{9}$ or 2.22

The perimeter of the figure equals 20s, which you know because there are 20 sides of length s. Since there are 9 squares and the area of each square is s^2 (just s times s) the total area is $9s^2$. Set the perimeter equal to the area to get the following equation: $20s = 9s^2$. Divide both sides by s to get $20 = 9s$. Divide both sides by 9 to get $s = \dfrac{20}{9}$.

SECTION 8

1. **C**   After 12 minutes, the fraction of the ride completed is $\dfrac{12}{72}$. This fraction reduces down to $\dfrac{1}{6}$, answer (C).

2. **A**   In a linear function, the $f(x)$—or y-value—changes by the same amount for each unit change in x. Here, the $f(x)$ value increases by 7 each time the x value increases by 1. Because $f(x)$ is 16 when x is 2, $f(x)$ is $16 + 7$ when x is 3, and $t = 23$. (A) is correct.

3. **C**   The basketball has 4 times the diameter of the racquetball. Make up diameters to work with: Let's start with the smaller ball: if the racquetball has a diameter of 2, the larger ball, the basketball, will have a diameter 4 times larger, $2 \times 2 = 8$. The diameters of the basketball and the racquetball have a ratio of 8 : 2. The radius is half the diameter, so the radii have a ratio of 4 : 1, answer (C). The actual diameter of a basketball is 9 inches, while a racquetball's is 2.25 inches, but when you come up with your own numbers on the SAT, always pick numbers that are easy to work with.

4. **A**   The first step is to find the number of students who turned in Detective stories for this assignment. 20% of 60 students is $\dfrac{20}{100} \times 60 = 12$ students. There are 6 assignments during the semester: $12 \times 6 = 72$.

5. **E**   First translate the words into math: if Sam produced p paintings, then Janet produced $3p + 4$ paintings. This matches (E). You could also make up a number for p. If Sam produced 2 paintings ($p = 2$), then Janet produced 10 paintings, which is 4 more than three times the number Sam produced. Plugging $p = 2$ into all five answer choices shows that only (E) gives an answer of 10.

6. **D**   Assign numbers to c and d that will satisfy the inequality. If $c = 5$, then d must be a negative number, such as -2, in order for $c - d$ to be greater than 5. This pair of numbers allows you to eliminate (A), (C) and (E). To choose between (B) and (D), try picking a negative number for c, such as -5. Now, d must be a negative number less than -5, such as -7, in order for $c - d$ to be greater than -5. So, eliminate (B).

7. **C** Rotate your test booklet clockwise 270 degrees (or counterclockwise 90 degrees) and take note of how the figure in the question looks. The L-shaped figure is at the bottom left corner, in the proper direction as a capital L would face. Only (C) has the L shape in that spot. If you selected (D), you rotated the original figure in the wrong direction.

8. **B** Test out some of your own numbers for a and b, and eliminate answer choices that are not always true. Try different sets of numbers until only one answer remains. If you try $a = 2$ and $b = -2$, you will be able to eliminate (C), (D), and (E). If you try $a = 3$ and $b = -4$, you will be able to eliminate (A). Basically the information given tells you that a is positive and b is negative. (B) is correct because dividing a positive number by a negative number always gives you a negative number.

9. **A** Line f has a negative slope, so eliminate (C), (D), and (E). Because the slope is steeper than a slope of -1, eliminate (B). You may also solve the slopes. Because the two lines are perpendicular, the slope of line f will be the negative reciprocal of the slope of line g. To find the slope of line g, identify the two points that are easily discernable—those at the intercepts. The x-intercept is $(-4, 0)$ and the y-intercept is $(0, 2)$. Thus, the slope of line g is $\dfrac{2-0}{0-(-4)}$, which reduces to $\dfrac{1}{2}$. The negative reciprocal is -2.

10. **D** There is a lot of information in the question. We know there are two flavors of heart-shaped candy and gumballs, and the ratio of hearts to gumballs is 5:1. We then learn that there are 4 times more vanilla hearts than chocolate hearts. Finally we are given the actual number of vanilla hearts: 16. Since there are 4 times more vanilla hearts than chocolate hearts, there must be 4 chocolate hearts. Now we know the total number of heart candies is $16 + 4 = 20$. To find out the total number of pieces of candy we need to know the number of gumballs. There are 5 times more heart candies than gumballs: $20 \div 5 = 4$. So there are 16 vanilla hearts, 4 chocolate hearts, and 4 gumballs, for a total of 24 pieces of candy.

11. **C** Try to come up with numbers that fit all three equations. If $a = 2$, $b = 4$, and $c = 1$, all three equations work. Now all you have to do is multiply. Another way to solve the problem is to multiply the three equations together to see what happens. On the left, you will have ($a^2\ b^2\ c^2$), and on the right you will have 64. Take the square root of each side, which gives you $abc = 8$, answer (C). If you picked answer choice (E), you left out the final step of taking the square root of each side.

12. **E** Translate this into a math sentence: $4n - 6 \geq -2$. Solve for n to see that $n \geq 1$. Eliminate answers (A), (B), and (C) because they include numbers less than 1. Between (D) and (E), (E) is correct because a solid indicates that the number is included in the set of values (*greater than or equal to*), while a hollow dot shows that the number is not included in the set (*greater than*).

13. **B** Start drawing figures, and look for a pattern. If you draw a four-sided figure with equal sides and angles (a square), you can draw only one diagonal from any vertex. For the equivalent five-sided figure, you can draw two; for the six-sided figure, three. By now, you can see the pattern: from any given point in a equilateral polygon, it has three fewer diagonals than it has sides. Thus, if the polygon has four diagonals from a single vertex, it must have seven sides.

14. **D** An easy way to start this problem is to make up a number for n. Let's say $n = 2$. Then $m = 9 + 3^4 = 90$. $3^2 = 9$. So when we Plug In $m = 90$, we should get 9. (D) is the only answer that works.

15. **B** The first thing to do is draw this triangle. If $AC = 5$, and the perimeter is 13, then AB and BC add up to 8. Since the problem says that AB and BC are equal, then $AB = BC = 4$. We have a triangle with sides 4, 4, and 5. If it were an equilateral triangle, and $AC = 4$, then x would equal 60. But $AC > 4$, and as a side on a triangle gets larger, the opposite angle gets larger. So $x > 60$. Cross off (A). Now if this were a triangle with sides 3, 4, and 5, then x would equal 90. But since $AC \neq 3$, then $x \neq 90$. Cross off (C). So we've got a triangle that's somewhere between an equilateral triangle and a right triangle. Which means that x is larger than 60, but smaller than 90, answer (B).

16. **C** Plug In numbers for a and b. Since we know ab must equal 20, since that's the area, $a = 5$ and $b = 4$ would work well. The length of fencing used is therefore $4 + 4 + 4 + 5 + 5 = 22$. Plug In 4 for b in the answer choices, and only (C) works out to be the target answer of 22. To solve the problem algebraically, first find a in terms of b. Because $ab = 20$, you know that $a = \dfrac{20}{b}$. The overall length of fence used on the window is $2a + 3b$. If you replace a with $\dfrac{20}{b}$, you get answer choice (C). If you chose answer choice (A), you found $a + b$. If you chose answer choice (B), you found $2a + b$.

SECTION 9

1. **C** Since we have a colon in the sentence, the first part of the sentence should have the same meaning as the second part. In the second part of the of the sentence, the clues *no idea* and *did not actually exist* indicate that the blank must contain a word along the lines of "false plot" or "false scheme". Therefore, answer choice (C) is correct.

2. **A** Because *Donald* is *involved in the affairs of others*, his *reputation* should describe "someone who would become *involved*." For the first blank, only (A) and (B) have words close to this meaning. We also have the word *and*, which tells us that the second blank should mean something similar to the first blank. (A) has a closer meaning to the blank than (B).

3. **A** The clue for the blank is that Devon was *viewed as undependable and easily swayed*. The words

despite the fact tell us that the blank should mean something opposite the clue. In addition, right before the blank we see another clue: *reliable.* The following word *and* tells us the blank should follow this is meaning. So, a good word to put into the blank would be something that means "reliable." The closest meaning is (A).

4. **B** The clue for the first blank, *superior protective structures,* must mean that the *helmet designs* were well-received. This allows only (B) and (C) to be possible answer choices. For the second blank, the words *even though,* tell us that the meaning will be opposite of the first blank. Since the clue for the second blank is *unreliable materials,* we can assume that the meaning of that blank should be close to "unreliable." Between *precarious and advantageous,* (B) is the better answer.

5. **E** The clue *lack of evidence or testimony to support* tells us that the blank must mean something close to "supporting evidence." None of the answer choices mean close to this except (E). (B) may be appealing because it is a word used in courtroom settings, but has no relationship to the sentence.

6. **E** The words *in spite of* tell us that blank will be opposite the clue *unhappy and detached.* The blank should then mean something like happy and social. None of the choices are close except for (E).

7. **E** Use Process of Elimination. William and Mr. Hunsden are not *enemies* as far as we know, so eliminate (A). They're not *coworkers,* so eliminate (B). They don't seem to be *friends,* so eliminate (C). They're not *brothers,* so eliminate (D). The correct answer is (E).

8. **C** The passage states that *any human being, worthy of the name, will row long against wind and tide before he allows himself to cry out, "I am baffled!"* In other words, he will keep going before admitting a mistake. (C) is a good paraphrase of this point. The other answers are not supported by the passage.

9. **B** The *primary objection* William has is *the antipathy which had sprung up between myself and Mr. Crimsworth* (his brother). Answer choice (B) refers to this fact. (D) is true, but doesn't answer the question, because it's not his *primary* objection (he specifically states that the work *was a dry and tedious task enough, but had that been all, I should long have borne with the nuisance*). The other answers are not supported by the passage.

10. **C** We know that William is characterized by his *punctuality and industry* (he's on time and works hard), and that he has a *degree of education* (he's educated). Furthermore, Edward finds this cause for *envy* (he's jealous). Answer choice (C) expresses this situation accurately. (A) is too strong, and while William might be condescending and scornful, we don't really know. (B) is false according to the passage. (D) and (E) are not indicated inn the passage.

11. **D** Always read a few lines above and below the line reference. After William says *I am no fossil,* Mr. Hunsden supports his argument by noting how William does the same thing, day after day, never doing anything new or interesting. Thus, he's *desensitized by his unvarying routine.* None of the other answers are supported by the passage.

12. **A** Mr. Hunsden responds by stating that *your case and mine are diametrically different, and it is non-*

sense attempting to draw a parallel. (A) summarizes this statement nicely. The other answers are not supported by the passage.

13.   **A**   Mr. Hunsden is unsure about *the conclusion to be drawn* (about William's character) because it *depends upon the nature of the motives that guide your conduct.* Therefore, he's *uncertain about the reasons underlying William's actions* (A). The other answers are not supported by the passage.

14.   **D**   Mr. Hunsden tells William he'll never make any money, and his only chance is to marry someone wealthy. But a few lines later, he notes that *even that is hopeless.* Thus, he's offering a *prediction of a bleak future* (D).

15.   **E**   William's response is that he'll leave such plans to those who come up with them, meaning he won't seriously consider such a plan. (E) paraphrases this nicely. He doesn't say anything about *a goal* (A); he's not *uncertain* as far as we know (B); there's no indication that he views Mr. Hunsden's idea as *promising* (C); he offers no opinion about whether the idea is *unlikely to succeed* (D).

16.   **C**   *Shifts* refers to Mr. Hunsden's idea of *marrying a rich widow, or...an heiress.* William regards this as a devious plan, or *scheme* (C). The other answers are not supported by the context of the passage.

17.   **C**   Mr. Hunsden states that William is *not bold and venturesome...nor handsome and fascinating.* In (C), *timid* is a good antonym for *bold*, and *bland* is a good antonym for *fascinating*.

18.   **B**   In context, *Fortune has cheated Nature* is used to suggest that William *should have been a nobleman*, because he's no good as a tradesmen. (B) paraphrases this point nicely. The other answers are not supported by the passage.

19.   **D**   At the beginning of the passage, William states that his brother is a hard and grinding master...an inexorable tyrant. Mr. Hunsden also notes that William's boss has treated (him) like a dog. Thus, they both agree that *William is treated poorly by his employer* (D). Choice (B) is tempting, but extreme, and we don't know if William thinks he'll never succeed as a tradesman; we just know he made a bad choice and hates his particular job (and employer).

SECTION 10

1.   **C**   This question is testing conjunctions; you need to choose the answer that most clearly connects the two parts of the sentence. (A) and (B) don't show a relationship between the two parts, (E) doesn't make sense, and (C) is better than (D) because the word *therefore* implies a stronger cause-effect relationship than the sentence gives us.

2.   **C**   The sentence as written is a fragment, so eliminate (A). (D) and (E) are passive constructions, so get rid of those. (B) uses the wrong form of the verb and also uses *being*, which is almost always wrong. You're left with (C).

3. **D**   The sentence as written contains a comma splice—two clauses that stand on their own as complete sentences must be joined by a semicolon or other conjunction. (B) has a semicolon, but *it consisting* causes the phrase after the semicolon to be an incomplete sentence. (C) uses the future tense while the question is in the present. (E) still has the comma splice and a problem with pronoun agreement. Only (D) links the description of the exhibit in the second phrase with *exhibit* in the first phrase.

4. **A**   The sentence is correct as written. (B) uses *its* instead of *they*, and (C), (D), and (E) are unclear compared to (A).

5. **C**   The sentence as written is awkward and ambiguous due to *it*. There are two things that must be done to the *Halloween costume*: it must be *determined* and *critiqued* and to be parallel, these verbs must be in the same form. (C) is the only answer with the verbs in parallel structure.

6. **C**   The sentence has an idiom error: the comparison begins, using the *as...as* construction, but does not finish correctly. Both (C) and (D) begin with *as*, but only (C) has a structure parallel to the beginning of the sentence.

7. **E**   The sentence as written is passive and wordy; also, since the phrase that starts the sentence describes *Agatha Christie*, her name should follow the comma. Only (E) does this. (D) might look close, but the subject is actually the *disappearance*, not *Agatha Christie*.

8. **D**   (A) has a misplaced modifier and is also in the passive voice. (B) and (C) both have pronoun errors—a *platypus* cannot be referred to as *who*. (C) also creates a fragment. (D) is in the active voice and lacks the pronoun error. Also, the introductory modifying clause correctly modifies *platypus*. (E) is awkward and incorrectly uses *which*.

9. **E**   Start by comparing the verbs in this one. You want *pilots believed*, because the sentence is in past tense; get rid of (A), (B), and (C). From there, you want to make the list of nouns parallel with *the importance of discipline*: we need *the authority of their commanding officers* and *demonstration of national pride*, which matches only (E).

10. **B**   The underlined portion is awkwardly phrased. Comparisons are correct when the terms are parallel to each other. An adjective-plural noun combo that matches *internal states* is the best solution, and (B) *external events* has this construction.

11. **C**   (A) is a sentence fragment; the part after the comma is incomplete. (B) is wordy and awkward. (D) uses *which* too much and is a fragment. (E) is also a fragment and uses the -ing word *being*, which is unnecessary here.

12. **E**   The sentence as written has a misplaced modifier or faulty comparison: this sentence is saying that *Frank Capra* is a *film*. (B) and (C) create incomplete sentences. (D) changes the meaning of the sentence. (E) fixes the modifier/comparison problem by making the subject *the films of Frank Capra* and the verb and pronoun agree with the plural subject *films*.

13. **A**   The sentence is correct as written. (C) and (E) incorrectly use the word *being* (which is usually wrong). (B) has a redundant *with*. (D) has a double negative. (E) is redundant. (A) has none of these problems.

14. **D**   As written, the sentence compares the *painting style of Picasso* to his contemporaries, but it should compare styles to styles. (A), (B), (C), and (E) don't fix the original problem. In (D), *that of* stands in for *styles* and creates a parallel comparison.

Chapter 12
Practice Test 5

Your Name (print) _____

Last   First   Middle

Date _____

IMPORTANT: The following codes should be copied onto your answer sheet exactly as shown.

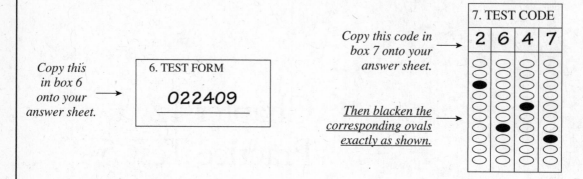

Copy this in box 6 onto your answer sheet. →

6. TEST FORM

022409

Copy this code in box 7 onto your answer sheet.

Then blacken the corresponding ovals exactly as shown. →

7. TEST CODE
2 6 4 7

General Directions

You will have three hours and 20 minutes to work on this objective test designed to familiarize you with all aspects of the SAT.

This test contains five 25-minute sections, two 20-minute sections, one 10-minute section, and one 25-minute essay. The supervisor will tell you when to begin and end each section. During the time allowed for each section, you may work only on that particular section. If you finish your work before time is called, you may check your work on that section, but you are not to work on any other section.

You will find specific directions for each type of question found in the test. **Be sure you understand the directions before attempting to answer any of the questions.**

YOU ARE TO INDICATE ALL YOUR ANSWERS ON THE SEPARATE ANSWER SHEET:

1. The test booklet may be used for scratchwork. However, no credit will be given for anything written in the test booklet.

2. Once you have decided on an answer to a question, darken the corresponding space on the answer sheet. Give only one answer to each question.

3. There are 40 numbered answer spaces for each section; be sure to use only those spaces that correspond to the test questions.

4. **Be sure each answer mark is dark and completely fills the answer space.** Do not make any stray marks on your answer sheet.

5. If you wish to change an answer, erase your first mark completely—an incomplete erasure may be considered an intended response—and blacken your new answer choice.

Your score on this test is based on the number of questions you answer correctly minus a fraction of the number of questions you answer incorrectly. Therefore, it is improbable that random or haphazard guessing will alter your score significantly. There are no deductions for incorrect answers on the student-produced response questions. However, if you are able to eliminate one or more of the answer choices on any question as wrong, it is generally to your advantage to guess at one of the remaining choices. Remember, however, not to spend too much time on any one question.

Diagnostic Test Form

Use a No. 2 pencil only. Be sure each mark is dark and completely fills the intended oval. Completely erase any errors or stray marks.

1 Your Name:

(Print)

Last   First   M.I.

Signature: _____ Date ___/___/___

Home Address: _____

Number and Street   City   State   Zip Code

E-Mail: _____ School: _____ Class: _____

(Print)

2 YOUR NAME

Last Name (First 4 Letters) | FIRST INIT | MID INIT

3 PHONE NUMBER

IMPORTANT: Fill in items 6 and 7 exactly as shown on the preceding page.

6 TEST FORM
(Copy from back of test book)

7 TEST CODE

4 DATE OF BIRTH

MONTH	DAY	YEAR
JAN		
FEB		
MAR	0 0	0
APR	1 1	1
MAY	2 2	2
JUN	3 3	3
JUL	4	4
AUG	5 5	5
SEP	6 6	6
OCT	7 7	7
NOV	8 8	8
DEC	9 9	9

8 OTHER
1 Ⓐ Ⓑ Ⓒ Ⓓ Ⓔ
2 Ⓐ Ⓑ Ⓒ Ⓓ Ⓔ
3 Ⓐ Ⓑ Ⓒ Ⓓ Ⓔ

5 SEX
○ MALE
○ FEMALE

OpScan iNSIGHT™ forms by Pearson NCS EM-253760-3:654321   Printed in U.S.A.   © TPR Education IP Holdings, LLC

PLEASE DO NOT WRITE IN THIS AREA

SERIAL #

THIS PAGE INTENTIONALLY LEFT BLANK

SECTION 1

IMPORTANT: **USE A NO. 2 PENCIL. DO NOT WRITE OUTSIDE THE BORDER!**
Words written outside the essay box or written in ink **WILL NOT APPEAR** in the copy sent to be scored and your score will be affected.

Begin your essay on this page. If you need more space, continue on the next page.

Continue on the next page, if necessary.

SECTION 2

1 Ⓐ Ⓑ Ⓒ Ⓓ Ⓔ　11 Ⓐ Ⓑ Ⓒ Ⓓ Ⓔ　21 Ⓐ Ⓑ Ⓒ Ⓓ Ⓔ　31 Ⓐ Ⓑ Ⓒ Ⓓ Ⓔ
2 Ⓐ Ⓑ Ⓒ Ⓓ Ⓔ　12 Ⓐ Ⓑ Ⓒ Ⓓ Ⓔ　22 Ⓐ Ⓑ Ⓒ Ⓓ Ⓔ　32 Ⓐ Ⓑ Ⓒ Ⓓ Ⓔ
3 Ⓐ Ⓑ Ⓒ Ⓓ Ⓔ　13 Ⓐ Ⓑ Ⓒ Ⓓ Ⓔ　23 Ⓐ Ⓑ Ⓒ Ⓓ Ⓔ　33 Ⓐ Ⓑ Ⓒ Ⓓ Ⓔ
4 Ⓐ Ⓑ Ⓒ Ⓓ Ⓔ　14 Ⓐ Ⓑ Ⓒ Ⓓ Ⓔ　24 Ⓐ Ⓑ Ⓒ Ⓓ Ⓔ　34 Ⓐ Ⓑ Ⓒ Ⓓ Ⓔ
5 Ⓐ Ⓑ Ⓒ Ⓓ Ⓔ　15 Ⓐ Ⓑ Ⓒ Ⓓ Ⓔ　25 Ⓐ Ⓑ Ⓒ Ⓓ Ⓔ　35 Ⓐ Ⓑ Ⓒ Ⓓ Ⓔ
6 Ⓐ Ⓑ Ⓒ Ⓓ Ⓔ　16 Ⓐ Ⓑ Ⓒ Ⓓ Ⓔ　26 Ⓐ Ⓑ Ⓒ Ⓓ Ⓔ　36 Ⓐ Ⓑ Ⓒ Ⓓ Ⓔ
7 Ⓐ Ⓑ Ⓒ Ⓓ Ⓔ　17 Ⓐ Ⓑ Ⓒ Ⓓ Ⓔ　27 Ⓐ Ⓑ Ⓒ Ⓓ Ⓔ　37 Ⓐ Ⓑ Ⓒ Ⓓ Ⓔ
8 Ⓐ Ⓑ Ⓒ Ⓓ Ⓔ　18 Ⓐ Ⓑ Ⓒ Ⓓ Ⓔ　28 Ⓐ Ⓑ Ⓒ Ⓓ Ⓔ　38 Ⓐ Ⓑ Ⓒ Ⓓ Ⓔ
9 Ⓐ Ⓑ Ⓒ Ⓓ Ⓔ　19 Ⓐ Ⓑ Ⓒ Ⓓ Ⓔ　29 Ⓐ Ⓑ Ⓒ Ⓓ Ⓔ　39 Ⓐ Ⓑ Ⓒ Ⓓ Ⓔ
10 Ⓐ Ⓑ Ⓒ Ⓓ Ⓔ　20 Ⓐ Ⓑ Ⓒ Ⓓ Ⓔ　30 Ⓐ Ⓑ Ⓒ Ⓓ Ⓔ　40 Ⓐ Ⓑ Ⓒ Ⓓ Ⓔ

SECTION 3

1 Ⓐ Ⓑ Ⓒ Ⓓ Ⓔ　11 Ⓐ Ⓑ Ⓒ Ⓓ Ⓔ　21 Ⓐ Ⓑ Ⓒ Ⓓ Ⓔ　31 Ⓐ Ⓑ Ⓒ Ⓓ Ⓔ
2 Ⓐ Ⓑ Ⓒ Ⓓ Ⓔ　12 Ⓐ Ⓑ Ⓒ Ⓓ Ⓔ　22 Ⓐ Ⓑ Ⓒ Ⓓ Ⓔ　32 Ⓐ Ⓑ Ⓒ Ⓓ Ⓔ
3 Ⓐ Ⓑ Ⓒ Ⓓ Ⓔ　13 Ⓐ Ⓑ Ⓒ Ⓓ Ⓔ　23 Ⓐ Ⓑ Ⓒ Ⓓ Ⓔ　33 Ⓐ Ⓑ Ⓒ Ⓓ Ⓔ
4 Ⓐ Ⓑ Ⓒ Ⓓ Ⓔ　14 Ⓐ Ⓑ Ⓒ Ⓓ Ⓔ　24 Ⓐ Ⓑ Ⓒ Ⓓ Ⓔ　34 Ⓐ Ⓑ Ⓒ Ⓓ Ⓔ
5 Ⓐ Ⓑ Ⓒ Ⓓ Ⓔ　15 Ⓐ Ⓑ Ⓒ Ⓓ Ⓔ　25 Ⓐ Ⓑ Ⓒ Ⓓ Ⓔ　35 Ⓐ Ⓑ Ⓒ Ⓓ Ⓔ
6 Ⓐ Ⓑ Ⓒ Ⓓ Ⓔ　16 Ⓐ Ⓑ Ⓒ Ⓓ Ⓔ　26 Ⓐ Ⓑ Ⓒ Ⓓ Ⓔ　36 Ⓐ Ⓑ Ⓒ Ⓓ Ⓔ
7 Ⓐ Ⓑ Ⓒ Ⓓ Ⓔ　17 Ⓐ Ⓑ Ⓒ Ⓓ Ⓔ　27 Ⓐ Ⓑ Ⓒ Ⓓ Ⓔ　37 Ⓐ Ⓑ Ⓒ Ⓓ Ⓔ
8 Ⓐ Ⓑ Ⓒ Ⓓ Ⓔ　18 Ⓐ Ⓑ Ⓒ Ⓓ Ⓔ　28 Ⓐ Ⓑ Ⓒ Ⓓ Ⓔ　38 Ⓐ Ⓑ Ⓒ Ⓓ Ⓔ
9 Ⓐ Ⓑ Ⓒ Ⓓ Ⓔ　19 Ⓐ Ⓑ Ⓒ Ⓓ Ⓔ　29 Ⓐ Ⓑ Ⓒ Ⓓ Ⓔ　39 Ⓐ Ⓑ Ⓒ Ⓓ Ⓔ
10 Ⓐ Ⓑ Ⓒ Ⓓ Ⓔ　20 Ⓐ Ⓑ Ⓒ Ⓓ Ⓔ　30 Ⓐ Ⓑ Ⓒ Ⓓ Ⓔ　40 Ⓐ Ⓑ Ⓒ Ⓓ Ⓔ

CAUTION 　Grid answers in the section below for SECTION 2 or SECTION 3 only if directed to do so in your test book.

Student-Produced Responses 　ONLY ANSWERS THAT ARE GRIDDED WILL BE SCORED. YOU WILL NOT RECEIVE CREDIT FOR ANYTHING WRITTEN IN THE BOXES.

Quality Assurance Mark ●

9　10　11　12　13

14　15　16　17　18

SECTION 4

1 Ⓐ Ⓑ Ⓒ Ⓓ Ⓔ   11 Ⓐ Ⓑ Ⓒ Ⓓ Ⓔ   21 Ⓐ Ⓑ Ⓒ Ⓓ Ⓔ   31 Ⓐ Ⓑ Ⓒ Ⓓ Ⓔ
2 Ⓐ Ⓑ Ⓒ Ⓓ Ⓔ   12 Ⓐ Ⓑ Ⓒ Ⓓ Ⓔ   22 Ⓐ Ⓑ Ⓒ Ⓓ Ⓔ   32 Ⓐ Ⓑ Ⓒ Ⓓ Ⓔ
3 Ⓐ Ⓑ Ⓒ Ⓓ Ⓔ   13 Ⓐ Ⓑ Ⓒ Ⓓ Ⓔ   23 Ⓐ Ⓑ Ⓒ Ⓓ Ⓔ   33 Ⓐ Ⓑ Ⓒ Ⓓ Ⓔ
4 Ⓐ Ⓑ Ⓒ Ⓓ Ⓔ   14 Ⓐ Ⓑ Ⓒ Ⓓ Ⓔ   24 Ⓐ Ⓑ Ⓒ Ⓓ Ⓔ   34 Ⓐ Ⓑ Ⓒ Ⓓ Ⓔ
5 Ⓐ Ⓑ Ⓒ Ⓓ Ⓔ   15 Ⓐ Ⓑ Ⓒ Ⓓ Ⓔ   25 Ⓐ Ⓑ Ⓒ Ⓓ Ⓔ   35 Ⓐ Ⓑ Ⓒ Ⓓ Ⓔ
6 Ⓐ Ⓑ Ⓒ Ⓓ Ⓔ   16 Ⓐ Ⓑ Ⓒ Ⓓ Ⓔ   26 Ⓐ Ⓑ Ⓒ Ⓓ Ⓔ   36 Ⓐ Ⓑ Ⓒ Ⓓ Ⓔ
7 Ⓐ Ⓑ Ⓒ Ⓓ Ⓔ   17 Ⓐ Ⓑ Ⓒ Ⓓ Ⓔ   27 Ⓐ Ⓑ Ⓒ Ⓓ Ⓔ   37 Ⓐ Ⓑ Ⓒ Ⓓ Ⓔ
8 Ⓐ Ⓑ Ⓒ Ⓓ Ⓔ   18 Ⓐ Ⓑ Ⓒ Ⓓ Ⓔ   28 Ⓐ Ⓑ Ⓒ Ⓓ Ⓔ   38 Ⓐ Ⓑ Ⓒ Ⓓ Ⓔ
9 Ⓐ Ⓑ Ⓒ Ⓓ Ⓔ   19 Ⓐ Ⓑ Ⓒ Ⓓ Ⓔ   29 Ⓐ Ⓑ Ⓒ Ⓓ Ⓔ   39 Ⓐ Ⓑ Ⓒ Ⓓ Ⓔ
10 Ⓐ Ⓑ Ⓒ Ⓓ Ⓔ   20 Ⓐ Ⓑ Ⓒ Ⓓ Ⓔ   30 Ⓐ Ⓑ Ⓒ Ⓓ Ⓔ   40 Ⓐ Ⓑ Ⓒ Ⓓ Ⓔ

SECTION 5

1 Ⓐ Ⓑ Ⓒ Ⓓ Ⓔ   11 Ⓐ Ⓑ Ⓒ Ⓓ Ⓔ   21 Ⓐ Ⓑ Ⓒ Ⓓ Ⓔ   31 Ⓐ Ⓑ Ⓒ Ⓓ Ⓔ
2 Ⓐ Ⓑ Ⓒ Ⓓ Ⓔ   12 Ⓐ Ⓑ Ⓒ Ⓓ Ⓔ   22 Ⓐ Ⓑ Ⓒ Ⓓ Ⓔ   32 Ⓐ Ⓑ Ⓒ Ⓓ Ⓔ
3 Ⓐ Ⓑ Ⓒ Ⓓ Ⓔ   13 Ⓐ Ⓑ Ⓒ Ⓓ Ⓔ   23 Ⓐ Ⓑ Ⓒ Ⓓ Ⓔ   33 Ⓐ Ⓑ Ⓒ Ⓓ Ⓔ
4 Ⓐ Ⓑ Ⓒ Ⓓ Ⓔ   14 Ⓐ Ⓑ Ⓒ Ⓓ Ⓔ   24 Ⓐ Ⓑ Ⓒ Ⓓ Ⓔ   34 Ⓐ Ⓑ Ⓒ Ⓓ Ⓔ
5 Ⓐ Ⓑ Ⓒ Ⓓ Ⓔ   15 Ⓐ Ⓑ Ⓒ Ⓓ Ⓔ   25 Ⓐ Ⓑ Ⓒ Ⓓ Ⓔ   35 Ⓐ Ⓑ Ⓒ Ⓓ Ⓔ
6 Ⓐ Ⓑ Ⓒ Ⓓ Ⓔ   16 Ⓐ Ⓑ Ⓒ Ⓓ Ⓔ   26 Ⓐ Ⓑ Ⓒ Ⓓ Ⓔ   36 Ⓐ Ⓑ Ⓒ Ⓓ Ⓔ
7 Ⓐ Ⓑ Ⓒ Ⓓ Ⓔ   17 Ⓐ Ⓑ Ⓒ Ⓓ Ⓔ   27 Ⓐ Ⓑ Ⓒ Ⓓ Ⓔ   37 Ⓐ Ⓑ Ⓒ Ⓓ Ⓔ
8 Ⓐ Ⓑ Ⓒ Ⓓ Ⓔ   18 Ⓐ Ⓑ Ⓒ Ⓓ Ⓔ   28 Ⓐ Ⓑ Ⓒ Ⓓ Ⓔ   38 Ⓐ Ⓑ Ⓒ Ⓓ Ⓔ
9 Ⓐ Ⓑ Ⓒ Ⓓ Ⓔ   19 Ⓐ Ⓑ Ⓒ Ⓓ Ⓔ   29 Ⓐ Ⓑ Ⓒ Ⓓ Ⓔ   39 Ⓐ Ⓑ Ⓒ Ⓓ Ⓔ
10 Ⓐ Ⓑ Ⓒ Ⓓ Ⓔ   20 Ⓐ Ⓑ Ⓒ Ⓓ Ⓔ   30 Ⓐ Ⓑ Ⓒ Ⓓ Ⓔ   40 Ⓐ Ⓑ Ⓒ Ⓓ Ⓔ

CAUTION   Grid answers in the section below for SECTION 4 or SECTION 5 only if directed to do so in your test book.

Student-Produced Responses   ONLY ANSWERS THAT ARE GRIDDED WILL BE SCORED. YOU WILL NOT RECEIVE CREDIT FOR ANYTHING WRITTEN IN THE BOXES.

Quality Assurance Mark ●

9   10   11   12   13

14   15   16   17   18

COMPLETE MARK ● EXAMPLES OF INCOMPLETE MARKS Ⓐ Ⓑ ⊖ Ⓓ Ⓐ Ⓑ ⊘ Ⓓ

You must use a No. 2 pencil and marks must be complete. Do not use a mechanical pencil. It is very important that you fill in the entire circle darkly and completely. If you change your responses, erase as completely as possible. Incomplete marks or erasures may affect your score.

SECTION 6

1 Ⓐ Ⓑ Ⓒ Ⓓ Ⓔ
2 Ⓐ Ⓑ Ⓒ Ⓓ Ⓔ
3 Ⓐ Ⓑ Ⓒ Ⓓ Ⓔ
4 Ⓐ Ⓑ Ⓒ Ⓓ Ⓔ
5 Ⓐ Ⓑ Ⓒ Ⓓ Ⓔ
6 Ⓐ Ⓑ Ⓒ Ⓓ Ⓔ
7 Ⓐ Ⓑ Ⓒ Ⓓ Ⓔ
8 Ⓐ Ⓑ Ⓒ Ⓓ Ⓔ
9 Ⓐ Ⓑ Ⓒ Ⓓ Ⓔ
10 Ⓐ Ⓑ Ⓒ Ⓓ Ⓔ

11 Ⓐ Ⓑ Ⓒ Ⓓ Ⓔ
12 Ⓐ Ⓑ Ⓒ Ⓓ Ⓔ
13 Ⓐ Ⓑ Ⓒ Ⓓ Ⓔ
14 Ⓐ Ⓑ Ⓒ Ⓓ Ⓔ
15 Ⓐ Ⓑ Ⓒ Ⓓ Ⓔ
16 Ⓐ Ⓑ Ⓒ Ⓓ Ⓔ
17 Ⓐ Ⓑ Ⓒ Ⓓ Ⓔ
18 Ⓐ Ⓑ Ⓒ Ⓓ Ⓔ
19 Ⓐ Ⓑ Ⓒ Ⓓ Ⓔ
20 Ⓐ Ⓑ Ⓒ Ⓓ Ⓔ

21 Ⓐ Ⓑ Ⓒ Ⓓ Ⓔ
22 Ⓐ Ⓑ Ⓒ Ⓓ Ⓔ
23 Ⓐ Ⓑ Ⓒ Ⓓ Ⓔ
24 Ⓐ Ⓑ Ⓒ Ⓓ Ⓔ
25 Ⓐ Ⓑ Ⓒ Ⓓ Ⓔ
26 Ⓐ Ⓑ Ⓒ Ⓓ Ⓔ
27 Ⓐ Ⓑ Ⓒ Ⓓ Ⓔ
28 Ⓐ Ⓑ Ⓒ Ⓓ Ⓔ
29 Ⓐ Ⓑ Ⓒ Ⓓ Ⓔ
30 Ⓐ Ⓑ Ⓒ Ⓓ Ⓔ

31 Ⓐ Ⓑ Ⓒ Ⓓ Ⓔ
32 Ⓐ Ⓑ Ⓒ Ⓓ Ⓔ
33 Ⓐ Ⓑ Ⓒ Ⓓ Ⓔ
34 Ⓐ Ⓑ Ⓒ Ⓓ Ⓔ
35 Ⓐ Ⓑ Ⓒ Ⓓ Ⓔ
36 Ⓐ Ⓑ Ⓒ Ⓓ Ⓔ
37 Ⓐ Ⓑ Ⓒ Ⓓ Ⓔ
38 Ⓐ Ⓑ Ⓒ Ⓓ Ⓔ
39 Ⓐ Ⓑ Ⓒ Ⓓ Ⓔ
40 Ⓐ Ⓑ Ⓒ Ⓓ Ⓔ

SECTION 7

1 Ⓐ Ⓑ Ⓒ Ⓓ Ⓔ
2 Ⓐ Ⓑ Ⓒ Ⓓ Ⓔ
3 Ⓐ Ⓑ Ⓒ Ⓓ Ⓔ
4 Ⓐ Ⓑ Ⓒ Ⓓ Ⓔ
5 Ⓐ Ⓑ Ⓒ Ⓓ Ⓔ
6 Ⓐ Ⓑ Ⓒ Ⓓ Ⓔ
7 Ⓐ Ⓑ Ⓒ Ⓓ Ⓔ
8 Ⓐ Ⓑ Ⓒ Ⓓ Ⓔ
9 Ⓐ Ⓑ Ⓒ Ⓓ Ⓔ
10 Ⓐ Ⓑ Ⓒ Ⓓ Ⓔ

11 Ⓐ Ⓑ Ⓒ Ⓓ Ⓔ
12 Ⓐ Ⓑ Ⓒ Ⓓ Ⓔ
13 Ⓐ Ⓑ Ⓒ Ⓓ Ⓔ
14 Ⓐ Ⓑ Ⓒ Ⓓ Ⓔ
15 Ⓐ Ⓑ Ⓒ Ⓓ Ⓔ
16 Ⓐ Ⓑ Ⓒ Ⓓ Ⓔ
17 Ⓐ Ⓑ Ⓒ Ⓓ Ⓔ
18 Ⓐ Ⓑ Ⓒ Ⓓ Ⓔ
19 Ⓐ Ⓑ Ⓒ Ⓓ Ⓔ
20 Ⓐ Ⓑ Ⓒ Ⓓ Ⓔ

21 Ⓐ Ⓑ Ⓒ Ⓓ Ⓔ
22 Ⓐ Ⓑ Ⓒ Ⓓ Ⓔ
23 Ⓐ Ⓑ Ⓒ Ⓓ Ⓔ
24 Ⓐ Ⓑ Ⓒ Ⓓ Ⓔ
25 Ⓐ Ⓑ Ⓒ Ⓓ Ⓔ
26 Ⓐ Ⓑ Ⓒ Ⓓ Ⓔ
27 Ⓐ Ⓑ Ⓒ Ⓓ Ⓔ
28 Ⓐ Ⓑ Ⓒ Ⓓ Ⓔ
29 Ⓐ Ⓑ Ⓒ Ⓓ Ⓔ
30 Ⓐ Ⓑ Ⓒ Ⓓ Ⓔ

31 Ⓐ Ⓑ Ⓒ Ⓓ Ⓔ
32 Ⓐ Ⓑ Ⓒ Ⓓ Ⓔ
33 Ⓐ Ⓑ Ⓒ Ⓓ Ⓔ
34 Ⓐ Ⓑ Ⓒ Ⓓ Ⓔ
35 Ⓐ Ⓑ Ⓒ Ⓓ Ⓔ
36 Ⓐ Ⓑ Ⓒ Ⓓ Ⓔ
37 Ⓐ Ⓑ Ⓒ Ⓓ Ⓔ
38 Ⓐ Ⓑ Ⓒ Ⓓ Ⓔ
39 Ⓐ Ⓑ Ⓒ Ⓓ Ⓔ
40 Ⓐ Ⓑ Ⓒ Ⓓ Ⓔ

CAUTION Grid answers in the section below for SECTION 6 or SECTION 7 only if directed to do so in your test book.

Student-Produced Responses ONLY ANSWERS THAT ARE GRIDDED WILL BE SCORED. YOU WILL NOT RECEIVE CREDIT FOR ANYTHING WRITTEN IN THE BOXES.

Quality Assurance Mark

9 10 11 12 13

14 15 16 17 18

(Grids each contain: / / fraction bars, ... decimal points, and digits 0 1 2 3 4 5 6 7 8 9 in four columns)

SECTION 8

1 Ⓐ Ⓑ Ⓒ Ⓓ Ⓔ	11 Ⓐ Ⓑ Ⓒ Ⓓ Ⓔ	21 Ⓐ Ⓑ Ⓒ Ⓓ Ⓔ	31 Ⓐ Ⓑ Ⓒ Ⓓ Ⓔ
2 Ⓐ Ⓑ Ⓒ Ⓓ Ⓔ	12 Ⓐ Ⓑ Ⓒ Ⓓ Ⓔ	22 Ⓐ Ⓑ Ⓒ Ⓓ Ⓔ	32 Ⓐ Ⓑ Ⓒ Ⓓ Ⓔ
3 Ⓐ Ⓑ Ⓒ Ⓓ Ⓔ	13 Ⓐ Ⓑ Ⓒ Ⓓ Ⓔ	23 Ⓐ Ⓑ Ⓒ Ⓓ Ⓔ	33 Ⓐ Ⓑ Ⓒ Ⓓ Ⓔ
4 Ⓐ Ⓑ Ⓒ Ⓓ Ⓔ	14 Ⓐ Ⓑ Ⓒ Ⓓ Ⓔ	24 Ⓐ Ⓑ Ⓒ Ⓓ Ⓔ	34 Ⓐ Ⓑ Ⓒ Ⓓ Ⓔ
5 Ⓐ Ⓑ Ⓒ Ⓓ Ⓔ	15 Ⓐ Ⓑ Ⓒ Ⓓ Ⓔ	25 Ⓐ Ⓑ Ⓒ Ⓓ Ⓔ	35 Ⓐ Ⓑ Ⓒ Ⓓ Ⓔ
6 Ⓐ Ⓑ Ⓒ Ⓓ Ⓔ	16 Ⓐ Ⓑ Ⓒ Ⓓ Ⓔ	26 Ⓐ Ⓑ Ⓒ Ⓓ Ⓔ	36 Ⓐ Ⓑ Ⓒ Ⓓ Ⓔ
7 Ⓐ Ⓑ Ⓒ Ⓓ Ⓔ	17 Ⓐ Ⓑ Ⓒ Ⓓ Ⓔ	27 Ⓐ Ⓑ Ⓒ Ⓓ Ⓔ	37 Ⓐ Ⓑ Ⓒ Ⓓ Ⓔ
8 Ⓐ Ⓑ Ⓒ Ⓓ Ⓔ	18 Ⓐ Ⓑ Ⓒ Ⓓ Ⓔ	28 Ⓐ Ⓑ Ⓒ Ⓓ Ⓔ	38 Ⓐ Ⓑ Ⓒ Ⓓ Ⓔ
9 Ⓐ Ⓑ Ⓒ Ⓓ Ⓔ	19 Ⓐ Ⓑ Ⓒ Ⓓ Ⓔ	29 Ⓐ Ⓑ Ⓒ Ⓓ Ⓔ	39 Ⓐ Ⓑ Ⓒ Ⓓ Ⓔ
10 Ⓐ Ⓑ Ⓒ Ⓓ Ⓔ	20 Ⓐ Ⓑ Ⓒ Ⓓ Ⓔ	30 Ⓐ Ⓑ Ⓒ Ⓓ Ⓔ	40 Ⓐ Ⓑ Ⓒ Ⓓ Ⓔ

SECTION 9

1 Ⓐ Ⓑ Ⓒ Ⓓ Ⓔ	11 Ⓐ Ⓑ Ⓒ Ⓓ Ⓔ	21 Ⓐ Ⓑ Ⓒ Ⓓ Ⓔ	31 Ⓐ Ⓑ Ⓒ Ⓓ Ⓔ
2 Ⓐ Ⓑ Ⓒ Ⓓ Ⓔ	12 Ⓐ Ⓑ Ⓒ Ⓓ Ⓔ	22 Ⓐ Ⓑ Ⓒ Ⓓ Ⓔ	32 Ⓐ Ⓑ Ⓒ Ⓓ Ⓔ
3 Ⓐ Ⓑ Ⓒ Ⓓ Ⓔ	13 Ⓐ Ⓑ Ⓒ Ⓓ Ⓔ	23 Ⓐ Ⓑ Ⓒ Ⓓ Ⓔ	33 Ⓐ Ⓑ Ⓒ Ⓓ Ⓔ
4 Ⓐ Ⓑ Ⓒ Ⓓ Ⓔ	14 Ⓐ Ⓑ Ⓒ Ⓓ Ⓔ	24 Ⓐ Ⓑ Ⓒ Ⓓ Ⓔ	34 Ⓐ Ⓑ Ⓒ Ⓓ Ⓔ
5 Ⓐ Ⓑ Ⓒ Ⓓ Ⓔ	15 Ⓐ Ⓑ Ⓒ Ⓓ Ⓔ	25 Ⓐ Ⓑ Ⓒ Ⓓ Ⓔ	35 Ⓐ Ⓑ Ⓒ Ⓓ Ⓔ
6 Ⓐ Ⓑ Ⓒ Ⓓ Ⓔ	16 Ⓐ Ⓑ Ⓒ Ⓓ Ⓔ	26 Ⓐ Ⓑ Ⓒ Ⓓ Ⓔ	36 Ⓐ Ⓑ Ⓒ Ⓓ Ⓔ
7 Ⓐ Ⓑ Ⓒ Ⓓ Ⓔ	17 Ⓐ Ⓑ Ⓒ Ⓓ Ⓔ	27 Ⓐ Ⓑ Ⓒ Ⓓ Ⓔ	37 Ⓐ Ⓑ Ⓒ Ⓓ Ⓔ
8 Ⓐ Ⓑ Ⓒ Ⓓ Ⓔ	18 Ⓐ Ⓑ Ⓒ Ⓓ Ⓔ	28 Ⓐ Ⓑ Ⓒ Ⓓ Ⓔ	38 Ⓐ Ⓑ Ⓒ Ⓓ Ⓔ
9 Ⓐ Ⓑ Ⓒ Ⓓ Ⓔ	19 Ⓐ Ⓑ Ⓒ Ⓓ Ⓔ	29 Ⓐ Ⓑ Ⓒ Ⓓ Ⓔ	39 Ⓐ Ⓑ Ⓒ Ⓓ Ⓔ
10 Ⓐ Ⓑ Ⓒ Ⓓ Ⓔ	20 Ⓐ Ⓑ Ⓒ Ⓓ Ⓔ	30 Ⓐ Ⓑ Ⓒ Ⓓ Ⓔ	40 Ⓐ Ⓑ Ⓒ Ⓓ Ⓔ

SECTION 10

1 Ⓐ Ⓑ Ⓒ Ⓓ Ⓔ	11 Ⓐ Ⓑ Ⓒ Ⓓ Ⓔ	21 Ⓐ Ⓑ Ⓒ Ⓓ Ⓔ	31 Ⓐ Ⓑ Ⓒ Ⓓ Ⓔ
2 Ⓐ Ⓑ Ⓒ Ⓓ Ⓔ	12 Ⓐ Ⓑ Ⓒ Ⓓ Ⓔ	22 Ⓐ Ⓑ Ⓒ Ⓓ Ⓔ	32 Ⓐ Ⓑ Ⓒ Ⓓ Ⓔ
3 Ⓐ Ⓑ Ⓒ Ⓓ Ⓔ	13 Ⓐ Ⓑ Ⓒ Ⓓ Ⓔ	23 Ⓐ Ⓑ Ⓒ Ⓓ Ⓔ	33 Ⓐ Ⓑ Ⓒ Ⓓ Ⓔ
4 Ⓐ Ⓑ Ⓒ Ⓓ Ⓔ	14 Ⓐ Ⓑ Ⓒ Ⓓ Ⓔ	24 Ⓐ Ⓑ Ⓒ Ⓓ Ⓔ	34 Ⓐ Ⓑ Ⓒ Ⓓ Ⓔ
5 Ⓐ Ⓑ Ⓒ Ⓓ Ⓔ	15 Ⓐ Ⓑ Ⓒ Ⓓ Ⓔ	25 Ⓐ Ⓑ Ⓒ Ⓓ Ⓔ	35 Ⓐ Ⓑ Ⓒ Ⓓ Ⓔ
6 Ⓐ Ⓑ Ⓒ Ⓓ Ⓔ	16 Ⓐ Ⓑ Ⓒ Ⓓ Ⓔ	26 Ⓐ Ⓑ Ⓒ Ⓓ Ⓔ	36 Ⓐ Ⓑ Ⓒ Ⓓ Ⓔ
7 Ⓐ Ⓑ Ⓒ Ⓓ Ⓔ	17 Ⓐ Ⓑ Ⓒ Ⓓ Ⓔ	27 Ⓐ Ⓑ Ⓒ Ⓓ Ⓔ	37 Ⓐ Ⓑ Ⓒ Ⓓ Ⓔ
8 Ⓐ Ⓑ Ⓒ Ⓓ Ⓔ	18 Ⓐ Ⓑ Ⓒ Ⓓ Ⓔ	28 Ⓐ Ⓑ Ⓒ Ⓓ Ⓔ	38 Ⓐ Ⓑ Ⓒ Ⓓ Ⓔ
9 Ⓐ Ⓑ Ⓒ Ⓓ Ⓔ	19 Ⓐ Ⓑ Ⓒ Ⓓ Ⓔ	29 Ⓐ Ⓑ Ⓒ Ⓓ Ⓔ	39 Ⓐ Ⓑ Ⓒ Ⓓ Ⓔ
10 Ⓐ Ⓑ Ⓒ Ⓓ Ⓔ	20 Ⓐ Ⓑ Ⓒ Ⓓ Ⓔ	30 Ⓐ Ⓑ Ⓒ Ⓓ Ⓔ	40 Ⓐ Ⓑ Ⓒ Ⓓ Ⓔ

SECTION 1
ESSAY
Time — 25 minutes

Turn to Section 1 of your answer sheet to write your essay.

The essay gives you an opportunity to show how effectively you can develop and express ideas. You should, therefore, take care to develop your point of view, present your ideas logically and clearly, and use language precisely.

Your essay must be written on the lines provided on your answer sheet—you will receive no other paper on which to write. You will have enough space if you write on every line, avoid wide margins, and keep your handwriting to a reasonable size. Remember that people who are not familiar with your handwriting will read what you write. Try to write or print so that what you are writing is legible to those readers.

You have twenty-five minutes to write an essay on the topic assigned below. DO NOT WRITE ON ANOTHER TOPIC. AN OFF-TOPIC ESSAY WILL RECEIVE A SCORE OF ZERO.

Think carefully about the issue presented in the following excerpt and the assignment below.

> There are times when it is easier to lie than it is to tell the truth. The truth may cause someone harm—financially, emotionally, or even physically—and so may do far greater damage than the damage of a lie, which harms only a person's trust.

Assignment: Are there instances when lying is the more appropriate action than telling the truth? Plan and write an essay in which you develop your point of view on this issue. Support your position with reasoning and examples taken from your reading, studies, experience, or observations.

DO NOT WRITE YOUR ESSAY IN YOUR TEST BOOK. You will receive credit only for what you write on your answer sheet.

BEGIN WRITING YOUR ESSAY IN SECTION 1 OF THE ANSWER SHEET.

S T O P
If you finish before time is called, you may check your work on this section only.
Do not turn to any other section in the test.

SECTION 2
Time — 25 minutes
24 Questions

Turn to Section 2 of your answer sheet to answer the questions in this section.

Directions: For each question in this section, select the best answer from among the choices given and fill in the corresponding circle on the answer sheet.

Each sentence below has one or two blanks, each blank indicating that something has been omitted. Beneath the sentence are five words or sets of words labeled A through E. Choose the word or set of words that, when inserted in the sentence, <u>best</u> fits the meaning of the sentence as a whole.

Example:

Desiring to ------- his taunting friends, Mitch gave them taffy in hopes it would keep their mouths shut.

(A) eliminate   (B) satisfy   (C) overcome
    (D) ridicule   (E) silence

(A)(B)(C)(D)●

1. Ellie looked on ------- as Tom described his encounter with Bigfoot; she doubted such a creature even existed.

    (A) erroneously   (B) awkwardly   (C) miraculously
        (D) skeptically   (E) maliciously

2. Always looking for ------- theories, Hector was as eager to explore new possibilities as the more narrow minded scientists were to ------- them.

    (A) enlightening . . develop
    (B) relative . . disregard
    (C) innovative . . belittle
    (D) provocative . . study
    (E) exciting . . support

3. Despite painter Jean Michel Basquiat's ------- rise to prominence, he just as quickly ------- to the pressures of fame and died before turning thirty.

    (A) unprecedented . . appealed
    (B) swift . . yielded
    (C) graceful . . aspired
    (D) hasty . . ascended
    (E) lethal . . subsided

4. After he had been bitten by a jungle insect, Kei experienced a dull, pervasive discomfort rather than an -------, localized pain.

    (A) unstudied   (B) acute   (C) invasive
        (D) elevated   (E) obvious

5. Andy's best feature is his -------: he will always stick to his principles, no matter how daunting the opposition.

    (A) munificence   (B) efficacy   (C) intensity
        (D) tenacity   (E) eccentricity

6. Procrastination is often tempting, but circumstances sometimes demand ------- action.

    (A) prompt   (B) reckless   (C) caustic
        (D) protracted   (E) fallacious

7. In public, Chris is an amiable and generous donor, who gives freely of his time and money, yet his stinginess and ------- in private ------- this benevolent public image.

    (A) callousness . . belie
    (B) immorality . . display
    (C) perniciousness . . evaluate
    (D) austerity . . alleviate
    (E) contentment . . contradict

8. Nurses who work in emergency medicine departments are accustomed to handling urgent trauma situations in which every task must be performed with great -------.

    (A) passivity   (B) ineptitude   (C) alacrity
        (D) morbidity   (E) consternation

GO ON TO THE NEXT PAGE

Directions: Each passage below is followed by questions based on its content. Answer the questions on the basis of what is <u>stated</u> or <u>implied</u> in each passage and in any introductory material that may be provided.

Questions 9-12 are based on the following passages.

Passage 1

The twentieth century will be remembered as one hundred years of great upheaval. All the major changes wrought in this century—from Picasso's paintings to James Joyce's novel
Line *Ulysses*—were profoundly influenced by Albert Einstein.
5 Einstein's theory of special relativity debunked the notions of Absolute Rest and Absolute Time, therefore implying that both time and space were subject to relative forces. Artists and writers applied this idea to their craft. Did all novels have to have plot, did all paintings have to be representational? The
10 answer of the twentieth century was an emphatic "no."

Passage 2

Just as the Renaissance pulled Europe out of the Middle Ages, ideas of the twentieth century radically altered the ways that people think, interact, and live. While several aspects of the twentieth century are unique, there are still startling
15 parallels between the Renaissance and the last hundred years of the past millennium. Both time periods saw great advances in science; Copernicus caused as much furor as Einstein. Exploration—whether of the New World or of new world markets—led to trade expansion. Art moved in startlingly
20 different directions, away from the Gothicism of the fifteenth century and the dogmatic Realism of the nineteenth. It seems the twentieth century was not so different from the world of Shakespeare.

9. According to the author of Passage 1, which of the following is true of the twentieth century?

(A) There was a synthesis of ideas across various disciplines.
(B) Einstein proved the existence of Absolute Rest.
(C) Picasso was younger than Einstein.
(D) Literature was completely different from nineteenth century works.
(E) Einstein dabbled in art as well as science.

10. It can be inferred from Passage 2 that

(A) Realism was a precursor to both the Renaissance and the twentieth century
(B) the Renaissance and the twentieth century saw similar advances in science
(C) Shakespeare was a Renaissance figure
(D) the Renaissance saw the beginnings of capitalism
(E) advances during both the Renaissance and the twentieth century were mainly centered in Europe

11. The authors of both passages would probably agree with which of the following statements?

(A) Art and science are inextricably linked.
(B) Picasso was indirectly influenced by ideas of Copernicus.
(C) Einstein was one of the most important thinkers of the twentieth century.
(D) The twentieth century could not have existed without the model of the Renaissance.
(E) Classical music did not change much in the twentieth century.

12. How would each passage incorporate the ideas of the nineteenth century into its argument?

(A) Passage 1 would focus on parallels in ideas; Passage 2 would see the nineteenth century as an extension of the Renaissance.
(B) Passage 1 would establish contrasts; Passage 2 would explore links between the nineteenth century and a similar historical period.
(C) Passage 1 would discuss economic advances; Passage 2 would discuss art theory.
(D) Both passages would mention the importance of immigration.
(E) Both passages would discuss Shakespeare's influence on the nineteenth century.

GO ON TO THE NEXT PAGE

Questions 13-24 are based on the following passage.

In this excerpt from "Stride Toward Freedom," Martin Luther King, Jr. discusses the condition of the African American in American society. Written in 1958, it presents a number of problems facing African Americans and points the way to a solution.

Ever since the signing of the Declaration of Independence, America has manifested a schizophrenic personality on the question of race. She has been torn between selves—a self
Line in which she has proudly professed democracy and a self in
5 which she has sadly practiced the antithesis of democracy. The reality of segregation, like slavery, has always had to confront the ideals of democracy and Christianity. Indeed, segregation and discrimination are strange paradoxes in a nation founded on the principle that all men are created equal.
10 This contradiction has disturbed the consciences of whites both North and South, and has caused many of them to see that segregation is basically evil.

Climaxing this process was the Supreme Court's decision outlawing segregation in the public schools. For all men of
15 good will, May 17, 1954 marked a joyous end to the long night of enforced segregation. In unequivocal language the court affirmed that "separate but equal" facilities are inherently unequal, and that to segregate a child on the basis of his race is to deny that child equal protection of the law. This decision
20 brought hope to millions of disinherited Negroes who had formerly dared only to dream of freedom. It further enhanced the Negro's sense of dignity and gave him even greater determination to achieve justice.

This determination of Negro Americans to win freedom
25 from all forms of oppression springs from the same deep longing that motivates oppressed peoples all over the world. The rumblings of discontent in Asia and Africa are expressions of a quest for freedom and human dignity by people who have long been the victims of colonialism and
30 imperialism. So in a real sense the racial crisis in America is a part of the larger world crisis.

But the numerous changes which have culminated in a new sense of dignity on the part of the Negro are not of themselves responsible for the present crisis. If all men
35 accepted these historical changes in good faith there would be no crisis. The crisis developed when the collective pressures to achieve fair goals for the Negro met with tenacious and determined resistance. Then the emerging new order, based on the principle of democratic equalitarianism, came face
40 to face with the older order, based on the principles of paternalism and subordination. The crisis was not produced by outside agitators, NAACP'ers, Montgomery Protestors, or even the Supreme Court. The crisis developed, paradoxically, when the most sublime principles of American democracy—
45 imperfectly realized for almost two centuries—began fulfilling themselves and met with the brutal resistance of forces seeking to contract and repress freedom's growth.

The resistance has risen at times to ominous proportions. Many states have reacted in open defiance. The legislative
50 halls of the South still ring loud with such words as "interposition" and "nullification." Many public officials are using the power of their offices to defy the law of the land. Through their irresponsible actions, their inflammatory statements, and the dissemination of distortion and half-
55 truths, they have succeeded in rousing abnormal fears and morbid antipathies within the minds of underprivileged and uneducated whites, leaving them in such a state of excitement and confusion that they are led to acts of meanness and violence that no normal person would commit.

60 The present crisis in race relations has characteristics that come to the forefront in any period of social transition. The guardians of the status quo lash out with denunciation against the person or organization that they consider most responsible for the emergence of the new order. Often this denunciation
65 rises to major proportions. In the transition form slavery to restricted emancipation Abraham Lincoln was assassinated. In the present transition from segregation to desegregation the Supreme Court is castigated and the NAACP is maligned and subjected to extralegal reprisals.

70 This is a great hour for the Negro. The challenge is here. To become the instruments of a great idea is a privilege that history gives only occasionally. Arnold Toynbee says in *A Study of History* that it may be the Negro who will give the new spiritual dynamic to Western civilization that it so
75 desperately needs to survive. I hope this is possible. The spiritual power that the Negro can radiate to the world comes from love, understanding, good will, and nonviolence, so to challenge the nations of the world that they will seriously seek an alternative to war and destruction. In a day when
80 Sputniks and Explorers dash through outer space and guided ballistic missiles are carving highways of death through the stratosphere, nobody can win a war. Today the choice is no longer between violence and nonviolence. It is either nonviolence or nonexistence. The Negro may be God's appeal
85 to this age—an age drifting rapidly to its doom. The eternal appeal takes the form of a warning: "All who take the sword will perish by the sword."

13. The author's description of America's "schizophrenic personality" (line 2) refers to his belief that

(A) racial inequality can be viewed as an American disease

(B) this nation is dramatically split on the issue of racial segregation

(C) the practice of segregation is contradictory to the ideals of democracy that define America

(D) segregation is immoral, and therefore America must transform itself into an ethical society

(E) segregation is an illusion that has clouded the judgment of many otherwise well-meaning individuals

GO ON TO THE NEXT PAGE

14. In the first paragraph, the contradiction that "disturbed the consciences of whites" (line 10) was

(A) the inconsistency of Dr. King's attitude as the leader of the Civil Rights movement

(B) the fact that the Supreme Court internally advocated desegregation, but passed laws that perpetuated segregation

(C) the fact that the principles of democracy and Christianity have little in common

(D) the fact that discrimination is rampant in a society that outwardly preaches equality

(E) differences in the attitudes of African Americans towards segregation in the North and the South

15. The passage suggests that as a result of the Supreme Court's decision (lines 13-14)

(A) the Civil Rights movement could be temporarily suspended

(B) schools were prevented from excluding students on the basis of skin color

(C) African Americans, inspired by the decision, became more involved in the educational system

(D) the political discontent in Asia and Africa intensified and spread to other regions

(E) the number of white supremacist groups in the South increased

16. In line 19 "deny" most nearly means

(A) dispute

(B) contradict

(C) disbelieve

(D) withhold from

(E) declare untrue

17. The third paragraph (lines 24-31) primarily emphasizes that

(A) society needs to concentrate on international issues before addressing domestic concerns

(B) the problems in Asia and Africa have received more international attention than the struggle for racial equality in America

(C) in order for freedom and human dignity to flourish, discontent needs to be suppressed

(D) the motivations for freedom are universal since the struggles in Africa and Asia are virtually identical

(E) the African Americans' struggle is not an isolated occurrence

18. The feature that distinguishes the "new order" (line 38) from the "older order" (line 40) is best described as which of the following?

(A) The older order has less democratic perceptions, believing that certain groups should be controlled by others.

(B) The new order is interested only in seizing social and political power by nonviolent means.

(C) The older order concerns itself only with issues that apply to the domestic situation and ignores matters of international importance.

(D) The new order consists of members whose affiliation with the NAACP and Montgomery Protesters has heightened their respectability.

(E) The older order cannot understand the arch-traditionalists who endorse a more resistant approach to minorities.

19. The author would consider which of the following responsible for the crisis mentioned in line 41 ?

(A) Supreme Court decisions that were unpopular with the majority of Americans

(B) conflict between the ideals of democracy and the realities of segregated society

(C) oppressed African Americans who stood up for the equal rights they deserved

(D) legislation that might have prevented the violence but was vetoed by the President

(E) intentional sabotage by alienated church leaders

20. In line 48, "resistance" most nearly means

(A) denial

(B) opposition

(C) underground

(D) distinction

(E) power

21. According to the author, "underprivileged and uneducated whites" (lines 56-57) act against integration by

(A) subtly ignoring the African American community in hopes that it might disintegrate

(B) engaging in haphazard acts of cruelty and destruction

(C) petitioning against any governmental agency that talks of "interposition"

(D) abusing officials who spread lies and half-truths that mislead the public

(E) issuing pleas to the government to block integration laws that would lead to mixed communities

GO ON TO THE NEXT PAGE

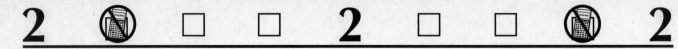

22. It can be inferred that the author compares the assassination of Abraham Lincoln with the castigation of the Supreme Court (lines 65-69) in order to

(A) indicate that absence of morality during the Civil War

(B) denounce white supremacists as racists who are unwilling to change in spite of recent constitutional amendments

(C) prove that the Supreme Court justices installed during Lincoln's tenure were exemplary

(D) warn the Supreme Court justices about possible assassination attempts

(E) emphasize that the current response to the change in race relations is similar to that of the past

23. The author cites Toynbee's *A Study of History* in order to

(A) suggest that African Americans may contribute something of value to Western civilization

(B) predict the imminent destruction of American civilization

(C) extol the efforts of Abraham Lincoln to abolish slavery

(D) demonstrate that spirituality is a direct result of nonviolent resistance

(E) establish that the constant pressures of discrimination have suppressed the spirituality of African Americans

24. The author would be most likely to agree with which of the following?

(A) Abraham Lincoln was assassinated because he advocated restrictions on emancipation.

(B) The threat of "war and destruction" is due to the racist policies of the United States.

(C) The principles of American democracy will never be perfectly realized.

(D) The Supreme Court's decision to desegregate public schools had impacts outside of the field of education.

(E) Public officials are irresponsible and can no longer be trusted to be honest with citizens.

STOP

If you finish before time is called, you may check your work on this section only.
Do not turn to any other section in the test.

NO TEST MATERIAL ON THIS PAGE.

SECTION 3
Time — 25 minutes
20 Questions

Turn to Section 3 of your answer sheet to answer the questions in this section.

Directions: For this section, solve each problem and decide which is the best of the choices given. Fill in the corresponding circle on the answer sheet. You may use any available space for scratchwork.

Notes

1. The use of a calculator is permitted.

2. All numbers used are real numbers.

3. Figures that accompany problems in this test are intended to provide information useful in solving the problems. They are drawn as accurately as possible EXCEPT when it is stated in a specific problem that the figure is not drawn to scale. All figures lie in a plane unless otherwise indicated.

4. Unless otherwise specified, the domain of any function f is assumed to be the set of all real numbers x for which $f(x)$ is a real number.

Reference Information

  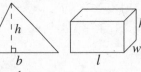 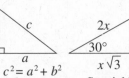

$A = \pi r^2$ $A = lw$ $A = \frac{1}{2}bh$ $V = lwh$ $V = \pi r^2 h$ $c^2 = a^2 + b^2$

Special Right Triangles

The number of degrees of arc in a circle is 360.

The sum of the measures in degrees of the angles of a triangle is 180.

1. If $3x + 1 = 19$, then $6x - 2 =$

   (A)   6
   (B)   12
   (C)   34
   (D)   38
   (E)   40

2. The average (arithmetic mean) of a student's grades on four history tests is 86. If the student received two grades of 83 and one of 85, what grade did the student receive on the fourth test?

   (A)   95
   (B)   93
   (C)   90
   (D)   89
   (E)   88

GO ON TO THE NEXT PAGE

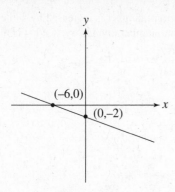

3. Which of the following equations defines the line in the *xy* coordinate system above?

(A) $y = -\dfrac{1}{3}x - 2$

(B) $y = -\dfrac{1}{2}x - 3$

(C) $y = -2x - 3$

(D) $y = -2x + 3$

(E) $y = -3x - 2$

4. Set *A* consists of all integers such that each element is equal to its square. How many elements are in set *A* ?

(A) Zero
(B) One
(C) Two
(D) Three
(E) Four

5. If $a^3 = 4$, what is the value of a^6 ?

(A) 8
(B) 10
(C) 12
(D) 16
(E) 64

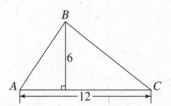

6. If the area of $\triangle ABC$ above is equal to the area of a square with side of length *x*, then *x* =

(A) 6
(B) $6\sqrt{2}$
(C) 9
(D) 12
(E) $12\sqrt{3}$

GO ON TO THE NEXT PAGE

7. If $x > 0 > y$, which of the following inequalities must be true?

(A) $x^3 > y^3$

(B) $x^2 < y^2$

(C) $x - y < 0$

(D) $\dfrac{1}{x^2} < \dfrac{1}{y^2}$

(E) $\dfrac{1}{x} < \dfrac{1}{y}$

8. If $f(x) = |x - 4|$, which of the following has the LEAST value?

(A) $f(8)$
(B) $f(4)$
(C) $f(0)$
(D) $f(-4)$
(E) $f(-8)$

9. When a certain number is increased by 4, the result is equal to that number divided by 7. What is the number?

(A) $-\dfrac{14}{3}$

(B) $-\dfrac{2}{3}$

(C) $\dfrac{4}{7}$

(D) $\dfrac{2}{3}$

(E) $\dfrac{14}{3}$

10. In square $PQRS$, point T is the midpoint of side $\overline{QR}$. If the area of $PQRS$ is 3, what is the area of quadrilateral $PQTS$?

(A) $\dfrac{3}{2}$

(B)   2

(C) $\dfrac{9}{4}$

(D) $\dfrac{3\sqrt{3}}{2}$

(E) $2\sqrt{3}$

GO ON TO THE NEXT PAGE →

11. Ron has a bucket of red, white, and blue marbles. The number of red marbles is two more than the number of blue marbles, and the number of white marbles is twice the number of red marbles. Which of the following could be the total number of marbles?

(A) 24
(B) 25
(C) 26
(D) 27
(E) 28

12. If $a = f - 2$ and $b = 4f + 5$, which of the following is an expression for b in terms of a ?

(A) $4a - 4$
(B) $4a$
(C) $4a + 2$
(D) $4a + 7$
(E) $4a + 13$

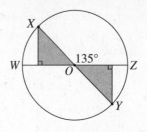

13. In the circle with center O, $\overline{WZ}$ and $\overline{XY}$ are diameters with lengths of 12. What is the area of the shaded region?

(A) 36
(B) 30
(C) 18
(D) 12
(E)   9

14. If x and y are positive integers, $(3^x)^y = 81$, and $3^x + 3^y = 84$, which of the following could be the value of x ?

(A) 2
(B) 3
(C) 4
(D) 5
(E) 6

GO ON TO THE NEXT PAGE

15. A triangle has vertices at points A, B, and C, which are located at $(1, 0)$, $(-3, 0)$, and $(0, 5)$ respectively. What is the distance from the midpoint of $\overline{AB}$ to point C ?

(A) 3

(B) 5

(C) $\sqrt{26}$

(D) $\sqrt{29}$

(E) $\dfrac{\sqrt{26} + \sqrt{34}}{2}$

16. In the function $f(x) = \left(x^c\right)\left(x^{\frac{1}{c}}\right)$, c is a nonzero constant. If $f(2) = 4\sqrt{2}$, what is the value of c ?

(A)   2
(B)   3
(C)   4
(D)   16
(E)   32

17. The cost for coal from a certain company is \$15 for the first pound plus \$6 for each additional pound of coal. Which of the following functions gives the total cost, in dollars, for p pounds of coal?

(A) $C(p) = 6p - 15$
(B) $C(p) = 6p - 9$
(C) $C(p) = 6p$
(D) $C(p) = 6p + 9$
(E) $C(p) = 6p + 15$

18. If the members of set A are all the odd single-digit positive integers and the members of set B are all the prime integers, which of the following is the set of numbers common to both set A and set B ?

(A) $\{1, 3, 5, 7\}$
(B) $\{1, 3, 5, 7, 9\}$
(C) $\{2, 3, 5, 7\}$
(D) $\{3, 5, 7\}$
(E) $\{3, 5, 7, 9\}$

GO ON TO THE NEXT PAGE

19. The sum of 8 positive integers is 31. If no individual integer value can appear more than twice in the list of 8 integers, what is the greatest possible value one of these integers can have?

(A) 16
(B) 15
(C) 10
(D) 9
(E) 7

20. Line q is given by the equation $y = -x + 8$, and line r is given by the equation $4y = 3x - 24$. If line r intersects the y-axis at point A, line q intersects the y-axis at point B, and both lines intersect the x-axis at point C, what is the area of $\triangle ABC$?

(A) 14
(B) 24
(C) 48
(D) 56
(E) 112

STOP

If you finish before time is called, you may check your work on this section only.
Do not turn to any other section in the test.

SECTION 4
Time — 25 minutes
35 Questions

Turn to Section 4 of your answer sheet to answer the questions in this section.

Directions: For each question in this section, select the best answer from among the choices given and fill in the corresponding circle on the answer sheet.

The following sentences test correctness and effectiveness of expression. Part of each sentence or the entire sentence is underlined; beneath each sentence are five ways of phrasing the underlined material. Choice A repeats the original phrasing; the other four choices are different. If you think the original phrasing produces a better sentence than any of the alternatives, select choice A; if not, select one of the other choices.

In making your selection, follow the requirements of standard written English; that is, pay attention to grammar, choice of words, sentence construction, and punctuation. Your selection should result in the most effective sentence—clear and precise, without awkwardness or ambiguity.

EXAMPLE:

Bobby Flay baked his first cake <u>and he was thirteen years old then</u>.

(A) and he was thirteen years old then
(B) when he was thirteen
(C) at age thirteen years old
(D) upon the reaching of thirteen years
(E) at the time when he was thirteen

1. The teacher's enthusiasm and obvious passion for the subject inspired <u>students and before they had never been interested in Shakespeare</u>.

   (A) students and before they had never been interested in Shakespeare
   (B) students, and they had never before been interested in Shakespeare
   (C) students; before that they had never been interested in Shakespeare
   (D) students who had never before been interested in Shakespeare
   (E) students that Shakespeare had never before interested them

2. In the last twenty years, despite the chauvinism of European connoisseurs, California wines <u>are respected throughout the world</u>.

   (A) are respected throughout the world
   (B) are becoming better respected throughout the world
   (C) which have gained respect throughout the world
   (D) have gained respect throughout the world
   (E) have since become respected throughout the world

3. In an effort to rouse her unconscious son, <u>Mrs. Simpson shaked him and called out his name</u>.

   (A) Mrs. Simpson shaked him and called out his name
   (B) shaking him, Mrs. Simpson called out his name
   (C) Mrs. Simpson shook him and called out his name
   (D) he was shaken and his name was called out by Mrs. Simpson
   (E) he was shaken by Mrs. Simpson, who called out his name

4. <u>As it is best known for its winter activities, which include skiing, skating, and sledding</u>, the resort also has a complete summer program.

   (A) As it is best known for its winter activities, which include skiing, skating, and sledding
   (B) Best known for its winter activities, which include both skiing and skating, as well as sledding
   (C) Best known for its winter activities, which include skiing, skating, and the riding of sleds
   (D) By being best known for its winter activities, which include skiing, skating, and sledding
   (E) Best known for its winter activities, which include skiing, skating, and sledding

5. Because the flight was non-stop, <u>and so they were able to sleep for a number of hours</u>.

   (A) and so they were able to sleep for a number of hours
   (B) therefore for a number of hours they slept
   (C) they were able to sleep for a number of hours
   (D) therefore they were sleeping for a number of hours
   (E) sleeping for a number of hours was possible for them

GO ON TO THE NEXT PAGE

6. Although the director closes it on Sundays during the summer <u>and conducting tours only twice a week</u>, the museum is still a popular tourist attraction.

   (A) and conducting tours only twice a week
   (B) and is conducting tours only twice a week
   (C) and conducts tours twice a week
   (D) and twice a week conducts tours only
   (E) and conducts tours only twice a week

7. If mixed with a weak acid in a sealed container, <u>you can get an explosion from baking soda.</u>

   (A) you can get an explosion from baking soda
   (B) baking soda can explode
   (C) you could be getting an explosion from baking soda
   (D) baking soda, it can explode
   (E) then baking soda could be exploding

8. <u>Manet's work had a profound impact on his contemporaries</u>, including famous Impressionists such as Monet and Renoir.

   (A) Manet's work had a profound impact on his contemporaries
   (B) Manet's work had profoundly impacted his contemporaries
   (C) Manet profoundly influenced his contemporaries through his work
   (D) The work of Manet was profound on his contemporaries in its impact
   (E) Many of his contemporaries had felt the profound impact of the work of Manet

9. The testing procedures of the Food and Drug Administration <u>is an obstacle course which any new drug and its makers must run</u> before the drug is approved for sale to the public.

   (A) is an obstacle course which any new drug and its makers must run
   (B) are like an obstacle course through which any new drug and its maker must run
   (C) are an obstacle course run by its makers
   (D) which must be run as an obstacle course by any new drug
   (E) runs an obstacle course for any new drug

10. <u>Having lived there as a child, the street looked vaguely familiar to Judy.</u>

   (A) Having lived there as a child, the street looked vaguely familiar to Judy.
   (B) Having lived there as a child, Judy found the street to be vaguely familiar.
   (C) Living there as a child, the street was found by Judy to be vaguely familiar.
   (D) Living there as a child, Judy found the street vaguely familiar to her.
   (E) Judy lived there as a child, so to her the street was found to be vaguely familiar.

11. The major areas of medicine in which lasers are effective <u>is in the cutting and closing of blood vessels, and in the destruction of tumors</u>.

   (A) is in the cutting and closing of blood vessels, and in the destruction of tumors
   (B) are the cutting and closing of blood vessels, and also the case of destroying tumors
   (C) are the cutting, closing of blood vessels, and in the destroying of tumors
   (D) are the cutting and closing of blood vessels, and the destroying of tumors
   (E) is in the cutting and closing of blood vessels, and the destruction of tumors

GO ON TO THE NEXT PAGE

The following sentences test your ability to recognize grammar and usage errors. Each sentence contains either a single error or no error at all. No sentence contains more than one error. The error, if there is one, is underlined and lettered. If the sentence contains an error, select the one underlined part that must be changed to make the sentence correct. If the sentence is correct, select choice E. In choosing answers, follow the requirements of standard written English.

EXAMPLE:

The <u>other</u> players and <u>her</u> <u>significantly</u> improved
    A   B   C

the game plan <u>created by</u> the coaches. <u>No error</u>
               D   E

Ⓐ ● Ⓒ Ⓓ Ⓔ

12. <u>Considering</u> how close the cafe was to his house, it is
   A

   <u>surprising that</u>, even though <u>he enjoyed</u> the ambiance,
      B   C

   Chris hardly <u>never visited</u> it. <u>No error</u>
              D   E

13. The trees <u>in</u> Bob's backyard <u>are</u> much
        A   B

   <u>taller and greener</u> than <u>Henry</u>. <u>No error</u>
      C   D   E

14. <u>To understand fully</u> William Shakespeare's body of work
     A

   we must analyze <u>not only</u> his most famous plays such
             B

   as *Hamlet*, <u>but also</u> his <u>lesser known</u> plays, poems, and
            C   D

   sonnets. <u>No error</u>
         E

15. <u>Last night</u> was not the first time Charles was exposed
     A

   <u>to her culinary</u> skills; Christine, a first-rate chef,
        B

   <u>has cooked</u> for him last week <u>as well</u>. <u>No error</u>
      C   D   E

16. Although the advertised price of a car may

   <u>seem reasonable</u>, <u>the addition of</u> dealer preparation fees,
      A   B

   required options, <u>taxes, and delivery</u> charges may make
                 C

   the actual cost less attractive to a <u>prospective</u> buyer.
                            D

   <u>No error</u>
     E

17. <u>Also allowed</u> by the newer and more liberal investment
     A

   law <u>was</u> tax shelters, now <u>commonly used</u> by people
       B   C

   <u>of all classes</u>. <u>No error</u>
      D   E

18. <u>While it may</u> appear that stewardesses are
     A

   <u>concerned solely to</u> passengers' comfort, they <u>are in fact</u>
      B   C

   extensively <u>schooled</u> in flight safety. <u>No error</u>
           D   E

19. <u>After</u> dining on fish <u>from both</u> the Atlantic and Pacific
     A   B

   oceans, <u>I have decided</u> that Seattle's fish are superior to
         C

   Cape Cod. <u>No error</u>
     D   E

GO ON TO THE NEXT PAGE →

20. <u>Whenever</u> Diana returns to the office after a long
      A

    vacation, <u>she</u> finds <u>it</u> disorganized, dirty, and
           B   C

    <u>an ugly place.</u> <u>No error</u>
        D   E

21. <u>While</u> the United States <u>may be lagging</u> behind Asia
      A   B

    in the electronics market and Europe in the automobile

    market, <u>we are</u> still a <u>leading</u> agricultural nation.
            C   D

    <u>No error</u>
      E

22. The newspaper reporter enjoys reading the essays

    <u>of</u> Orwell <u>during</u> his free time for <u>their</u> clarity,
    A   B   C

    conciseness, and <u>because they are persuasive.</u> <u>No error</u>
                      D   E

23. After we had skipped <u>our</u> second class of the week,
                    A

    the <u>principal</u> called <u>Thomas and I</u> down to her office
        B   C

    <u>for a conference.</u> <u>No error</u>
      D   E

24. Students who wish to become <u>a doctor</u> must begin
                   A

    planning <u>their</u> studies <u>long before</u> they <u>apply to</u>
         B   C   D

    medical school. <u>No error</u>
               E

25. During the past several decades, <u>as</u> "super stores"
                        A

    and national franchises have gained popularity, many

    <u>locally owned</u> small businesses <u>are closing</u> <u>because of</u>
      B   C   D

    the overwhelming competition. <u>No error</u>
                        E

26. Although <u>his term</u> <u>was much shorter</u> <u>than that of later</u>
            A   B   C

    presidents, <u>President Lincoln instituted</u> the income tax,
               D

    the draft, and the Thanksgiving holiday. <u>No error</u>
                          E

27. The <u>recently lowered</u> interest <u>rates allowed</u> my
         A   B

    <u>wife and me</u> to buy a <u>larger home</u> for our family.
      C   D

    <u>No error</u>
      E

28. Neither of America's major political parties <u>are interested</u>
                            A

    <u>in making</u> the <u>trade balance</u> an important issue
      B   C

    <u>in the recent</u> elections. <u>No error</u>
      D   E

29. Only after the Air Force <u>had ran</u> out of
                    A

    <u>other options</u> did it consider <u>launching</u> the new satellite
      B   C

    <u>from the space shuttle.</u> <u>No error</u>
      D   E

GO ON TO THE NEXT PAGE

Directions: The following passage is an early draft of an essay. Some parts of the passage need to be rewritten.

Read the passage and select the best answers for the questions that follow. Some questions are about particular sentences or parts of sentences and ask you to improve sentence structure or word choice. Other questions ask you to consider organization and development. In choosing answers, follow the requirements of standard written English.

Questions 30-35 are based on the following passage.

(1) Starting on January 1, Bakersfield High School is planning to implement a dress code. (2) The administration has printed out a list of those items that students will be allowed to wear to school and those that will be considered unacceptable. (3) Even though I understand that the school had good intentions, I think that it is a bad idea overall.

(4) There are a number of problems with the dress code. (5) The rule against clothes that are "torn, ripped, or cut off" discriminates against many students. (6) Some students cannot afford to buy new clothes every year. (7) In the late spring and early summer, students forced to wear long pants will be so uncomfortable that they will not be able to concentrate on their studies. (8) Although girls can stay cool in skirts and dresses, boys have no such option.

(9) Even so, a dress code violates students' freedom of expression. (10) Students should be able to dress themselves in a way that expresses their tastes and creativity. (11) It is only through making decisions about ourselves and how we choose to present ourselves that we will grow into mature, independent adults.

30. In context, which version of the underlined section of sentence 2 (reproduced below) is the best?

    The administration has printed out a list of those items that students will be allowed to wear to <u>school and those that will be considered unacceptable</u>.

    (A) (as it is now)
    (B) school. Those that will be considered unacceptable
    (C) school; others that will be considered unacceptable
    (D) school as well as unacceptable clothing
    (E) school, and others that will not be considered acceptable

31. In sentence 3, the word "it" could best be replaced with which of the following?

    (A) the administration
    (B) the dress code
    (C) the list
    (D) the intention
    (E) the school

32. Which of the following is the best version of the underlined portion of sentence 9 (reproduced below)?

    Even so, a dress code violates students' freedom of expression.

    (A) (As it is now)
    (B) Most importantly,
    (C) To the extent that
    (D) It is true that
    (E) That notwithstanding,

33. Which of the following, if added immediately after sentence 11, would provide the best concluding sentence for the passage?

    (A) As near-adults, we should be allowed to decide how to dress ourselves.
    (B) In today's society, teenagers are required to make decisions about a number of extremely important issues.
    (C) Thus, the dress code will ultimately impede the educational process rather than aid it.
    (D) It is for a student and his or her parents to decide what clothing a student should wear, not a school administration.
    (E) If we must have a dress code, it should be one that does not discriminate against students on the basis of their gender or income level.

GO ON TO THE NEXT PAGE

34. The author's argument would be more balanced if it included a section on which of the following?

   (A) An outline of the steps that students will take to overturn the dress code, should it be implemented

   (B) A list of other bureaucratic policies that have angered students in the past

   (C) A discussion of the author's own clothing preferences

   (D) An acknowledgment of the positive aspects of the dress-code policy

   (E) The suggestion that the dress code be limited to ninth graders

35. In context, which of the following is the best way to revise the underlined wording in order to combine sentences 5 and 6 ?

The rule against clothes that are "torn, ripped or cut off" discriminates <u>against many students. Some students cannot afford to buy new clothes every year.</u>

   (A) against many students, some students cannot afford to buy new clothes every year.

   (B) against many of those students who cannot buy new clothes every year because they cannot afford it.

   (C) against students, many of which cannot afford to buy new clothes every year.

   (D) against those students who cannot afford to buy new clothes every year.

   (E) against many of the students being unable to afford to buy new clothes every year.

STOP

If you finish before time is called, you may check your work on this section only.
Do not turn to any other section in the test.

SECTION 5
Time — 25 minutes
18 Questions

Turn to Section 5 of your answer sheet to answer the questions in this section.

Directions: This section contains two types of questions. You have 25 minutes to complete both types. For questions 1-8, solve each problem and decide which is the best of the choices given. Fill in the corresponding circle on the answer sheet. You may use any available space for scratchwork.

Notes

1. The use of a calculator is permitted.

2. All numbers used are real numbers.

3. Figures that accompany problems in this test are intended to provide information useful in solving the problems. They are drawn as accurately as possible EXCEPT when it is stated in a specific problem that the figure is not drawn to scale. All figures lie in a plane unless otherwise indicated.

4. Unless otherwise specified, the domain of any function f is assumed to be the set of all real numbers x for which $f(x)$ is a real number.

Reference Information

  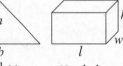 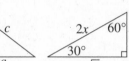

$A = \pi r^2$ $A = lw$
$C = 2\pi r$ $A = \frac{1}{2}bh$ $V = lwh$ $V = \pi r^2 h$ $c^2 = a^2 + b^2$ Special Right Triangles

The number of degrees of arc in a circle is 360.

The sum of the measures in degrees of the angles of a triangle is 180.

6, 12, 24, 48, . . .

1. Which of the following expressions represents the nth term in the sequence above?

(A) $2 \cdot 6^n$
(B) $2 \cdot 6^{n-1}$
(C) $6 \cdot 2^{n-1}$
(D) $6 \cdot n$
(E) $6 \cdot n^2$

2. If $3d - 2q = 17$ and $2d + 2q = -32$, what is the value of $10d$?

(A)   3
(B)   −3
(C)   −13
(D)   −15
(E)   −30

GO ON TO THE NEXT PAGE

3. Which of the following has the same area as a circle with an area of 16π ?

   (A) A circle with a radius of 4π
   (B) A circle with a circumference of 32π
   (C) A circle with a radius of 8
   (D) A circle with a diameter of 4
   (E) A circle with a circumference of 8π

$$f(x) = x^2 - 5$$

4. If $y = f(x)$, which of the following represents all possible values of y ?

   (A) $y < 5$
   (B) $y \geq -5$
   (C) $y < -5$
   (D) $y > 5$
   (E) All real numbers

5. Set A consists of all even integers from 1 to 100, inclusive. If a number is selected at random from set A, what is the probability that the number is less than 40 ?

   (A) $\dfrac{19}{50}$

   (B) $\dfrac{39}{100}$

   (C) $\dfrac{2}{5}$

   (D) $\dfrac{31}{50}$

   (E) $\dfrac{9}{10}$

6. In a certain game, different colored tokens are worth different numbers of points. A blue token and a red token together are worth a total of 12 points, a blue token and a green token together are worth a total of 13 points, and a red token and a green token together are worth a total of 15 points. How many points is a blue token worth?

   (A) 5 points
   (B) 6 points
   (C) 7 points
   (D) 8 points
   (E) 9 points

GO ON TO THE NEXT PAGE

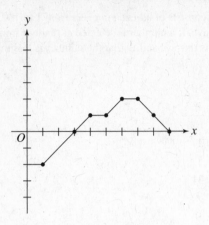

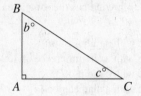

Note: Figure not drawn to scale.

7. The figure above shows the graph of $y = f(x)$, where f is a function. If $f(c) = f\left(\dfrac{c}{3}\right)$, which of the following could be the value of c ?

(A) 3
(B) 5
(C) 6
(D) 8
(E) 9

8. In $\triangle ABC$ above, $AB < AC$. Which of the following must be true?

(A) $AC > BC$
(B) $AC = BC$
(C) $b > c$
(D) $b = 90$
(E) $c = 45$

GO ON TO THE NEXT PAGE ➡

Directions: For Student-Produced Response questions 9-18, use the grids at the bottom of the answer sheet page on which you have answered questions 1-8.

Each of the remaining 10 questions requires you to solve the problem and enter your answer by marking the circles in the special grid, as shown in the examples below. You may use any available space for scratch work.

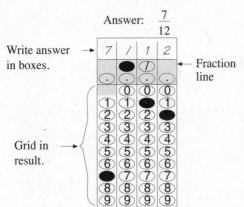

Answer: $\frac{7}{12}$

Write answer in boxes.

Fraction line

Grid in result.

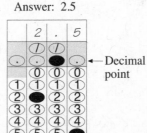

Answer: 2.5

Decimal point

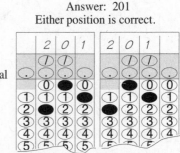

Answer: 201
Either position is correct.

Note: You may start your answers in any column, space permitting. Columns not needed should be left blank.

• Mark no more than one circle in any column.

• Because the answer document will be machine-scored, **you will receive credit only if the circles are filled in correctly.**

• Although not required, it is suggested that you write your answer in the boxes at the top of the columns to help you fill in the circles accurately.

• Some problems may have more than one correct answer. In such cases, grid only one answer.

• No question has a negative answer.

• **Mixed numbers** such as $3\frac{1}{2}$ must be gridded as

3.5 or 7/2. (If [3 1 / 2] is gridded, it will be

interpreted as $\frac{31}{2}$, not $3\frac{1}{2}$.)

• **Decimal Answers:** If you obtain a decimal answer with more digits than the grid can accommodate, it may be either rounded or truncated, but it must fill the entire grid. For example, if you obtain an answer such as 0.6666..., you should record your result as .666 or .667. **A less accurate value such as .66 or .67 will be scored as incorrect.**

Acceptable ways to grid $\frac{2}{3}$ are:

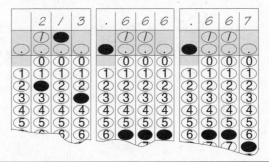

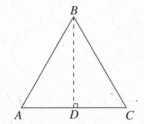

Note: Figure not drawn to scale.

9. If the area of $\triangle ABC$ is 40 and $AC = 10$, what is BD ?

10. If $f(x) = 2x - 10$, then $f(5) =$

GO ON TO THE NEXT PAGE ⟹

11. Sixty percent of Gateway High School's 300 students are female, and sixty percent of Riverdale High School's 400 students are male. How many more female students attend Gateway than attend Riverdale?

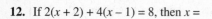

12. If $2(x + 2) + 4(x - 1) = 8$, then $x =$

13. If $3^{x+1} = 9^2$, what is the value of x^2 ?

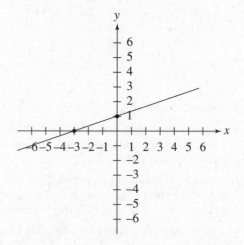

14. What is the slope of the line in the xy-coordinate system above?

GO ON TO THE NEXT PAGE ➡

15. If $n + \dfrac{n}{2} = \dfrac{n+1}{2}$, then $n =$

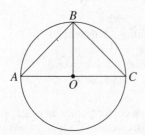

Note: Figure not drawn to scale.

16. In the figure above, $\overline{AC}$ is a diameter of the circle with center O. If the circumference of the circle is 32π, and the length of $\overline{AB}$ is 16, what is the degree measure of $\angle BAC$? (Disregard the degree symbol when gridding your answer.)

17. It took Garth $1\dfrac{1}{2}$ times as long to drive to the beach as it took him to drive home. If the trip was 60 miles in each direction and the total driving time for the round trip was $3\dfrac{1}{3}$ hours, what was Garth's average speed in miles per hour on the way to the beach?

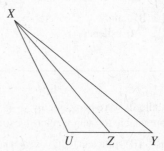

Note: Figure not drawn to scale.

18. If the length of $\overline{UZ}$ is 30 percent of the length of $\overline{UY}$ and the area of ΔXYZ is 210, what is the area of ΔUXZ ?

STOP

If you finish before time is called, you may check your work on this section only.
Do not turn to any other section in the test.

SECTION 6
Time — 25 minutes
24 Questions

Directions: For each question in this section, select the best answer from among the choices given and fill in the corresponding circle on the answer sheet.

Each sentence below has one or two blanks, each blank indicating that something has been omitted. Beneath the sentence are five words or sets of words labeled A through E. Choose the word or set of words that, when inserted in the sentence, <u>best</u> fits the meaning of the sentence as a whole.

Example:

Desiring to ------- his taunting friends, Mitch gave them taffy in hopes it would keep their mouths shut.

(A) eliminate   (B) satisfy   (C) overcome
  (D) ridicule   (E) silence

Ⓐ Ⓑ Ⓒ Ⓓ ●

---

1. The new landlords were hampered by ------- resources and therefore unable to finance extensive improvements.

   (A) various   (B) sufficient   (C) inadequate
     (D) invalid   (E) fiscal

2. It was Mrs. Smedley's opinion that her daughter would ------- herself by marrying someone so obviously beneath her.

   (A) confuse   (B) indulge   (C) glorify
     (D) insinuate   (E) demean

3. The director did not consider her film ------- because her depiction of the sensitive topic was -------: it presented both sides of the issue fairly.

   (A) biased . . equitable
   (B) noteworthy . . balanced
   (C) challenging . . skewed
   (D) bombastic . . unconvincing
   (E) slanted . . apathetic

4. When Western contemporary art was first shown in Japan, Japanese artists were ------- it and sought to ------- its bold expressiveness.

   (A) oblivious to . . acquire
   (B) attracted to . . disclose
   (C) incensed by . . parallel
   (D) impressed by . . emulate
   (E) astonished by . . overrun

5. Nurses with ------- personalities were welcomed during the war because of their ability to uplift the dejected soldiers who were disabled.

   (A) winsome   (B) practical   (C) capricious
     (D) multifaceted   (E) cantankerous

GO ON TO THE NEXT PAGE

Directions: Each passage below is followed by questions based on its content. Answer the questions on the basis of what is <u>stated</u> or <u>implied</u> in each passage and in any introductory material that may be provided.

Questions 6-7 are based on the following passage.

Though most people know the definition of the word "boycott," few know its origin. Named for Captain Charles Boycott, the word as we know it owes less to him than to Irish
Line nationalist Charles Parnell. Parnell organized Irish farmers
5 and convinced them to fix their rent rates. When Boycott refused, Parnell unleashed the power of the people. A band of hostile peasants forced the Captain's servants to leave. There were no laborers to gather the harvest and no stablemen to care for the animals. Boycott was not allowed to enter stores
10 or make purchases. Eventually, Boycott and his wife fled Ireland, and Parnell was hailed as the workingman's hero.

6. The passage is best summarized by which of the following?

    (A) The origin of a word is explored, and an explanation for its popularity is given.
    (B) A word is introduced, and a history of its usage is related.
    (C) The origin of a word is explored, and an unrelated story is told.
    (D) A word is introduced, and the history of its coining is related.
    (E) An event is described as the reason behind a shift in a word's meaning.

7. It can be most reasonably inferred from the passage that

    (A) Boycott's land was not harvested that year
    (B) the townspeople referred to were sympathetic to the farmers
    (C) Parnell was popular among all Irishmen
    (D) the farmers threatened Boycott with physical harm
    (E) the farmers would never have organized without Parnell's help

Questions 8-9 are based on the following passage.

Hans Christian Andersen's story, "The Little Mermaid," contrary to popular perception, doesn't end happily. Instead of marrying her prince, the mermaid fails and is changed into
Line sea foam. The fate of this character mirrors that of many of
5 Andersen's fairy tales; throughout the years, his works have changed dramatically. As in the children's game of telephone, multiple translations altered both the words and meanings of the texts. In addition, the tales were bowdlerized to meet Victorian standards: risqué situations and inappropriate
10 language were cut. Finally, publishers edited them to fit in illustrations. While there is no one cause for the many changes to Andersen's stories, the original meanings departed as surely as sea foam on the shore.

8. What is the main idea of the passage?

    (A) Unscrupulous publishers changed the story of "The Little Mermaid."
    (B) There are many different reasons that Andersen's tales have changed through the years.
    (C) Due to a number of factors, there can be no accurate version of a fairy tale.
    (D) The Victorians insisted that Andersen's stories be changed to suit their standards.
    (E) Happy endings in fairy tales are deceiving, as evidenced by "The Little Mermaid."

9. Sea foam is mentioned twice in the passage in order to

    (A) mirror Andersen's obsession with sea imagery through allegory
    (B) highlight a prevalent theme of loss and disappearance in the work of Hans Christian Andersen
    (C) suggest that Hans Christian Andersen's fairy tales disappeared quickly after they were written in the Victorian age
    (D) create a metaphor with the second citation which evokes the first time the word is used
    (E) prove that the modern ending of "The Little Mermaid" is as arbitrary as the original ending

GO ON TO THE NEXT PAGE

Questions 10-15 are based on the following passage.

The following passage describes one battle in the bloody Anglo-Zulu War of 1879.

On a windswept hillside near a towering fortress of rock known to the Zulu as Isandlwana, a proletarian army from the world's foremost capitalist nation was defeated by a part-time
Line force of peasant farmers in a short, bloody, and eventually
5 inconclusive battle that rocked the British empire to its core. The Zulus attacked the red-coated British because they feared for their land and their independence. The British soldiers, drawn from the very poorest level of the working classes, fought back because they had been lured, like Private Moss
10 from Wales, to "take the Queen's shilling," thus placing a strain on royal finances.

Neither side had a clue as to why they were involved in desperate battle, not even the officers—on either side. In the words of an old soldier's song; "We're here because we're
15 here."

With the hindsight of history, it is perhaps simplest to say that the African peasants were fighting to stop themselves from becoming the same as their red-coated adversaries: the working class of a new capitalist South Africa modeled
20 on Britain. Most of the British dearly wished they were somewhere else, like the private who wrote to his family: "I repent the day I took the shilling. I have not had a bed since I left England. We have only one blanket, and are out every night in the rain—no shelter."

25 For the British officers, most of them from the landed classes and raised at dehumanizing boarding schools such as Tom Brown's Rugby, the war in the far-flung corners of the empire was more of a game than a serious instrument of imperial policy. For the Zulu, it was a war fought to defend
30 land, homes and families against unprovoked aggression by the most powerful military force in the world.

A British army sergeant who arrived at the battlefield later "could not help crying to see so many of our poor comrades lying dead on the ground, when only a few hours before that
35 we left them all well and hearty. Oh, father, such a sight I never witnessed in my life before. I could not help crying to see how the poor fellows were massacred."

His use of the word "massacre" gives another insight to the colonial view of the war—in which Zulu victories were
40 usually referred to as "massacres"; while the British won "victories" over their enemies—destroying homesteads, shooting down thousands with volley fire or blowing them to bloody rags with artillery.

Nevertheless, the British authorities were hard put to
45 explain how an army of "savages" had inflicted such a shattering defeat on their forces, and the myth was created that, because of a lack of screwdrivers, soldiers were unable to open reserve ammunition boxes—whose lids were secured by as many as nine screws, some "rusted into the wood." In
50 truth, the lids of the Mark V and VI ammunition boxes used in the campaign were each secured by only a single brass screw.

It is unlikely many of the working class soldiers who died at Isandlwana would have agreed with such myths. A
55 better tribute to them and the Zulu dead was paid by Bishop Colenso in a sermon after the battle: "We ourselves have lost very many precious lives, and widows and orphans, parents, brothers, sisters, friends are mourning bitterly their sad bereavements. But are there no griefs—no relatives that
60 mourn their dead—in Zululand? Have we not heard how the wail has gone up in all parts of the country for those who have bravely and nobly died in repelling the invader and fighting for the King and fatherland? And shall we kill ten thousand more to avenge that dreadful day?"

10. The primary purpose of the passage is to

   (A) trace the specific reasons for British military action in South Africa
   (B) describe the British-Zulu conflict and discuss the motivations of both parties
   (C) disprove the myth that British-Zulu relations were amicable
   (D) point to the factors that incited strong loyalty on both sides of the British-Zulu conflict
   (E) present the history of British-Zulu relations

11. The author gives which of the following reasons for the lure felt by British soldiers such as Private Moss, in lines 7-11 ?

   (A) The thrill of battling the primitive Zulu tribe
   (B) The opportunity to show their loyalty to the Queen
   (C) The fear that the Zulus might seize their land and independence
   (D) The chance to make money from the country
   (E) The fact that war could be both a game and a serious instrument of imperial policy

GO ON TO THE NEXT PAGE

12. The author cites which of the following reasons for the appropriateness of the lyric, "We're here because we're here," mentioned in lines 14-15 ?

(A) The seemingly eternal nature of the war was paralleled in the repetition of the lyric.
(B) Blind obedience to superior officers caused the soldiers to regard their position as unchanging.
(C) The song served to rally the troops behind the Queen, enabling them to go forth to victory.
(D) The British soldiers' uncertainty about the reasons for their participation in the war.
(E) The song had once been the rallying cry of the Zulus.

13. The fourth paragraph primarily serves to illustrate the fact that

(A) war was a dehumanizing reality for both the British and the Zulus
(B) while the British officers saw the war as a diversion, the Zulus took the conflict quite seriously
(C) the British military force consisted mainly of aristocrats while the Zulu army was comprised of homeowners and family men
(D) Zulu tradition did not call for mourning of the dead
(E) the Zulus were prepared to continue the war until 10,000 more British soldiers had been slain

14. The British device of calling Zulu victories "massacres," mentioned in lines 39-40, points to

(A) the appalling brutality of the Zulus
(B) the need on the part of the British to elevate their stature above that of the Zulus
(C) the British tendency to avoid excessive violence when dealing with civilians
(D) the British inability to win strategic battles
(E) the Zulu's superior weaponry

15. In can be inferred that the "myth" mentioned in line 46 was created in order to

(A) appease the defeated Zulus and advocate for more funds for the military
(B) explain the uncivilized actions of the Zulu forces
(C) mollify those in England who could not comprehend that a less powerful army could defeat the British
(D) explain the British soldiers' inability to utilize all of their ammunition during the Anglo-Zulu war
(E) cast doubt on the accuracy of the author's description of British atrocities

GO ON TO THE NEXT PAGE

Questions 16-24 are based on the following passage.

The following passage discusses critical reactions, both contemporary and modern, to Russian writer Karolina Pavlova's A Double Life, *an innovative literary work.*

Published in 1848, *A Double Life* was Karolina Pavlova's most successful original work among critics and readers alike. Although her translations were highly praised throughout
Line her literary career, her poetry was usually greeted by critical
5 reviews. Even admiration of her verse was often mixed with personal ridicule. A woman poet who took her work as seriously as any man was, to put it mildly, an oddity. Parodies of Pavlova were not uncommon and were usually satires of *her* rather than of her poetry. For example, the poet and publisher
10 Nikolay Nekrasov, one of Pavlova's more disdainful critics, bemoaned "the possibility that women might want to give up jelly-boiling and pickle-making for philosophy and literature."

Apart from the problems that Pavlova faced as a female poet in a male-dominated literary world, she was also forced
15 to contend with the general animosity that the utilitarian literary critics of the time had for many poets. The golden age of romanticism, these critics claimed, had come to an end in the 1830s, and the 1840s were heralded by Belinsky as the "era of action." Other critics such as Nekrasov, Panaev, and
20 Dobrolyubov felt that poetry should be useful and that people had lost their taste for dreamy, escapist poetry. Those poets who did not address contemporary issues in their verse or whose poetry was distinguished more by the beautiful sounds of the words rather than the poetic content were treated
25 harshly by critics. Thus Pavlova wrote *A Double Life* at a difficult time for poetry in general.

While it is true that many poets of the 1840s were still closely bound to the romantic tradition, their work was nevertheless developing, surmounting its romantic beginnings
30 and striving toward more objective narration and the new possibilities of revealing the lyric "I" in poetry. The direction in which poetry was moving revealed how intense an influence prose had on poetry. The appearance of so-called "stories in verse" helped to keep poetry alive in a prose-
35 oriented literary world.

A Double Life encompasses several themes and contains a wide variety of poetic styles. It is a reasonably successful marriage of prose and verse—not a "story in verse" exactly, but rather a work within which poetry is on equal footing
40 with prose, with neither truly subordinate to the other. In *A Double Life*, Pavlova has plenty of room to create "art for art's sake" as well as to address a contemporary social problem for her generation: the education of society women. The main criticism that *A Double Life* received from both nineteenth-
45 and twentieth-century critics was that it lacked "substance." Critics did not consider the problem of women's education to be a problem at all, and certainly not of the same import as the oppression of Russia's peasant class, a popular topic among writers of the time. These critics obviously overlooked the point
50 of Pavlova's work. The issues Pavlova raises are not relevant only to women, but speak more generally to the intellectual shortcomings and spiritual emptiness of members of her class.

16. According to the passage, Pavlova was most successful as

(A) an innovator of poetic forms
(B) an economic revolutionary
(C) a cook and a baker
(D) a translator of others' work
(E) a teacher of philosophy and literature

17. It can be inferred that Panaev (line 19) would most likely prefer a literary work that

(A) was not written by a woman
(B) created an alternative reality superior to the actual one
(C) contained lots of action and exciting plot twists
(D) had harsh, discordant sounds and images
(E) sought to offer solutions to current social problems

18. All of the following are true about the poets of the 1840s (line 27) EXCEPT

(A) their work was judged differently than it would have been a decade earlier
(B) they were unwilling to develop beyond the romantic tradition
(C) they were interested in both lyrical and objective aspects of poetry
(D) they had strong roots in the romantic past
(E) their poetry was often influenced by contemporary trends in prose

19. What is the function of the third paragraph (lines 27-35) ?

(A) It stresses the way in which Pavlova's work stood out from that of her contemporaries.
(B) It establishes that the 1840s was an extremely difficult time in which to write poetry.
(C) It lists what the utilitarians considered to be the attributes of poetry that lacks "substance."
(D) It creates an artistic background within which to understand *A Double Life*.
(E) It emphasizes the difficulties Pavlova faced as a female writer.

GO ON TO THE NEXT PAGE

20. According to the passage, a "story in verse" (line 38)

(A) was less objectionable to romantic critics than traditional poetry

(B) contains elements drawn from non-poetical works

(C) stresses class over issues such as gender and religion

(D) focuses on the narrative "I" to the exclusion of other characters

(E) was the most popular form of literature in the 1840s

21. It can be inferred that the critics mentioned in the final paragraph (lines 36-52) would have preferred Pavlova's work if she had

(A) written about the education of female peasants rather than society women

(B) focused more on artistic issues and ignored intellectual questions

(C) focused on issues such as class and politics

(D) been more concerned with goading the upper class into action

(E) explored the religious issues that were currently affecting Russia

22. In line 42, "address" most nearly means

(A) attend to

(B) situate in

(C) send to

(D) speak with

(E) leave space

23. Which of the following is a reason that the author disagrees with the criticism of Pavlova's work?

(A) The fact that the critics did not recognize the utilitarian thrust of Pavlova's work

(B) The critics' escapist attitude toward the realities of life for Russian peasants

(C) The critics' insistence that women are unable to write poetry as well as men

(D) The fact that the critics did not recognize Pavlova's skills as a translator

(E) The critics' inability to recognize Pavlova's wide ranging artistic and social interests

24. Which of the following, if true, would weaken the criticism leveled on *A Double Life*?

(A) The discovery that well-educated Russian society women were more concerned about the plight of the peasant class

(B) The fact that it was the most disdained blending of poetry and prose of any work of the 1840s

(C) A survey of readers of novels about society women that discovered the readers did not complain of spiritual emptiness

(D) A complaint by a peasant woman that *A Double Life* did not pertain to her life

(E) Proof that readers of the work were inspired to institute educational reform

STOP

If you finish before time is called, you may check your work on this section only.
Do not turn to any other section in the test.

SECTION 8
Time — 20 minutes
16 Questions

Directions: For this section, solve each problem and decide which is the best of the choices given. Fill in the corresponding circle on the answer sheet. You may use any available space for scratchwork.

Notes

1. The use of a calculator is permitted.

2. All numbers used are real numbers.

3. Figures that accompany problems in this test are intended to provide information useful in solving the problems. They are drawn as accurately as possible EXCEPT when it is stated in a specific problem that the figure is not drawn to scale. All figures lie in a plane unless otherwise indicated.

4. Unless otherwise specified, the domain of any function f is assumed to be the set of all real numbers x for which $f(x)$ is a real number.

Reference Information

$A = \pi r^2$ $A = lw$ $A = \frac{1}{2}bh$ $V = lwh$ $V = \pi r^2 h$ $c^2 = a^2 + b^2$ Special Right Triangles

The number of degrees of arc in a circle is 360.

The sum of the measures in degrees of the angles of a triangle is 180.

---

1. Which of the following numbers disproves the statement "A number that is divisible by 4 and 8 is also divisible by 12" ?

(A) 24
(B) 36
(C) 40
(D) 48
(E) 60

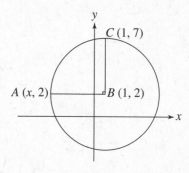

2. In the figure above, $\overline{AB}$ and $\overline{BC}$ are radii of the circle with center B. What is the value of x ?

(A) −5
(B) −4
(C) −3
(D) 3
(E) 7

GO ON TO THE NEXT PAGE

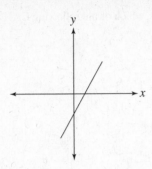

3. Which of the following equations could be represented by the line above?

(A) $y = 2x + 1$
(B) $y = 2x - 1$
(C) $y = -2x + 1$
(D) $y = -2x - 1$
(E) $y = -2x$

4. If, at a certain clothing store, three pairs of dress socks and four pairs of athletic socks cost a total of $27 and four pairs of dress socks and three pairs of athletic socks cost a total of $29, what is the combined cost of one pair of dress socks and one pair of athletic socks?

(A) $56
(B) $28
(C) $16
(D) $8
(E) $2

5. When the organizers of a bake sale sell brownies for $1.50 each, they sell 7 brownies every hour. When the brownies are sold for $2.00 each, 5 brownies are sold each hour. If x is the price per brownie in dollars, and f is the number of brownies sold per hour, then which of the following could represent f as a function of x?

(A) $f(x) = 4x + 1$
(B) $f(x) = 6x - 7$
(C) $f(x) = -3x + 11$
(D) $f(x) = -4x + 13$
(E) $f(x) = -6x + 16$

6. If $a < -1$ and $-1 < b < 0$, what are all of the possible values of ab?

(A) All negative numbers
(B) All negative numbers between -1 and 0
(C) All positive numbers less than 1
(D) All positive numbers greater than 1
(E) All positive numbers

GO ON TO THE NEXT PAGE

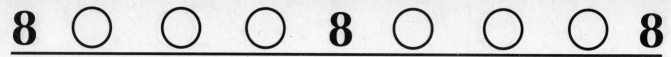
7. If p items can be purchased for 60 dollars, how many items can be purchased for w dollars?

(A) $\dfrac{wp}{60}$

(B) $\dfrac{w}{60p}$

(C) $\dfrac{60p}{w}$

(D) $\dfrac{60}{wp}$

(E) $\dfrac{60w}{p}$

9. If $f(-3) = 1$, which of the following CANNOT be $f(x)$?

(A) $f(x) = x^2 - 8$

(B) $f(x) = x^2 + 2x - 4$

(C) $f(x) = \dfrac{x^2 - 3}{-2x}$

(D) $f(x) = x^2 + 3x + 1$

(E) $f(x) = |x - 3| - 5$

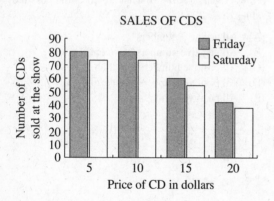

SALES OF CDS

Number of CDs sold at the show
Price of CD in dollars

Friday
Saturday

8. A musician goes on tour and sells CDs of his music. He varied the price of the CD on a nightly basis, kept track of how many were sold, and put this information in the graph above. Which of the following conclusions is best supported by the graph?

(A) Reducing the price of a CD will always increase the number of CDs sold.

(B) Above a certain price level, reducing the price of a CD will increase the number of CDs sold. Below that level reducing the price has no effect.

(C) The price of a CD has no effect on the number of CDs sold.

(D) Reducing the price of a CD will decrease the number of CDs sold.

(E) The price of the CD should be raised.

10. On her biology test, Cathy answered $\dfrac{5}{6}$ of the questions correctly. If Cathy answered 18 of the first 27 questions correctly, then the total number of questions on the test must be at <u>least</u>

(A) 32
(B) 36
(C) 45
(D) 48
(E) 54

GO ON TO THE NEXT PAGE

11. A rectangular box is constructed from ten square tiles, each of which has a perimeter of 24 centimeters. If the box is formed so that the tiles do not overlap, what is the volume of the box in cubic centimeters?

- A) 432
- (B) 288
- (C) 240
- (D) 216
- (E) 36

12. If $\dfrac{2x+10\sqrt{x}+12}{\sqrt{x}+3} = 3\sqrt{x}$, what is the value of x ?

- (A) 0
- (B) 2
- (C) 4
- (D) 9
- (E) 16

13. In a list of four positive even numbers, the mean, median, and mode are all equal. Which of the following CANNOT be done to the list if the mean, median, and mode are to remain equal?

- (A) Add one number to the list.
- (B) Add one number to the list that is greater than the mean.
- (C) Add two distinct numbers to the list.
- (D) Add 2 to each number in the list.
- (E) Remove the first and last numbers from the list.

14. Points L, M, and N lie in a plane. If the distance between L and M is 4, and the distance between M and N is 9, which of the following could be the distance between L and N ?

- I. 5
- II. 8
- III. 13

- (A) I only
- (B) II only
- (C) III only
- (D) I and III
- (E) I, II, and III

GO ON TO THE NEXT PAGE

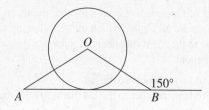

15. In the figure above, $\overline{AB}$ is tangent to the circle with center O, and $\overline{AO}$ is congruent to $\overline{OB}$. If the radius of the circle is 6, what is the area of $\triangle AOB$?

    (A) $18\sqrt{2}$
    (B) $18\sqrt{3}$
    (C) $36\sqrt{2}$
    (D) $36\sqrt{3}$
    (E) It cannot be determined from the information given.

16. Which of the following graphs could represent the equation $|y+1| = x + 3$?

    (A)
    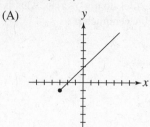

    (B)
    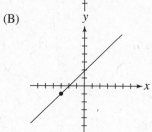

    (C)
    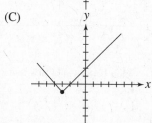

    (D)
    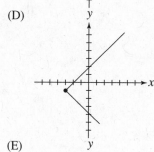

    (E)
    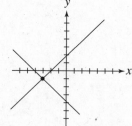

STOP
If you finish before time is called, you may check your work on this section only.
Do not turn to any other section in the test.

NO TEST MATERIAL ON THIS PAGE.

SECTION 9
Time — 20 minutes
19 Questions

Turn to Section 9 of your answer sheet to answer the questions in this section.

Directions: For each question in this section, select the best answer from among the choices given and fill in the corresponding circle on the answer sheet.

Each sentence below has one or two blanks, each blank indicating that something has been omitted. Beneath the sentence are five words or sets of words labeled A through E. Choose the word or set of words that, when inserted in the sentence, best fits the meaning of the sentence as a whole.

Example:

Desiring to ------- his taunting friends, Mitch gave them taffy in hopes it would keep their mouths shut.

(A) eliminate   (B) satisfy   (C) overcome
    (D) ridicule   (E) silence

---

1. Many people find coyotes to be ------- creatures because their high-pitched and piercing howl tends to trigger humans' primordial fears.

    (A) unnerving   (B) anthropological   (C) sacrosanct
        (D) haughty   (E) suspicious

2. Lemony Snicket is only -------; the real name of the author of the popular children's book is Daniel Handler.

    (A) a hyperbole   (B) a prevarication   (C) a pseudonym
        (D) an epigram   (E) a non sequitur

3. Valued in traditional Chinese culture for its purifying qualities, the Quan Yin symbol is believed to ------- an environment after an argument or disagreement has occurred.

    (A) unsettle   (B) harmonize   (C) preserve
        (D) amplify   (E) pollute

4. Heather felt ------- regarding her work for the class, but Ms. Shockey was -------; she did not find Heather's essay particularly exceptional.

    (A) satisfied . . unconcerned
    (B) malcontent . . pleased
    (C) confident . . indifferent
    (D) glum . . impressed
    (E) energized . . soured

5. The seemingly ------- policy changes eventually resulted in a severe economic downturn, prompting critics to wonder if the intent of the changes was more ------- than once thought.

    (A) informed . . unintended
    (B) sinister . . malicious
    (C) obsolete . . fortuitous
    (D) harmless . . beneficial
    (E) benign . . pernicious

6. The editor refused to approve the story because the reporter had included some ------- statements that could not be verify by experts in the field.

    (A) substantiated   (B) serious   (C) ingenuous
        (D) indubitable   (E) specious

GO ON TO THE NEXT PAGE

Directions: Each passage below is followed by questions based on its content. Answer the questions on the basis of what is <u>stated</u> or <u>implied</u> in each passage and in any introductory material that may be provided.

Questions 7-19 are based on the following passages.

The following passages review the Shakespearean actors David Garrick and Charles Macklin. Passage 1, written by Thomas Davies in 1741, describes Garrick's abilities on the stage; Passage 2, written by James Boaden in 1849, compares Macklin's performing abilities with Garrick's.

Passage 1

On the 19th of October 1741, David Garrick acted Richard the Third, for the first time, at the playhouse in Goodman's Fields. So many idle persons, under the title of gentlemen
Line acting for their diversion, had exposed their incapacity at that
5 theatre, and had so often disappointed the audiences, that no very large company was brought together to see the new performer. However, several of his own acquaintance, many of them persons of good judgment, were assembled at the usual hour; though we may well believe that the greater part
10 of the audience was stimulated rather by curiosity to see the event, than invited by any hopes of rational entertainment.

An actor, who, in the first display of his talents, undertakes a principal character, has generally, amongst other difficulties, the prejudices of the audience to struggle with,
15 in favor of an established performer. Here, indeed, they were not insurmountable: Cibber, who had been much admired in Richard, had left the stage. Quin was the popular player; but his manner of heaving up his words, and his labored action, prevented his being a favorite Richard.

20 Mr. Garrick's easy and familiar, yet forcible style in speaking and acting, at first threw the critics into some hesitation concerning the novelty as well as propriety of his manner. They had been long accustomed to an elevation of the voice, with a sudden mechanical depression of its tones,
25 calculated to excite admiration, and to entrap applause. To the just modulation of the words, and concurring expression of the feature from the genuine workings of nature, they had been strangers, at least for some time. But after he had gone through a variety of scenes, in which he gave evident proofs
30 of consummate art, and perfect knowledge of character, their doubts were turned into surprise and astonishment, from which they relieved themselves by loud and reiterated applause. They were more especially charmed when the actor, after having thrown aside the hypocrite and politician,
35 assumed the warrior and the hero. When news was brought to Richard, that the Duke of Buckingham was taken, Garrick's look and action, when he pronounced the words,

—Off with his head!
So much for Buckingham!

40 were so significant and important, from his visible enjoyment of the incident, that several loud shouts of approbation proclaimed the triumph of the actor and satisfaction of the audience. The death of Richard was accompanied with the loudest gratulations of applause.

Passage 2

45 As I paid much attention to Macklin's performances, and personally knew him, I shall endeavor to characterize his acting, and discriminate it from that of others. If Macklin really was of the old school, that school taught what was truth and nature. His acting was essentially manly—there was
50 nothing of trick about it. His delivery was more level than modern speaking, but certainly more weighty, direct, and emphatic. His features were rigid, his eye cold and colorless; yet the earnestness of his manner, and the sterling sense of his address, produced an effect in Shylock, that has remained
55 to the present hour unrivalled. Macklin, for instance, in the trial scene, "stood like a TOWER," as Milton has it. He was "not bound to please" anybody by his pleading; he claimed a right, "grounded upon LAW," and thought himself as firm as the Rialto. To this remark it may be said, "You are here
60 describing SHYLOCK." True; I am describing Macklin. If this perfection be true of him, when speaking the language of Shakespeare, it is equally so, when he gave utterance to his own. Macklin was the author of *Love à la Mode* and the *Man of the World*. His performance of the two true born Scotsmen
65 was so perfect, as though he had been created expressly to keep up the prejudice against Scotland. The late George Cooke was a noisy Sir Pertinax compared with Macklin. He talked of *booing*, but it was evident he took a credit for suppleness that was not in him. He was rather Sir Giles than
70 Sir Pertinax. Macklin could inveigle as well as subdue; and modulated his voice, almost to his last year, with amazing skill.

It has been commonly considered that Garrick introduced a mighty change in stage delivery: actors had never, until his
75 time, been natural. If Macklin at all resembled his masters, as it is probable he did, he can certainly not be obnoxious to a censure of this kind. He abhorred all trick, all start and ingenious attitude; and his attacks upon Mr. Garrick were always directed to the restless abundance of his action and his
80 gestures, by which, he said, rather than by the fair business of the character, he caught and detained all attention to himself.

With respect to the alleged unfairness of Garrick in engrossing all attention to himself, a charge often repeated, it may, perhaps, be true, that this great master converged the
85 interest of the whole too much about his particular character; and willingly dispensed with any rival attraction, not because he shunned competition with it as *skill*, but because it might encroach upon, delay or divide that palm for which he labored—public applause.

GO ON TO THE NEXT PAGE

7. In line 6, the reference to "no very large company" is intended to convey that

    (A) the cast of actors was very small
    (B) the theatre received little support from businesses
    (C) the audience was not very big
    (D) the new performer's audition was seen by few of the theatre's producers
    (E) the theatre was extremely understaffed

8. From lines 8-11, we may assume that the author of Passage 1 believes that the audience

    (A) was assembled with high hopes of viewing a superior performance
    (B) expected a mediocre performance
    (C) had little enthusiasm for a careful, competent performance
    (D) had never attended a theatrical event and was curious to see what it entailed
    (E) was a rival of Garrick's who intended to distract the performers

9. The reference in line 22 to "novelty as well as propriety" is used to

    (A) explain the critics' reluctance to embrace Garrick's unfamiliar acting style
    (B) explain the enthusiasm the audience felt toward Garrick's exciting portrayal
    (C) show that Garrick was not a serious actor, but a dilettante who rejected a studied performance in favor of haphazard indifference
    (D) indicate that Garrick's naturalistic approach was inappropriate to the portrayal of King Richard III
    (E) reinforce the notion that Garrick had no intention of giving a serious performance, since the critical community was determined to see him fail

10. The applause mentioned in the last sentence of Passage 1 signifies that

    (A) the audience was thoroughly pleased with Garrick's portrayal of Richard
    (B) the audience so disliked Garrick's portrayal that it cheered his death
    (C) Richard's death scene was spectacularly gruesome
    (D) the lengthy play had finally reached its conclusion
    (E) the death of a principal character was customarily applauded in the eighteenth century

11. In line 49, "manly" most nearly means

    (A) virile
    (B) deceptive
    (C) honest
    (D) powerful
    (E) emphatic

12. In line 52, Macklin's facial expressions while playing Shylock can best be described as

    (A) colorfully animated
    (B) difficult to understand
    (C) easy to misinterpret
    (D) stoic and unfeeling
    (E) free and relaxed

13. Which of the following , if true, would most weaken the contention in lines 73-75 that "Garrick introduced . . . natural"?

    (A) In Shakespeare's time, productions of his work were characterized in many cases by unexaggerated, lifelike performances.
    (B) In the original productions of Shakespeare's plays, female parts were always played by boys.
    (C) Shakespearean actors working before Garrick were taught to speak Shakespeare's words in a stilted and forced manner.
    (D) Many modern productions of Shakespeare's plays emphasize a naturalistic, non-stylized approach to the language.
    (E) Garrick was unwilling to teach his acting method to other Shakespearean actors of his time.

GO ON TO THE NEXT PAGE

14. In Passage 2, Macklin's main problem with Garrick concerns

(A) Garrick's tendency to be overly reserved in movement, and to focus too intently on his lines

(B) Garrick's dynamic physicality, which unjustly drew focus away from the other characters

(C) Garrick's emphasis on a more natural stage delivery

(D) Garrick's inability to make his body rigid and his demeanor stern in his portrayal of Shylock

(E) Garrick's lack of concern for the audience's approval

15. The author of Passage 2 views Macklin's criticism of Garrick as

(A) irrelevant, despite Garrick's outspoken scorn for the public

(B) justly forgotten, because of Macklin's strong prejudice against Scotland

(C) justifiable, even in light of Garrick's talents

(D) based primarily upon Macklin's groundbreaking portrayal of Shylock

(E) profoundly influential on the younger Garrick

16. In line 88, "palm" most nearly means

(A) promotion

(B) part of the hand

(C) leaf

(D) money

(E) symbol of triumph

17. The author of Passage 2 may have had a more favorable regard for the actor described in Passage 1 had the author

(A) viewed the actor's flexibility on stage

(B) seen first-hand a performance in which the audience's applause was the not the overriding impetus for Garrick's actions

(C) viewed a critically acclaimed production of Richard III

(D) seen the version of Richard IIII performed by Garrick's company before Garrick joined it

(E) taken into consideration "the old school's" influence on the actor

18. The author of Passage 1 describes Garrick's acting style as "familiar" (line 20) and the author of Passage 2 describes it as "natural" (line 75). What is the significance of these references?

(A) The adjectives refer to a style of acting that was not commonly used by actors prior to Garrick.

(B) Actors were becoming personally acquainted with their audiences.

(C) Acting was becoming an easier craft as playwrights improved their manuscripts.

(D) Performers were becoming better known to their audiences.

(E) No new plays were being written, so the actors knew their parts thoroughly.

19. Which of the following references from Passage 1 could that author present to support the statement in lines 73-75 ("It has been . . . natural") ?

(A) "Mr. Garrick's easy and familiar . . . manner." (lines 20-23)

(B) "An actor, who in the first . . . performer." (lines 12-15)

(C) "On the nineteenth . . . Fields" (lines 1-3)

(D) "The death of Richard . . . applause." (lines 43-44)

(E) "However several of his . . . entertainment." (lines 7-11)

STOP

If you finish before time is called, you may check your work on this section only.
Do not turn to any other section in the test.

SECTION 10
Time — 10 minutes
14 Questions

Turn to Section 10 of your answer sheet to answer the questions in this section.

Directions: For each question in this section, select the best answer from among the choices given and fill in the corresponding circle on the answer sheet.

The following sentences test correctness and effectiveness of expression. Part of each sentence or the entire sentence is underlined; beneath each sentence are five ways of phrasing the underlined material. Choice A repeats the original phrasing; the other four choices are different. If you think the original phrasing produces a better sentence than any of the alternatives, select choice A; if not, select one of the other choices.

In making your selection, follow the requirements of standard written English; that is, pay attention to grammar, choice of words, sentence construction, and punctuation. Your selection should result in the most effective sentence—clear and precise, without awkwardness or ambiguity.

EXAMPLE:

Bobby Flay baked his first cake <u>and he was thirteen years old then</u>.

(A) and he was thirteen years old then
(B) when he was thirteen
(C) at age thirteen years old
(D) upon the reaching of thirteen years
(E) at the time when he was thirteen

1. <u>Since one should not count</u> out the Yankees early in the season, as they always get stronger by the middle of August.

   (A) Since one should not count
   (B) One ought not to count
   (C) Since one ought not count
   (D) One had ought not to count
   (E) One should not be counting

2. Historian Mike Wallace founded the Gotham Center for New York History in 200 <u>with the goal being to generate</u> greater interest in the city's wealth of historic spaces.

   (A) with the goal being to generate
   (B) and the goal was generating
   (C) to generate
   (D) therefore to generate
   (E) he generated

3. The new bill is a move <u>to take the responsibility for welfare allocation from the federal government and that give</u> it to the state administration.

   (A) to take the responsibility for welfare allocation from the federal government and that give
   (B) to take the responsibility for welfare allocation from the federal government and give
   (C) to take the responsibility for welfare allocation from the federal government for giving
   (D) which takes the responsibility for welfare allocation from the federal government to give
   (E) taking the responsibility for welfare allocation from the federal government and that give

4. In 1982, the Go-Go's <u>became the first all-woman band</u> to have a number-one album, garnering an enduring victory for women in popular music.

   (A) became the first all-woman band to have
   (B) are the first all-woman band that have had
   (C) were the first all-woman band that had
   (D) was the first all-woman band that had
   (E) came to be the first all-woman band to receive

5. After moving farther away from downtown, <u>Ryan's commute being less time consuming than it had been was surprising to him</u>.

   (A) Ryan's commute being less time consuming than it had been was surprising to him
   (B) it was surprising to Ryan that his commute was less time consuming than it had been
   (C) surprisingly, Ryan's commute was less time consuming than it had been
   (D) Ryan was surprised that his commute was less time consuming than it had been
   (E) taking less time than it had, Ryan's commute surprised him

---

GO ON TO THE NEXT PAGE ➡

6. During one of the worst mudslides in California history, what began as flash flood soon raged out of control <u>and it roared downhill at 35 miles per hour, consuming everything in its path</u>.

   (A) and it roared downhill at 35 miles per hour, consuming everything in its path
   (B) and it roared downhill at 35 miles per hour, everything in its path having been consumed
   (C) and the roaring downhill was at 35 miles per hour, consuming everything in its path
   (D) and roared downhill at 35 miles per hour, consuming everything in its path
   (E) and roaring at 35 miles per hour downhill; consuming everything in its path

7. Carrying an assortment of bats, balls, and helmets in several cumbersome bags, <u>the equipment manager's search for assistance was desperate</u>.

   (A) the equipment manager's search for assistance was desperate
   (B) the equipment manger's desperate search was for assistance
   (C) assistance was what the equipment manager desperately searched for
   (D) assistance for which the equipment manager desperately searched
   (E) the equipment manager searched desperately for assistance

8. Members of the squash family include not only the pumpkin, <u>but the butternut, the Hubbard, and the acorn squash as well</u>.

   (A) but the butternut, the Hubbard, and the acorn squash as well
   (B) but also the butternut, Hubbard squash, and the acorn squash
   (C) but also the butternut, Hubbard, and acorn squash
   (D) and the butternut, Hubbard, and acorn as well
   (E) and the butternut, Hubbard, and acorn squashes as well

9. College admission officers suggest that before submitting <u>your application, prospective students should proofread one's essay</u> carefully.

   (A) your application, prospective students should proofread one's essay
   (B) their application, a prospective applicant should proofread their essay
   (C) their applications, proofread the essays
   (D) their applications, prospective students should proofread their essays
   (E) one's application, you should proofread your essay

10. The clear blue water off the coast of Fiji is home to aquatic life of such beauty and <u>variedness and the water has appealed</u> to both fisherman and underwater photographers alike.

    (A) variedness and the water has appealed
    (B) variety and the water has appeals
    (C) variety and the water having appeal
    (D) variety that have appealed
    (E) variety that it appeals

11. The male weaverbird builds a nest of green grass and then clings, shrieking and fluttering, to his new home, attracting <u>what females, if any, that are</u> in his vicinity.

    (A) what females, if any, that are
    (B) any females
    (C) females, if there might be any
    (D) the females, so that if any are
    (E) whatever females that are or may be

12. The problem of food and aid <u>distribution, frequently compounded in certain countries because</u> corrupt officials and poor infrastructure making accessing the neediest people all the more challenging.

    (A) distribution, frequently compounded in certain countries because
    (B) distribution, frequently compounded in certain countries and
    (C) distribution, frequently compounded in certain countries when
    (D) distribution is frequently compounded in certain countries where
    (E) distribution is frequently compounded in certain countries and

GO ON TO THE NEXT PAGE

13. Since the early 1980s, many musicians have chosen to make themselves known mainly through <u>music videos, and playing small clubs affords</u> musicians a better opportunity to build a loyal fan base.

(A) music videos, and playing small clubs affords

(B) music videos, but playing small clubs is good in that in affords

(C) music videos; however, playing small clubs affords

(D) music videos, playing small clubs affording

(E) music videos, when playing small clubs afford

14. The delicious and vast menu choices <u>contribute to the popularity of the Ethiopian restaurant, as does</u> the authentic and quaint decor.

(A) contribute to the popularity of the Ethiopian restaurant, as does

(B) contributes to the popularity of the Ethiopian restaurant as greatly as

(C) contributes as greatly to the popularity of the Ethiopian restaurant as do

(D) contribute to the popularity of the Ethiopian restaurant, so do

(E) contribute greatly to the popularity of the Ethiopian restaurant, as it also comes from

STOP

**If you finish before time is called, you may check your work on this section only.
Do not turn to any other section in the test.**

NO TEST MATERIAL ON THIS PAGE.

PRACTICE TEST 5: ANSWER KEY

2 Reading	3 Math	4 Writing	5 Math	6 Reading	8 Math	9 Reading	10 Writing
1. D	1. C	1. D	1. C	1. C	1. C	1. A	1. B
2. C	2. B	2. D	2. E	2. E	2. B	2. C	2. C
3. B	3. A	3. C	3. E	3. A	3. B	3. B	3. B
4. B	4. C	4. E	4. B	4. D	4. D	4. C	4. A
5. D	5. D	5. C	5. A	5. A	5. D	5. E	5. D
6. A	6. A	6. E	6. A	6. D	6. E	6. E	6. D
7. A	7. A	7. B	7. E	7. B	7. A	7. C	7. E
8. C	8. B	8. A	8. C	8. B	8. B	8. B	8. C
9. A	9. A	9. B	9. 8	9. D	9. B	9. A	9. D
10. C	10. C	10. B	10. 0	10. B	10. E	10. A	10. E
11. C	11. C	11. D	11. 20	11. D	11. A	11. C	11. B
12. B	12. E	12. D	12. $\frac{4}{3}$ or 1.33	12. D	12. E	12. D	12. D
13. C	13. C	13. D	13. 9	13. B	13. B	13. A	13. C
14. D	14. C	14. E	14. $\frac{1}{3}$ or .333	14. B	14. E	14. B	14. A
15. B	15. C	15. C	15. $\frac{1}{2}$ or .5	15. C	15. D	15. C	
16. D	16. A	16. E	16. 60	16. D	16. D	16. E	
17. E	17. D	17. B	17. 30	17. E		17. B	
18. A	18. D	18. B	18. 90	18. B		18. A	
19. B	19. B	19. D		19. D		19. A	
20. B	20. D	20. D		20. B			
21. B		21. C		21. C			
22. E		22. D		22. A			
23. A		23. C		23. E			
24. D		24. A		24. A			
		25. C					
		26. C					
		27. E					
		28. A					
		29. A					
		30. A					
		31. B					
		32. B					
		33. C					
		34. D					
		35. D					

SAT SCORING WORKSHEET

For directions on how to score your SAT practice test, see pages 10–11.

SAT Writing Section

Total Writing Multiple-Choice Questions Correct:

—

Total Writing Multiple-Choice Questions Incorrect: _____ ÷ 4 =

Grammar Raw Score:

Grammar Scaled Subscore

+

Compare the Grammar Raw Score with the Writing Multiple-Choice Subscore Conversion Table on page 424 to find the Grammar Scaled Subscore.

Your Essay Score (2–12): _____ × 2 =

Writing Raw Score:

Compare Raw Score with SAT Score Conversion Table on page 424 to find the Writing Scaled Score.

Writing Scaled Score

SAT Critical Reading Section

Total Critical Reading Questions Correct:

—

Total Critical Reading Questions Incorrect: _____ ÷ 4 =

Critical Reading Raw Score:

Compare Raw Score with SAT Score Conversion Table on page 424 to find the Critical Reading Scaled Score.

Critical Reading Scaled Score

SAT Math Section

Total Math Grid-In Questions Correct:

+

Total Math Multiple-Choice Questions Correct:

—

Total Math Multiple-Choice Questions Incorrect: _____ ÷ 4 =

Don't include wrong answers from grid-ins!

Math Raw Score:

Compare Raw Score with SAT Score Conversion Table on page 424 to find the Math Scaled Score.

Math Scaled Score

SAT SCORE CONVERSION TABLE

Raw Score	Writing Scaled Score	Reading Scaled Score	Math Scaled Score	Raw Score	Writing Scaled Score	Reading Scaled Score	Math Scaled Score	Raw Score	Writing Scaled Score	Reading Scaled Score	Math Scaled Score
73	800			47	590–630	600–640	660–700	21	400–440	410–450	440–480
72	790–800			46	590–630	590–630	650–690	20	390–430	400–440	430–470
71	780–800			45	580–620	580–620	650–690	19	380–420	400–440	430–470
70	770–800			44	570–610	580–620	640–680	18	370–410	390–430	420–460
69	770–800			43	570–610	570–610	630–670	17	370–410	380–420	410–450
68	760–800			42	560–600	570–610	620–660	16	360–400	370–410	400–440
67	760–800	800		41	560–600	560–600	610–650	15	350–390	360–400	400–440
66	760–800	770–800		40	550–590	550–590	600–640	14	340–380	350–390	390–430
65	750–790	760–800		39	540–580	550–590	590–630	13	330–370	340–380	380–420
64	740–780	750–790		38	530–570	540–580	590–630	12	320–360	340–380	360–400
63	730–770	740–780		37	530–570	530–570	580–620	11	320–360	330–370	350–390
62	720–760	730–770		36	520–560	530–570	570–610	10	310–350	320–360	340–380
61	710–750	720–760		35	510–550	520–560	560–600	9	300–340	310–350	330–370
60	700–740	710–750		34	500–540	520–560	560–600	8	290–330	300–340	320–360
59	690–730	700–740		33	490–530	510–550	550–590	7	280–320	300–340	310–350
58	680–720	690–730		32	480–520	500–540	540–580	6	270–310	290–330	300–340
57	680–720	680–720		31	470–510	490–530	530–570	5	260–300	280–320	290–330
56	670–710	670–710		30	470–510	480–520	520–560	4	240–280	270–310	280–320
55	660–720	670–710		29	460–500	470–510	520–560	3	230–270	250–290	280–320
54	650–690	660–700	760–800	28	450–490	470–510	510–550	2	230–270	240–280	270–310
53	640–680	650–690	740–780	27	440–480	460–500	500–540	1	220–260	220–260	260–300
52	630–670	640–680	730–770	26	430–470	450–490	490–530	0	210–250	200–240	250–290
51	630–670	630–670	710–750	25	420–460	440–480	480–520	−1	200–240	200–230	230–270
50	620–660	620–660	690–730	24	410–450	430–470	470–510	−2	200–230	200–220	220–260
49	610–650	610–650	680–720	23	410–450	430–470	460–500	−3	200–220	200–210	200–240
48	600–640	600–640	670–710	22	400–440	420–460	450–490				

WRITING MULTIPLE-CHOICE SUBSCORE CONVERSION TABLE

Grammar Raw Score	Grammar Scaled Subscore	Grammar Raw Score	Grammar Scaled Subscore	Grammar Raw Score	Grammar Scaled Subscore	Grammar Raw Score	Grammar Scaled Subscore	Grammar Raw Score	Grammar Scaled Subscore
49	78–80	38	67–71	27	55–59	16	42–46	5	30–34
48	77–80	37	66–70	26	54–58	15	41–45	4	29–33
47	75–79	36	65–69	25	53–57	14	40–44	3	28–32
46	74–78	35	64–68	24	52–56	13	39–43	2	27–31
45	72–76	34	63–67	23	51–55	12	38–42	1	25–29
44	72–76	33	62–66	22	50–54	11	36–40	0	24–28
43	71–75	32	61–65	21	49–53	10	35–39	−1	22–26
42	70–74	31	60–64	20	47–51	9	34–38	−2	20–23
41	69–73	30	59–63	19	46–50	8	33–37	−3	20–22
40	68–72	29	58–62	18	45–49	7	32–36		
39	68–72	28	56–60	17	44–48	6	31–35		

Chapter 13
Practice Test 5:
Answers and
Explanations

SECTION 2

1. **D**   Because Ellie *doubted* Tom's story, the blank means something like "with doubt" (D) *skeptically* comes closest to this meaning.

2. **C**   Start with the second blank. Hector is willing to *explore new possibilities,* which is different from how the *more narrow-minded scientists* feel about it. A good word for the second blank is "reject." Only (B) and (C) are appropriately negative Eliminate (A), (D), and (E) Because Hector is *eager to explore new possibilities,* "new" is a good word for the first blank, and only (C) matches both blanks.

3. **B**   The phrase near the second blank, *he just as quickly* indicates that we need a word for the first blank that means "quick." Only (B) *swift* and (D) *hasty* have a meaning close to "quick." *Despite* indicates that the second blank will mean the opposite of *rise*, so "fell" is be a good word for the blank. Between (B) *yielded* and (D) *ascended* only (B) fits the meaning of both blanks.

4. **B**   We know that Kai's pain was *dull* rather than whatever goes in the blank, so we need a word that means something like "sharp." Only (B) *acute* means "sharp."

5. **D**   The colon indicates that the description following the punctuation is the meaning of the blank. We need a word that means "firmly sticking to one's principles," and (D) *tenacity* means "the quality of keeping a firm hold on something." These answers have some tough vocab, so look up any unfamiliar words.

6. **A**   The word *but* indicates that the second part of the sentence will mean the opposite of *Procrastination*. The opposite of putting things off is "immediate" *action*. Eliminate any words that don't mean "immediate," leaving only (A) *prompt*.

7. **A**   The word *and* indicates that the first blank will mean something close to *stinginess*. Eliminate (E)—all the other words describe someone mean or stingy. The second blank must be a word that describes his contrasting *public image* and his *private* behavior, so "go against" is a good meaning for the blank. Both (A) *belie* and (E) *contradict* fit this meaning, but only (A) matches the meaning of both blanks.

8. **C**   Because the department handles *urgent situations* these are tasks which must be *performed with great* "urgency," or great speed. Only (C) *alacrity* fits this meaning.

9. **A**   The main idea of Passage 1 is that Einstein's theories affected the works of artists and writers. This is paraphrased in (A). The opposite of (B) is true: Einstein *debunked,* or disproved *Absolute Rest*. (C), (D), and (E) are not mentioned in the passage.

10. **C** The passage is about the *startling parallels between the Renaissance* and the twentieth century and sums up by stating that *the twentieth century was not so different from the world of Shakespeare*, thus making (C) the only answer supported by the passage. *Realism* (A) is not mentioned in the passage. While both eras *saw great advances in science* the advances themselves were not necessarily similar, as in (B). There was *trade expansion* in the Renaissance, but not necessarily *capitalism* as in (D). There is no evidence that the advances were centered mainly in Europe as in (E). Remember, even an inference question must be supported by text in the passage.

11. **C** Both passages mention Einstein's influence on the twentieth century. While both passages are generally about science and art, (A) is too strong: art and science are somewhat linked in Passage 1, but not at all in Passage 2. There is no evidence in either passage for (B).

12. **B** Neither passage mentions the nineteenth century, but finding the main ideas of each passage will show how each would make a relevant use of the nineteenth century. Passage 1 is about how the twentieth century is one of *upheaval* and *major changes*, though it doesn't give any examples of life before the change. Passage 2 is about *startling parallels* between the twentieth century and another era. (B) is the best answer: *contrasts* would show the differences between the nineteenth and twentieth centuries, while *links between the nineteenth century and another period* does for the nineteenth century what Passage 2 did for the twentieth.

13. **C** The first paragraph discusses how America *proudly professed democracy* but acted against that belief. (C) is correct, because it addresses this *contradictory* practice that goes against the *ideals of democracy*. (A) has a trap answer in its mention of *disease*. The *nation's* feelings about *segregation* (B) are not mentioned in the passage. (D) may be true, but it doesn't address the issue of believing one thing and doing the opposite. (E) segregation was not *an illusion* and the answer does not address the split of belief and action needed to explain the *schizophrenic personality*.

14. **D** As with question 13, this *contradiction* is the difference between what is professed and actual actions of the nation: the passage states *segregation and discrimination are strange paradoxes in a nation founded on the principle that all men are created equal*, and this is paraphrased well in (D). (A) is not true—Dr. King is the author of the passage. The *Supreme Court* mentioned in (B) is in the passage, but doesn't relate to the *disturbed consciences* asked about in the question. (C) is not mentioned in the passage, and many people may be offended if the SAT considered this a true or correct answer. (E) is also not mentioned in the passage.

15. **B** The *Supreme Court's decision* outlawed segregation in schools. (A) is the opposite, while (C), (D), and (E) are not mentioned in the passage. (B) is a good paraphrase of the desegregation schools.

16. **D** Go back to the passage and use the context to come up with a word to replace *deny*. In the passage, segregation is described as *inherently unequal* and "does not allow" a child to have *equal protection of the law*. The correct answer should be something like "does not allow." While many of the answers do address certain meanings of *deny* only (D) *withhold from* matches the context of the passage.

17.   E   The main idea of the third paragraph is that the issues involved in segregation as the same as those *all over the world* and that the *racial crisis…is a part of the larger world crisis.* This is best reflected in (E), that this struggle *is not an isolated occurrence* since it is something addressed around the world. There is no evidence in the passage for any of the other answers.

18.   A   From the passage, the *new order* is based on democratic equality, while the *older order* is based on *subordination,* or keeping people down. (A) best reflects this, stating that the *older order* is *less democratic* and believes *certain groups should be controlled by others.* (B) and (C) are extreme, due to their use of *only.* (D) is much too specific, and not supported by the passage. (E) contradicts the passage: those of the *older order* are the traditionalists.

19.   B   The *crisis* mentioned in line 41 is explained in the rest of the paragraph: it is the *paradox* of the *principles of American democracy* clashing with the actions of people who would *repress freedom's growth.* This is paraphrased in (B) the *conflict between the ideals…and realities.* This also fits in with the main idea of the passage as a whole. (A) and (C) are contradicted by lines 41–43. (D) and (E) are not mentioned at all in the passage.

20.   B   Go back to the passage and use the context to come up with a word to replace *resistance.* In the passage the *principles of American democracy* came up against people who wanted the opposite, to *repress freedom.* (A) and (B) are both close, but in context, (A) *denial of forces* either means that those forces themselves were denied, or perhaps they just ignored what was going on, which does not fit with *brutal.* (B) *opposition* fits better, because it shows direct action of the part of the forces.

21.   B   The passage states in lines 57–59 that the *uneducated whites* were in a state of *confusion* that led them to commit *acts of meanness and violence.* This is paraphrased in (B). None of the other answers are mentioned in the passage.

22.   E   The author brings up *Lincoln* and the *castigation of the Supreme Court* to support the idea at the beginning of the paragraph: that there are *characteristics that come to the forefront in any period of social transition.* Therefore, these are two instances that have similarities, paraphrased best in (E). The rest of the answers are unsupported by evidence in the passage.

23.   A   The point of Toynbee's *A Study of History* is that African Americans have something to give that *Western civilization…desperately needs to survive.* This is best paraphrased in (A). (B) is the opposite of what's stated in the passage. (C), (D), and (E) are unsupported in the passage.

24.   D   There is no line reference, so go through the answers one by one to see if it is supported by the passage as a whole. (A) actually is the opposite of Lincoln's stance on emancipation. In (B) the connection is unsupported by the passage. (C) is too strong due to the use of *never* and (E) is also extreme in its implication that all *public officials* share the qualities listed. Only (D) is supported: the passage discusses how the Supreme Court's decision caused *resistance* by *older orders* of people who believed in segregation, not just of schools but as a general principle.

SECTION 3

1. **C** Manipulate the first equation to find that $3x = 18$. We don't have to solve for x itself, because we can multiply both sides by 2 to see that $6x = 36$. $36 - 2 = 34$, choice (C). There are trap answers in (A), which is the value of x, and in (D) which is the result if 2 is added to rather than subtracted from 36.

2. **B** The average on four tests is 86, so the total of all four tests added together is 344. Now we can subtract the actual values of the three tests we know the scores of: $344 - 83 - 83 - 85 = 93$. So the fourth test had a score of 93, answer (B).

3. **A** In the line formula, $y = mx + b$, b is the y-intercept. In the graph, the line crosses the y-axis at -2, so eliminate (B), (C), and (D) because they have a different y-intercept. The m value is the slope, so using the slope formula $\dfrac{y_2 - y_1}{x_2 - x_1}$ we get $\dfrac{(-2) - 0}{0 - (-6)} = -\dfrac{1}{3}$, which matches (A). (E) has the x and y values reversed.

4. **C** There are very few numbers that are equal to their square. Only 0 and 1 have this property: $0 \times 0 = 0$ and $1 \times 1 = 1$. -1 does not work, because a negative times a negative is a positive: $-1 \times -1 = 1$. Only two integers work; (C) is correct.

5. **D** When a number with an exponent is raised to another power, multiply the two exponents. Since we are given $a^3 = 4$, and we can get the value of a^6 by raising both sides of the equation to the second power. $(a^3)^2 = 4^2$ so $a^6 = 16$.

6. **A** The first step is to find the area of the triangle: Area of a triangle $= \dfrac{1}{2}bh$. $\dfrac{1}{2} \times 12 \times 6 = 36$. This is also the area of the square we need to find the side of. A square with sides of length 6 would have an area of 36, so (A) 6 is the correct answer.

7. **A** From the statement $x > 0 > y$, we know that x is positive and y is negative. The easiest way to solve this is to Plug In numbers for x and y and test out each answer. If $x = 3$ and $y = -2$, (A) and (D) are both true, while (B), (C), and (E) can be eliminated. If we change the numbers so that $x = 2$ and $y = -2$, (A) is still true, but (D) is no longer true, since $\dfrac{1}{4} = \dfrac{1}{4}$. The correct answer is (A).

8. **B** To solve this, try out all the answer choices: for (A) $8 - 4 = 4$, since the answer is positive, the absolute value is also 4. For (B) $4 - 4 = 0$, and the absolute value is also 0. For (C), $0 - 4 = -4$, which has an absolute value of 4. (D) gives 8 and (E) gives 12, leaving (B) as the lowest value. Because absolute value is always positive 0 is the lowest value that can be obtained.

9.   **A**   This can be solved algebraically by translating the question to $x + 4 = \dfrac{x}{7}$. Multiply both sides by 7:

$7x + 28 = x$. Get the variables on one side and the numbers on the other: $6x = -28$, then solve for x:

$x = -\dfrac{28}{6}$ which simplifies to $-\dfrac{14}{3}$ answer (A). This can also be solved by trying out each answer

choice. In (A) $-\dfrac{14}{3} + 4 = -\dfrac{14}{3} + \dfrac{12}{3} = -\dfrac{2}{3}$. Now we need to see if we get the same result when

we divide $-\dfrac{14}{3}$ by 7: $-\dfrac{14}{3} \times \dfrac{1}{7} = -\dfrac{14}{21}$ which reduces to $-\dfrac{2}{3}$, making (A) correct.

10.   **C**   When a question describes a figure but doesn't show it, draw it yourself. Square *PQRS* has an area

of 3. Now add *T*, the midpoint of *QR*. Drawing the line from point *T* to point *S* forms the fourth

side of quadrilateral *PQTS*. It also creates a triangle that is $\dfrac{1}{4}$ of the area of the square. This means

that quadrilateral *PQTS* is $\dfrac{3}{4}$ of the area of the square: $\dfrac{3}{4} \times 3 = \dfrac{9}{4}$, answer (C).

11.   **C**   To solve this try out some numbers for the marbles: it's easiest to start with red. If red is 6, blue
must be two less than red, so that's 4. White is twice red, so that's 12. 6 + 4 + 12 = 22, which is
too low for any of the answers. Trying red = 8, then blue = 6, and white = 16. 8 + 6 + 16 = 30, too
big for anything on our list. That leaves only 7 as a possible value for red (we can't have half of a
marble). 7 + 5 + 14 = 26, answer (C).

12.   **E**   Because there is an *f* in each of the equations, we can make up our own number for *f* and find
values for *a* and *b* that agree with each other. If *f* = 5, then *a* must equal 3. Now use the second
equation to find *b*: *b* + 4(5) + 5, so *b* + 25. The question asks us to find the value of *b*, so replace
each *a* in the answers with 3, and the correct answer will be the one that gives our value for *b*, 25.
(A) gives 12, so eliminate it. (B) gives 8, so that's out. (C) is 14, (D) is 19, and only (E) gives the
number we were looking for, 25.

13. **C**   The triangles within the circle are special right triangles. Because we are given a measure of 135° in the top half of the circle, the angle within the triangle must measure 45°, making the triangle a 45-45-90 triangle. The legs of these triangles have a ratio of $x : x : x\sqrt{2}$. We know that the hypotenuse is 6, because XY is a diameter, and each triangle takes up half the diameter of 12. If $6 = x\sqrt{2}$, then x, the legs of the triangles, each equal $\dfrac{6}{\sqrt{2}}$. The triangles together form a square, and the sides are $\dfrac{6}{\sqrt{2}}$, so to find the area of the shaded region, we just need to square $\dfrac{6}{\sqrt{2}}$:

$$\dfrac{6}{\sqrt{2}} \times \dfrac{6}{\sqrt{2}} = \dfrac{36}{2} = 18, \text{ answer (C)}.$$

14. **C**   We can use exponent rules here or simply try out some of the answer choices by substituting them in for x. If $x = 4$, the first equation becomes $3^{4y} = 81$, or $3^{4y} = 3^4$. Because the bases are equal, the exponents are equivalent, so $4y = 4$, which yields $y = 1$. $3^4 + 3^1 = 81 + 3 = 84$, so the answer is (C).

15. **C**   When a question describes a figure but doesn't show it, draw it yourself. We know that A is at $(1, 0)$ and B is at $(-3, 0)$, and we need the midpoint of that. Since the distance between A and B is 4, the midpoint is at $(-1, 0)$. The question asks for the distance between $(-1, 0)$ and point C, which is at $(0, 5)$ If you have drawn the figure, you can see that the line we need to find the distance of is the hypotenuse of a triangle with legs of 1 and 5, so we can use the Pythagorean theorem to find the distance: $a^2 + b^2 + c^2$, so $1^2 + 5^2 = 26$, and the distance of the hypotenuse is $\sqrt{26}$, answer (C).

16. **A**   For this question we need to use each of the answers and see which, when used as a replacement for c gives $4\sqrt{2}$ when $x = 2$. Using $c = 2$, as in (A) we get $\left(2^2\right)\left(2^{\frac{1}{2}}\right)$. A fractional exponent means that the base number is raised by the numerator of the fraction, and the root taken is determined by the denominator. Therefore, an exponent of $\dfrac{1}{2}$ means to take the square root of the base number. $\left(2^2\right)\left(\sqrt{2}\right) = 4\sqrt{2}$, the number given in the question for $f(2)$, so c must equal 2, answer (A). None of the other answer choices used as c give a result of $4\sqrt{2}$ when $x = 2$.

17. **D**   It costs \$15 to buy one pound of coal and \$6 for each additional pound, represented by p. So each pound after the first would cost $6(p - 1)$. The total cost for al the coal would be \$15 + \$6$(p - 1)$, which simplifies to $15 + 6p - 6$, or $6p + 9$. The answer is (D).

18.   **D**   The members of set A are {1, 3, 5, 7, 9}. The members of set B are {2, 3, 5, 7, 11,...} There are more prime numbers, but since we need to find the elements the two sets have in common, and set A has only single-digit numbers, we've gone far enough. The numbers that these sets have in common are {3, 5, 7}, answer (D).

19.   **B**   The question asks for the greatest possible value of one of the integers in the group of 8 integers, so come up with the smallest numbers possible for the first 7 integers that fit the description given in the question. We can use numbers up to 2 times each, so $1 + 1 + 2 + 2 + 3 + 3 + 4 = 16$. We can find the value of the eighth (and largest possible) number by subtracting this from the sum of all 8 numbers: $31 - 16 = 15$, answer (B).

20.   **D**   When an equation is in the $y = mx + b$ format, b is the y-intercept. To find point A, put the equation for line r in $y = mx + b$:

$$4y = 3x - 24$$
$$y = \frac{3}{4}x - 6$$

This means that point A is located at $(0, -6)$. As line q is already in the right format, point B is located at $(0, 8)$, and the distance between points A and B is 14. To find point C, which is the x-intercept of both lines, using line q, substitute 0 for y in the equation of line q:

$$y = -x + 8$$
$$0 = -x + 8$$
$$x = 8$$

This means that point C is located at $(8, 0)$. Therefore, we have a triangle with a base of 14 and a height of 8, so solve for area: Area = $\frac{1}{2}$ (14)(8) = 56, answer (D).

SECTION 4

1.   **D**   The sentence as written uses a conjunction that awkwardly links the two parts of the sentence; eliminate (A). The addition of a comma in (B) does not fix the error. In (C) it is unclear what the pronoun *that* refers to. The pronoun *that* in (E) seemingly refers to *the students*, and thus should be *who*. (D) simplifies and clarifies the sentence by using the pronoun *who* to refer to *the students*. The correct answer is (D).

2.   **D**   The sentence as written has a verb tense error: *the last twenty years* does not agree with *are*. Eliminate (A) and (B). (C) is an incomplete sentence, and *since* in (E) is redundant, as the time frame is already established in the sentence. This leaves only (D), which properly uses the present perfect tense as the correct answer.

3. **C** The sentence as written uses the incorrect past tense of "shake:" *shaked* should be *shook*. Eliminate (A). (B) has an awkward construction. Both (D) and (E) have a misplaced modifier. Only (C) uses the correct verb construction without adding any further errors.

4. **E** The word *As* should be used when describing a cause-and-effect relationship or two events happening at the same time. Neither is the case in the sentence as written, so eliminate (A). (B) fixes this, but should simply list the activities rather than using the *both…as well as* construction. The list of activities in (C) is not parallel. In (D), the phrase *By being* indicates a cause-and-effect relationship that does not exist in the sentence. Only (E) creates a sentence that has the correct relationship between the *winter* and *summer* at *the resort* and has all the activities in a parallel list.

5. **C** The word *Because* sets up a cause-and-effect relationship, but this is disrupted by *and so* in the sentence as written, so eliminate (A). In (B) and (D), *therefore* is redundant since *Because* already establishes the relationship between the two parts of the sentence. (E) is awkward and passive, leaving only (C), which eliminates the unnecessary *and so*.

6. **E** In the sentence as written, the verbs *closes* and *conducting* should be in parallel form. Eliminate (A) and (B). (C) eliminates the necessary *only* that is part of the contrast set up by the sentence, while (D) puts *only* in the wrong place, which changes the meaning. Only (E) correctly puts the verbs in parallel form and introduces no other errors.

7. **B** The sentence as written has a misplaced modifier; the first word after the comma needs to be something that could be *mixed with a weak acid*. Eliminate (A) and (C). Both (D) and (E) are awkwardly phrased. Only (B) correctly puts *baking soda* immediately after the comma without introducing any other errors.

8. **A** The sentence is correct as written. The word *impacted* in (B) is not the correct form of the verb and since the end of the sentence describes the *contemporaries*, that is the word that should come before the comma, so (C), (D), and (E) are incorrect.

9. **B** The sentence as written has a subject-verb agreement error: *procedures* is plural while *is* is singular. The pronoun *its* in (C) is ambiguous, and seems to refer to *the course*, which changes the meaning of the sentence. (D) creates an incomplete sentence. The verb *runs* (E) confuses the sentence: *The testing procedures* could not run an obstacle course. Only (B) corrects the misplaced modifier and clearly shows the comparison of *the testing procedures* and *an obstacle course*.

10. **B** The sentence as written has a misplaced modifier, as does (C). (D) indicates that *Judy* is still a child, which changes the meaning of the sentence. (E) is awkwardly constructed and confuses the meaning of the sentence. Only (B) corrects the misplaced modifies and clearly describes the relationship between *Judy* and the street.

11. **D** The sentence as written has a subject-verb agreement error. Eliminate (A) and (E) for using the singular *is* with the plural *areas*. The areas listed in (B) and (C) are not in parallel form. (D) is correct because it uses the proper verb and has the list in parallel form.

12. **D**   There is a double negative in (D). The correct construction is *hardly ever.*

13. **D**   (D) creates a comparison error, the *trees* should not be compared to *Henry.* The correct construction is *than those in Henry's.*

14. **E**   The sentence is correct as written. Don't just go by how things sound: check each underlined part for errors.

15. **C**   The verb construction *has cooked* in (C) is not appropriate for the past tense established by *last week.*

16. **E**   The sentence is correct as written. The list is in parallel form, and the verbs have correct constructions and tenses.

17. **B**   (B) creates a subject-verb agreement error: *was* is singular while *tax shelters* is plural.

18. **B**   (B) uses the wrong preposition with *concerned.* While prepositions *for* or *about* could be used with *concerned,* depending on context, *to* is never correct.

19. **D**   *Cape Cod* in (D) creates a comparison error: it should be parallel to *Seattle's.*

20. **D**   The list is not in parallel form: (D) should simply be *ugly* to fit in with the adjectives in the rest of the list.

21. **C**   The pronoun *we* in (C) is incorrect: *The United States* is a singular, collective noun. *It* would be the appropriate pronoun to use in this case.

22. **D**   The list is not in parallel form: (D) should be *persuasiveness* to fit in with the nouns in the rest of the list.

23. **C**   The pronoun *I* in (C) is in the incorrect case. If *Thomas and* were not part of the sentence, it would read *the principal called I.* This makes it more evident that the pronoun should be "me."

24. **A**   The sentence has a noun agreement error: *Students* is plural, so *a doctor* should also be plural. All the students cannot become a single doctor, they must wish to become doctors.

25. **C**   The sentence has a verb tense error in (C). The time is given as *the past several decades* so the present perfect *have closed* is the appropriate verb construction in the sentence since the time frame is an unspecified point before now.

26. **C**   Because the *later presidents* had more than one term among them, the singular pronoun *that* in (C) is incorrect; it should be the plural *those.*

27. **E**   There is no error in this sentence. (C) might be tempting, but if *my wife and* is removed from the sentence, it is clear that the correct pronoun case is being used.

28. **A**   *Neither* is a singular, and needs to be followed with "is" rather than *are* as seen in (A).

29. A   (A) uses the incorrect verb construction, the past perfect "had run" is appropriate in the sentence since this is an action completed before something else that happened in the past.

30. A   The sentence is fine as it is. (B) and (C) are incomplete sentences. (D) is unclear, and makes it sound as if the students are allowed to wear unacceptable clothing. (E) is wordier than the original, and it also creates a run on, since a complete idea does not follow the comma.

31. B   While each of the nouns in the answer choices are mentioned in the passage, the context makes it clear that what is being discussed in the first paragraph is *the dress code*.

32. B   This is part of the list of problems begun in sentence 4. *Even so* indicates something opposite, when what we need is something that indicates a continuation, as *Most importantly* in (B) does.

33. C   A conclusion should tie in to the previous sentence, and effectively end the passage. *Thus* in (C) is a conjunction that connects two thoughts together in a cause and effect relationship, and the content of (C) and sentence 11 work together well in that sentence 11 is about how *making decisions about...* what to wear helps students *grow into mature adults* and (C) continues the theme in suggesting that this choice is part of *an educational process* that the lack of choice would *impede*. The other choices do not connect as well to 11 or introduce new ideas.

34. D   The argument as presented is pretty one-sided. It is overwhelmingly negative in its presentation of dress codes. Addressing some positive aspects of dress codes would be a more balanced argument, and would be more persuasive as it shows the author has weighed both pros and cons in coming to a thoughtful decision about whether dress codes are good or bad overall. Only (D) adds information that would create a more balanced argument.

35. D   (A) creates a comma splice. (B) is wordy. (C) uses the incorrect pronoun to refer to *students*: *which* should be *whom*. (E) is awkward: beware of sentences that use the word "being;" it's usually bad news on the SAT. Only (D) clearly identifies the students with the correct pronoun and includes no other errors.

SECTION 5

1. C   We want to know which expression gives the value of the nth term. There are four examples above the question. The 1st term ($n = 1$) has a value of 6; the 2nd term ($n = 2$) has a value of 12; the 3rd term ($n = 3$) has a value of 24 . Plug In each value of n into the answers and eliminate expressions that do not give the value of that term. Eliminate (A) and (B) because they don't give 6 when $n = 1$. Eliminate (E) because it doesn't give 12 when $n = 2$. Eliminate (D) because it doesn't give 24 when $n = 1$. Only (C) works with all the numbers.

2.   E   You can find the value of 10*d* by using simultaneous equations. By placing one equation on top of the other and adding the two equations, you are left with $5d = -15$.

$$\begin{array}{r} 3d - 2q = 17 \\ +\ 2d + 2q = -32 \\ \hline 5d \qquad = -15 \end{array}$$

Now multiply the resulting equation by 2 on both sides to obtain $10d = -30$. You don't even have to solve for *d*!

3.   E   A circle with an area of 16π has a radius of 4. (A) and (C) are too big. The circle in (B) has a radius of 16. The one in (D) has a radius of 2. (E) is correct because the formula for circumference is $2\pi r$, so a circle with a circumference of 8π has a radius of 4.

4.   B   Test out numbers for *x*. If $x = 0$, x^2 is also 0, and $y = -5$. Eliminate (C) and (D). Because the square of any integer other than zero is positive, *y* can never be negative, so eliminate (E) since negative numbers are real numbers. If $x = 10$, then $y = 95$, which rules out (A). (B) is correct.

5.   A   There are 50 even integers in set *A* since the question states that 100 is included in the list. The word *inclusive* is not applied *to less than 40* so we need to know how many numbers are 38 or below. From 2 through 38 there are 19 even integers out of the total of 50, so the probability is (A) $\dfrac{19}{50}$.

6.   A   The answer choices represent the point value of the blue token. Since we are given the point values for blue and red together (12) and blue and green together (13) we can subtract the value in each answer to find the points for red and green separately, and see if they add to 15 as stated in the question. (A) is correct: subtracting 5 blue from 12 red leaves 7 red. 5 blue from 13 green leaves 8 green. $7 + 8 = 15$.

7.   E   Use the graph. Where are the *y*-coordinates the same? There are two where $y = 2$, three where $y = 1$, and two where $y = 0$. Now check to see if the *x*-value of one point is 3 times the value of another at the same *y*-value. The answer is (E). If $c = 9$, we get $f(9) = f(3)$, which is true because both have a *y*-value of 0.

8.   C   Small sides are opposite small angles and big sides are opposite big angles. Eliminate (A) and (B) because *BC* is the hypotenuse: it's across from the biggest angle. Neither *b* nor *c* can be equal to or larger than 90°, eliminate (E). The question states that $AB < AC$, *b* must be bigger than *c*, so eliminate (E), in which $b = c$. (C) is correct.

9.   8   The formula for area of a triangle is $\dfrac{1}{2}bh$. We are given the area (40) and *AC* is the base, so $b = 10$. Now we can solve for height, since $h = BD$. $40 = \dfrac{1}{2}(10)h$, so $40 = 5h$ and $h = 8$.

10.   0   Plug $x = 5$ into the function. $2(5) - 10 = 10 - 10 = 0$.

11. **20** Be careful! The question asks only about the number of female students at the two schools, though the data is given for the females at Gateway, and the males at Riverdale. For Gateway we are told that 60% of 300 students are female. We can translate this into math: $\frac{60}{100} \times 300 = 180$ female students. Because we are told that 60% of Riverdale's students are male, we know that 40% of the 400 students are female: $\frac{40}{100} \times 400 = 160$. $180 - 160 = 20$, so there are 20 more female students at Gateway than at Riverdale.

12. $\frac{4}{3}$ **or 1.33**

Remember to distribute the number in front of the parentheses to all parts within the parentheses:

$$2(x + 2) + 4(x - 1) = 8$$
$$2x + 4 + 4x - 4 = 8$$
$$6x = 8$$

so $x = \frac{8}{6}$. If you grid in an equivalent, such as $\frac{4}{3}$ or 1.33, you also get credit for the question.

13. **9** The question asks for x^2, so find x first. In $3^{x+1} = 9^2$, we can turn 9 into a number with a base number of 3 to simplify the comparison: $3^{x+1} = (3^2)^2$, so $3^{x+1} = 3^4$. Because the bases are the same, we know that $x + 1 = 4$, so $x = 3$. We need to find x^2, so the answer is 9.

14. $\frac{1}{3}$ **or .333**

The slope formula is $\frac{y_2 - y_1}{x_2 - x_1}$. The points in the graph are at $(-3, 0)$ and $(0, 1)$ so $\frac{1-0}{0-(-3)} = \frac{1}{3}$. The slope formula can be simplified as $\frac{rise}{run}$ so if you see that the line rises 1 unit up while it runs 3 units sideways, you also get $\frac{1}{3}$.

15. $\frac{1}{2}$ **or .5**

Simplify the equation by multiplying everything by 2 to get rid of the fractions: $n + \frac{n}{2} = \frac{n+1}{2}$ becomes $2n + n = n + 1$. Get n by itself: $3n = n + 1$, so $2n = 1$ and $n = \frac{1}{2}$.

16. **60** The formula for circumference is 2π, so a circle with a circumference of 32π has a radius of 16. We know that $AB = 16$, so triangle ABO, made up of two radii and AB is actually equilateral (remember, the figure is not drawn to scale). Since all angles of an equilateral triangle are 60°, and angle BAC is an angle of that triangle, the answer is 60.

17. **30** It is easier to deal with minutes than with fractions of hours. $3\frac{1}{3}$ hours × 60 minutes = 200 minutes. So the trip to the beach + the trip home = 200 minutes. If we make the way home is x, then the way to the beach is $1\frac{1}{2}x$. Solve for x: $1\frac{1}{2}x + x = 200$, so $\frac{5}{2}x = 200$, $5x = 400$, and $x = 80$. So now we know that x (the way home) took 80 minutes and the way to the beach took $1\frac{1}{2}$ times that, or 120 minutes. Now we know that the 60 miles to the beach took 2 hours, for a rate of 30 miles per hour.

18. **90** Notice that the height for both triangles is the same (it would be a line straight down from point X). The base is the only difference between the triangles. The areas of the triangles are proportional to the bases of the triangles. Since UZ is 30 percent of UY, the area of triangle UXZ is 30 percent of triangle UXY. That makes the area of triangle XYZ 70 percent of the area of triangle UXY. The question states that XYZ has an area of 210. Set up a proportion: $\frac{30}{70} = \frac{x}{210}$. Solve for x: $x = 90$.

SECTION 6

1. **C** The *landlords* were *unable to finance* what they wanted to do, so they do not have enough *resources*. We need a word for the blank that means "not enough." Only (C), *inadequate* has a close meaning.

2. **E** Mrs. Smedley's worry is that the daughter is marrying *beneath her*. The blank and *herself* refers to the daughter, so "lower" is a good word for the blank. If you don't know all the words, eliminate answers that have words you know couldn't mean "lower." Only (E) *demean* matches in meaning.

3. **A** We know that the words for the blanks must be opposite, because *the director did not* consider the description in the first blank to be correct, and the second blank is the director's (opposite) opinion of her film. The part of the sentence after the colon lets us know the director believes her movie is *fair*: a good word for the second blank, so the first blank must mean "unfair". Only (A) *biased… equitable* matches "unfair"…"fair."

4. **D** Finding the correct answer depends on the relationship between the blanks. If the *Japanese artists* were liked *Western contemporary art* they would "copy" its *bold expressiveness*. If they disliked the art, they would "reject" its traits. For the second blank, neither (B) disclose or (E) overrun makes sense in either case, and (A), (C), and (D) are all somewhat close to "copy" so we need to find a match for the first blank that indicates "liking" the art. (A) and (C) are negative, leaving only (D) as a match for both blanks.

5.   **A**   The nurses were able to *uplift* sad people, so they must have "uplifting" or "upbeat" *personalities.* There is some tough vocab in the answers. (A) *winsome,* which means "charming; winning; engaging" is correct.

6.   **D**   The passage describes the history of the word "boycott." (A) is incorrect, because the passage doesn't state why the word is *popular.* (B) is incorrect, because it tells about the incident that inspired the word, not the history of its *usage.* There is no *unrelated story* (C) here, and no *shift* in the word's meaning is given.

7.   **B**   Inference questions must be supported by evidence in the passage. Eliminate (A) because Boycott may have done it himself or found someone who wasn't protesting. (B) is true: the townspeople refused Boycott service and so were taking the farmers' side. The *all* in (C) and *never* in (E) is extreme. (D) *physical harm* is not mentioned in the passage.

8.   **B**   The passage is about how and why "The Little Mermaid" changed over time. No *unscrupulous publishers* are mentioned so eliminate (A). (B) is true: reasons for the changes are given. (C) is extreme and too broad. (D) is mentioned, but it is not the main point. (E) is not supported by the passage.

9.   **D**   The first mention of *sea foam* in line 4 states what happened at the end of the fairy tale, and the second mention in line 14 describes what happened to Andersen's *original meanings* so there is a comparison being made, using a phrase from one of his stories. (A) *obsession* is too strong. (B) is incorrect, because we are told only of one work, not enough to discover *a prevalent theme* among his stories. There is no evidence for (C), and (E) *prove* is too strong. (D) is correct, a *metaphor* is a figure of speech that compares one thing to another.

10.   **B**   A *primary purpose* question like this one asks "Why did the author write this passage?" The passage talks about both the British and Zulu sides of the war without taking one side over the other. The second through fourth paragraphs in particular discuss why some British soldiers decided to join the war, and also why the Zulu took part. This is paraphrased nicely in (B). (A) does not mention the Zulu at all. The *myths* in the passage refer to reasons why the British were defeated, not about *relations* so eliminate (C). (D) is incorrect because *loyalty* is not the main focus of the passage and (E) is much broader that what's covered in this short text.

11.   **D**   Private Moss joined the war *for the Queen's shilling,* or in other words, for the money. Only (D) mentions *money.*

12.   **D**   The paragraph that contains the quote from the question begins *Neither side had a clue as to why they were involved,* and (D) captures this with *uncertainty about the reasons for their participation.* None of the other answers address the soldiers' cluelessness about *why they were involved.*

13. **B** The fourth paragraph is primarily about the attitudes of the British officers compared to that of the Zulu. The British thought it was a *game* and the Zulu *fought to defend land, homes, and families.* These are opposite, so eliminate (A) because *both* describes similarity. (B) paraphrases "game vs. defense" well. Eliminate (C) because *aristocrats* describes only the officers, not the whole *military force.* (D) and (E) come from other parts of the passage, and the question is only about the fourth paragraph.

14. **B** Lines 38–43 describe how *massacre* and *victory* mean the same thing, but *massacre* is used to avoid saying that the Zulu had won a victory. (B) comes closest: the word *massacre* makes it sound like the Zulu are doing something particularly bad or evil, when the British are doing the exact same thing. (A) goes against the passage: the British are described as *brutal* in the paragraph. (C) is opposite of what is stated in the passage. There is no evidence for (D) or (E).

15. **C** The *myth* was the reasons that were created to explain how the British could be defeated by a supposedly inferior force. This is paraphrased best in (C). (D) may be tempting, but it describes the myth itself, not why it was created.

16. **D** Lines 3 and 4 state that *her translations were highly praised throughout her literary career,* making (D) the correct answer. (A) may be tempting, but her poetry had a negative reception, so eliminate (A).

17. **E** In line 19, *Panaev* is described as a *utilitarian* critic who felt poetry should be *useful.* Of all the answers, only (E) *offer solutions* could be considered *useful.*

18. **B** Only (B) *unwilling to develop* contradicts the passage. Lines 27–29 state that these poets still were part of the romantic tradition, but *their work was nevertheless developing.*

19. **D** The third paragraph is about how poets' works were developing, then *A Double Life* is given as an example of a work that encompasses these trends. This is best described in (D). (A) is incorrect: it tell how Pavlova's work was like her contemporaries'. There is no support for (B) or (E), and (C) is opposite of what is stated in the passage.

20. **B** The "stories in verse" *helped keep poetry alive* when readers preferred prose. Adding the elements of a story to poetry is best paraphrased in (B) that it drew *from non-poetical works.*

21. **C** The passage states that the critics *did not consider* the issue of women's education to be a problem. They are more concerned with *the oppression of Russia's peasant class.* (A) seems close because it mentions *peasants,* but *education* is too specific a focus; the critics are more concerned with *oppression.* (B), (D), and (E) are not mentioned in the passage. Only (C) discusses *class.*

22. **A** Go back to the passage and use the context to come up with a word to replace *address.* A good phrase might be "focus on." The only answer that works in the context of the passage is (A) *attend to.*

23.   E   The *main criticism* of *A Double Life* was that is *lacked substance* (lines 43–45) and did not focus on class. The author states that *these critics obviously overlooked the point* of her work and describes that it did indeed evoke *her class*. The phrase "*overlooked* qualities of her writing" can be paraphrased as *inability to recognize* seen in (E). There is no evidence in the passage for the other answers.

24.   A   The critics were concerned that Pavalova's work took focus away from the peasant class. Only (A) and (D) mention anything about the peasant class, but (D) would actually strengthen the criticism, rather than weaken it as the question states. This makes (A) the best answer.

SECTION 8

1.   C   First eliminate any number that does not fulfill the first part of the statement. All of the numbers are divisible by 4, but (B) and (E) are not divisible by 8, so eliminate them. Now that we have just the numbers that are divisible by 4 and 8, we can disprove the statement by finding one that is not divisible by 12. (A) and (D) are both divisible by 12, but (C) 40 is not. (C) is correct.

2.   B   All radii are equal, so since BC has a length of 5 (the distance between y-values of 2 and 7) AB must also have a length of 5. The distance between the x-values of x and 1 must be 5, and x is a negative number, so $x = -4$, answer (B).

3.   B   The equations in the answers are in the $y = mx + b$ format. From the image, we know that the y-intercept (b) is negative. Eliminate (A) and (C) because they show a positive y-intercept, and eliminate (E) because it shows none. The slope of the line (m) is pointing up, and is positive, so eliminate (D) for having a negative slope. (B) is correct.

4.   D   We need to translate this word problem into math. If dress socks is d and athletic socks are a, we want to find $a + b$. We can show the first statement as $3d + 4a = 27$ and the second as $4d + 3a = 29$. If we stack these equations on top of one another and add them together to get the same number of dress and athletic socks:

$$3d + 4a = 27$$
$$\underline{+ \ 4d + 3a = 29}$$
$$7d + 7a = 56$$

Divide all parts of the final equation by 7 to see that $a + b = 8$, answer (D).

5. **D** We know the variables for x and f are the price and number of brownies per hour, respectively. Because f is the y-value on the coordinate plane, sketch the line they make on the coordinate plane. Selling brownies that cost $1.50 at a rate of 7 brownies an hour gives a coordinate pair of (1.5, 7), and selling brownies that cost $2.00 at a rate of 5 brownies an hour gives a coordinate pair of (2, 5). The line that connects these points slants downward, so it has a negative slope. The $f(x)$ in the answers can be replaced by y, and then it's more clear that the answers are the equation of a line, $y = mx + b$. Eliminate (A) and (B) because they show a positive slope. The slope formula can be simplified as $\dfrac{rise}{run}$, with the difference in y-values as the rise, and the difference in x values as the run. The negative slope means we need the negative difference between 5 and 7 as our rise. The run is positive 0.5: $\dfrac{-2}{0.5} = -4$. Eliminate (C) and (E). (D) is correct because is has a slope of -4.

6. **E** Come up with some numbers that fulfill the statements in the question, and see which answers you can eliminate. Both a and b must be negative, and a negative times a negative is positive, so that eliminates (A), and (B). If $a = -2$ and $b = -\dfrac{1}{2}$, then $ab = 1$. That gets rid of (C) and (D) because they don't include 1, only (E) is left, and it is the correct answer.

7. **A** Use your own numbers to replace the variables to make this problem easier to solve. If $p = 4$ and $w = 30$ that means we can purchase 4 items for $60, and we need to find out how many items we can purchase for $30. For half the amount of money, we can get half the number of items, so we can get 2 items. Now replace the variables in the answers with $p = 4$ and $w = 30$, and the answer that gives 2 is correct. Only (A) gives 2, while (B) and (D) are too small and (C) and (E) are too large.

8. **B** Get rid of the answers that are not true based on information in the graph. Eliminate (A) because reducing from $10 to $5 resulted in the same number of sales. (C) is not true, because there is a difference in sales based on price. (D) states the opposite of what is seen in the graph. (E) can not be confirmed from the chart's information. (B) is true: between $20 and $10, the lower the price, the higher the sales. A lower price than $10 did not change sales. (B) is a good paraphrase of this.

9. **B** Replace the x in the answer choices and eliminate any that give a result of 1—we're looking for what CANNOT be $f(x)$. (A), (C), (D), and (E) all give 1, but (B) gives -1. (B) is correct.

10. **E** Out of the 27 questions Cathy answered, she has missed 9 questions. Since we want to find out the least number of questions on the test, so we won't add any more misses. If $\frac{5}{6}$ of the answers are correct, then $\frac{1}{6}$ were missed. 9 is $\frac{1}{6}$ of what? Translate that question into $9 = \frac{1}{6}x$ and solve for x: $x = 54$, (E).

11. **A** The 10 tiles form a box without overlapping, so there are 2 tiles on each of the 4 sides, and one tile each at top and bottom. Each tile has a perimeter of 24, so the edge of each tile is 6. If the box is 2 tiles tall, that's a height of 12 centimeters. The bottom is one tile, so that's a width and depth of 6 for each dimension. $12 \times 6 \times 6 = 432$, answer (A).

12. **E** The easiest way to solve this is to use each of the answers in place of x and see which makes the equation true. Since we are taking a square root, the easiest answers to check are those that are perfect squares (A) gives $4 = 0$ which is not true. Hold on to (B) since its root is not an integer. (C) gives $8 = 6$ which is not true. (D) gives $10 = 9$ which is not true. (E) gives $12 = 12$ which is correct. (No need to go back to check (B) now.)

13. **B** Come up with some numbers to serve as an example of the situation described to figure this one out. One example of a list in which mean, median and mode are all equal is {2, 4, 4, 6}. If we add a 4 to the list, it changes nothing, thereby eliminating (A). If we add a 0 and an 8 to the list, it also adds nothing, thereby eliminating (C). Adding 2 to each number leaves us with {4, 6, 6, 8}, which has a mean of 6, mode of 6, and median of 6, which lets us get rid of (D). Removing the first and last numbers would leave us with {4, 4}, which is fine; therefore, eliminate (E). Remember, we're looking for the thing that CANNOT be done to the original list. Adding a number such as 11 does change the mean to a 7, while the mode is still 4, so (B) definitely is the correct answer.

14. **E** Draw out the possibilities: If points L, M, and N are in a straight line in that order, LN has a length of 13. Statement III is true, so eliminate (A) and (B) because they have no III. If L is between M and N, the whole line has a length of 9, LM takes up 4 of that, leaving LN to be 5 units long. Statement I is true; eliminate (C) because it had no I. Statement 2 is true: If LMN is a triangle, we know that one side is 4 and another is 9. The third-side rule is that the length of the third side of the triangle must be less than the sum of the other two legs (13) but greater than the difference between the legs (5). Since 8 is between 5 and 13, II is true and (E) is correct.

15. **D** The radius of the circle is also the height of the triangle. A line that is tangent to a circle is perpendicular to the radius of the circle, so drawing the height splits *AOB* into two 30-60-90 triangles. Angle *B* must be 30° because *AB* is a line, so angle *B* added to the 150° shown must add up to 180°. A 30-60-90 triangle has sides in the ratio of $x : x\sqrt{3} : 2x$, respectively. Since the height of 6 is opposite the 30° angle, the base of each 30-60-90 triangle is $6\sqrt{3}$. Since we want to find the area of the larger triangle *AOB*, double the base of the 30-60-90 triangle and use the area formula: $\frac{1}{2}bh = \frac{1}{2}(12\sqrt{3})(6) = 36\sqrt{3}$ and (D) is correct.

16. **D** Because *y* + 1 is within the absolute value brackets, that means the correct graph will have 2 *y*-values for every *x* value, a positive *y* and a negative *y*. For example, if *x* = 0, then $|y+1| = 3$. The value within the brackets could be 3 or –3, which means that the correct graph shows *y* as 2 and –4 when *x* is 0. (A), (B), and (D) show only one of these points. Now go back to the equation, but this time make *y* = 0. The inside of the brackets is positive, as is absolute value, so *x* can be 2 only when *y* = 0. Eliminate (E) because it shows (–2, 0) and (–4, 0). (D) is correct.

SECTION 9

1. **A** *Piercing* and *primordial fears* indicate something unpleasant. Only (A) fits. (C) is positive; (B) and (D) are neutral; (E) is negative but not unpleasant.

2. **C** The phrase *the real name…is Daniel Handler* indicates that the blank must mean "not a real name." Only (C) *a pseudonym* means "fake name."

3. **B** The *Quan Yin symbol* is known for its *purifying qualities*, and it is used *after an argument or disagreement* so the symbol can "remove bad feelings from" *an environment*. We need a word that means something similar to "remove bad feelings from." That's a positive quality, so we can eliminate (A) and (E) for being negative. (B) *harmonize* means "to bring into harmony, accord, or agreement" so it removes *disagreement*.

4. **C** The word *but* indicates that *Heather* and *Ms. Shockey* feel differently about something. The portion of the sentence after the colon indicates that Ms. Shockey *did not find Heather's essay particularly exceptional* so the second blank means "not impressed." Eliminate (A) (neutral) and (B) and (D) (positive). (C) and (E) both have negative words, but only (C) *indifferent* is close in meaning to "not impressed." We need a positive word for the first blank and *confident* fits well. (C) is correct.

5. E   The *policy changes* resulted in something bad. The word *seemingly* indicates that the first blank means something positive and the bad result of the changes let us know that the second blank is something negative. The first word in (B) and (C) are negative, so eliminate them. The second word in (D) is positive so eliminate it. The words in (A) are neither positive nor negative, while (E) fits the positive negative pattern. (E) is correct.

6. E   The clue *could not be verified* indicates that the blank should mean "not verified" or "untrue." (E) *specious* is the only choice that means "untrue." (A) *substantiated* and (D) *indubitable* mean the opposite of untrue.

7. C   The *company* refers to the audience, the people there *to see the new performer*. Only (C) talks about the audience.

8. B   The passage describes the audience as *stimulated by curiosity* but having no hopes for good entertainment. This is paraphrased in (B) *expected a mediocre performance*. (A) and (C) are the opposite of what's indicated by the passage because they describe the show positively. There is no evidence for (D) or (E).

9. A   The *novelty and propriety* of Garrick's acting style *threw the critics into some hesitation* because it was different from common acting styles of the day. (A) is a good paraphrase of this. The rest of the answers are not supported by the passage.

10. A   The paragraph that describes *the applause* also mentions *the triumph of the actor*, so it was a good show and the audience liked it. Only (A) describes this situation.

11. C   Go back to the passage and use the context to come up with a word to replace *manly*. The word is defined after the dash: *there was nothing of the trick about it*. So *honest* (C) is a good replacement. Some of the other words are meanings for "manly" but they do not fit the context of the passage.

12. D   The facial expressions are described as *rigid, cold,* and *colorless* this is closest to (D) *stoic and unfeeling*.

13. A   The passage indicates that *never until his time* did anyone act like Garrick. (A) describes a time before Garrick during which actors acted in the same way, which would weaken the idea that Garrick *introduced* the style. (C) strengthens the argument, while (B), (D), and (E) don't have any bearing on the argument.

14. B   The passage states that Macklin criticized Garrick because he used *action and his gestures* to draw attention to himself. This is paraphrased in (B).

15. C   In the last paragraph of Passage 2, the author agrees with Macklin that Garrick called too much attention to himself, and gives a reason for why Garrick was motivated to do so. Only (C) *justifiable* indicates agreement with Macklin's opinion.

16. **E** The passage gives *public applause* as the *palm* Garrick desired. This is closest to *symbol of triumph* (E). (B) and (C) are overly literal meanings of *palm* and do not fit the context.

17. **B** The author of Passage 2 criticizes Garrick for hogging the spotlight. If the author saw Garrick perform and he did not try to hog the spotlight, the author would like Garrick better. This is paraphrased in (B).

18. **A** The descriptions *familiar* and *natural* are part of larger descriptions that state that this acting style had not been seen before Garrick. Only (A) captures this. The other answers do not mention Garrick's style of acting.

19. **A** The statement referred to in the question is about Garrick being the first person to act in a natural style. The closest match to this is (A), from the portion of Passage 1 that describes how Garrick surprised the critics with this novel acting style.

SECTION 10

1. **B** The word *Since* at the beginning of the sentence conflicts with the conjunction *as* after the comma. Eliminate (A) and (C). In (E) *be counting* creates an awkward and wordy. (B) is correct; it is shorter and clearer than (D).

2. **C** Keep the sentence short and simple. The underlined part explains why Wallace founded the group. (C) gets that across simply. (A) is wordy and uses an incorrect idiom, (B) lacks a comma before *and*, which makes it sound like the goal was doing the generating, (D) adds the unnecessary *therefore*, and (E) loses the meaning and incorrectly links the phrases.

3. **B** The word *that* is unnecessary and prevents the sentence from being parallel. (B) removes *that* and so is correct. (C) changes the meaning of the sentence. (D) and (E) are not parallel.

4. **A** The sentence is correct as written. The phrase *In 1982* indicates that the verb needs to be in the past tense. Eliminate (B) because it is in the present tense. (C) and (D) are in the past tense, but *was* and *were* indicate that a different band was *the first* in other years, which is not true: the first to do something is always the first. (E) changes the meaning of the sentence.

5. **D** The sentence as written has a misplaced modifier. The subject right after the comma is what is described before the comma, so we need *Ryan* not *Ryan's commute*. Only (D) starts with *Ryan*.

6. **D** The underlined portion of the sentence contains the redundant pronoun *it*. (B) has the same problem. (C) and (E) use a verb form, *roaring,* that does not agree with the rest of the sentence. (D) removes the unnecessary *it* and remains in the proper tense.

7. **E** The sentence as written has a misplaced modifier. The subject right after the comma should be someone who can carry something, not the *manager's search*. Only in (E) is a person mentioned: *the equipment manager*. (E) is correct.

8. **C** (A), (D), and (E) all lack the necessary part of the idiomatic phrase "but also." (B) is wordy, redundant, and lacks parallelism. (C) corrects all of these problems.

9. **D** The sentence switches pronouns, using both *your* and *one's*. Eliminate (A); (E) has the same problem. In (B), *their* doesn't agree with *a prospective applicant*. (C) lacks a subject for *proofread*. In (D), *their applications* and *their essays* agree with *prospective students*.

10. **E** The noun *variedness* is incorrect: *variety* matches the form of *beauty*, the other quality of *aquatic life*. Only (E) finishes the idiom *such…that* and the verb is in the present tense as it is in the non-underlined portion of the sentence.

11. **B** The sentence as written is wordy and redundant. Most of the answer choices share this problem, but (B) is short and simple while giving us all the information we need.

12. **D** This is an incomplete sentence: the comma begins a descriptive phrase in (A), (B), and (C), but never finishes the idea that was begun before the comma. (E) uses an inappropriate conjunction *and*. Only (D) is a complete sentence that correctly uses *where* to link the actions described in the second part of the sentence to *certain countries*.

13. **C** This sentence uses the wrong transition *and*. The second part of the sentence describes a situation opposite to that described in the first part, so we need a transition that shows an opposing relationship. This is seen in (B) *but* and (C) *however*. (B) is unnecessarily wordy, so (C) is correct.

14. **A** There are no errors in the sentence as it is written. As you can tell from the way the first word of each answer choice switches between *contributes* to *contribute*, the first issue you need to deal with is subject-verb agreement. The subject of the sentence is *choices*, which is plural. Therefore, we need the plural verb *contribute*. Eliminate (B) and (C). (E) incorrectly uses the pronoun *it*; it is unclear to what it is referring, so eliminate (E). The big difference between (A) and (D) is the verb *do*. (A) uses the singular verb *does*, while (D) uses the plural verb *do*. The subject of this verb is the singular noun *decor*, so (A) is correct.

Chapter 14
Practice Test 6

IMPORTANT: The following codes should be copied onto your answer sheet exactly as shown.

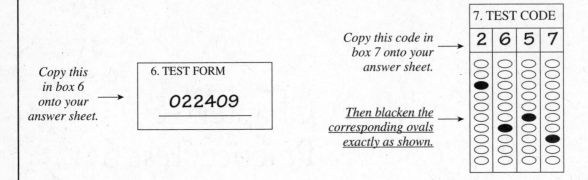

Copy this in box 6 onto your answer sheet.

6. TEST FORM

022409

Copy this code in box 7 onto your answer sheet.

Then blacken the corresponding ovals exactly as shown.

7. TEST CODE

2 6 5 7

General Directions

You will have three hours and 20 minutes to work on this objective test designed to familiarize you with all aspects of the SAT.

This test contains five 25-minute sections, two 20-minute sections, one 10-minute section, and one 25-minute essay. The supervisor will tell you when to begin and end each section. During the time allowed for each section, you may work only on that particular section. If you finish your work before time is called, you may check your work on that section, but you are not to work on any other section.

You will find specific directions for each type of question found in the test. **Be sure you understand the directions before attempting to answer any of the questions.**

YOU ARE TO INDICATE ALL YOUR ANSWERS ON THE SEPARATE ANSWER SHEET:

1. The test booklet may be used for scratchwork. However, no credit will be given for anything written in the test booklet.

2. Once you have decided on an answer to a question, darken the corresponding space on the answer sheet. Give only one answer to each question.

3. There are 40 numbered answer spaces for each section; be sure to use only those spaces that correspond to the test questions.

4. **Be sure each answer mark is dark and completely fills the answer space.** Do not make any stray marks on your answer sheet.

5. If you wish to change an answer, erase your first mark completely—an incomplete erasure may be considered an intended response—and blacken your new answer choice.

Your score on this test is based on the number of questions you answer correctly minus a fraction of the number of questions you answer incorrectly. Therefore, it is improbable that random or haphazard guessing will alter your score significantly. There are no deductions for incorrect answers on the student-produced response questions. However, if you are able to eliminate one or more of the answer choices on any question as wrong, it is generally to your advantage to guess at one of the remaining choices. Remember, however, not to spend too much time on any one question.

Diagnostic Test Form

Use a No. 2 pencil only. Be sure each mark is dark and completely fills the intended oval. Completely erase any errors or stray marks.

1 Your Name:

(Print)

Last   First   M.I.

Signature: _____ Date ___/___/___

Home Address: _____

Number and Street   City   State   Zip Code

E-Mail: _____ School: _____ Class: _____

(Print)

2 YOUR NAME

Last Name (First 4 Letters) | FIRST INIT | MID INIT

3 PHONE NUMBER

0	0	0	0	0	0	0
1	1	1	1	1	1	1
2	2	2	2	2	2	2
3	3	3	3	3	3	3
4	4	4	4	4	4	4
5	5	5	5	5	5	5
6	6	6	6	6	6	6
7	7	7	7	7	7	7
8	8	8	8	8	8	8
9	9	9	9	9	9	9

4 DATE OF BIRTH

MONTH	DAY		YEAR	
○ JAN				
○ FEB				
○ MAR	0	0		0
○ APR	1	1		1
○ MAY	2	2		2
○ JUN	3	3		3
○ JUL		4		4
○ AUG		5	5	5
○ SEP		6	6	6
○ OCT		7	7	7
○ NOV		8	8	8
○ DEC		9	9	9

5 SEX
○ MALE
○ FEMALE

IMPORTANT: Fill in items 6 and 7 exactly as shown on the preceding page.

6 TEST FORM
(Copy from back of test book)

7 TEST CODE

0	0	0	0
1	1	1	1
2	2	2	2
3	3	3	3
4	4	4	4
5	5	5	5
6	6	6	6
7	7	7	7
8	8	8	8
9	9	9	9

8 OTHER
1 Ⓐ Ⓑ Ⓒ Ⓓ Ⓔ
2 Ⓐ Ⓑ Ⓒ Ⓓ Ⓔ
3 Ⓐ Ⓑ Ⓒ Ⓓ Ⓔ

PLEASE DO NOT WRITE IN THIS AREA

SERIAL #

THIS PAGE INTENTIONALLY LEFT BLANK

SECTION 1

IMPORTANT: **USE A NO. 2 PENCIL. DO NOT WRITE OUTSIDE THE BORDER!**
Words written outside the essay box or written in ink **WILL NOT APPEAR** in the copy sent to be scored and your score will be affected.

Begin your essay on this page. If you need more space, continue on the next page.

Continue on the next page, if necessary.

SECTION 2

1. Ⓐ Ⓑ Ⓒ Ⓓ Ⓔ
2. Ⓐ Ⓑ Ⓒ Ⓓ Ⓔ
3. Ⓐ Ⓑ Ⓒ Ⓓ Ⓔ
4. Ⓐ Ⓑ Ⓒ Ⓓ Ⓔ
5. Ⓐ Ⓑ Ⓒ Ⓓ Ⓔ
6. Ⓐ Ⓑ Ⓒ Ⓓ Ⓔ
7. Ⓐ Ⓑ Ⓒ Ⓓ Ⓔ
8. Ⓐ Ⓑ Ⓒ Ⓓ Ⓔ
9. Ⓐ Ⓑ Ⓒ Ⓓ Ⓔ
10. Ⓐ Ⓑ Ⓒ Ⓓ Ⓔ

11. Ⓐ Ⓑ Ⓒ Ⓓ Ⓔ
12. Ⓐ Ⓑ Ⓒ Ⓓ Ⓔ
13. Ⓐ Ⓑ Ⓒ Ⓓ Ⓔ
14. Ⓐ Ⓑ Ⓒ Ⓓ Ⓔ
15. Ⓐ Ⓑ Ⓒ Ⓓ Ⓔ
16. Ⓐ Ⓑ Ⓒ Ⓓ Ⓔ
17. Ⓐ Ⓑ Ⓒ Ⓓ Ⓔ
18. Ⓐ Ⓑ Ⓒ Ⓓ Ⓔ
19. Ⓐ Ⓑ Ⓒ Ⓓ Ⓔ
20. Ⓐ Ⓑ Ⓒ Ⓓ Ⓔ

21. Ⓐ Ⓑ Ⓒ Ⓓ Ⓔ
22. Ⓐ Ⓑ Ⓒ Ⓓ Ⓔ
23. Ⓐ Ⓑ Ⓒ Ⓓ Ⓔ
24. Ⓐ Ⓑ Ⓒ Ⓓ Ⓔ
25. Ⓐ Ⓑ Ⓒ Ⓓ Ⓔ
26. Ⓐ Ⓑ Ⓒ Ⓓ Ⓔ
27. Ⓐ Ⓑ Ⓒ Ⓓ Ⓔ
28. Ⓐ Ⓑ Ⓒ Ⓓ Ⓔ
29. Ⓐ Ⓑ Ⓒ Ⓓ Ⓔ
30. Ⓐ Ⓑ Ⓒ Ⓓ Ⓔ

31. Ⓐ Ⓑ Ⓒ Ⓓ Ⓔ
32. Ⓐ Ⓑ Ⓒ Ⓓ Ⓔ
33. Ⓐ Ⓑ Ⓒ Ⓓ Ⓔ
34. Ⓐ Ⓑ Ⓒ Ⓓ Ⓔ
35. Ⓐ Ⓑ Ⓒ Ⓓ Ⓔ
36. Ⓐ Ⓑ Ⓒ Ⓓ Ⓔ
37. Ⓐ Ⓑ Ⓒ Ⓓ Ⓔ
38. Ⓐ Ⓑ Ⓒ Ⓓ Ⓔ
39. Ⓐ Ⓑ Ⓒ Ⓓ Ⓔ
40. Ⓐ Ⓑ Ⓒ Ⓓ Ⓔ

SECTION 3

1. Ⓐ Ⓑ Ⓒ Ⓓ Ⓔ
2. Ⓐ Ⓑ Ⓒ Ⓓ Ⓔ
3. Ⓐ Ⓑ Ⓒ Ⓓ Ⓔ
4. Ⓐ Ⓑ Ⓒ Ⓓ Ⓔ
5. Ⓐ Ⓑ Ⓒ Ⓓ Ⓔ
6. Ⓐ Ⓑ Ⓒ Ⓓ Ⓔ
7. Ⓐ Ⓑ Ⓒ Ⓓ Ⓔ
8. Ⓐ Ⓑ Ⓒ Ⓓ Ⓔ
9. Ⓐ Ⓑ Ⓒ Ⓓ Ⓔ
10. Ⓐ Ⓑ Ⓒ Ⓓ Ⓔ

11. Ⓐ Ⓑ Ⓒ Ⓓ Ⓔ
12. Ⓐ Ⓑ Ⓒ Ⓓ Ⓔ
13. Ⓐ Ⓑ Ⓒ Ⓓ Ⓔ
14. Ⓐ Ⓑ Ⓒ Ⓓ Ⓔ
15. Ⓐ Ⓑ Ⓒ Ⓓ Ⓔ
16. Ⓐ Ⓑ Ⓒ Ⓓ Ⓔ
17. Ⓐ Ⓑ Ⓒ Ⓓ Ⓔ
18. Ⓐ Ⓑ Ⓒ Ⓓ Ⓔ
19. Ⓐ Ⓑ Ⓒ Ⓓ Ⓔ
20. Ⓐ Ⓑ Ⓒ Ⓓ Ⓔ

21. Ⓐ Ⓑ Ⓒ Ⓓ Ⓔ
22. Ⓐ Ⓑ Ⓒ Ⓓ Ⓔ
23. Ⓐ Ⓑ Ⓒ Ⓓ Ⓔ
24. Ⓐ Ⓑ Ⓒ Ⓓ Ⓔ
25. Ⓐ Ⓑ Ⓒ Ⓓ Ⓔ
26. Ⓐ Ⓑ Ⓒ Ⓓ Ⓔ
27. Ⓐ Ⓑ Ⓒ Ⓓ Ⓔ
28. Ⓐ Ⓑ Ⓒ Ⓓ Ⓔ
29. Ⓐ Ⓑ Ⓒ Ⓓ Ⓔ
30. Ⓐ Ⓑ Ⓒ Ⓓ Ⓔ

31. Ⓐ Ⓑ Ⓒ Ⓓ Ⓔ
32. Ⓐ Ⓑ Ⓒ Ⓓ Ⓔ
33. Ⓐ Ⓑ Ⓒ Ⓓ Ⓔ
34. Ⓐ Ⓑ Ⓒ Ⓓ Ⓔ
35. Ⓐ Ⓑ Ⓒ Ⓓ Ⓔ
36. Ⓐ Ⓑ Ⓒ Ⓓ Ⓔ
37. Ⓐ Ⓑ Ⓒ Ⓓ Ⓔ
38. Ⓐ Ⓑ Ⓒ Ⓓ Ⓔ
39. Ⓐ Ⓑ Ⓒ Ⓓ Ⓔ
40. Ⓐ Ⓑ Ⓒ Ⓓ Ⓔ

CAUTION Grid answers in the section below for SECTION 2 or SECTION 3 only if directed to do so in your test book.

Student-Produced Responses

ONLY ANSWERS THAT ARE GRIDDED WILL BE SCORED. YOU WILL NOT RECEIVE CREDIT FOR ANYTHING WRITTEN IN THE BOXES.

Quality Assurance Mark ●

Grids 9, 10, 11, 12, 13, 14, 15, 16, 17, 18 — each with columns for digits 0–9 and fraction/decimal markers.

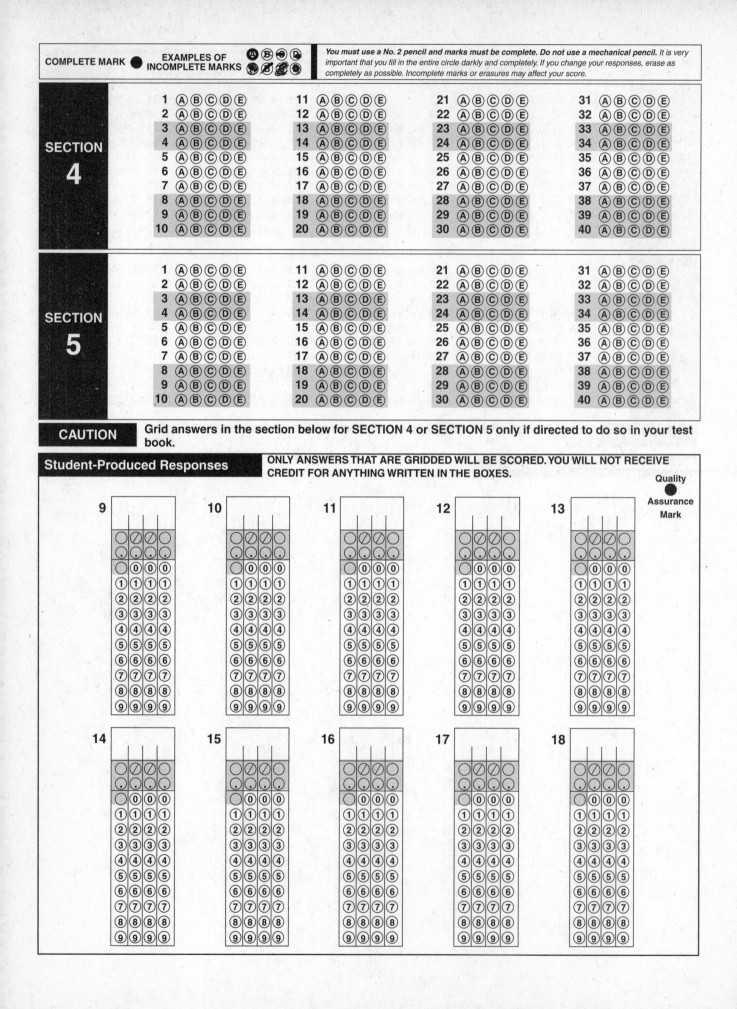

COMPLETE MARK ●   EXAMPLES OF INCOMPLETE MARKS Ⓐ Ⓑ ⊜ Ⓓ ⊗ ⊘ ⊖ ⊕

SECTION 6

1 Ⓐ Ⓑ Ⓒ Ⓓ Ⓔ   11 Ⓐ Ⓑ Ⓒ Ⓓ Ⓔ   21 Ⓐ Ⓑ Ⓒ Ⓓ Ⓔ   31 Ⓐ Ⓑ Ⓒ Ⓓ Ⓔ
2 Ⓐ Ⓑ Ⓒ Ⓓ Ⓔ   12 Ⓐ Ⓑ Ⓒ Ⓓ Ⓔ   22 Ⓐ Ⓑ Ⓒ Ⓓ Ⓔ   32 Ⓐ Ⓑ Ⓒ Ⓓ Ⓔ
3 Ⓐ Ⓑ Ⓒ Ⓓ Ⓔ   13 Ⓐ Ⓑ Ⓒ Ⓓ Ⓔ   23 Ⓐ Ⓑ Ⓒ Ⓓ Ⓔ   33 Ⓐ Ⓑ Ⓒ Ⓓ Ⓔ
4 Ⓐ Ⓑ Ⓒ Ⓓ Ⓔ   14 Ⓐ Ⓑ Ⓒ Ⓓ Ⓔ   24 Ⓐ Ⓑ Ⓒ Ⓓ Ⓔ   34 Ⓐ Ⓑ Ⓒ Ⓓ Ⓔ
5 Ⓐ Ⓑ Ⓒ Ⓓ Ⓔ   15 Ⓐ Ⓑ Ⓒ Ⓓ Ⓔ   25 Ⓐ Ⓑ Ⓒ Ⓓ Ⓔ   35 Ⓐ Ⓑ Ⓒ Ⓓ Ⓔ
6 Ⓐ Ⓑ Ⓒ Ⓓ Ⓔ   16 Ⓐ Ⓑ Ⓒ Ⓓ Ⓔ   26 Ⓐ Ⓑ Ⓒ Ⓓ Ⓔ   36 Ⓐ Ⓑ Ⓒ Ⓓ Ⓔ
7 Ⓐ Ⓑ Ⓒ Ⓓ Ⓔ   17 Ⓐ Ⓑ Ⓒ Ⓓ Ⓔ   27 Ⓐ Ⓑ Ⓒ Ⓓ Ⓔ   37 Ⓐ Ⓑ Ⓒ Ⓓ Ⓔ
8 Ⓐ Ⓑ Ⓒ Ⓓ Ⓔ   18 Ⓐ Ⓑ Ⓒ Ⓓ Ⓔ   28 Ⓐ Ⓑ Ⓒ Ⓓ Ⓔ   38 Ⓐ Ⓑ Ⓒ Ⓓ Ⓔ
9 Ⓐ Ⓑ Ⓒ Ⓓ Ⓔ   19 Ⓐ Ⓑ Ⓒ Ⓓ Ⓔ   29 Ⓐ Ⓑ Ⓒ Ⓓ Ⓔ   39 Ⓐ Ⓑ Ⓒ Ⓓ Ⓔ
10 Ⓐ Ⓑ Ⓒ Ⓓ Ⓔ   20 Ⓐ Ⓑ Ⓒ Ⓓ Ⓔ   30 Ⓐ Ⓑ Ⓒ Ⓓ Ⓔ   40 Ⓐ Ⓑ Ⓒ Ⓓ Ⓔ

SECTION 7

1 Ⓐ Ⓑ Ⓒ Ⓓ Ⓔ   11 Ⓐ Ⓑ Ⓒ Ⓓ Ⓔ   21 Ⓐ Ⓑ Ⓒ Ⓓ Ⓔ   31 Ⓐ Ⓑ Ⓒ Ⓓ Ⓔ
2 Ⓐ Ⓑ Ⓒ Ⓓ Ⓔ   12 Ⓐ Ⓑ Ⓒ Ⓓ Ⓔ   22 Ⓐ Ⓑ Ⓒ Ⓓ Ⓔ   32 Ⓐ Ⓑ Ⓒ Ⓓ Ⓔ
3 Ⓐ Ⓑ Ⓒ Ⓓ Ⓔ   13 Ⓐ Ⓑ Ⓒ Ⓓ Ⓔ   23 Ⓐ Ⓑ Ⓒ Ⓓ Ⓔ   33 Ⓐ Ⓑ Ⓒ Ⓓ Ⓔ
4 Ⓐ Ⓑ Ⓒ Ⓓ Ⓔ   14 Ⓐ Ⓑ Ⓒ Ⓓ Ⓔ   24 Ⓐ Ⓑ Ⓒ Ⓓ Ⓔ   34 Ⓐ Ⓑ Ⓒ Ⓓ Ⓔ
5 Ⓐ Ⓑ Ⓒ Ⓓ Ⓔ   15 Ⓐ Ⓑ Ⓒ Ⓓ Ⓔ   25 Ⓐ Ⓑ Ⓒ Ⓓ Ⓔ   35 Ⓐ Ⓑ Ⓒ Ⓓ Ⓔ
6 Ⓐ Ⓑ Ⓒ Ⓓ Ⓔ   16 Ⓐ Ⓑ Ⓒ Ⓓ Ⓔ   26 Ⓐ Ⓑ Ⓒ Ⓓ Ⓔ   36 Ⓐ Ⓑ Ⓒ Ⓓ Ⓔ
7 Ⓐ Ⓑ Ⓒ Ⓓ Ⓔ   17 Ⓐ Ⓑ Ⓒ Ⓓ Ⓔ   27 Ⓐ Ⓑ Ⓒ Ⓓ Ⓔ   37 Ⓐ Ⓑ Ⓒ Ⓓ Ⓔ
8 Ⓐ Ⓑ Ⓒ Ⓓ Ⓔ   18 Ⓐ Ⓑ Ⓒ Ⓓ Ⓔ   28 Ⓐ Ⓑ Ⓒ Ⓓ Ⓔ   38 Ⓐ Ⓑ Ⓒ Ⓓ Ⓔ
9 Ⓐ Ⓑ Ⓒ Ⓓ Ⓔ   19 Ⓐ Ⓑ Ⓒ Ⓓ Ⓔ   29 Ⓐ Ⓑ Ⓒ Ⓓ Ⓔ   39 Ⓐ Ⓑ Ⓒ Ⓓ Ⓔ
10 Ⓐ Ⓑ Ⓒ Ⓓ Ⓔ   20 Ⓐ Ⓑ Ⓒ Ⓓ Ⓔ   30 Ⓐ Ⓑ Ⓒ Ⓓ Ⓔ   40 Ⓐ Ⓑ Ⓒ Ⓓ Ⓔ

CAUTION Grid answers in the section below for SECTION 6 or SECTION 7 only if directed to do so in your test book.

Student-Produced Responses   ONLY ANSWERS THAT ARE GRIDDED WILL BE SCORED. YOU WILL NOT RECEIVE CREDIT FOR ANYTHING WRITTEN IN THE BOXES.

Quality Assurance Mark ●

9, 10, 11, 12, 13, 14, 15, 16, 17, 18

Each grid contains columns with ⊘ (slash) and decimal point in the top rows, followed by digits 0 through 9.

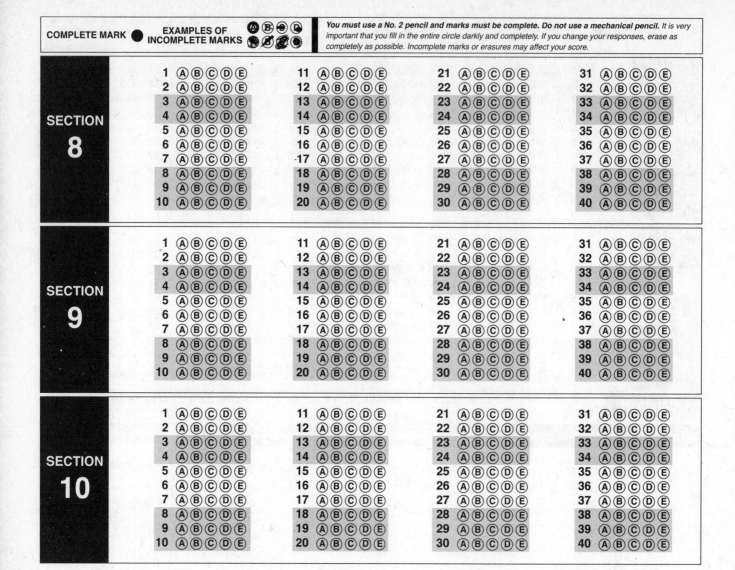

SECTION 1
ESSAY
Time — 25 minutes

Turn to Section 1 of your answer sheet to write your essay.

The essay gives you an opportunity to show how effectively you can develop and express ideas. You should, therefore, take care to develop your point of view, present your ideas logically and clearly, and use language precisely.

Your essay must be written on the lines provided on your answer sheet—you will receive no other paper on which to write. You will have enough space if you write on every line, avoid wide margins, and keep your handwriting to a reasonable size. Remember that people who are not familiar with your handwriting will read what you write. Try to write or print so that what you are writing is legible to those readers.

You have twenty-five minutes to write an essay on the topic assigned below. DO NOT WRITE ON ANOTHER TOPIC. AN OFF-TOPIC ESSAY WILL RECEIVE A SCORE OF ZERO.

Think carefully about the issue presented in the following excerpt and the assignment below.

> The "Scholastic Election," conducted since 1940 by polling children, claims to have predicted every presidential election correctly with two exceptions: Truman's win over Dewey in 1948—when many individual Dewey supporters, encouraged by widespread victory projections, felt less motivated to vote— and Kennedy's win over Nixon in 1960—when Nixon won the popular vote, despite losing the electoral college. While large numbers of voters in other polls report that they are "undecided" as election day approaches, this survey of children produces almost invariably reliable results.

Assignment: Are children's political opinions an echo of those espoused by their parents? Plan and write an essay in which you develop your point of view on this issue. Support your position with reasoning and examples taken from your reading, studies, experience, and observations.

DO NOT WRITE YOUR ESSAY IN YOUR TEST BOOK. You will receive credit only for what you write on your answer sheet.

BEGIN WRITING YOUR ESSAY IN SECTION 1 OF THE ANSWER SHEET.

STOP
If you finish before time is called, you may check your work on this section only.
Do not turn to any other section in the test.

SECTION 2
Time — 25 minutes
24 Questions

Turn to Section 2 of your answer sheet to answer the questions in this section.

Directions: For each question in this section, select the best answer from among the choices given and fill in the corresponding circle on the answer sheet.

Each sentence below has one or two blanks, each blank indicating that something has been omitted. Beneath the sentence are five words or sets of words labeled A through E. Choose the word or set of words that, when inserted in the sentence, best fits the meaning of the sentence as a whole.

Example:

Desiring to ------- his taunting friends, Mitch gave them taffy in hopes it would keep their mouths shut.

(A) eliminate   (B) satisfy   (C) overcome
   (D) ridicule   (E) silence

Ⓐ Ⓑ Ⓒ Ⓓ ●

---

1. Some behavior theorists argue that in human relationships the absence of love is not hatred, but rather -------, in which a person shows little or no passion.

    (A) apathy   (B) assurance   (C) sensibility
       (D) skepticism   (E) irascibility

2. The class thought the new student was -------: her haughty and dismissive attitude made many of her classmates angry.

    (A) opulent   (B) conceded   (C) arrogant
       (D) ominous   (E) agile

3. In the late 1980s there was a sudden ------- of interest in the work of Frida Kahlo; her paintings escalated in price as more and more people sought to purchase them.

    (A) decline   (B) assessment   (C) fluctuation
       (D) moderation   (E) burgeoning

4. Many people are stunned at how ------- the personalities of twins can be, even of those who look -------.

    (A) interchangeable . . identical
    (B) perplexing . . secretive
    (C) contradictory . . unrelated
    (D) veracious . . handsome
    (E) dissimilar . . alike

5. Even though it is by no means -------, Carol Gilligan's research into the influence of gender differences in moral development is particularly essential because work in this area has been so -------.

    (A) riveting . . impartial
    (B) irrelevant . . unfocused
    (C) grandiose . . ambivalent
    (D) exhaustive . . sparse
    (E) current . . abundant

6. Richard's new friends were so ------- by his charming manner that it continued to captivate them even as they began to realize that it was, in fact -------.

    (A) disarmed . . candid
    (B) enamored . . earnest
    (C) repulsed . . insincere
    (D) placated . . inadvertent
    (E) beguiled . . calculated

7. While the medical profession was once strictly the ------- of men, more than half the students at many American medical schools are now women.

    (A) conscription   (B) gratification   (C) concourse
       (D) province   (E) refuge

8. The publisher was compelled to ------- the author's vivid description of life in the combat zone; the atrocities he depicted were more gruesome than his readers could bear.

    (A) expurgate   (B) corroborate   (C) appropriate
       (D) propagate   (E) plagiarize

GO ON TO THE NEXT PAGE

> **Directions:** Each passage below is followed by questions based on its content. Answer the questions on the basis of what is <u>stated</u> or <u>implied</u> in each passage and in any introductory material that may be provided.

Questions 9-10 are based on the following passage.

Although the first internal-combustion-powered vehicle was created in 1885, automotive history did not begin until 1907. That was the year that Henry Ford's revolutionary
Line assembly line began churning out his Model T automobiles.
5 Ford's grand vision was to make the car an integral par t of the American lifestyle, and his mass production techniques allowed him to sell his Model T at unbelievably low prices— the cost of the car was $950 in 1907 and had dropped to under $300 by 1926. Soon, there were more cars in the United States
10 than households. A new era of freedom and mobility had begun.

9. It may be inferred from the passage that

   (A) Ford's refinements to automobile technology allowed him to produce better quality, cheaper cars.

   (B) most Americans owned a Model T by 1926

   (C) one of Ford's contributions to automobile history was the introduction of the assembly line

   (D) the price of the Model T continued to drop after 1926

   (E) no significant innovations in automobile technology occurred between 1885 and 1907

10. The author most likely views Henry Ford as

   (A) an industrialist who ushered in a new era of working conditions

   (B) an innovator who revolutionized automobile structure and design

   (C) a tycoon who made his fortune by selling a necessary product

   (D) a salesman who ingeniously marketed his new product

   (E) a visionary who changed American culture

Questions 11-12 are based on the following passage.

Existentialism has become so associated with Jean-Paul Sartre that for the latter part of the twentieth century, many have overlooked the contributions of his intellectual and
Line literary contemporary, Albert Camus. The two writers met
5 and collaborated during the German occupation of France and became overnight celebrities after liberation. Sartre's enthusiastic support for Joseph Stalin eventually caused a rift in the writers' friendship because Camus viewed the Communists as ideologues with little regard for the human
10 condition. Though derided by his peers as too conservative, Camus eventually became the youngest Nobel Prize winner for literature in 1957.

11. With which of the following statements would the author most agree?

   (A) Sartre's fame was highly unwarranted.

   (B) Existentialism was caused by the horrors of WWII.

   (C) Existentialism ignored the human condition.

   (D) Camus' work was superior to Sartre's.

   (E) Camus deserved more acclaim than he initially received.

12. It can be inferred from the passage that Camus believed that Communism

   (A) was not primarily concerned with people's welfare

   (B) would be doomed to failure

   (C) was too liberal a philosophy

   (D) was incompatible with Existentialism

   (E) was responsible for France's occupation

GO ON TO THE NEXT PAGE

Questions 13-24 are based on the following passage.

The following passage examines the relationship between the creative elements of a film and the emotional response of the viewer.

Emotions represented within a film interact as parts of the film's total system. For example, a grimace of pain might be reinforced by the contortions of a comedian's body. Or,
Line a cheerful scene might stand in contrast to a mournful one.
5 A tragic event might be undercut by humorous editing or music. All of the emotions present in a film may be seen as systematically related to one another through that film's form*.

The spectator's emotional response to the film is related
10 to form as well. Often this form in artwork appeals to ready-made reactions, already formulated emotions: fear of darkness or heights, or even stereotyped reactions to certain images (sexuality, race, social class). But form can create new responses as easily as it can refer to old ones. Just as formal
15 conventions often lead us to suspend our normal sense of real-life experience, so they may lead us to override our everyday emotional responses. Why else would people whom we would despise in life become spell-binding as characters in a film? How can we watch a film about a subject that normally
20 repels us and find it fascinating? The answer lies in the systematic quality of our involvement in form. In *The Wizard of Oz* we might, for example, find the land of Oz far more attractive than Kansas. But because the film's form leads us to sympathize with Dorothy in her desire to go home, we feel
25 great satisfaction when she finally returns to Kansas.

It is foremost the dynamic process of form that engages our feelings. Expectation, for instance, spurs emotion. To wonder about "what happens next" is to invest some emotion in the situation. Delayed fulfillment of an expectation may
30 produce anxiety, sympathy, concern, or suspense. (Will the detective find the criminal? Will the boy get the girl?) Cheated expectations may produce puzzlement or keener interest. (So he isn't the detective? This isn't a romance story?) Gratified expectations may produce a feeling of satisfaction
35 or relief. (The mystery is solved, and the boy does get the girl.) Note that all of these possibilities may occur. There is no general recipe by which a novel or film can be concocted to produce the "correct" emotional response. It is all a matter of context—that is, of the individual system that is each
40 artwork's overall form. All we can say for certain is that the emotion felt by the spectator will emerge from the formal relationships in the work. This is one reason that we should try to perceive as many formal relations as possible in a film, for on these perceptions rest our reaction to that film.

45 Taken in context, the relations between the feelings represented in the film and those felt by the spectator can be quite complex. In Frank Capra's *It's a Wonderful Life*, young George Bailey's dream of college is shattered by the untimely death of his father, the president of the Bedford Falls
50 Building and Loan. When the board of trustees convenes, the villainous Potter assails the business acumen of the elder Bailey in an effort to guarantee the closing of the Building and Loan. After an impassioned speech in support of his father's impractical but generous business practices, George
55 Bailey departs for college. At the last moment, the board reveals that they have overturned Potter's bid to close the Building and Loan. At that moment the emotional structure shifts. While the viewer feels some sadness because George looks so stricken, he or she also feels joy since the Building
60 and Loan has been saved and the diabolical Potter thwarted. This example illustrates how emotions on screen and our response to them are dependent on form.

* *form* refers to the specific elements used by a filmmaker to create a coherent story.

13. The primary purpose of this passage is to

(A) examine how a film's form and emotion shape a viewer's experience
(B) discuss the ways a film's form control a viewer's emotion
(C) explain the viewer's impact on the form of a film
(D) highlight an actor's ability to direct his emotions to a viewer
(E) provide a history of film form in the 20th century

14. Which of the following would NOT be considered a "ready-made" emotion (line 11) ?

(A) Fear of a dark deserted alley
(B) Anxiety at a job interview
(C) Reverence for a war hero
(D) Joy at a family reunion
(E) Relief when bank robbers aren't caught

15. The examples mentioned in the first paragraph are all examples of

(A) pairings of actions and emotions used in all films
(B) contrasting emotional scenes that heighten the emotional investment in a film
(C) unexpected settings for tragic scenes
(D) various emotions, scenery, settings and action that may comprise a films' form
(E) film forms that use actors' emotions and scenes or music to manipulate the viewer's emotions

GO ON TO THE NEXT PAGE ▷

16. In line 15, "suspend" most nearly means

(A) hold up
(B) push further
(C) withhold
(D) excite
(E) expel

17. The questions in lines 17-20 chiefly serve to emphasize that

(A) film forms are preferable to real life because fictional characters are not as easily despised as real people
(B) people are tricked by film form into liking people they would normally hate
(C) if life were more like the movies, then people would get along better
(D) film form allows viewers to transcend the assumptions they have when experiencing real life
(E) film forms are well defined while real-life forms are ambiguous

18. Which of the following best illustrates and emotional response similar to that illustrated by the example of *The Wizard of Oz* (lines 21-25) ?

(A) Appreciating the beauty of rural farm scenery when one lives in a city
(B) Being happy for the heroine even though she's made many mistakes
(C) Feeling joy when two characters admit they're in love with each other
(D) Feeling compassion for a tyrannical dictator when he is reunited with his son
(E) Feeling bad when the heroine messes up her 5th job interview

19. Which of the following is an example of a "gratified expectation" (lines 34-35) ?

(A) Not discovering who the killer is by the end of the movie
(B) Sympathizing with the killer because of his tough childhood
(C) Being surprised at whom the heroine ends up marrying
(D) Seeing the tyrannical king overthrown by the commoners
(E) Finding out the killer was the detective in disguise

20. Which of the following, if true, would most weaken the author's assertion in lines 37-38 ("There is no . . . response") ?

(A) Many filmmakers have found ways to provoke a wide range of emotions in audiences without ever showing an image that would elicit a response from audience members in real life?
(B) Sometimes film scenes intended to be serious or tragic instead provoke laughter in audience members.
(C) Certain movies have a more profound emotional effect on contemporary audiences than they had on audiences of their time.
(D) Audiences viewing a film in a movie theater often respond more strongly to it than do those viewing the same film on television.
(E) Certain types of films effectively evoke a predictable set of emotions from audiences by adhering closely to a "formula" for romance movies.

21. It can be inferred from the audience's response to the emotional complexity of George's situation that

(A) Capra's style of filmmaking creates a complex emotional response
(B) the notion of an appropriate reaction is fallacious
(C) George is making an unselfish decision
(D) fantasy is often harsher than reality
(E) Capra is interested in shamelessly manipulating the viewer's emotions

22. Which of the following, if true, would most weaken the author's statement in lines 40-42 ("All we can say for certain is . . . work.") ?

(A) A spectator sympathizes with the grave robber because it is revealed during the film that the grave robber is seeking a special amulet that was stolen from his mother.
(B) A spectator laughs at an emergency room scene because the characters are faking their injuries to cover up for an employee who risks losing his job.
(C) A spectator cries throughout a scene about a big wedding and family reunion because the most beloved family member is off fighting a meaningless war.
(D) A spectator is filled with joy when the scary alien tramples through town because the alien is going to join his ship.
(E) A spectator cries throughout a film that was intended to be a comedy because the spectator has just lived through a terrible experience that was similar to the situation in the comedy.

GO ON TO THE NEXT PAGE

23. The description of *It's a Wonderful Life* in the final paragraph primarily serves to

(A) summarize a plot
(B) support an assertion
(C) describe an ideal
(D) trace a character's history
(E) analyze an actor's methods

24. In the context of the passage, the "elder Bailey" (lines 51-52) is best described as

(A) villainous and offensive
(B) sad and stricken
(C) idealistic yet charitable
(D) joyous yet disappointed
(E) anxious then ecstatic

STOP

**If you finish before time is called, you may check your work on this section only.
Do not turn to any other section in the test.**

NO TEST MATERIAL ON THIS PAGE.

SECTION 4
Time — 25 minutes
20 Questions

Turn to Section 4 of your answer sheet to answer the questions in this section.

Directions: For this section, solve each problem and decide which is the best of the choices given. Fill in the corresponding circle on the answer sheet. You may use any available space for scratchwork.

Notes

1. The use of a calculator is permitted.

2. All numbers used are real numbers.

3. Figures that accompany problems in this test are intended to provide information useful in solving the problems. They are drawn as accurately as possible EXCEPT when it is stated in a specific problem that the figure is not drawn to scale. All figures lie in a plane unless otherwise indicated.

4. Unless otherwise specified, the domain of any function f is assumed to be the set of all real numbers x for which $f(x)$ is a real number.

Reference Information

$A = \pi r^2$ $A = lw$ $A = \frac{1}{2}bh$ $V = lwh$ $V = \pi r^2 h$ $c^2 = a^2 + b^2$ Special Right Triangles

$C = 2\pi r$

The number of degrees of arc in a circle is 360.

The sum of the measures in degrees of the angles of a triangle is 180.

---

1. When 28 is divided by 8, the remainder is the same as that obtained when 53 is divided by which of the following numbers?

(A) 3
(B) 4
(C) 5
(D) 6
(E) 7

2. A 20-gallon water tank is filled to capacity. If 8 gallons of water are pumped out of the tank, what percent of the tank is now filled?

(A) 20%
(B) 40%
(C) 50%
(D) 60%
(E) 70%

GO ON TO THE NEXT PAGE

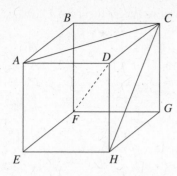

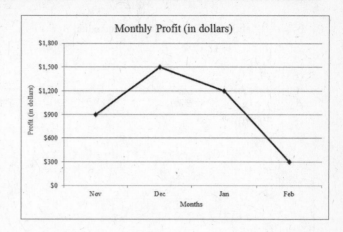

3. In the cube shown above, the length of $\overline{EG}$ (not shown) is less than the length of which of the following?

(A) $\overline{EH}$

(B) $\overline{AB}$

(C) $\overline{CH}$

(D) $\overline{GH}$

(E) $\overline{DF}$

5. The graph above shows the monthly profit at a mountain climbing supplies store over a four-month period. What is the difference between the greatest and least monthly profits, in dollars, over the 4 months?

(A) $300

(B) $600

(C) $1,200

(D) $1,400

(E) $1,500

4. The hypotenuse of an isosceles triangle has endpoints (4, 3) and (9, 8). What is the length of one of the legs of the triangle?

(A) 3

(B) 5

(C) 7

(D) 9

(E) 11

6. Which of the following is the distance between the points (7, 3) and (11, 0) in the *xy*-coordinate plane?

(A) 4

(B) 5

(C) 6

(D) 7

(E) 8

GO ON TO THE NEXT PAGE

7. If $\dfrac{x}{2} < 12$ and $y = x - 4$, then (x, y) could equal

(A) (5, 9)
(B) (19, 23)
(C) (20, 17)
(D) (22, 18)
(E) (30, 26)

8. Which of the following expressions represents $b - 3a$ subtracted from twice the sum of $2a$ and $5b$?

(A) $-9b - 7a$
(B) $-4b - a$
(C) $4b + a$
(D) $7b + 3a$
(E) $9b + 7a$

9. If x is a positive integer, all of the following are equal to $(4^3)^x$ EXCEPT

(A) 4^{3x}
(B) $2^{4x}(4^x)$
(C) $4^x(4^{3x})$
(D) $4^x(4^{2x})$
(E) 8^{2x}

10. If $-3 \le x \le 4$, which of the following is not a possible value for $f(x)$ in the function $f(x) = x^2 - 2$?

(A) -2
(B) 5
(C) 7
(D) 14
(E) 16

GO ON TO THE NEXT PAGE

11. What is the value of b if $1 - \dfrac{4}{b} = \dfrac{5}{3}$?

(A) –6

(B) –2

(C) $\dfrac{1}{4}$

(D) $\dfrac{2}{3}$

(E) 6

12. Theresa is comparing the length of four magazine articles. The first article begins on page 1 and ends on page 7. The second article begins on page 17 and ends on page 24. The third article begins on page 28 and ends on page 31, and the fourth article begins on page 52 and ends on page 56. What is the median number of pages in these articles?

(A) 4
(B) 5
(C) 6
(D) 7
(E) 8

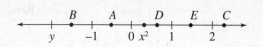

13. Which of the lettered points on the number line above could represent the result of $x + y$?

(A) A
(B) B
(C) C
(D) D
(E) E

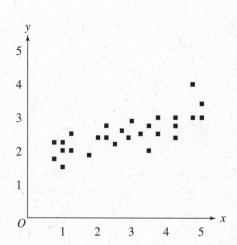

14. For the scatter plot graph above, which of the following equations is most likely the line of best fit?

(A) $y = 3x + 2$

(B) $y = \dfrac{1}{3}x + 2$

(C) $y = -\dfrac{1}{3}x + 2$

(D) $y = -2x + 3$

(E) $y = -3x + 2$

GO ON TO THE NEXT PAGE

15. If $a^b = 0$, $c^b = c$, $bc \neq 0$, and $c \neq 1$, what must be the value of bc^a ?

(A) 0
(B) 1
(C) a
(D) a^b
(E) c

17. If a, b, and c are consecutive even integers, such that $0 < a < b < c$, what is $c^2 - a^2$ in terms of a ?

(A) $8a + 16$
(B) $4a + 4$
(C) $8a$
(D) $4a + 16$
(E) $4a$

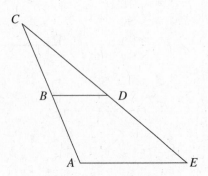

Note: Figure not drawn to scale.

16. In the figure above, $AB = BC = CD = DE = 5$. If $BD = 3$, what is the perimeter of quadrilateral $ABDE$?

(A) 13
(B) 16
(C) 19
(D) 26
(E) 31

18. There are four colors of lottery tickets in a hat. If $\frac{1}{10}$ of the tickets in the hat are green, $\frac{1}{2}$ are white, $\frac{1}{4}$ are blue.

and the remaining 30 tickets are pink, what is the number

of blue tickets in the hat?

(A) 25
(B) 50
(C) 75
(D) 120
(E) 200

GO ON TO THE NEXT PAGE

19. The members of set R are the integer solutions of $|y| < 10$, and the members of set S are the even integer solutions of $|x| > 5$. Which of the following includes all the members common to both set R and set S ?

(A) $\{-8, -6, 6, 8\}$
(B) $\{-9, -8, -7, -6, -5, 5, 6, 7, 8, 9\}$
(C) $\{-9, -8, -7, -6, 6, 7, 8, 9\}$
(D) $\{6, 8\}$
(E) $\{6, 7, 8, 9\}$

20. What is the area of a circle that is circumscribed around a square that has sides of length 6?

(A) 6π
(B) 18π
(C) $18\sqrt{2}\pi$
(D) 36π
(E) 72π

STOP
If you finish before time is called, you may check your work on this section only.
Do not turn to any other section in the test.

SECTION 5
Time — 25 minutes
35 Questions

Turn to Section 5 of your answer sheet to answer the questions in this section.

Directions: For each question in this section, select the best answer from among the choices given and fill in the corresponding circle on the answer sheet.

The following sentences test correctness and effectiveness of expression. Part of each sentence or the entire sentence is underlined; beneath each sentence are five ways of phrasing the underlined material. Choice A repeats the original phrasing; the other four choices are different. If you think the original phrasing produces a better sentence than any of the alternatives, select choice A; if not, select one of the other choices.

In making your selection, follow the requirements of standard written English; that is, pay attention to grammar, choice of words, sentence construction, and punctuation. Your selection should result in the most effective sentence—clear and precise, without awkwardness or ambiguity.

EXAMPLE:

Bobby Flay baked his first cake <u>and he was thirteen years old then</u>.

(A) and he was thirteen years old then
(B) when he was thirteen
(C) at age thirteen years old
(D) upon the reaching of thirteen years
(E) at the time when he was thirteen

Ⓐ●ⒸⒹⒺ

1. <u>The complex contradictions of the human mind providing</u> one of mankind's greatest enigmas to psychologists.

   (A) The complex contradictions of the human mind providing
   (B) The human mind with its complex contradictions having provided
   (C) Providing that the complex contradictions of the human mind is
   (D) It is the complex contradictions of the human mind providing
   (E) The complex contradictions of the human mind provide

2. <u>The requirements for becoming an astronaut is</u> knowledge of physics and physical fitness rather than simple bravery and a sense of adventure.

   (A) The requirements for becoming an astronaut is
   (B) An astronaut, it requires
   (C) The job of an astronaut requires
   (D) In becoming an astronaut is required
   (E) As for becoming an astronaut

3. Since environmental issues have become so <u>important is the reason that many states have passed pollution control laws</u>.

   (A) important is the reason that many states have passed pollution control laws
   (B) important, many states have passed pollution control laws
   (C) important, pollution control laws have been passed by many states
   (D) important is the reason that pollution control laws have been passed in many states
   (E) important, they have passed pollution control laws in many states

4. During World War II, the French resistance movement was an underground group of French nationalists and freedom <u>fighters, it helped</u> fight the occupying Nazis.

   (A) fighters, it helped
   (B) fighters and helping
   (C) fighters that helped
   (D) fighters to attempt to help
   (E) fighters, thus attempting to help

GO ON TO THE NEXT PAGE

5. Mr. Phelps contends that although most schools have succeeded in educating future technicians, <u>their neglect is in their not training</u> humanities students in the ways of technical thought.

   (A) their neglect is in their not training
   (B) their neglect they have is in their not training
   (C) they neglected not to train
   (D) they have neglected to train
   (E) neglecting in their training of

6. Gloria Feldon is <u>almost as talented a singer as she is a songwriter</u>.

   (A) almost as talented a singer as she is a songwriter
   (B) almost equally talented, whether a singer or a songwriter
   (C) of the same talent as a singer and as a songwriter, almost
   (D) a talented songwriter, with almost as much talent in singing
   (E) talented as a songwriter and almost so talented in singing

7. The state of the house came <u>as a shock to her, in that the furniture in it being</u> much dirtier than she had recalled.

   (A) as a shock to her, in that the furniture in it being
   (B) as a shock to her, the furniture in it is
   (C) to her as a shock, being that the furniture in it was
   (D) to her as a shock; with the furniture in it being
   (E) as a shock to her; the furniture in it was

8. It is often hard to know whether a product is successful because <u>someone discovers the consumer's needs or because they are intelligently creating them</u>.

   (A) someone discovers the consumer's needs or because they are intelligently creating them
   (B) of the discovery of the consumer's needs or intelligently creating those needs
   (C) someone has discovered the consumer's needs or because someone has intelligently creating those needs
   (D) of discovering the consumer's needs or because they are intelligently creating those needs
   (E) someone has discovered the consumer's needs or has intelligently created them

9. <u>Unlike 100 years ago, schoolteachers nowadays</u> usually aspire to earn a good living.

   (A) Unlike 100 years ago, schoolteachers nowadays
   (B) Unlike 100 years ago, in contemporary society, schoolteachers
   (C) Unlike their counterparts 100 years ago, schoolteachers today
   (D) Differing to their counterparts 100 years ago, today's schoolteachers
   (E) Schoolteachers today, opposed to 100 years ago

10. Besides being thought the most attractive of all tropical flowers, <u>the gardenia is used in many communities for cooking, cleansing, and perfume making</u>.

    (A) the gardenia is used in many communities for cooking, cleansing, and perfume making
    (B) many communities use the gardenia for cooking, cleansing, and perfume making
    (C) the gardenia's many uses include many communities using them for cooking, cleansing, and perfume making
    (D) cooking, cleansing, and perfume making are many communities' uses for the gardenia
    (E) in many communities the gardenia being used for cooking, cleansing, and perfume making

11. A filmmaker who stunningly captured the moods of a society, <u>Frank Capra's films depict the idealistic world of early twentieth-century America</u>.

    (A) Frank Capra's films depict the idealistic world of early twentieth-century America
    (B) the films of Frank Capra depict the idealistic world of early twentieth-century America
    (C) Frank Capra in his films depicting the idealistic world of early twentieth-century America
    (D) Frank Capra depicts in his films the idealistic world of early twentieth-century America
    (E) Frank Capra's idealistic world of early twentieth-century America is depicted in his films

GO ON TO THE NEXT PAGE

The following sentences test your ability to recognize grammar and usage errors. Each sentence contains either a single error or no error at all. No sentence contains more than one error. The error, if there is one, is underlined and lettered. If the sentence contains an error, select the one underlined part that must be changed to make the sentence correct. If the sentence is correct, select choice E. In choosing answers, follow the requirements of standard written English.

EXAMPLE:

The other players and her significantly improved
    A   B   C

the game plan created by the coaches. No error
             D   E

Ⓐ ● Ⓒ Ⓓ Ⓔ

12. A superb designer, Coco Chanel blended the extremely
                                A   B

different styles of traditional and modern fashion more

easily as any contemporary designer ever has. No error
       C   D   E

13. I cleaned the house by the time my parents come home
    A   B

from their vacation in Mexico. No error
       C   D   E

14. Joanna took great pleasure in remembering the times
                   A

where her family spent summers at her grandmother's
  B   C   D

farm. No error
      E

15. By 2076, the United States will have been a nation for
    A

three hundred years, while, by the same year, China
                       B

has been a nation for almost four thousand years.
  C   D

No error
  E

16. Placement of students in unchallenging learning
                A

environments frequently creates frustration, boredom,
           B   C

and sometimes other problems. No error
D   E

17. People that avoid eating foods high in cholesterol
       A

and saturated fat are less likely to suffer from heart
            B   C   D

disease, diabetes, and other life-threatening diseases.

No error
E

18. Carmen Smith's novel *Hope* sheds light on the
                       A

character Anita, who as a young woman has scarcely no
                                  B

memory of her own upbringing. No error
  C   D   E

19. If your body reacts adversely to inexpensive metal
  A   B

earrings, you should only wear gold, sterling silver, or
                C

wear other hypoallergenic materials. No error
D   E

20. Many actions of young children are frequently similar to
                         A   B

ones that he or she has seen on television. No error
     C   D   E

GO ON TO THE NEXT PAGE →

21. <u>Many of those</u> involved <u>were</u> professionals who,
　　　　　A　　　　　　　　B

in <u>recognition</u> of their accomplishments in previous
　　　C

projects, <u>had been given</u> new assignments. <u>No error</u>
　　　　　　　　D　　　　　　　　　　　　　E

22. A brand new committee of residents and business

owners <u>have spoken with</u> the town board <u>to express</u>
　　　　　　A　　　　　　　　　　　　　　　B

its <u>feelings about</u> <u>proposals for</u> a new park in the
　　　　C　　　　　　D

neighborhood. <u>No error</u>
　　　　　　　　E

23. John <u>has become aware</u> that he can display his emotions
　　　　　　A

more easily <u>through</u> <u>his</u> music <u>and not</u> through his
　　　　　　　B　　　C　　　　D

artwork. <u>No error</u>
　　　　　　E

24. The council members proposed many new ideas,

including taking parking privileges <u>away from</u> county
　　　　　　　　　　　　　　　　　　A

employees and opening <u>more</u> lots, <u>but</u> the chairman
　　　　　　　　　　　　B　　　　C

would not <u>approve it</u>. <u>No error</u>
　　　　　　　D　　　　E

25. <u>Though it began</u> as <u>a protest on</u> traditional theology, the
　　　　A　　　　　　　B

Protestant Reformation <u>created</u> a new set of traditions
　　　　　　　　　　　　　C

<u>in its</u> own era. <u>No error</u>
　　D　　　　　E

26. Frank Hessler's map of North America, which

<u>was discovered</u> in 1928, is the third <u>recorded</u> map
　　A　　　　　　　　　　　　　　　B

<u>where</u> Canada and Mexico are depicted as <u>distinct from</u>
　　C　　　　　　　　　　　　　　　　　　D

the U.S. <u>No error</u>
　　　　E

27. An amateur painter <u>herself</u>, the teacher offered <u>to help</u>
　　　　　　　　　A　　　　　　　　　　　B

the artist <u>with his essays</u> on theory, complicated as
　　　　　　C

<u>they were</u> by his bizarre system of note-taking. <u>No error</u>
　　D　　　　　　　　　　　　　　　　　E

28. The critic <u>tasting</u> the dishes offered by the restaurant
　　　　　　A

<u>found</u> that the variety of entrees <u>were</u> fairly good but
　　B　　　　　　　　　　　　C

<u>somewhat</u> unusual. <u>No error</u>
　　D　　　　　E

29. Because the manner in which the existentialists <u>viewed</u>
　　　　　　　　　　　　　　　　　　　A

this issue differed <u>from the nihilists</u>, their philosophies
　　　　　　　B

<u>mirrored each other</u> only <u>slightly</u>. <u>No error</u>
　　C　　　　　　　　D　　　E

GO ON TO THE NEXT PAGE

Directions: The following passage is an early draft of an essay. Some parts of the passage need to be rewritten.

Read the passage and select the best answers for the questions that follow. Some questions are about particular sentences or parts of sentences and ask you to improve sentence structure or word choice. Other questions ask you to consider organization and development. In choosing answers, follow the requirements of standard written English.

Questions 30-35 are based on the following passage.

(1) Our city needs more activity and help centers for teens. (2) Living in a society where loneliness surrounds us, it is vital that we develop places that are warm and nurturing so that teens can talk about their goals and problems. (3) It is easy to do more than you might think with negligible cost to the local government. (4) An empty house can become a cozy place for activities and counseling.

(5) And, buying a lot of fancy furniture and media equipment for teenagers to use is not necessary. (6) You can create a fun environment for kids with little cash. (7) Some folding chairs and an old curtain rod can provide the setting for a small theater group. (8) Simply replace any curtain rings that are broken, then hang it over a wide entryway with some old drapes. (9) Put the folding chairs in rows in front of the curtains. (10) Excellent way to encourage creativity!

(11) Teenagers can learn new ways to express themselves by writing and acting in short plays. (12) Parents and local business owners could donate other useful items for the teen center. (13) We ought to do such things because teenagers need havens from this alienated society we inhabit. (14) This may not be easy, but if people cooperate and they will have given financial and emotional support, a lot can be achieved.

30. Which of the following is the best way to rewrite the underlined portion of sentence 2 (reproduced below) ?

Living in a society where loneliness surrounds us, it is vital that we develop places that are warm and nurturing so that teens can talk about their goals and problems.

(A) Living in a society in which loneliness surrounds us, the vital thing is to

(B) Surrounded by a society full of loneliness, we need to

(C) Surrounding us with a society full of loneliness, we need to

(D) Being surrounded by a society full of loneliness, it is vital to

(E) We live in a society where loneliness surrounds us, it is vital that we

31. Which of the following is the best way to rewrite sentence 3 (reproduced below) ?

It is easy to do more than you might think with negligible cost to the local government.

(A) (As it is now)

(B) With negligible local government cost, more than you might think to do is easy.

(C) It is easy to make the cost to the local government negligible by doing more than you might think.

(D) With negligible cost to the local government, it is easy to do more than you might think you can do.

(E) Causing the local government a negligible amount, it is easy to do more than you might think.

32. Of the following words, which would be the best to use in place of "And" at the start of sentence 5 (reproduced below) ?

And, buying a lot of fancy furniture and media equipment for teenagers to use is not necessary.

(A) Rather

(B) But

(C) Moreover

(D) Contrastingly

(E) Yet

33. Which of the following versions of the underlined portion of sentence 8 (reproduced below) best conveys the intended meaning?

Simply replace any curtain rings that are broken, then hang it over a wide entryway with some old drapes.

(A) (as it is now)

(B) it should be hung

(C) hang this thing

(D) the rod is to be hanged

(E) hang the rod

GO ON TO THE NEXT PAGE

34. Which of the following is the best way to rewrite sentence 10 (reproduced below) so that it is a complete sentence?

Excellent way to encourage creativity!

(A) That is an excellent way to encourage creativity!
(B) This kind of project is an excellent way to encourage creativity!
(C) This excellent way encourages creativity!
(D) This is creatively encouraging!
(E) This will be encouraging creativity!

35. To most improve the clarity of sentence 13, the phrase "do such things" could be replaced by which of the following?

(A) achieve our goals
(B) help these teens
(C) discuss other options
(D) develop these centers
(E) have fresh ideas

STOP

If you finish before time is called, you may check your work on this section only.
Do not turn to any other section in the test.

SECTION 6
Time — 25 minutes
18 Questions

Turn to Section 6 of your answer sheet to answer the questions in this section.

Directions: This section contains two types of questions. You have 25 minutes to complete both types. For questions 1-8, solve each problem and decide which is the best of the choices given. Fill in the corresponding circle on the answer sheet. You may use any available space for scratchwork.

Notes

1. The use of a calculator is permitted.

2. All numbers used are real numbers.

3. Figures that accompany problems in this test are intended to provide information useful in solving the problems. They are drawn as accurately as possible EXCEPT when it is stated in a specific problem that the figure is not drawn to scale. All figures lie in a plane unless otherwise indicated.

4. Unless otherwise specified, the domain of any function f is assumed to be the set of all real numbers x for which $f(x)$ is a real number.

Reference Information

   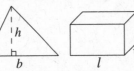 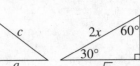

$A = \pi r^2$ $A = lw$
$C = 2\pi r$ $A = \frac{1}{2}bh$ $V = lwh$ $V = \pi r^2 h$ $c^2 = a^2 + b^2$ Special Right Triangles

The number of degrees of arc in a circle is 360.

The sum of the measures in degrees of the angles of a triangle is 180.

1. If 3 times y is decreased by 4, then which of the following must be true?

    (A) $4(3 - y)$
    (B) $3(4 - y)$
    (C) $3(y - 4)$
    (D) $4 - 3y$
    (E) $3y - 4$

2. Nora has 10 fewer than twice the number of CDs that Deborah has. If n represents the number of Nora's CDs, and d represents the number of Deborah's CDs, which of the following is a correct equation relating n and d ?

    (A) $n = 2d - 10$
    (B) $n = 2(d - 10)$
    (C) $n = 10 - 2d$
    (D) $n = 2(10 - d)$
    (E) $n = 10 - (d + 2)$

GO ON TO THE NEXT PAGE

3. If $f(x) = |x| + 2$, which of the following is the LEAST possible value of $f(x)$?

(A) −2
(B) −1
(C)   0
(D)   1
(E)   2

4. If $\dfrac{2x}{x^2 + 1} = \dfrac{2}{x + 2}$, what is the value of x ?

(A) $-\dfrac{1}{4}$

(B) $\dfrac{1}{4}$

(C) $\dfrac{1}{2}$

(D) 0

(E) 2

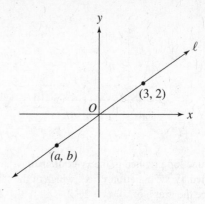

5. In the figure above, line ℓ passes through the origin. What is the value of $\dfrac{b}{a}$?

(A) 6

(B) $\dfrac{3}{2}$

(C) $\dfrac{2}{3}$

(D) $-\dfrac{2}{3}$

(E) $-\dfrac{3}{2}$

6. If $x - y = 5$ and $x^2 + y^2 = 15$, what is the value of xy ?

(A) −25
(B) −5
(C) −3
(D)   3
(E)   25

GO ON TO THE NEXT PAGE

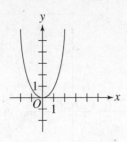

7. If the function graphed in the xy-coordinate system above is defined by the equation $y = x^2$, which of the following could be the graph of $y = (x + 2)^2$?

(A)

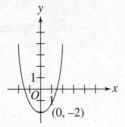

(0, –2)

(B)

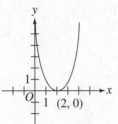

(2, 0)

(C)

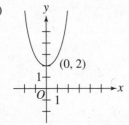

(0, 2)

(D)

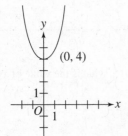

(0, 4)

(E)

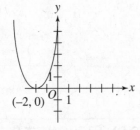

(–2, 0)

8. A rectangular solid that has a width of 8, a length of 8, and a height of 12 is divided into 12 cubes, each of equal volume. What is the length of the edge of one of these cubes?

(A)   4
(B)   6
(C)   8
(D)   12
(E)   64

GO ON TO THE NEXT PAGE

Directions: For Student-Produced Response questions 9-18, use the grids at the bottom of the answer sheet page on which you have answered questions 1-8.

Each of the remaining 10 questions requires you to solve the problem and enter your answer by marking the circles in the special grid, as shown in the examples below. You may use any available space for scratch work.

Answer: $\frac{7}{12}$

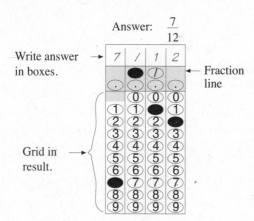

Write answer in boxes.

Fraction line

Grid in result.

Answer: 2.5

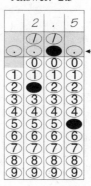

Decimal point

Answer: 201
Either position is correct.

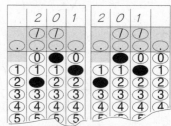

Note: You may start your answers in any column, space permitting. Columns not needed should be left blank.

- Mark no more than one circle in any column.

- Because the answer document will be machine-scored, **you will receive credit only if the circles are filled in correctly.**

- Although not required, it is suggested that you write your answer in the boxes at the top of the columns to help you fill in the circles accurately.

- Some problems may have more than one correct answer. In such cases, grid only one answer.

- No question has a negative answer.

- **Mixed numbers** such as $3\frac{1}{2}$ must be gridded as

  3.5 or 7/2. (If $\boxed{3 \ 1 \ / \ 2}$ is gridded, it will be

  interpreted as $\frac{31}{2}$, not $3\frac{1}{2}$.)

- **Decimal Answers:** If you obtain a decimal answer with more digits than the grid can accommodate, it may be either rounded or truncated, but it must fill the entire grid. For example, if you obtain an answer such as 0.6666..., you should record your result as .666 or .667. **A less accurate value such as .66 or .67 will be scored as incorrect.**

Acceptable ways to grid $\frac{2}{3}$ are:

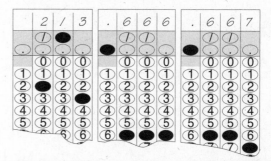

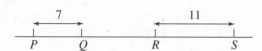

9. In the figure above, if $\overline{QS}$ has a length of 20, what is *PR*?

Candy	Pieces per box
Chocolate	36
Licorice	8
Sour Chewies	8

10. What is the total number of pieces of candy that Meredith buys if she buys 20 boxes of Sour Chewies and 10 boxes of chocolate?

GO ON TO THE NEXT PAGE →

11. The product of two positive numbers is 24 and their difference is 5. What is the sum of the two numbers?

12. A researcher found that the average (arithmetic mean) amount of sleep that she allows her mice to get is inversely proportional to the number of errors the mice make in a maze test. If mice that get 2 hours of sleep make 3 errors in the maze test, how many errors would mice with 5 hours of sleep make on average?

13. The value of k is an integer between 50 and 90 and is a multiple of 4. When k is divided by 5, the remainder is 3. When k is divided by 3, the remainder is 2. What is the value of k ?

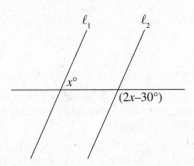

14. In the figure above, if $\ell_1 \| \ell_2$, then $x =$

GO ON TO THE NEXT PAGE

15. If $a + b = 27$, $c = 13 - b$, and $c = 20 - a$, what is $a + b + c$?

16. If $2x^2 - 68 = 10(x + 10)$, what is one possible value for x?

17. There are 400 people at a baseball game. If there are 40 more adults than children, and 40 more adult men than adult women, how many adult men are there at the game?

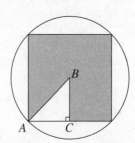

18. In the figure above, the square is inscribed in the circle with center B. If $AB = 3\sqrt{2}$ and $AC = CB$, then what is the area of the shaded region?

STOP

**If you finish before time is called, you may check your work on this section only.
Do not turn to any other section in the test.**

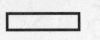
SECTION 7
Time — 25 minutes
24 Questions

Turn to Section 7 of your answer sheet to answer the questions in this section.

Directions: For each question in this section, select the best answer from among the choices given and fill in the corresponding circle on the answer sheet.

Each sentence below has one or two blanks, each blank indicating that something has been omitted. Beneath the sentence are five words or sets of words labeled A through E. Choose the word or set of words that, when inserted in the sentence, best fits the meaning of the sentence as a whole.

Example:

Desiring to ------- his taunting friends, Mitch gave them taffy in hopes it would keep their mouths shut.

(A) eliminate   (B) satisfy   (C) overcome
    (D) ridicule   (E) silence

Ⓐ Ⓑ Ⓒ Ⓓ ●

---

1. In contrast to the luxury of Mexico's coastal resort areas, the ------- that characterizes many of its urban centers is striking.

   (A) splendor   (B) vibrancy   (C) opulence
       (D) cacophony   (E) poverty

2. George's grandparents kept a kitchen so full of ------- aromas and flavorful exotic foods that merely entering their kitchen made him feel ------- at the thought of sitting down to eat.

   (A) enticing . . ravenous
   (B) rancid . . sophisticated
   (C) bland . . hungry
   (D) illusory . . nauseous
   (E) recognizable . . bloated

3. The judicial system should strive for ------- penalties, rather than haphazardly enforcing the current arbitrary and ------- criminal statutes.

   (A) distinct . . irrelevant
   (B) uniform . . inconsistent
   (C) detailed . . onerous
   (D) harsher . . subjective
   (E) appropriate . . refined

4. The scientist's success was a direct result of her -------; she refused to quit even when her efforts appeared futile.

   (A) conceit   (B) intellect   (C) foolhardiness
       (D) steadfastness   (E) inconsistency

5. When people habitually read or study with music playing in the background, they unfortunately cultivate "passive hearing," which is the very ------- of listening, a process that is essentially active.

   (A) presage   (B) antithesis   (C) circumstance
       (D) pinnacle   (E) illumination

GO ON TO THE NEXT PAGE

Directions: Each passage below is followed by questions based on its content. Answer the questions on the basis of what is <u>stated</u> or <u>implied</u> in each passage and in any introductory material that may be provided.

Questions 6-9 are based on the following passages.

Passage 1

The riders in a race do not stop short when they reach the goal. There is a finishing canter before coming to a standstill. There is time to say to oneself, "The work is done." But just as one says that, the answer comes, "The race is over, but the work is never done while the power to work remains" and so I end with a line from a Latin poet who uttered the message more than fifteen hundred years ago, "Death plucks my ear and says: Live—I am coming."

Line
5

Passage 2

First, girls, don't smoke—that is, don't smoke to excess. I am seventy three and one-half years old, and I have been smoking seventy three of them. But I never smoke to excess. That is, I smoke in moderation—only one cigar at a time. Second, don't drink—that is, don't drink to excess. Third don't marry—I mean, to excess. Now, if you will have all the virtues that anyone will honor and respect.

10

15

6. The style of Passage 2 can best be described as

(A) factual
(B) debauched
(C) solemn
(D) tongue-in-cheek
(E) unscrupulous

7. What does Passage 1 contain that Passage 2 does not?

(A) Advice for living
(B) An analogy
(C) Exaggeration
(D) An audience
(E) Satire

8. The advice in both Passage 1 and Passage 2 can be described as

(A) poetic
(B) somber
(C) indirect
(D) dubious
(E) straightforward

9. The author of Passage 1 would most disagree with Passage 2's use of

(A) tobacco
(B) allusion
(C) levity
(D) commands
(E) vice

GO ON TO THE NEXT PAGE

Questions 10-15 are based on the following passage.

The following passage recounts scientist and contemporary author Carl Sagan's feelings upon viewing Paul Broca's brain on display at a museum in Paris, France.

Paul Broca was a major figure in the development of both medicine and anthropology in the mid-nineteenth century. He performed distinguished work on cancer pathology and
Line treatment of aneurysms, and made a landmark contribution
5 to understanding the origins of aphasia—an impairment of the ability to articulate ideas. Broca was a superb brain anatomist and made important investigations of the limbic region, earlier called the rhinencephalon (the "smell brain"), which we know to be profoundly involved in human emotion.
10 But Broca is today probably best-known for his discovery of a small region in the third convolution of the left frontal lobe of the cerebral cortex, a region known as Broca's area. Articulate speech, it turns out, as Broca inferred from only fragmentary evidence, is to an important extent localized
15 in and controlled by Broca's area. It was one of the first discoveries of a separation of function between the left and right hemispheres of the brain. But most important, it was one of the first indications that specific brain functions exist in particular locales in the brain that there is a connection
20 between the anatomy of the brain and what the brain does, and activity sometimes described as "mind."

Paul Broca died in 1880, perhaps of the very sort of aneurysm that he had studied so brilliantly. At the moment of his death he was working on a comprehensive study of brain
25 anatomy.

It was difficult to hold Broca's brain without wondering whether in some sense Broca was still *in* there—his wit, his skeptical mien, his abrupt gesticulations when he talked, his quiet and sentimental moments. Might there be preserved in
30 the configuration of neurons before me a recollection of the triumphant moment when he argued before the combined medical faculties (and his father, overflowing with pride) on the origins of aphasia? Where do we go when we die? Is Paul Broca still there in his formalin-filled bottle? Perhaps
35 the memory traces have decayed, although there is good evidence from modern brain investigations that a given memory is redundantly stored in many different places in the brain. Might it be possible at some future time, when neurophysiology has advanced substantially, to reconstruct the
40 memories or insights of someone long dead? And would that be a good thing? It would be the ultimate breach of privacy. But it would also be a kind of practical immortality, because, especially for a man like Broca, our minds are clearly a major aspect of who we are.

10. From the discussion of Broca's research on articulate speech (lines 12-15), it can be inferred that

(A) Broca would have arrived at a different conclusion had he not relied on fragmentary evidence
(B) Broca's inference was too localized and fragmentary and was therefore incomplete
(C) Broca was successful in locating the part of the brain responsible for articulate speech
(D) due to fragmentary evidence, Broca was unable to localize articulate speech
(E) despite its validity, Broca's biggest achievement was never fully accepted in the scientific community

11. The "discoveries" (line 15) are best described as

(A) the convolutions of the human brain
(B) the separation of thoughts and brain structure
(C) the abilities of humans to articulate ideas
(D) the physical connections between the left and the right hemispheres
(E) the link between physical parts of the brain and certain tasks

12. In what way was Paul Broca's death ironic?

(A) Although he studied infant mortality for many years, he died an old man.
(B) He was killed by the very people that he was trying to save.
(C) After devoting most of his life to medicine, he made an unexpected switch to anthropology.
(D) He seems to have been killed by the very disorder he was studying.
(E) He studied aneurysms brilliantly, yet he died with a decaying mind.

13. The questions posed in lines 29-34 demonstrate the author's interest in

(A) the physical preservation of memory and identity within the brain
(B) Broca's victory over the combined medical faculties in the debate over aphasia
(C) the appreciation of Broca's father in neurophysiology
(D) the configuration of neurons that eventually causes aphasia
(E) a cherished memory that the author of the passage shared with Broca

GO ON TO THE NEXT PAGE ➤

14. It can be inferred from the passage that

(A) before Broca's discovery the scientific community had not seen a lot of evidence of the localization of functionality in the brain

(B) the scientific community was hesitant to accept Broca's theory of localization of functionality in the brain

(C) the discovery that specific brain functions exist in particular brain locales was the first indication of separation of function between the left and right hemispheres of the brain

(D) the discovery of the "mind" was the first indication that specific brain functions exist in particular locales in the brain

(E) the functionality of the limbic region was not known before Broca's discovery

15. The phrase "practical immortality" (line 42) can best be understood to mean that

(A) memories and insights are what keep us alive

(B) reconstructing memories and insights could bring someone back to life because if the mind is alive, then the body is alive

(C) if a mind's memories and insights are revived, it could revive the body

(D) physical being is not the only indication of viable life

(E) reviving memories and insights could be considered immortality because our minds primarily define who we are

GO ON TO THE NEXT PAGE

Questions 16-24 are based on the following passage.

The following passage describes the reasons for the formation of NATO and how the fear of Soviet and U.S. supremacy was particularly responsible for Western European participation. The passage was written in 1983.

NATO was formed in April 1949 because of a fear by its original signatories—Belgium, Canada, Denmark, France, Iceland, Italy, Luxembourg, the Netherlands, Norway,
Line Portugal, the United Kingdom, and the United States—that
5 the Soviet Union posed a major threat to their security. Its central provision is Article 5, which states: "The parties agree that an armed attack against one or more of them in Europe or North America shall be considered an attack against them all."
10 NATO is a grand alliance. It is, however, a grand alliance different from earlier alliances. When grand alliances were formed in the past—such as those that put down Napoleon, Kaiser Wilhelm, and Adolph Hitler—they were formed after an act of aggression occurred. The purpose of NATO
15 is twofold: deterrence and defense. The very act of forming a peacetime alliance, it was believed, would serve to deter aggression by the Soviet Union. If deterrence failed, however, the alliance would be politically united and militarily strong so as to protect its members from a Soviet victory.
20 Certain factors underlay the formation of NATO. These involved supremacy of the United States as a nuclear power, the fear of Soviet policies, and the economic conditions of the Europeans. First, in April 1949, the United States had a monopoly of nuclear weapons. The United States could carry
25 those weapons to the Soviet Union itself by relying on its air bases in Western Europe and Africa. NATO members could believe that the American nuclear forces offered a credible deterrent to Soviet aggression.
Second, it seemed to NATO members that the Soviet
30 Union in particular and communism in general posed a threat to Western security. The post-World War II period was characterized by such apparent threats as a civil war in Greece, communist takeover in France and Italy, a Soviet-inspired communist takeover of Czechoslovakia in 1948, and
35 a blockade of allied surface routes to Berlin in 1948.
Third, Western Europe was devastated by World War II. It depended upon the United States for its economic support. The Marshall Plan of 1947, in which the United States committed nearly $15 billion of economic aid to its Western
40 European allies, was a reflection of that economic bond.
In the more than 35 years since NATO came into existence, there have been many changes in the conditions underlying NATO and in the character of the alliance itself. No longer does the United States possess a monopoly of
45 nuclear weapons, as it did until the 1960s. During the Cuban missile crisis of 1962, the Soviet Union had about seventy long-range missiles that took 10 hours to fuel. This made Soviet missiles easily vulnerable to an American attack before they could be launched. Even as late as the Yom Kippur war
50 of 1973, the United States had a superiority of about 8 to 1 in nuclear warheads.

In addition, NATO's membership grew. Greece and Turkey joined the alliance in 1952, and West Germany entered in 1955. West German entrance into NATO was
55 the immediate cause of the establishment in 1955 of the equivalent Soviet alliance defense organization—the Warsaw Pact. In 1982, Spain became the sixteenth member of NATO.

16. The primary purpose of the passage is to

(A) portray the Soviet Union as an aggressive force that could be controlled only by an alliance of world powers

(B) describe the influence the Marshall Plan of 1947 had on the creation of NATO

(C) identify the conditions that led to the creation of NATO and outline the subsequent changes it has undergone

(D) discuss the nuclear superiority of the United States

(E) question the necessity of the NATO alliance following the breakup of the Soviet Union

17. In line 15, the word "deterrence" refers to

(A) the discouragement of attack by other nations, especially the Soviet Union

(B) the size of the NATO alliance relative to that of earlier alliances

(C) the strength of the NATO member nations with regard to the rest of Europe

(D) the possible aggressive behavior of the Soviet Union

(E) the high moral purpose of earlier alliances as opposed to the superficial purpose of NATO

18. The purpose of the second paragraph (lines 10-19) in relation to the rest of the passage is to

(A) introduce the factors underlying the formation of NATO

(B) highlight a factor distinguishing NATO from other pacts

(C) define the term "deterrence" relative to the functionality of NATO

(D) describe the provisional aspects of the NATO treaty

(E) identify the aggressors prompting the formation of NATO

GO ON TO THE NEXT PAGE

19. The author mentions Napoleon, Kaiser Wilhelm, and Adolph Hitler (lines 12-13) in order to emphasize which point about the NATO alliance?

(A) It was specifically intended to stop the barbarism promoted by Adolph Hitler.
(B) It was a peacetime alliance established to deter future aggression.
(C) The Soviet Union's inclusion was a result of its military strength.
(D) It was the first alliance in which both the United States and the United Kingdom were members.
(E) The military alliance was politically united and militarily strong.

20. In context, lines 20-40 suggest that the formation of NATO occurred for all of the following reasons EXCEPT

(A) democratic uprisings in France
(B) military strength of the United States
(C) European need for monetary support
(D) apprehension about the spread of communism
(E) belief that weaker members of NATO could be defended by stronger members

21. The author uses the example of the Cuban missile crisis (lines 45-47) in order to establish that

(A) the United States' superiority in nuclear weaponry ended in the late 1960s
(B) in the aftermath of the Cuban missile crisis the number of nuclear weapons manufactured in the United States was reduced
(C) Soviet advances in nuclear technology were considered a threat to NATO, but the United States' ingenuity saved the alliance
(D) while the United States no longer had a monopoly on nuclear weapons, the weapons it had were superior to those of the Soviet Union
(E) the Cuban missile crisis marked the end of the United States' domination of world affairs

22. According to the passage, the "Warsaw Pact" (lines 56-57)

(A) was formed as an immediate reaction to the formation of NATO
(B) was a direct result of World War II
(C) prompted the formation of NATO
(D) was a reaction to West Germany's joining NATO
(E) was created by Soviet political figures

23. The Warsaw Pact is similar to NATO in that

(A) its formation was a peacetime reaction to a potential threat
(B) it was formed as a response to aggressive behavior on the part of many Western European nations
(C) it was established in the same year that the NATO alliance was formed
(D) Warsaw Pact member nations have a correspondingly strong commitment to democracy
(E) it too was created as a reaction to imperialistic maneuvering on the part of certain European nations

24. The primary function of the final paragraph is to

(A) demonstrate how the formation of NATO caused the creation of the Warsaw Pact
(B) summarize the details surrounding Spain's entrance into NATO
(C) summarize the details surrounding Greece's and West Germany's entrance into NATO
(D) detail the provisions of the Warsaw Pact
(E) cite additional examples of how NATO has changed since its formation

STOP

If you finish before time is called, you may check your work on this section only.
Do not turn to any other section in the test.

SECTION 8
Time — 20 minutes
16 Questions

Turn to Section 8 of your answer sheet to answer the questions in this section.

Directions: For this section, solve each problem and decide which is the best of the choices given. Fill in the corresponding circle on the answer sheet. You may use any available space for scratchwork.

Notes

1. The use of a calculator is permitted.

2. All numbers used are real numbers.

3. Figures that accompany problems in this test are intended to provide information useful in solving the problems. They are drawn as accurately as possible EXCEPT when it is stated in a specific problem that the figure is not drawn to scale. All figures lie in a plane unless otherwise indicated.

4. Unless otherwise specified, the domain of any function f is assumed to be the set of all real numbers x for which $f(x)$ is a real number.

Reference Information

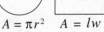

$A = \pi r^2$
$C = 2\pi r$

$A = lw$

$A = \frac{1}{2}bh$

$V = lwh$

$V = \pi r^2 h$

$c^2 = a^2 + b^2$

Special Right Triangles

The number of degrees of arc in a circle is 360.

The sum of the measures in degrees of the angles of a triangle is 180.

1. If $\sqrt{x+3}+3=9$, then $x=$

(A) 3
(B) 33
(C) 39
(D) 69
(E) 75

2. Ninety people work in a certain office. If the ratio of men to women is 7:8, how many more women than men work in the office?

(A) 1
(B) 2
(C) 4
(D) 6
(E) 15

GO ON TO THE NEXT PAGE

3. Faisel watches television for a total of three hours. During the first hour, he has his choice of three shows. For each of the second and third hours, he can choose from two shows. How many different schedules of shows can Faisel watch?

(A)   3
(B)   6
(C)   7
(D)   8
(E)   12

4. If $x > 0$ and 20 percent of x is 30 percent of y, which of the following represents 80 percent of x ?

(A) $0.5y$
(B) $0.8y$
(C) $0.9y$
(D) y
(E) $1.2y$

5. If x and y are integers, how many distinct ordered pairs (x, y) satisfy the equation $2x + 4y = 17$?

(A)   None
(B)   One
(C)   Two
(D)   Three
(E)   Four

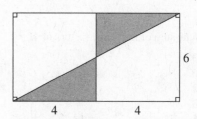

Note: Figure not drawn to scale.

6. What is the probability that a randomly selected point will fall within one of the shaded regions?

(A) $\dfrac{1}{8}$

(B) $\dfrac{1}{4}$

(C) $\dfrac{1}{2}$

(D) $\dfrac{2}{3}$

(E) $\dfrac{3}{4}$

GO ON TO THE NEXT PAGE

7. For any two distinct negative integers c and d, which of the following must be less than cd ?

   (A) $cd + 1$
   (B) $(-cd)^2$
   (C) $d(c - 2)$
   (D) $(c - 1)(d - 1)$
   (E) $(c + 1)(d + 1)$

8. What is the sum of the prime factors of 42 ?

   (A) 3
   (B) 6
   (C) 12
   (D) 13
   (E) 76

9. The average (arithmetic mean) of three consecutive even integers a, b, and c is 8. What is the median of a, b, c, and 20 ?

   (A) 8
   (B) 9
   (C) 10
   (D) 11
   (E) 12

10. If n is an integer, which of the following must be true about $12n + 3$?

    I. It is even
    II. It is odd
    III. It is divisible by 3

    (A) I only
    (B) II only
    (C) III only
    (D) II and III only
    (E) I, II, and III

GO ON TO THE NEXT PAGE

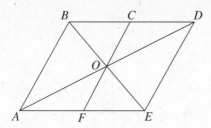

Note: Figure not drawn to scale.

11. In the figure above, points C and F are the midpoints of $\overline{BD}$ and $\overline{AE}$, respectively. If $BC = 3$ and the area of parallelogram $ABDE$ is 48, what is the area of triangle AOF?

(A) 6
(B) 8
(C) 10
(D) 12
(E) 14

12. Stephanie, Damon, and Karissa have been contracted to paint an office building that contains 72 rooms. If Stephanie paints half as many rooms as Karissa and 12 more than Damon, how many rooms does Karissa paint?

(A) 9
(B) 21
(C) 30
(D) 42
(E) 48

13. If $q = \dfrac{1}{s}$ and $qs \neq 0$, what is the result of $\dfrac{(1+q)}{(1+s)}$?

(A) 0
(B) $-q$
(C) 1
(D) s
(E) q

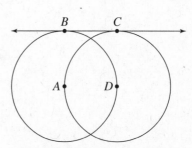

Note: Figure not drawn to scale.

14. In the figure above, A and D are the centers of circles with radii of r. If $\overline{BC}$ is tangent to both circles and $\overline{BC} = \overline{AD} = r$, what is the area of quadrilateral $ABCD$ (not shown) in terms of r ?

(A) $4r^2$
(B) $4r$
(C) $2r^2$
(D) $2r$
(E) r^2

GO ON TO THE NEXT PAGE

x	f(x)
−2	3
−1	0
0	−2
1	−3
2	1
3	4

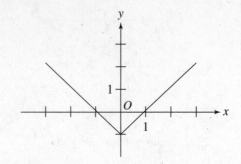

15. The table above shows several values for function f. If the function h is defined by $h(x) = f\left(\dfrac{2}{x} + 2\right)$, what is the value of $h(-2)$?

(A) −3
(B) −2
(C)   0
(D)   2
(E)   3

16. If the graph of $f(x)$ is shown in the figure above, and $f(a) = 1$, then which of the following must be true?

(A) $f(f(a)) = 0$
(B) $f(f(a)) = 1$
(C) $a = f(a)$
(D) $a = 0$
(E) $a = 1$

STOP
If you finish before time is called, you may check your work on this section only.
Do not turn to any other section in the test.

NO TEST MATERIAL ON THIS PAGE.

SECTION 9
Time — 20 minutes
19 Questions

Turn to Section 9 of your answer sheet to answer the questions in this section.

Directions: For each question in this section, select the best answer from among the choices given and fill in the corresponding circle on the answer sheet.

Each sentence below has one or two blanks, each blank indicating that something has been omitted. Beneath the sentence are five words or sets of words labeled A through E. Choose the word or set of words that, when inserted in the sentence, best fits the meaning of the sentence as a whole.

Example:

Desiring to ------- his taunting friends, Mitch gave them taffy in hopes it would keep their mouths shut.

(A) eliminate   (B) satisfy   (C) overcome
    (D) ridicule   (E) silence

1. The senator's chances of winning another term in office are -------, since she has consistently broken promises and let people down.

    (A) cogent   (B) remote   (C) frivolous
        (D) disastrous   (E) veritable

2. Monet's first Impressionist works were met with widespread ------- by art critics, but throughout the twentieth century the pieces' visually striking and unconventional style was consistently celebrated and -------.

    (A) ridicule . . revered
    (B) scorn . . reviled
    (C) acclaim . . admired
    (D) notice . . imitated
    (E) distraction . . esteemed

3. Predictably, it is ------- among sports fans who become most distraught when owners ------- traditional practices in favor of more profitable new ones.

    (A) dissenters . . compromise
    (B) commentators . . undermine
    (C) moderates . . institute
    (D) fanatics . . welcome
    (E) purists . . forsake

4. Thomas showed little interest in making conversation with people he barely knew; consequently, his manner often struck people as impolite, even -------.

    (A) vindictive   (B) devious   (C) apologetic
        (D) brusque   (E) banal

5. Although he was ------- throughout much of his life, his later years were characterized by a ------- lifestyle that kept him constantly moving from place to place.

    (A) stationary . . dormant
    (B) sedentary . . peripatetic
    (C) secular . . missionary
    (D) animated . . frenetic
    (E) obstinate . . unconventional

6. In order to meet the demands of its customers, the corporation had to remain -------: the inability to adjust to constant changes would spell disaster.

    (A) adroit   (B) homogeneous   (C) scrupulous
        (D) steadfast   (E) immutable

GO ON TO THE NEXT PAGE

Directions: Each passage below is followed by questions based on its content. Answer the questions on the basis of what is <u>stated</u> or <u>implied</u> in each passage and in any introductory material that may be provided.

Questions 7-19 are based on the following passages.

The following passages present two views of the differences between the left and the right side of the brain. Passage 1 discusses scientific evidence of this phenomenon, called cerebral asymmetry. Passage 2, written in 1979, presents an analysis of cultural stereotypes related to the dominance of the left and right hemispheres of the brain

Passage 1

While hunting and foraging, particularly among trees, early man found it necessary to use his arms independently of each other. That required an asymmetric arrangement
Line between brain hemispheres different from such symmetric
5 activities such as swimming, walking, postural adjustments, and so on. As one arm or hand started being used in preference to another, the hemispheres began to "specialize" further. In this way specialization and lateralization progressed in tandem over thousands of years.
10   As it turns out, the asymmetry of our hands and our brains is very much part of the natural order of things. Right- and left-handed sugar molecules differ in their geometry, a quality that can be taken advantage of in a weight-reduction program. Since our body cells accept only right-handed sugars, the
15 left-handed sugars become capable of sweetening our food without burdening us with needless calories. The situation is reversed when it comes to amino acids, the building blocks of proteins, which can be used by the body only if the amino acids are left-handed.
20   Autopsy examinations of the human brain show clear-cut asymmetries in the area of speech. In the left hemisphere, this portion, the *planum temporale*, is decidedly larger in two-thirds of the brains examined. This difference has even been shown in a thirty-one-week-old fetus.
25   X-ray studies using CAT scans reveal the same kinds of asymmetry in adults. The *Sylvian fissure* (a deep cleft in the outer area of the brain around which the major speech areas are located) is longer and more horizontally placed in the left hemisphere than in the right. In some left-handed people the
30 tendency for acute angulation on the right hemisphere is less marked, the first demonstration ever of a difference between the brain structures of right- and left-handed persons.
Since the *Sylvian fissure* leaves a pattern on the inner surface of the skull, it is possible to trace these asymmetries
35 backward in time. Harvard neuroradiologist Marjorie Lee May examined the skull of a Neanderthal man thirty thousand to fifty thousand years old and the skull of a Peking man three hundred thousand years old. She found an asymmetry in the *Sylvian fissures* similar to that in brains
40 examined in the 1980s, an indication that cerebral asymmetry and left-hemisphere dominance for language are not recent events in human evolution.

Passage 2

Words and phrases concerning concepts of left and right permeate our language and thinking: The right hand
45 (meaning also the left hemisphere) is strongly connected with what is good, just, moral, proper. The left hand (therefore the right hemisphere) is strongly linked with concepts of anarchy and feelings that are somehow out of conscious control— somehow bad, immoral, dangerous.
50   Throughout human history, terms with connotations of *good* for the right hand/left hemisphere and connotations of *bad* for the left hand/right hemisphere appear in many languages around the world. The Latin word for left is *sinister*, meaning "bad," "ominous," "sinister." The Latin
55 word for right is *dexter* from which comes our word "dexterity" meaning "skill" or "adroitness." In English, "left" comes from the Anglo-Saxon *lyft*, meaning "weak" or "worthless." The left hand of most right-handed people is in fact weaker than the right, but the original word also implied
60 lack of moral strength. The derogatory meaning of "left" may reflect the prejudice of a right-handed majority against a minority of people who were different, that is, left-handed.
Along with the opposite connotations of left and right in our language, concepts of the *duality*, or two-sidedness,
65 or human nature and thought have been postulated by philosophers, teachers and scientists from many different times and cultures. The key idea is that there are two different ways of knowing.
The main divisions are, for example, between thinking
70 and feeling, intellect and intuition, objective analysis and subjective insight. Inside our skulls, therefore, we have a double brain with two ways of knowing. As each of our hemispheres gathers in the same sensory information, each half of our brains may handle the information in different
75 ways: the task may be divided between the two hemispheres, each handling the part suited to its style.
The left hemisphere analyzes, abstracts, counts, marks time, plans step-by-step procedures, verbalizes, makes rational statements based on logic. On the other hand, we
80 have a second way of knowing: the right-hemisphere mode. We "see" things in this mode that may be imaginary or recall things that may be real. Using the right hemisphere, we understand metaphors, we dream, we create new combinations of ideas. The right hemisphere mode is the
85 intuitive, subjective, relational, holistic, time-free mode. This is also the disdained, weak, left-handed mode which in our culture has been generally ignored.

GO ON TO THE NEXT PAGE

7. The author mentions "hunting and foraging" (line 1) in order to

   (A) provide a reason for hemisphere specialization
   (B) trace the history of human development
   (C) defend the abilities of a brain with symmetrical structure
   (D) divide human activities into two types
   (E) differentiate between ancient and modern human activities

8. In line 12, "geometry" most nearly means

   (A) structural configuration
   (B) molecular weight
   (C) chemical origin
   (D) angle measure
   (E) integral formula

9. In Passage 1 the reference to "Right- and left-handed sugar molecules" (lines 11-12) serves to

   (A) prove that asymmetry pertains to all human beings at the molecular level
   (B) replicate the structural nature of sugar molecules
   (C) provide an example of asymmetry as it appears in nature
   (D) emphasize the practical applications of left-handed molecules
   (E) determine the relationship between sugar intake and weight gain

10. In discussing the nature of the *Sylvian fissure* (lines 25-32), the author of Passage 1 suggests that

    (A) CAT scans are capable of revealing abnormalities in a human adult brain
    (B) minor speech centers occupy specific locales within the adult brain
    (C) the *planum temporale* is a precursor of the *Sylvian fissure*
    (D) there is a physical difference between the brains of right-handed and left-handed individuals
    (E) there are no differences between the right and the left hemispheres of the brain

11. In lines 43-49 of Passage 2, the connection between physical function and hemisphere dominance is described in which of the following ways?

    (A) The left cerebral hemisphere is related to control of the right hand.
    (B) The right cerebral hemisphere controls all of the functions on the right side of the body.
    (C) The right cerebral hemisphere tends to control right-handedness.
    (D) The left cerebral hemisphere tends to control all of the functions on the right side of the body.
    (E) Dominance by the left cerebral hemisphere has traditionally had negative physical repercussions.

12. The second paragraph of Passage 2 (lines 50-62) primarily serves to

    (A) clarify two commonly confused terms
    (B) explore the historical meanings of two opposing terms
    (C) weigh the merits of two distinctively different concepts
    (D) explain how the definitions for a particular term vary widely among languages
    (E) discuss the development of the brain into two hemispheres

13. Passage 2 makes a distinction between left- and right-handedness (lines 50-63) in order to

    (A) analyze the psychological impact of a social phenomenon
    (B) prove that left-handed individuals are more creative than right-handed people
    (C) demonstrate the necessity for a change of attitude among educators
    (D) give credence to the popular view that right-handed society is purposefully impeding the progress of culture
    (E) illustrate the social implications of a physical variation

14. The "duality" described in the passage in line 64 can best be described as

    (A) the difference between the right and left cerebral hemispheres
    (B) a representation of the weakness of human nature
    (C) the juxtaposition of emotion and reason
    (D) the skills of an ambidextrous individual
    (E) the physiological basis for right- or left-handedness

GO ON TO THE NEXT PAGE ⇒

15. The author of Passage 1 would most likely make which argument in support of the observations made by the author of Passage 2 in lines 69-76 ?

(A) People who are left handed are more likely to rely on rational thinking and logical coherence.

(B) The asymmetry of the human brain is responsible for the cultural prejudices exhibited in negative connotations of left-handedness.

(C) Human beings developed an ability to think in different ways only after the separateness between the right and left hand was established.

(D) The dual nature of our mental faculties, similar to our physical asymmetry, most likely evolved to serve the needs of early man.

(E) Traces of the separate functions of the left and right hemispheres can be seen in the remnants of the *Sylvian fissure* impressed on the inner skull.

16. From the information presented in Passage 2 it can be inferred that a student who relied mainly on the right side of her brain would be likely to choose which of the following disciplines as an academic concentration?

(A) Creative writing
(B) Biochemistry
(C) Anthropology
(D) Art history
(E) Mathematics

17. The authors of Passages 1 and 2 would most likely agree about which of the following?

(A) Acute angulation of the *Sylvian fissure* in left-handed people is responsible for the extreme awkwardness of their manual operations.

(B) Speech is a process controlled primarily by the physical functions of the left side of the brain.

(C) Asymmetries in the area of speech determine the verbal acuity of infants up to thirty-one weeks old.

(D) Cerebral lateralization is responsible for the varying cultural attitudes toward left and right.

(E) Discrimination is not a recent event in human evolution.

18. The author of Passage 1 would most likely explain the "duality" referred to by the author of Passage 2 as

(A) lacking anthropological proof
(B) impossible to prove without psychological evidence
(C) related to the asymmetry of the brain
(D) one result of increased angulation in the *Sylvian fissure*
(E) an essential part of the cerebral lateralization and specialization processes

19. Which of the following best summarizes the structure of the two passages?

(A) Passage 1 remains objective in discussing nature's asymmetry while Passage 2 displays a tendency for the cultural preferences it argues against.

(B) Passage 1 uses reason and the archaeological record to argue the interchangeability of the brain's hemispheres while Passage 2 relies on circumstantial and unproven evidence.

(C) Passage 2 attempts to refute the arguments made in Passage 1 concerning the reliability of using fragmentary evidence gleaned from ancient human remains.

(D) Passage 2 develops its argument of the linguistic recognition of the duality of right and left from the examination of the speech areas of the brain in Passage 1.

(E) Passage 1 focuses on the brain's asymmetry while Passage 2 discusses cultural manifestations of that symmetry.

STOP

If you finish before time is called, you may check your work on this section only.
Do not turn to any other section in the test.

SECTION 10
Time — 10 minutes
14 Questions

Turn to Section 10 of your answer sheet to answer the questions in this section.

Directions: For each question in this section, select the best answer from among the choices given and fill in the corresponding circle on the answer sheet.

The following sentences test correctness and effectiveness of expression. Part of each sentence or the entire sentence is underlined; beneath each sentence are five ways of phrasing the underlined material. Choice A repeats the original phrasing; the other four choices are different. If you think the original phrasing produces a better sentence than any of the alternatives, select choice A; if not, select one of the other choices.

In making your selection, follow the requirements of standard written English; that is, pay attention to grammar, choice of words, sentence construction, and punctuation. Your selection should result in the most effective sentence—clear and precise, without awkwardness or ambiguity.

EXAMPLE:

Bobby Flay baked his first cake <u>and he was thirteen years old then</u>.

(A) and he was thirteen years old then
(B) when he was thirteen
(C) at age thirteen years old
(D) upon the reaching of thirteen years
(E) at the time when he was thirteen

○●○○○

1. Because studies show that stomach ulcers are caused by acute microbial infections, physicians may soon have the option <u>of common antibiotics being prescribed to combat</u> ulcers in their patients.

(A) of common antibiotics being prescribed to combat
(B) of prescribing common antibiotics to combat
(C) of the prescription of common antibiotics for combating
(D) by which common antibiotics are employed to combat
(E) that they prescribe common antibiotics in combating

2. Machiavelli's *The Prince* is frequently studied in philosophy <u>courses and it is</u> an example of rational politics.

(A) courses and it is
(B) courses, when it is
(C) courses as
(D) courses; moreover as
(E) courses whereas it is

3. Salvador Dali has been described by some as <u>the most controversial artist and also the most treasured of them</u> in the modern age.

(A) the most controversial and also the most treasured of them
(B) not only the most controversial artist, but also more treasured than any
(C) the most controversial artist at the same time as he is the most treasured artist
(D) at once the most controversial and also the most treasured of them
(E) the most controversial and yet the most treasured of artists

4. Given the decisions that the new vice president has made since he was hired, <u>many employees at the advertising agency are wishing earnest for a change</u>.

(A) many employees at the advertising agency are wishing earnest for a change
(B) many employees at the advertising agency have a wish for change that is earnest
(C) many employees at the advertising agency earnestly wish for a change
(D) many employees at the advertising agency earnestly have a wish for changes
(E) an earnest wish for change was been brought about for many employees at the advertising agency

5. Annie Sullivan firmly admonished her young charge Helen <u>that the crockery must not be thrown by her</u> during family mealtimes in the Keller household.

(A) that the crockery must not be thrown by her
(B) she must not be throwing the crockery
(C) not to throw the crockery
(D) not to throw her the crockery
(E) that the crockery must not be thrown by herself

GO ON TO THE NEXT PAGE

6. Under Alexander the Great, the Hellenistic Empire ruled parts of Europe, Africa, and Asia, <u>as well as bringing</u> its famed Greek architectural wisdom across the known world.

   (A) as well as bringing
   (B) as well as they brought
   (C) additionally bringing
   (D) they also brought
   (E) and brought

7. The camera obscura, a sixteenth-century precursor of the modern camera, <u>produced a picture in much the same way that modern overhead projectors shows images</u>.

   (A) produced a picture in much the same way that modern overhead projectors shows images
   (B) was able to produce a picture in much the same way that modern overhead projectors often show many images
   (C) produced a picture in exactly the same way that modern overhead projectors can show images
   (D) produced a picture like the modern overhead projectors show images
   (E) produced a picture in much the same way that a modern overhead projector shows and image

8. Though they have a <u>chemical composition similar to that of the common chrysoberyl</u>, flawless emeralds are so rare that they are prized above any other gems except perfect rubies.

   (A) chemical composition similar to that of the common chrysoberyl
   (B) chemical composition that is like the common chrysoberyl's
   (C) chemical composition the same as the common chrysoberyl's
   (D) similar chemical composition to the common chrysoberyl
   (E) similar chemical composition to the chrysoberyl's

9. Confessions of violent crimes nationwide skyrocketed last year, <u>but in some towns it</u> remained steady or decreased.

   (A) but in some towns it
   (B) but in some towns they
   (C) although in some towns they would have
   (D) yet in some towns such confessions would have
   (E) but in some towns such confessions

10. The average adult American in the 1970s read more novels <u>than</u> the 1980s and 1990s.

    (A) than
    (B) than did
    (C) than the average adults of
    (D) than with the average adults in
    (E) than did the average adult in

11. Lashonda enjoyed her trip to Puerto Rico last summer <u>just like she had on her visit in 1994</u>.

    (A) just like she had on her visit in 1994
    (B) just like her 1994 visit
    (C) just as she had in 1994
    (D) just as she had enjoyed it in 1994
    (E) just like 1994

12. For many people, <u>being in good health is more important</u> than being rich and famous.

    (A) being in good health is more important
    (B) having good health is more important
    (C) there is more importance in being healthy
    (D) healthiness is more important
    (E) to have good health is more important

13. Alexei urges his art students <u>to go beyond creating technically proficient drawings, they should imbue</u> their two-dimensional sketches with emotional depth.

    (A) to go beyond creating technically proficient drawings, they should imbue
    (B) going beyond creating technically proficient drawings to imbuing
    (C) to go beyond creating technically proficient drawing to imbue
    (D) to go beyond technically proficient drawing creation, so as to imbue
    (E) going beyond technically proficient drawing creation, imbuing

14. <u>A native Californian, Jeff McDonald's first play received</u> a Tony award in 1975.

    (A) A native Californian, Jeff McDonald's first play received
    (B) A native Californian, the first play by Jeff McDonald received
    (C) The first play by Jeff McDonald, a native Californian, received
    (D) Jeff McDonald, a native Californian, wrote his first play and he received
    (E) A native Californian, Jeff McDonald as well as his first play received

STOP
**If you finish before time is called, you may check your work on this section only.
Do not turn to any other section in the test.**

PRACTICE TEST 6: ANSWER KEY

2 Reading	4 Math	5 Writing	6 Math	7 Reading	8 Math	9 Reading	10 Writing
1. A	1. E	1. E	1. E	1. E	1. B	1. B	1. B
2. C	2. D	2. C	2. A	2. A	2. D	2. A	2. C
3. E	3. E	3. B	3. E	3. B	3. E	3. E	3. E
4. E	4. B	4. C	4. C	4. D	4. E	4. D	4. C
5. D	5. C	5. D	5. C	5. B	5. A	5. B	5. C
6. E	6. B	6. A	6. B	6. D	6. B	6. A	6. E
7. D	7. D	7. E	7. E	7. B	7. E	7. A	7. E
8. A	8. E	8. E	8. A	8. C	8. C	8. A	8. A
9. C	9. C	9. C	9. 16	9. C	9. B	9. C	9. E
10. E	10. E	10. A	10. 520	10. C	10. D	10. D	10. E
11. E	11. C	11. D	11. 11	11. E	11. A	11. A	11. C
12. A	12. C	12. C	12. $\frac{6}{5}$ or 1.2	12. D	12. D	12. B	12. A
13. A	13. B	13. A	13. 68	13. A	13. E	13. E	13. C
14. E	14. B	14. B	14. 70	14. A	14. E	14. C	14. C
15. D	15. B	15. C	15. 30	15. E	15. A	15. D	
16. C	16. C	16. E	16. 12	16. C	16. A	16. A	
17. D	17. A	17. A	17. 130	17. A		17. B	
18. D	18. B	18. B	18. $\frac{63}{2}$ or 31.5	18. B		18. C	
19. D	19. A	19. D		19. B		19. E	
20. E	20. B	20. C		20. A			
21. A		21. E		21. D			
22. E		22. A		22. D			
23. B		23. D		23. A			
24. C		24. D		24. E			
		25. B					
		26. C					
		27. E					
		28. C					
		29. B					
		30. B					
		31. A					
		32. C					
		33. E					
		34. B					
		35. D					

SAT SCORING WORKSHEET

For directions on how to score your SAT practice test, see pages 10–11.

SAT Writing Section

Total Writing Multiple-Choice Questions Correct: ⬚

−

Total Writing Multiple-Choice Questions Incorrect: _____ ÷ 4 = ⬚

Grammar Raw Score: ⬚

Grammar Scaled Subscore

⬚

Compare the Grammar Raw Score with the Writing Multiple-Choice Subscore Conversion Table on page 504 to find the Grammar Scaled Subscore.

+

Your Essay Score (2–12): _____ × 2 = ⬚

Writing Raw Score: ⬚

Compare Raw Score with SAT Score Conversion Table on page 504 to find the Writing Scaled Score.

Writing Scaled Score

⬚

SAT Critical Reading Section

Total Critical Reading Questions Correct: ⬚

−

Total Critical Reading Questions Incorrect: _____ ÷ 4 = ⬚

Critical Reading Raw Score: ⬚

Compare Raw Score with SAT Score Conversion Table on page 504 to find the Critical Reading Scaled Score.

Critical Reading Scaled Score

⬚

SAT Math Section

Total Math Grid-In Questions Correct: ⬚

+

Total Math Multiple-Choice Questions Correct: ⬚

−

Total Math Multiple-Choice Questions Incorrect: _____ ÷ 4 = ⬚

Don't include wrong answers from grid-ins!

Math Raw Score: ⬚

Compare Raw Score with SAT Score Conversion Table on page 504 to find the Math Scaled Score.

Math Scaled Score

⬚

SAT SCORE CONVERSION TABLE

Raw Score	Writing Scaled Score	Reading Scaled Score	Math Scaled Score	Raw Score	Writing Scaled Score	Reading Scaled Score	Math Scaled Score	Raw Score	Writing Scaled Score	Reading Scaled Score	Math Scaled Score
73	800			47	590–630	600–640	660–700	21	400–440	410–450	440–480
72	790–800			46	590–630	590–630	650–690	20	390–430	400–440	430–470
71	780–800			45	580–620	580–620	650–690	19	380–420	400–440	430–470
70	770–800			44	570–610	580–620	640–680	18	370–410	390–430	420–460
69	770–800			43	570–610	570–610	630–670	17	370–410	380–420	410–450
68	760–800			42	560–600	570–610	620–660	16	360–400	370–410	400–440
67	760–800	800		41	560–600	560–600	610–650	15	350–390	360–400	400–440
66	760–800	770–800		40	550–590	550–590	600–640	14	340–380	350–390	390–430
65	750–790	760–800		39	540–580	550–590	590–630	13	330–370	340–380	380–420
64	740–780	750–790		38	530–570	540–580	590–630	12	320–360	340–380	360–400
63	730–770	740–780		37	530–570	530–570	580–620	11	320–360	330–370	350–390
62	720–760	730–770		36	520–560	530–570	570–610	10	310–350	320–360	340–380
61	710–750	720–760		35	510–550	520–560	560–600	9	300–340	310–350	330–370
60	700–740	710–750		34	500–540	520–560	560–600	8	290–330	300–340	320–360
59	690–730	700–740		33	490–530	510–550	550–590	7	280–320	300–340	310–350
58	680–720	690–730		32	480–520	500–540	540–580	6	270–310	290–330	300–340
57	680–720	680–720		31	470–510	490–530	530–570	5	260–300	280–320	290–330
56	670–710	670–710		30	470–510	480–520	520–560	4	240–280	270–310	280–320
55	660–720	670–710		29	460–500	470–510	520–560	3	230–270	250–290	280–320
54	650–690	660–700	760–800	28	450–490	470–510	510–550	2	230–270	240–280	270–310
53	640–680	650–690	740–780	27	440–480	460–500	500–540	1	220–260	220–260	260–300
52	630–670	640–680	730–770	26	430–470	450–490	490–530	0	210–250	200–240	250–290
51	630–670	630–670	710–750	25	420–460	440–480	480–520	−1	200–240	200–230	230–270
50	620–660	620–660	690–730	24	410–450	430–470	470–510	−2	200–230	200–220	220–260
49	610–650	610–650	680–720	23	410–450	430–470	460–500	−3	200–220	200–210	200–240
48	600–640	600–640	670–710	22	400–440	420–460	450–490				

WRITING MULTIPLE-CHOICE SUBSCORE CONVERSION TABLE

Grammar Raw Score	Grammar Scaled Subscore	Grammar Raw Score	Grammar Scaled Subscore	Grammar Raw Score	Grammar Scaled Subscore	Grammar Raw Score	Grammar Scaled Subscore	Grammar Raw Score	Grammar Scaled Subscore
49	78–80	38	67–71	27	55–59	16	42–46	5	30–34
48	77–80	37	66–70	26	54–58	15	41–45	4	29–33
47	75–79	36	65–69	25	53–57	14	40–44	3	28–32
46	74–78	35	64–68	24	52–56	13	39–43	2	27–31
45	72–76	34	63–67	23	51–55	12	38–42	1	25–29
44	72–76	33	62–66	22	50–54	11	36–40	0	24–28
43	71–75	32	61–65	21	49–53	10	35–39	−1	22–26
42	70–74	31	60–64	20	47–51	9	34–38	−2	20–23
41	69–73	30	59–63	19	46–50	8	33–37	−3	20–22
40	68–72	29	58–62	18	45–49	7	32–36		
39	68–72	28	56–60	17	44–48	6	31–35		

Chapter 15
Practice Test 6:
Answers and
Explanations

SECTION 2

1. **A** The blank is followed by *in which*, words that indicate a definition. The blank means *shows little or no passion*. The best word for the blank will mean "without passion." Only (A) *apathetic* shares this meaning.

2. **C** *Haughty and dismissive* is the clue, indicating that "stuck up" is the meaning of the word in the blank. (C), *arrogant,* means stuck up. (B), *conceded,* is a trap answer because it sounds like *conceited,* but spelled *conceded,* it means "granted," and is therefore incorrect. (A) means "richly decorated," (D) means "threatening," and (E) means "coordinated," so none of these choices works, and (C) is the best answer.

3. **E** The *interest* must have either suddenly risen or dropped. In the second half of the sentence *more and more people* wanted them, so a word that means "explosion" or "quick growth" is needed for the blank. Only (E) *burgeoning* matches this definition.

4. **E** This sentence is a relationship-between-the blanks question, since there isn't really a clue. The trigger word *even* tells you that the blanks are going in opposite directions,. Eliminate (A), (B), and (C), since they contain words with similar meanings. (A) is also a trap answer, since you might associate the word *identical* with *twins*. The words in (D) are unrelated. Only answer choice (E) has words going in opposite directions, making it the best answer.

5. **D** The second blank is easier to start with. *Gilligan's research* is described as *particularly essential* so there must not be much *work* on the subject. A good word for the second blank is "neglected." (E) has the opposite meaning, Only (B) and (D) seem close. The first blank must be something positive, because the words immediately before the blank *Even though it is by no means* and the sentence goes on to say positive things about the research. (D) *exhaustive* is a positive quality while (B) *irrelevant* is negative. (D) is correct.

6. **E** A good word for the first blank is "charmed," since the blank indicates a reaction to *charming behavior*. Eliminate (C) and (D). The rest are all fairly close to meaning "charmed." For the second blank, the friends *began to realize* something negative: a good word for the blank is "false" or "an act." Both (C) *insincere* and (E) *calculated* fit this meaning, but only (E) matches for both blanks.

7. **D** There is a relationship between *once* and *now. Once* medicine was only for *men,* and *now women* are engaged in it. The word for the blank must mean "restricted to" or "only for." (D) *province* is closest, meaning "a sphere or field of activity or authority."

8. **A** The *depictions* were *more gruesome than his readers could bear* so the editor needed to remove the *vivid description*. The word that fits in the blank must mean "take out." (A) *expurgate* is the closest, meaning "removing words or passages deemed offensive or objectionable." There is a lot of tough vocab here: look up any unfamiliar words.

9. **C** The passage makes references to *churning out* and *mass production* and resulting *lower prices*. There is no mention of *better quality* as in (A). (B) is extreme due to *most*. The passage states that *automotive history began* when the *assembly line* got going, so (C) is supported by the passage. We don't know what happened after 1926, so eliminate (D). (E) is extreme due to *no*.

10. **E** The passage discusses Ford's *grand vision* and how it began *a new era of freedom and mobility*, so the author has a good opinion of Ford as someone who changed life in America. This is paraphrased best in (E). In (A), *working conditions* are not mentioned in the passage. (B) may be tempting because of *revolutionized* but *structure and design* are not mentioned in the passage. (C) misses the focus and tone of the passage. In (E), *marketing* is not mentioned in the passage.

11. **E** The statement that the author would agree with must match the main idea of the passage. The overall idea is that people associate Existentialism with Sartre, but his colleague Camus achieved more but was *overlooked*. This is best paraphrased in (E). (A) goes a little to far: the author is just trying to give Camus some recognition too. There is no evidence in the passage to support (B), (C) or (D).

12. **A** The passage states the *Camus viewed the Communists as ideologues with little regard for the human condition*. Even if *ideologues* is an unfamiliar word, the context is that Camus did not have a good opinion of Communism because of how it treated people. This is best paraphrased in (A). (B) and (C) are negative, but too extreme.

13. **A** The primary purpose of a passage will agree with the main idea of the passage, but it's really asking "why did the author write this passage?" or "what is the writer trying to accomplish in this passage?" The author from the beginning discusses *Emotions represented in a film* and goes on to discuss how *the spectator's emotional response to film is related to form* and ends with an example of how an audience reacts along with the emotions in one particular film. Thus, (A) best describes what the author accomplishes in the passage. In (B), *control* is extreme. In (C), a *viewer* cannot *impact* a film. Some characters of a film are mentioned, but no specific *actors* as in (D). (E) is too broad of a subject and ignores *emotions*.

14. **E** In the passage, the *ready-made reactions* are also referred to as *already formulated emotions* and *stereotyped reactions*, so we could say these are "typical" or "predictable" reactions. Since we want the situation that is not a ready-made reaction, look for the one that is abnormal or not what is usually predicted. (A), (B), (C), and (D) are all common reactions for the given situations, but (E) *relief* when *bank robber*s are on the loose is not normal.

15. **D** The examples in the first paragraph each describe *emotions present in a film* and how the parts of a film reinforce the emotions. This is best paraphrased in (D). (A) is extreme. In (B), *investment* is not mentioned in the passage. No *unexpectedness* is indicated in the passage, as in (C). There is no evidence to say viewers are *manipulated* as in (E).

16. **C** *Suspend* is a synonym for a couple of the terms in the answers, but make sure you always go back to the passage and determine the meaning from the context.

17. **D** The questions that begin with *Why else* emphasize the point that comes right before the hypothetical questions, that form *may lead us to override our everyday emotional responses.* (A) *preferable to real life* goes too far. In (B), *tricked* is too negative. (C) and (E) have no support in the passage. (D) *transcend assumptions* is a good paraphrase of what we were looking for.

18. **D** The example that follows states that many viewers find *Oz more attractive than Kansas*, but because we are so involved in Dorothy's viewpoint, we identify with her desire to be in Kansas, so we will need an answer that reflects an audience identifying with a character and experiencing an emotion opposite of how they usually would feel in a given situation. Only (D) describes a feeling (*compassion*) that is not the usual reaction to a *tyrannical dictator* (usually that would be more along the lines of fear).

19. **D** In the passage the examples given for *gratified expectations* are all stories that end the way we expect them to. (A) is an example of a *cheated expectation* (B) is an example of overriding everyday emotions. (C) and (E) are surprising, and only (D) gives a satisfying and expected end to a situation.

20. **E** From the passage, the author's assertion can be paraphrased as "there is no one right way" for a film to generate emotion. Thus, what would weaken this is a situation in which "one right way" is described. This is seen in (E) which describes a *formula* for evoking emotions.

21. **A** The passage discusses how the audience's emotions follow along with those experienced by *George*. Thus if *George* is going through some *emotional complexity* then the audience is too. The passage states that the audience's reaction is due to the form—the elements used by a filmmaker (according to the footnote). This is seen in (A). There is no support in the passage for the other answers, and (E) is extreme.

22. **E** From the passage, the author's statement can be paraphrased as "form is responsible for the emotions felt by the viewer." We want to <u>weaken</u> this statement, so look for an answer that shows something other than form as generating emotions. (E) best weakens the statement, because the form of the movie is that of a comedy meant to provoke laughter, while the spectator is focused on his or her own experience.

23. **B** According to the passage, the description of *It's a Wonderful Life* illustrates how emotions on screen and responses to them are dependent on form. That is the author's *assertion*, as mentioned in (B). The movie is a concrete example of how an audience's responses are provoked by a film. The example also supports the author's thesis that a film's form influences audience emotion (A) is incorrect because the *summarizing* is not the point, the author includes it to support his argument. (C) *ideal* is too strong to describe the passage. (D) is too broad for a description of a single scene of a film, and while characters and filmmakers are mentioned *actors*, as in (E), are not.

24. **C** The *elder Bailey* is the *father* described in lines 51–52 as *impractical but generous* is paraphrased in (C) *idealistic yet charitable.* (A) describes *Potter.* (B) (D), and (E) describes possible reactions to points in the film described.

SECTION 4

1. **E**   When 28 is divided by 8, 8 goes in evenly 3 times and there are 4 left over. Use each of the answer choices to divide 53 and see which gives a remainder of 4. The only one that matches is (E) When 53 is divided by 7, 7 goes in evenly 3 times and there are 4 left over.

2. **D**   If 8 gallons of the 20 gallons is pumped out $\frac{12}{20}$ of the tank is full. Percent means "out of 100," so since $\frac{12}{20} = \frac{60}{100}$, 60% of the tank is filled. (D) is correct.

3. **E**   In the image, EG is the diagonal of the base of the cube. A diagonal of a square is longer than any of the sides, so eliminate (A), (B), and (D) as these are all sides of the squares that make up the cube. In (C), CH is also a diagonal of one of the squares, and is equal to, not larger than EG. In (E), DF is longer than EG because DF is the diagonal of the cube. FH is the same length as EG, and it is clear that FH is a leg of a right triangle in which DF is the hypotenuse and thus the longest side of the triangle.

4. **B**   Sketch the triangle described by the question: Points (4, 3) and (9, 8) make a diagonal with a positive slope. The lowest y-value is 3, so the base of the triangle is a horizontal line that goes from (4, 3) to (9, 3), where a vertical line drops down from (9, 8). There is a difference of 5 between the x-values of the base, so the answer is (B) 5.

5. **C**   From the graph, the month in which the store earned the greatest profit was December with $1,500. The month with the least amount of profit was February with $300. Thus, the difference between the greatest and least profits is $1,200. The answer is (C).

6. **B**   The distance between two points can be found using the distance formula, $d = \sqrt{(x_2 - x_1)^2 + (y_2 - y_1)^2}$. Plugging In the values from the question we get: $d = \sqrt{(11-7)^2 + (0-3)^2} = \sqrt{(4^2)+(-3)^2} = \sqrt{16+9} = \sqrt{25} = 5$. Answer (B). You could also solve this by drawing a right triangle as described in the explanation for question 4 and using the Pythagorean theorem when you determine the lengths of the legs (3 and 4, which is a Pythagorean triplet 3 : 4 : 5).

7. **D**   Solve the inequality by multiplying both sides by 2. Since x is less than 24, we can eliminate (E). We are also told that y is 4 less than x. Of the remaining choices, this is true only of (D). Alternatively, you can simply substitute each answer choice for x and y in the given inequality and equation, and eliminate answers that don't make both of them true.

8.   E   Plug in! If you plug in $b = 2$ and $a = 3$, $b - 3a$, or $2 - 3(3)$, equals –7. Twice the sum of $2a$ and $5b$ is $2[2(3) + 5(2)]$, which equals 32. The question then asks us to subtract –7 from 32, which gives us a Target Value of 39. Therefore, after checking all answer choices, (E) is correct in that $9b + 7a$ is $9(2) + 7(3)$, or $18 + 21 = 39$.

9.   C   Simplify $(4^3)^x$. Remember that when a number is raised to a power, we multiply the exponents. One option is 4^{3x}, which is (A). Since this is an EXCEPT question, if it works, eliminate it. Eliminate (A). Another option in simplifying the original equation is that 4 becomes 2^2. So you have $(2^2)^3)^x$, or 2^{6x}. Rewrite the rest of the answers. (B) becomes $(2^{4x})(2^{2x})$. When you multiply like bases, add the exponents. This is 2^{6x}. Eliminate (B). (C) simplifies to 4^{4x}, which isn't either of our choices. The answer is (C).

10. E   Since the inequality in the question shows the possible values for x, try out numbers from the inequality to see what the highest and lowest possibilities are for $f(x)$. If x is –3, $f(x) = (-3)^2 - 2 = 7$. Since 7 is a possible value, we can eliminate (C). Although we used the lowest value for x, the lowest value for $f(x)$ comes when $x = 0$, which gives $f(x) = -2$: eliminate (A). Using $x = 4$ gives the highest value of $f(x)$, which is $4^2 - 2 = 14$. Eliminate (D), and also (B), since it falls between the highest and lowest values of $f(x)$. Only (E) 16 is not a possible value.

11. C   The easiest way to tackle this problem is to try out the answers in place of b in the equation and see which makes the equation true. Only –6 makes $1 - \frac{4}{b} = \frac{5}{3}$ true: $1 - \left(-\frac{4}{6}\right) = \frac{6}{6} + \frac{4}{6} = \frac{10}{6} = \frac{5}{3}$.

12. C   The first article has 7 pages. For the second article, don't just subtract 17 from 24, because the article is also on page 17, so the second article has 8 pages. The third article starts on page 28 and ends on 31, for a total of 4 pages. The fourth article begins on 52 and ends of 56 for a total of 5 pages. In numeric order, the total number of pages for each article is 4, 5, 7, 8. To find the median, add the two middle numbers and divide by 2: $\frac{5+7}{2} = 6$ answer (C).

13. B   The number line indicates that y is –2. We know that x^2 is positive, but x alone could be either positive or negative (for example, the square of both 2 and –2 = 4). Since x^2 looks to be at about $\frac{1}{4}$, x must be $\frac{1}{2}$ or $-\frac{1}{2}$. The result of $x + y$ is either $-\frac{1}{2} + (-2) = -2\frac{1}{2}$ or $\frac{1}{2} + (-2) = -1\frac{1}{2}$. Eliminate (D), (E), and (C) because they are positive. Eliminate (A), which is at $-\frac{1}{2}$. (B) is located at $-1\frac{1}{2}$.

14. **B** Sketch a line that follows the direction of the "cloud" of dots. This is definitely a positive slope, so eliminate (C), (D), and (E), which have negative slopes. The line created roughly passes through (1, 2) and (4, 3) so for every increase of 1 to the y-value, there is an increase of 3 to the x-value. That's a slope of $\frac{1}{3}$, as seen in (B). If your line gave you points that are pretty close, such as (1, 2) and (5, 3), you could still eliminate (A), because you would get a fractional slope of $\frac{1}{4}$, which is closer to the fractional slope in (B) than the whole number slope in (A).

15. **B** Since $a^b = 0$, $a = 0$. That's all we need to know in order to determine the value of bc^a. Any number raised to 0 is 1, so $bc^a = bc^0 = 1$, answer (B).

16. **C** Mark the dimensions given on the figure above the question. Since B is the same distance from A as D is from E, BD is parallel to AE, which means that triangle BCE, with sides 5, 5, and 3 is similar to triangle ACE with sides of 10, 10 and side AE that we need to find the perimeter of $ABDE$. Since the sides we know in ACE are twice the size of those in BCE, we know the third side is twice as big also, and $AE = 6$. $ABDE$ then is $6 + 5 + 3 + 5 = 19$, answer (C).

17. **A** Come up with some numbers that fit the rules given in the question, such as $a = 2$, $b = 4$, and $c = 6$. This means that $c^2 - a^2 = 6^2 - 2^2 = 36 - 4 = 32$. Replace the variables in the answers with $a = 2$. Only (A) gives 32. (B) gives 12; (C) and (D) give 16; (E) gives 8.

18. **B** Calculate the fraction of the tickets that are NOT pink: $\frac{1}{2} + \frac{1}{10} + \frac{1}{4} = \frac{17}{20}$. Since $\frac{17}{20}$ of the tickets are NOT pink, $\frac{3}{20}$ of the tickets are pink. Since we also know that 30 tickets are pink, that means the number 30 is $\frac{3}{20}$ of the total: $\frac{3}{20} \times x = 30$. Solve for x to find that there are 200 tickets total. Since $\frac{1}{4}$ of the tickets are blue: $\frac{1}{4} \times 200 = 50$. There are 50 blue tickets.

19. **A** We're looking for the set that has the integers common to both set R and set S. Because the absolute value bars appear around x and y, we need to consider both the positive and negative values. Set R is all positive integers less than 10, 0, and all negative integers greater than −10, so set R is $\{-9, -8, -7, -6, -5, -4, -3, -2, -1, 0, 1, 2, 3, 4, 5, 6, 7, 8, 9\}$. Set S is made up of all even integers greater than 5 or less than −5, so that's $\{\ldots-10, -8, -6, 6, 8, 10\ldots\}$. We could go on and on, but since we've gotten to a number higher than any in set R, no further numbers in set S would be common to both sets. The only common elements are $\{-8, -6, 6, 8\}$, as seen in (A).

20. **B** After drawing a square and labeling its sides with length 6, draw a circle around the square such that there are 4 points of intersection between the two shapes occur at the vertices of the square. In doing so, the diagonal of the square doubles as the diameter of the circle. Using $45°$–$45°$–$90°$ right triangle rules, the diagonal of this special right triangle is $6\sqrt{2}$, which would also then be the length of the diameter of the circle. The radius is then equal to $3\sqrt{2}$. Using the formula for the area of a circle, $A = \pi \cdot r^2$, the area of the circle is then equal to 18π. Thus, answer choice (B) is correct.

SECTION 5

1. **E** The sentence is incomplete as written due to *providing*, as are (B) and (D). (C) has a subject-verb agreement error. We need the simple present tense *provide* as in (E).

2. **C** The subject in (A), the *requirements*, needs the plural verb *are* rather than *is*. (B) and (D) are awkward. (E) lacks a subject, making it a sentence fragment.

3. **B** The sentence is redundant as it uses both *Since* and *is the reason*. Eliminate (A) and (D). (C) is passive and (E) contains the ambiguous pronoun *they*. (B) eliminates the redundancy without adding any errors.

4. **C** There is a comma splice in the sentence as written; two complete thoughts that could stand on their own as sentences cannot be separated only by a comma. Eliminate (A). In (B), *helping* does not match the tense of *was*. (C) correctly uses *that* to link the description after it to *the freedom fighters*. (D) changes the meaning, which (E) is overly wordy.

5. **D** The sentence is awkward and redundant. (B) is even worse. (C) contains a double negative and (E) is an incomplete sentence. (D) clarifies the sentence.

6. **A** The sentence is correct as written. It compares *singer* and *songwriter* in parallel ways.

7. **E** The word *being* is rarely correct on the SAT because sentences that use it tend to be wordy and passive, as this one is. Eliminate (A), (C), and (D). In (B), the verb *is* does not agree with *came*. (E) simplifies the sentence and uses the correct verb tense.

8. **E** The pronoun *they* does not agree with *someone* in the sentence as written. (B) and (D) are passive. (C) *creating* in not in the necessary verb tense. (E) put the elements of the sentence into parallel form.

9. **C** This sentence has a misplaced modifier *100 years ago* is not something a person could be *unlike*. (B) and (E) also contain this error. (D) is awkward in its use of *Differing to*. (C) correctly compares *counter parts* and *schoolteachers*.

10. **A** There is no error in the sentence as written. The other answers all contain misplaced modifiers.

11.   D   The sentence as written contains a misplaced modifier. *Frank Capra* is a filmmaker, not his *films*. Both (C) and (D) fix this error, but (C) is awkward and wordy while (D) is clear and concise.

12.   C   There is an idiom problem in (C). The correct idiom is *more…than. As* should be *than*.

13.   A   There is a verb agreement problem in (A) because *cleaned* is in the past while the rest of the sentence describes a time in the future.

14.   B   The word *where* refers only to specific location. The word *that* is more appropriate for (B).

15.   C   Verb tense should be consistent throughout a sentence. *Will have been* is future perfect continuous, while *has been* is present perfect continuous and should be changed to *will have been*.

16.   E   There is no error in the sentence as written.

17.   A   There is an error in (A) because the pronoun *that* does not refer to *people*. The pronoun *who* is correct.

18.   B   There is a double negative in (B). *Scarcely* should be removed.

19.   D   The use of *wear* in (D) is out of place in the list of materials.

20.   C   In this sentence, *children* is plural, but the phrase *he or she* in (C) refers to a single subject.

21.   E   There is no error in the sentence as written.

22.   A   There is a subject-verb agreement problem in the sentence. The *committee* is singular, but (A) contains a plural verb.

23.   D   The sentence has an idiom problem: the correct construction for the comparison is *more…than*, not *and not* as in (D).

24.   D   The pronoun *it* in (D) is singular and does not fit with the plural *new ideas*.

25.   B   (B) contains an idiom error: one can *protest against* but not *protest on*.

26.   C   The word *where* refers only to specific location, and in this case it refers to the map, not *Canada and Mexico*. The phrase *in which* is more appropriate for (C).

27.   E   There is no error in the sentence as written. Don't choose an answer just because it "sounds weird." Make sure you can name a specific error.

28.   C   In this sentence *the variety* is a singular noun, but *were* is a plural verb.

29.   B   There is a comparison error here: *the manner* of one group is compared to the other group itself (*the nihilists*). (B) should read *from that of the nihilists*.

30. **B** The original sentence has a misplaced modifier: the pronoun *we* needs to come directly after the comma since *we* is what the phrase before the comma is describing. (A) and (C) have misplaced modifiers. (D) does too, and also has the awkward word *being*. (E) contains a comma splice. Only (B) is without error.

31. **A** The sentence is correct as written. The rest of the answers change the meaning of the sentence or make it less clear.

32. **C** In the passage, the sentence is giving further ways the government can save money. (C) *Moreover* is close in meaning to *further*, while the rest of the transitions in the answers set up a relationship of two opposites.

33. **E** In the underlined portion, the pronoun *it* is ambiguous. (E) most clearly states what it is that should be hung over the entryway.

34. **B** The sentence as written is vague, and (A), (C), (D), and (E) are also too vague. (B) clarifies the sentence with *this kind of project*.

35. **D** The paragraph and the passage as a whole is about developing *teen centers*. Only (D) addresses *centers*.

SECTION 6

1. **E** Plug in! If $x = 2$, then the Target Value is 2. All answer choices except for (E) can then be eliminated. The answer is (E).

2. **A** If Nora had twice the number of CDs that Deborah has, it would be represented as $n = 2d$. Because Nora has 10 fewer than that number, we get $n = 2d - 10$.

3. **E** Absolute value can never be negative, so it is impossible for $f(x)$ to be anything less than 2, answer (E).

4. **C** When confronted with two fractions equal to each other, cross-multiply. This gives us $2x^2 + 4x = 2x^2 + 2$. Subtract $2x^2$ from both sides to get $4x = 2$ and divide both sides by 4 to get $x = \dfrac{1}{2}$, answer (C). Alternatively, you could try out the numbers in the answers in place of x and eliminate any answers that do not make the equation true.

5. **C** The line crosses through $(0, 0)$ and $(3, 2)$, and so has a slope of $\dfrac{2}{3}$. For every movement of 2 in the y direction, there is a movement of 3 in the x direction. Therefore, (a, b) is at $(-3, -2)$, and $\dfrac{-2}{-3} = \dfrac{2}{3}$, answer (C).

6. **B** We know that $x - y = 5$, and in the rest of the equation we have all the pieces for the quadratic equation of $(x - y)^2$, which, when FOILed out is $x^2 - 2xy + y^2$. Since $5^2 = 25$, $x^2 - 2xy + y^2 = 25$. We are told that $x^2 + y^2 = 15$, so $-2xy = 10$. We want to know the value of xy, so divide both sides by -2 to find that $xy = -5$, answer (B).

7. **E** Use a graphing calculator or apply the rules regarding the movement of curved graphs (parabolas). If a number is inside the parentheses, it moves the parabola left or right. Outside the parentheses, the number affects the up and down movement. The difference between the equations is within the parentheses, so eliminate (A), (C), and (D) since they move the graph up or down. Within the parentheses, a negative sign moves the graph to the <u>right</u>, and a positive sign moves the graph to the <u>left</u> which is opposite of the way things usually move on a number line. Since we have a positive 2 within the parentheses, the graph must move 2 units to the left, as it does in (E).

8. **A** Start by using the volume formula $V = l \times w \times h$ to find the volume of the rectangular solid. So, $V = 8 \times 8 \times 12 = 768$. Now, divide that result by 12 to find the volume of each cube, $768 \div 12 = 64$. Finally, use the formula for the volume of a cube, $V = s^3$, to find the length of an edge of one of the cubes: $64 = s^3$. So, $s = 4$.

9. **16** Since QS has a length of 20, and the image shows that RS has a length of 11, QR must have a length of 9. PR then must have a length of $7 + 9 = 16$.

10. **520** Because 10 boxes of chocolate candy has a total of 360 pieces of candy and 20 boxes of peanut butter candy has a total of 160 pieces of candy, the grand total of number of pieces of candy that Meredith buys is 520.

11. **11** Because the product of the two integers is 24, use the factors of 24. The two numbers could be 1 and 24, 2 and 12, 3 and 8, or 4 and 6. Now find the pair whose difference is 5. Only 3 and 8 work, and their sum is 11.

12. $\dfrac{6}{5}$ **or 1.2**

   Inversely proportional means that the product of *errors* and *hours of sleep* is always the same. Since in the first trial 2 *hours of sleep* results in 3 *errors*, 5 hours of sleep will result in fewer errors. We can set up an equation to see just how many errors the mice would make: $(2)(3) = (5)(x)$, so $6 = 5x$. Divide both sides by 5 to find that $x = \dfrac{6}{5}$ or 1.2.

13. **68** First, find the multiples of 4 between 50 and 90. They are 52, 56, 60, 64, 68, 72, 76, 80, 84, and 88. Next, find the members of this set that have a remainder of 3 when divided by five. That leaves 68 and 88. Finally, see which number has a remainder of 2 when divided by 3, leaving only 68.

14.   70   When two parallel lines are crossed by another line, big angles and small angles are created. The big angles are all equal to each other, the small angles are all equal to each other, and a big angle and a small angle add up to 180°. In the image, x is a small angle, and $(2x - 30)$ is a big angle, so $x + (2x - 30) = 180$, and we can solve for x. $3x - 30 = 180$, so $3x = 210$, and $x = 70$.

15.   30   Add the two values given for c together to see that $2c = (13 - b) + (20 - a)$, or $2c = 33 - a - b$. If we add a and b to both sides, we see that $a + b + 2c = 33$. The question states that $a + b = 27$, so don't solve for them individually: we just need to get c by itself so we can find $a + b + c$: $27 + 2c = 33$, and $2c = 6$, giving us $c = 3$. $a + b + c = 27 + 3 = 30$.

16.   12   First distribute the 10 to both parts of the parentheses on the right hand side of the equation to get $2x^2 - 68 = 10x + 100$. This simplifies to $2x^2 - 10x - 168 = 0$. Now we can factor out the 2 to see that $2(x^2 - 5x - 84) = 0$. Factor the quadratic equation to see that $2[(x + 7)(x - 12)] = 0$, which means that x can be either -7 or 12. Since negative numbers cannot be gridded in, 12 is correct.

17.   130   First divide the group of 400 into adults and children. There must be 40 more adults than children, so that's 220 adults and 180 children. Among the 220 adults there are 40 more men than women, so that's 130 men and 90 women. The answer is 130.

18. $\frac{63}{2}$ or 31.5

       The triangle in the figure is an isosceles right triangle, since $AC = CB$. A 45-45-90 triangle has a $1 : 1 : \sqrt{2}$ ratio of sides. That means that AC and CB each have length 3 and the square has sides of 6. We can now see that the area for the whole square is 36, and we need to subtract the area of the triangle. $\frac{1}{2} bh = \frac{1}{2}(3)(3) = 4.5$. The area of the shaded region is $36 - 4.5 = 31.5$ or $\frac{63}{2}$.

SECTION 7

1.   E   The phrase *in contrast to* indicates that the blank will mean the opposite of *luxury*. (A) and (C) are synonyms for luxury. Only (E) *poverty* means the opposite of *luxury*.

2.   A   The relationship between the blanks indicates that if the word that describes *aromas* in the first blank is positive, then the second blank will also be positive, indicating a desire *to eat*. If the first blank is negative, the second blank will be too. Only (A) has a similar relationship between its words.

3.   B   The phrase *rather than* indicates that the first blank will mean the opposite of *haphazardly enforcing*. A word like "systematic" is a good word for the first blank. Only (B) and maybe (E) come close. For the second blank, the word *and* indicates the second blank will be similar in meaning to *arbitrary*, or "random." Only (B) matches for both blanks.

4. **D** The semicolon acts like an equal sign; the second half of the sentence will be close in meaning to the first half. In this case, the second part of the sentence acts as the definition for the blank that appears immediately before the semicolon. We need a word that describes the quality of *refusing to quit* even when things seem *futile*. The only word in the answers that matches this definition is (D), *steadfastness*.

5. **B** The blank requires a word that shows the relationship between *passive hearing* and an *active process*, which are opposites. Only (B), *antithesis* means "opposite of."

6. **D** The second passage has kind of a humorous tone: the author indicates she's been smoking since she was a baby and undermines her advice after each dash in a joking manner. The best description of this is (D) *tongue-in-cheek*.

7. **B** Passage 2 has all the qualities listed in (A), (C), (D), and (E). Passage 2 does not have (B) *analogy* though Passage 1 does, in the comparison of living life to riding in a race. (B) is correct.

8. **C** (A) and (B) apply to the Passage 1, but not Passage 2. There is nothing in either passage to indicate that the advice is particularly bad, so eliminate (D). (C) *indirect* and (E) *straightforward* are essentially opposites. (C) is the best match because Passage 1 relates some thoughts about life, but uses an impersonal pronoun *one* rather than directly telling a person how to live. Passage 2 is written in a satirical manner, so though it seems to offer its advice directly, the twist that the humor and satire add prevent it from being *straightforward*.

9. **C** The main thing that is different between the passages is the tone: Passage 1 is very serious and somber, implying that the purpose of life is work while Passage 2 makes jokes. Making jokes fits with *levity*, (C). There is no evidence for the other answers.

10. **C** The passage states that *Broca inferred* the link between the brain region and articulate speech. The use of the words *it turns out* before *as Broca inferred*, indicate that he has since been proven correct. Only (C) *Broca was successful* fits with this. The other answers are not supported by the passage, and (B) is extreme.

11. **E** The *discoveries* are that there is a *separation of function between the let and right hemispheres of the brain*. The words *most important* highlight that *specific brain functions exist in particular locales*. This is a paraphrase of (E) that the *discoveries* were about *the link between physical parts of the brain and certain tasks*.

12. **D** Broca died *perhaps of the very sort of aneurysm that he studied*, which is best paraphrased in (D). The passage does not state how old he was, and there is no mention of *infant mortality* as in (A). There is also no evidence for *the people* in (B) causing his death, *anthropology* as mentioned in (C) or the *decaying mine* in (E).

13. **A** The question asked in the passage could be paraphrased as "is something of Broca's memory left in his physical brain after his death?" Only (A) mentions the *physical preservation of memory*. (E) also mentions memory, but in a very different sense from (A).

14. **A** (A) is supported by the passage, particularly in the first paragraph, which describes Broca's discoveries as *One of the first discoveries* and *one of the first indications* that brain functions are controlled by specific areas of the brain. (C) and (D) use a lot of words seen in the passage, but are extreme in saying that Broca's discovery was *the first indication*. There is no evidence for (B) or (D).

15. **E** The passage states that *it would be a kind of practical immortality,* and *it* is mentioned a couple lines before that: the ability to *reconstruct the memories or insights of someone long dead.* In (E), *reviving memories and insights* is a good paraphrase of this, and is further supported by lines 43–44, *our minds are clearly a major aspect of who we are.*

16. **C** The passage as a whole is informative and provides a description of how NATO was formed. (A) is too strong. (B) indicates that the main focus is the *Marshall Plan*, not *NATO*. (D) is too narrow and in (E) *question* does not reflect the informative tone of the passage. (C) is the best match.

17. **A** After line 15, the passage describes *deterrence* in that forming a *peacetime alliance* would *deter aggression by the Soviet Union.* So we need an answer that means "to preserve peace" or "prevent fighting." Only (A) *the discouragement of attacks* and specifically mentions *the Soviet Union.* The other answers are not supported by the passage.

18. **B** The second paragraph overall describes what makes NATO different from other alliances that came before. This is paraphrased in (B) *highlight a factor distinguishing NATO from other pacts.* (A) is mentioned in the next paragraph, but does not answer the question asked. The rest of the answers are not supported by the paragraph or the passage as a whole.

19. **B** In the passage, the three men are cited as leaders *put down* by a *grand alliances* that differed from NATO in that the *grand alliances* were formed specifically *after an act of aggression* to get rid of those leaders, whereas the NATO alliance was to form in peacetime to prevent any aggressive acts from occurring. This is paraphrased best in (B). (A) and (C) are contradicted by the passage, and there is no evidence for (D) or (E) in the passage.

20. **A** Go through each answer choice, and eliminate those supported by evidence in the passage. (A) is not a reason for the formation of NATO. While France is mentioned, it was not *democratic uprisings* but *communist political strength in France* that served as a reason that NATO was formed. The rest of the answers are paraphrases of the reasons listed in lines 20–40.

21. **D** (A) is not true: While the U.S. *no longer had a monopoly*, the passage states that the U.S. *had a superiority of about 8 to 1.* (D) gives a paraphrase of this, and is the correct answer. There is no evidence for (B) or (C), and (E) is too strong.

22. **D** The passage states that *West German entrance into NATO was the immediate cause of the establishment…of the Warsaw Pact.* This is seen in (D). (A) is incorrect: NATO was formed in 1949 while the Warsaw Pact came about in 1955—not immediately. (B) is not the reason given in the passage for the Warsaw Pact. (C) gives the reverse order of events. (E) is not mentioned in the passage.

23. **A** (B) is not true: there was no *aggressive behavior*: both were established in peacetime. (C) is not true: one was established in 1949 and the other in 1955. (D) is incorrect because the Warsaw Pact was a *Soviet alliance defense organization*, and so communist, not democratic. (E) is out: there is no evidence for *imperialism*.

24. **E** The last paragraph is about how *NATO's membership grew* and mentions the nations that joined after 1952. This is seen most closely in (E). The rest of the answers may be tempting, but these are narrow details of the paragraph. The primary purpose of the passage is stated in its first and last sentences.

SECTION 8

1. **B** To solve this equation, first simplify: $\sqrt{x+3} = 6$. Now square both sides: $x + 3 = 36$. Finally, isolate x to see that $x = 33$, choice (B). Another way to solve this is to replace x with each of the numbers in the answer choices to see which makes the equation true.

2. **D** The ratio of men to women is 7:8. If we add these together, we can see that in a group of 15 people, 7 will be men and 8 will be women. To see how many of these groups of 15 exist at the company, divide 90 by 15 to see that there are 6 groups of 7 men and 8 women. $7 \times 6 = 42$ men in the office and $8 \times 6 = 48$ women in the office. $48 - 42 = 6$ so there are 6 more women than men.

3. **E** In the three time slots described, there are 3 choices for the first hour, 2 in the second, and 2 in the third. Multiplying the possibilities for each slot gives the total number of possibilities: $3 \times 2 \times 2 = 12$, answer (E).

4. **E** Let's make $x = 10$. Set up the equation to solve for y: $\frac{20}{100} \times 90 = \frac{30}{100} y$. So $18 = \frac{30}{100} y$; and $\frac{1,800}{30} = y$ Thus, $y = 60$. Now find 80 percent of 90: $\frac{80}{100} \times 90 = 72$. Replace the y in each answer choice with 60 to find the choice that equals 72. The answer has to be (E): $1.2 \times 60 = 72$.

5. **A** No integers will work for x and y because 17 is odd. Since an integer x multiplied by 2 and an integer y multiplied by 4 will both be even, and an even added to an even must be even, there is no way that integer values for (x, y) could result in 17.

6. **B** The probability of a point landing in a shaded region is equal to the fraction of the figure that is shaded. The figure is a rectangle, as indicated by the right angle marks in each of the corners. The shaded area in each half of the rectangle is much smaller than the non-shaded portion, so the over-

all shaded portion of the figure must be less than $\frac{1}{2}$. Eliminate (C), (D), and (E). You can solve this visually by adding lines to the figure: drawing the other diagonal and a horizontal line where the diagonals cross divides the rectangle into 8 identical triangles, 2 of which are shaded. $\frac{2}{8} = \frac{1}{4}$. Mathematically, you can find the area of the whole rectangle ($8 \times 6 = 48$). Find the area of a shaded triangle: $A = \frac{1}{2}bh = \frac{1}{2}(4)(3) = 6$. Remember, there are 2 triangles so the area of the entire shaded portion is 12 out of 48, and $\frac{12}{48} = \frac{1}{4}$.

7. **E** Because both c and d are negative, cd must be positive, since a negative times a negative is positive. Only (E) is guaranteed to be either zero or negative, because c and d must be distinct. If we come up with some values for the variables, such as $c = -1$ and $d = -2$, this makes the expression in (E) equal 0 while the rest of the answers give positive numbers. If $c = -2$ and $d = -3$, (E) gives a negative result, and again all the rest are positive.

8. **C** The prime factors of a number can be found by listing all the factors of a number and eliminating any that are not prime numbers. The factors of 42 are 1, 42, 2, 21, 3, 14, 6, and 7. Of this list, only 2, 3, and 7 are prime (1 is not prime!). $2 + 3 + 7 = 12$, answer (C).

9. **B** Because the average is 8 and there are 3 items, the sum of a, b, and c is 24. Therefore, the three consecutive even integers are $a = 6$, $b = 8$, $c = 10$. This means that the list of numbers is 6, 8, 10, and 20. The median is between 8 and 10, so the correct answer is 9.

10. **D** Statement I is false, because $12n$ will always be even, but adding 3, an odd number, makes $12n + 3$ odd for any n. Thus, Statement II is always true. Statement III is also true, because you can factor a 3 out of $12n + 3$ to obtain $3(4n + 1)$. This number will always be divisible by 3, because it is clear that 3 is a factor. (D) is correct.

11. **A** We know the base of triangle AOF must be 3, since the opposite sides of a parallelogram are equal, and we know that C and F are both midpoints. Now we need the height of the triangle. We can find the height of the parallelogram, because the base must be 6 and we know the area is 48. This means the height is 8. The height of triangle AOF is half that, so now we can use the formula for the area of a triangle: $A = \frac{1}{2}bh = \frac{1}{2}(4)(3) = 6$ answer (A).

12. **D** Read carefully. The first sentence translates to $s + d + k = 72$. If Stephanie paints half as many rooms as Karissa, then $s = \frac{1}{2}k$. Stephanie also paints 12 more than Damon: $s = d + 12$ or $d = s - 12$. We can replace the s with $\frac{1}{2}k$ and write the equation in terms of k:

$$k + \frac{1}{2}k + \frac{1}{2}k - 12 = 72$$

$$2k - 12 = 72$$

$$2k = 84$$

$$k + 42, \text{ answer (D)}.$$

Want an easier way? You can also assign your own numbers to the variables using the numbers in the answer choices for k. Start with (C). If Karissa paints 30 rooms, then Stephanie paints 15, and Damon paints 3, that's only 48 rooms. Now try larger numbers and eliminate (A), (B), and (C). Try (D). If Karissa paints 42 rooms, Stephanie paints 21 and Damon paints 9. These numbers all add up to 72, so (D) is the correct answer.

13. **E** An easy approach is to create your own values for q and s. Try $q = \frac{1}{2}$ and $s = 2$, $\frac{\left(1 + \frac{1}{2}\right)}{1 + 2} = \frac{1}{2}$. Now replace q and s in the answer choices with the values you chose and figure out which one equals $\frac{1}{2}$. Only (E) works. Algebraically, replace s with $\frac{1}{q}$. Start by getting the expression into terms of q because there are two answers in terms of q: $\frac{(1+q)}{1 + \frac{1}{q}}$. Multiply by $\frac{q}{q}$: $\frac{(1+q)}{1 + \frac{1}{q}} \times \frac{q}{q} = q$, as seen in (E).

14. **E** When a question mentions a figure that is not shown, draw the figure. Adding the quadrilateral shows that each side of the quadrilateral (which we now know is a square) is the length of the radii of the circles. The area of a square is found by squaring the length of a side. The correct answer is r^2, as seen in (E).

15. **A** Substitute -2 into the expression for f to find that $h(-2) = f\left(\frac{2}{-2} + 2\right) = f(1)$ Now, look up the value of $f(1)$ —in other words, where $x = 1$—on the provided table to find that $f(1) = -3$. (A) is correct.

16. **A** The easiest way to solve this problem is to simplify the answers: we are told that $f(a) = 1$, so replace $f(a)$ in the answer choices with 1. This changes (A) to $f(1) = 0$, (B) to $f(1) = 1$ and (C) to $a = 1$. Now (C) and (E) are identical, and since there can be only one correct answer on the SAT, we can get rid of both (C) and (E). Now check the remaining answers against the graph. (A) works: it is true that $f(1) = 0$. On the graph, when $x = 1$, $y = 0$. Keep (A). (B) is not true: we know that when $x = 1$, $y = 0$, not $y = 1$. Eliminate (B). For (D) we can see if $a = 0$ by replacing a in the function given in the question. Does $f(0) = 1$? No: when $x = 0$, $y = -1$. Eliminate (D). Only (A) is always true.

SECTION 9

1. **B** A senator who broke *promises and let people down* is not likely to win reelection, so a good word for the blank is "unlikely." In this context, (B) *remote* matches this meaning best. (A), *cogent*, means "clear and precise." (C), *frivolous*, means "unnecessary." Although it might be *disastrous* to have a senator who breaks promises, there isn't evidence for this in the sentence, so (D) is out. (E), *veritable*, means "true," not "unlikely."

2. **A** The second blank is easier to fill in. The word *and* indicates that the second blank must mean something similar to *celebrated*. Eliminate (B) and (D) since these are not similar to *celebrated*. The word *but* indicates that the initial reaction was the opposite of the later views of Monet's work. Eliminate (C) since *acclaim* is positive. In (A), *ridicule* is a much stronger opposite to *celebrated* than is (E) *distraction*. (A) is correct.

3. **E** The words *traditional* and *new* are opposites, and the phrase *in favor of more* indicates that a good word for the second blank is something that means "trade" or "exchange." Eliminate (C) and (D). The rest of the answers have a second word that could possibly fit the meaning of the second blank. It is the *traditional* fans that would be upset when the *traditional practices*, so eliminate answers that don't have a first word meaning "traditional." Only (E) works for both blanks.

4. **D** The semicolon acts like an equal sign between the first and second parts of the sentence. Therefore, the meaning of the blank must fit the description in the first part of the sentence. The word *even* is an indication that the blank means something a little more serious than *impolite*. (C) and (E) are not close, so eliminate them. The rest of the answers are all negative, and are definitely worse than being impolite. Remember the first part of the sentence though. The blank must mean something related to not *making conversation*. (A) and (B) do not fit this meaning at all, while (D) *brusque* has the meaning " abrupt in manner; blunt; rough" and describes someone who would cut off a conversation impolitely.

5. **B** The second blank must mean *constantly moving*. There is some tough vocab here, but of the second words in the answers, only (B) *peripatetic* and (D) *frenetic* come close to this meaning. The word *Although* indicates that the first blank will mean the opposite of the second, so we need a word that means "staying still." Both (A) *stationary* and (B) *sedentary* mean this, making (B) the best match for both blanks.

6. **A** The word for the blank must mean something close to ability *to adjust to constant changes* since the opposite of this *would spell disaster*. A word like "agile" or "flexible" is necessary here. Only (A) *adroit* matches this meaning.

7. **A** The author mentions *hunting and foraging* as activities that *required an asymmetric arrangement* different from other activities, and as humans engaged in this, *specialization and lateralization* progressed. So it is an example of how our brains started to specialize and develop asymmetrically. (A) is a good paraphrase of this.

8. **A** The word *geometry* may describe many of the answers, but always go back to the passage and replace the word with one of your own, based on the context of the passage. The sentence discusses *right- and left-handed sugar molecules* and how they differ in their *geometry*. We know only that the molecules differ in their "arrangement" or "structure." Only (A) *structural configuration* fits the context of the passage.

9. **C** The *sugar molecules* are used in support of how *the asymmetry of our brains and hands* is part of *the natural order of things*. So the sugar molecules are another example of natural asymmetry. (C) is a good paraphrase of this. (A) is too extreme. There is no mention of *replication* as in (B) or *practical applications* in (D). (E) is mentioned in the passage, but is not the reason the author brought up the molecules.

10. **D** In the passage, the *Sylvian fissure* is brought up to show that there is a *difference between the brain structures of right- and left- handed people*. This is best paraphrased in (D). (A) and (B) are not mentioned, while (C) and (E) are opposite of what is stated in the passage.

11. **A** The *physical function* is what hand is used and *hemisphere dominance* is about what half of the brain makes it work. The first paragraph of Passage 2 states that *The right hand (meaning the left hemisphere)* and *The left hand (therefore the right hemisphere)* shows that the physical side of the body is operated by the opposite hemisphere of the brain. Only (A) shows this relationship. (B) and (C) are not true, (D) is extreme, and (E) is not mentioned at all.

12. **B** The second paragraph of Passage 2 discusses the words and meanings that have come from the words for *left* and *right throughout human history*. This is best paraphrased in (B). There are no *commonly confused terms* as in (A). Two distinct concepts are addressed, but their *merits* are not weighed. (D) is opposite of what is in the passage: the paragraph states how the words and meanings for *right* are more positive than left throughout history in a variety of languages. (E) is not mentioned in the second paragraph of Passage 2.

13. E Passage 2 is about how the left and right connotations and modes of thinking play out in society. This is best paraphrased in (E). It is not about a *social phenomenon* as in (A). (B) is not true and uses extreme language (*prove*). There is no evidence for (C) or (D).

14. C The *duality* is explained in the passage to mean that all humans have two sides to their nature. Eliminate (A), (D), and (E) because they have nothing to do with *human nature*. (B) mentions the phrase, *human nature* but there is nothing in the passage to support *weakness*. (C) is correct: the passage states that *there are two ways of knowing* and these are described as *between thinking and feeling*. This is represented by *emotion* and *reason* in (C).

15. D The first passage is about how the hemispheres of our brains developed in different ways to deal with the physical ways humans needed to deal with their environments. The second passage is about how "left-ness" and "right-ness" affect our feelings and mental processes. So both passages talk about asymmetry, just the physical vs. mental. Only (D) combines these. (A) and (B) deal with aspects found only in Passage 2, and don't involve the Passage 1 viewpoint that our brains changed to help humans work with their environment. There is no evidence that the physical changes happened before the mental changes, as in (C). In (E), the mention of the *Sylvian fissure* does not address the mental modes of the left and right hemispheres.

16. A Passage 2 states that the right hemisphere is in charge of imagination and intuition, while the left hemisphere is in charge of the step-by-step logical ways of thinking.

17. B Only (B) is supported by both passages. In Passage 1, lines 20–23 state that there are *clear-cut asymmetries in the area of speech* and indicates that *this portion* is located in the *left hemisphere*. Similarly, in Passage 2, line 78 states that the left hemisphere *verbalizes*, or creates speech.

18. C Any argument the author of Passage 1 would make must go along with the main idea of Passage 1. The main idea of Passage 1 is that our brain became asymmetrical and developed different physical functions to help humans better deal with their environment. The *duality* in Passage 2 refers to the different mental functions that each side of the brain is responsible for. (A) is out: the author of Passage 1 gave some of the human history or how our brain became asymmetrical, which is likely what led to the development of differing mental functions. (B) is extreme. (C) reflects the main idea of passage 1 in *the asymmetry of the brain*. There is no connection between the *duality* and the *Sylvian fissure*. (E) is not true: the author of Passage 1 did not mention the *duality* as coming before the lateralization process described in that passage, and therefore would not say that it was *essential to* lateralization.

19. E The main ideas of both passages are best captured in (E). There is no *cultural preferences* as in (A). There is no *circumstantial and unproven evidence* as mentioned in (B). Passage 1 and 2 are separate passages that both deal with the same subject. Passage 2 is not a reaction to Passage 1, as stated in (C). The *linguistics* that Passage 2 delves into is based on the history of the words for left and right, not a focus on a specific area of the brain as in (D).

SECTION 10

1. **B**   The sentence as written is passive. Eliminate (A). We do need the replacement to start with the idiomatically correct *of* following *option*, so eliminate (D) and (E). (B) is more active, clear and concise than (C).

2. **C**   The use of *it* in this sentence to refer to *The Prince* is redundant. Eliminate (A), (B), and (E). (D) is unnecessarily wordy, and the phrase that follows a semicolon must be able to stand on its own as a complete sentence. This is not true of (D). (C) is correct.

3. **E**   In the sentence as written, there is a contrast in the words *controversial* and *treasured* but the conjunction *also* indicates a similar relationship. Furthermore, the end of the sentence, *of them* is awkward. Eliminate (A). (B) is wordy, though it does set up an opposition with *but*. (C) is wordy and awkward. (D) has the awkward *of them* from the original. Only (E) sets up the opposition with *yet* and is clear and concise.

4. **C**   Because *are wishing* is a verb construction, it needs to be modified by an adverb, not the adjective *earnest*. Eliminate (A). In (B) it is unclear if the *wish* is earnest, or if the *change* is. (C) is more active and correctly modifies the verb with the adverb *earnestly*. In (D), *have a wish* is not as active as (C) while (E) is passive and awkward.

5. **C**   The sentence as written is passive. Eliminate (A). (B) is awkward and it is unclear which female *she* refers to; (D) changes the meaning of the sentence; (E) is passive and uses the wrong pronoun *herself*. Only (C) concisely fixes the passiveness of the sentence without introducing any further errors.

6. **E**   The verbs in (A) and (C) are not parallel with the verb *ruled*. (B) employs poor sentence structure. (D) needs a semicolon or conjunction before it to make the sentence whole. Only (E) is parallel and structurally sound.

7. **E**   There is a subject-verb agreement error in *projectors shows*, so eliminate (A). (B) is awkward and changes the meaning of the sentence with *many pictures*. (C) is unclear and changes the meaning of the sentence. (D) uses the word *like* in a way that makes the sentence unclear. Only (E) creates a clear comparison between the way one device worked in the past and the way that a modern device works.

8. **A**   The sentence is correct as written. The comparison in the rest of the answer choices do not correctly compare the same things.

9. **E**   (A) is incorrect because *it* is singular while both *confessions* and *violent crimes* are plural. (B) does not fix the problem because *they* is an ambiguous pronoun. A pronoun must refer clearly to only one noun. Here it is unclear if *they* refers to the *confessions* or the *crimes*. (B) and (C) both make this error. (D) incorrectly uses the verb tense *would have*, which also unnecessarily changes the meaning of the sentence. Only (E) clearly identifies what *remained steady* without introducing other errors.

10. **E** There is a comparison error in the sentence as written: it compares *the average adult American* to *1980s and 1990s*. We need to add something that makes the comparison between adults of one era and adults of the other. Eliminate (A) and (B). The comparison in (E) is correct because the focus is a single *average American* whereas in (C) and (D) there is a comparison between a single individual and plural individuals.

11. **C** The word *like* is used to compare two nouns, while *as* is used to compare actions. Eliminate (A), (B), and (E). In (D), the unnecessary words *enjoyed it* make the sentence wordy and somewhat unclear, due to the pronoun *it*. (C) is correct.

12. **A** In (B), *having good health* is not as correct as *being in good health*. (C) and (E) are not parallel and make the sentence wordier and more cumbersome. (D) is not parallel. (A) is the most concise and retains a parallel structure. This is a great example of *being* used correctly.

13. **C** The sentence as written contains a comma splice. Two phrases that could stand on their own as complete sentences cannot be joined by a comma. Eliminate (A). The *ing* words in (B) and (E) make the sentence less clear, since *going* makes it seem that the following words are part of a description of the students. The beginnings of (C) and (D) make it clear that what follows is what *Alexei* is encouraging his students to do. (D) is unnecessarily wordy, making (C) the correct answer.

14. **C** The sentence as written contains a misplaced modifier error. The phrase *A native Californian* refers to Jeff McDonald, not his play, as the original sentence suggests. We can eliminate (B) for this same reason. (D) isn't parallel in structure because it redundantly uses the pronoun *he* with the second verb *received*. This also makes it seem as if the award he received isn't connected to the first play he wrote. (E) also changes the meaning of the sentence by stating that both Jeff McDonald and his first play received Tony awards.

Chapter 16
Practice Test 7

Your Name (print) _____
                        Last   First   Middle

Date _____

IMPORTANT: The following codes should be copied onto your answer sheet exactly as shown.

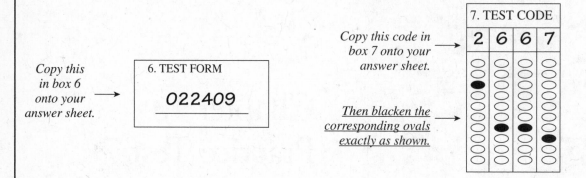

Copy this in box 6 onto your answer sheet. →
6. TEST FORM
022409

Copy this code in box 7 onto your answer sheet.

Then blacken the corresponding ovals exactly as shown.

7. TEST CODE
2 6 6 7

General Directions

You will have three hours and 20 minutes to work on this objective test designed to familiarize you with all aspects of the SAT.

This test contains five 25-minute sections, two 20-minute sections, one 10-minute section, and one 25-minute essay. The supervisor will tell you when to begin and end each section. During the time allowed for each section, you may work only on that particular section. If you finish your work before time is called, you may check your work on that section, but you are not to work on any other section.

You will find specific directions for each type of question found in the test. **Be sure you understand the directions before attempting to answer any of the questions.**

YOU ARE TO INDICATE ALL YOUR ANSWERS ON THE SEPARATE ANSWER SHEET:

1. The test booklet may be used for scratchwork. However, no credit will be given for anything written in the test booklet.

2. Once you have decided on an answer to a question, darken the corresponding space on the answer sheet. Give only one answer to each question.

3. There are 40 numbered answer spaces for each section; be sure to use only those spaces that correspond to the test questions.

4. **Be sure each answer mark is dark and completely fills the answer space.** Do not make any stray marks on your answer sheet.

5. If you wish to change an answer, erase your first mark completely—an incomplete erasure may be considered an intended response—and blacken your new answer choice.

Your score on this test is based on the number of questions you answer correctly minus a fraction of the number of questions you answer incorrectly. Therefore, it is improbable that random or haphazard guessing will alter your score significantly. There are no deductions for incorrect answers on the student-produced response questions. However, if you are able to eliminate one or more of the answer choices on any question as wrong, it is generally to your advantage to guess at one of the remaining choices. Remember, however, not to spend too much time on any one question.

Diagnostic Test Form

Use a No. 2 pencil only. Be sure each mark is dark and completely fills the intended oval. Completely erase any errors or stray marks.

1 Your Name:

(Print) _____

Last   First   M.I.

Signature: _____ Date ___/___/___

Home Address: _____

Number and Street   City   State   Zip Code

E-Mail: _____ School: _____ Class: _____

(Print)

2 YOUR NAME

Last Name (First 4 Letters) | FIRST INIT | MID INIT

3 PHONE NUMBER

IMPORTANT: Fill in items 6 and 7 exactly as shown on the preceding page.

6 TEST FORM (Copy from back of test book)

7 TEST CODE

4 DATE OF BIRTH

MONTH	DAY		YEAR	
JAN				
FEB				
MAR	0	0		0
APR	1	1		1
MAY	2	2		2
JUN	3	3		3
JUL		4		4
AUG		5	5	5
SEP		6	6	6
OCT		7	7	7
NOV		8	8	8
DEC		9	9	9

8 OTHER

1 Ⓐ Ⓑ Ⓒ Ⓓ Ⓔ
2 Ⓐ Ⓑ Ⓒ Ⓓ Ⓔ
3 Ⓐ Ⓑ Ⓒ Ⓓ Ⓔ

5 SEX

○ MALE
○ FEMALE

OpScan *i*NSIGHT™ forms by Pearson NCS EM-253760-3:654321   Printed in U.S.A.   © TPR Education IP Holdings, LLC

PLEASE DO NOT WRITE IN THIS AREA

SERIAL #

THIS PAGE INTENTIONALLY LEFT BLANK

Begin your essay on this page. If you need more space, continue on the next page.

Continue on the next page, if necessary.

SECTION 2

1 Ⓐ Ⓑ Ⓒ Ⓓ Ⓔ   11 Ⓐ Ⓑ Ⓒ Ⓓ Ⓔ   21 Ⓐ Ⓑ Ⓒ Ⓓ Ⓔ   31 Ⓐ Ⓑ Ⓒ Ⓓ Ⓔ
2 Ⓐ Ⓑ Ⓒ Ⓓ Ⓔ   12 Ⓐ Ⓑ Ⓒ Ⓓ Ⓔ   22 Ⓐ Ⓑ Ⓒ Ⓓ Ⓔ   32 Ⓐ Ⓑ Ⓒ Ⓓ Ⓔ
3 Ⓐ Ⓑ Ⓒ Ⓓ Ⓔ   13 Ⓐ Ⓑ Ⓒ Ⓓ Ⓔ   23 Ⓐ Ⓑ Ⓒ Ⓓ Ⓔ   33 Ⓐ Ⓑ Ⓒ Ⓓ Ⓔ
4 Ⓐ Ⓑ Ⓒ Ⓓ Ⓔ   14 Ⓐ Ⓑ Ⓒ Ⓓ Ⓔ   24 Ⓐ Ⓑ Ⓒ Ⓓ Ⓔ   34 Ⓐ Ⓑ Ⓒ Ⓓ Ⓔ
5 Ⓐ Ⓑ Ⓒ Ⓓ Ⓔ   15 Ⓐ Ⓑ Ⓒ Ⓓ Ⓔ   25 Ⓐ Ⓑ Ⓒ Ⓓ Ⓔ   35 Ⓐ Ⓑ Ⓒ Ⓓ Ⓔ
6 Ⓐ Ⓑ Ⓒ Ⓓ Ⓔ   16 Ⓐ Ⓑ Ⓒ Ⓓ Ⓔ   26 Ⓐ Ⓑ Ⓒ Ⓓ Ⓔ   36 Ⓐ Ⓑ Ⓒ Ⓓ Ⓔ
7 Ⓐ Ⓑ Ⓒ Ⓓ Ⓔ   17 Ⓐ Ⓑ Ⓒ Ⓓ Ⓔ   27 Ⓐ Ⓑ Ⓒ Ⓓ Ⓔ   37 Ⓐ Ⓑ Ⓒ Ⓓ Ⓔ
8 Ⓐ Ⓑ Ⓒ Ⓓ Ⓔ   18 Ⓐ Ⓑ Ⓒ Ⓓ Ⓔ   28 Ⓐ Ⓑ Ⓒ Ⓓ Ⓔ   38 Ⓐ Ⓑ Ⓒ Ⓓ Ⓔ
9 Ⓐ Ⓑ Ⓒ Ⓓ Ⓔ   19 Ⓐ Ⓑ Ⓒ Ⓓ Ⓔ   29 Ⓐ Ⓑ Ⓒ Ⓓ Ⓔ   39 Ⓐ Ⓑ Ⓒ Ⓓ Ⓔ
10 Ⓐ Ⓑ Ⓒ Ⓓ Ⓔ   20 Ⓐ Ⓑ Ⓒ Ⓓ Ⓔ   30 Ⓐ Ⓑ Ⓒ Ⓓ Ⓔ   40 Ⓐ Ⓑ Ⓒ Ⓓ Ⓔ

SECTION 3

1 Ⓐ Ⓑ Ⓒ Ⓓ Ⓔ   11 Ⓐ Ⓑ Ⓒ Ⓓ Ⓔ   21 Ⓐ Ⓑ Ⓒ Ⓓ Ⓔ   31 Ⓐ Ⓑ Ⓒ Ⓓ Ⓔ
2 Ⓐ Ⓑ Ⓒ Ⓓ Ⓔ   12 Ⓐ Ⓑ Ⓒ Ⓓ Ⓔ   22 Ⓐ Ⓑ Ⓒ Ⓓ Ⓔ   32 Ⓐ Ⓑ Ⓒ Ⓓ Ⓔ
3 Ⓐ Ⓑ Ⓒ Ⓓ Ⓔ   13 Ⓐ Ⓑ Ⓒ Ⓓ Ⓔ   23 Ⓐ Ⓑ Ⓒ Ⓓ Ⓔ   33 Ⓐ Ⓑ Ⓒ Ⓓ Ⓔ
4 Ⓐ Ⓑ Ⓒ Ⓓ Ⓔ   14 Ⓐ Ⓑ Ⓒ Ⓓ Ⓔ   24 Ⓐ Ⓑ Ⓒ Ⓓ Ⓔ   34 Ⓐ Ⓑ Ⓒ Ⓓ Ⓔ
5 Ⓐ Ⓑ Ⓒ Ⓓ Ⓔ   15 Ⓐ Ⓑ Ⓒ Ⓓ Ⓔ   25 Ⓐ Ⓑ Ⓒ Ⓓ Ⓔ   35 Ⓐ Ⓑ Ⓒ Ⓓ Ⓔ
6 Ⓐ Ⓑ Ⓒ Ⓓ Ⓔ   16 Ⓐ Ⓑ Ⓒ Ⓓ Ⓔ   26 Ⓐ Ⓑ Ⓒ Ⓓ Ⓔ   36 Ⓐ Ⓑ Ⓒ Ⓓ Ⓔ
7 Ⓐ Ⓑ Ⓒ Ⓓ Ⓔ   17 Ⓐ Ⓑ Ⓒ Ⓓ Ⓔ   27 Ⓐ Ⓑ Ⓒ Ⓓ Ⓔ   37 Ⓐ Ⓑ Ⓒ Ⓓ Ⓔ
8 Ⓐ Ⓑ Ⓒ Ⓓ Ⓔ   18 Ⓐ Ⓑ Ⓒ Ⓓ Ⓔ   28 Ⓐ Ⓑ Ⓒ Ⓓ Ⓔ   38 Ⓐ Ⓑ Ⓒ Ⓓ Ⓔ
9 Ⓐ Ⓑ Ⓒ Ⓓ Ⓔ   19 Ⓐ Ⓑ Ⓒ Ⓓ Ⓔ   29 Ⓐ Ⓑ Ⓒ Ⓓ Ⓔ   39 Ⓐ Ⓑ Ⓒ Ⓓ Ⓔ
10 Ⓐ Ⓑ Ⓒ Ⓓ Ⓔ   20 Ⓐ Ⓑ Ⓒ Ⓓ Ⓔ   30 Ⓐ Ⓑ Ⓒ Ⓓ Ⓔ   40 Ⓐ Ⓑ Ⓒ Ⓓ Ⓔ

CAUTION Grid answers in the section below for SECTION 2 or SECTION 3 only if directed to do so in your test book.

Student-Produced Responses

ONLY ANSWERS THAT ARE GRIDDED WILL BE SCORED. YOU WILL NOT RECEIVE CREDIT FOR ANYTHING WRITTEN IN THE BOXES.

Quality Assurance Mark ●

9   10   11   12   13

14   15   16   17   18

SECTION 4

1 Ⓐ Ⓑ Ⓒ Ⓓ Ⓔ	11 Ⓐ Ⓑ Ⓒ Ⓓ Ⓔ	21 Ⓐ Ⓑ Ⓒ Ⓓ Ⓔ	31 Ⓐ Ⓑ Ⓒ Ⓓ Ⓔ
2 Ⓐ Ⓑ Ⓒ Ⓓ Ⓔ	12 Ⓐ Ⓑ Ⓒ Ⓓ Ⓔ	22 Ⓐ Ⓑ Ⓒ Ⓓ Ⓔ	32 Ⓐ Ⓑ Ⓒ Ⓓ Ⓔ
3 Ⓐ Ⓑ Ⓒ Ⓓ Ⓔ	13 Ⓐ Ⓑ Ⓒ Ⓓ Ⓔ	23 Ⓐ Ⓑ Ⓒ Ⓓ Ⓔ	33 Ⓐ Ⓑ Ⓒ Ⓓ Ⓔ
4 Ⓐ Ⓑ Ⓒ Ⓓ Ⓔ	14 Ⓐ Ⓑ Ⓒ Ⓓ Ⓔ	24 Ⓐ Ⓑ Ⓒ Ⓓ Ⓔ	34 Ⓐ Ⓑ Ⓒ Ⓓ Ⓔ
5 Ⓐ Ⓑ Ⓒ Ⓓ Ⓔ	15 Ⓐ Ⓑ Ⓒ Ⓓ Ⓔ	25 Ⓐ Ⓑ Ⓒ Ⓓ Ⓔ	35 Ⓐ Ⓑ Ⓒ Ⓓ Ⓔ
6 Ⓐ Ⓑ Ⓒ Ⓓ Ⓔ	16 Ⓐ Ⓑ Ⓒ Ⓓ Ⓔ	26 Ⓐ Ⓑ Ⓒ Ⓓ Ⓔ	36 Ⓐ Ⓑ Ⓒ Ⓓ Ⓔ
7 Ⓐ Ⓑ Ⓒ Ⓓ Ⓔ	17 Ⓐ Ⓑ Ⓒ Ⓓ Ⓔ	27 Ⓐ Ⓑ Ⓒ Ⓓ Ⓔ	37 Ⓐ Ⓑ Ⓒ Ⓓ Ⓔ
8 Ⓐ Ⓑ Ⓒ Ⓓ Ⓔ	18 Ⓐ Ⓑ Ⓒ Ⓓ Ⓔ	28 Ⓐ Ⓑ Ⓒ Ⓓ Ⓔ	38 Ⓐ Ⓑ Ⓒ Ⓓ Ⓔ
9 Ⓐ Ⓑ Ⓒ Ⓓ Ⓔ	19 Ⓐ Ⓑ Ⓒ Ⓓ Ⓔ	29 Ⓐ Ⓑ Ⓒ Ⓓ Ⓔ	39 Ⓐ Ⓑ Ⓒ Ⓓ Ⓔ
10 Ⓐ Ⓑ Ⓒ Ⓓ Ⓔ	20 Ⓐ Ⓑ Ⓒ Ⓓ Ⓔ	30 Ⓐ Ⓑ Ⓒ Ⓓ Ⓔ	40 Ⓐ Ⓑ Ⓒ Ⓓ Ⓔ

SECTION 5

1 Ⓐ Ⓑ Ⓒ Ⓓ Ⓔ	11 Ⓐ Ⓑ Ⓒ Ⓓ Ⓔ	21 Ⓐ Ⓑ Ⓒ Ⓓ Ⓔ	31 Ⓐ Ⓑ Ⓒ Ⓓ Ⓔ
2 Ⓐ Ⓑ Ⓒ Ⓓ Ⓔ	12 Ⓐ Ⓑ Ⓒ Ⓓ Ⓔ	22 Ⓐ Ⓑ Ⓒ Ⓓ Ⓔ	32 Ⓐ Ⓑ Ⓒ Ⓓ Ⓔ
3 Ⓐ Ⓑ Ⓒ Ⓓ Ⓔ	13 Ⓐ Ⓑ Ⓒ Ⓓ Ⓔ	23 Ⓐ Ⓑ Ⓒ Ⓓ Ⓔ	33 Ⓐ Ⓑ Ⓒ Ⓓ Ⓔ
4 Ⓐ Ⓑ Ⓒ Ⓓ Ⓔ	14 Ⓐ Ⓑ Ⓒ Ⓓ Ⓔ	24 Ⓐ Ⓑ Ⓒ Ⓓ Ⓔ	34 Ⓐ Ⓑ Ⓒ Ⓓ Ⓔ
5 Ⓐ Ⓑ Ⓒ Ⓓ Ⓔ	15 Ⓐ Ⓑ Ⓒ Ⓓ Ⓔ	25 Ⓐ Ⓑ Ⓒ Ⓓ Ⓔ	35 Ⓐ Ⓑ Ⓒ Ⓓ Ⓔ
6 Ⓐ Ⓑ Ⓒ Ⓓ Ⓔ	16 Ⓐ Ⓑ Ⓒ Ⓓ Ⓔ	26 Ⓐ Ⓑ Ⓒ Ⓓ Ⓔ	36 Ⓐ Ⓑ Ⓒ Ⓓ Ⓔ
7 Ⓐ Ⓑ Ⓒ Ⓓ Ⓔ	17 Ⓐ Ⓑ Ⓒ Ⓓ Ⓔ	27 Ⓐ Ⓑ Ⓒ Ⓓ Ⓔ	37 Ⓐ Ⓑ Ⓒ Ⓓ Ⓔ
8 Ⓐ Ⓑ Ⓒ Ⓓ Ⓔ	18 Ⓐ Ⓑ Ⓒ Ⓓ Ⓔ	28 Ⓐ Ⓑ Ⓒ Ⓓ Ⓔ	38 Ⓐ Ⓑ Ⓒ Ⓓ Ⓔ
9 Ⓐ Ⓑ Ⓒ Ⓓ Ⓔ	19 Ⓐ Ⓑ Ⓒ Ⓓ Ⓔ	29 Ⓐ Ⓑ Ⓒ Ⓓ Ⓔ	39 Ⓐ Ⓑ Ⓒ Ⓓ Ⓔ
10 Ⓐ Ⓑ Ⓒ Ⓓ Ⓔ	20 Ⓐ Ⓑ Ⓒ Ⓓ Ⓔ	30 Ⓐ Ⓑ Ⓒ Ⓓ Ⓔ	40 Ⓐ Ⓑ Ⓒ Ⓓ Ⓔ

CAUTION   Grid answers in the section below for SECTION 4 or SECTION 5 only if directed to do so in your test book.

Student-Produced Responses   ONLY ANSWERS THAT ARE GRIDDED WILL BE SCORED. YOU WILL NOT RECEIVE CREDIT FOR ANYTHING WRITTEN IN THE BOXES.

Quality Assurance Mark ●

Grids: 9, 10, 11, 12, 13

Grids: 14, 15, 16, 17, 18

(Each grid contains digit columns 0–9 with fraction-slash and decimal-point options.)

COMPLETE MARK ● **EXAMPLES OF INCOMPLETE MARKS** Ⓐ Ⓑ Ⓒ Ⓓ Ⓐ Ⓑ Ⓒ Ⓓ

You must use a No. 2 pencil and marks must be complete. Do not use a mechanical pencil. It is very important that you fill in the entire circle darkly and completely. If you change your responses, erase as completely as possible. Incomplete marks or erasures may affect your score.

SECTION 6

1 Ⓐ Ⓑ Ⓒ Ⓓ Ⓔ	11 Ⓐ Ⓑ Ⓒ Ⓓ Ⓔ	21 Ⓐ Ⓑ Ⓒ Ⓓ Ⓔ	31 Ⓐ Ⓑ Ⓒ Ⓓ Ⓔ
2 Ⓐ Ⓑ Ⓒ Ⓓ Ⓔ	12 Ⓐ Ⓑ Ⓒ Ⓓ Ⓔ	22 Ⓐ Ⓑ Ⓒ Ⓓ Ⓔ	32 Ⓐ Ⓑ Ⓒ Ⓓ Ⓔ
3 Ⓐ Ⓑ Ⓒ Ⓓ Ⓔ	13 Ⓐ Ⓑ Ⓒ Ⓓ Ⓔ	23 Ⓐ Ⓑ Ⓒ Ⓓ Ⓔ	33 Ⓐ Ⓑ Ⓒ Ⓓ Ⓔ
4 Ⓐ Ⓑ Ⓒ Ⓓ Ⓔ	14 Ⓐ Ⓑ Ⓒ Ⓓ Ⓔ	24 Ⓐ Ⓑ Ⓒ Ⓓ Ⓔ	34 Ⓐ Ⓑ Ⓒ Ⓓ Ⓔ
5 Ⓐ Ⓑ Ⓒ Ⓓ Ⓔ	15 Ⓐ Ⓑ Ⓒ Ⓓ Ⓔ	25 Ⓐ Ⓑ Ⓒ Ⓓ Ⓔ	35 Ⓐ Ⓑ Ⓒ Ⓓ Ⓔ
6 Ⓐ Ⓑ Ⓒ Ⓓ Ⓔ	16 Ⓐ Ⓑ Ⓒ Ⓓ Ⓔ	26 Ⓐ Ⓑ Ⓒ Ⓓ Ⓔ	36 Ⓐ Ⓑ Ⓒ Ⓓ Ⓔ
7 Ⓐ Ⓑ Ⓒ Ⓓ Ⓔ	17 Ⓐ Ⓑ Ⓒ Ⓓ Ⓔ	27 Ⓐ Ⓑ Ⓒ Ⓓ Ⓔ	37 Ⓐ Ⓑ Ⓒ Ⓓ Ⓔ
8 Ⓐ Ⓑ Ⓒ Ⓓ Ⓔ	18 Ⓐ Ⓑ Ⓒ Ⓓ Ⓔ	28 Ⓐ Ⓑ Ⓒ Ⓓ Ⓔ	38 Ⓐ Ⓑ Ⓒ Ⓓ Ⓔ
9 Ⓐ Ⓑ Ⓒ Ⓓ Ⓔ	19 Ⓐ Ⓑ Ⓒ Ⓓ Ⓔ	29 Ⓐ Ⓑ Ⓒ Ⓓ Ⓔ	39 Ⓐ Ⓑ Ⓒ Ⓓ Ⓔ
10 Ⓐ Ⓑ Ⓒ Ⓓ Ⓔ	20 Ⓐ Ⓑ Ⓒ Ⓓ Ⓔ	30 Ⓐ Ⓑ Ⓒ Ⓓ Ⓔ	40 Ⓐ Ⓑ Ⓒ Ⓓ Ⓔ

SECTION 7

1 Ⓐ Ⓑ Ⓒ Ⓓ Ⓔ	11 Ⓐ Ⓑ Ⓒ Ⓓ Ⓔ	21 Ⓐ Ⓑ Ⓒ Ⓓ Ⓔ	31 Ⓐ Ⓑ Ⓒ Ⓓ Ⓔ
2 Ⓐ Ⓑ Ⓒ Ⓓ Ⓔ	12 Ⓐ Ⓑ Ⓒ Ⓓ Ⓔ	22 Ⓐ Ⓑ Ⓒ Ⓓ Ⓔ	32 Ⓐ Ⓑ Ⓒ Ⓓ Ⓔ
3 Ⓐ Ⓑ Ⓒ Ⓓ Ⓔ	13 Ⓐ Ⓑ Ⓒ Ⓓ Ⓔ	23 Ⓐ Ⓑ Ⓒ Ⓓ Ⓔ	33 Ⓐ Ⓑ Ⓒ Ⓓ Ⓔ
4 Ⓐ Ⓑ Ⓒ Ⓓ Ⓔ	14 Ⓐ Ⓑ Ⓒ Ⓓ Ⓔ	24 Ⓐ Ⓑ Ⓒ Ⓓ Ⓔ	34 Ⓐ Ⓑ Ⓒ Ⓓ Ⓔ
5 Ⓐ Ⓑ Ⓒ Ⓓ Ⓔ	15 Ⓐ Ⓑ Ⓒ Ⓓ Ⓔ	25 Ⓐ Ⓑ Ⓒ Ⓓ Ⓔ	35 Ⓐ Ⓑ Ⓒ Ⓓ Ⓔ
6 Ⓐ Ⓑ Ⓒ Ⓓ Ⓔ	16 Ⓐ Ⓑ Ⓒ Ⓓ Ⓔ	26 Ⓐ Ⓑ Ⓒ Ⓓ Ⓔ	36 Ⓐ Ⓑ Ⓒ Ⓓ Ⓔ
7 Ⓐ Ⓑ Ⓒ Ⓓ Ⓔ	17 Ⓐ Ⓑ Ⓒ Ⓓ Ⓔ	27 Ⓐ Ⓑ Ⓒ Ⓓ Ⓔ	37 Ⓐ Ⓑ Ⓒ Ⓓ Ⓔ
8 Ⓐ Ⓑ Ⓒ Ⓓ Ⓔ	18 Ⓐ Ⓑ Ⓒ Ⓓ Ⓔ	28 Ⓐ Ⓑ Ⓒ Ⓓ Ⓔ	38 Ⓐ Ⓑ Ⓒ Ⓓ Ⓔ
9 Ⓐ Ⓑ Ⓒ Ⓓ Ⓔ	19 Ⓐ Ⓑ Ⓒ Ⓓ Ⓔ	29 Ⓐ Ⓑ Ⓒ Ⓓ Ⓔ	39 Ⓐ Ⓑ Ⓒ Ⓓ Ⓔ
10 Ⓐ Ⓑ Ⓒ Ⓓ Ⓔ	20 Ⓐ Ⓑ Ⓒ Ⓓ Ⓔ	30 Ⓐ Ⓑ Ⓒ Ⓓ Ⓔ	40 Ⓐ Ⓑ Ⓒ Ⓓ Ⓔ

CAUTION Grid answers in the section below for SECTION 6 or SECTION 7 only if directed to do so in your test book.

Student-Produced Responses

ONLY ANSWERS THAT ARE GRIDDED WILL BE SCORED. YOU WILL NOT RECEIVE CREDIT FOR ANYTHING WRITTEN IN THE BOXES.

Quality Assurance Mark ●

9, 10, 11, 12, 13, 14, 15, 16, 17, 18 — grid boxes with columns of bubbles containing / / , . , 0 1 2 3 4 5 6 7 8 9

SECTION 8

1 Ⓐ Ⓑ Ⓒ Ⓓ Ⓔ 11 Ⓐ Ⓑ Ⓒ Ⓓ Ⓔ 21 Ⓐ Ⓑ Ⓒ Ⓓ Ⓔ 31 Ⓐ Ⓑ Ⓒ Ⓓ Ⓔ
2 Ⓐ Ⓑ Ⓒ Ⓓ Ⓔ 12 Ⓐ Ⓑ Ⓒ Ⓓ Ⓔ 22 Ⓐ Ⓑ Ⓒ Ⓓ Ⓔ 32 Ⓐ Ⓑ Ⓒ Ⓓ Ⓔ
3 Ⓐ Ⓑ Ⓒ Ⓓ Ⓔ 13 Ⓐ Ⓑ Ⓒ Ⓓ Ⓔ 23 Ⓐ Ⓑ Ⓒ Ⓓ Ⓔ 33 Ⓐ Ⓑ Ⓒ Ⓓ Ⓔ
4 Ⓐ Ⓑ Ⓒ Ⓓ Ⓔ 14 Ⓐ Ⓑ Ⓒ Ⓓ Ⓔ 24 Ⓐ Ⓑ Ⓒ Ⓓ Ⓔ 34 Ⓐ Ⓑ Ⓒ Ⓓ Ⓔ
5 Ⓐ Ⓑ Ⓒ Ⓓ Ⓔ 15 Ⓐ Ⓑ Ⓒ Ⓓ Ⓔ 25 Ⓐ Ⓑ Ⓒ Ⓓ Ⓔ 35 Ⓐ Ⓑ Ⓒ Ⓓ Ⓔ
6 Ⓐ Ⓑ Ⓒ Ⓓ Ⓔ 16 Ⓐ Ⓑ Ⓒ Ⓓ Ⓔ 26 Ⓐ Ⓑ Ⓒ Ⓓ Ⓔ 36 Ⓐ Ⓑ Ⓒ Ⓓ Ⓔ
7 Ⓐ Ⓑ Ⓒ Ⓓ Ⓔ 17 Ⓐ Ⓑ Ⓒ Ⓓ Ⓔ 27 Ⓐ Ⓑ Ⓒ Ⓓ Ⓔ 37 Ⓐ Ⓑ Ⓒ Ⓓ Ⓔ
8 Ⓐ Ⓑ Ⓒ Ⓓ Ⓔ 18 Ⓐ Ⓑ Ⓒ Ⓓ Ⓔ 28 Ⓐ Ⓑ Ⓒ Ⓓ Ⓔ 38 Ⓐ Ⓑ Ⓒ Ⓓ Ⓔ
9 Ⓐ Ⓑ Ⓒ Ⓓ Ⓔ 19 Ⓐ Ⓑ Ⓒ Ⓓ Ⓔ 29 Ⓐ Ⓑ Ⓒ Ⓓ Ⓔ 39 Ⓐ Ⓑ Ⓒ Ⓓ Ⓔ
10 Ⓐ Ⓑ Ⓒ Ⓓ Ⓔ 20 Ⓐ Ⓑ Ⓒ Ⓓ Ⓔ 30 Ⓐ Ⓑ Ⓒ Ⓓ Ⓔ 40 Ⓐ Ⓑ Ⓒ Ⓓ Ⓔ

SECTION 9

1 Ⓐ Ⓑ Ⓒ Ⓓ Ⓔ 11 Ⓐ Ⓑ Ⓒ Ⓓ Ⓔ 21 Ⓐ Ⓑ Ⓒ Ⓓ Ⓔ 31 Ⓐ Ⓑ Ⓒ Ⓓ Ⓔ
2 Ⓐ Ⓑ Ⓒ Ⓓ Ⓔ 12 Ⓐ Ⓑ Ⓒ Ⓓ Ⓔ 22 Ⓐ Ⓑ Ⓒ Ⓓ Ⓔ 32 Ⓐ Ⓑ Ⓒ Ⓓ Ⓔ
3 Ⓐ Ⓑ Ⓒ Ⓓ Ⓔ 13 Ⓐ Ⓑ Ⓒ Ⓓ Ⓔ 23 Ⓐ Ⓑ Ⓒ Ⓓ Ⓔ 33 Ⓐ Ⓑ Ⓒ Ⓓ Ⓔ
4 Ⓐ Ⓑ Ⓒ Ⓓ Ⓔ 14 Ⓐ Ⓑ Ⓒ Ⓓ Ⓔ 24 Ⓐ Ⓑ Ⓒ Ⓓ Ⓔ 34 Ⓐ Ⓑ Ⓒ Ⓓ Ⓔ
5 Ⓐ Ⓑ Ⓒ Ⓓ Ⓔ 15 Ⓐ Ⓑ Ⓒ Ⓓ Ⓔ 25 Ⓐ Ⓑ Ⓒ Ⓓ Ⓔ 35 Ⓐ Ⓑ Ⓒ Ⓓ Ⓔ
6 Ⓐ Ⓑ Ⓒ Ⓓ Ⓔ 16 Ⓐ Ⓑ Ⓒ Ⓓ Ⓔ 26 Ⓐ Ⓑ Ⓒ Ⓓ Ⓔ 36 Ⓐ Ⓑ Ⓒ Ⓓ Ⓔ
7 Ⓐ Ⓑ Ⓒ Ⓓ Ⓔ 17 Ⓐ Ⓑ Ⓒ Ⓓ Ⓔ 27 Ⓐ Ⓑ Ⓒ Ⓓ Ⓔ 37 Ⓐ Ⓑ Ⓒ Ⓓ Ⓔ
8 Ⓐ Ⓑ Ⓒ Ⓓ Ⓔ 18 Ⓐ Ⓑ Ⓒ Ⓓ Ⓔ 28 Ⓐ Ⓑ Ⓒ Ⓓ Ⓔ 38 Ⓐ Ⓑ Ⓒ Ⓓ Ⓔ
9 Ⓐ Ⓑ Ⓒ Ⓓ Ⓔ 19 Ⓐ Ⓑ Ⓒ Ⓓ Ⓔ 29 Ⓐ Ⓑ Ⓒ Ⓓ Ⓔ 39 Ⓐ Ⓑ Ⓒ Ⓓ Ⓔ
10 Ⓐ Ⓑ Ⓒ Ⓓ Ⓔ 20 Ⓐ Ⓑ Ⓒ Ⓓ Ⓔ 30 Ⓐ Ⓑ Ⓒ Ⓓ Ⓔ 40 Ⓐ Ⓑ Ⓒ Ⓓ Ⓔ

SECTION 10

1 Ⓐ Ⓑ Ⓒ Ⓓ Ⓔ 11 Ⓐ Ⓑ Ⓒ Ⓓ Ⓔ 21 Ⓐ Ⓑ Ⓒ Ⓓ Ⓔ 31 Ⓐ Ⓑ Ⓒ Ⓓ Ⓔ
2 Ⓐ Ⓑ Ⓒ Ⓓ Ⓔ 12 Ⓐ Ⓑ Ⓒ Ⓓ Ⓔ 22 Ⓐ Ⓑ Ⓒ Ⓓ Ⓔ 32 Ⓐ Ⓑ Ⓒ Ⓓ Ⓔ
3 Ⓐ Ⓑ Ⓒ Ⓓ Ⓔ 13 Ⓐ Ⓑ Ⓒ Ⓓ Ⓔ 23 Ⓐ Ⓑ Ⓒ Ⓓ Ⓔ 33 Ⓐ Ⓑ Ⓒ Ⓓ Ⓔ
4 Ⓐ Ⓑ Ⓒ Ⓓ Ⓔ 14 Ⓐ Ⓑ Ⓒ Ⓓ Ⓔ 24 Ⓐ Ⓑ Ⓒ Ⓓ Ⓔ 34 Ⓐ Ⓑ Ⓒ Ⓓ Ⓔ
5 Ⓐ Ⓑ Ⓒ Ⓓ Ⓔ 15 Ⓐ Ⓑ Ⓒ Ⓓ Ⓔ 25 Ⓐ Ⓑ Ⓒ Ⓓ Ⓔ 35 Ⓐ Ⓑ Ⓒ Ⓓ Ⓔ
6 Ⓐ Ⓑ Ⓒ Ⓓ Ⓔ 16 Ⓐ Ⓑ Ⓒ Ⓓ Ⓔ 26 Ⓐ Ⓑ Ⓒ Ⓓ Ⓔ 36 Ⓐ Ⓑ Ⓒ Ⓓ Ⓔ
7 Ⓐ Ⓑ Ⓒ Ⓓ Ⓔ 17 Ⓐ Ⓑ Ⓒ Ⓓ Ⓔ 27 Ⓐ Ⓑ Ⓒ Ⓓ Ⓔ 37 Ⓐ Ⓑ Ⓒ Ⓓ Ⓔ
8 Ⓐ Ⓑ Ⓒ Ⓓ Ⓔ 18 Ⓐ Ⓑ Ⓒ Ⓓ Ⓔ 28 Ⓐ Ⓑ Ⓒ Ⓓ Ⓔ 38 Ⓐ Ⓑ Ⓒ Ⓓ Ⓔ
9 Ⓐ Ⓑ Ⓒ Ⓓ Ⓔ 19 Ⓐ Ⓑ Ⓒ Ⓓ Ⓔ 29 Ⓐ Ⓑ Ⓒ Ⓓ Ⓔ 39 Ⓐ Ⓑ Ⓒ Ⓓ Ⓔ
10 Ⓐ Ⓑ Ⓒ Ⓓ Ⓔ 20 Ⓐ Ⓑ Ⓒ Ⓓ Ⓔ 30 Ⓐ Ⓑ Ⓒ Ⓓ Ⓔ 40 Ⓐ Ⓑ Ⓒ Ⓓ Ⓔ

SECTION 1
ESSAY
Time — 25 minutes

Turn to Section 1 of your answer sheet to write your essay.

The essay gives you an opportunity to show how effectively you can develop and express ideas. You should, therefore, take care to develop your point of view, present your ideas logically and clearly, and use language precisely.

Your essay must be written on the lines provided on your answer sheet—you will receive no other paper on which to write. You will have enough space if you write on every line, avoid wide margins, and keep your handwriting to a reasonable size. Remember that people who are not familiar with your handwriting will read what you write. Try to write or print so that what you are writing is legible to those readers.

You have twenty-five minutes to write an essay on the topic assigned below. DO NOT WRITE ON ANOTHER TOPIC. AN OFF-TOPIC ESSAY WILL RECEIVE A SCORE OF ZERO.

Think carefully about the issue presented in the following excerpt and the assignment below.

> A sense of the past is an essential part of our identity. The past is in many respects a foreign country, but on the premise that travel broadens the mind, this is all the more reason to go there.
>
> Adapted from Rosamond McKitterick, *History and Its Audiences*

Assignment: Do we need knowledge of the past to fully understand the present? Plan and write an essay in which you develop your point of view on this issue. Support your position with reasoning and examples taken from your reading, studies, experience, or observations.

DO NOT WRITE YOUR ESSAY IN YOUR TEST BOOK. You will receive credit only for what you write on your answer sheet.

BEGIN WRITING YOUR ESSAY IN SECTION 1 OF THE ANSWER SHEET.

S T O P
If you finish before time is called, you may check your work on this section only.
Do not turn to any other section in the test.

SECTION 3
Time — 25 minutes
20 Questions

Turn to Section 3 of your answer sheet to answer the questions in this section.

Directions: For this section, solve each problem and decide which is the best of the choices given. Fill in the corresponding circle on the answer sheet. You may use any available space for scratchwork.

Notes

1. The use of a calculator is permitted.

2. All numbers used are real numbers.

3. Figures that accompany problems in this test are intended to provide information useful in solving the problems. They are drawn as accurately as possible EXCEPT when it is stated in a specific problem that the figure is not drawn to scale. All figures lie in a plane unless otherwise indicated.

4. Unless otherwise specified, the domain of any function f is assumed to be the set of all real numbers x for which $f(x)$ is a real number.

Reference Information

     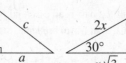

$A = \pi r^2$
$C = 2\pi r$
$A = lw$
$A = \frac{1}{2}bh$
$V = lwh$
$V = \pi r^2 h$
$c^2 = a^2 + b^2$

Special Right Triangles

The number of degrees of arc in a circle is 360.

The sum of the measures in degrees of the angles of a triangle is 180.

---

1. If Jonas has already run 4 miles in a 20-mile race, what fraction of the race has he already run?

(A) $\dfrac{1}{80}$

(B) $\dfrac{1}{24}$

(C) $\dfrac{1}{8}$

(D) $\dfrac{1}{6}$

(E) $\dfrac{1}{5}$

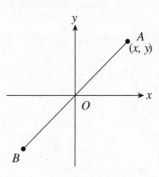

2. Line $\overline{AB}$ is shown in the xy-plane above. What are the coordinates of B if $\overline{BO} = \overline{AO}$?

(A) $(-x, -y)$
(B) $(-x, y)$
(C) $(x, -y)$
(D) (x, y)
(E) $(y, -x)$

GO ON TO THE NEXT PAGE

3. If 3 kilograms of rose petals are needed to produce 5 grams of perfume, how many kilograms of rose petals are needed to produce 870 grams of perfume?

(A)   290
(B)   522
(C)   870
(D) 1,450
(E) 2,610

5. A field contains 4,500 flowers that are either roses, daisies, or daffodils. If 18% are daisies and 18% are daffodils, what percent of the flowers are roses?

(A)   18%
(B)   36%
(C)   46%
(D)   64%
(E)   82%

4. The only way to purchase Brand X muffins is to buy one or more boxes that each contain 6 muffins. Each box costs $1.50. If Alejandro needs at least 20 muffins, what is the least amount of money he could spend?

(A) $3.00
(B) $4.50
(C) $6.00
(D) $7.50
(E) $30.00

6. In $\triangle EFG$, the length of $\overline{EF}$ is 9 and the length of $\overline{EG}$ is 12. Each of the following could be the length of side $\overline{FG}$ EXCEPT

(A)   20
(B)   16
(C)   8
(D)   4
(E)   2

GO ON TO THE NEXT PAGE

7. On a map, 1 centimeter represents 6 kilometers. A square on the map with a perimeter of 16 centimeters represents a region with what area?

    (A) 64 km^2
    (B) 96 km^2
    (C) 256 km^2
    (D) 576 km^2
    (E) 8216 km^2

8. If the sum of two negative integers is –15 and the product of the two integers is less than 40, then which of the following could be one of the two integers?

    (A)   –8
    (B)   –7
    (C)   –5
    (D)   –4
    (E)   –3

9. If c is positive, what percent of $3c$ is 9 ?

    (A) $\dfrac{c}{100}$

    (B) $\dfrac{100c}{3}$

    (C) $\dfrac{9}{c}$

    (D)   3

    (E) $\dfrac{300}{c}$

GO ON TO THE NEXT PAGE

10. Max realized that the longer he runs, the slower his pace becomes. Which of the following could be the graph of Max's pace by his distance?

(A)

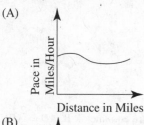

(B)

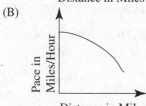

(C)

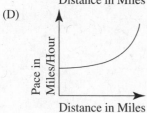

(D)

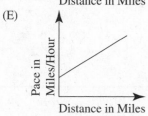

(E)

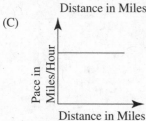

11. If $n = \dfrac{3m+2}{2}$ and the value of m is decreased by 4, then the value of n is decreased by how much?

(A) 4
(B) 6
(C) 8
(D) 14
(E) 18

12. The graph of $y = x - 2$ is drawn on a set of coordinate axes. If the graph of $y = x + 7$ is then drawn on the same axes, how does the second graph compare to the first?

(A) The second graph will be 9 units above the first.
(B) The second graph will be 3 units above the first.
(C) The second graph will be 5 units below the first.
(D) The second graph will be 9 units below the first.
(E) The second graph will have a greater slope than the first.

GO ON TO THE NEXT PAGE

Tuesday's Bread Sales

Weight of loaf in ounces	Number of loaves sold
8	140
12	20
16	110
24	30

13. A bakery sells bread in loaves weighing 8, 12, 16, or 24 ounces. On Tuesday, the bakery sold a total of 300 loaves as shown in chart above. What was the median weight, in ounces, of a loaf of bread sold on Tuesday?

(A) 16
(B) 15
(C) 14
(D) 12
(E) 8

14. A certain box contains only black, blue, and red pens. If a pen is chosen at random from the box, the probability of choosing a black pen is $\frac{1}{4}$ and the probability of choosing a blue pen is $\frac{1}{6}$. What is the probability of choosing a red pen?

(A) $\frac{1}{24}$

(B) $\frac{1}{12}$

(C) $\frac{7}{12}$

(D) $\frac{3}{4}$

(E) It depends on the number of pens in the box.

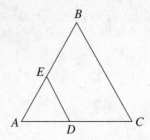

15. Both $\triangle ABC$ and $\triangle AED$ are equilateral. If $AD = \frac{2}{3} DC$, then the perimeter of $\triangle AED$ is what fraction of the perimeter of $\triangle ABC$?

(A) $\frac{1}{3}$

(B) $\frac{2}{5}$

(C) $\frac{3}{5}$

(D) $\frac{2}{3}$

(E) $\frac{4}{5}$

16. If in a certain sequence the first term is 8 and every subsequent term is determined by adding 15 to the previous term, what is the value of the 50th term?

(A) 743
(B) 750
(C) 753
(D) 758
(E) 773

GO ON TO THE NEXT PAGE

17. If $x - y = 10$ and $x^2 - y^2 = 40$, then $y =$

(A) 14
(B)   7
(C)   4
(D) –3
(E) –6

18. The length and width of a certain rectangle are both decreased by 50 percent. If the length and width of the new rectangle are then increased by 40 percent, the area of the resulting rectangle is what percent less than the area of the original rectangle?

(A) 10%
(B) 45%
(C) 49%
(D) 51%
(E) 90%

19. A circle with radius r is inscribed in a square. If a point within the square is randomly selected, what is the probability that the point will not be within the circle?

(A) $\dfrac{\pi}{4}$

(B) $\dfrac{\pi - 4}{4}$

(C) $\dfrac{4 - \pi}{4}$

(D) πr

(E) $4r$

$$-7, -5, -3, -1, 0, 1, 3, 5, 7$$

20. How many distinct products can be obtained by multiplying pairs of numbers from the list above?

(A)   9
(B) 17
(C) 19
(D) 21
(E) 31

STOP

**If you finish before time is called, you may check your work on this section only.
Do not turn to any other section in the test.**

SECTION 4
Time — 25 minutes
24 Questions

Turn to Section 4 of your answer sheet to answer the questions in this section.

Directions: For each question in this section, select the best answer from among the choices given and fill in the corresponding circle on the answer sheet.

Each sentence below has one or two blanks, each blank indicating that something has been omitted. Beneath the sentence are five words or sets of words labeled A through E. Choose the word or set of words that, when inserted in the sentence, <u>best</u> fits the meaning of the sentence as a whole.

Example:

Desiring to ------- his taunting friends, Mitch gave them taffy in hopes it would keep their mouths shut.

(A) eliminate   (B) satisfy   (C) overcome
    (D) ridicule   (E) silence

1. Unable to cross the bridge because it was in ill-repair, Clarissa ------- a makeshift one from a fallen log.

   (A) claimed   (B) devised   (C) hesitated
       (D) exulted   (E) perished

2. The corn farmers are worried about today's weather forecast since the ------- hailstorm will have a ------- effect on this year's crop.

   (A) minor . . lasting
   (B) unpredictable . . negative
   (C) approaching . . beneficial
   (D) terrible . . brief
   (E) imminent . . harmful

3. The poet's most recent collection has been very well-received; a recent ------- article in *The New York Times* was only the latest in a long line of accolades for the book.

   (A) austere   (B) laudatory   (C) cursory
       (D) vituperative   (E) accessible

4. Countries in the twenty-first century are not -------, but -------; every war, every treaty, and every trade that takes place anywhere in the world can affect them all.

   (A) dependable . . changing
   (B) enlarging . . expanding
   (C) inaccessible . . imperfect
   (D) isolated . . interdependent
   (E) bellicose . . peaceful

5. The vagabond seemed content with his ------- lifestyle, but he secretly longed for the ------- of a permanent home.

   (A) serene . . passivity
   (B) transient . . innocuousness
   (C) peripatetic . . stability
   (D) commendable . . inertia
   (E) reprehensible . . audacity

6. Her political slogans were actually forgotten clichés revived and ------- with new meaning.

   (A) fathomed   (B) imbued   (C) distilled
       (D) instigated   (E) foreshadowed

7. The surprisingly precise measurement of the circumference of the earth made by the early Greeks ------- some of our beliefs about the simplistic nature of ancient mathematics.

   (A) belies   (B) assuages   (C) clarifies
       (D) redoubles   (E) obscures

8. The character Don Quixote is perhaps best known for his -------; he was constantly embarking upon wild and fanciful expeditions.

   (A) impiety   (B) vagaries   (C) gluttony
       (D) evanescence   (E) narcissism

GO ON TO THE NEXT PAGE

Directions: Each passage below is followed by questions based on its content. Answer the questions on the basis of what is <u>stated</u> or <u>implied</u> in each passage and in any introductory material that may be provided.

Questions 9-10 are based on the following passage.

The Food and Drug Administration's guidelines for labeling food are outdated, critics say, and don't reflect the actual contents of the package. Often, nutritional information
Line regarding fat, calories, and sodium are listed for a single
5 serving, though two or more servings can be offered in one package. The result? Consumers cannot get correct nutritional information without a calculator and a detailed study of what they plan to eat. Food companies claim they've done nothing illegal, though intentionally confusing
10 consumers is unethical. Until the FDA changes its rules, consumers should be vigilant about reading labels.

9. It can be inferred from the passage that

(A) mislabeled packages have caused America's obesity problem
(B) packaged food is unhealthful to consume
(C) the confusion caused by food labels may not be unintentional
(D) the FDA's guidelines aren't strict enough
(E) consumers are unlikely to look at nutritional information on packaging

10. The author suggests that people seeking nutritional information on packaging should be

(A) critical
(B) anxious
(C) suspicious
(D) attentive
(E) dubious

Questions 11-12 are based on the following passage.

Flannery O'Connor was a prolific fiction writer who often spoke about her craft. She once wrote: "The writer's business is to contemplate experience, not to be merged in it. . . The
Line fact is that anybody who has survived his childhood has
5 enough information about life to last him the rest of his days." I try not to think of these words when I am trekking the trails of Yellowstone and touring the villas in Tuscany, searching in vain for the seeds of a short story.

11. The author most likely says, "I try not to think of these words" (line 6) because

(A) he disagrees with O'Connor's philosophy of writing
(B) he doesn't want to be distracted while doing research
(C) he doesn't think his childhood is very interesting subject material
(D) his actions conflict with O'Connor's philosophy of writing
(E) he doesn't want to be influenced by O'Connor's writing

12. According to the quote on lines 2-5 ("The writer's business… the rest of his days"), O'Connor would probably agree with which of the following statements?

(A) Childhood provides adults with many of life's lessons.
(B) Everyone who has survived to adulthood is capable of writing well.
(C) Children tend to observe life, not participate in it.
(D) The best writers usually write about childhood.
(E) Writers must write about their childhood to be considered accomplished.

GO ON TO THE NEXT PAGE

Questions 13-24 are based on the following passage.

The following passage is a selection from a history of jazz. Its subject is Duke Ellington, a pioneer and innovator in modern jazz forms.

Duke Ellington's Orchestra is a complex configuration of many spiritual and musical elements. To be sure, it was Duke Ellington's music that was created here, but it was just
Line as much the music of each individual member of the band.
5 Many Ellington pieces were genuine collective achievements, but it was Ellington who headed the collective. Attempts have been made to describe how Ellington recordings have come into being, but the process is so subtle that verbalization appears crude. Duke, or his alter ego, the late arranger and
10 jazz composer, Billy Strayhorn, or one of the members of the band would come to the studio with a theme. Ellington would play on the piano. The rhythm section would fall in. One or another of the horn men would pick it up. Baritone saxophonist Harry Carney might improvise a solo on it. The
15 brass would make up a suitable background for him. And Ellington would sit at the piano and listen, gently accenting the harmonies—and suddenly he'd know: This is how the piece should sound and no other way. Later, when it was transcribed, the note paper only happened to retain what was,
20 in the real meaning of the word, improvised into being.

The dynamic willpower with which Ellington stamped his ideas on his musicians, while giving them the impression that he was only helping them to unfold and develop their hidden powers, was one of his many great gifts. Owing to
25 the relationship between Duke and his musicians, which can barely be put into words, everything he had written seemed to be created for him and his orchestra—to such a degree that hardly anyone can copy it.

When Ellington was eighteen, he wanted to become a
30 painter. By becoming a musician he only seemed to have abandoned painting. He painted not in colors but in sounds. His compositions, with their many colors of timbre and harmony, are musical paintings. Sometimes this is revealed by the titles: "The Flaming Sword," "Beautiful Indians,"
35 "Portrait of Bert Williams," "Sepia Panorama," "Country Girl," "Dusk in the Desert," "Mood Indigo," and so forth. Even as a conductor, Ellington remained the painter: in the grand manner in which he confronted the orchestra and, with a few sure movements of the hand, placed spots of color on a
40 canvas made of sounds.

It may be due to this that he perceived his music as "the transformation of memories into sounds." Ellington said, "The memory of things gone is important to a jazz musician. I remember I once wrote a sixty-four-bar piece about a memory
45 of when I was a little boy in bed and heard a man whistling on the street outside, his footsteps echoing away."

Again and again Ellington has expressed his pride in the color of his skin. Many of his larger works took their themes from black history: "Black, Brown, and Beige," the
50 tone painting of the American Negro who was "black" when he came to the New World, became "brown" in the days of slavery, and today is "beige"—not only in his color, but in

his being as well; "Liberian Suite," a work in six movements commissioned by the small republic on the west coast of
55 Africa for its centennial; "Harlem," the work in which the atmosphere of New York's black city has been captured; "Deep South Suite," which reminds us of the locale of the origins of jazz, or "New World A-comin'," the work about a better world without racial discrimination.

60 Many critics have said that Ellington often comes too close to European music. They point to his concern with larger forms. But in this very concern is revealed an insufficiency in the molding of these forms which is certainly not European: an astonishing, amiable naïveté. This naïveté
65 was also present in those medleys—long series of his many successful tunes—with which Duke again and again upset many of his more sophisticated fans at his concerts. Ellington simply failed to see why the idea of the hit medley should be alien to an artistic music.

70 The jungle style is one of the four styles identified with Duke Ellington. The other three are (in a somewhat simplistic but synoptically clear grouping) "mood style," "concerto style," and "standard style," which came rather directly from Fletcher Henderson, the most important band leader of the
75 twenties, and initially did not contribute much that was new. What it did have to offer, though, was clothed in typically Ellingtonian colors and sounds. In addition, of course, there is every imaginable mixture of these styles.

The history of Duke Ellington is the history of the
80 orchestra in jazz. No significant big band—and this includes commercial dance bands—has not been directly or indirectly influenced by Duke. The list of innovations and techniques introduced by Ellington and subsequently picked up by other orchestras or players is unrivaled.

---

13. Which of the following best describes the "process" (line 8) of Ellington and his band in the composition of new pieces?

(A) Ellington's primary concern was to help his band members realize their full potential as composers.

(B) Ellington exploited the talents of his band in order to further his own career as a composer.

(C) Ellington and his band collaborated as equals in the development of new compositions.

(D) Ellington used his band's improvisations as inspiration for his compositions.

(E) Ellington based his compositions on early recordings by his band members.

14. In line 16, "accenting" most nearly means

(A) fashioning
(B) emphasizing
(C) improving
(D) enunciating
(E) reworking

GO ON TO THE NEXT PAGE

15. The descriptions given in lines 47-59 provide the reader with which of the following?

(A) an understanding of Ellington's youth
(B) a sense of the momentum behind Ellington's earlier work
(C) a history of Ellington's social conscience
(D) the reasons behind Ellington's long-lived popularity
(E) the inspirations for some of Ellington's compositions

16. According to the author, which of the following is true of "Black, Brown, and Beige" (line 49) ?

(A) It tells the story of several major black historical figures.
(B) Its title refers to color both literally and metaphorically.
(C) It is comprised of three distinct sections.
(D) It was inspired by a series of paintings.
(E) It was written on commission for a national celebration.

17. The author implies that the "origins of jazz" (line 58) can be traced to

(A) Harlem
(B) the American South
(C) the west coast of Africa
(D) Europe
(E) Liberia

18. Which of the following attributes does the author mention in response to the criticisms leveled in lines 60-61 ?

(A) Ellington's pride in the color of his skin
(B) Ellington's European sensibility
(C) Ellington's grasp of timbre and harmony
(D) Ellington's genuine innocence
(E) Ellington's ability to write hit songs

19. According to the passage, some "fans" (line 67) of Ellington were

(A) critical of one of Ellington's presentation formats
(B) unfamiliar with more classical forms of music
(C) lacking in the naïveté required to understand Ellington's medleys
(D) dismayed by Ellington's use of European musical forms
(E) close-minded in their dismissal of Ellington's work

20. The author mentions all of the following as sources of inspiration for Ellington's work EXCEPT

(A) famous paintings
(B) childhood memories
(C) ethnic heritage
(D) orchestral improvisations
(E) regional ambiance

21. The phrase in parentheses (lines 71-72) serves to

(A) introduce the styles the author most appreciates
(B) offer a new definition for a widely accepted term
(C) summarize the process by which music is categorized
(D) enhance the reader's perception of jungle style's heritage
(E) justify what may be perceived as an oversimplification

22. It can be inferred from the passage that "Fletcher Henderson" (line 74)

(A) was a stylistic influence on Duke Ellington
(B) composed in a style that was inspired by the work of Duke Ellington
(C) was a contemporary of Duke Ellington
(D) created music that was not particularly memorable
(E) wrote music that had much in common with Ellington's jungle style

23. Which of the following questions could be answered based on information in the passage?

(A) At what age did Ellington achieve success as a musician?
(B) What musical devices did Ellington use to convey color?
(C) By what process did Ellington develop his orchestral compositions?
(D) What are the characteristics of Ellington's jungle style?
(E) What is considered Ellington's best-known composition?

24. The final paragraph of the passage focuses on which of the following aspects of Duke Ellington's work?

(A) its commercial success
(B) its versatility
(C) its legacy
(D) its creativity
(E) its sources

STOP
**If you finish before time is called, you may check your work on this section only.
Do not turn to any other section in the test.**

SECTION 5
Time — 25 minutes
18 Questions

Turn to Section 5 of your answer sheet to answer the questions in this section.

Directions: This section contains two types of questions. You have 25 minutes to complete both types. For questions 1-8, solve each problem and decide which is the best of the choices given. Fill in the corresponding circle on the answer sheet. You may use any available space for scratchwork.

Notes

1. The use of a calculator is permitted.

2. All numbers used are real numbers.

3. Figures that accompany problems in this test are intended to provide information useful in solving the problems. They are drawn as accurately as possible EXCEPT when it is stated in a specific problem that the figure is not drawn to scale. All figures lie in a plane unless otherwise indicated.

4. Unless otherwise specified, the domain of any function f is assumed to be the set of all real numbers x for which $f(x)$ is a real number.

Reference Information

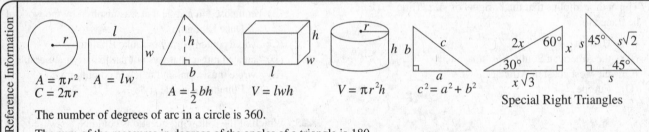

$A = \pi r^2$
$C = 2\pi r$
$A = lw$
$A = \frac{1}{2}bh$
$V = lwh$
$V = \pi r^2 h$
$c^2 = a^2 + b^2$
Special Right Triangles

The number of degrees of arc in a circle is 360.

The sum of the measures in degrees of the angles of a triangle is 180.

---

1. If $2x + 10 = 16$, what is the value of $2x - 10$?

(A) -4
(B) -3
(C) 3
(D) 4
(E) 6

2. In $\triangle ABC$, $\overline{AB} = \overline{BC}$ and $\overline{AB} \perp \overline{BC}$, if $BC = 10$, what is the area of the triangle?

(A) $10\sqrt{2}$
(B) 25
(C) 50
(D) $50\sqrt{2}$
(E) 100

GO ON TO THE NEXT PAGE

3. On the *xy*-coordinate plane, moving the graph of $y = x - 5$ three units upward would result in the graph of which of the following functions?

   (A) $y = x - 8$
   (B) $y = x - 3$
   (C) $y = x - 2$
   (D) $y = x + 3$
   (E) $y = x + 5$

5. The number of students who order hot lunch by the month at the Tucker Elementary School varies directly with the number of times pizza appears on the lunch menu during that month. If 135 students order hot lunch when pizza appears three times on the menu, how many students order hot lunch when pizza appears eight times on the menu?

   (A) 260
   (B) 295
   (C) 325
   (D) 360
   (E) 405

4. If $f(c) = \dfrac{9}{5}c + 32$, then what is the value of $f(25)$?

   (A) 13
   (B) 46
   (C) 77
   (D) 103
   (E) 113

GO ON TO THE NEXT PAGE

Car Model	Selling Price	Number of Cars Sold
Convertible Sports Car	$60,000	500
Minivan	$30,000	1,500
Family Sedan	$20,000	3,000

6. A certain car manufacturer sells only three models of cars. The chart above shows the selling price for each model, along with the quantity of each model sold in one year. Which of the following graphs most correctly shows the relationship between the price of a model and the number of that model sold?

(A)
Number of Cars Sold

Selling Price

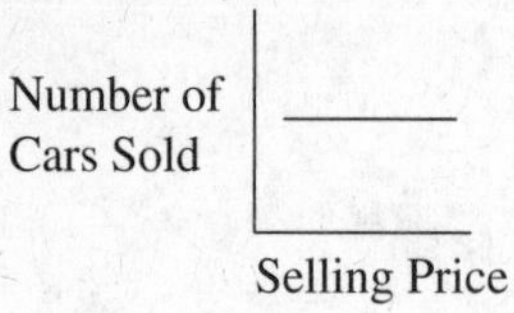

(B)
Number of Cars Sold

Selling Price

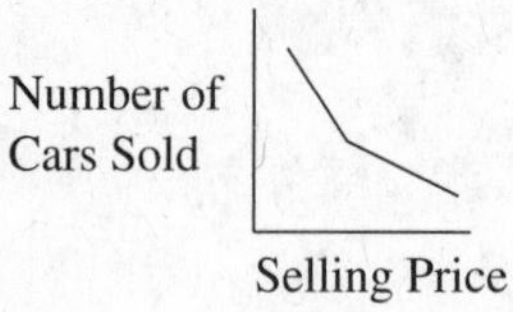

(C)
Number of Cars Sold

Selling Price

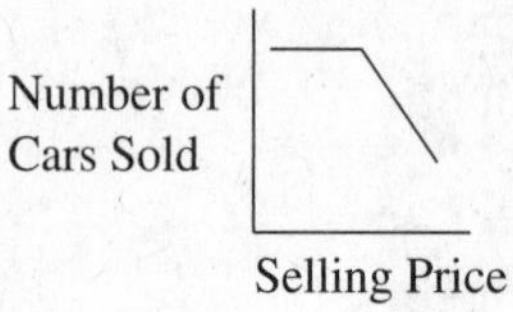

(D)
Number of Cars Sold

Selling Price

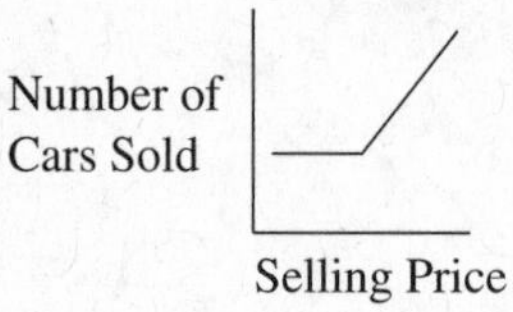

(E)
Number of Cars Sold

Selling Price

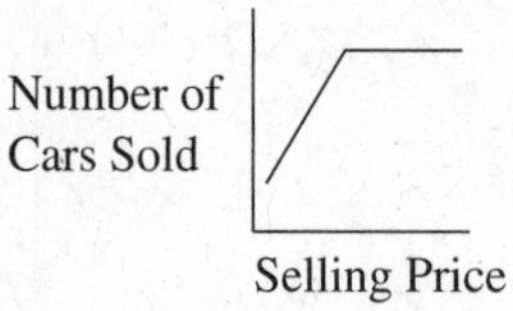

7. Which of the following is equivalent to $\dfrac{x^2+4x+3}{-3-x}>0$?

(A) $x<-1$ and $x \neq -3$
(B) $x>-1$
(C) $x>-1$ and $x \neq 3$
(D) $-3<x<-1$
(E) $x<-1$ or $x>3$

8. If the price of a certain product is increased by 15 percent, by approximately what percent must the new price be reduced to obtain the original price?

(A) 13
(B) 15
(C) 17
(D) 85
(E) 115

GO ON TO THE NEXT PAGE

Directions: For Student-Produced Response questions 9-18, use the grids at the bottom of the answer sheet page on which you have answered questions 1-8.

Each of the remaining 10 questions requires you to solve the problem and enter your answer by marking the circles in the special grid, as shown in the examples below. You may use any available space for scratch work.

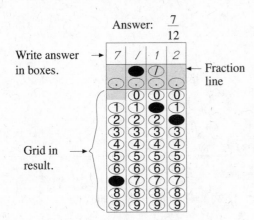

Answer: $\frac{7}{12}$

Write answer in boxes.

Fraction line

Grid in result.

Answer: 2.5

Decimal point

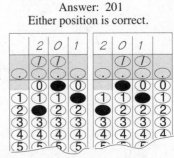

Answer: 201
Either position is correct.

Note: You may start your answers in any column, space permitting. Columns not needed should be left blank.

• Mark no more than one circle in any column.

• Because the answer document will be machine-scored, **you will receive credit only if the circles are filled in correctly.**

• Although not required, it is suggested that you write your answer in the boxes at the top of the columns to help you fill in the circles accurately.

• Some problems may have more than one correct answer. In such cases, grid only one answer.

• No question has a negative answer.

• **Mixed numbers** such as $3\frac{1}{2}$ must be gridded as 3.5 or 7/2. (If [3 1 / 2] is gridded, it will be interpreted as $\frac{31}{2}$, not $3\frac{1}{2}$.)

• **Decimal Answers:** If you obtain a decimal answer with more digits than the grid can accommodate, it may be either rounded or truncated, but it must fill the entire grid. For example, if you obtain an answer such as 0.6666..., you should record your result as .666 or .667. **A less accurate value such as .66 or .67 will be scored as incorrect.**

Acceptable ways to grid $\frac{2}{3}$ are:

9. If $5x - 4 = x - 1$, what is the value of x?

10. A rectangular packing crate has a height of 4.5 inches and a base with an area of 18 square inches. What is the volume of the crate in cubic inches?

GO ON TO THE NEXT PAGE

11. A box of donuts contains 3 plain, 5 cream-filled, and 4 chocolate donuts. If one of the donuts is chosen at random from the box, what is the probability that it will NOT be cream-filled?

13. The Tyler Jackson Dance Company plans to perform a piece that requires two dancers. If there are 7 dancers in the company, how many different pairs of dancers could perform the piece?

14. If $2\sqrt{a} = 3$, what is the value of a ?

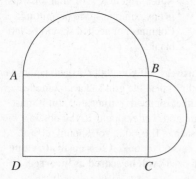

12. In the figure above, if semicircular $\overset{\frown}{AB}$ has length 6π and semicircular $\overset{\frown}{BC}$ has length 4π, what is the area of rectangle $ABCD$?

GO ON TO THE NEXT PAGE

SPICE PRICES OF DISTRIBUTOR D

Spice	Price per Pound
Cinnamon	$8.00
Nutmeg	$9.00
Ginger	$7.00
Cloves	$10.00

15. The table above shows the price per pound that Distributor D charges for spices. The owner of a spice store buys 3 pounds each of cinnamon, nutmeg, ginger, and cloves from Distributor D. She then sells all of the spices at $2.00 per ounce. What, in dollars, is her total profit? (1 pound = 16 ounces) (Disregard the $ sign when gridding your answer.)

16. What is the length of the diagonal of the rectangle which has vertices located at (a, b), $(9, 2)$, $(9, 8)$ and $(1, 8)$ in the xy-coordinate system?

17. A right triangle with area 24 has vertices at $(-3, 2)$, $(5, 2)$, and $(5, b)$, where $b > 0$. What is the value of b ?

18. The faces of a rectangular solid have areas 6, 10, and 15. If the dimensions of the rectangular solid are all integers, what is its volume?

STOP
If you finish before time is called, you may check your work on this section only.
Do not turn to any other section in the test.

SECTION 6
Time — 25 minutes
35 Questions

Turn to Section 6 of your answer sheet to answer the questions in this section.

Directions: For each question in this section, select the best answer from among the choices given and fill in the corresponding circle on the answer sheet.

The following sentences test correctness and effectiveness of expression. Part of each sentence or the entire sentence is underlined; beneath each sentence are five ways of phrasing the underlined material. Choice A repeats the original phrasing; the other four choices are different. If you think the original phrasing produces a better sentence than any of the alternatives, select choice A; if not, select one of the other choices.

In making your selection, follow the requirements of standard written English; that is, pay attention to grammar, choice of words, sentence construction, and punctuation. Your selection should result in the most effective sentence—clear and precise, without awkwardness or ambiguity.

EXAMPLE:

Bobby Flay baked his first cake <u>and he was thirteen years old then</u>.

(A) and he was thirteen years old then
(B) when he was thirteen
(C) at age thirteen years old
(D) upon the reaching of thirteen years
(E) at the time when he was thirteen

1. <u>Though accepting multiple points of view</u>, the students were unable to either assess or justify them.

   (A) Though accepting multiple points of view
   (B) Multiple points of view being accepted
   (C) Having been accepting of multiple points of view
   (D) They accepted multiple points of view
   (E) Their accepting multiple points of view

2. <u>If everyone would have contributed</u>, we might have raised enough money to save the old landmark from developers.

   (A) If everyone would have contributed
   (B) Had everyone contributed
   (C) If there was a contribution from everyone
   (D) Since everyone has contributed
   (E) If everyone contributes

3. <u>Consumed in massive quantities for decades, Americans have only recently begun to limit their intake of sugar.</u>

   (A) Consumed in massive quantities for decades, Americans have only recently begun to limit their intake of sugar.
   (B) Americans have only recently begun to limit their intake of sugar after having consumed it in massive quantities for decades.
   (C) Americans, consuming massive quantities of it for decades, have only recently begun to limit their intake of sugar.
   (D) Americans, consuming massive quantities for decades, are recently beginning to limit their intake of sugar.
   (E) Consumed in massive quantities for decades, the intake of sugar by Americans had only recently been limited.

4. Despite its excellent reputation, students found the novel <u>to be dense, long, and boring to them</u>.

   (A) to be dense, long, and boring to them
   (B) to be dense, long, and boring as well
   (C) as being dense, long, and boring
   (D) as dense, long, and boring to them
   (E) dense, long, and boring

5. Albert Einstein <u>made a bold leap, adopted</u> as his fundamental premise a paradox that had been ignored by other physicists.

   (A) made a bold leap, adopted
   (B) making the bold leap of adopting
   (C) made a bold leap and he adopted
   (D) made a bold leap; he adopted
   (E) made a bold leap while he adopted

GO ON TO THE NEXT PAGE ➡

6. The play contains four acts, <u>and each one of them commences with an identical setting at the beginning</u>.

  (A) and each one of them commences with an identical setting at the beginning
  (B) commencing with an identical setting each time
  (C) with an identical setting to begin each
  (D) each of which commences with an identical setting
  (E) having an identical setting at the beginning of each

7. For centuries, children's fables have been written to teach universal lessons of morality, but <u>there are few that equal Aesop</u>.

  (A) there are few that equal Aesop
  (B) few written equal to Aesop
  (C) there are few to equal Aesop
  (D) few are equal to those written by Aesop
  (E) few equaling Aesop

8. The giant seaplane "Spruce Goose" has 100-yard long wings that <u>provide it with stability and carry its eight massive engines</u>.

  (A) provide it with stability and carry its eight massive engines
  (B) provide it with stability and carry their eight massive engines
  (C) stabilized it and carried its eight massive engines
  (D) provides its stability and carries its eight massive engines
  (E) provides them with stability and carries their eight massive engines

9. It may be that the conflicts between parents and their children are indications <u>of their need for dependence versus their desire for independence</u>.

  (A) of their need for dependence versus their desire for independence
  (B) that they need dependence, but desire independence
  (C) of how much they need dependence but desire independence
  (D) of the children's need for dependence as against their desire for independence
  (E) of the children's need for dependence but desire for independence

10. Environmentalists will find it difficult to discover <u>which is most to blame for the disaster—the</u> company workers who dumped the chemicals or the mayor who allowed the dumping.

  (A) which is most to blame for the disaster—the
  (B) who is to blame for this disaster, the
  (C) who is more to blame for the disaster—the
  (D) what caused the most harm in this disaster—the
  (E) whether the disaster was the fault of the

11. Sociologists believe that an individual requires a certain amount of conflict, and therefore cannot cope <u>either with an overcrowded environment nor with a desolate one</u>.

  (A) either with an overcrowded environment nor with a desolate one
  (B) neither with the overcrowding of the environment nor with making it more desolate
  (C) either with an overcrowded environment or with a desolate one
  (D) neither with an overcrowded environment or with a desolate one
  (E) either with or without an overcrowded or desolate environment

GO ON TO THE NEXT PAGE

The following sentences test your ability to recognize grammar and usage errors. Each sentence contains either a single error or no error at all. No sentence contains more than one error. The error, if there is one, is underlined and lettered. If the sentence contains an error, select the one underlined part that must be changed to make the sentence correct. If the sentence is correct, select choice E. In choosing answers, follow the requirements of standard written English.

EXAMPLE:

The other players and her significantly improved
  A   B   C

the game plan created by the coaches. No error
                 D   E

Ⓐ●ⒸⒹⒺ

12. Bradley insists how the music used in the television
          A   B

commercial cannot possibly be Gershwin's
             C

composition, *Rhapsody in Blue*. No error
    D   E

13. When Odysseus and crew encountered the Sirens, his
    A   B

fellow sailors stuffed their own ears with wax, but
                C

Odysseus decided to listen to it. No error
                   D   E

14. Constantly recognized by hordes of adoring fans,
    A   B

movie stars have taken to wearing disguises to avoid
              C

excessive attention. No error
    D   E

15. We have read your proposed amendment to the club's
     A   B

bylaws and have decided to change our mind about the
                 C   D

eligibility requirements for membership. No error
                         E

16. America's primary asset is their teachers, who educate
                     A   B

and inspire future generations of responsible citizens.
     C   D

No error
 E

17. The professor suggested that her students purchase
                                    A

Fareed Zakaria's new book if they have not read his
                      B

articles when they appeared in *Newsweek*. No error
      C   D   E

18. Many critics now suspect that Shakespeare is not the
                             A

only playwright who was involved in the writing of
  B   C

those works popularly attributed to him. No error
               D   E

19. As unemployment in certain metropolitan areas
  A

increase to depression levels, the federal government
  B

will be forced to address the problem. No error
   C   D   E

20. The chairman, after conferring with his closest aides,
                 A   B

signaled his acceptance on the bill. No error
      C   D   E

GO ON TO THE NEXT PAGE

21. As skilled a dancer as he is a DJ, Belli found that his
     A   B   C

skills were in high demand at nightclubs across the
                          D

town. No error
       E

22. Angela was curious about the unopened letter on the
          A   B

table and wondered for whom it was meant. No error
                C   D   E

23. The restaurant's recently-updated computer system

can automatically look up a customer's address when
A   B   C

calling to place a take-out order. No error
   D   E

24. Two jurors believed that there were, notwithstanding the
                A   B

testimony of numerous experts and witnesses, questions

that had not been answered by the prosecuting attorney.
C   D

No error
 E

25. In the event that any one of the main circuits are
         A   B   C

knocked out, we can resort to reserve power cells.
              D

No error
 E

26. Jim finds his fear of the dark worse than heights since
                     A   B   C

he can more easily avoid high places. No error
               D   E

27. The symphony contains many difficult passages where
                                A

the novice instrumentalist may have trouble keeping up
    B

with the more experienced player. No error
     C   D   E

28. A noisy, unwieldy crowd of onlookers were jostling
     A   B

and milling around at the scene of the accident,
    C

impeding the progress of the medical technicians.
 D

No error
 E

29. As finalists, Mark and I were both shocked by the
                     A

decision; it seemed to us that the winner of the contest
     B

was far less talented than we. No error
    C   D   E

GO ON TO THE NEXT PAGE

Directions: The following passage is an early draft of an essay. Some parts of the passage need to be rewritten.

Read the passage and select the best answers for the questions that follow. Some questions are about particular sentences or parts of sentences and ask you to improve sentence structure or word choice. Other questions ask you to consider organization and development. In choosing answers, follow the requirements of standard written English.

Questions 30-35 are based on the following student essay.

(**1**) E.O. Smith High School's wrestling team has always been all male. (**2**) This has never before been a problem, since no girls expressed an interest in competitive wrestling. (**3**) In the past, female athletes were contentedly participating in athletics through the girls' soccer, basketball, field hockey, volleyball, and gymnastics teams. (**4**) However, recently one unconventional girl has come forward to challenge the assumption that contact sports are only suitable for boys.

(**5**) It all started at the first meeting of the wrestling team this year. (**6**) Jodie McGillis showed up and announced that she wanted to join. (**7**) She surprised the entire school. (**8**) At first, Coach Houston thought it was a prank, but after a few minutes, she convinced him that her intentions were earnest. (**9**) He explained that this matter was beyond his realm of authority, and that she would have to discuss it with the administration. (**10**) The matter is still pending.

(**11**) It is easy to understand what some of the fears might be about having a girl on an all-male team. (**12**) This is particularly true of a team that places such an emphasis on direct physical contact. (**13**) It hardly seems fair to exclude a student from a school activity on the basis of gender. (**14**) If Jodie wants to wrestle, she should be given the opportunity to do so. (**15**) Although this might seem like a trivial matter to some, the larger civil rights issues at stake are actually extremely important.

30. In context, which of the following versions of the underlined part of sentence 3 (reproduced below) is the best?

In the past, female athletes were contentedly participating *in athletics through the girls' soccer, basketball, field hockey, volleyball, and gymnastics teams*

(A) (as it is now)
(B) are contented and participated
(C) would be content to participate
(D) were content to participate
(E) contentedly participating

31. Which of the following sentences could best be omitted from the passage, without sacrifice to content or flow?

(A) Sentence 1
(B) Sentence 2
(C) Sentence 8
(D) Sentence 11
(E) Sentence 13

32. How could the author most effectively revise and combine the underlined portions of sentences 11 and 12 (reproduced below)?

It is easy to understand what some of the fears might be about having a girl on an all-male team. This is particularly true of a team *that places such an emphasis on direct physical contact.*

(A) team, however true it may be of a team
(B) team, particularly one
(C) team: a team, in particular,
(D) team, this being particularly true because it is a team
(E) team, an all-male team more particularly

33. The meaning of sentence 15 could be made more clear by replacing "this" with which of the following?

(A) the right to wrestle
(B) Jodie McGillis
(C) civil rights issues
(D) the matter
(E) emphasis on physical contact

34. What would be the most appropriate subject for a paragraph immediately following sentence 15?

(A) A description of the training of a competitive wrestler
(B) The results of a student poll on the situation
(C) An explanation of the civil rights issues involved in the situation
(D) A report on the results of an interview with Jodie McGillis
(E) A discussion of the ways in which other schools have dealt with similar situations

35. Which of the following changes to the underlined part of sentence 13 makes the transition from sentence 12 to sentence 13 more clear (reproduced below)?

It hardly seems fair to exclude a student from a school activity on the basis of gender.

(A) (as it is now)
(B) Because it hardly seems fair
(C) However, it hardly seems fair
(D) And, it hardly seems fair
(E) Hardly does it seem fair

STOP

If you finish before time is called, you may check your work on this section only.
Do not turn to any other section in the test.

NO TEST MATERIAL ON THIS PAGE.

SECTION 7
Time — 25 minutes
24 Questions

Turn to Section 7 of your answer sheet to answer the questions in this section.

Directions: For each question in this section, select the best answer from among the choices given and fill in the corresponding circle on the answer sheet.

Each sentence below has one or two blanks, each blank indicating that something has been omitted. Beneath the sentence are five words or sets of words labeled A through E. Choose the word or set of words that, when inserted in the sentence, best fits the meaning of the sentence as a whole.

Example:

Desiring to ------- his taunting friends, Mitch gave them taffy in hopes it would keep their mouths shut.

(A) eliminate   (B) satisfy   (C) overcome
  (D) ridicule   (E) silence

Ⓐ Ⓑ Ⓒ Ⓓ ●

---

1. Clint Eastwood is considered a _____ filmmaker; his body of work stretches over four decades and covers numerous genres.

   (A) gifted
   (B) visionary
   (C) natural
   (D) prolific
   (E) limited

2. Rachel Carson's *Silent Spring*, which graphically exposed the ------- of the indiscriminate use of pesticides, is widely credited with having ------- the modern environmental movement.

   (A) advantages . . inaugurated
   (B) hazards . . defused
   (C) benefits . . inspired
   (D) deaths . . contained
   (E) dangers . . launched

3. Anoxemia, a condition in which the normally highly oxygenated blood cells undergo an abnormal reduction in oxygen content, has so few ------- symptoms that the disease is often -------.

   (A) recognizable . . undiagnosed
   (B) irreversible . . prolonged
   (C) remarkable . . revealed
   (D) distinguishable . . fatal
   (E) treatable . . concealed

4. The process of maturing is defined by psychologists as a person's growth away from insecurity and dependency toward self-assurance and -------.

   (A) callowness   (B) ascendancy   (C) obstinacy
     (D) despotism   (E) autonomy

5. The advertising agency was known for its skilled use of ------- in the commercials it produced; these emotional appeals were particularly successful for political candidates.

   (A) jargon   (B) pathos   (C) stoicism
     (D) bombast   (E) acrimony

GO ON TO THE NEXT PAGE

Directions: Each passage below is followed by questions based on its content. Answer the questions on the basis of what is <u>stated</u> or <u>implied</u> in each passage and in any introductory material that may be provided.

Questions 6-9 are based on the following passages.

Passage 1

But there is something I must say to my people: In the process of gaining our rightful place we must not be guilty of wrongful deeds. Let us not satisfy our thirst for freedom
Line by drinking from the cup of bitterness and hatred. We must
5 forever conduct our struggle on the high plane of dignity and discipline. We must not allow our creative protest to degenerate into physical violence. Again and again we must rise to the majestic heights of meeting physical force with soul force.

Passage 2

10 I cite these various revolutions, brothers and sisters, to show you that you don't have a peaceful revolution. There's no such thing as a nonviolent revolution: revolution is bloody, revolution is hostile, revolution knows no compromise, revolution overturns and destroys everything that gets in its
15 way. In a revolution, you don't do any singing, you're too busy swinging. A revolutionary wants land so he can set up his own nation, an independent nation.

6. The conflict between the views in Passage 1 and Passage 2 can best be described as

(A) dignity versus iniquity
(B) derision versus hatred
(C) populism versus individualism
(D) racial equality versus racial superiority
(E) pacifism versus militancy

7. Which of the following would the author of Passage 1 most likely mention in order to weaken the author of Passage 2's assertion that nonviolent revolution doesn't exist (line 12) ?

(A) Both men share a common enemy.
(B) Gandhi led a successful and nonviolent revolution.
(C) Revolution is not the best way to progress as a nation.
(D) There is no more room to expand the country's borders.
(E) Violence can lead only to more violence.

8. The author of Passage 1 refers to "wrongful deeds" (line 3) in order to

(A) dissuade his followers from acting violently
(B) condone violence as a solution to the problem
(C) point out that all people have committed wrongful acts
(D) blame his enemies for all of society's wrongs
(E) underscore his disagreements with his enemies

9. On which of the following points would the authors of both passages most likely agree?

(A) The actions of the other are incompatible with the movement's goals.
(B) There is a need for social change.
(C) History records only the words of the winner.
(D) It is better to shed another's blood than one's own.
(E) Change is impossible without unity in a movement.

GO ON TO THE NEXT PAGE

Questions 10-18 are based on the following passage

The following excerpt from the memoir of a Japanese-American journalist and short fiction writer is set in 1920s California.

For some reason, part of the first grade was spent in another school, and I remember the last day there. In the excitement we rush pell-mell through the long closet to grab
Line our sweaters and lunchpails on the way out. In the mad
5 scramble, my hip collides sharply with the corner of a stored desk. The pain makes me stop and cry. The summoned teacher is moved to pick me up and carry me back into the classroom. She sits down in one of the children's seats, cradles me on her lap and cuddles me. "Ah," she explains to the
10 children who are gathering around us in curiosity. "The poor dear, she's crying because it's the last day of school!" Her own inner bruise transferred to me, she rocks me tenderly. She gives me a picture book to take home for my very own, such sweet consolation.
15 It was not outright fraud, you know. I do not think my English at six was flexible enough to go into the details of the situation. But there is more than one lesson connected with that incident. The value of dissembling? The value of silence? The realization that there were some teachers who
20 truly loved teaching, for whom the prospect of school vacation was a desolation? Or maybe only the side benefits of being wounded.

It was at this same school that I spent the longest day of my whole life. I think it was Memorial Day and the bus
25 must have come to pick us up in the morning because I don't know how else I would have gotten to school. The project was for the whole student body to walk over to the ocean with flowers, in order to pay tribute to those who had died at sea. I straggled along with the others all right and got to the pier,
30 from where we threw our posies to float on the water. But somehow, as I made my way back to school, everyone else seemed to drop away, one by one, and I arrived back at achool all by myself. And the school building was locked.

It gradually came to me that there was to be no school
35 that day, that there would be no bus coming to take me home, that I was marooned with no help in sight. I must not have understood the entire announcement the previous day. So I remained there the rest of the afternoon, maybe changing my seat occasionally from one side of the cement stairs to the
40 other, maybe playing hopscotch on the sidewalk from time to time, maybe going up to the school entrance and peering in. I don't recall anyone passing by. But eventually my father came in the car, looking for me, and I was rescued at last.

It was in the cafeteria of this same school that I saw an
45 older dark-haired girl praying before and after she ate, making some odd gestures in front of her face, then holding her hands together, then making the same gestures again. Because of this ritual, she even seemed to eat reverently, and out of the corner of my eye I watched her slow mastication with
50 great admiration, stowing any questions about her irregular behavior in that pigeonhole in the back of my mind.

I think it was about the third grade, back at South School, that I first encountered the joy of being read to. *Dr. Doolittle* and *The Wizard of Oz* burst into my consciousness in this
55 way, and even now I can't distinguish between the excitement of hearing these stories read aloud and the sheer rapture of anticipating the next chapter.

Meanwhile, I was also learning other things from the anger of my teachers. Once, during an art session, I was
60 distracted by some old mucilage that had been left to dry on my desk by a previous occupant. I tried to remove the dried flakes of paste, ever so gingerly lifting at them with the tip of my scissors. Engrossed in this delicate task, I suddenly became aware that the teacher was standing right over me.
65 There was fire in her eye. In front of the class I was held up as an example of the worst kind of vandal, a destroyer of school property, and made to sit alone off to one corner of the room. I still did not trust my English enough to explain the reason for my seeming criminality. But i did not weep,
70 however. I clowned, making faces for the enjoyment of my classmates when they looked toward the seat of my disgrace. After awhile, the teacher reluctantly allowed me to resume my regular seat. I sensed that she did not think I was taking my punishment seriously. But deep down, I was thoroughly
75 humiliated and never attempted to clean school property again.

10. As used in the passage, "pell-mell" (line 3) most nearly means

   (A) simple and childish
   (B) dangerous and reckless
   (C) careless and hurried
   (D) angry and loud
   (E) fearful and diffident

GO ON TO THE NEXT PAGE

11. The author most likely uses the phrase "inner bruise" (line 12) to indicate the teacher's

(A) cruel need to hurt others
(B) precarious emotional state
(C) discomfort with crying children
(D) fragile physical health
(E) individual psychological pain

12. It can be inferred that the author asserts "It was not outright fraud" (line 15) because she

(A) worries about being seen as a liar
(B) wants to explore the consequences of her action
(C) is confused by the definition of "dissembling"
(D) did not speak enough English to explain her injury
(E) feels lastingly humiliated by the memory of the incident

13. What is the primary reason that the author uses the description "the longest day of my whole life" (lines 23-24) ?

(A) Her family abandoned her.
(B) She was tired out by her long walk.
(C) She was frightened and alone due to a misheard announcement.
(D) It was the first time she realized how many had lost their lives at sea.
(E) She was excited because she did not have to attend class and could play games instead.

14. The "older dark-haired girl" (line 45) had an impact on the author because she

(A) suggested the richness of cultural diversity
(B) inspired her religious zeal
(C) taught her proper table manners and etiquette
(D) was a role model in all ways
(E) repelled the author with her incongruity

15. The author's attitude toward reading can best be described as

(A) ambivalent, due to her incomplete mastery of English
(B) suspicious, because she did not trust her teachers to clearly explain assignments
(C) hostile, because she preferred to be seen as a clown
(D) positive, because she loved thinking about what plot twists would occur
(E) affirmative, due to her enjoyment in learning about other cultures

16. The primary purpose of the passage is to

(A) argue that children should be encouraged to clean school property and respect their environments
(B) illustrate the difficulties bilingual children encounter while attending school
(C) demonstrate a child's increasing awareness of others
(D) present a series of significant childhood impressions
(E) explain her academic bent

17. The author uses phrases such as "for some reason" (line 1) and "I don't . . . to school" (lines 25-26) to emphasize

(A) her confusion at school due to her poor English
(B) that these events are far past and she does not remember them clearly
(C) that a child's memory tends to be made up of falsifications and outright lies
(D) that she paid little attention to school events
(E) that the impression of the events, rather than their specific details, is what is important

18. Which of the following statements about her childhood teachers would the author most likely agree with?

(A) Her teachers tended to be authoritarian and dismissive of her efforts to help.
(B) She found all of her teachers to be caring.
(C) One of her childhood discoveries was that teachers, too, had varying motives for their actions.
(D) The pathos of her school years resulted from an inability to understand her teachers.
(E) Only because of her teachers was she able to become the success that she is today.

GO ON TO THE NEXT PAGE

Questions 19-24 are based on the following passages.

The following excerpt was taken from a 1995 book of essays which includes current scientific observations.

Whether in life or after death, Vincent van Gogh has never been a painter of moderation. He painted ferociously, drank great quantities of the potent liqueur absinthe, went
Line for days without eating, slashed off his left earlobe, and
5 committed suicide at the age of thirty-seven. And since his suicide, in 1890, the great post-impressionist has been the subject of no fewer than 152 posthumous medical diagnoses. Doctors poring over van Gogh's paintings and his extensive correspondence have preposterously claimed that he suffered
10 temporal lobe epilepsy, a brain tumor, glaucoma, cataracts, manic depression, schizophrenia, magnesium deficiency, and poisoning by digitalis—which once was given as a treatment for epilepsy and can cause yellow vision —thus explaining, the story goes, van Gogh's penchant for brilliant yellows.
15 The latest entries in the Van Gogh malaise-of-the-month club are part of a continuing exercise that certain aesthetically minded doctors engage in, either for cerebral sport or for a better understanding of the natural history of diseases. The game is called "Diagnosing the Canvas." In one approach,
20 physicians attempt to identify an artist's illness or to chart its progression by considering suggestive details in the artist's work, like color choice, perspective, and subject matter. That sort of analysis has yielded the proposal that Claude Monet's near-blinding cataracts and eventual eye surgery deeply
25 influenced the evolution of his water lily series.
In the second version of the pastime, doctors study abnormal or deformed subjects portrayed in works of art and attempt to explain a figure's anomalous appearance by making a medical diagnosis. Noting the distinctively gnarled
30 hand of the woman shown in Corot's painting "Girl with Mandolin," two physicians and an art student have suggested that the musician had rheumatoid arthritis, a crippling autoimmune condition relatively common among young women.
35 Most art-loving doctors say they engage in diagnosing canvases less for scientific reasons than because it is an irresistible diversion. They feel a kinship with artists, since a good diagnostician, like a good painter, observes the tiny, revealing details that ordinary eyes usually miss. So when
40 doctors see artists paying attention to the same clues in their paintings, they can't help regarding the canvas as a patient, silently awaiting their professional opinion.
For all the pleasure it affords, however, the temptation to pin a syndrome to an artist the doctor has never met, or to
45 diagnose a painted figure unable to so much as say where it hurts, has led to outlandish notions about art and artists. In 1913, Parisian doctors suggested that El Greco* painted his elongated figures because he may have had astigmatism, a vision problem in which the eyeball is shaped more like a
50 football than a sphere. In some types of astigmatism that have been corrected with glasses, objects may appear slightly elongated in one direction and squashed in the other.

But as ophthalmologists and others have repeatedly argued in the intervening years, the theory about El Greco
55 is nonsense. To begin with, an astigmatic whose vision is not corrected with glasses doesn't see objects as elongated, but merely as blurs, and there were no corrective lenses for astigmatism in El Greco's day. In any case, X-ray images taken of El Greco's painting show that beneath the painted
60 figures are drawings of a more naturalistic composition, indicating that the artist consciously chose to stretch out his images when he applied paint, very likely to lend them an ethereal quality.

* A Spanish painter who lived from 1541 to 1614.

19. As used in line 8, "poring over " most nearly means

(A) imagining
(B) contrasting
(C) redressing
(D) critiquing
(E) scrutinizing

20. The passage suggests that some believe that "van Gogh's penchant for brilliant yellows " (line 14) was caused by

(A) magnesium deficiency
(B) cataracts
(C) large quantities of absinthe
(D) digitalis
(E) epilepsy

21. The phrase "malaise-of-the-month club" (lines 15-16) conveys the

(A) author's irritation with the number of outlandish theories about Van Gogh put forth by modern doctors
(B) extensive research done by the author chronicling each theory of Van Gogh 's medical condition
(C) author's admiration for the skill that doctors seem to have for diagnosing disease from artwork
(D) purely frivolous nature of the "game" doctors play when evaluating a canvas for clues to an artist's health
(E) author's attempt to add humor to an otherwise disturbing account of physical and mental illness

GO ON TO THE NEXT PAGE ⟶

22. Which example most accurately illustrates what is being described in lines 26-29 ?

(A) A doctor recommends that a contemporary painter be examined for an eye disease which may be disrupting her field of vision.

(B) Observing the bulging eye on a Mayan sculpture, a doctor suggests that the subject had a tumorous eye cancer.

(C) Using existing photos, scientists hypothesize that Abraham Lincoln had Marfan's syndrome, a disease resulting in excessively elongated bones.

(D) A psychiatrist theorizes that the painter Chagall may have been unable to distinguish dreams from reality.

(E) From a study of Picasso's paintings, a sociologist suggests that Picasso distorted the features of his models as a statement about women in society.

23. The author believes that the doctors mentioned in lines 34-36 ("Most art-loving...diversion.")

(A) regard artworks as patients awaiting diagnosis

(B) feel that diagnosing artwork is the only way they can understand it

(C) feel a connection to the art, not the artist

(D) view artists as amateur physicians

(E) view themselves as modern-day artists

24. In the discussion of El Greco, the author implies which of the following?

(A) Corrective lenses for astigmatism were in existence in Paris in 1913.

(B) Astigmatism was not yet discovered in El Greco's day.

(C) El Greco's elongated figures are visible only on X-ray images of his paintings.

(D) An astigmatic with uncorrected vision sees objects as squashed.

(E) Parisian doctors in El Greco's day misunderstood the painter's ailment.

S T O P
If you finish before time is called, you may check your work on this section only.
Do not turn to any other section in the test.

SECTION 8
Time — 20 minutes
16 Questions

Turn to Section 8 of your answer sheet to answer the questions in this section.

Directions: For this section, solve each problem and decide which is the best of the choices given. Fill in the corresponding circle on the answer sheet. You may use any available space for scratchwork.

Notes

1. The use of a calculator is permitted.

2. All numbers used are real numbers.

3. Figures that accompany problems in this test are intended to provide information useful in solving the problems. They are drawn as accurately as possible EXCEPT when it is stated in a specific problem that the figure is not drawn to scale. All figures lie in a plane unless otherwise indicated.

4. Unless otherwise specified, the domain of any function f is assumed to be the set of all real numbers x for which $f(x)$ is a real number.

Reference Information

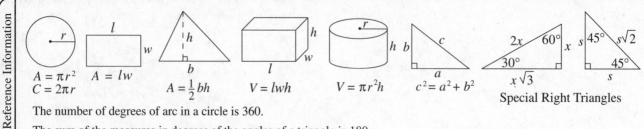

$A = \pi r^2$
$C = 2\pi r$

$A = lw$

$A = \frac{1}{2}bh$

$V = lwh$

$V = \pi r^2 h$

$c^2 = a^2 + b^2$

Special Right Triangles

The number of degrees of arc in a circle is 360.

The sum of the measures in degrees of the angles of a triangle is 180.

1. In a certain game, words earn points based on the letters in each word. The letters a, s, and k are each worth 8 points, and all other letters are worth 2 points each. How many points would the word "sandblaster" earn in this game?

(A) 10
(B) 22
(C) 28
(D) 38
(E) 46

2. If $p > 0$, then $p^3 \left(\dfrac{1}{p} - \dfrac{1}{p} \right) =$

(A) 0
(B) 1
(C) p
(D) p^2
(E) p^3

GO ON TO THE NEXT PAGE

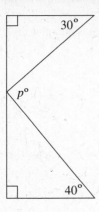

Note: Figure not drawn to scale.

3. In the figure above, what is the value of *p* ?

(A) 20
(B) 35
(C) 60
(D) 70
(E) 90

4. David has 4 less than one-half the number of balloons that Katie has. If David has *d* balloons, and Katie has *k* balloons, which of the following equations correctly expresses the relationship between *d* and *k* ?

(A) $d = \frac{1}{2}(k+4)$

(B) $d = \frac{1}{2}(k-4)$

(C) $d = \frac{1}{2}k + 4$

(D) $d = \frac{1}{2}k - 4$

(E) $d = 2(k-4)$

5. The charge for the first quarter-mile of a taxi ride is $1.40, and the charge for each additional quarter-mile is $0.20. If the total charge for a certain taxi ride is $5.00, what is the length of this ride, in miles?

(A) $4\frac{1}{2}$

(B) $4\frac{3}{4}$

(C) $5\frac{1}{2}$

(D) 19

(E) 25

6. If *a* is 4 greater than *b* and $a^2 + b^2 = 10$, what is the value of *ab* ?

(A) 13
(B) 6
(C) 3
(D) −3
(E) −6

GO ON TO THE NEXT PAGE

7. If lines $\overline{BC}$ and $\overline{BD}$ are each perpendicular to line $\overline{AB}$, which of the following must be true?

   (A) $\overline{AB} \perp \overline{CD}$
   (B) $\overline{AB} \perp \overline{AC}$
   (C) $\overline{AC} \perp \overline{AD}$
   (D) $\overline{AB} \parallel \overline{CD}$
   (E) $\overline{BC} \perp \overline{BD}$

8. The total monthly cost, c to send x text messages is given by the function $C(x) = 0.05x - 2.5$ for all $x \geq 51$. If Hannah received a bill for \$10.50 for sending text messages last month, how many text messages did she send?

   (A) 60
   (B) 125
   (C) 160
   (D) 225
   (E) 260

9. If $\dfrac{(a+b)}{(a-b)} = \dfrac{3}{7}$, what is the value of $\dfrac{a}{b}$?

   (A) $-\dfrac{5}{2}$

   (B) -1

   (C) $-\dfrac{2}{5}$

   (D) $\dfrac{2}{5}$

   (E) $\dfrac{5}{2}$

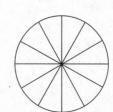

10. In the circle above, if some of the sectors are colored yellow and the rest are colored blue, which of the following cannot be the ratio of yellow sectors to blue sectors?

    (A) 1 : 11
    (B) 1 : 5
    (C) 1 : 4
    (D) 1 : 3
    (E) 1 : 2

GO ON TO THE NEXT PAGE

11. If $a = b^{-2}$ and $b = m^{\frac{1}{2}}$, what is a in terms of m ?

(A) $\dfrac{1}{m}$

(B) $\sqrt{\dfrac{1}{m}}$

(C) m^2

(D) $\sqrt{m}$

(E) $-m$

12. If $f(x) = 4x - 8$ and $g(x) = 3x^2 + 7$, then $f(g(3)) =$

(A) 26
(B) 55
(C) 95
(D) 128
(E) 344

13. A fire fighter with a 52-foot ladder approaches a burning building, which rests on level ground. If the top of the ladder must be at least 48 feet above ground level, what is the maximum possible distance, in feet, from the exact <u>middle</u> of the ladder to the wall of the building?

(A) 0
(B) 5
(C) 10
(D) 15
(E) 20

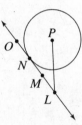

Note: Figure not drawn to scale.

14. P is the center of the above circle, and points L, M, N, and O are all equally spaced along $\overline{LO}$, which is tangent to the circle at point N. If $MN = 4$ and $LP = \dfrac{5}{6}LO$, what is the area of the circle?

(A) 16π
(B) 25π
(C) 36π
(D) 64π
(E) It cannot be determined from the information provided.

GO ON TO THE NEXT PAGE

15. Which of the following graphs represents the equation $|y| = |x|$?

(A)

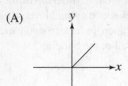

(B)

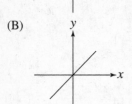

(C)

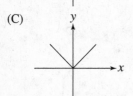

(D)

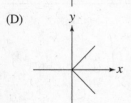

(E)

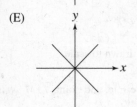

16. If the variables a, b, c, d, and e have distinct values and are listed in order from least to greatest, which of the following could be true?

    I. b is the arithmetic mean
   II. e is one of the modes
  III. d is the median

(A) I only
(B) II only
(C) I and II
(D) I and III
(E) I, II, and III

STOP
If you finish before time is called, you may check your work on this section only.
Do not turn to any other section in the test.

NO TEST MATERIAL ON THIS PAGE.

SECTION 9
Time — 20 minutes
19 Questions

Turn to Section 9 of your answer sheet to answer the questions in this section.

Directions: For each question in this section, select the best answer from among the choices given and fill in the corresponding circle on the answer sheet.

Each sentence below has one or two blanks, each blank indicating that something has been omitted. Beneath the sentence are five words or sets of words labeled A through E. Choose the word or set of words that, when inserted in the sentence, best fits the meaning of the sentence as a whole.

Example:

Desiring to ------- his taunting friends, Mitch gave them taffy in hopes it would keep their mouths shut.

(A) eliminate   (B) satisfy   (C) overcome
    (D) ridicule   (E) silence

Ⓐ Ⓑ Ⓒ Ⓓ ●

1. Many young musicians who are praised for their mastery of difficult pieces often play -------, with little understanding of the emotional content of the music they perform.

   (A) begrudgingly   (B) tirelessly   (C) mechanically
       (D) opportunistically   (E) impeccably

2. Although the colonists resented British rule, they ------- it as long as England did not ------- it too strenuously.

   (A) rejected . . define
   (B) amended . . follow
   (C) tolerated . . enforce
   (D) defied . . interpret
   (E) welcomed . . violate

3. Judith Rich Harris' ------- theory that parents play only a minor role in their children's social development is one of the most controversial in modern psychology; many scholars remain ------- her findings.

   (A) learned . . fearful of
   (B) atypical . . intimidated by
   (C) idiosyncratic . . supportive of
   (D) provocative . . skeptical of
   (E) infamous . . confused by

4. Because the author's unflattering references to her friends were so -------, she was surprised that her ------- were recognized.

   (A) congratulatory . . styles
   (B) obvious . . anecdotes
   (C) oblique . . allusions
   (D) critical . . eulogies
   (E) apparent . . motives

5. The Inquisition branded Galileo's works as ------- since they went against the teachings of medieval religious institutions.

   (A) dogmatic   (B) credible   (C) heretical
       (D) esoteric   (E) ideological

6. Accustomed to the desert conditions of Arizona, Anna did not expect to be so ------- after a day of sightseeing under the Egyptian sun.

   (A) sonorous   (B) enervated   (C) abashed
       (D) venerated   (E) placated

GO ON TO THE NEXT PAGE

Directions: Each passage below is followed by questions based on its content. Answer the questions on the basis of what is <u>stated</u> or <u>implied</u> in each passage and in any introductory material that may be provided.

Questions 7-19 are based on the following passage.

In 63 B.C., after losing an election for the Roman senate, the politician Catiline attempted, with the help of a band of co-conspirators, to take the office by force. When Cicero, the great Roman orator and philosopher who had defeated Catiline in election, heard of this plot, he arrested and put to death five of the conspirators. Catiline, however, had already fled. He escaped execution, but died in battle in Pistoia a month later. The first of the following passages is a speech by Catiline to his conspirators. The second is a speech against Catiline by Cicero to the Roman senate.

Passage 1

As I have, on many remarkable occasions, experienced your bravery and attachment to me, I have ventured to engage in a most important and glorious enterprise. I am aware, too,
Line that whatever advantages or evils affect you, the same affect
5 me; and to have the same desires and the same aversions is assuredly a firm bond of friendship.

What I have been meditating you have already heard separately. But my ardor for action is daily more and more excited when I consider what our future condition of life must
10 be unless we ourselves assert our claims to liberty. For since the government has fallen under the power and jurisdiction of a few, kings and princes have constantly been their tributaries; nations and states have paid them taxes; but all the rest of us have been regarded as a mere mob, without interest or
15 authority. Hence all influence, power, honor, and wealth, are in their hands, or where they dispose of them; to us they have left only insults, dangers, persecutions, and poverty. To such indignities, O bravest of men, how long will you submit?

But success (I call gods and men to witness!) is in our own
20 hands. Our years are fresh, our spirit is unbroken; among our oppressors, on the contrary, through age and wealth a general debility has been produced. We have, therefore, only to make a beginning; the course of events will accomplish the rest.

Will you not, then, awake to action? Behold that liberty,
25 that liberty for which you have so often wished, with wealth, honor, and glory, are set before your eyes. Let the enterprise itself, then, let the opportunity, let your property, your dangers, and the glorious spoils of war, animate you far more than my words. Use me either as your leader or your fellow
30 soldier; neither my heart nor my hand shall be wanting to you. These objects I hope to effect, in concert with you, in the character of consul*; unless, indeed, my expectation deceives me, and you prefer to be slaves rather than masters.

Passage 2

When, O Catiline, do you mean to cease abusing our
35 patience? Do not the mighty guards placed on Palatine Hill— does not the alarm of the people, and the union of all good men—does not the precaution taken of assembling the senate in this most defensible place—do not the looks and countenances of this venerable body here present, have
40 any effect upon you? Do you not see that your conspiracy is already arrested and rendered powerless by the knowledge which everyone here possesses of it?

Shame on the age and on its principles! The senate is aware of these things; the consul sees them; and yet this man
45 lives. Lives! aye, he comes even into the senate. He takes a part in the public deliberations; he is watching and marking down and checking off for slaughter every individual among us. And we, gallant men that we are, think that we are doing our duty to the republic if we keep out of the way of his
50 frenzied attacks.

You ought, O Catiline, long ago to have been led to execution by command of the consul. You are summoning to destruction and devastation the temples of the immortal gods, the houses of the city, the lives of all the citizens; in
55 short, all Italy. Wherefore, since I do not yet venture to do that which is the best thing, and which belongs to my office and to the discipline of our ancestors, I will do that which is more merciful if we regard its rigor, and more expedient for the state. For if I order you to be put to death, the rest of
60 the conspirators will still remain in the republic; if, as I have long been exhorting you, you depart, your companions, these worthless dregs of the republic, will be drawn off from the city too. Do you ask me, Are you to go into banishment? I do not order it; but if you consult me, I advise it.

65 For what is there, O Catiline, that can now afford you any pleasure in this city? For there is no one in it, except that band of profligate conspirators of yours, who does not fear you—no one who does not hate you. What brand of domestic baseness is not stamped upon your life? Is there one youth,
70 when you have once entangled him in the temptations of your corruption, to whom you have not held out a sword for audacious crime, or a torch for licentious wickedness?

Since, then, this is the case, do you hesitate, O Catiline, if you cannot remain here with tranquility, to depart to some
75 distant land? Make a motion, say you, to the senate (for that is what you demand), and if this body votes that you ought to go into banishment, you say that you will obey. I will not make such a motion, it is contrary to my principles, and yet I will let you see what these men think of you. Do you not perceive, do
80 you not see the silence of these men? They permit it, they say nothing; why wait you for the authority of their words, when you see their wishes in their silence?

* one of the chief magistrates of the Roman Republic

GO ON TO THE NEXT PAGE

7. Which of the following best describes the contrast between the portrayal of Catiline in Passage 1 and that in Passage 2 ?

   (A) Passage 1 portrays him as a leader of men, while Passage 2 claims that even his co-conspirators do not subscribe to his beliefs.
   (B) Passage 1 portrays him as a proponent of peaceful change, while Passage 2 portrays him as warlike.
   (C) Passage 1 portrays him as a threat to society, while Passage 2 portrays him as a crusader for the oppressed.
   (D) Passage 1 portrays him as a liberator, while Passage 2 portrays him as corrupt and dangerous.
   (E) Passage 1 portrays him as selfless, while Passage 2 portrays him as one eager to rule.

8. In Passage 1, the speaker's observation that "whatever . . . affect me," (lines 4-5) is intended to support his belief that

   (A) individuals are more alike than different
   (B) people's feelings are determined by their environment
   (C) common aspirations encourage friendship
   (D) courage is often rewarded with loyalty
   (E) human desires and aversions are universal

9. Catiline's question, "O bravest . . . submit?" (line 18) is most likely intended to

   (A) determine how dedicated his listeners are to the rebellion
   (B) diminish the aggressiveness and pride of his audience
   (C) inspire his listeners to take action against their oppressors
   (D) cast doubt on the bravery of his own countrymen
   (E) encourage his audience to consider an opposing view

10. The speaker in Passage 1 advances which of the following as a reason for his belief that the rebellion he urges will succeed?

   (A) The gods are on the side of the rebellion.
   (B) The people in power have no honor or courage.
   (C) Age and prosperity have weakened those who govern.
   (D) A cause that is just must always prevail.
   (E) The government has fallen under the power of kings.

11. In line 28, the word "animate" most nearly means

   (A) illustrate
   (B) motivate
   (C) enliven
   (D) direct
   (E) elevate

12. Which of the following, if true, would most seriously undermine the speaker in Passage 1's claim of assured success?

   (A) Inherent in youth is arrogant strength that will serve to conquer their oppressors.
   (B) In order to overcome the enemy, agility, and fortitude are necessary.
   (C) Power, honor, and wealth can serve to weaken defenses.
   (D) Youth and determination are necessary to, but not guarantors of, success.
   (E) Older and affluent forces always have the experience and resources necessary to triumph.

13. What is the speaker of Passage 2 referring to when he talks about the "countenances of this venerable body" (line 39) ?

   (A) The powers possessed by Cicero
   (B) The intelligence of the speaker
   (C) The expressions of the senators
   (D) The conspiracy of Cataline and his followers
   (E) The size of the opposition

14. The measures listed by the orator of Passage 2 in lines 35-42 serve to

   (A) suggest that rebellion is impossible in an armed society
   (B) demonstrate that the city has opposed itself to Cataline's conspiracy
   (C) exploit Cataline's growing sense of isolation
   (D) alert the people of the city to Cataline's subversive actions
   (E) appeal to Cataline's remaining national pride

GO ON TO THE NEXT PAGE

15. It can be inferred from the passage that the orator in Passage 2 chooses not to call for Catiline's execution because

  (A) the execution of criminals and rebels is against his morals

  (B) the senators have concluded that banishment is more prudent than execution

  (C) he fears that Catiline's death could anger the senate

  (D) he believes that an alternative punishment is more beneficial to the state

  (E) the large number of Catiline's followers makes his execution dangerous

16. In line 65, "afford" most nearly means

  (A) encourage

  (B) purchase

  (C) spare

  (D) promote

  (E) provide

17. According to the orator in Passage 2, the "silence" (line 80) of the senators indicates which of the following?

  (A) Their hostility toward Catiline

  (B) Their unwillingness to execute Catiline

  (C) Their inability to reach consensus

  (D) Their concern with morality

  (E) Their disagreement with the orator

18. The orator in Passage 1 would most likely respond to the accusation in Passage 2 that "You are summoning . . . all Italy" (lines 52-55) by

  (A) indicating that, as slaves, his people were unable to cause true change

  (B) claiming that his goal was justice through nonviolent revolution

  (C) insisting on the right of citizens to arm themselves against oppressive rulers

  (D) demonstrating that the subjugation of his people would inevitably lead to such drastic action

  (E) swearing that his true allegiance lay with those having power, honor, and wealth

19. Which of the following best describes the society suggested by BOTH of the speeches?

  (A) An uneasy society contemplating its current political situation

  (B) An enlightened democracy in which crime and dissent are rare

  (C) A polarized society divided along economic lines

  (D) A tyrannical society in which the expression of opinions is forbidden

  (E) A society on the verge of sweeping political change

STOP

If you finish before time is called, you may check your work on this section only.
Do not turn to any other section in the test.

SECTION 10
Time — 10 minutes
14 Questions

Turn to Section 10 of your answer sheet to answer the questions in this section.

Directions: For each question in this section, select the best answer from among the choices given and fill in the corresponding circle on the answer sheet.

The following sentences test correctness and effectiveness of expression. Part of each sentence or the entire sentence is underlined; beneath each sentence are five ways of phrasing the underlined material. Choice A repeats the original phrasing; the other four choices are different. If you think the original phrasing produces a better sentence than any of the alternatives, select choice A; if not, select one of the other choices.

In making your selection, follow the requirements of standard written English; that is, pay attention to grammar, choice of words, sentence construction, and punctuation. Your selection should result in the most effective sentence—clear and precise, without awkwardness or ambiguity.

EXAMPLE:

Bobby Flay baked his first cake <u>and he was thirteen years old then</u>.

(A) and he was thirteen years old then
(B) when he was thirteen
(C) at age thirteen years old
(D) upon the reaching of thirteen years
(E) at the time when he was thirteen

Ⓐ●ⒸⒹⒺ

1. One of the best-selling books of all time, <u>Margaret Mitchell wrote *Gone With the Wind*</u>.

   (A) Margaret Mitchell wrote *Gone With the Wind*
   (B) Margaret Mitchell was the writer of *Gone With the Wind*
   (C) the writer of *Gone With the Wind* was Margaret Mitchell
   (D) *Gone With the Wind,* was written by Margaret Mitchell
   (E) Margaret Mitchell's *Gone With the Wind* was written

2. New buildings in earthquake-prone areas must be heavily reinforced <u>or else they may otherwise collapse in a strong quake</u>.

   (A) or else they may otherwise collapse in a strong quake
   (B) or they may collapse in a strong quake
   (C) so as not to collapse in a strong quake
   (D) not to collapse in a strong quake
   (E) or else it may collapse in a strong quake

3. Fully one-third of registered voters, according to recent polls, <u>believes that character is the first</u> consideration in assessing the worth of a politician.

   (A) believes that character is the first
   (B) believes that character is first a
   (C) believes that character is at first
   (D) believe that character is at first
   (E) believe that character is the first

4. <u>Since 1945, when World War II ended</u>, the American family has become increasingly nuclearized.

   (A) Since 1945, when World War II ended
   (B) Since 1945, when there was an end to World War II
   (C) From 1945, the end of World War II
   (D) After 1945, when there was an ending to World War II
   (E) From 1945, which was the end of World War II

5. Cognitive science is a relatively new field <u>where aspects of several different</u> disciplines are brought together to help better understand the mind.

   (A) where aspects of several different
   (B) in which aspects of several different
   (C) whereby aspects of several different
   (D) and the reason is the several aspects of different
   (E) because in it several aspects of different

GO ON TO THE NEXT PAGE

6. The curator claimed that while few modern blacksmiths have made enough money to support themselves, <u>their success has been in preserving</u> an ancient art form.

(A) their success has been in preserving
(B) they have succeeded in preserving
(C) succeeding in preserving
(D) the success is with their preserving
(E) the preservation was a success of

7. <u>Jane took many of the same art classes in high school as Kate did, and she</u> has just announced her upcoming art exhibition.

(A) Jane took many of the same art classes in high school as Kate did, and she
(B) Taking many of the same art classes in high school were Jane and Kate, and they
(C) Jane took many of the same art classes in high school with Kate, and this is why she
(D) Jane, who took many of the same art classes in high school as Kate did,
(E) The taking of many of the same high school art classes with Kate, Jane

8. <u>Outside the window under the eaves is a nest full of swallows that recently hatched.</u>

(A) Outside the window under the eaves is a nest full of swallows that recently hatched.
(B) Outside the window under the eaves are a nest full of swallows that recently hatched.
(C) Outside the window under the eaves would be a nest full of swallows that are recently hatched.
(D) Outside the window under the eaves a nest full of swallows could be found recently hatching.
(E) Outside the window under the eaves you can see a nest full of swallows who recently hatched.

9. Many critics consider the prose of Baudelaire <u>equally intoxicating and his poetry is</u> beautiful.

(A) equally intoxicating and his poetry is
(B) equally intoxicating as his poetry
(C) as intoxicating as his poetry is
(D) as intoxicating and their poetry is
(E) as intoxicating as their poetry is

10. The violin is one of the oldest instruments still played <u>considering that it combines both beauty and a portable size</u>.

(A) considering that it combines both beauty and a portable size
(B) considering that it combines beauty and portability
(C) because it combines beauty and portability
(D) because it will combine not only beauty but also a portable size
(E) provided that it will combine both beauty and portability

11. Dieticians disagree about the best way to lose weight, but most <u>are in agreement that dieters must abstain from not eating</u> when they are no longer hungry.

(A) are in agreement that dieters must abstain from not eating
(B) are in agreement that they must abstain from not eating
(C) agree that dieters must abstain from not eating
(D) agree that dieters must abstain from eating
(E) agree that abstaining from eating

GO ON TO THE NEXT PAGE

12. Without taking detailed notes in class and studying diligently for the final exam, <u>a good grade cannot be expected to be received</u> in the course.

   (A) a good grade cannot be expected to be received
   (B) you cannot expect to receive a good grade
   (C) your good grade cannot be expected to be received
   (D) by not receiving a good grade
   (E) they will not give you a good grade

13. The reason Mr. Gomez's students are being honored in the assembly <u>is because their project won the science fair</u>.

   (A) is because their project won the science fair.
   (B) is that their project won the science fair.
   (C) is that the science fair project was won by them.
   (D) is that their project won the science fair for them.
   (E) is because the science fair was won by them with their project.

14. <u>When the cello is played by Yo-Yo Ma, an audience knows that they are</u> listening to one of the greatest concert virtuosos of our time.

   (A) When the cello is played by Yo-Yo Ma, an audience knows that they are
   (B) When the cello is played by Yo-Yo Ma, an audience knows that it is
   (C) When Yo-Yo Ma is playing the cello, an audience knows that they are
   (D) When Yo-Yo Ma plays the cello, an audience knows that it is
   (E) When Yo-Yo Ma plays the cello, an audience knows that they are

STOP

If you finish before time is called, you may check your work on this section only.
Do not turn to any other section in the test.

NO TEST MATERIAL ON THIS PAGE.

PRACTICE TEST 7: ANSWER KEY

3 Math	4 Reading	5 Math	6 Writing	7 Reading	8 Math	9 Reading	10 Writing
1. E	1. B	1. A	1. A	1. D	1. E	1. C	1. D
2. A	2. E	2. C	2. B	2. E	2. A	2. C	2. B
3. B	3. B	3. C	3. B	3. A	3. D	3. D	3. E
4. C	4. D	4. C	4. E	4. E	4. D	4. C	4. A
5. D	5. C	5. D	5. D	5. B	5. B	5. C	5. B
6. E	6. B	6. B	6. D	6. E	6. D	6. B	6. B
7. D	7. A	7. A	7. D	7. B	7. A	7. D	7. D
8. E	8. B	8. A	8. A	8. A	8. E	8. C	8. A
9. E	9. C	9. $\frac{3}{4}$ or .75	9. E	9. B	9. A	9. C	9. C
10. B	10. D	10. 81	10. C	10. C	10. C	10. C	10. C
11. B	11. D	11. $\frac{7}{12}$ or .583	11. C	11. E	11. A	11. B	11. D
12. A	12. A	12. 96	12. A	12. B	12. D	12. E	12. B
13. D	13. D	13. 21	13. D	13. C	13. C	13. C	13. B
14. C	14. B	14. $\frac{9}{4}$ or 2.25	14. E	14. A	14. C	14. B	14. D
15. B	15. E	15. 282	15. D	15. D	15. E	15. D	
16. A	16. B	16. 10	16. B	16. D	16. A	16. E	
17. D	17. B	17. 8	17. B	17. E		17. A	
18. D	18. D	18. 30	18. A	18. C		18. C	
19. C	19. A		19. B	19. E		19. A	
20. B	20. A		20. D	20. D			
	21. E		21. E	21. A			
	22. A		22. E	22. B			
	23. C		23. D	23. A			
	24. C		24. E	24. A			
			25. C				
			26. B				
			27. A				
			28. B				
			29. E				
			30. D				
			31. B				
			32. B				
			33. A				
			34. C				
			35. C				

SAT SCORING WORKSHEET

For directions on how to score your SAT practice test, see pages 10–11.

SAT Writing Section

Total Writing Multiple-Choice Questions Correct: ☐

−

Total Writing Multiple-Choice Questions Incorrect: _____ ÷ 4 = ☐

Grammar Raw Score: ☐

Grammar Scaled Subscore ☐

+

Compare the Grammar Raw Score with the Writing Multiple-Choice Subscore Conversion Table on page 582 to find the Grammar Scaled Subscore.

Your Essay Score (2–12): _____ × 2 = ☐

Writing Raw Score: ☐

Writing Scaled Score ☐

Compare Raw Score with SAT Score Conversion Table on page 582 to find the Writing Scaled Score.

SAT Critical Reading Section

Total Critical Reading Questions Correct: ☐

−

Total Critical Reading Questions Incorrect: _____ ÷ 4 = ☐

Critical Reading Raw Score: ☐

Critical Reading Scaled Score ☐

Compare Raw Score with SAT Score Conversion Table on page 582 to find the Critical Reading Scaled Score.

SAT Math Section

Total Math Grid-In Questions Correct: ☐

+

Total Math Multiple-Choice Questions Correct: ☐

−

Total Math Multiple-Choice Questions Incorrect: _____ ÷ 4 = ☐

Don't include wrong answers from grid-ins!

Math Raw Score: ☐

Math Scaled Score ☐

Compare Raw Score with SAT Score Conversion Table on page 582 to find the Math Scaled Score.

SAT SCORE CONVERSION TABLE

Raw Score	Writing Scaled Score	Reading Scaled Score	Math Scaled Score	Raw Score	Writing Scaled Score	Reading Scaled Score	Math Scaled Score	Raw Score	Writing Scaled Score	Reading Scaled Score	Math Scaled Score
73	800			47	590–630	600–640	660–700	21	400–440	410–450	440–480
72	790–800			46	590–630	590–630	650–690	20	390–430	400–440	430–470
71	780–800			45	580–620	580–620	650–690	19	380–420	400–440	430–470
70	770–800			44	570–610	580–620	640–680	18	370–410	390–430	420–460
69	770–800			43	570–610	570–610	630–670	17	370–410	380–420	410–450
68	760–800			42	560–600	570–610	620–660	16	360–400	370–410	400–440
67	760–800	800		41	560–600	560–600	610–650	15	350–390	360–400	400–440
66	760–800	770–800		40	550–590	550–590	600–640	14	340–380	350–390	390–430
65	750–790	760–800		39	540–580	550–590	590–630	13	330–370	340–380	380–420
64	740–780	750–790		38	530–570	540–580	590–630	12	320–360	340–380	360–400
63	730–770	740–780		37	530–570	530–570	580–620	11	320–360	330–370	350–390
62	720–760	730–770		36	520–560	530–570	570–610	10	310–350	320–360	340–380
61	710–750	720–760		35	510–550	520–560	560–600	9	300–340	310–350	330–370
60	700–740	710–750		34	500–540	520–560	560–600	8	290–330	300–340	320–360
59	690–730	700–740		33	490–530	510–550	550–590	7	280–320	300–340	310–350
58	680–720	690–730		32	480–520	500–540	540–580	6	270–310	290–330	300–340
57	680–720	680–720		31	470–510	490–530	530–570	5	260–300	280–320	290–330
56	670–710	670–710		30	470–510	480–520	520–560	4	240–280	270–310	280–320
55	660–720	670–710		29	460–500	470–510	520–560	3	230–270	250–290	280–320
54	650–690	660–700	760–800	28	450–490	470–510	510–550	2	230–270	240–280	270–310
53	640–680	650–690	740–780	27	440–480	460–500	500–540	1	220–260	220–260	260–300
52	630–670	640–680	730–770	26	430–470	450–490	490–530	0	210–250	200–240	250–290
51	630–670	630–670	710–750	25	420–460	440–480	480–520	–1	200–240	200–230	230–270
50	620–660	620–660	690–730	24	410–450	430–470	470–510	–2	200–230	200–220	220–260
49	610–650	610–650	680–720	23	410–450	430–470	460–500	–3	200–220	200–210	200–240
48	600–640	600–640	670–710	22	400–440	420–460	450–490				

WRITING MULTIPLE-CHOICE SUBSCORE CONVERSION TABLE

Grammar Raw Score	Grammar Scaled Subscore	Grammar Raw Score	Grammar Scaled Subscore	Grammar Raw Score	Grammar Scaled Subscore	Grammar Raw Score	Grammar Scaled Subscore	Grammar Raw Score	Grammar Scaled Subscore
49	78–80	38	67–71	27	55–59	16	42–46	5	30–34
48	77–80	37	66–70	26	54–58	15	41–45	4	29–33
47	75–79	36	65–69	25	53–57	14	40–44	3	28–32
46	74–78	35	64–68	24	52–56	13	39–43	2	27–31
45	72–76	34	63–67	23	51–55	12	38–42	1	25–29
44	72–76	33	62–66	22	50–54	11	36–40	0	24–28
43	71–75	32	61–65	21	49–53	10	35–39	–1	22–26
42	70–74	31	60–64	20	47–51	9	34–38	–2	20–23
41	69–73	30	59–63	19	46–50	8	33–37	–3	20–22
40	68–72	29	58–62	18	45–49	7	32–36		
39	68–72	28	56–60	17	44–48	6	31–35		

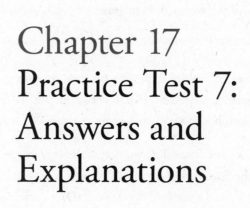

Chapter 17
Practice Test 7:
Answers and
Explanations

SECTION 3

1. **E** Jonas has run 4 out of 20 miles, or $\dfrac{4}{20}$ of the race. This fraction reduces to $\dfrac{1}{5}$, answer (E).

2. **A** Point A is in the quadrant where the x and y coordinates are positive. The x and y coordinates of point B must both be negative. Only (A) has a coordinate pair in which both x and y are negative.

3. **B** We can set up a proportion to solve this one: the question states that 3 kg of petals make 5 grams of perfume, and the ratio is the same for the greater number of grams of perfume. Solving for x will give the number of kilograms of petals needed for 870 grams of perfume: $\dfrac{3}{5} = \dfrac{x}{870}$, so $5x = 2{,}610$. Divide both sides by 5 to find that $x = 522$, answer (B).

4. **C** Since there are 6 muffins per box, 3 boxes give 18 muffins, which is not enough for 20 muffins. There is a little more than needed in the 4th box, but four boxes are necessary to make 20 muffins. Each box is $1.50, so 4 boxes costs $6.00, answer (C).

5. **D** The important information is the percentage of each flower, since we need to find the percent of the flowers that are roses. The non-roses total 36%, so the roses must make up 64%, the rest of the 100% of the whole flower bed. (D) is correct.

6. **E** We can find the third side of a triangle when two of the sides are known. The third side must be less than the sum of the two other sides. In this case, the third side must be less than $12 + 9 = 21$ and greater than $12 - 9 = 3$. This is an EXCEPT question, so we need the answer that is not possible. All of the answers are between 3 and 21 except (E) 2.

7. **D** A square with a perimeter of 16 cm has sides of 4 cm. The question states that 1 cm = 6 km, so each side of the square represents 24 km. The area is $24^2 = 576$ km^2, answer (D).

8. **E** The easiest way to solve this one is to test out the answer choices. It's good to start with the middle value in (C): If -5 is one number, the other negative number must be -10 to add to -15. The product of -5 and -10 is 50, which is not less than 40 as required by the question. We need a smaller number; If one number is -4 as in (D), the other number is -11 which results in a product of 44. So only (E) -3 works: -3 and -12 have a sum of -15 and a product of 36, which fits all the requirements of the question.

9. **E** To solve algebraically, translate the sentence into math: $\frac{x}{100} \times 3c = 9$. Solve for x: divide both sides by 100 so $x \times 3c = 900$. To get x alone, divide both sides by $3c$ to get $x = \frac{900}{3c}$ which reduces to $\frac{300}{c}$, answer (E). The other option is to come up with a number for c. We can pick a number that makes dealing with percents easier, such as 100. The question then becomes what percent of 30 is 9? This can be translated to $\frac{x}{100} \times 300 = 9$, which becomes $3x = 9$, and $x = 3$, giving the number that the correct answer will provide when c is replaced by 100 in the answer choices. (A) gives 1, (B) gives $\frac{10,000}{3}$, (C) gives $\frac{9}{100}$, (D) gives 3 as does (E). We can change the number for c and recheck (D) and (E). If $c = 10$, then $\frac{x}{100} \times 30 = 9$. This makes $30x = 900$, and $x = 30$. (D) is now incorrect while (E) gives 30.

10. **B** We need a graph that shows an increasingly lower pace the longer that Max exercises. Only (B) shows this relationship. In (A) Max gets faster after a while. In (C) his pace never changes. In (D) and (E) he gets faster with greater distance.

11. **B** The easiest way to solve this problem is to come up with a number for m that is greater than 4, so we can see what the difference is between the values for n. If $m = 8$, then $n = \frac{3(8)+2}{2} = 13$. Subtracting 4 from m gives $m = 4$. Now $n = \frac{3(4)+2}{2} = 7$. $13 - 7 = 6$, answer (B).

12. **A** The difference between the two equations given is in the amount added to x^2. This value determines the y-distance between the two parabolas. The equation $y = x^2$ forms a parabola in which the bottom curve touches the origin. The first equation is for a graph with the bottom of its curve at –2, or 2 below the origin, and the second equation is for one with the bottom of its curve at 7 above the origin. The parabola in the second equation is 9 units higher than the parabola in the second equation, as described in answer (A). If you can't remember the rules for how parabolas move, just Plug In points for x and y in each equation and sketch the parabolas to see the difference between them.

13. **D** Read the chart carefully. The 8-ounce loafs are the 140 lowest-weight loaves. Added together, the 16-ounce and 24-ounce loaves make up the 140 highest-weight loaves. The 12-ounce loaves make up the 20 loaves in the middle of the 300 total loaves, so the median must be 12, answer (D).

14. **C**   Come up with a number that can be divided by both 4 and 6, as indicated by the fractions in the question. If there are 12 pens in the box, then 3 of them are black since there is a probability of $\frac{1}{4}$ that the chosen pen is black. There must be 2 blue pens, since the probability of choosing one is $\frac{1}{6}$.

$12 - 3 - 2 = 7$, so there must be 7 red pens out of the 12, giving a probability of $\frac{7}{12}$ that a red pen would be chosen, answer (C).

15. **B**   Come up with some numbers for the sides of the triangles based on the ratios given in the question. If AD is 2, then DC is 3. The triangles are equilateral, so the perimeter of triangle AED is 6. The side of triangle ABC is 5, so the perimeter is 15. The perimeter of triangle AED is $\frac{6}{15}$, or $\frac{2}{5}$, that of triangle ABC.

16. **A**   List out the values for as many terms as you need to in order to discover the pattern: The first term is 8, the second is $(8 + 15)$ the third is $(8 + 30)$, the fourth is $(8 + 45)$, so the list would be 8, 23, 38, 53… All the odd-numbered terms end in 8, while all the even-numbered terms end in 3. The term we're looking for, the 50th, is an even-numbered term and must end in 3, so eliminate (B) and (D). Since three of the answers end with 3, we need to do some more work. We are continually adding 15 more to the first term of 8, and when we get to the 50th term we have added 15 to the number 49 times. $15 \times 49 = 735$, so the 50th term is $735 + 8 = 743$, answer (A).

17. **D**   We have a quadratic equation to factor here. $x^2 - y^2 = (x + y)(x - y) = 40$. We know from the question that $x - y = 10$, so $x + y = 4$. Beware of answer (C), it's a partial answer. To find the value of y, first add the two equations together:

$$\begin{array}{r} x + y = 4 \\ + \quad x - y = 10 \\ \hline 2x \quad\quad = 14 \end{array}$$

Now we know that $x = 7$, but beware of answer (B); we are looking the value of y. Since $x + y = 4$, $7 + y = 4$ and $y = -3$, answer (D). You could also try out the different values in the answer choices to replace y. Only (D) -3 works in both equations of the question.

18. **D** The easiest way to solve this question is to make up your own numbers for the length and width of the *certain rectangle*. A square is a rectangle, so let's make the length 10 and the width 10 also. This gives an area of 100, so it will be easy to work out how much less the percent of the resulting rectangle is than the original. If the original has sides 10 by 10, then when the length and width are each reduced by 50%, the sides have length 5. This now must be increased by 40%. $\frac{40}{100} = \frac{2}{5}$, so 40% of 5 is 2. Increasing the sides of the square by 2 gives sides of 7 and an area of 49. $100 - 49$ gives 51, so the new rectangle is 51% less than the original rectangle, answer (D).

19. **C** To find the area of the square not occupied by the circle, find the area of both shapes and subtract the area of the circle from the square. The probability is given in a fraction where the difference is the numerator and the area of the square is the denominator. Algebraically, the area of the square is $2r \times 2r = 4r^2$. The area of the circle is πr^2. The difference over the area of the square is $\frac{4r^2 - \pi r^2}{4r^2}$. The r^2 can be factored out: $\frac{r^2(4 - \pi)}{4r^2} = \frac{4 - \pi}{4}$, answer (C). Alternately, you could make up your own number for the radius, and because all the values involving r cancel out, the fraction still reduces to $\frac{4 - \pi}{4}$.

20. **B** Watch your signs and be sure to count only *distinct* products. Be methodical, start at the left and multiply that number by each of the other numbers, then do the same for the next number; don't write down any products that aren't distinct:

    –7: 35, 21, 7, 0, –7, –21, –35, –49
    –5: 15, 5, –5, –15, –25
    –3: 3, –3, –9
    0: (no distinct products)
    1: –1
    3, 5, and 7 have no distinct products.

    The number of distinct products is 17.

SECTION 4

1. **B** Clarissa was *unable to cross the bridge*, and the word *makeshift* indicates that she "made" one. Only (B) *devised* is close in meaning to "made."

2. **E** It's easier to start with the second blank on this one. The word *worried* is a clue that something "bad" is going to happen: eliminate (A), (C), and (D) because they don't mean "bad." The first word in (E) works best, because the farmers are *worried about today's weather forecast,* so the *imminent* bad weather was predicted, and is thus not *unpredictable,* as in (B).

3. **B** The semicolon is like an equal sign between the word before it and the description that follows it. We know that the work was *well-received* so the article must have been a positive one. This is backed up by the description of the article as an *accolade*. Only (B) *laudatory* describes the high praise the sentence describes.

4. **D** The word *but* between the two blank indicates that we need a pair of opposites for the two blanks. (B) has a pair of synonyms, and the words in (C) are not opposites, so eliminate them. The rest could be consider opposites. The phrase *can affect them all* indicates that the second blank must mean "connected," and since the first must be opposite to that, it must mean something like "alone." (D) best shows this relationship.

5. **C** (C) is the correct answer because the clue for the first blank is *vagabond…lifestyle*. A good word for this blank is "wandering." That eliminates (A), (D), and (E). Looking at the two remaining choices, we cross out (B) because *innocuousness*, or harmlessness, does not fit. *Stability*, (C), is very different from a vagabond's nomadic life and goes well with the concept of a permanent home.

6. **B** The word for the blank must fit with the word *revived*, "filled" *with new meaning* would be a good thing, and (B) *imbued* is close to this meaning. None of the other words fit the meaning of the blank. There's some tough vocab here. Be sure to look up any unfamiliar words.

7. **A** The *surprisingly precise measurements* disproves the idea of that *ancient mathematics* had a *simplistic nature*. The word "disproves" would be a good word for the blank, and matches (A): *belies* means "shows to be false; contradicts."

8. **B** The semicolon indicates that what follows it is very closely related to what comes immediately before the semicolon. Since what follows describes his *expeditions*, Don Quixote is probably known for his *expeditions,* or "travels." Only (B) *vagaries* matches this meaning.

9. **C** Read the whole short reading passage, then go through the answers one by one to eliminate those that are not supported by the passage. (A) is too strong. (B) is extreme because not <u>all</u> packaged food is likely to be unhealthful. (C) is supported by lines 8–10 and the reaction of the *Food companies*. (D) is incorrect: the passage mentions the guidelines are *outdated*, but doesn't mention their *strictness*. (E) is not mentioned in the passage.

10. **D** The author mentions that consumers looking for nutritional information need a *calculator* and *a detailed study*, which suggests that the labels can be complicated. The last sentence says that *consumers should be vigilant*. These suggest that someone seeking nutritional information from a package should be *attentive* (D).

11. **D** The author is going against O'Connor's advice by seeking out *the seeds of a story* rather than rely on personal events already experienced. Only (D) captures this rejection of advice. (A) is not necessarily true, (B) is not mentioned in the passage, (C) is not a reflection of what the quote means. There is no evidence in the passsage for (E) as an interpretation of the author's statement.

12. **A** The quote could be paraphrased as "childhood is all the material you need to be a writer." The correct answer will agree with this. (A) looks close, but always check all the answers. (B) is extreme; and (C), (D), and (E) don't reflect the meaning of the quote. (A) is the best answer.

13. **D** The *process* was one of collaboration, with different people bringing in ideas until the song is *improvised into being*, although *it was Ellington who headed the collective*. Only (C) and (D) come close to the description in the passage, and (C) can be ruled out because the members band were not *equals*—Ellington was definitely the leader.

14. **B** Go back to the passage and use the context to come up with a word to replace *accenting*. In the passage, Ellington is "bringing out" the melodies of the piece from the *background*. This is closest to (B) emphasizing. More to the point, there is no evidence for the rest of the answers in the passage.

15. **E** The description in the fifth paragraph provides some of the ideas behind some of Ellington's works. This is best paraphrased in (E). The rest of the answers are not supported by the passage.

16. **B** The paragraph describes the colors of the title in two ways, as the colors of people's skin and *not only in color, but in his being as well*, using color describing the state of the world as a *metaphor*. This is reflected best in (B).

17. **B** The *origins of jazz* in the passage is a reference to the work *Deep South Suite*. Since that work is intended to remind listeners *of the locale of the origins* this is evidence that (B) *the American South* is the place referred to. There is no evidence for the other choices.

18. **D** The author follows the description of the *criticisms* with a discussion about Ellington's *astonishing, amiable naïveté* and gives examples of how Ellington *failed to see* that his choices were not sophisticated. This sense of *naïveté* is best captured in the *innocence* in (D). (A) is not mentioned in the correct part of the passage to answer this question. (B) is the actual criticism, not the author's response to it.

19. **A** Always go back to the passage: we need to find out how the attitude of the *fans* is described. The fans were *upset* by Ellington's use of *medleys of his successful tunes*. This is best summarized in (A). There is no evidence for (B); (C) is extreme and attributes *naïveté* to the wrong individuals; (D) is the attitude of the *critics*, not the *fans*. (E) is judgmental of the *fans* and is not supported by the passage.

20. **A** Only (A), *famous paintings,* is not mentioned in the passage. (B) is in lines 44–46, (C) is in lines 48–49, (D) is in lines 9–18, and (E) is in 55–58.

21. **E** The phrase in the parentheses states that what follows is *simplistic* but *clear.* So it is an attempt to diffuse criticism that what the author is about to say is too simplistic. (E) *justification* for the potential *oversimplification* fits best. The rest of the choices are not supported by the passage.

22. **A** *Fletcher Henderson* is mentioned as the person from whom Ellington *rather directly* got three of his four styles. So Henderson was an inspiration or model for Ellington. This is best captured in (A) *influence on.* (B) reverses the relationship. It is clear that Henderson came first, so they were not *contemporaries* as in (C). (D) goes against the main idea of the passage. (E) is not supported by the passage.

23. **C** While the passage mentions Ellington's age at the time he wanted to become a painter, it does not give the age at which he became a musical success: eliminate (A). Ellington's use of colors in his song titles is mentioned, but not how he expressed the colors musically: eliminate (B). The *jungle style* is mentioned, but not described in detail: eliminate (D). The passage does not provide the title of Ellington's best-known composition; eliminate (E). Only the question in (C) could be answered by information in the passage.

24. **C** The final paragraph states how all the significant bands had been *influenced by Duke,* so we need a word that indicates *lasting influence,* making (C) *its legacy* the best match.

SECTION 5

1. **A** From the first equation, $2x - 10 = 16$, we can see that $2x = 6$. Now we can find the value of $2x - 10$. $6 - 10 = -4$, answer (A).

2. **C** Draw the figure: From the information in the question we know we have right triangle *ABC*, with equal legs of 10. Since it is a right triangle, the two legs are the base and height. Use the Area formula for a triangle: $\frac{1}{2} bh = \frac{1}{2} \times 10 \times 10 = 50$, answer (C).

3. **C** When a number is added to an *x* value or to an expression in parentheses, the graph shifts up that number of units, and if a number is subtracted, the graph shifts down. Moving $y = x - 5$ upward three units adds 3 to the equation, $y = x - 5 + 3$ becomes $y = x - 2$, answer (C). You can also come up with your own numbers for *x* and *y* and sketch a graph. The first graph should cross the *y*-axis at $(0, -5)$ and when moved up, it should cross at $(0, -2)$.

4. **C** Replace *c* with 25 in the function and solve. $f(25) = \frac{9}{5}(25) + 32$, and $45 + 32 = 77$, answer (C).

5. **D** The phrase *varies directly* indicates that we can use a proportion to solve the problem. Putting the number of times pizza is on the menu on top of the fractions and the number of students on the bottom, we get $\frac{3}{35} = \frac{8}{x}$. Cross-multiply and solve for x. $3x = 1080$, and $x = 360$, answer (D).

6. **B** In general, the chart shows that as prices go up, the sales go down. All of the graphs, except (B), have a flat portion that indicates no change in the number of sales at two price points.

7. **A** Try out numbers from the answer choices in place of x to find which make the expression greater than 0. In the inequality, x cannot be -3 because the denominator would be zero. Eliminate (E) because it shows that -3 is possible. If x is -1, the numerator is 0. The answers have a choice between greater than -1 and less than -1. If x is less than -1, such as -5, the fraction is positive: $\frac{(-5)^2 + 4(-5) + 3}{-3 - (-5)} = \frac{25 - 20 + 3}{-3 + 5} = \frac{8}{2}$. Eliminate (B), (C), and (D) because they don't show -5. Only (A) shows all the possibilities.

8. **A** Use x for the price of the product. When the price is increased by 15 percent, the new price becomes $x + 0.15x$, or $1.15x$. To get back to the original price, the new price needs to lose $0.15x$. The percent will be the decrease divided by the total, or $\frac{0.15x}{115}$. This is approximately 0.13, or 13 percent. Another option is to create a value for the original price. Try 100 for the original price. Now increase 100 by 15 percent. Since we're starting with 100, just add 15. The new price is 115. To get back to 100 we need to know the percent change from 115 to 100. This should be the amount decreased divided by the total, $\frac{15}{115}$. Use your calculator to get the value of 0.13043. This is approximately 13 percent.

9. $\frac{3}{4}$ **or .75**

    Simplify the given equation to $4x = 3$. Divide both sides by 4 to get x by itself to see that $x = \frac{3}{4}$.

10. **81** Volume is found by multiplying the length by the width by the height. We already know the area of the base ($l \times w = 18$), so to get the volume multiply 18 by the height, 4.5: $18 \times 4.5 = 81$.

11. $\frac{7}{12}$ **or .583**

    The probability is a fraction with the number of donuts <u>not</u> cream-filled as the numerator and the total number of donuts as the denominator. There are 3 plain and 4 chocolate, so there are 7 <u>not</u> cream-filled donuts out of 12 donuts total, or $\frac{7}{12}$.

12. **96** The semicircle made of arc AB is half of a circle with a circumference of 12π. The circumference formula is $C = 2\pi r$ or πd, so its diameter, $\overline{AB}$, is 12. Now we have the length of rectangle $ABCD$ Semicircle BC is 4π and is half of a circle with a circumference of 8π. Its diameter, $\overline{BC}$, is 8. Multiply the height by the length to get the area of the rectangle: $12 \times 8 = 96$.

13. **21** There are two spots in the piece, so 7 of the dancers could potentially be the first chosen, leaving 6 dancers to be chosen for the second spot. Just multiplying 7×6 is not enough, because order doesn't matter. If the dancers are *A, B, C, D, E, F,* and *G,* then the pair *AB* is the same as pair *BA.* The way to get rid of that is to divide by the factorial of the number of spots, in this case, 2! : $\frac{7 \times 6}{1 \times 2} = \frac{42}{2} = 21$. Alternately, you could write out the pairs: first match A with the other numbers to get *AB, AC, AD, AE, AF,* and *AG. A* will repeat after those 6 matches, so it's out. *B* forms 5 pairs (*BC, BD, BE, BF,* and *BG*), *C* forms 4 pairs, *D* forms 3 pairs, *E* forms 2 pairs and *F* forms 1 pair. $6 + 5 + 4 + 3 + 2 + 1 = 21$.

14. $\frac{9}{4}$ **or 2.25**

    Manipulate the equation to get *a* by itself. First divide $2\sqrt{a} = 3$ by 2 on each side: $\sqrt{a} = \frac{3}{2}$. Square each side to get rid of the square root to get $a = \frac{9}{4}$.

15. **282** First find the total cost for 3 pounds of each spice: Cinnamon = \$24, Nutmeg = \$27, Ginger = \$21, Cloves = \$30, for a total cost of \$102. The shop owner sells the spices for \$2/ounce, so since there are 16 ounces in a pound, that's \$32/pound. The owner purchased 12 pounds of spices, so 32×12 = \$384. Subtract the amount the store owner paid the distributor to find the total profit: $384 - 102 = 282$.

16. **10** Draw the figure and fill in the information given in the problem. The points (1, 8) and (9, 8) form the top side of a rectangle with a length of 8. Points (9, 8) and (9, 2) form the right side of the rectangle with a length of 6. To find the length of the diagonal, we can use the information we have to use the Pythagorean theorem or recognize the 6-8-10 Pythagorean triple to see that the length of the diagonal must be 10.

17. **8** Draw the figure. The base of the triangle should be 8, since that is the distance from the point at $(-3, 2)$ to the point at $(5, 2)$. Since the area equals 24 and the base equals 8, the height has to equal 6. *Area* $= \frac{1}{2} bh$, So since $\frac{1}{2} \times 8 \times h = 24$, $h = 6$. So the other coordinate, $(5, b)$, must be 6 above the base, or at $(5, 8)$.

18.   **30**   The sides with an area of 6 have dimensions of 2×3. The sides with an area of 10 have dimensions of 2×5. The sides with an area of 15 have dimensions of 3×5. The dimensions of the rectangular solid are then $2 \times 3 \times 5$, which give a volume of 30.

SECTION 6

1.   **A**   The sentence is correct as written. The word *being* is usually incorrect, as in (B). (C) is wordy and awkward. (D) creates a comma splice. The pronoun *Their* is unwarranted in the sentence in (E).

2.   **B**   The first part of the sentence needs the past tense *had* rather than *would have*. This is seen in (B). (C) is passive; (D) shifts the meaning of the sentence; and (E) has the wrong verb tense.

3.   **B**   The sentence as written has a misplaced modifier. *Americans* are not being consumed, *sugar* is. (B) clearly describes the relationship of who is consuming what. (C) has the unclear pronoun *it*. (D) is not clear about what is being consumed. (E) is passive.

4.   **E**   The sentence as written, and many of the answers, contains unnecessary words. After the phrase *found the novel* no extra words need follow the description that comes after the noun. The phrase *to them* is also an unnecessarily redundant use of the pronoun. Only (E) eliminates all the errors.

5.   **D**   The conjunction is missing in the sentence as written. (B) is not a complete sentence; (C) creates a run-on sentence. The use of *while* in (E) does not work in the sentence. Only (D) connects the parts of the sentence using a semicolon.

6.   **D**   In the sentence as written, *commences* and *beginning* are redundant. Only (D) clearly arranges the ideas so that the phrase immediately after the comma directly relates to the noun *acts* immediately before the comma.

7.   **D**   The comparison between *children's fables* and *Aesop* is not correct. The sentence should refer to Aesop's fables, not the author himself. This is seen in (D) in the phrase *those written by Aesop*.

8.   **A**   The sentence is correct as written. An incorrect pronoun, *their,* is used in (B). (C) uses the past tense, which does not match with *has* in the sentence. In (D) and (E), the singular verbs *provides* and *carries* do not agree with the plural subject *wings*.

9.   **E**   The pronoun *their* cannot definitely be connected to either *children* or *parents*. The same error appears in (A), (B), and (C). (D) uses an unidiomatic phrase *as against*. Only (E) clearly identifies whose needs and desires these are.

10.   **C**   The pronoun *which* is incorrect here: we're dealing with people, so we need to use *who*. Between (B) and (C), (C) is correct because (B) changes the meaning of the sentence.

11. C The word *either* needs to be matched with *or*, not *nor*: eliminate (A). In (B) and (D) *neither* creates a double negative with *cannot*. The phrase *with or without* is unnecessary in (E). Only (C) fixes the either/nor error without introducing any new errors.

12. A The incorrect adverb *how* in (A) should be the pronoun *that*.

13. D The pronoun *it* is ambiguous in (D) and makes it seem that Odysseus is listening to *wax*.

14. E There is no error in the sentence as written.

15. D The single noun *mind* does not agree with the plural possessive pronoun *our*. (D) should be the plural *minds*.

16. B *America* is a singular noun, and agrees with the singular possessive pronoun *its*, not *their* as in (B).

17. B The verb *suggested* is in the past tense, and *when they appeared* also suggests the past tense. (B) *have* does not match the past tense. The sentence needs *did* in place of *have*.

18. A The sentence is set in the past, but *is not* does not match *was not* later in the sentence. Shakespeare has been dead for several centuries, so he should be referred to in the past tense.

19. B The noun *unemployment* is single, but the verb *increase* is plural. (B) should be replaced with the singular verb *increases*.

20. D The sentence has an idiom error: the phrase in (D) should be *acceptance of* not *acceptance on*.

21. E There is no error in the sentence as written.

22. E There is no error in the sentence as written. The pronoun *whom* may sound a little odd, but it is correct to use an object case pronoun (whom, him, her, us) after the preposition *to*.

23. D In the sentence as written, it seems that the computer is calling for take-out. In (D) the phrase should read *when someone calls to place*.

24. E There is no error in the sentence as written. Notwithstanding may sound odd, but don't go by your ear. Make sure you can identify an error before you select your answer.

25. C The sentence has a subject-verb agreement error. *One* is singular while *are* is plural. (C) should contain the verb *is*.

26. B There is an improper comparison in the sentence *fear of the dark* is compared to *heights* in (B) when the sentence should read *fear of heights*.

27. A The adverb *where* is used only for specific, physical locations. In (A), the phrase should read "in which."

28. **B** The collective noun *crowd* is a singular noun, but *were jostling* agrees with a plural subject. (B) should read *was jostling.*

29. **E** There is no error in the sentence as written. The *we* in (D) may sound strange, but the subject pronoun is correct here.

30. **D** The phrase *content to* is closer to the meaning of the passage: that women were not interested in sports beyond those in which they were already engaged. The phrase *contentedly playing* in the original suggests that the women are actively playing those games in a spirit of happiness, which does not fit the meaning of the passage.

31. **B** Sentence 1 cannot be eliminated, because the *This* at the beginning of sentence 2 indicates something has come before. The paragraph works fine and no essential information is lost if sentence 2 is eliminated, and (B) is correct. The rest of the sentences are crucial to understanding the passage.

32. **B** The last word of sentence 11 is *team* and sentence 12 also mentions the *team*, so we need to connect the sentences in a way that eliminates this redundancy. Eliminate (A), (C), (D), and (E) because they all contain the redundancy. (B) is the short and simple way to join the sentences.

33. **A** The word *this* is too vague in a conclusion sentence. We need a replacement that relates to the subject of the passage, such as *the right to wrestle.* (B), (C), and (E) are all mentioned in the passage, but none make sense as a replacement for *this.* (D) is redundant and no more specific than *this.*

34. **C** The end of the final sentence of the passage discusses *the larger civil rights issues*, but does not explain or give details. A paragraph after sentence 15 would be the place to go into *the civil rights issues involved in the situation,* (C).

35. **C** Sentences 11 and 12 are reasons why some fear the prospect of having females on predominantly male teams. Sentence 13 mentions that the exclusion is unfair, so we need a conjunction that indicates a change of direction. The transition in (C) *However,* correctly indicates a change of direction in a sentence.

SECTION 7

1. **D** The clues for this sentence are "stretches over four decades" and "numerous genres," so the missing word in the blank must be similar to "produces a lot of work." (A) and (C) might seem like tempting answers given the question but are not supported by the clues. (B) is a trap since "filmmaker" could be associated with being a visionary. (E) is the opposite of "a lot of work"; thus, (D) is correct since prolific most closely means "producing many works."

2. **E** The first blank must mean something like "problems with." Eliminate (A) and (C) for being positive. Although (D) *deaths* is not positive, the word does not fit the sentence in connection with the *use of pesticides.* For the second blank we need a word that means "started." In (B), the second word means calmed down, leaving (E) as a match for both blanks.

3. A   The phrase *so few symptoms* indicates that the disease may go unnoticed. In the answers, the second word in both (A) and (E) could mean "go unnoticed." The first blank must mean something like "visible" or "obvious" since it supports the idea that there are *few symptoms* to indicate the disease. (A) is much closer in meaning to "obvious" than is (E).

4. E   The pair of phrases *away from* and *toward* indicate that the actions involve two opposite ideas. The blank must mean the opposite of *dependence* so "independence" is a good word for the blank. Only (E) *autonomy* is close in meaning to independence.

5. B   The semicolon indicates that the ideas in the two parts of the sentence are very close in meaning. The pronoun *these* indicates that what is discussed in the first part of the sentence is *emotional appeals*. This is a good word for the blank. In the answer choices, only (B) *pathos,* which means "the power to evoke a feeling of pity or compassion," matches *emotional appeals.*

6. E   Passage 1 is anti-violence, while Passage 2 is pro-violence. The pair of words in (E) *pacifism* and *militancy* is a good match for anti- and pro-violence.

7. B   The statement in (B) does the most to weaken the idea that nonviolent revolution doesn't exist because it is an example of nonviolent revolution that was successful. Whether the men had *a common enemy* in (A) is irrelevant to nonviolent revolution. (C) is out because nonviolent revolution is still pro-revolution, it just seeks a peaceful way to bring about revolution. (D) is irrelevant to the discussion and (E) doesn't address the assertion in the question.

8. A   The author of Passage 1 mentions *wrongful deeds* in order to support the main idea of the rest of the passage. The main idea is that people should not act in revenge, they should rise above acting in the same violent way. This is best paraphrased in (A). (B) is false, (C) is extreme; there is no support for *blame* in (D) or *disagreements with enemies* in (E).

9. B   Both passages are different views of the best way to bring about necessary change. This is best represented in (B). There is no evidence for (A); (C) is extreme, (D) is not mentioned in Passage 1, and (E) is not addressed in the passage.

10. C   The question asks us to substitute our own word, using contextual clues. We know that the author was in a *rush* and engaged in a *mad scramble* that resulted in an injury (lines 3–6). (C) is correct, because the author rushed, and bumped her hip because she was not careful. There is nothing in the passage to support (A), although it is a story about a child. (B) is very strong, but while the author was reckless, a bumped hip is not all that dangerous. (D) depends on the reader taking *mad* out of context, and (E) references the tears that happened after the excitement.

11. **E**   The author is talking about her own physical bruise and pain, and says that the teacher, who was upset about school ending, transferred *her own inner bruise...to me*—that is, she interpreted the narrator's crying as a response to the end of school. In other words, the teacher projected her own sadness onto the narrator. (E) paraphrases this best. (A) is not supported; the teacher was nurturing rather than hurtful. (B) is very strong, but *precarious*—dangerously insecure or unstable—is way too extreme: The teacher was sad, but probably not on the edge of a breakdown. There is nothing in the passage to support (C), since the teacher took the crying child onto her lap. (D) is also not supported by the passage.

12. **B**   Why does the author start the paragraph by saying she was not deliberately lying? This sentence is a bridge between the end of the first paragraph—in which the narrator didn't correct the teacher who misinterpreted her tears—and the rest of the second paragraph, which first offers support for her contention that she wasn't trying to lie—*I do not think my English at six was flexible enough to go into the details of the situation*—and then uses the word *But* to shift into explaining the importance of the event in her life (lines 15–22). In other words, the function of the sentence is to provide a transition between describing an event and exploring its lessons. (B) expresses this. (A) is too literal (it's unlikely that a reader would consider a six-year-old a deliberate liar for not correcting an upset teacher) and doesn't express the real purpose of the sentence. (C) and (D) both reference the narrator's limited English, which is mentioned but not the point of this transition (and has no relationship to the author's fluent written English, which includes using the word *dissembling*, or "concealing"). This is not the incident that especially humiliated the narrator (that's at the end of the passage), so eliminate (E).

13. **C**   To answer this question, we must think about why this experience was so memorable for the author. The sentences immediately after the phrase *the longest day of my whole life* describe the beginning of the day, but don't provide a satisfying explanation for why it felt so long. We hit pay dirt in the next paragraph: The narrator was confused, alone, and stranded at school because she had misunderstood an announcement. When she says, *I remained there the rest of the afternoon, maybe changing my seat occasionally...maybe playing hopscotch on the sidewalk...maybe going up to the school entrance and peering in. I don't recall anyone passing by*, the day starts to seem really, really long. It didn't end until *eventually* she was *rescued* by her father (lines 37–43). (C) expresses the author's feelings of being stranded and alone, having no control over when the long wait will end, and needing rescue. (A) misinterprets the event. Her family did not abandon her; rather, she misunderstood what was going on. (B) and (D) are both events that happened during the day, but the author does not spend most of her time describing them, or the impact they had on her. (E) is not an accurate description of the author's attitude; she was worried (and probably bored), not excited.

14. **A**   This question directs us to the fifth paragraph, in which the author describes watching another student's *odd* actions with great interest and *admiration* (lines 46–50). (A) is the correct answer, since the narrator admired and was very interested in the new culture she encountered through this girl. (B) and (C) both focus on the girl's actions (her religious ritual and *reverent* eating) rather than what impact these actions had on the author, who does not indicate that she copied the girl's actions in any way. (D) goes further than the passage does, since the narrator was interested in the other girl, but didn't necessarily use her as a role model. (E) is the opposite of the narrator's interest and admiration.

15. **D**   The sixth paragraph directly describes the narrator's feelings about reading. The author's tone is very positive, and she mentions her *excitement* at hearing stories read aloud and her *rapture* in *anticipating the next chapter* (lines 52–57). Therefore, (D) is the best answer. Because the narrator loved reading, we can eliminate (A), (B) and (C), all of which describe negative or ambivalent attitudes. Although the fifth paragraph describes the narrator's curiosity about other cultures, this interest isn't mentioned as part of her love of reading, so eliminate (E).

16. **D**   This question asks about the general purpose of the passage. Note that the author lists a number of different experiences in a fragmented manner, and emphasizes the lessons and feelings she gained from each one. (D) best sums this up. (A) focuses very literally on only the final paragraph, and ignores the main purpose of the passage. While several of the incidents relate to the author's struggles to express herself, this is not the sole focus as in (B). (C) also focuses on some of the incidents, such as the author's fascination with the older girl's religious ritual, but not on all of them. Although the narrator was curious and loved to read, nothing suggests that studying and class work were of particular interest to her, so eliminate (E).

17. **E**   These phrases are used when the author doesn't remember a detail: why she went to a different school for part of first grade, and how she got to school on Memorial Day. Because this is a fairly difficult question, we'll keep in mind the overall purpose of the passage, as discussed in the answer to question 22: The author lists a number of different experiences in a fragmented manner and emphasizes the lessons and feelings she gained from each one. (E) is the best answer, because she spends more time talking about what each incident meant to her than what actually happened in each one. (A) is attractive, because the author mentions her difficulty in understanding instructions or announcements several times, but the cited phrases do not describe these moments. (B) is tempting but too extreme, because she does remember many aspects of these events. (C) is attractive, because it mimics phrases from the second paragraph, but the passage nowhere suggests that the author is making up the events. (D) is the opposite of the overall impression of the passage, since these events at school were important enough to her that she records them.

18. **C** To answer this question, we should review the two incidents in which teachers figured: the first, when the teacher misunderstood the narrator's tears and ascribed her own feelings to the narrator, who then realized how much some teachers enjoy school (lines 8–21), and the second, in which the teacher mistook the author's picking paste off the desk for vandalism and punished her (lines 59–68). (C) refers to the narrator's realization in the first incident *that there were some teachers who truly loved teaching, for whom the prospect of school vacation was a desolation*, without contradicting anything that happened in the second incident. (A) recalls only the second incident, and does not give an overall statement. (B) is very attractive, because the second part is true, but it is unlikely that she found *all* of her teachers, including the one who reprimanded her for trying to clean the paste, caring. The passage mentions her difficulties in expressing herself in English several times, but it does not say she had trouble understanding her teachers as in (D). There is nothing in the passage about her becoming a success due to her teachers, so eliminate (E).

19. **E** Go back to the passage to read the sentence that contains *poring over*. What's a word would fit in the blank if *poring over* were gone? Something like "examining" would work since the *Doctors* are looking for evidence for their diagnoses. (E) *scrutinizing* comes closest in meaning. (C) redressing, might be something that doctors do, since it means "to set right or remedy," but the word does not fit the context of the sentence.

20. **D** While most of the answers among the choices are mentioned as afflictions that van Gogh suffered, the only one that *can cause yellow vision* is the item listed before the dash—*digitalis*, (D).

21. **A** The statement is pretty sarcastic: the author is dismissive of the activities of the diagnostic *games* of *aesthetically minded doctors*. The best paraphrase of this is (A). (D) may be tempting, but the *games* are not *purely frivolous*; in line 17–18, the author mentions that one reason the doctors engage in the activity is *a better understanding of…diseases*, which is more professional than frivolous. The phrase tells us more about the author than it does the people he is writing about.

22. **B** In lines 29–33, the subjects of artwork, rather than the artists who created the works, are the focus of diagnoses. Therefore, we need to find the example that shows a diagnoses of a figure of a work of art. Eliminate (A); it's a diagnosis for a painter. (B) gives a diagnosis based on the appearance of a sculpted figure, so hold onto that. (C) is out because it is a diagnosis of a historical person. Eliminate (D) and (E) because they use artwork to form a psychological impression of artists.

23. **A** At the end of the paragraph that begins with the quote from the question, the passage states that the doctors *can't help regarding the canvas as a patient silently awaiting their professional opinion*. (A) paraphrases this well. (B) is extreme due to the word *only*. (C) is not true: in line 36, the passage states that doctors *feel a kinship with artists*. (D) and (E) are not supported by the passage.

24.   **A**   The discussion about El Greco, a sixteenth-century painter, begins on line 45. In 1913, the idea came about that the artist may have had astigmatism. In 1913, they had enough information about the causes of astigmatism and its effects on vision to recognize the difference between corrected and uncorrected vision, so there is evidence in the passage for (A). (B) is not supported: Although the passage mentions that there were *no corrective lenses for astigmatism in El Greco's day,* there is no evidence that astigmatism was unknown then. (C) is untrue. (D) is the opposite of the description given in lines 54–57. There is no evidence that doctors *misunderstood* an ailment as in (E).

SECTION 8

1.   **E**   Write out the word sandblaster, and then write the value for each letter beneath the letter. Add the values up: $8 + 8 + 2 + 2 + 2 + 2 + 8 + 8 + 2 + 2 + 2 = 46$.

2.   **A**   The value in the parenthesis is always 0, no matter what the value of p is. Therefore $p^3 \times 0 = 0$, answer (E).

3.   **D**   We know two of the three measures for the triangles in the figure. In the top triangle, the third angle is $180° - 90° - 30° = 60°$. In the bottom triangle, the third angle is $180° - 90° - 40° = 50°$. The straight line on the left of the figure has a measure of 180°, so $60 + 50 + p = 180$, and $p = 70$.

4.   **D**   Translate the words into math: $d = \frac{1}{2} k - 4$. You can also make sure of the correct answer by coming up with your own numbers for the values in the question. If David has 10 balloons, that is equal to half the number of Katie's balloons minus 4. Setting up the equation to solve for k, you will see $10 = \frac{1}{2} k - 4$, which is pretty much what you see in (D).

5.   **B**   One way to solve this is to try out the answers. It's most helpful to start with the middle value: If the length of the trip is $5\frac{1}{2}$ miles as in (C), that is 22 quarter-miles. The first quarter-mile is $1.40, and the remaining 21 quarter-miles cost $0.20: $1.40 + 21(0.20) = 1.40 + 4.20 = 5.60. That number is too high for the $5.00 cost of the trip given in the question. Try a lower number such as (B): $4\frac{3}{4}$ miles is 19 quarter-miles: $1.40 + 18(0.20) = 1.40 + 3.60 = 5.00. (B) is correct: none of the other choices will result in a fare of $5.00.

6.   **D**   This question can be answered algebraically: from the question we know that $a = b + 4$. We can rearrange that to be $a - b = 4$ and square both sides, we get $(a - b)^2 = 4^2$, which gives $a^2 - 2ab + b^2 = 16$. Rearranging this to $a^2 + b^2 - 2ab = 16$ makes it obvious that we can replace $a^2 + b^2$ with 10, so $10 - 2ab = 16$, $-2ab = 6$. Finally divide both sides by -2 to find that $ab = -3$, answer (D). A quicker option might be to try out the answers: only (D) works with all the requirements of the question.

7. **A** Draw any figure that is discussed in a question but is not shown. Since the letter B appears in all pairs of letters, that is where the three lines come together. $\overline{BC}$ and $\overline{BD}$ form a straight line $\overline{CD}$ that is perpendicular to $\overline{AB}$, so (A) is true.

8. **E** To find the number of text messages that Hannah sent, try the answer choices for x until you find the one that produces a bill of \$10.50. For (E), $C(260) = (260)(.05) - 2.5 = 13 - 2.5 = 10.5$. Alternatively, you could replace $C(x)$ with 10.50 and solve for x: $10.5 = .05x - 2.5$, so $13 = .05x$, and dividing both sides by .05 gives 260, answer (E).

9. **A** We can take the numerator and denominator values as two equations to let us find the value of a and b. If we add the two equations together, we get:

$$a + b = 3$$
$$\underline{+ \quad a - b = 7}$$
$$2a \quad\quad = 10, \text{ so } a = 5.$$

We can replace a with 5 in the equation $a + b = 3$ to get $5 + b = 3$ and $b = -2$. Finally, replace a and b with these values in the fraction $\dfrac{a}{b}$ to get $\dfrac{5}{-2}$, which is equal to (A).

10. **C** There are 12 parts to the circle. The numbers in the ratios must add up to 12 or a factor of 12 (such as 2, 3, 4, or 6). (A) works: $1 + 11 = 12$. (B) adds up to 6, (C) adds up to 5, which is not a factor of 12. (D) adds to 4 and (E) adds to 3. Only (C) gives a sum that is not a factor of 12.

11. **A** One way to solve this question is to come up with your own values for the variables. If $b = 2$, then a is $\dfrac{1}{2^2}$. (A negative exponent means that we need the reciprocal of the positively exponented base). In simplified form, $a = \dfrac{1}{4}$, and the correct answer will result in $\dfrac{1}{4}$ when m is replaced with its value. We must also use $b = 2$ to find the value of m. The fractional exponent in $m^{\frac{1}{2}}$ means that we need to take the square root of m, so $2 = \sqrt{m}$, and $m = 4$. Now we have a real number to replace the variables in the answers, and the one that gives the value we found for a is the correct answer. (A) gives $\dfrac{1}{4}$; (B) gives $\dfrac{1}{2}$; (C) gives 16, (D) gives 2, and (E) gives -2. Only (A) matches.

12. **D** Begin by working with the innermost function $g(3)$: $g(3) = 3(3^2) + 7 = 27 + 7 = 34$. Now that $g(3)$ can be replaced with 34, the value of $f(34)$ must be determined: $f(34) = 4(34) - 8 = 136 - 8 = 128$. Thus, answer choice (D) is correct.

13.   C   The ladder makes a triangle with the wall and the ground. Draw it out and label the information from the question. The hypotenuse (the leaning ladder) is given first at 52, and the height is 48. We need to know the width at the middle of the ladder, so we really need the base of a triangle with half the height and half the hypotenuse. The smaller numbers will also make the Pythagorean theorem easier to work with: $24^2 + b^2 = 26^2$. You can go on to solve for b, or recognize that this is a 5-12-13 Pythagorean triplet, only twice as big. The values of 2 times 12 and 13 are accounted for, so the missing value is the 5, which means that $b = 10$, as in (C).

14.   C   A line tangent to a circle is always perpendicular to the radius, *NP,* which we need to find in order to answer the question. After we draw *NP* on the figure, we are dealing with a right triangle. The question states that *MN* = 4, and that the points on the line are equally spaced, so we know the base of the triangle, *LN* is 8. We can also find the hypotenuse, *LP* because it is equal to $\frac{5}{6}$ of *LO.* There are 3 segments to *LO,* each of which has length 4. *LO* has a length of 12, and $\frac{5}{6} \times 12 = 10$. You can use the Pythagorean theorem and solve for a in $a^2 + 8^2 = 10^2$, or recognize the 6-8-10 Pythagorean triplet to see that the radius is 6, and thus, the area of the circle is $\pi r^2 = \pi 6^2 = 36\pi$ as seen in (C).

15.   E   To solve this problem, test out some points that work with the equation given in the question then determine if the points work on the graphs provided in the answer choices. Some pairs that work with the equation are (2, 2), (–2, 2), (2, –2), (–2, –2). This combination of positive and negative values is seen in (E) only. The rest of the graphs are missing 2 or more of the points that must be included on the correct graph.

16.   A   Evaluate the information in the passage and check out the three statements. The question states that the five variables have *distinct* values. The easiest to check are statements II and III. Statement II is false: because no two of the numbers are the same, there is no mode in the list. Eliminate (B) and (E) because they contain II. Statement III is false because c, the middle value must be the median. This eliminates (C) and (D), leaving only (A) as the correct answer. We know that the numbers are already in order from smallest to largest, and we can select numbers that would make statement I true: in the list –11, –2, 0, 1, 2, the value for b, –2, is the arithmetic mean (average).

SECTION 9

1. **C** The blank must mean something like "without emotion" since the sentence states that the *musicians* have *little understanding of the emotional content*. Only (C) *mechanically* is close to this meaning.

2. **C** The word *although* signals that the first blank means something the opposite of *resented*. The opposite action would be to not so anything against the resented situation, so "put up with" is a good meaning for the first blank. This eliminates (A), (B), and (D). Since both (C) and (D) work for the first blank, check the second word in each to see which makes the most sense. (C) is correct, *enforce* is a more logical thing for England to do with its rules, while *violate* would better describe the colonists.

3. **D** The first blank describes the *theory* that is described later as one of the most *controversial*. The word controversial is synonymous to the word that belongs in the first. Eliminate (A) *learned* and (B) *atypical* and (C) *idiosyncratic*, which means "having a habit or mannerism that is peculiar to an individual" (D) and (E) could legitimately mean "controversial." The semicolon means that the second part of the sentence continues the ideas in the first part. A *controversial* theory would split people into a side that agrees with it and a side that does not. (D) *skeptical of* fits (as might *supportive of*), but (E) *confused by* does not fit the meaning of the sentence. Only (D) fits the meaning of both blanks.

4. **C** The first part of the sentence mentions the *references to her friends*, and "references" is a good word to fill in the second blank. Eliminate (A) *styles*, (D) *eulogies* and (E) *motives* because they do not match "references" at all. The author was *surprised that her* "references" *were recognized*, so the first blank must mean something like "well-hidden" or "unrecognizable." Only (C) *oblique* fits in with this, as it means "not straight or direct," and so not easily grasped.

5. **C** This short sentence describes Galileo's works with a blank and with the description *went against the teachings*. Only (C), *heretical* matches this meaning. There are some tough vocabulary words here. Look up any unfamiliar words, and you'll see that their meanings are all quite different than "going against teachings."

6. **B** *Anna* is *accustomed to desert conditions*, so she probably expected to be fine in the heat of *Egyptian sun*. The phrase *did not expect* indicates that Anna did not do so well in Egypt's climate. The only word that has a negative meaning that makes sense in the sentence is *enervated* which means "weakened." There are a lot of tough vocab words here: look up any that are unfamiliar.

7. **D** Both passages describe Catiline, to find the difference or *contrast*, between them, look for the main idea of the passages. Passage 1 is by Catiline, and he speaks of wanting to bring people to liberty and freedom. Passage 2 describes Catiline as someone who is alarming the people (line 36) and should be executed (52) and whose followers are considered *worthless dregs*. This is best paraphrased in (D). The other answers do not have the correct relationship to the ideas expressed in the passage.

8. **C** The quote is of the speaker stating that he has the same *advantages and evils* as those experienced by his listeners. The end of the first paragraph states that *to have the same desires and aversions* is a *bond of friendship*. This is best summarized in (C) *common aspirations encourage friendship*. The other answers are not supported by text in the passage.

9. **C** The question is rhetorical, and not meant to be answered, so eliminate (A). The purpose of a rhetorical question is to emphasize the speaker's main point. The speech as a whole is an attempt to rally followers to rebel against the people in charge. Just before the question, Catiline mentions how those in the government have all the *power, honor, and wealth*, while the common people that he is trying to gather to fight have only *insults, dangers, persecutions, and poverty*. The question is supposed to inspire the people to fight the unjust situation he described. This is best paraphrased in (C).

10. **C** In the third paragraph, the speaker tells why he thinks they will *succeed*: his side is *fresh* and *unbroken* while the other side has a *debility* caused by *age* and *wealth*. This is paraphrased in (C). There is no evidence for *gods* as in (A); in lines 19–20 the speaker mentions that success *is in our own hands*. (B) and (D) are extreme. (E) *kings* is mentioned in the passage, but not in relation to the success of Catiline and his followers.

11. **B** Go back to the passage and use the context to come up with a word to replace *animate*. The speaker is telling the audience of the benefits the people will gain if they join him in the *enterprise*. Catiline is trying to "tempt" or "motivate" the people to join him. While the answer choices contain more than one definition for *animate*, only *motivate* (B) fits in the context of the actual sentence.

12. **E** The speaker gives his opponents' age and wealth as the reason for his assured success. What would make the speaker wrong, and undermine his argument is if age and wealth are things that assure success. (A) strengthens, not undermines, the claim. (B) does not involve either age or wealth. (C) would weaken the speaker's opponents, and so would not undermine his claim. (D) weakens the speaker's claim a little, but not as much as (E) does with the idea that *older and affluent forces* always triumph.

13. **C** The *venerable body* mentioned in line 39 are the senators in *the senate* that the speaker in Passage 2 describes as a place that Catiline has the freedom be in despite his personal beliefs and actions. The clue *looks and countenances,* mentioned in the passage just before the quote in the question, helps explain what is referred to. The look on a person's face is a clue to their emotions, such as an angry look or a pleased look. It turns out that the word *countenance* actually does have the meaning of "face," but *look* may be enough to identify that we are talking about emotion or *expressions* as in (C).

14. **B** In lines 34–42 the orator lists the things that should be convincing Catiline that he is in the wrong and has been defeated by those in charge of the city. This is best paraphrased in (B). The statement in (A) is a little too broad. There is no evidence of *isolation,* for the orator to *exploit* in (C). In fact, later, the orator even mentions the freedoms that Catiline is allowed. There are *alarmed people* mentioned in the passage but the measures listed are not meant to *alert* them. The list is about things that should be making Catiline feel remorseful for his actions, not to *appeal to his national pride* as in (E).

15. **D** The evidence for why the orator is against executing Catiline is in lines 59–64: The speaker states that the followers would stick around causing trouble, but if Catiline is alive and leaves the state, his followers would leave along with him. So the orator gets more of what he seeks if Catiline stays alive. This is paraphrased in (D). (A) is not true: the blurb mentions that Cicero had previously ordered executions. There is no evidence that the reason involved the *senators* in (B), or angering the senate as in (C). There is no evidence for the *large number* in (E), nor that the followers would make the *execution dangerous.* Cicero is concerned about the followers staying in town after Catiline died.

16. **E** Go back to the passage and use the context to come up with a word to replace *afford.* In the passage, the orator is implying that nothing could "give" Catiline any pleasure, because everyone in the city hated him. Only (E) *provide* has a meaning close to give. (B) *purchase* is a word that connects with a different meaning of *afford* and does not fit into the context of the sentence in the passage.

17. **A** In lines 79–82, the orator points out the silence of the senators to show that they agree with him in his condemnation of Catiline and his activities. The orator's speech is pretty harsh on Catiline, so the correct answer indicates that the senators feel negatively toward Catiline. (A) is the best match. Although (B) also mentions Catiline, the silence had nothing to do with their willingness to execute him. There is no evidence for (C) or (D), and (E) is the opposite of what is presented in the passage.

18. **C** The orator in Passage 1 is pro-Catiline (he *is* Catiline) and would respond in way that agrees with the main idea of Passage 1. Passage 1 was about how the people were being unfairly treated by those in power, and the people needed to rise up and claim their liberty and right to wealth and power. There is no evidence that the speaker and his followers were *slaves* as in (A). Violence is advocated in Passage 1, so (B) is not true, (C) invokes the unfairness (*oppressiveness*) of the situation and mentions the rights of citizens, so it is a good match. (D) is out because *inevitably* is too strong and impossible to *demonstrate* in the situation described. (E) is the opposite of what is expressed in Passage 1.

19. **A**   See what you can eliminate. (B) is out: the situation described in the blurb and passages indicate that there is a struggle for power between groups that have different ideas, or *dissent* about how things should be run. Only Passage 1 brings up the point in (C). (D) is shown to be untrue in the second paragraph of Passage 2, in which the freedoms that are allowed even to those who express disagreement are mentioned. (E) is not correct because it is impossible to say if things will change drastically or if the current situation will simply be strengthened or stabilized.

SECTION 10

1. **D**   The sentence has a misplaced modifier. What comes after the comma should be the book, not *Margaret Mitchell* as in (A), (B), and (C). Between (D) and (E), (D) is stronger because it puts the book first, and clearly states that Margaret Mitchell wrote it. (E) is passive, and does not actively attribute writing it to Margaret Mitchell. The phrase *was written* doesn't provide much useful information, and should serve as a link to identify the person who performed the action.

2. **B**   The use of the word *otherwise* is redundant in the phrase with *or else*. (B) eliminates both *else* and *otherwise*, and still makes sense. In (C) the phrase *so as not to* changes the meaning of the sentence and is not as clear as (B) which uses a pronoun to identify what is in danger of collapsing. (D) also lacks the pronoun. (E) has an agreement problem between *buildings* and *it*.

3. **E**   A fraction can modify a singular or a plural noun; the rest of the sentence should agree with the noun. In this case, since the fraction modifies *voters* in the non-underlined portion of the sentence, the rest of the sentence should be plural: *voters* goes with *believe*. This leaves only (D) and (E). (D) is incorrect because *at* seems to make the sentence incomplete.

4. **A**   There is no error in the sentence as written. (B), (D), and (E) are wordy and unclear, and *From* in (C) does not clearly establish the time period that would require *has become*. *Since*, in the original sentence, clearly establishes a time that is still continuing and needs the present perfect *has*.

5. **B**   The word *where* should be used only when referring to a physical location. In this case, the *field* is not a physical location; it's the study of *cognitive science*. The correct replacement for *where* is *in which*, as seen in (B).

6. **B**   This sentence has a misplaced modifier: we need the portion after the comma to be about the blacksmiths themselves, not *their success*, as in (A). Eliminate (C), (D), and (E). (B) is correct because the pronoun *they* refers directly to *the blacksmiths*.

7. **D**   *She* in (A) is ambiguous, since it could refer to either *Kate* or *Jane*. In (B), the plural pronoun *they* does not agree with the singular verb *has*. (C) changes the meaning of the original sentence, implying that taking the same art classes as Kate did in high school has caused Jane to announce her art exhibition. (E) contains a fragment.

8.   **A**   The sentence is correct as written. (B) has a subject-verb problem between *nest* and *are*. (C) unnecessarily uses the construction *would be*. In (D) the passive *could be found* makes it unclear who or what is hatching. The use of *you* in (E) is unwarranted, and *who* should be *that*.

9.   **C**   (A) changes the meaning and is illogical: It is not clear what the critics consider as intoxicating as the prose of Baudelaire. In (B), *equally as* is the incorrect idiom: We can use *equally* or *as* in a comparison, but not both. (C) contains the correct idiom *as...as*, but (D) fails to include it. The pronoun *their* in (E) changes the meaning, suggesting that the critics consider their own poetry as beautiful as Baudelaire's prose is intoxicating.

10.   **C**   Only (C) and (D) correctly join both halves of the sentence with the conjunction *because*. (D), however, incorrectly changes the tense of the verb *combine* to the future, by preceding it with the word *will*.

11.   **D**   The pair of words *agree* and *disagree* should be in parallel form. Eliminate (A) and (B) for using *agreement*. The double negative in (C) changes the meaning of the sentence; the added *not* does not fit in the context of the sentence. (E) is unclear because the people who should be abstaining (the dieters) are not identified. Only (D) fixes the original error without introducing any new errors.

12.   **B**   (A), (C), and (E) contain misplaced modifiers, since neither *a good grade*, *your good grade*, nor *they* are *taking...notes...and studying*. (D) creates a fragment. Only (B) contains the correct meaning, since *you* are the one who must study and take notes.

13.   **B**   This sentence is redundant in using both *The reason* and *because*. The phrase should be structured *The reason...is that*. Eliminate (A) and (E) for using *because*. Of the remaining three, (C) is passive, (D) is attributes the action to the *project* rather than the students. (B) is correct.

14.   **D**   The sentence as written is passive. We need an answer in which Yo-Yo Ma is the active subject, so eliminate (A) and (B). The *ing* form of verbs makes a sentence awkward and less active than they should be, so eliminate (C). (D) is correct. There is a noun-pronoun agreement problem in (E) between *an audience* which is a singular collective noun, and the plural pronoun *they*.

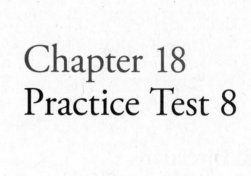

Chapter 18
Practice Test 8

Your Name (print) _____

Last   First   Middle

Date _____

IMPORTANT: The following codes should be copied onto your answer sheet exactly as shown.

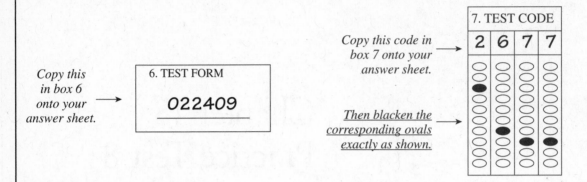

Copy this in box 6 onto your answer sheet. →

6. TEST FORM

022409

Copy this code in box 7 onto your answer sheet. →

Then blacken the corresponding ovals exactly as shown. →

7. TEST CODE

2 6 7 7

General Directions

You will have three hours and 20 minutes to work on this objective test designed to familiarize you with all aspects of the SAT.

This test contains five 25-minute sections, two 20-minute sections, one 10-minute section, and one 25-minute essay. The supervisor will tell you when to begin and end each section. During the time allowed for each section, you may work only on that particular section. If you finish your work before time is called, you may check your work on that section, but you are not to work on any other section.

You will find specific directions for each type of question found in the test. **Be sure you understand the directions before attempting to answer any of the questions.**

YOU ARE TO INDICATE ALL YOUR ANSWERS ON THE SEPARATE ANSWER SHEET:

1. The test booklet may be used for scratchwork. However, no credit will be given for anything written in the test booklet.

2. Once you have decided on an answer to a question, darken the corresponding space on the answer sheet. Give only one answer to each question.

3. There are 40 numbered answer spaces for each section; be sure to use only those spaces that correspond to the test questions.

4. **Be sure each answer mark is dark and completely fills the answer space.** Do not make any stray marks on your answer sheet.

5. If you wish to change an answer, erase your first mark completely—an incomplete erasure may be considered an intended response—and blacken your new answer choice.

Your score on this test is based on the number of questions you answer correctly minus a fraction of the number of questions you answer incorrectly. Therefore, it is improbable that random or haphazard guessing will alter your score significantly. There are no deductions for incorrect answers on the student-produced response questions. However, if you are able to eliminate one or more of the answer choices on any question as wrong, it is generally to your advantage to guess at one of the remaining choices. Remember, however, not to spend too much time on any one question.

Diagnostic Test Form

Use a No. 2 pencil only. Be sure each mark is dark and completely fills the intended oval. Completely erase any errors or stray marks.

1 Your Name:

(Print) _____

Last   First   M.I.

Signature: _____ Date ___ / ___ / ___

Home Address: _____

Number and Street   City   State   Zip Code

E-Mail: _____ School: _____ Class: _____
(Print)

2 YOUR NAME

Last Name (First 4 Letters) | FIRST INIT | MID INIT

Columns with ovals: –, ', ○, A–Z

3 PHONE NUMBER

Seven columns of ovals 0–9

4 DATE OF BIRTH

MONTH	DAY		YEAR	
○ JAN				
○ FEB				
○ MAR	0	0		0
○ APR	1	1		1
○ MAY	2	2		2
○ JUN	3	3		3
○ JUL		4		4
○ AUG		5	5	5
○ SEP		6	6	6
○ OCT		7	7	7
○ NOV		8	8	8
○ DEC		9	9	9

5 SEX

○ MALE
○ FEMALE

IMPORTANT: Fill in items 6 and 7 exactly as shown on the preceding page.

6 TEST FORM

(Copy from back of test book)

7 TEST CODE

Four columns of ovals 0–9

8 OTHER

1 Ⓐ Ⓑ Ⓒ Ⓓ Ⓔ
2 Ⓐ Ⓑ Ⓒ Ⓓ Ⓔ
3 Ⓐ Ⓑ Ⓒ Ⓓ Ⓔ

OpScan iNSIGHT™ forms by Pearson NCS EM-253760-3:654321   Printed in U.S.A.   © TPR Education IP Holdings, LLC

PLEASE DO NOT WRITE IN THIS AREA

SERIAL #

THIS PAGE INTENTIONALLY LEFT BLANK

SECTION 1

IMPORTANT: **USE A NO. 2 PENCIL. DO NOT WRITE OUTSIDE THE BORDER!**
Words written outside the essay box or written in ink **WILL NOT APPEAR** in the copy sent to be scored and your score will be affected.

Begin your essay on this page. If you need more space, continue on the next page.

Continue on the next page, if necessary.

Continuation of ESSAY Section 1 from previous page. Write below only if you need more space.
IMPORTANT: DO NOT START on this page—if you do, your essay may appear blank and your score may be affected.

SECTION 2

1 Ⓐ Ⓑ Ⓒ Ⓓ Ⓔ   11 Ⓐ Ⓑ Ⓒ Ⓓ Ⓔ   21 Ⓐ Ⓑ Ⓒ Ⓓ Ⓔ   31 Ⓐ Ⓑ Ⓒ Ⓓ Ⓔ
2 Ⓐ Ⓑ Ⓒ Ⓓ Ⓔ   12 Ⓐ Ⓑ Ⓒ Ⓓ Ⓔ   22 Ⓐ Ⓑ Ⓒ Ⓓ Ⓔ   32 Ⓐ Ⓑ Ⓒ Ⓓ Ⓔ
3 Ⓐ Ⓑ Ⓒ Ⓓ Ⓔ   13 Ⓐ Ⓑ Ⓒ Ⓓ Ⓔ   23 Ⓐ Ⓑ Ⓒ Ⓓ Ⓔ   33 Ⓐ Ⓑ Ⓒ Ⓓ Ⓔ
4 Ⓐ Ⓑ Ⓒ Ⓓ Ⓔ   14 Ⓐ Ⓑ Ⓒ Ⓓ Ⓔ   24 Ⓐ Ⓑ Ⓒ Ⓓ Ⓔ   34 Ⓐ Ⓑ Ⓒ Ⓓ Ⓔ
5 Ⓐ Ⓑ Ⓒ Ⓓ Ⓔ   15 Ⓐ Ⓑ Ⓒ Ⓓ Ⓔ   25 Ⓐ Ⓑ Ⓒ Ⓓ Ⓔ   35 Ⓐ Ⓑ Ⓒ Ⓓ Ⓔ
6 Ⓐ Ⓑ Ⓒ Ⓓ Ⓔ   16 Ⓐ Ⓑ Ⓒ Ⓓ Ⓔ   26 Ⓐ Ⓑ Ⓒ Ⓓ Ⓔ   36 Ⓐ Ⓑ Ⓒ Ⓓ Ⓔ
7 Ⓐ Ⓑ Ⓒ Ⓓ Ⓔ   17 Ⓐ Ⓑ Ⓒ Ⓓ Ⓔ   27 Ⓐ Ⓑ Ⓒ Ⓓ Ⓔ   37 Ⓐ Ⓑ Ⓒ Ⓓ Ⓔ
8 Ⓐ Ⓑ Ⓒ Ⓓ Ⓔ   18 Ⓐ Ⓑ Ⓒ Ⓓ Ⓔ   28 Ⓐ Ⓑ Ⓒ Ⓓ Ⓔ   38 Ⓐ Ⓑ Ⓒ Ⓓ Ⓔ
9 Ⓐ Ⓑ Ⓒ Ⓓ Ⓔ   19 Ⓐ Ⓑ Ⓒ Ⓓ Ⓔ   29 Ⓐ Ⓑ Ⓒ Ⓓ Ⓔ   39 Ⓐ Ⓑ Ⓒ Ⓓ Ⓔ
10 Ⓐ Ⓑ Ⓒ Ⓓ Ⓔ   20 Ⓐ Ⓑ Ⓒ Ⓓ Ⓔ   30 Ⓐ Ⓑ Ⓒ Ⓓ Ⓔ   40 Ⓐ Ⓑ Ⓒ Ⓓ Ⓔ

SECTION 3

1 Ⓐ Ⓑ Ⓒ Ⓓ Ⓔ   11 Ⓐ Ⓑ Ⓒ Ⓓ Ⓔ   21 Ⓐ Ⓑ Ⓒ Ⓓ Ⓔ   31 Ⓐ Ⓑ Ⓒ Ⓓ Ⓔ
2 Ⓐ Ⓑ Ⓒ Ⓓ Ⓔ   12 Ⓐ Ⓑ Ⓒ Ⓓ Ⓔ   22 Ⓐ Ⓑ Ⓒ Ⓓ Ⓔ   32 Ⓐ Ⓑ Ⓒ Ⓓ Ⓔ
3 Ⓐ Ⓑ Ⓒ Ⓓ Ⓔ   13 Ⓐ Ⓑ Ⓒ Ⓓ Ⓔ   23 Ⓐ Ⓑ Ⓒ Ⓓ Ⓔ   33 Ⓐ Ⓑ Ⓒ Ⓓ Ⓔ
4 Ⓐ Ⓑ Ⓒ Ⓓ Ⓔ   14 Ⓐ Ⓑ Ⓒ Ⓓ Ⓔ   24 Ⓐ Ⓑ Ⓒ Ⓓ Ⓔ   34 Ⓐ Ⓑ Ⓒ Ⓓ Ⓔ
5 Ⓐ Ⓑ Ⓒ Ⓓ Ⓔ   15 Ⓐ Ⓑ Ⓒ Ⓓ Ⓔ   25 Ⓐ Ⓑ Ⓒ Ⓓ Ⓔ   35 Ⓐ Ⓑ Ⓒ Ⓓ Ⓔ
6 Ⓐ Ⓑ Ⓒ Ⓓ Ⓔ   16 Ⓐ Ⓑ Ⓒ Ⓓ Ⓔ   26 Ⓐ Ⓑ Ⓒ Ⓓ Ⓔ   36 Ⓐ Ⓑ Ⓒ Ⓓ Ⓔ
7 Ⓐ Ⓑ Ⓒ Ⓓ Ⓔ   17 Ⓐ Ⓑ Ⓒ Ⓓ Ⓔ   27 Ⓐ Ⓑ Ⓒ Ⓓ Ⓔ   37 Ⓐ Ⓑ Ⓒ Ⓓ Ⓔ
8 Ⓐ Ⓑ Ⓒ Ⓓ Ⓔ   18 Ⓐ Ⓑ Ⓒ Ⓓ Ⓔ   28 Ⓐ Ⓑ Ⓒ Ⓓ Ⓔ   38 Ⓐ Ⓑ Ⓒ Ⓓ Ⓔ
9 Ⓐ Ⓑ Ⓒ Ⓓ Ⓔ   19 Ⓐ Ⓑ Ⓒ Ⓓ Ⓔ   29 Ⓐ Ⓑ Ⓒ Ⓓ Ⓔ   39 Ⓐ Ⓑ Ⓒ Ⓓ Ⓔ
10 Ⓐ Ⓑ Ⓒ Ⓓ Ⓔ   20 Ⓐ Ⓑ Ⓒ Ⓓ Ⓔ   30 Ⓐ Ⓑ Ⓒ Ⓓ Ⓔ   40 Ⓐ Ⓑ Ⓒ Ⓓ Ⓔ

CAUTION Grid answers in the section below for SECTION 2 or SECTION 3 only if directed to do so in your test book.

Student-Produced Responses ONLY ANSWERS THAT ARE GRIDDED WILL BE SCORED. YOU WILL NOT RECEIVE CREDIT FOR ANYTHING WRITTEN IN THE BOXES.

Quality Assurance Mark ●

9, 10, 11, 12, 13

14, 15, 16, 17, 18

(Grid answer bubbles 0–9 for each response section)

COMPLETE MARK ●   **EXAMPLES OF INCOMPLETE MARKS** Ⓐ Ⓑ Ⓒ Ⓓ / Ⓢ Ⓒ Ⓔ Ⓒ

You must use a No. 2 pencil and marks must be complete. Do not use a mechanical pencil. It is very important that you fill in the entire circle darkly and completely. If you change your responses, erase as completely as possible. Incomplete marks or erasures may affect your score.

SECTION 4

1 Ⓐ Ⓑ Ⓒ Ⓓ Ⓔ   11 Ⓐ Ⓑ Ⓒ Ⓓ Ⓔ   21 Ⓐ Ⓑ Ⓒ Ⓓ Ⓔ   31 Ⓐ Ⓑ Ⓒ Ⓓ Ⓔ
2 Ⓐ Ⓑ Ⓒ Ⓓ Ⓔ   12 Ⓐ Ⓑ Ⓒ Ⓓ Ⓔ   22 Ⓐ Ⓑ Ⓒ Ⓓ Ⓔ   32 Ⓐ Ⓑ Ⓒ Ⓓ Ⓔ
3 Ⓐ Ⓑ Ⓒ Ⓓ Ⓔ   13 Ⓐ Ⓑ Ⓒ Ⓓ Ⓔ   23 Ⓐ Ⓑ Ⓒ Ⓓ Ⓔ   33 Ⓐ Ⓑ Ⓒ Ⓓ Ⓔ
4 Ⓐ Ⓑ Ⓒ Ⓓ Ⓔ   14 Ⓐ Ⓑ Ⓒ Ⓓ Ⓔ   24 Ⓐ Ⓑ Ⓒ Ⓓ Ⓔ   34 Ⓐ Ⓑ Ⓒ Ⓓ Ⓔ
5 Ⓐ Ⓑ Ⓒ Ⓓ Ⓔ   15 Ⓐ Ⓑ Ⓒ Ⓓ Ⓔ   25 Ⓐ Ⓑ Ⓒ Ⓓ Ⓔ   35 Ⓐ Ⓑ Ⓒ Ⓓ Ⓔ
6 Ⓐ Ⓑ Ⓒ Ⓓ Ⓔ   16 Ⓐ Ⓑ Ⓒ Ⓓ Ⓔ   26 Ⓐ Ⓑ Ⓒ Ⓓ Ⓔ   36 Ⓐ Ⓑ Ⓒ Ⓓ Ⓔ
7 Ⓐ Ⓑ Ⓒ Ⓓ Ⓔ   17 Ⓐ Ⓑ Ⓒ Ⓓ Ⓔ   27 Ⓐ Ⓑ Ⓒ Ⓓ Ⓔ   37 Ⓐ Ⓑ Ⓒ Ⓓ Ⓔ
8 Ⓐ Ⓑ Ⓒ Ⓓ Ⓔ   18 Ⓐ Ⓑ Ⓒ Ⓓ Ⓔ   28 Ⓐ Ⓑ Ⓒ Ⓓ Ⓔ   38 Ⓐ Ⓑ Ⓒ Ⓓ Ⓔ
9 Ⓐ Ⓑ Ⓒ Ⓓ Ⓔ   19 Ⓐ Ⓑ Ⓒ Ⓓ Ⓔ   29 Ⓐ Ⓑ Ⓒ Ⓓ Ⓔ   39 Ⓐ Ⓑ Ⓒ Ⓓ Ⓔ
10 Ⓐ Ⓑ Ⓒ Ⓓ Ⓔ   20 Ⓐ Ⓑ Ⓒ Ⓓ Ⓔ   30 Ⓐ Ⓑ Ⓒ Ⓓ Ⓔ   40 Ⓐ Ⓑ Ⓒ Ⓓ Ⓔ

SECTION 5

1 Ⓐ Ⓑ Ⓒ Ⓓ Ⓔ   11 Ⓐ Ⓑ Ⓒ Ⓓ Ⓔ   21 Ⓐ Ⓑ Ⓒ Ⓓ Ⓔ   31 Ⓐ Ⓑ Ⓒ Ⓓ Ⓔ
2 Ⓐ Ⓑ Ⓒ Ⓓ Ⓔ   12 Ⓐ Ⓑ Ⓒ Ⓓ Ⓔ   22 Ⓐ Ⓑ Ⓒ Ⓓ Ⓔ   32 Ⓐ Ⓑ Ⓒ Ⓓ Ⓔ
3 Ⓐ Ⓑ Ⓒ Ⓓ Ⓔ   13 Ⓐ Ⓑ Ⓒ Ⓓ Ⓔ   23 Ⓐ Ⓑ Ⓒ Ⓓ Ⓔ   33 Ⓐ Ⓑ Ⓒ Ⓓ Ⓔ
4 Ⓐ Ⓑ Ⓒ Ⓓ Ⓔ   14 Ⓐ Ⓑ Ⓒ Ⓓ Ⓔ   24 Ⓐ Ⓑ Ⓒ Ⓓ Ⓔ   34 Ⓐ Ⓑ Ⓒ Ⓓ Ⓔ
5 Ⓐ Ⓑ Ⓒ Ⓓ Ⓔ   15 Ⓐ Ⓑ Ⓒ Ⓓ Ⓔ   25 Ⓐ Ⓑ Ⓒ Ⓓ Ⓔ   35 Ⓐ Ⓑ Ⓒ Ⓓ Ⓔ
6 Ⓐ Ⓑ Ⓒ Ⓓ Ⓔ   16 Ⓐ Ⓑ Ⓒ Ⓓ Ⓔ   26 Ⓐ Ⓑ Ⓒ Ⓓ Ⓔ   36 Ⓐ Ⓑ Ⓒ Ⓓ Ⓔ
7 Ⓐ Ⓑ Ⓒ Ⓓ Ⓔ   17 Ⓐ Ⓑ Ⓒ Ⓓ Ⓔ   27 Ⓐ Ⓑ Ⓒ Ⓓ Ⓔ   37 Ⓐ Ⓑ Ⓒ Ⓓ Ⓔ
8 Ⓐ Ⓑ Ⓒ Ⓓ Ⓔ   18 Ⓐ Ⓑ Ⓒ Ⓓ Ⓔ   28 Ⓐ Ⓑ Ⓒ Ⓓ Ⓔ   38 Ⓐ Ⓑ Ⓒ Ⓓ Ⓔ
9 Ⓐ Ⓑ Ⓒ Ⓓ Ⓔ   19 Ⓐ Ⓑ Ⓒ Ⓓ Ⓔ   29 Ⓐ Ⓑ Ⓒ Ⓓ Ⓔ   39 Ⓐ Ⓑ Ⓒ Ⓓ Ⓔ
10 Ⓐ Ⓑ Ⓒ Ⓓ Ⓔ   20 Ⓐ Ⓑ Ⓒ Ⓓ Ⓔ   30 Ⓐ Ⓑ Ⓒ Ⓓ Ⓔ   40 Ⓐ Ⓑ Ⓒ Ⓓ Ⓔ

CAUTION

Grid answers in the section below for SECTION 4 or SECTION 5 only if directed to do so in your test book.

Student-Produced Responses

ONLY ANSWERS THAT ARE GRIDDED WILL BE SCORED. YOU WILL NOT RECEIVE CREDIT FOR ANYTHING WRITTEN IN THE BOXES.

Quality Assurance Mark ●

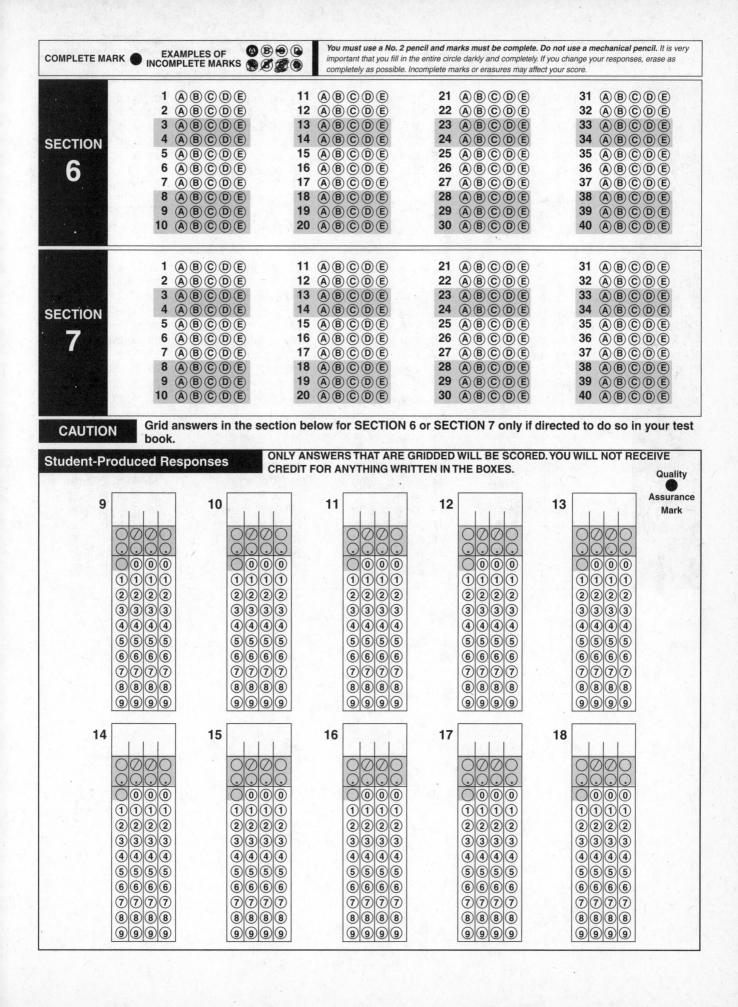

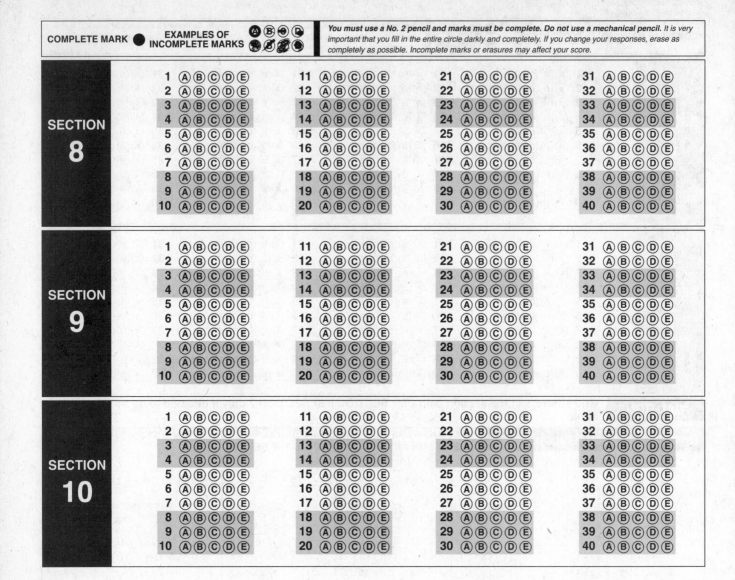

SECTION 1
ESSAY
Time — 25 minutes

Turn to Section 1 of your answer sheet to write your essay.

The essay gives you an opportunity to show how effectively you can develop and express ideas. You should, therefore, take care to develop your point of view, present your ideas logically and clearly, and use language precisely.

Your essay must be written on the lines provided on your answer sheet—you will receive no other paper on which to write. You will have enough space if you write on every line, avoid wide margins, and keep your handwriting to a reasonable size. Remember that people who are not familiar with your handwriting will read what you write. Try to write or print so that what you are writing is legible to those readers.

You have twenty-five minutes to write an essay on the topic assigned below. DO NOT WRITE ON ANOTHER TOPIC. AN OFF-TOPIC ESSAY WILL RECEIVE A SCORE OF ZERO.

Think carefully about the issue presented in the following excerpt and the assignment below.

> Making decisions is something we all struggle with. We worry that we need more time to think things through, or that we need more information, or that we will simply make the wrong decision regardless. But inaction gets you nowhere. Even a bad decision can teach us something valuable.
>
> Adapted from Alicia Smith

Assignment: Is making a bad decision better than making no decision at all? Plan and write an essay in which you develop your point of view on this issue. Support your position with reasoning and examples taken from your reading, studies, experience, or observations.

DO NOT WRITE YOUR ESSAY IN YOUR TEST BOOK. You will receive credit only for what you write on your answer sheet.

BEGIN WRITING YOUR ESSAY IN SECTION 1 OF THE ANSWER SHEET.

S T O P
If you finish before time is called, you may check your work on this section only.
Do not turn to any other section in the test.

SECTION 2
Time — 25 minutes
20 Questions

Turn to Section 2 of your answer sheet to answer the questions in this section.

Directions: For this section, solve each problem and decide which is the best of the choices given. Fill in the corresponding circle on the answer sheet. You may use any available space for scratchwork.

Notes

1. The use of a calculator is permitted.

2. All numbers used are real numbers.

3. Figures that accompany problems in this test are intended to provide information useful in solving the problems. They are drawn as accurately as possible EXCEPT when it is stated in a specific problem that the figure is not drawn to scale. All figures lie in a plane unless otherwise indicated.

4. Unless otherwise specified, the domain of any function f is assumed to be the set of all real numbers x for which $f(x)$ is a real number.

Reference Information

$A = \pi r^2$ $A = lw$ $A = \frac{1}{2}bh$ $V = lwh$ $V = \pi r^2 h$ $c^2 = a^2 + b^2$ Special Right Triangles
$C = 2\pi r$

The number of degrees of arc in a circle is 360.
The sum of the measures in degrees of the angles of a triangle is 180.

1. If $y + 4 = 13$, then $y - 2 =$

   (A) 7
   (B) 8
   (C) 9
   (D) 10
   (E) 11

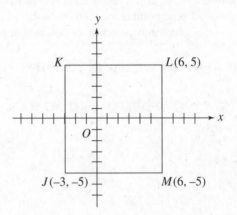

2. In the figure above, *JKLM* is a rectangle. What is the perimeter of *JKLM* ?

   (A) 18
   (B) 33
   (C) 38
   (D) 45
   (E) 55

GO ON TO THE NEXT PAGE

3. Of 650 vehicles in a parking lot, $\dfrac{1}{5}$ are trucks. How many of the vehicles are <u>not</u> trucks?

(A) 65
(B) 130
(C) 325
(D) 420
(E) 520

4. If $x = -3$, then $\big\| x - 2 \big| - \big| 2 + x \big\| =$

(A) −3
(B) 0
(C) 1
(D) 2
(E) 4

5. A certain fraction is equivalent to $n\%$, where n is an integer. Which of the following could be the value of that fraction?

(A) $\dfrac{1}{25}$

(B) $\dfrac{1}{12}$

(C) $\dfrac{1}{8}$

(D) $\dfrac{1}{6}$

(E) $\dfrac{1}{3}$

6. How much greater than 15% of z is 30% of z ?

(A) 15z
(B) 2z
(C) 1.5z
(D) z
(E) 0.15z

GO ON TO THE NEXT PAGE

7. Every year the population of Northville is $\frac{3}{4}$ of what it was 10 years earlier. If there are currently 800 people living in Northville, how many people will live there in 20 years?

(A) 10
(B) 200
(C) 400
(D) 450
(E) 600

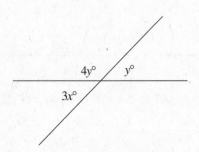

Note: Figure not drawn to scale.

8. In the figure above, what is the value of x ?

(A) 12
(B) 15
(C) 20
(D) 24
(E) 36

9. $\left(60\times10^4\right)+\left(60\times10^2\right) =$

(A) 606×10^3
(B) 606×10^2
(C) 120×10^6
(D) 66×10^4
(E) 60×10^6

Numbers of Books Read	Number of Students Who Read This Many Books
10	18
20	24
30	3

10. Forty-five students participated in a summer reading program to raise money for charity, as shown in the chart above. For every book read, fifty cents was donated to the charity. How much money was raised altogether?

(A) $300
(B) $375
(C) $450
(D) $750
(E) $900

GO ON TO THE NEXT PAGE

11. The square of b is equal to the sum of b and 12. Which of the following equations could be used to find the value of b ?

(A) $b^2 + 12b = 0$
(B) $b^2 - 12b = 0$
(C) $b^2 + b + 12 = 0$
(D) $b^2 - b + 12 = 0$
(E) $b^2 - b - 12 = 0$

12. A bowl contains punch made from pineapple juice, orange juice, and seltzer, in a ratio of $2 : 3 : 1$, respectively. If the bowl contains 2 liters of seltzer, how many liters of punch does the bowl contain?

(A)   6
(B)   8
(C)   10
(D)   12
(E)   14

13. If $wx = y$, $xy = z$, and $wxyz \neq 0$, which of the following is equal to w ?

(A) xz

(B) xz^2

(C) $\dfrac{x}{z}$

(D) $\dfrac{z}{x}$

(E) $\dfrac{z}{x^2}$

14. If Duane were to give Gregg \$14, they would each have the same amount of money. If Duane has \$45, how much money does Gregg have?

(A) \$10
(B) \$17
(C) \$24
(D) \$31
(E) \$38

GO ON TO THE NEXT PAGE

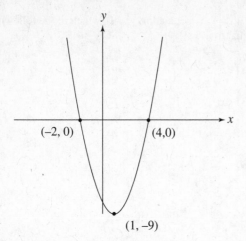

15. If the graph shown above is that of $y = f(x)$, which of the following functions could be $f(x)$?

(A) $f(x) = (x+1)^2 - 9$
(B) $f(x) = (x-2)^2 - 10$
(C) $f(x) = (x-1)^2 - 8$
(D) $f(x) = (x+1)^2 - 6$
(E) $f(x) = (x-1)^2 - 9$

16. Three lines intersect within a circle. What is the greatest number of separate, nonoverlapping regions that can be formed inside the circle by the intersection of the lines?

(A) Four
(B) Five
(C) Six
(D) Seven
(E) Eight or more

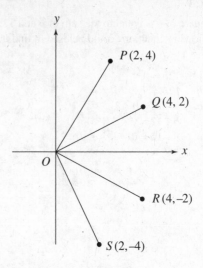

17. In the figure above, what is the average (arithmetic mean) of the slopes of $\overline{OP}$, $\overline{OQ}$, $\overline{OR}$, and $\overline{OS}$?

(A) −2

(B) −1

(C) 0

(D) $\dfrac{1}{2}$

(E) 1

18. If m and n are integers and $(x + m)(x + n) = x^2 + 11x + c$, what is the greatest possible value of c ?

(A) 22
(B) 24
(C) 28
(D) 30
(E) 33

GO ON TO THE NEXT PAGE

19. If x and y are distinct prime numbers, which of the following has exactly four distinct factors?

   (A) x^2
   (B) xy
   (C) xy^2
   (D) $(x+y)^2$
   (E) $(x-y)^2$

20. The length of the diagonal of a square is $j + 3$. Which of the following represents the area of the square?

   (A) $j^2 + 9$

   (B) $j^2 + 6j + 9$

   (C) $(j^2 + 9)\sqrt{2}$

   (D) $\dfrac{j^2 + 9}{2}$

   (E) $\dfrac{j^2 + 6j + 9}{2}$

STOP
If you finish before time is called, you may check your work on this section only.
Do not turn to any other section in the test.

SECTION 3
Time — 25 minutes
24 Questions

Turn to Section 3 of your answer sheet to answer the questions in this section.

Directions: For each question in this section, select the best answer from among the choices given and fill in the corresponding circle on the answer sheet.

Each sentence below has one or two blanks, each blank indicating that something has been omitted. Beneath the sentence are five words or sets of words labeled A through E. Choose the word or set of words that, when inserted in the sentence, best fits the meaning of the sentence as a whole.

Example:

Desiring to ------- his taunting friends, Mitch gave them taffy in hopes it would keep their mouths shut.

(A) eliminate   (B) satisfy   (C) overcome
  (D) ridicule   (E) silence

---

1. The baseball coaches were stunned by the ------------- of skills shown by the prospect; he repeatedly missed ground balls and overthrew the first baseman by several feet.

   (A) assortment
   (B) absence
   (C) visibility
   (D) effortlessness
   (E) expertise

2. However ------- were Marvin Gaye's beginnings as a member of his father's church choir, he became a famous and ------- performer.

   (A) modest . . esteemed
   (B) popular . . unqualified
   (C) inspiring . . notorious
   (D) humble . . spiritual
   (E) powerful . . wealthy

3. Juliana's ------- in solving logic puzzles made her a top ------- at the state-wide contest.

   (A) dispassion . . competitor
   (B) disappointment . . challenger
   (C) skill . . personality
   (D) handicap . . contributor
   (E) alacrity . . contender

4. The professor, in effect, discouraged ------- behavior when he announced that his grading system would put all the students in the course in competition with each other for the highest grades.

   (A) academic   (B) selfish   (C) rhetorical
      (D) mischievous   (E) congenial

5. The graduate students in the global studies course were surprised at their professor's ------------- take on the material, in that he only addressed issues associated with the United States.

   (A) international
   (B) sonorous
   (C) myopic
   (D) nonchalant
   (E) diffident

GO ON TO THE NEXT PAGE

Directions: Each passage below is followed by questions based on its content. Answer the questions on the basis of what is <u>stated</u> or <u>implied</u> in each passage and in any introductory material that may be provided.

Questions 6-9 are based on the following passages.

The following passages briefly discuss the concept of the labyrinth and its mythical and historical origin.

Passage 1

A labyrinth is not a maze; there are no dead ends or forks in the road. Instead, there is one path that winds to the center, a path which symbolizes a journey to the center of the self.
Line Following the path back out is a rebirth into the world. The
5 most famous labyrinth is perhaps the thirteenth-century labyrinth on the cathedral floor at Chartres, France, although the ancient Greeks utilized labyrinths as early as 2500 B.C. Today labyrinths can be found in parks, hospitals, schools, and even jails. This millennia-old meditation is thought to
10 increase community spirit, and provide people with a peaceful centering experience.

Passage 2

From Ancient Greek mythology comes the story of the Minotaur—a half man, half bull—imprisoned in the Labyrinth under orders of King Minos. Although today we
15 think of a labyrinth mainly as an impossibly intricate maze, the word *labyrinth* actually comes from the word "labrys" which means "double-ax." According to legend, "House of the Double Ax" commonly referred to the dynasty of King Minos. Archeologists excavating the site of the city of
20 Knossos on Crete have found many images of double axes. Records exist that travelers of the ancient world told tales about a palace or temple here that had a complex system of corridors.

6. The author of Passage 1 most likely includes the first two sentences in order to

(A) discriminate between a common misconception and the subject to be discussed

(B) set a mystical tone that is appropriate for a spiritual discussion

(C) begin a list of directions of how to meditate on a walk through a labyrinth

(D) convince the reader of the healthful and spiritual benefits of labyrinths

(E) begin an inspiring passage with a dark and melancholy sentiment

7. In Passage 2, the author's purpose in mentioning the "Archeologists" (line 19) is to

(A) support the credibility of legends recorded by ancient historians

(B) identify what is believed to be the oldest known labyrinth

(C) conclusively prove the authenticity of Greek myths

(D) give evidence of a link between the city of Knossos and King Minos

(E) detail recent archaeological excavations in the area

8. Which pair of phrases best describes the labyrinth as presented in Passage 1 and Passage 2, respectively?

(A) Chartres, France and King Minos

(B) A meditation aid and a prison

(C) A path and a thread

(D) A fork in the road and a double-ax symbol

(E) A jail and an archeologist's excavation

9. As compared to the author of Passage 1, the author of Passage 2 is more interested in

(A) labyrinth construction methods

(B) etymology of the word "labyrinth"

(C) the spirituality of the labyrinth

(D) historical examples of labyrinths

(E) a community's enthusiasm for meditation

GO ON TO THE NEXT PAGE

Questions 10–15 are based on the following passage.

The following passage is excerpted from a contemporary American novel.

William was completely lost, that much he knew. Unfortunately, that was all he knew.

Of course, he hated to admit it when he was lost, so
Line much so that when he did get lost, it would inevitably create
5 a tragic episode of the grandest proportions, rather than a minor inconvenience. In a way, that made it easier for him to explain his tardiness to others. It was certainly easier to evade responsibility for a huge, unforeseeable mishap than for a series of small, yet obvious, errors.

10 These situations always started out the same way. William would be setting out to drive to a business appointment. Before leaving he would verify that he had everything he needed for the day. First he checked to see that he had his briefcase. He then checked and rechecked the contents of the
15 briefcase to see that every possible document he might need was there, not to mention extra pens, notepads, a calculator, spare calculator batteries, his cell phone, and spare cell phone battery.

He even insisted upon carrying a miniature tape recorder,
20 and spare batteries for that, as well. The inclusion of this last item was particularly perplexing to his coworkers, as there was no possible use for it in his work. When casually queried about the tape recorder, William merely responded, "I might need it." That much, certainly, was evident, and they let the
25 matter drop. To be sure, his insistence on traveling with a tape recorder for which he had no need was not the oddest thing about William, as far as his coworkers were concerned. Although his hygiene and grooming were impeccable, his clothing seemed remarkably similar, if not identical, from one
30 day to the next. His coworkers surmised that he owned several suits and ties, all of the same cut, in just two colors, navy blue and brown.

As he began his trip, William would have the directions to his destination neatly written out in his own, extremely
35 precise handwriting (the only handwriting he could dependably read, he would say). The directions would be hung on the dashboard within easy view, on a miniature clipboard. William didn't actually need the directions at that point, since he had already committed them to memory. In fact, if
40 you were in the car with him on such occasions (a practical impossibility since William would never drive with anyone in the car during business hours, not that anyone was anxious to, of course), you would hear him muttering a litany of lefts and rights; chanting his mantra, street names and route numbers
45 in their proper order.

Everything would be going fine until something would distract William, perhaps a flock of birds flying in formation, or an out-of-state license plate he didn't recognize. Several minutes would pass, and he would slowly realize that he
50 might have missed a turn. He would remain, however, in relatively calm denial of this possibility, until he had driven many more miles and passed several other turns. "This road doesn't look like it goes the right way," he would grumble. "Too many other people are turning off here; I don't want
55 to get stuck in traffic." And maybe, just maybe, he *hadn't* missed his turn, and it was going to appear around the next bend in the road. "No way to find out but to keep on going." Obviously, the sensible thing to do would be to pull over, and consult a map, or perhaps use the cell phone to
60 call for assistance. Neither of these things was an option as far as William was concerned. The cell phone, as he put it, "should be used only in emergencies." Since nothing that ever happened to him constituted an "emergency" in his mind, he never once actually used the phone.

65 As to maps, he never carried one. He claimed that most of them were useless to him, as they were "organized and planned so badly." In any event, what need did he have for maps when he always had his directions written out so carefully?

70 So on and on he drove, hoping that some type of resolution would eventually reveal itself to him, that it would suddenly occur to him where to turn around, what to do. On one occasion, he drove through three different states before finding his way back to the office, well after dark, his suit
75 rumpled, but his blue necktie still flying proudly.

10. The attitude of William's coworkers toward him can best be described as

(A) mildly curious
(B) coldly indifferent
(C) overtly condescending
(D) deeply intrigued
(E) moderately disturbed

GO ON TO THE NEXT PAGE

11. William's answer to his coworkers' questions about his tape recorder (lines 19-25) implies that he

  (A) knows much more about the applications of technology in business than they do
  (B) records business conversations in order to have proof of what was discussed
  (C) believes it is best to be prepared for any contingency
  (D) regrets not having had a tape recorder on a previous occasion
  (E) feels that their questions are rude and intrusive

12. William's preparations for his business meetings are best described as

  (A) professional
  (B) careless
  (C) useful
  (D) fruitless
  (E) tiresome

13. The reference to maps (line 65) implies that William

  (A) has much to learn about navigation
  (B) relies more on instinct than reason
  (C) questions the mapmaker's eye for detail
  (D) does not trust the orderliness of most maps
  (E) often forgets his maps at home

14. The author refers to William's "blue necktie" (line 75) in order to suggest

  (A) the length and duration of his journey to work
  (B) the importance William places on his hygiene and grooming
  (C) his ability to display dignity despite his mistakes
  (D) the lack of variety in his wardrobe
  (E) his obliviousness to the fact the he caused his own tardiness

15. The primary purpose of the passage is to

  (A) recount the mishaps of a man driving to a business meeting
  (B) chronicle the idiosyncrasies of a traveling businessman
  (C) provide a detailed description of a day in the life of a salesperson
  (D) explain a man's lateness to his co-workers
  (E) give insight into the mentally ill

GO ON TO THE NEXT PAGE

Questions 16-24 are based on the following passage.

The following passage is excerpted from a book by a naturalist who studied the behavior of coyotes living in Yellowstone Park. Canis latrans refers to the species of coyote she observed.

I had not solved the problem of how to obtain photographic evidence of the "loving" and "cooperative" behavior of my subjects, though in making notations I now
Line freely referred to my band of coyotes as a "pack." I knew that
5 objections might be raised to my use of this term. A number of knowledgeable people have thought that coyotes, since they do not depend on one another to obtain food, never had the need to evolve such a complex social unit as is implied by the word "pack." Wolves, by contrast, have had to band
10 together to kill animals sufficiently large to provide them with adequate nourishment. A wolf can weigh five times more than a coyote, and therefore a wolf is unable to subsist entirely on a diet of small rodents.

One support of the prevailing view of the coyote as a loner
15 is the undeniable fact that he is almost always observed singly or in pairs. A winter study by Robert Chesness in northern Minnesota reported 61 percent of the animals sighted traveling alone and 34 percent in the company of only one other animal. In winter observations, only once did Chesness
20 observe as many as four coyotes together.

But these figures cannot possibly tell the complete story. I too, more frequently than not, observed coyotes hunting alone or in pairs, especially in winter. But often after watching a particular animal for many hours, I would see it be joined
25 by others or would catch sight of coyotes mousing nearby. To *Canis latrans*, 1,000 yards or more is not a separation. Togetherness cannot be determined by human standards.

And now, in spring, the coyotes I was watching were positively wolf-like in their tendency to form exclusive
30 relationships with one another. They recognized and greeted "accepted" individuals and expelled all others from what seemed to be delineated territories. They also cooperated in the rearing of the young. And often in the early evening I observed as many as six of my subjects convene on Miller
35 Butte, enjoy a good howl, and then, just like wolves, set off together as if to hunt game. Upon arriving at their destination, usually the marsh, they would simply scatter and individually begin to look for mice. Thereafter they would pay no further heed to one another.

40 I was by no means the first to notice that coyotes sometimes "pack-up" for seemingly no purpose than to enjoy one another's company. Explorers who visited the Far West during the nineteenth century (Audubon included) reported coyotes to be more sociable than wolves. J. Frank
45 Dobie, noting that in recent years such behavior was not being reported, tried to reconcile past and present trends by postulating that the versatile coyote may have been forced to adapt himself to a more solitary life to survive the advance of civilization. He wrote: "Had they, bison-like, persisted in
50 following an inherited instinct for gregariousness, they would by now have been eliminated from much of their territory."

Perhaps, then, my Miller Butte coyotes, living as they did on a protected refuge, had reverted to the more gregarious lifestyle once natural to the species. Or perhaps all coyotes
55 become clannish in the spring of the year when pups are born. Such behavior would certainly have high survival value.

It might even help to explain how *Canis latrans* has managed to survive the efforts aimed at its extermination. For should Redlegs and Gray Dog both be killed, their
60 three pups would undoubtedly be raised by Harness Marks or Brownie, or the two together. Nature had provided the litter with surrogate parents. At the same time, Brownie and Harness Marks were enjoying the advantage of serving an apprenticeship in pup-rearing for the day when they would
65 produce a litter of their own.

Then again, perhaps the pack association I was observing was only temporary. Certainly Mama's growing intolerance of Brownie suggested that the bond between these two females was weakening. Might not the dynamics of coyote survival
70 demand that these two animals sever their relationship? Miller Butte could not support an indefinite number of coyote litters, and therefore Brownie's maturation would ultimately present a threat to the well-being of any future pups born to Mama Redlegs. But since coyotes are rarely able to reproduce before
75 their second year, the rupture between these two females might not occur before the younger one had served for a season as "nursemaid" to the other's whelps.

16. The author discounts the findings of Robert Chesness on the grounds that

(A) Chesness incorrectly used the term "pack"
(B) the study may have been biased toward a human understanding of closeness
(C) Chesness' observations merely support the prevailing view
(D) some species cannot be understood solely through observation
(E) 1,000 yards or more is too great a distance to allow communication between coyotes

GO ON TO THE NEXT PAGE

17. The author mentions nineteenth-century explorers (lines 42-43) in order to

   (A) denounce a traditional custom
   (B) prove a controversial theory
   (C) illustrate a scientific conundrum
   (D) explain a temporary phenomenon
   (E) provide evidence supporting a claim

18. The author quotes the writings of J. Frank Dobie (lines 44-45) in order to

   (A) provide an alternative perspective in order to resolve an apparent inconsistency
   (B) show how another species benefited from a characteristic similar to that of coyotes
   (C) suggest that coyotes' gregariousness will lead to their inevitable extinction
   (D) advocate that certain animal behaviors should not be continued indefinitely
   (E) bring the ultimate fate of the bison into public awareness

19. The "protected refuge" (line 53) is given as a possible reason for the coyotes'

   (A) population explosion
   (B) lower birthrate
   (C) expected extinction
   (D) apparent ruthlessness
   (E) increased companionship

20. In line 56, "such behavior" can best be described as

   (A) ruthless
   (B) sociable
   (C) insightful
   (D) uncomplicated
   (E) primitive

21. The author would most likely agree with which of the following?

   (A) Coyotes are more frequently cooperative than has been commonly believed.
   (B) Robert Chessness' studies have no merit when regarding coyote observations.
   (C) Wolves are likely more dangerous animals than coyotes.
   (D) The cooperation amongst coyotes is a fleeting phenomenon.
   (E) Yellowstone Park is the ideal location for coyote observation.

22. In lines 61-62, the author's characterization of "nature" suggests that

   (A) coyotes don't raise their own young
   (B) coyotes hunt in pairs
   (C) coyotes will nurture orphaned pups
   (D) Brownie is the mother of a litter of pups
   (E) coyotes travel in packs in order to protect their young

23. It can be inferred from the passage that coyotes in North America have

   (A) become less numerous since the nineteenth Century
   (B) flourished in the protected refuge of Yellowstone Park
   (C) resorted to traveling in packs for survival
   (D) failed to adapt to environmental changes
   (E) always hunted small rodents alone

24. Based on the passage, which of the following questions cannot be explicitly answered?

   (A) What characteristics of wolves make them more likely to hunt in packs than coyotes?
   (B) What conditions exist in Yellowstone Park that allowed coyotes to revert to their natural lifestyle?
   (C) What do the observations of this naturalist tell us about the future of the coyote population at Miller Butte?
   (D) What did Audubon report about the sociability of coyotes in the Far West during the nineteenth century?
   (E) What are the reasons for some scientists to believe that coyotes have not had the need to form complex social units called "packs"?

STOP
If you finish before time is called, you may check your work on this section only.
Do not turn to any other section in the test.

SECTION 5
Time — 25 minutes
24 Questions

Turn to Section 5 of your answer sheet to answer the questions in this section.

Directions: For each question in this section, select the best answer from among the choices given and fill in the corresponding circle on the answer sheet.

Each sentence below has one or two blanks, each blank indicating that something has been omitted. Beneath the sentence are five words or sets of words labeled A through E. Choose the word or set of words that, when inserted in the sentence, best fits the meaning of the sentence as a whole.

Example:

Desiring to ------- his taunting friends, Mitch gave them taffy in hopes it would keep their mouths shut.

(A) eliminate   (B) satisfy   (C) overcome
   (D) ridicule   (E) silence

Ⓐ Ⓑ Ⓒ Ⓓ ●

1. The newly published research study on the effects of sleep disorders is so ------- that it leaves no aspect of the issue unexamined.

  (A) comprehensive   (B) rewarding   (C) insignificant
    (D) problematic   (E) imprecise

2. The actress ------- her parents when she failed to ------- their contributions to her career during her award acceptance speech.

  (A) honored . . recognize
  (B) cheated . . accept
  (C) chagrined . . acknowledge
  (D) avoided . . understand
  (E) grieved . . dismiss

3. Though frequently read in college literature courses, the writer's novels are generally thought of as ------- ; critics feel they do not display any true originality.

  (A) unique   (B) insightful   (C) trite
    (D) elusive   (E) arid

4. Until he studied Picasso's works and realized how the painter's ------- revealed an emotional reality that bespoke pure -------, the art critic had believed that a traditional rendering of reality was the hallmark of greatness.

  (A) realism . . genius
  (B) ingenuity . . brilliance
  (C) pedantry . . recognition
  (D) novelty . . popularity
  (E) fancy . . opulence

5. The audience members at the illusionist's latest show were -------; they could not believe the spectacle they had just witnessed.

  (A) incredulous   (B) irresolute   (C) diverted
    (D) persistent   (E) pernicious

6. Though the article was meant to be an ------- analysis of the President's life and politics, some actually interpreted it as a ------- criticism of his term in office.

  (A) intrusive . . satirical
  (B) incendiary . . provocative
  (C) indifferent . . disinterested
  (D) impartial . . prosaic
  (E) objective . . partisan

7. Warned by teachers that further disturbances would result in his dismissal from school, Kevin struggled daily to avoid altercations and keep his ------- nature in check.

  (A) duplicitous   (B) irascible   (C) serene
    (D) scrupulous   (E) smarmy

8. During the war, coffee beans were scarce due to restrictions on international shipping; many people had to drink an ------- brew, made of roasted dandelion roots or chicory.

  (A) intermediate   (B) insufficient   (C) aesthetic
    (D) ersatz   (E) enervating

GO ON TO THE NEXT PAGE ▷

Directions: Each passage below is followed by questions based on its content. Answer the questions on the basis of what is <u>stated</u> or <u>implied</u> in each passage and in any introductory material that may be provided.

Questions 9-10 are based on the following passage.

Alexander Calder is known today for his massive mobiles, sculptures, and "stabiles." The sheer magnitude of these objects makes them seem worthy and significant; it is not
Line
surprising that scientist Albert Einstein once spent almost an
5 hour watching one of Calder's models revolve. Yet Calder's reputation was initially built on a seemingly trivial interest: the circus. Engrossed by the movement and balance of circus performers, Calder created hundreds of minute performers and animals from materials such as wire, felt, wood, leather,
10 nuts, and bolts. Small as each piece was, his collection eventually grew so large that he had to use five suitcases to tote it from place to place.

9. According to the passage, Calder created all of the following EXCEPT

(A) miniature animals
(B) moving sculptures
(C) immense pieces of visual art
(D) human figurines
(E) mechanical circus models

10. The passage suggests that one reason for Einstein's interest in Calder's artwork was its

(A) lack of seriousness
(B) numerous components
(C) immense dimensions
(D) use of scientific formulas
(E) depiction of trivial themes

Questions 11-12 are based on the following passage.

In the 1950s, a California doctor named Lawrence Craven published in an obscure scientific journal what would turn out to be a ground breaking paper. While tracking the health
Line
of his patients to whom he had prescribed a daily dose of
5 aspirin, he had discovered that aspirin was beneficial to the cardiac system. Since the end of the nineteenth century, one of the great fears about aspirin had been that it would weaken the heart, so Craven's results rehabilitated aspirin within the medical community. Along with aspirin's new benefits,
10 however, came problems; aspirin can also cause ulcers, hemorrhages, and internal bleeding. Using it to prevent heart disease is, as one researcher put it, like doing surgery with a hatchet.

11. The author mentions Craven's discovery in order to

(A) introduce the twofold nature of a medical treatment
(B) suggest that he should have chosen a more popular journal
(C) prove how little people knew about aspirin before the 1950s
(D) question aspirin's efficacy for cardiac health
(E) castigate Craven's eagerness to promote aspirin

12. The author uses the simile "like . . . a hatchet" (lines 12-13) to illustrate which point?

(A) There are better methods for preventing heart disease than administering aspirin.
(B) Surgery, like aspirin, has evolved a great deal since the 1950s.
(C) Aspirin is ultimately the most effective way to prevent heart disease.
(D) Aspirin's benefits are counterbalanced by its dangerous side effects.
(E) Researchers often exaggerate the negative aspects of new medical treatments.

GO ON TO THE NEXT PAGE

Questions 13-24 are based on the following passage.

The following passage, excerpted from Trudier Harris's book Black Women in the Fiction of James Baldwin, *attempts to analyze Baldwin's female characters.*

The black women James Baldwin creates in his works play a number of roles, several of which overlap. Whatever their role, most of the women believe themselves to be guilty of
Line some crime or condition of existence that demands penance.
5 At times the women are spiritual outcasts, psychological ghetto dwellers in a familial, sexual, religious world where their suffering does not lead to redemption.

The sense of guilt the women feel is often tied to their desire to break away from roles that have been defined for
10 them, or their failure to fulfill a role. Almost all of the roles in which we find black women in Baldwin's fiction are traditional ones—mothers, sisters, lovers, wives—and almost all of them are roles of support for the male characters.

The most prominent women we associate with Baldwin's
15 fiction are those who are solely within the tradition of the fundamentalist church as it exists in black communities. These women may be classified as churchgoers and appear from *Go Tell it on the Mountain* to *Just Above My Head*. The women in this category come closer to being stereotypes
20 than perhaps any others in Baldwin's works. They are usually described as large, buxom and middle-aged or older. On rare occasions, these women in the church extend their roles beyond those of support to ones of leadership. Praying Mother Washington has a recognized position of respect in *Go Tell*
25 *It on the Mountain*; she is "a powerful evangelist and very widely known."

Baldwin's portrayal of mothers overlaps with his portrayal of churchgoers. Indeed, many of the women in the church who have no children of their own assume the role of mother
30 to the young people in their churches. Several of the mothers, like the churchgoing women, are long-suffering. They range from hypersensitive Elizabeth, from whom her son John must sense her moods and desires, to supportive Sharon Rivers in *If Beale Street Could Talk*. The most attractive mothers are the
35 ones who would give everything for their children.

Few of these women in Baldwin's works are able to move beyond the bounds of the traditional roles that have been cut out for them. There are, nonetheless, a few iconoclasts. Florence expresses more independence than is usual with
40 anyone in Baldwin's early fiction, and Sharon Rivers is certainly unusual in her nonreligious approach to sacrificing for her children.

In terms of the work they do, though, few women in Baldwin's works are nontraditional. Even Florence, who values
45 independence so much, still has a very traditional job as a domestic. Ida, in her bid to be a singer, has a profession that started in tradition and has moved beyond it. Like many women in Baldwin's works, she started out singing in her church; her desire to be a blues singer in nightclubs is the added dimension.
50 But it is Julia who has the atypical career for women in Baldwin's fiction; she is a model. Mention of her work seems more a device for allowing Julia and Hall to meet again than to emphasize the intrinsic value of the work; but it is different from that in which most of the other women engage.

55 Different categories can mean that the black women are treated differently and that Baldwin has varying degrees of positive or negative responses to them. It is a function of their guilt as well as of their creation that most of the black female characters in Baldwin's fiction have been subordinated to the
60 males; they are in a supportive, serving position in relation to the males and male images in their lives. They serve their neighbors; they serve their children and their husbands and they serve God.

How the characters in the fiction are revealed to us is
65 important for understanding Baldwin's progression in the treatment of them as well as for seeing more clearly the place he has assigned to them. Most of the women are revealed through omniscient narration or through male narrators in a third-person, limited point of view. The only female who
70 narrates a story or a novel is Tish in *Beale Street*. Like Hall Montana in *Just Above My Head*, she often ventures into omniscience in picturing scenes at which she is not present, in recreating conversations she has not heard, and in revealing thoughts of other characters when those thoughts have not
75 been verbalized to her. For the male narrators, it is often necessary to consider their personalities and sympathies as well as what they present about the women characters who appear through their narrations. Black women we see in Baldwin's fiction, then, are usually twice removed—by way
80 of Baldwin and narrators—and are sometimes distanced through other layers as well.

13. The author suggests that the "sense of guilt the women feel" (line 8) can be attributed to

(A) disappointment or character flaws
(B) role playing or human nature
(C) aspiration or lack of success
(D) lack of definition or stereotypes
(E) lack of fulfillment or shame

GO ON TO THE NEXT PAGE

14. It can be inferred from the passage that the author sees the churchgoing women in Baldwin's fiction as

(A) always being middle-aged
(B) leaders in the black community
(C) having strong views that are worth consideration
(D) typical of many of the women found elsewhere in Baldwin's fiction
(E) interchangeable with the mothers in Baldwin's fiction

15. Which of the following descriptions best characterizes typical churchgoers in Baldwin's fiction?

(A) "stereotypes" (line 19)
(B) "spiritual outcasts" (line 5)
(C) "subordinated to the males" (lines 59-60)
(D) "omniscient" (line 68)
(E) "widely known" (line 26)

16. The author mentions Praying Mother Washington (lines 23-24) in order to

(A) give an example of the typical female churchgoer found in Baldwin's fiction
(B) demonstrate the wide range of women characters portrayed by Baldwin
(C) prove that women were not important in Baldwin's works
(D) point out an exception to the typical female churchgoer presented by Baldwin
(E) discuss the opportunities missed by the women in Baldwin's novels

17. The characters of Mother Washington and Ida are similar in that

(A) both women played a role within the tradition of the fundamentalist church
(B) both women are widely known
(C) both women sing in the church choir
(D) both women fit the stereotypical roles of women in Baldwin's fiction
(E) neither woman are able to extend their roles beyond those of supporting a man

18. Which best captures the meaning of the word "assume" on line 29 ?

(A) To take for granted
(B) To guess
(C) To take on
(D) To presuppose
(E) To nurture

19. Judging from lines 31-33, Baldwin's character John apparently

(A) resents his mother
(B) must be vigilant to Elizabeth's whims
(C) lives in fear
(D) gets support from Sharon Rivers
(E) attends church regularly

20. The word "iconoclasts," as used in line 38, most nearly means

(A) defendants
(B) images
(C) nonconformists
(D) conservatives
(E) pictures

21. The author mentions Julia in lines 50-54 to provide an example of

(A) a lucrative career choice for some women in Baldwin's novels
(B) an unusual career for a female character in Baldwin's works
(C) Baldwin's belief that all women belonged either at home or in church
(D) the redundancy of traditional careers for women in Baldwin's fiction
(E) the fact that Baldwin's major characters had less traditional roles than his minor ones had

22. The author's stated reason for the subordination of the women in Baldwin's fiction to the men suggests that Baldwin

(A) portrays women as having underlying feelings of remorse
(B) believes men are naturally superior to women
(C) relies on stereotypes rather than imagination
(D) always depicts women as having traditional occupations
(E) lacks a true understanding of his women contemporaries

GO ON TO THE NEXT PAGE

23. The reference to the character "Tish" (line 70) serves as

(A) a counterpoint to a prior assumption

(B) a termination of a trend previously dominant in Baldwin's literature

(C) a criticism of the assumptions underlying a popular belief

(D) an exception that refutes an earlier argument

(E) an exception to one of Baldwin's literary conventions

24. The author argues that female characters in Baldwin's fiction are distanced from the reader because

(A) their thoughts are never presented firsthand

(B) Baldwin restricts them to nontraditional roles

(C) Baldwin appears unwilling to portray a strong female who does not fit into a traditional category

(D) they are almost always depicted by a male narrator who is created by a male author

(E) they do not play a major role in most of Baldwin's novels

STOP

If you finish before time is called, you may check your work on this section only.
Do not turn to any other section in the test.

NO TEST MATERIAL ON THIS PAGE.

SECTION 6
Time — 25 minutes
18 Questions

Turn to Section 6 of your answer sheet to answer the questions in this section.

Directions: This section contains two types of questions. You have 25 minutes to complete both types. For questions 1-8, solve each problem and decide which is the best of the choices given. Fill in the corresponding circle on the answer sheet. You may use any available space for scratchwork.

1. The use of a calculator is permitted.

2. All numbers used are real numbers.

3. Figures that accompany problems in this test are intended to provide information useful in solving the problems. They are drawn as accurately as possible EXCEPT when it is stated in a specific problem that the figure is not drawn to scale. All figures lie in a plane unless otherwise indicated.

4. Unless otherwise specified, the domain of any function f is assumed to be the set of all real numbers x for which $f(x)$ is a real number.

Reference Information

$A = \pi r^2$
$C = 2\pi r$

$A = lw$

$A = \frac{1}{2}bh$

$V = lwh$

$V = \pi r^2 h$

$c^2 = a^2 + b^2$

Special Right Triangles

The number of degrees of arc in a circle is 360.

The sum of the measures in degrees of the angles of a triangle is 180.

---

1. If $10a + 8b = 4x$, then, in terms of x, $5a + 4b =$

   (A) $8x$

   (B) $4x$

   (C) $2x$

   (D) x

   (E) $\frac{x}{2}$

2. A scientist found that time, in seconds, a mouse required to complete a maze test successfully varied inversely with the number of hours of sleep the mouse had the previous night, such that $time = \frac{320}{sleep}$. If the mouse had 8 hours of sleep the night before a maze test, how long, in seconds, would the mouse take to complete the maze test?

   (A)   40
   (B)   160
   (C)   320
   (D) 1,280
   (E) 2,560

GO ON TO THE NEXT PAGE

3. One box of muffin mix is sufficient to bake six large muffins or ten mini-muffins. How many boxes are needed to bake 180 muffins, 120 of which are large muffins and the rest of which are mini-muffins?

(A) 18
(B) 20
(C) 22
(D) 26
(E) 28

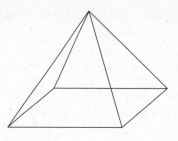

5. In the pyramid shown above, the base is a square with an area of 49. If each triangular face has a height of 12, what is the area of one of the triangular faces?

(A) 21
(B) 28
(C) 35
(D) 42
(E) 56

4. If $a = \dfrac{4}{3}$, then $\dfrac{4}{a} - \dfrac{a}{a-1} =$

(A) −3

(B) −1

(C) $\dfrac{3}{4}$

(D) 1

(E) 3

GO ON TO THE NEXT PAGE

Questions 6-7 refer to the following chart and information.

Airline	Coach Class	First Class
W	$305	$350
X	$225	$280
Y	$260	$315
Z	$320	$375

The chart above gives fare information for the cost of flights between two cities on four different airlines, W, X, Y, and Z.

6. What is the least expensive combination of flights available?

(A) Coach Class on Airline X and First Class on Airline Z
(B) First Class on Airline Y and Coach Class on Airline Y
(C) First Class on Airline X and Coach Class on Airline Z
(D) First Class on Airline Y and Coach Class on Airline W
(E) Coach Class on Airline Z and Coach Class on Airline Z

7. What is the quotient of the mode of the differences in price between First Class and Coach Class for each airline and the average (arithmetic mean) of the four airlines' First Class prices?

(A) $\frac{1}{6}$

(B) $\frac{1}{5}$

(C) $\frac{1}{4}$

(D) 3

(E) 6

8. The integer 90 can be expressed as the sum of z consecutive integers. The value of z could be any of the following EXCEPT

(A) 3
(B) 4
(C) 5
(D) 6
(E) 9

GO ON TO THE NEXT PAGE

Directions: For Student-Produced Response questions 9-18, use the grids at the bottom of the answer sheet page on which you have answered questions 1-8.

Each of the remaining 10 questions requires you to solve the problem and enter your answer by marking the circles in the special grid, as shown in the examples below. You may use any available space for scratch work.

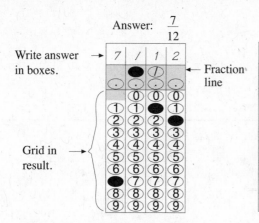

Answer: $\frac{7}{12}$

Write answer in boxes.

← Fraction line

Grid in result.

Answer: 2.5

← Decimal point

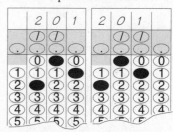

Answer: 201
Either position is correct.

Note: You may start your answers in any column, space permitting. Columns not needed should be left blank.

• Mark no more than one circle in any column.

• Because the answer document will be machine-scored, **you will receive credit only if the circles are filled in correctly.**

• Although not required, it is suggested that you write your answer in the boxes at the top of the columns to help you fill in the circles accurately.

• Some problems may have more than one correct answer. In such cases, grid only one answer.

• No question has a negative answer.

• **Mixed numbers** such as $3\frac{1}{2}$ must be gridded as

3.5 or 7/2. (If [3 1 / 2] is gridded, it will be

interpreted as $\frac{31}{2}$, not $3\frac{1}{2}$.)

• **Decimal Answers:** If you obtain a decimal answer with more digits than the grid can accommodate, it may be either rounded or truncated, but it must fill the entire grid. For example, if you obtain an answer such as 0.6666..., you should record your result as .666 or .667. **A less accurate value such as .66 or .67 will be scored as incorrect.**

Acceptable ways to grid $\frac{2}{3}$ are:

9. If $\frac{x}{14} = \frac{5}{y} = \frac{4}{8}$, what is the value of $x + y$?

10. Four consecutive odd integers have a sum of 80. What is the least of these integers?

GO ON TO THE NEXT PAGE

11. The sum of five integers is 190. If one of these numbers is removed, the average (arithmetic mean) of the four remaining numbers is between 34.5 and 36, inclusive. What is one possible value for the number that was removed?

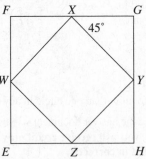

12. In the coordinate plane above, what is the slope of $\overline{AB}$?

13. If $3^{5x} = 27^4$, what is the value of x ?

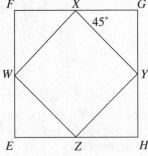

14. If the perimeter of square *WXYZ* above is $16\sqrt{2}$, what is the area of square *EFGH* ?

GO ON TO THE NEXT PAGE

15. For all numbers k, where $k \neq 4$, let $f(k) = \dfrac{k+8}{4-k}$.

If $f(k) = \dfrac{5}{2}$, what is the value of k?

16. A rectangular box has a length of 6 and a width of 4. If the volume of the box is numerically equal to its surface area, what is the height of the box?

17. In a box of tickets, there are 50 blue tickets and 15 red tickets. After a certain number of red tickets are added to the box, the probability of randomly choosing a red ticket is $\dfrac{2}{3}$. How many red tickets were added to the box?

18. Pierre receives a weekly allowance of $8, plus $3 for each chore he completes during the week. Armand receives a weekly allowance of $6, plus $8 for each chore he completes during the week. Neither of them receive any other money. In a certain week, if they both complete the same number of chores, but Armand receives twice as much money as Pierre, then what is the total dollar amount that Armand receives in that week? (Disregard the dollar sign when gridding your answer.)

STOP
If you finish before time is called, you may check your work on this section only.
Do not turn to any other section in the test.

SECTION 7
Time — 25 minutes
35 Questions

Turn to Section 7 of your answer sheet to answer the questions in this section.

Directions: For each question in this section, select the best answer from among the choices given and fill in the corresponding circle on the answer sheet.

The following sentences test correctness and effectiveness of expression. Part of each sentence or the entire sentence is underlined; beneath each sentence are five ways of phrasing the underlined material. Choice A repeats the original phrasing; the other four choices are different. If you think the original phrasing produces a better sentence than any of the alternatives, select choice A; if not, select one of the other choices.

In making your selection, follow the requirements of standard written English; that is, pay attention to grammar, choice of words, sentence construction, and punctuation. Your selection should result in the most effective sentence—clear and precise, without awkwardness or ambiguity.

EXAMPLE:

Bobby Flay baked his first cake <u>and he was thirteen years old then</u>.

(A) and he was thirteen years old then
(B) when he was thirteen
(C) at age thirteen years old
(D) upon the reaching of thirteen years
(E) at the time when he was thirteen

1. Last year the apple harvest was rather small, in contrast to that of the previous year, which <u>would be</u> quite bountiful.

   (A) would be
   (B) was being
   (C) has been
   (D) had been
   (E) will be

2. To make a good strawberry cake, you must use a bag of fresh flour, a cup of finely sifted sugar, and <u>a fresh strawberry container</u>.

   (A) a fresh strawberry container
   (B) containers with fresh strawberries
   (C) fresh strawberries in a container
   (D) strawberries freshly in a container
   (E) a container of fresh strawberries

3. William McKinley's family, who moved to Poland, Ohio, when he was nine years old, <u>were accepted quickly</u> by the townspeople and general community in Poland.

   (A) were accepted quickly
   (B) quickly having been accepted
   (C) were quick to be accepted
   (D) was quick to accept
   (E) was quickly accepted

4. *Anna Karenina* is a classic tale <u>when the doomed love affair between the rebellious Anna and the dashing Count Vronsky create</u> a dynamic imbalance, playing out all the variations on love and family happiness.

   (A) when the doomed love affair between the rebellious Anna and the dashing Count Vronsky create
   (B) when the doomed love affair between the rebellious Anna and the dashing Count Vronsky creates
   (C) in that the doomed love affair between the rebellious Anna and the dashing Count Vronsky creates
   (D) in which the doomed love affair between the rebellious Anna and the dashing Count Vronsky creates
   (E) in which the doomed love affair between the rebellious Anna and the dashing Count Vronsky create

GO ON TO THE NEXT PAGE

5. If more young people voted, politicians <u>would pay more attention to what young people thought</u>.

(A) would pay more attention to what young people thought

(B) will pay more attention to what young people think

(C) would pay more attention to what young people think

(D) would pay attention to what young people thought more

(E) will pay more attention to those thoughts of young people

6. <u>Los Angeles's freeways, usually busier and more crowded than those of other cities,</u> are clogged almost twenty-four hours a day, contributing to the city's pollution problem.

(A) Los Angeles's freeways, usually busier and more crowded than those of other cities,

(B) The freeways of Los Angeles, which are usually busier and more crowded with cars than other cities,

(C) The freeways of Los Angeles, usually busier and more crowded than other cities,

(D) The freeways of Los Angeles, usually busier and crowding with cars than other cities,

(E) Usually busier and more crowded than other cities, the freeways of Los Angeles

7. In the predawn crispness of a September morning, the conjunction of Mars and Venus thrilled the amateur astronomer <u>like on the first occasion he had seen it</u>.

(A) like on the first occasion he had seen it

(B) like he did the first time of his seeing it

(C) as when he was thrilled the first time

(D) like the thrill when he first saw it

(E) as it had the first time he saw it

8. Francisca is not only running cross country this year, <u>but she is going to play on the tennis team as well</u>.

(A) but she is going to play on the tennis team as well

(B) but she also plays tennis

(C) but she is also playing on the tennis team

(D) and she is also going to play on the tennis team

(E) and playing tennis is something she will also do

9. The most efficient way for cells to harvest energy stored in food is through <u>cellular respiration, this is part of the process by which</u> adenosine triphosphate (ATP) is produced.

(A) cellular respiration, this is part of the process by which

(B) cellular respiration, a part of the process by which

(C) cellular respiration; a part of the process where

(D) cellular respiration, a part of the process where

(E) cellular respiration, which is defined as a part of the process by which

10. Smoking cigarettes is not only <u>dangerous, but they are also a waste of money.</u>

(A) dangerous, but they are also a waste of money

(B) dangerous, but they are also wasting money

(C) dangerous, it is also wasting money

(D) dangerous but also financially wasteful

(E) dangerous but also it is a money waster

11. Looking up into the night sky, <u>almost all of the stars people can see</u> are bigger and brighter than our sun.

(A) almost all of the stars people can see

(B) people see mostly stars that

(C) almost all of the stars that people see

(D) people can almost see all of those stars that

(E) many of the stars that people see

GO ON TO THE NEXT PAGE

The following sentences test your ability to recognize grammar and usage errors. Each sentence contains either a single error or no error at all. No sentence contains more than one error. The error, if there is one, is underlined and lettered. If the sentence contains an error, select the one underlined part that must be changed to make the sentence correct. If the sentence is correct, select choice E. In choosing answers, follow the requirements of standard written English.

EXAMPLE:

The other players and her significantly improved
    A   B   C

the game plan created by the coaches. No error
            D   E

Ⓐ ● Ⓒ Ⓓ Ⓔ

12. Laurel wanted to go out to the movies that night,
          A   B

   and so her friend Ben wanted to stay home and study.
     C   D

   No error
    E

13. All of the stamps in Tony's collection is valuable,
    A   B

   especially those from foreign countries. No error
     C   D   E

14. John's schedule is so packed that he scarcely has no
         A   B

   time to get from one appointment to the next.
         C   D

   No error
    E

15. The telephone, one of the most life-changing
           A   B

   inventions of the past 150 years, are now present in
                     C

   nearly every American home. No error
    D   E

16. Every few years extensive rains come, and the desert,
            A   B

   which normally has hardly no plant life, blooms with
    C   D

   brilliant color. No error
         E

17. Neither Susan nor Jacob likes to relax and watch the
                A   B   C

   grass grows. No error
      D   E

18. The instructor, a mountaineer named Sophie, prepared
                            A

   us well for our first expedition; she was quick to correct
        B

   them when we slipped on the climbing wall. No error
    C   D   E

19. One of the children on the playground is eating ice
    A   B

   cream, while the others are enjoying the see-saw.
        C   D

   No error
    E

GO ON TO THE NEXT PAGE

20. Insects had been living on land for millions of years by
      A   B

the time the first fish crawled out of the sea. No error
         C   D   E

21. Julietta went to the National Park and swims across the
          A   B

lake every day to get her exercise. No error
              C   D   E

22. During the recent earthquake, all of Luissa's pictures
      A

fell off the mantel, having left many of them shattered
   B   C   D

beyond repair. No error
           E

23. Xavier, never one to remain sedentary, preferred riding
              A   B   C

his bicycle to driving a car, as the exercise made him
                                 D

feel energized. No error
           E

24. It is difficult to drive safe when traveling at night to
    A   B   C

an unknown destination, especially if it is snowing or
                      D

raining. No error
       E

25. Mrs. Johnson gave the assignment to Paul and I , and
           A   B

we decided to work together. No error
 C   D   E

26. Surprisingly, when botanists study plants, classification

as either flowers or weeds are often based upon noting
  A   B

how easily a given plant grows without assistance.
   C   D

No error
  E

27. With their long, fancy, and colorful tails, the male guppy
             A   B

is the most beautiful of all the fish in my aquarium.
     C   D

No error
  E

28. Regardless of which person wins the race, they
     A   B   C

will have earned the victory. No error
    D   E

29. One should try to avoid breaking rules, not only because
    A

doing so is wrong, but also because you do not
  B   C

know whether you will be caught. No error
    D   E

GO ON TO THE NEXT PAGE

Directions: The following passage is an early draft of an essay. Some parts of the passage need to be rewritten.

Read the passage and select the best answers for the questions that follow. Some questions are about particular sentences or parts of sentences and ask you to improve sentence structure or word choice. Other questions ask you to consider organization and development. In choosing answers, follow the requirements of standard written English.

Questions 30-35 refer to the following passage.

(1) Most people underestimate the importance of a cover letter. (2) Probably people avoid taking the time to write a quality one because it takes too much time. (3) But copious employers look at the cover letter even more than resumes to get a sense of who the applicant is.

(4) A hopeful candidate should fill the letter with quality content. (5) You should say specifically why you'd be viable for the job and give examples of your prior work experiences as proof. (6) That way the employer gets better acquainted with you. (7) Never come across as desperate, unqualified, or incompetent. (8) Always make the letter specific to the job.

(9) Formality and presentation are essential. (10) Many employers want to see if you put your best foot forward to get the job. (11) Indicators include structure, grammar, spelling, and your ability to convey confidence in your ability. (12) Do not mix up "from" and "form."

(13) If the employer feels that the content and quality of the cover letter are right for the position, they will contact the applicant for an interview. (14) Now the applicant has won the desired prize and has a chance to impress with personality as well as words. (15) To many employers, the resumé is less significant because it's been carefully edited and typed; they know few spend the same time on a cover letter.

30. Which of the following is the best way to combine the underlined portions of sentences 5 and 6 (reproduced below) ?

    You should say specifically why you'd be viable for the job and give examples of your prior work experiences as proof. That way the employer gets better acquainted with you.

    (A) proof, that way the employer gets
    (B) proof so that the employer gets
    (C) proof that shows why the employer should get
    (D) proof, but that way the employer gets
    (E) (There is no way to combine the sentences)

31. In context, which is the best replacement for the underlined words in sentence 5 (reproduced below) ?

    You should say specifically why you'd be viable for the job and give examples of your prior work experiences as proof.

    (A) dominating
    (B) mediocre at
    (C) necessary for
    (D) networked into
    (E) appropriate for

32. In context, which of the following phrases placed before sentence 9 best connects the second and third paragraphs?

    (A) Despite their time-consuming nature,
    (B) In cover letters,
    (C) In addition to content,
    (D) Although they may seem superficial,
    (E) Along with being specific,

33. Which sentence would least disrupt the flow of the essay if it were removed?

    (A) Sentence 3
    (B) Sentence 5
    (C) Sentence 9
    (D) Sentence 12
    (E) Sentence 13

34. In context, where would sentence 15 be placed most effectively in the essay?

    (A) (As it is now)
    (B) After sentence 3
    (C) After sentence 8
    (D) After sentence 10
    (E) After sentence 13

35. Which of the following sentences most logically follows sentence 15 ?

    (A) Therefore, when looking for a job, make sure the cover letter gets the attention it deserves.
    (B) Thus, the resumé is does not require the same amount of attention as the cover letter.
    (C) So most bosses won't even look at your resume.
    (D) After you send the cover letter, it is important to follow it up with a phone call.
    (E) Regardless of the extent of your work experience, the cover letter should mention all relevant skills.

STOP
If you finish before time is called, you may check your work on this section only.
Do not turn to any other section in the test.

NO TEST MATERIAL ON THIS PAGE.

SECTION 8
Time — 20 minutes
19 Questions

Turn to Section 8 of your answer sheet to answer the questions in this section.

Directions: For each question in this section, select the best answer from among the choices given and fill in the corresponding circle on the answer sheet.

Each sentence below has one or two blanks, each blank indicating that something has been omitted. Beneath the sentence are five words or sets of words labeled A through E. Choose the word or set of words that, when inserted in the sentence, <u>best</u> fits the meaning of the sentence as a whole.

Example:

Desiring to ------- his taunting friends, Mitch gave them taffy in hopes it would keep their mouths shut.

(A) eliminate   (B) satisfy   (C) overcome
   (D) ridicule   (E) silence

---

1. The baseball coaches chose Mack over the other talented players for the final spot on the team due to his ------- : he can play every position.

    (A) passion   (B) physique   (C) versatility
       (D) endurance   (E) credibility

2. The hurricane was a ------- event, leaving in its wake millions of dollars in damage.

    (A) calamitous   (B) banal   (C) minuscule
       (D) precipitous   (E) heralded

3. Weakened by his bout with pneumonia, Gary found himself virtually incapacitated, ------- to ------- the energy necessary to run a marathon.

    (A) ardent . . salvage
    (B) unable . . muster
    (C) disinclined . . squander
    (D) eager . . exert
    (E) hesitant . . enervate

4. Despite her ------- schedule, Karen amazed everyone with her seemingly unlimited -------.

    (A) episodic . . vitality
    (B) hectic . . acuity
    (C) strenuous . . alacrity
    (D) busy . . sanctity
    (E) precise . . energy

5. The oracle at Delphi purposely made ------- prophecies so that they could be interpreted in more than one way.

    (A) equivocal   (B) vacuous   (C) mirthful
       (D) omnipotent   (E) meager

6. The lake was found to be so ------- that state environment officials were forced to investigate and temporarily ------- all recreational swimming and boating.

    (A) placid . . prohibit
    (B) polluted . . urge
    (C) brimming . . evade
    (D) noxious . . proscribe
    (E) shallow . . promote

GO ON TO THE NEXT PAGE

Directions: Each passage below is followed by questions based on its content. Answer the questions on the basis of what is <u>stated</u> or <u>implied</u> in each passage and in any introductory material that may be provided.

Questions 7-19 are based on the following passages.

George Washington's legendary reputation tends to overshadow the human being behind those legends. The following two passages were written by noted historians in an attempt to discuss the "real" George Washington.

Passage 1

At the end of his own time and for generations thereafter, he was acclaimed at home and abroad as the founder of the American nation. He achieved sainthood in the minds of the
Line Americans who came after him. There was a tendency to look
5 upon him as an archangel who possessed the genius of Caesar, the vision of Moses, and the morals of Galahad. A change came. Later Americans gave more and more attention to their rights, less and less to the man who was the principal begetter of those rights. Scholars and teachers in America offered
10 more and more praise to men of the era of the Revolution who talked and wrote on behalf of liberty, to those who labored at European capitals for independence, to those who remodeled American institutions, to Thomas Paine, Thomas Jefferson, Benjamin Franklin, Alexander Hamilton, and James
15 Madison. There was also in the twentieth century a school of biographical "debunkers" who discovered that great men and women, American as well as European, were inconstant and incontinent, addicted to profanity, and menaced by insanity. Among them were writers who sought to destroy the hallowed
20 Washington, to reduce him to mortal or smaller proportions. They found sin in the saint. So doing, they tended to make the Father of His Country into an important scamp. It was often forgotten that the sword can be more potent than the pen, that the bayonet can speak more decisively than the tongue
25 of the diplomat, that Washington was the one man essential to the triumph of the Patriots in the War of Independence, to the creation of the American union, and perhaps even to the success of the democratic revolution throughout the world.

It is no secret that Washington was not born to the
30 imperial purple. Nor was he by birth a member of the First Families of Virginia, the fabled Virginia aristocracy. He opened his eyes without fanfare of trumpets, with modest hereditary prestige, in a brick house near the junction of Pope's Creek with the Potomac River in Westmoreland
35 County, Virginia, at 10 A.M. on February 11, 1732—a day of the month that became February 22 when Britain and the British empire afterward condescended to strike eleven days from their defective calendar to match it with that of the remainder of the Western world. He was later duly baptized
40 in the Episcopal church. He was not christened after King George III, who came into the world six years later. It has been urged that he was named after a George Eskridge, a benefactor of Washington's mother. It is not unlikely that the parents had King George II in mind.

Passage 2

45 On April 14, 1789, Washington received formal notification of his election. He set out in his coach "with more anxious and painful sensations than I have words to express."

Among the worries that now bothered him was a fear that the people might resent his return to public office after
50 his promise that he would never do so. The enthusiasm with which he was greeted on the road not only extinguished this fear but raised its opposite. As he moved, he could not see the countryside because of the dust churned up by the horsemen who in relays surrounded his carriage. At every
55 hamlet there were speeches; at every city he had to lead a parade and be toasted at a sumptuous dinner; everywhere and always people were jostling him, shaking his hand, cheering and cheering until his ears ached. Throughout the jubilations that stretched down the long days and late into the nights,
60 Washington sensed a hysteria which he found "painful." How easily and with what frenzy could this irrational emotion turn, if the government did not immediately please, "into equally extravagant (though I will fondly hope unmerited) censures. So much is expected, so many untoward circumstances may
65 intervene, in such a new and critical situation that I feel an insuperable diffidence in my own abilities."

The task which he was now approaching was both more uncertain and infinitely more important than that which had lain before him when in 1775 he had ridden north to take
70 command of the Continental Army. His duty then had been to win military victory. Since such victories had been won ten thousand times, there was no philosophical reason to doubt that success was possible. And, if he did fail, the result would be sad for America, catastrophic perhaps for himself and his
75 companions, but no more than a tiny footnote in the history of mankind.

Washington's present mission might change all history. As he himself put it, "the preservation of the sacred fire of liberty and the destiny of the republican model of government
80 are justly considered as deeply, perhaps as finally, staked on the experiment entrusted to the hands of the American people." He was on his way to lead an enterprise which, if it succeeded, would prove to all the world, and for the future to time immemorial, the falsity of the contention that men were
85 "unequal to the task of governing themselves and therefore made for a master." That contention had, down the ages, been accepted by many of the greatest thinkers. Supposing the failure of the American experiment should seem to prove them right? How long would it be before this "awful
90 monument " to the death of liberty would be forgotten, before the experiment was tried again? And if, through inability or misunderstanding, Washington contributed to the catastrophe, how deep and eternal would be his personal guilt?

GO ON TO THE NEXT PAGE

7. The author of Passage 1 objects to the attitudes of certain "Later Americans" (lines 7-9) for which of the following reasons?

(A) Their admiration for Caesar, Moses, and Galahad was unjustified.

(B) They tended to ignore the achievements of Washington.

(C) Their misconceptions of Washington could have been easily avoided.

(D) They took their personal rights for granted.

(E) They forgot that Washington had been the first president of the U.S.

8. According to the author of Passage 1, the "biographical 'debunkers'" described in line 16 were responsible for

(A) discovering the greatness of American and European men and women

(B) expanding awareness of such historical figures as Jefferson and Franklin

(C) writing inaccurate portrayals of Washington's patriotism

(D) reducing Washington to a less than heroic status

(E) comparing Washington to other historical heroes like Caesar and Galahad

9. In Passage 1, the reference to the "imperial purple" (line 30) is used to

(A) indicate that Washington came from a wealthy family

(B) indicate Washington's humble lineage

(C) provide an idea of the color of clothing worn by the Virginia aristocracy

(D) imply that Washington resented his family and aspired for greatness

(E) draw a comparison between Washington and King George III

10. In the second paragraph of Passage 1 (lines 29-44), the author explains that George Washington's birthday is celebrated on February 22 because of

(A) its proximity to Abraham Lincoln's birthday

(B) a change in the British calendar

(C) a discrepancy about Washington's actual date of birth

(D) the Epsicopal church's decision to change the Western world's calender

(E) a misprint on Washington's birth certificate

11. In lines 58-66, the author of Passage 2 implies that the wildly supportive crowd

(A) could help Washington succeed by supporting his policies

(B) could be a powerful ally to Washington by opposing his challengers

(C) could quickly turn on Washington if he did not satisfy their needs

(D) would ignore Washington's shortcomings because of their overwhelming allegiance

(E) would not endorse a president about whom they knew so little

12. In line 66, the phrase "insuperable diffidence" refers to

(A) Washington's lack of self-confidence

(B) the disparity between Washington's own beliefs and the beliefs of his constituents

(C) the extraordinary importance of the creation of a new nation

(D) Washington's unwavering self-assurance in the face of adversity

(E) Washington's firm convictions about how the country must be run

13. The distinction between Washington's potential success in his "task" (line 67) and his command of the Continental Army might be best expressed in which of the following ways?

(A) The first had historical precedent, the second did not.

(B) The first was more easily accomplished than the second.

(C) The first was a hypothetical situation, the second was not.

(D) The first was as yet untried by Washington, the second was familiar and possible.

(E) The first was Washington's responsibility, the second was not.

14. Which pair of words best describes the author's view in Passage 2 of Washington's "duty" (line 70) in the continental Army and Washington's presidency?

(A) Abrasive and contentious

(B) Impatial and disinterested

(C) Trivial and ineffective

(D) Unremarkable and momentous

(E) Uncertain and doubtful

GO ON TO THE NEXT PAGE

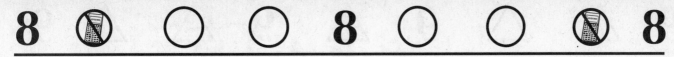

15. According to the author of Passage 2, which of the following is true about the statement that men "were 'unequal to the task of governing themselves and therefore made for a master'" (lines 85-86) ?

(A) It was not a commonly held belief.
(B) It was believed only by pessimistic philosophers.
(C) It would be disproved if Washington was successful.
(D) It was British propaganda used to combat the rebellion.
(E) It was Washington's credo.

16. Which of the following statements is true of Passage 2, but not of Passage 1 ?

(A) The passage deals largely with Washington's youth.
(B) The passage portrays George Washington as a perfectionist.
(C) The passage shows only George Washington's confidence in his abilities.
(D) The passage discusses the unfairness of historians.
(E) The passage includes a direct quotation of Washington's.

17. The author of Passage 2 would most probably describe Washington's feelings towards the accomplishments mentioned in lines 25 - 28 of Passage 1 as

(A) enthusiastic
(B) confident
(C) curious
(D) wary
(E) morose

18. Which of the following best describes the primary difference between Passage 1 and Passage 2 ?

(A) Passage 1 describes the myths surrounding Washington's life, while Passage 2 presents Washington's view of his place in history.
(B) Passage 1 presents an objective view of Washington, while Passage 2 attempts to show Washington as a perfect leader.
(C) Passage 1 focuses on Washington's achievements after the Revolutionary War, while Passage 2 discusses his military successes.
(D) Passage 1 gives a personal view of Washington, while Passage 2 shows how academics have recently changed their opinion of Washington's success as president.
(E) Passage 1 focuses on reactions others have had to Washington, while Passage 2 strives to show Washington as an unconfident and inept leader.

19. With which of the following statements would the authors of BOTH passages agree?

(A) Washington's failure may have caused the United States to abandon a democratic system of government.
(B) Although not without flaw, Washington was indispensable to the success of world democracy.
(C) Washington's lack of confidence contributed to historian's criticisms of him.
(D) Washington, like other great men and women, was often inconstant and incontinent.
(E) Washington played a formative role at a pivotal point in the history of the United States.

STOP
If you finish before time is called, you may check your work on this section only.
Do not turn to any other section in the test.

SECTION 9
Time — 20 minutes
16 Questions

Turn to Section 9 of your answer sheet to answer the questions in this section.

Directions: For this section, solve each problem and decide which is the best of the choices given. Fill in the corresponding circle on the answer sheet. You may use any available space for scratchwork.

Notes

1. The use of a calculator is permitted.

2. All numbers used are real numbers.

3. Figures that accompany problems in this test are intended to provide information useful in solving the problems. They are drawn as accurately as possible EXCEPT when it is stated in a specific problem that the figure is not drawn to scale. All figures lie in a plane unless otherwise indicated.

4. Unless otherwise specified, the domain of any function f is assumed to be the set of all real numbers x for which $f(x)$ is a real number.

Reference Information

$A = \pi r^2$
$C = 2\pi r$

$A = lw$

$A = \frac{1}{2} bh$

$V = lwh$

$V = \pi r^2 h$

$c^2 = a^2 + b^2$

Special Right Triangles

The number of degrees of arc in a circle is 360.

The sum of the measures in degrees of the angles of a triangle is 180.

1. If $3a + 3b + c = 26$ and $a + b = 6$, then $c =$

    (A) 8
    (B) 14
    (C) 20
    (D) 32
    (E) 44

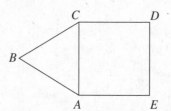

2. In the figure above, $\triangle ABC$ is equilateral and $ACDE$ is a square. If $AC = 3n$, what is the perimeter of polygon $ABCDE$?

    (A)   6n
    (B)   9n
    (C) 12n
    (D) 15n
    (E) 21n

GO ON TO THE NEXT PAGE

3. For which of the following lists of numbers is the mode equal to the average (arithmetic mean) ?

(A) 10, 10, 10, 50, 70
(B) 10, 20, 25, 30, 40
(C) 15, 35, 35, 35, 55
(D) 10, 20, 25, 35, 45
(E) 5, 15, 25, 25, 50

5. Peter's income is directly proportional to the amount of time he works. If he earns \$27.00 for every 90 minutes of work, how many hours must he work to earn \$162.00 ?

(A) 6
(B) 9
(C) 16.2
(D) 18
(E) 27

4. A line of plastic ducks moves across a conveyor belt at a shooting gallery. The color of each duck follows the repeating pattern orange, green, red, blue, yellow, purple, orange, green, red, blue, yellow, purple, continuing indefinitely. If the first duck is orange, what is the color of the 50th duck?

(A) Green
(B) Red
(C) Blue
(D) Yellow
(E) Purple

6. If $7 + x < 5$ and $3 + x < 0$, which of the following could be the value of x ?

(A) 3
(B) 2
(C) 0
(D) −3
(E) −4

GO ON TO THE NEXT PAGE

7. There are an equal number of dogs and cats at a clinic. After 2 dogs and 8 cats are taken home, there are three times as many dogs as cats still at the clinic. How many cats are still at the clinic?

(A) Three
(B) Four
(C) Six
(D) Eight
(E) Nine

8. If $ab \neq 0$, which of the following must equal $\dfrac{a}{b}$?

(A) $\dfrac{a^2}{b^2}$

(B) $\dfrac{a^3}{b^3}$

(C) $\dfrac{1}{\dfrac{a}{b}}$

(D) $\dfrac{\dfrac{a}{5}}{\dfrac{b}{5}}$

(E) $\dfrac{a+1}{b+1}$

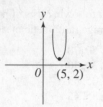

9. The graph of $y = f(x)$ is shown in the figure above. Which of the following could be the graph of $y = f(x+5) - 2$?

(A)

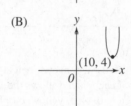

(0, 0)

(B)

(10, 4)

(C)

(10, 0)

(D)

(3, 7)

(E)

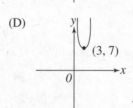

(4, 0)

GO ON TO THE NEXT PAGE

INGREDIENTS IN A SINGLE CHEESE PIZZA

	Dough	Sauce	Cheese
Small	1 pound	$1\frac{1}{2}$ cups	2 cups
Medium	$1\frac{1}{4}$ pounds	$1\frac{3}{4}$ cups	$2\frac{1}{3}$ cups
Large	$1\frac{1}{2}$ pounds	2 cups	$2\frac{2}{3}$ cups

NUMBER OF CHEESE PIZZAS SOLD

	Small	Medium	Large
Take out	3	8	7
Delivery	7	16	11

10. The tables above show the amount of each ingredient needed to make various sizes of cheese pizzas at a certain restaurant, and the number of each size of cheese pizza sold by the restaurant for take out or delivery. What is the sum of the number of cups of sauce and the number of cups of cheese used in the cheese pizzas that the restaurant sold?

(A)   93
(B)   124
(C)   196
(D)   217
(E)   284

11. A square, stained-glass window pane is composed of 36 individual squares of colored glass. Some individual squares are red and others are blue. Which of the following is NOT a possible ratio of red to blue squares in the window?

(A) 1 : 35
(B) 1 : 7
(C) 2 : 7
(D) 5 : 7
(E) 4 : 5

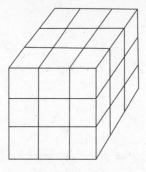

12. The figure above shows a solid cube with an edge of length 3, which is made up of small white cubes with edges of length 1. Every face of the large cube is painted black, and the large cube is disassembled. What is the probability that a small cube chosen at random will have an odd number of its faces painted black?

(A) $\frac{1}{3}$

(B) $\frac{4}{9}$

(C) $\frac{13}{27}$

(D) $\frac{14}{27}$

(E) $\frac{2}{3}$

13. If xy^2z^3 is negative, which of the following must be negative?

(A) xy
(B) xz
(C) yz
(D) x^2z
(E) xz^2

GO ON TO THE NEXT PAGE

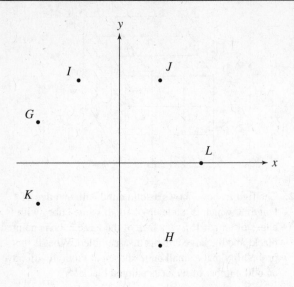

14. In the figure above, if point *G* has coordinates $(-2b, -a)$, then which of the following points could have coordinates $(b, -2a)$?

(A) *H*
(B) *I*
(C) *J*
(D) *K*
(E) *L*

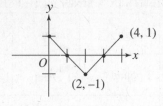

15. A portion of the graph of $g(x)$ is shown in the figure above. If $g(x) = g(x - 4)$ for all real values of *x*, then which of the following is true?

(A) $g(7) - g(6) = g(1)$
(B) $g(6) - g(5) = g(1)$
(C) $g(5) - g(4) = g(6)$
(D) $2 \times g(6) = g(12)$
(E) $g(-2) = -g(2)$

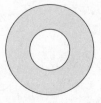

16. In the figure above, the two circles share the same center, and the shaded region has an area twice that of the inner circle. What is the ratio of the radius of the inner circle to that of the outer circle?

(A) $1 : \sqrt{2}$
(B) $1 : \sqrt{3}$
(C) $\sqrt{2} : 3$
(D) $2 : 1$
(E) $1 : 3$

STOP
**If you finish before time is called, you may check your work on this section only.
Do not turn to any other section in the test.**

NO TEST MATERIAL ON THIS PAGE.

SECTION 10
Time — 10 minutes
14 Questions

Turn to Section 10 of your answer sheet to answer the questions in this section.

Directions: For each question in this section, select the best answer from among the choices given and fill in the corresponding circle on the answer sheet.

The following sentences test correctness and effectiveness of expression. Part of each sentence or the entire sentence is underlined; beneath each sentence are five ways of phrasing the underlined material. Choice A repeats the original phrasing; the other four choices are different. If you think the original phrasing produces a better sentence than any of the alternatives, select choice A; if not, select one of the other choices.

In making your selection, follow the requirements of standard written English; that is, pay attention to grammar, choice of words, sentence construction, and punctuation. Your selection should result in the most effective sentence—clear and precise, without awkwardness or ambiguity.

EXAMPLE:

Bobby Flay baked his first cake <u>and he was thirteen years old then</u>.

(A) and he was thirteen years old then
(B) when he was thirteen
(C) at age thirteen years old
(D) upon the reaching of thirteen years
(E) at the time when he was thirteen

Ⓐ●ⒸⒹⒺ

1. <u>The notion that children should be seen and not heard prevailed for much of the last century.</u>

(A) The notion that children should be seen and not heard prevailed for much of the last century.
(B) The notion that prevailed about children for much of the last century was that of being seen and not heard.
(C) For much of the last century, they had a prevalent notion that children should be seen and not heard.
(D) Prevalent as a notion for much of the last century was for children to be seen and not heard.
(E) Prevalent for much of the last century, they thought that children should be seen and not heard.

2. The benefit of exercise on all the body systems <u>are becoming increasingly acknowledged</u>.

(A) are becoming increasingly acknowledged
(B) is increasing in acknowledgement
(C) is becoming increasingly acknowledged
(D) are increasingly well acknowledged
(E) has increased in acknowledgement

3. Recognized <u>as a hero of the Civil Rights Movement, the legacy of the Rev. Dr. Martin Luther King Jr. is an inspiration to many Americans</u>.

(A) as a hero of the Civil Rights Movement, the legacy of the Rev. Dr. Martin Luther King Jr. is an inspiration to many Americans
(B) for being a hero of the Civil Rights Movement, the legacy of the Rev. Dr. Martin Luther King Jr. is an inspiration to many Americans
(C) for being a Civil Rights Movement hero, is the legacy of the Rev. Dr. Martin Luther King Jr., and he is an inspiration to many Americans
(D) as a hero of the Civil Rights Movement, the Rev. Dr. Martin Luther King Jr. is an inspiration to many Americans
(E) as a hero of the Civil Rights Movement, the Rev. Dr. Martin Luther King Jr. is seen by many Americans as an inspiration

4. <u>An airplane trip is</u> less fuel-efficient than driving an electric hybrid car.

(A) An airplane trip is
(B) Flying in an airplane is
(C) To drive an airplane is
(D) Traveling by airplanes are
(E) Trips made in an airplane is

GO ON TO THE NEXT PAGE

5. Until recently, all railroad tracks consisted of only three materials: steel, <u>wood, and stones</u>.

   (A)   wood, and stones
   (B)   woods, and stones
   (C)   wood, and stone
   (D)   pieces of wood, and stones
   (E)   and pieces of wood and stone

6. When you write a research paper, you should first create a rough <u>outline and then that outline will be modified</u> as you develop your thesis.

   (A)   outline and then that outline will be modified
   (B)   outline and then modify that outline
   (C)   outline, modifying that outline then
   (D)   outline, then you modify that outline
   (E)   outline, you modify that outline

7. <u>Far longer a distance than most birds go,</u> the arctic tern flies from the Arctic to the Antarctic and back every year.

   (A)   Far longer a distance than most birds go,
   (B)   Although it is far longer than most birds,
   (C)   Even though most birds have shorter routes,
   (D)   With a migration route far longer than that of most birds,
   (E)   One of the longest bird migration routes belongs to it,

8. Disneyland in California <u>was the first Disney theme park, but today there are also</u> Disney World in Florida and Euro Disney outside Paris.

   (A)   was the first Disney theme park, but today there are also
   (B)   is the first Disney theme park, but today there is also
   (C)   was the first Disney theme park; but today you also have
   (D)   is the first Disney theme park; but today there are also
   (E)   was the first Disney theme park but today there is also

9. The Greeks are often credited with the creation of drama, <u>and the Romans should be credited for</u> bringing drama to the masses.

   (A)   and the Romans should be credited for
   (B)   and the Romans should be credited with
   (C)   until the Romans were credited with
   (D)   though the Romans were credited for
   (E)   though the Romans should be credited with

10. <u>During his presidency, John Quincy Adams, who was known for his formal nature, was often lonely and isolated.</u>

   (A)   During his presidency, John Quincy Adams, who was known for his formal nature, was often lonely and isolated.
   (B)   Known for his formal nature, John Quincy Adams' presidency was often lonely and isolated.
   (C)   Often lonely and isolated, during his presidency John Quincy Adams was known for his formal nature.
   (D)   John Quincy Adams was a president that was known for his formal nature as well as for being lonely and isolated.
   (E)   Often lonely and isolated during his presidency, John Quincy Adams, who was known for his formal nature.

11. The birch bark documents of Novgorod enable scholars to partially reconstruct everyday life in twelfth-century Russia <u>and they can study</u> literacy patterns among common people.

   (A)   and they can study
   (B)   as well as studying
   (C)   so they could study
   (D)   and a study of
   (E)   and to study

12. In the past hurricanes were all given <u>women's names, now they are</u> given names of both men and women.

   (A)   women's names, now they are
   (B)   womens' names now they are
   (C)   women's names; now they are
   (D)   womens' names, now being
   (E)   women's names; now they are being

GO ON TO THE NEXT PAGE

13. In most parts of Sri Lanka it rains only from June to September <u>during the monsoon season; the clear skies the rest</u> of the year make it difficult to farm.

   (A)   during the monsoon season; the clear skies the rest
   (B)   while the monsoons take place; the clear skies the rest
   (C)   during the monsoon season however the clear skies the rest
   (D)   while the monsoons are taking place, and the clear skies the rest
   (E)   during the monsoon season because the clear skies the rest

14. After the 1950s, film adaptations of musical theatre became less and less common, <u>although the success of 2002's *Chicago* led some people to believe it</u> would see a revival that has yet to materialize.

   (A)   although the success of 2002's *Chicago* led some people to believe it
   (B)   and then the success of 2002's *Chicago*, some people thought, meant they
   (C)   but the success of 2002's *Chicago* would lead them to believe that they
   (D)   whereas some people were led to believe by the success of 2002's *Chicago* that such adaptations
   (E)   although the success of 2002's *Chicago* led some people to believe that such adaptations

STOP

If you finish before time is called, you may check your work on this section only.
Do not turn to any other section in the test.

NO TEST MATERIAL ON THIS PAGE.

PRACTICE TEST 8: ANSWER KEY

2 Math	3 Reading	5 Reading	6 Math	7 Writing	8 Reading	9 Math	10 Writing
1. A	1. B	1. A	1. C	1. D	1. C	1. A	1. A
2. C	2. A	2. C	2. A	2. E	2. A	2. D	2. C
3. E	3. E	3. C	3. D	3. E	3. B	3. C	3. D
4. E	4. E	4. B	4. B	4. D	4. C	4. A	4. B
5. A	5. C	5. A	5. D	5. C	5. A	5. B	5. C
6. E	6. A	6. E	6. B	6. A	6. D	6. E	6. B
7. D	7. D	7. B	7. A	7. E	7. B	7. A	7. D
8. A	8. B	8. D	8. D	8. C	8. D	8. D	8. A
9. A	9. B	9. E	9. 17	9. B	9. B	9. A	9. E
10. B	10. A	10. C	10. 17	10. D	10. B	10. D	10. A
11. E	11. C	11. A	11. 46, 47, 48,	11. B	11. C	11. B	11. E
12. D	12. D	12. D	49, 50, 51,	12. C	12. A	12. D	12. C
13. E	13. A	13. C	or 52	13. B	13. D	13. B	13. A
14. B	14. C	14. D	12. $\frac{7}{3}$ or 2.33	14. B	14. D	14. C	14. E
15. E	15. B	15. A	13. $\frac{12}{5}$ or 2.4	15. C	15. C	15. C	
16. D	16. B	16. D	14. 64	16. D	16. E	16. B	
17. C	17. E	17. A	15. $\frac{4}{7}$ or .571	17. D	17. D		
18. D	18. A	18. C	16. 12	18. C	18. A		
19. B	19. E	19. B	17. 85	19. E	19. E		
20. E	20. B	20. C	18. 46	20. E			
	21. A	21. B		21. A			
	22. C	22. A		22. C			
	23. A	23. E		23. E			
	24. C	24. D		24. B			
				25. B			
				26. B			
				27. A			
				28. C			
				29. A			
				30. B			
				31. E			
				32. C			
				33. D			
				34. B			
				35. A			

SAT SCORING WORKSHEET

For directions on how to score your SAT practice test, see pages 10–11.

SAT Writing Section

Total Writing Multiple-Choice Questions Correct: [ ]

−

Total Writing Multiple-Choice Questions Incorrect: _____ ÷ 4 = [ ]

Grammar Raw Score: [ ]

Grammar Scaled Subscore [ ]

Compare the Grammar Raw Score with the Writing Multiple-Choice Subscore Conversion Table on page 666 to find the Grammar Scaled Subscore.

+

Your Essay Score (2–12): _____ × 2 = [ ]

Writing Raw Score: [ ]

Compare Raw Score with SAT Score Conversion Table on page 666 to find the Writing Scaled Score.

Writing Scaled Score [ ]

SAT Critical Reading Section

Total Critical Reading Questions Correct: [ ]

−

Total Critical Reading Questions Incorrect: _____ ÷ 4 = [ ]

Critical Reading Raw Score: [ ]

Compare Raw Score with SAT Score Conversion Table on page 666 to find the Critical Reading Scaled Score.

Critical Reading Scaled Score [ ]

SAT Math Section

Total Math Grid-In Questions Correct: [ ]

+

Total Math Multiple-Choice Questions Correct: [ ]

−

Total Math Multiple-Choice Questions Incorrect: _____ ÷ 4 = [ ]

Don't include wrong answers from grid-ins!

Math Raw Score: [ ]

Compare Raw Score with SAT Score Conversion Table on page 666 to find the Math Scaled Score.

Math Scaled Score [ ]

SAT SCORE CONVERSION TABLE

Raw Score	Writing Scaled Score	Reading Scaled Score	Math Scaled Score	Raw Score	Writing Scaled Score	Reading Scaled Score	Math Scaled Score	Raw Score	Writing Scaled Score	Reading Scaled Score	Math Scaled Score
73	800			47	590–630	600–640	660–700	21	400–440	410–450	440–480
72	790–800			46	590–630	590–630	650–690	20	390–430	400–440	430–470
71	780–800			45	580–620	580–620	650–690	19	380–420	400–440	430–470
70	770–800			44	570–610	580–620	640–680	18	370–410	390–430	420–460
69	770–800			43	570–610	570–610	630–670	17	370–410	380–420	410–450
68	760–800			42	560–600	570–610	620–660	16	360–400	370–410	400–440
67	760–800	800		41	560–600	560–600	610–650	15	350–390	360–400	400–440
66	760–800	770–800		40	550–590	550–590	600–640	14	340–380	350–390	390–430
65	750–790	760–800		39	540–580	550–590	590–630	13	330–370	340–380	380–420
64	740–780	750–790		38	530–570	540–580	590–630	12	320–360	340–380	360–400
63	730–770	740–780		37	530–570	530–570	580–620	11	320–360	330–370	350–390
62	720–760	730–770		36	520–560	530–570	570–610	10	310–350	320–360	340–380
61	710–750	720–760		35	510–550	520–560	560–600	9	300–340	310–350	330–370
60	700–740	710–750		34	500–540	520–560	560–600	8	290–330	300–340	320–360
59	690–730	700–740		33	490–530	510–550	550–590	7	280–320	300–340	310–350
58	680–720	690–730		32	480–520	500–540	540–580	6	270–310	290–330	300–340
57	680–720	680–720		31	470–510	490–530	530–570	5	260–300	280–320	290–330
56	670–710	670–710		30	470–510	480–520	520–560	4	240–280	270–310	280–320
55	660–720	670–710		29	460–500	470–510	520–560	3	230–270	250–290	280–320
54	650–690	660–700	760–800	28	450–490	470–510	510–550	2	230–270	240–280	270–310
53	640–680	650–690	740–780	27	440–480	460–500	500–540	1	220–260	220–260	260–300
52	630–670	640–680	730–770	26	430–470	450–490	490–530	0	210–250	200–240	250–290
51	630–670	630–670	710–750	25	420–460	440–480	480–520	–1	200–240	200–230	230–270
50	620–660	620–660	690–730	24	410–450	430–470	470–510	–2	200–230	200–220	220–260
49	610–650	610–650	680–720	23	410–450	430–470	460–500	–3	200–220	200–210	200–240
48	600–640	600–640	670–710	22	400–440	420–460	450–490				

WRITING MULTIPLE-CHOICE SUBSCORE CONVERSION TABLE

Grammar Raw Score	Grammar Scaled Subscore	Grammar Raw Score	Grammar Scaled Subscore	Grammar Raw Score	Grammar Scaled Subscore	Grammar Raw Score	Grammar Scaled Subscore	Grammar Raw Score	Grammar Scaled Subscore
49	78–80	38	67–71	27	55–59	16	42–46	5	30–34
48	77–80	37	66–70	26	54–58	15	41–45	4	29–33
47	75–79	36	65–69	25	53–57	14	40–44	3	28–32
46	74–78	35	64–68	24	52–56	13	39–43	2	27–31
45	72–76	34	63–67	23	51–55	12	38–42	1	25–29
44	72–76	33	62–66	22	50–54	11	36–40	0	24–28
43	71–75	32	61–65	21	49–53	10	35–39	–1	22–26
42	70–74	31	60–64	20	47–51	9	34–38	–2	20–23
41	69–73	30	59–63	19	46–50	8	33–37	–3	20–22
40	68–72	29	58–62	18	45–49	7	32–36		
39	68–72	28	56–60	17	44–48	6	31–35		

Chapter 19
Practice Test 8:
Answers and
Explanations

SECTION 2

1. **A** First solve for y: $y + 4 = 13$, so subtract 4 from both sides to see that $y = 9$. Replace the y in the second equation with 9 to see that $9 - 2 = 7$, answer (A).

2. **C** Find the length of side $\overline{JM}$ by subtracting the smaller x value from the larger x value: $6 - (-3) = 9$. Find the length of side $\overline{LM}$ by subtracting the smaller y value from the larger y value: $5 - (-5) = 10$. This is a rectangle, so opposite sides have equal length. The perimeter is $9 + 9 + 10 + 10 = 38$, (C).

3. **E** The question asks how many vehicles are <u>not</u> trucks, but gives the fraction of the vehicles that are trucks. If $\dfrac{1}{5}$ of the vehicles are trucks, then $\dfrac{4}{5}$ of the 650 vehicles are <u>not</u> trucks. $\dfrac{4}{5}(650) = 520$, (E). Be careful; (B) is the number of trucks.

4. **E** Start in the innermost pair of absolute values and replace x with -3: $\big\||-3-2|-|2+(-3)|\big\| = \big\||-5|-|-1|\big\| = |5-1| = |4| = 4$, (E).

5. **A** To find the percent equivalent of each fraction, divide the numerator by the denominator and multiply by 100. (A) gives 4%; (B) gives 8.33%; (C) gives 12.5%; (D) gives 16.67%; and (E) gives 33.3%. Only (A) has an integer value.

6. **E** Make up your own number for z. Since we are dealing with percents, making $z = 100$ will help keep things simple: 15% of 100 = 15, and 30% of 100 = 30. There is a difference of 15 between the two numbers. The correct answer will equal 15 when z is replaced with 100. (A) results in 1500, (B) results in 200, (C) results in 150, (D) results in 100 and (E) results in 15. Only (E) matches the target number.

7. **D** In 10 years, $\dfrac{3}{4}$ of the 800 people will live in Northville: $\dfrac{3}{4} \times 800 = 600$. In another 10 years, $\dfrac{3}{4}$ of those 600 people will live there: $\dfrac{3}{4} \times 600 = 450$, answer (D). Beware of (E); that is a partial answer.

8. **A** We can find the value of y because the straight line of 180° is made up of angles measuring $4y$ and y. The total, $5y$, equals 180, so $y = 36$. Because the angles labeled $3x$ and y are vertical angles, $3x = y$, so $3x = 36$, and $x = 12$, answer (A).

9. **A** Simplify the statement by multiplying the expressions within the parentheses: $(60 \times 10^4) + (60 \times 10^2) = (60 \times 10,000) + (60 \times 100) = 600,000 + 6,000 = 606,000$. This can be written as 606×10^3, as seen in (A).

10. **B** Use the numbers in the chart to determine how much money was raised by each level of readers. 18 students read 10 books each for a total of 180 books. Since each book read earned fifty cents, the first level earned $180 \times .50 = \$90$. 24 students read 20 books each for a total of 480 books, so the second level earned $480 \times .50 = \$240$. 3 students read 30 books each for a total of 90 books, so the third level earned $90 \times .50 = \$45$. Now add up the three amounts earned: $90 + 240 + 45 = 375$, answer (B).

11. **E** Translate the question into math. The equation described is written $b^2 = b + 12$. The equations in the answer choices all equal 0, so we need to rearrange the equation we came up with so that it equals 0. Subtracting b and 12 from the left side of the equation gives: $b^2 - b - 12 = 0$, the equation in (E). This quadratic equation can be factored into $(b + 3)(b - 4) = 0$, which tells us that b can be either −3 or 4.

12. **D** If we add the parts of the 2 : 3 : 1 ratio together, we find the total number of liters in one batch of all the ingredients combined. In this case, 2 parts pineapple + 3 parts OJ + 1 part seltzer gives 6 parts per set. Since there are two liters of seltzer used, the number of liters for all ingredients is 2 times that of one batch, for a total of 12 liters, answer (D).

13. **E** Plug In some numbers of your own for w, x, y, and z. Because $wxyz \neq 0$, we know that none of the numbers can possibly be 0. If $w = 2$ and $x = 3$, then y must be 6 and z must be 18. We need to know which of the answers is equal to the value of w, so our target number is 2. (A) is too large: $xz = 3 \times 18$. (B) is even larger, since it is the value in (A) but z is squared. (C) gives $\dfrac{3}{18}$, (D) gives $\dfrac{18}{3} = 6$. (E) gives $\dfrac{18}{9} = 2$, the number we were looking for. Algebraically, $wx \times xy = y \times z$ and $wx^2y = yz$. Divide both sides by y to get $wx^2 = z$. Finally, divide both sides by x^2 to get $w = \dfrac{z}{x^2}$, as seen in (E).

14. **B** In the situation described in the question, Gregg gets \$14, and Duane loses the \$14 he gives away. If Duane lost \$14, he would have $\$45 - \$14 = \$31$. This the amount Gregg should have if he gains \$14. The answer choices reflect the amount of money that Gregg starts with. Test out the answers by adding 14 and look for the one whose total equals \$31. Only (B) $\$17 + \$14 = \$31$.

15. **E** To solve this problem, take points from the figure and test them out in the equations in the answer choices, replacing x with the x value and $f(x)$ with the y value. If an equation is not true with the point from the graph, eliminate that answer. Using point (1, 9) works only in (B) and (E). Use another point from the graph to test out just these two answers. Using point (4, 0) does not work in (B), but it does create a true equation in (E).

16. **D** Use a pencil to draw geometric figures that are mentioned but not shown. If all three lines intersect in the center of the circle, the circle is broken into 6 regions. This eliminates (A) and (B), but try to arrange the three lines in a different pattern of intersection that creates more regions. If the three lines form a triangle at the center of the circle, that creates 7 regions, answer (D). There is no way to create 8 regions with 3 lines.

17. **C** The slope is the difference in y values of two points on a line over the difference in x values for those two points. Since all four lines intersect the origin, all we have to do is put the y value on top of the x value for each point. OP has a slope of $\frac{4}{2}$ or 2. OQ has a slope of $\frac{2}{4}$ or $\frac{1}{2}$. OR has a slope of $\frac{-2}{4}$, or $-\frac{1}{2}$. OS has a slope of $-\frac{4}{2}$ or -2. Now add up the four slopes and divide by 4 to find the average slope. $2 + \frac{1}{2} + (-\frac{1}{2}) + (-2) = 0$, and $\frac{0}{4} = 0$, answer (C).

18. **D** When the two values in parentheses are FOILed out, the numbers that are multiplied together to get c will add up to 11. This gives us a choice of 5 pairs: 1 and 10; 2 and 9; 3 and 8; 4 and 7; and 5 and 6. These give products of 10, 18, 24, 28, and 30, respectively. The greatest value that we obtained for c was 30, answer (D).

19. **B** The easiest way to solve this problem is to use two prime numbers in place of x and y. If $x = 3$ and $y = 5$, (A) is not correct because $x^2 = 9$, which has only three distinct factors (1, 3, 9). (B) is correct because $xy = 15$, which has four distinct factors (1, 3, 5, 15). In (C) $xy^2 = 75$, which has six distinct factors (1, 3, 5, 15, 25, 75). In (D) $(x + y)^2 = 64$, which has 7 distinct factors (1, 2, 4, 8, 16 32, 64). In (E) $(x - y)^2 = 4$ which has three distinct factors (1, 2, 4).

20. **E** Draw the square that is described in the question. The diagonal is $j + 3$, and we can use the proportions of the 45-45-90 triangle to find the lengths of the sides in the square that we can use to find the area of the square. The proportion of the legs to the hypotenuse is $s : s : s\sqrt{2}$. The diagonal is the hypotenuse, so $s\sqrt{2} = j + 3$, and $s = \frac{j+3}{\sqrt{2}}$. Find the area of the square of this value: $\frac{(j+3)(j+3)}{(\sqrt{2})(\sqrt{2})} = \frac{j^2 + 6j + 9}{2}$ as seen in (E). To avoid having to FOIL values in parentheses, you can come up with a number for j, such as 2, so the diagonal is 5 and the sides of the squares are $\frac{5}{\sqrt{2}}$, which when squared gives $\frac{25}{2}$. The only answer choice that gives this result when j is replaced with 2 is (E). (A) gives 13; (B) gives 25; (C) gives $13\sqrt{2}$; (D) gives $\frac{13}{2}$.

SECTION 3

1. **B**   The clue in this sentence is that the prospect *missed ground balls and overthrew the first baseman by several feet.* Therefore, the prospect had a severe "lack" of skills. Only (B) matches this meaning.

2. **A**   Start with the second blank. We know that Marvin Gaye is *famous,* so the blank is going to mean something close to *famous.* Eliminate (B) and (D). (C) should also be eliminated because *notorious* means "famous for a bad reason," which is not indicated in the sentence. For the first blank, the word *however* tells you to choose something that is the opposite of famous. *Powerful* is not the opposite of famous, so eliminate (E) and choose (A).

3. **E**   The second blank is easier to fill in: Since Juliana is in a *contest* she is a "contestant." Eliminate (C) and (D) because their second words do not match "contestant." *Competitor, challenger,* and *contender* are all reasonably close. Juliana is the *top* contestant in the contest, so "skillfulness" or "ability" is the meaning for the first blank that should describe how Juliana does at *solving puzzles.* Only (C) *skill* and (E) *alacrity* are words that describe the ability to do something well, making (E) the only answer that matches both blanks.

4. **E**   The professor's grading system put the students into competition with one another. Since he encourages competitiveness, he would discourage something like "working together." Only (E) *congenial* matches this definition. (B) *selfish* is the opposite of what we are looking for.

5. **C**   The clues for this sentence are *surprised* and *only addressed issues associated with the United States,* so you should therefore find the answer choice that best matches "limited," since the professor is teaching a global studies course. (A) is a trap since it is very similar to *global.* (B) is close since it means "superficial," but that does not mean "limited." (D) nonchalant is not supported because there is no evidence to indicate how much he cares —or doesn't care— about the topic. (E) should be eliminated because *diffident* means "shy."

6. **A**   The first sentence states what a labyrinth is not, while the second sentence describes the reality of a labyrinth's structure. The author probably includes the first sentence to clear up false ideas people might believe, and the second to clarify the qualities of the subject the author intends to discuss. This is paraphrased in (A). (B) is incorrect because there is nothing *mystical* implied in the first two sentences. The sentences do not form a list, so eliminate (C). No *healthful or spiritual benefits* are mentioned so eliminate (D). (E) is incorrect because there is nothing *dark* or *melancholy* about these informative sentences.

7. **D**   The passage states that the *archeologists excavating the city of Knossos* have found many images of a double ax. This is a *link* between the city and *King Minos,* because Minos was the one who possessed the Labyrinth, which is a word that comes from the word for "double-ax" lines 16–17). Furthermore, the passage states in lines 17-19 that *according to legend,* the dynasty of Minos was referred to as *house of the Double Ax* (D), *link between Knossos and King Minos* is the most supported.

(A) is kind of true, but (D) is more specific. (B) is not stated. The phrase *conclusively prove* in (C) is extreme. (E) is incorrect because there is nothing in the passage that states when the excavation happened. The reference is used to support the author's point that a mythological story may have basis in some factual details, not merely to provide details of the excavation for their own sake.

8. **B** (A) gives a pair of words that is mentioned in each passage, but they don't *describe* the labyrinths. The phrase *meditation aid* in (B) is supported in lines 3–4 *a path which symbolizes a journey to the center of the self*, and *prison* is supported by lines 13–14 *imprisoned in the Labyrinth*. There is no evidence in the passage for the other answers.

9. **B** Go through the answer choices and eliminate those that do not have a stronger presence in Passage 2 than in Passage 1. (A) is not mentioned in either passage. (B) is correct: Passage 2 discusses where the word *labyrinth* comes from, and Passage 1 does not address this. The topic of *spirituality*, (C), is addressed in Passage 1, not in Passage 2, which is the opposite of what the question asks for. There is no evidence for (D) or (E) in Passage 2.

10. **A** William's *coworkers* are mentioned in line 21 and find William's behavior *perplexing*. In the next mention of the coworkers in line 27, it states in the coworkers' viewpoint that the tape recording is *not the oddest thing* about William. Since the *coworkers surmised* (line 30) the reason for his dressing in identical clothes every day indicates that they have been interested enough to discuss his behavior and want to understand why he does things in his peculiar way. The coworkers seem *mildly curious*, (A). The emotion in (B) *coldly indifferent* is not supported by the passage. There is no evidence of the coworkers being *condescending*, (C). (D) *deeply intrigued* is too strong compared to the level of interest expressed in the passage. There is no evidence that the coworkers are *disturbed* as in (E).

11. **C** William's answer is that he *might need* the tape recorder. There is no mention of knowledge of *technology* in (A). (B) is incorrect because the passage states that *there was no possible use for it in his work*. Bringing something that one *might need* is a way of being prepared, so hold on to (C) and check the other two answers. There is no mention in the passage of *previous occasions* in (D). There is no evidence that William feels the questions are rude as in (E).

12. **D** William's preparations are painstaking: he *checks and rechecks* his possessions, his directions are *neatly written out*, but it's all for nothing. William has packed useless items, and he never gets to use any of his meeting supplies because he doesn't make it to the meeting; his neatly written directions get him lost. The useless energy put into preparations "all for nothing" situation is best described by *fruitless* (D), which means "useless or unproductive." (A) *professional* is incorrect, because William's coworkers wouldn't think he was *odd* if he were acting professionally. While William does not pay attention on his way and gets lost, his *preparations* themselves are not *careless*, (B). The preparations are not *useful*, (C), because William has unnecessary items and doesn't get where he plans to go. There is no evidence that William or anyone else thought his preparations were *tiresome*, or "annoying."

13. **A** The best supported answer is (A). Although William *says* that he doesn't use maps because they lack organization, it is implied that the actual reason is that William doesn't understand how to use them—it seems unlikely that all the map-makers are wrong and William is right. William also states that he doesn't need maps because he has the directions written down. These directions end up getting him lost, so it is further evidence that William *has much to learn about navigation*.

14. **C** The *blue necktie* is still flying proudly despite William's disastrous day and the poor state of the rest of his clothes. Just as in a sentence completion, the word *but* indicates the opposite of what comes before. In this case, the necktie is a positive symbol in contrast to the other aspects of William's behavior. (D) is too literal: this isn't about the variety of his wardrobe.

15. **B** The primary purpose of a passage is what the author is trying to accomplish in his or her writing. This is a fictional piece, written to tell a story and the focus from the very first sentence is about how an individual with odd habits is always lost and late. (A) does not mention how weird some of William's behavior is. (B) is good because *chronicles* means to tell a story, and it mentions *idiosyncrasies* of a *salesman*. (C) does not mention any weirdness about the day or the salesperson. The passage is not directed to William's coworkers as in (D)—they're fictional! (E) is too strong: There is no evidence of mental illness.

16. **B** The *study by Robert Chesness* is mentioned in the second paragraph. The author begins *discounting* Chesness's findings with the word *But* in the next paragraph, and concludes with the sentence *Togetherness cannot be determined by human standards*. This fits best with (B), biased toward a human understanding of closeness. (A) is incorrect: the author herself uses the term *pack* for coyotes. (C) may be true, but does not tell what the author states as a reason to reject Chesness's findings.

17. **E** In the passage, the paragraph that mentions *nineteenth-century explorers* begins with the statement *I was by no means the first*. The first sentence is often a good clue to the main focus of a paragraph. The rest of the paragraph tells how *nineteenth-century explorers* noted that they found coyotes to be very *sociable*, which supports the author's main point. This purpose is seen in (E), *provide evidence supporting a claim*. There is no mention of *custom*, (A), in relation to the explorers. The word *proof* is too strong, and the phrases *controversial theory, scientific conundrum, and temporary phenomenon* don't describe this author's observations about wildlife, so (B), (C), and (D) are out, and furthermore, the point is not to *explain* as in (D) it is to support.

18. **A** The quote from *J. Frank Dobie* suggests that it is true that coyotes are more solitary than they once were, and theorizes that coyotes may have changed from sociable to solitary in order to survive in a changed environment. The author uses this idea to reason that the coyotes that he observes are sociable because they have a protected environment. The quote provides an explanation for why some researchers record solitary behavior while the author and early observers recorded sociable behaviors. This is best summarized in (A). There is no *benefit* mentioned between species. (C) and (E) mention details from the paragraph, but are not the reason why the author cites the quote. There is no evidence for (D).

19. **E** The *protected refuge* is mentioned as a reason that the coyotes that he observes are sociable while others have described coyotes as solitary. It comes after the quote from *J. Frank Dobie* indicating that coyotes once were sociable, but the modern environment makes them solitary. The *protected refuge* is more like the coyote's natural environment where they can be sociable, as in (E) *increased companionship.*

20. **B** In the passage, *Such behavior* refers to the *gregarious lifestyle* and the way coyotes *become clannish* exhibited by the coyotes the author observes. Something like "friendly" describes this behavior, and *sociable,* (B), is a match. None of the other answers have a meaning close to that of friendly.

21. **A** Since the author's main point in this passage is that the traditional theory on coyotes-as-loners may be incorrect, (A) successfully states her view. (B) is extreme since it says *no merit,* while (C) and (E) are not supported in the passage. (D) may seem acceptable since the final paragraph shows some of the author's doubts to her observations, but there is no evidence that the coyotes eventually break their cooperative nature.

22. **C** In lines 61–62, the word *Nature* starts off the sentence that *Nature had provided them with surrogate parents,* so the correct answer must indicate that coyotes will raise the pups of other coyotes if something happens to the parents. This is seen in (C), with *orphaned pups.* It is not that coyote *don't raise their own young,* as in (A); it just means that other coyotes step in if necessary. (B) is mentioned elsewhere in the passage, but not in the discussion of nature. (D) is unrelated to the characterization of nature, and there is no mention of *travel* as in (E).

23. **A** Only (A) is supported by the passage. (B) *flourished* is too strong; we know only that they are more social than some studies indicate. (C) contradicts that passage: coyotes are now less likely to be seen in packs, not more so. (D) contradicts the passage, which states that the coyotes are solitary now because they have adapted to environmental change. Though there is mention of coyotes breaking apart from each other to hunt mice, there is no evidence in the passage to support that coyotes *always* hunt alone, as in (E).

24. **C** Since the question asks for the question that <u>cannot</u> be answered, go through the answer choices, and find the spot in the passage that contains the necessary information. (A) can be answered in lines 9–13. (B) can be answered in lines 52–54. (C) cannot be answered: there is no indication of the future. (D) can be answered in lines 42–44. (E) can be answered in lines 26–39.

SECTION 5

1. **A** The study *leaves no aspect of the issue unexamined*, so a good word for the blank would be "thorough." The word in (A), *comprehensive* means this exactly. The rest of the words could describe a *sleep theory*, but none of the other answers make sense with the part of the sentence following the blank.

2. **C** The actress is making a *speech*, so her parents' *contributions* are something that could be "mentioned" in a speech. We need a word for the second blank that means "mentioned". Eliminate answers (B), (D), and (E); only *recognize* and *acknowledge*. If the parents' contributions were neglected, they would not be too pleased, so "upset" is a good meaning for the first blank. Between (A) *honored* and (C) *chagrined*, definitely pick (C), even if you don't know what *chagrin* (disappointment or humiliation) means, because *honored* is a positive emotion.

3. **C** The semicolon is an indication that the phrase immediately following the semicolon is a description of the word that comes immediately before it. In this case, what comes immediately before the semicolon is the blank. The description, *does not display true originality* means a word that means "unoriginal" is a good match for the blank. (C) *trite* fits, as it means "ineffective due to overuse or excessive repetition; stale:" Eliminate (A) because *unique* is the opposite of unoriginal. None of the other answers mean "unoriginal."

4. **B** The word *Until* indicates a separation of two time periods, and indicates that something has changed between the two times. Later in the sentence the phrase *had believed traditional reality was great* lets us know how thing were *until he studied Picasso's works*. Afterward, he was different, so he must now believe that "anti-reality" or "non-realism" is great. The correct word for the first blank means something like "non-realism," so eliminate (A) *realism* immediately: it's the opposite of what we're looking for. It may be hard to eliminate any of the other answers based on the first word. There is some tough vocab here. The second blank describes the artist, and since this was a perspective-changing encounter, we need a word that shows the artist's work is really amazing. Both *genius* and *brilliance* from the second word in the answers would work, but the rest of the answers are not related. Only the pair of words in (B) fit into both blanks.

5. **A** The phrase that follows the semicolon describes the word immediately before it. The sentence states that the audience *could not believe*, so the blank must mean something like "disbelieving." (A) *incredulous* is a synonym for disbelieving. None of the other words match in meaning. There is some tough vocab here, so look up any unfamiliar words.

6. **E** The word *though* and *meant be* indicate that the how the article is *actually interpreted* differs from what the article planned to say. The first blank describes *analysis*. A good analysis would be *analytical*, so eliminate answers in which the first word is not close in meaning to "analytical." Only (D) *impartial* and (E) fit. The second blank is the opposite, and describes *criticism*. Criticism suggests that the author of the article took a one-sided (negative) view of the President, "biased" is a good meaning for the second blank. Between (D) *prosaic* (commonplace or dull) and (E) *partisan* (showing a biased, emotional allegiance) (E) is much closer.

7. **B** The blank describes Kevin's *nature*, so look for evidence in the sentence to come up with a word to describe him. Kevin causes *disturbances*, *struggles to avoid altercations*, or fights. This sounds like someone who is aggressive and angry. (C) *serene* and (D) *scrupulous*, are the opposite of what we're looking for. (E) *smarmy* is unrelated in meaning. (B) is correct because *irascible* means "easily provoked to anger."

8. **D** The sentence states that *coffee beans were scarce*, and the semicolon indicates that the second part of the sentence is closely related to the ideas in the first part. The second part the sentence describes all the things the people are drinking in place of coffee, so we need a word to indicate non-coffee, such as "imitation." The answers include some tough vocabulary. Look up any unfamiliar words! (D) is correct because *ersatz* means "an often inferior substitute."

9. **E** The items listed in (A) and (D) are mentioned in lines 8–9. (B) is mentioned in line 2, and (C) is mentioned in line 1. Only (E) *mechanical circus models*, is not mentioned. This is a tricky one, because the passage does mention that Calder used the circus as a theme in his work, but the models were not *mechanical*.

10. **C** In the same sentence that mentions Einstein, right before the semicolon, the passage states that the *sheer magnitude* of Calder's work made it *seem worthy and significant*. Only (C), *immense dimensions* refers to size. The other answer choices involve science and art, but do not relate to why Einstein spent a long time looking at one of Calder's works.

11. **A** Craven's discovery is described as *Craven's results* in line 8 of the passage. The text mentions that this use of aspirin had *benefits, however* it caused other kinds of *problems*. (A) *twofold nature* is an abstraction of aspirin's two opposing qualities. There is no evidence for any of the other answers.

12. **D** The phrase *like doing surgery with a hatchet* means that in trying to do something beneficial, the treatment causes major damage. (A) is out because we don't need another method; (B) is true, but has nothing to do with benefits or damage, (C) is the opposite of what is stated in the passage and extreme. (D) mentions *benefits* and *dangerous side effects*, so it matches what we were looking for. (E) definitely does not match: there is no evidence for *exaggeration*.

13. **C** According to the passage, the *sense of guilt* is *tied to their desire to break away* or *their failure to fulfill a role*. Only (C) addresses both of these points. There is no evidence for (A) (B, or (D). The word *shame* in (E) is much too strong.

14. **D** The word *always* in (A) makes it too extreme, *usually* would be true, but *always* is impossible. There is no evidence in the passage for (B) or (C). (D) is correct because the passage's first two paragraphs establish that black women in Baldwin's work have many overlapping roles, the most prominent of which is the churchgoing black female. The passage gives two examples of specific Baldwin works that feature this characterization.

15. **A** The *typical churchgoer* in Baldwin's fiction is described in the third paragraph. The sentence in lines 19–20 states that *The women in this category come closer to being stereotypes than perhaps any others in Baldwin's works.* This is what is described in (A). The word *outcasts,* in (B), does not describe the *churchgoers*: the mention of outcasts is too far away in the passage from where the *churchgoers* are discussed. The description of being *subservient to males* in (C) is also too far from the *churchgoers,* and in the passage is describing Baldwin's female characters in general. (D) *omniscient* describes the narration style, and (E) *widely known* refers to *Praying Mother Washington.*

16. **D** The author mentions *Praying Mother Washington* as an example of the type of character she has just described in lines 23–24: the kind who *extend their roles* to *leadership* that appear in Baldwin's fiction *On rare occasions.* (D) is a good paraphrase of this. (A) is the opposite of what we are looking for: the churchgoer is the typical female in Baldwin's fiction. Baldwin's fiction does not have a *wide range* of women characters, as in (B). (C) is not true. (E) is not supported by evidence in the passage.

17. **A** In lines 14–16, the passage states that *the most prominent women* in Baldwin's fiction *are solely within the tradition of the fundamentalist church.* Praying Mother Washington, first mentioned in lines 23–24, has *a recognized position of respect,* and is a *powerful evangelist.* Ida is first mentioned in line 46. All we know about her is that she wants to be a blues singer, she started out singing in her church, that she began in a tradition and *moved beyond* it. This is best captured in (A), which addresses the role of the church in both women's lives. (B) is about only Mother Washington. (C) is about only Ida. (D) is the opposite of what we're looking for: these women are the rare exceptions, not the stereotype. (E) is also opposite of what we're looking for.

18. **C** Go back to the passage and use the context to come up with a word to replace *assume.* In the passage, women who have no children "take on" the role of mother. "Take on" is closest to (C). While some of the answer choices are definitions for other meaning of *assume,* these do not fit in the context of the passage.

19. **B** In the passage. John is described as someone who *must sense* the *moods and desires* of Elizabeth. That's really all we know about him. This is best paraphrased in (B). (A) is not stated in the passage. There is no evidence for (C). (D) is not true, and (E) is not mentioned in the passage.

20. **C** Go back to the passage and use the context to come up with a word to replace *iconoclasts.* Beginning in line 37, the passage states that few women break free of the *bounds of traditional roles.* Those few that do are referred to as *iconoclasts,* so *iconoclasts* means "people that do things differently than most people do." Only (C), *nonconformists* fits this definition.

21. **B** In the passage, Julia is mentioned in line 50, and it states that *it is Julia who has the atypical career for women in Baldwin's fiction.* This is paraphrased in (B). (A) is out because money is not mentioned in relation to Julia. There is no evidence for (C) or (D). (E) is not mentioned in the passage.

22. **A** The phrase *subordination of women* is referred to in line 65. The reason is given in lines 57–58: *It is a function of their guilt…that most…have been subordinated to males.* Only (A) mentions *guilt* (in *remorse*) There is no evidence for (B) or (C). (D) is incorrect because *always* makes it extreme. (E) is not mentioned in the passage.

23. **E** The reason that the author mentions *Tish* in line 70 as an example of *The only female who narrates a story or novel.* The fact that she is *the only one* indicates that she is different from most of Baldwin's female characters. Both (D) and (E) use a word, *exception* to indicate this difference, but (E) is a stronger answer because she does not refute anything, as mentioned in (D).

24. **D** That the female characters are *distanced* from the reader is described at the end of the last paragraph, in lines 78–81. Black women are *twice removed*—seen through a filter of male narrators and a male author (A) is extreme due to its use of *never*. (B) is not true. (C) is untrue: the passage gives examples of strong women in Baldwin's fiction. (D) is correct; it matches the male narrator and author suggested by *twice removed*. (E) is contradicted by evidence in the passage of women who play major roles in Baldwin's fiction.

SECTION 6

1. **C** If you notice that the value the question asks for, $5a + 4b$ is half the value of the equation $10a + 8b = 4x$, then you can divide the result of the equation by 2 to see that the value of $5a + 4b$ must be $2x$, answer (C). Alternately, you can come up with your own answers for a and b, such as $a = 2$ and $b = 5$. We need to find the value for x: since it appears in the answers. We can use the first equation to find x. $10a + 8b = 4x$, so $10(2) + 8(5) = 4x$, and $20 + 40 = 4x$. Since $4x = 60$, $x = 15$. Because $5a + 4b$ has a value of 30, the correct answer will also result in 30 when x is replaced with 15. (A) gives $8(15) = 120$. (B) gives $4(15) = 60$. (C) matches because $2(15) = 30$. (D) gives 15, and (E) gives $\frac{15}{2}$.

2. **A** The term *varies inversely* means that the product of two numbers is always the same. If this constant product is represented by k, the equation looks like this: $y = \dfrac{k}{x}$, or $xy = k$. The information in the question is structured like the version that contains a fraction. The question states that the mouse had 8 hours of sleep, so *time* $= \dfrac{320}{8} = 40$, answer (A).

3. **D** One box of mix makes 6 large muffins. We need 120 large muffins, so $\frac{120}{6}$ = 20 boxes of mix needed to make the large muffins. Beware of (B); it's a partial answer. We need 180 muffins total, so that's 60 mini-muffins that we need boxes of mix for. One box makes 10 mini-muffins, so $\frac{60}{10}$ = 6 boxes of mix necessary for mini-muffins, for a total of 26 boxes of mix, as seen in (D).

4. **B** We are told that $a = \frac{4}{3}$ so we can replace each instance of a in the equation we need to solve with $\frac{4}{3}$. This changes the expression to $\frac{4}{\frac{4}{3}} - \frac{\frac{4}{3}}{\frac{4}{3} - 1}$. The rule for dividing by a fraction is "Don't ask why, just flip it over and multiply." If we do that with the first fraction in the expression, we get $(4 \times \frac{3}{4})$ = 3. We can simplify the second fraction to $\frac{\frac{4}{3}}{\frac{1}{3}}$ to get $\frac{4}{3} \times \frac{3}{1}$ = 4. Now we can find that $3 - 4 = -1$, answer (B).

5. **D** The formula for the area of a triangle is $Area = \frac{1}{2}bh$. We are given a height of 12 for each triangular face, and we can find the base because were are given the area of the square base of the triangle. The area of the base is 49, which is the square of 7, so the base of the triangle is 7. The area of a triangular face is $\frac{1}{2}$(7)(12), or $\frac{1}{2}$(84), which is 42, answer (D).

6. **B** Go through the list of answer choices, and add up how much the two tickets would cost. In (A), although Airline *X* does have the lowest Coach fare at $225, it is paired with Airline *Z*, which has the highest First Class fare, at $375, for a total of $600. In (B), First Class on Airline *Y* is $315 and Coach on Airline *Y* is $260, for a total of $575. In (C) First on Airline *X* is $280 and Coach on Airline *Z* is $320 for a total of $600. In (D), First on Airline *Y* is $315 and Coach on Airline *W* is $305 for a total of $620. While it might seem tempting to pick (E) because the tickets are both for Coach on Airline *Z*, the cost per ticket is $320, for a total of $640. The lowest total is the $575 of answer (B); the other answers are all $600 or over.

7. **A** To answer this question we first need to find the difference in price between First and Coach for each airline. Airline *W* has a difference of $45. Airline *X* has a difference of $55, Airline *Y* has a difference of $55, and Airline *Z* has a difference of $55. Since $55 occurs the most times in the four numbers, $55 is the mode. Now find the average, of the first-class prices: The total cost of a ticket

from each airline is 350 + 280 + 315 + 375 = 1,320. To get the average, divide by 4: 1,320 ÷ 4 = 330. Finally, what we need to do is answer the question, *What is the quotient of the mode* and *average* we found? The quotient is the answer to a division operation. Divide the first number by the second to get the quotient: $\dfrac{55}{330}$, which is not in the answer choices as is, but reduced becomes $\dfrac{1}{6}$, answer (A).

8. **D** Plug In numbers! This one may take some time, but we will eventually find the answer. Three numbers: 29 + 30 + 31 = 90; eliminate (A). Four numbers: 21 + 22 + 23 + 24 = 90; eliminate (B). Five numbers: 16 + 17 + 18 + 19 + 20 = 90; eliminate (C). Nine numbers: 6 + 7 + 8 + 9 + 10 + 11 + 12 + 13 + 14 = 90; eliminate (E). No six consecutive integers add up to 90; choose (D).

9. **17** The question shows a fraction that has x as a numerator as equal to a fraction without variables, so we can get a value for x: $\dfrac{x}{14} = \dfrac{4}{8}$. Reduce $\dfrac{4}{8}$ to $\dfrac{1}{2}$, an easier number to work with: $\dfrac{x}{14} = \dfrac{1}{2}$, so $x =$ 7. Now find a value for y: $\dfrac{5}{y} = \dfrac{1}{2}$ so $y = 10$. 7 + 10 = 17.

10. **17** If four numbers add up to 80, then their average must be 20 (80 ÷ 4 = 20). Since all the numbers must be consecutive odd integers, we should choose 4 odd consecutive numbers around 20. If we pick 19, 21, 23, and 25, the sum is too large (88), so let's try smaller numbers. If we pick 17, 19, 21, and 23, the sum is 80. Therefore the least of the integers is 17.

11. **46, 47, 48, 49, 50, 51, or 52**
    Multiply the higher average of the four remaining integers by four and do the same for the lower average to find the range of possible sums of the four integers. The total for the four integers is between 138 and 144, inclusive. The question states that when there were five integers, their sum was 190. Find the difference between the original and the lower average sum: 190 − 138 = 52. Now find the difference between the original and the higher average sum: 190 − 144 = 46. The number that was removed could therefore be 46, 47, 48, 49, 50, 51, or 52. Any one of these integers is correct.

12. $\dfrac{7}{3}$ **or 2.33**

    The formula for slope is $\dfrac{y_2 - y_1}{x_2 - x_1}$. We can Plug In values from the points for A and B shown in the figure: $\dfrac{4 - (-3)}{5 - 2} = \dfrac{7}{3}$.

13. $\frac{12}{5}$ or 2.4

The rules of exponents can be applied once the numbers have the same base. $3^{5x} = 27^4$ can be converted to $3^{5x} = (3^3)^4$, since $3^3 = 27$. An exponent raised to another power is multiplied, so $3^{5x} = 3^{12}$. Since the bases are the same, we know that $5x = 12$. $x = \frac{12}{5}$

14. 64

The perimeter of the smaller square is $16\sqrt{2}$, so divide by 4 to find the length of each side of $WXYZ$ is $4\sqrt{2}$. The corners of the larger square each form the right angle of a 45-45-90 triangle in which a side of $WXYZ$ is the hypotenuse. The ratio of sides in a 45-45-90 triangle is $1 : 1 : \sqrt{2}$. Since the hypotenuse is $4\sqrt{2}$, the legs must each have length of 4. The sides of $EFGH$ are made up of two legs of the 45-45-90 triangles, so $EFGH$ has sides of 8 and an area of 64.

15. $\frac{4}{7}$ or .571

$\frac{k+8}{4-k} = \frac{5}{2}$, so cross-multiply to get $2k + 16 = 20 - 5k$. Then, solve for k: Add $5k$ to both sides and get $7k + 16 = 20$. Now, subtract 16 from both sides: $7k = 4$. Divide by 7 and $k = \frac{4}{7}$ or 0.571.

16. 12

We need to know the height of the box. Call it n for now, then we can use the formulas for surface area and volume to solve for n. The formula for volume is *length × width × height,* or $6 \times 4 \times n = 24n$. The surface area is the area of all 6 sides of the box added together. There are 2 sides with dimensions 4 by 6, so $2(4 \times 6) = 48$. There are 2 sides with dimensions 4 by x, so $2(4 \times n) = 8n$. There are 2 sides with dimensions n by 6, so $2(n \times 6) = 12n$. Add the three products together. The surface area is $48 + 20n$, and is equal to the area of $24n$. Since $48 + 20n = 24n$, then $48 = 4n$ and $n = 12$.

17. 85

In the box there were originally 50 blue tickets and 15 red tickets. The question asks how many red tickets there are in order for the number of red tickets to make up $\frac{2}{3}$ of the tickets. If red makes up $\frac{2}{3}$, then blue makes up $\frac{1}{3}$ of the total number of tickets, and we know that we have 50 blue tickets. Solve for x to find the total number of tickets: $\frac{50}{x} = \frac{1}{3}$, so there are 150 tickets in the box, 100 of which are red. The question asks how many red tickets have been added. Since there were 15 red tickets originally, $100 - 15 = 85$.

18. 46

First, turn the given information into an algebraic equation. If x is the number of chores that each of them completes (you are told that it's the same number for both of them, so use x in both cases), then Pierre receives $(8 + 3x)$ dollars. Armand receives $(6 + 8x)$ dollars. Since Armand receives twice what Pierre does, $(6 + 8x) = 2(8 + 3x)$. Solving for x gives you $x = 5$, but you're not done. The questions asks for the amount that Armand receives, so plug $x = 5$ into $(6 + 8x)$: $6 + 8(5) = 46$.

SECTION 7

1. **D** The sentence first discusses something from *Last year*, and the verb is in the past tense. The underlined verb is an action that occurred in the *previous year* so we need the past perfect form of the verb *be* to express that one action happened before another in a specific time in the past. The past perfect is the form that uses "had" with a verb's past tense, so (D) *had been* is the correct answer.

2. **E** The list in the sentence is not in parallel form. In the underlined portion, *container* should come first, and connect to the contents with *of*, as does everything else on the list. This makes (E) *container of fresh strawberries* the correct choice. (B) has the plural *containers* when all the other containers are singular, although it does put *container* and *strawberries* in the correct order.

3. **E** The subject of the sentence is *family*, a collective noun that is singular. The subject is separated from the verb it belongs with by a descriptive phrase set off by commas. The verb *were* is plural, which is incorrect: it should read the family *was*. Eliminate (A), (B), and (C) for using the incorrect verb form. (D) changes the meaning of the sentence in indicating that the *family* was doing the accepting, not the town. (E) is correct.

4. **D** The word *when* does not make sense in this sentence. Eliminate (A) and (B). The rest of the sentence describes the plot of the book, so the phrase that would connect the title of the book to a description of what's in it is *in which*. Eliminate (C). Between (D) and (E), (D) is better: (E) has a subject-verb agreement problem between *affair*, which is singular, and *create* which is plural.

5. **C** The verb *thought* is in the wrong tense. We need the verb to be in the present tense: think. Eliminate (A). In the answers, two of the remaining choices begin *would pay* and two begin *will pay*. The *if…would* construction is correct, so eliminate (B) and (E). Between (C) and (D), choice (C) is stronger because the verb in (D) is in the past tense, and also changes the meaning by moving the modifier *more*.

6. **A** The sentence is correct as written. (B), (C), and (E) have a parallelism problem. The freeways of Los Angeles should be compared with the freeways of other cities, not the cities themselves. (D) incorrectly uses the phrase *crowding with cars*.

7. **E** When two actions are compared, the correct word to use is *as*, not *like*. Only (C) and (E) use *as*. (E) correctly compares the two actions (it thrilled him . . . as it had), but (C) incorrectly compares the action with *when* and is repetitive.

8. **C** The idiom that uses *not only* is *not only…but also*. Eliminate (A) for using *as well* instead of *also*. The idiom in (B) is correct, but has the wrong verb form: to be parallel with *running*, the verb *plays* should be *playing*. (C) has the correct idiom and it has a parallel form to the first part of the sentence. (D) and (E) have the wrong conjunction, *and*.

9. **B** The sentence as written contains a comma splice: two phrases that could stand on their own as sentences cannot be joined by a mere comma. (B) is good because it changes the phrase to a one that describes *cellular respiration* by changing *this is* to *a*. (C) and (D) are incorrect because they use *where*, which should only be used for physical locations, not for a *process*. (E) is incorrect because it is unnecessarily wordy.

10. **D** The subject of the sentence is the act of *Smoking cigarettes*. This is singular, just as if the action were replaced with the words "the action" which is more understandable to be singular. This makes the pronoun *they* incorrect: eliminate (A) and (B). Answer choice (C) is incorrect because it does not follow the proper construction of the idiom *not only....but also*, which is one of ETS' most commonly tested idioms. Therefore, answer choice (D) is correct because it contains the proper construction of the idiom and the correct parallel structure as *financially wasteful* corresponds with *dangerous*.

11. **B** This sentence has a misplaced modifier. When a descriptive phrase is set off by a comma, the first word after the comma is what is described by the phrase. As written, it seems that the *stars* are looking up: eliminate (A). The answers that begin with a noun capable of the action of *looking up* are (B) and (D). (B) is the better choice because while (D) puts *people* after the comma, it is overly wordy and changes the meaning of the sentence with *almost see*.

12. **C** The sentence has the incorrect conjunction, *and*, in (C). Laurel wanted to go out but Ben wanted to stay in, so we need a conjunction that indicates that the idea that what follows will be moving in an opposite direction from the first part of the sentence, such as "but" or "however."

13. **B** The beginning of the sentence starts with *All of the stamps*, which makes the subject plural. The verb *is* is incorrect in (B), because while *is* is the proper verb to modify *collection,* in the sentence the verb *is* is actually describing the *stamps*.

14. **B** There is a double negative in (B). To eliminate the double negative, the phrase should read *scarcely has any.*

15. **C** The subject of the sentence is *The telephone*, which is singular. There is incorrect verb agreement in (C); the verb should be the singular *is*, not *are*.

16. **D** There is a double negative in (D). Using the word *any* in place of *no* to read *scarcely any* would fix the sentence.

17. **D** The verb *grows* in the sentence should be *grow*, because the grass is not the subject. It is not doing the action in the sentence so the verb is not supposed to agree with *grass*. The people are performing the action *watch* which needs to be followed by the infinitive verb form of whatever they are watching.

18. **C** The pronoun *them* in (C) does not agree with the pronoun *us* used earlier in the sentence.

19. **E** There is no error in the sentence as written.

20. E   There is no error in the sentence as written. Make sure you can identify and name a specific error before selecting an answer.

21. A   The past tense verb *went* in (A) does not agree with the present tense verb *swims*. The verb *went* should be *goes*.

22. C   The verb form in (C) does not match the setting of the sentence; *having left* is unclear and seems to attribute the action of leaving to the pictures, rather than Luissa. To be correct, the sentence should read *leaving* instead of *having left*.

23. E   There is no error in the sentence as it is written.

24. B   Only adverbs can modify verbs, so the adjective *safe* in (B) cannot modify *drive*. The sentence needs the adverb *safely*.

25. B   There is a pronoun error in (B). If Paul were not involved in this sentence at all, the speaker would say that *Mrs. Johnson gave the assignment to me*, which is the object pronoun that should appear in (B). After a preposition, such as *to* always use an object pronoun.

26. B   The sentence has a subject-verb agreement between *classification*, which is singular, and *are* in (B) which is a plural verb. The verb should be *is*.

27. A   There is a pronoun error in (A). *Their* is plural, but the underlined portion of (B) refers to a singular *the male guppy*. Which is correct, singular, or plural? The sentence should be singular, because the singular verb *is* is not underlines, and therefore must be correct. The error is in (A).

28. C   There is going to be only one person who wins the race. The error is in (C) because *they* is a plural pronoun. The way to use a singular pronoun when the gender of the person is unknown is with the construction *he or she*.

29. A   Watch out for the pronouns *one* and *you*. ETS often uses these pronouns incorrectly. Whenever you see one of them underlined, check the rest of the sentence for them. The rule is you must use only one or the other, not both. The sentence uses the pronoun *you* twice (and it's not underlined, so it must be right); therefore, we cannot use the pronoun *one* in (A). The phrase *but also* in (C) is correct because it follows the phrase *not only* and completes the idiom.

30. B   The combination in (A) creates a comma splice. (B) is correct. (C) is redundant in its use of *proof* and *that shows*. (D) uses the wrong conjunction. (E) is incorrect: there definitely is a way to combine the sentences, and (B) is correct.

31. E   To replace the word *viable for* we need something positive, since the goal is to convince an employer to hire us. Eliminate (B) because it is not very positive. (A) *dominating* is not really appropriate for a professional situation. (C) *necessary* is close, but too strong. (D) refers to business, but does not make sense as a replacement in this context. (E) *appropriate for* is correct.

32.   C   The second paragraph is about the content of the letter. The third paragraph is about the presentation needed for the letter. The only answer that brings both these ideas into the first sentence of the third paragraph is (C). None of the other answers mention the *content* that is the subject of the second paragraph.

33.   D   The only non-essential sentence in the list is sentence 12, (D). Sentence 12 contains a tiny detail about grammar that is too small to matter much and does nothing to enhance the author's point.

34.   B   Sentence 15 is a specific detail about a cover letter. While the whole passage is about cover letters, this sentence is explaining why a cover letter is important. The other place in the passage that discusses why cover letters are important to employers is in the first paragraph, so eliminate any locations that are not in the first paragraph: (A) is incorrect: the sentence is definitely out of place where it is at. Only (B) is part of the first paragraph, the rest all come later in the passage.

35.   A   After sentence 15, we need a sentence that wraps up this essay that was written to tell people about what goes into successful cover letters. (A) works pretty well, but check the rest of the answers. (B) is incorrect: just because the cover letter is important doesn't mean that the resume is not important. (C) takes this to an even greater extreme. (D) is irrelevant: we want to keep the focus on cover letters. (E) is a small detail that belongs in the content section, not as the summary sentence of the whole passage.

SECTION 8

1.   C   The colon is like an equal sign between the word before the colon and the phrase after the colon. In this case, the blank is immediately before the colon, and we need a word that describes someone who *can play every position*. Eliminate choices that definitely don't mean something close to "ability to do everything." (A) is out. (B) and (D) may be tempting because they are related to athletics, but they do not fit the idea of being flexible to do well in all the positions. (E) does not describe the ability to do many things. Only (C), *versatile,* matches the meaning we were looking for.

2.   A   Something that does *millions of dollars in damage* is pretty bad; "terrible" is a good word for the blank. (A) *calamitous* matches best. (B) means "commonplace." (C) means "tiny." (D) may be tempting because it is close to precipitation, but *precipitous* means "steep." (E) *heralded* is positive.

3.   B   Gary doesn't sound like someone who is about to run a marathon. Because he is *weakened* and *incapacitated*, he won't be able to run. The word "unable" is a good word for the first blank. That is in the answer choices, but *disinclined* and *hesitant* would work too. We can eliminate (A) and (D), however. The second blank needs to be something like "raise" *the energy to run*. Of the three answers we have left, *squander* and *enervate* are more like opposites to "raise." (B) *muster* means "to gather, summon, rouse," which is much closer to "rise."

4. **C** For the first blank, if Karen is *amazing* people, she must be putting up with a pretty harsh schedule. Eliminate (A) and (E) because they don't indicate having a tough schedule. *Hectic, strenuous,* and *busy* could all work. Let's look at the second blank. What is amazing people is something that is unlikely in someone in a tough situation, so a good word for the second blank is "cheerfulness" or "energy." (C) *alacrity* fits this meaning. Its definition is "cheerful readiness, promptness, or willingness." The second word in (B) means "sharpness" and *sanctify* in (D) means "to make holy."

5. **A** We need a word for the blank that describes prophecies *that could be interpreted in more than one way*. Something like "vague" or "indefinite." The vocab in the answers is pretty tough, but the only word that matches the meaning we came up with based on context is (A) *equivocal* which means "allowing the possibility of several different meanings," just as the prophecies are described in the sentence. Look up the definitions of any words you are not familiar with.

6. **D** The *environment officers* would be concerned only if something bad were happening in the lake, so "dirty" is a good meaning for the first blank. Both (B) *polluted* and (D) *noxious* are words that indicate that this is water people shouldn't be swimming in. Eliminate the rest of the answers because the first word in each pair could describe water, but does not address the "bad" aspect of the first blank. Swimming or boating in bad water is unhealthy, so the officers would probably "stop" these activities. Between (B) and (D), (D) is the better choice because *proscribe* means "prohibit." (B) is incorrect because *urge* means the opposite of what we are looking for.

7. **B** The sentence that begins with *Later Americans* describes them as people who enjoy their rights but forget about the person (Washington) who established some of those rights. This is best paraphrased in (B). *They tended to ignore* Washington. There is no evidence in the passage for any of the other answers.

8. **D** The *debunkers* are people who tried to find out improper things about the people we hold up as examples of goodness in order to *destroy* or *reduce* them. This is expressed in (D) *reducing to a less than heroic status*. (A) is the opposite of what the debunkers are doing. (B) is not negative enough to describe the debunkers' activities. (C) is incorrect because the focus is not about Washington's *patriotism* but his very character. (E) is incorrect because it is much too positive.

9. **B** The passage states that Washington was not born to the imperial purple, and goes on to say he was not a member of the aristocracy, in fact he had a *modest* start in life. (B) is correct: *modest* is very close in meaning to *humble*. (A) is the opposite of what we're looking for. (C) is too literal: the expression in the passage is meant to be figurative. In (D) there is no evidence in the passage to support *resented*. King George III is mentioned later in the passage, but there is no comparison being made like the one described in (E).

10. **B** The part of the second paragraph of Passage 1 that discusses Washington's birthday mentions that he was born on February 11, but 11 days were removed from the calendar to match up with the day in the rest of Europe. Only (B) mentions the *calendar*. There is no mention of *Lincoln's birthday*, (A). There is no mention of a discrepancy about when he was born as in (C): the author seems pretty clear about the dates before and after the calendar change. (D) is incorrect because the Episcopal Church is mentioned as where Washington was baptized, but had nothing to do with ordering the time change. Also Britain changed to catch up to the rest of the Western world. The Western world did not change. (E) is not mentioned at all in the passage.

11. **C** In the paragraph that mentions the *wildly supportive crowd* the author describes their *hysteria* and then asks *How easily and with what frenzy could* the emotion turn if the *government did not please*. So he's worried that the crowd could *turn* on him, and be the opposite of supportive if the government doesn't do what the people want. Only (C) reflects this.

12. **A** Go back to the passage where *insuperable diffidence* is mentioned. This is the end of the paragraph in which Washington is worrying about whether he'll do a good enough job as president to keep the people from turning on him. He's worried he won't measure up to his duties, so a good word for the spot that *insuperable diffidence* is taking up is "insecurity." In (A) *lack of self-confidence* is a good match for insecurity. There is no difference in belief mentioned in the paragraph. (C) is out because we need a word to describe how Washington feels about his ability to lead. Eliminate (D) and (E) because they are the opposite of what we're looking for.

13. **D** The *task* is described in the passage as *more uncertain* and *important* than his Continental Army command. He felt about the Continental Army role that there was no *reason to doubt that success was possible*. Only (D) indicates that Washington was *untried* or uncertain about the first situation and that the second was *possible*. (A) is the opposite of what we're looking for. (B) is not mentioned in the passage. (C) is not true. (E) is not true because the responsibility in both cases definitely belonged to Washington.

14. **D** The pair of words that best describes Washington's Continental Army *duty* and the presidency that Washington is about to assume in the passage is (D) *Unremarkable and momentous*. The Army duty is described in lines 71–72 *had been won ten thousand times*, which supports *unremarkable*. The author describes the presidency in line 77 as *Washington's present mission* as something *that might change all history*, which supports *momentous*. None of the other answers are supported by the passage.

15. **C** In Passage 2, the quote is mentioned as something that Washington will prove untrue if his presidency is a success. (A) is unrelated to Washington proving anything. (B) is out because the passage mentions that the idea had been accepted by *many of the greatest thinkers*, not just pessimistic ones. (C) mentions that the quote *would be disproved* if he was *successful*, so it is a very good match. (D) is not mentioned in the passage, and there is no evidence that the quote was Washington's *credo* as in (E): in fact, it was something that he wanted to disprove.

16.   E   In Passage 1 the first part talks generally about how Washington was a great individual, then discusses how writers try to tear down popular figures, and finally gives details about Washington's early life. Passage 2 is about Washington's feelings as he is about to take office as president. We want to find something in the answers that is in Passage 2 but not in Passage 1. (A) is out because it tells us something about Passage 1. There is no evidence for (B), (C) or (D) in the passages. (E) is easy to check for in Passage 2: there are quotation marks in line 60, but not enough to be considered a *quote* from Washington. Just a little further down there are more quotation marks on line 62 and line 66 and between them is a quote from Washington, proving that (E) is true.

17.   D   Washington is seen throughout Passage 2 as doubtful of himself, shown primarily in lines 65-66 where he states that he feels "an insuperable diffidence in my own abilities." Since many of his triumphs are listed in lines 25-28, we need to find a word that matches "doubtful" or "unsure." Thus, answer choices (A) and (B) are eliminated. (C) *curious* is a neutral word, so it does not fit. (E) *morose* means "gloomy" and is too extreme. Therefore, (D) *wary* means "showing caution" and is therefore the correct answer.

18.   A   (A) best describes the main difference between the passages. The most striking thing in the second passage is that it tells about the beginning of the American presidency in a reflective way from Washington's view of the event. Looking just at the descriptions of Passage 2 in the answers, eliminate any that are not close to the main point of Passage 2. We can keep (A) for *Washington's view of his place in history*. In (B) *perfect* has no support from the passage. (C) is incorrect because Passage 2 is about worries at the time of becoming president, not *military successes*. (D) is wrong because there is no mention of academics changing their position in Passage 2. (E) is incorrect; the passage does not *strive to show Washington as unconfident*. It is reporting that Washington was worried about the kind of job he'd do, but *strive* is much too strong. This leaves only (A), and the first part of the answer, *describes the myths* does actually reflect what is happening in Passage 1.

19.   E   Both passages support the statement in (E): Passage 1 mentions that *Washington was the one man essential to the triumph...to the creation* of America, and *the success of the democratic revolution* (lines 25–28). Passage 2 mentions that *Washington's present mission might change all history* (line 77). (B) is extreme, and there is no support in the passage for any of the other answers.

SECTION 9

1.   A   Come up with your own numbers for a and b that add up to 6, such as $a = 4$ and $b = 2$. Replacing a and b in the first equation, we get $3(4) + 3(2) + c = 26$, which simplifies to $12 + 6 + c = 26$, and $c = 8$, answer (A).

2.   D   The line *AC* is one side of the square as well as one side of the equilateral triangle. This means that all sides of the figure have length 3*n*. Polygon *ABCDE* has 5 sides, so the perimeter is 5 × 3*n* = 15*n*, as in answer (D). Alternately, you could come up with your own number for *n*, such as *n* = 2, then use that to solve the problem: all sides would have a length of 6, the perimeter of *ABCDE* is 30, and the correct answer will be the one to give a value of 30 when *n* is replaced by 2. It is true that only (D) gives a value of 30.

3.   C   First find the mode for each of the answer choices: it's easiest to find because you just have to notice which number is in the list most frequently. (A) has a mode of 10, (C) has a mode of 35, and (B), (D), and (E) all lack a mode because all their numbers appears only once. The mean of (A) must be greater than 10, because there are no numbers smaller than 10, and 2 numbers greater than 10 in the list. (C) does have a mean that matches its mode, 35. We really just have to see if the average of the numbers in the list that are not 35 (the 15 and the 55) have an average of 35. $\frac{15+55}{2} = \frac{70}{2} = 35$. (C) is correct.

4.   A   Write out the pattern: you can use letters instead of writing out the whole color name. The colors of the ducks are in a repeating pattern of 6: O, G, R, B, Y, P. The closest multiple of 6 closest to the number that we want (#50) is 48. The 48th duck will be purple. We want the duck that is two after the purple duck, which would be the green duck, answer (A).

5.   B   The term *directly proportional* lets us know that we can set up the values in the problem as a proportion. We know how much Peter makes in 90 minutes, but we want an answer in hours, so set up your proportion with the amount of money earned on top and the number of hours worked on the bottom. We get the equivalent fractions $\frac{27}{1.5} = \frac{162}{x}$. Cross-multiply and solve for *x* to find out how many hours Peter worked in order to earn $162: 27*x* = 243. *x* = $\frac{243}{27}$ = 9, answer (B).

6.   E   Use the numbers in the answer choices to see which of them makes the equation true. It's not (A): it is untrue that 7 + 3 < 5. In fact, it is now clear that we need a negative number to get a value less than 5. Eliminate (A), (B), and (C). Try (D), –3: 7 + (–3) = 4, which is less than 5. It doesn't hold up in the next equation though: It is not true that 3 + (–3) < 0; it is exactly 0. Only (E) –4 works for both equations.

7.   A   The easiest way to solve this problem is to try out the numbers in the answers. Start with the middle value in order to save time: if (C) is not correct, you may gain a hint about whether the number should be smaller or larger. If there are 6 cats still at the clinic, then we can multiply by 3 (since there are three times the number of dogs as there are cats) to find that there are 18 dogs left. We are supposed to have the same number of cats and dogs left, but if we add back the 2 dogs and 8 cats

that were already taken we get 20 dogs, which is not equal to 14 cats. Only (A) works: if there are 3 cats left, then there are 9 dogs. Adding in the first animals taken 9 + 2 = 11 dogs and 3 + 8 = 11 cats.

8. **D** Come up with your own numbers for *a* and *b*. Any number except 0 will do. If *a* = 3 and *b* = 2, then we are looking for an answer that is equivalent to $\frac{3}{2}$. (A) gives $\frac{9}{4}$; eliminate it. (B) gives $\frac{27}{8}$; eliminate it; (C) gives $\frac{\frac{1}{3}}{2}$; which is simplified to $\frac{2}{3}$; eliminate (C). (D) works: $\frac{\frac{3}{5}}{\frac{2}{5}} = \frac{3}{5} \times \frac{5}{2} = \frac{15}{10} = \frac{3}{2}$. (E) is incorrect, it gives $\frac{4}{3}$.

9. **A** The number added to or subtracted from the *x* inside the parentheses moves the graph left and right. Adding to *x* causes the graph to move left, while subtracting moves the graph that many units to the right. A number added outside the parentheses makes the graph move up that many units and a number subtracted outside the parentheses moves the graph down that many units. The equation $y = f(x + 5) - 2$ means that the graph in the figure should move down 2 units and 5 units to the left. This means that the point at (5, 2) in the image above the question would be at the origin. This is seen in (A). No other graph has the bottom point of the parabola at (0, 0).

10. **D** This is a long question, but what it really wants us to find is the number of cups of sauce on all the pizzas plus the number of cups of cheese on all the pizzas. First add up the number of small, medium, and large pizzas from take-out and delivery. There are 10 small, 24 medium, and 18 large pizzas. Convert the mixed fractions from the table into improper fractions for easier multiplying and find the number of cups of sauce that was used: $10(\frac{3}{2}) + 24(\frac{7}{4}) + 18(2) = 15 + 42 + 36 = 93$ cups of sauce. Now find the number of cups of cheese: $10(2) + 24(\frac{7}{3}) + 18(\frac{8}{3}) = 20 + 56 + 48 = 124$ cups of cheese. The total number of cups of sauce and cups of cheese is 93 + 124 = 217, answer (D).

11. **B** Because there are 36 panes of glass, the numbers in the ratios in the answers must add to a factor of 36. Check all the answer choices for the one that adds to a number that does not divide 36 evenly. (A) works because 1 + 35 = 36. (B) does not work: 1 + 7 = 8, and 36 divided by 8 gives 4.5. All the other answers give factors of 36: (C) gives 9, (D) gives 12, and (E) gives 9. The correct answer is (B).

12. **D** In the cube shown, there would be an odd number of faces painted on the corner pieces. There are 8 corners on the cube. The other type of piece that has an odd number of faces painted are the center cubes of each face that have one side painted. There are 6 faces, so there are 6 cubes painted on one side. The total number of cubes with an odd number of faces painted is $8 + 6 = 14$. The probability is the number that fulfils the rules over the total number of possibilities. In this case, since there are a total of 27 cubes, the probability that one chosen at random has an odd number of sides painted is $\dfrac{14}{27}$, as seen in (D).

13. **B** Because the question asks which must be negative, if we can make an answer give a positive we can eliminate it. (B) is the only answer that must be negative, because if xy^2z^3 is negative, then either x or z is negative, but both cannot be negative. A negative times a positive is negative. The value for both x and y can be positive or negative, so eliminate (A). The same is true of z and y, so eliminate (C). The value of x^2 is positive, even if x itself is negative. If x is negative, then z is positive, creating a positive, so eliminate (D) The same is true if the z value is squared, so eliminate (E).

14. **C** Look at point G in the figure. It has a negative x value and a positive y value. The question states that the coordinates of point G are $(-2b, -a)$. For a negative x value, b must be positive. For a positive y value, a must be negative. Now we can find the point at $(b, -2a)$ because we know it has a positive x value and a positive y value. Only point J fits this, answer (C).

15. **C** In the graph, points $(4, 1)$ and $(2, -1)$ are labeled. Point $(0, 1)$ is easily identifiable and also fits into the pattern described in the question, that $g(x) = g(x - 4)$: $g(4)$ and $g(0)$ both give a y-value of 1. In fact, any time the x value is a multiple of 4, the y value is 1. $g(12) = g(8) = g(4) = g(0) = 1$. We can work out from the graph that $y = 0$ when $x = 1$, $y = -1$ when $x = 2$, and $y = 0$ when $x = 3$. A particular y value should be repeated every four x values since $g(x) = g(x - 4)$ for all values of x. This gives us a list of $g(0) = 1$, $g(1) = 0$, $g(2) = -1$, $g(3) = 0$, $g(4) = 1$, $g(5) = 0$, $g(6) = -1$, $g(7) = 0$, $g(8) = 1$. That's enough to be able to evaluate the answers. Replace the $g(x)$ in each answer with the value from the list above: (A) gives $0 - (-1) = 0$, which is not true. (B) gives $(-1) - 0 = 1$ which is not true. (C) gives $0 - 1 = -1$, which is true. (D) gives $2 \times (-1) = 1$, which is not true. (E) gives $(-1) = -(-1)$, which is not true.

16. **B** If the shaded area is twice the area of the inner circle, then the area of the larger, outer circle is three times the area of the small circle. If we make the area of the small circle equal to 1π, then the radius of the small circle is 1. The area of the larger circle must then be 3π, so the radius of the large circle is $\sqrt{3}$. The ratio of the small radius to the large radius is $1 : \sqrt{3}$, as seen in (B).

SECTION 10

1. **A**   The sentence is correct as written. (B) and (D) are passive; (C) and (E) contain ambiguous pronouns.

2. **C**   The sentence as written has a subject-verb agreement error between the singular *benefit* and the plural verb *are*. Eliminate (A) and (D) for their plural verbs. (B) and (E) change the meaning of the sentence, leaving only (C), which is correct.

3. **D**   The sentence has a misplaced modifier. As the sentence is written, it is *the legacy* that is *Recognized as a hero*. This error also appears in (B) and (C). (D) correctly places MLK immediately after the comma. (E) also fixes the modifier problem, but the rest of the sentence is passive, making (D) the stronger choice.

4. **B**   The sentence as written lacks parallelism. The first part of the sentence about the *airplane trip* must have a structure parallel to *driving an electric car*. Only (B) and (D) have the *ing* form of a verb, which is necessary for it to be parallel to *driving*. (D) contains a subject-verb error in *Traveling…are*, making (B) the stronger choice.

5. **C**   The elements in a list need to be as close in form to each other as possible. The list following the colon could be more parallel than it is, so eliminate (A). Making *stones* singular for *steel, wood, and stone* would make all parts of the list about the material in general. The plural *stones* in the original references many individual stones rather than a situation in which a wall is made of stone, for example. Only (C) refers to the materials in this way. (B) has two plurals, which are not parallel to *steel*. (D) and (E) add words and are no longer parallel.

6. **B**   The sentence as written has a passive construction in *will be modified*. The verb should be in the form *modify* to fit in with the directive form of the verbs in the rest of the sentence. Only (B), (D), and (E) have the correct form of modify. Of these three answers, (B) is strongest because both (D) and (E) contain a comma splice.

7. **D**   The sentence has a misplaced modifier. Because the *tern* is the noun immediately after the comma, the descriptive phrase before the comma must describe the *tern*. Only (D), which begins with *With*, modifies the *tern*.

8. **A**   The sentence is correct as written. The plural verb *are* is appropriate, because two single items joined by *and* becomes a plural subject.

9. **E**   The sentence as written contains an idiom error: the preposition that goes with *credited* is *with*. Only (B), (C), and (E) have the correct idiom, *credited with*. We need a conjunction that indicates that the second part of the sentence is giving an exception to the information in the first part of the sentence. The conjunction *and* indicates that more of the same is coming, so eliminate (B). *Until* does not indicate that a change is coming, but (E) *though the Romans should be credited* does set up the exception we need, providing an exception to the Greeks getting all the credit.

10. **A**   The sentence is correct as written. (B) has a misplaced modifier. (C) changed the meaning of the sentence. (D) uses *that* when *who* is needed to refer to a person. (E) is a sentence fragment.

11. **E**   The verbs in the sentence are not in parallel form: *they can study* needs to be in the same form as *to partially reconstruct*. The correct answer will have *to study,* which is seen only in (E).

12. **C**   The sentence as written contains a comma splice. Two phrases that could stand on their own as complete sentences are too strong to be joined by a mere comma. (B) is a run-on sentence. (C) corrects the comma splice problem by replacing the comma with a semicolon, which is the punctuation that is strong enough to hold two related complete sentences together. (D) contains a comma splice. Although (E) correctly uses a semicolon to separate two phrases, the second phrase is unnecessarily wordy.

13. **A**   The sentence is correct as written. (C) is a run-on sentence. (D) is unnecessarily wordy. (E) changes the meaning of the sentence.

14. **E**   There is an ambiguous pronoun, *it*, in the sentence as written. (B) is awkward; (C) contains an unclear pronoun *them*. (D) is unnecessarily wordy. (E) clearly replaces *it* with *that such adaptations*. (E) is correct.

Chapter 20
Practice Test 9

Your Name (print) _____

Last   First   Middle

Date _____

IMPORTANT: The following codes should be copied onto your answer sheet exactly as shown.

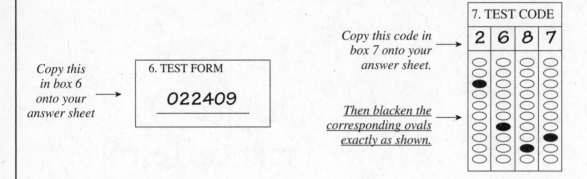

Copy this in box 6 onto your answer sheet → **6. TEST FORM** *022409*

Copy this code in box 7 onto your answer sheet. → **7. TEST CODE** 2 6 8 7

Then blacken the corresponding ovals exactly as shown. →

General Directions

You will have three hours and 20 minutes to work on this objective test designed to familiarize you with all aspects of the SAT.

This test contains five 25-minute sections, two 20-minute sections, one 10-minute section, and one 25-minute essay. The supervisor will tell you when to begin and end each section. During the time allowed for each section, you may work only on that particular section. If you finish your work before time is called, you may check your work on that section, but you are not to work on any other section.

You will find specific directions for each type of question found in the test. **Be sure you understand the directions before attempting to answer any of the questions.**

YOU ARE TO INDICATE ALL YOUR ANSWERS ON THE SEPARATE ANSWER SHEET:

1. The test booklet may be used for scratchwork. However, no credit will be given for anything written in the test booklet.

2. Once you have decided on an answer to a question, darken the corresponding space on the answer sheet. Give only one answer to each question.

3. There are 40 numbered answer spaces for each section; be sure to use only those spaces that correspond to the test questions.

4. **Be sure each answer mark is dark and completely fills the answer space.** Do not make any stray marks on your answer sheet.

5. If you wish to change an answer, erase your first mark completely—an incomplete erasure may be considered an intended response—and blacken your new answer choice.

Your score on this test is based on the number of questions you answer correctly minus a fraction of the number of questions you answer incorrectly. Therefore, it is improbable that random or haphazard guessing will alter your score significantly. There are no deductions for incorrect answers on the student-produced response questions. However, if you are able to eliminate one or more of the answer choices on any question as wrong, it is generally to your advantage to guess at one of the remaining choices. Remember, however, not to spend too much time on any one question.

Diagnostic Test Form

Use a No. 2 pencil only. Be sure each mark is dark and completely fills the intended oval. Completely erase any errors or stray marks.

1 Your Name:

(Print)

Last   First   M.I.

Signature: _____   Date __/__/__

Home Address: _____

Number and Street   City   State   Zip Code

E-Mail: _____   School: _____   Class: _____

(Print)

2 YOUR NAME

Last Name (First 4 Letters) | FIRST INIT | MID INIT

3 PHONE NUMBER

(0)(1)(2)(3)(4)(5)(6)(7)(8)(9) columns

IMPORTANT: Fill in items 6 and 7 exactly as shown on the preceding page.

6 TEST FORM
(Copy from back of test book)

7 TEST CODE

(0)(1)(2)(3)(4)(5)(6)(7)(8)(9)

4 DATE OF BIRTH

MONTH	DAY		YEAR
JAN			
FEB			
MAR	(0)	(0)	(0)
APR	(1)	(1)	(1)
MAY	(2)	(2)	(2)
JUN	(3)	(3)	(3)
JUL		(4)	(4)
AUG		(5)	(5) (5)
SEP		(6)	(6) (6)
OCT		(7)	(7) (7)
NOV		(8)	(8) (8)
DEC		(9)	(9) (9)

8 OTHER

1 (A)(B)(C)(D)(E)
2 (A)(B)(C)(D)(E)
3 (A)(B)(C)(D)(E)

5 SEX

◯ MALE
◯ FEMALE

OpScan iNSIGHT™ forms by Pearson NCS EM-253760-3:654321   Printed in U.S.A.

PLEASE DO NOT WRITE IN THIS AREA

SERIAL #

THIS PAGE INTENTIONALLY LEFT BLANK

Begin your essay on this page. If you need more space, continue on the next page.

Continue on the next page, if necessary.

SECTION 2

1 Ⓐ Ⓑ Ⓒ Ⓓ Ⓔ   11 Ⓐ Ⓑ Ⓒ Ⓓ Ⓔ   21 Ⓐ Ⓑ Ⓒ Ⓓ Ⓔ   31 Ⓐ Ⓑ Ⓒ Ⓓ Ⓔ
2 Ⓐ Ⓑ Ⓒ Ⓓ Ⓔ   12 Ⓐ Ⓑ Ⓒ Ⓓ Ⓔ   22 Ⓐ Ⓑ Ⓒ Ⓓ Ⓔ   32 Ⓐ Ⓑ Ⓒ Ⓓ Ⓔ
3 Ⓐ Ⓑ Ⓒ Ⓓ Ⓔ   13 Ⓐ Ⓑ Ⓒ Ⓓ Ⓔ   23 Ⓐ Ⓑ Ⓒ Ⓓ Ⓔ   33 Ⓐ Ⓑ Ⓒ Ⓓ Ⓔ
4 Ⓐ Ⓑ Ⓒ Ⓓ Ⓔ   14 Ⓐ Ⓑ Ⓒ Ⓓ Ⓔ   24 Ⓐ Ⓑ Ⓒ Ⓓ Ⓔ   34 Ⓐ Ⓑ Ⓒ Ⓓ Ⓔ
5 Ⓐ Ⓑ Ⓒ Ⓓ Ⓔ   15 Ⓐ Ⓑ Ⓒ Ⓓ Ⓔ   25 Ⓐ Ⓑ Ⓒ Ⓓ Ⓔ   35 Ⓐ Ⓑ Ⓒ Ⓓ Ⓔ
6 Ⓐ Ⓑ Ⓒ Ⓓ Ⓔ   16 Ⓐ Ⓑ Ⓒ Ⓓ Ⓔ   26 Ⓐ Ⓑ Ⓒ Ⓓ Ⓔ   36 Ⓐ Ⓑ Ⓒ Ⓓ Ⓔ
7 Ⓐ Ⓑ Ⓒ Ⓓ Ⓔ   17 Ⓐ Ⓑ Ⓒ Ⓓ Ⓔ   27 Ⓐ Ⓑ Ⓒ Ⓓ Ⓔ   37 Ⓐ Ⓑ Ⓒ Ⓓ Ⓔ
8 Ⓐ Ⓑ Ⓒ Ⓓ Ⓔ   18 Ⓐ Ⓑ Ⓒ Ⓓ Ⓔ   28 Ⓐ Ⓑ Ⓒ Ⓓ Ⓔ   38 Ⓐ Ⓑ Ⓒ Ⓓ Ⓔ
9 Ⓐ Ⓑ Ⓒ Ⓓ Ⓔ   19 Ⓐ Ⓑ Ⓒ Ⓓ Ⓔ   29 Ⓐ Ⓑ Ⓒ Ⓓ Ⓔ   39 Ⓐ Ⓑ Ⓒ Ⓓ Ⓔ
10 Ⓐ Ⓑ Ⓒ Ⓓ Ⓔ   20 Ⓐ Ⓑ Ⓒ Ⓓ Ⓔ   30 Ⓐ Ⓑ Ⓒ Ⓓ Ⓔ   40 Ⓐ Ⓑ Ⓒ Ⓓ Ⓔ

SECTION 3

1 Ⓐ Ⓑ Ⓒ Ⓓ Ⓔ   11 Ⓐ Ⓑ Ⓒ Ⓓ Ⓔ   21 Ⓐ Ⓑ Ⓒ Ⓓ Ⓔ   31 Ⓐ Ⓑ Ⓒ Ⓓ Ⓔ
2 Ⓐ Ⓑ Ⓒ Ⓓ Ⓔ   12 Ⓐ Ⓑ Ⓒ Ⓓ Ⓔ   22 Ⓐ Ⓑ Ⓒ Ⓓ Ⓔ   32 Ⓐ Ⓑ Ⓒ Ⓓ Ⓔ
3 Ⓐ Ⓑ Ⓒ Ⓓ Ⓔ   13 Ⓐ Ⓑ Ⓒ Ⓓ Ⓔ   23 Ⓐ Ⓑ Ⓒ Ⓓ Ⓔ   33 Ⓐ Ⓑ Ⓒ Ⓓ Ⓔ
4 Ⓐ Ⓑ Ⓒ Ⓓ Ⓔ   14 Ⓐ Ⓑ Ⓒ Ⓓ Ⓔ   24 Ⓐ Ⓑ Ⓒ Ⓓ Ⓔ   34 Ⓐ Ⓑ Ⓒ Ⓓ Ⓔ
5 Ⓐ Ⓑ Ⓒ Ⓓ Ⓔ   15 Ⓐ Ⓑ Ⓒ Ⓓ Ⓔ   25 Ⓐ Ⓑ Ⓒ Ⓓ Ⓔ   35 Ⓐ Ⓑ Ⓒ Ⓓ Ⓔ
6 Ⓐ Ⓑ Ⓒ Ⓓ Ⓔ   16 Ⓐ Ⓑ Ⓒ Ⓓ Ⓔ   26 Ⓐ Ⓑ Ⓒ Ⓓ Ⓔ   36 Ⓐ Ⓑ Ⓒ Ⓓ Ⓔ
7 Ⓐ Ⓑ Ⓒ Ⓓ Ⓔ   17 Ⓐ Ⓑ Ⓒ Ⓓ Ⓔ   27 Ⓐ Ⓑ Ⓒ Ⓓ Ⓔ   37 Ⓐ Ⓑ Ⓒ Ⓓ Ⓔ
8 Ⓐ Ⓑ Ⓒ Ⓓ Ⓔ   18 Ⓐ Ⓑ Ⓒ Ⓓ Ⓔ   28 Ⓐ Ⓑ Ⓒ Ⓓ Ⓔ   38 Ⓐ Ⓑ Ⓒ Ⓓ Ⓔ
9 Ⓐ Ⓑ Ⓒ Ⓓ Ⓔ   19 Ⓐ Ⓑ Ⓒ Ⓓ Ⓔ   29 Ⓐ Ⓑ Ⓒ Ⓓ Ⓔ   39 Ⓐ Ⓑ Ⓒ Ⓓ Ⓔ
10 Ⓐ Ⓑ Ⓒ Ⓓ Ⓔ   20 Ⓐ Ⓑ Ⓒ Ⓓ Ⓔ   30 Ⓐ Ⓑ Ⓒ Ⓓ Ⓔ   40 Ⓐ Ⓑ Ⓒ Ⓓ Ⓔ

CAUTION Grid answers in the section below for SECTION 2 or SECTION 3 only if directed to do so in your test book.

Student-Produced Responses

ONLY ANSWERS THAT ARE GRIDDED WILL BE SCORED. YOU WILL NOT RECEIVE CREDIT FOR ANYTHING WRITTEN IN THE BOXES.

Quality Assurance Mark ●

9, 10, 11, 12, 13

14, 15, 16, 17, 18

(Each grid: boxes with fraction bars and decimal points; columns of bubbles numbered 0 through 9.)

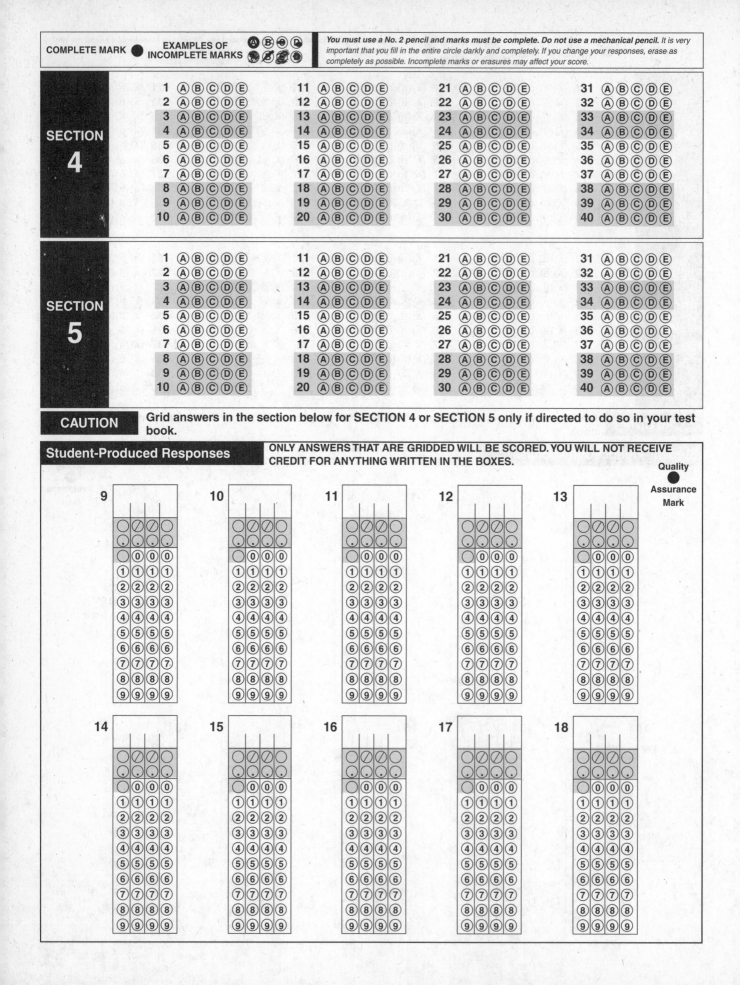

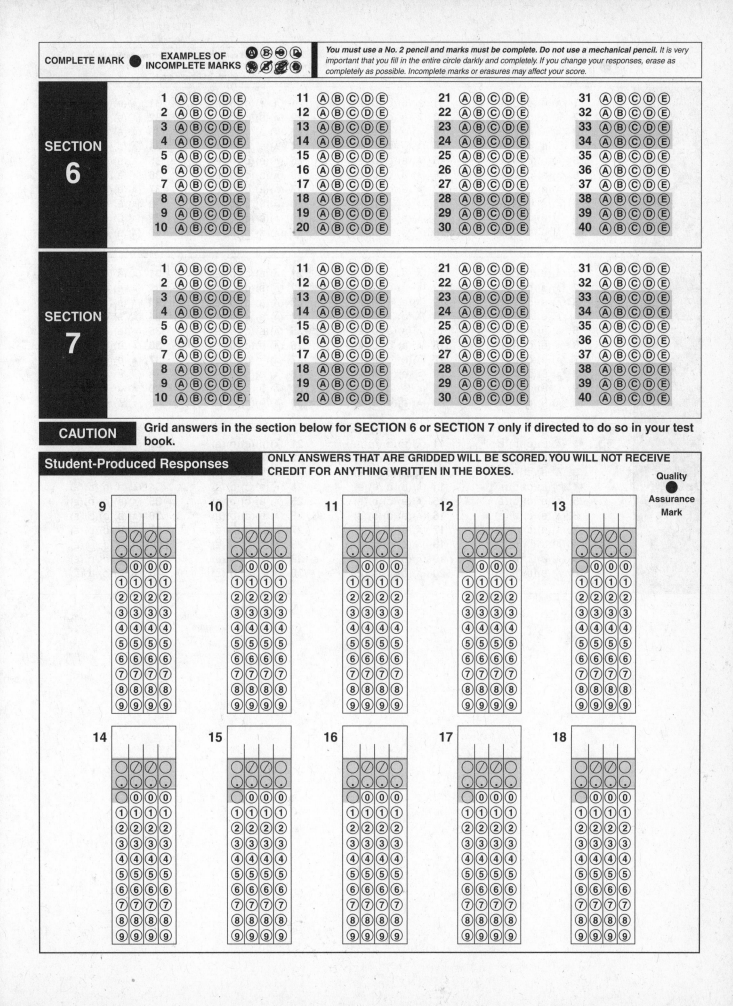

SECTION 8

1 Ⓐ Ⓑ Ⓒ Ⓓ Ⓔ
2 Ⓐ Ⓑ Ⓒ Ⓓ Ⓔ
3 Ⓐ Ⓑ Ⓒ Ⓓ Ⓔ
4 Ⓐ Ⓑ Ⓒ Ⓓ Ⓔ
5 Ⓐ Ⓑ Ⓒ Ⓓ Ⓔ
6 Ⓐ Ⓑ Ⓒ Ⓓ Ⓔ
7 Ⓐ Ⓑ Ⓒ Ⓓ Ⓔ
8 Ⓐ Ⓑ Ⓒ Ⓓ Ⓔ
9 Ⓐ Ⓑ Ⓒ Ⓓ Ⓔ
10 Ⓐ Ⓑ Ⓒ Ⓓ Ⓔ

11 Ⓐ Ⓑ Ⓒ Ⓓ Ⓔ
12 Ⓐ Ⓑ Ⓒ Ⓓ Ⓔ
13 Ⓐ Ⓑ Ⓒ Ⓓ Ⓔ
14 Ⓐ Ⓑ Ⓒ Ⓓ Ⓔ
15 Ⓐ Ⓑ Ⓒ Ⓓ Ⓔ
16 Ⓐ Ⓑ Ⓒ Ⓓ Ⓔ
17 Ⓐ Ⓑ Ⓒ Ⓓ Ⓔ
18 Ⓐ Ⓑ Ⓒ Ⓓ Ⓔ
19 Ⓐ Ⓑ Ⓒ Ⓓ Ⓔ
20 Ⓐ Ⓑ Ⓒ Ⓓ Ⓔ

21 Ⓐ Ⓑ Ⓒ Ⓓ Ⓔ
22 Ⓐ Ⓑ Ⓒ Ⓓ Ⓔ
23 Ⓐ Ⓑ Ⓒ Ⓓ Ⓔ
24 Ⓐ Ⓑ Ⓒ Ⓓ Ⓔ
25 Ⓐ Ⓑ Ⓒ Ⓓ Ⓔ
26 Ⓐ Ⓑ Ⓒ Ⓓ Ⓔ
27 Ⓐ Ⓑ Ⓒ Ⓓ Ⓔ
28 Ⓐ Ⓑ Ⓒ Ⓓ Ⓔ
29 Ⓐ Ⓑ Ⓒ Ⓓ Ⓔ
30 Ⓐ Ⓑ Ⓒ Ⓓ Ⓔ

31 Ⓐ Ⓑ Ⓒ Ⓓ Ⓔ
32 Ⓐ Ⓑ Ⓒ Ⓓ Ⓔ
33 Ⓐ Ⓑ Ⓒ Ⓓ Ⓔ
34 Ⓐ Ⓑ Ⓒ Ⓓ Ⓔ
35 Ⓐ Ⓑ Ⓒ Ⓓ Ⓔ
36 Ⓐ Ⓑ Ⓒ Ⓓ Ⓔ
37 Ⓐ Ⓑ Ⓒ Ⓓ Ⓔ
38 Ⓐ Ⓑ Ⓒ Ⓓ Ⓔ
39 Ⓐ Ⓑ Ⓒ Ⓓ Ⓔ
40 Ⓐ Ⓑ Ⓒ Ⓓ Ⓔ

SECTION 9

1 Ⓐ Ⓑ Ⓒ Ⓓ Ⓔ
2 Ⓐ Ⓑ Ⓒ Ⓓ Ⓔ
3 Ⓐ Ⓑ Ⓒ Ⓓ Ⓔ
4 Ⓐ Ⓑ Ⓒ Ⓓ Ⓔ
5 Ⓐ Ⓑ Ⓒ Ⓓ Ⓔ
6 Ⓐ Ⓑ Ⓒ Ⓓ Ⓔ
7 Ⓐ Ⓑ Ⓒ Ⓓ Ⓔ
8 Ⓐ Ⓑ Ⓒ Ⓓ Ⓔ
9 Ⓐ Ⓑ Ⓒ Ⓓ Ⓔ
10 Ⓐ Ⓑ Ⓒ Ⓓ Ⓔ

11 Ⓐ Ⓑ Ⓒ Ⓓ Ⓔ
12 Ⓐ Ⓑ Ⓒ Ⓓ Ⓔ
13 Ⓐ Ⓑ Ⓒ Ⓓ Ⓔ
14 Ⓐ Ⓑ Ⓒ Ⓓ Ⓔ
15 Ⓐ Ⓑ Ⓒ Ⓓ Ⓔ
16 Ⓐ Ⓑ Ⓒ Ⓓ Ⓔ
17 Ⓐ Ⓑ Ⓒ Ⓓ Ⓔ
18 Ⓐ Ⓑ Ⓒ Ⓓ Ⓔ
19 Ⓐ Ⓑ Ⓒ Ⓓ Ⓔ
20 Ⓐ Ⓑ Ⓒ Ⓓ Ⓔ

21 Ⓐ Ⓑ Ⓒ Ⓓ Ⓔ
22 Ⓐ Ⓑ Ⓒ Ⓓ Ⓔ
23 Ⓐ Ⓑ Ⓒ Ⓓ Ⓔ
24 Ⓐ Ⓑ Ⓒ Ⓓ Ⓔ
25 Ⓐ Ⓑ Ⓒ Ⓓ Ⓔ
26 Ⓐ Ⓑ Ⓒ Ⓓ Ⓔ
27 Ⓐ Ⓑ Ⓒ Ⓓ Ⓔ
28 Ⓐ Ⓑ Ⓒ Ⓓ Ⓔ
29 Ⓐ Ⓑ Ⓒ Ⓓ Ⓔ
30 Ⓐ Ⓑ Ⓒ Ⓓ Ⓔ

31 Ⓐ Ⓑ Ⓒ Ⓓ Ⓔ
32 Ⓐ Ⓑ Ⓒ Ⓓ Ⓔ
33 Ⓐ Ⓑ Ⓒ Ⓓ Ⓔ
34 Ⓐ Ⓑ Ⓒ Ⓓ Ⓔ
35 Ⓐ Ⓑ Ⓒ Ⓓ Ⓔ
36 Ⓐ Ⓑ Ⓒ Ⓓ Ⓔ
37 Ⓐ Ⓑ Ⓒ Ⓓ Ⓔ
38 Ⓐ Ⓑ Ⓒ Ⓓ Ⓔ
39 Ⓐ Ⓑ Ⓒ Ⓓ Ⓔ
40 Ⓐ Ⓑ Ⓒ Ⓓ Ⓔ

SECTION 10

1 Ⓐ Ⓑ Ⓒ Ⓓ Ⓔ
2 Ⓐ Ⓑ Ⓒ Ⓓ Ⓔ
3 Ⓐ Ⓑ Ⓒ Ⓓ Ⓔ
4 Ⓐ Ⓑ Ⓒ Ⓓ Ⓔ
5 Ⓐ Ⓑ Ⓒ Ⓓ Ⓔ
6 Ⓐ Ⓑ Ⓒ Ⓓ Ⓔ
7 Ⓐ Ⓑ Ⓒ Ⓓ Ⓔ
8 Ⓐ Ⓑ Ⓒ Ⓓ Ⓔ
9 Ⓐ Ⓑ Ⓒ Ⓓ Ⓔ
10 Ⓐ Ⓑ Ⓒ Ⓓ Ⓔ

11 Ⓐ Ⓑ Ⓒ Ⓓ Ⓔ
12 Ⓐ Ⓑ Ⓒ Ⓓ Ⓔ
13 Ⓐ Ⓑ Ⓒ Ⓓ Ⓔ
14 Ⓐ Ⓑ Ⓒ Ⓓ Ⓔ
15 Ⓐ Ⓑ Ⓒ Ⓓ Ⓔ
16 Ⓐ Ⓑ Ⓒ Ⓓ Ⓔ
17 Ⓐ Ⓑ Ⓒ Ⓓ Ⓔ
18 Ⓐ Ⓑ Ⓒ Ⓓ Ⓔ
19 Ⓐ Ⓑ Ⓒ Ⓓ Ⓔ
20 Ⓐ Ⓑ Ⓒ Ⓓ Ⓔ

21 Ⓐ Ⓑ Ⓒ Ⓓ Ⓔ
22 Ⓐ Ⓑ Ⓒ Ⓓ Ⓔ
23 Ⓐ Ⓑ Ⓒ Ⓓ Ⓔ
24 Ⓐ Ⓑ Ⓒ Ⓓ Ⓔ
25 Ⓐ Ⓑ Ⓒ Ⓓ Ⓔ
26 Ⓐ Ⓑ Ⓒ Ⓓ Ⓔ
27 Ⓐ Ⓑ Ⓒ Ⓓ Ⓔ
28 Ⓐ Ⓑ Ⓒ Ⓓ Ⓔ
29 Ⓐ Ⓑ Ⓒ Ⓓ Ⓔ
30 Ⓐ Ⓑ Ⓒ Ⓓ Ⓔ

31 Ⓐ Ⓑ Ⓒ Ⓓ Ⓔ
32 Ⓐ Ⓑ Ⓒ Ⓓ Ⓔ
33 Ⓐ Ⓑ Ⓒ Ⓓ Ⓔ
34 Ⓐ Ⓑ Ⓒ Ⓓ Ⓔ
35 Ⓐ Ⓑ Ⓒ Ⓓ Ⓔ
36 Ⓐ Ⓑ Ⓒ Ⓓ Ⓔ
37 Ⓐ Ⓑ Ⓒ Ⓓ Ⓔ
38 Ⓐ Ⓑ Ⓒ Ⓓ Ⓔ
39 Ⓐ Ⓑ Ⓒ Ⓓ Ⓔ
40 Ⓐ Ⓑ Ⓒ Ⓓ Ⓔ

SECTION 1
ESSAY
Time — 25 minutes

Turn to Section 1 of your answer sheet to write your essay.

The essay gives you an opportunity to show how effectively you can develop and express ideas. You should, therefore, take care to develop your point of view, present your ideas logically and clearly, and use language precisely.

Your essay must be written on the lines provided on your answer sheet—you will receive no other paper on which to write. You will have enough space if you write on every line, avoid wide margins, and keep your handwriting to a reasonable size. Remember that people who are not familiar with your handwriting will read what you write. Try to write or print so that what you are writing is legible to those readers.

You have twenty-five minutes to write an essay on the topic assigned below. DO NOT WRITE ON ANOTHER TOPIC. AN OFF-TOPIC ESSAY WILL RECEIVE A SCORE OF ZERO.

Think carefully about the issue presented in the following excerpt and the assignment below.

> We are predisposed to regard any conflict as a clash between good and evil rather than as simply a clash between conflicting interests. We must learn to explore all of the options and possibilities that confront us in a complex and rapidly changing world and to welcome rather than fear the voices of dissent. If we are to act wisely and creatively upon the new realities of our time, we must think and talk about our problems with perfect freedom.
>
> Adapted from U.S. Senator James Fulbright, "Old Myths and New Realities"

Assignment: Is disagreement necessary to progress? Plan and write an essay in which you develop your point of view on this issue. Support you position with reasoning and examples taken from your reading, studies, experience, or observations.

DO NOT WRITE YOUR ESSAY IN YOUR TEST BOOK. You will receive credit only for what you write on your answer sheet.

BEGIN WRITING YOUR ESSAY ON SECTION 1 OF THE ANSWER SHEET.

STOP
**If you finish before time is called, you may check your work on this section only.
Do not turn to any other section in the test.**

SECTION 2
Time — 25 minutes
20 Questions

Turn to Section 2 of your answer sheet to answer the questions in this section.

Directions: For this section, solve each problem and decide which is the best of the choices given. Fill in the corresponding circle on the answer sheet. You may use any available space for scratchwork.

Notes

1. The use of a calculator is permitted.

2. All numbers used are real numbers.

3. Figures that accompany problems in this test are intended to provide information useful in solving the problems. They are drawn as accurately as possible EXCEPT when it is stated in a specific problem that the figure is not drawn to scale. All figures lie in a plane unless otherwise indicated.

4. Unless otherwise specified, the domain of any function f is assumed to be the set of all real numbers x for which $f(x)$ is a real number.

Reference Information

 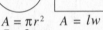   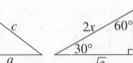

$A = \pi r^2$
$C = 2\pi r$ $A = lw$ $A = \frac{1}{2}bh$ $V = lwh$ $V = \pi r^2 h$ $c^2 = a^2 + b^2$ Special Right Triangles

The number of degrees of arc in a circle is 360.

The sum of the measures in degrees of the angles of a triangle is 180.

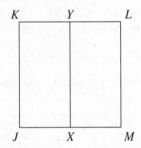

1. In the figure above, *JKLM* is a square, and *X* and *Y* are the midpoints of $\overline{JM}$ and $\overline{KL}$, respectively. If rectangle *JKYX* has a perimeter of 12, what is *JK* ?

(A) 1
(B) 2
(C) 3
(D) 4
(E) 5

2. If $5k + 8 = -7 + 2k$, what is the value of $3k$?

(A) -15

(B) -5

(C) $\dfrac{-15}{7}$

(D) 5

(E) 15

GO ON TO THE NEXT PAGE

3. If k is an even integer, which of the following <u>must</u> be an odd integer?

(A) $k + 2$
(B) $3k$
(C) $3k + 2$
(D) $k(k - 1)$
(E) $(k + 1)(k - 1)$

<u>Note:</u> Figure not drawn to scale.

4. In the figure above, what is the value of z ?

(A) 70
(B) 74
(C) 77
(D) 79
(E) 83

$8 - a, \ 8, \ 8 + a$

5. What is the average (arithmetic mean) of the numbers in the list above?

(A) 4
(B) 8
(C) 16
(D) $a + 4$
(E) $2a$

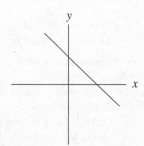

<u>Note:</u> Figure not drawn to scale.

6. Which of the following could be the equation of the line represented in the graph above?

(A) $y = 2x + 4$
(B) $y = 2x - 4$
(C) $y = -2x - 1$
(D) $y = -2x - 4$
(E) $y = -2x + 4$

GO ON TO THE NEXT PAGE

7. Set *C* consists of all of the positive integer multiples of 5 that are less than 20. Set *D* consists of all of the factors of 20. Which of the following is the union of Set *C* and Set *D* ?

(A) {1, 2, 4, 5, 10, 15, 20}
(B) {2, 4, 5, 10, 15}
(C) {5, 10}
(D) {5, 10, 15, 20}
(E) {2, 4, 5, 10}

8. If every student in Mr. McNabb's class enjoys making masks, which of the following must be true?

(A) If a student enjoys making masks, then the student is not in Mr. McNabb's class.
(B) If a student enjoys making masks, then the student is in Mr. McNabb's class.
(C) If a student does not enjoy making masks, then the student is not in Mr. McNabb's class.
(D) If a student is not in Mr. McNabb's class, then the student does not enjoy making masks.
(E) If a student is in Mr. McNabb's class, then the student does not enjoy making masks.

9. If $6s - 2t = 10$ and $s - 5t = 14$, what is the value of $5s + 3t$?

(A) 24
(B) 4
(C) $\dfrac{5}{7}$
(D) −4
(E) −7

10. If 299 is divisible by 2*B*, and *B* represents a positive digit, what is the value of *B* ?

(A) 2
(B) 3
(C) 4
(D) 6
(E) 9

GO ON TO THE NEXT PAGE

11. In a jar of cookies, $\frac{1}{8}$ of the cookies are oatmeal raisin, $\frac{1}{4}$ are peanut butter, $\frac{1}{2}$ are chocolate chip, and the remaining 12 cookies are mint. How many peanut butter cookies are in the jar?

(A) 24
(B) 28
(C) 32
(D) 48
(E) 50

12. Given a sequence of integers where every third term is a multiple of 3 and every second term is a multiple of 2, which of the following could be the value of the 144th term in the sequence?

(A) 15
(B) 44
(C) 81
(D) 114
(E) 206

13. For how many ordered pairs of positive integers (a, b) is $5a + 7b < 20$?

(A) One
(B) Two
(C) Three
(D) Four
(E) More than four

14. If the ratio of a to b is 2 to 5, and the ratio of b to c is 1 to 4, what is the ratio of a to c?

(A) $1:2$
(B) $1:10$
(C) $5:8$
(D) $5:4$
(E) $5:2$

GO ON TO THE NEXT PAGE

15. A 1,000 square meter parcel of land is bought for $300,000 and then divided into five equally sized plots. The first four plots are then sold at a price of $320 per square meter. If the overall profit is to be at least 20%, what is the minimum selling price of the fifth plot?

(A) $64,000
(B) $68,000
(C) $80,000
(D) $96,000
(E) $104,000

16. At a certain grocery store, a customers each spend an average of $30 every b hours. In dollars, how much do customers spend at this store in c hours?

(A) $\dfrac{30c}{ab}$

(B) $\dfrac{bc}{30a}$

(C) $\dfrac{30bc}{a}$

(D) $\dfrac{30ac}{b}$

(E) $\dfrac{30b}{ac}$

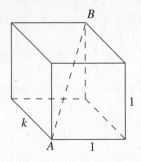

17. In the rectangular box above with dimensions 1 by 1 by k, what is the length of diagonal $\overline{AB}$ in terms of k ?

(A) $1+\sqrt{1+k^2}$

(B) $\sqrt{2+k^2}$

(C) $2+k$

(D) $\sqrt{3k}$

(E) $\sqrt{2k}$

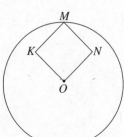

18. In the figure above, O is the center of the circle. If the area of square $KMNO$ is 50, and vertex M is on the circle, what is the area of the circle?

(A) 100π
(B) 50π
(C) 25π
(D) $10\sqrt{2}\pi$
(E) $5\sqrt{2}\pi$

GO ON TO THE NEXT PAGE

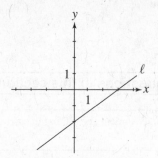

19. In the figure above, which of the following coordinates would lie on line ℓ after it had been reflected across both the y-axis and the x-axis?

(A) $(0, -2)$
(B) $(3, 4)$
(C) $(-4, 3)$
(D) $(3, 0)$
(E) $(-3, 4)$

20. In the xy plane above, point R lies in the center of a circle which is tangent to the x–axis. What is the measurement of $\overline{PR}$ (not shown) ?

(A) 20
(B) $2\sqrt{205}$
(C) $6\sqrt{20}$
(D) 36
(E) It cannot be determined from the information given.

STOP
If you finish before time is called, you may check your work on this section only.
Do not turn to any other section in the test.

SECTION 3
Time — 25 minutes
24 Questions

Turn to Section 3 of your answer sheet to answer the questions in this section.

Directions: For each question in this section, select the best answer from among the choices given and fill in the corresponding circle on the answer sheet.

Each sentence below has one or two blanks, each blank indicating that something has been omitted. Beneath the sentence are five words or sets of words labeled A through E. Choose the word or set of words that, when inserted in the sentence, best fits the meaning of the sentence as a whole.

Example:

Desiring to ------- his taunting friends, Mitch gave them taffy in hopes it would keep their mouths shut.

(A) eliminate (B) satisfy (C) overcome
  (D) ridicule (E) silence

---

1. Great personal danger is one of the few things that will force a lion to relinquish its prey; carnivores will ------- a meal only at the point where self-preservation outweighs hunger.

   (A) consume (B) camouflage (C) forgo
     (D) inspect (E) balance

2. The miser was so afraid of losing money that he was willing to pass up a -------- opportunity rather than ------- what he already possessed.

   (A) profitable . . earn
   (B) lucrative . . risk
   (C) hazardous . . secure
   (D) shrewd . . waste
   (E) fortunate . . discredit

3. One can argue that the scientific process is a constant, because despite numerous ------- in the instruments used, the steps that scientists follow have been ------- for centuries.

   (A) losses . . converted
   (B) refinements . . atypical
   (C) drawbacks . . intact
   (D) advances . . unaltered
   (E) improvements . . unreliable

4. Health experts have found that the use of antibiotics, while beneficial when used with -------, may actually be ------- in the long term.

   (A) constraint . . advantageous
   (B) moderation . . detrimental
   (C) dispatch . . beneficial
   (D) excess . . pernicious
   (E) exactness . . excruciating

5. Some early American pioneers were so ------- to be beholden to others that they refused any favors or offers of help.

   (A) fervent (B) brazen (C) resolved
     (D) prudent (E) loath

6. His parents fostered in him such a sense of self-worth that when he became a prisoner of war, the ------- treatment by his captors failed to make him feel -------.

   (A) genteel . . humiliated
   (B) morose . . bewildered
   (C) corrupt . . praiseworthy
   (D) demeaning . . inferior
   (E) reverential . . venerated

7. Viki's tendency to aggressively exaggerate her case was not to her advantage; her ------- manner often angered her superiors.

   (A) overblown (B) callow (C) inane
     (D) refined (E) belligerent

8. When the president's misdeed was finally uncovered, the press called for his indictment, but he insisted that his action was merely a ------- which he need not have disclosed.

   (A) windfall (B) plot (C) lapse
     (D) malfeasance (E) calamity

GO ON TO THE NEXT PAGE

Directions: Each passage below is followed by questions based on its content. Answer the questions on the basis of what is <u>stated</u> or <u>implied</u> in each passage and in any introductory material that may be provided.

Questions 9-12 are based on the following passages.

Passage 1

When great changes occur in history, when great principles are involved, as a rule the majority is wrong. The minority is usually right. In every age there have been a few
Line heroic souls who have been in advance of their time, who
5   have been misunderstood, maligned, persecuted—sometimes put to death. Long after their martyrdom, monuments were erected to them and garlands woven for their graves, the men and women who have been in advance, who have had new ideas, new ideals, who have had the courage to attack
10 the established order of things, have all had to pay the same penalty.

Passage 2

Life is growth, life is progress, and progress depends on new ideas; there can be no conquest to the man who dwells in the narrow and small environment of a groveling life, and
15 there can be no vision to the man the horizon of whose vision is limited by the bounds of self. But the great things of the world, the great accomplishments of the world, have been achieved by those singular men who had high ideals and who received great visions. The path is not easy, the climbing
20 is rugged and hard, but the glory of the vision at the end is worthwhile.

9. What is the primary difference in the tones of Passages 1 and 2 ?

(A) Passage 1 is flippant, while Passage 2 is inspired.
(B) Passage 2 is graver than Passage 1.
(C) Passage 2 is more hopeful than Passage 1.
(D) Passage 1 is serious, while Passage 2 is sardonic.
(E) Passage 2 is more partisan than Passage 1.

10. The authors of both passages would most likely agree with which of the following?

(A) All great ideas were at first attacked by the majority.
(B) Travel brings with it new ways of seeing the world.
(C) Politicians are unlikely to advance humanity's interests.
(D) Change is essential for human progress.
(E) Men are more likely to discover new ideas when they are exercising.

11. What is the difference in how the authors view people who enact change?

(A) Passage 1 sees them as victims; Passage 2 sees them as explorers.
(B) Passage 1 sees them as dangerous; Passage 2 sees them as hermits.
(C) Passage 1 mourns their inevitable deaths; Passage 2 scorns their fears.
(D) Passage 1 envies them; Passage 2 admires them.
(E) Passage 1 views them as unnecessary sacrifices; Passage 2 supports them.

12. Both passages indicate that people who advance humanity

(A) have political motivations
(B) go to great lengths to protect their lives
(C) are few in number
(D) are usually men
(E) are philosophically inclined

GO ON TO THE NEXT PAGE

Questions 13-24 are based on the following passage.

Printmaking advanced the art world as well as the realm of communication. The following passage, written in 1985, discusses its history.

"Printmaker!" The connotation of this word, curiously absent from other languages, began to have some meaning only after World War II. Surely, before the war, and often in
Line the long, splendid history of prints, there had been artists who
5 created nothing but prints. However, in most cases the artists drew a composition before going to the plate or block of stone, rather than working directly on these materials exclusively. Even this is not the entire distinction between earlier artists like Callot and Meryon and those followers of Hayter who
10 could be called only "printmakers." Callot and Meryon made prints that, following the original object of working in a multiple medium, were meant to be printed in large numbers for wide distribution of the image. Indeed, many painters made prints for this sole reason. But the printmakers of the
15 second half of the twentieth century have found that creating in a print medium is itself totally satisfying; they often care not at all if no more than a few copies are made before they go on to the next image. It is the complex techniques of printmaking that entrance them. In the words of Sylvan Cole,
20 former Director of Associated American Artists (AAA, the largest print gallery in America and publisher of over 1,500 prints since 1934), "The change that was taking place was the breakup with the artist/painter (or Abstract Expressionist) who was not interested in printmaking, and out of this came
25 a man called a printmaker, people like Karl Schrag, Peterdi, Lasansky, Misch Kohn—who built their reputations as printmakers."

Before the war, artists made considerable numbers of prints. This was their only work; no doubt it was often a
30 matter of survival, not preference. Dozens of prints in a relatively new medium, silkscreen, were turned out for the adornment of schools and other government buildings.

The G.I. Bill filled the colleges, universities, and art schools of post-war America during a period of prosperity
35 that encouraged such institutions to enlarge their facilities or open new ones, particularly those devoted to the arts. Many veterans who would never have had the opportunity to attend college if they had not been drafted had little direction— were "lost," so to speak—and found that the unrestrained
40 atmosphere of the post-war art schools and art departments represented just the sort of freedom they needed after years of military conformity. (Many others, of course, had profited from the organized lifestyle of the military and sought it in more disciplined fields such as law, medicine, and business.
45 The famous "Organization Man" could hardly have had such success if this less independent group had not also made a major contribution to post-war society.) In the late 1940s, then, one could observe the beginnings of a phenomenal expansion of art education in institutions of higher learning,
50 where art departments attracted returning G.I.s who had completed their undergraduate work before the war, and in older, established art schools that were filled to capacity with those who had finished only high school. Students who fell under the spell of Lasansky during his first years at the State
55 University of Iowa went on to found print workshops in other universities. Soon students of these workshops pioneered others, so that in a very short time there were facilities for the study of printmaking in most universities in the United States.

The proliferation of places where printmaking was
60 taught and the subsequent increase in the number of printmakers led to the birth of ancillary institutions: the Brooklyn Museum's annual National Print Exhibition, an open exhibition, in contrast with the traditional invitational showings of the Society of Etchers (note that these artists
65 referred to themselves as etchers, not printmakers) or the other one-medium groups such as the National Serigraph Society; the International Group Arts Society, a membership/ subscription organization the purpose of which was to publish and sell prints by new artists of less conservative nature than
70 those sponsored by AAA; and regional and international exhibitions devoted exclusively to prints, such as the Northwest Printmakers Society, the Philadelphia Print Club, and international biennials of prints in Cincinnati, Ljubljana, and Tokyo. Thus, in the United States and elsewhere, the need
75 to show and distribute the outpourings of the print workshops produced new organizations that in turn further encouraged the creation of prints.

13. In lines 10-13, the author asserts that Callot and Meryon

(A) collaborated with Hayter in pioneering the role of "printmaker"

(B) were more concerned with producing vast quantities of prints than Hayter's disciples had been

(C) were painters who regarded printmaking as an inferior vocation

(D) found complete satisfaction in the creating art through a print medium

(E) were difficult to distinguish from earlier artists, like Hayter

14. The author contends that "printmakers of the . . . twentieth century" (lines 14-15)

(A) were more concerned with the quantity of their prints than with the intricacy of their work

(B) were often distracted from their primary intention by the complexity of printmaking

(C) were fulfilled by the act of printmaking itself, while mass production was a secondary concern

(D) faced a production quota of prints which became an insurmountable handicap for most artists

(E) wanted to achieve international recognition for their groundbreaking work

GO ON TO THE NEXT PAGE

15. The author quotes Sylvan Cole in lines 22-27 in order to

(A) demonstrate how Cole changed the art of printmaking during the turn of the century

(B) pay homage to a notable pioneer of the art of printmaking

(C) introduce the term "Abstract Expressionist" and examine its place in the art movement

(D) explain the relationship between printmaking and painting

(E) provide support for his assertions about the new developments in printmaking

16. The purpose of the second paragraph (lines 28-32) in relation to the passage is to

(A) provide support for the idea that modern printmaking emerged only after World War II

(B) acquaint the reader with the long established history of printmaking as a distinct art form

(C) question the originality of such artists as Callot and Meryton who claimed to have invented modern printmaking

(D) argue for the recognition of artists who were forced to create prints for the government

(E) lament the deplorable situation of those artists who could find no other opportunity for expression than printmaking

17. In line 32, "adornment" most nearly means

(A) distribution

(B) inundation

(C) decoration

(D) enjoyment

(E) construction

18. The purpose of the G.I. Bill, mentioned in line 33, was to

(A) allow veterans to bypass college in order to concentrate on artistic pursuits

(B) allow veterans to attend colleges or specialized schools by offering assistance after the war

(C) provide the "lost" veterans with a place to study

(D) open new facilities or strengthen already established art institutions

(E) discourage veterans uninterested in any type of artistic endeavor

19. In line 39, "lost" most nearly means

(A) unfound

(B) denied

(C) desperate

(D) aimless

(E) aberrant

20. The author suggests that an "Organization Man" (line 45) is

(A) one who resisted entering the military in order to focus on more structured pursuits

(B) one who benefited from the infusion of former soldiers into the white-collar workforce

(C) a college student who helped enlarge facilities such as art schools

(D) a failed attempt by an elected member to organize the artists into a more formal union

(E) a veteran who bridged the gap between the gap between 'lost' artist and successful business man

21. The author attributes the "phenomenal expansion of art education" (lines 48-49) primarily to

(A) increased membership in the military

(B) the appeal of art departments both to veterans who had graduated from college and to those who had not

(C) Lasansky's trickery in brainwashing students

(D) the State University of Iowa's groundbreaking work in recruiting students

(E) the influence in the late 1940s of the famous "Organization Man"

22. In the final paragraph, the author cites which of the following effects of the "proliferation of places where printmaking was taught" (line 59) in the United States?

(A) The increased opportunities to display printmakers' work encouraged the production of more prints.

(B) The financial success of the AAA encouraged many businesses to establish their own institutions.

(C) Attempts to expose the public to the works of less conservative artists produced a backlash against all printmakers.

(D) Printmakers desperate to entice more artists into printmaking neglected their own work.

(E) Increased publicity spurred a rise in public appreciation and financial support.

GO ON TO THE NEXT PAGE

23. The author's description in the final paragraph of the new organizations indicates that

(A) while printmaking ceases to be an actively pursued art, many institutes still display old prints

(B) etchers are being neglected because of the extraordinary popularity of printmakers

(C) today, exhibitions of prints can be found around the world

(D) the demand for prints has grown beyond all expectations

(E) older organizations were reluctant to display prints because they didn't consider printmaking to be a true art form

24. All of the following could be expected of a disciple of Lasanky EXCEPT

(A) advocating that artists work in multiple medium formats

(B) establishing new programs in universities devoted to printmaking

(C) forgoing the composition stage in the creation of new art

(D) caring little for the mass production or distribution of new prints

(E) viewing the intricacies of print production as a vital part of their art

STOP
**If you finish before time is called, you may check your work on this section only.
Do not turn to any other section in the test.**

NO TEST MATERIAL ON THIS PAGE.

SECTION 4
Time — 25 minutes
35 Questions

Turn to Section 4 of your answer sheet to answer the questions in this section.

Directions: For each question in this section, select the best answer from among the choices given and fill in the corresponding circle on the answer sheet.

The following sentences test correctness and effectiveness of expression. Part of each sentence or the entire sentence is underlined; beneath each sentence are five ways of phrasing the underlined material. Choice A repeats the original phrasing; the other four choices are different. If you think the original phrasing produces a better sentence than any of the alternatives, select choice A; if not, select one of the other choices.

In making your selection, follow the requirements of standard written English; that is, pay attention to grammar, choice of words, sentence construction, and punctuation. Your selection should result in the most effective sentence—clear and precise, without awkwardness or ambiguity.

EXAMPLE:

Bobby Flay baked his first cake <u>and he was thirteen years old then</u>.

(A) and he was thirteen years old then
(B) when he was thirteen
(C) at age thirteen years old
(D) upon the reaching of thirteen years
(E) at the time when he was thirteen

1. Increasingly concerned about the loss of both customers and revenue, the airline <u>has hired a team of creative advertisers to lure new passengers</u>.

   (A) has hired a team of creative advertisers to lure new passengers
   (B) has hired a team of advertisers creatively to lure new passengers
   (C) has made a hire, a team of creative advertisers to lure new passengers
   (D) has made a team of creative advertisers to lure new passengers
   (E) have hired a creative team of advertisers to lure new passengers

2. Communications and echo ranging are two general types of <u>sonar use, and the sonar must generate its own signal in it</u>.

   (A) sonar use, and the sonar must generate its own signal in it
   (B) sonar use in which the sonar must generate its own signal
   (C) sonar use generating its own signal
   (D) sonar use, its own signal must be generated in it
   (E) sonar use in which its own signal must be generated by the sonar

3. <u>John Stuart Mill developed no unique theories, his writings are little more than the borrowings of other thinkers.</u>

   (A) John Stuart Mill developed no unique theories, his writings are little more than the borrowings of other thinkers.
   (B) John Stuart Mill, who developed no unique theories, primarily borrowing the thoughts of other writers.
   (C) With none of his own unique theories developed by John Stuart Mill, it was the ideas of other thinkers that he borrowed.
   (D) None of his theories were developed by John Stuart Mill; they were the borrowings of other thinkers.
   (E) John Stuart Mill developed no unique theories; he did little more than borrow ideas from other thinkers.

4. To the French, business is considered more a necessity <u>and not a skill or trade</u>.

   (A) and not a skill or trade
   (B) and not considered a skill or trade
   (C) instead of a skill or trade
   (D) than considered to be a skill or trade
   (E) than a skill or trade

GO ON TO THE NEXT PAGE

5. Although they are the wiser of the sexes, it is thought that women are the more emotional.

- (A) Although they are the wiser of the sexes, it is thought that women are the more emotional.
- (B) Although they are the wisest of the sexes, it is thought that women are the most emotional.
- (C) Although the wiser of the sexes, women are thought to be the more emotional.
- (D) Although the wiser of the sexes, women are more emotional, it is thought.
- (E) Although they are the wiser of the sexes, a woman is thought to be the more emotional.

6. New York City's nightlife is exhilarating and expensive, which exhausts one's energy as well as one's money.

- (A) exhilarating and expensive, which exhausts
- (B) exhilarating, expensive, and exhausting
- (C) exhilarating and expensive, it exhausts
- (D) exhilarating and expensive, exhausting
- (E) exhilarating and expensive, and thus exhausting

7. It is terrifying to observe how indifferent people have remained to the irreversible contamination of our environment.

- (A) indifferent people have remained to
- (B) indifferently people have remained to
- (C) indifferently people have remained from
- (D) indifferently people have been to
- (E) with such indifference, people have remained to

8. Just as cameras and recording equipment was prohibited, as were bottles and cans.

- (A) equipment was prohibited, as were bottles and cans
- (B) equipment were prohibited, so too were bottles and cans
- (C) equipment were prohibited, and so were bottles and cans
- (D) equipment was prohibited, and bottles and cans were prohibited too
- (E) equipment was prohibited, also prohibiting bottles and cans

9. The National Weather Service forecast indicated that a chance of thundershowers was possible.

- (A) indicated that a chance of thundershowers was possible
- (B) had an indication of a chance of thundershowers
- (C) indicated that a chance of thundershowers were possible
- (D) indicated a chance of thundershowers
- (E) indicated a possible chance of thundershowers

10. William has resolved to have completed his Ph.D. in astronomy by the time Halley's Comet returns.

- (A) to have completed
- (B) to being completed with
- (C) having completed
- (D) to be completing with
- (E) to completing

11. *The American* and *The Bostonians* are two Henry James novels of whom film versions have been as successful as their book versions.

- (A) novels of whom film versions have been as successful as their book versions
- (B) novels whose film versions have been as successful as its book versions
- (C) novels, the film versions of which have been as successful as the book versions
- (D) novels of which film versions have been successful like their book versions
- (E) novels of which film versions have been as successful as its book versions

GO ON TO THE NEXT PAGE

The following sentences test your ability to recognize grammar and usage errors. Each sentence contains either a single error or no error at all. No sentence contains more than one error. The error, if there is one, is underlined and lettered. If the sentence contains an error, select the one underlined part that must be changed to make the sentence correct. If the sentence is correct, select choice E. In choosing answers, follow the requirements of standard written English.

EXAMPLE:

<u>The other</u> players and <u>her</u> <u>significantly</u> improved
   A   B   C

the game plan <u>created by</u> the coaches. <u>No error</u>
           D   E

(A) ● (C) (D) (E)

12. Developed by Richard Feynman, the theory of quantum

electrodynamics <u>explaining</u> <u>how</u> light <u>interacts with</u>
              A   B   C

atoms and <u>their</u> electrons. <u>No error</u>
        D   E

13. Most of <u>the characters in</u> *The Lone Ranger and Tonto*
         A

Fistfight in Heaven, a short story collection <u>written by</u>
                                B

Sherman Alexie, <u>lives on</u> a Spokane reservation
              C

<u>in Washington state.</u> <u>No error</u>
    D   E

14. Anyone <u>thinking of</u> buying a used car should <u>consider</u>
        A   B

not only the sale price of <u>your</u> purchase, but also the
                   C

<u>cost of</u> repairing the vehicle. <u>No error</u>
  D   E

15. Rachael <u>was able</u> to make her high school's varsity cross
      A

country team <u>as a freshman</u> because <u>she</u> ran 5 miles
          B   C

every morning and <u>had done</u> 100 sit-ups a day. <u>No error</u>
              D   E

16. The creative schedules <u>that</u> were <u>created by</u> Jeannie
                A   B

<u>has</u> allowed Bettina and Elise more free time to spend
C

<u>watching</u> foreign films. <u>No error</u>
  D   E

17. Tibet, one of several Asian regions <u>partially covered by</u>
                         A

mountains, <u>contain</u>, <u>in addition</u>, fertile areas <u>in which</u>
         B   C   D

grains and vegetables grow. <u>No error</u>
               E

18. When one wants <u>to do well</u> on an upcoming test, <u>they</u>
           A   B

should review <u>a little</u> bit each day, <u>rather than</u> all at
          C   D

once. <u>No error</u>
    E

19. The bikini, <u>invented</u> forty years ago, derived <u>its</u> name
        A   B

<u>from</u> the tiny Pacific atoll <u>on which</u> the United States
C   D

conducted early nuclear tests. <u>No error</u>
                E

20. <u>Because</u> Kamm has decided that <u>he needs</u> to
  A   B

supplement his income <u>this year</u>, he <u>raised</u> wheat.
               C   D

<u>No error</u>
  E

GO ON TO THE NEXT PAGE →

21. Although its name is not <u>as recognized</u> as it <u>once was</u>,
                                    A   B

the college is proud of <u>their</u> graduates, many of whom
                         C

have gone on <u>to earn</u> national honors. <u>No error</u>
             D   E

22. Because of the recent <u>increase in</u> property values,
                               A

<u>how</u> <u>one</u> can find inexpensive housing <u>within a week</u>
 B   C   D

is a puzzle to me. <u>No error</u>
                E

23. Tricia's chances <u>of finding</u> her lost dog <u>depend</u>
                   A   B

<u>as much</u> on luck as <u>they</u> do on persistence. <u>No error</u>
 C   D   E

24. <u>The newest</u> State Department survey, a 300-page list
   A

of figures, tables, and other statistics, <u>show</u> that the
                                   B

<u>average American</u> is more likely to die in his own
   C

bathtub than <u>to be killed</u> in a car accident. <u>No error</u>
            D   E

25. Each weekend my father taught my sister and <u>I</u>
                                    A

<u>how</u> to play the banjo <u>until</u> our skills <u>surpassed</u> his.
 B   C   D

<u>No error</u>
 E

26. The artist's <u>fascination about</u> the natural world around
                 A

her <u>has inspired</u> her <u>great passion</u> for <u>painting</u>
   B   C   D

landscapes. <u>No error</u>
        E

27. <u>After learning</u> to knit, Karen made a long wool scarf and
   A

matching hat, and <u>proudly</u> <u>wore it</u> <u>to school</u> every day
                 B   C   D

this past winter. <u>No error</u>
            E

28. <u>When</u> the hometown crowd <u>realized</u> that its team
   A   B

<u>was about to</u> lose the game, <u>they</u> started to leave the
   C   D

stadium. <u>No error</u>
      E

29. Neither Keith nor Anthony <u>has</u> finished <u>their</u> science
                     A   B

project <u>in time for</u> Professor Chiu's exhibition <u>today</u>.
      C   D

<u>No error</u>
 E

GO ON TO THE NEXT PAGE

Directions: The following passage is an early draft of an essay. Some parts of the passage need to be rewritten.

Read the passage and select the best answers for the questions that follow. Some questions are about particular sentences or parts of sentences and ask you to improve sentence structure or word choice. Other questions ask you to consider organization and development. In choosing answers, follow the requirements of standard written English.

Questions 30-35 refer to the following passage.

(1) I've always watched skiing on television. (2) I thought that it looked like fun. (3) So, naturally, when my friend suggested that we go skiing over Christmas vacation, I agreed. (4) Even though I was never on the slopes before, I assumed that I'd be able to catch on pretty quickly. (5) After all, how hard could it be to slide down a mountain?

(6) By the time we got out of the lift at the top of the mountain, I was starting to get nervous. (7) But the slope looked unbelievably steep and treacherous. (8) I asked George if we could take the lift back down, and start out with something a little bit tamer. (9) He just laughed and told me that this was the beginner slope. (10) I screwed up my courage, and pushed off.

(11) I felt a wave of relief and exhilaration. (12) This is easy, I thought. (13) Unfortunately, my musing was rudely interrupted when my skis suddenly began to fly out in opposite directions, and I hit the snow underneath me, almost losing my ski pants in the process. (14) It took me about ten minutes to stand up: I just did not have enough hands to hold my poles, brace myself, and keep my skis pointing in the same direction.

(15) I wish I could say that I soon got my bearings, and sailed confidently down the mountain. (16) I ended up taking two hours to walk, slide, and slip down what should have been a half-hour slope. (17) Maybe sometime I will go back and try to ski again, but for now, I am content to watch skiing on television, with a new respect for the skiers who sail so effortlessly down the slopes.

30. Which of the following sentences could best be omitted from the paragraph without sacrifice to the meaning or flow of the paragraph?

(A) sentence 3
(B) sentence 8
(C) sentence 10
(D) sentence 13
(E) sentence 15

31. Which of the following is the most effective way to combine the underlined portion of sentences 1 and 2 (reproduced below) ?

I've always watched skiing on underlined television. I thought that it looked like fun.

(A) television; however, I thought that it looked
(B) television, it looking, I thought,
(C) television, and I thought that it looked
(D) television, thinking it was looking
(E) television because I think that it looks

32. Which of the following is the best version of the underlined portion of sentence 4 (reproduced below)?

Even though I was never on the slopes before, I assumed that I'd be able to catch on pretty quickly.

(A) was not
(B) could not have been
(C) never had not been
(D) have not been
(E) had never been

33. Replacing the underlined portion of sentence 3 (reproduced below) with which of the following would best resolve the ambiguity in sentence 8?

So, naturally, when my friend suggested that we go skiing over Christmas vacation, I agreed.

(A) my friend, an experienced skier, suggested
(B) my friend George suggested
(C) my oldest and best friend suggested
(D) my friend suggested with great enthusiasm
(E) my friend, who could talk me into anything, suggested

GO ON TO THE NEXT PAGE

34. Which of the following words could best be omitted from sentence 14 without sacrifice to the meaning or flow of the sentence?

   (A) same
   (B) myself
   (C) enough
   (D) in
   (E) up

35. Which of the following sentences, if inserted between sentence 16 and sentence 17, would provide the best transition?

   (A) I felt as if I were flying.
   (B) Unfortunately, this was not the case.
   (C) Everyone around me seemed to be skiing effortlessly.
   (D) Getting down the slope was certainly more difficult than I had imagined.
   (E) After that, I could not believe that anyone really enjoyed skiing.

STOP

If you finish before time is called, you may check your work on this section only.
Do not turn to any other section in the test.

SECTION 5
Time — 25 minutes
18 Questions

Turn to Section 5 of your answer sheet to answer the questions in this section.

Directions: This section contains two types of questions. You have 25 minutes to complete both types. For questions 1-8, solve each problem and decide which is the best of the choices given. Fill in the corresponding circle on the answer sheet. You may use any available space for scratchwork.

Notes

1. The use of a calculator is permitted.

2. All numbers used are real numbers.

3. Figures that accompany problems in this test are intended to provide information useful in solving the problems. They are drawn as accurately as possible EXCEPT when it is stated in a specific problem that the figure is not drawn to scale. All figures lie in a plane unless otherwise indicated.

4. Unless otherwise specified, the domain of any function f is assumed to be the set of all real numbers x for which $f(x)$ is a real number.

Reference Information

  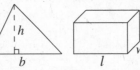 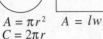 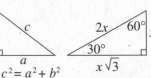

$A = \pi r^2$ $A = lw$ $A = \frac{1}{2}bh$ $V = lwh$ $V = \pi r^2 h$ $c^2 = a^2 + b^2$ Special Right Triangles

$C = 2\pi r$

The number of degrees of arc in a circle is 360.

The sum of the measures in degrees of the angles of a triangle is 180.

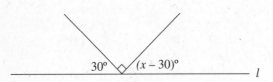

1. In the figure above, what is the value of x ?

(A) 30
(B) 60
(C) 70
(D) 80
(E) 90

2. If $\dfrac{\sqrt{x}}{2} = 2\sqrt{2}$, what is the value of x ?

(A) 4
(B) 16
(C) $16\sqrt{2}$
(D) 32
(E) 64

GO ON TO THE NEXT PAGE

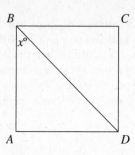

3. If $\overline{BD}$ bisects $\angle ABC$ and $ABCD$ is a rectangle, $x =$

(A) 15
(B) 30
(C) 45
(D) 60
(E) 90

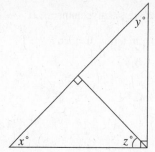

Note: Figure not drawn to scale.

5. In the figure above, if $y = 2x$, what is the value of z ?

(A) 30
(B) 45
(C) 60
(D) 75
(E) 90

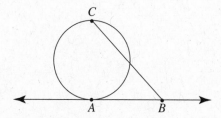

4. In the figure above, $\overline{AB}$ is tangent to the circle at point A. The circle has an area of 25π. If AB is 10 and AC is a diameter, what is BC ?

(A) 5
(B) $5\sqrt{2}$
(C) 10
(D) $10\sqrt{2}$
(E) 15

6. For all real numbers, $f(x) = \dfrac{(x^2 + 1)}{2}$. If $f(a) = 25$ and $f(11) = b$, which of the following could be the value of $a - b$?

(A) −14
(B) 36
(C) 68
(D) 77
(E) 86

GO ON TO THE NEXT PAGE

7. Both c and d are positive numbers. If $\dfrac{x-d}{cx} = \dfrac{5}{2}$, what is the value of x in terms of c and d ?

(A) $10(5-d) + c$

(B) $10(5+d) - c$

(C) $5cd$

(D) $-\dfrac{2d}{5c-2}$

(E) $\dfrac{2d}{5c-2}$

8. The number of instances of illness that a person has in one year is inversely proportional to the average (arithmetic mean) number of hours that person sleeps per night. If last year Lori slept an average of 8 hours per night and was ill 3 times, how many times would she have been ill if she had slept an average of 6 hours per night?

(A) 2.25
(B) 3
(C) 3.5
(D) 4
(E) 4.75

GO ON TO THE NEXT PAGE

Directions: For Student-Produced Response questions 9-18, use the grids at the bottom of the answer sheet page on which you have answered questions 1-8.

Each of the remaining 10 questions requires you to solve the problem and enter your answer by marking the circles in the special grid, as shown in the examples below. You may use any available space for scratch work.

Answer: $\frac{7}{12}$

Write answer in boxes.

Grid in result.

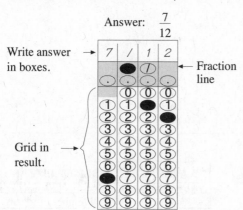

Answer: 2.5

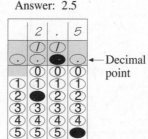

Answer: 201
Either position is correct.

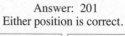
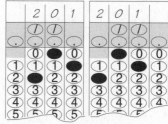

Note: You may start your answers in any column, space permitting. Columns not needed should be left blank.

• Mark no more than one circle in any column.

• Because the answer document will be machine-scored, **you will receive credit only if the circles are filled in correctly.**

• Although not required, it is suggested that you write your answer in the boxes at the top of the columns to help you fill in the circles accurately.

• Some problems may have more than one correct answer. In such cases, grid only one answer.

• No question has a negative answer.

• **Mixed numbers** such as $3\frac{1}{2}$ must be gridded as 3.5 or 7/2. (If ⬚ is gridded, it will be interpreted as $\frac{31}{2}$, not $3\frac{1}{2}$.)

• **Decimal Answers:** If you obtain a decimal answer with more digits than the grid can accommodate, it may be either rounded or truncated, but it must fill the entire grid. For example, if you obtain an answer such as 0.6666..., you should record your result as .666 or .667. **A less accurate value such as .66 or .67 will be scored as incorrect.**

Acceptable ways to grid $\frac{2}{3}$ are:

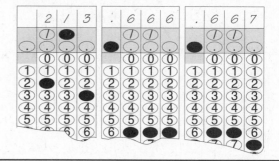

9. On a certain map, 100 miles is represented by 1 inch. What is the number of miles represented by 2.4 inches on this map?

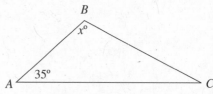

Note: Figure not drawn to scale.

10. In △ABC above, if AB = BC, then x =

GO ON TO THE NEXT PAGE

11. In a list of five real numbers, 30 is the greatest number, 10 is the least number, 15 is the number that occurs most often, and 18 is the average (arithmetic mean). What is the median of the five numbers?

12. In a large city, the number of people with pets was 6 percent greater in February than it was in January. If 2,400 people had pets in January, how many had pets in February?

13. $\overline{XZ}$ is the diagonal of square *WXYZ* and has a length of $7\sqrt{2}$. What is the perimeter of square *WXYZ*?

AVERAGE NUMBER OF PIZZAS CONSUMED PER PERSON PER YEAR	
Year	Number of Pizzas
1960	2.45
1970	4.86
1980	8.12
1990	15.6

14. According to the table above, the number of pizzas consumed per person in 1990 was what multiple, rounded to the nearest integer, of the number of pizzas consumed per person in 1960?

GO ON TO THE NEXT PAGE

15. How many integers between 1 and 100 contain the digit 5 ?

16. If $x^2 \leq 25$ and $y^2 \geq 16$, what is the least possible value of $(x - y)^2$?

17. Admission to an amusement park costs $7 for a child and $15 for an adult. If 96 tickets were sold for a total of $800, what was the ratio of the number of adult's tickets sold to the number of children's tickets sold?

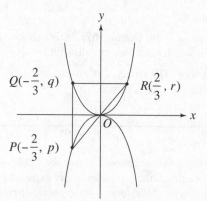

Note: Figure not drawn to scale.

18. In the figure above, points Q and R lie on the graph of $y = ax^2$, and point P lies on the graph of $y = -ax^2$, where a is a positive constant. If the area of $\triangle PQR$ is 16, what is the value of a ?

STOP
If you finish before time is called, you may check your work on this section only.
Do not turn to any other section in the test.

SECTION 7
Time — 25 minutes
24 Questions

Turn to Section 7 of your answer sheet to answer the questions in this section.

Directions: For each question in this section, select the best answer from among the choices given and fill in the corresponding circle on the answer sheet.

Each sentence below has one or two blanks, each blank indicating that something has been omitted. Beneath the sentence are five words or sets of words labeled A through E. Choose the word or set of words that, when inserted in the sentence, best fits the meaning of the sentence as a whole.

Example:

Desiring to ------- his taunting friends, Mitch gave them taffy in hopes it would keep their mouths shut.

(A) eliminate   (B) satisfy   (C) overcome
(D) ridicule   (E) silence

---

1. After the governor announced that she would refrain from smear tactics in the campaign, many expressed hope that this action would restore ------- to public discourse.

   (A) civility   (B) abstraction   (C) monotony
       (D) partiality   (E) tension

2. Schubert exclaimed with ------- when he realized that the one ------- error he made in calculation had accidentally given him the solution he had been seeking for years.

   (A) dismay . . appalling
   (B) elation . . significant
   (C) dread . . involuntary
   (D) jubilation . . intentional
   (E) exultation . . audible

3. The project manager ------- his presentation with an excessively optimistic outlook and flowery language in an effort to win the director's approval.

   (A) appeased   (B) embellished   (C) conceived
       (D) disdained   (E) derived

4. At the science fair, Joanna was stunned when what she thought was ------- entry received ------- score from the judges.

   (A) an outstanding . . a differential
   (B) a blemished . . a contemptible
   (C) a mediocre . . a superlative
   (D) an extremist . . an atrocious
   (E) a laudable . . a gratifying

5. The prisoner's looming execution date gave defense attorneys added ------- to analyze new DNA evidence that might exonerate their client.

   (A) discretion   (B) certitude   (C) acuity
       (D) enmity   (E) impetus

GO ON TO THE NEXT PAGE

Directions: Each passage below is followed by questions based on its content. Answer the questions on the basis of what is <u>stated</u> or <u>implied</u> in each passage and in any introductory material that may be provided.

Questions 6-7 are based on the following passage.

Although humans have hunted many species nearly to extinction, few imperiled animals have received as much international attention as have the whales. The International *Line* Whaling Commission was established by the world's fourteen
5 major whaling countries in order to preserve sufficient stocks of whales. The Commission now boasts 51 members, including such landlocked and minor maritime powers as Switzerland, which obviously joined the Commission in order to support the strong Swiss whaling industry. What was once
10 viewed as a merely regulatory body for one industry is now perceived as an open forum for discussing a globally relevant issue.

6. In discussing Switzerland, the author uses irony in order to

(A) provide a description of new members
(B) discredit the actions of certain members
(C) explain the expansion of an organization's membership
(D) emphasize the initial goals of an organization
(E) suggest that not all members have the same motivations

7. It can be most reasonably inferred from the passage that

(A) the International Whaling Commission successfully manages the whaling industry and preserves sufficient stocks of whales
(B) countries are not required to have a major whaling industry in order to join the International Whaling Commission
(C) Switzerland joined the International Whaling Commission in order to oppose the whaling industry
(D) the International Whaling Commission no longer regulates the whaling industry but merely serves as a forum for discussion
(E) international commissions are the most effective way to raise awareness about the hunting of endangered species

Questions 8-9 are based on the following passage.

In 1801 astronomer William Herschel posited that one hundred years of recording solar activity showed that periods with few sunspots coincided with the highest wheat prices. *Line* The connection was recently confirmed when a study of
5 wheat prices in England between 1259 and 1702 showed that the price peaks occurred at the same intervals as low points in a typical cycle of sunspot activity. Additionally, chemical analysis of Greenland's ice cores shows that in the seventeenth century high levels of cosmic rays, which indicate
10 low solar activity, peaked in the same cycles as wheat prices.

8. Which of the following statements, if true, does the most to strengthen the link between wheat price and sunspot activity?

(A) Research carried out since the 1700s proves the existence of an eleven-year sunspot cycle.
(B) Nineteenth-century scientists had little proof of the effect of sunspots on the earth's weather.
(C) Meticulous records have been kept for hundreds of years on the market price of corn.
(D) Low sunspot activity causes cooler, rainy weather in England, resulting in lower crop yields.
(E) Scientists have been unable to find a reliable pattern of peaks and lows in sunspot activity.

9. According to information in the passage, all of the following methods have been used to determine the effects of sunspot activity EXCEPT

(A) examination of centuries of records of market prices for wheat
(B) analysis of radiation levels in past centuries utilizing ice core samples
(C) use of scientific equipment near the sun's atmosphere that measures cosmic rays
(D) detailed observation by astronomers over decades
(E) a comparison of wheat prices to two methods of documenting sunspot activity

GO ON TO THE NEXT PAGE >

Questions 10-18 refer to the following passage.

In this passage, the author, Virginia Woolf, describes the process by which she discovered her own voice as a writer.

My story is a simple one. You have only got to figure to yourselves a girl in a bedroom with a pen in her hand.
She had only to move that pen from left to right—from ten
Line o'clock to one. Then it occurred to her to do what is simple
5 and cheap enough after all—to slip a few of those pages into an envelope, fix a penny stamp in the corner, and drop the envelope into the red box at the corner. It was thus that I became a journalist; and my effort was rewarded on the first day of the following month—a very glorious day it was for
10 me—by a letter from an editor containing a cheque for one pound ten shillings and sixpence.

What could be easier than to write articles? But wait a moment. Articles have to be about something. Mine, I seemed to remember, was about a novel by a famous man.
15 And while I was writing this review, I discovered that if I were going to review books I should need to do battle with a certain phantom. And the phantom was a woman, and when I came to know her better I called her after the heroine of a famous poem, "The Angel in the House." It was she who
20 used to come between me and my paper when I was writing reviews. It was she who bothered me and wasted my time and so tormented me that at last I killed her. I will describe her as shortly as I can. She was intensely sympathetic. She was immensely charming. She was utterly unselfish. She excelled
25 in the difficult arts of family life. She sacrificed herself daily. She was so constituted that she never had a mind or a wish of her own, but preferred to sympathize with the minds and wishes of others. Above all—I need not say it —she was pure. In those days every house had its Angel. And when I
30 came to write I encountered her with the very first words. The shadow of her wings fell on my page; I heard the rustling of her skirts in the room. Directly, that is to say, I took my pen in hand to review that novel by a famous man, she slipped behind me and whispered: "My dear, you are a young woman.
35 You are writing about a book that has been written by a man. Be sympathetic; be tender; flatter; deceive; use all the arts and wiles of our sex. Never let anybody guess that you have a mind of your own. Above all, be pure." And she made as if to guide my pen. I now record the one act for which I take
40 some credit to myself. I turned upon her and caught her by the throat. I did my best to kill her. My excuse, if I were to be had up in a court of law, would be that I acted in self-defense. Had I not killed her she would have killed me. She would have plucked the heart of my writing. For, as I found, directly I put
45 pen to paper, you can not even review a novel without having a mind of your own, without expressing what you think to be the truth about human relations, morality, sex. And all these questions, according to the Angel in the House, cannot be dealt with freely and openly by women; they must charm,
50 they must conciliate, they must—to put it bluntly—tell lies if

they are to succeed. Thus, whenever I felt the shadow of her wing or the radiance of her halo upon my page, I took up the inkpot and flung it at her. She died hard. Her fictitious nature was of great assistance to her. It is far harder to kill a phantom
55 than a reality.

10. The author most likely describes "a girl in a bedroom" (line 2) in order to

   (A) bring to light the limits placed on young female journalists

   (B) present a picture of herself as a fledgling writer

   (C) describe the vulnerability of young woman writers

   (D) demonstrate the economic feasibility of entering a career as a writer

   (E) encourage the reader to empathize with the hardships faced by female writers

11. The question "What could . . . articles?" (line 12) serves to

   (A) begin a description of the facility with which the author was able to write freely and openly

   (B) commence a discourse on writer's block and its causes

   (C) point out how quickly and effortlessly the author produced news features

   (D) suggest how easy it was to write with the help of the Angel in the House

   (E) introduce a discussion of the difficulties the author had disregarding a phantom influence

12. In line 26, "constituted" most nearly means

   (A) formally composed

   (B) creative and imaginative

   (C) devoted to being pure

   (D) physically strong

   (E) committed to writing

13. The description of the Angel in the House in lines 19-29 ("She was . . . she was pure.") reflects the author's

   (A) desire to model herself after the Angel

   (B) inability to achieve the ideal represented by the Angel

   (C) feeling that the Angel's positive characteristics could be seen in a negative light

   (D) gratitude for the Angel's assistance in becoming a writer

   (E) impression of her mother as an incarnation of the Angel

GO ON TO THE NEXT PAGE ⟶

14. In line 28, the author uses the expression "I need not say it" in order to suggest that

(A) she has no obligation to describe the Angel's character

(B) the Angel's purity is too delicate a subject to discuss

(C) although the Angel lacked free will, the author does not

(D) she presumes that readers will know the Angel was pure

(E) she is reluctant to admit that she is not as pure as the Angel

15. The word "directly," as it is used in lines 32 and 44, could be replaced with which of the following words or phrases without a change in meaning?

(A) unswervingly

(B) as soon as

(C) in a straight line

(D) honestly

(E) in a straightforward manner

16. For what reason does the author fear the Angel's effect on her writing?

(A) She recognizes that the Angel could prevent her from expressing her opinions honestly.

(B) She feels that the Angel could induce her to focus on stereotypically feminine subjects.

(C) She thinks the Angel would deem writing an inappropriate career for a woman.

(D) She believes that the Angel will influence the plots of the stories she writes.

(E) She sees that the Angel could prevent her from writing about books that matter to her.

17. The author would most likely agree with which of the following statements?

(A) Social expectations placed upon women during the nineteenth century kept women from being successful writers.

(B) A writer is justified in committing acts of violence when her art is threatened.

(C) Writing requires an independence not compatible with traditional ideas of femininity.

(D) A woman writer should not always be completely truthful in her work.

(E) Woman writers must inevitably work harder than male writers to achieve success.

18. In the last sentence of the passage, the author implies that

(A) one's imagination can be a powerful adversary

(B) woman writers must overcome their hesitation to flout traditional roles

(C) she came to realize that the Angel ultimately helped her succeed as a writer

(D) the influence of the Angel could never be escaped

(E) it was difficult to distinguish between fantasy and reality

GO ON TO THE NEXT PAGE

Questions 19-24 are based on the following passage.

The modern atomic theory of matter was not developed until the twentieth century. The following passage discusses an atomistic theory developed by the classical Greek thinker Democritus.

Democritus was fascinated by the question of what principle underlay the material universe and developed a solution that revealed the brilliance of his thought. Every
Line material thing, Democritus believed, is made up of a finite
5 number of discrete particles, or atoms, as he called them, whose joining together and subsequent separation account for the coming to be of things and for their passing away. The atoms themselves, he said, are infinite in number and eternal. They move, according to a necessary motion, in the void,
10 which we would call space.

Most of the main tenets of the atomism of Democritus were astonishingly modern. First, the atoms were invisibly small. They were all of the same stuff, or nature, but they came in a multitude of different shapes and sizes. Though
15 impermeable (Democritus did not know that atoms could be split), they acted upon one another, aggregating and clinging to one another so as to produce the great variety of bodies that we see. The space outside the atoms was empty, a concept that most of Democritus's contemporaries could not accept.
20 Second, the atoms were in perpetual motion, in every direction, throughout empty space. There is no above or below, before or behind, in empty space, said Democritus. In modern terms, empty space did not vary according to direction. This was an extremely sophisticated notion.
25 Third, the continual motion of the atoms was inherent. They possessed what we would call inertial mass. The notion that the atoms kept on moving without being pushed, besides being another remarkable intellectual concept, was not acceptable to Aristotle and others. Only the celestial bodies,
30 Aristotle thought, kept on moving of and by themselves, because they were divine. The general refusal by Aristotle and his influential followers to accept the law of inertia stood as an obstacle to the development of physics for two thousand years.
35 Fourth, weight or gravity was not a property of atoms or indeed of aggregates thereof. Here Democritus was as wrong as wrong could be.

Whether Democritus was right or wrong about a fifth point is not definitely decided to this day. He held that the
40 soul is breath and because breath is material, and therefore made up of atoms, so must the soul be. He maintained that, because the soul is a physical thing, it must be determined by physical laws; it cannot be free. Even the hardy thinkers who claim to accept this theory do not act as if they do. They
45 may deny the innate freedom of others, but they act as if they believe in their own.

The tension built up by this antinomy has proved to be fruitful over the centuries. However, the notion that the soul was material proved so unacceptable to both the Aristotelians
50 and the Christians that for nearly two millennia the atomic hypothesis languished.

19. In line 5, "discrete" most nearly means

(A) separate
(B) subtle
(C) restrained
(D) obvious
(E) careful

20. According to Democritus, empty space

(A) does not exist with regard to atoms
(B) is directionless with regard to the movement of atoms
(C) is an erroneous notion concerning atoms
(D) possesses inertial mass
(E) is an illusion when viewed at the atomic level

21. The author discusses the beliefs of Aristotle and his followers (lines 26-34) in order to

(A) support the validity of Democritus's theories
(B) show the history that led up to the development of the theory of atomism
(C) note that influential individuals delayed the acceptance of scientific truth
(D) highlight the accuracy of certain parts of Democritus's theory
(E) add an element of philosophy into an otherwise scientific discussion

22. It can be inferred from Democritus's inclusion of the soul in his theories of the material universe (lines 39-46) that

(A) philosophy, religion, and science were not always thought of as separate fields
(B) scientists are often unsuccessful in making philosophical theories
(C) he was attempting to align his thinking with that of Aristotle
(D) his line of thinking was essentially unsound
(E) while his initial theories were accurate, his later theories were proven wrong

GO ON TO THE NEXT PAGE

23. Democritus would most likely believe that which of the following would explain the life cycle of a flower?

(A) A unique type of matter is drawn to a point in the void and takes root.

(B) The constant motion of atoms produces the illusion of a flower.

(C) The splitting of atoms leads to the creation of new cells which form the flower.

(D) The same material that composes the soul also breathes life into plants.

(E) Atoms come together as the flower grows and disperse as it dies.

24. Which is most analogous to a "hardy thinker's" (line 43) view of the soul?

(A) A politician's practice of using public transportation because that is how everyone in his city travels

(B) A doctor's recommendation that his patient quit smoking to improve the patient's health while the doctor smokes a pack a day

(C) A mother taking her daughter to ballet practice every day because the mother never had that opportunity as a child

(D) A teacher showing all his students the proper way to do a math problem and then doing nothing while the students solve a set of problems

(E) A museum curator deciding not to run an exhibition because he believes the public will not enjoy it

STOP

If you finish before time is called, you may check your work on this section only.
Do not turn to any other section in the test.

SECTION 8
Time — 20 minutes
16 Questions

Turn to Section 8 of your answer sheet to answer the questions in this section.

Directions: For this section, solve each problem and decide which is the best of the choices given. Fill in the corresponding circle on the answer sheet. You may use any available space for scratchwork.

Notes

1. The use of a calculator is permitted.

2. All numbers used are real numbers.

3. Figures that accompany problems in this test are intended to provide information useful in solving the problems. They are drawn as accurately as possible EXCEPT when it is stated in a specific problem that the figure is not drawn to scale. All figures lie in a plane unless otherwise indicated.

4. Unless otherwise specified, the domain of any function f is assumed to be the set of all real numbers x for which $f(x)$ is a real number.

Reference Information

 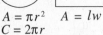   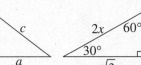

$A = \pi r^2$ $\quad$ $A = lw$ $\quad$ $A = \frac{1}{2}bh$ $\quad$ $V = lwh$ $\quad$ $V = \pi r^2 h$ $\quad$ $c^2 = a^2 + b^2$

$C = 2\pi r$ $\qquad\qquad\qquad\qquad\qquad\qquad\qquad\qquad\qquad\qquad\qquad$ Special Right Triangles

The number of degrees of arc in a circle is 360.

The sum of the measures in degrees of the angles of a triangle is 180.

---

1. If a store sells n newspapers on each of 5 days, which of the following represents the total number of newspapers sold?

   (A) $5n$
   (B) $5 + n$
   (C) $n - 5$
   (D) n^5
   (E) 5^n

2. If $\dfrac{a}{b} = \dfrac{7}{4}$, and $\dfrac{b}{c} = \dfrac{8}{6}$, then $\dfrac{a}{c} =$

   (A) $\dfrac{3}{7}$

   (B) $\dfrac{4}{7}$

   (C) $\dfrac{16}{21}$

   (D) $\dfrac{21}{16}$

   (E) $\dfrac{7}{3}$

GO ON TO THE NEXT PAGE

3. If a rectangular rug measures 72 inches by 96 inches, what is its area in square feet? (1 foot = 12 inches)

(A) 864
(B) 576
(C) 336
(D) 144
(E) 48

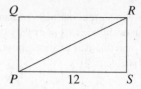

Note: Figure not drawn to scale.

5. In the figure above, the area of rectangle *PQRS* is 96. What is the perimeter of triangle *PQR* ?

(A) $20+4\sqrt{6}$ (approximately 29.80)
(B) $20+4\sqrt{13}$ (approximately 34.42)
(C) 20
(D) 40
(E) 48

4. The cost of a meal including a 20 percent tip is $30. What was the cost of the meal before the tip was added?

(A) $10.00
(B) $24.00
(C) $25.00
(D) $29.80
(E) $36.00

6. What is the slope of a line with the equation $y + 3 = 5(x - 2)$?

(A) 7
(B) 5
(C) 3
(D) 10
(E) 13

GO ON TO THE NEXT PAGE

7. Stephanie has ten shirts, four pairs of pants, and five pairs of shoes. If an outfit consists of exactly one shirt, one pair of pants, and one pair of shoes, how many different outfits could she wear?

(A) 19
(B) 95
(C) 105
(D) 190
(E) 200

8. At a certain store, the price of a new compact disc is five times the price of a used compact disc. The difference between the two prices is ten dollars. What would be the total price of three used compact discs and two new compact discs at this store?

(A) $26.00
(B) $30.00
(C) $32.50
(D) $42.50
(E) $45.00

9. Points E and F lie in the xy-coordinate plane at $(0, 10)$ and $(6, 0)$, respectively. Which of the following is the midpoint of $\overline{EF}$?

(A) $(5, 3)$
(B) $(3, 5)$
(C) $(3, 10)$
(D) $(10, 3)$
(E) $(6, 10)$

10. If $r = \dfrac{2s^3}{t}$, what happens to the value of t when both r and s are doubled?

(A) t is halved.
(B) t is doubled.
(C) t is tripled.
(D) t is multiplied by 4.
(E) t is multiplied by 8.

GO ON TO THE NEXT PAGE

11. A jar contained red and green marbles in a ratio of 3 to 4. After 6 red marbles are added to the jar, the ratio becomes 3 to 2. How many green marbles does the jar now contain?

(A)   3
(B)   4
(C)   6
(D)   8
(E)   14

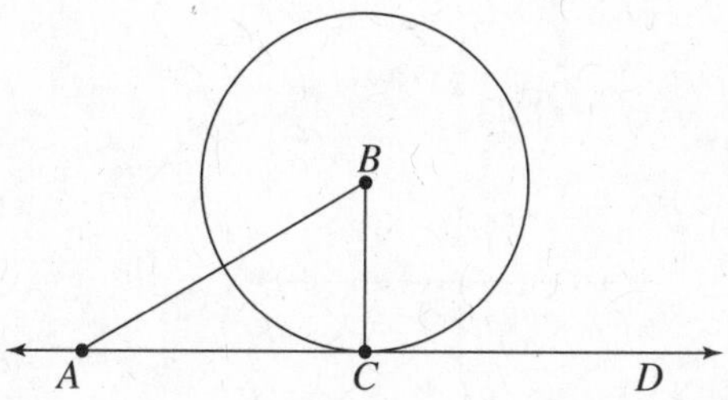

13. If $\dfrac{b^x}{2} = 8$ then $b^{\frac{x}{2}} =$

(A)   1
(B)   2
(C)   4
(D)   8
(E)   16

12. In the figure above, $\overline{AD}$ is tangent to the circle with center B at point C. If the area of the circle is 16π and $AB = 8$, what is AC ?

(A)   2
(B) $2\sqrt{3}$
(C)   4
(D) $4\sqrt{2}$
(E) $4\sqrt{3}$

14. In a sequence of numbers, the first term is 6. Each term after the first is calculated by adding 2 to the previous term and then dividing by −1. What is the value of the 101st term subtracted from the 70th term?

(A)   31
(B)   14
(C)   −2
(D)   −14
(E)   −31

GO ON TO THE NEXT PAGE

15. The number of baseball cards in Caleb's collection doubles every three months. If after 9 months he has b baseball cards, then which of the following is an expression for the number of baseball cards in his collection after y years?

(A) $2^y b$

(B) $2^{4y\,3} b$

(C) $2^{4y} b$

(D) $2b^{4y\,3}$

(E) $2^y b^{y+2}$

16. Which of the following graphs shows the line defined by the equation $\frac{5}{3}y - 5 = x$ in the xy coordinate system?

(A)

(B)

(C)

(D)

(E)

STOP

If you finish before time is called, you may check your work on this section only.
Do not turn to any other section in the test.

NO TEST MATERIAL ON THIS PAGE.

SECTION 9
Time — 20 minutes
19 Questions

Turn to Section 9 of your answer sheet to answer the questions in this section.

Directions: For each question in this section, select the best answer from among the choices given and fill in the corresponding circle on the answer sheet.

Each sentence below has one or two blanks, each blank indicating that something has been omitted. Beneath the sentence are five words or sets of words labeled A through E. Choose the word or set of words that, when inserted in the sentence, best fits the meaning of the sentence as a whole.

Example:

Desiring to ------- his taunting friends, Mitch gave them taffy in hopes it would keep their mouths shut.

(A) eliminate   (B) satisfy   (C) overcome
    (D) ridicule   (E) silence

Ⓐ Ⓑ Ⓒ Ⓓ ●

1. Once relegated to only a few outlets such as television and radio, advertising now confronts us everywhere; it has become ------- presence in our lives.

    (A) an offensive   (B) an insensible   (C) an urbane
        (D) a ubiquitous   (E) an ineffective

2. Considering Desiree's ------- on the basketball court, it was surprising that her younger brother was so -------: whereas she moved with ease and skill, he was rather uncoordinated.

    (A) grace . . superior
    (B) agility . . clumsy
    (C) haughtiness . . nimble
    (D) sportsmanship . . temperamental
    (E) ineptitude . . blundering

3. After the first week of the semester, students in the accounting course found the subject more ------- and thought-provoking than ------.

    (A) academic . . scholarly
    (B) suspicious . . gracious
    (C) interesting . . intriguing
    (D) riveting . . wearisome
    (E) stale . . interesting

4. The conversation between the fierce competitors quickly degenerated from restrained and playful taunts to aggressively ------- insults.

    (A) vituperative   (B) professional   (C) inscrutable
        (D) noisome   (E) vapid

5. Although Sumi sincerely wanted her team to succeed, she refused to ------- her teammate's plan to cheat during the championship game.

    (A) proscribe   (B) hamper   (C) obfuscate
        (D) endorse   (E) meander

6. Though Nina believes her argument to be a ------- one, her verbose explanations and exclusive reliance on her own obscure experiences make it more ------- than she realizes.

    (A) pithy . . obtuse
    (B) passionate . . insipid
    (C) petulant . . approachable
    (D) strident . . vociferous
    (E) tremulous . . terse

GO ON TO THE NEXT PAGE

Directions: Each passage below is followed by questions based on its content. Answer the questions on the basis of what is <u>stated</u> or <u>implied</u> in each passage and in any introductory material that may be provided.

Questions 7-19 are based on the following passages.

The following passages discuss the use of alum, an inorganic compound, in paper making.

Passage 1

Alum has been used since before 2000 B.C.E., and was, historians believe, first used by the Egyptians; it has a colorful history which includes important roles in papal
Line edicts, religious warfare, and power struggles. Originally used
5 as a mordant* to set dyes in textiles, alum came to be used in papermaking in more recent eras. It was used as a finisher in the papermaking process in the seventeenth, eighteenth, and nineteenth centuries. Alum exists as a naturally-occurring compound, similar to the aluminum sulfate that eventually
10 replaced it in the twentieth century. James Whatman used alum in his famous eighteenth-century paper mill, and Class I paper (a highly durable paper) in the nineteenth century used alum mixed with a type of gelatin as a finisher. The alum acted as a strengthener for the gelatin, bonding it to
15 the paper and preventing mold growth. This coating process, called sizing, kept the paper from being too porous, inhibiting ink from spreading. The paper made in this way still holds up 200 years later, largely undamaged and more robust than most modern paper. Unfortunately, alum is held in low repute
20 today among some printmakers who base their opinion of the compound on inferior samples of alum-treated paper. Alum that was mixed with rosin, for example, protected paper only for the short term, so paper thus treated now appears brittle and discolored.

 * a chemical that fixes a dye in or on a substance by combining with the dye to form an insoluble compound

Passage 2

25   The compound alum has been valuable to the tanning, textile, and papermaking industries for centuries. Early in its history, the compound was manufactured by boiling crude rock (alum stone, shale, or schist) with ammonia, then allowing the liquid to crystallize. Today aluminum sulfate is
30 often used in place of the original compound. The original compound alum is considered an adequate finisher in the papermaking process, although too much of it can damage the strength of the paper. Nonetheless, a few printers still use excessive amounts of alum to prevent bubbles in the paper
35 and stickiness in the papermaking presses. These maverick printers obviously also enjoy the historic cachet of the compound, but they ignore its acidity and the deteriorating effect it has on the paper. Alum isn't particularly acidic itself, but it combines with ingredients such as chlorine in the paper
40 to form aluminum chloride. Under some conditions it even forms hydrochloric acid, which is detrimental to the cellulose in most paper. This problem doesn't occur when alum is used in small quantities and as an additive to aid the function of other finishing compounds.

7. According to Passage 1, "sizing" (line 16) was used to

 (A) combine alum with a gelatin mixture
 (B) keep the dye in textiles from spreading
 (C) protect papal edicts
 (D) make paper less porous
 (E) set dyes in textiles

8. In line 18, "robust" most nearly means

 (A) durable
 (B) undamaged
 (C) stout
 (D) healthy
 (E) fragile

9. Which feature is characteristic of an "inferior" (line 21) sample of alum-treated paper?

 (A) stickiness
 (B) bubbles
 (C) discoloration
 (D) acidity
 (E) mold growth

10. In line 36 "cachet" most nearly means

 (A) hiding place
 (B) storage
 (C) infamy
 (D) distinction
 (E) notoriety

11. The author of Passage 2 characterizes alum as all of the following EXCEPT

 (A) a component of an acidic compound
 (B) a compound that reduces porosity in paper
 (C) a compound that has a deteriorating effect
 (D) a compound that prevents stickiness
 (E) a compound that can aid the function of other compounds

12. According Passage 1, it can be inferred that alum mixed with rosin

 (A) is often used in place of the original compound
 (B) protected paper for 200 years
 (C) stopped dye from spreading in textiles
 (D) protected paper for fewer than 200 years
 (E) is detrimental to the cellulose in most paper

GO ON TO THE NEXT PAGE

13. Which application of alum mentioned in Passage 2 is NOT mentioned in Passage 1?

   (A) Paper finishing
   (B) Preventing mold growth
   (C) Preventing fading of inks
   (D) Forming hydrochloric acid
   (E) Aiding the function of other compounds

14. In Passage 1, the author characterizes alum as all of the following EXCEPT

   (A) an ingredient that prevents mold growth
   (B) an agent that assists in the function of other finishing agents
   (C) a substance with an unduly positive reputation
   (D) a finisher that is sometimes unable to prevent damage and discoloration
   (E) a natural compound for which other compounds can be substituted

15. The author of Passage 2 criticizes some modern papermakers for

   (A) using excessive amounts of alum
   (B) awareness of the acidity of alum and its deteriorating effect on paper
   (C) using an ineffective substitute for alum
   (D) discounting the importance of alum's popular history
   (E) failing to prevent bubbles and stickiness in the paper during printing

16. The authors of the two passages seem to agree on alum's

   (A) value as a preventative against mold growth
   (B) importance as the most effective paper finisher on record
   (C) ability to preserve paper and prevent deterioration
   (D) effectiveness when combined with some other finishers
   (E) relatively low level of acidity

17. The author of Passage 1 would most likely agree with the all the following EXCEPT

   (A) paper made with alum 200 years ago is still undamaged and robust
   (B) alum safely combines with the chlorine contained in paper
   (C) aluminum sulfate is now used as a substitute for alum
   (D) modern criticism of alum stems from samples treated with rosin
   (E) modern printmakers rarely use alum in printing

18. According to Passage 2, a "maverick printer" (lines 35-36) is one who

   (A) produces monographs on the history of papermaking
   (B) prefers using aluminum and chlorine compounds
   (C) applies a superfluous amount of alum in the printmaking process
   (D) inadvertently experiments with volatile acids in printmaking
   (E) decides what chemicals to use based on historical precedents instead of new technologies

19. Which if the following is NOT mentioned in either passage as a function of alum in papermaking?

   (A) Minimizing the incidence of bubbles
   (B) Inhibiting mold production
   (C) Coating paper to decrease absorbency
   (D) Preventing stickiness in pulp
   (E) Homogenizing the texture of paper

STOP

If you finish before time is called, you may check your work on this section only.
Do not turn to any other section in the test.

NO TEST MATERIAL ON THIS PAGE.

SECTION 10
Time — 10 minutes
14 Questions

Turn to Section 10 of your answer sheet to answer the questions in this section.

Directions: For each question in this section, select the best answer from among the choices given and fill in the corresponding circle on the answer sheet.

The following sentences test correctness and effectiveness of expression. Part of each sentence or the entire sentence is underlined; beneath each sentence are five ways of phrasing the underlined material. Choice A repeats the original phrasing; the other four choices are different. If you think the original phrasing produces a better sentence than any of the alternatives, select choice A; if not, select one of the other choices.

In making your selection, follow the requirements of standard written English; that is, pay attention to grammar, choice of words, sentence construction, and punctuation. Your selection should result in the most effective sentence—clear and precise, without awkwardness or ambiguity.

EXAMPLE:

Bobby Flay baked his first cake <u>and he was thirteen years old then</u>.

(A) and he was thirteen years old then
(B) when he was thirteen
(C) at age thirteen years old
(D) upon the reaching of thirteen years
(E) at the time when he was thirteen

1. Michael was widely considered the best swimmer in the <u>competition; however, he was beaten decisively</u> in two of his eight races.

   (A) competition; however, he was beaten decisively
   (B) competition, for he was beaten decisively, however,
   (C) competition; however, being beaten decisively
   (D) competition, having been beaten decisively
   (E) competition, but was being beaten decisively

2. Although the sun often shines twelve hours a day on the orchids, <u>causing them to grow no more</u> than a few inches a year.

   (A) causing them to grow no more
   (B) and yet they grow no more
   (C) it does not cause them to grow more
   (D) and it does not cause them to grow more
   (E) yet causing them to grow no more

3. Even the play's most evil villains are portrayed with convincing pathos, <u>this artistic choice results in a very ambiguous message</u>.

   (A) this artistic choice results in a very ambiguous message
   (B) with this artistic choice resulting in a very ambiguous message
   (C) and a very ambiguous message being the result of this artistic choice
   (D) an artistic choice that results in a very ambiguous message
   (E) a very ambiguous message results from this artistic choice

4. The adage that <u>you can catch flies with more honey than vinegar</u> is often invoked with respect to business and politics.

   (A) you can catch flies with more honey than vinegar
   (B) honey can catch more flies than vinegar
   (C) you can catch more flies with honey than with vinegar
   (D) you can catch flies with honey much more than vinegar
   (E) you can catch flies with honey much more than with vinegar

5. Armando was surprised by the film because he thought <u>not only that it was entertaining but that it raised provocative questions as well</u>.

   (A) not only that it was entertaining but that it raised provocative questions as well
   (B) not only that it was entertaining and also that it raised provocative questions as well
   (C) that it was entertaining but in addition that it raised provocative questions as well
   (D) that it was entertaining but it also raised provocative questions
   (E) that it was entertaining and he also thought that it raised provocative questions

GO ON TO THE NEXT PAGE ⟩

6. In the early years of the twentieth century, New York debutante <u>Caresse Crosby refusing to be constrained by corsets and customs: she invented</u> the first brassiere and sold the design to Warner's for $1500.

    (A) Caresse Crosby refusing to be constrained by corsets and customs: she invented
    (B) Caresse Crosby, angrily refusing to be constrained by corsets and customs, invented
    (C) Caresse Crosby was refusing to be constrained by corsets and customs because she invented
    (D) Caresse Crosby refused to be constrained by corsets and customs: she invented
    (E) Caresse Crosby was a debutante who often refused to be constrained by corsets and customs, and she invented

7. <u>The requirement for a healthful vegetarian diet during childhood and adolescence is</u> sufficient iron and plenty of protein from plant, rather than animal, sources.

    (A) The requirement for a healthful vegetarian diet during childhood and adolescence is
    (B) To have a healthful vegetarian diet during childhood and adolescence it requires
    (C) A healthful vegetarian diet during childhood and adolescence requires
    (D) In healthful vegetarian diets during childhood and adolescence is required
    (E) As for healthful vegetarian diet during childhood and adolescence

8. Study-abroad programs often involve a semester spent with a host family <u>which they</u> can experience the local way of life firsthand.

    (A) which they
    (B) during which a student
    (C) through which they
    (D) and a student
    (E) where a student

9. Some students regard mathematics as the subject they find most <u>challenging; others regard it as</u> a means to improve their reasoning skills.

    (A) challenging; others regard it as
    (B) challenging, to others it is
    (C) challenging; for others regarding it as
    (D) challenging, but it is regarded by others to be
    (E) challenging, but regarding it, others are

10. <u>Being that he is a gifted entertainer</u>, Odds Bodkin brings to life stories such as *The Odyssey* and King Arthur's adventures using only his voice, a harp, and a hand drum.

    (A) Being that he is a gifted entertainer
    (B) In being a gifted entertainer
    (C) A gifted entertainer
    (D) Although he is a gifted entertainer
    (E) Entertaining giftedly,

11. A study of stocks and bonds <u>reveal interest earned on corporate and municipal bonds tend to be</u> lower than earnings from stocks, but bond interest is virtually guaranteed.

    (A) reveal interest earned on corporate and municipal bonds tend to be
    (B) reveals interest earned on corporate and municipal bonds tends to be
    (C) reveal interest earned on corporate and municipal bonds that tend to be
    (D) is revealing corporate and municipal bond interest tending to be
    (E) reveals that interest earned on corporate and municipal bonds tends to be

12. <u>Viewing the context of the book</u>, the words "impulsive" and "blunt" are supposed to put the senator in a bad light.

    (A) Viewing the context of the book
    (B) In the context of the book
    (C) When the book's context is viewed
    (D) Taking into account its context
    (E) Examining the book's context

GO ON TO THE NEXT PAGE ⟩

13. By the 1980s, most large corporations had come to depend on a bloated corps of middle managers, <u>each of whom were servants</u> as much to his or her individual profit as to that of the company.

    (A) each of whom were servants
    (B) each of whom was a servant
    (C) each being servants
    (D) all a servant
    (E) which were all servants

14. For over forty years, Newbery Award-winning <u>Madeleine L'Engle, author of scores of books, is married to Hugh Franklin, the actor</u> who played Dr. Charles Tyler in the series *All My Children* until his death.

    (A) Madeleine L'Engle, author of scores of books, is married to Hugh Franklin, the actor

    (B) Madeleine L'Engle, author of scores of books, married actor Hugh Franklin,

    (C) Madeleine L'Engle, who is the proud author of a multitude of books, was married to Hugh Franklin, the actor

    (D) Madeleine L'Engle, author of scores of books, was married to Hugh Franklin, the actor

    (E) Madeleine and Hugh Franklin, the married actor

STOP
If you finish before time is called, you may check your work on this section only.
Do not turn to any other section in the test.

NO TEST MATERIAL ON THIS PAGE.

PRACTICE TEST 9: ANSWER KEY

2 Math	3 Reading	4 Writing	5 Math	7 Reading	8 Math	9 Reading	10 Writing
1. D	1. C	1. A	1. E	1. A	1. A	1. D	1. A
2. A	2. B	2. B	2. D	2. B	2. E	2. B	2. C
3. E	3. D	3. E	3. C	3. B	3. E	3. D	3. D
4. C	4. B	4. E	4. D	4. C	4. C	4. A	4. C
5. B	5. E	5. C	5. C	5. E	5. B	5. D	5. D
6. E	6. D	6. D	6. C	6. E	6. B	6. A	6. D
7. A	7. A	7. A	7. D	7. B	7. E	7. D	7. C
8. C	8. C	8. B	8. D	8. D	8. C	8. A	8. B
9. D	9. C	9. D	9. 240	9. C	9. B	9. C	9. A
10. B	10. D	10. A	10. 110	10. B	10. D	10. D	10. C
11. A	11. A	11. C	11. 15	11. E	11. D	11. B	11. E
12. D	12. C	12. A	12. 2,544	12. C	12. E	12. D	12. B
13. C	13. B	13. C	13. 28	13. C	13. C	13. D	13. B
14. B	14. C	14. C	14. 6	14. D	14. D	14. C	14. D
15. E	15. E	15. D	15. 19	15. B	15. B	15. A	
16. D	16. A	16. C	16. 0	16. A	16. E	16. D	
17. B	17. C	17. B	17. $\frac{1}{5}$ or .2	17. C		17. B	
18. A	18. B	18. B	18. 27	18. A		18. C	
19. B	19. D	19. E		19. A		19. E	
20. A	20. B	20. D		20. B			
	21. B	21. C		21. C			
	22. A	22. E		22. A			
	23. C	23. E		23. E			
	24. A	24. B		24. B			
		25. A					
		26. A					
		27. C					
		28. D					
		29. B					
		30. E					
		31. C					
		32. E					
		33. B					
		34. E					
		35. D					

SAT SCORING WORKSHEET

For directions on how to score your SAT practice test, see pages 10–11.

SAT Writing Section

Total Writing Multiple-Choice Questions Correct: [   ]

Total Writing Multiple-Choice Questions Incorrect: _____ ÷ 4 = [   ]

Grammar Raw Score: [   ]

Your Essay Score (2–12): _____ × 2 = [   ]

Writing Raw Score: [   ]

Grammar Scaled Subscore [   ]

Compare the Grammar Raw Score with the Writing Multiple-Choice Subscore Conversion Table on page 752 to find the Grammar Scaled Subscore.

Writing Scaled Score [   ]

Compare Raw Score with SAT Score Conversion Table on page 752 to find the Writing Scaled Score.

SAT Critical Reading Section

Total Critical Reading Questions Correct: [   ]

Total Critical Reading Questions Incorrect: _____ ÷ 4 = [   ]

Critical Reading Raw Score: [   ]

Critical Reading Scaled Score [   ]

Compare Raw Score with SAT Score Conversion Table on page 752 to find the Critical Reading Scaled Score.

SAT Math Section

Total Math Grid-In Questions Correct: [   ]

Total Math Multiple-Choice Questions Correct: [   ]

Total Math Multiple-Choice Questions Incorrect: _____ ÷ 4 = [   ]

Don't include wrong answers from grid-ins!

Math Raw Score: [   ]

Math Scaled Score [   ]

Compare Raw Score with SAT Score Conversion Table on page 752 to find the Math Scaled Score.

SAT SCORE CONVERSION TABLE

Raw Score	Writing Scaled Score	Reading Scaled Score	Math Scaled Score	Raw Score	Writing Scaled Score	Reading Scaled Score	Math Scaled Score	Raw Score	Writing Scaled Score	Reading Scaled Score	Math Scaled Score
73	800			47	590–630	600–640	660–700	21	400–440	410–450	440–480
72	790–800			46	590–630	590–630	650–690	20	390–430	400–440	430–470
71	780–800			45	580–620	580–620	650–690	19	380–420	400–440	430–470
70	770–800			44	570–610	580–620	640–680	18	370–410	390–430	420–460
69	770–800			43	570–610	570–610	630–670	17	370–410	380–420	410–450
68	760–800			42	560–600	570–610	620–660	16	360–400	370–410	400–440
67	760–800	800		41	560–600	560–600	610–650	15	350–390	360–400	400–440
66	760–800	770–800		40	550–590	550–590	600–640	14	340–380	350–390	390–430
65	750–790	760–800		39	540–580	550–590	590–630	13	330–370	340–380	380–420
64	740–780	750–790		38	530–570	540–580	590–630	12	320–360	340–380	360–400
63	730–770	740–780		37	530–570	530–570	580–620	11	320–360	330–370	350–390
62	720–760	730–770		36	520–560	530–570	570–610	10	310–350	320–360	340–380
61	710–750	720–760		35	510–550	520–560	560–600	9	300–340	310–350	330–370
60	700–740	710–750		34	500–540	520–560	560–600	8	290–330	300–340	320–360
59	690–730	700–740		33	490–530	510–550	550–590	7	280–320	300–340	310–350
58	680–720	690–730		32	480–520	500–540	540–580	6	270–310	290–330	300–340
57	680–720	680–720		31	470–510	490–530	530–570	5	260–300	280–320	290–330
56	670–710	670–710		30	470–510	480–520	520–560	4	240–280	270–310	280–320
55	660–720	670–710		29	460–500	470–510	520–560	3	230–270	250–290	280–320
54	650–690	660–700	760–800	28	450–490	470–510	510–550	2	230–270	240–280	270–310
53	640–680	650–690	740–780	27	440–480	460–500	500–540	1	220–260	220–260	260–300
52	630–670	640–680	730–770	26	430–470	450–490	490–530	0	210–250	200–240	250–290
51	630–670	630–670	710–750	25	420–460	440–480	480–520	−1	200–240	200–230	230–270
50	620–660	620–660	690–730	24	410–450	430–470	470–510	−2	200–230	200–220	220–260
49	610–650	610–650	680–720	23	410–450	430–470	460–500	−3	200–220	200–210	200–240
48	600–640	600–640	670–710	22	400–440	420–460	450–490				

WRITING MULTIPLE-CHOICE SUBSCORE CONVERSION TABLE

Grammar Raw Score	Grammar Scaled Subscore	Grammar Raw Score	Grammar Scaled Subscore	Grammar Raw Score	Grammar Scaled Subscore	Grammar Raw Score	Grammar Scaled Subscore	Grammar Raw Score	Grammar Scaled Subscore
49	78–80	38	67–71	27	55–59	16	42–46	5	30–34
48	77–80	37	66–70	26	54–58	15	41–45	4	29–33
47	75–79	36	65–69	25	53–57	14	40–44	3	28–32
46	74–78	35	64–68	24	52–56	13	39–43	2	27–31
45	72–76	34	63–67	23	51–55	12	38–42	1	25–29
44	72–76	33	62–66	22	50–54	11	36–40	0	24–28
43	71–75	32	61–65	21	49–53	10	35–39	−1	22–26
42	70–74	31	60–64	20	47–51	9	34–38	−2	20–23
41	69–73	30	59–63	19	46–50	8	33–37	−3	20–22
40	68–72	29	58–62	18	45–49	7	32–36		
39	68–72	28	56–60	17	44–48	6	31–35		

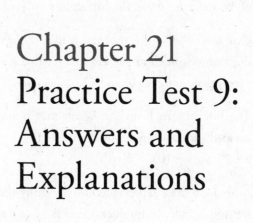

Chapter 21
Practice Test 9:
Answers and
Explanations

SECTION 2

1. **D** The perimeter of rectangle *JKYX* is made from two sides the same length as the sides of the square and two sides that are half the length of the sides of the square. We want to find *JK*, the length of the side of the square. Make *s* is the side of the square, and use the given perimeter of *JKYX* = 12: $s + s + \frac{1}{2}s + \frac{1}{2}s = 12$, so $3s = 12$ and $s = 4$, answer (D).

2. **A** Simplify the original equation: $5k + 8 = -7 + 2k$ becomes $3k = -15$. The question asks for the value of $3k$, so we are done; the correct answer is (A) –15.

3. **E** One way to solve this problem is to come up with your own number for *k*. Any even integer will do, and we can eliminate any answer that gives an even value. If $k = 4$, (A), (B), (C) and (D) give even values of 6, 12, 14 and 12, respectively. (E) gives a value of 15, and is the only odd answer.

4. **C** The information from the figure that is important is the straight line beneath the triangle is divided into two angles of *z*° and 103°. There are 180° in a straight line, so $z + 103 = 180$ and $z = 77$, answer (C).

5. **B** Add up all three expressions and divide by the number of expressions (3) to find the average. Alternatively, think of a number line: 8 is exactly at the midpoint of $8 - a$ and $8 + a$, so it is the average value. You can verify this by substituting an easy number for *a*. (B), 8 is correct.

6. **E** The equation of a line is $y = mx + b$. The *b* value is the *y*-intercept. In this case, we know from the figure that the *y*-intercept is positive. Eliminate answers with a negative *y*-intercept: (B), (C), and (D). The difference between (A) and (E) is in the *m* value, which represents the slope of the line. The line points downward to the right, so it has a negative slope. Eliminate (A); (E) has the negative slope.

7. **A** Set *C* is {5, 10, and 15} and set *D* is {1, 2, 4, 5, 10, 20}. The *union* of a set includes all of the numbers in one or both sets. The union of set *C* and set *D* is {1, 2, 4, 5, 10, 15, 20}. Only (A) includes all the members of both sets.

8. **C** Based on information in the statement about the class, (A) is not possible. (B) is not necessarily true, (C) is true, because we know that *every student* in the class *enjoys making masks*, there is no one in the class who does not enjoy masks. (D) is not necessarily true, and (E) contradicts the statement in the question.

9. **D** We have two equations, so stack them and see if adding or subtracting the equations will lead to $5s + 3t$. In this case we want to subtract:

$$6s - 2t = 10$$
$$\underline{- \; (s - 5t = 14)}$$

which, when the subtraction sign is distributed is

$$6s - 2t = 10$$
$$\underline{-s + 5t = -14}$$
$$5s + 3t = -4, \text{ answer (D)}.$$

10. **B** Try out the answers in place of B in the question. The correct answer is the unit's digit of a number that divides evenly into 299. In (A), $299 \div 22$ does not give an integer. In (B) $299 \div 23 = 13$, an integer. None of the other answers result in an integer.

11. **A** Start with a full jar: 1. From the 1 full jar subtract $\frac{1}{8}$, then subtract $\frac{1}{4}$, then subtract $\frac{1}{2}$. We're left with $\frac{1}{8}$ of a jar of cookies, and the remaining 12 cookies are mint. So $\frac{1}{8}$ of the jar is mint. Translate: $\frac{1}{8} \times$ (# in jar) = 12. Solve to get 96 cookies total in the jar. We need to know the number of peanut butter cookies: $\frac{1}{4}$ of the cookies in the jar are peanut butter, so $\frac{1}{4}(96) = 24$, (A).

12. **D** The only rule we know is that the third term is a multiple of 3 and every second term must be a multiple of 2. A list of numbers such as 1, 2, 3, 4, 5, 6, 7, 8, 9,... fits this rule. While in this list, the 144th term would be 144, that answer is not among the choices. The number 144 is even and obviously a multiple of 2, but it is also divisible by 3. Thus, every 6th term is divisible by 6. The only number in the answer choices that is also divisible by both 2 and 3 is (D) 114. The rest of the answers are either not even or not divisible by 3.

13. **C** Try plugging numbers into the given equation, but be careful to use the right kind of numbers. The values a and b must be positive integers, so don't use negative integers or zero. Start with $a = 1$: What values of b can work? Start with $5(1) + 7b < 20$, and subtract 5 from both sides. Now we know that $7b < 15$. The inequality allows b to be either 1 or 2, so there are at least two ordered pairs that work: (1, 1) and (1, 2). Now make $a = 2$. Now what values of b can work? The inequality now allows only b to equal 1: $5(2) + 7(1) < 20$. No other positive integer works, so (2, 1) is our third ordered pair. Can $a = 3$? If so, we have $5(3) + 7b < 20$. Subtract 15 from both sides to get $7b < 5$. There are no integer values of b that satisfy the inequality. Therefore, there are three ordered pairs that satisfy the inequality, answer (C).

14. **B** Be careful of answer (A): you can't just take the values of a and c; the b value must be the same in each relationship. The first ratio is $a : b$, which equals 2 : 5. If b is 5 in the ratio of $b : c$, we get 5 : 20. Now we can see that $a : b : c = 2 : 5 : 20$, and $a : c = 2 : 20$, or 1 : 10 as in answer (B).

15. E To find the price of the minimum selling price of the fifth plot, we have to perform several steps. The amount of money that the first four plots is sold for is given per square meters. The first sentence says that the land was 1000 square meters and divided into 5 equal plots, so each plot is 200 square meters. At $320 per square meter means that each plot was sold for $64,000, and the total selling price of the four plots is $256,000. There needs to be a profit of at least 20% of the amount originally paid for the land, so 120% of $300,000 = $\frac{120}{100} \times 300,000$ = $360,000. This is the minimum total of the selling price of the fifth plot and the selling price of the first four plots. $360,000 – $256,000 = $104,000, as in answer (E).

16. D One easy approach to this problem is to plug in values for the variables. For instance, try $a = 8$, $b = 2$, and $c = 3$. Eight customers each spend $30 every 2 hours, which is $240 in two hours, or $120 per hour. Therefore, in 3 hours, the store will make $360. Use the same variables in the answers to see which equals $360. (A) is $5\frac{5}{8}$, (B) is $\frac{1}{40}$, (C) $22\frac{1}{2}$, (D) is 360, and (E) is $2\frac{1}{2}$, so (D) is the only one that works.

17. B To find the diagonal of a cube or rectangular solid, you can find the diagonal of the base by using the Pythagorean theorem with the sides of the base. You can then use the Pythagorean theorem with the height and the diagonal of the base as legs to find the hypotenuse that is also the diagonal of the solid. In this case, our dimensions are k, 1, and 1. It is easiest to come up with a value for k to work with. If $k = 5$, then the dimensions of the base are 1 by 5, so $1^2 + 5^2 = c^2$. This means that $c^2 = 26$. Don't worry about finding the value of c: we'll be using the squared value in the second. The height is 1, so $b^2 + c^2 = d^2$, and $1 + 26 = d^2$, and $d = \sqrt{27}$. Replace the k in the answers with 5, and the correct answer will result in $\sqrt{27}$. (A) gives $1 + \sqrt{26}$, (B) gives $\sqrt{27}$ —a match. (C) gives 7; (D) gives $\sqrt{15}$ and (E) gives $\sqrt{10}$. Algebraically, using the "Super Pythagorean" equation of $a^2 + b^2 + c^2 = d^2$ and replacing with values we get $1^2 + 1^2 + k^2 = d^2$, or $2 + k^2 = d^2$. Solving for d by taking the root of both sides gives the equation seen in (B): $\sqrt{2 + k^2}$.

18. A We know the area of square $KMNO$ is 50, so the square root of 50, or $5\sqrt{2}$, is the length of the sides of the square. Line MO is a radius of the circle, and it creates two 45-45-90 right triangles. The ratio of sides in this special right triangle is $1 : 1 : \sqrt{2}$. The legs in this case are $5\sqrt{2}$, so multiply all the values in the ratio by $5\sqrt{2}$ to find that $MO = 10$. This is also the radius of the circle, so now we can answer the question about the circle's area. Area = πr^2 = 100π, (A).

19.　**B**　The line, after it had been reflected about the *x*- and *y*-axes would be parallel to the line in the figure, but higher up on the *y*-axis. Draw this out on the figure: the first reflection, about the *y*-axis should pass through (0, −2), where the original line crosses the *y*-axis, and through (−3, 0). Now reflect this new line about the *x*-axis. This third line passes through (−3, 0), where the second line passes through the *x*-axis and through (0, 2). This line has a slope of $\frac{2}{3}$. Only the point in (B) and another point in the twice-reflected line, such as (−3, 0), have a slope of $\frac{2}{3}$. (A) is the point at where the original line and the first reflection cross. (C) is out because the *x*-value of the line is positive when the *y* value is positive. (D) is in the original line, and (E) is impossible because the twice-reflected line passes through (−3, 0).

20.　**A**　*QR* has a length of 20 and is the diameter of the circle, so we know that the radius is 10. We can form a triangle and use the Pythagorean theorem to find the value of hypotenuse *PR*. From the center of the circle to the *x* axis is 10, and the distance from the *x*-axis to the base of the triangle is 6, so the height of this triangle is 16. The base is 12 (6 from the width of the small square and another 6 to the diameter of the circle). $16^2 + 12^2 = c^2$, and *PR* = 20, answer (A). This is a multiple of the 3:4:5 Pythagorean triplet. You can also use the distance formula $\sqrt{(x_2 - x_1)^2 + (y_2 - y_1)^2}$.

SECTION 3

1.　**C**　The semicolon is like an equal sign between the first and second parts of the sentence. Like the first part, the second describes a situation that would cause a lion *to relinquish* its food. The word from the answer choices that is closest to *relinquish*, or "go without," is (C), *forgo*.

2.　**B**　The miser is *afraid of losing money* so he would rather not "give up" *what he already possessed*. Eliminate choices in which the second word does not describe losing something: (A) and, (B) are out. The first blank must describe a situation that had the potential to make money, which is the definition of *lucrative*, in (B), which works well with *risk* in the sentence.

3. **D** The word *because* in the sentence indicates that there is a similarity between what comes before and after. After, the sentence explains why the scientific process is *constant*, which is the meaning of the second blank. Scientific steps *have been* "the same" for centuries. Eliminate answers in which the word for the second blank is not close in meaning to "the same." (B) and (E) are out. The first blank is influenced by the word *despite*, which indicates that what comes after is the opposite of what comes before, so a good word for the first blank is "changes." (B), (D), and (E) are all close, but only (D) *advances...unaltered* is a match for both blanks.

4. **B** The words *while beneficial* and *may actually* indicate that the second blank means something that is the opposite of beneficial. Look for answers with a negative second word. Keep (B), (D), and (E). The other two are positive. For the first blank, we need something that limits the danger of the antibiotic, such as "caution." Of the three choices we have left, only *moderation* (B) fits.

5. **E** We need a word for the blank that means that the *pioneers* were "not wanting" *to be beholden*: they didn't want to owe anyone any favors. The only answer close in meaning to not wanting something is *loath*, which means "unwilling; reluctant." (E) is correct.

6. **D** There is a relationship between the blanks. The phrase *failed to make* indicates that the blanks are similar, so that "good" *treatment failed to make him feel* "good," or "bad" *treatment failed to make him feel* "bad." The context of the sentence indicates the first blank is a negative word, so eliminate (A) and (E). The sentence states that the man had a strong sense of *self worth*, so the treatment failed to make him feel a "lack of self worth." Only *inferior* matches from the three choices we had left, so (D) is correct.

7. **A** The semicolon is like an equal sign between the parts of the sentence; each part explains or describes the same ideas as the other. The *tendency* and the *manner* are the same thing, so we need a word for the blank that means "*aggressively exaggerating.*" (A) *overblown* comes closest in meaning. Many of the words in the answers are negative, but don't specifically relate to the *aggressive exaggeration*.

8. **C** The word *merely* indicates that the word in the blank means "something insignificant" that is not worth an *indictment*. Eliminate (D) and (E) because these are strongly negative words. (A) *windfall* is a very positive thing, and doesn't make sense here. A *lapse* is more insignificant than a *plot*, which takes some effort, so (C) is correct.

9. **C** In (A) *flippant*, or "frivolously disrespectful" is not an apt description for Passage 1. (B) is out; both passages describe the *grave* situations that face people who come up with new ideas. (C) is correct: Passage 2 can be seen as more hopeful in the final lines of the passage. Passage 1 states that *those who have courage...pay the same penalty*. Passage 2 end with *the glory of the vision at the end is worthwhile*. There is no evidence for (D) or (E) in the passage.

10.   **D**   The authors are similar in the idea that a person who has a new idea will have a rough time, but these ideas are important to society. (A) is extreme because of the word *All*. There is no mention of *travel* as in (B). The *politicians* in (C) do not relate strongly to either passage. (D) is correct because it indicates that new ideas are essential for human progress. (E) may be true, but there is no evidence in either passage to support whether the authors would agree with the statement.

11.   **A**   Passage 1 indicates that people who enact change have to *pay the penalty*, even though after they die, their ideas may be celebrated. Passage 2 describes these people as those with *high ideals* who can stick to a *rugged and hard path*. (A) is pretty close to these ideas: *victims* indicates the unfair treatment they received for ideas later celebrated and *explorers* is captured by Passage 2, especially earlier in the passage, when the author describes those who enact change as those who get beyond *the bounds of self* and deal with the *world*. In (B) *dangerous* is extreme and there is no evidence for *hermits*. Eliminate (C) because *mourning* is not mentioned in Passage 1, although *deaths* is. There is no proof of *envy,* so eliminate (D). There is no support that the sacrifices were *unnecessary*; Passage 1 indicates that the ideas are so important that their originators are celebrated after their deaths for them.

12.   **C**   Look for evidence in the passage for each answer as a description of *people who advance humanity*: There is no mention of (A), (B), or (E) the passage. (C) is correct because *the minority is always right* in line 3 of passage 1 and *those singular men* in line 17 of Passage 2 indicate that the people who have great ideas are rare. (D) is incorrect: Passage 1 mentions both women and men, and *men* in Passage 2 generally refers to "humankind."

13.   **B**   The assertion is that *Callot and Meryon made prints that…were meant to be printed in large numbers.* Eliminate (A): the term *printmakers* represents the "other side" in a distinction between *Callot and Meyron* and *those followers of Hayter*. (B) is correct because it addresses the *large numbers* of prints. (C) is not mentioned in the passage. The *complete satisfaction* in (D) is extreme. (E) is incorrect: a distinction is provided in lines 8–13.

14.   **C**   In the passage in lines 14–17, the *printmakers* are described as having *found that creating in a print medium is…totally satisfying.* This is best paraphrased in (C), *fulfilled*. There is no evidence for the other answers in the passage.

15.   **E**   In lines 22–27, the quote of Sylvan Cole describes *this change that was taking place* which was from printmaking for mass production, and the artistic printmaking practice of making few prints. The pronoun *this* indicates that the change was mentioned previously, and in fact the whole paragraph has been discussing how printmaking changed between one era and another. The passage does not indicate that *Cole,* in (A) changed anything; he just explains it. There is also *no homage to a notable pioneer*, as in (B). (C) is incorrect because *Abstract Expressionism* is mentioned only in line 23, not *examined*. There is a relationship between painting and printmaking described in the quote, but the question asks why the author includes it. The reason is that it is support from an expert about the changes in printmaking that the whole essay so far has been discussing. This is paraphrased in (E).

16. **A** The question asks what the second paragraph does to help the passage. The short paragraph discusses that *Before the war* printmakers made only prints, and made lots of them. In the first paragraphs, the point was made that there was a big change from prolific printmaking for mass distribution to smaller runs of prints as art. The third paragraph discusses how the number of people studying printmaking changed drastically because of programs for those who fought in the war. We need an answer that mentions both *war* and that printmaking changed. (A) mentions both of these and seems reasonable, but take a quick look at the rest of the answers: (B) is the opposite of what we are looking for. *Callot and Meryon* in (C) were only discussed in the first paragraph. (D) is not mentioned in the passage, and (E) is extreme and without evidence from the passage.

17. **C** Go back to the passage and use the context to come up with a word to replace *adornment*. In the passage, *adornment* describes the use of artwork in schools and government buildings. While many of the answers could refer to prints, in this case, these visual artworks are more for *decoration* than just for *enjoyment* so (C) is closest.

18. **B** The passage, states that the G.I. Bill gave veterans *the opportunity to attend college* (lines 37–38). This is stated to be *during a period of prosperity* (line 34), so it meant that *opportunity* was that the government paid the schools the money for the veterans' education. (B) is the best paraphrase of these elements. The opposite of (A) is true. The G.I. Bill was not just for *lost* veterans. (D) has the wrong chronology: students using the GI Bill directed money to institutions that used the funds to expand. There is no evidence for (E) in the passage.

19. **D** Go back to the passage and use the context to come up with a word to replace *lost*. In lines 38–39 of the passage, the *"lost"* are described as those that *had little direction*—they didn't know what to do with themselves. The word *aimless* in (D) describes this quality best. While *lost* can have the meaning of some of the other words in the answers, these do not fit in the context of the passage.

20. **B** In the passage, the *Organization Man* is described as one who had *great success* because of the contribution of the *less independent group* of veterans who enjoyed the *organized lifestyle* of the military. This is best paraphrased in (B). There is no support for any of the other answers in the passage.

21. **B** The *phenomenal expansion* in the passage is that of *art education*. One reason mentioned is that the *atmosphere* of art departments was appealing, and in lines 47–53, the *expansion* is described at two levels: new and advanced programs for those with college degrees at *institutions of higher learning*, and older, established schools for beginning students that were *filled to capacity*. This is all addressed in the education experiences listed in (B). The membership of the army (A) is not a reason, but the number of those using the G.I. Bill to obtain art education. (C) is extreme, (D) is not mentioned, and (E) does not refer to art at all.

22. **A** The best supported answer is (A). The effect of the *proliferation* is mentioned in lines (59–77) the passage as causing an increase in the number of printmakers, which in turned caused more *institutions* whose purpose was to *exhibit* and *publish and sell* prints. To fill all this demand, more organizations were created in order to *encourage the creation of prints*. There is no evidence for (B), (D), and (E), and (C) is extreme due to the use of *all*.

23. **C** The descriptions of the *new organizations* are both *regional and international groups* that span a wide range of specific areas of printmaking. (A) is not mentioned in the passage. There is no proof that either (B) or (E) is true. (D) is mentioned in the passage, but not in the final paragraph. This leaves (C) as the correct answer, which is supported by lines 70–77 in the passage.

24. **A** (A) describes *Callot and Meryon,* not Lasansky. There is evidence in the passage for all the other answers as descriptions of Lasansky. (B) is in lines 56–58. (C) is in lines 14–16. (D) is in lines 16–18. (E) is in lines 18–19.

SECTION 4

1. **A** The sentence is correct as written. (B) changes the meaning. (C) is wordy. In (D), changing *hired* to *made* makes the sentence less precise. In (E) *creative* describes the team, but it should describe the *advertisers*.

2. **B** The sentence is wordier than in needs to be and contains the unnecessary reference *it*. (B) is correct because it eliminates *it* and clarifies the sentence. (C) changes the meaning. (D) contains the unnecessary pronoun *it*. The multiple use of *sonar* in (E) is redundant.

3. **E** The sentence as written contains a comma splice. (B) and (D) are more passive than is typically correct on the SAT. (C) is awkward in its use of *his* before *Mill* is mentioned. (E) is correct. The semicolon is used to connect two closely related ideas in two phrases that could each stand on its own as a sentence. Both phrases have Mill as the active subject.

4. **E** There is an idiom error in the sentence. The word *than* should be used with more instead of *and*. Eliminate (A), (B), and (C). Of the remaining two, (E) is correct because *a skill or trade* is parallel in construction to *a necessity*.

5. **C** The sentence as written uses an unnecessary pronoun, *they*, and the awkward construction *it is*. (B) uses an improper comparison words *wisest* and *most* when only two possibilities exist. (C) is correct because the phrase before the comma describes *women*, and *women* is the word that follows directly after the comma. (D) is awkward with the ending, *it is thought*. (E) has a pronoun agreement error between *they* and *a woman*.

6. **D** The comma and the word *which* indicate that the phrase after it describes *expensive* instead of *nightlife*. (B) changes the meaning of the sentence. The comma joins two phrases in (C) that could stand on their own as sentences, which is a comma splice. (D) is correct: both *exhilarating and exhausting* are in parallel form and refer to *nightlife*. In (E), if *thus* should be used with *exhausts*, not *exhausting*.

7. **A** The sentence is correct as written. (B), (C), and (D) improperly use the adverb form when the word is meant to be an adjective that still describes *people*. (E) is much more awkward than (A).

8. **B** The sentence as written has a subject-verb agreement problem between the plural subject and *was*. Eliminate (A), (D), and (E). The correct idiom is *just as...so too*. (B) is correct because (C) improperly includes *and* as well.

9. **D** The sentence is redundant because it includes *a chance* and *is* possible. (B) *had an indication* is wordy and passive. There is a subject-verb agreement in (C) between *a chance* and *were*, and it retains the redundancy problem. (D) is correct. (E) is redundant.

10. **A** The sentence is correct as written. The verb construction may seem strange, but it joins the time periods and events correctly. The other answer choices are not as strong: their *ing* constructions make the sentence less direct and active.

11. **C** The wording is unclear in the sentence as written: *of whom* should refer to a person, but it seems that in (A) it refers to a book. The pronoun *its* in (B) does not agree with the multiple works referred to. (C) is correct; *of which* correctly indicates objects rather than people. (D) is not parallel, and (E) becomes unclear when *of which* moves to after *novels*, and changes the meaning of the sentence.

12. **A** The *ing* form of *explaining* in (A) creates a sentence fragment. It should be *explains*.

13. **C** There is a subject-verb agreement between *characters* and *lives* in (C). The descriptive phrase gets between the subject and verb and makes it difficult to see the error. (C) should be *live on*.

14. **C** The pronoun *you* in (C) does not agree with *Anyone*. (C) should be *his or her*.

15. **D** The verbs in the sentence are not parallel: *had done* in (D) should agree with *ran*, and therefore should be *did*.

16. **C** There is a subject-verb agreement problem between *schedules* and *has* in (C), which should be *have*.

17. **B** Tibet is a singular subject, and so *contain* in (B) should be *contains* in order to agree with *Tibet*.

18. **B** The pronouns *one* and *they* do not agree. The error is in (B).

19. **E** There is no error in the sentence as written. The phrase in (D) may sound a little odd, but it is correct and uses the proper idiom *test on*.

20. **D** Wheat is a plant, so Kamm *grew* it. The word *raised* is correctly used with livestock, not crops.

21. **C** Check that pronoun agree with nouns. *Their...graduates* refers to the college's graduates. Because *college* is singular, the pronoun in (C) should be *its*.

22. **E** There is no error in the sentence as written.

23. **E** There is no error in the sentence as written. Make sure you can identify and name a specific error before selecting an answer.

24. **B** The subject of the sentence is *survey*, which does not agree with the verb *show* in (B). The plural *statistics* right before *show* makes the verb "sound" alright, but *statistics* is just part of a phrase describing the *survey*.

25. **A** The pronoun *I* in (A) should be the object pronoun *me*. If *my sister* were not in the sentence, it would be more obvious that *my father taught me* is correct.

26. **A** There is an idiom error in (A). The correct idiom is *fascination with*.

27. **C** There are multiple items referred to—a scarf and a hat—so they become a plural subject. The pronoun *it* in (C) should be *them*.

28. **D** There is a pronoun error in (D). The subject is *the crowd*, which is singular, so *they* should be *it*.

29. **B** The word *Neither* agrees with singular pronouns because it refers to the two people separately. The pronoun *their* should be *his*. The error is in (B).

30. **E** Check out each sentence in the passage and determine how necessary it is to the passage. Eliminate (A); sentence 3 is part of the main idea. Eliminate (B); 8 is connected to sentence 9. Eliminate (C); sentence 10 is a good transition to the next paragraph. Eliminate (D) because it tells that the author fell, which is necessary information. (E) is correct: it's disposable because sentence 14 transitions well into sentence 16.

31. **C** The conjunction in (A) *however*, is incorrect. (B) has an awkward structure. (C) is clear and concise. (D) has too many *ing* words that weaken it. (E) changes the meaning of the sentence.

32. **E** In (A) *was not* does not put the action far enough into the past. (B) changes the meaning of the sentence. (C) contains a double negative. (D) uses a verb tense that does not agree with *I'd*. (E) is correct because *had* does agree with *I'd*.

33. **B** In sentence 8, *George* comes out of nowhere. The ambiguity of the sentence can be eliminated by mentioning George earlier in the passage. Only (B) identifies George as *my friend*.

34. **E** Check each word in the sentence and see which one we can live without. (A) *same* is necessary to know which *direction*. (B) *myself* is necessary, or we don't know what gets *braced*. (C) *enough* is necessary for describing *hands*. In (D) *in* is a necessary preposition. (E) is correct because *stand* alone works fine without *up*.

35. **D** To determine which answer would best link sentences 16 and 17, first see what the two sentences are about. Sentence 16 describes the rough time had by the author. Sentence 17 is about how the author might ski again someday, but watching it on TV is enough for him. (A) is the opposite of how things are described in sentence 16. (B) doesn't make sense, because the author just reported on his day of skiing. (C) is possible, but doesn't work very well with sentence 17. (D) is correct because it fits in the theme that skiing was difficult for the author. (E) does not work because it doesn't fit in with the idea in 17 that he has a *newfound respect* for skiers.

SECTION 5

1. **E** We know that there are 180° in a straight line, and this is divided among the 3 angles. $30 + 90 + (x - 30) = 180$, so $(x - 30) = 60$. Add 30 to both sides, and $x = 90$, as in (E).

2. **D** To simplify the equation $\frac{\sqrt{x}}{2} = 2\sqrt{2}$, multiply both sides by 2 to get $\sqrt{x} = 4\sqrt{2}$. Squaring both sides gives $x = \left(4\sqrt{2}\right)^2$, so $x = 32$, answer (D).

3. **C** Because *ABCD* is a rectangle, all the corners = 90°. *BD* cuts the angle in half, so $x = 45$, answer (C).

4. **D** A line that is tangent to a circle forms a 90° angle with a radius or diameter. Draw diameter *AB* to form right triangle *ABC*. Because the circle has an area of 25π, the circle has a radius of 5, and a diameter of 10. The question states that $AC = 10$, so we have an isosceles right triangle, or a 45-45-90 triangle. The sides have a ratio of $1 : 1 : \sqrt{2}$. Because the legs are 10, the sides are $10 : 10 : 10\sqrt{2}$. Side *BC*, the hypotenuse, is $10\sqrt{2}$, answer (D).

5. **C** There are 180° in a triangle. We know this is a right triangle, so 90° are spoken for, and $x + y = 90$. The question states that $y = 2x$, so if we replace *y* with 2*x*, we have $x + 2x = 90$, so $3x = 90$ and $x = 30$. Now we have enough information to find *z* because we have a right triangle: $x + 90 + z = 180$, so replacing *x* we get $30 + 90 + z = 180$, and $z = 60$, answer (C).

6. **C** Solve for *a* first. $25 = \frac{(x^2 + 1)}{2}$, which simplifies to $x^2 = 49$, which means $x = \pm 7$. For *b*, $\frac{(11^2 + 1)}{2} = \frac{122}{2} = 61$. The two possibilities for answers are $61 - 7$ and $61 - (-7)$, which yield 54 and 68, respectively. However, only 68 is a choice. (C) is correct.

7. **D** Because we have two fractions, we can cross-multiply and isolate x: $\dfrac{x-d}{cx} = \dfrac{5}{2}$, so $5cx = 2x - 2d$. Get all the x values on one side to get $5cx - 2x = -2d$, then $x(5c - 2) = -2d$, and $x = \dfrac{-2d}{5c - 2}$, which is seen in (D). This problem, can also be solved by making up a value for x that is larger than 5, and finding values for c and d, but the cross-multiplication may be easier.

8. **D** The term *inversely proportional* means that the product of two numbers is always the same. This means that as one number goes down, the other goes up. The product of the hours of sleep and times being ill is the same in any case, so using the numbers from the problem, we see that $8 \times 3 = 6x$, and $24 = 6x$, so $x = 4$, answer (D).

9. **240** The information in this problem can be put into a proportion of miles over inches to find the number of miles represented by 2.4 inches. $\dfrac{100}{1} = \dfrac{x}{2.4}$. Cross-multiply to see that $240 = x$.

10. **110** If a figure has the note "not drawn to scale," redraw the figure. The question is talking about an isosceles triangle: $AB = BC$, so $\angle A = \angle C$. There are 180 degrees in a triangle, so $35 + 35 + x = 180$, and $x = 110$.

11. **15** If 15 occurs most often, it could occur as either two or three of the missing numbers. Plugging in 15 for all three makes the average of all five numbers (10, 15, 15, 15, 30) into 17, which disagrees with the given information. So 15 must be two of the three missing numbers. Call the remaining missing number x. If the average of all 5 numbers is 18, then $\dfrac{10 + 15 + 15 + 30 + x}{5} = 18$, and x is 20. Arranging the numbers in increasing order (10, 15, 15, 20, 30) shows you that the median (middle number) is 15. A shortcut: If *exactly* two of the numbers are 15, then the missing number is not 15, but it must be greater than 10 and less than 30 (from the given information). Thus, arranging the numbers in increasing order will give you either 10, 15, 15, x, 30 or 10, x, 15, 15, 30. Either way, 15 is the median.

12. **2,544** Use the percent increase/decrease formula. $\dfrac{\textit{difference}}{\textit{original}} \times 100 = \%$ change. The original is 2,400 and the percent increase is 6. Put these values into the equation, and solve for the difference, which is 144. Because the question asks for the total number of people with pets, not the difference, add the difference, 144, to the original, 2,400, to get 2,544.

13. **28** Draw any geometric figure that is described but not shown. A diagonal of a square forms two 45-45-90 right triangles. The ratio of sides in this special right triangle is $1 : 1 : \sqrt{2}$, and we know the hypotenuse is $7\sqrt{2}$, so the legs must have a length of 7. The legs are made of the sides of the square, so the four sides of the square each have length 7. The perimeter is thus $4 \times 7 = 28$.

14. **6** The number of pizzas consumed in 1960 is 2.45 and the number consumed in 1990 is 15.6. We want to find out what number multiplied by 2.45 equals 15.6. Because the question asks for a rounded number, we'll get close enough and make life easier by using 2.5 and 16 instead: $2.5 \times n = 16$. Then $n = 6.4$, or, rounded, about 6.

15. **19** We can break this down by tens, since most, but not all sets of 10 consecutive numbers have one number that includes the digit 5. In the 1–10 range, there's only 5. In the 11–20 range there's only 15. In the 21–30 range, there's only 25. In the 31–40 range there's only 35. In the 41–50 range, there are two: 45 and 50. In the 51–60 range there are nine: 51, 52, 53, 54, 55, 56, 57, 58, and 59. In the 61–70 range, there's only 65. In the 71–80 range, there's only 75. In the 81–90 range, there's only 85. In the 91–100 range, there's only 95. So $1 + 1 + 1 + 1 + 2 + 9 + 1 + 1 + 1 + 1 = 19$.

16. **0** Because the value $(x - y)$ is squared, it can never be negative. Since we want the lowest value possible, we should aim for 0 if the restrictions placed on the variables by the inequalities allow it. The question states that x^2 is less than or equal to 25, and y^2 is greater than or equal to 16. Solving for x and y gives $-5 \le x \le 5$ and $y \ge 4$ or $y \le -4$. We can make $x = y$ if $x = 4$ and $y = 4$. This gives a value of $(4 - 4)^2 = 0^2 = 0$.

17. $\dfrac{1}{5}$ **or .2**

Translate the information given. Let's say that a represents the number of adult tickets and c represents the number of children's tickets. We know that 96 tickets were sold. So $a + c = 96$. We also know that the total sales was $800, which means that $15a + 7c = 800$. You have simultaneous equations, so stack them and see if adding or subtracting the equations will get a or b by itself. In this case we want to multiply $a + c = 96$ by 7 and subtract:

$$15a + 7b = 800$$
$$- \ 7(a + b \ = 96)$$

which, when the subtraction sign and 7 are distributed is

$$15a + 7b = 800$$
$$\underline{-7a -7b \ = -672}$$
$$8a \qquad = 128$$

So, you know that $8a = 128$; and $a = 16$. Now put 16 back into the first equation: $16 + c = 96$; $c = 80$. The ratio of $a : c$ is $16 : 80$, or $\dfrac{16}{80}$, which reduces to $\dfrac{1}{5}$ or .2.

18. **27** From the formula for a triangle area, we get $A = \dfrac{1}{2} bh = \left(\dfrac{1}{2}\right)\left(\dfrac{4}{3}\right)(q - p) = 16$. Because $p = -q$, this simplifies to $\left(\dfrac{1}{2}\right)\left(\dfrac{4}{3}\right)(2q) = \dfrac{4}{3}q = 16$. Get q by itself and find that $q = 12$. Point Q lies on the graph $y = ax^2$, so you can replace q with 12 to find the coordinates $(-\dfrac{2}{3}, 12)$, and then use those coordinates to solve for a: $12 = a\left(\dfrac{2^2}{3}\right) = \dfrac{4}{9}a$. Since $12 = \dfrac{4}{9}a$, $a = 27$.

SECTION 7

1. **A** Many *expressed hope* that something good will come from the lack of *smear tactics*. The only word in the answers that is somewhat positive is *civility*, (A) which describes the opposite situation of one in which candidates attack each other with *smear tactics*. None of the other answers relate to acting in ways related to good *public discourse*.

2. **B** That Schubert had gotten a *solution he had been seeking for years*, his exclamation was probably a happy one. Eliminate any answers in which the first word is not positive. (A) *dismay*, and (C) *dread* are both the opposite of what we're looking for. The second blank describes the *error*, and of the remaining answer choices, (B) *significant* is the best match for both blanks. (D) *intentional* is the opposite of an *error* and there is no support for (E) *audible* in the sentence.

3. **B** The blank must be a word that indicates incorporating an *excessively optimistic outlook and flowery language* into a *presentation*. (A) *appeased* means "soothed." (B) *embellished* means "added ornamentation," which could describe the whistles and bells the manager added to the presentation. (C) *conceived* means "formed." (D) *disdained* means "despised." (E) *derived* means "obtained from," making (B) the best match.

4. **C** There is a relationship between the blanks in this question. Because *Joanna was stunned*, the score was the opposite of what she thought it was going to be. We can't tell whether she is *stunned* in a positive or negative way, but the words for the blanks must have an opposite relationship. Eliminate (A) and (D) because the words are not related. Eliminate (B) and (E) because the pairs of words are similar rather than opposite. (C) is correct because *mediocre* and *superlative* are negative and positive words.

5. **E** The word *looming* indicates that something is "nearing." If the *attorneys* have only until the execution to work to save the prisoner, so they have to act fast. A good word for the blank is "incentive." Only (E) *impetus* matches this meaning. There is some tough vocab in the answers: look up any unfamiliar words.

6. **E** The mention of *the strong Swiss whaling industry* is ironic because the country is *landlocked*, so Switzerland must have had another reason to join than *to preserve sufficient stocks of whales*, and the passages sums up with describing the Commission as an *open forum* for issues. This is best paraphrased in (E). There is no *description* as in (A). In (B) *discredit* is too strong. The sentence does not *explain* anything. The sentence is ironic; (D) would be true if the sentence were straightforward, but in this case the author is saying something that is not actually true in order to make a point.

7. **B** There is no evidence for the *success* in (A). (B) is supported because *landlocked* Switzerland is a member. There is no proof for (C), we know only that Switzerland's reason was not about *the strong Swiss whaling industry*. There is no proof that the Commission *no longer regulates*, as in (D); the group may now have *an open forum*, in addition to regulating. (E) is extreme due to the word *most*.

8. **D**   The *link between wheat price and sunspot activity* is described in the passage as *high price = low sun-spot activity*. If a price is high, it indicates that supplies are scarce, so low sunspot activity causes the wheat to not grow so well. We need an answer that provides more evidence to back up this relationship. (A) mentions sunspots, but not wheat growth. (B) is irrelevant, and doesn't mention wheat growth. (C) discusses *corn*, and is irrelevant to the question. (D) works, because it mentions both *sunspots* and *crop yield*. (E) is out because it is not true, and does not mention wheat growth.

9. **C**   Only (C) is not mentioned in the passage. (A) is in lines 4–5. (B) is in lines 7–8. (D) is in lines 1–2. (E) is in lines 5–7 and 10.

10. **B**   The *girl in a bedroom* in mentioned in the passage where the author describes her life as a beginning writer. This is best paraphrased in (B). There are no *limits* mentioned, as in (A). There is no proof of *vulnerability* as in (C). The *economic feasibility*, (D) is not why the author mentions the girl. This part of the passage is about how she *became a journalist*, not about *hardships*.

11. **E**   The author poses the question at the beginning of the second paragraph because she is going to discuss what troubles she did have *writing articles*. The *But wait* in the passage indicates that (A), (C) and (D) are the opposite of what we're looking for. (B) is incorrect because the author is not *blocked*; she is struggling between being honest and being nice. (E) is correct because it does *introduce difficulty*.

12. **C**   Go back to the passage and use the context to come up with a word to replace *constituted*. In the passage, *constituted* refers to *the Angel* who is described as *charming* and *unselfish,* who *sacrifices herself*. Eliminate (A); it describes writing. (B) describes a writer. (C) describes *the Angel*, so hold onto it. *The Angel* is only in the author's imagination, so *physical strength* is not possible, as in (D). (E) describes the author. (C) is correct.

13. **C**   The author is describing something that *bothered me and wasted my time and so tormented me,* so although the author is listing qualities that are generally considered positive, she is using them as evidence that *the Angel* is a negative force in the author's life. This is reflected best in (C). There is no proof for (A). That the author *tried to kill* The Angel indicates that the author was not trying *to achieve the ideal*. The author does not believe that The Angel is ideal. (D) is not true and (E) is not mentioned in the passage.

14. **D**   In the passage, immediately after *I need not say it*, the author states *she was pure*. This indicates that the author assumes that the reader would find it obvious that the Angel is pure. Only (D) addresses the *presumed* knowledge of the audience. (A) is out, because the author did describe The Angel's character. (B) is disproved, again because the author did describe The Angel in detail. There is no proof for *free will* in (C). (E) gets too far away from what is stated in the passage.

15. **B** Go back to the passage and use the context to come up with a word to replace *directly* in the two locations in the passage. In the first instance, the author is saying that the Angel *slipped in behind* her immediately when the author began to write. In the second instance, the phrase "exactly when" could easily replace *directly*. (B) *as soon as* is the best match. None of the other answers make sense as a replacement for *directly*.

16. **A** The gist of the passage is that the author is worried that the Angel will prevent her from writing honestly. This is best summarized in (A). The Angel's effect on the author's choice of *subject* (B) is not mentioned in the passage. The Angel tries to influence how the author writes, not to stop her from doing so, so (C) is out. The passage states that the author is writing reviews, not stories with plots. (E) is not true.

17. **C** There were successful women authors in the nineteenth century, so (A) is untrue. There is no mention of *committing violence* in the passage, so (B) is out. (C) is best supported by the passage, because the Angel possesses all the traditional ideas of femininity, and this influence threatens to force the author to not write the truth. The point of the passage is the opposite of (D). (E) is unrelated to the main idea of the passage, so we can't say how the author would feel about this.

18. **A** At the end of the passage, the author states that the Angel *died hard* and *was harder to kill...than reality*. This is paraphrased in (A). (B) is not mentioned. (C) is not true. (D) is disproved by the passage, because it states the author was successful at killing the Angel in the end. (E) is too literal.

19. **A** Go back to the passage and use the context to come up with a word to replace *discrete*. The sentence is talking about how something is *made up of* smaller "individual" parts. While all of the answers except *obvious* could be a synonym for *discrete*, the context of the passage supports the meaning only for "individual" or *separate*, (A).

20. **B** *Empty space* is mentioned in line 21, and is described in lines 20–24. (A) is not true, because *Democritus* is the one who said it existed; his *contemporaries* could not accept it. There is evidence for (B) in the passage in lines 23–24. (C) and (E) contradict the main idea of the passage, which is that Democritus's theories about atoms were correct. The phrase *inertial mass* in (D) is mentioned in the passage, but is out of context in regards to *empty space*.

21. **C** The reason the author mentions *Aristotle and others* is to show that the idea of *inertial mass* was a complicated concept now known to be true that *was not acceptable to Aristotle*. This is best captured in (C), *Aristotle* was an *influential individual* who this not *accept scientific truth*. The opposite of (A) is true. (B) is too broad. (D) is not true: Aristotle did not believe Democritus. (E) is incorrect because although the passage mentions *the divine*, which could be considered *philosophical*, this is not why the author mentions Aristotle.

22. **A** Today, the question of the soul is not included when we consider the physical laws that govern our experience. We would consider it a religious or philosophical question, not scientific. In Democritus's time, the division of what was physical and what was philosophical were not defined the way they are today, as mentioned in lines 38-46, so (A) is the best supported answer. There is no proof for (B). (C) makes too big a leap from the information provided in the passage. (D) and (E) are disproved in lines 38–39: we don't know whether Democritus was right or wrong.

23. **E** In the first paragraph, the passage states that *Democritus believed* that the *joining together and subsequent separation* of atoms *account for* the existence of things and *for their passing away.* This is best paraphrased in (E). There is no proof for (A) and (D), and these two answers do not mention atoms. There is no proof in the passage that the flower is an *illusion,* as in (B). (C) is incorrect, because Democritus was not aware of the process of *splitting atoms.*

24. **B** The *hardy thinker's view of the soul* is described in the passage in lines 43–46. That they accept the view that *the soul cannot be free,* but only for other people: they believe their own souls are free. There is an element of hypocrisy here, that is seen only in (B), in which the doctor gives advice that he himself does not follow. None of the other relationships in the answers has this element of hypocrisy.

SECTION 8

1. **A** Come up with your own numbers for *n*. If *n* = 7, then every day for 5 days the store sells 7 newspapers for a total of 35 papers over the 5 days. Replace *n* with 7 in the answers, and only (A) yields 35.

2. **E** To find the equivalent values of *a* and *c*; the *b* value must be the same in each relationship. The first fraction is $\frac{a}{b} = \frac{7}{4}$. This fraction can be multiplied by 2 on the top and the bottom to create an equivalent fraction in which the *b* value is 8 as it is in the second pair of equivalent fractions. So now we know that $\frac{a}{b} = \frac{14}{8}$ and $\frac{b}{c} = \frac{8}{6}$, so $\frac{a}{c} = \frac{14}{6}$, or $\frac{7}{3}$, as in (E).

3. **E** Because the question asks about square feet in the end, convert the inches to feet right away. Divide the dimensions given in inches by 12. The rug that measures 72 inches by 96 inches has dimensions in feet of 6 by 8. This means that the rug has an area of 48 square feet, answer (E).

4. **C** The easiest way to solve this problem is to try out the answers in the question and see which one works. Start with the middle value in order to save time: if (C) is not correct, you may gain a hint about whether the number should be smaller or larger. If the cost of a meal is $25, and the tip is 20%, or $\frac{1}{5}$ of the $25, then $25 + $5 =$30, which is the amount that the question says is supposed to be the total. We're done! (C) is the answer. (A) and (B) add up to less than $30, and (D) and (E) add up to more than $30.

5. **B** We need to find the perimeter of triangle *PQR*. Even though the figure is not drawn to scale, we are told that this is a rectangle, so *Area = bh*, and we know the area and the base: $96 = (12)h$, and $h = 8$. Now we know the two legs of the triangle are 12 and 8. The angles of a rectangle are all 90°, so we can use the Pythagorean theorem to find the hypotenuse and add up the three sides to find the perimeter of the triangle. $12^2 + 8^2 = c^2$, so $144 + 64 = c^2$, $c^2 = 208$, so take the square root of both sides to find that $c = \sqrt{208}$. If we leave the hypotenuse as is for now, the perimeter is $12 + 8 + \sqrt{208}$, or $20 + \sqrt{208}$. Only (A) and (B) are close to this, and if we simplify the square root we see that (B) is the correct answer: $208 = 16 \times 13$, so $\sqrt{208} = 4\sqrt{13}$.

6. **B** The equation of a line with slope *m* and *y*-intercept *b* is $y = mx + b$. Manipulate the given equation into that form to get $y = 5x - 13$. The slope is 5, answer (B).

7. **E** Find the total number of possible combinations by multiplying the number of shirts times the number of pants times the number of pairs of shoes. $10 \times 4 \times 5 = 200$, answer (E).

8. **C** Translate the words into math: A new disc is 5 times the price of a used one, so $n = 5u$. The second sentence states that the difference in prices is \$10, so we know that $n - u = 10$. To find the value of *u*, we can replace *n* with $5u$ in the second equation to see that $5u - u = 10$, so $4u = 10$ and $u = \$2.50$. Since a new disk is 5 times the price, $n = 5 \times 2.50 = \$12.50$. The total of 3 used and 2 new compact disks is $3(2.50) + 2(12.50) = 7.50 + 25 = \$32.50$, answer (C).

9. **B** To find *x* value of the midpoint, find the distance between the *x* values of the two points given and divide by 2: From 0 to 6 is 6 units, and dividing by 2 gives 3. Only (B) and (C) have an *x* value of 3, so eliminate (A), (D), and (E). The distance between the *y* values of the two points given is 10, so the midpoint has a *y* value of 5. Only (B) matches both values. Be careful of (A): it has the values of *x* and *y* reversed.

10. **D** To solve this problem, make up some values for *s* and *t* to determine *r*, and see how *t* is affected after following the directions to double *r* and *s*. If at first $s = 3$ and $t = 4$, then $r = \dfrac{2(3^3)}{4} = \dfrac{27}{2}$. Now double *r* and *s* to see what happens to *t*: $27 = \dfrac{2(6^3)}{t}$, so $27t = 432$, and *t* now equals 16. At first, $t = 4$, so now it is 4 times bigger, as stated in (D).

11. **D** The answer choices are the number of green marbles the jar now contains. Since at the end there is a 3 : 2 ratio of red to green marbles, we can use the number of green marbles to determine how many red marbles there are. Then take away 6 red marbles and see if the ratio is equal to the original ratio of 3 : 4. Start with the middle value in (C): If there are 6 green then a 3 : 2 ratio of red to green would be 9 : 6. If we took 6 red marbles away, we would have a ratio of 3 : 6, which does not equal 3 : 4. Try (D). If there are 8 green then a 3 : 2 ratio of red to green would be 12 : 8. If we took 6 red marbles away, we would have a ratio of 6 : 8, which does equal 3 : 4. (D) is correct.

12. **E** A line that is tangent to a circle forms a 90° angle with a radius or diameter, so radius BC is one leg of a right triangle. Because the area of the circle is 16π, the radius must be 4. We are told that AB, the hypotenuse of the triangle, is 8, so we can use the Pythagorean theorem to solve for the other leg, side AC: $4^2 + b^2 = 8^2$, so $16 + b^2 = 64$, and $b^2 = 48$. $AC = \sqrt{48} = 4\sqrt{3}$, as in (E). Seeing that the hypotenuse is twice the length of one of the legs may help you realize that you have a 30-60-90 special right triangle here, with sides in the ratio of $1 : \sqrt{3} : 2$, which also gives $4\sqrt{3}$ for side AC.

13. **C** Multiply both sides of the equation by 2 to get $b^x = 16$. The denominator of a fractional exponent represents taking the root of a number. In this case, the second (square) root, so $b^{\frac{x}{2}} = \sqrt{b^x} = \sqrt{16}$, which is 4, answer (C).

14. **D** Start by writing out the first few terms of the sequence and look for a pattern. The first term is 6, the second term is $(6 + 2) \div (-1) = 8 \div (-1) = -8$. The third term is $(-8 + 2) \div (-1) = 6$. The pattern is 6, –8, 6, –8,… Notice that all the odd-numbered terms are 6 and all the even-numbered terms are –8. 101 is an odd number, so the 101st term will be 6. And the 70th term will be –8. So, $-8 - 6 = -14$, as seen in (D). Make sure you don't do $6 - (-8) = 14$. (B) is a trap answer.

15. **B** Make up your own numbers for the variables. Use 3 in place of b, and 2 in place of y. If Caleb has 3 cards at the end of 9 months, he'll have 6 cards three months later, which is the end of the first year. He'll have 12 cards after 15 months, 24 cards after 18 months, 48 cards after 21 months, and 96 cards after two years. Now replace b with 3 and y with 2 in the answer choices and see which one yields 96. Only (B) yields 96 as an answer.

16. **E** First put the equation given for the line into the $y = mx + b$ format: $\frac{5}{3}y - 5 = x$ becomes $\frac{5}{3}y = x + 5$, and multiplying both sides by $\frac{3}{5}$ gives $y = \frac{3}{5}x + 3$. Now it is clear that we are looking for a graph that has a slope of $\frac{3}{5}$ and a y intercept of 3. Only (E) shows a graph with a y-intercept of 3.

SECTION 9

1. **D**   The semicolon indicates that the two phrases on either side are so close in meaning that they had to be joined, even though each could stand on its own as a complete sentence. The word *it* in the second phrase refers to *advertising* in the first part. The word for the blank must be something that *confronts us everywhere*. Among the answers, the word *ubiquitous* in (D) means "existing everywhere." None of the other words describe "everywhere."

2. **B**   The colon is like an equal sign between the two parts of the sentence. The first blank describes *Desiree*, and the second part of the sentence states that *she moved with ease*. The first blank must mean something close to "easiness." Eliminate (E), *ineptitude* is the opposite of what we are looking for. The second blank describes the skill of her younger brother, and the word *surprising* indicates that the blank will mean the opposite of the first. A word like "uncoordinated" would fit well. In the answers, *clumsy* and *blundering* are both close to uncoordinated, but only (B) *agility* and *clumsy* fit the context of the sentence.

3. **D**   The first blank must be positive, because it is linked to *thought-provoking* by *and*. Eliminate the answer choices in which the first word is not similar to *thought-provoking*. (B) and (C) are definitely out. The second blank is the opposite of *thought-provoking* due to the words *rather than*. Something like "boring" is a good word for the blank, which matches only *wearisome* in (D). You can also use the relationship between the blanks to help find the right answer: The blanks in the sentence are opposites with a positive to negative relationship. The pairs in (A) and (C) have a synonymous relationship. The pairs in (B) and (E) have a negative to positive relationship.

4. **A**   The sentence describes how the conversation *degenerated from* something *playful* to something *aggressive* and *insulting*. A good word for the blank will mean something like "mean." Eliminate (B) *professional* because it describes the opposite of the behavior. There is a lot of tough vocab here, so look up any unfamiliar words. When you do, you'll see that *vituperative* means "marked by harshly abusive criticism," which fits with *aggressive insults*.

5. **D**   The word *although* indicates that Sumi wanted to win, but not in a dishonest way. So she refused to "go along with" the teammates plan to cheat. Only (D) *endorse* has a meaning close to "go along with." Look up any of the words that you cannot define.

6. **A**   The word *Though* at the beginning of the sentence indicates that there is a relation of opposites. The first blank describes how Nina *believes* her arguments to be, and the second blank is how they really come across. The part of the sentence that describes *verbose explanations* and *obscure experience* indicates that the second blank means "wordy and unclear," so the first blank must mean "clear and concise." The vocab in the answers is pretty tough, but (A) *pithy . . obtuse* matches these definitions perfectly. None of the other pairs fit the context of the sentence.

7. **D** According to lines 16–17 of the passage, *sizing kept the paper from being too porous, inhibiting ink from spreading.* (A) tells what is in sizing, not what it does. (B) discusses *textiles* rather than *paper*. (C) *papal edicts* are mentioned in line 4, but is not related to the discussion on *sizing.* (D) is correct because it mentions porous paper. (E) is incorrect.

8. **A** Go back to the passage and use the context to come up with a word to replace *robust.* The passage states that paper was *largely undamaged and robust,* so robust here means "able to avoid damage" or "sturdy." This is closest in meaning to *durable* (A). In (B), *undamaged* doesn't indicate any qualities of the paper to stand up to damage, just that damage hasn't occurred. (E) is the opposite of what we were looking for.

9. **C** The description of the *inferior* alum paper is in lines 21–24 and it *appears brittle and discolored.* (A) and (B) are mentioned in Passage 2, not Passage 1. (C) is correct because it mentions *discoloration.* (D) and (E) are not mentioned in the part of the passage that describes the *inferior* qualities.

10. **D** Go back to the passage and use the context to come up with a word to replace *cachet.* The passage states that the printers *enjoy the historic cachet* so we need some positive word close in meaning to "importance." (A) and (B) are meanings of *cachet* in some contexts, but not this one. (C) and (E) are close in meaning to important, but in a negative way. (D) *distinction* is a positive word that means that something is held in special regard.

11. **B** Go through the answers and eliminate any that can be proved with text from Passage 2. (B) is mentioned in Passage 1, not Passage 2. All the rest of the answers are in Passage 2: (A) is in lines 38–41. (B) is in lines 16–17. (C) is mentioned in lines 37-38. (D) is in line 34, and (E) is in lines 42–44.

12. **D** In lines 19–24, the paper made with the alum/rosin mix is described as *inferior…protected only for the short term…brittle, discolored.* Eliminate (A) because we don't know how often. Eliminate (B), because that describes alum without rosin. Eliminate (C) because the mixture was used with paper, not textiles. (D) is correct, because *less than 200 years* fits with *protected for the short term.* There is no proof for (E).

13. **D** Go through the answers and eliminate any that can be proved with text from Passage 1. (A) is in line 6. (B) is in line 15. (C) is mentioned in line 5 and the footnote. (D) is correct because it is mentioned only in Passage 2, not passage 1. (E) is mentioned in line 14.

14. **C** Go through the answers and eliminate any that can be proved with text from Passage 1. (A) is in line 15. (B) is in lines 13–15 and 21–24. (C) is the opposite of what is stated in the passage, which describes alum as held *in low repute* in line 19. (D) is in lines 23-24 and (E) is in lines 8–10.

15. **A** (A) is correct: in lines 33–34, Passage 2 states that *a few printers still use excessive amounts of alum.* The papermakers are not criticized for *awareness.* There is no *substitute* mentioned for alum in Passage 2. (D) is contradicted in Passage 2: line 36 states that they *enjoyed the historical cachet.* The *bubbles and stickiness* is what alum prevents, not what the papermakers are criticized for.

16. **D** (A) is not mentioned in Passage 2. In (B), the word *most* makes the answer extreme. The beneficial qualities in (C) are mentioned only in Passage 1; the author of Passage 2 disagrees: at best he says alum is *adequate, can damage the strength* of the paper, and is good only *in small quantities and as an additive.* (D) is correct: in lines 13–15 in Passage 1 and lines 42–44 in Passage 2 both describe alum as effective when combined with other compounds. (E) contradicts Passage 2 and is not mentioned in Passage 1.

17. **B** The *chlorine* in (B) is not mentioned in Passage 1 at all, so we can't know the author's opinion. There is evidence in the passage that the author would agree with all the other answers: (A) in lines 17–19; (C) in lines 8–10; (D) in lines 19–24; and (E) in lines 8–10.

18. **C** In Passage 2 in lines 35–36, *These maverick printers* are described as those who use too much alum. This is best paraphrased in (C). (A) is not mentioned in either passage. (B) is mentioned in the passage, but not in relation to *maverick printers.* (D) is extreme and not true in either passage. (E) in not mentioned in Passage 2.

19. **E** Go through the answer choices and identify the place in the passage where each is found. Only (E) is not supported by any evidence in the passage. (A) is in Passage 2 in line 34. (B) is in Passage 1 in line 15. (C) is in Passage 1 in lines 15–17. (D) is in Passage 2 in lines 35.

SECTION 10

1. **A** The sentence is correct as written. (B) has a same-direction conjunction *for* when the opposite-direction *however* is more appropriate. The phrase after a semicolon should function as a complete sentence, but (C) creates an incomplete sentence. (D) changes the meaning and (E) has a verb tense error.

2. **C** The sentence as written is incomplete because of the *ing* word *causing.* The word *Although* indicates that we have a relationship that is opposite or unexpected. If the sun shines a lot, the flowers should grow a lot. So *Although* the sun shines a lot, the orchids do not grow much. (B) has an unnecessary conjunction *and yet.* (C) is correct because *it* refers to the action of the sun shining, and *not cause them to grow* acknowledges the opposite effect we were looking for. (D) has the unnecessary conjunction *and,* (E) creates a sentence fragment.

3. **D** In the sentence as written the comma joins two phrases that could stand on their own as sentences, which is a comma splice. (B) and (C) incorrectly use *ing* words, which are typically passive or wordy and weaken a sentence. (D) correctly uses *this artistic choice* to take the place of what is described in the first phrase. (E) contains a comma splice.

4. **C** There is a parallelism error in the sentence as written because of *more* should modify *flies*, not *honey*. (B) changes the meaning so that *honey* is catching the flies rather than *you*. (C) fixes the parallelism error with *more flies with honey than with vinegar*. (D) contains a faulty comparison. (E) changes the meaning of the sentence.

5. **D** There is an idiom phrase error in (A) and (B) *not only...but that...as well*: the correct idiom is *not only...but also*, as seen in (D). (C) is redundant in its use of *in addition* and *as well*. (E) changes the meaning of the sentence.

6. **D** The *ing* word *refusing* is a tip-off that this sentence is not as clear or active as it should be. The sentence as written contains a colon, and there needs to be a phrase that can stand on its own as a complete sentence on each side of the colon. This does not happen in (A). Introducing *angrily* in (B) assumes too much and changes the meaning of the sentence. The construction *was refusing* in (C) is passive and weak. (D) is correct because there is a complete sentence on each side of the colon and the sentence is clear. The use of *was a debutante* is redundant with the non-underlined portion of the sentence.

7. **C** There is more than one *requirement* listed in the sentence as written In (A), the subject and verb should be plural. (B) is incorrect because *To* and *it* are unnecessary. The correct answer, (C) is concisely worded. (D) is awkward and employs a passive verb. (E) is wordy, awkward, and is a fragment.

8. **B** *Semester* refers to a length of time, so *during which* in answer choice (B) is the correct idiom. (A) and (C) contain the pronoun *they,* implying that *programs...can experience*. In (D), *and* does not express the logical connection between the two clauses. (E) is incorrect because *where* cannot be used to refer to *a semester* (or *a host family*), only to an actual physical location.

9. **A** There are no errors in the sentence as written. (B), (C), (D), and (E) are not parallel to the first clause. Also, (B) uses the unidiomatic *to others*, rather than *for others*. Only independent clauses or lists containing commas may follow a semicolon, so (C) is wrong. (D) is passive and uses an improper idiom (*regarded...to be*). (E) is completely illogical, since students cannot be a means to improve their own reasoning skills while they look at mathematics.

10. **C** Sentences that contain the word *being* should always be suspect on the SAT: *being* usually makes a sentence wordier and more passive than it should be. We can eliminate (A) and (B). (C) correctly creates a phrase that clearly and concisely describes *Odds Bodkin*. There is no need for the conjunction *Although*, in (D). The *ing* construction *Entertaining giftedly* is an awkward way to describe someone.

11. **E** *A study* is a singular subject and requires the singular verb *reveals*. Thus, (A) and (C) are incorrect. The correct idiom in this sentence is *reveals that*, so (B) and (D) are wrong. (E) uses the proper subject-verb agreement; the singular *interest* agrees with the singular *tends*.

12. **B** The sentence as written incorrectly implies that someone is viewing the book, though the sentence makes no mention of any such person and therefore is awkward. (C), (D), and (E) all repeat this error. Only (B) correctly removes this error.

13. **B** There is a subject-verb agreement problem in the sentence as written between *each,* which indicates a singular, and the plural verb *were.* This is corrected in (B) *each…was.* In (C) there is disagreement between the singular *each* and the plural *servants.* (D) has a disagreement between the plural *all* and singular *servant.* (E) is incorrect because *which* refers to objects whereas people are referred to here, so we need *who* or *whom.*

14. **D** The phrase *For over forty years…until his death* indicates a specific length of time in the past. The verb *is* in the sentence as written is in the wrong tense: we need *was.* The lack of *was* in (B) causes a verb agreement problem in *For over forty years…married*, because getting married is done at one point in time, not continuously for forty years (that's *being* married). In (C) the phrase *proud author* changes the meaning of the sentence. (D) is uses the correct construction *was married.* (E) indicates that both people won the Newberry, which changes the meaning of the sentence.

Chapter 22
Practice Test 10

Your Name (print) _____

Last   First   Middle

Date _____

IMPORTANT: The following codes should be copied onto your answer sheet exactly as shown.

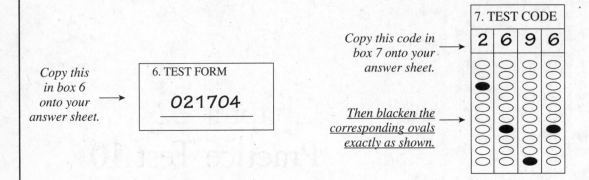

Copy this in box 6 onto your answer sheet.

6. TEST FORM

021704

Copy this code in box 7 onto your answer sheet.

Then blacken the corresponding ovals exactly as shown.

7. TEST CODE

2 6 9 6

General Directions

You will have three hours and 20 minutes to work on this objective test designed to familiarize you with all aspects of the SAT.

This test contains five 25-minute sections, two 20-minute sections, one 10-minute section, and one 25-minute essay. The supervisor will tell you when to begin and end each section. During the time allowed for each section, you may work only on that particular section. If you finish your work before time is called, you may check your work on that section, but you are not to work on any other section.

You will find specific directions for each type of question found in the test. **Be sure you understand the directions before attempting to answer any of the questions.**

YOU ARE TO INDICATE ALL YOUR ANSWERS ON THE SEPARATE ANSWER SHEET:

1. The test booklet may be used for scratchwork. However, no credit will be given for anything written in the test booklet.

2. Once you have decided on an answer to a question, darken the corresponding space on the answer sheet. Give only one answer to each question.

3. There are 40 numbered answer spaces for each section; be sure to use only those spaces that correspond to the test questions.

4. **Be sure each answer mark is dark and completely fills the answer space.** Do not make any stray marks on your answer sheet.

5. If you wish to change an answer, erase your first mark completely—an incomplete erasure may be considered an intended response—and blacken your new answer choice.

Your score on this test is based on the number of questions you answer correctly minus a fraction of the number of questions you answer incorrectly. Therefore, it is improbable that random or haphazard guessing will alter your score significantly. There are no deductions for incorrect answers on the student-produced response questions. However, if you are able to eliminate one or more of the answer choices on any question as wrong, it is generally to your advantage to guess at one of the remaining choices. Remember, however, not to spend too much time on any one question.

Diagnostic Test Form

Use a No. 2 pencil only. Be sure each mark is dark and completely fills the intended oval. Completely erase any errors or stray marks.

1 **Your Name:**

(Print)

Last   First   M.I.

Signature: _____ Date ___/___/___

Home Address: _____

Number and Street   City   State   Zip Code

E-Mail: _____ School: _____ Class: _____

(Print)

2 **YOUR NAME**
Last Name
(First 4 Letters)   FIRST INIT   MID INIT

3 **PHONE NUMBER**

IMPORTANT: Fill in items 6 and 7 exactly as shown on the preceding page.

6 **TEST FORM**
(Copy from back of test book)

7 **TEST CODE**

4 **DATE OF BIRTH**

MONTH	DAY		YEAR	

JAN, FEB, MAR, APR, MAY, JUN, JUL, AUG, SEP, OCT, NOV, DEC

8 **OTHER**
1 (A)(B)(C)(D)(E)
2 (A)(B)(C)(D)(E)
3 (A)(B)(C)(D)(E)

5 **SEX**
MALE
FEMALE

OpScan *i*NSIGHT™ forms by Pearson NCS EM-253760-3:654321   Printed in U.S.A.   © TPR Education IP Holdings, LLC

PLEASE DO NOT WRITE IN THIS AREA

SERIAL #

THIS PAGE INTENTIONALLY LEFT BLANK

Begin your essay on this page. If you need more space, continue on the next page.

Continue on the next page, if necessary.

Continuation of ESSAY Section 1 from previous page. Write below only if you need more space.
IMPORTANT: DO NOT START on this page—if you do, your essay may appear blank and your score may be affected.

SECTION 2

1 Ⓐ Ⓑ Ⓒ Ⓓ Ⓔ
2 Ⓐ Ⓑ Ⓒ Ⓓ Ⓔ
3 Ⓐ Ⓑ Ⓒ Ⓓ Ⓔ
4 Ⓐ Ⓑ Ⓒ Ⓓ Ⓔ
5 Ⓐ Ⓑ Ⓒ Ⓓ Ⓔ
6 Ⓐ Ⓑ Ⓒ Ⓓ Ⓔ
7 Ⓐ Ⓑ Ⓒ Ⓓ Ⓔ
8 Ⓐ Ⓑ Ⓒ Ⓓ Ⓔ
9 Ⓐ Ⓑ Ⓒ Ⓓ Ⓔ
10 Ⓐ Ⓑ Ⓒ Ⓓ Ⓔ

11 Ⓐ Ⓑ Ⓒ Ⓓ Ⓔ
12 Ⓐ Ⓑ Ⓒ Ⓓ Ⓔ
13 Ⓐ Ⓑ Ⓒ Ⓓ Ⓔ
14 Ⓐ Ⓑ Ⓒ Ⓓ Ⓔ
15 Ⓐ Ⓑ Ⓒ Ⓓ Ⓔ
16 Ⓐ Ⓑ Ⓒ Ⓓ Ⓔ
17 Ⓐ Ⓑ Ⓒ Ⓓ Ⓔ
18 Ⓐ Ⓑ Ⓒ Ⓓ Ⓔ
19 Ⓐ Ⓑ Ⓒ Ⓓ Ⓔ
20 Ⓐ Ⓑ Ⓒ Ⓓ Ⓔ

21 Ⓐ Ⓑ Ⓒ Ⓓ Ⓔ
22 Ⓐ Ⓑ Ⓒ Ⓓ Ⓔ
23 Ⓐ Ⓑ Ⓒ Ⓓ Ⓔ
24 Ⓐ Ⓑ Ⓒ Ⓓ Ⓔ
25 Ⓐ Ⓑ Ⓒ Ⓓ Ⓔ
26 Ⓐ Ⓑ Ⓒ Ⓓ Ⓔ
27 Ⓐ Ⓑ Ⓒ Ⓓ Ⓔ
28 Ⓐ Ⓑ Ⓒ Ⓓ Ⓔ
29 Ⓐ Ⓑ Ⓒ Ⓓ Ⓔ
30 Ⓐ Ⓑ Ⓒ Ⓓ Ⓔ

31 Ⓐ Ⓑ Ⓒ Ⓓ Ⓔ
32 Ⓐ Ⓑ Ⓒ Ⓓ Ⓔ
33 Ⓐ Ⓑ Ⓒ Ⓓ Ⓔ
34 Ⓐ Ⓑ Ⓒ Ⓓ Ⓔ
35 Ⓐ Ⓑ Ⓒ Ⓓ Ⓔ
36 Ⓐ Ⓑ Ⓒ Ⓓ Ⓔ
37 Ⓐ Ⓑ Ⓒ Ⓓ Ⓔ
38 Ⓐ Ⓑ Ⓒ Ⓓ Ⓔ
39 Ⓐ Ⓑ Ⓒ Ⓓ Ⓔ
40 Ⓐ Ⓑ Ⓒ Ⓓ Ⓔ

SECTION 3

1 Ⓐ Ⓑ Ⓒ Ⓓ Ⓔ
2 Ⓐ Ⓑ Ⓒ Ⓓ Ⓔ
3 Ⓐ Ⓑ Ⓒ Ⓓ Ⓔ
4 Ⓐ Ⓑ Ⓒ Ⓓ Ⓔ
5 Ⓐ Ⓑ Ⓒ Ⓓ Ⓔ
6 Ⓐ Ⓑ Ⓒ Ⓓ Ⓔ
7 Ⓐ Ⓑ Ⓒ Ⓓ Ⓔ
8 Ⓐ Ⓑ Ⓒ Ⓓ Ⓔ
9 Ⓐ Ⓑ Ⓒ Ⓓ Ⓔ
10 Ⓐ Ⓑ Ⓒ Ⓓ Ⓔ

11 Ⓐ Ⓑ Ⓒ Ⓓ Ⓔ
12 Ⓐ Ⓑ Ⓒ Ⓓ Ⓔ
13 Ⓐ Ⓑ Ⓒ Ⓓ Ⓔ
14 Ⓐ Ⓑ Ⓒ Ⓓ Ⓔ
15 Ⓐ Ⓑ Ⓒ Ⓓ Ⓔ
16 Ⓐ Ⓑ Ⓒ Ⓓ Ⓔ
17 Ⓐ Ⓑ Ⓒ Ⓓ Ⓔ
18 Ⓐ Ⓑ Ⓒ Ⓓ Ⓔ
19 Ⓐ Ⓑ Ⓒ Ⓓ Ⓔ
20 Ⓐ Ⓑ Ⓒ Ⓓ Ⓔ

21 Ⓐ Ⓑ Ⓒ Ⓓ Ⓔ
22 Ⓐ Ⓑ Ⓒ Ⓓ Ⓔ
23 Ⓐ Ⓑ Ⓒ Ⓓ Ⓔ
24 Ⓐ Ⓑ Ⓒ Ⓓ Ⓔ
25 Ⓐ Ⓑ Ⓒ Ⓓ Ⓔ
26 Ⓐ Ⓑ Ⓒ Ⓓ Ⓔ
27 Ⓐ Ⓑ Ⓒ Ⓓ Ⓔ
28 Ⓐ Ⓑ Ⓒ Ⓓ Ⓔ
29 Ⓐ Ⓑ Ⓒ Ⓓ Ⓔ
30 Ⓐ Ⓑ Ⓒ Ⓓ Ⓔ

31 Ⓐ Ⓑ Ⓒ Ⓓ Ⓔ
32 Ⓐ Ⓑ Ⓒ Ⓓ Ⓔ
33 Ⓐ Ⓑ Ⓒ Ⓓ Ⓔ
34 Ⓐ Ⓑ Ⓒ Ⓓ Ⓔ
35 Ⓐ Ⓑ Ⓒ Ⓓ Ⓔ
36 Ⓐ Ⓑ Ⓒ Ⓓ Ⓔ
37 Ⓐ Ⓑ Ⓒ Ⓓ Ⓔ
38 Ⓐ Ⓑ Ⓒ Ⓓ Ⓔ
39 Ⓐ Ⓑ Ⓒ Ⓓ Ⓔ
40 Ⓐ Ⓑ Ⓒ Ⓓ Ⓔ

CAUTION Grid answers in the section below for SECTION 2 or SECTION 3 only if directed to do so in your test book.

Student-Produced Responses

ONLY ANSWERS THAT ARE GRIDDED WILL BE SCORED. YOU WILL NOT RECEIVE CREDIT FOR ANYTHING WRITTEN IN THE BOXES.

Quality Assurance Mark ●

9, **10**, **11**, **12**, **13** — grids with digits 0–9

14, **15**, **16**, **17**, **18** — grids with digits 0–9

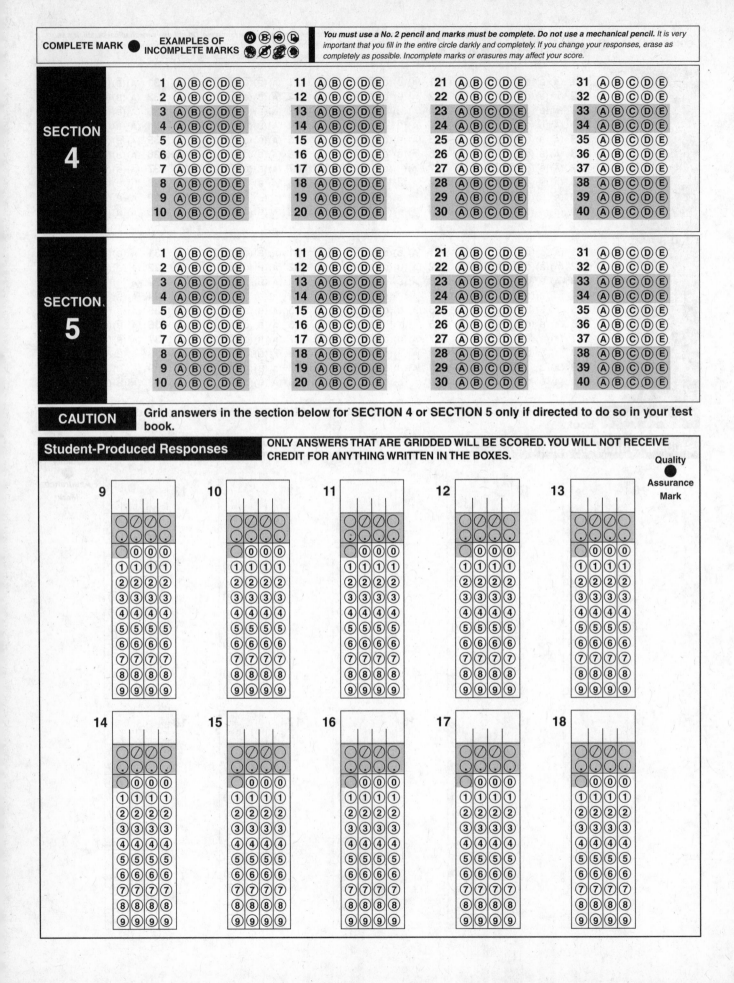

SECTION 6

1 Ⓐ Ⓑ Ⓒ Ⓓ Ⓔ   11 Ⓐ Ⓑ Ⓒ Ⓓ Ⓔ   21 Ⓐ Ⓑ Ⓒ Ⓓ Ⓔ   31 Ⓐ Ⓑ Ⓒ Ⓓ Ⓔ
2 Ⓐ Ⓑ Ⓒ Ⓓ Ⓔ   12 Ⓐ Ⓑ Ⓒ Ⓓ Ⓔ   22 Ⓐ Ⓑ Ⓒ Ⓓ Ⓔ   32 Ⓐ Ⓑ Ⓒ Ⓓ Ⓔ
3 Ⓐ Ⓑ Ⓒ Ⓓ Ⓔ   13 Ⓐ Ⓑ Ⓒ Ⓓ Ⓔ   23 Ⓐ Ⓑ Ⓒ Ⓓ Ⓔ   33 Ⓐ Ⓑ Ⓒ Ⓓ Ⓔ
4 Ⓐ Ⓑ Ⓒ Ⓓ Ⓔ   14 Ⓐ Ⓑ Ⓒ Ⓓ Ⓔ   24 Ⓐ Ⓑ Ⓒ Ⓓ Ⓔ   34 Ⓐ Ⓑ Ⓒ Ⓓ Ⓔ
5 Ⓐ Ⓑ Ⓒ Ⓓ Ⓔ   15 Ⓐ Ⓑ Ⓒ Ⓓ Ⓔ   25 Ⓐ Ⓑ Ⓒ Ⓓ Ⓔ   35 Ⓐ Ⓑ Ⓒ Ⓓ Ⓔ
6 Ⓐ Ⓑ Ⓒ Ⓓ Ⓔ   16 Ⓐ Ⓑ Ⓒ Ⓓ Ⓔ   26 Ⓐ Ⓑ Ⓒ Ⓓ Ⓔ   36 Ⓐ Ⓑ Ⓒ Ⓓ Ⓔ
7 Ⓐ Ⓑ Ⓒ Ⓓ Ⓔ   17 Ⓐ Ⓑ Ⓒ Ⓓ Ⓔ   27 Ⓐ Ⓑ Ⓒ Ⓓ Ⓔ   37 Ⓐ Ⓑ Ⓒ Ⓓ Ⓔ
8 Ⓐ Ⓑ Ⓒ Ⓓ Ⓔ   18 Ⓐ Ⓑ Ⓒ Ⓓ Ⓔ   28 Ⓐ Ⓑ Ⓒ Ⓓ Ⓔ   38 Ⓐ Ⓑ Ⓒ Ⓓ Ⓔ
9 Ⓐ Ⓑ Ⓒ Ⓓ Ⓔ   19 Ⓐ Ⓑ Ⓒ Ⓓ Ⓔ   29 Ⓐ Ⓑ Ⓒ Ⓓ Ⓔ   39 Ⓐ Ⓑ Ⓒ Ⓓ Ⓔ
10 Ⓐ Ⓑ Ⓒ Ⓓ Ⓔ   20 Ⓐ Ⓑ Ⓒ Ⓓ Ⓔ   30 Ⓐ Ⓑ Ⓒ Ⓓ Ⓔ   40 Ⓐ Ⓑ Ⓒ Ⓓ Ⓔ

SECTION 7

1 Ⓐ Ⓑ Ⓒ Ⓓ Ⓔ   11 Ⓐ Ⓑ Ⓒ Ⓓ Ⓔ   21 Ⓐ Ⓑ Ⓒ Ⓓ Ⓔ   31 Ⓐ Ⓑ Ⓒ Ⓓ Ⓔ
2 Ⓐ Ⓑ Ⓒ Ⓓ Ⓔ   12 Ⓐ Ⓑ Ⓒ Ⓓ Ⓔ   22 Ⓐ Ⓑ Ⓒ Ⓓ Ⓔ   32 Ⓐ Ⓑ Ⓒ Ⓓ Ⓔ
3 Ⓐ Ⓑ Ⓒ Ⓓ Ⓔ   13 Ⓐ Ⓑ Ⓒ Ⓓ Ⓔ   23 Ⓐ Ⓑ Ⓒ Ⓓ Ⓔ   33 Ⓐ Ⓑ Ⓒ Ⓓ Ⓔ
4 Ⓐ Ⓑ Ⓒ Ⓓ Ⓔ   14 Ⓐ Ⓑ Ⓒ Ⓓ Ⓔ   24 Ⓐ Ⓑ Ⓒ Ⓓ Ⓔ   34 Ⓐ Ⓑ Ⓒ Ⓓ Ⓔ
5 Ⓐ Ⓑ Ⓒ Ⓓ Ⓔ   15 Ⓐ Ⓑ Ⓒ Ⓓ Ⓔ   25 Ⓐ Ⓑ Ⓒ Ⓓ Ⓔ   35 Ⓐ Ⓑ Ⓒ Ⓓ Ⓔ
6 Ⓐ Ⓑ Ⓒ Ⓓ Ⓔ   16 Ⓐ Ⓑ Ⓒ Ⓓ Ⓔ   26 Ⓐ Ⓑ Ⓒ Ⓓ Ⓔ   36 Ⓐ Ⓑ Ⓒ Ⓓ Ⓔ
7 Ⓐ Ⓑ Ⓒ Ⓓ Ⓔ   17 Ⓐ Ⓑ Ⓒ Ⓓ Ⓔ   27 Ⓐ Ⓑ Ⓒ Ⓓ Ⓔ   37 Ⓐ Ⓑ Ⓒ Ⓓ Ⓔ
8 Ⓐ Ⓑ Ⓒ Ⓓ Ⓔ   18 Ⓐ Ⓑ Ⓒ Ⓓ Ⓔ   28 Ⓐ Ⓑ Ⓒ Ⓓ Ⓔ   38 Ⓐ Ⓑ Ⓒ Ⓓ Ⓔ
9 Ⓐ Ⓑ Ⓒ Ⓓ Ⓔ   19 Ⓐ Ⓑ Ⓒ Ⓓ Ⓔ   29 Ⓐ Ⓑ Ⓒ Ⓓ Ⓔ   39 Ⓐ Ⓑ Ⓒ Ⓓ Ⓔ
10 Ⓐ Ⓑ Ⓒ Ⓓ Ⓔ   20 Ⓐ Ⓑ Ⓒ Ⓓ Ⓔ   30 Ⓐ Ⓑ Ⓒ Ⓓ Ⓔ   40 Ⓐ Ⓑ Ⓒ Ⓓ Ⓔ

CAUTION Grid answers in the section below for SECTION 6 or SECTION 7 only if directed to do so in your test book.

Student-Produced Responses ONLY ANSWERS THAT ARE GRIDDED WILL BE SCORED. YOU WILL NOT RECEIVE CREDIT FOR ANYTHING WRITTEN IN THE BOXES.

Quality Assurance Mark ●

SECTION 8

1 Ⓐ Ⓑ Ⓒ Ⓓ Ⓔ
2 Ⓐ Ⓑ Ⓒ Ⓓ Ⓔ
3 Ⓐ Ⓑ Ⓒ Ⓓ Ⓔ
4 Ⓐ Ⓑ Ⓒ Ⓓ Ⓔ
5 Ⓐ Ⓑ Ⓒ Ⓓ Ⓔ
6 Ⓐ Ⓑ Ⓒ Ⓓ Ⓔ
7 Ⓐ Ⓑ Ⓒ Ⓓ Ⓔ
8 Ⓐ Ⓑ Ⓒ Ⓓ Ⓔ
9 Ⓐ Ⓑ Ⓒ Ⓓ Ⓔ
10 Ⓐ Ⓑ Ⓒ Ⓓ Ⓔ

11 Ⓐ Ⓑ Ⓒ Ⓓ Ⓔ
12 Ⓐ Ⓑ Ⓒ Ⓓ Ⓔ
13 Ⓐ Ⓑ Ⓒ Ⓓ Ⓔ
14 Ⓐ Ⓑ Ⓒ Ⓓ Ⓔ
15 Ⓐ Ⓑ Ⓒ Ⓓ Ⓔ
16 Ⓐ Ⓑ Ⓒ Ⓓ Ⓔ
17 Ⓐ Ⓑ Ⓒ Ⓓ Ⓔ
18 Ⓐ Ⓑ Ⓒ Ⓓ Ⓔ
19 Ⓐ Ⓑ Ⓒ Ⓓ Ⓔ
20 Ⓐ Ⓑ Ⓒ Ⓓ Ⓔ

21 Ⓐ Ⓑ Ⓒ Ⓓ Ⓔ
22 Ⓐ Ⓑ Ⓒ Ⓓ Ⓔ
23 Ⓐ Ⓑ Ⓒ Ⓓ Ⓔ
24 Ⓐ Ⓑ Ⓒ Ⓓ Ⓔ
25 Ⓐ Ⓑ Ⓒ Ⓓ Ⓔ
26 Ⓐ Ⓑ Ⓒ Ⓓ Ⓔ
27 Ⓐ Ⓑ Ⓒ Ⓓ Ⓔ
28 Ⓐ Ⓑ Ⓒ Ⓓ Ⓔ
29 Ⓐ Ⓑ Ⓒ Ⓓ Ⓔ
30 Ⓐ Ⓑ Ⓒ Ⓓ Ⓔ

31 Ⓐ Ⓑ Ⓒ Ⓓ Ⓔ
32 Ⓐ Ⓑ Ⓒ Ⓓ Ⓔ
33 Ⓐ Ⓑ Ⓒ Ⓓ Ⓔ
34 Ⓐ Ⓑ Ⓒ Ⓓ Ⓔ
35 Ⓐ Ⓑ Ⓒ Ⓓ Ⓔ
36 Ⓐ Ⓑ Ⓒ Ⓓ Ⓔ
37 Ⓐ Ⓑ Ⓒ Ⓓ Ⓔ
38 Ⓐ Ⓑ Ⓒ Ⓓ Ⓔ
39 Ⓐ Ⓑ Ⓒ Ⓓ Ⓔ
40 Ⓐ Ⓑ Ⓒ Ⓓ Ⓔ

SECTION 9

1 Ⓐ Ⓑ Ⓒ Ⓓ Ⓔ
2 Ⓐ Ⓑ Ⓒ Ⓓ Ⓔ
3 Ⓐ Ⓑ Ⓒ Ⓓ Ⓔ
4 Ⓐ Ⓑ Ⓒ Ⓓ Ⓔ
5 Ⓐ Ⓑ Ⓒ Ⓓ Ⓔ
6 Ⓐ Ⓑ Ⓒ Ⓓ Ⓔ
7 Ⓐ Ⓑ Ⓒ Ⓓ Ⓔ
8 Ⓐ Ⓑ Ⓒ Ⓓ Ⓔ
9 Ⓐ Ⓑ Ⓒ Ⓓ Ⓔ
10 Ⓐ Ⓑ Ⓒ Ⓓ Ⓔ

11 Ⓐ Ⓑ Ⓒ Ⓓ Ⓔ
12 Ⓐ Ⓑ Ⓒ Ⓓ Ⓔ
13 Ⓐ Ⓑ Ⓒ Ⓓ Ⓔ
14 Ⓐ Ⓑ Ⓒ Ⓓ Ⓔ
15 Ⓐ Ⓑ Ⓒ Ⓓ Ⓔ
16 Ⓐ Ⓑ Ⓒ Ⓓ Ⓔ
17 Ⓐ Ⓑ Ⓒ Ⓓ Ⓔ
18 Ⓐ Ⓑ Ⓒ Ⓓ Ⓔ
19 Ⓐ Ⓑ Ⓒ Ⓓ Ⓔ
20 Ⓐ Ⓑ Ⓒ Ⓓ Ⓔ

21 Ⓐ Ⓑ Ⓒ Ⓓ Ⓔ
22 Ⓐ Ⓑ Ⓒ Ⓓ Ⓔ
23 Ⓐ Ⓑ Ⓒ Ⓓ Ⓔ
24 Ⓐ Ⓑ Ⓒ Ⓓ Ⓔ
25 Ⓐ Ⓑ Ⓒ Ⓓ Ⓔ
26 Ⓐ Ⓑ Ⓒ Ⓓ Ⓔ
27 Ⓐ Ⓑ Ⓒ Ⓓ Ⓔ
28 Ⓐ Ⓑ Ⓒ Ⓓ Ⓔ
29 Ⓐ Ⓑ Ⓒ Ⓓ Ⓔ
30 Ⓐ Ⓑ Ⓒ Ⓓ Ⓔ

31 Ⓐ Ⓑ Ⓒ Ⓓ Ⓔ
32 Ⓐ Ⓑ Ⓒ Ⓓ Ⓔ
33 Ⓐ Ⓑ Ⓒ Ⓓ Ⓔ
34 Ⓐ Ⓑ Ⓒ Ⓓ Ⓔ
35 Ⓐ Ⓑ Ⓒ Ⓓ Ⓔ
36 Ⓐ Ⓑ Ⓒ Ⓓ Ⓔ
37 Ⓐ Ⓑ Ⓒ Ⓓ Ⓔ
38 Ⓐ Ⓑ Ⓒ Ⓓ Ⓔ
39 Ⓐ Ⓑ Ⓒ Ⓓ Ⓔ
40 Ⓐ Ⓑ Ⓒ Ⓓ Ⓔ

SECTION 10

1 Ⓐ Ⓑ Ⓒ Ⓓ Ⓔ
2 Ⓐ Ⓑ Ⓒ Ⓓ Ⓔ
3 Ⓐ Ⓑ Ⓒ Ⓓ Ⓔ
4 Ⓐ Ⓑ Ⓒ Ⓓ Ⓔ
5 Ⓐ Ⓑ Ⓒ Ⓓ Ⓔ
6 Ⓐ Ⓑ Ⓒ Ⓓ Ⓔ
7 Ⓐ Ⓑ Ⓒ Ⓓ Ⓔ
8 Ⓐ Ⓑ Ⓒ Ⓓ Ⓔ
9 Ⓐ Ⓑ Ⓒ Ⓓ Ⓔ
10 Ⓐ Ⓑ Ⓒ Ⓓ Ⓔ

11 Ⓐ Ⓑ Ⓒ Ⓓ Ⓔ
12 Ⓐ Ⓑ Ⓒ Ⓓ Ⓔ
13 Ⓐ Ⓑ Ⓒ Ⓓ Ⓔ
14 Ⓐ Ⓑ Ⓒ Ⓓ Ⓔ
15 Ⓐ Ⓑ Ⓒ Ⓓ Ⓔ
16 Ⓐ Ⓑ Ⓒ Ⓓ Ⓔ
17 Ⓐ Ⓑ Ⓒ Ⓓ Ⓔ
18 Ⓐ Ⓑ Ⓒ Ⓓ Ⓔ
19 Ⓐ Ⓑ Ⓒ Ⓓ Ⓔ
20 Ⓐ Ⓑ Ⓒ Ⓓ Ⓔ

21 Ⓐ Ⓑ Ⓒ Ⓓ Ⓔ
22 Ⓐ Ⓑ Ⓒ Ⓓ Ⓔ
23 Ⓐ Ⓑ Ⓒ Ⓓ Ⓔ
24 Ⓐ Ⓑ Ⓒ Ⓓ Ⓔ
25 Ⓐ Ⓑ Ⓒ Ⓓ Ⓔ
26 Ⓐ Ⓑ Ⓒ Ⓓ Ⓔ
27 Ⓐ Ⓑ Ⓒ Ⓓ Ⓔ
28 Ⓐ Ⓑ Ⓒ Ⓓ Ⓔ
29 Ⓐ Ⓑ Ⓒ Ⓓ Ⓔ
30 Ⓐ Ⓑ Ⓒ Ⓓ Ⓔ

31 Ⓐ Ⓑ Ⓒ Ⓓ Ⓔ
32 Ⓐ Ⓑ Ⓒ Ⓓ Ⓔ
33 Ⓐ Ⓑ Ⓒ Ⓓ Ⓔ
34 Ⓐ Ⓑ Ⓒ Ⓓ Ⓔ
35 Ⓐ Ⓑ Ⓒ Ⓓ Ⓔ
36 Ⓐ Ⓑ Ⓒ Ⓓ Ⓔ
37 Ⓐ Ⓑ Ⓒ Ⓓ Ⓔ
38 Ⓐ Ⓑ Ⓒ Ⓓ Ⓔ
39 Ⓐ Ⓑ Ⓒ Ⓓ Ⓔ
40 Ⓐ Ⓑ Ⓒ Ⓓ Ⓔ

SECTION 1
ESSAY
Time — 25 minutes

Turn to Section 1 of your answer sheet to write your essay.

The essay gives you an opportunity to show how effectively you can develop and express ideas. You should, therefore, take care to develop your point of view, present your ideas logically and clearly, and use language precisely.

Your essay must be written on the lines provided on your answer sheet—you will receive no other paper on which to write. You will have enough space if you write on every line, avoid wide margins, and keep your handwriting to a reasonable size. Remember that people who are not familiar with your handwriting will read what you write. Try to write or print so that what you are writing is legible to those readers.

You have twenty-five minutes to write an essay on the topic assigned below. DO NOT WRITE ON ANOTHER TOPIC. AN OFF-TOPIC ESSAY WILL RECEIVE A SCORE OF ZERO.

Think carefully about the issue presented in the following excerpt and the assignment below.

> Despite the dazzling successes of modern technologies, they suffer from a common and catastrophic fault. Although they provide us with a bountiful supply of food, with great industrial plants, with high-speed transportation, and with military weapons of unprecedented power, they also threaten our very survival.
>
> Adapted from Barry Commoner, *Science and Survival*

Assignment: Do the costs of technology sometimes outweigh the benefits? Plan and write an essay in which you develop your point of view on this issue. Support your position with reasoning and examples taken from your reading, studies, experience, or observations.

DO NOT WRITE YOUR ESSAY IN YOUR TEST BOOK. You will receive credit only for what you write on your answer sheet.

BEGIN WRITING YOUR ESSAY IN SECTION 1 OF THE ANSWER SHEET.

STOP

If you finish before time is called, you may check your work on this section only.
Do not turn to any other section in the test.

SECTION 2
Time — 25 minutes
24 Questions

Turn to Section 2 of your answer sheet to answer the questions in this section.

Directions: For each question in this section, select the best answer from among the choices given and fill in the corresponding circle on the answer sheet.

Each sentence below has one or two blanks, each blank indicating that something has been omitted. Beneath the sentence are five words or sets of words labeled A through E. Choose the word or set of words that, when inserted in the sentence, best fits the meaning of the sentence as a whole.

Example:

Desiring to ------- his taunting friends, Mitch gave them taffy in hopes it would keep their mouths shut.

(A) eliminate   (B) satisfy   (C) overcome
  (D) ridicule   (E) silence

Ⓐ Ⓑ Ⓒ Ⓓ ●

1. Although the student insisted his essay was an original, his teacher was -------, since she remembered reading the exact same paper last year.

   (A) circumspect   (B) ambivalent   (C) skeptical
       (D) stoic   (E) sanguine

2. Marie was ------- to disappointment, having weathered numerous instances of -------.

   (A) imperceptive . . affluence
   (B) unused . . misfortune
   (C) habituated . . contentment
   (D) accustomed . . disillusionment
   (E) resigned . . beneficence

3. Despite the fact that the docudrama was not entirely -------, historians extolled its production as -------.

   (A) factual . . meritorious
   (B) fabricated . . specious
   (C) prodigious . . exhaustive
   (D) theoretical . . naive
   (E) cordial . . dogmatic

4. Many fear that the ------- of more lenient rules regarding tobacco advertising could be detrimental to public health.

   (A) withdrawal   (B) ratification   (C) provocation
       (D) elocution   (E) elucidation

5. In low-pressure air systems, clouds can contain large amounts of moisture, which allow them to ------- enough precipitation to make for damp and ------- weather.

   (A) produce . . sunny
   (B) generate . . inclement
   (C) advance . . humid
   (D) agitate . . chilly
   (E) evaporate . . foggy

6. The coach does not expect his players to be -------, that is, lacking energy before an important game.

   (A) irksome   (B) complacent   (C) listless
       (D) idle   (E) vital

7. Professional critics derided the actor's performance as lacking subtlety and depth, and predicted that his fame would be -------.

   (A) esoteric   (B) ephemeral   (C) dramatic
       (D) lucrative   (E) pejorative

8. The ------- of the wax museum's statues astounded us; the Elvis sculpture appeared so lifelike that I half expected it to speak.

   (A) verisimilitude   (B) integrity   (C) placidity
       (D) fecundity   (E) deviousness

GO ON TO THE NEXT PAGE

Directions: Each passage below is followed by questions based on its content. Answer the questions on the basis of what is <u>stated</u> or <u>implied</u> in each passage and in any introductory material that may be provided.

Questions 9-10 are based on the following passage.

Why is the Dead Sea so salty? Although the Dead Sea is fed by the Jordan River and a number of smaller tributaries, the sea has no outlet. Therefore, any water that flows into the
Line Dead Sea stays in the Dead Sea, at least until the process of
5 evaporation takes effect. The heat of the region causes the water to evaporate at a high rate. Any mineral deposits remain during the process and, as a result, the liquid turns brackish. Though no marine life or vegetation can survive in this salty concoction, humans can often be found laying back and
10 relaxing without the use of rafts or inner tubes.

9. According to the passage, the rate of evaporation is increased when

(A) marine life is threatened
(B) saline levels decrease
(C) mineral deposits remain
(D) high temperatures prevail
(E) water flows from tributaries

10. The function of the passage as a whole is to

(A) probe a unique phenomenon
(B) introduce an irksome concept
(C) challenge a long-held assumption
(D) question a misunderstood fact
(E) propose a viable solution

Questions 11-12 are based on the following passage.

Sumerian history may be divided into three main periods. The first, from roughly 3360 B.C. to 2400 B.C., was characterized primarily by incessant wars between rival
Line city-states. Sargon I, the king of the city of Akkad, marked
5 the beginning of the second main phase of Sumerian history around 2350 B.C. by building a stable empire after conquering the majority of the Sumerian city-states. Akkadian rule lasted about 200 years until the Gutians, a Sumerian mountain people, overthrew the Akkadian monarch, a great-grandson
10 of Sargon I. This event ushered in the third and final period of Sumerian history, the "neo-Sumerian" period, so called because of the return of native Sumerian rule to the lands.

11. Which of the following may be properly concluded from the passage?

(A) Prior to Sargon I, no Sumerian warlord had succeeded in conquering a majority of Sumerian city-states.
(B) The Sumerian civilization was at some points in its history ruled by non-Sumerian monarchs.
(C) Sumerian history was marked by incessant warfare between the Gutians and Akkadians.
(D) The second phase of Sumerian history, from 2350 B.C. to approximately 2150 B.C., was the shortest of the three main periods.
(E) All Sumerian monarchs passed their titles down to their sons and grandsons.

12. According to the passage, the Gutians

(A) were the only people willing to challenge the reigning Akkadian monarch
(B) were responsible for restoring native rule to the Sumerian civilization
(C) established a dynasty similar to the type of dynasty that characterized the first phase of Sumerian history
(D) were able to maintain a stable empire after overthrowing the great-grandson of Sargon I
(E) called the third period of Sumerian history the "neo-Sumerian" period

GO ON TO THE NEXT PAGE

Questions 13-24 are based on the following passage.

In the following fiction passage, the narrator reflects on an incident from his adolescence.

Up on the bandstand, framed by the giant pines that
towered over the crumbling barn, a quartet played
provincial songs, ones that were easily recognizable to
everyone in the valley. We had heard them throughout our
childhood, tunes that celebrated our land and its people, in
this unique place that had yet to be touched by the strife and
growing dangers of the outside world. The lilting melodies
made some of the older women sob softly. They dabbed
their handkerchiefs at the corners of their eyes and looked
longingly at their sons. I wondered if Mother, if she were still
with us, would have allowed herself to show such emotion.
Her stoic presence on the farm had always struck my brothers
as distant, but I knew she had cared for us in ways that were
deep and ineffable. The thought passed as quickly as it came,
and my attention turned to the movement of the dancers and
the noise of the chatter that bounced between Ralph and
Michael. The pair were surveying the moonlit crowd and
talking nervously about a plan Ralph had devised earlier in
the week. One of us, he claimed, would fall in love that night.

We sipped our drinks—sickly sweet lemonade pressed by
hand and tainted with heaps of sugar—and eyed the bourgeois
girls who had come in from the city in their opulent motorcars
and garish dresses. So innocent and frightened we were!
Michael admitted he did not have the courage to utter a word
to any of the female strangers who stood before us now. But
Ralph was resolute. He had boasted all week that he would
find the most beautiful girl who ventured into his orbit, whisk
her onto the matted grass, and dance madly with her until she
broke into a smile. The plan was delicious in its simplicity,
but the enthusiasm I had felt earlier had greatly diminished
in the face of what seemed like a cruel reality. Who were we
to think that any of these urbane ladies, with their perfumed
hair and nimble ankles, would tolerate our shabby attire and
callused hands?

Like an eel, Ralph weaved through the jostling crowd,
now ebullient since the band members had picked up the
rhythm and were playing their instruments with vigor. We
scurried behind him, keeping just enough distance between us
not to look suspicious. He was navigating toward a tall, thin
angel with blonde curls and tiny hands. When Ralph finally
reached her, I was not ten paces from him, yet his proposal
was barely audible over the din of the crowd. He gestured
wildly with his arms, miming what appeared to be a waltz.
Although I could not hear her response, it was obvious that
she had demurred. The blood from Ralph's face drained away
and he sulked for a moment, perhaps hoping she would relent.
When it was clear that she had no intention of waltzing with
him, Ralph meandered back towards Michael and me. "She'll
have none of it . . ." his voice trailed off. "Silly girl. I'm the
best dancer in the county!"

Michael and I said nothing. We looked at our shoes and
pushed the dirt around in circles as if to indicate resignation.
I found myself thinking of Mother once more. If she were
here, had her health not failed her last winter, she would have
introduced me to Sylvia, who was unlike any of the girls
at the dance, with their painted faces and insensible shoes.
Mother had always spoken highly of Sylvia. Her family was
of good stock, she said, and according to Mother, that counted
more than wealth or possessions. Yet here I was, standing
beneath the pines, the music of my childhood reaching its
crescendo, with only Ralph's foolish plan and Michael's
lethargy to guide me. I looked up and saw a cloud appear
across the moon, and for a moment, I felt the distinct chill of
autumn descending on the valley.

13. In lines 4-7, the author suggests that the songs played by
the quartet had special meaning, because

(A) the people of the region recognized local themes in
the music
(B) the melodies made the elders of the valley feel sad
about the future
(C) the area produced unique musicians that could be
found only in the valley
(D) the children at the dance were the only ones to
recognize their value
(E) the women in attendance were eager to dance to the
music

14. In line 20 "sickly" most nearly means

(A) unhealthily
(B) weakly
(C) overpoweringly
(D) amazingly
(E) deliciously

15. The narrator's assertion about a "cruel reality" in lines
29-34 would be most weakened if which of the following
were true?

(A) The valley was widely considered to be inferior to
the city.
(B) Naive young men were less desirable than urbane
young men.
(C) A person's ability to dance was more important than
wealth or privilege.
(D) Wealthy young women came to the valley to meet
boys of humble origins.
(E) Outward appearances were crucial in measuring a
person's worth.

GO ON TO THE NEXT PAGE

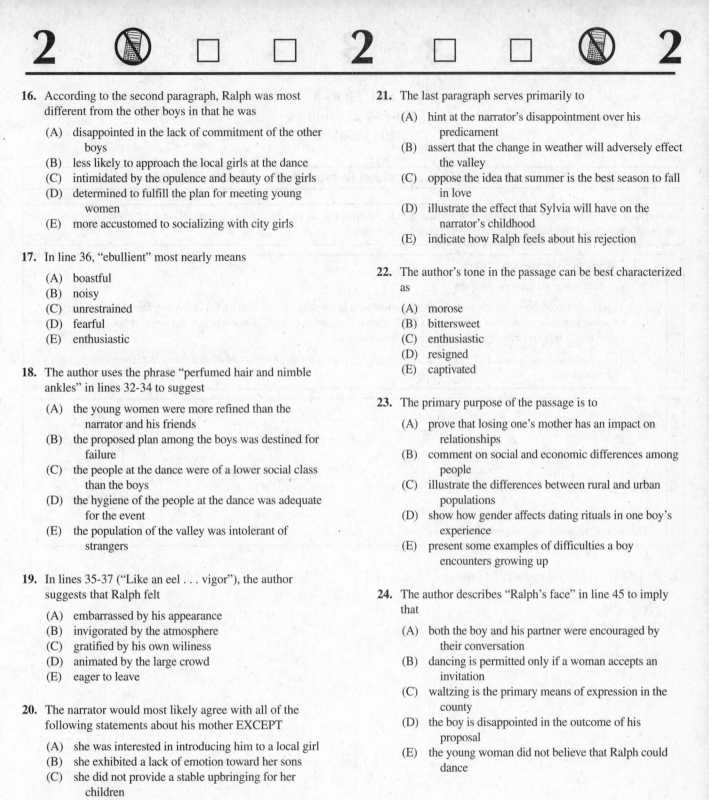
16. According to the second paragraph, Ralph was most different from the other boys in that he was

(A) disappointed in the lack of commitment of the other boys
(B) less likely to approach the local girls at the dance
(C) intimidated by the opulence and beauty of the girls
(D) determined to fulfill the plan for meeting young women
(E) more accustomed to socializing with city girls

17. In line 36, "ebullient" most nearly means

(A) boastful
(B) noisy
(C) unrestrained
(D) fearful
(E) enthusiastic

18. The author uses the phrase "perfumed hair and nimble ankles" in lines 32-34 to suggest

(A) the young women were more refined than the narrator and his friends
(B) the proposed plan among the boys was destined for failure
(C) the people at the dance were of a lower social class than the boys
(D) the hygiene of the people at the dance was adequate for the event
(E) the population of the valley was intolerant of strangers

19. In lines 35-37 ("Like an eel . . . vigor"), the author suggests that Ralph felt

(A) embarrassed by his appearance
(B) invigorated by the atmosphere
(C) gratified by his own wiliness
(D) animated by the large crowd
(E) eager to leave

20. The narrator would most likely agree with all of the following statements about his mother EXCEPT

(A) she was interested in introducing him to a local girl
(B) she exhibited a lack of emotion toward her sons
(C) she did not provide a stable upbringing for her children
(D) she believed one's worth was based on character
(E) she had deep feelings for her children and their well-being

21. The last paragraph serves primarily to

(A) hint at the narrator's disappointment over his predicament
(B) assert that the change in weather will adversely effect the valley
(C) oppose the idea that summer is the best season to fall in love
(D) illustrate the effect that Sylvia will have on the narrator's childhood
(E) indicate how Ralph feels about his rejection

22. The author's tone in the passage can be best characterized as

(A) morose
(B) bittersweet
(C) enthusiastic
(D) resigned
(E) captivated

23. The primary purpose of the passage is to

(A) prove that losing one's mother has an impact on relationships
(B) comment on social and economic differences among people
(C) illustrate the differences between rural and urban populations
(D) show how gender affects dating rituals in one boy's experience
(E) present some examples of difficulties a boy encounters growing up

24. The author describes "Ralph's face" in line 45 to imply that

(A) both the boy and his partner were encouraged by their conversation
(B) dancing is permitted only if a woman accepts an invitation
(C) waltzing is the primary means of expression in the county
(D) the boy is disappointed in the outcome of his proposal
(E) the young woman did not believe that Ralph could dance

STOP

If you finish before time is called, you may check your work on this section only.
Do not turn to any other section in the test.

SECTION 3
Time — 25 minutes
20 Questions

Turn to Section 3 of your answer sheet to answer the questions in this section.

Directions: For this section, solve each problem and decide which is the best of the choices given. Fill in the corresponding circle on the answer sheet. You may use any available space for scratchwork.

Notes

1. The use of a calculator is permitted.

2. All numbers used are real numbers.

3. Figures that accompany problems in this test are intended to provide information useful in solving the problems. They are drawn as accurately as possible EXCEPT when it is stated in a specific problem that the figure is not drawn to scale. All figures lie in a plane unless otherwise indicated.

4. Unless otherwise specified, the domain of any function f is assumed to be the set of all real numbers x for which $f(x)$ is a real number.

Reference Information

 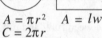 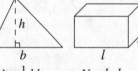 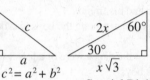

$A = \pi r^2$
$C = 2\pi r$
$A = lw$
$A = \frac{1}{2}bh$
$V = lwh$
$V = \pi r^2 h$
$c^2 = a^2 + b^2$

Special Right Triangles

The number of degrees of arc in a circle is 360.

The sum of the measures in degrees of the angles of a triangle is 180.

---

1. If $(0.008)x = 0.032$, then what is the value of $0.08x$?

(A)   0.032
(B)   0.32
(C)   3.2
(D)   32
(E)   320

2. If $|x+3| > 5$, which of the following is a possible value of x ?

(A)   −9
(B)   −8
(C)   −3
(D)   1
(E)   2

GO ON TO THE NEXT PAGE

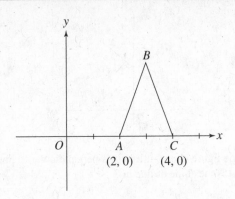

3. Isosceles $\triangle ABC$, shown above, has an area of 4. If $AB = BC$, what is the coordinate of point B ?

(A) (3, 2)
(B) (3, 4)
(C) (4, 4)
(D) (4, 3)
(E) (0, 3)

4. Five people stand in line: three men, Denzel, Melvin, and Aneet, and two women, Janine and Susan. The order in which they stand must match the following conditions:

  (1) A man is not first in line.
  (2) Denzel is ahead of Janine in the line.
  (3) A woman must stand fourth in line.
  (4) Melvin cannot stand next to Denzel.

In which position does Melvin stand in the line?

(A) First
(B) Second
(C) Third
(D) Fourth
(E) Fifth

5. If $x < y < z$ and the average (arithmetic mean) of x, y, and z is y, which of the following must be true?

(A) $z - y = 2$
(B) $x + y + z = 3y$
(C) $x + y < z$
(D) $x + y = z$
(E) $2z = 3y$

6. After selling $\dfrac{1}{3}$ of the muffins he made for the school bake sale, Alan then sold an additional 10 muffins, leaving him with $\dfrac{1}{2}$ of the number of muffins he started with. How many muffins did Alan start with?

(A) 30
(B) 42
(C) 50
(D) 60
(E) 75

GO ON TO THE NEXT PAGE

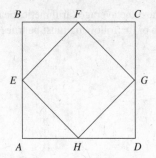

7. In the figure above, *E, F, G,* and *H* are the midpoints of $\overline{AB}$, $\overline{BC}$, $\overline{CD}$, and $\overline{DA}$, respectively, and *ABCD* is a square with perimeter 16. What is the perimeter of *EFGH* ?

(A)   2

(B)   4

(C)   8

(D) $2\sqrt{2}$

(E) $8\sqrt{2}$

8. $\left(-3a^2b^5\right)^3 =$

(A) $-3a^5b^8$

(B) $-3a^6b^{15}$

(C) $-27a^5b^8$

(D) $-27a^6b^{15}$

(E) $27a^6b^{15}$

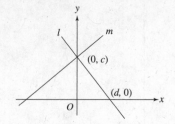

9. In the figure above, if line *m* is perpendicular to line *l*, what is the slope of line *m* ?

(A) $-\dfrac{d}{c}$

(B) $\dfrac{d}{c}$

(C) $\dfrac{c}{d}$

(D) $-\dfrac{1}{cd}$

(E) $-\dfrac{c^2}{d}$

10. If $|3x - 6| = 36$, what is one possible value of *x* ?

(A)   −30

(B)   −14

(C)   −10

(D)   0

(E)   10

GO ON TO THE NEXT PAGE

11. If the ratio of *a* to *b* is equal to the ratio of 2*a* to *b*, and *b* ≠ 0, which of the following must be true?

    I. $b = 2a$
   II. $a = 0$
  III. $b = 2b$

(A) I only
(B) II only
(C) III only
(D) I and II
(E) II and III

12. If $3y^4 + xy - x^2 = y^2 - 25$ and $y = 0$, how many possible values of *x* are there?

(A) 0
(B) 1
(C) 2
(D) 3
(E) 4

13. If *w* is a positive odd integer, which of the following gives a possible value of the product of one more than *w* and 2 less than *w* ?

(A)   0
(B)   10
(C)   18
(D)   28
(E)   54

ACRES OF FOREST LAND DEVELOPED

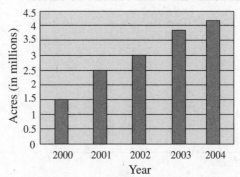

14. The chart above shows acres of forest land that were developed for each of five years. Which of the following is the closest approximation of the median number of acres developed from 2001 to 2004 ?

(A) 1.2
(B) 2.5
(C) 3.0
(D) 3.4
(E) 4.1

GO ON TO THE NEXT PAGE

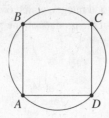

15. In the figure above, square *ABCD* is inscribed in the circle. If the perimeter of *ABCD* is 4, what is the circumference of the circle?

(A) $\dfrac{\pi}{2}$

(B) π

(C) $\dfrac{\sqrt{2}}{2}\pi$

(D) $\sqrt{2}\pi$

(E) 2π

16. The members of set *A* are the single digit prime numbers. Two numbers are selected at random from set *A*. What is the probability that the average (arithmetic mean) of the two selected numbers is even?

(A) 0

(B) $\dfrac{1}{6}$

(C) $\dfrac{1}{3}$

(D) $\dfrac{1}{2}$

(E) 1

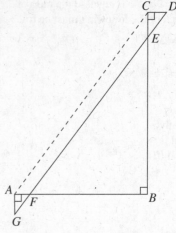

Note: Figure not drawn to scale.

17. In the figure above, *AGF, BEF,* and *CDE* are all isosceles right triangles. If $BE = 2x$, and $GF = ED = x\sqrt{2}$, what is *AC* in terms of *x* ?

(A) $3x\sqrt{2}$

(B) $4x$

(C) $2x\sqrt{2}$

(D) $3x$

(E) $x\sqrt{3}$

18. If *r* is a positive even integer and *s* is a prime integer, then all of the following are factors of *rs* EXCEPT

(A) *r*

(B) *s*

(C) *2s*

(D) *2r*

(E) 2

GO ON TO THE NEXT PAGE

19. The Brighton High School Marching Band has x members. The Brighton Drum Corp has y members. If the Monroe County All-Star Drum Line consists of all the members of the Brighton High School Marching Band and all the members of the Brighton Drum Corp except for the p common members ($p > 0$), then how many members does the Monroe County All-Star Drum Line have in terms of x, y, and p ?

(A) $x + y$
(B) $x + y - p$
(C) $x + y + 2p$
(D) $x + y - 2p$
(E) $2x + 2y - p$

20. a, b, c, d, and e are all integers, where $a < b < c < d < e$. If c, d, and e are each greater than the product of the next two smaller values (for example, $d > bc$), and $e = 6$, which of the following could equal zero?

(A) a only
(B) b only
(C) b or c only
(D) a, b, or c only
(E) a, b, c, or d only

STOP

If you finish before time is called, you may check your work on this section only.
Do not turn to any other section in the test.

SECTION 4
Time — 25 minutes
24 Questions

Turn to Section 4 of your answer sheet to answer the questions in this section.

Directions: For each question in this section, select the best answer from among the choices given and fill in the corresponding circle on the answer sheet.

Each sentence below has one or two blanks, each blank indicating that something has been omitted. Beneath the sentence are five words or sets of words labeled A through E. Choose the word or set of words that, when inserted in the sentence, best fits the meaning of the sentence as a whole.

Example:

Desiring to ------- his taunting friends, Mitch gave them taffy in hopes it would keep their mouths shut.

(A) eliminate   (B) satisfy   (C) overcome
    (D) ridicule   (E) silence

Ⓐ Ⓑ Ⓒ Ⓓ ●

---

1. The precision and significant breadth of her revised essay showcased Latricia's ------- writing skill, whereas her first draft was ------- and obviously rushed.

   (A) formidable . . practiced
   (B) factual . . thorough
   (C) linguistic . . creative
   (D) considerable . . scattered
   (E) polished . . effective

2. One cannot help but be moved by Theresa's ------- struggle to overcome a devastating and debilitating accident.

   (A) heartrending   (B) provoked   (C) belated
       (D) therapeutic   (E) brief

3. The Louvre museum houses many paintings that likely will never be -------, because the Louvre's ownership rights to them are virtually -------.

   (A) viewed . . variable
   (B) released . . incomprehensible
   (C) maintained . . laudable
   (D) devalued . . regrettable
   (E) transferred . . inalienable

4. Lincoln made his Gettysburg Address concise by using only the most ------- language possible and by relying on the compact power of the few lines he chose to deliver.

   (A) celebratory   (B) timorous   (C) succinct
       (D) solemn   (E) glorious

5. The evidence strongly suggested the suspect was guilty, but the jury found no such -------.

   (A) exoneration   (B) juxtaposition   (C) acquittal
       (D) manifestation   (E) culpability

GO ON TO THE NEXT PAGE

Directions: Each passage below is followed by questions based on its content. Answer the questions on the basis of what is <u>stated</u> or <u>implied</u> in each passage and in any introductory material that may be provided.

Questions 6-9 are based on the following passages.

Passage 1

No major political election in the United States has ever been decided by one vote. In fact, a single vote contributes only about one millionth of the total result of the average
Line statewide election. Considering how numerically insignificant
5 a single vote is, is there any rational justification for an individual to vote? In order to answer this question, one must look past the mere numerical value of a vote. An individual's vote is valuable as a measure of that individual's belief in the system of government, which likewise indicates the degree to
10 which a person feels included in the greater social order.

Passage 2

When recently asked whom he voted for in the last presidential election, a friend of mine replied, "I didn't bother." With a rather bored shrug, and little embarrassment, my friend continued, "It's not like it matters. My vote
15 wouldn't have changed the outcome." I couldn't help thinking then that the argument was uncannily persuasive. If I had stayed in bed that morning, the result would likewise be exactly the same. But the argument does not hold up under scrutiny. If democracy means rule by the people, and not
20 by any one individual, then why should the vote of just one person determine the outcome of an election? No person, no matter who he is, should be able to change the greater will of a collected group. The idea of doing so is simply undemocratic.

6. Which of the following, if true, would most strengthen the hypothesis of the author of Passage 1 concerning voting behavior?

   (A) Historical documents reveal that many local elections have been decided by a single vote.
   (B) A new study finds that many Americans feel that voting is a burdensome inconvenience.
   (C) A poll of American citizens indicates that most citizens consider voting an important communal duty.
   (D) Voting records show that most people who vote participate in both national and local elections.
   (E) People who vote once tend to continue to vote in other elections.

7. The author of Passage 1 would most likely conclude which of the following about the "friend" described in Passage 2 (line 12) ?

   (A) The friend likely feels that he is disconnected from the society in which he lives.
   (B) Unless he changes the outcome of an election, the friend is unlikely to ever vote.
   (C) The number of people today who act as the friend does indicates a fundamental flaw in society.
   (D) The friend distrusts his government and the elected officials.
   (E) People who don't feel the need to vote are generally satisfied with life as it is.

8. Both passages serve to discourage the

   (A) inclination of Americans to invent excuses for not voting
   (B) reliance on elections as a means of choosing leaders
   (C) tendency of voters to avoid making difficult decisions
   (D) valuation of a vote by its ability to decide an election
   (E) apathy that some voters feel about the lack of real choices

9. The final sentence of Passage 2 serves to

   (A) explain the rationale behind a behavior pattern
   (B) denounce the actions of those who do not vote
   (C) show the subtle irony of the friend's argument
   (D) offer a solution to a pressing problem
   (E) remind people of the original intent of the Constitution

GO ON TO THE NEXT PAGE

Questions 10-18 are based on the following passage.

The following passage concerns the Irish author James Joyce and investigates the literary significance of his longtime self-imposed exile to his work.

The Irish author James Joyce (1882-1941) created some of the most unique and personal, yet controversial and inaccessible, literature of the last century. With his modernist,
Line experimental narrative style, his close attention to the details
5 of ordinary life, his novel technical innovations, and his recurring themes of isolation and exile, Joyce created fictional worlds at once stark and foreign, yet simultaneously rich and familiar.

In order to better decipher the seemingly endless
10 conundrum of Joyce's meanings and messages, it is worth turning one's attention to events in Joyce's life that may help the reader understand some of the sources of his creative inspiration. While studies of Joyce have considered the importance of Joyce's years in exile to his writing, few have
15 made explicit the connections between Joyce's writing and the specific contexts of his time abroad; Richard Ellman's definitive 1959 treatment and John McCourt's more recent work are the exceptions rather than the rule in this regard. The parallels between the reality of Joyce's life and the
20 fictional worlds he created are too frequent to ignore.

Joyce first fled Dublin in 1904 with his lifelong love, Nora Barnacle, for reasons both personal and professional. Joyce and Barnacle were then unmarried, and their relationship was the target of social condemnation. So, too, was Joyce driven
25 out of Ireland by the Catholic Church's harsh criticism of his early writings in which he clearly rejected what he felt to be the Church's oppressive spiritual controls. For eleven years, the couple lived in the major Mediterranean seaport of Trieste, then an Austrian imperial city. Trieste was a melting
30 pot of mercantile, religious, and cultural activity, and its language, Triestino (which Joyce came to speak beautifully) was an amalgamation of blended words and sounds from many languages. Joyce's exposure to Triestino directly influenced Joyce's fashioning of his own potpourri language
35 for his final novel *Finnegan's Wake*; the composite dialect of the work harkened back to its English origins, but also incorporated diverse elements of many tongues.

As Joyce's most famous biographer, Ellman, notes, every moment of an author's waking life may manifest itself in the
40 author's work, and Joyce himself encouraged his audience to read his works autobiographically. However, ferreting out the autobiographical elements from Joyce's work involves much more than such a superficial survey of literary images. The relationship between an author's writings and the author's life
45 experiences is not as transparent as it may seem. A writer's life may be reflected in his work, but this reflection is almost always distorted to some degree, sometimes purposefully, and sometimes inadvertently.

This situation leaves both the reader and the critic at an
50 intriguing impasse: when can we know when a seemingly autobiographical image in a fictional work is actually meaningful? When, in *Ulysses,* Joyce's literary alter ego Stephen Dedalus muses on whether Shakespeare's characters were all based on actual people that he knew, is this an
55 example of Joyce commenting indirectly on Shakespeare, or of Joyce alluding to his own work? Regardless of how tempting it may be for the reader to read *Ulysses* or *A Portrait of the Artist as a Young Man* solely through the biography of Joyce, such a technique is fraught with danger, since we can
60 ultimately never be sure exactly what any author means to express through his or her art.

10. It can be inferred that Joyce left Dublin and went into exile to

(A) find literary inspiration
(B) attain greater artistic and personal freedom
(C) accept a job as a writer
(D) escape Nora's parents' disapproval
(E) raise a family in a richer cultural environment

11. The description of Joyce's work in the first paragraph provides information about all of the following EXCEPT

(A) when Joyce wrote his first novel
(B) the style in which Joyce wrote
(C) the degree of critical acclaim Joyce has received
(D) some of the themes of Joyce's writing
(E) when Joyce lived

12. In line 10, "conundrum" most nearly means

(A) stratagem
(B) conception
(C) intuition
(D) parody
(E) puzzle

GO ON TO THE NEXT PAGE

13. Which of the following best describes the organization of the passage?

(A) The author makes a specific claim, offers evidence to support this claim, and ends by expanding the discussion to a more general, but related, idea.
(B) The author states the main point, offers three theories that may support this point, and ends by selecting the theory that provides the best evidence.
(C) The author puts forth an idea, supports it with evidence, but ends by completely rejecting the original idea.
(D) The author makes a claim, shows that other writers also make this claim, and ends by criticizing the others' research methods.
(E) The author summarizes scholarly literature about James Joyce, then concludes that Joyce isn't as great a writer as originally claimed.

14. The author mentions Joyce's viewpoint ("Joyce himself . . . autobiographically") in lines 40-41 to emphasize

(A) how tempting it may be to read Joyce's work as a reflection of his life
(B) that Joyce and Ellman influenced each other in significant ways
(C) that Joyce intended to fool the reader all along
(D) that Joyce had to fight with his critics to have his work interpreted this way
(E) that Joyce always spoke directly through one of the characters in his books

15. The comment in lines 47-48 ("sometimes purposefully, and sometimes inadvertently") suggests that

(A) writers are usually writing about themselves
(B) writers can't tell fact from fiction
(C) writers may misrepresent an actual event in a fictional work without realizing it
(D) readers should not trust writers who write autobiographically
(E) readers don't always interpret a novel the way the author intended

16. According to the ideas presented in the final paragraph, which of the following is the most appropriate interpretation of Dedalus's claim regarding Shakespeare?

(A) Joyce had no real opinions about Shakespeare.
(B) The character of Dedalus was a literary critic.
(C) Joyce expressed this controversial belief through Dedalus to protect his career.
(D) Joyce may have believed Shakespeare's characters were based on real people.
(E) Dedalus was based on a person Joyce knew personally.

17. The last two paragraphs in the passage function primarily to

(A) partially refute the author's thesis
(B) support the author's main contention
(C) allow the reader to better appreciate Joyce's unique writing style
(D) make the claim that Joyce's work was not, in fact, autobiographical
(E) expand the scope of the passage to include other writers

18. All of the following could be considered autobiographical elements in Joyce's writing EXCEPT

(A) themes of isolation and exile
(B) a character who worked as a sailor in Trieste
(C) a character who is a writer
(D) a character who is persecuted for his religious beliefs
(E) the character of Stephen Dedalus

GO ON TO THE NEXT PAGE

Questions 19-24 are based on the following passage.

This passage describes the effects of geomagnetic storms on the earth.

The idea that the sun has an almost unambiguously benign effect on our planet appears, on the surface, to be an incontrovertible one. Few people realize, however, that
Line certain events on the sun can have disastrous consequences
5 for life here on Earth. The geomagnetic storm is one such phenomenon. These storms begin on the surface of the sun when a group of sunspots creates a burst of electromagnetic radiation. These bursts thrust billions of tons of ionized gas, known as plasma, into space; scientists refer to these
10 solar projections as coronal mass ejections (CMEs). After this initial explosion, the CME gets caught up in a shower of particles, also known as a "solar wind," that continuously rains down on the Earth from the sun.

The last recorded instance of a major CME occurred in
15 1989, when the resulting geomagnetic storm knocked out an entire electrical power grid, depriving over six million energy consumers of power for an extended period. As we become increasingly dependent on new technologies to sustain ourselves in our day-to-day activities, the potential havoc
20 wrought by a major CME becomes even more distressing. Scientists conjecture that a "perfect storm" would have the potential to knock out power grids across the globe and create disruptions in the orbit of low-altitude communication satellites, rendering such satellites practically useless.

25 What troubles scientists most about these "perfect storms" is not only their potential for interstellar mischief, but also the fact that they are so difficult to forecast. For one thing, remarkable though these solar occurrences might be, they are still a relatively rare phenomenon, and the few existing
30 records regarding major CMEs provide researchers with scant information from which to draw conclusions about their behavior. Solar storm watchers are frustrated by yet another limitation: time. CMEs have been known to travel through space at speeds approaching 5 million miles per hour, which
35 means they can cover the 93 million miles between the sun and the Earth in well under 20 hours. (Some have been known to travel the same distance in as little as 14 hours.) The difficulties created by this narrow window of opportunity are compounded by the fact that scientists are able to determine
40 the orientation of a CMEs magnetic field only about 30 minutes before it reaches the atmosphere, giving them little or no time to predict the storm's potential impact on the surface.

Some world governments hope to combat this problem by placing a satellite in orbit around the sun to monitor activity
45 on its surface, in the hopes that this will buy scientists more time to predict the occurrence and intensity of geomagnetic storms. In the meantime, many energy providers are responding to the CME threat by installing voltage control equipment and limiting the volume of electricity generated by
50 some power stations.

19. The primary purpose of this passage is

(A) to describe the chilling potential effects of a "perfect storm"
(B) to inform readers about CMEs and their effects on electrical circuitry on Earth
(C) to persuade readers that CMEs are a problem that both governments and individual citizens need to combat
(D) to inform readers about a potentially dangerous phenomenon and the difficulties in addressing that danger
(E) to convince readers that cultural dependence on electricity jeopardizes everyone

20. Which of the following can most reasonably be inferred about the significant CME that took place in 1989 ?

(A) Because of the hysteria caused by this storm, scientists and world leaders are more fearful of future storms than they are willing to express publicly.
(B) The next geomagnetic storm that occurs will be much worse.
(C) The window of opportunity for foreseeing similar storms in the future is even smaller now.
(D) Its effects were limited to knocking out a power grid, depriving customers of power for a week.
(E) A geomagnetic storm of similar magnitude could easily cause more extensive damage and hardship in today's society.

21. In line 31, "scant" most nearly means

(A) multifaceted
(B) limited
(C) exhaustive
(D) excessive
(E) appropriate

22. The author uses the term "compounded by" (line 39) to

(A) emphasize the fact that these researchers face even more stringent time limits than those already mentioned
(B) assert that the scientists working to predict CMEs are not given adequate time to do so successfully
(C) disprove the notion that the orientation of CMEs affects the length of time available for scientific inquiry into this phenomenon
(D) contribute further to a list of challenges that stand in the way of researchers working to disprove CMEs
(E) caution readers that speculations of energy providers might heighten the uncertainty raised by CMEs

GO ON TO THE NEXT PAGE ⟩

23. Which of the following were mentioned as factors contributing to the difficulty of forecasting CMEs?

    I.   Limited available reaction time in which to determine orientation

    II. The tendency of voltage controls to be overridden by electrical surges

    III. Insufficient data upon which to base assessments of past behavior

(A) I only
(B) I and II only
(C) I and III only
(D) II and III only
(E) I, II, and III

24. With which of the following statements would the author of this article be most likely to agree?

(A) CMEs are a subject of interest but little practical importance, because there is nothing that can be done to minimize their impact.

(B) Individuals should join in the fight to protect today's energy-dependent society from the harm caused by CMEs by raising money to support research.

(C) In the next decade, a "perfect storm" will interrupt power supplies and cause extensive inconvenience and loss of services.

(D) We should learn more about the potential dangers of CMEs, but few steps can be taken to alter such storms' effects.

(E) Each of us should view a significant CME as a real possibility but should also expect that leaders will have effective protective measures in place before such an event.

STOP

If you finish before time is called, you may check your work on this section only.
Do not turn to any other section in the test.

SECTION 5
Time — 25 minutes
18 Questions

Turn to Section 5 of your answer sheet to answer the questions in this section.

Directions: This section contains two types of questions. You have 25 minutes to complete both types. For questions 1-8, solve each problem and decide which is the best of the choices given. Fill in the corresponding circle on the answer sheet. You may use any available space for scratchwork.

Notes

1. The use of a calculator is permitted.

2. All numbers used are real numbers.

3. Figures that accompany problems in this test are intended to provide information useful in solving the problems. They are drawn as accurately as possible EXCEPT when it is stated in a specific problem that the figure is not drawn to scale. All figures lie in a plane unless otherwise indicated.

4. Unless otherwise specified, the domain of any function f is assumed to be the set of all real numbers x for which $f(x)$ is a real number.

Reference Information

$A = \pi r^2$ $A = lw$ $A = \frac{1}{2}bh$ $V = lwh$ $V = \pi r^2 h$ $c^2 = a^2 + b^2$ Special Right Triangles
$C = 2\pi r$

The number of degrees of arc in a circle is 360.

The sum of the measures in degrees of the angles of a triangle is 180.

1. Mr. Barua teaches for 3.5 hours on each day that he is scheduled to teach. If he teaches d days per year, then which of the following is an expression for the total number of hours he teaches per year?

(A) $3.5d$

(B) $365d$

(C) $d + 3.5$

(D) $\dfrac{d}{3.5}$

(E) $\dfrac{3.5}{d}$

2. If $3x = 10 - 2x$, then $(5x)(5x) =$

(A) 2
(B) 4
(C) 20
(D) 25
(E) 100

GO ON TO THE NEXT PAGE

3. Points P, Q, R, S, and T lie on a line in that order. If $PR = 6$ and $PQ = QR = RS = ST$, then $PT =$

(A) 3
(B) 6
(C) 9
(D) 12
(E) 24

$$\begin{array}{r} 83 \\ -AB \\ \hline 31 \end{array}$$

4. In the correctly solved subtraction problem above, A and B represent digits. What is the value of $A \times B$?

(A) 2
(B) 5
(C) 7
(D) 10
(E) 52

5. If $|x - 6| = x^2$, then x could equal which of the following?

(A) −3
(B) −2
(C) 3
(D) 4
(E) 9

6. The circle with center P shown above has a circumference of 10π. If $XY = 6$, what is the area of the shaded region?

(A) 24

(B) $25\pi - 24$

(C) $50\pi - 48$

(D) $24 - \dfrac{25\pi}{2}$

(E) $\dfrac{25\pi}{2} - 24$

GO ON TO THE NEXT PAGE

7. If $j, k, l, m,$ and n are consecutive integers and $j < k < l < m < n$, then what is the value of $(j + n) - (k + m)$?

(A) 0
(B) 1
(C) 2
(D) 4
(E) It cannot be determined from the information given.

8. If $f(x) = 2x^2 - 4x - 16$ and $g(x) = x^2 - 3x - 4$, which of the following is an expression for $\dfrac{f(x)}{g(x)}$?

(A) $\dfrac{22}{3}$

(B) $x^2 - x - 12$

(C) $x^2 + \dfrac{4}{3}x + 4$

(D) $\dfrac{2x + 4}{x + 1}$

(E) $\dfrac{2x - 4}{x - 1}$

GO ON TO THE NEXT PAGE

Directions: For Student-Produced Response questions 9-18, use the grids at the bottom of the answer sheet page on which you have answered questions 1-8.

Each of the remaining 10 questions requires you to solve the problem and enter your answer by marking the circles in the special grid, as shown in the examples below. You may use any available space for scratch work.

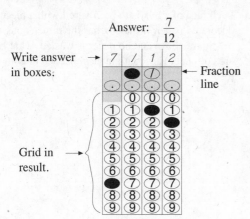

Answer: $\frac{7}{12}$

Write answer in boxes.

← Fraction line

Grid in result.

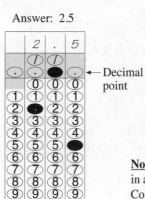

Answer: 2.5

← Decimal point

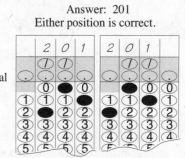

Answer: 201
Either position is correct.

Note: You may start your answers in any column, space permitting. Columns not needed should be left blank.

- Mark no more than one circle in any column.

- Because the answer document will be machine-scored, **you will receive credit only if the circles are filled in correctly.**

- Although not required, it is suggested that you write your answer in the boxes at the top of the columns to help you fill in the circles accurately.

- Some problems may have more than one correct answer. In such cases, grid only one answer.

- No question has a negative answer.

- **Mixed numbers** such as $3\frac{1}{2}$ must be gridded as

  3.5 or 7/2. (If 3 1 / 2 is gridded, it will be

  interpreted as $\frac{31}{2}$, not $3\frac{1}{2}$.)

- **Decimal Answers:** If you obtain a decimal answer with more digits than the grid can accommodate, it may be either rounded or truncated, but it must fill the entire grid. For example, if you obtain an answer such as 0.6666..., you should record your result as .666 or .667. **A less accurate value such as .66 or .67 will be scored as incorrect.**

Acceptable ways to grid $\frac{2}{3}$ are:

9. A rectangle has a perimeter of 10. If the lengths of the sides are all integer values, what is one possible value for the area of the rectangle?

10. If $(5 \times 10^5) - (4 \times 10^4) = b \times 10^5$, what is the value of b?

GO ON TO THE NEXT PAGE

PERCENT OF APPLES PICKED
BY MIRANDA AND FRIENDS

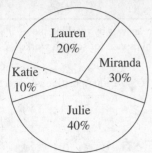

11. Miranda picked apples with her friends. If Miranda picked 15 apples, according to the information in the graph above, what was the total number of apples picked?

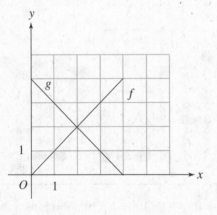

12. The graphs of functions f and g are lines as shown above. For which value of x does $f(x) = g(x)$?

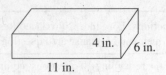

13. Each face of a box is to be covered with a piece of decorated paper. If the box has the dimensions shown in the figure above and no paper is wasted, what is the total area of paper (in square inches) needed to complete the job?

14. Reynaldo is building a model car. He can choose up to three of the following accessories to enhance it: glow-in-the-dark hubcaps, moveable windshield wipers, smiling passengers. If he chooses at least one accessory, how many different combinations of accessories can he choose?

15. If A is the set of all positive integers less than 300 that are divisible by 3, and B is the set of all prime numbers, the intersection of set A and set B has how many elements?

GO ON TO THE NEXT PAGE ⟶

16. Megan buys two sweaters that have each been discounted by 20% from their regular prices. If the regular price of the less expensive sweater is $25 and the second regularly costs 40% more than the first, how much does Megan pay for the more expensive sweater? (Disregard the $ sign when you grid your answer.)

AVERAGE CD PRICES BY GENRE

	2002	2003	2004
Jazz	$10	$11	$12
Blues	$8	$9	$10
Folk	$8	$10	$12

CD PURCHASES BY YEAR

	Jazz	Blues	Folk
2002	12	5	5
2003	15	8	7
2004	25	12	15

17. Jack purchases new CDs every year. The chart on the top shows the average prices that he pays for each type of CD for three different years. The chart below shows how many of each type of CD that he purchased in those three different years. The total amount that Jack spent on CDs in 2004 is what percent greater than the total amount that he spent in 2002 ? (Disregard the % symbol when you grid your answer.)

18. In year y, the value in dollars, v, of a certain painting created in 1970 is given by the equation $v = (r - 6(y - 1970))^2$, where q and r are constants. If the painting reached its lowest value in 1990, when it was worth $500, what was the painting's value, in dollars, in the year 2000 ?

STOP
If you finish before time is called, you may check your work on this section only.
Do not turn to any other section in the test.

SECTION 6
Time — 25 minutes
35 Questions

Turn to Section 6 of your answer sheet to answer the questions in this section.

Directions: For each question in this section, select the best answer from among the choices given and fill in the corresponding circle on the answer sheet.

The following sentences test correctness and effectiveness of expression. Part of each sentence or the entire sentence is underlined; beneath each sentence are five ways of phrasing the underlined material. Choice A repeats the original phrasing; the other four choices are different. If you think the original phrasing produces a better sentence than any of the alternatives, select choice A; if not, select one of the other choices.

In making your selection, follow the requirements of standard written English; that is, pay attention to grammar, choice of words, sentence construction, and punctuation. Your selection should result in the most effective sentence—clear and precise, without awkwardness or ambiguity.

EXAMPLE:

Bobby Flay baked his first cake <u>and he was thirteen years old then</u>.

(A) and he was thirteen years old then
(B) when he was thirteen
(C) at age thirteen years old
(D) upon the reaching of thirteen years
(E) at the time when he was thirteen

---

1. Numerous companies are decreasing production and focusing on managing a limited supply of inventory <u>so that they will not be required in adding</u> additional warehouse space.

   (A) so that they will not be required in adding
   (B) so that they will not be required to be adding
   (C) so that they will not be required to add
   (D) because it would required the adding
   (E) because it would be requiring them to add

2. Children who do not crawl before they walk may <u>not only have difficulty with reading skills, creating speech problems</u>.

   (A) not only have difficulty with reading skills, creating speech problems
   (B) not only have reading skills difficulties but also creating speech problems
   (C) not only have difficulty with reading skills but may also experience speech problems
   (D) not only have reading difficulties; it creates speech problems too
   (E) not only have difficulty with reading skills; speech problems are also created by it

3. The American poet John Banister Tabb was reminiscent of many seventeenth-century English devotional poets, <u>being that his works focused on topics like nature and being religious</u>.

   (A) being that his works focused on topics like nature and being religious
   (B) being that his works were about nature and religion
   (C) since his works focused on topics such as nature and religion
   (D) since his works are focusing on topics like nature and religion
   (E) if his works focus on natural and religious topics

4. Today's computers, equipped with word-processing programs, are <u>superior than the typewriters of the 1960s</u>.

   (A) superior than the typewriters of the 1960s
   (B) superior from the typewriters of the 1960s
   (C) superior to those of typewriters of the 1960s
   (D) superior to what a typewriter was in the 1960s
   (E) superior to the typewriters of the 1960s

GO ON TO THE NEXT PAGE ⟩

5. For many office employees, e-mail is thought of as more of a burden <u>and not</u> a help in expediting communications.

   (A) and not
   (B) instead of actually being
   (C) instead of being thought of as
   (D) than
   (E) and not thought of as

6. The talk show host contends that rock-and-roll songs, regardless of <u>its theme, is not the cause of teenage violence or behavioral problems</u>.

   (A) its theme, is not the cause of teenage violence or behavioral problems
   (B) their theme, is not the cause of teenage violence or behavioral problems
   (C) its theme, are not the cause of teenage violence or behavioral problems
   (D) its themes, are not the cause of teenage violence or behavioral problems
   (E) their themes, are not the cause of teenage violence or behavioral problems

7. The team of flight mechanics, <u>four who</u> are certified electricians, work on all of the interior mechanical malfunctions reported by the flight crews.

   (A) four who
   (B) four that
   (C) four of whom
   (D) four which
   (E) four of which

8. DVD technology, <u>providing better quality video than VHS cassettes, are continuing to gain in</u> popularity.

   (A) providing better quality video than VHS cassettes, are continuing to gain in popularity
   (B) which provides better quality video than do VHS cassettes, continues to gain in popularity
   (C) which provides better quality video than do VHS cassettes, continue to gain in popularity
   (D) with better quality video than VHS cassettes, continuing to gain in popularity
   (E) with its better quality video over VHS cassettes, continue gaining in popularity

9. Either the president or the vice president of the student council, who both participate in multiple activities, <u>is always present at committee meetings</u>.

   (A) is always present at committee meetings
   (B) are always present at committee meetings
   (C) is always attending committee meetings
   (D) are always in attendance at committee meetings
   (E) are always there at committee meetings

10. The brokerage firm made a very sizeable trade in a particular mutual fund, <u>even though they were being monitored closely</u> by the federal agents.

    (A) even though they were being monitored closely
    (B) even though they were monitored closely
    (C) even though the firm was monitored closely
    (D) even though the firm were monitored closely
    (E) even though the firm is monitored closely

11. The issue of who will be in charge of the committee is <u>just between Sharon and I</u>.

    (A) just between Sharon and I
    (B) just among Sharon and me
    (C) just between Sharon and me
    (D) among just Sharon and I
    (E) between only Sharon and my own self

GO ON TO THE NEXT PAGE

The following sentences test your ability to recognize grammar and usage errors. Each sentence contains either a single error or no error at all. No sentence contains more than one error. The error, if there is one, is underlined and lettered. If the sentence contains an error, select the one underlined part that must be changed to make the sentence correct. If the sentence is correct, select choice E. In choosing answers, follow the requirements of standard written English.

EXAMPLE:

The other players and her significantly improved
   A   B   C

the game plan created by the coaches. No error
            D   E

Ⓐ ● Ⓒ Ⓓ Ⓔ

12. Him and her ran hurriedly to catch the ferry because
     A   B   C

the boat was the last one until tomorrow. No error
                  D   E

13. Although early forms of the roller skate had appeared
                                 A

as early as 1860, the ball-bearing skate were not
  B   C

invented until the 1880s. No error
  D   E

14. The founder of Georgia, James Edward Oglethorpe,

served as chairman of a committee charged with
  A

investigating prison conditions, which led him to take a
                      B   C

special interest in the plight of debtors. No error
      D   E

15. At first, Funny Cide, a horse co-owned by three racing
                A

amateurs, was thought to have a chance at the Triple
                B

Crown, but a wet, sloppy track at Belmont made for a
             C

difficult third race and thus ends his chances. No error
               D   E

16. UNESCO, an office of the United Nations who has
                        A

its office in Paris, was chartered in 1945 and became
B   C   D

an official agency of the United Nations in 1946.

No error
E

17. Birds of the Madagascan species are sometimes called
  A   B

false sunbirds because of their common diet, habitat,
          C   D

and appearance. No error
        E

18. When he decides to retire and move to a quiet rural
                  A

village, an all-star professional athlete often does not
                      B

realize that, for better or worse, they will be the talk of
                  C   D

the town. No error
      E

19. If you plan to participate in a marathon, you need to
  A

realize that many athletes, even those in top physical
                  B

condition, find it difficult to finish such a long race; by
                  C

the end of a marathon you will run twenty-six miles.
              D

No error
E

GO ON TO THE NEXT PAGE →

20. The zoologist <u>worried over</u> the sick elephant; <u>if</u> the
A B

elephant did not survive, her young calf <u>could</u>
C

<u>perish from</u> starvation or depression. <u>No error</u>
D E

21. While some pundits assert that the total amount of money

the United States spends on foreign aid <u>is</u> excessive,
A

<u>another argues</u> that <u>compared to</u> other economically
B C

powerful countries, the United States <u>contributes</u> an
D

insignificant fraction of its budget to this cause. <u>No error</u>
E

22. The controversial magazine <u>has been criticized</u> for
A

<u>being partial</u>, in every article, <u>of</u> the most <u>conservative</u>
B C D

causes. <u>No error</u>
E

23. The clever grandmother, concerned because her

grandsons seemed to resent their new baby sister, elected

not <u>to take</u> a stern approach but rather to win
A

<u>their heart</u> by saying how much <u>their sister</u>
B C

<u>would adore</u> them. <u>No error</u>
D E

24. The senator <u>will either</u> decide to vote against the
A

legislation <u>or risk</u> angering the farmers <u>by taking away</u>
B C

the water rights <u>they deserve</u>. <u>No error</u>
D E

25. She <u>dried</u> the dishes when, all of a sudden, the
A

phone rang; <u>startled, she</u> dropped a plate to the
B

floor, <u>whereupon</u> it <u>shattered</u>. <u>No error</u>
C D E

26. Nadir Shah, a <u>warlord that</u> is generally considered the
A

<u>last of</u> the great Asian conquerors, <u>founded</u> a kingdom
B C

that <u>lasted for</u> only thirteen years. <u>No error</u>
D E

27. When crafting our lobster trap nets, Maine

<u>lobstermen and I</u> cannot agree whether <u>to use</u> cotton yarn,
A B

<u>which</u> quickly erodes in the harsh sea water, <u>or</u> synthetic
C D

material, which is nonbiodegradable. <u>No error</u>
E

28. Students in the literature course will explore ways

<u>in which</u> medieval authors <u>represented</u> themes of their
A B

time, and <u>will be reading</u> Augustine's *Confessions*,
C

Boccaccio's *Decameron*,and <u>Heloise and Abelard's</u>
D

Letters. <u>No error</u>
E

29. Typically, professors <u>instruct</u> students
A

<u>to complete</u> all background reading by the due date,
B

<u>making the assumption</u> that this will save <u>them</u> time
C D

during class. <u>No error</u>
E

GO ON TO THE NEXT PAGE ➡

Directions: The following passage is an early draft of an essay. Some parts of the passage need to be rewritten.

Read the passage and select the best answers for the questions that follow. Some questions are about particular sentences or parts of sentences and ask you to improve sentence structure or word choice. Other questions ask you to consider organization and development. In choosing answers, follow the requirements of standard written English.

Questions 30-35 are based on the following passage.

(1) Working with the elderly is better than most teenagers realize. (2) This summer I started working at a retirement home for my community service project for my high school. (3) At first I was really scared. (4) Besides with my grandparents, I had never been around other older people. (5) I thought they might assume I was rude or not like my clothes. (6) Surely, we wouldn't have anything to talk about.

(7) When I arrived on the first day, I looked around me. (8) I had never seen so many old people in one place before. (9) But one thing: there weren't any hospital beds. (10) Two ladies were watching television in the front lobby, another coming in to sign up for a lecture on computers. (11) Several walked by discussing a play. (12) Another gentleman was waiting for a taxi next to his luggage.

(13) I discovered that older people often move to retirement homes to live in a community with people of the same age with good services, not because they are sick. (14) These people were healthy and active. (15) Though, I found I shared more in common with the residents than I thought. (16) There is a chess club. (17) Several take art classes like me. (18) Many of them travel. (19) One couple just returned from Greece. (20) The retirees were excited to have a young person with them to explain computers, talk about books, or tell them what I'm reading at school. (21) They just want to have friends and to learn new things, like anybody else.

30. In the context of the passage, which of the following is the best revision of sentence 4 (reproduced below) ?

Besides with my grandparents, I had never been around other older people.

(A) (As it is now)
(B) I had spent little time around older people other than my grandparents.
(C) I had spent little time around other older people, but with my grandparents.
(D) I had never been around older people, unlike my grandparents.
(E) Other than being around my grandparents, I had never been around other people.

31. Which of the following is the best way to revise the underlined portion of sentence 9 (reproduced below) in order to improve the logical flow of the passage?

But one thing: there weren't any hospital beds.

(A) One thing surprised me, though: not
(B) But one thing, there weren't
(C) One thing: there weren't
(D) One thing, though: there weren't
(E) One thing surprised me, though: I didn't see

32. In context, which of the following is the best revision of the underlined portion of sentence 10 (reproduced below) ?

Two ladies were watching television in the front lobby, another coming in to sign up for a lecture on computers.

(A) (As it is now)
(B) lobby, another would be coming in
(C) lobby; another would be coming in
(D) lobby; soon another resident came in
(E) lobby, soon another resident had come in

33. Which of the following sentences would, if inserted before sentence 13, most greatly improve the logical flow of the passage as a whole?

(A) I soon learned that I had been wrong to believe stereotypes about retirement homes and older people.
(B) This first day was a life-changing experience; I will never be the same.
(C) My view of older people changed entirely based on my experiences at the retirement home.
(D) My time at the retirement home changed my belief system dramatically.
(E) I enjoyed my time volunteering at the retirement in more ways than I could have imagined before I arrived.

GO ON TO THE NEXT PAGE

34. In context, which of the following is the best way to revise and combine the underlined portion of sentences 18 and 19 (reproduced below) ?

Many of them travel. One couple just returned from Greece.

(A) (As it is now)
(B) Many of the residents travel; in fact, one couple I met there had just returned
(C) Many of them travel; one couple was just returning
(D) Many of them travel, in fact, one couple just returned
(E) Many of the residents travel, and some even returned recently

35. Which of the following could replace "Though" in sentence 15 to clarify the relationship between sentences 14 and 15 ?

(A) Furthermore
(B) Therefore
(C) Nevertheless
(D) So
(E) Still

STOP
If you finish before time is called, you may check your work on this section only.
Do not turn to any other section in the test.

SECTION 8
Time — 20 minutes
16 Questions

Turn to Section 8 of your answer sheet to answer the questions in this section.

Directions: For this section, solve each problem and decide which is the best of the choices given. Fill in the corresponding circle on the answer sheet. You may use any available space for scratchwork.

Notes

1. The use of a calculator is permitted.

2. All numbers used are real numbers.

3. Figures that accompany problems in this test are intended to provide information useful in solving the problems. They are drawn as accurately as possible EXCEPT when it is stated in a specific problem that the figure is not drawn to scale. All figures lie in a plane unless otherwise indicated.

4. Unless otherwise specified, the domain of any function f is assumed to be the set of all real numbers x for which $f(x)$ is a real number.

Reference Information

    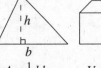

$A = \pi r^2$ $A = lw$ $A = \frac{1}{2}bh$ $V = lwh$ $V = \pi r^2 h$ $c^2 = a^2 + b^2$ Special Right Triangles
$C = 2\pi r$

The number of degrees of arc in a circle is 360.

The sum of the measures in degrees of the angles of a triangle is 180.

---

1. If $\sqrt{x} = \dfrac{x}{10}$ and $x > 0$, what is the value of x ?

   (A)   −1
   (B)   1
   (C)   10
   (D)   100
   (E) 1,000

2. In the figure above, $\overline{AB}$ and $\overline{CD}$ are parallel and intersected by $\overline{EF}$. What is the value of $w + y + z$?

   (A) 180
   (B) 240
   (C) 260
   (D) 280
   (E) 300

GO ON TO THE NEXT PAGE ⇨

3. If $x = y + 2$ and $y = 4$, then $\frac{3}{2}x =$

(A) 2
(B) 9
(C) 12
(D) 18
(E) 24

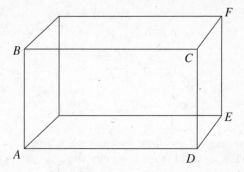

5. In the figure above, *ABCDEF* is a rectangular solid. If $\overline{AB} = 5$ and $\overline{AD} = 12$ and the area of face *ABCD* is twice that of face *CDEF*, what is the volume of *ABCDEF* ?

(A) 30
(B) 60
(C) 324
(D) 360
(E) 720

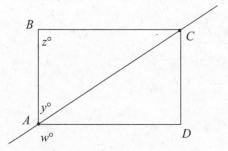

Note: Figure not drawn to scale.

4. In the figure above *ABCD* is a rectangle. If $w = 100$, then $y + z =$

(A) 90
(B) 100
(C) 120
(D) 170
(E) 180

6. If $10 + \sqrt{x} = 154$, then $10\sqrt{x} =$

(A) 12
(B) 120
(C) 144
(D) 1,200
(E) 1,440

GO ON TO THE NEXT PAGE

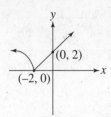

7. The graph of $y = h(x)$ is shown above. Which of the following could be the graph of $y = h(2x)$?

(A)
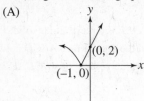

(B)
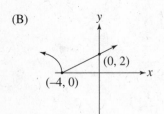

(C)
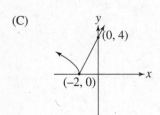

(D)
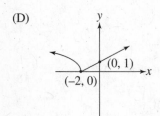

(E)
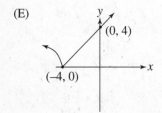

PERCENT BODY FAT BY WEIGHT

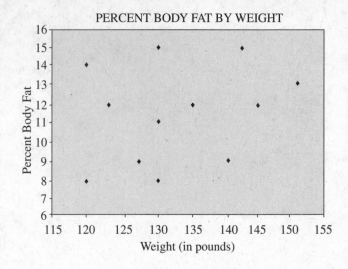

8. The chart above shows the body weights and percent body fat for the 12 members of a wrestling team. What is the median percent body fat for the members of the team?

(A)   9
(B)   11
(C)   12
(D)   120
(E)   130

GO ON TO THE NEXT PAGE ⟶

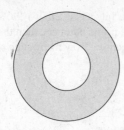

9. In the figure above, the circumference of the larger circle is 6π and the circumference of the smaller circle is 4π. What fractional portion of the larger circle is shaded?

(A) $\dfrac{1}{3}$

(B) $\dfrac{4}{9}$

(C) $\dfrac{1}{2}$

(D) $\dfrac{5}{9}$

(E) $\dfrac{2}{3}$

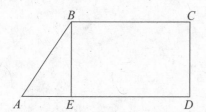

Note: Figure not drawn to scale.

10. In the figure above, *EBCD* is a rectangle. *AE* = 9, *AB* = 15, and the perimeter of *EBCD* = 40. What is the area of *EBCD* ?

(A) 48
(B) 54
(C) 96
(D) 108
(E) 150

11. Stephan takes 240 minutes to draw 20 pictures. Pavel draws three times as fast as Stephan. How many pictures can Pavel draw in 6 hours?

(A) 30
(B) 40
(C) 60
(D) 90
(E) 120

12. If $(x + y)(x - y) + (4 - y)(2 - y) = 0$, then what is the value of *y* when *x* equals 8 ?

(A) 12

(B) $-9\dfrac{1}{3}$

(C) 6

(D) $9\dfrac{1}{3}$

(E) 12

GO ON TO THE NEXT PAGE

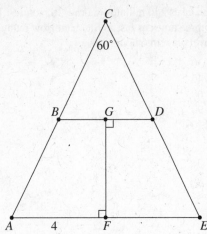

Note: Figure not drawn to scale.

13. In the figure above, B is the midpoint of $\overline{AC}$, D is the midpoint of $\overline{CE}$, F is the midpoint of $\overline{AE}$, and G is the midpoint of $\overline{BD}$. If $CB = CD$, what is FG ?

(A) $2\sqrt{2}$

(B) $2\sqrt{3}$

(C) $3\sqrt{2}$

(D) $3\sqrt{3}$

(E) $4\sqrt{2}$

14. If the set of four integers n, $2n$, $n + 2n$, and $n + 4n$ consists only of prime numbers, then the set is called a "prime convergence." How many such sets exist?

(A) None

(B) One

(C) Three

(D) Four

(E) More than four

GO ON TO THE NEXT PAGE

15. For the annual school fundraiser, Santiago has p pledges each for c cents per lap that he jogs. If his school track has 4 laps per mile and Santiago raises a total of d dollars, how many miles did he jog in terms of p, c, and d ?

(A) $\dfrac{25d}{pc}$

(B) $\dfrac{4pc}{d}$

(C) $\dfrac{100d}{pc}$

(D) $4pcd$

(E) $25pcd$

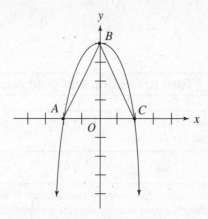

16. The figure above shows the graph of $y = f - |gx^3|$, where f and g are positive constants and triangle ABC. If $AB = 2\sqrt{5}$ and $AC = 4$, what is the value of g ?

(A) $\dfrac{1}{2}$

(B) 1

(C) $\sqrt{2}$

(D) 2

(E) 4

STOP

If you finish before time is called, you may check your work on this section only.
Do not turn to any other section in the test.

SECTION 9
Time — 20 minutes
19 Questions

Turn to Section 9 of your answer sheet to answer the questions in this section.

Directions: For each question in this section, select the best answer from among the choices given and fill in the corresponding circle on the answer sheet.

Each sentence below has one or two blanks, each blank indicating that something has been omitted. Beneath the sentence are five words or sets of words labeled A through E. Choose the word or set of words that, when inserted in the sentence, best fits the meaning of the sentence as a whole.

Example:

Desiring to ------- his taunting friends, Mitch gave them taffy in hopes it would keep their mouths shut.

(A) eliminate   (B) satisfy   (C) overcome
   (D) ridicule   (E) silence

---

1. The environmental organization disagreed with David's unsound proposal to use the local river as a dumping site for the chemical plant he managed; it claimed that his proposal would cause ------- of the local drinking water.

   (A) a dispersal   (B) a purification   (C) a contamination
      (D) an enforcement   (E) a polarization

2. To show them how to recognize when a thunderstorm was ------- and would soon strike, Mrs. Hauser taught her sixth-grade science students to spot cumulonimbus clouds, or thunderheads.

   (A) voluble   (B) imminent   (C) saturating
      (D) mercurial   (E) perilous

3. Although the company claimed responsibility for the environmental disaster, management executives showed little -------; in fact, many environmental groups were outraged by the lack of -------.

   (A) inspiration . . repentance
   (B) contrition . . regret
   (C) deception . . integrity
   (D) compunction . . inhumanity
   (E) resentment . . competence

4. When Helena won the Worst Dressed Award at the Halloween party, she was utterly -------, because she hadn't even worn a costume.

   (A) attired   (B) incompetent   (C) obscured
      (D) mortified   (E) rambunctious

5. Reacting to the chemical company's several decades of ------- dumping industrial waste, the government has ordered a cleanup of Onondaga Lake; however, company executives counter that the ------- costs of a thorough cleanup will bankrupt them.

   (A) imprecise . . fiscal
   (B) molecular . . excessive
   (C) volatile . . pecuniary
   (D) unconscionable . . remunerative
   (E) indiscriminate . . exorbitant

6. Despite mounting evidence that the researcher's findings were faked, the researcher himself staunchly ------- such claims.

   (A) verified   (B) repudiated   (C) disseminated
      (D) embellished   (E) insinuated

GO ON TO THE NEXT PAGE

Directions: Each passage below is followed by questions based on its content. Answer the questions on the basis of what is <u>stated</u> or <u>implied</u> in each passage and in any introductory material that may be provided.

Questions 7-19 are based on the following passages.

The first passage is an essay that presents a look at suburban culture in modern American society. The second passage discusses an attempt to limit suburban sprawl by the State of New Jersey.

Passage 1

Pull up to a traffic light in Anytown, U.S.A. and look around. On one side sits a franchised burger joint or a national clothing retailer; on the other, an expansive set of cookie-
Line cutter homes separated by perfectly trimmed lawns and wide
5 streets named for bucolic features of the landscape long since obliterated. In front and behind lie endless streams of red brake lights and bright white headlights emanating from blue, silver, and red hunks of steel.

Welcome to Suburbia. While suburbs offer their residents
10 convenient shopping and generally comfortable standards of living, they concomitantly promote a uniformity that is a disservice to all. American suburbs arose in the 1940s as a way to effectively utilize large tracts of land needed to house a booming population. While the suburban building
15 frenzy did make home ownership more accessible to the average American, the resulting communities are mainly characterized by hyper-organization and uniformity. But at what cost? Suburban culture and its principles of residential planning, instead of improving our condition of
20 life as intended, have in fact diminished our standing as an inquisitive, expressive people.

Identical-looking, prefabricated houses have robbed us of hundreds of years of original and beautiful home design; simple, efficient construction has trumped all. Suburban
25 sprawl has engulfed the natural landscape, a practice that has laid the groundwork for a hotbed of consumerism made manifest in strip malls, gas stations, fast-food restaurants, and chain music and video stores. Family-owned businesses and independent merchants who specialize in the sale of
30 handcrafts and locally made products have been swept away, unable to compete economically against national and multinational corporate conglomerates. The ultimate results of such rampant growth are communities with no center, no soul, few social bonds, and no reason to exist other than to
35 consume.

It is perhaps too much of a stretch to claim the growth of suburbia is responsible for all of today's problems; crime, pollution, and other social problems constitute more immediate and pervasive threats. Nevertheless, suburban
40 culture, with its emphasis on standardization and ubiquity, has proven to be a sore spot for a culture hungry for individual expression in the way it shops, dresses, lives, and dreams.

Passage 2

Difficult problems call for creative answers. Critics of suburban growth point to a variety of problems caused by
45 the seemingly quickening pace of so-called "sprawl," a derisive term that refers to the spread of suburban housing developments onto farms and unused plots of land. While many of these complaints border on the histrionic, one must concede that sprawl does detract from the beauty of the
50 landscape and decrease the amount of open space available for public use.

Despite alarming forecasts enumerating the damage to be wrought if growth is not stemmed, sprawl has shown few signs of relenting, primarily because of the public's appetite
55 for big suburban homes and easy access to shopping centers. In an attempt to address the problem of sprawl, the state of New Jersey proposed a program intended to stem the tide of sprawl before it was too late. The plan would allow the state to use taxpayer money to protect remaining open land—for
60 years and years to come—from mall builders, three-bedroom house owners, or anyone else, for that matter.

Through a statewide referendum, the state successfully earned the support of its citizens to buy back up to one million acres of land; the measure passed in 1998 with 66
65 percent voter assent and was signed into law in June 1999. For 10 years from the signing of the Garden State Preservation Trust Act, the state promised to spend $98 million a year to repurchase land. Residents, eager to maintain the beauty of their areas, voted for the referendum, despite the eventual
70 increase in their own taxes required by the act.

The "Garden State," known as much for its boundless suburban tracts as its beautiful beaches, farms, and pinelands, has demonstrated that it is possible to control sprawl without unduly hurting economic growth or the fiscal health of the
75 state. Homeowners are reminded through green-and-blue road signs that their tax dollars are preserving the beauty of the state. The tourism industry has a new draw for visitors. And all residents of the state may now rest assured that the state's natural charms will not soon disappear.

7. In the first paragraph of Passage 1, the author uses the term "Anytown, U.S.A." (line 1) to

(A) indicate that the described conditions are commonly found in the United States
(B) introduce the reader to a specific place
(C) suggest that the description of the suburban condition is mostly imaginary
(D) encourage the reader to visit as many suburban towns as possible
(E) imply that suburbia is common only in the United States

GO ON TO THE NEXT PAGE ⟩

8. In the context of Passage 1, "concomitantly" (line 11) most nearly means

(A) belligerently
(B) simultaneously
(C) in a widespread way
(D) with greedy intent
(E) ostentatiously

9. The first sentence in the final paragraph of Passage 1 (lines 39-42) serves to

(A) clarify the extent to which the author believes suburbs are a problem
(B) exemplify the primary argument of suburbia's effects
(C) summarize the collection of prior points about suburban sprawl
(D) rebut a popular misconception about the benefits of suburbia
(E) modify a previously made argument about standardized housing

10. The author of Passage 1 asserts that, to some degree, suburban sprawl is responsible for

(A) a desire for individuality
(B) an increase in conformity
(C) an upswing in burglaries
(D) air pollution
(E) a million acres of farmland and open space

11. According to Passage 2, which of the following people would most likely be considered "anyone else" (line 61) ?

(A) A factory worker
(B) The governor
(C) A New Jersey resident
(D) A principal of a school
(E) A fast-food restaurant owner

12. Which of the following relationships is most similar to that between the government of New Jersey and suburban sprawl legislation as described in Passage 2 ?

(A) An adult lion protecting her cub
(B) A homeowner purchasing a fence to keep out destructive animals
(C) A man depositing money into his bank account
(D) A postal worker delivering mail
(E) A locksmith changing the lock on a door

13. According to Passage 2, all of the following statements about the "Garden State" are true EXCEPT

(A) Its governor authorized the repurchase of land through executive order.
(B) It is well known for topographical features such as pinelands.
(C) Its implementation of an anti-sprawl effort has been considered a success.
(D) This nickname, perhaps referring to its attractions to farmers, refers to New Jersey.
(E) Evidence of a land repurchase program is visible to the state's residents.

14. The author's tone in Passage 2 is one of

(A) florid exuberance
(B) unbounded criticism
(C) rational optimism
(D) benign neglect
(E) restrained regret

15. The author of Passage 1 and the author of Passage 2 are similar in that both

(A) argue the construction of typical suburban houses has no benefit to homeowners
(B) agree suburban sprawl has a negative impact on the aesthetics of an area
(C) feel efforts to curb suburban sprawl have been effective
(D) feel suburban sprawl has been detrimental to American culture
(E) feel the voters of New Jersey have made a positive step toward limiting sprawl

16. Which of the following statements about suburban sprawl is supported by both passages?

(A) Government interference is necessary to limit suburban sprawl.
(B) Reducing sprawl will have a negative impact on the American economy.
(C) American culture has been devastated by suburban sprawl.
(D) Housing preferences and consumer needs primarily cause suburban sprawl.
(E) Local businesses benefit from suburban sprawl.

GO ON TO THE NEXT PAGE →

17. What would the author of Passage 2 most likely say about the arguments posed in the third paragraph of Passage 1?

(A) They rely too heavily on a faulty premise.
(B) They make too many false assumptions.
(C) They are excessively vague.
(D) They ignore the underlying problems associated with the topic.
(E) They are excessively dramatic or emotional.

18. Which best describes the relationship between Passage 1 and Passage 2 ?

(A) Passage 2 argues for changes described in Passage 1.
(B) Passage 2 debunks the arguments made in Passage 1.
(C) Passage 2 describes one solution to a problem described in Passage 1.
(D) Passage 2 provides a theoretical argument that offsets the practical argument provided in Passage 1.
(E) Passage 2 responds to a question posed in Passage 1.

19. The author of Passage 1 would most probably consider the last sentence of Passage 2 to be

(A) pessimistic
(B) perceptive
(C) cautious
(D) exaggerated
(E) flagrant

STOP
If you finish before time is called, you may check your work on this section only.
Do not turn to any other section in the test.

SECTION 10
Time — 10 minutes
14 Questions

Turn to Section 10 of your answer sheet to answer the questions in this section.

Directions: For each question in this section, select the best answer from among the choices given and fill in the corresponding circle on the answer sheet.

The following sentences test correctness and effectiveness of expression. Part of each sentence or the entire sentence is underlined; beneath each sentence are five ways of phrasing the underlined material. Choice A repeats the original phrasing; the other four choices are different. If you think the original phrasing produces a better sentence than any of the alternatives, select choice A; if not, select one of the other choices.

In making your selection, follow the requirements of standard written English; that is, pay attention to grammar, choice of words, sentence construction, and punctuation. Your selection should result in the most effective sentence—clear and precise, without awkwardness or ambiguity.

EXAMPLE:

Bobby Flay baked his first cake <u>and he was thirteen years old then</u>.

(A) and he was thirteen years old then
(B) when he was thirteen
(C) at age thirteen years old
(D) upon the reaching of thirteen years
(E) at the time when he was thirteen

Ⓐ ● Ⓒ Ⓓ Ⓔ

1. When asked to identify the most memorable day of their lives, <u>their wedding day would probably be chosen by many adults</u>.

   (A) their wedding day would probably be chosen by many adults
   (B) chosen by many adults would probably be their wedding day
   (C) their wedding day would most likely get the majority of choices
   (D) adults—at least many of them—select their wedding day
   (E) many adults would most likely select their wedding days

2. <u>The weather forecast for most eastern cities are</u> high winds and cold temperatures throughout the week.

   (A) The weather forecast for most eastern cities are
   (B) The weather forecast for most eastern cities, they say
   (C) The weather forecast for most eastern cities is
   (D) Most eastern cities' weather forecast are
   (E) In forecasting weather for most eastern cities

3. My grandmother, president of the watercolor association for many <u>years, and she won first prize in the competition for her painting of my mother's pet goldfish</u>.

   (A) years, and she won first prize in the competition for her painting of my mother's pet goldfish
   (B) years, won first prize in the competition for her painting of my mother's pet goldfish
   (C) years, winning first prize in the competition, which she won for her painting of my mother's pet goldfish
   (D) years, her painting of my mother's pet goldfish winning her first prize in the competition
   (E) years, winning first prize in the competition for her painting of my mother's pet goldfish

4. The comet has recently changed direction toward Jupiter, <u>which is leading scientists to wonder about</u> the composition of the object.

   (A) which is leading scientists to wonder about
   (B) this development leading scientists to wonder about
   (C) and with it scientists' wonder of
   (D) a development leading scientists to wonder about
   (E) this leading scientists to wonder on

5. <u>Despite being</u> found in only one place on earth, a cemetery in Australia, Majors Creek leek orchids are now protected by a government agency.

   (A) Despite being
   (B) Because of being
   (C) Because they are
   (D) Whenever they are
   (E) Though only

GO ON TO THE NEXT PAGE →

6. Aspiring directors often mimic the visual style of well-established ones, <u>some of whom are</u> not even from the same country as their protégés.

   (A) some of whom are
   (B) and some are
   (C) some are
   (D) of whom there are some
   (E) there are some who are

7. In testing, each of the company's new washing machines <u>works so intermittently that the engineers may have to redesign</u> the entire product line.

   (A) works so intermittently that the engineers may have to redesign
   (B) works so intermittently; the engineers may have redesigned
   (C) work very intermittently; so engineers having to redesign
   (D) work so intermittently that the engineers may have to redesign
   (E) work so intermittently that the engineers may redesign

8. <u>A lover of sugar is Michelle, being my friend, who still chooses it over artificial sweeteners.</u>

   (A) A lover of sugar is Michelle, being my friend, who still chooses it over artificial sweeteners.
   (B) My friend Michelle is still loving sugar, she chooses it over artificial sweeteners.
   (C) Although not chosen over real ones, my friend Michelle, she still loves sugar, and that more than artificial sweeteners.
   (D) My friend Michelle, a sugar lover, still chooses sugar over artificial sweeteners.
   (E) Many people choosing artificial sweeteners over real ones, my friend Michelle still loves the latter.

9. Perhaps the most compelling new idea introduced to explain mysterious bursts of gamma rays, <u>the hypernova theory, which is supported by astrophysicists who believe</u> the bursts to be caused by the explosion of supermassive stars.

   (A) the hypernova theory, which is supported by astrophysicists who believe
   (B) the hypernova theory, supported by astrophysicists, believes
   (C) the hypernova theory, is supported by astrophysicists, believing
   (D) the hypernova theory is supported by astrophysicists who believe
   (E) astrophysicists support the hypernova theory who believe

10. Last year, a few teachers in the district participated in <u>workshops that increased</u> their interest in mathematics.

    (A) workshops that increased
    (B) workshops for the increase of
    (C) workshops being able to increase
    (D) workshops, for it increased
    (E) workshops in which it increased

11. <u>Less than half of his students could correctly identify Nigeria on an unmarked map,</u> the fifth-grade teacher devoted substantial class time to the study of African geography.

    (A) Less than half of his students could correctly identify Nigeria on an unmarked map,
    (B) Less than half of his students could correctly identify Nigeria on an unmarked map, therefore
    (C) Less than half of his students could correctly identify Nigeria on an unmarked map, yet
    (D) Because less than half of his students could correctly identify Nigeria on an unmarked map,
    (E) Whenever less than half of his students could correctly identify Nigeria on an unmarked map,

12. <u>The layout of streets in most older cities are</u> in a grid formation as opposed to the more organic design of city streets created after World War II.

    (A) The layout of streets in most older cities are
    (B) In the layout of streets in most older cities, they are
    (C) The layout of streets in most older cities is
    (D) In laying out streets in most older cities, they designed
    (E) The layout of most older cities are

13. In 1999, shopkeepers sold more widgets <u>than</u> 1998.

    (A) than
    (B) than did
    (C) then shopkeepers in
    (D) than with shopkeepers in
    (E) than did shopkeepers in

14. <u>The list of ingredients on a product's package are</u> in order of concentration, with the higher quantity ingredients coming first.

    (A) The list of ingredients on a product's package are
    (B) The list of ingredients are
    (C) The listing of ingredients, they are
    (D) The list of ingredients on a product's package is
    (E) In listing ingredients

STOP
If you finish before time is called, you may check your work on this section only.
Do not turn to any other section in the test.

PRACTICE TEST 10: ANSWER KEY

2 Reading	3 Math	4 Reading	5 Math	6 Writing	8 Math	9 Reading	10 Writing
1. C	1. B	1. D	1. A	1. C	1. D	1. C	1. E
2. D	2. A	2. A	2. E	2. C	2. D	2. B	2. C
3. A	3. B	3. E	3. D	3. C	3. B	3. B	3. B
4. B	4. E	4. C	4. D	4. E	4. B	4. D	4. D
5. B	5. B	5. E	5. A	5. D	5. D	5. E	5. C
6. C	6. D	6. C	6. E	6. E	6. E	6. B	6. A
7. B	7. E	7. A	7. A	7. C	7. A	7. A	7. A
8. A	8. D	8. D	8. D	8. B	8. C	8. B	8. D
9. D	9. B	9. C	9. 4 or 6	9. A	9. D	9. A	9. D
10. A	10. C	10. B	10. 4.6	10. C	10. C	10. B	10. A
11. B	11. B	11. A	11. 50	11. C	11. D	11. E	11. D
12. B	12. C	12. E	12. 2	12. A	12. E	12. B	12. C
13. A	13. C	13. A	13. 268	13. C	13. B	13. A	13. E
14. C	14. D	14. A	14. 7	14. E	14. A	14. C	14. D
15. D	15. D	15. C	15. 1	15. D	15. A	15. B	
16. D	16. D	16. D	16. 28	16. A	16. A	16. D	
17. E	17. A	17. A	17. 200	17. E		17. E	
18. A	18. D	18. B	18. 4,100	18. C		18. C	
19. B	19. D	19. D		19. D		19. D	
20. C	20. B	20. E		20. A			
21. A		21. B		21. B			
22. B		22. A		22. C			
23. E		23. C		23. B			
24. D		24. D		24. E			
				25. A			
				26. A			
				27. E			
				28. C			
				29. D			
				30. B			
				31. E			
				32. D			
				33. A			
				34. B			
				35. A			

SAT SCORING WORKSHEET

For directions on how to score your SAT practice test, see pages 10–11.

SAT Writing Section

Total Writing Multiple-Choice Questions Correct: ☐

−

Total Writing Multiple-Choice Questions Incorrect: _____ ÷ 4 = ☐

Grammar Raw Score: ☐ ── **Grammar Scaled Subscore** ☐

+

Compare the Grammar Raw Score with the Writing Multiple-Choice Subscore Conversion Table on page 832 to find the Grammar Scaled Subscore.

Your Essay Score (2–12): _____ × 2 = ☐

Writing Raw Score: ☐

Compare Raw Score with SAT Score Conversion Table on page 832 to find the Writing Scaled Score.

Writing Scaled Score ☐

SAT Critical Reading Section

Total Critical Reading Questions Correct: ☐

−

Total Critical Reading Questions Incorrect: _____ ÷ 4 = ☐

Critical Reading Raw Score: ☐

Compare Raw Score with SAT Score Conversion Table on page 832 to find the Critical Reading Scaled Score.

Critical Reading Scaled Score ☐

SAT Math Section

Total Math Grid-In Questions Correct: ☐

+

Total Math Multiple-Choice Questions Correct: ☐

−

Total Math Multiple-Choice Questions Incorrect: _____ ÷ 4 = ☐

Don't include wrong answers from grid-ins!

Math Raw Score: ☐

Compare Raw Score with SAT Score Conversion Table on page 832 to find the Math Scaled Score.

Math Scaled Score ☐

SAT SCORE CONVERSION TABLE

Raw Score	Writing Scaled Score	Reading Scaled Score	Math Scaled Score	Raw Score	Writing Scaled Score	Reading Scaled Score	Math Scaled Score	Raw Score	Writing Scaled Score	Reading Scaled Score	Math Scaled Score
73	800			47	590–630	600–640	660–700	21	400–440	410–450	440–480
72	790–800			46	590–630	590–630	650–690	20	390–430	400–440	430–470
71	780–800			45	580–620	580–620	650–690	19	380–420	400–440	430–470
70	770–800			44	570–610	580–620	640–680	18	370–410	390–430	420–460
69	770–800			43	570–610	570–610	630–670	17	370–410	380–420	410–450
68	760–800			42	560–600	570–610	620–660	16	360–400	370–410	400–440
67	760–800	800		41	560–600	560–600	610–650	15	350–390	360–400	400–440
66	760–800	770–800		40	550–590	550–590	600–640	14	340–380	350–390	390–430
65	750–790	760–800		39	540–580	550–590	590–630	13	330–370	340–380	380–420
64	740–780	750–790		38	530–570	540–580	590–630	12	320–360	340–380	360–400
63	730–770	740–780		37	530–570	530–570	580–620	11	320–360	330–370	350–390
62	720–760	730–770		36	520–560	530–570	570–610	10	310–350	320–360	340–380
61	710–750	720–760		35	510–550	520–560	560–600	9	300–340	310–350	330–370
60	700–740	710–750		34	500–540	520–560	560–600	8	290–330	300–340	320–360
59	690–730	700–740		33	490–530	510–550	550–590	7	280–320	300–340	310–350
58	680–720	690–730		32	480–520	500–540	540–580	6	270–310	290–330	300–340
57	680–720	680–720		31	470–510	490–530	530–570	5	260–300	280–320	290–330
56	670–710	670–710		30	470–510	480–520	520–560	4	240–280	270–310	280–320
55	660–720	670–710		29	460–500	470–510	520–560	3	230–270	250–290	280–320
54	650–690	660–700	760–800	28	450–490	470–510	510–550	2	230–270	240–280	270–310
53	640–680	650–690	740–780	27	440–480	460–500	500–540	1	220–260	220–260	260–300
52	630–670	640–680	730–770	26	430–470	450–490	490–530	0	210–250	200–240	250–290
51	630–670	630–670	710–750	25	420–460	440–480	480–520	–1	200–240	200–230	230–270
50	620–660	620–660	690–730	24	410–450	430–470	470–510	–2	200–230	200–220	220–260
49	610–650	610–650	680–720	23	410–450	430–470	460–500	–3	200–220	200–210	200–240
48	600–640	600–640	670–710	22	400–440	420–460	450–490				

WRITING MULTIPLE-CHOICE SUBSCORE CONVERSION TABLE

Grammar Raw Score	Grammar Scaled Subscore	Grammar Raw Score	Grammar Scaled Subscore	Grammar Raw Score	Grammar Scaled Subscore	Grammar Raw Score	Grammar Scaled Subscore	Grammar Raw Score	Grammar Scaled Subscore
49	78–80	38	67–71	27	55–59	16	42–46	5	30–34
48	77–80	37	66–70	26	54–58	15	41–45	4	29–33
47	75–79	36	65–69	25	53–57	14	40–44	3	28–32
46	74–78	35	64–68	24	52–56	13	39–43	2	27–31
45	72–76	34	63–67	23	51–55	12	38–42	1	25–29
44	72–76	33	62–66	22	50–54	11	36–40	0	24–28
43	71–75	32	61–65	21	49–53	10	35–39	–1	22–26
42	70–74	31	60–64	20	47–51	9	34–38	–2	20–23
41	69–73	30	59–63	19	46–50	8	33–37	–3	20–22
40	68–72	29	58–62	18	45–49	7	32–36		
39	68–72	28	56–60	17	44–48	6	31–35		

Chapter 23
Practice Test 10:
Answers and
Explanations

SECTION 2

1. **C** The clue is *remembered reading the exact same paper last year*. The word *although* indicates that the teacher doubts the student is being truthful. (C) most nearly expresses this doubt. (A), *circumspect*, means "prudent and cautious." (B), *ambivalent*, means "indifferent." (D), *stoic*, means "impassive." (E), *sanguine*, means "optimistic."

2. **D** The clue for the first blank is *numerous instances;* we need a word there that touches on the meaning of something having happened before. The clues for the second blank are *weathered* and *disappointment*, so we need something similar in meaning to disappointment. The clue for the first blank eliminates (A) and (B); the clues for the second eliminate (C) and (E). (D) provides *accustomed*, or "being used to," and *disillusionment*, which is similar to "disappointment."

3. **A** The clue is *historians extolled its production*. To *extol* means "to praise," so this statement combined with *despite...not* means the docudrama must have contained some objective facts or truths, or at least something historians would like. Using these two clues allows us to eliminate all the other choices. (A) gives us exactly what we are looking for: *factual* for the first blank and *meritorious*, which means "worthy of praise," for the second.

4. **B** The clue is *lenient rules...could be detrimental*. A good word for the blank would be "approval." (A) is the opposite of "approval," and (C), (D), and (E) are unrelated to "approval." (B), *ratification*, means "to approve formally."

5. **B** The clue for the first blank is *enough precipitation to make for,* and the clue for the second blank is *damp*. Based on the first clue, we want something meaning "to make" or "to create": (C), (D), and (E) don't fit. Based on the second clue, we want a word meaning or related to damp weather; eliminate (A). (E) is a trap answer because the words are weather-related terms. The words in (B) fit perfectly; *generate* means "to make or create," and *inclement* refers to bad weather.

6. **C** The clue is *lacking energy*. (D), *idle*, is not specific enough; one can be full of energy and still be idle. (A), *irksome* ("annoying"), and (B), *complacent* ("unconcerned or self-satisfied"), are unrelated. (E), *vital* ("full of life"), has the opposite meaning.

7. **B** The performance is criticized, and the actor's fame is not likely to last. (C), *dramatic,* and (D), *lucrative* ("profitable"), are concepts often associated with acting, but are trap answers. Neither (A), *esoteric* ("known to only select few"), nor (E), *pejorative* ("belittling"), fit here either. (B), *ephemeral*, means "short-lived," and that fits nicely.

8. **A** The clue in the sentence is *so lifelike*. (A) is correct because *verisimilitude* means "realism." (B), *integrity,* means "morally sound or whole." (C), *placidity,* means "calmness." (D), *fecundity,* means "fertile." (E), *deviousness,* means "deceptive or not straightforward."

9. **D** The passage states that the heat of the region causes evaporation to occur at a high rate. (B) is incorrect because saline levels have no effect on evaporation. (A) and (C) are results, not causes, of evaporation. (E) is unrelated to the increase in evaporation rates.

10. **A** The passage explores the reasons why the Dead Sea is salty. The concept is not *irksome* or irritating, as mentioned in (B). There are no *assumptions* made in the passage, as stated in (C). There is no *misunderstood fact*, as stated in (D). The passage does not offer a *solution*, nor does it present a problem, as implied in (E).

11. **B** The passage states that the neo-Sumerian period was so named because it marked the return of Sumerian rule to Sumer. Thus, it may be inferred that at times, Sumer was not ruled by Sumerians. (A) is incorrect because the passage never specifically says that Sargon was the first warlord to conquer the city-states. (C) is wrong because the passage mentions only one instance of Gutian-Akkadian conflict. No information is provided about the length of the third phase, so we cannot infer (D). (E) states that *all Sumerian monarchs* engaged in this practice; however, the passage mentions only Sargon (who wasn't even Sumerian).

12. **B** (B) is correct, based on the final lines of the passage. The overthrow of the Akkadians by the Gutians *ushered in* the final phase of Sumerian history and returned rule of Sumer to native Sumerians. (A), (C), and (D) are wrong because this information is not mentioned in the passage. (E) is incorrect because the Gutians did not name the period.

13. **A** The passage notes that the songs are *provincial*, or local, that they are about the *land and its people*, and that everyone recognizes them. The older women might be sad, but the future is never mentioned as asserted in (B). It is never mentioned that the musicians can be found only in the valley, as stated in (C). (D) is never mentioned in the passage. (E) might be true, but does not answer the question.

14. **C** *Sickly* means "overpowering" or "too much." (A) and (B) are the trap answers; *sickly* can mean either of these, but not in this context. (D) and (E) are not definitions of the word in context.

15. **D** The *cruel reality* was that city girls would not be at all interested in less sophisticated country boys. However, if girls came from the city to the country to meet boys like the narrator, with *shabby attire and callused hands*, then there would be no cruel reality, weakening the narrator's assertion. (A), (B), and (E) would all strengthen the narrator's assertion. One's ability to dance is not part of the cruel reality, as stated in (C).

16. **D** The passage suggests Ralph was *resolute* toward the plan. (A) is not mentioned in the passage. (B) and (C) are true of the other boys, not of Ralph. Although Ralph may have been boastful, the passage does not mention he is more experienced in socializing with girls, as stated in (E).

17. **E** The word *ebullient* means "excited" or "enthusiastic," the effect that the lively music has on the crowd. (B) is a trap; the music may have been loud, but the word *ebullient* doesn't also mean "loud." (C) is a trap; the crowd may be jostling, but it's not necessarily *unrestrained*. (A) and (D) are not supported by the passage.

18. **A**   The description of the girls indicates that they are different from the narrator and his friends. (B) is too strong. At this point in the passage it is not clear the plan will fail. The suggestion in (C) is not mentioned and is the opposite of what the phrase indicates. Neither (D) nor (E) is mentioned in the passage.

19. **B**   Ralph is described as *ebullient since the band members had picked up the rhythm*. In other words, he's excited by what he hears and sees. This is best expressed in (B). While the boys are described as appearing *shabby* (line 33) there's no indication that Ralph is embarrassed, so eliminate (A). (C) is incorrect because, although Ralph is surely gratified, it's not the reason that he is wily, or sly (although since eels could be considered wily, this is an answer that might be attractive if we haven't read carefully). Eliminate (D) because it's the band, not the large crowd, that excites Ralph. He's moving toward the dance floor, not the door, so (E) is also out.

20. **C**   The passage neither implies nor mentions that Mother did not provide a stable upbringing for the children. The others are all mentioned in the passage: (A), lines 53–59; (B), lines 10–14; (D), lines 57–59; and (E), lines 13–14.

21. **A**   The paragraph gives examples of the narrator's unease and leads the reader to believe he is disappointed. The information in (B) is never mentioned. For (C), the paragraph does not favor one season over another. Although Sylvia is mentioned, the paragraph does not actually show how she would affect the narrator's childhood, as stated in (D). There is no indication of Ralph's feelings in this paragraph, as stated in (E).

22. **B**   The narrator speaks longingly, with some happiness, regret, and nostalgia. (A) is extreme. The narrator is not overly sad. (C) is partly right. The narrator is *enthusiastic* about meeting girls, but is also disappointed. (D) is also partly right. The narrator is somewhat *resigned* at the end but not throughout. (E) is extreme. The narrator is not totally *captivated*.

23. **E**   The passage talks about one boy and his friends, his difficulty with meeting girls, and his ways of dealing with the loss of his mother. Although (A) might be true, it is not the central focus of the passage. The passage does touch on the *social and economic differences among people*, as seen in (B), but it's only part of the larger narrative. Similarly, while the passage does talk about *rural and urban* areas, as stated in (C), it is only part of the narrative. (D) is not part of the narrative.

24. **D**   When Ralph is rejected, he goes pale. (A) is the opposite of what the phrase indicates. (B) is not supported by the passage. *Expression* is not mentioned as stated in (C). (E) may be true but does not answer the question.

SECTION 3

1. **B** To turn 0.008 into 0.08, you need to move the decimal point one place to the right. As long as you move the decimal point in 0.032 one place to the right as well, you have not changed the equality. So, $0.08x = 0.32$. To do this problem mathematically, multiply both sides by 10.

2. **A** Try each of the answers until you find one that works. For (A), you get $|-9 + 3| > 5$, which is a true statement since $|-6| > 5$. To solve the equation, remember that $x + 3 > 5$ or $x + 3 < -5$. Solving both inequalities gives $x > 2$ or $x < -8$. Only (A) meets one of those conditions.

3. **B** Since this is an isosceles triangle, the two sides $\overline{AB}$ and $\overline{BC}$ have the same length. Therefore, point B's x-coordinate will be in the exact middle of the other two points, and so will be 3. This eliminates (C), (D), and (E). Since the area is 4 and the base is 2 (the distance from A to C), $4 = \frac{1}{2}(2)(h)$. The height is 4, which should be the y-coordinate.

4. **E** Try to figure out the order. No man stands first, and since a woman stands fourth, the two women must be first and fourth, so eliminate (A) and (D). Since Denzel stands in front of Janine, Janine can't be first, so she must be fourth. That leaves Susan standing first. Denzel must be in front of Janine, so he must now be in spot 2 or 3. Since Denzel can't stand next to Melvin, the only place for Melvin to stand is in the fifth place, and that's answer choice (E).

5. **B** Try some numbers and use the Process of Elimination. For example, x, y, and z could be 1, 2, and 3, respectively. Note that the average of these numbers is 2, which the problem requires. (A) and (C) can be eliminated. Now, try spacing the numbers a little further apart. For example, try 1, 5, and 9. Note that the middle number is still the average. Now, (D) and (E) can be eliminated.

6. **D** Try Plugging In the answers. If Alan started with 50 muffins, he can't sell one-third of them because 50 is not evenly divisible by 3, so eliminate (C). Try other answers until we find the one that works. Try (D). If he starts with 60, that means he sells one-third, or 20, muffins, then an additional 10, leaving him with 30, which is half the number he started with.

7. **E** Since the perimeter of $ABCD$ is 16, each of the sides of the larger square has length 4. EBF (and the triangles like it) is an isosceles right triangle with two sides of length 2 and a hypotenuse of length $2\sqrt{2}$. So, $EFGH$ is a square with sides of length $2\sqrt{2}$ and a perimeter of $8\sqrt{2}$.

8. **D** Remember that the exponent outside of the parentheses applies to each item within the parentheses. When raising a power to a power, we multiply the exponents. So, $(-3a^2b^5)^3 = (-3)^3 \times (a^2)^3 \times (b^5)^3 = -27a^6b^{15}$.

9. **B** First, determine the slope of line l since two points are provided for that line. The slope of l is given by $\frac{0-c}{d-0} = -\frac{c}{d}$. Since line m is perpendicular to line l, the slope of line m will be the negative reciprocal of the slope of line l. So, the slope of line m is $\frac{d}{c}$.

10. **C** Since this is an absolute value question, there will be two answers, one for $3x - 6 = 36$, and one for $3x - 6 = -36$. Solve both of these equations for x to get 14 and –10. Since –10 shows up in the answers, (C) is correct.

11. **B** Set up the ratio as a proportion: $\frac{a}{b} = \frac{2a}{b}$. Because the bottoms of these proportions are the same and cannot be 0, the tops must be equal. So, $a = 2a$. The only number that makes this true is $a = 0$, so statement II is true. Statement I cannot be true because b cannot be 0. Statement III cannot be true because b cannot be 0 and that is the only number that would make the statement true. (B) has II only.

12. **C** If the equation is going to work out for $y = 0$, Plug In 0 for y and see if the equation simplifies. $3(0)^4 + x(0) - x^2 = (0)^2 - 25$, which simplifies to $x^2 = 25$. Therefore there are 2 possible values for x: 5 and –5.

13. **C** Translate "the product of one more than w and 2 less than w" into $(w + 1)(w - 2) = w^2 - w - 2$. Try possible values for w that are odd. Start with 1, and the product is –2, which isn't an answer choice. Next try 3, for which the product is 4—also not an answer choice. If 5 is used, the product is 18, so (C) is correct.

14. **D** Since the numbers are already in numerically ascending order, just average the numbers for the years 2002 and 2003 from the chart. For 2002, the chart shows 3 million acres developed. For 2003, the chart shows about 3.8 million acres developed. The median is therefore 3.4. If you picked (C), be careful. The question didn't ask for the median for all 5 years shown.

15. **D** If the perimeter of the square is 4, the length of one of the 4 sides is $\frac{4}{4} = 1$. To find the circumference, find the radius. Draw in a diameter connecting A and C. This creates a right triangle with two sides of length equal to 1. It is a 45°-45°-90° triangle because two of the sides are equal. The ratio of the sides is $1:1:\sqrt{2}$, which means $AC = \sqrt{2}$. The radius is half the diameter, so $r = \frac{\sqrt{2}}{2}$. Circumference is $2\pi r$, so $2\pi\left(\frac{\sqrt{2}}{2}\right) = \sqrt{2}\pi$. Also, $C = \pi d$, so save a step and go directly to $\sqrt{2}\pi$.

16. **D** Set A = {2, 3, 5, 7}. Since there are only six different selections of numbers possible, it's easiest just to list out the possibilities: 2 + 3, 2 + 5, 2 + 7, 3 + 5, 3 + 7, 5 + 7. Of those selections, only 3 + 5, 3 + 7, and 5 + 7 are even. So, the probability that the sum of the two selected numbers is even is $\frac{3}{6} = \frac{1}{2}$.

17. **A** The sides of isosceles right triangles have a ratio of $x : x : x\sqrt{2}$. This ratio will provide all the lengths needed. *CE* is *x*, since the hypotenuse of that triangle is $x\sqrt{2}$. So if *CE* is *x*, and *BE* = 2*x*, *BC* is 3*x*, as is *AB*; thus *AC* is $3x\sqrt{2}$.

18. **D** A good approach to this problem is to Plug In values for the variables. For instance, try *r* = 4 and *s* = 7. The product of *rs* is 28 and all of the answers are factors of 28 except (D).

19. **D** Assign some numbers to the variables so that it's easier to see what's going on. Suppose that there are *x* = 10 members of the Brighton High School Marching Band and that there are *y* = 12 members of the Brighton Drum Corp. Finally, let there be *p* = 4 common members. To find the total membership of the Monroe County All-Star Drum Line, add the members of the marching band and drum corp. However, now you've counted the four common members twice and you weren't supposed to count them at all. You'll need to subtract out twice the number of the common members: 10 + 12 − 8 = 14. (D) evaluates to 14 with the chosen numbers.

20. **B** If *a* = 0, *b* must be at least 1, *c* must be at least 2, and *d* must be at least 3. This does not work because *e* = 6, which is not greater than *cd* (2 × 3). Since *a* cannot equal 0, eliminate (A), (D), and (E) because they contain *a*. Eliminate (C) because *c* cannot equal 0, since *a* and *b* would then both be negative, so *ab* would be positive and, therefore, not less than *c*.

SECTION 4

1. **D** The clues for the first blank, *precision*, *significant breadth*, and *revised essay*, suggest that we need a positive word in that blank. Eliminate (B) and (C). The clues *obviously rushed* and *whereas* imply a change in direction; therefore, we want a negative word in the second blank. (D) is best. All the other choices for the second blank have positive meanings.

2. **A** (A) is correct because *be moved* is the clue. *Heartrending* agrees with that clue. (D), *therapeutic*, relates to recovering from an accident and so is intended to be a trap answer. None of the other choices captures the meaning of being moved emotionally.

3. **E** In this kind of sentence completion, there are no clues to help us find the answers. Instead, the words in the blanks are similar in meaning. The word *inalienable* means "incapable of being *transferred*," exactly the relationship required here. No other pair shares meaning in this way. In (A), *variable* rights do not suggest that the paintings will never be *viewed*. In (B), knowing that the rights are *incomprehensible* does not suggest that the paintings cannot be *released*. In (C), having *laudable* ("worthy of praise") rights does not suggest that they can't be *maintained*. In (D), if the paintings can never be *devalued*, owning them would not be *regrettable*.

4.   **C**   A good word for the blank is "precise" or "brief," based on the clue words *concise, compact,* and *few.* (C), *succinct,* describes speech that is clear and concise. (B), *timorous,* means "timid," which is not the right meaning needed here. (A), (D), and (E) are trap answers as they are adjectives often associated with the Gettysburg Address.

5.   **E**   The clue is *guilty. But* acts to switch the direction of the sentence. However, *no* then switches it back. Thus, we need a word that means "guilt" in the blank, and *culpability* means "guilt." (A) and (C) both imply a lack of guilt. (D), *manifestation* ("an indication of something's existence or reality"), is close, but lacks a clear link with guilt, making (E) the better answer. (B), *juxtaposition,* means "placed next to or close to something."

6.   **C**   The author believes that voting is more a measure of civil allegiance than a purely numerical exercise. Thus, (C) is the best answer because a poll indicating that citizens value *communal duty* would strengthen the argument. (A) is not correct—the author feels opposite of this. (B) is extreme—the author is not attacking democracy. The author does not introduce a complex problem, nor claim that there are no rational explanations. The question posed does not emphasize this fact about elections. Neither (D) nor (E) is addressed in the passage.

7.   **A**   The main point of Passage 1 is that the real value of voting is in how it shows an individual's belief in his or her government and how included he or she feels in society. The story about the friend is meant to give an example of someone who doesn't vote because he feels it doesn't matter. Since the friend thinks voting is not worth his time, the author of Passage 1 would conclude that the friend does not feel he is included in society. This is best expressed in (A). (B) is unrealistic and extreme. We cannot say that because he did not vote, he is unlikely ever to vote in the future. (C) is outside the range of these passages; we have no idea how many people do not vote, or what this means to the society at large. (D) is also extreme; it is clear he doesn't think much of the electoral process, but we do not know if that means he distrusts the government. (E) is outside the range of these passages; we know only that some people don't vote, and we know nothing else of what their lives are like.

8.   **D**   To answer this question, keep in mind the main point of each passage and eliminate answers that do not agree with both passages. (D) best agrees with both passages; both authors say we should not think that the worth of a single vote lies in its ability to change an election result. Passage 1 never mentions the excuses that people make not to vote, so (A) cannot be correct. Neither passage indicates that people shouldn't vote, so (B) cannot be correct. There is no evidence that Americans do not vote because they don't like making difficult decisions, so (C) is not correct. Although both passages allude to voter apathy, there is no indication that the apathy is caused by a lack of choices, so (E) is not correct.

9. **C**   To answer this question, consider this sentence's role in the context of the passage. The author refutes the argument that because one's vote would not change an election's outcome, one doesn't need to vote by showing that by the definition of democracy, one person should not be able to change the will of a greater group of people; instead one should vote to be part of a group of people. The final sentence states that thinking one can change an election is undemocratic. (C) best expresses the relationship. *Subtle irony* refers to the incongruity between the understanding of the value of a vote and the meaning of democracy, which grants us the vote. It may be easier on this question to simply eliminate the other four answers, and arrive at this one by default. The final sentence offers no reason for why people do or do not vote, so (A) cannot be correct. (B) is too extreme for Passage 2; the author doesn't criticize anyone. This sentence offers no solution to getting people to vote, so (D) cannot be correct. (E) is out of scope; the Constitution is never mentioned in Passage 2, so this cannot be correct.

10. **B**   (B) is correct, as Joyce fled for *reasons both personal and professional* (line 22). (A) is wrong because while Joyce did find inspiration abroad, the passage offers other reasons for his leaving. (C), (D), and (E) are wrong because they are not mentioned in the passage. (B) is the best paraphrase of the two reasons.

11. **A**   (A) is not mentioned. Eliminate (B) because Joyce wrote in a *modernist, experimental narrative style*. (C) is incorrect because the passage tells us that Joyce is regarded as one of the greatest writers ever. (D) is incorrect, since Joyce wrote about *isolation and exile*. Eliminate (E) because Joyce lived between 1882 and 1941.

12. **E**   A *conundrum* is a predicament or a puzzling statement. The word *inaccessible* in the first sentence supports this idea. (E), *puzzle,* is closest to this meaning.

13. **A**   The author of the passage claims that the reader can understand a writer's work by studying that person's biography. Then he or she describes elements from James Joyce's life in Trieste that are reflected in his writing. Lastly, the author moves from a discussion of Joyce's work to pose a more general question about how to interpret autobiographical elements in a writer's work. This structure most closely agrees with (A). (B) is incorrect because three theories are not mentioned. Eliminate (C), since the author does not reject an idea. (D) is wrong; the author doesn't criticize other writers. Finally, eliminate (E), since the author never says this.

14. **A**   (C) is not indicated and is too extreme. (B) is wrong because Ellman wrote about Joyce after Joyce died; there is no indication they knew each other. There is no mention that Joyce's critics were against an autobiographical interpretation of his work, so eliminate (D). Joyce may have spoken through the character of Dedalus, but it is too extreme to say this always occurred, so (E) is wrong.

15. **C**   The word *inadvertently* means the author may misrepresent reality without meaning to do so. (A) and (B) are not mentioned. Both (D) and (E) are about readers, but the statement at issue is about writers.

16. **D** (D) may be one way to interpret Dedalus's claim. (A) and (B) are wrong because the author states we can't know for sure exactly what Joyce meant here, and we aren't given any information about Dedalus's profession. For (C), even if Joyce used Dedalus to voice an opinion, nowhere does it say that he had reason to fear making this claim. There is no evidence in the passage for (E).

17. **A** The author begins by claiming that knowing a writer's biography helps the reader to understand his work, but ends by saying that this may not be true. The last paragraphs present an opposing, not a supporting, idea, so eliminate (B). (C) is wrong because the end of the passage does not make this claim. (D) is extreme; according to the passage, some parts of Joyce's works were in fact autobiographical. Another writer (Shakespeare) is mentioned, but not to serve the purpose given in (E).

18. **B** Joyce was not a sailor (the passage says he's an author), so such a character would not be autobiographical. (A), (C), and (D) are described in the passage as characteristics of Joyce's life. As for (E), Stephen Dedalus is described as Joyce's *literary alter ego* (line 52), meaning the character through whom Joyce speaks in this book.

19. **D** (D) accurately reflects both the author's effort to inform and warn readers about CMEs and the author's explanation of the challenges researchers are facing. (A) and (B) accurately describe only one part of the passage. (C) and (E) are wrong because most of the passage is not persuasive in style.

20. **E** The 1989 storm is described as a major CME. The author also states that since our society is increasingly dependent on technology, the potential havoc wrought by a major CME becomes even more distressing. (A), (B), and (D) are all answers that are not supported by the passage. (C) is also not mentioned anywhere; it garbles different pieces of the passage.

21. **B** The researchers have *scant information* about the CMEs because there are *few existing records*. Therefore, we're looking for a word that means only a few, or not enough. (B) fits the bill. (C) and (D) are opposites (and distracting). (A) and (E) simply don't have the meaning we're looking for.

22. **A** *Compounded* means "increased or added to." Scientists' inability *to determine the orientation of a CME's magnetic field* more than *30 minutes before it reaches the atmosphere* increases, or adds to, the *difficulties* of prediction. (A) best expresses this problem. (B) is close but not quite right. The author already says that there is little time to predict CMEs, and just uses *compounded by* to show that the situation is even worse than previously asserted. (C) is incorrect because the author does not try to *disprove* this idea. Nor are scientists working to discredit CMEs, so eliminate (D). There is nothing in the passage to support (E).

23. **C** To answer this question, we must determine the truth of the given statements and rely upon Process of Elimination. The second-to-last paragraph discusses how rare CMEs are, and therefore, how little data exists that would allow scientists to predict future occurrences. III is therefore true, so eliminate (A) and (B). The same paragraph also mentions how little time there would be to react to and study a CME, so I is true. This eliminates (D). II is false because the passage doesn't discuss this phenomenon, so eliminate (E).

24. **D**   The author of this passage shows an interest in informing readers about CMEs. But the author also explains that scientists (and, implicitly, readers) can do little to predict these storms or prevent the damage they cause. (A) is extreme: The author cites countermeasures in the final paragraph, so there are some things that can be done to minimize impact. The author never urges individuals to do anything, so (B) is out. (C) is extreme: The author has not provided evidence that identifies so precisely the time or effects of future CMEs. (E) The first half of the answer is reasonable, but the second half overstates the author's view of how prepared our society will be.

SECTION 5

1. **A**   A good approach to this problem is to Plug In a value for the variable. For instance, try $d = 10$. Then Mr. Barua works 35 hours in a year. Plug In 10 for d in the answers. Only (A) equals 35. Algebraically, if he teaches d days, and each day teaches 3.5 hours, he teaches $3.5d$ hours altogether.

2. **E**   Add $2x$ to both sides of the equation to get $5x = 10$. Multiply 10 by itself to get 100.

3. **D**   Draw a figure to see that R is the midpoint of $\overline{PT}$. Since PR is 6, double it to get PT, which is 12. Alternatively, if $PQ = QR$, then Q is the midpoint of $\overline{PR}$ (which has length 6), and PQ is therefore 3. Therefore, all four lengths that are given as equal to PQ must be 3 units long. So $PT = 3 + 3 + 3 + 3$, or 12.

4. **D**   Read the question carefully. A and B are not variables; they are digits (the integers between 0 and 9 inclusive). For B, what number subtracted from 3 gives 1? 2. For A, since there's no carrying, what number subtracted from 8 gives 3? 5. Double check: Does 83 minus 52 equal 31? Yes. Another way to think about this problem would be to reverse the operation: $83 - 31 =$ what? 52. The final step is to multiply the two digits together, giving us 10.

5. **A**   Try Plugging In the answer choices: $|-3 - 6| = |-9| = 9 = (-3)^2$. Note: 2 is another solution. However, 2 does not appear among the answer choices.

6. **E**   Since the circumference is 10π, the diameter is 10. $XY = 6$, and $\angle XYZ$ is marked as a right angle in the figure, so $\triangle XYZ$ is a 6:8:10 right triangle. The base and height of a triangle are perpendicular, so we can use the legs of length 6 and 8 as the triangle's base and height. The area of $\triangle XYZ$ is therefore $A = \frac{1}{2}bh = \frac{1}{2}(6)(8) = 24$. If the diameter of the circle is 10, the radius is 5. Therefore, the area of the circle is $A = \pi r^2 = \pi(5)^2 = 25\pi$. The area of the top half of the circle is thus $\frac{25\pi}{2}$. Now subtract the area of the triangle (the unshaded region) from the circle to get the area of the shaded region: $\frac{25\pi}{2} - 24$.

7.   **A**   A good approach to this problem is to Plug In values for the variables. For instance, try 1, 2, 3, 4, and 5 for j, k, l, m, and n, respectively. $(j + n) - (k + m) = (1 + 5) - (2 + 4) = 0$.

8.   **D**   Start by putting the expression for $f(x)$ over the expression for $g(x)$ to create two equivalent frac-

tions: $\dfrac{f(x)}{g(x)} = \dfrac{2x^2 - 4x - 16}{x^2 - 3x - 4}$. Now, factor the top and bottom of the new expression to get the

most reduced form. So, $\dfrac{f(x)}{g(x)} = \dfrac{2x^2 - 4x - 16}{x^2 - 3x - 4} = \dfrac{(x-4)(2x+4)}{(x-4)(x+1)} = \dfrac{2x+4}{x+1}$.

9.   **4 or 6**   The perimeter of the rectangle is 10, and $(2 \times base) + (2 \times height)$ = perimeter. So, possible lengths of the sides are 1 and 4 or 2 and 3. Then, to find area, plug the values for base and height into the formula: *area = base × height*.

10. **4.6**   Use your calculator to solve the left side of the equation. We find that $460,000 = b \times 10^5$. Divide both sides by 10^5 to find that $b = 4.6$.

11. **50**   15 is 30% of the total number of apples picked. So, $15 = \dfrac{30}{100}x$. Multiply both sides of the equa-

tion by $\dfrac{100}{30}$ to find that $x = 50$.

12. **2**   The question wants to know the value of the x-coordinate that makes the y-coordinates of the two lines equal. In other words, look for the point of intersection on the graph. The x-coordinate of the point of intersection for the two lines is $x = 2$.

13. **268**   Find the surface area of the box to find how much paper is needed. To find the surface area, find the area of all the faces. $4 \times 6 = 24$, $6 \times 11 = 66$, and $4 \times 11 = 44$. Then add the area of each face together and remember that there are two of each. So, $24 + 24 + 66 + 66 + 44 + 44 = 268$.

14. **7**   The simplest way to solve this problem is to list out all the possibilities. Remember, 1, 2, or 3 items are possible. So, the options are H, W, P, HW, HP, WP, HWP. There are 7 different combinations. The tricky part in this problem is the phrase *up to*, meaning this isn't a simple $3 \times 2 \times 1$ type of problem.

15. **1**   3 is the only number that is an element of both sets. Any other multiple of 3 is by definition not prime, since it equals 3 times another integer.

16. **28**   Start by determining the regular price of the more expensive sweater: $25 + \dfrac{40}{100}(25) = \$35$. Now,

remember that Megan buys the sweater when it is on sale for 20% off. So, $35 - \dfrac{20}{100}(35) = \$28$.

17. **200**   Start by figuring out how much Jack spent on CDs in 2002 and 2004. For 2002, he spent $(\$10 \times 12) + (\$8 \times 5) + (\$8 \times 5) = \$200$. For 2004, he spent $(\$12 \times 25) + (\$10 \times 12) + (\$12 \times 15) = \$600$. To find the percentage increase, use the formula: % increase $= \dfrac{\text{change}}{\text{original}} \times 100 = \dfrac{600 - 200}{200} \times 100 = 200\%$.

18. **4,100** The minimum value of any real number squared is 0, since $0^2 = 0$ and anything else squared is positive. So the minimum value of the expression in parentheses is 0. The lowest value (v) of the painting must therefore be equal to q and, since it occurred in 1990, $(r - 6(1990 - 1970))^2 = 0$. Therefore, $(r - 6(1990 - 1970)) = 0$. Solving this equation for r yields $r = 120$. Since the dollar value of the painting in 1990 is 500, $q = 500$. Now Plug In 2000 for the year, and solve for v: $v = 500 + (120 - 6(2000 - 1970))^2 = 4,100$.

SECTION 6

1. **C** (A) and (D) lack the correct idiom, "required to." (B) uses an *-ing* verb (generally avoided on the SAT) and is less concise than (C). (D) and (E) contain an ambiguous pronoun: *it*.

2. **C** (A) is missing the conjunction "but also" after the comma; *not only* needs to be paired with "but also." (B) contains this pair, but lacks parallelism. (D) and (E) not only lack the necessary *not only…but also,* but make reference to an ambiguous *it*. Only (C) fixes the conjunction problem without adding new errors.

3. **C** This choice correctly fixes not only the parallelism problem, but also changes *being* to *since*, showing cause and effect. (A) both ignores parallelism and uses *being*. (B) repeats *being*. (D) changes the verb to present tense. (E) changes the meaning of the sentence.

4. **E** (E) correctly uses the idiom and maintains parallel construction. (A) and (B) contain incorrect idioms; the correct form is "superior to." (C) suggests that typewriters have word-processing programs. (D) correctly uses the idiom but is wordy and is not parallel; *today's computers* should be compared with *the typewriters of the 1960s*.

5. **D** The idiom is "more…than." Only (D) has the correct idiom. (B), (C), and (E) are all too wordy as well.

6. **E** (E) has correct agreement in both the pronoun *their* and the verb *are*, which agree with *rock-and-roll songs*. The use of *its* in (A), (C), and (D) does not correctly refer to *songs*, which is plural. (A) and (B) also lack subject-verb agreement since the verb should agree with *songs*.

7. **C** (A) incorrectly uses the subject pronoun *who*, instead of the object pronoun *whom*. (B) should be eliminated because *that* is not a good choice to use when referring to people. Both (D) and (E), which use *which*, should be eliminated for the same reason.

8. **B** The subject of the sentence, *DVD technology*, is singular, so the verb must also be singular. Therefore, the correct form of the verb is *continues*. Only (B) contains the proper form of the verb.

9. **A** (B), (D), and (E) do not have subject-verb agreement since the verb must agree with *vice president*, which is singular. Remember, in an *either…or* scenario, the verb of the sentence should agree with the last subject listed. (C) has subject-verb agreement, but it is best to stay away from verbs ending in *-ing*.

10. **C** (C) uses the correct pronoun and verb. (A) and (B) incorrectly use the plural pronoun *they* in reference to the singular subject, the *brokerage firm*. The form of the verb in (D) is incorrect—it should be *was*. The verb in (E) changes the tense to present and, therefore, should be eliminated.

11. **C** Prepositions need to be followed by object pronouns. (C) is correct since it uses the object pronoun *me*. (A) and (D) incorrectly use the subject pronoun *I* and should be eliminated. (B) uses the object pronoun but the wrong preposition, since *among* is used only with more than two things. (E) is cumbersome and uses the wrong pronoun.

12. **A** The subject of the sentence should be written with the subject case. The sentence should start with *He and she*. Try removing half the subject to see it more clearly. We would never say "Him ran hurriedly," we'd say "He ran hurriedly."

13. **C** The verb *were* is plural and therefore does not agree with the singular subject *skate*.

14. **E** This sentence is correct as written.

15. **D** *Ends* (present tense) should be changed to *ended* (past tense) to agree with *made for* (past tense).

16. **A** The *office* should take the pronoun *that*, not *who*.

17. **E** This sentence is correct as written. The items in the list are parallel and the verb *are* correctly agrees with the subject *birds*.

18. **C** The words *he* and *athlete* are singular, but the word *they*, which should agree, is plural. (C) should read *he*.

19. **D** (D) incorrectly uses the future tense of *run*. When checking a verb for tense errors, look at both the context of the sentence and other verbs that are not underlined. The sentence is talking about a hypothetical situation that has just ended (you have just finished the race); therefore, we cannot use the simple future tense because the action has theoretically ended. The sentence should have used *will have run*.

20. **A** *Worried over* is the colloquial and incorrect version of the idiom "worried about."

21. **B** In this sentence, *another,* which is singular, needs to be parallel to *some,* which is plural. (B) should be *others argue*.

22. **C** The sentence incorrectly uses the preposition *of* with the adjective *partial*. This is an idiom, a pairing of a preposition with another part of speech. The correct idiom is *partial to*. Always check underlined prepositions (short words that show place) for idiom errors.

23. **B** The word *grandsons* is plural, so anything that refers to them should be plural in number. In the phrase *their heart*, while *their* is plural, *heart* is not; it should be *hearts*. (The phrase *their sister*, however, is correct: *Sister* is singular because the boys share the same sister.)

24. **E** This sentence is correct as written.

25. **A** *Dried* is past tense, and yet the sentence indicates an ongoing action that was interrupted; therefore, we need the past continuous, which is *was drying*. This, then, agrees with the sudden interruption indicated by *dropped* (past tense).

26. **A** When referring to a person, one should always use *who* rather than *that*. (A) should read *warlord who*.

27. **E** (A) correctly uses the pronoun *I*. An easy way to tell if it should be *I* or *me* is to remove the other part of the subject. There are no errors in (B), (C), or (D). Be careful not to pick *which* just because it sounds strange. So (E) is correct.

28. **C** The verb *will explore* is in the future tense. *Will be reading* is the future continuous tense and should be changed to the future tense *will read*. Remember: When faced with a list of verbs, be sure they are in the same form and have the same tense.

29. **D** The plural pronoun *them* could refer to professors or students, and therefore is ambiguous.

30. **B** (A) is incorrect. In the original sentence, the word *with* is unnecessary and the word *other* is redundant because of the word *besides*. (B) eliminates both of these problems. The word *but,* as used in (C), does not have the same meaning as the word *besides,* which it replaces. (D) and (E) both change the meaning of the sentence.

31. **E** Here the writer's assumptions about the retirement home start to crumble, and adding *surprised me* shows this change more clearly. Also, this statement is the beginning of a list of the writer's own observations, so saying *I didn't see* fits better than the broad statement *there weren't* any hospital beds. In (A), the word *not* would make the last half of the sentence a fragment. (B), (C), and (D) are not as strong as (E) because the phrase *one thing* lacks clarity without additional information.

32. **D** The word *another* is unclear without *resident*. Also, watching television is an extended activity, whereas one person entering a room is brief and defined; adding the word *soon* and changing the verb to *came in* both provide a clearer picture of this action. (A) is incorrect because the word *another* is unclear as written; it could refer to a single resident, another lady, or another pair of two ladies. (B) and (C) have the same lack of clarity; furthermore, nothing in the sentence suggests that the verb form should change to *would be coming in*. (E) also includes a needless change in verb tense. Also, a semicolon is better than a comma here: Each half of the sentence could stand by itself as a complete sentence, and so a comma is not sufficient to link these two halves.

33. **A** This sentence introduces the two new pieces of information presented in this paragraph (what retirement homes and older people are truly like). Also, the word *stereotypes* hints at the larger theme of this passage, which is that many teenagers hold false beliefs about retirees. (B) is too extreme: Nothing in the passage indicates such a broad change. (C) not only includes extreme language but also suggests that this paragraph only discusses the writer's view of older people, which is too limited. The writer's belief system (religion, faith, personal principles) has not been changed by these experiences, so (D) is wrong. (E) is close, but this paragraph shows the writer learning and enjoying.

34.　**B**　A semicolon is a good way to link these two sentences, which share different but related ideas. Adding *of the residents* and clarifying which couple went to Greece strengthen this sentence; saying that the writer *met* this couple (past) goes hand in hand with changing the next verb to *had just returned* (before they met). (A) is choppy and vague, and (D) is incorrect because simply replacing the period after *travel* with a comma is not correct. (C) is vague: *Them* is unclear, and it changes the meaning of the sentence. (E) is grammatically sound, but *some* lacks precision.

35.　**A**　Sentence 15 is intended to extend the point of sentence 14: The writer overcomes preconceptions about the elderly. (A) accomplishes this transition. (C) and (E), like the original sentence, express a contrast, which is not what the writer intends. (B) and (D) wrongly imply that health and activity were the only common elements between the writer and the elderly, thus ignoring the context (that is, the other examples of similarity provided in the rest of the paragraph).

SECTION 8

1.　**D**　The easiest way to solve this question is to simply try the answers until you find one that works. For (D), you'd get $\sqrt{100} = 10$ on the left side of the equation and $\frac{100}{10} = 10$ on the right side of the equation. Exactly what you need! To actually solve the equation, square both sides to get: $x = \frac{x^2}{100}$. Cross-multiply to find that $100x = x^2$. Dividing both sides by x gives you $x = 100$.

2.　**D**　When lines are parallel, any line that crosses them both creates two kinds of angles, large and small; w and y are "large" angles that each equal 100°. Since a line has 180°, we can find out the measure of the small angle—80°. So add the measures of the two large and one small angle together. $100° + 100° + 80° = 280°$.

3.　**B**　$x = 6$, so $\frac{3}{2}x = 9$.

4.　**B**　The angle created by the intersection of $\overline{AD}$ with $\overline{AC}$ is the complement to w and therefore measures 80°. Thus, $y = 10$. Since z is a right angle, $z + y = 100$.

5.　**D**　Start by finding the area of face *ABCD*, which is given by $l \times w$ or, in this case $5 \times 12 = 60$. Since the area of face *CDEF* is half that of *ABCD*, the area of *CDEF* is 30. Side $CD = 5$, so $DE = 6$. Finally, use the volume formula ($V = lwh$) to find the volume of the solid: $V = 5 \times 12 \times 6 = 360$.

6.　**E**　We know that 10 plus something gives 154, so that something equals 144, or $\sqrt{x} = 144$, so $10 \times 144 = 1,440$. Don't solve for x! It isn't necessary here—make sure to do only what is needed to answer the question. This question has a classic trick in it: $\sqrt{x} = 144$ is not the same as $x = \sqrt{144} = 12$.

7. **A** Easy points to check are the *y*-intercept and the *x*-intercept. The graph of $h(2x)$ should have the same *y*-intercept as the graph of $h(x)$, since $h(2(0)) = h(0)$. Eliminate (C), (D), and (E). The *x*-intercept of the new graph should be half as far from the origin as that of the original graph, since $h(2(1)) = h(2)$. Eliminate (B).

8. **C** To find the median, you need to list the data points from the chart. Start at the lowest numbers for the body fat percentage (the values on the *y*-axis). Two wrestlers have a body fat percentage of 8, two have 9, etc. The list of data points is: 8, 8, 9, 9, 11, 12, 12, 12, 13, 14, 15, 15. Since the median is the average of the two middle numbers when the number of items in the list is even, you need to average the two middle numbers, 12 and 12 in this case. So, the median is 12.

9. **D** First, find the radius of each circle by using the circumference formula, $C = 2\pi r$. For the larger circle: $6\pi = 2\pi r$ and the $r = 3$. For the smaller circle: $4\pi = 2\pi r$ and the $r = 2$. Now, find the area of each circle. For the larger circle: $A = \pi(3)^2 = 9\pi$. For the smaller circle: $A = \pi(2)^2 = 4\pi$. The shaded area is given by $9\pi - 4\pi = 5\pi$. Finally, form the fraction: $\dfrac{5\pi}{9\pi} = \dfrac{5}{9}$.

10. **C** *ABE* is a 3:4:5 triangle with each side multiplied by 3, and $BE = 12$. The perimeter of *EBCD* is 40, so $BC = 8$. The area of $EBCD = 8 \times 12 = 96$.

11. **D** To find Stephan's rate: $\dfrac{20 \text{ pictures}}{240 \text{ minutes}} = \dfrac{1 \text{ picture}}{12 \text{ minutes}}$. So, Stephan draws 5 pictures every hour. That means that Pavel will draw 15 pictures every hour, since he draws three times faster than Stephan. So, Pavel will draw $15 \times 6 = 90$ pictures in 6 hours.

12. **E** Plug In $x = 8$, and solve the equation for *y*. $(8 + y)(8 - y) + (4 - y)(2 - y) = 0$ simplifies to $64 - y^2 + 8 - 6y + y^2 = 0$, or $6y = 72$. Thus $y = 12$.

13. **B** Since $CB = CD$, angle $B \cong$ angle D, and angle *C* is 60°, then angles *B* and *D* must also be 60°. So, $\triangle BCD$ is equilateral. The same logic applies to triangle *ACE*: It is also equilateral. Therefore, all of the line segments other than *FG* have lengths of 4. Next, find the heights of triangles *ACE* and *BCD*—the difference between the two will be *FG*. Using the 30°-60°-90° triangle rule, we know that the height of $\triangle ACE$ is $4\sqrt{3}$, and the height of $\triangle BCD$ is $2\sqrt{3}$. The difference is $2\sqrt{3}$, which gives us *FG*.

14. **A** Since the first term must be prime, the smallest value that *n* can have is 2. The second term will always be even, and therefore the set could never be a "prime convergence."

15. **A** Try Plugging In values for the variables presented. For instance, try $p = 20$, $c = 10$, and $d = 40$.

(20 pledges) × (10 cents/lap) × (4 laps/mile) × (1 dollar/100 cents) × (number of miles) = $40.

$\frac{800}{100}$ × (number of miles) = $40. Number of miles = $\frac{\$40}{8} = 5$. If we then Plug In $p = 20$, $c = 10$,

and $d = 40$ into the answers, only (A) gives us 5. Algebraically, $p\left(\frac{c}{1}\right)\left(\frac{4}{1}\right)\left(\frac{1}{100}\right)(x \text{ miles}) = d$.

16. **A** For all variables m and n, where n is a positive integer, $|m^n| = |(-m)^n|$, absolute value functions of a single variable to a single positive integer exponent all have symmetry across the vertical line that passes through their absolute maximum/minimum. In this case, the graph of $y = f - |gx^3|$ is symmetric across the y-axis. Because of this symmetry, since $AC = 4$, A and C are each at a distance of 2 from the origin. The maximum value of the function is f, since the graph reaches its maximum height when $|gx^3| = 0$, and everywhere else a positive number will be subtracted from f. Using the right triangle formed by A, B, and the origin, utilize the Pythagorean theorem to find the y-coordinate of B, which, as stated above, must equal f: $2^2 + f^2 = \left(2\sqrt{5}\right)^2$, so $f = 4$. Thus, we know our function looks like $y = 4 - |gx^3|$. Now Plug In the coordinates of point A or C into $y = 4 - |gx^3|$: Using the coordinates of C yields $0 = 4 - |g \times 2^3|$, or $0 = 4 - |8g|$, so $g = \pm\frac{1}{2}$. Since the question states that g is positive, $g = \frac{1}{2}$.

SECTION 9

1. **C** The clue *dumping site for the chemical plant* tells us that the blank should refer to "polluting." The closest to this meaning is (C) *a contamination* of. (B) means the opposite, and (A), (D), and (E) have nothing to do with dumping chemicals; therefore (C) is the best answer.

2. **B** The best answer is (B). The clue *would soon strike* tells us that a thunderstorm is near, so we can put "about to happen" in the blank. This is the meaning of (B) *imminent*. A thunderstorm could be *saturating,* (C), or *perilous,* (E), but these words don't mean "about to happen." (A) and (D) look like they might have to do with weather, but *voluble* means "talkative," and *mercurial* means "fickle," so they won't work in this sentence.

3. **B** The word *Although* indicates that there is an opposite relationship between the fact that *the company claimed responsibility* and what they *showed little of.* The semicolon and the words *in fact* tell us that the second part of the sentence is something that continues or illustrates the first part of the sentence/ The second blank means the same as the first blank: the *environmental groups* are upset at *a lack of* the thing that *the company showed little of.* A word that means "regret" is needed for both the first and second blanks. Only (B) *contrition* and *regret* fit the definition of "regret."

4. **D**   The best answer is (D). The clue is *Worst Dressed Award…hadn't even worn a costume.* We ask ourselves how someone would feel in this case. "Shocked and embarrassed" is a good expression to write in the blank; this is the meaning of *mortified.* (A) means "dressed," (B) means "incapable," (C) means "hidden," and (E) means "unruly," so we can eliminate these choices.

5. **E**   The second blank should mean "very expensive," as we see from the clue *costs…will bankrupt them.* Both (B) and (E) could work; we can eliminate the other choices because (A) and (C) are both related to money, but do not indicate an excess, and (D) has to do with paying back. Looking at the first blank of the two answer choices we have left, we see that (E), which means "unlimited," works better because the first blank needs to describe *dumping.* Although (B), *molecular,* refers to chemicals, it is unrelated to *dumping,* so the only choice for which both words work is (E); (E) is the best answer.

6. **B**   The clue is *findings were faked. Despite* suggests the researcher was against the claims, which makes (B) the best answer. *Repudiated* means "denied." (A), *verified,* means "proven true," the opposite of what is needed here. (C), *disseminated,* means "spread or scattered." (D), *embellished,* means "decorated." (E), *insinuated,* means "introduced an idea," usually in a bad way.

7. **A**   The term *Anytown, U.S.A.,* implies that the conditions described could be found in practically any town in the United States. (A) captures exactly what the term implies, while (B) expresses the opposite. For (C), while *Anytown* may be imaginary, this is not the author's point. For (D), the author does not make any recommendations to the reader in this passage. (E) is incorrect because the author does not discuss whether suburbs are common outside the United States.

8. **B**   If we cross out the word we're trying to understand, what word could we put in its place? The sentence suggests that suburbs offer some good things, but also offer some bad things at the same time. Thus, we're looking for a word that means "also or at the same time." (B) best expresses this meaning. (A) means "warlike"—eliminate it. (B) means "at the same time"—keep it! (C), *widespread,* and (D), *greedy,* may describe suburbia, but they don't mean "also or at the same time," so eliminate them. (E) means "in a showy fashion"—not what we're looking for, so eliminate it.

9. **A**   The author uses the phrase *too much of a stretch* (line 36) to show his or her belief that all modern problems are not caused by suburbia. (A) captures the meaning for which we are looking. (B) is wrong because nothing in this answer is reflected in the author's statements. (C) and (E) are incorrect, since the list of problems on these lines was not mentioned before, so the list isn't a summary or a modification of a previous argument. (D) is wrong because there is no misconception about the benefits of suburbia in the passage.

10. **B**   (B), suburban conformity, is what Passage 1 is all about. (A), (D), and (E) are mentioned in the passage, but not as results of *suburban sprawl.* For (C), the word *robbed* is used in line 22, but prefabricated houses are robbing, not *being robbed.*

11. **E** Like *mall builders*, fast-food restaurant owners would likely want the land the state wants to protect from commercial interests, so (E) is correct. (B) is illogical. The governor is looking to save land and would not likely be grouped with a list of people who wish to build on unused land. (A), (C), and (D) all describe people who have less reason than would a restaurant owner to want to use land protected by the state.

12. **B** A homeowner spends money to limit property damage, just as the government spends money to protect state land from the potential damage of suburban sprawl, so (B) is correct. A mother lion protects her cub out of instinct; the New Jersey government is not acting on instinct, so eliminate (A). The New Jersey government is trying to save something but not in the sense of putting money in a safe place to earn interest that can be spent later; eliminate (C). There's no similarity to mail delivery; eliminate (D). The government's action is not like changing a lock; rather, it is like putting a lock on where none existed. Therefore, eliminate (E).

13. **A** Four of the answer choices are mentioned in the passage; we're looking for the one that is not. (B) is incorrect because the pinelands are mentioned in line 72. (C) is wrong since line 73 states the anti-sprawl effort *has demonstrated that it is possible to control sprawl*. We can eliminate (D) based on lines 71–72, and (E) based on lines 75–77. As line 69 shows, New Jersey residents voted for the measure in a referendum; it was not implemented through executive order.

14. **C** The author is hopeful, in an intelligent way. (C) best expresses this. (A) is too extreme; there is nothing *florid* ("flowery") about the prose in the passage. (B) is negative, but we know the author is somewhat hopeful. (D) refers to an indifferent attitude. (E) is wrong because nothing in the passage indicates that the author regrets New Jersey's program to purchase land.

15. **B** The author of Passage 1 laments that suburban sprawl has *robbed us of hundreds of years of original and beautiful home design* (lines 22–23) and the author of Passage 2 *must concede that sprawl does detract from the beauty of the landscape* (lines 48–50). (B) best sums up these concerns. (A) is extreme—neither author argues that there's no benefit whatsoever to suburban construction. The author of Passage 1 would disagree with (C), the author of Passage 2 would disagree with (D), and the first passage doesn't discuss New Jersey specifically, so eliminate (E).

16. **D** Passage 1 refers to *convenient shopping and generally comfortable standards of living* (lines 10–11) and Passage 2 mentions *the public's appetite for big suburban homes and easy access to shopping centers* (lines 54–55). (D) paraphrases this similarity between the two passages. Passage 1 doesn't discuss government solutions, so (A) is out. (B) contradicts Passage 2's assertion that reducing sprawl doesn't have to impact the economy. (C) is too extreme to be supported by Passage 1. According to Passage 1, sprawl hurts *family-owned businesses and independent merchants*, so eliminate (E).

17. **E** The author of Passage 2 says that complaints about sprawl—like the ones in Passage 1—*border on the histrionic* (line 48), which means "excessively emotional or dramatic." (A), (B), (C), and (D) are not specifically mentioned in Passage 2, and don't describe the criticism we're looking for.

18. **C** Passage 1 outlines, in vivid detail, the problem posed by suburban sprawl. Passage 2 describes how New Jersey fought back. This is most like (C). Passage 1 doesn't advocate specific changes, so strike (A). While Passage 2 contradicts parts of Passage 1, it doesn't *debunk*, or "expose the falseness or ridiculousness of," Passage 1, so eliminate (B). (D) is wrong because it reverses the two arguments (Passage 1 is more *theoretical* while Passage 2 is more concrete and *practical*). Passage 1 does not pose any questions for Passage 2 to answer, so get rid of (E).

19. **D** According to the passage, *all residents of the state may now rest assured that the state's natural charms will not soon disappear.* All residents can breathe easy? The charms definitely won't disappear? The pessimistic author of Passage 1 would probably think this was extreme, unjustified optimism, so (D) is the best answer. Passage 2 is just the opposite of *pessimistic*, so strike out (A). Since the author of Passage 1 would disagree with the statement, he or she is unlikely to find it *perceptive*, so cross out (B). The statement expresses almost passionate conviction, not *caution*, so eliminate (C). *Flagrant* describes something deliberately conspicuous or shocking, so (E) is incorrect.

SECTION 10

1. **E** The original sentence contains a misplaced modifier error. The phrase *When asked to identify the most memorable day of their lives* should be followed by the subject this phrase is talking about: *adults.* (B) and (C) repeat this error. (D) is awkward and therefore not as good as (E). (A), (B), (C), and (D) also contain a noun-agreement error: *adults* have wedding *days.*

2. **C** This question contains a subject-verb agreement problem. The singular noun *forecast* is paired with the plural verb *are.* (D) repeats this error. (B) and (E) incorrectly omit the verb altogether.

3. **B** The subject of the sentence is *my grandmother,* so the pronoun *she* (A) is redundant. (C), (D), and (E) contain fragments. Also, in (C), *winning...she won* is redundant.

4. **D** (A) contains a misplaced modifier suggesting that Jupiter is leading scientists to wonder. (B), (C), and (E) create fragments. (C) and (E) employ the improper idioms *wonder of/wonder on.* Also, *this* in (E) is ambiguous, since it is unclear to what it refers. While the phrase *a development* in (D) is unnecessary, it is not grammatically incorrect, and thus (D), while not perfect, is clearly the least bad choice.

5. **C** (C) correctly employs the conjunction *because* to express the cause and effect intended by the writer of this sentence. (A) and (E), alternatively, use conjunctions that would be appropriate only to express contrasting ideas. (D) changes the intended meaning: *Whenever...are now* is illogical. (B) uses an *-ing* word, which is generally incorrect on the SAT.

6. **A** In (B), *some* is ambiguous because it could refer to either *aspiring* or *well-established* directors. (C) and (E) contain comma splices. (D) is wordy and awkward. In the more concise version provided by (A), the pronoun *whom* clearly replaces *well-established ones.*

7. **A** The grammatical subject *each* is always singular and therefore requires the singular verb *works,* so (C), (D), and (E) are wrong. (B) creates a fragment. (A) uses correct subject-verb agreement and expresses the intended meaning, which is that the poor performance of the machines is causing the engineers to rethink their designs.

8. **D** (A) is passive. (B) contains a comma splice. (C) includes a misplaced modifier because it implies that *Michelle* is *not chosen over real ones.* (E) is introduced by a fragment rather than the required dependent clause.

9. **D** (A) and (C) create fragments. (B) implies that *the hypernova theory…believes,* which is not the intended meaning. (C), too, warps the meaning by implying that the theory is supported by all astrophysicists. (E) contains two misplaced modifiers: *Astrophysicists* are described as a *compelling new idea* by the introductory phrase, and *the hypernova theory who believe* suggests that the theory itself has an opinion. Although (D) uses the passive voice, there is no other answer without grammatical errors, so (D) is the best answer.

10. **A** (B) is passive, and *increase of* is idiomatically a bad choice ("increase in" is the proper idiom). In (D) and (E), the singular pronoun *it* does not agree with the plural noun *workshops.* (C) changes the intended meaning, suggesting that the *workshops* themselves had abilities. (A) correctly introduces the subordinate clause with *that,* indicating that the workshops were responsible for the increase.

11. **D** The original sentence is a run-on. (D) best corrects this error by using the conjunction *because* to link the two halves of the sentence in the most sensible way. (B) isn't bad but is not as good an answer as is (D). (C) and (E) change the meaning of the sentence.

12. **C** The error in this question is one of subject-verb agreement. The subject of the sentence is the singular noun *layout,* but the verb is the plural *are.* (E) repeats this error. (D) and (B) incorrectly use the ambiguous pronoun *they* to refer to no one.

13. **E** The original sentence contains a comparison error, since we are comparing how many widgets were sold in 1999 with those sold in 1998. Remember the two things being compared must be the same. (D) repeats this error. (B) incorrectly omits the noun *shopkeepers,* making it sound as if the year 1998 sold widgets. (C) uses the incorrect word *then.*

14. **D** This question contains a subject-verb agreement problem. The plural verb *are* incorrectly refers to the singular noun *list.* (B) repeats this error. (E) incorrectly omits the verb altogether. (C) introduces the pronoun *they,* which changes the meaning of the sentence to suggest the ingredients are in order of concentration and not the entire list.

Part III
PSAT Practice Test

Chapter 24
Practice Test 11

IMPORTANT: The following codes should be copied onto your answer sheet exactly as shown.

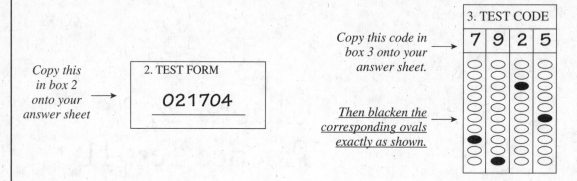

Copy this in box 2 onto your answer sheet →

2. TEST FORM

021704

Copy this code in box 3 onto your answer sheet. →

Then blacken the corresponding ovals exactly as shown. →

3. TEST CODE

7 9 2 5

General Directions

You will have two hours and 10 minutes to work on this objective test designed to familiarize you with all aspects of the PSAT.

This test contains four 25-minute sections, and one 30-minute section. During the time allowed for each section, you may work only on that particular section. If you finish your work before time is called, you may check your work on that section, but you are not to work on any other section.

You will find specific directions for each type of question found in the test. **Be sure you understand the directions before attempting to answer any of the questions.**

YOU ARE TO INDICATE ALL YOUR ANSWERS ON THE SEPARATE ANSWER SHEET:

1. The test booklet may be used for scratchwork. However, no credit will be given for anything written in the test booklet.

2. Once you have decided on an answer to a question, darken the corresponding space on the answer sheet. Give only one answer to each question.

3. There are 40 numbered answer spaces for each section; be sure to use only those spaces that correspond to the test questions.

4. **Be sure each answer mark is dark and completely fills the answer space.** Do not make any stray marks on your answer sheet.

5. If you wish to change an answer, erase your first mark completely—an incomplete erasure may be considered an intended response—and blacken your new answer choice.

Your score on this test is based on the number of questions you answer correctly minus a fraction of the number of questions you answer incorrectly. Therefore, it is improbable that random or haphazard guessing will alter your score significantly. There are no deductions for incorrect answers on the student-produced response questions. However, if you are able to eliminate one or more of the answer choices on any question as wrong, it is generally to your advantage to guess at one of the remaining choices. Remember, however, not to spend too much time on any one question.

PSAT

UR NAME: _____
(Print)   Last   First   M.I.

GNATURE: _____ DATE: _____ / _____ / _____

OME ADDRESS: _____
(Print)   Number and Street

E-MAIL: _____

City   State   Zip

ONE NO.: _____ SCHOOL: _____ CLASS OF: _____
(Print)

IMPORTANT: Please fill in these boxes exactly as shown on the back cover of your text book.

F-17982-PRP   P3 2803 628 5 4 3 2 1

© TPR Education IP Holdings, LLC

5. YOUR NAME

First 4 letters of last name				FIRST INIT	MID INIT
Ⓐ	Ⓐ	Ⓐ	Ⓐ	Ⓐ	Ⓐ
Ⓑ	Ⓑ	Ⓑ	Ⓑ	Ⓑ	Ⓑ
Ⓒ	Ⓒ	Ⓒ	Ⓒ	Ⓒ	Ⓒ
Ⓓ	Ⓓ	Ⓓ	Ⓓ	Ⓓ	Ⓓ
Ⓔ	Ⓔ	Ⓔ	Ⓔ	Ⓔ	Ⓔ
Ⓕ	Ⓕ	Ⓕ	Ⓕ	Ⓕ	Ⓕ
Ⓖ	Ⓖ	Ⓖ	Ⓖ	Ⓖ	Ⓖ
Ⓗ	Ⓗ	Ⓗ	Ⓗ	Ⓗ	Ⓗ
Ⓘ	Ⓘ	Ⓘ	Ⓘ	Ⓘ	Ⓘ
Ⓙ	Ⓙ	Ⓙ	Ⓙ	Ⓙ	Ⓙ
Ⓚ	Ⓚ	Ⓚ	Ⓚ	Ⓚ	Ⓚ
Ⓛ	Ⓛ	Ⓛ	Ⓛ	Ⓛ	Ⓛ
Ⓜ	Ⓜ	Ⓜ	Ⓜ	Ⓜ	Ⓜ
Ⓝ	Ⓝ	Ⓝ	Ⓝ	Ⓝ	Ⓝ
Ⓞ	Ⓞ	Ⓞ	Ⓞ	Ⓞ	Ⓞ
Ⓟ	Ⓟ	Ⓟ	Ⓟ	Ⓟ	Ⓟ
Ⓠ	Ⓠ	Ⓠ	Ⓠ	Ⓠ	Ⓠ
Ⓡ	Ⓡ	Ⓡ	Ⓡ	Ⓡ	Ⓡ
Ⓢ	Ⓢ	Ⓢ	Ⓢ	Ⓢ	Ⓢ
Ⓣ	Ⓣ	Ⓣ	Ⓣ	Ⓣ	Ⓣ
Ⓤ	Ⓤ	Ⓤ	Ⓤ	Ⓤ	Ⓤ
Ⓥ	Ⓥ	Ⓥ	Ⓥ	Ⓥ	Ⓥ
Ⓦ	Ⓦ	Ⓦ	Ⓦ	Ⓦ	Ⓦ
Ⓧ	Ⓧ	Ⓧ	Ⓧ	Ⓧ	Ⓧ
Ⓨ	Ⓨ	Ⓨ	Ⓨ	Ⓨ	Ⓨ
Ⓩ	Ⓩ	Ⓩ	Ⓩ	Ⓩ	Ⓩ

TEST FORM

_____

DATE OF BIRTH

MONTH		DAY		YEAR	
○ JAN					
○ FEB					
○ MAR	⓪	⓪	⓪	⓪	
○ APR	①	①	①	①	
○ MAY	②	②	②	②	
○ JUN	③	③	③	③	
○ JUL		④	④	④	
○ AUG		⑤	⑤	⑤	
○ SEP		⑥	⑥	⑥	
○ OCT		⑦	⑦	⑦	
○ NOV		⑧	⑧	⑧	
○ DEC		⑨	⑨	⑨	

3. TEST CODE / 4. PHONE NUMBER

(Columns of bubbles 0–9)

7. SEX

○ MALE
○ FEMALE

8. OTHER

1 Ⓐ Ⓑ Ⓒ Ⓓ Ⓔ
2 Ⓐ Ⓑ Ⓒ Ⓓ Ⓔ
3 Ⓐ Ⓑ Ⓒ Ⓓ Ⓔ

1 READING

1 Ⓐ Ⓑ Ⓒ Ⓓ Ⓔ   8 Ⓐ Ⓑ Ⓒ Ⓓ Ⓔ   15 Ⓐ Ⓑ Ⓒ Ⓓ Ⓔ   22 Ⓐ Ⓑ Ⓒ Ⓓ Ⓔ
2 Ⓐ Ⓑ Ⓒ Ⓓ Ⓔ   9 Ⓐ Ⓑ Ⓒ Ⓓ Ⓔ   16 Ⓐ Ⓑ Ⓒ Ⓓ Ⓔ   23 Ⓐ Ⓑ Ⓒ Ⓓ Ⓔ
3 Ⓐ Ⓑ Ⓒ Ⓓ Ⓔ   10 Ⓐ Ⓑ Ⓒ Ⓓ Ⓔ   17 Ⓐ Ⓑ Ⓒ Ⓓ Ⓔ   24 Ⓐ Ⓑ Ⓒ Ⓓ Ⓔ
4 Ⓐ Ⓑ Ⓒ Ⓓ Ⓔ   11 Ⓐ Ⓑ Ⓒ Ⓓ Ⓔ   18 Ⓐ Ⓑ Ⓒ Ⓓ Ⓔ
5 Ⓐ Ⓑ Ⓒ Ⓓ Ⓔ   12 Ⓐ Ⓑ Ⓒ Ⓓ Ⓔ   19 Ⓐ Ⓑ Ⓒ Ⓓ Ⓔ
6 Ⓐ Ⓑ Ⓒ Ⓓ Ⓔ   13 Ⓐ Ⓑ Ⓒ Ⓓ Ⓔ   20 Ⓐ Ⓑ Ⓒ Ⓓ Ⓔ
7 Ⓐ Ⓑ Ⓒ Ⓓ Ⓔ   14 Ⓐ Ⓑ Ⓒ Ⓓ Ⓔ   21 Ⓐ Ⓑ Ⓒ Ⓓ Ⓔ

2 MATHEMATICS

1 Ⓐ Ⓑ Ⓒ Ⓓ Ⓔ   8 Ⓐ Ⓑ Ⓒ Ⓓ Ⓔ   15 Ⓐ Ⓑ Ⓒ Ⓓ Ⓔ
2 Ⓐ Ⓑ Ⓒ Ⓓ Ⓔ   9 Ⓐ Ⓑ Ⓒ Ⓓ Ⓔ   16 Ⓐ Ⓑ Ⓒ Ⓓ Ⓔ
3 Ⓐ Ⓑ Ⓒ Ⓓ Ⓔ   10 Ⓐ Ⓑ Ⓒ Ⓓ Ⓔ   17 Ⓐ Ⓑ Ⓒ Ⓓ Ⓔ
4 Ⓐ Ⓑ Ⓒ Ⓓ Ⓔ   11 Ⓐ Ⓑ Ⓒ Ⓓ Ⓔ   18 Ⓐ Ⓑ Ⓒ Ⓓ Ⓔ
5 Ⓐ Ⓑ Ⓒ Ⓓ Ⓔ   12 Ⓐ Ⓑ Ⓒ Ⓓ Ⓔ   19 Ⓐ Ⓑ Ⓒ Ⓓ Ⓔ
6 Ⓐ Ⓑ Ⓒ Ⓓ Ⓔ   13 Ⓐ Ⓑ Ⓒ Ⓓ Ⓔ   20 Ⓐ Ⓑ Ⓒ Ⓓ Ⓔ
7 Ⓐ Ⓑ Ⓒ Ⓓ Ⓔ   14 Ⓐ Ⓑ Ⓒ Ⓓ Ⓔ

3 READING

25 Ⓐ Ⓑ Ⓒ Ⓓ Ⓔ   33 Ⓐ Ⓑ Ⓒ Ⓓ Ⓔ   41 Ⓐ Ⓑ Ⓒ Ⓓ Ⓔ
26 Ⓐ Ⓑ Ⓒ Ⓓ Ⓔ   34 Ⓐ Ⓑ Ⓒ Ⓓ Ⓔ   42 Ⓐ Ⓑ Ⓒ Ⓓ Ⓔ
27 Ⓐ Ⓑ Ⓒ Ⓓ Ⓔ   35 Ⓐ Ⓑ Ⓒ Ⓓ Ⓔ   43 Ⓐ Ⓑ Ⓒ Ⓓ Ⓔ
28 Ⓐ Ⓑ Ⓒ Ⓓ Ⓔ   36 Ⓐ Ⓑ Ⓒ Ⓓ Ⓔ   44 Ⓐ Ⓑ Ⓒ Ⓓ Ⓔ
29 Ⓐ Ⓑ Ⓒ Ⓓ Ⓔ   37 Ⓐ Ⓑ Ⓒ Ⓓ Ⓔ   45 Ⓐ Ⓑ Ⓒ Ⓓ Ⓔ
30 Ⓐ Ⓑ Ⓒ Ⓓ Ⓔ   38 Ⓐ Ⓑ Ⓒ Ⓓ Ⓔ   46 Ⓐ Ⓑ Ⓒ Ⓓ Ⓔ
31 Ⓐ Ⓑ Ⓒ Ⓓ Ⓔ   39 Ⓐ Ⓑ Ⓒ Ⓓ Ⓔ   47 Ⓐ Ⓑ Ⓒ Ⓓ Ⓔ
32 Ⓐ Ⓑ Ⓒ Ⓓ Ⓔ   40 Ⓐ Ⓑ Ⓒ Ⓓ Ⓔ   48 Ⓐ Ⓑ Ⓒ Ⓓ Ⓔ

The Princeton Review
PSAT

MATHEMATICS

21 Ⓐ Ⓑ Ⓒ Ⓓ Ⓔ
22 Ⓐ Ⓑ Ⓒ Ⓓ Ⓔ
23 Ⓐ Ⓑ Ⓒ Ⓓ Ⓔ
24 Ⓐ Ⓑ Ⓒ Ⓓ Ⓔ

25 Ⓐ Ⓑ Ⓒ Ⓓ Ⓔ
26 Ⓐ Ⓑ Ⓒ Ⓓ Ⓔ
27 Ⓐ Ⓑ Ⓒ Ⓓ Ⓔ
28 Ⓐ Ⓑ Ⓒ Ⓓ Ⓔ

ONLY ANSWERS ENTERED IN THE OVALS IN EACH GRID AREA WILL BE SCORED.
YOU WILL NOT RECEIVE CREDIT FOR ANYTHING WRITTEN IN THE BOXES ABOVE THE OVALS.

29 30 31 32 33

34 35 36 37 38

WRITING SKILLS

1 Ⓐ Ⓑ Ⓒ Ⓓ Ⓔ
2 Ⓐ Ⓑ Ⓒ Ⓓ Ⓔ
3 Ⓐ Ⓑ Ⓒ Ⓓ Ⓔ
4 Ⓐ Ⓑ Ⓒ Ⓓ Ⓔ
5 Ⓐ Ⓑ Ⓒ Ⓓ Ⓔ
6 Ⓐ Ⓑ Ⓒ Ⓓ Ⓔ
7 Ⓐ Ⓑ Ⓒ Ⓓ Ⓔ
8 Ⓐ Ⓑ Ⓒ Ⓓ Ⓔ
9 Ⓐ Ⓑ Ⓒ Ⓓ Ⓔ
10 Ⓐ Ⓑ Ⓒ Ⓓ Ⓔ
11 Ⓐ Ⓑ Ⓒ Ⓓ Ⓔ
12 Ⓐ Ⓑ Ⓒ Ⓓ Ⓔ
13 Ⓐ Ⓑ Ⓒ Ⓓ Ⓔ

14 Ⓐ Ⓑ Ⓒ Ⓓ Ⓔ
15 Ⓐ Ⓑ Ⓒ Ⓓ Ⓔ
16 Ⓐ Ⓑ Ⓒ Ⓓ Ⓔ
17 Ⓐ Ⓑ Ⓒ Ⓓ Ⓔ
18 Ⓐ Ⓑ Ⓒ Ⓓ Ⓔ
19 Ⓐ Ⓑ Ⓒ Ⓓ Ⓔ
20 Ⓐ Ⓑ Ⓒ Ⓓ Ⓔ
21 Ⓐ Ⓑ Ⓒ Ⓓ Ⓔ
22 Ⓐ Ⓑ Ⓒ Ⓓ Ⓔ
23 Ⓐ Ⓑ Ⓒ Ⓓ Ⓔ
24 Ⓐ Ⓑ Ⓒ Ⓓ Ⓔ
25 Ⓐ Ⓑ Ⓒ Ⓓ Ⓔ
26 Ⓐ Ⓑ Ⓒ Ⓓ Ⓔ

27 Ⓐ Ⓑ Ⓒ Ⓓ Ⓔ
28 Ⓐ Ⓑ Ⓒ Ⓓ Ⓔ
29 Ⓐ Ⓑ Ⓒ Ⓓ Ⓔ
30 Ⓐ Ⓑ Ⓒ Ⓓ Ⓔ
31 Ⓐ Ⓑ Ⓒ Ⓓ Ⓔ
32 Ⓐ Ⓑ Ⓒ Ⓓ Ⓔ
33 Ⓐ Ⓑ Ⓒ Ⓓ Ⓔ
34 Ⓐ Ⓑ Ⓒ Ⓓ Ⓔ
35 Ⓐ Ⓑ Ⓒ Ⓓ Ⓔ
36 Ⓐ Ⓑ Ⓒ Ⓓ Ⓔ
37 Ⓐ Ⓑ Ⓒ Ⓓ Ⓔ
38 Ⓐ Ⓑ Ⓒ Ⓓ Ⓔ
39 Ⓐ Ⓑ Ⓒ Ⓓ Ⓔ

SECTION 1
Time — 25 minutes
24 Questions

Directions: For each question in this section, select the best answer from among the choices given and fill in the corresponding circle on the answer sheet.

Each sentence below has one or two blanks, each blank indicating that something has been omitted. Beneath the sentence are five words or sets of words labeled A through E. Choose the word or set of words that, when inserted in the sentence, *best* fits the meaning of the sentence as a whole.

Example:

Desiring to ------- his taunting friends, Mitch gave them taffy in hopes it would keep their mouths shut.

(A) eliminate   (B) satisfy   (C) overcome
    (D) ridicule   (E) silence

1. Scientists predict that the next volcano to erupt in North America will have a ------- impact: it will cause dramatic environmental changes in the immediate area while creating lasting climate changes in far-flung regions.

    (A) financial   (B) focused   (C) meaningless
        (D) widespread   (E) mediocre

2. A new computer system cannot be ------- without first running extensive tests to ------- the effectiveness and accuracy of the system.

    (A) installed . . compensate
    (B) compromised . . ensure
    (C) designed . . undermine
    (D) dismantled . . illustrate
    (E) implemented . . evaluate

3. The miser was so afraid of losing money that he was willing to pass up a ------- opportunity rather than ------- what he already possessed.

    (A) replete . . chance
    (B) futile . . make
    (C) lucrative . . risk
    (D) brusque . . enhance
    (E) facile . . discredit

4. The editor claimed that great effort was being expended to check each fact, lest the book be ------- because of ------- details.

    (A) commended . . inappropriate
    (B) disparaged . . indisputable
    (C) revived . . unforgettable
    (D) invalidated . . impeccable
    (E) challenged . . inaccurate

5. Stick insects have elongated, twig-shaped bodies that enable them to be ------- when they alight on shrubbery.

    (A) devoured   (B) foliated   (C) nurtured
        (D) camouflaged   (E) acclimated

6. Ten years ago, Representative Dooley successfully ------- the many problems that had plagued previous administrations by responding to requests from various leaders in each community that she be more ------- in her policy development.

    (A) eluded . . economical
    (B) evaded . . inclusive
    (C) subverted . . prepared
    (D) foretold . . decorous
    (E) penetrated . . divisive

7. Even though Jennifer seems -------, her desk ------- her orderly image.

    (A) disoriented . . contradicts
    (B) unkempt . . disproves
    (C) materialistic . . verifies
    (D) structured . . validates
    (E) organized . . belies

8. The notion that a woman could become president of the United States gained ------- with the nomination of Geraldine Ferraro as a vice-presidential candidate.

    (A) credence   (B) resolve   (C) veracity
        (D) kudos   (E) distinction

GO ON TO THE NEXT PAGE

The passages below are followed by questions based on their content; questions following a pair of related passages may also be based on the relationship between the paired passages. Answer the questions on the basis of what is <u>stated</u> or <u>implied</u> in the passage and in any introductory material that may be provided.

Questions 9-10 are based on the following passage.

One name that would be certain to appear on any list of controversial figures of the twentieth century is that of Malcolm X. A self-educated man from humble beginnings *Line* and with a checkered past, Malcolm X was able to appeal to
5 his listeners by using universal imagery. Many of his most famous speeches centered on startling images designed to capture the hearer's imagination. By using this rhetorical device, he was able to communicate with his listeners on a personal and emotional level rather than on a merely
10 academic one.

9. The author describes Malcolm X as being "able to communicate with his listeners on a personal and emotional level" (lines 8-9) due primarily to his

   (A) use of creative description
   (B) simple origins in life
   (C) complex knowledge of psychiatry
   (D) widespread fame
   (E) frequent academic allusions

10. The author's conclusion regarding the use of imagery in Malcolm X's speeches would be most strongly supported by which of the following pieces of information?

   (A) A literary critique of Malcolm X's style showing the accuracy of his literary imagery
   (B) A thorough analysis of historical oration showing how the use of imagery in speeches developed
   (C) Examples of other speakers, from a variety of time periods, who have used imagery
   (D) Eyewitness accounts of people responding emotionally to speeches using imagery
   (E) An excerpt from Malcolm X's autobiography detailing how he educated himself

Questions 11-12 are based on the following passage.

The biological processes that allow us to hear are marvelously complex and, to some degree, still mysterious. When a sound of a particular frequency reaches the ear it *Line* stimulates a group of nerves located in the inner ear. This
5 cluster of nerves sends the signal deeper into the brain, almost as if a miniature keyboard were being played inside the ear, to the hindbrain. The hindbrain translates the frequency to a diatonic scale and relays it to the inferior colliculi. From there, the sound passes to the auditory cortex, where the signal is
10 translated into the final form that the mind hears.

11. The author's tone may best be described as

   (A) awed
   (B) neutral
   (C) skeptical
   (D) incredulous
   (E) dumbfounded

12. The image of the "miniature keyboard" (line 6) serves to

   (A) equate the hearing process with the diatonic scales found on a keyboard
   (B) provide an approximation of the process by which nerve cells send an auditory signal to the hindbrain
   (C) indicate the similarity of the nerve structures of the ear to the parts of a keyboard
   (D) link the ability to hear with the ability to differentiate tones on a keyboard
   (E) describe how the ear naturally tends to interpret sounds in terms of a keyboard

GO ON TO THE NEXT PAGE

Questions 13-24 are based on the following passages.

The term "black hole" comes from the notion that a stellar body can become completely nonreflective over time; that is, it emits no light. The following two passages outline the conventional, historical justification for the existence of black holes and present a radical new theory by renowned astrophysicist Stephen Hawking.

Passage 1

The concept of black holes is not really all that new, because it also arises in Newtonian gravity. Laplace pointed out as early as 1824 that if a star contains enough mass in a small enough package, the velocity needed to escape from
5 its surface is greater than that of light. No light can then get out, though light and matter can fall in. Simply add the speed limit of *c* from special relativity, and you have a one-way ticket into the universe; nothing that goes in can ever get out.

Of course in general relativity, unlike Laplace's case, the
10 light does not just fall back. It simply travels on curved paths smaller than the size of the star. The star is, for all intents and purposes, plucked out of space-time.

The density of matter required is phenomenal. Our sun would have to be only a few miles in diameter to become a
15 black hole. The pressure generated by the nuclear "flame" in its heart prevents it from collapsing. Even when the sun finally exhausts its fuel, we do not expect it to become a black hole but simply to collapse to a compact form called a white dwarf.

20 But a star 5 to 10 times heavier than our sun would have gravity enough to pull it down through the white-dwarf stage, through another form known as a neutron star or pulsar (which is essentially one huge atomic nucleus), to the black-hole stage.

Whether heavy stars actually do this is anyone's guess.
25 Stellar collapse usually leads to an explosion, a supernova such as the one that launched Tycho Brahe's career. The greater part of the star's mass is blown away, and whether enough remains to make a black hole is hard to say. But we do know that enough often remains to form a neutron star;
30 there is one in the center of the Crab Nebula, the debris of a supernova recorded by Chinese astronomers in 1054. Since the minimum mass for a black hole is not all that much greater than for a neutron star, it is an odds-on bet that they do sometimes form.

35 For obvious reasons, however, a black hole is well nigh impossible to detect. Our best bet is to catch one that is absorbing matter at a substantial rate. This can happen if the black hole has a nearby binary partner. The black hole draws in hot gases from its companion's atmosphere. As they fall,
40 the tremendous acceleration makes the gases radiate light; the higher the acceleration, the greater the frequency. A black hole has strong enough gravity to make x-rays come out.

Passage 2

Stephen Hawking, an English astrophysicist, has suggested the existence of mini black holes, the size of pinheads. There
45 is no observational evidence for a mini hole, but they are theoretically plausible. Hawking has deduced that small black holes can seem to emit energy in the form of elementary particles (neutrinos and so forth). The mini holes would thus evaporate and disappear. This may seem to contradict the
50 concept that mass can't escape from a black hole. But when we consider effects of quantum mechanics, the simple picture of a black hole that we have discussed up to this point is not sufficient. Hawking suggests that a black hole so affects the space near it that a pair of particles—a nuclear particle and
55 its antiparticle—can form simultaneously. The antiparticle disappears into the black hole, and the remaining particle reaches us. Photons, which are their own antiparticles, appear too.

Emission from a black hole is significant only for the
60 smallest mini black holes, for the amount of radiation increases sharply as we consider less and less massive black holes. Only mini black holes up to the mass of an asteroid— far short of stellar masses—would have had time to disappear since the origin of the universe. Hawking's ideas set a lower
65 limit on the size of black holes now in existence, since we think the mini black holes were formed only in the first second after the origin of the universe by the tremendous pressures that existed then.

On the other extreme of mass, we can consider what a
70 black hole would be like if it contained a very large number, that is, thousands or millions, of solar masses. Thus far, we have considered only black holes the mass of a star or smaller. Such black holes form after a stage of high density. But the more mass involved, the lower the density needed for a black
75 hole to form. For a very massive black hole, the density would be fairly low when the event horizon* formed, approaching the density of water. For even higher masses, the density would be lower yet. We think such high masses occur in the centers of active galaxies and quasars.

80 Thus if we were traveling through the universe in a spaceship, we couldn't count on detecting a black hole by noticing a volume of high density. We could pass through the event horizon of a high-mass black hole without even noticing. We would never be able to get out, but it might be hours on
85 our watches before we would notice that we were being drawn into the center at an accelerating rate.

---
* Event horizon—the border between the edge of a black hole and the rest of the universe

GO ON TO THE NEXT PAGE

13. The author of Passage 1 refers to Laplace in order to

(A) discuss general relativity
(B) show that the idea of black holes is not a new one
(C) portray light as something that travels on curved paths
(D) explain the formation of a supernova
(E) show how one can escape a black hole

14. According to Passage 1, all of the following are reasons our own sun will not become a black hole in the immediate future EXCEPT

(A) its diameter is too large
(B) when it collapses, it will become a white dwarf instead
(C) the "nuclear flame" at its core prevents it from collapsing
(D) its gravitational pull is too strong
(E) it is not dense enough

15. In line 17, the word "exhausts" most nearly means

(A) uses up
(B) squanders
(C) fatigues
(D) emits
(E) creates

16. The author of Passage 1 refers to the Crab Nebula in order to

(A) discuss relevant Chinese astronomers
(B) provide an example of minimum mass
(C) give an example of what leftover star mass can form
(D) describe the process a star goes through to become a black hole
(E) prove the existence of black holes

17. It can be inferred from Passage 1 that the best way to find a black hole is to

(A) measure the density of a star
(B) search for x-ray emissions
(C) locate a white dwarf
(D) send up a manned space probe
(E) find two planets next to each other

18. In line 47, the word "elementary" most nearly means

(A) easy
(B) scholastic
(C) theoretical
(D) electric
(E) basic

19. Which of the following best describes the contradiction mentioned in lines 49-50 ?

(A) Mini black holes do not possess the same physical characteristics as do their larger counterparts.
(B) Hawking's theory contains a principle that contradicts the accepted black hole theories.
(C) The principles of quantum mechanics are in direct opposition to Hawking's theory of mini black holes.
(D) Mini black holes cannot be as small as pinheads because existing equipment could not detect so tiny a configuration in space.
(E) It is highly unlikely that particles and antiparticles could exist simultaneously.

20. It can be inferred that the emission from mini black holes is significant only for the smallest black holes (lines 59-62) because

(A) since the origin of the universe, few black holes have been created
(B) nearly all notable astronomers have attempted to disprove the trend
(C) larger black holes disappear before they have a chance to emit radiation
(D) emissions from black holes are inversely proportional to the size of black holes
(E) the amount of radiation released by mini black holes is minuscule compared to that emitted by larger black holes

GO ON TO THE NEXT PAGE

21. The primary purpose of Passage 2 is to

(A) discuss the theoretical existence of black holes of extreme sizes

(B) explain the ratio of mass to density within mini black holes

(C) describe Stephen Hawking's significance as a premier physicist

(D) argue the existence of black holes outside the known universe

(E) cite the many different mini black holes observed by astronomers

22. The last paragraph of Passage 2 uses the spaceship scenario to

(A) illustrate an abstract theory with some concrete details

(B) prove the existence of a much-discussed hypothetical phenomenon

(C) warn future theorists of the danger of tenuous evidence

(D) add credence to an otherwise flimsy hypothesis

(E) validate a theory by solving a conundrum

23. The authors of Passage 1 and Passage 2 would probably agree that which of the following is an identifying factor of a star capable of becoming a black hole?

(A) The number of asteroids nearby

(B) Its color

(C) The presence of quasars

(D) Its mass and density

(E) The pathway of the emitted light

24. In which of the following ways would the author of Passage 2 dispute the statement put forth on lines 6-9 in Passage 1 ?

(A) It is possible for only extraordinarily powerful energy emissions to escape black holes.

(B) While nothing can escape a black hole, it is unlikely that any matter can go in.

(C) It is faulty to assume that black holes exist in the first place.

(D) Black holes do exist, but it is impossible to theorize about their gravitational pull.

(E) Hawking theorized that matter can, in fact, escape a mini black hole.

STOP

If you finish before time is called, you may check your work on this section only.
Do not turn to any other section in the test.

SECTION 2
Time — 25 minutes
20 Questions

Directions: For this section, solve each problem and decide which is the best of the choices given. Fill in the corresponding circle on the answer sheet. You may use any available space for scratchwork.

Notes

1. The use of a calculator is permitted.

2. All numbers used are real numbers.

3. Figures that accompany problems in this test are intended to provide information useful in solving the problems. They are drawn as accurately as possible EXCEPT when it is stated in a specific problem that the figure is not drawn to scale. All figures lie in a plane unless otherwise indicated.

4. Unless otherwise specified, the domain of any function f is assumed to be the set of all real numbers x for which $f(x)$ is a real number.

Reference Information

 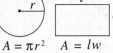   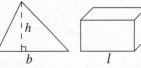

$A = \pi r^2$ $A = lw$
$C = 2\pi r$ $A = \frac{1}{2}bh$ $V = lwh$ $V = \pi r^2 h$ $c^2 = a^2 + b^2$

Special Right Triangles

The number of degrees of arc in a circle is 360.

The sum of the measures in degrees of the angles of a triangle is 180.

	ABC	DEF
1	2	3
GHI	JKL	MNO
4	5	6
PRS	TUV	WXY
7	8	9

1. In the keypad shown above, each digit from 2 through 9 can be represented by any of three certain letters. If each digit in a number is replaced by a letter, a "word" is formed. Which of the following "words" could NOT be formed from the four-digit number 7283 ?

(A) RATE
(B) PAVE
(C) SCUD
(D) RAID
(E) PATE

2. If a gallon of lemonade requires 3 pints of lemon juice, how many pints of lemon juice would be needed to make z gallons of lemonade?

(A) $z - 3$

(B) $z + 3$

(C) $\dfrac{z}{3}$

(D) $3z$

(E) z^3

GO ON TO THE NEXT PAGE

3. Janice bought four shirts that cost $12.90, $16.00, $18.00, and $21.90, respectively. If she made an initial down payment of one half of the total amount and paid the rest in 4 equal payments, how much was each of the 4 payments?

   (A) $ 8.60
   (B) $ 9.20
   (C) $ 9.45
   (D) $ 17.20
   (E) $ 34.40

4. A certain system of numbers uses dots and lines to represent two-digit numbers. The lines represent the tens digit and the dots represent the units digit. For example,

   $$73 = \text{⊬} \; \| \; \vdots$$
   $$68 = \text{⊬} \; | \; \vdots \; \vdots$$

   What is the value of the following expression?

   $$\text{⊬} \; \vdots \vdots \; - \; \|\| \; \vdots\vdots$$

   (A) $| \; \vdots$
   (B) $\| \; \vdots$
   (C) $\||| \; \cdot$
   (D) $\||| \; \vdots$
   (E) $\|||| \; \cdot$

5. If $4j - k = 11$ and $k = 3j$, then $j =$

   (A) $\dfrac{1}{11}$

   (B) $\dfrac{7}{11}$

   (C) $\dfrac{11}{7}$

   (D) $\dfrac{11}{4}$

   (E) 11

6. If a right circular cylinder has a volume of 144π and a height of 9, what is the area of its base?

   (A) 4π
   (B) 8π
   (C) 16π
   (D) 25π
   (E) 32π

GO ON TO THE NEXT PAGE

7. Which of the following equations represents this information: "Mr. Johnson distributed 85 beakers among the z students in his science class. Each student received 5 beakers?"

(A) $z = \dfrac{5}{85}$

(B) $85 \times 5 = z$

(C) $5 = \dfrac{z}{85}$

(D) $85z = 5$

(E) $5z = 85$

8. On a map, $\dfrac{1}{2}$ inch represents 15 miles. If the distance between Dover and Portland is 50 miles, what is the distance, in inches, between the two cities on the map?

(A) 1

(B) $1\dfrac{2}{3}$

(C) $2\dfrac{1}{2}$

(D) $3\dfrac{1}{3}$

(E) $6\dfrac{2}{3}$

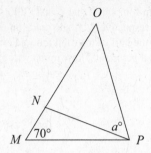

Note: Figure not drawn to scale.

9. In the figure above, if $MO = OP$ and $MP = NP$, then $a =$

(A) 30
(B) 40
(C) 50
(D) 55
(E) 70

COSTS OF LEMONADE PRODUCTION					
Number of Pitchers	1	2	3	4	5
Total Cost	$3	$5	$7	$9	$11

10. Merrily's costs for producing lemonade are shown in the table above. If c represents the cost, in dollars, of producing n pitchers of lemonade, then which of the following equations best expresses the relationship between c and n ?

(A) $c = 2n + 1$
(B) $c = 3n$
(C) $c = 4n - 1$
(D) $c = n^2 + 2$
(E) $c = 2n^2 + 1$

GO ON TO THE NEXT PAGE

11. If $r \neq -s$, what is the value of $\dfrac{(r-s)(r-s-r+s)}{(r+s)}$?

    (A) 0
    (B) 1
    (C) 2
    (D) $r+s$
    (E) $2(r-s)$

13. For $x \neq -1$, $\dfrac{x-2}{x+1} + \dfrac{x+3}{x+1} =$

    (A) 1

    (B) 2

    (C) x

    (D) $\dfrac{2x+1}{x+1}$

    (E) $\dfrac{2x+1}{2x+2}$

12. At a certain hour, a lamppost that stands 108 inches tall casts a shadow 27 inches long. Sue is f inches tall. In terms of f, how many inches long is her shadow at the same hour?

    (A) $3\sqrt{f}$

    (B) $f+81$

    (C) $\dfrac{f}{4}$

    (D) $4f$

    (E) $\left(\dfrac{f}{3}\right)^2$

14. The square root of the product of 4 and a number is 6. What is the number?

    (A) 2
    (B) $\sqrt{6}$
    (C) 9
    (D) 24
    (E) 36

GO ON TO THE NEXT PAGE

$$A4B7$$
$$- \underline{A4B}$$
$$5CA7$$

15. In the subtraction problem of a three-digit number from a four-digit number above, *A*, *B*, and *C* represent three different digits. What digit does *C* represent?

(A) 0
(B) 2
(C) 4
(D) 7
(E) 8

---

a, b , m, c , d

16. In the set of five distinct numbers ordered from smallest to largest above, *m* is the median. Which of the following must be FALSE?

(A) $bm > am$
(B) $b - a > d - c$
(C) $m - b > c - m$
(D) $a + d > b + c$
(E) $a + b > c + d$

$(0.4)(0.6)(0.8) = 0.192$

17. In the multiplication problem above, if each of the three decimals on the left is divided by *r* , the new product is 24. What is the value of *r* ?

(A) 0.08
(B) 0.02
(C) 0.8
(D) 0.2
(E) 2

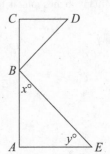

18. In the figure above, $\overline{CD}$ and $\overline{AE}$ are both perpendicular to $\overline{AC}$, and $\overline{BD}$ is perpendicular to $\overline{BE}$. If $x = y$, the length of $\overline{BD}$ is 4, and the length of $\overline{BE}$ is 6, what is the length of $\overline{AC}$?

(A) $5\sqrt{2}$
(B) $6\sqrt{2}$
(C) $10\sqrt{2}$
(D) $2\sqrt{3}$
(E) $10\sqrt{3}$

GO ON TO THE NEXT PAGE

19. How many integers between 100 and 999 inclusive have a units digit of 7 ?

(A)   10
(B)   70
(C)   81
(D)   90
(E)   100

20. The minute hand of a clock has a length of l from its point of rotation to the point at the end of the arrow. What is the total distance traveled by the point at the end of the arrow in m minutes?

(A) $\dfrac{m\pi}{60l}$

(B) $\dfrac{lm\pi}{30}$

(C) $120lm\pi$

(D) $2l\pi$

(E) $\dfrac{30l\pi}{m}$

STOP

If you finish before time is called, you may check your work on this section only.
Do not turn to any other section in the test.

SECTION 3
Time — 25 minutes
24 Questions

Directions: For each question in this section, select the best answer from among the choices given and fill in the corresponding circle on the answer sheet.

Each sentence below has one or two blanks, each blank indicating that something has been omitted. Beneath the sentence are five words or sets of words labeled A through E. Choose the word or set of words that, when inserted in the sentence, best fits the meaning of the sentence as a whole.

Example:

Hoping to ------- the dispute, negotiators proposed a compromise that they felt would be ------- to both labor and management.

(A) enforce . . useful
(B) end . . divisive
(C) overcome . . unattractive
(D) extend . . satisfactory
(E) resolve . .acceptable

25. Together, Angela and Ed built the park's new castle, a ------- effort to give city kids a place to play and imagine.

(A) stratified   (B) cooperative   (C) disregarded
(D) conclusive   (E) diverting

26. The conflict between the two political groups that arose during the meeting was not -------; these groups have often ------- each other on key issues.

(A) surprising . . supported
(B) unusual . . copied
(C) explicit . . evaluated
(D) unique . . opposed
(E) expected . . encountered

27. The archaeologist enjoyed the ------- life she led while gathering artifacts; she never stayed at any one site long enough to get bored.

(A) stealthy   (B) nomadic   (C) clamorous
(D) indiscreet   (E) rustic

28. The effects of this event have been -------: the conflagration forced most people to ------- their homes in the middle of the night.

(A) important . . desert
(B) gratifying . . celebrate in
(C) significant . . leave
(D) devastating . . abandon
(E) negative . . fortify

29. The Indo-Hispanic *vaquero*, a precursor of the cowboy, left ------- imprint on the early Southwest, which is reflected in poems, legends, and stories.

(A) a solicitous   (B) a meager   (C) an indelible
(D) a dubious   (E) an incredulous

GO ON TO THE NEXT PAGE

The passages below are followed by questions based on their content; questions following a pair of related passages may also be based on the relationship between the paired passages. Answer the questions on the basis of what is <u>stated</u> or <u>implied</u> in the passage and in any introductory material that may be provided.

Questions 30-33 are based on the following passages.

Passage 1

In the beginning years of the twentieth century, Maria Montessori developed a method of learning in which children were given freedom to engage in meaningful activities in an
Line environment of mental stimulation and were provided with
5 opportunities to develop self-esteem. This regimen proved so effective that when "directors" following Montessori's techniques provided students from a Roman slum with a specially prepared environment in which to freely explore and interact, the students took on new and more difficult
10 tasks with amazing results. These children could read and write before their fifth birthdays, could concentrate intensely for prolonged periods of time, and even preferred working productively to playing.

Passage 2

One of the most revolutionary concepts within modern
15 educational theory is that of "scaffolding." Though initially met with skepticism, scaffolding now is taught in universities across the world. Scaffolding is based upon the sociocultural theories of Lev Vygotsky, specifically his concept of the "zone of proximal development" (ZPD). Vygotsky defines
20 the ZPD as "the distance between what children can do by themselves and the next learning that they can be helped to achieve with competent assistance." Vygotsky's theory contends that the central factor in a student's learning is how effectively the teacher can provide a structured environment
25 in which the student can challenge herself.

30. Both authors would most likely agree with which of the following statements?

(A) Children should have the freedom to learn only what they want while they are in school.
(B) Children are born "blank slates" onto which any behavior or talent can be inscribed freely.
(C) Each human being is born with levels of skill and aptitudes that cannot be altered.
(D) Providing the proper setting for learning is important for a child's development.
(E) If a child can read and write at age four, he or she should be sent to a Montessori school.

31. Based on the description of her educational practices, graduates of Montessori's early childhood program are likely to have all of the following characteristics EXCEPT

(A) inquisitiveness
(B) intelligence
(C) omnipotence
(D) creativity
(E) industriousness

32. Which of the following pairs of phrases best captures the theories presented in Passage 1 and Passage 2, respectively?

(A) "regimen" (line 5) and "theory" (line 15)
(B) "difficult" (line 9) and "skepticism" (line 16)
(C) "prolonged" (line 12) and "revolutionary" (line 14)
(D) "explore" (line 8) and "structured" (line 24)
(E) "self-esteem" (line 5) and "modern" (line 14)

33. As used in Passage 2, the word "contends" (line 23) most nearly means

(A) disputes
(B) asserts
(C) disproves
(D) imagines
(E) proves

GO ON TO THE NEXT PAGE

Questions 34-39 are based on the following passage.

In this passage, the author reminisces about her father, Kenneth Hamilton, and compares his independence to that of Paul Robeson, one of the first black actors and singers in America to achieve renown for his many talents.

Like many Americans, my father must have heard Paul Robeson sing over the radio at one time or another. He must have read about Robeson's extraordinary feats of daring and
Line skill on the football fields of Rutgers. "I imagine," Kenneth
5 Hamilton would begin, "that Mr. Paul Robeson woke up one morning to find there was more to the day than playing football. I know I did (Kenneth Hamilton played football for Iowa State). I imagine he looked around him. He saw that plenty of his people already were preachers; there were
10 enough morticians to reach from here to kingdom come. I imagine Mr. Robeson decided then and there he would be what there never had been before. And he was."

I don't recall Kenneth Hamilton ever saying what it was Paul Robeson became besides a football star. But surely he
15 was referring to Robeson's powerful singing voice. Yet what came through clearly to me at the time was this: If one were to become anything, it would have to be not only the best but wholly original, a new idea. This concept sank deep into my consciousness. Imperceptibly, I grew up yearning for the
20 unusual, seeking something unique in myself. I longed not just to write, but to newly write and like no one else. Kenneth Hamilton wanted no less for his youngest child.

"Like no one else," he had been no less himself. Graduating from Iowa State Business College in the early
25 1890s when it was an achievement when a black man completed high school, he began his search for employment.

One day, the banker for whom his mother worked as a cook asked that young Kenneth be sent around to the bank, where there was a suitable job for him. Kenneth Hamilton
30 hurried over to the bank, absolutely amazed at this sudden stroke of luck. Dressed in starched collar and gray business suit, he wondered what would he become.

Kenneth Hamilton passed under the marble facade into the bank and was promptly handed a mop and a bucket. He
35 threw both the length of the establishment and turned on his heel, never to return. Perhaps he should have accepted that first mop and bucket, but I'm rather glad his imagination wouldn't permit him. For now I have the pleasure of remembering him as a man who would not allow mind or
40 body to be limited by another's reality. I could have wanted no less for a father.

34. According to lines 4-12, Kenneth Hamilton and Paul Robeson were similar because they

(A) both played football for Iowa State
(B) were both talented singers
(C) both, at one time, aspired to be preachers
(D) both had aspirations for things greater than collegiate sports
(E) were both more privileged than many blacks of the time

35. The passage might best be characterized as which of the following?

(A) An excerpt from Paul Robeson's autobiography
(B) An analysis of Paul Robeson's performing career
(C) A critique of Paul Robeson's success as a performer
(D) A personal narrative discussing a role model
(E) A criticism of Kenneth Hamilton's admiration of Paul Robeson

36. Which of the following best exemplifies the "wholly original, a new idea" (line 18) to which the author refers?

(A) Kenneth Hamilton's decision to play football
(B) Paul Robeson's determination that he would not be a preacher
(C) The author's choice to write about her past experiences
(D) The author's life as a writer
(E) The author's resolve to be unlike any other writer

37. In lines 23-26 the author implies that

(A) few people graduated from high school in the late nineteenth century
(B) Kenneth Hamilton had no possibility of obtaining employment
(C) not many black males graduated from college in the 1890s
(D) it was impossible for high school graduates to find employment during the 1890s
(E) Kenneth Hamilton entered business school immediately after high school

GO ON TO THE NEXT PAGE

38. The story about Kenneth Hamilton's search for employment in the last two paragraphs is included by the author to

   (A) emphasize the policy of bigotry in banking institutions of the 1890s
   (B) illustrate the author's admiration for her father
   (C) stress Kenneth Hamilton's aptitude for janitorial work
   (D) suggest that the author was capable of far more than menial labor
   (E) explain how her father came upon his eventual great success

39. The passage suggests that the author's admiration for her father stems from

   (A) his unwillingness to submit to society's expectations of him
   (B) the similarities between Paul Robeson and her father
   (C) the realistic expectations he placed on his mind and body
   (D) the imaginative way in which he undertook his daily assignments
   (E) his courage in seeking a bank job in the 1890s

GO ON TO THE NEXT PAGE

Questions 40-48 are based on the following passage.

The following is a childhood remembrance written by Eudora Welty, a twentieth-century Southern writer who is best known for such short stories as "Why I Live at the P.O." and "The Robber Bridegroom."

When I was six or seven, I was taken out of school and put to bed for several months for an ailment the doctor described as "fast-beating heart." I felt all right—perhaps I felt too good.
Line It was the feeling of suspense. At any rate, I was allowed to
5 occupy all day my parents' double bed in the front upstairs bedroom.

I was supposed to rest, and the little children didn't get to run in and excite me often. Davis School was as close as across the street. I could keep up with it from the window
10 beside me, hear the principal ring her bell, see which children were tardy, watch my classmates eat together at recess: I knew their sandwiches. I was homesick for school; my mother made time for teaching me arithmetic and hearing my spelling.

An opulence of story books covered my bed; it was the
15 "Land of Counterpane." As I read away, I was Rapunzel, or the Goose Girl, or the Princess Labam in one of the *Thousand and One Nights* who mounted the roof of her palace every night and of her own radiance faithfully lighted the whole city just by reposing there, and I daydreamed I could light Davis
20 School from across the street.

But I never dreamed I could learn as long as I was away from the schoolroom, and that bits of enlightenment far-reaching in my life went on as ever in their own good time. After they'd told me goodnight and tucked me in—although
25 I knew that after I'd finally fallen asleep they'd pick me up and carry me away—my parents draped the lampshade with a sheet of the daily paper, which was tilted, like a hatbrim, so that they could sit in their rockers in a lighted part of the room and I could supposedly go to sleep in the protected dark
30 of the bed. They sat talking. What was thus dramatically made a present of to me was the secure sense of the hidden observer. As long as I could make myself keep awake, I was free to listen to every word my parents said between them.

I don't remember that any secrets were revealed to me,
35 nor do I remember any avid curiosity on my part to learn something I wasn't supposed to—perhaps I was too young to know what to listen for. But I was present in the room with the chief secret there was—the two of them, father and mother, sitting there as one. I was conscious of this secret and
40 of my fast-beating heart in step together, as I lay in the slant-shaded light of the room, with a brown, pear-shaped scorch in the newspaper shade where it had become overheated once.

What they talked about I have no idea, and the subject was not what mattered to me. It was no doubt whatever a
45 young married couple spending their first time privately in each other's company in the long, probably harried day would talk about. It was the murmur of their voices, the back-and-forth, the unnoticed stretching away of time between my bedtime and theirs, that made me bask there at my distance.
50 What I felt was not that I was excluded from them but that I was included, in—and because of—what I could hear of their voices and what I could see of their faces in the cone of yellow light under the brown-scorched shade.

I suppose I was exercising as early as then the turn of
55 mind, the nature of temperament, of a privileged observer; and owing to the way I became so, it turned out that I became the loving kind.

A conscious act grew out of this by the time I began to write stories: getting my distance, a prerequisite of my
60 understanding of human events, is the way I begin work. Just as, of course, it was an initial step when, in my first journalism job, I stumbled into making pictures with a camera. Frame, proportion, perspective, the values of light and shade, all are determined by the distance of the observing
65 eye.

I have always been shy physically. This in part tended to keep me from rushing into things, including relationships, headlong. Not rushing headlong, though I may have wanted to, but beginning to write stories about people, I drew near
70 slowly; noting and guessing, apprehending, hoping, drawing my eventual conclusions out of my own heart, I did venture closer to where I wanted to go. As time and my imagination led me on, I did plunge.

40. The primary purpose of the passage is to

(A) evoke a scene of carefree family life from the writer's childhood
(B) list the elements that are necessary to enable a child to develop into a writer
(C) describe early events that eventually shaped the author's approach to writing
(D) contrast the author's education at home with her education at school
(E) explain the way in which an early illness led to the author's physical fragility

GO ON TO THE NEXT PAGE

41. In line 4, "the feeling of suspense" describes the

(A) author's anxiety over her illness

(B) author's excitement about being allowed to miss school

(C) physical sensation that the author felt as a symptom of her ailment

(D) concern that the author felt about missing several months of school

(E) author's fear that she may become more ill

42. The second paragraph suggests that the author

(A) experienced profound sadness as a result of her isolation from her classmates during her illness

(B) became jealous of the other children while she was confined

(C) felt that her mother's instruction was vastly inferior to that which she received from her teacher at school

(D) looked forward to the time when her confinement was over, and she could return to her life a schoolchild

(E) was frequently visited by her classmates

43. It can be inferred from the phrase in lines 15-16 ("I was Rapunzel, or the Goose Girl") that the author

(A) had an overactive imagination

(B) had difficulty differentiating between fantasy and reality

(C) occupied herself during her illness by writing stories

(D) wanted to pursue a career as an actress

(E) became extremely engaged in the books that she read

44. In lines 31-32, the author describes herself as a "hidden observer" because

(A) her parents were unable to see her in the darkened area of the bedroom

(B) she could understand her parents' conversation despite its sophisticated nature

(C) after her parents put her to sleep in their bed, they conversed as if they were alone

(D) by pretending to be asleep, the author could hear her parents' secrets

(E) she was able to watch her schoolmates unseen from the window of her room

45. What is the "chief secret" to which the author refers in line 38 ?

(A) Her parents' concerns about her health

(B) The nature of her parents' interactions

(C) The content of her parents' conversations

(D) The disharmony in her parents' relationship

(E) The fact that she was not really asleep

46. In line 54, the word "exercising" most nearly means

(A) focusing

(B) utilizing

(C) overcoming

(D) training

(E) imagining

47. The author compares writing stories with "making pictures" (line 62) in order to do which of the following?

(A) Emphasize the creative aspects of both activities

(B) Present the differences between the role of the writer and the photographer

(C) Show how writing stresses distance and photography stresses understanding

(D) Highlight the importance of perspective in both activities

(E) Demonstrate how the author was able to overcome illness through artistic endeavors

48. It can be inferred from the last paragraph that the author's shyness

(A) prevented her from having personal relationships as an adult

(B) remains an obstacle in her creative endeavors

(C) was an impediment that she eventually overcame

(D) led her to pursue her interest in photojournalism

(E) forced her to overcome her childhood fears

STOP

If you finish before time is called, you may check your work on this section only.
Do not turn to any other section in the test.

SECTION 4
Time — 25 minutes
18 Questions

Directions: For this section, solve each problem and decide which is the best of the choices given. Fill in the corresponding circle on the answer sheet. You may use any available space for scratchwork.

Notes

1. The use of a calculator is permitted.

2. All numbers used are real numbers.

3. Figures that accompany problems in this test are intended to provide information useful in solving the problems. They are drawn as accurately as possible EXCEPT when it is stated in a specific problem that the figure is not drawn to scale. All figures lie in a plane unless otherwise indicated.

4. Unless otherwise specified, the domain of any function f is assumed to be the set of all real numbers x for which $f(x)$ is a real number.

Reference Information

  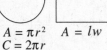 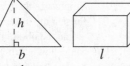 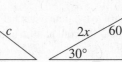

$A = \pi r^2$ $A = lw$ $A = \frac{1}{2}bh$ $V = lwh$ $V = \pi r^2 h$ $c^2 = a^2 + b^2$

Special Right Triangles

$C = 2\pi r$

The number of degrees of arc in a circle is 360.

The sum of the measures in degrees of the angles of a triangle is 180.

---

21. If $5x + 8 = 18$, what is the value of $10x$?

(A)　2
(B)　4
(C)　10
(D)　12
(E)　20

22. Which of the following values of c satisfies the equation

$$\sqrt{\frac{2c}{5}} - 2\sqrt{2} = 0 \ ?$$

(A)　$\sqrt{10}$
(B)　5
(C)　8
(D)　20
(E)　40

GO ON TO THE NEXT PAGE

23. If $\dfrac{a^{10}}{a^f} = a^2$ and $(a^6)^g = a^{18}$, what is the value of $g - f$?

(A) −5
(B) −2
(C) 4
(D) 7
(E) 10

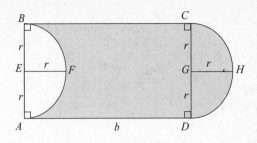

25. In the figure above, what is the area of the shaded region?

(A) br

(B) $2br$

(C) $2br - \dfrac{\pi r^2}{2}$

(D) $2br + \dfrac{\pi r^2}{2}$

(E) $2br + \pi r^2$

24. Set F contains 5 consecutive even integers. Set G contains all the numbers that result from adding 5 to each of the elements of set F and also all the numbers that result from subtracting 5 from each of the elements of set F. Set G has how many more elements than set F ?

(A) 0
(B) 2
(C) 5
(D) 6
(E) 10

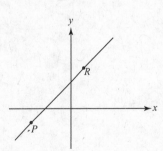

26. Which of the following could be the equation of $\overleftrightarrow{PR}$ in the figure above?

(A) $y = x + 2$
(B) $y = 2x + 1$
(C) $y = 2x + 2$
(D) $y = 2x + 3$
(E) $y = 3x$

GO ON TO THE NEXT PAGE →

27. If $x^{\frac{a+2}{3}} = 4$, then $x^{\frac{a+2}{2}}$ could equal

(A) 6
(B) 8
(C) 10
(D) 14
(E) 64

28. On March 17, a town had an average snow base of x inches. Then, the weather warmed, and the snow began to melt. At the end of each day, $\frac{1}{5}$ of the snow base left from the previous day had melted. Four days later on March 21, what was the remaining snow base in inches?

(A) $\frac{1}{5}x$

(B) $\frac{64}{125}x$

(C) $\frac{256}{625}x$

(D) $\frac{300}{625}x$

(E) $\frac{4}{5}x$

GO ON TO THE NEXT PAGE

Directions for Student-Produced Response Questions

Each of the remaining 10 questions requires you to solve the problem and enter your answer by marking the ovals in the special grid, as shown in the examples below. You may use any available space for scratch work.

Answer: $\frac{7}{12}$

Write answer in boxes. → Fraction line

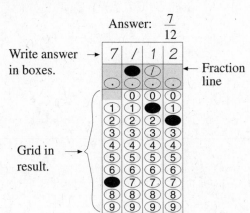

Grid in result. →

Answer: 2.5

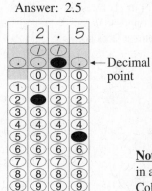

← Decimal point

Answer: 201
Either position is correct.

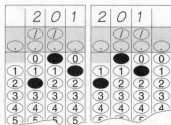

Note: You may start your answers in any column, space permitting. Columns not needed should be left blank.

• Mark no more than one circle in any column.

• Because the answer sheet will be machine-scored, **you will receive credit only if the circles are filled in correctly.**

• Although not required, it′is suggested that you write your answer in the boxes at the top of the columns to help you fill in the circles accurately.

• Some problems may have more than one correct answer. In such cases, grid only one answer.

• No question has a negative answer.

• **Mixed numbers** such as $3\frac{1}{2}$ must be gridded as

3.5 or 7/2. (If [3 1 / 2] is gridded, it will be

interpreted as $\frac{31}{2}$, not $3\frac{1}{2}$.)

• **Decimal Answers:** If you obtain a decimal answer with more digits than the grid can accommodate, it may be either rounded or truncated, but it must fill the entire grid. For example, if you obtain an answer such as 0.6666..., you should record your result as .666 or .667. **A less accurate value such as .66 or .67 will be scored as incorrect.**

Acceptable ways to grid $\frac{2}{3}$ are:

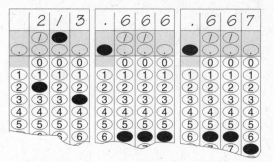

---

29. If $\frac{x}{y} = 1$, then $2x - 2y =$

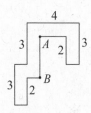

30. If all of the angles in the figure above are right angles, what is the length of $\overline{AB}$?

GO ON TO THE NEXT PAGE ⟩

31. The cube above has a number on each of its six faces. If the sum of the numbers on each pair of opposite faces is 10, what is the sum of the numbers on the faces <u>not</u> shown?

32. At a clothing store, the price of a cashmere sweater is three times the price of a cotton sweater. If the store sold 25 cashmere sweaters for a total of $1,500, and the combined sales of cashmere and cotton sweaters totaled $1,800, how many cotton sweaters were sold?

33. The weight of the tea in a box of 100 identical tea bags is 8 ounces. What is the weight, in ounces, of the tea in one bag?

34. What is the product of all of the positive integer factors of 10 ?

GO ON TO THE NEXT PAGE

35. If point P lies on $\overline{TR}$ such that $TP = 2$ and $PR = 1$, what is the probability that a randomly selected point on $\overline{TR}$ will lie on $\overline{TP}$?

_____

36. If $n \neq 0$ and $125n^x$ is equal to n^{x+3}, then $125n =$

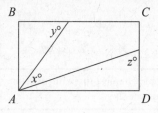

37. In rectangle $ABCD$, if $x = 40$, then $y + z =$

_____

38. If a varies inversely as b, and $a = 3$ when $b = 4$, then what is the value of b when $a = 48$?

STOP
If you finish before time is called, you may check your work on this section only.
Do not turn to any other section in the test.

SECTION 5
Time — 30 minutes
39 Questions

Directions: For each question in this section, select the best answer from among the choices given and fill in the corresponding circle on the answer sheet.

The following sentences test correctness and effectiveness of expression. Part of each sentence or the entire sentence is underlined; beneath each sentence are five ways of phrasing the underlined material. Choice A repeats the original phrasing; the other four choices are different. If you think the original phrasing produces a better sentence than any of the alternatives, select choice A; if not, select one of the other choices.

In making your selection, follow the requirements of standard written English; that is, pay attention to grammar, choice of words, sentence construction, and punctuation. Your selection should result in the most effective sentence—clear and precise, without awkwardness or ambiguity.

EXAMPLE:

Bobby Flay baked his first cake <u>and he was thirteen years old then</u>.

(A) and he was thirteen years old then
(B) when he was thirteen
(C) at age thirteen years old
(D) upon the reaching of thirteen years
(E) at the time when he was thirteen

1. Many parents and children argue often about responsibility; this would be avoided if <u>they have more trust in them</u>.

    (A) they have more trust in them
    (B) their trust in them was more
    (C) their trust were more
    (D) their parents had more trust in them
    (E) parents had more trust in their children

2. <u>When reading</u> the reviews of his recently published romantic novel, Father O'Malley threw his manuscript into the blazing fireplace.

    (A) When reading
    (B) Having to read
    (C) After he read
    (D) When he reads
    (E) Reading

3. Today's computers <u>are becoming not only more varied and powerful, but also less expensive</u>.

    (A) are becoming not only more varied and powerful, but also less expensive
    (B) not only are becoming more varied and powerful, they cost less
    (C) become not only more varied and powerful, they become less expensive
    (D) becoming more varied and powerful, but also less expensive
    (E) become more varied and powerful, not only, but also less expensive

4. To get through an emergency, <u>it demands remaining calm</u> and collected.

    (A) it demands remaining calm
    (B) it demands calmness
    (C) one is demanded to remain calm
    (D) one should remain calm
    (E) demands one to remain calm

5. <u>After getting off the chairlift, Neil adjusted his boot buckles, polished his goggles, and skied down the slope.</u>

    (A) After getting off the chairlift, Neil adjusted his boot buckles, polished his goggles, and skied down the slope.
    (B) He got off the chairlift, Neil adjusted his boot buckles, polished his goggles, and skied down the slope.
    (C) After getting off the chairlift, Neil adjusted his boot buckles, polished his goggles, and then he skiing down the slope.
    (D) Neil, after getting off the chairlift, adjusted his boot buckles, polished his goggles, and was skiing down the slope.
    (E) Getting off the chairlift, Neil adjusted his boot buckles, polished his goggles, and skied down the slope.

GO ON TO THE NEXT PAGE

6. It is easy for a person to get an entry-level position at the company, but <u>you will find it difficult to advance rapidly</u>.

   (A) you will find it difficult to advance rapidly
   (B) you will find rapid advancement a difficulty
   (C) rapid advancing is difficult
   (D) rapid advancement is difficult
   (E) rapidly advancing is a difficulty

7. My parents told me that <u>in France they sometimes</u> do not wear bathing suits on the beach.

   (A) in France they sometimes
   (B) in France some people
   (C) some French people
   (D) in France there are people, some of whom
   (E) in France, men not women

8. <u>When first implicated in it, Nixon denied any wrongdoing in the Watergate scandal, but soon the evidence against him was overwhelming.</u>

   (A) When first implicated in it, Nixon denied any wrongdoing in the Watergate scandal, but soon the evidence against him was overwhelming.
   (B) When Nixon was first implicated in the Watergate scandal, he denied any wrongdoing and the evidence against him was soon overwhelming.
   (C) When first implicated in the Watergate scandal, the evidence against Nixon was soon overwhelming but he denied any wrongdoing.
   (D) When he was first implicated in the Watergate scandal, Nixon denied any wrongdoing, but soon he was overwhelmed by the evidence against him.
   (E) Nixon first denied any wrongdoing in it, but soon the overwhelming evidence implicated him in the Watergate scandal.

9. Having spent hours developing the essay questions, <u>the professor was extremely annoyed by the students' lack of preparation for the final examination</u>.

   (A) the professor was extremely annoyed by the students' lack of preparation for the final examination
   (B) the students' lack of preparing for the final examination was an extreme annoyance to the professor
   (C) that the students did not prepare for the final examination annoyed the professor extremely
   (D) the professor's extreme annoyance resulted from the students not preparing for the final examination
   (E) the professor's annoyance at the students' lack of preparing for the final examination was extreme

10. Kate is known not only for the creativity of her works of sculpture, but <u>also her</u> spirit of compassion.

    (A) also her
    (B) she has a
    (C) also for her
    (D) also she has a
    (E) having also a

11. <u>By being both low-cost and highly flexible and also light in weight</u>, plastic is often regarded as an excellent material for plumbing applications.

    (A) By being both low-cost and highly flexible and also light in weight
    (B) With its low cost, high degree of flexibility and being light in weight
    (C) Because of its low cost, high degree of flexibility, and light weight
    (D) Having a low cost, a high degree of flexibility, as well as a light weight
    (E) Having a low cost, a high degree of flexibility, and its weight is light

12. Roger will lead the management team for our new <u>project, for in recent months he has been superbly able to do it</u>.

    (A) project, for in recent months he has been superbly able to do it
    (B) project, his ability to do this was superb in recent months
    (C) project, he has been superbly able in recent months in this
    (D) project; his ability to coordinate company meetings having been superb in recent months
    (E) project, for his ability to coordinate company meetings has been superb in recent months

13. The purpose of learning history may be to show us how the world works and how humans behave instead of <u>what some think it is: to make us memorize facts and then repeat them</u>.

    (A) what some think it is: to make us memorize facts and then repeat them
    (B) what some think it is, the making of our memorization and repetition of facts
    (C) what some think it does, which is to make us memorize facts and then repeat them
    (D) what some think it does, to make us memorize facts and then repeat them
    (E) making us memorize facts and then repeat them, what some think it does

GO ON TO THE NEXT PAGE

14. Practical arts courses often include activities <u>by which they</u> can put their knowledge to use immediately.

   (A) by which they
   (B) that they
   (C) and during this, students
   (D) during which students
   (E) where they

15. <u>Unless they become more responsible</u> about investing money, many college students will soon rebel against their administrations.

   (A) Unless they become more responsible
   (B) Unless becoming more responsible
   (C) Unless colleges become more responsible
   (D) Unless it becomes more responsible
   (E) Unless more responsibility is shown

16. Although the entertainer <u>was trained in dancing</u>, he won acclaim as a singer.

   (A) was trained in dancing
   (B) was trained to dance
   (C) had trained to dance
   (D) was trained as a dancer
   (E) had trained in dancing

17. Goethe's poetry is different <u>from any others</u> in the way it lyrically expresses profound thoughts.

   (A) from any others
   (B) from that of any other poet
   (C) from any other poet
   (D) than anyone else's
   (E) than anyone else

18. Vacationing in foreign countries provides one not only with relaxing experiences but also <u>cultures different from theirs are better understood</u>.

   (A) cultures different from theirs are better understood
   (B) a better understanding of cultures different from theirs
   (C) with a better understanding of different cultures
   (D) better understood are cultures different from theirs
   (E) cultures, although different, are better understood

19. Unprepared for such a strong rebuttal, the <u>lawyer's attempt at winning the case failed</u>.

   (A) lawyer's attempt at winning the case failed
   (B) lawyer's attempt failed to win the case
   (C) lawyer failed to win the case
   (D) lawyer failed in his attempt to win the case
   (E) lawyer attempted to win his case, but failed

20. <u>One should eat more vegetables if they want to develop strong bodies and maintain their health.</u>

   (A) One should eat more vegetables if they want to develop strong bodies and maintain their health.
   (B) One should eat more vegetables to develop strong bodies and maintain their health.
   (C) One should eat more vegetables if one wants to develop a strong body and maintain one's health.
   (D) One, wishing to develop a strong body and maintain one's health, should eat more vegetables.
   (E) One should eat more vegetables in order to develop strong bodies and maintain their health.

GO ON TO THE NEXT PAGE ⟶

The following sentences test your ability to recognize grammar and usage errors. Each sentence contains either a single error or no error at all. No sentence contains more than one error. The error, if there is one, is underlined and lettered. If the sentence contains an error, select the one underlined part that must be changed to make the sentence correct. If the sentence is correct, select choice E. In choosing answers, follow the requirements of standard written English.

EXAMPLE:

The other players and her significantly improved
    A   B   C

the game plan created by the coaches. No error
             D   E

21. A good teacher should not only convey information
               A   B

and should also instill in his students a love for
C   D

learning. No error
       E

22. Psychologists have long debated the connection
             A   B

between violence on television plus actual crime.
              C   D

No error
E

23. Of the nominees for the Nobel Prize in Literature
A   B

this year, few are as qualified as the English novelist
        C   D

Anthony Powell. No error
           E

24. Revered as one of the world's most versatile geniuses,
A

Leonardo da Vinci excelled in everything he attempted
                   B

and serving as a prototype for the Renaissance man.
    C   D

No error
E

25. The twins wanted to be a member of the team, but the
              A   B

captain had already made her selections. No error
       C   D   E

26. The crowd of onlookers grew larger as the veterans
       A   B

which were picketing the White House began shouting.
C   D

No error
E

27. When Ms. Ruiz arrived at the holiday sale, she realized
          A

that she had left her wallet at home and must go back
B   C   D

to get it. No error
      E

28. My art history professors prefer Michelangelo's painting
            A

to viewing his sculpture, although Michelangelo himself
B   C

was more proud of the latter. No error
          D   E

GO ON TO THE NEXT PAGE

29. A number of scientists <u>have begun</u> to speculate <u>whether</u>
                                     A   B

life <u>actually began</u> as crystals of clay rather <u>than</u> as
         C   D

organic molecules. <u>No error</u>
                    E

30. The <u>continual</u> improvements in athletic training
           A

methods <u>has made</u> performances <u>that would have been</u>
          B   C

considered impossible <u>a generation ago</u> everyday
                         D

occurrences. <u>No error</u>
            E

31. Pilot carelessness, <u>rather than</u> equipment failure,
                 A

<u>was</u> <u>responsible for</u> the <u>near disaster</u> at the local
B   C   D

airport. <u>No error</u>
       E

32. Dieting and exercise <u>is</u> not the answer <u>to</u> all weight
                     A   B

problems, but they <u>should</u> do the trick <u>for most</u>
               C   D

waistlines. <u>No error</u>
          E

33. Rome is an <u>exceedingly</u> beautiful city <u>largely</u> because
             A   B

<u>they have</u> successfully blended <u>the modern</u> with the
C   D

ancient. <u>No error</u>
      E

34. <u>Unless</u> scientists discover new ways to increase food
    A

production, the Earth <u>is not</u> be able to satisfy the food
                B

needs <u>of</u> all <u>its</u> inhabitants. <u>No error</u>
   C   D   E

GO ON TO THE NEXT PAGE →

Directions: The following passage is an early draft of an essay. Some parts of the passage need to be rewritten.

Read the passage and select the best answers for the questions that follow. Some questions are about particular sentences or parts of sentences and ask you to improve sentence structure or word choice. Other questions ask you to consider organization and development. In choosing answers, follow the requirements of standard written English.

Questions 35-39 are based on the following passage.

(1) Our town needs to make more of an effort to make its museums accessible to children. (2) Raised with frequent exposure to sculpture and paintings, it is much more likely that young people will mature into artists and patrons of the arts.

(3) It is often quite easy to accomplish a great deal simply. (4) Placed slightly lower on the walls, paintings are more easily enjoyed by children. (5) But extensive programs to encourage children to appreciate art are often not a necessity. (6) Children have a natural enjoyment of art. (7) A museum is an excellent place for a child. (8) We must only understand that these young museum patrons cannot help acting like them. (9) Children should not be asked to be silent, or to spend long periods of time in front of any one piece. (10) If necessary, museums should set up special "children's times" during which young people may roam through the building, enjoying the artwork in their own way. (11) A wonderful learning experience! (12) Children can have a great time, and at the same time gain an appreciation of art. (13) Precautions can be taken to make sure that no damage is done.

(14) This is necessary because places like museums must be available to everyone. (15) These changes cannot happen overnight, but if we volunteered and were helping to make these changes in our town's museums, we can realize the goal of making them accessible to people of all ages.

35. Which of the following is the best way to revise the underlined portion of sentence 2 (reproduced below) ?

Raised with frequent exposure to sculpture and paintings, it is much more likely that young people will mature into artists and patrons of the arts.

(A) Raised being frequently exposed to sculpture and paintings, the likelihood is that young people will
(B) If they grow up with frequent exposure to sculpture and paintings, young people are much more likely to
(C) Grown up with exposure frequently to sculpture and paintings, young people are much more likely to
(D) Being raised frequently exposed to sculpture and painting, it is much more likely for young people to
(E) They grow up with frequent exposure to sculpture and paintings, it is much more likely that young people

36. Which version of the underlined portion of sentence 8 provides the most clarity?

We must only understand that these young museum patrons can not help acting like them.

(A) (as it is now)
(B) like it
(C) as if they were
(D) like what they are
(E) like children

37. Sentence 13 could be best improved if the author were to

(A) describe possible damage
(B) explain the precautions to be taken
(C) give a historic precedent
(D) extend her argument to include other institutions
(E) explain the mission of a museum

38. Sentence 14 would be clearer if the words "This is" were replaced with

(A) These precautions are
(B) Efforts such as these are
(C) Museums are
(D) Appreciation of art is
(E) Educating children is

39. Which of the following is the best version of the underlined portion of sentence 15 (reproduced below)?

These changes cannot happen overnight, but if we volunteered and were helping to make these changes in our town's museums, we can realize the goal of making them accessible to people of all ages.

(A) (as it is now)
(B) so if we volunteer and we help change
(C) but if we volunteer to help make these changes
(D) yet if we will volunteer and also help with changing
(E) although if we would volunteer and would help make changes

STOP

If you finish before time is called, you may check your work on this section only.
Do not turn to any other section in the test.

PRACTICE TEST 11 ANSWER KEY

Section 1	Section 2	Section 3	Section 4	Section 5	
1. D	1. D	25. B	21. E	1. E	31. E
2. E	2. D	26. D	22. D	2. C	32. A
3. C	3. A	27. B	23. A	3. A	33. C
4. E	4. A	28. D	24. C	4. D	34. B
5. D	5. E	29. C	25. B	5. A	35. B
6. B	6. C	30. D	26. A	6. D	36. E
7. E	7. E	31. C	27. B	7. B	37. B
8. A	8. B	32. D	28. C	8. D	38. B
9. A	9. A	33. B	29. 0	9. A	39. C
10. D	10. A	34. D	30. 3	10. C	
11. A	11. A	35. D	31. 16	11. C	
12. B	12. C	36. E	32. 15	12. E	
13. B	13. D	37. C	33. $\frac{4}{50}$, $\frac{2}{25}$, or .08	13. A	
14. D	14. C	38. B		14. D	
15. A	15. D	39. A	34. 100	15. C	
16. C	16. E	40. C	35. $\frac{2}{3}$, .666, or .667	16. D	
17. B	17. D	41. C		17. B	
18. E	18. A	42. D	36. 625	18. C	
19. B	19. D	43. E	37. 130	19. C	
20. D	20. B	44. C	38. $\frac{4}{16}$, $\frac{1}{4}$, or .25	20. C	
21. A		45. B		21. C	
22. A		46. B		22. D	
23. D		47. D		23. E	
24. E		48. C		24. C	
				25. A	
				26. C	
				27. D	
				28. B	
				29. E	
				30. B	

You will find a detailed explanation for each question beginning on page 896.

SCORING YOUR PRACTICE PSAT

Critical Reading

After you have checked your answers against the answer key, you can calculate your score. For the two Critical Reading sections (Sections 1 and 3), add up the number of correct answers and the number of incorrect answers. Enter these numbers on the worksheet on the next page. Multiply the number of incorrect answers by .25 and subtract this result from the number of correct answers. Then round this to the nearest whole number. This is your Critical Reading "raw score." Next, use the conversion table to convert your raw score to a scaled score.

Math

Figuring your Math score is a bit trickier, because some of the questions have 5 answer choices (for these, the incorrect answer deduction is .25), and some are Grid-Ins (which have no deduction for wrong answers).

First, check your answers to all of the problem-solving questions on Sections 2 and 4. For Section 2 and questions 21–28 of Section 4, put the number of correct answers and the number of incorrect answers into the worksheet on the next page. Multiply the number of incorrect answers by .25 and subtract this total from the number of correct answers. For questions 29–38 of Section 4, the Grid-In questions, simply put in the number of correct answers. Now, add up the totals for both types of math questions to give you your total Math raw score. Then you can use the conversion table to find your scaled score.

Writing Skills

The Writing Skills section should be scored just like the Critical Reading sections. Add up the number of correct answers and the number of incorrect answers from Section 5, and enter these numbers on the worksheet on the next page. Multiply the number of incorrect answers by .25 and subtract this result from the number of correct answers. Then round this to the nearest whole number. This is your Writing Skills raw score. Next, use the conversion table to convert your raw scores to scaled scores.

WORKSHEET FOR CALCULATING YOUR SCORE

Critical Reading

	Correct	Incorrect

A. Sections 1 and 3 _____ − (.25 × _____) =

[   ] A

B. Total rounded Critical Reading raw score

[   ] B

Math

	Correct	Incorrect

C. Section 2 and Section 4—Problem Solving _____ − (.25 × _____) =

[   ] C

D. Section 4—Grid-Ins _____ =

[   ] D

E. Total unrounded Math raw score (C + D)

[   ] E

F. Total rounded Math raw score

[   ] F

Writing Skills

Section 5 _____ − (.25 × _____) =

[   ]

Total rounded Writing Skills raw score

[   ]

SCORE CONVERSION TABLE

Math Raw Score	Math Scaled Score	Critical Reading Raw Score	Critical Reading Scaled Score	Writing Skills Raw Score	Writing Skills Scaled Score
0	26	0	25	0	29
1	29	1	27	1	30
2	30	2	29	2	31
3	32	3	30	3	32
4	34	4	32	4	33
5	35	5	33	5	35
6	36	6	34	6	36
7	38	7	36	7	37
8	39	8	37	8	39
9	40	9	38	9	40
10	41	10	39	10	41
11	42	11	40	11	43
12	43	12	41	12	44
13	44	13	42	13	45
14	45	14	43	14	46
15	46	15	44	15	48
16	47	16	45	16	49
17	48	17	46	17	50
18	50	18	47	18	51
19	51	19	48	19	52
20	52	20	49	20	54
21	53	21	50	21	55
22	54	22	51	22	56
23	55	23	52	23	57
24	57	24	53	24	59
25	58	25	54	25	60
26	59	26	54	26	62
27	60	27	55	27	63
28	61	28	56	28	65
29	62	29	57	29	66
30	64	30	58	30	68
31	65	31	59	31	69
32	66	32	60	32	71
33	68	33	61	33	73
34	70	34	62	34	74
35	72	35	62	35	76
36	74	36	63	36	77
37	77	37	64	37	78
38	80	38	66	38	80
		39	67	39	80
		40	68		
		41	69		
		42	71		
		43	72		
		44	74		
		45	76		
		46	78		
		47	80		
		48	80		

Chapter 25
Practice Test 11:
Answers and
Explanations

SECTION 1

1. **D**   The clues *changes in the immediate area* and *in far-flung regions* make "wide-ranging" a good phrase for the blank. It has nothing to do with money, so eliminate (A). (B) is the opposite of what we want. (C) and (E) are at odds with *dramatic*. (D) comes closest to "wide-ranging."

2. **E**   The clue *new...system* makes "started" a good word for the first blank. (B), (C), and (D) are not close in meaning to "started," and therefore are eliminated. The clue for the second blank, *without first running...tests*, could mean "check out," which eliminates (A), (B), (C), and (D), leaving only (E). (E), *implemented* and *evaluate*, fits with both blanks.

3. **C**   The clue *afraid of losing money* makes it unlikely the miser would *risk* it. (B), (D), and (E) are eliminated because the meaning of the second word in each is not close to *risk*. "Money-making" is a good phrase for the first blank. (C) is correct because *lucrative* is closest in meaning to "money-making."

4. **E**   The clue for the second blank *effort...to check each fact* makes "incorrect" a good word for the second blank. (B), (C), and (D) can be eliminated because they don't mean "incorrect." A negative word, like "rejected," goes in the first blank. (A) is positive, and therefore wrong. (E) most closely matches the meanings for both blanks.

5. **D**   The clue *twig-shaped* lets us know the insect would be "hidden," a good word for the blank, if it were on a branch of *shrubbery*. The insect was not eaten, as in (A), nor does it grow leaves, as in (B). (C) and (E) are not related at all to the sentence's meaning. Only (D) matches the meaning of "hidden."

6. **B**   The clues *successfully* and *had plagued previous administrations* make "avoided" a good word for the first blank. (D) and (E) do not match "avoided" and can therefore be eliminated. The clue for the second blank, *responding to requests from various leaders in each community*, makes "collaborative" a good word for the second blank. Of the three remaining choices (B) *inclusive* is closest in meaning to "collaborative."

7. **E**   The clue *orderly* is a good word for the first blank. (A), (B), and (C) are not close in meaning to *orderly* and are therefore incorrect. The phrase *even though* indicates a change in direction, so the word "negates" is a good word for the second blank. (E) is closest in meaning to "negates."

8. **A**   "Believability" is a good word for the blank because a female vice president makes the idea of a female president more likely. This eliminates (B), (D), and (E). (A), *credence*, is closer in meaning to "believability" than (C), *veracity*, which is closer in meaning to "truthfulness." (A) is therefore the correct answer.

9.   **A**   (A) is correct because the phrase *by using this rhetorical device* (lines 7–8) indicates that *startling images, designed to capture the hearer's imagination* (lines 6–7), are what gave Malcolm X's speeches their power. (B) is very tempting, as Malcolm X is described as being from humble beginnings in the same sentence as being *able to appeal to his listeners* (lines 4–5). But that sentence indicates it was the *universal imagery*, not his humble beginnings, that was appealing. (A) comes closest to *startling images*. While (B) and (D) are true about Malcolm X, they are not reasons for his communicative abilities. There is no evidence for choice (C). (E) contradicts the passage.

10. **D**   (D) is correct because the author's conclusion that Malcolm X communicated on an emotional level with his use of imagery would be most strongly supported by people who had actually experienced his speeches. (A), (B), and (C) mention imagery but not the listeners' emotions. (E) mentions neither imagery nor emotions.

11. **A**   (A) is correct because phrases such as *marvelously complex* and *still mysterious* indicate that the author is amazed by the process of hearing, yet realizes much is unknown. (A), *awed*, describes a mix of reverence, dread, and wonder. (B) is incorrect because the author expresses an emotion. There is no evidence for (C) or (D); *skeptical* or *incredulous* indicates the author disputes what's known about the process of hearing. (E) is incorrect because *dumbfounded* indicates that the author doesn't understand anything about hearing.

12. **B**   (B) is correct because the passage uses this metaphor to show that the nerve cells send a signal to the hindbrain. (A) is not correct because diatonic scales are mentioned to show communication between hindbrain and the inferior colliculi. There is no evidence in the passage for (C), (D), or (E).

13. **B**   (A), (C), and (D) are mentioned later on in the passage, but have no relation to Laplace. (E) contradicts the passage. (B) is correct because in the first paragraph, the passage states that the concept of black holes is not all that new; Laplace pointed them out in 1824.

14. **D**   There is evidence for four of the choices in the passage: (A), lines 13–15, *Our sun would have to be only a few miles in diameter to become a black hole.* It isn't, therefore it won't become a black hole; (B), lines 20–21; (C), lines 15–16; and (E), lines 13–15. (D) is correct because it is the only one NOT in the passage. Indeed, the opposite of this is true: The sun would have to be heavier to have enough gravity to pull it down to a black hole, suggesting that its gravitational pull is not enough to make a black hole.

15. **A**   Try replacing the word *exhausts* with what would make sense in the sentence. A good phrase to replace *exhausts* is "uses all." (A), *uses up,* comes closest to this meaning. None of the other answer choices comes close. (B) means "to spend or use up senselessly." (C) means "to tire or make weary." (D) means "to give off or send out."

16. **C**   (A) and (B) are both mentioned in the passage, but neither is the reason why the author mentions the Crab Nebula. There is no evidence for (D) or (E) in the passage. The author mentions the Crab Nebula in conjunction with the *neutron star* (lines 30–34).

17. **B** There is no evidence for any of the answer choices in the passage except (B). (B) is correct because of evidence in the last paragraph of the passage. Lines 41–42 state that black holes have *enough gravity to make x-rays come out.*

18. **E** The clue to the meaning of *elementary particles* refers to the smallest units that make up neutrons, protons, and electrons. (A), (B), (C), and (D) can thus be eliminated. (Think *elementary* school, which is basic compared to high school or college.)

19. **B** The passage states in line 47 that in Hawking's theory, the mini black holes *can seem to emit energy,* which contradicts the notion that nothing can escape from a black hole. (A) is very tempting, but we don't really know about the comparative physical characteristics (other than size). (C) and (E) are false according to the passage, while (D) is a jumble of other ideas. The relevant part of the passage is best summed up by (B).

20. **D** (A), (B), (C), and (E) take bits and pieces from the passage, so they all "sound" pretty good. However, we're asked to select what can be *inferred*; that is, what do we know for a fact based on the passage? (D) is correct because the passage states in lines 60–62 that *the amount of radiation increases sharply as we consider less and less massive black holes.* This is an inverse relationship, since the more radiation, the smaller the size.

21. **A** (B), (C), and (D) are mentioned in the passage as details, but none is the main idea of the whole passage. (E) contradicts the passage; the mini black holes have not been observed. (A) is correct because Passage 2 is about the theory that mini black holes exist.

22. **A** (A) is correct because the paragraph describes the experience *you* would have on the edge of a black hole, incorporating such mundane details as checking the time. (B) is too strong—scientific proof takes more than an analogy. There is no evidence of warning, as in (C). (D) is insulting to the author. There is no evidence for (E) in the passage.

23. **D** Lines 3–4 in Passage 1 state that *mass in a small enough package* is a black hole, and go on to discuss why our sun is not likely to become a black hole because of its density. The second paragraph of Passage 2 also discusses mass and density. There is no evidence in either passage that (A), (B), (C), or (E) are capable of identifying a star that is capable of becoming a black hole. (D) matches the statements noted.

24. **E** Passage 1 states, in lines 7–8, that black holes are a *one-way ticket*—matter goes in, but doesn't come out. There is no evidence for (A) or (C) in the passage. (B) and (D) are contradicted by information in the passage. (E), Hawking's theory of mini black holes, does the most to dispute the statement.

SECTION 2

1. **D** See what letters are possible for each digit of 7,283. 7 gives PRS. All the words begin with those letters, so nothing is eliminated. 2 gives ABC. All the words have those letters second, so nothing is eliminated. 8 gives TUV. So (D), RAID, is not possible.

2. **D** Plug in a number for z. If $z = 2$ gallons, then a proportion can be set up: 3 pints of lemon juice make 1 gallon of lemonade, so 6 pints of lemon juice make 2 gallons of lemonade. Our target number is 6; only choice (D) gives us 6. Algebraically, if 3 pints make 1 gallon, multiply both by z: $3z = z$ gallons.

3. **A** Work this problem step by step. First add to find the total of all the shirts, which is $68.80. The down payment is half the total, which is $34.40. Be careful of choice (E)—it's a partial answer. The remainder is divided into four equal payments, which is $8.60. This is what the question asks us to find, so (A) is correct. Be careful of choice (D). If we skipped the step of dividing the total by 2 for the down payment, we would get (D).

4. **A** First, convert the lines and dots to real numbers. $59 - 46 = 13$, so we're looking for the symbols that represent 13, which we find in (A).

5. **E** The question asks for the value of j. We are told $4j - k = 11$ and that $k = 3j$. Replace the k with $3j$. $4j - 3j = 11$, so $j = 11$.

6. **C** The volume for a cylinder is the area of the circular base multiplied by the height $(\pi r^2 h)$. We are given a height of 9, so $\pi r^2 9 = 144\pi$. Divide both sides by 9, and we see that $\pi r^2 = 16\pi$. Go no further; that is the base of the cylinder.

7. **E** If Mr. Johnson is dividing the 85 beakers among his z students, we would divide 85 by z to find 5. So, $\frac{85}{z} = 5$. Multiply each side by z to find $5z = 85$.

8. **B** Set up a proportion and solve for x. $\frac{(0.5)}{15} = \frac{x}{50}$. Cross-multiply, so $25 = 15x$. $x = \frac{25}{15}$, which reduces to $1\frac{2}{3}$.

9. **A** Redraw figures not drawn to scale. Triangle MOP is isosceles, and so is triangle MNP. Equal sides are opposite equal angles, so the angles of the smaller triangle can thus be figured out: $\angle MNP$ measures 70°, $\angle MPN$ measures 40°. Since we know $\angle MPO$ measures 70°, a is 30.

10. **A** Plug in the numbers from the chart into the equations in the answer choices until we find the one that always works. Only (A) always produces the correct cost when the values for n (the number of pitchers) are plugged in.

11. **A** Try using an easy number. No matter what numbers we plug in for r and s (as long as $r \neq -s$, as stated in the question), the numerator has a value of 0. In $(r - s - r + s)$, each value is canceled out by its opposite.

12. **C** Plug in and make a proportion for height to shadow. If $f = 20$, then $\dfrac{108}{27} = \dfrac{20}{\text{Sue's shadow}}$. $108 \div 27 = 4$. So if Sue is 20 inches tall, her shadow must be 5 inches long. Plug 20 into the answer choices and only (C) gives the target number 5. Algebraically, let x = length of Sue's shadow. Then set up a proportion and solve for x: $\dfrac{108}{27} = \dfrac{f}{x}$. $27f = 108x$. $x = \dfrac{27f}{108} = \dfrac{f}{4}$.

13. **D** Plug in a number for x. If $x = 2$, then add the fractions $\dfrac{0}{3}$ and $\dfrac{5}{3}$, which equals $\dfrac{5}{3}$. Only (D) gives us $\dfrac{5}{3}$. Algebraically, since both expressions are divided by $(x + 1)$, we can add the numerators. $\dfrac{(x-2)+(x+3)}{(x+1)} = \dfrac{2x+1}{x+1}$.

14. **C** Translate first; then we can solve or plug in the answer choices. The square root of $4n = 6$, so $4n = 36$, which makes $n = 9$.

15. **D** Note that the letters are standing in for one-digit numbers, not variables. If $7 - B = 7$, B must represent 0. Now the problem is $A407 - A40 = 5CA7$. If we carry a one from the 4 to the 0, we get $10 - 4 = A$, which means A is equal to 6. Now we have $6407 - 640 = 5C67$. Once we calculate from here, we get $C = 7$.

16. **E** Since the question asks which must be FALSE, if we can plug in any numbers that make a statement in the answer choices true, we can eliminate that choice. (E) never works because the question states that the numbers are distinct and correctly ordered (that is, from lowest to highest). Since a and b are lower values than c and d, this means that $a + b$ can never be higher than $c + d$.

17. **D** Try solving by plugging in the answer choices. Only (D) works. $0.4 \div 0.2 = 2$; $0.6 \div 0.2 = 3$; $0.8 \div 0.2 = 4$. Since $2 \times 3 \times 4 = 24$, (D) is the correct answer. Algebraically, $\dfrac{0.4}{r} \times \dfrac{0.6}{r} \times \dfrac{0.8}{r} = 24$, so $\dfrac{0.192}{r^3} = 24$, and multiplying both sides by r^3 gives $24r^3 = 0.192$. Thus, $r^3 = 0.008$ and taking the cube root of both sides to get $r = 0.2$.

18. **A** Because $\overline{CD}$ and $\overline{AE}$ are perpendicular to $\overline{AC}$, we have two right triangles. Triangle BCD has a hypotenuse of 4, while triangle ABE has a hypotenuse of 6. Because $x = y$, triangle ABE is a 45°-45°-90° triangle. Triangle BCD is also 45°-45°-90° since $x = 45°$, $\overline{BD}$ is perpendicular to $\overline{BE}$, and there are 180° in a straight line. Now we can use special right triangles. Since the hypotenuse of triangle BCD is 4, then $4 = s\sqrt{2}$, and each leg is $\dfrac{4}{\sqrt{2}}$. Since the hypotenuse of triangle ABE is 6, $6 = s\sqrt{2}$, and each leg is $\dfrac{6}{\sqrt{2}}$. AC is thus $\dfrac{10}{\sqrt{2}}$, which simplifies to $5\sqrt{2}$ when we multiply numerator and denominator by $\sqrt{2}$.

19. **D** Write out on pattern questions until the pattern is clear: 107, 117, 127, 137. There are 10 integers with a 7 in the units place between 100 and 199. Since we have 9 sets of these from 100 to 999, there are 90 integers with a units digit of 7.

20. **B** Rotation questions are often about circumference, $C = 2\pi r$. Pick any number for l, but if we plug in for m, pick a number of minutes that is an easy fraction of an hour (except for 60 or 30 because those are in the answer choices). If $l = 5$ and $m = 15$, the whole circumference is 10π. Fifteen minutes is $\dfrac{1}{4}$ of an hour, so the minute hand will move $\dfrac{1}{4}$ of the circumference, which is 2.5π. Plug into the answer choices. Only (B) gives us 2.5π.

SECTION 3

25. **B** The clue in the sentence is *together*, making "joint" a good word for the blank. (A) means "layered," so it doesn't fit. (C) and (D) don't fit, as we don't know whether the castle was *disregarded*, and *conclusive* doesn't make logical sense. (E) means "to direct attention elsewhere," so that can be eliminated. (B), *cooperative*, comes closest to "joint."

26. **D** The clues are *not* and *have often;* a good word for the first blank is "rare," which eliminates answer choices (C) and (E). *Conflict* is the clue for the second blank, making the phrase "conflicted with" useful (why make up a clue when we can recycle?). (D), *opposed*, comes closest to conflict, so eliminate (A) and (B).

27. **B** The clue *never stayed at any one site long enough* makes "mobile" a good word for the blank. (A) means "quietly," or "in a sneaky manner," while (C), *clamorous,* means "noisy." (D) means "blatantly" or "openly," and (E) means "country-like." None of those means the same as "mobile." (B), *nomadic,* describes a person who moves frequently.

28. **D** Clues such as *conflagration* and *middle of the night* indicate that a sudden bad event has occurred, which make "disastrous" a good word for the first blank; eliminate (A), (B), and (C). "Evacuate" would be a good word for the second blank, eliminating (B) and (E). (D) matches both words most closely.

29. **C** The vaquero's acts were recorded, so they must have left an imprint. "Strong" or "significant" would be a good word for the first blank. This eliminates (A), (B), (D), and (E), leaving only (C).

30. **D** The language in (A) and (B)—*only what they want to* and *any behavior or talent*—is too strong. (C) is contradicted by both passages. There is no evidence for (E) in Passage 1, and it does not address Passage 2. (D) is correct because it describes both the Montessori method and *scaffolding*.

31. **C** There is evidence in the passage that the Montessori program develops the characteristics noted in (A), (B), (D), and (E), but we're looking for the answer to an EXCEPT question. (C) is correct because *omnipotence* means "all knowing"; the passage does not indicate that it's possible to develop *omnipotence*.

32. **D** The primary difference between the two passages is that Passage 1 focuses on student-driven learning (*freedom to engage in meaningful activities*) and Passage 2 on teacher-driven learning (*provide a structured environment*). While mentioned in Passage 1, *regimen* is more along the lines of Passage 2, so eliminate (A). (B) is unsupported, since *skepticism* is not important to the theory presented in Passage 2; it's how *scaffolding* was first received. Neither word in (C) is supported by the passages. (E) is close, as *self-esteem* works well for Passage 1, but there is nothing necessarily *modern* about Passage 2.

33. **B** It's helpful to treat these vocabulary-in-context questions like sentence completions. Since Vygotsky would be in favor of providing *a structured environment*, the word *contends* must mean something like "agrees with," so eliminate (A), (C), and (E). (D) is unsupported, as there is no reason to think that Vygotsky only *imagines*.

34. **D** (A) and (B) are each half right; only Hamilton played for Iowa, and the passage mentions only Robeson's singing. There is no evidence in the passage for (C) or (E). (D) is correct because the passage states Robeson believed there was more to the day than playing football, and Hamilton agrees.

35. **D** (A), (B), and (C) all focus on Robeson rather than on Hamilton. (E) is incorrect because there is no indication of criticism, only of admiration. (D) is correct because according to the blurb, the passage is by an author reminiscing about her father, later identified as Kenneth Hamilton.

36. E (A) and (B) focus on characters other than the author. (B) is a trap answer, as the passage does imply that Mr. Robeson did not want to be a preacher, but doesn't answer the question. Neither (C) nor (D) indicates anything new or like no one else. (E) is correct because the passage states in line 21 that the author longed not just to write, but to newly write and like no one else.

37. C (A) does not indicate the specific situation of black men at that time. (B) and (D) use extreme language such as *no possibility* and *impossible*, for which there is no evidence in the passage. There is no evidence for (E) in the passage. (C) is correct because the passage states that Hamilton graduated college when just finishing high school was an achievement for black men.

38. B (A) does not illustrate the author's purpose. (C) is contradicted by the passage. There is no evidence in the passage for (D) or (E). (B) is correct because after relating the incident, the author states that she's *rather glad* he refused the job and that she *could have wanted no less for a father*, indicating the purpose is to show admiration for him.

39. A There is no evidence for (B) or (C) in the passage. (D) and (E) are actions that reflect the father's belief in individuality but are too specific to be the root of the author's admiration. (A) is correct because throughout the passage the author states the importance of independence to her father, as well as her agreement with his belief, and ends the passage happy to remember him as not allowing himself to be *limited by another's reality*.

40. C (A) is incorrect because the reason for evoking the author's childhood is to show how it influenced her as a writer. (B) is incorrect because the passage refers only to Welty's experience, not to things necessary for *all* children or *all* writers. (D) is only a small part of the passage. (E) is half right, but the passage indicates the illness led to the author's writing style, not her fragility (lines 54–60). (C) is correct because most of the passage describes the author's childhood, and the rest of the passage describes how this influenced the kind of writer she became.

41. C (A) is incorrect because there is no indication of anxiety. (B) and (D) are incorrect because the author describes herself as homesick for school. There is no evidence in the passage for (E). (C) is correct because the author uses the phrase to describe what the physical symptoms of a *fast-beating heart* felt like to her.

42. D There is no evidence for the *profound sadness* in (A). (B) is too strong; Welty was interested but is not described as *jealous*. (C) is incorrect because although Welty seems to prefer school to her mother's lessons, there is no evidence they are *vastly inferior*. (E) is incorrect because the author states in lines 7–8 that children *didn't get to…excite me often*. (D) is correct because the author describes herself as *homesick for school*, wishing she were back with her classmates.

43. E There is no evidence for (B); the author states that she is daydreaming, and therefore knows the difference. (C) is incorrect; writing isn't discussed until later in the passage. There is no evidence in the passage for (D). (E) is correct because the author is identifying with the characters in the books she reads.

44. **C** (A) contradicts the passage; her parents knew she was there. There is no evidence in the passage for (B). (D) is incorrect because she didn't have to pretend to be asleep. (E) is discussed elsewhere in the passage. (C) is correct because the scene describes overhearing her parents talk in the lighted part of the bedroom, while she is supposed to sleep in the darkened part.

45. **B** (A) and (C) refer to specific information in the parents' conversation, but she doesn't understand it. There is no evidence for (D) or (E) in the passage. (B) is correct because the chief secret was *father and mother, sitting...as one*—not any specific information.

46. **B** We have to find the meaning of the word in context. If we crossed out *exercising*, what could we put in its place? The word "using" would be a good replacement for *exercising* in the sentence. (D) is a trap answer, since exercise can be associated with *training*, but that is not the sense in which *exercising* is being used in the sentence. (B), *utilizing*, most closely matches using. None of the other answer choices means "using."

47. **D** When the author discusses writing, she mentions *distance*; when she discusses *making pictures* or photography, she mentions the *observing eye*. (A) is incorrect as the author stresses *observation*, not *creative aspects*. The author emphasizes similarities, not *differences*, so eliminate (B) and (C). (E) may be true but is not why the author mentions writing and photography.

48. **C** (C) is correct because the last paragraph states that the author wanted to write stories, but *drew near slowly*. In the end, she followed her imagination and did plunge into writing. (A) is incorrect; the passage states that she didn't rush, but there is no evidence she was prevented from building relationships. (B) is incorrect because she did eventually plunge into her desire to write. (D) is wrong because photojournalism is not mentioned in the last paragraph. There is no evidence for (E) in the passage.

SECTION 4

21. **E** Subtract 8 from both sides of the equation, and we're left with $5x = 10$. Since we are asked for $10x$, simply multiply by 2, and we see that $10x = 20$. Read the question carefully; $x = 2$, so (A) is a trap answer.

22. **D** Simplify first; then solve or plug in the answer choices. The two terms given are equal to each other since one subtracted from the other equals 0. Add $2\sqrt{2}$ to both sides. Then, square each side of the equation to get rid of the root signs. Now we have $\frac{2c}{5} = 8$. $2c = 40$, so $c = 20$.

23. **A** The problem tests the ability to work with exponents when the bases are the same. For example, when we multiply the numbers, we add the exponents; if we divide the numbers, we subtract the exponents; and if we take the number to a power, we multiply the exponents. $10 - f = 2$, so $f = 8$. $6g = 18$, so $g = 3$. Therefore, $g - f = 3 - 8 = -5$.

24. **C** Use easy numbers to figure this out! Make a list of five consecutive even integers for set F, such as 2, 4, 6, 8, 10. Make a list for set G: Adding 5 to each number in set F gives 7, 9, 11, 13, 15; subtracting 5 gives –3, –1, 1, 3, 5 for a total of ten integers in set G, which is 5 more than in set F.

25. **B** We know the semicircles on the inside and outside of the rectangle are identical because they each have a radius of r; therefore, we need to find only the area of the rectangle that has length b and width $2r$. Length times width gives $2br$. Plugging In also works here. For example, we could try 5 for b and 2 for r, and solve with numbers. The rectangle would have an area of 20 (*length* × *width*). Note: The area for each semicircle is $\frac{\pi r^2}{2}$ or 2π. This is added to obtain the rectangle plus the shaded area on the right, but then subtracted to carve out the left-hand end. We don't need it at all, either way!

26. **A** Make up a couple of numbers for x in each of the answer choices to see if the y forms a coordinate pair that would be on the line. (A) produces the pairs (–2, 0), (–1, 1), (0, 2), (1, 3), and (2, 4). These numbers could fit on $\overline{PR}$. All the other choices give some coordinate pairs that conflict with $\overline{PR}$. Try sketching them out.

27. **B** Try an easy number. If $a = 4$, then $x^{\frac{a+2}{3}} = x^2 = 4$, so $x = 2$ or –2. Plug in 4 for a and 2 for x into $x^{\frac{a+2}{2}}$, which simplifies to 2^3, which equals 8. There is no need to try –2.

28. **C** Be careful! Each day the snow is reduced by $\frac{1}{5}$ of what is left *from the previous day*, NOT $\frac{1}{5}$ of the total. (A) is a trap answer. Essentially, each day there is $\frac{4}{5}$ of the previous day's snow. It is safest to plug in. If $x = 100$, that's the measurement on March 17. Multiply by $\frac{4}{5}$ to find March 18 has 80 inches. Multiply that by $\frac{4}{5}$ (or 0.8) to find March 19 has 64 inches. Multiply that by 0.8 to find March 20 has 51.2 inches. Multiply that by 0.8 to find March 21 has 40.96 inches. This is the target answer, what the answer choice should yield when we put our chosen numbers in. Plug in the value for x into the answer choices, and only (C) gives 40.96. Be careful; (B) gives the result for March 20.

29. **0** Because $\dfrac{x}{y} = 1$, $x = y$. Therefore, any numbers we plug in will result in $2x - 2y = 0$.

30. **3** Because all angles are 90°, draw on the given figure to see more clearly the rectangles and squares within. This is helpful because opposite sides of rectangles are equal. A line parallel to $\overline{AB}$ from the bottom of the right-hand side of the figure shows that the top portion of $\overline{AB}$ is 2 units long. A line parallel to $\overline{AB}$ from point B shows that the rest of $\overline{AB}$ is 1 unit long, for a total of 3 units.

31. **16** Since opposite sides add up to 10, the three unseen sides are 8 (10 − 2), 2 (10 − 8), and 6 (10 − 4), which add up to 16.

32. **15** Do this problem one step at a time. 25 cashmere sweaters cost $1,500, so each is $60. Cashmere is three times the cost of cotton, so cotton sweaters are $20. The total cost of all the sweaters is $1,800, $1,500 of which is cashmere, leaving $300 worth of cotton. $300 ÷ $20 = 15.

33. $\dfrac{4}{50}$, $\dfrac{2}{25}$, **or .08**

Eight ounces of tea must be divided evenly into 100 parts. $\dfrac{8}{100}$ can be reduced or converted into a decimal, 0.08.

34. **100** First list the factors of ten: {1, 10, 2, 5}. Then multiply. 10 × 2 × 5 = 100.

35. $\dfrac{2}{3}$, **.666, or .667**

Draw figures whenever they are described but not given, since it can often be helpful to understanding what's happening. TP is $\dfrac{2}{3}$ of TR; there is a $\dfrac{2}{3}$ chance of a random point landing on $\overline{TP}$.

36. **625** Try working this problem with an easy number, using the exponent rules (see question 23) to solve for n. If $x = 2$, then $125n^2 = n^5$. Divide both sides by n^2. $125 = n^3$, so $n = 5$. $125n$ therefore is 625. We can't plug in values for both x and n. One of the values must be determined by the relationship of the equation.

37. **130** Let's try using our own numbers. Since $ABCD$ is a rectangle, each corner has a value of 90°. As stated in the problem, $x = 40$. $\angle C$ measures 90°. There are 360° in any 4-sided figure, so make up appropriate values for the remaining corners of the diamond-shaped figure within the rectangle. Then we can use the rule of 180° in a straight line to find values for x and y. If the corner of the diamond next to y is 100°, then y is 80°. The corner of the diamond next to x must then be 130° (because of the 360° in a four-sided figure), thus x is 50°. We find that 80 + 50 = 130.

38. $\dfrac{4}{16}$, $\dfrac{1}{4}$, **or .25**

The formula for inverse variation is $a_1 b_1 = a_2 b_2$. Plug the original values for a and b into the first part of the equation to find that $12 = a_2 b_2$. Since the value $a = 48$ is given for the second part of the equation, solve for b. $12 = 48b$. Thus, $b = .25$.

SECTION 5

1. **E** Avoid ambiguity. (A), (B), (C), and (D) are not clear as to whom the *them* refers—parents or children. (E) makes the sentence clear.

2. **C** The verb *threw* is not underlined in the sentence and indicates that all action happened in the past. Be very suspicious of *-ing* verb forms! (A), (B), and (E) are all incorrect. (D) implies that every time O'Malley reads reviews, he throws the manuscript into the fire. Only (C) is in the past tense.

3. **A** The correct construction is *not only...but also*. (B) and (C) are missing the *but also* portion. (D) is missing the *not only* portion. (E) is jumbled and poorly written. Only (A) has the correct construction.

4. **D** As written, the sentence is not clear as to *who* remains *calm and collected*. (A) and (B) are missing a subject. (E) puts a comma between the subject (*to get*) and the verb (*demands*). (C) uses passive voice. Only (D) corrects the original error without introducing another one.

5. **A** (B) is a run-on sentence. (C) and (D) have parallelism errors. (E) indicates that Neil executed all these actions at the exact same time.

6. **D** The pronoun *you* does not agree with its noun *a person*. (A) and (B) both have this error. (C) and (E) both use *-ing* form of the verb, which is always suspicious. (D) is the most direct and clear.

7. **B** Avoid ambiguity. (A) is unclear as to *who* does not wear bathing suits. (C) does not specify the location as France; French people can be anywhere, but nude beaches are not. (D) is unnecessarily wordy. (E) indicates that no one wears bathing suits in France! (B) is the only option that clears up the ambiguity.

8. **D** (A) is wordy. (B) uses the conjunction *and*, when *but* is needed. (C) has a misplaced modifier, which indicates that the evidence was implicated rather than Nixon. (E) is awkward; it is conventional to mention a noun (*Watergate scandal*) before referring to it as a pronoun. Only (D) is without error.

9. **A** Only *the professor* could have *spent hours developing the essay questions*, so (A) is the correct answer. The other choices all contain modification errors.

10. **C** Since the proper idiom is *not only...but also*, you can eliminate (B). (A), (D), and (E) all violate parallelism. Only (C) completes the sentence in accordance with parallelism: *not only for x but also for y*.

11. **C** All items in a list must be parallel, so (B), (D), and (E) are incorrect. (A) includes the unidiomatic *both x...and y...and also z* construction. (C) uses correct parallelism.

12.   **E**   (A) The pronoun *it* is ambiguous. (B) and (C) both contain a comma splice. A fragment follows the semicolon in (D), but a clause is required. (E) correctly uses *for* to introduce a clause that explains why *Roger will lead the management team*.

13.   **A**   The pronoun *it* stands for *purpose*. So, to achieve parallelism, the construction *purpose may be* must be followed by a form of the verb "to be" (*what some think it is*) rather than some form of the verb "to do" (*what some think it does*). Thus, you can eliminate (C), (D), and (E). Parallelism also requires that the sentence include infinitive verbs: "The purpose of *x* is to *y* instead of to *z*." (A) uses this structure, but (B) does not, and can therefore be eliminated.

14.   **D**   In the versions of the sentence suggested by (A), (B), and (E), the pronoun *they* seems to refer to *courses*, which obviously cannot *put their knowledge to use*. (C) includes the singular pronoun *this*, which has no reference at all. Only (D) uses the correct idiom, since the students can put their knowledge to use during activities, and *which* is the pronoun best suited to replace *activities*.

15.   **C**   As written, the sentence structure implies that the students need to become more responsible about investing, since *students* comes right after the introductory phrase. This doesn't make any sense. This error is found in (A), (B), (D), and (E), along with some other errors. Only (C) correctly identifies who needs to be more responsible.

16.   **D**   Watch out for parallelism errors. Since *won acclaim as a singer* is not underlined, it must be correct. Only (D), *was trained as a dancer*, matches with *won acclaim as a singer*. Jumbling up the tenses in the other answer choices is a trap.

17.   **B**   Faulty comparison. Poetry must be compared to poetry, not to people. (A) compares *poetry* to *others*; (C) compares *poetry* to a *poet*. *Different than* in (D) and (E) is incorrect; the correct construction is *different from*. Only (B) has no errors.

18.   **C**   As written, this sentence has inconsistent use of pronouns—*one* does not agree with *theirs*. (A), (B), and (D) all contain this error. (E) is jumbled and unclear.

19.   **C**   The *attempt* was not unprepared, the *lawyer* was. This is a misplaced modifier problem. (A) and (B) repeat this error. (D) is wordy, and (E) is redundant—we know the lawyer failed, so it is clear that he attempted to succeed without using the word *attempted*. Only (C) corrects the error without introducing another one.

20.   **C**   A pronoun must agree with the subject. *The average person* needs a single subject. (A) and (B) each has a plural pronoun. The action of (D) is not as direct as that in (C). (E) does not have agreement in number: only one body per person!

21.   **C**   *And* is not the correct conjunction to use here. The correct construction is *not only…but also*.

22.   **D**   When comparing two things, the correct construction is *between…and*. The word *plus* is never used in this case.

23. **E** This sentence is correct as written.

24. **C** Since the non-underlined verb *excelled* is in the past tense, *serving* is incorrect. *Served* would be better because it maintains consistent tense in the sentence.

25. **A** There must be agreement between nouns that refer to the same thing. Since *twins* is plural, they want to be *members* of the team.

26. **C** When referring to people, always use *who* or *whom,* not *which* if you use a pronoun. The sentence would also be correct if the underlined portion of (C) were eliminated altogether.

27. **D** Verb agreement requires all verbs to be in the past tense. Replacing *and must* with *and had to* shows the necessity as well as the proper tense.

28. **B** This is a faulty comparison. The professors prefer Michelangelo's *painting* to his *sculpture.* The verb *viewing* should be deleted to preserve the proper comparison.

29. **E** This sentence is correct as written.

30. **B** Because *improvements* is plural, we need *have made.* Be careful when there are lots of words between the subject and the verb.

31. **E** This sentence is correct as written.

32. **A** When two singular subjects are joined by *and,* the subject is plural. The pronoun *they* supports this, as well. The verb *are* is required here.

33. **C** Rome is a city and is singular. Therefore, *it has* would be correct here.

34. **B** This sentence requires the future tense *will not,* since it refers to something that has not happened but will need to happen in the future to avoid an unpleasant situation.

35. **B** As written, the sentence is in the passive voice. (A) and (D) are no better; *being* can usually be replaced by more active verbs. (C), *Grown up,* is not a verb; it is an adjective. (E) is missing the word *if,* which is necessary in order for the sentence to make sense.

36. **E** (A) and (B) are ambiguous as to whom the *them* refers, *children* or *patrons.* (C) and (D) are wordy and not much more specific. (E) is specific and clear.

37. **B** Mentioning specific precautions would connect to the main idea of the passage (what the town can do to make museums more accessible). In (A), the emphasis is on results of misbehavior. Neither (C) nor (D) connects to the main idea of the passage. (E) would not fit in with the context of the paragraph.

38. **B** This is the topic sentence of the conclusion, and thus should sum up the passage. (A) is too specific, although it would be a good transition to a paragraph all about precautions. (C), (D), and (E) make the sentence less clear than the original sentence; none creates a reasonable cause-and-effect relationship indicated by *because* in the sentence.

39. **C** As the original sentence is written in choice (A), the verbs do not agree with each other: All verbs should be in the present tense after *but if*. The conjunction *so* in (B) does not fit the meaning of the sentence. (D) and (E) do not have the correct verb forms.

SAT INSIDER

The Princeton Review's Bonus Materials

PART 1: 25 TIPS FOR FINANCIAL AID

PART 2: HOW TO WRITE YOUR COLLEGE
ADMISSIONS ESSAY

PART 3: PLANNING THE PERFECT COLLEGE VISIT

Part 1

25 Tips for Getting Financial Aid, Scholarships, and Grants and for Paying Less for College

by Kalman A. Chany, author of
Paying for College Without Going Broke
(Random House/Princeton Review Books)

GETTING FINANCIAL AID

1.   Learn how the financial aid process works. The more and the sooner you know about the process, the better you can take steps to maximize your aid eligibility.

2.   Apply for financial aid no matter what your circumstances. Some merit-based aid can only be awarded if the applicant has submitted financial aid application forms.

3.   Don't wait until you receive your acceptance letter to your top choice school to apply for financial aid. Do it when applying for admission.

4.   Complete all the required aid applications. All students seeking aid must submit the FAFSA (Free Application for Federal Student Aid); however, other forms may also be required by individual schools. Check with each college to see what's required and when.

5.   Get the best scores you can on the SAT or ACT. They are used not only in decisions for admission but also financial aid. If your scores and other stats exceed the school's admission criteria, you are likely to get a better aid package than a marginal applicant.

6.   Apply strategically to colleges. Your chances of getting aid will be better at schools that have generous financial aid budgets.

7.   Don't rule out any school as too expensive. A generous aid award from a pricey private school can make it less costly than a public school with a lower sticker price.

8.   Take advantage of education tax benefits. A dollar saved on taxes is worth the same as a dollar in scholarship aid. Look into Coverdells, education tax credits, and loan deductions.

SCHOLARSHIPS AND GRANTS

9.   Get your best possible score on the PSAT: It is the National Merit Scholarship Qualifying Test and is also used in the selection of students for other scholarships and recognition programs.

10. Check your eligibility for grants and scholarships from your state. Some (but not all) states will allow you to use such funds out of state.

11. Look for scholarships locally. Find out if your employer offers scholarships or tuition assistance plans for employees or family

members. Also look into scholarships from your church, community groups, and high school.

12. Look for outside scholarships realistically: they account for less than five percent of aid awarded. Research them at princetonreview.com or other free sites. Steer clear of scholarship search firms that charge fees and "promise" scholarships.

PAYING FOR COLLEGE

13. Invest wisely. Considering a 529 plan? Compare your own state's plan which may have tax benefits with other states' programs. Get info at savingforcollege.com.

14. If you have to borrow, first pursue federal education loans (Perkins, Stafford, PLUS). Avoid private loans at all costs.

15. Never put tuition on a credit card. The debt is more expensive than ever given recent changes to interest rates and other fees some card issuers are now charging.

16. Try not to take money from a retirement account or 401(k) to pay for college. In addition to likely early distribution penalties and additional income taxes, the higher income will reduce your aid eligibility.

PAYING LESS FOR COLLEGE

17. Attend a community college for two years and transfer to a pricier school to complete the degree. Plan ahead: Be sure the college you plan to transfer to will accept the community college credits.

18. Look into "cooperative education" programs. Over 900 colleges allow students to combine college education with a job. It can take longer to complete a degree this way but graduates generally owe less in student loans and have a better chance of getting hired.

19. Take as many Advanced Placement (AP) courses as possible and get high scores on AP exams. Many colleges award course credits for high AP scores. Some students have cut a year off their college tuition this way.

20. Earn college credit via "dual enrollment" programs available at some high schools. These allow students to take college level courses during their senior year.

21. Earn college credits by taking CLEP (College-Level Examination Program) exams. Depending on the college, a qualifying score on any of the thirty-three CLEP exams can earn students three to twelve college credits. (See Princeton Review's *Cracking the CLEP*—5th Edition.)

22. Stick to your college and your major. Changing colleges can result in lost credits. Aid may be limited/not available for transfer students at some schools. Changing majors can mean paying for extra courses to meet requirements.

23. Finish college in three years if possible. Take the maximum number of credits every semester, attend summer sessions, and earn credits via online courses. Some colleges offer three-year programs for high-achieving students.

24. Let Uncle Sam pay for your degree. ROTC (Reserve Officer Training Corps) programs available from U.S. Armed Forces branches (except the Coast Guard) offer merit-based scholarships up to full tuition via participating colleges in exchange for military service after you graduate.

25. Better yet: Attend a tuition-free college!

Part 2

8 Essential Tips for Writing Your College Essay

Most selective colleges require you to submit an essay or personal statement. It may sound daunting to represent your best self in only a few hundred words, and it will certainly take a substantial amount of work. But it's also a unique opportunity that can make a big difference at decision time. Admissions committees put the most weight on your high school grades and your test scores. However, colleges receive applications from many worthy students, so they use your essay (along with your letters of recommendation and extracurricular activities) to find out what sets you apart from the other talented candidates.

1. What does set you apart?

Your background, interests and personality are things that make you more than just a GPA and a standardized test score. The best way to tell your story is to write a personal, thoughtful essay about something that has meaning for you. Be honest and genuine, and your unique qualities will shine through.

2. Sound like yourself!

For examples of strong application essays, check out The Princeton Review's book, *College Essays that Made a Difference.*

Admissions counselors have to read an unbelievable number of essays. Many students try to sound smart rather than sounding like themselves. Others write about a subject that they don't care about, but that they think will impress admissions brass. Don't write about the same subjects as every other applicant. You don't need to have started a company or discovered a lost Mayan temple. Colleges are simply looking for thoughtful, motivated students who will add something to the freshman class.

3. Write about something that's important to you.

It could be an experience, a person, a book–anything that has had an impact on your life. Don't just recount–reflect! Anyone can write about how they won the big game or the time they spent in Rome. Describe what you learned from the experience and how it changed you.

4. Predict the future!

You can also write about your future. Why do you want to attend this school, over any other? Steer clear of generalities (e.g., "to get a good liberal arts education") and stay specific (e.g., "I'm a future doctor and your science department has a terrific reputation"). Colleges are more likely to admit students who can articulate why the school is a good fit for them.

5. Be consistent, and avoid redundancies.

What you write in your application essay or personal statement should not contradict any other part of your application–nor should it repeat it. This isn't the place to list your awards or discuss your grades or test scores. Answer the question being asked. Don't reuse an answer to a similar question from another application.

6. Use humor with caution!

Being funny is a challenge. A student who can make an admissions officer laugh never gets lost in the shuffle. But beware: What you think is funny and what an adult working in a college thinks is funny might be very different. We caution against one-liners, limericks and anything off-color.

7. Start early and write several drafts.

Set the essay aside for a few days and read it again. Put yourself in the shoes of an admissions counselor: Is the essay interesting? Do the ideas flow logically? Does it reveal something about the applicant? Is it written in the applicant's own voice?

8. Ask for feedback!

Have at least one other person edit your essay—a teacher or college counselor is best. And before you send it off, triple check to make sure your essay is free of spelling or grammar errors. We recommend asking a second person to proofread your essay, as spellcheck and grammar software won't pick up every typo. It can be tricky to spot mistakes in your own work, especially after you've spent so much time writing and rewriting.

Part 3

Planning the Perfect College Visit: Advice for Before You Go & Questions to Ask When You're There

By The Staff of The Princeton Review

INTRODUCTION

If you're reading this book, you're probably either embarking on or in the middle of your college search. You've likely been swamped with information about how to pick a school—rankings, academic specialties, financial aid, location, et cetera—and your mailbox has been flooded with glossy promotional brochures. These are all great tools for weighing potential schools, but when it comes to researching, there's nothing more useful than an actual college visit. No website, guidebook, or testimonial will give you a better feel for a school than you'll get by actually showing up!

This section is intended to be a short, helpful guide to planning and getting the most out of your college visits. Inside, you'll find information about why a college visit is important, what you should look for while on campus, and what your observations can tell you about the students and culture there.

You'll also find useful information about the logistics of planning a visit, such as when to go, and learn what you should ask when you get there. At the end of the book, we provide a list of the most essential questions you should find answers for—you can use this as an easy, quick reference while you're visiting, or to help jump-start your own question-asking process.

Whether you're considering which colleges to apply to or trying to decide between schools where you're already accepted, a campus tour is a great—in fact, we'd say the best—way to get a sense of what life at a school will actually be like for you as a student. Best of luck—and have fun!

— The Editors of The Princeton Review

WHY SHOULD YOU DO A CAMPUS VISIT?

A campus visit won't tell you everything you need to know about life at your prospective college, but it will give you a richer, more detailed view than you would get from surfing websites, browsing brochures, watching videos, or reading college guides. Every school has its own culture, its own unique way of doing things, and you can't divine it from a brochure! And even though you won't learn all there is to know from a brief visit, you'll get a sense of the "big picture" issues that define life on a campus. You'll probably get enough of a sense of those issues to determine whether the school is a good fit for you.

Spend a weekday on campus while classes are in session and you'll get a feel for the rhythm of life there, the attitudes of the students towards their studies, and—if you get the chance to attend a few classes—some idea of the atmosphere in the school's classrooms. Visit over a weekend and you'll experience the school's social life (or lack thereof). You'll also find students relaxing and taking it easy, making it easier to approach them with any questions about the school that you may have.

Let's look at some of the benefits of a campus visit:

You'll get a feel for the academic atmosphere and whether it's a good fit for you

Academics are the primary reason you're attending college, so you want to know whether you and the school you're considering are a good academic fit. The quality of the school's academic life and the intensity of student-teacher relationships will strongly impact your experience at college. Look for clues about both during your campus visit.

If possible, attend a class or two during your visit (make sure to arrange for this with the LC well in advance of your visit). If asked for your preference, request to sit in on a class that is required for all freshmen so that you'll get a better sense of what your first year will be like—or, alternatively, try to pick a low-level class within the subject you're planning to major in, if you've already decided that. When you're there, keep your eyes and ears open. Are the classes huge or small? Is the teacher a full professor or a graduate student? Is the class format lecture, lab, discussion, or a hybrid of several formats? Are students' contributions to the class interesting? Are students furiously scribbling notes? Are they asking questions? Is "Will this be on the test?" the only question any of them asks? Answer these questions and you'll get a pretty good sense of how students approach their studies at the school and whether you'll be comfortable with that approach.

If you can't attend a class, at least take time to walk around campus and to observe the students and faculty. Pay close attention to students as they travel to and from class. Are they in a hurry? Do they look stressed? Or are they walking at a leisurely pace, conversing, and laughing? Do faculty members talk with students as they walk across campus? Do you even see faculty members walking across campus, or are they missing from the picture? If faculty members are conspicuously absent, it could mean that they have numerous commitments off campus (e.g., conferences, serving on corporate boards, or teaching at more than one school) that would leave them less time to devote to undergraduates on campus.

You'll get a feel for the type of student who attends the school

For many students, whom they go to school with is just as important as where they go to school and what they study. You may think this is a frivolous concern, but it's not; your fellow students will be your peers, friends, competitors, and, in some cases, rivals throughout your tenure at the school. If you're a bad fit with the student body, you could be in for four miserable years (fewer, probably, because most "bad fits" eventually transfer out; regardless, being the "sore thumb" at a school is an unpleasant scenario that you'll probably want to avoid).

There are lots of different issues to consider as you assess a student body. First, note the degree of similarity among students. Do they all look alike, or is the population diverse? Consider not just racial diversity but also economic diversity, religious diversity, and diversity of personality types. Are you more comfortable surrounded by people just like yourself, or do you want a college that will give you the opportunity to encounter people with different backgrounds and perspectives? More specifically, think about:

- *Class/Status:* Is the parking lot filled with new sports cars and SUVs? Or are most of the cars clunkers (if they are, make sure you haven't stumbled onto the faculty parking lot by mistake!)? Do students dress as though they do all their shopping at high-priced, name-brand stores? Do the men and women seem especially fashion-conscious? Are they outfitted in nice but affordable clothing? Are students flashing a lot of high-priced gadgets or the newest, hottest technology? Ask yourself, "Can I envision myself a part of this community?" For many students, answering this question means having to think about class issues and the social circles they feel the most comfortable navigating.

- **Personality type:** Do you see lots of students in sweats and sneakers? Or are most students decked out in alpaca sweaters, skinny jeans, or pearls? Is the campus an ocean of polo shirts? The way students dress can tell you about more than their economic status; it can also tell you about the group or personality type with which they associate. You'll be surprised at how many students you will immediately identify as jocks, hippies, preps, nerds, etc. You've probably encountered most of these personality types in high school. Which type reigns supreme on campus, if any? Is this a group you're comfortable spending four years among? Keep in mind, of course, that you can't judge a book entirely by its cover. Before you draw any definitive conclusions about students' personalities, talk with some students. You may well find that college students don't fit your assumptions as neatly as do your peers in high school.

- **Intellectualism:** Observe students in class, at the library, and in conversation as they walk across campus. Do you get the sense that students study primarily for the sake of learning? Or is their primary goal to score a high-paying job? If you're the type who wants to stay up all night discussing Plato, you won't likely be happy at a school full of pre-professionals with little interest in pure academics. Conversely, if your only goal is to get great grades in order to get into the best med, law, or b-school, you probably won't be happy at a school with a bunch of philosophizing dreamers.

- **Religion:** Are students religious? Are there frequent and obvious demonstrations of religious belief across campus? Deeply religious students may find the rampant secularism of many college campuses off-putting. Students with a more secular bent will likely have a hard time adjusting to life on deeply religious campuses, particularly those with strict behavioral codes or those where students openly proselytize.

- **Sexuality/Gender Issues:** To what extent do couples display affection on campus? Do you see indicators of an active and accepted gay community (e.g., posters for GLBT events)? Here's another area where it can be important to find a good personal fit. Socially conservative students may be uncomfortable on a campus with a large and active gay community, such as New York University or Smith. Conversely, gay students may be uncomfortable on campuses with profoundly conservative social attitudes.

While it's important for the school's academic program to be the right fit for you, it's just as important for the campus community to be a good fit, too. A college visit, even a brief one, will give you a good sense of who your classmates will be and whether you'll be comfortable among them. Yes, it's true: You really can't know exactly what a school is going to be like until you get there. Even your own opinion of your college experience will change as you grow more accustomed to being on campus. In the meantime, as you're searching, trust your instincts. The real "scoop" lies not so much in the specific information you receive, as the applicability of the information to your interests, needs, and wants.

So know your priorities. Exactly what type of atmosphere are you looking for? Urban or rural? Big or small? Laid-back or focused? Getting a handle on what will make you, specifically, a happy individual at college is half the battle.

You'll get a feel for extracurricular life

Your college experience will consist of more than studying and hanging out with friends. There will be all sorts of clubs and organizations available for participation, and you may want to join one or more. That's why it's important to explore the extracurricular life of a school. What do students do when they're not in class, in the library, or hanging around the dorms with friends? A campus visit can give you an idea, especially if you plan an overnight stay. As you make your inspection, look for evidence of the following:

- *Active clubs and organizations:* All schools have some clubs and organizations, but what those are exactly will vary from school to school. You can find out which clubs are registered on campus by visiting the student activity center, where a list of the school's organizations is usually posted. In addition, most schools list all their clubs and organizations on their websites; many provide separate sites for each group. Look for posters announcing meetings and events to determine which groups are most active.

- *Greek organizations:* Does the school have a Greek scene? How active is it? Is it simply one aspect of campus life, or is it the dominant feature? Are lots of students wearing T-shirts and sweatshirts emblazoned with the names of their houses? Are there posters around campus announcing upcoming parties at Greek houses? Ask students—Greeks and independents alike—about the school's fraternity and sorority scene. Their answers will reveal what you can expect from the social scene on campus.

- **The party scene:** The Greek scene and the party scene are synonymous at some schools, but not at all of them. Some schools have no Greek organizations. Others place strict restrictions on Greek parties, forcing the party scene elsewhere. At many schools the Greek houses are the locus of parties for underclassmen, while students of drinking age prefer local bars or even smaller parties at their apartments or houses. And some schools have minimal party scenes: military academies, single-sex schools, and religious schools are the most likely candidates, but small schools with large commuter populations or a large in-state population (at some schools, in-state students leave campus for the weekend immediately after their last class of the week) can also be relatively party-free. Whether you're looking for a year-round Mardi Gras, a cloister, or something in between, you should consider the school's party scene when choosing your undergraduate institution. Even if you have no interest in partying—especially if you have no interest in partying, really—the intensity of the party scene will have a big impact on your life at school. Don't wait until your roommate is vomiting on your bed to figure this out! During your visit, survey the campus for evidence of an active party scene: dumpsters full of empties, posters advertising huge blowout parties, bleary-eyed students in pajamas straggling across campus in the early afternoon, etc. Better still, schedule a weekend visit so you can experience the party scene firsthand.

- **The arts:** Some schools house well-known museums and frequently host touring theatrical, musical, and dance productions. Others host regular student theatrical and musical productions, galleries displaying student and faculty art, and a steady diet of movies, old and new. Still others have practically no arts scene at all; there's no interest on campus, so it doesn't exist. If your idea of fun is a Truffaut double feature or a night of experimental theatre, make sure you find a school that can accommodate you. Scan the bulletin boards for notices about upcoming arts events. Survey the campus map for evidence of student galleries, art and dance studios, concert halls, etc.

- **Athletics:** Most schools have some form of an athletic program, but the degree to which athletics are a major campus focal point varies greatly from school to school. At some schools, football or basketball season is the high point of the school year; students are passionate about their teams and build their schedules around games, camping out to get tickets and tailgating enthusiastically for hours before the start of an event. You'll see evidence of students' devotion at these sports-happy schools in the form of banners, pennants, bumper stickers, T-shirts, etc. At other schools, athletics are an afterthought, and if you ask students about the football team they're likely to respond, "We have a football team?" If college athletics are important to you, you probably shouldn't attend such a school.

- ***The neighborhood around campus and the school's hometown:*** Try to save time to tour the town or city in which the school is located. If you can't, at least take a walk around the surrounding neighborhood to see what sort of off-campus housing, restaurants, clubs, and retail shops are easily accessible. If you visit enough schools, you'll probably notice that campus life is generally much more active in schools located in smaller towns. At big-city schools—schools in New York City, Boston, and Chicago, for example—students tend to seek their fun off-campus, and for good reason: Few schools could compete with all the options that a big city offers.

WHEN IS THE BEST TIME TO VISIT COLLEGES?

There are two timing issues to consider in this question: the best time in the school's schedule, and the best time in your tenure as a high schooler. Let's look at both.

Best Times To Visit During The College Academic Year

The best time to visit a school is when the school is in session. Yes, it's probably easier to visit schools during the summer when you're on vacation, but the trouble is that the school is on break then, too. You'll be able to see the campus and take a tour, but you won't be able to attend classes (summer classes are nothing like classes held during the regular academic year), and you won't get to see what the campus looks like when it's full of students. You won't get to see the students (or most of the professors and administrators, for that matter), so you won't be able to get a sense of how well you'll fit into the campus community. You won't get a good feel for the school, so you'll be missing out on the most important part of your campus visit.

During the school year, avoid visiting during school holidays such as Thanksgiving and Spring Break. Also, try not to visit during exam periods or reading periods (the few days or week of study time that precedes final exams, during which no classes are scheduled). It'll be difficult to attend a class during those times, and students will be preoccupied with exams and probably a little frazzled. They won't be in the mood to chat with you about their school, because they won't have the time. Visit during these periods and you'll get a skewed impression of the school. You'll probably walk away thinking the students are all basket cases!

Fitting a College Visit Into Your High School Schedule

Exploit your vacation time and off days. When is your spring break? Use it to visit colleges that aren't on break at the same time. Check your school's calendar for three-day weekends; some colleges don't observe national holidays and you can use those weekends for a Sunday overnight visit and attend some college classes on Monday. And remember that overnight visits should be scheduled well in advance, as they require extra planning both on your part and on the part of the school.

As for your own high school schedule, when is the best time in your high school career to visit colleges? The short answer is that, essentially, any time after you start seriously considering college choices is good. In practice this can depend on what your goals for the trips are, where you already are in the college application process, and, of course, financial constraints.

Some students prefer to wait until they've already applied and have heard back from schools, and use college visits to help make their decision between schools where they've already been accepted. This can also help avoid "wasting" money on visiting a school where they aren't accepted. In this case, you'd necessarily need to plan visits in the spring of your senior year.

In an ideal world, though, you could visit schools earlier in the process in order to decide where you want to apply. During your sophomore year and the autumn semester of your junior year, you should try to visit lots of different types of schools—big schools, small schools, urban campuses, suburban/rural campuses, private liberal arts schools, public universities— to see what options are available to you. Intensify your efforts during the spring semester of junior year and throughout senior year, and also intensify your focus; hone in on those schools about which you are most serious. While you're a junior and during the autumn semester of senior year, you should try to pay daytime visits to all the schools on your short list, and you should try to schedule overnight visits for at least some of the schools that interest you most.

When you reach the end of your visits and it comes time to compare the schools you visited, remember to take into account the time of year of your visit. Most campuses are at their most alluring in the early autumn and late spring. Conversely, some schools can be pretty austere, even forbidding, in the height of winter. Don't let the season of your visit unduly influence your final decision positively or negatively.

HOW TO ASK THE RIGHT QUESTIONS

No matter how the information session is organized, at some point you'll get a chance to ask questions. Do so! It gives you a chance to learn about something that truly interests you and it provides an opportunity to impress the session leader with what an articulate and thoughtful person you are.

Lots and lots of questions are listed later, but here are a few rules of thumb when asking questions:

Ask about something that is of particular interest to you

Do you hope to study abroad in a particular country? Ask about the availability of international education programs. Are you interested in pursuing independent study in a particular field? Ask about the opportunities and resources that will be available to you. Would you like to get related work/internship experience while at school? Ask about available cooperative learning programs.

Don't ask about data and other information that can be easily found in the school's promotional material

Asking about average SAT scores, the number of volumes in the school library, the student:teacher ratio, etc., communicates that you are too lazy to find this readily accessible information yourself. It also suggests that you're asking a question simply for the sake of asking a question, which fails to demonstrate genuine interest in attending that particular school.

If you are accompanied by your parents, politely suggest that they let you ask most of the questions

The school is considering you for admission, not your parents. Parents who ask long-winded questions designed mostly to show off how much they know about the school may think they are making a good impression, but their effect is actually the opposite.

Be polite

Present yourself well; don't slouch, don't chew gum, and speak politely. If your parents have accompanied you, don't bicker with them. And for goodness' sake, don't tell the person conducting the information session that the school is your "safety" or that you'll only attend if you receive a monster scholarship (true stories). Remember: tact is key.

GUIDELINES FOR PARENTS

Be supportive, be positive, be patient: A college visit is a stressful time for everyone. Behave in a way most likely to minimize stress.

Schedule plenty of extra time in the itinerary

Nothing creates stress more effectively than running late for important appointments. Plan to spend at least three hours on each campus you visit. Build plenty of buffer time into your travel plans to and from campuses and to and from appointments on campus. Follow these guidelines and you shouldn't find yourself constantly rushing from one place to the next. Worst case scenario, you have some extra time on one of the campuses you're visiting—that's a win-win. Use the extra time to check out popular campus hangout spots.

Don't try to run the show

From the planning of the trip through its execution, consult with your child about the itinerary. Is s/he ready for on-campus interviews? How many campuses does s/he feel capable of assimilating in one day? Once on campus, resist the temptation to advocate for your child or to manage your child's on-campus experience. Give your child plenty of opportunities to explore on his or her own. And under no circumstances should you try to participate in your child's on-campus interview. It sends a terrible message to the school (i.e., our child is not self-sufficient enough to handle this experience) and almost always produces bad results.

Utilize your child's free time efficiently

While your child is exploring campus on his or her own, make your own inquiries. Check out the surrounding area to see whether it looks safe. Search for reasonably priced restaurants and shopping near campus. Visit dormitories, dining halls, computer labs, science labs, arts facilities, and whatever else might be of interest to your child.

Take pictures

Let's face it—this is way too embarrassing for your kid to be seen doing (your students will be focused on fitting in, not standing out!), but you, on the other hand, can snap away without any embarrassment. These photos will go a long way toward helping your child compare schools later.

Talk to other parents

Find out what other parents think about the school, what concerns they have, and what their questions are. Listening to them will help clarify some of your own concerns—you may even learn about a new scholarship, a new college financing program, or the name of another great school for your child to consider!

GUIDELINES FOR STUDENTS

Set goals in advance

What exactly do you hope to learn from your visit? Know before you go and you'll get a lot more out of it. Make a list of questions you want to answer during your trip (and check out the lists provided for you at the end of this book). You may not get to ask all your questions, but just having listed them will help focus your observations while on campus.

Wear comfortable shoes, but dress nicely

You'll be doing a lot of walking, so choose shoes that won't turn your feet into hamburger meat. Otherwise, dress nicely; remember, you're a guest in someone else's home and you should carry yourself accordingly. That means behaving in a respectful manner, which includes dressing well. A presentable outfit is especially important if you've scheduled an on-campus interview.

Don't be afraid to ask questions during your tour

Don't be shy. You're on campus to find out what you need to know; asking questions is the best way to get that done. Don't hog the tour guide's attention, but don't be a wallflower either.

Don't be unduly influenced by the tour guide

Your tour guide may seem really cool, or he/she may seem like a total dork. Either way, the guide is just one of many students who attend the school; don't judge the school based on this one person. Try to meet as many other students as you can to get a broad picture of the student body. Visit the student center and the dining hall. Introduce yourself to students and ask if they wouldn't mind answering questions. If possible, schedule an overnight visit with a stay in a host student's dorm room (many colleges offer this—just talk to the admissions office when you're scheduling your visit).

Keep a journal

We don't mean you actually have to take notes while you're visiting campus…although it's not a bad idea! At the very least, you should record your observations and insights about each campus you visit at the end of each day of visiting. You'll probably be visiting a lot of campuses. A journal will help you remember what you liked and didn't like about each school you visited.

Snap a few pictures

Maybe you can recruit your parents to be the "real" tourists, but even if not, snap a few pictures of things about the campus that you really like so you can look back on the day when it's time to make decisions about which schools to take off your list.

9 STEPS TO A SUCCESSFUL VISIT

The logistics of organizing a multi-stop, multi-day trip is a daunting task. Following the nine steps outlined below makes it a lot easier.

Step 1: Determine when you are free to take a trip

Check your school calendar to figure out when you have weeks off, three-day weekends, etc. If you plan to miss a day or two of school in order to accommodate your trip, figure out when your exams are scheduled and make sure you're not traveling during those days or during the week before.

Step 2: Identify all the schools you want to visit and then group them by geographic area

Collate the academic schedules of the schools you wish to visit with the dates of your planned trip. If possible, plan to visit the geographic region whose schools mesh best with your travel days. Try to avoid visiting campuses during holidays (e.g., Thanksgiving, Christmas, and Spring Break), reading periods, and exam periods.

Step 3: Create an itinerary

Map out the locations of the schools you plan to visit. If you have to fly to visit colleges, try to coordinate general geographic regions, and figure out if you'll be able to rent a car to drive between locations. If driving, try to map a course that connects the schools in a single loop, as this will minimize driving time. Even if you're interested in three schools within a half-hour of each other, plan to visit no more than two schools per day.

Step 4: Tinker with the itinerary

Now that you know where you're going, look closely at the map. Are there other schools you might consider that are along your route? Make a note to squeeze in a quick visit to one or more schools. Also, take time to find out whether there are some fun sights to see along your route. Yeah, this trip is about seeing schools, but that doesn't mean you can't have a little fun, time permitting.

Step 5: Call the admissions offices of the schools you plan to visit

Schedule an interview if you choose to. Find out what time tours begin and end. If you're scheduling more than one campus visit per day, make sure to leave extra time at each school to wander around campus, talk with students, and explore the neighborhood and town surrounding the school.

Step 6: Create a daily schedule

Start with the appointments you've made. Then figure out when you have to arrive and leave each school in order to make it to all your appointments. Use an online itinerary planner (such as Google Maps, randmcnally.com, or mapquest.com) to estimate your travel time between schools.

Step 7: Make your overnight arrangements

Find places to stay. If you're planning on staying on campus, make sure to contact the school and make arrangements at least two weeks in advance. Calling a month in advance is better; two months in advance, better still. If you travel with your parents, they will probably need to find a place to stay off campus. Contact the school to ask for recommendations. Schools sometimes have prearranged discount rates with local hotels and motels.

Step 8: Write out or print out your entire itinerary

Be sure it includes maps to and from schools and hotels, driving directions, all the phone numbers you may need, etc. Research any local dining and shopping establishments you're interested in visiting and print out their names, addresses, and telephone numbers.

Step 9: Write out a list of questions you want to ask at the schools

This is the only way to avoid that "Rats, I wish I'd asked about…" feeling that comes about an hour after you've left the campus. We have lists and lists of questions at the end of this book to help you make sure you get all the information you need—be sure to read them through and then add any questions particular to *you*.

When you finally hit the road, don't forget to enjoy yourself. Yes, college visits are important and should be taken seriously, but they are also wonderful adventures to new and exciting places. Soak it all in and be grateful that you're smart enough and capable enough to be looking forward to a college education. It's easy to take all that for granted, but you don't have to step back too far to gain some perspective and realize what a fortunate position you're in. So don't be afraid to have a little fun on your trip; you've earned it!

KEY PLACES TO VISIT

Remember to leave time after the tour/information session to walk around campus on your own. Although the promotional material, the tour, and the information session will all be helpful, they all represent an image of the school packaged by public relations professionals. You want to spend some time seeing the school without that filter. Visit whatever buildings you can access without school identification. High on your list of "must visit" places should be the main freshman dormitory (you'll probably be living there if you attend), the dining hall (buy lunch and try to imagine eating this food every day of the week; also, try to work your way into a group of current students chatting among themselves on campus so you can ask them about the school); finally, make sure you visit the general information library (this is where books for required courses will be on reserve and thus is a place where you could spend a lot of your freshman year). You should also check out the student union, the athletic facilities, and any other facilities you expect to use. Are all these facilities up-to-date and well maintained? Can you imagine yourself happy in this setting? You should also spend some time exploring the neighborhood around campus.

You should try to attend at least one class while on campus. This will require some extra planning, as you will probably need to schedule your classroom visit in advance with the admissions office. Ideally, the school will send you to a class that's required for all freshmen. Unless the professor calls specifically on you, do not try to participate in the class. You are just there to observe, not to overwhelm your future classmates with your brilliance. Stay for the entire class no matter how boring it is; it's rude to get up and leave a class that's in session. And this may go without saying, but please remember to turn off your cell phone before you enter the classroom!

That's a whole lot of activity to cram into one visit, which is one of the reasons admissions professionals advise against visiting more than two campuses in one day. The other reason is sensory overload—visit more than two schools in a day and they all start to blend into one amorphous blob-school! Take notes during your visits (or immediately after) so that you can remember what you liked and disliked about each school. If you visit a lot of schools you will have a hard time remembering which details pertain to which school if you don't take notes.

Your campus visit presents an incredible opportunity to get the skinny on life at college from the real experts—the students in attendance. Don't be shy about going up to a student and asking them the tough questions—you'll be happy you did.

THE ESSENTIAL TIP LIST FOR GETTING THE MOST OUT OF YOUR COLLEGE VISIT

Since sometimes it's helpful to have everything boiled down to the basics, this section condenses our most essential tips for getting the most out of your college visit into one place. If your college visits are spread out over a long period of time and you don't have time to go back and re-read a section, or you want a quick reminder about what to look for right before you hit a campus, just visit this section for a refresher!

Visit as many colleges as you can

If possible, visit every college that you are strongly considering. Many students change their minds after a college visit. That's great—it means the visit has done its job. And this is obviously preferable to changing your mind after you enroll!

Mind the calendar

Schedule your visit while school is in session. You won't get a realistic idea of student life in August (or if you attend during a special event like Spring Fling).

Meet the experts

Talk to the current students—they may soon be your peers. If they have a problem or grievance, they will probably share it with you. If they love their school, they won't be shy about it either. Specific questions yield far more interesting (and helpful) answers. Here are a few questions to ask:

- What are the best reasons to go here?
- Why made you choose this school over others that you were considering?
- What do you do on weekends?
- What do you love about this college?
- What things frustrate you about this college?
- What do students complain about most?
- Did you have friends that were going here before you?
- Have you changed your major? (If so, why?)
- Are students friendly?

Meet the other experts

Stop by the admissions office and introduce yourself. Let them know what interests you about the school so they can direct you to the best place for further investigation. Collect contact information and send a brief, friendly email thanking them for taking the time to talk to you. If there is a sign-up sheet, add your name! Colleges do keep track of which applicants have demonstrated genuine interest in the school. A visit is a great way to demonstrate your interest. Some schools will let you interview with an admissions rep during your campus visit. If this opportunity is available, don't pass it up.

Take the campus tour

Although it's the most obvious thing to do, the official campus tour is worth your while. (Find out if you need to register to get a spot.) It gives the school a chance to show its best face, like the brand-spankin' new theater or their rooftop planetarium. While you're walking around, check out the flyers and bulletin boards and pick up a school newspaper to get a sense of what's going on … then venture out on your own. The official tour will probably steer you clear of the school's less attractive features, like the shoddy dining hall or the tiny gymnasium. Take your own unofficial tour by wandering around campus. If there are any facilities that are important to you, find them and have a look for yourself. Make sure your destinations include the freshmen dormitories.

Be a student for a day (or night)

Some schools sponsor overnight programs in which you can stay with a current student. This is a great opportunity to get a deeper sense of campus life and interact with your potential future friends and roommates. Even if you don't stay over, most schools will allow you to sit in on lectures. Browse the course catalogue before you arrive, or ask the admissions office what classes are in session that day.

Save the best for last

You'll get better at visiting colleges with practice. As you compare schools, you pick up on the aspects you like and the aspects you're not so fond of. You also figure out the right questions to ask, as well as the best campus spots to gauge student life. For that reason, visit your favorite schools last, so you'll be in the best position to make comparisons to the others on your list.

Don't rush to judgment

Be careful not to rush to judgment if the weather's bad or the class you attended is boring. There are bound to be sunny days and more interesting classes. At the same time, trust your gut. Sometimes it's love at first sight. Other times, something feels wrong (even if you can't put your finger on it).

Keep a record of every college visit

We recommend jotting down a few notes after every college visit. This may seem pointless, but trust us—after visiting the ninth or tenth school, you'll have a hard time remembering which one had the killer cafeteria or the great library. Keep track of the details you like and the stuff that you don't like, and when more questions arise (as they most definitely will) you can fire off an email for an answer rather than visiting a second time. Your notes will be helpful when you decide where to apply (and, after you're admitted, where to go). They should be candid and real. They're for you—not your parents or college counselor. Be honest with yourself and trust your gut.

CHEAT SHEET: THE MOST IMPORTANT QUESTIONS TO ASK WHILE ON CAMPUS

We've compiled some of the most useful questions to ask while you're visiting colleges, grouped by subject. Some are no-brainers—you're going to need to know about dorms pretty much everywhere—but not all of these questions will apply for every school, and you may also already be familiar with the answers from a college's admissions brochure.

We encourage you to read through the lists below and use them both as checklists and as jumping-off points for thinking about the *specific* questions you might have. Your college-specific questions can be prompted either by the particular features of a school (for instance, is there a program that appealed to you in the college brochure that you want to know more about?) or about how you might fit in there (i.e., if your hobby is photography, do you want to know if there's a darkroom available on campus?). Feel free to photocopy this list and take it with you when you're visiting schools. Use the space underneath each question as well as the sidebars to write in your answer. Even if you don't want to take actual notes while touring the campus, looking through it on your way back from a visit can help you recall what you saw and heard before it slips your mind.

Applying/Admissions

- Does the school recommend the ACT or the SAT?

- Is the writing portion of the ACT or SAT required?

- Is there an early action or early decision option?

- How much weight is given to essays and interviews?

- What does the school look for in an applicant?

- How many students apply for how many positions?

- What are my options if I'm waitlisted?

- What else goes with the application (transcript, essay, recommendations, etc.)?

Academics

- What are the most prominent majors and programs?

- Are those majors more difficult to get accepted into?

- Do they offer the major in my area of interest?

- How large or small are the classes?

- What is the student/faculty ratio (especially for the freshman class)?

- Are there freshman seminars?

- How much contact is there between students and professors?

- Are professors required to teach undergraduate courses or do they mostly focus on research?

- Are classes taught by graduate students, especially freshman classes?

- Are there research opportunities with professors?

- What is the Honors Program like?

- Is there a special winter or summer term?

- Who are the best professors?

- What is the quality of the student advising?

- Is there tutoring help on campus?

- How do we contact the office that helps students with learning disabilities?

- How do we contact the office that helps international students?

Administration

- How hard/easy is it to work with the administration?

- How hard/easy is it to work with the financial aid office?

- Does it seem like there is a lot of red tape or bureaucracy?

- How hard/easy is it to register for classes?

- How hard/easy is it to change classes/majors/departments?

- Is it easy to get face-time with administrators?

Dorm/Housing

- How many dorms are there?

- How are the dorms different from each other?

- What are the options (co-ed, suite-style, freshman, houses, honors)?

- Are students required to live on campus?

- Do most freshmen live on campus?

- Is there guaranteed housing for freshmen?

- What's the off-campus housing situation like?

- How are roommates paired up?

- What if that roommate doesn't work out?

- How many roommates per room for different dorms?

- What are the laundry facilities like?

- Are there curfews?

- What kind of security/entry is there for dorms?

- Are there refrigerators/microwaves/group kitchens?

- Are there dedicated study areas?

- Are there dorm events?

- Do the dorms close down during holidays?

Food

- What are the on-campus food options?

- What are the hours for the on-campus food options?

- What are the local/off-campus food options?

- Are there vegetarian/vegan options?

- How much of the food is bought locally?

- Is there a meal plan?

- How does the meal plan work (like debit card or per meal)?

- How much is the meal plan?

- How is the amount for the meal plan billed/paid for?

Extracurricular and Social Activities

- How many clubs, activities, and athletics are at the college?

- How do you sign up for clubs?

- What are the most popular student groups on campus?

- What is there to do on the weekends?

- Are there fraternities and sororities?

- How prominent are fraternities and sororities on campus?

- How prominent is drinking on campus?

- How prominent are drugs on campus?

- What activities are there that don't involve drinking and drugs?

- What kind of events are planned by the campus activities board?

- Are there lots of religious events?

- What kinds of events are school-sponsored?

- What kinds of speakers come to campus?

- What kinds of bands come to campus?

- Do students hang out on campus on the weekends, or do they hit up local venues?

- Are there many student theater productions?

Athletics

- What kind of intercollegiate sports are prominent on campus?

- How do you purchase student tickets for sports events?

- What kind of intramural sports are prominent on campus?

- What kinds of sports facilities are available on campus?

- How much scholarship money goes for student athletes?

- What kinds of sports facilities and activities are there in the local community?

- Do athletes have special housing?

- Are admissions requirements different for athletes?

Technology

- How much of campus is Wi-Fi enabled?

- Are classrooms set up for laptops?

- Are there online classes?

- Do professors generally post class notes?

- How much of teacher-student interaction is online?

- How many computer labs are there on campus?

- Are computer labs 24 hours?

- Are textbooks available as ebooks?

Surrounding Town

- How well does the college get along with the surrounding town?

- What is the local social scene like?

- What is the crime rate in town?

- What are the job prospects like in the local town?

- What are the larger companies in town?

- Do they recruit interns from this college?

- What kinds of public transportation are available in town?

- Where is the local shopping center?

- Where is the closest grocery store?

- What other area colleges are around here?

- What other towns/cities are around here?

Transportation

- Are freshmen allowed to have cars on campus?

- What is parking like?

- How much commuter parking is there?

- How much residential parking is there?

- How much does parking cost?

- Are there trolley or bus routes on campus?

- Is there transportation from campus to local areas?

- How late does that transportation run?

- Is there a bike-share program on campus?

- Is theft from cars a problem on campus?

- Is a car necessary to get around the town?

- How much will parking tickets cost?

- Is there a shuttle from campus to the airport?

- Are there late-night shuttles or taxis available?

- Is there a car-share program on campus (Zipcar)?

Study Abroad

- What percentage of students study abroad at some point during their four years?

- What countries do students go to?

- How do you sign up for study abroad?

- How do those credits count toward graduation?

- About how much does it cost?

- Does financial aid cover study abroad?

Financial

- How much is tuition?

- What other charges are there (room and board, fees, computers, etc)?

- What types of scholarships or financial aid is available?

- When are the deadlines for the forms?

- What do you need to do to apply?

- Are there jobs available on or near campus, if you want to work? How easy or difficult is it to secure one?

Internships/Career

- What percentage of students receive jobs in their field of interest after graduation?

- Is there a job or career placement program?

- What internship programs or opportunities are available?

Politics

- Are students mostly conservative on campus?

- Are students mostly liberal on campus?

- Are students very politically active on campus?

Religion

- How actively religious are students on campus?

- What is the dominant religion on campus?

- How strict are the rules on campus?

- How tolerant are students of non-religious students?

Holidays/Festivities

- What is the holiday schedule for the school?

- Are the dorms closed over long holidays?

- Are there options for holiday housing?

- What are the Homecoming festivities like?

- What are holiday festivities like?

- What are some of the campus traditions?

Campus Media

- Is there a college radio station?

- Is there a campus newspaper or new website?

- Are there other student publications?

Students

- How happy are students?

- How nice are students?

- How much diversity is there on campus?

- Are students athletic-minded?

- Are students arts-minded?

- Are students involved in lots of clubs and activities?

- Is this mainly a commuter campus?

- Do students generally stay around campus on weekends?

- How tolerant are students of LGBT students?

- Where can I find the best food/coffee on campus?

- What is the school's best-kept secret?

- Can I get anything for free on campus?

- How often do you attend campus events?

Alumni

- How involved are alumni with students?

- How active is the alumni association?

- Are there alumni mentors for students?

Campus/Facilities

- Is the campus safe and secure?

- Is there a blue light system or a late-night escort system available?

- Is there a library on campus that is open 24 hours?

- How many bookstores are on campus?

- Is there a post office on campus?

- How accessible is the campus for students with disabilities?

FINAL THOUGHTS

It's important to remember that most students end up liking where they go to college. The student who is crushed to have been rejected by Princeton ends up loving Oberlin and being happy that the fate kept her from being accepted by what had once been her first-choice school. In many ways, the most important thing about college is the one characteristic that virtually all colleges have in common: They are communities of young people living on their own without many serious responsibilities. You'll never get another chance to live this way, and you'll probably enjoy it almost anywhere you have a chance. Where you go to college can be very important. In addition to determining where you spend the next four years of your life, where you go to school can determine where you work after graduation, whom you marry, where you live, and who your lifelong friends are. A degree from Wharton really can make it easier to get a good job after graduation; however, spending four years in a glamorous state like Colorado or Hawaii really can be a lot of fun. You should make your college decision carefully and with a clear head. Don't make your decision simply to please (or infuriate) someone else. If you begin to think that you won't be able to go on living unless you get into (let's say) Yale, get hold of Yale's faculty directory and see where its professors went to college. You'll see that some of them went to Yale, some to Harvard, and some to other Ivy League schools, but that many of them went to exactly the sort of colleges that you may think are "beneath" you. If those colleges are good enough for Yale, might they not also be good enough for you? You should approach college selection thoughtfully, but not with a conviction that your entire life hangs in the balance.

Because, let's be honest, it doesn't. No matter the college, the education you will get out of it largely depends on what you put into it. No one can tell you what you want or need. Not your parents, not your guidance counselor, not your teachers, not your older brother or sister, not us. Students who end up enrolling in colleges based on the wants, needs, or expectations of others often regret it. You should certainly listen to the advice all these people have to give you, but you need to do your own soul-searching and research because only you can figure out what attributes of college are most important to you.

No matter where you go for your college research help or where you end up actually going to college, we sincerely hope that it's the right school for you. Best of luck!

NOTES

Score Your Best on Both of the Tests

Get proven prep for the SAT and ACT at **PrincetonReviewBooks.com**

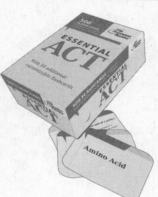

More SAT Guides:

Essential SAT Vocabulary (Flashcards)
978-0-375-42964-4
$16.99/$21.99 Can.

11 Practice Tests for the SAT and PSAT, 2014 Edition
978-0-307-94616-4
$24.99/$27.95 Can.

 July 2013!

Cracking the SAT, 2014 Edition
978-0-307-94561-7
$21.99/$24.95 Can.
eBook: 978-0-307-94588-4

Cracking the SAT with DVD, 2014 Edition
978-0-307-94562-4
$34.99/$39.95 Can.

Crash Course for the SAT, 4th Edition
978-0-375-42831-9
$9.99/$10.99 Can.

Math Workout for the SAT, 3rd Edition
978-0-375-42833-3
$16.99/$18.99 Can.

Reading and Writing Workout for the SAT, 2nd Edition
978-0-375-42832-6
$16.99/$18.99 Can.

Crack the ACT, Too!

Cracking the ACT, 2013 Edition
978-0-307-94535-8
$19.99/$23.99 Can.
eBook: 978-0-307-94540-2

Cracking the ACT with DVD, 2013 Edition
978-0-307-94536-5
$31.99/$37.99 Can.

Crash Course for the ACT, 4th Edition
978-0-375-42762-6
$9.99/$11.99 Can.

Essential ACT (Flashcards)
978-0-375-42806-7
$17.99/$19.99 Can.

Admissions Advice from the Experts:

The Best 378 Colleges, 2014 Edition
978-0-307-94605-8
$23.99/$26.99 Can.

 August 2013!

Paying for College Without Going Broke, 2013 Edition
978-0-307-94532-7
$20.00/$24.00 Can.

The Best Value Colleges, 2013 Edition
978-0-307-94598-3
$21.99/$25.99 Can.

The Complete Book of Colleges, 2014 Edition
978-0-307-94628-7
$26.99/$31.00 Can.

 August 2013!